"Wonderfully readable. . . . [*Gettysburg*] marries scholarly rigor to a sense of narrative that rivals that of a novel."   —*The Daily Beast*

"In this consistently riveting book, Allen Guelzo makes us feel that we are hearing the epic story of the Civil War's most famous battle for the first time. . . . This is, simply, the best book about Gettysburg that has yet been written. It is hard, if not impossible, to imagine that there will ever be a better one."   —Fergus M. Bordewich, author of *America's Great Debate*

"What is there left to say about Gettysburg? In Allen Guelzo's deft, scholarly hands, plenty. *Gettysburg: The Last Invasion* is fresh, fascinating, and compellingly provocative. It is a marvelous book that deserves to be read and savored. And it deserves to be on the bookshelf of all Civil War buffs."   —Jay Winik, author of *April 1865*

"An extraordinary work of thorough scholarship combined with a lifetime of judgment about historic events. . . . Everyone interested in the decisive moment in freedom's struggle should read Guelzo's simply extraordinary book."   —Newt Gingrich, former Speaker of the House
and coauthor of *Gettysburg: A Novel of the Civil War*

"Despite all that has been written about the battle of Gettysburg, Allen Guelzo provides new information and insights in this stirring account. . . . Readers will find much to think about in this book."
—James M. McPherson,
Pulitzer Prize–winning author of *Battle Cry of Freedom*

"Guelzo has composed a narrative that is detailed and compelling on a human level but easy to follow on an operational and tactical one. . . . A triumph of source use and presentation, engaging enough for the general reader but rigorous enough for the scholar."   —*Library Journal*

"Guelzo's entry identifies key controversies, trenchantly advocates its interpretations, and rests on a sensible foundation, the confusion of a Civil War battle. . . . [*Gettysburg*] reads like the battle might have been experienced. . . . Guelzo demonstrates versatile historical skill in this superior treatment of Gettysburg."   —*Booklist* (starred review)

"Stirring . . . robust, memorable reading that will appeal to Civil War Buffs, professional historians, and general readers alike."
—*Kirkus Reviews* (starred review)

Allen C. Guelzo

Gettysburg

Allen C. Guelzo is the Henry R. Luce Professor of the Civil War Era and Director of Civil War Era Studies at Gettysburg College. He is the author of *Lincoln's Emancipation Proclamation: The End of Slavery in America* and *Abraham Lincoln: Redeemer President*, both winners of the Lincoln Prize. Guelzo's essays, reviews, and articles have appeared in publications ranging from *The American Historical Review* and *The Wilson Quarterly* to newspapers such as *The Philadelphia Inquirer* and *The Wall Street Journal*.

Gettysburg

Gettysburg

THE LAST INVASION

Allen C. Guelzo

VINTAGE CIVIL WAR LIBRARY
VINTAGE BOOKS
A Division of Random House LLC
New York

FIRST VINTAGE BOOKS EDITION, FEBRUARY 2014

Copyright © 2013 by Allen C. Guelzo

All rights reserved. Published in the United States by Vintage Books, a division
of Random House LLC, New York, and in Canada by Random House of Canada
Limited, Toronto, Penguin Random House companies. Originally published in
hardcover in the United States by Alfred A. Knopf, a division of
Random House LLC, New York, in 2013.

Vintage is a registered trademark and Vintage Civil War Library and colophon are
trademarks of Random House LLC.

The Library of Congress has cataloged the Knopf edition as follows:
Guelzo, Allen C.
Gettysburg : the last invasion / by Allen C. Guelzo.—First edition.
pages cm
Includes bibliographical references and index.
1. Gettysburg, Battle of, Gettysburg, Pa., 1863. I. Title.
E475.53.G875 2013
973.7'349— dc23 2012047013

Vintage Trade Paperback ISBN: 978-0-307-74069-4
eBook ISBN: 978-0-385-34964-2

Maps by Robert Bull
Book design by Maggie Hinders

www.vintagebooks.com

Printed in the United States of America
10 9 8 7 6 5 4 3 2 1

To 2nd Lieutenant Jonathan E. Guelzo, U.S. Army,

in remembrance of all the days we have walked

the fields of Gettysburg together

Contents

Gettysburg

O Pride of the days in prime of the months
Now trebled in great renown,
When before the ark of our holy cause
Fell Dagon down—
Dagon foredoomed, who, armed and targed,
Never his impious heart enlarged
Beyond that hour; God walled his power,
And there the last invader charged.

He charged, and in that charge condensed
His all of hate and all of fire;
He sought to blast us in his scorn,
And wither us in his ire.
Before him went the shriek of shells—
Aerial screamings, taunts and yells;
Then the three waves in flashed advance
Surged, but were met, and back they set:
Pride was repelled by sterner pride,
And Right is a strong-hold yet.

Before our lines it seemed a beach
Which wild September gales have strown
With havoc on wreck, and dashed therewith
Pale crews unknown—
Men, arms, and steeds. The evening sun
Died on the face of each lifeless one,
And died along the winding marge of fight
And searching-parties lone.

Sloped on the hill the mounds were green,
Our centre held that place of graves,
And some still hold it in their swoon,
And over these a glory waves.
The warrior-monument, crashed in fight,
Shall soar transfigured in loftier light,
A meaning ampler bear;
Soldier and priest with hymn and prayer
Have laid the stone, and every bone
Shall rest in honor there.

—HERMAN MELVILLE

Acknowledgments

ACKNOWLEDGMENTS are supposed to be the altar of gratitude. However, I cannot help noticing how often they serve more or less the same purpose as the cocktail party to the social climber, as a place to issue noisy salutes to a checklist of celebrities with whom one is eager to be associated. I have no such parade of cultural mandarins to wave up onto my little stage, and probably not even much of a stage. But this makes me all the more uncommonly grateful to those from whom help has unstintingly come. I single out in particular my office staffers in Civil War Era Studies at Gettysburg College: Cathy Bain first, and then my faithful note-card transcribers, Lauren Roedner and Tim Koenig. I have benefited delightfully from discussions and exchanges of documents with John Rudy, Eric Wittenberg, Scott Mingus, and Charles Tarbox. Troy Harman, John Heiser, and Scott Hartwig of the Gettysburg National Military Park have been unflaggingly helpful. And for patience beyond the measure of Job, I must thank the happy few who read through each chapter for me as they appeared, and commented on them: Scott Bowden, Joe Bilby, Charles Teague, Gregory Urwin, and Ted Alexander. Zack Fry and Jason Frawley freely allowed me to use research material that is, as yet, unpublished by them. William A. Frassanito not only provided me with access to a number of the rare photographs in his collection, but also gave highly useful advice on the selection of images as a whole.

I want also to hail the cooperation of a number of libraries and collections in accessing manuscript collections, including the Houghton Library at Harvard University, the Alderman Library at the University of Virginia, the Southern Historical Collection at the University of North Carolina at Chapel Hill, the Library of Congress, the Museum of the Confederacy, the New-York Historical Society, the Virginia Historical Society, Special Collections in the Musselman Library at Gettysburg College, the Adams County

Historical Society, the Western Reserve Historical Society, the library of the Gettysburg National Military Park, and Bowdoin College. Gettysburg College and Princeton University united in funding a yearlong sabbatical during the 2010–11 academic year, during which I served as the William Garwood Visiting Professor in the Department of Politics at Princeton. Bringing the manuscript out of its chrysalis state and into full wingspread has been the unceasing labor of my glorious agent, Michele Rubin of Writers House, and Andrew Miller, my editor at Random House. The *Gettysburg Magazine* published an early version of some of my thinking on the tactical context of the battle as "Some Unturned Corners of the Battle of Gettysburg" in its July 2011 issue.

Above all, I salute as gracefully and handsomely as I can the patience and good humor of my beloved wife, Debra, and our three now-grown children, Jerusha Mast, Alexandra Fanucci, and Jonathan Guelzo, all of whom have tolerated days, weeks, and months of an unresponsive and abstracted paterfamilias, his mind wandering somewhere over rocky hills and golden fields, toward a small knot of trees on a distant horizon.

This is a book about a nineteenth-century battle. That fact alone calls forward a number of caveats, beginning with the arrangement of hours and minutes in these chapters. America in the 1860s knew nothing about synchronized time. Clocks and watches were set by light and dark; there were no time zones, no standardized time-measurement schemes. Even meticulous timekeepers relied on the sound of church bells or public clocks for uniformity. Of course, in the middle of the battle, few people were noticing bells, if they were being rung at all, and few were likely to be listening for the cheerful chiming of a courthouse clock. Soldiers set their personal watches by their own estimates, and in battle, those lacking watches were reduced to little more than a hazardous guess about the time. This is a long way of saying that the times cited in this book are entirely the reckoning and responsibility of the author; but the vagaries of timekeeping in 1863 were so great that even I must protest having to share too much of the responsibility. The participants themselves tried to establish some rough sense of the timing of the battle's events, and sometimes I have accepted their estimates or time notations, but always with the question in mind: *Could this really have happened at that time?*

The same is true concerning the maps that appear in this book; they, too, are entirely the reckoning and responsibility of the author. But they, too, suffer from the uncertainties of the battle's participants about where they were and what landmarks were nearby. Maps in both armies were in short and uncoordinated supply, and local place-names were swapped around by soldiers with an unsteady abandon (it is estimated that Little Round Top was called by as many as nine different names in after-action reports, simply because the officers composing those reports had only the most slender information about what names the locals attached to them). Names for local landmarks shifted from telling to telling: the Lutheran Theological Seminary was frequently mistaken for Pennsylvania College, and vice versa; the road leading southwest from Gettysburg is usually known as the Fairfield Road, but sometimes is referred to as the Hagerstown Road, while the road leading west to Cashtown is frequently called the Cashtown Pike *and* the Chambersburg Pike; the road from the northeast used by Jubal Early's division on July 1st was alternately referred to as the Old Harrisburg Road *and* the Heidlersburg Road (I have opted to use the latter); Baltimore Street in the town of Gettysburg becomes the Baltimore Pike as soon as it leaves the environs of Gettysburg, just as York Street becomes the York Pike. The greatest confusion is liable to occur concerning the Cashtown Pike versus Chambersburg Pike usage, so let me say here that I have simply settled on calling the west road the Cashtown Pike. Other geographical points also suffer from name-swapping: Herbst's Woods is frequently spoken of as McPherson's Woods, but in fact, the woods belonged to John Herbst and only bordered the Edward McPherson property. Oak Hill is a large prominence north and west of Gettysburg, but it has a south-running spur known as Oak Ridge which is geologically distinct, and so I have rigorously segregated the *Hill* for the hill and the *Ridge* for the ridge. The same distinction applies to the more famous Cemetery *Hill* and Cemetery *Ridge*.

The vagaries of postwar memory did not help this uncertainty. The 1,324 monuments, markers, statues, and plaques which dot the six thousand acres of the modern Gettysburg battlefield look like they ought to offer some reliable guidance to the placement of soldiers on the ground. But for a variety of reasons, even these fixed stars of the battlefield are not entirely to be relied upon. Veterans wishing to erect monuments to their stand frequently petitioned the Gettysburg Battlefield Memorial Association for locations near the battlefield's roadways, rather than where they actually fought, so that their monuments would be more easily visible to tourists (so that Freeman McGilvery's artillery line is marked by placements along modern-day Hancock Avenue, some two hundred yards *east* of where they surely parked themselves in the desperate twilight combat of July 2, 1863). One unit's veterans (those of the 72nd Pennsylvania) actually waged a successful battle in the Pennsylvania courts to have their monument placed on a spot which reflected better their claims to valor and courage rather than the rear-echelon position the GBMA planned for them. Although there are at least three atlases devoted exclusively to maps of the Gettysburg battlefield (by Bradley Gottfried, Philip Laino, and Steven Stanley), none of the unit positions marked in these volumes can possibly hope to claim absolute accuracy, and so neither will I. My maps must serve as general guides to the reader, alongside the text, and not be viewed as testimony worth fighting over.

That uncertainty also reaches through to the sources I have used for this book. The literature on the Gettysburg battle is enormous—the 2004 edition of Richard Sauers' *The Gettysburg Campaign, June 3–August 1, 1863: A Comprehensive, Selectively Annotated Bibliography* lists 6,193 books, articles, chapters, and pamphlets on the battle; an entire biannual magazine, *The Gettysburg Magazine,* has been published since 1989 focusing in exacting detail on various facets of the battle, and ponderous volumes have appeared from distinguished university presses, dividing the story of the battle into single days, parts of days, and finally to quarter hours or so. I have spent most of my time in pursuit of the accounts written by the veterans of the battle themselves, in the form of autobiographies, lectures, pamphlets, dedicatory speeches, ill-tempered newspaper articles, self-aggrandizing memoirs, and that most peculiar of American literary genres, the regimental history. The further in time from the battle these recollections were written, the less reliability is sure to be attached to these reminiscences. But that is not a fixed rule. There are regimental histories published immediately after the war which show little sign that the authors saw or understood most of the battle they had fought through, whereas numerous writers, even long after the fact, came up with nuggets of reminiscence so vivid that time has clearly been no dimmer of them.

Nor is there any easy refuge from false lead to be found in self-limiting one's curiosity to unpublished manuscripts. There is no authoritative census of Gettysburg-related manuscript sources, although Sauers includes a fifty-two-page listing, by unit, of letters, papers, and diaries. But even letters written from the field frequently betray little comprehension of what had been happening around the writers, and an old soldier can be as forgetful of detail after a day as after a decade. And, as Richard Holmes discovered as a correspondent during the Falklands War in 1982, it took no long time before veterans, hearing other veterans, incorporated a certain agreed-upon story line into their own accounts. Holmes was amazed to interview Falklands veterans, and discover how "a carapace of accepted fact hardened almost before my eyes." The temptation would always be to make the experience of battle more reasoned, more synchronous with others' experiences, than it had ever seemed at the moment. One of the greatest collections of manuscript materials on the battle is the vast heap of letters and accounts (mostly Union) solicited by John Badger Bachelder, the battle's first great remembrancer, and finally published in 1994–95 as *The Bachelder Papers* by David and Audrey Ladd in three volumes. But even within *The Bachelder Papers,* the old veterans advance conflicting accounts, rehearse old grievances, debate large-scale tactical pictures which they could never have known about at the time, and defend pet theories with only slightly less vehemence than that which they employed in the battle itself. The same is true of John Warwick Daniel, who essayed to be the Confederate Bachelder. In the end, the chronicler of Gettysburg has little to take for a final guide than the refined twitching of common sense, and a willingness to endure the arrows of outraged fortune hunters who have planned to make that fortune from this or that presumably pristine version of events. Again, the same question posed to me by timing has to be posed about sources, no matter how immediate: *Could this really have happened at that time?*

Nor is there any way that these sources could finally settle the great controversies of the battle:

- Did J.E.B. Stuart lose the battle before it even started by galloping off on a senseless joyride with the Confederate cavalry, and thus deprive the Confederates of intelligence-gathering capacity?
- Did Richard Ewell lose the battle because he lacked the energy and the ruthlessness to press his successes on July 1st to the point of driving the battered Union forces off Cemetery Hill and Culp's Hill?
- Did Dan Sickles force George Meade to stay and fight at Gettysburg on July 2nd, as Sickles claimed after the war?
- Was James Longstreet criminally negligent by insolently refusing to mount the Confederate attacks on July 2nd and 3rd with the appropriate spirit Lee demanded?

These are only the most prominent of the Gettysburg controversies, and I put forward the answers I do with the resigned confidence that neither reason nor reasonableness is guaranteed certainty of success over self-interest and braggadocio.

Occasionally, I have taken my own counsel as the only way to make sense of certain problems in the Gettysburg narrative. It puzzles me why the ridgeline which forms the western boundary of John Rose's wheat field is routinely called "the Stony Hill," when it is perfectly obvious to the naked eye that it is a ridge, like the other undulating waves of ridges running eastward from South Mountain, and so I have determined to call it "the stony ridge." Likewise, it makes no sense to replicate the ethnic tone-deafness of nineteenth-century

Americans in spelling Alexander Schimmelpfennig's name as *Schimmelfen-
ning* or *Schimmelfennig* (or, as his grave monument indecorously renders it,
Schimmelfinnig), and so Schimmelpfennig he stays.

Books about battles are not in high fashion, since they frequently engender
suspicion in prominent places that an interest in war—even a war as distant
as the American Civil War—panders to an unhappy streak of destructiveness
in the American psyche, and by rights should be stuffed into some genie's
bottle lest it entice more of the naïve to serve it. By contrast, in the middle
of the nineteenth century, war was considered (and not just by unbalanced
psychotics) to be "the highest, most exalted art; the art of freedom and of
right, of the blessed condition of Man and of humanity—the Principle of
Peace." A century and a half later, the lure of the Civil War remains strong,
but dealing with its battles has acquired among my academic peers a reputation close to pornography. This, despite the nagging reality that aggression is
an instinctive form of human self-preservation; despite the curiosity, for those
of a Marxist bent, that no more efficient repudiation of liberal individualism
(another ideology now on-the-town) exists than the collectivity of war and
combat; and despite Susan Sontag's ironic reminder that "war was and still is
the most irresistible—and picturesque—news." However, a generation of professional historians whose youth was dominated by the Vietnam War has not
been eager to embrace *any* war after that experience, except perhaps for the
purpose of demonstrating the atrocious malevolence with which American
soldiers are habitually supposed to wage it or the pitiful pall of death which it
spreads across the land.

   This book will not offer much comfort to those persuasions, if only
because we cannot talk about the American nineteenth century without talking about the Civil War, and we cannot talk about the Civil War without
acknowledging, even grudgingly, that the Civil War era's singular event was a
war, and that all the other issues hung ineluctably on the results achieved by
large numbers of organized citizens attempting to kill one another. But even
more contrary to the grain, the American Civil War—and the battle of Gettysburg in particular—were conducted with an amateurism of spirit and an
innocence of intent which would be touching if that same amateurism had
not also contrived to make it so bloody. And it was remembered by its veterans
as the occasion for a great ratification "of freedom and of right." Although it
has become commonplace to speak shudderingly of the Civil War as the "first
modern war" or the "first total war," there are few things more impressive
than the sheer *lack* of totality in both the battle of Gettysburg and the Civil
War as a whole, and few things more humiliating than the bewildered, small-

town incompetence with which American soldiers addressed themselves to the task of managing, directing, and commanding the mammoth citizen-armies they had called forth.

The best testimony to that lack of totality is the silent witness of places like Gettysburg, where almost all of the buildings that sat in the path of the battle are still here. The technology of nineteenth-century warfare, even as advanced as it was over that of the Napoleonic Wars, was simply too limited to knock them down. It is difficult to understand the "modernity" of a war fought with single-shot muzzle-loading weapons, under the direction of commanders whose chief credential was a diploma from a military engineering school, and on battlefields where it was still reasonably safe to stand up. The principal historical cognates of Gettysburg and the American Civil War are not the Western Front or My Lai, but the Crimean War, the North Italian War of 1859, the Schleswig-Holstein War of 1864, the Austro-Prussian and Franco-Prussian Wars, and the Taiping Rebellion—none of which are more modern than high-button shoes and pince-nez. The same is true of the concept of war which still prevailed among the Civil War armies, a concept which still accepted the "bracketing" of war from civil life as a sort of idealized joust between sovereigns who possessed a monopoly on state violence. Because the sovereigns in the Civil War were the peoples of the Union and the Confederacy, the Civil War holds the portents of mass, popular wars in which no result could be acceptable but the total defeat of an enemy. But these were still only portents, just as the popular resistance of the French people after the debacle at Sedan in 1870 made the Franco-Prussian War a similar portent of such conflicts.

A book on the battle of Gettysburg will also lose contact with fashion because Gettysburg does not touch on emancipation and has almost nothing to say on the subject of African-American agency. There were, to be sure, several thousand black people involved in the campaign, perhaps as many as thirty thousand. But they came as slaves, as the logistical underpinning of the rebel army, and left only the most passing traces. Nor is there much agency to be celebrated in slaves who were compelled to work for those who were defending slavery. There were no black troops at Gettysburg, and most of the free black inhabitants of the town of Gettysburg had fled to avoid capture and enslavement by the Confederate invaders. (If there was malevolence anywhere in this story, it was here—but it was the sort of malevolence which had been going on for 250 years, and not an expression of some newfound embrace of "total war.") A few black Gettysburgians would end up serving in the Union armies—and I call the roll here of Andrew Meads, James Russell, and Stewart Woods, the latter serving in the 54th Massachusetts and miraculously surviving both the 54th's decimation at Battery Wagner two weeks after Gettysburg and the Confederate prison camp at Andersonville—but otherwise, Gettysburg was almost univocally a battle for the Union, and it was made all the more so by Lincoln's famous address, which contains no allusion to slavery, and casts the battle entirely in the context of the preservation of liberal democracy.

Of course, for many of the Civil War's cultured despisers, the Union is old hat and liberal democracy the listless desert of history's last—and very dull—man. Emancipation makes a better story for our times. But emancipation cannot be so easily detached from union (which is another way of saying that racial justice and liberal democracy rise or fall with each other). Lincoln insisted that the Civil War was being fought by the United States in order to restore the constitutionally mandated union of those states, and the Gettysburg Address was his most eloquent declaration that the ultimate purpose of the war was the test it afforded of the practical viability of democracy. This was not because race, slavery, and emancipation were unimportant to Lincoln, but because the Union (and the liberal democracy it represented) and emancipation were not, after all, mutually exclusive goals. Unless the Union was restored, there would be no practical possibility of emancipation, since the overwhelming majority of American slaves would, in that case, end up living in a foreign country, and beyond the possible grasp of Lincoln's best antislavery intentions.

But by the same token, restoring the Union would be a hollow accomplishment unless the blot of race-based slavery was wiped from the Union's escutcheon, and in that there was as much black agency at work at Gettysburg as on any other Civil War battlefield, because no democracy worth its name could continue to drag the burden of slavery around after it. "Under which of the old tyrannical governments of Europe is every sixth man a slave, whom his fellow-creatures may buy and sell and torture?" asked a sarcastic Sydney Smith, from his English perch, a full forty years before the war,

> what right has the American, a scourger and murderer of slaves, to compare himself with the least and lowest of the European nations?—much more with this great and humane country, where the greatest lord dare not lay a finger upon the meanest peasant? What is freedom, where all are not free? where the greatest of God's blessings is limited, with impious caprice, to the colour of the body?

This was the question which chilled the blood of every American who was not actually a slaveowner, and more than a few who were. It was the best of news to European aristocrats who looked upon the United States as the one disturbing testimony against the Romantic revival of absolutism. "If the United States go wrong what hope have we of the civilized world in our turn?" asked Richard Cobden, the figurehead of the Manchester School and the principal star (along with John Bright) of English liberalism.

Preventing that wrong turn was what the preservation of the Union was about. Emancipating American slaves would remove the cause of that wrong, and make the Union worth preserving. But neither of them would be possible without the triumph of the Union armies. And Gettysburg would be the place where the armies of the Union would receive their greatest test, and the Union its last invasion.

Gettysburg

Prologue

ANYONE WHO TOOK THE TROUBLE on one of the few fair days in late
June of the year 1863 to climb the winding forest trail to the old Indian
lookout on South Mountain would have enjoyed a sweet reward for his trouble. Looking to the east and north, across central Maryland and south-central
Pennsylvania, a watcher at the lookout stood high above a plain, full of pleats
and tucks, rolling effortlessly eastward to the Susquehanna River. Only a last
chain of hills in the blue distance hid the vista that led southeast, down to
Washington, or northeast, to Harrisburg. Laid across this expanse were spin-
neys of forest—white and red oak, black walnut, sycamore, chestnut, hickory,
alder, elm—whose tree crowns would have shimmered in the humid, golden
sunlight. Between the fingers of forest lay green and gold patches of grassy
farmland, irregularly dotted with small white barns and houses.

If the watcher shifted and looked to the west, the slopes of South Mountain fell away into the lengthening shadows of the Cumberland Valley, before
pitching sharply upward again to the ranges of the Tuscarora and Blue mountain and the vast, pine-covered spines of the Appalachians, now turning
cobalt in the late afternoon haze.

South Mountain is the first outlier of the Appalachians, and it runs on an
axis that tilts northeast from the Blue Ridge Mountains in Virginia (another
outlier chain of the Appalachians) to the west bank of the Susquehanna near
Harrisburg. On the western side of South Mountain, the fertile Shenandoah
and Cumberland valleys could take a traveler without too much difficulty
from Lexington, Virginia, down to the Potomac and across into the Cumberland Valley and to Carlisle or Harrisburg—some 220 miles. But on South

Mountain's eastern face, the ground drops sharply to the rich green farmlands of the plain. This plain itself subsides into a series of low-lying ridges that parallel South Mountain itself as though they were undulations from the mountain's upthrust, until one by one they gradually expend their height and their force sixty miles away at the Susquehanna. The roadways which cut across the plain conformed themselves to the undulations, and ran mostly north to south. Only two major east–west roads bored their way horizontally through South Mountain, one stretching from Philadelphia, through Lancaster and York, to the Cashtown Gap, and the other reaching up from Washington, across Maryland to Turner's and Fox's gaps, and thence to Harpers Ferry.

Those upfolded north–south ridges were really the jammed-together lips of great cracks in an enormous underlying sill of granitelike rock. In places, the jamming had been so violent that ungainly masses of stone, gray and coarse-grained, pushed up through the soils, sometimes forming cone-shaped hills that punctuated the ridgelines. But the soils themselves were soft, thick loam, and in 1863 a farming family could support itself on as little as 150 acres. A long time before, the heirs of William Penn, the original feudal proprietor of Pennsylvania, struggled to prevent the dissipation of this rich, wrinkled plain into a sprawl of small farms, and even tried to set aside a 43,500-acre tract as a manor. But as so often happened to the Penn family's plans for Pennsylvania, the German Lutherans and Scots-Irish Presbyterians who overleaped the Susquehanna simply dismissed the proprietors' restrictions. The Penns had neither sufficient interest nor sufficient power to curb the demand for cutting up their "manor" into disposable farmland, and by the 1760s the broad plain between the Susquehanna and South Mountain had passed into the hands of the farmers and speculators. In 1797, the new Pennsylvania state government dissolved all title to the "manor" in favor of those who had squatted on it.[1]

One of these farmers' sons, James Gettys, turned speculator himself. Sizing up the growth of the region and the prospects for trade between the mountains and the Susquehanna, Gettys shrewdly bought 116 acres from his father at the point where the principal north–south road to Harrisburg crossed the east–west road heading toward South Mountain and the Cashtown Gap. There were already two taverns there, doing a roaring business, and it seemed to James Gettys that a good deal more could be made out of this intersection. He laid out 210 lots for a town, built around a central square (or "diamond"), and without any excess of modesty named it for himself.[2]

From the vantage point of the watcher on South Mountain, Gettysburg lay at the north edge of the horizon, although a good brass naval telescope could bring it pretty easily into view. But on that late June afternoon, the watcher's attention would be captured, not by James Gettys' distant town, or by the newly cut mounds of grass and hay, or by the fields of full-grown wheat and the knee-high cornstalks, spread out like yellow aprons on the plain below. Instead, if the watcher looked to the west in the oncoming twilight, the darkening shadows over the Cumberland Valley quickly became pinpricked with a carpet of fire lights. Or, if the watcher looked east, what caught the eye was an interminably long snake of traffic—white canvas-topped wagons, horses, men on foot, ambulances, more and more men on foot with the sun glinting sharply off the rifle barrels perched on their shoulders, big-wheeled cannon, flags (some huge and square, some small and swallow-tailed, the Stars and Stripes, state flags, headquarters flags)—all stopping and starting, and stopping again, and then sluggishly moving again, and all of it headed north, toward Gettysburg. The watcher was beholding something never seen before from this spot, and never seen again—two great armies, bound for the greatest and most violent collision the North American continent had ever seen.

PART 1

———— ❖ ————

The March Up

CHAPTER ONE

People who will not give in

THE AMERICAN CIVIL WAR had been raging for just a little more than two years when the armies came into the view of the Indian lookout. "Neither party," Abraham Lincoln would say later, "expected for the war, the magnitude, or the duration, which it has already attained." Hardly ever has any nation fallen into the abyss of war less prepared to wage it, or with less foresight of the costs it would have to pay. From the moment they took a republic rather than a monarchy as the shape of their government, Americans prided themselves on being a nation of peace, dedicated to the arts of commerce rather than the rapacity of empire and "the spirit of war." Americans hadn't entirely given up on the call to arms—there was a war with Britain in 1812, then a war with Mexico in 1846, and ongoing flashes of conflict with uncooperative tribes of Creeks, Choctaw, Shawnee, Comanche, Kiowa, and Sioux. But none of these occurred on any great scale, and all of them could be explained away as regrettable but necessary defensive measures for the good of the republic. There would invariably be Americans who gloried in war and killing, just as there would be anywhere. But the numbers of the bloodlusters would not be great. Even one of the small cadre of professionally trained officers produced by the republic's military academy at West Point, Oliver Otis Howard, admitted to deep religious uneasiness about the glorification of war. "We cannot well exaggerate . . . the horrors, the hateful ravages, and the countless expense of war," Howard wrote long after the Civil War's guns had fallen silent. And stories of war serve only one purpose, to "show plainly to our children that war, with its embodied woes and furies must be avoided."[1]

This ambivalence toward wars and soldiering lent strength to the penury of the Federal Congress, which routinely set military expenditures and military personnel to a level befitting a national constabulary. At the first shot of the Civil War, the United States Army comprised only 16,357 officers and men, almost none of whom were grouped together in one place in any formidable size. Nor was there any professional association equivalent to Britain's Royal United Services Institution to foster thinking on new weapons and tactical schemes. "Nearly the whole of my eleven years' service," wrote one West Pointer of the class of 1850, "has been with my company on the frontier of Texas," and Richard Stoddert Ewell, who would wear a Confederate lieutenant general's stars at Gettysburg in 1863, confessed that during his twenty years' service as a cavalry officer, "he had learned all about commanding fifty United States dragoons, and forgotten everything else."[2]

Even this minuscule army was too much for Horace Greeley, the madhatter editor of the country's most widely read newspaper, the *New-York Tribune.* "Of all solecisms, a Standing Army in a Republic of the XIXth Century is the most indefensible," Greeley announced in 1858. "We have no more need of a Standing Army than of an order of nobility."[3] In the event of any national emergency, the states would put their part-time militias into Federal hands, like the Prussian *Landwehr* in 1813, and *they* would provide the manpower which the Regular Army could deploy. The officers would emerge, like Napoleon's generals, as corporals with field marshals' batons in their packs. "It was the fashion to sneer at those who had made the profession of arms their study," complained a contributor to the *Army and Navy Journal,* and "experience in Congress was apparently regarded as a more essential qualification to command than a course of study at West Point." One lonely voice, Henry Wager Halleck (who himself had left the army in despair and gone quite profitably into law and banking), warned that "disorganized and frantic masses" were not likely to provide "as good a defense against invasion as the most disciplined and experienced." But it was easier to believe otherwise, and cheaper, too. In 1857, a Democratic-controlled Congress spent more money on Federal judges than on "armories, arsenals, and munitions of war," more on customhouses and warehouses than on "Fortifications, and other works of defence," and more on the General Post Office building in Washington than on West Point.[4]

Congressional parsimony continued to be the rule even after the Civil War began. Rather than enlist hundreds of thousands of recruits as long-service Regulars, Congress turned to an expedient it had tried once before, in the Mexican War—the enlistment of half a million state "volunteers" for two- or three-year terms. *Volunteers* were a category of military service borrowed from British practice in the Napoleonic Wars, as a less costly way of protecting the home islands without relying on county militias or paying for a greatly expanded regular army. In like manner, American volunteers in 1861 would be recruited by the states into regiments bearing state designations (83rd Pennsylvania, 75th Ohio, and so on) and carrying state colors as well as the Stars and Stripes, and with officers elected by the regiments themselves and appointed by state governors. They would be paid and equipped by the Federal government and march under the orders and articles of war of federally appointed general officers (drawn mostly from the ranks of the Regular Army), but without any long-service commitments from either the volunteers or the government. The Confederate government, strapped by even greater financial problems, adopted the same state-based volunteer system, keeping the state designations in place even after it instituted a compulsory draft.[5]

What these volunteer regiments contributed in numbers was often sacrificed in efficiency. Unlike the British soldiers of the Crimean War of 1854–56, who already had an average of seven years' service under their cross-belts, the Civil War volunteer was a temporary soldier, long on self-esteem and very, very short on experience. He "entertained the idea that he was little, if any, inferior to Napoleon, in his capabilities and possibilities," and was "never ready to submit to the routine duty and discipline of the camp or the march." Few of them grasped what *discipline* meant, and fewer still saw any sense in unquestioningly following orders. "Many of the men seem to think they should never be spoken to unless the remarks are prefaced by some words of deferential politeness," raged one Michigan officer. "Will the gentlemen who compose the first platoon have the kindness to march forward, or will they please to halt, &c. is abt. what some of them seem to expect." It was the privilege of "the old Confederate soldier" always to believe that he "would decide some questions for himself," wrote Carlton McCarthy, who served in the Richmond Howitzers. "To the last he maintained the right of private judgment, and especially on the field of battle."[6]

Not that the volunteers' officers were much superior to the men they commanded. "None of the officers or men had any military education," wrote a volunteer in the 11th Virginia, "and were all, officers and men, quite green and inexperienced in military affairs generally." John S. Mosby, who went from being a Virginia lawyer to a cavalry private to the most famous partisan officer of the war, conceded that "I could never repeat the formulas of the regulations." A soldier in the 147th New York chuckled sardonically to himself at the ineptness of his company's captain. He "went out with us on Battalion Drill yesterday and got so befuddled he could not do anything, so we drilled or skedaddled about for half an hour, then came back to camp." In the 31st Illinois, a private who had seen some service in the Mexican War had to give instruction to his officers in company drill. Thomas Hyde was surprised to find himself elected major of the 7th Maine, but then again, "I was the only man in the regiment" who knew how to "drill a company." Even so, Hyde had to stay one drill lesson ahead by "studying by candle light."[7]

This bumbling was not helped by the culture gaps formed by large numbers of immigrants in the volunteer ranks, whose principal motivation for enlistment might be a uniform, bounties, pay, and something besides unemployment and penury. German and Irish immigrants made up slightly less than a third of the Federal volunteer forces, with some units—the 39th New York (the "Garibaldi Guard"), 58th New York (the "Polish Legion"), and the five regiments of the "Irish Brigade" (63rd, 69th, 88th New York, 28th Massachusetts, and 116th Pennsylvania)—marching under the red-white-and-green banner of Italian unification, the green-and-gold of Ireland, and the black-red-and-gold of the German Revolution of 1848. The Confederacy recruited proportional numbers of German immigrants, and its most dreaded regiment, the 1st Louisiana Special Battalion (the "Louisiana Tigers"), was supposed to be composed entirely of Irish wharf rats from the New Orleans docks. In some ways, it was not a bad thing in a democracy to have such a diverse army. On the other hand, the immigrants often spoke no English—in the 27th Pennsylvania, "the intercourse between officers as well as men is in German"—and the foreign-born officers were just as likely to have their expertise thrown back in their faces by resentful native-born Americans. (Ironically, that resentment did not extend to foreign military *dress:* given the reputation of the French Army as the embodiment of military dash and sizzle, volunteer regiments like the 18th Massachusetts and 74th New York or the 23rd and 114th Pennsylvania borrowed the patterns of French specialty units and kitted themselves out as chasseurs, in "red pants, white leggings, blue jacket, with broad red chevrons and shoulder knots, and cap with blue band, red above and blue top," or as Zouaves, the elite shock troops of France's Armeé d'Afrique, with rounded monkey jackets, two rows of brass buttons, and baggy trousers "in broad folds" and a "pleated waist.")[8]

The Regular officers who were embedded with the volunteers to give them some professional stiffening privately regarded them as uncontrollable adolescents who kicked off every back-home restraint the moment they were on campaign. During the Mexican War, austere General Winfield Scott complained to the secretary of war that "our militia & volunteers, if a tenth of what is said be true, have committed atrocities—horrors—in Mexico, sufficient to make Heaven weep, & every American, of Christian morals, blush for his country." What Scott meant by *atrocities* was not the torture, mauling, or execution of enemy combatants, but an epidemic of petty theft, happy-go-lucky foraging, and a general spirit of carnival whenever the volunteers felt like it. They learned to let the admonitions of the professionals at headquarters go in one ear and out the other, and it was no different a decade and a half later. "Whenever we stop for twenty-four hours," wrote one horrified Confederate medical officer in the 13th South Carolina, "every corn field and orchard within two or three miles is completely stripped. The troops not only rob the fields, but they go to houses and insist on being fed, until they eat up everything about a man's premises which can be eaten."[9]

Judged beside the volunteers, the Regulars were the apex of military professionalism; judged beside their counterparts in the European armies, they seemed little better than the volunteers. The prewar Regular Army had almost nothing in the way of an administrative staff (the Confederate armies had an average of only five staff officers at each command level, as compared to fifty for the armies of Napoleon Bonaparte), and few staff officers were expected to serve as more than glorified orderlies. Staff appointments often went to relatives and favorites, and routine staff functions, from provost guards to company clerks, had to be improvised from scratch by robbing personnel from the ordinary regimental rolls. In the Prussian service, staff officers were trained to be "land artists" and the chief of the Prussian general staff, Helmuth von Moltke, created a comprehensive map system of the Prussian kingdom which he used for war gaming, lecturing, and strategic planning. But in America, the best prewar map of Virginia was a nine-sheet affair with a scale of only five miles to the inch that was first published in 1827. Even on their own ground in Virginia, complained Richard Taylor, a Confederate general and the son of onetime U.S. president Zachary Taylor, "the Confederate commanders . . . were without maps, sketches, or proper guides" and "knew no more about the topography of the country than they did about Central Africa."

Nor did they have any concept of the transportation requirements for armies which could easily amount to more than 50,000 men, nor any sense of how the railroads and telegraph lines (which had only begun to spread their webs over the American landscape in the 1840s) might be brought to bear on directing them. Regimental medical staffs might include a doctor and one or two orderlies, but their practical function was to prevent "shirkers" from absenting themselves from duty, not provide medical care. Sanitary inspection was beyond consideration. One Union scout later remarked that "awful bad air" was a sure giveaway of the nearness of Confederate soldiers, since "the smell simply indicated the presence of the rebel army in the neighborhood." A Pennsylvania civilian remarked sourly that "a column" of Confederate cavalry "can be smelled as far as a slave ship."[10]

Under such circumstances, what was it that kept the volunteers to their task as they twined their way northward toward Gettysburg in that long summer of 1863? It was certainly not that they "liked to fight just for the fun of it; I did not for one, I well know," recalled a member of the 11th Virginia. His opposite number in the 155th Pennsylvania agreed: "The anxiety for battle and thirst for gore and terms so freely used by descriptive writers, belongs to the domain of fiction, and describes a sentiment far from the truth."

For most in the Union Army, the war was a campaign to save liberal democracy from a conspiracy to replant European-style aristocracy in America. Augustus Horstmann, a German-born captain in the 45th New York, thought the war in America was "much the same as it is in Germany, the free and industrious people of the North are fighting against the lazy and haughty Junker spirit of the South." "Freedom is the same everywhere," agreed a Danish-born captain in the 15th Massachusetts, when he spoke of the American Union as the keystone of a universal desire for the cause of freedom. "I cheerfully give my life in its defense. I would give more if I had it." And then there was slavery. The war might have begun "for the preservation of the Union," wrote a soldier in the 10th Massachusetts, but "all were equally aware that it could not continue a very great while without trouble over the slavery question," and by 1863 that "question" had already induced President Lincoln to issue an Emancipation Proclamation as "the [death] knell of the institution of slavery in this Country."[11]

Moreover, as citizen-volunteers, they fought "in obedience to the dictates of duty and of patriotism," not in "personal hatred toward those who for the time they call enemies." Thomas Hyde remembered riding out on the Union picket lines along the Rappahannock River, and seeing "a tall lank rebel dressed in 'butternut' . . . step out from his picket post in the woods across the river and gravely present arms, while I scrupulously returned the salute." These volunteers were neither indifferent praetorians nor soulless cosmopolitans. Leonidas Torrance of the 13th North Carolina writing home to answer his sister's questions about what Yankees were like merely replied that "If you were to see a yankey you would think it was a man too. (They are nothing more than other men.)" They occupied a shifting arena which was part chivalry and part piracy, an amalgam of prankster, protector, and avenger, capable at one moment of self-interested thievery and at another of self-limiting innocence, and they invested their struggle with a tragic nobility, because defending their republic meant estranging themselves from the anti-aristocratic values which formed its soul.[12]

Defending slavery deprived the Confederate soldier of the same claim to nobility, but not to tragedy. "I have seen men who have spent their whole lives in affluent circumstances and in rural pursuits, men who have led quiet and peaceable lives," said the Marquess of Hartington (the leader of the Liberal Party) in the House of Commons, after visiting the Confederacy in 1862,

I have seen them serving as privates in regiments of their States, serving badly clothed, badly fed, perhaps hardly with shoes upon their feet. . . . I

have seen men who have lived all their lives in poverty, who you would say have nothing to lose and nothing to gain, who had no interest in slavery, but who have joined with as much readiness as those who had the ranks of the army—I have seen these men in their camps as cheerful as possible, and asking for nothing but again to be led to battle with the enemy. . . . I say surely a people animated with such a feeling . . . [are] not a people who are going to give in.

Like their Union counterparts, many Confederates saw themselves as fighting for home and county, or for "sectional and financial interests," and some "for the inestimable right of self-government." Harry Handerson, who enlisted in the 9th Louisiana, was actually born and educated in the North, but emigrated to Louisiana in 1859 to become a tutor in a plantation family. "All my interests lay in the South and with Southerners, and if the seceding States, in one of which I resided, chose deliberately to try the experiment of self-government, I felt quite willing to give them such aid as lay in my feeble power." At the same time, there is no use denying that many quite frankly fought to protect slavery, which laid on the survivors of the rebel armies an incubus to which few were willing to admit in later years. More than one out of three Confederates whose campfires dotted South Mountain in the June dusk owned slaves or were the sons of households owning slaves, and more than half of their officers were slave owners. And they brought slaves with them on campaign to tend to the menial jobs that, in the Union armies, had to be performed by enlisted men or civilian hires. They were touchy, disinclined to take advice, and pulled between religious imaginings and creek-bank carousing. The slave system had invested them with an instinctive impulse for domestic dictatorship; they could brawl, stab, and shoot, in and out of race tracks and saloons, and still assume that they were God's natural aristocrats. Alexis de Tocqueville, in his sojourn through the United States in 1831, found Southerners "high-minded, prompt, irascible, ardent in his desires, impatient of obstacles," but also "easy to discourage if he cannot triumph with the first stroke."[13]

What carried these particular Confederates as far as they had come also had a great deal to do with their confidence and adulation for the man who commanded them—"the idol of his soldiers & the Hope of His Country," and the "only man living in whom they would unreservedly trust all power for the preservation of their independence," who "combines the organizing capacity of a Marlborough, the intuition of a Turenne, the celerity of a Napoleon, and the tenacity of a Wellington." His name was Robert E. Lee.[14]

CHAPTER TWO

There were never such men in an army before

MARLBOROUGH WAS FIFTY-FOUR at the time of his victory over the French at Blenheim; Wellington was forty-six at Waterloo. At fifty-five, Robert Edward Lee was older than either in the summer of 1863, but the impression he made on soldiers and spectators easily rivaled the image of the great dukes. "He is six feet in height, weighs about one hundred and ninety pounds; is erect, well formed, and of imposing appearance," wrote a Confederate journalist. He had grown a beard at the beginning of the war (a military fashion popularized by the British Army in the Crimean War), although both that and the jet-black hair and mustache he had in 1861 quickly turned gray, and then silvered over to white. "He is exceedingly plain in his dress," sometimes wearing "a long linen duster, which so enveloped his uniform as to make it invisible, topped off with "a wide-brimmed straw hat," and sometimes in a "well-worn long gray jacket, a high black felt hat, and blue trousers tucked into his Wellington boots." He wore none of the usual Confederate officer's gold braiding on his sleeves to indicate his rank, only "three stars on his collar" and "a military cord around the crown" of the hat. "No man," wrote a Richmond newspaper, "is superior in all that constitutes a soldier and the gentleman—no man more worthy to head our forces and lead our army."[1]

This was a judgment that few people would have been inclined to make only two years before. "When Gen. Lee took command there was really very little known of him generally," admitted Edward Porter Alexander, who would later become one of Lee's most talented officers. He was the fifth child of one of George Washington's favorite devil-may-care cavalrymen, "Light-Horse Harry" Lee, and Anne Hill Carter. Light-Horse Harry was a spendthrift and a rake, and when he abandoned them, one step ahead of his creditors, Robert, his siblings, and his mother were thrown back on the resources of their Carter relations. He learned from that to prefer "my own kith & kin to any one elses," and when he married, it was to one of his cousins, Mary Anna Custis.[2]

Lee entered West Point in 1825 and went on to graduate second in his class, without a single behavioral demerit. But any gloating was buried beneath self-discipline, a punctiliousness about paying debts, and a reserve which made him seem to Mary Chesnut, the greatest of Confederate diary keepers, to be "so cold and quiet and grand."[3] And although the Custis marriage settled Robert Lee financially and put a permanent roof over his head in the form of the Custis mansion, Arlington, Lee stayed with the army rather than earn the reputation of a sponger. During the Mexican War, he made an immediate and admiring impression on his commanding officer, Winfield Scott. Lee was "the very best soldier I ever saw in the field," Scott wrote to the secretary of war in 1857, and Scott later prophesied that Lee "is the greatest soldier now living, and if he ever gets the opportunity, he will prove himself the greatest captain of history."[4]

Lee never indulged much hope for the future for slavery. "In this enlightened age, there are few I believe, but what will acknowledge, that slavery as an institution, is a moral & political evil in any Country," Lee wrote in 1856. But in his mind, emancipation "will sooner result from the mild & melting influence of Christianity, than the storms & tempests of fiery controversy." And so Lee deplored slavery—and still held slaves, rented slaves, and on one occasion whipped them. As the Union began to tear itself apart over slavery in the winter of 1860–61, Lee felt a similar ambivalence. His long service in the army, and in so many different locales, made it obvious to him that the American republic "contained no North, no South, no East no west, but embraced the broad Union, in all its might and strength, present and future." But when Virginia finally made up its mind to join the Confederacy in April 1861, Lee was pulled in the other direction by the enormous debts he owed to the "kith and kin" who had kept him afloat in his youth. Lee had never owned a square inch of Virginia soil in his own name, and thought of the Lower South fire-eaters as a malignant political cancer; but Virginia's people had been the single safety net that his mother and her children had known, and to that intervention Lee owed everything.[5]

Despite the pleas of Winfield Scott, and an offer of high command from Abraham Lincoln, Lee resigned from the only professional world he had ever known. He was promptly commissioned as a brigadier general of Virginia state volunteers and adopted by Jefferson Davis, the Confederate president, as his chief military adviser. But he was only too well aware of the likely consequences, both for himself and the South. Arlington was immediately occupied by Federal troops, rendering him homeless and penniless at the same time. Nor did he have much confidence that the Confederacy could summon enough military vigor to resist the pounding the industrial North was likely to give it. "When this war began, I was opposed to it, bitterly opposed to it," Lee remarked to his son, "and I told these people that, unless every man should do whole duty, they would repent it." But even if they did that duty, the odds remained long ones. If there was any chance for victory, it would come through invading the North and so demoralizing Northern public opinion that "a revolution among their people" would force the Lincoln government to give up.[6]

But in 1861, invading the North was not the strategy preferred by Southerners who wanted to portray the Confederacy as the injured party in this war. Confederate troops instead stood inertly on the defensive in both the West, in Tennessee, and in the East, in northern Virginia, and field command of the Confederate troops in Virginia went instead to an old friend of Lee's from West Point, Joseph E. Johnston, who likewise preferred to wait, defensively, for the Federal forces to act. When they did, Johnston merely fell back farther, ignoring Lee's advice "to turn against Washington" and attack "with his whole force." As a Federal invasion finally did appear, and crept closer to the Confederate capital at Richmond in the spring of 1862, Johnston was severely wounded at the battle of Seven Pines, and into his place Jefferson Davis thrust Lee.[7]

From that moment, people saw another man, the aggressive, temperamental, almost reckless Lee, the long repressed son of Light-Horse Harry. Just after Lee's appointment to field command, Porter Alexander remembered being brought up short by a colleague for wondering if Lee had the aggressiveness needed to drive back the Federal invaders. "Alexander," he was told, "if there is one man in either army, Federal or Confederate, who is, head & shoulders, far above every other one in either army in audacity that man is Gen. Lee. . . . Lee is audacity personified." Jefferson Davis discovered the same thing—"Lee's natural temper was combative"—and so did an English journalist who watched Lee prepare to take on the Federal hosts. "No man who, at the terrible moment, saw his flashing eyes and sternly-set lips, is ever like to forget them" or "the light of battle . . . flaming in his eyes." Lee was, said John Mosby, the "most aggressive man I met in the war, and was always ready for any enterprise," never happier than when he could cast his doubts and the scabbard away together.[8]

The enterprise immediately at hand was to reshape the sprawling force he inherited from Joe Johnston and use it to save the threatened Confederate capital. Johnston had already found it necessary to begin sorting the multi-

tude of Confederate volunteer regiments into brigades (of four or more regiments) and then divisions (of three or more brigades). Now, taking charge
of an army which had grown to almost 92,000 men, Lee organized the force
into two *corps d'armée*, and put these corps into the hands of the two most
aggressive officers he could find, the South Carolina–born James Longstreet
and a onetime Virginia Military Institute instructor, Thomas Jonathan Jackson, who had earned the first great nickname of the war—"Stonewall." And
he made official the name by which this army would be known until it surrendered its last banner—the Army of Northern Virginia.[9]

On June 26, 1862, Lee and the Army of Northern Virginia uncoiled and
struck. Over the course of one week, Lee crowded the Federal army back to
the James River in a series of deadly battles in Richmond's outlying towns—
Mechanicsville, Gaines' Mill, Savage's Station, Frayser's Farm, Malvern
Hill—bounded aggressively up into northern Virginia to wallop another
Federal force twenty miles outside Washington, and then bolted across the
Potomac into Maryland, aimed at Pennsylvania. This miraculous reversal of
fortune was carried along by Lee's belief that only by shifting the fighting
onto Northern soil and transferring "this campaign from the banks of the
James to those of the Susquehanna" could the Confederacy hope to collapse
Northern public confidence to the point of demanding a negotiated peace.
But Lee's invasion plans were thwarted when a copy of his campaign orders
fell into Federal hands, and he was forced to fight an outnumbered battle at
Antietam Creek in September 1862. He withdrew sullenly back to Virginia.
But he never stopped hoping to carry the war northward. "If I could do so,
I would again cross the Potomac and invade Pennsylvania," Lee insisted. "I
believe this to be our true policy." Not only would an invasion of Pennsylva-
nia in 1862 have given "our people an opportunity to collect supplies" in an
untouched enemy granary, but "we would have been in a few days' march of
Philadelphia, and the occupation of that city would have given us peace."

He would have moved sooner in that direction but for two more determined Federal thrusts toward Richmond. Lee stopped them both, at Fredericksburg in December 1862, and at Chancellorsville in May 1863. But he knew
that defensive victories won on Virginia's soil would only end up wearing
down Confederate resistance. "At Fredericksburg," Lee admitted, "our people
were greatly elated" but "I was much depressed. We had really accomplished
nothing; we had not gained a foot of ground, and I knew the enemy could
easily replace the men he had lost." The same thing happened after Chancellorsville. "Our people were wild with delight—I, on the contrary, was more
depressed than after Fredericksburg; our loss was severe, and again we had
gained not an inch of ground and the enemy could not be pursued." Sitting

on the defensive in Virginia also spelled deterioration for his army's discipline. Northern Virginia was "so cleaned out that one can forage to no purpose now," and as commissary officers and ordinary men in the ranks scavenged the Old Dominion's depleted fields and pastures ever more desperately, they would gradually disintegrate into what one Alabama officer described as "little better than an armed mob."[10]

But the ultimate proof of the folly of a defensive war was the death of Stonewall Jackson at Chancellorsville. Accidentally wounded by fire from his own corps, Jackson lingered for eight days until he died on May 10, 1863. With this awkward, blue-eyed, relentlessly devout Presbyterian from the western Virginia mountains, Lee had developed an almost intuitive rapport. His death was "a terrible loss. . . . Such an executive officer the sun never shone on. I have but to show him my design, and I know that if it can be done it will be done." Jackson's death was also a warning that the attrition of war would only keep grinding up the Confederacy's best officers and men unless the torch was made to burn on Northern soil and Northerners became disheartened enough to quit. "As far as I can judge," Lee wrote to Confederate secretary of war James A. Seddon, "there is nothing to be gained by this army remaining quietly on the defensive. . . . I am aware that there is difficulty & hazard in taking the aggressive with so large an army in its front," but a new offensive aimed at the North was "worth a trial" rather than sitting and waiting to be overwhelmed. "All our military preparations and organizations should now be pressed forward with the greatest vigor." If so, then "next fall there will be a great change in public opinion in the North" and "the friends of peace will become so strong" that a "distinct and independent national existence" would finally be conceded to the Confederacy.[11]

The death of Stonewall Jackson had one silver opportunity concealed within its black folds, and that was a further reorganization of the command structure of the Army of Northern Virginia "to simplify the mechanism . . . as much as possible." Under Jackson and Longstreet, Lee had created two corps large enough (with 30,000 to 35,000 men each, in four or five divisions) for both men to use their own discretion and judgment without requiring Lee to overseeing the tactical details of battles. As Lee himself explained to the Prussian engineer and military observer Justus Scheibert, "I plan and work with all my might to bring the troops to the right place at the right time; with that I have done my duty." From that point on, it was his corps commanders who must take charge: "It is my generals' turn to perform their duty." Happily, in Jackson and Longstreet, Lee had officers who could fill that bill. But in anyone else's hands, a corps the size of Jackson's or Longstreet's might prove so big as to become clumsy, or worse, might call for a degree of micromanagement that Lee and his diminutive staff might not be able to deliver. "Some of our divisions exceed the army Genl Scott entered the city of Mexico with, & our brigades are larger than his divisions," Lee explained, and that created stupendous headaches in "causing orders & req[uisitio]ns to be obeyed."[12]

Rather than merely appoint a successor to Jackson, Lee peeled off brigades from Jackson's and Longstreet's old commands, and together with the addition of new levies from North Carolina, created an entirely new third corps in the Army of Northern Virginia. Each corps in the Army of Northern Virginia would now contain three divisions, or about 25,000 to 30,000 infantrymen, and each division between three and five brigades. There would necessarily be a good deal of shuffling and reshuffling—new staffs would have to be created, old ones redistributed, colonels in command of regiments would find themselves scratching heads over the manner and personalities of new brigade commanders, and so on up the ladder—but Lee felt no unease over the ordinary soldiers' ability to adjust. "There were never such men in an army before," Lee believed. "They will go anywhere and do anything if properly led."[13]

But this, of course, was the catch. "Nothing prevented my proposing to you to reduce" the size of the army's corps as far back as the winter, he told Davis, "but my inability to recommend commanders." At least in the case of James Longstreet, the senior corps commander, he had "a Capital soldier" who was already "the Staff of my right hand." Longstreet was forty-two years old that summer, an imposing six-feet, two-inches tall and a bulky 220 pounds, with a heavy brown beard, and a short Austrian-style gray officer's jacket "on the collar of which the devices indicating his rank were scarcely distinguishable." He had pig's-eyes, vigilant and inspecting, was grudgingly deferential, and "a man of very few words." But he had the knack, rare in the Civil War armies, of knowing how to "handle and arrange large numbers of troops . . . and he seems to manage a division of eight or ten thousand men with as much ease as he would a company of fifty men." His weakness was a streak of "obstinacy and self-assertion," and his "jealousy of advice was so great that really at times it seemed as if he preferred that of the enemy rather than to take it from one of his subordinates." But even if he could not take advice, Longstreet could certainly take orders, and along with that, he had a slugger's instinct for knowing how to drive into an enemy where it hurt most. In 1862, it was Longstreet who urged Lee to keep attacking the Federal army at Malvern Hill, despite the superior position the Federals had on the hilltop, and at Antietam, Lee hailed him as "my old *war-horse!*" His soldiers regarded him as "a bully general" and "real bulldog fighter" who "drives the Yankees whenever he meets them," and they loaded him with nicknames—"Old Peter" and the "Bull of the Woods." In the estimate of the Austro-Hungarian soldier-of-fortune Bela Estvàn, Longstreet was simply "one of the ablest generals of the Confederate army."[14]

Filling the slots for the other two corps was a dicier affair. Richard Stoddert Ewell and Ambrose Powell Hill were next in seniority among the Army of Northern Virginia's generals, and both had served as division commanders under Stonewall Jackson. But Powell Hill, a nervous, wiry man with a persistent chip of underappreciation on his shoulder and a bevy of chronic illnesses when under stress, had managed to antagonize nearly everyone else in Jackson's corps, including Jackson himself, whom Hill denounced as "that crazy old Presbyterian fool." The pity was that Powell Hill was precisely the kind of cantankerous, combative officer that Lee wanted in command; at Antietam, Hill had driven his division unmercifully on the roads up from Harpers Ferry, hit the Federals by surprise, and saved the Army of Northern Virginia from destruction. Lee thought Powell Hill was "upon the whole . . . the best soldier of his grade with me." But Jackson's staff neither forgot nor forgave Hill's "very hot-headed and badly disciplined temper," and so it was easier, both in terms of seniority and personalities, to let Jackson's old corps go to Richard Ewell, and assign Hill to command the newly minted third corps.[15]

Not that Dick Ewell was everyone's first choice, either. Ewell was another West Pointer, two years ahead of Longstreet and seven ahead of Powell Hill, who had served in Mexico and in Arizona, chasing Apaches, and who was accounted on all hands to be "a superb rider" and "upright, brave and devoted." But he was also "a queer character, very eccentric," with a peculiar pop-eyed look and a bald, domelike head which gave him something of the appearance of a nervous pigeon. Under Jackson (who took all prizes for eccentricity), Ewell developed into a first-rate division commander, and during Jackson's lightning campaign in the Shenandoah Valley in 1862, Ewell showed a commendable willingness to take matters into his own hands by attacking the Federal defenders of Winchester "without instructions" from Stonewall. But Jackson could be a quixotic master. (Ewell once complained that he never knew when his next orders would be for a march on the North Pole.) What this taught Ewell was to use his own judgment when he was on his own, but to wait for point-by-point orders when his superiors were close at hand and he could determine whether or not "his advice will be ungraciously received & perhaps his interference rebuked." It did not help Ewell's sense of self-reliance that he had been out of action for ten months, after a Federal bullet crushed his left kneecap and splintered the bone below at the second battle of Bull Run. All of the leg from thigh downward had to be amputated, and he now got around mostly on crutches or with an "ill-contrived" wooden prosthesis.[16]

As a result, all that Robert E. Lee saw in Ewell was a "want of decision."

But he could not vault Powell Hill over Ewell's place on the army list, and he quieted his reservations with the reflection that Ewell was "an honest, brave soldier, who has always done his duty well." It would not have given Lee more ease if he had known that Ewell had reservations of his own about both the war and his aptness for corps command. "I don't feel up to a separate command," he wrote, with more humility than his record under Jackson justified, and after the trauma of the amputation Ewell had no desire to "see the carnage and shocking sights of another field of battle." Still, Ewell was "the choice of all the soldiers as well as the officers" of Jackson's corps. And Lee did not have a large pool of experienced division commanders from which to choose. Jubal Early, who had also commanded a division under Jackson and who now became the senior division commander under Ewell, was "active, enterprising, and diligent," but also "never blessed with popular or captivating manners" and generally regarded as sarcastic, brusque, and irascible. (It was probably Early who, "looking at the Yankees with a dark scowl on his face, exclaimed most emphatically, 'I wish they were all dead,'" only to earn the rebuke from Lee, "I wish they were all at home, attending to their own business, leaving us to do the same.")[17]

The reorganization of the Army of Northern Virginia would eventually boost more (and better) up-and-coming officers from brigade to division command, but it would take time for them to prove themselves equal to their new rank, much less one beyond it, and it would sometimes make for serious misjudgments. Harry Heth was a particular example of this. Heth's grandfather and father had fought in the Revolution and the War of 1812, and the family's coal-mining business gave the young Harry expensive tastes. But when his father's death spelled the end of the Heth family's good living, Harry was packed off for an education to West Point, where he enjoyed the reputation of a "gay reveler" and an abominable student. He managed only two promotions between graduating in 1847 and the outbreak of the Civil War and then spent most of his time in garrison duties and in the West. But Heth had a certain aristocratic dash and charm that took the notice of Jefferson Davis and he became a particular protégé of Lee's. In February 1863, Heth was given a brigade to command in Powell Hill's division, and then promoted again to division command in Hill's new corps.

This was a mistake. Heth had little experience under fire, and an earlier petition for Heth's promotion had been turned down by the Confederate Senate. His primary strength, apart from Lee's sponsorship, was that he was one of the few people who could call Powell Hill a friend. William Dorsey Pender, a serious, pious North Carolinian who had only graduated from West Point in 1854, was also given one of Hill's divisions, and also partly because Pender and Hill got along. But much as Pender was recommended by Lee "on account of valour & skill displayed on many fields, & particularly at the battle of Chancellorsville," Lee had also erupted at Pender after Chancellorsville for failing to pursue the retreating Federals. "That is what you young men always do," Lee upbraided him. "You allow these people to get away. I tell you what to do, but you don't do it."[18]

It did nothing to ease the friction between the army's personalities to discover that the Army of Northern Virginia was a divided house in political respects, as well. Its name made it a Virginia army, and its commanding general was a Virginian, and so were the commanding general's personal and general staff. (Even Lee's personal military escort were two companies from the 39th Virginia Cavalry Battalion.) But Virginia's forty-three regiments amounted to less than a quarter of the Confederate infantry on the march up to Gettysburg in 1863; Georgia contributed thirty-six regiments, Mississippi eleven, distant Louisiana ten, and North Carolina outstripped them all (including Virginia) with forty-four. Nevertheless, the two new corps appointments went to Virginians, which made for "no little discontent" and a "serious feeling" of what James Longstreet called "too much Virginia" on the part of the rest of the army. "Do you know," asked one of Longstreet's division commanders, a Georgian, that "there is a strong feeling growing among the Southern troops against Virginia, caused by the jealousy of her own people for those from every other state? . . . No matter how trifling the deed may be which a Virginian performs it is heralded at once as the most glorious of modern times."[19]

Added to these slights was the growing suspicion directed by the Richmond government at the political steadiness of the army's Georgia and North Carolina troops. Georgia's governor, Joseph E. Brown, was notoriously critical of Jefferson Davis, and by the summer of 1863 a "sudden lukewarmness had come over many of our people," to the point where "the State will stand a chance of being handed over to the Lincoln government." North Carolinians were made to feel that their state had been "slow to leave the old Government" (or "did not secede quite soon enough to suit some other slave states") and remained a "source of Unionism." True enough, some of the North Carolina regiments were not all that tactful about suggesting that "the State of South Carolina ought to be sunk" because that "was where the trouble started." But that meant, in turn, that pro-secession partisans like John Bell Hood, who commanded a division in Longstreet's corps, professed "no confidence in his Carolinians."[20]

The chill of suspicion cast in the direction of North Carolina was exacerbated by "a most disgraceful spirit of desertion" in North Carolina regiments. Leonidas Torrance in the 13th North Carolina gloomily reported on the embarrassing seepage of deserters from North Carolina units in the spring of 1863. "There was 4 men run the gantlet [i.e., whipping by the whole regiment] in the 5th N.C. Regt the Saturday before . . . for going Home with out lief," and "one of them died the 8th day after he was whipped." In his own regiment, Torrance could count "14 of this Regt in the guard house for the same crime." In the 43rd North Carolina, an anxious captain wrote that "men are running away very bad," as poor whites from the western mountains, with a much lower investment in defending slavery, registered their dissent by taking French leave and deserting "in squads, with their arms." But the response of the Richmond government was to appoint politically reliable secession enthusiasts like Alfred Iverson to command North Carolina brigades, and to practice "a studied exclusion of all ones termed anti-secessionists" from promotion. "If these facts taken together do not constitute a class of suspicion against the great body of our people," complained North Carolina's governor, Zebulon Vance, "I am unable to conceive what would."[21]

Governor Vance's worry about the play of politics in the Army of Northern Virginia was, as it turned out, hugely overmatched by the political travails of the Federal army camped opposite Lee on the north bank of the Rappahannock River. "Unquestionably," wrote Horace Greeley, the first six months of 1863 were "the darkest hours of the National Cause," in both political and military terms. The Democratic opposition in the U.S. Congress had found a new voice to rally around, that of Clement Vallandigham, the charismatic congressman from Ohio who was boosted to the level of near-martyr in May 1863 when Federal troops arrested him, after a campaign rally in his native Ohio, for denouncing this "wicked, cruel, and unnecessary war." The great campaign to capture Richmond in 1862 had fizzled into failure, and with only a brief respite at Antietam it had stumbled bloodily into defeat again at Fredericksburg and Chancellorsville. A massive naval assault on Charleston harbor in April likewise fizzled despite the use of new ironclad warships. Lincoln's Emancipation Proclamation and the first authorization to recruit black soldiers for the Union Army had been met with howling indignation by white Northerners who imagined that the war was being waged solely for the purpose of national reunion. "I am a strong union man," insisted one Massachusetts artilleryman, "but I am not willing to shed one drop of blood to fight Slavery up or down." In the West, Federal forces were plagued by "the wholesale desertion of the troops who leave a hundred at a time."[22]

Predictably, Northern voters punished Lincoln and the Republicans in the fall 1862 midterm elections. The Republican majority in the House of Representatives shrank by thirty-one seats, and Republican governors were unseated by antiwar Democrats in New York and New Jersey. Abraham Lincoln's longtime political friend Orville Hickman Browning (one of those Republicans in the Senate whose head went off in the elections), "thinks our cause hopeless" and believed "we were upon the brink of ruin." War-weariness "looks like a great, sweeping revolution of public sentiment," moaned the New York Republican lawyer George Templeton Strong. "All is up. . . . The Historical Society should secure an American flag at once for its museum of antiquities." Even more unpopular was the new national draft law, passed by the lame-duck Congress on March 3, 1863, which was denounced across New York and Pennsylvania as "oppressive, unjust, and unconstitutional," and "openly threatened" with riot when enrollment of eligible draftees would begin in June and July. One New York politician-turned-general wailed that "an impression, almost a belief, gains ground that for military, economical, and political reasons the success of the North is doubtful." Robert E. Lee had not been seeing visions when he predicted that one more firm, aggressive— and this time, successful—Confederate invasion of the North might be all that was needed to bring the Lincoln administration to the negotiating table. "No bright spark seems to arise," lamented a soldier in the 142nd Pennsylvania on May 21st. "All is dark and gloomy."[23]

A great deal of the trouble lay at the very top of the Federal Army. At the beginning of the war, the 30,000 militia and volunteers who rallied around Washington to defend the capital had marched confidently into Virginia, only to have their noses bloodied in an embarrassingly lame defeat at a meandering little creek called Bull Run. Determined to put this host back on its feet, Lincoln called in the one man whom Winfield Scott had rated even above Robert E. Lee, the talented and elegant George Brinton McClellan. Born to an upper-crust Philadelphia family, second in his class at West Point, tapped for staff service with Scott in Mexico and as the junior member of the military commission sent to Europe in 1855 to report on the state of the European armies, and then (after leaving the army in 1857) vice president of the Illinois Central Railroad, McClellan glittered as he rode into the dispirited army camps around Washington in the late summer of 1861. He sorted them into brigades, divisions, and corps, trained and drilled them, and gave them, on the French pattern, their own name—the Army of the Potomac. "McClellan had the most extraordinary results in the organization and discipline of his troops," wrote an appreciative Pennsylvania politico, Alexander McClure, "and there was every reason to believe that the Army of the Potomac was a most efficient military force, and that it had the one commander best fitted to lead it to victory." And the army, in turn, adored McClellan. "He was one of those few men in history who had the faculty of making his men love him," remembered a veteran of a New York regiment. He became "the idol of the old soldiers," who regarded him as "the greatest strategist the war brought to the front."[24]

The problem was, as a soldier in the 71st Pennsylvania afterward reflected, that McClellan "loved the army better [than] he loved the Cause . . . which he was engaged for." McClellan could not contain a silver-spoon contempt for Lincoln as "the *original gorilla*" and "an idiot," and for the Republicans in Congress and the cabinet as "imbeciles." And as a Democrat, he displayed only lukewarm interest in emancipation, and picked quarrels with Lincoln over the political loyalties of the officers appointed to corps command. "You know McClellan as well as I do," wrote one unsympathetic officer to Treasury Secretary Salmon Chase, "& I will not describe him further than to say that Jeff Davis has not a greater repugnance to, nor less confidence in, Republicans than has McClellan." And there would always remain some question about the extent to which McClellan allowed his military judgments to be influenced by his political ones, especially after he took it upon himself to use the prisoner of war exchange system to invite clandestine negotiations for peace between himself and the Richmond government. The Young Napoleon might have gotten away with more of this, had he not turned out to be considerably less talented as a field commander in battle than he was as an organizer and cheerleader. The campaign he designed against Richmond in the spring of 1862 failed nervelessly in the face of Robert E. Lee's aggressive hounding. Although McClellan partially redeemed himself by cornering Lee at Antietam, he failed to pursue Lee with anything that looked like eagerness, and balked for a month after Lincoln issued the preliminary version of the Emancipation Proclamation before publishing it as a general order to the Army of the Potomac. Lincoln finally sacked him in November 1862.[25]

But the Army of the Potomac never lost its affection for McClellan. "Little Mac," recalled the veterans of the 42nd Pennsylvania, "possessed the hearts of nine out of every ten." Nor did political bickering over emancipation in the army cease with McClellan's departure. The ineffectiveness of the army "lies in the personal rivalries and more than doubtful policies of some of its . . . corps commanders," complained the abolitionist newspaper *Wilkes' Spirit of the Times*. These McClellanites "had a sort of fealty to McClellan . . . and would not permit a new man to rise to glory over his eclipse." One captain in the 2nd Wisconsin remembered that "many officers talked open treason, while in the ranks men reviled the Government, and nearly all seemed to agree that the war for the Union had degenerated into a 'war for the nigger.'" Lincoln hoped to placate the McClellanites by appointing as McClellan's successor a close friend of McClellan's, Ambrose Burnside. But Burnside nearly bled the army to death at Fredericksburg, and unforgiving McClellan loyalists turned on Burnside as though the two men had never known each other. Since appeasement didn't work, Lincoln turned next to the most bitter anti-McClellanite general in the army, the maniacally ambitious Joseph Hooker, who "was violent in his denunciation of McClellan" and had grown conveniently ardent in support of emancipation.[26]

Hooker was a loud-mouthed bruiser with blazing bright eyes who projected a confidence which he did not, in the hollow core of his personality, really have. He promised to do as McClellan had *not* done, and force Lee and the Army of Northern Virginia to "either ingloriously fly, or come out from behind his defenses and give us battle on our own ground, where certain destruction awaits him." Instead, Hooker allowed Lee to swing a gigantic left hook (in the form of Stonewall Jackson's corps) through the tangled woods around Chancellorsville and send one of Hooker's corps fleeing in confusion. He then abandoned a key high-ground position in the center of his defensive line at Hazel Grove, only to suffer a concussion when a solid ball fired from Confederate artillery that had occupied Hazel Grove smashed into a porch pillar Hooker had been leaning against. Without even bothering to call up two unused corps of his army, the dazed and unhinged Hooker decreed yet another retreat. At once, the same knives which had been used on Burnside were turned on him. Darius Couch, the Army of the Potomac's senior corps commander, resigned in disgust over Hooker's failure, and the McClellanites, who "had against him the double grievance of his military judgments and of his political opinions," agitated for his "overthrow." Lincoln heard enough lewd rejoicing over Hooker's downfall that he had to warn him "that some of your corps and Division Commanders are not giving you their entire confidence." Even the men in the ranks of the 2nd Rhode Island hissed at Hooker as he rode past on the line of march, calling out, "Pull the Chancellorsville Murderer off that horse."[27]

One could, in fact, plot the political loyalties of the seven infantry corps of the Army of the Potomac on a rough line which, corps by corps and commander by commander, ran from the most pro-McClellan and anti-emancipation to the most pro-Lincoln and antislavery. Chief among the McClellanites was Winfield Scott Hancock, "one of McClellan's devoted friends and admirers," who inherited command of the 2nd Corps from the departing Darius Couch. John Sedgwick, commanding the 6th Corps, fell in behind Hancock, affirming that "I mean to stand or fall with McClellan"; Sedgwick even proposed passing the hat through the army to raise a "testimonial" to McClellan "to show that he still retains the love and confidence of the Army of the Potomac." And at the top of the 5th Corps, McClellan's fellow Philadelphian George Gordon Meade expressed "great confidence personally in McClellan—know him well—know he is one of the best men we have to handle large armies," and was perfectly happy to "make terms of some kind with the South." They were a crowd who frequented McClellan's headquarters, where they "talked freely, abused the civil administration and drank champagne out of a wooden bucket." Even on the division level, John Gibbon in Hancock's 2nd Corps frankly admitted that he "was a pro-slavery man," and in Sedgwick's 6th Corps, William Newton likewise conceded that "in argument the south had the better side of it." It was tempting for the McClellanites to imagine that they were the target of deep antislavery conspiracies: Hancock's wife was convinced that the War Department was planting spies among her household help, and Edward Cross of the 5th New Hampshire, who commanded a brigade in the 2nd Corps, hotly resented Lincoln's "attempt to make an abolition war," and believed that "the Army is full of Abolition spies, under the guise of tract distributors, State Agents—chaplains, Sanitary Commission Agents" and "correspondents of the Abolition papers."[28]

On the other hand, the McClellanites did not entirely rule the roost in the army. Hooker succeeded in weeding out a number of McClellan's favorites and replacing them with generals more favorable to the Lincoln administration. The commander of the 3rd Corps, the raffish New York ex-congressman Daniel Sickles, was a lifelong Democrat, but he also took a gratifyingly strong line on prosecuting the war. "The South must feel the overwhelming power of the Union," Sickles insisted, "and when they are compelled to acknowledge its supremacy, they will lay down their arms and not until then." Sickles was already "advocating the re-nomination and reelection of Abraham Lincoln" for 1864. Oliver Otis Howard, commanding the 11th Corps, was an ardent New England evangelical, an abolitionist, and a Republican. At the head of the 12th Corps, Henry Warner Slocum (although not exactly a friend of Joe Hooker's) was also a Republican and also no friend of McClellan's, and made his mark at West Point, "when it cost so much to do so," by his "free expression of opinon . . . as an opponent of human slavery." The "Hooker ring"—and especially its card-carrying Republican members—returned the paranoia of the McClellanites in spades. "There have been pro-slavery cliques controlling that army," complained one Republican general, "composed of men who, in my opinion, would not have been unwilling to make a compromise in favor of slavery, and who desired to have nobody put in authority except those who agreed with them on that subject." If these halfhearts had the chance, added George Templeton Strong, "they will all come together and agree on some compromise or adjustment, turn out Lincoln and his 'Black Republicans' and use their respective armies to enforce their decision North and South."[29]

Somewhere in the middle of the army's political spectrum was John Fulton Reynolds and his 1st Corps. Reynolds was a Pennsylvania Democrat who had once compared Lincoln to a "baboon," and believed that McClellan's removal was "as unwise and injudicious as it was uncalled for." Nevertheless, he was also a serious, unbending professional who, unlike McClellan, actually lived by the principle of "obedience to the powers that be." Consequently, Reynolds, "almost alone of all the corps commanders, had not been to Washington to instruct the authorities there how to organize and to operate the Army of the Potomac," and Reynolds' staffer Joseph Rosengarten admired Reynolds' policy of holding "stoutly aloof from all personal or partisan quarrels, and keeping guardedly free from any of the heart-burnings and jealousies that did so much to cripple the usefulness and endanger the reputation of many gallant officers."[30]

Moreover, Reynolds' 1st Corps had originally been a component of the short-lived Army of Virginia, an alternative to the Army of the Potomac organized under the abolitionist Major General John Pope in 1862, and all three of Reynolds' divisions were commanded by some of the Army's most fervent abolitionists—Abner Doubleday, James S. Wadsworth, and John Cleveland Robinson. Wadsworth had actually been the Republican candidate in the New York gubernatorial race in 1862, only to be denounced by New York Democrats as a "malignant Abolition disorganizer" and by George McClellan as "a pseudo-fanatic." Doubleday, with a large Johnsonian face that sagged like a sinking battleship, had been a lieutenant in the tiny garrison of Fort Sumter when the Confederates bombarded the post into submission, and from the first he had expected that his antislavery credentials would guarantee a rise to the top of Lincoln's army. What he discovered was (as his father had howled to the radical Republican senator Zachariah Chandler) that there were "not more than twenty avowed Republican Officers in the U.S. Army," and none of them was going to be welcomed to senior command. "Slavery had so long dominated every thing with a rod of iron that . . . all the avenues of promotion in the army and navy, lay in that direction." For the men in the ranks, "It is enough to make one sick, to see what fools we have for *Generals,*" wrote a soldier in Sickles' 3rd Corps. "I am about tired of Generals who are too afraid to be conquered to fight hard to conquer." A major in the 7th Ohio bewailed the "two years of marches, counter-marches, sieges, and battles" the Army of the Potomac had endured, with "but little territory . . . gained, and the possession of this little being constantly disputed by a well-organized and gallant" Confederate Army. From Lincoln's perspective, "the army is one vast hot-bed of bickerings, heart-burnings and jealousies." Marsena Patrick, the army's provost marshal general, almost expected "that this Army will be broken up, that it is so thoroughly McClellan as to be dangerous."[31]

That is, if it didn't disintegrate on its own. In the wake of McClellan's dismissal in November 1862, and the debacle at Fredericksburg in December, desertions from the Army of the Potomac reached hemophiliac proportions—200 a day by one estimate, and over 25,000 by the end of January. Joe Hooker had, in a surprisingly skillful display of both carrot and stick,

managed to restore and rebuild the army through the spring of 1863, bringing the number of deserters down to only 2,000 and ensuring that the army
was well fed and well equipped. But the promises of victory that Hooker so
lavishly spread around came to nothing at Chancellorsville in May; and what
was worse, approximately 30,000 of the men in the ranks of the Army of the
Potomac had been enlisted for two-year terms, rather than the customary
three-year volunteer service, or else had signed up for nine months' service
during the panic which greeted Lee's invasion of Maryland in the fall of 1862.
Those enlistments were due to expire in May and June 1863, taking away what
seemed to one Minnesota soldier to be "fully one-half of the fighting strength
of the old Army of the Potomac." This was the rankers' view; in terms of
actual numbers, the army could still field between 85,000 and 94,000 men
(allowing for sickness, leaves, and assignment to rear-echelon duties). More
serious damage was done to the inner workings of the army, which lost units
and officers that had otherwise been part of the day-to-day machinery of divisions and corps. John Reynolds' 1st Corps was reduced from 16,000 to 9,000
men, and within the 1st Corps, James Wadsworth's division was shrunk from
four to two brigades and John Cleveland Robinson's division from three to
two. Dan Sickles' 3rd Corps was downsized from three divisions to two. Not
even the commanders stayed still: not a single one of the major generals who
would command a corps at Gettysburg had been in command ten and a half
months before at Antietam; sixteen of the Army of the Potomac's nineteen
divisions got new commanding officers between Antietam and Gettysburg.[32]

And yet, the army survived its battering at Chancellorsville in far better
shape than it had Fredericksburg. "A sort of fatality had . . . settled down upon
the Army of the Potomac," the sense expressed by a corporal in the 71st Pennsylvania "that the Soldiers . . . must depend Only on themselves for fighting
out an honorable peace." A soldier in the 5th Maine rebuked the plea of his
wife in a letter ("don't go in to another battle for my sake") by telling her that
he wouldn't be worth having back "if we are called upon to go in to battle to
leave the ranks and fall back in the rear if I am able to go with them." And
they would fight with increasing clarity, resolved Oliver Edwards, a captain in
the 37th Massachusetts, "to leave the blessing of freedom to our children" in a
nation cleansed from "the foul blot of slavery." It almost surprised Edwards to
hear himself think this way. "You see," he added, "I am now a thorough 'Black
Republican' Abolitionist. Well, this war is a good school to make them."[33]

CHAPTER THREE

This Campaign is going to end this show

O UR MEN seem to be in the spirit and feel confident," wrote the newly promoted Confederate division commander William Dorsey Pender. "I wish we could meet Hooker and have the matter settled at once." But it was a good question whether Pender was likely to get his wish (or Lee to get his to invade Pennsylvania) so long as the military fortunes of the Confederacy were sagging in so many other places. In the West, the Confederacy had staked out ambitious ground for itself, planting rebel flags in western Kentucky, turning Missouri into a battleground, and choking off Northerners' access to the great economic throughway of the Ohio and Mississippi river valleys. This ambition quickly came unsprung. Federal troops successfully cleared Missouri and penetrated northern Arkansas by the spring of 1862. At the same time, still more Federal troops and river gunboats seized the vital Confederate posts on the Cumberland and Tennessee rivers in western Tennessee, forcing the principal Confederate army in the West to abandon Kentucky and most of Tennessee. The Federal Navy blew open the defenses of New Orleans at the far end of the Mississippi, and by the end of 1862 Confederate control of the Mississippi had shrunk to a single stretch of river between Port Hudson (in Louisiana) and Vicksburg. Three times, a Confederate field army tried to recover the lost territory in Tennessee and Kentucky, in battles at Shiloh, Perryville, and Murfreesboro. All three times it failed, and now the Confederacy was left barely clinging to the southeast corner of Tennessee, while a Union army was fastening its grip on Vicksburg. If these points were lost, nothing would stand between the Union forces and the vital economic intestines of the Confederacy in Georgia and Alabama, and the Confederacy would be as good as finished, no matter what happened in the East.

Even now, in the spring of 1863, an entire Federal infantry corps (the 9th Corps, under the unfortunate Ambrose Burnside) was being transferred to the Ohio River, and in Richmond it looked to Jefferson Davis as though a hammer blow was being prepared for the Confederacy on the other side of the Appalachians. Davis had only two aces to play in the West—the Confederate garrison holding Vicksburg, under John C. Pemberton, and the lone Confederate field army in the West, the Army of Tennessee, under Braxton Bragg. Overall Western command was in the hands of the now recovered Joe Johnston, and Johnston did not hesitate to tell Davis that concentration of Confederate military strength in the West was "our true system of warfare." The Confederacy could "beat the enemy here, and then reconquer the country beyond it which he might have gained in the mean time." In the same key, the *Charleston Mercury* insisted that an "invasion of Kentucky . . . can be made with a force of thirty or forty thousand men at least. A single great victory won by such a force over Burnside would roll the war back at once beyond Louisville and to the very banks of the Ohio."[1]

In March 1863, Jefferson Davis called Lee to Richmond to discuss the suggestion that Lee "detach a corps for service in the West" from the Army of Northern Virginia. Lee's response was cagey—a good idea, but "an unexpected activity has been exhibited by the enemy in Northern Virginia" which made it impossible for the moment. When Davis pressed him again two weeks later, Lee was still evasive. Joe Hooker's army, "from the zealous manner of guarding their lines, and the systematic propagation of reports of an intended advance of their armies on the Rappahannock," required keeping the Army of Northern Virginia together. In fact, Lee added, he was hoping "to make some aggressive movements" of his own, in the form of "a blow at Milroy, which I think will draw General Hooker out, or at least prevent further re-enforcements being sent to the west." (The Milroy in question was Robert H. Milroy, the commander of the Federal garrison at Winchester, Virginia, and it is with this casual reference to Winchester that the first dim outline of what would become the Gettysburg campaign makes its appearance.) Unappeased, Secretary of War Seddon pressed Lee: "I am . . . unwilling to send beyond your command any portion even of the forces here without your counsel and approval," but would Lee not at least consider parting with "two or three brigades"?[2]

The answer, of course, was *no*. Robert E. Lee had thrown away a lifelong career, thrown away, in fact, an oath sworn on his honor, for the sake of Virginia and all of the Virginians like his Carter cousins—"my relatives, my children, my home." Virginia was his all, and Virginia's success was the only hope he had of recouping all he had ventured for the Old Dominion's sake. What he would not give up for Winfield Scott and Abraham Lincoln, he was certainly not going to endanger for the sake of Jefferson Davis and James A. Seddon. "Save in defense of my native State, I never desire again to draw my sword"—those words, which Lee wrote to Scott back in the springtime of the war, had as much application to the Richmond government as to Winfield Scott. Besides, Lee already had other plans in mind for the use of the Army of Northern Virginia in 1863, plans which he had discussed with no one in Richmond, but which had first taken shape back in February, when Stonewall Jackson had, without any further explanation, instructed his chief topographical engineer, Jedediah Hotchkiss, to "prepare a map of the [Shenandoah] Valley of Virginia extended to Harrisburg, Pa., and then on to Philadelphia." Hotchkiss had been warned to keep "the preparations . . . a profound secret," and Jackson's prize mapmaker quietly slipped his engineering staff across the Potomac in civilian dress "to examine the Country in and around Harrisburg." Once in Pennsylvania, "plenty of fine horses and cattle, with the means of their support, could easily be procured" for an invading army; and Lee could "maneouver & alarm the enemy, threaten their cities" and generally encourage the peace party to demand an end to the war. And if Lee could lure the Army of the Potomac into "a pitched battle" on ground and timing of his own choosing, the Union forces "would be seriously disorganized and forced to retreat across the Susquehanna—an event which would give him control of Maryland and Western Pennsylvania, and . . . would very likely cause the fall of Washington city and the flight of the Federal government."[3]

None of this was explained to Davis and Seddon, however, and so on May 9th, while the dying Stonewall Jackson was preparing to cross his last river, the mystified Confederate secretary of war wired Lee in cipher to ask why Pickett's division could not be spared for Pemberton and the relief of Vicksburg. Lee stubbornly refused. "The adoption of your proposition is hazardous, and it becomes a question between Virginia and the Mississippi," and he informed Seddon that he would obey only if he received a direct order. Seddon was very nearly ready to give up on persuading Lee when Jefferson Davis interposed and invited Lee to Richmond again to have this all out in person on May 14th. No minutes of the conference survive, but when Davis and Seddon afterward met with the Confederate cabinet, both of them had evidently been persuaded by Lee to shelve any plans for reinforcing Joe Johnston with troops from Virginia.

The only other dissent Lee had to cope with came, surprisingly, from within the circle of his corps commanders, from James Longstreet. Joe Johnston had been Longstreet's commanding officer in 1861–62 for almost as long as Lee had been in 1862–63, and Longstreet retained a stubborn loyalty to Johnston, which Longstreet believed was widely shared in the army. When Johnston took up department command in the West, Longstreet offered to ask for a transfer if Johnston wanted him. (Longstreet may have even sought out Seddon in Richmond on May 6th precisely to propose such a transfer.) He was surprised to discover that Seddon was thinking along the same lines, and promptly offered not only himself for transfer but "the two divisions of my command" which had missed the Chancellorsville battle. But when he repeated the proposition to Lee, the army commander refused: he was already planning a new offensive and could "spare nothing from this army to re-enforce in the West." Like Seddon, Longstreet relented—but only with Lee's assurance that the Army of Northern Virginia would conduct any pitched battle during this invasion on the *tactical* defensive. "We were not to deliver an offensive battle, but to so maneuver that the enemy should be forced to attack us . . . offensive strategy, but defensive tactics." (Or at least that was how Longstreet would remember the agreement years later.)[4]

Lee had won the first battle of his campaign. The next battle would be with the Union army.

What would this battle look like? The great British historian Thomas Arnold warned in 1874 that "the part which unprofessional men can least understand" about military affairs "is what is technically called tactic," about which "the commonest sergeant, or the commonest soldier, knows infinitely more of the matter than he does."[5] But even with that caveat in mind, the appearance of Civil War battle—soldiers standing up, elbow to elbow, firing single-shot muzzleloaders by volley, in neat parade-ground lines, as though they were consciously imitating the battles of Napoleon and Frederick the Great—seems to pass all understanding. The fact that these same armies were employing weapons—in the form of the rifle musket and rifled artillery—which hugely increased the range and accuracy of fire combat over the eighteenth century's short-range smoothbore musket and pop-gun cannon, *and* hugely increased the Civil War's casualty lists, makes the Civil War look like an exercise in raw stupidity equivalent to the slaughters of the Western Front.

Arnold's "commonest sergeant" would not have thought those lines of battle so unwise. For a long time, it was customary for Civil War historians to speak of the rifle musket and rifled artillery in awed tones, as though rifling were a prototype of the machine gun, or so novel that Civil War officers were unable to come to grips with its implications. The legendary Bruce Catton summed this up about as well as anyone could when he wrote in 1953 that:

the generals had been brought up wrong. The tradition they had learned was that of close-order fighting in open country, where men with bayonets bravely charged a line of men firing smooth-bore muskets. . . . But the rifle came in and changed all of that. The range at which charging men began to be killed was at least five times as great as it used to be, which meant that about five times as many of the assailants were likely to be hit.[6]

But by 1863, there was nothing novel about the improvements in accuracy and range produced by rifling. The Minié rifle musket system (the brainchild of French weapons innovator Claude-Etienne Minié) had actually made its debut in the Crimea in 1854 in the form of both the Minié rifle and its British-made counterpart, the Pattern 1853 Enfield rifle musket, and from there, the rifle musket become the weapon of choice for both the British infantry in the Indian Mutiny in 1857 and the French and Austrian infantry in the North Italian War in 1859. Two brigade commanders at Gettysburg, Cadmus Wilcox and George Lamb Willard, had actually written pretty lucidly on the uses of the rifle musket before the war, and the practical lessons which Wilcox, Willard, and many others took out of the rifle's debut in the 1850s were about its limitations as much as its advantages.[7]

Rifling bestowed greater range and accuracy on a musket, but it did so at the price of forming a trajectory for the bullet which "dropped" rather than went straight to a target. To hit a target thus required exact knowledge of the speed and distance of a target, something which in battle was rarely available. "A very good marksman, by placing his piece in the more careful manner, generally at a dead rest . . . and firing usually not more than once in five minutes," might very well be able to "strike a half-dollar tolerably often," wrote the future Confederate general Raleigh Colston in 1858. But how often did such conditions prevail in battle? And if those targets got close enough that the rifleman had no time to reload, then the targets' bayonets, not the rifle musket, would be what decided the encounter. Despite the oft-touted ability of the soldier to load and fire three aimed shots in a minute, in practice the rate of fire produced by muzzleloading rifle muskets by regiments in line of battle (just like its smoothbore counterpart) was actually closer to one every four and a half minutes. "Tacticians talk, no doubt, about firing four and five shots in a minute," snorted one British officer, but these were "miserable puerilities, not worth discussing." At Montebello, in northern Italy, the battle had been won by French infantry *bayonets,* not by long-range rifle musket fire or rifled artillery, and won so successfully that the Austrian Army thereafter cast off any hope of the rifle musket dominating battlefields. The British had learned much the same lesson in India in 1857.[8]

Whatever the gains bestowed by the technology of the rifle musket and rifled artillery, those improvements were only apparent under ideal conditions (which is to say, not in the middle of a firefight). "On the target-ground," warned a British officer, it was possible to concentrate entirely on perfect shooting, and exclude "the least disturbance that may distract the attention." But "how will it be in the ranks at volley-firing or file-firing" when men are "excited to the highest degree, cannon-balls decimating the ranks, shells and bullets whistling their infernal tune overhead"? Under that kind of stress, "it will matter little; the soldier will simply raise his rifle to the horizontal, and fire without aiming." Nor was the technology itself foolproof. The black powder which continued in use as a propellant through the Civil War blanketed a battlefield in rolling clouds of smoke. Soldiers on the firing lines quickly found "the smoke from their rifles hanging about them in clouds," and it was not uncommon for officers to have to get down on all fours to peer under the smoke bank to confirm enemy troop positions. At Fredericksburg, artillery gun crews ran laps around their guns, waving their arms, in an effort to dispel the powder smoke from the guns' discharge.[9] No improvements in accuracy or range could trump blindness. The black powder itself quickly packed the rifle's grooves with residue from firing, and the need to load the rifle by ramming home each charge from the muzzle with a ramrod, whose banging about nicked and chipped the muzzle at the very point where the bullet was expelled, further degraded the accuracy of the rifle in use.

Another limitation on the impact of rifled weapons in battle was field communications. In 1863, there could be only the most primitive synchronization of actions on different portions of a battlefield, because orders had to be delivered personally, through couriers or aides, a process which could require up to an hour between army headquarters and corps headquarters, another thirty minutes from corps to division, and another twenty from division to the fundamental unit of Civil War combat, the brigade. Once engaged in combat, the noise of battle was "absolutely impenetrable by the voice to any distance," and "orders have to be so multiplied and repeated, that the genius of a Napoleon would get entangled on a day of battle." Officers on the line of battle responded to situations by herding their men within earshot of drums, bugles, and their officers' own voices rather than dispersing them; sometimes they were reduced to using the most basic visual signs, or the position of the regimental colors. Hence, in the context of nineteenth-century battle, the elbow-to-elbow line was still the best way to concentrate fire or coordinate movement, and the bayonet remained, quite reasonably, the queen of the battlefield.[10]

But the ultimate limitation of the rifle revolution in the Civil War was the meager training imparted to volunteer soldiers by the volunteers' officers, who

were often incapable of superintending much more than basic drill movements. "I found it far more difficult to make officers than soldiers," wrote
crusty Edward Cross, especially when officers in regiments like the 1st Minnesota "brought their books to the drill grounds and prompted themselves or
corrected their errors by referring to the books." Even the West Point–trained
officers "who came to us, & who were invaluable to us, were very green,"
admitted a Virginia cavalryman. Target practice and instruction in how to
move to the attack under fire went by the boards. When one Illinois regiment
lined up to target-shoot at a barrel 180 yards away, only 4 shots out of 160 tries
hit the barrel. In the 5th Connecticut forty men firing at a barn fifteen feet
high from only 100 yards' distance managed to score a mere four hits, and
only one below the height of a man. At First Bull Run, William Buel Franklin
was exasperated even by the Regulars of his 12th U.S. Infantry: "It is my firm
belief that a great deal of the misfortune of the day at Bull Run is due to the
fact that the troops knew very little of the principles and practice of firing. . . .
Ours was very bad, the rear files sometimes firing into and killing the front
ones." William Izlar of the 1st South Carolina remembered a fierce exchange
of volleys at a distance of no more than 100 yards in which the chief casualties were "the needles and cones from the extreme top" of the pine trees all
around them. He guessed that only one round in 500 ever hit anyone. A Federal captain watched in disbelief as his men fired off "at an angle of forty-five
degrees," hitting little or nothing, "and the instances of their firing into each
other are by no means rare." What ran up the Civil War's enormous casualty
lists was not expert marksmanship or highly refined weapons, but the inability of poorly trained officers to get their poorly trained volunteers to charge
forward and send the enemy flying before the bayonet, instead of standing up
and blazing away for an hour or two in close-range firefights where the sheer
volume of lead in the air killed enough people to be noticed.[11]

But the technology of nineteenth-century warfare only accounts for the
physical constraints placed on tactics at Gettysburg. The armies at Gettysburg were also restrained by a body of tactical doctrine with long roots back
to the 1790s, and the great debate over the virtues of "column" and "line" in
combat. It is a risky simplification to suggest that the line of battle was the
British tactic—the "mode of attack peculiarly suited to British infantry." But
it was characteristic of British training to maximize the power of single-shot,
muzzleloading firearms by spreading a unit (in the British case, the 250-to-
350-man regiment) out into two or three lines which allowed the full play
of musket fire along its front. It would be equally risky to suggest that the
column was the *French* tactic, the massing of troops behind a narrow front
that, like swinging a ram, could smash into, and disrupt, an enemy infantry
formation and make it run for its life. But this was, in general, how matters

had played out in the Napoleonic Wars. The great virtue of a British line was its ability to deliver musket fire by volley and its relative invulnerability to artillery fire, since artillery rounds could not hurt more than a handful even in the event of a direct hit; the great defect of line was that it was very difficult to get it to move together or to move swiftly, especially over uneven ground.[12] A French column, on the other hand, could move very fast and very easily, and develop tremendous forward momentum, which was a decided plus in reducing the amount of time an attacking force was exposed to enemy musket fire; the defect of column, however, was that it presented an enormously fat target to artillery, which could do hideous damage to a tightly packed column with just a few well-placed rounds.[13]

Column's principal reliance was on the bayonet rather than volley fire, since most of a column's body would have no clear field of fire; but a solid column, moving at collision speed and tipped with the menacing steel shanks of bayonets, could spike through a terrified line like a javelin through cardboard. "The *bullet* will lose its way," was the rule in the Crimean War, "the *bayonet*, never!" Column was also flexible; attack columns could be formed of regimental columns stacked by company lines, or division columns stacked by brigade. The introduction of the rifle musket had comparatively little effect on either column or line as attack formations; if anything, the rifle encouraged an entirely separate formation, in the shape of clouds of open-order skirmishers which were thrown out like curtains in front of big infantry formations. They could use the rifle's accuracy and distance to better effect at picking off enemy artillerymen and officers. "A battery can keep back or destroy masses of the enemy," wrote one Maine artillery officer, but "it cannot successfully contend with a line of skirmishers. To resist them would be like shooting mosquitoes with musket balls." It was artillery more than infantry that felt the sting of the rifle; artillery now had to be bracketed by supporting wings of infantry, or kept well to the rear to fire over the heads of infantry lines.

But good skirmishing required a higher level of training, and this, too, was something which the Civil War armies greatly lacked. In 1862, the Confederate government authorized the creation of "sharpshooter" battalions to provide specialized skirmish details, and two entire regiments of sharpshooters were raised for the Army of the Potomac by Hiram Berdan in 1862. But beyond these units, actual training in skirmish tactics remained painfully limited. "It is a melancholy fact that three out of four who entered the service" received no instruction in skirmishing, lamented Francis Walker, the chief of staff to Winfield Hancock's 2nd Corps. "Indeed, most regiments in the service had as little idea of skirmishing as an elephant."[14]

And so the debate between column and line continued through the 1850s and beyond the Civil War. At the Alma in 1854, the Russian infantry preferred to fight in column, and they were amazed when Lord Raglan deployed his two British divisions into line of battle and moved to attack the heights behind the Alma River straight ahead in line. "We had never before seen troops fight in lines of two deep," wrote a Polish officer (who ended up fighting in the Civil War, too), "nor did we think it possible for men to be found with sufficient firmness of morale to be able to attack in this apparently weak formation" and rout their enemy. The French, meanwhile, continued to fight in regimental columns, stacked two companies at a time, as did the allied German armies which invaded France in 1870; at Solferino in 1859, the French emperor Napoleon III piled up columns three regiments deep, so that an attack column could be composed of as many as eighteen ranks of infantry-men, sometimes only a yard behind one another. All of this, Civil War generals had to read, mark, and digest.[15]

Where the Civil War battlefield differed most from European battlefields was the absence of cavalry. The most basic rule of nineteenth-century battle since Napoleon had been:

> *Artillery prepares the victory;*
> *Infantry achieves it;*
> *Cavalry completes it, and secures its fruits.*

But for all of the romance attached to the U.S. cavalry in the Indian Wars of the later nineteenth century, most of the American military's first century of existence minimized the use of cavalry (in the Revolution, Washington had used his cavalry contingents mostly for reconnaissance and raiding, when he used them at all). There were, in fact, no Regular cavalry units in the army until Congress authorized two regiments of dragoons in 1833 and 1836. Even though American cavalry officers were eventually sent to the French cavalry school at Saumur to learn the intricacies of cavalry tactics, the army never pushed development of its mounted arm to include a heavy cavalry regiment (for direct use against infantry) or lancers (to exploit the disintegration of enemy infantry formations already on the run).[16]

One reason for this odd reluctance to invest in a fully operational mounted service was symbolic: just as the American republican tradition sat uneasily beside the notion of permanent professional armies, nothing made Americans more uneasy than the image of the mounted soldier (the vision of the Manchester and Salford Yeomanry hacking down protesters with their sabers in the Peterloo Massacre in 1819 remained a toxic one for cavalry through much of the nineteenth century). But just as persuasive a reason for minimizing cavalry in the U.S. Army was its sheer cost. Mounted troops were enormously expensive to maintain, requiring at least six months to train just in riding drill. Beyond that, admitted one veteran officer, another "three years had been regarded as necessary to transform a recruit into a good cavalryman," all of which cost money with no sign of immediate return on the investment. Cavalry horses were even more costly. A cavalry brigade in the Crimea consumed 20,000 pounds of fodder a day (in addition, each horse required five gallons of water), and that did not even begin to reckon with the cost of the horses themselves or their attrition (in a six-month period in 1854–55, British cavalry in the Crimea lost 932 of its 2,216 horses to sickness). It was easier for budget-conscious American Congresses to stint the cavalry, authorizing only light cavalry regiments.[17]

Moreover, the heavily forested terrain of North America did not lend itself very easily to the kind of line-breaking charges of heavy cavalry that distinguished European battlefields. Although some sporadic attempt was made at the beginning of the Civil War to diversify both Union and Confederate cavalry (the most signal example being the creation of "Rush's Lancers"—the 6th Pennsylvania Cavalry—at the prompting of George McClellan), the sudden onset of the war not only found the U.S. Army shy of an officer cadre which could train diversified cavalry units, but with neither the time nor the inclination to create them. "Our cavalry are too often satisfied with a few discharges of their pistols and carbines, and then 'retire' to give the infantry a chance," complained a Confederate infantryman in 1863. "An idea that cavalry are only fit for spying out the enemy's position, picketing, and opening the fight, seems to prevail." The proof was in the numbers: at Waterloo, the ratio of Wellington's infantry to cavalry was approximately four to one; in the Crimea, Raglan's army had thirty infantry battalions and ten cavalry regiments; at Sedan in 1870, MacMahon's Army of Chalons had an infantry–cavalry ratio of six to one; at Gettysburg, Lee's ratio of infantry to cavalry was ten to one.[18]

The hard result in the Civil War was that, as Francis Lippett complained in 1865, "neither side had a sufficient force of true cavalry to enable it to complete a victory, to turn a defeat into a rout, and drive the enemy effectually from the field." By the end of the Civil War, the light cavalry forces of both armies finally concentrated on providing wide-ranging screens that concealed infantry movments from prying eyes, or on behind-the-lines raiding missions to interdict the flow of enemy supplies. "The Americans in their vast country . . . used cavalry wisely in sending it off on distant forays to cut communications, make levies, etc.," wrote the keen French military analyst Ardant du Picq, in 1870. Significantly, there are comparatively few instances in the Civil War where worthwhile intelligence was garnered by cavalry operations. Cavalry screens might provide some limited amount of news, but screening was primarily a protective operation, and any information the screening units might produce was usually limited to scrapings against the enemy's cavalry screens. At Chancellorsville, James Ewell Brown Stuart had provided Lee with the key information that Joe Hooker's right flank was dangling, unprotected, in the air; but Stuart had been able to contribute this vital tip because Hooker's cavalry had galloped itself out of reach and supplied no cloak against Stuart's probing. Even then, it was not Stuart, but two of the locals—Jackson's chaplain, Beverly Tucker Lacy, and Charles Wellford—who supplied Lee with the crucial information about access roads for an attack. "Raiding," and not intelligence collection, "was Stuart's hobby," wrote one of Stuart's staff officers, and "it was urged with all the earnestness which characterized him whenever his heart was set on any particular object." In the Army of the Potomac, intelligence collection was being done by a tightly knit cadre of operatives attached to Col. George Sharpe's Bureau of Military Information. Sharpe's scouts, in turn, were supported by Signal Corps detachments which could establish chains of flag stations from Harpers Ferry to "South Mountain, Monterey, Greencastle . . . up to Parnell's Knob, in the Cumberland Valley," and by networks of civilian spies and "scouts" (who were scarcely more than spies).[19]

As the task of cavalry on the Civil War battlefield shrank, the task of artillery expanded. The U.S. Army's artillery in 1861 had fallen off considerably from "the high reputation which it had gained in Mexico. . . . There was no chief nor special administration for that arm, and no regulation for its government." Experience soon changed that, in both the Army of the Potomac and the Army of Northern Virginia. Americans might be, as John Ropes wrote, "an unmilitary people," but in the mechanical attractions artillery offered a nation of tinkerers, "the American soldier seems, in fact, to take naturally to artillery." In 1805, Napoleonic armies deployed something less than 2 artillery pieces per 1,000 infantrymen; seven years later, at Borodino, Napoleon had expanded his artillery to 5 guns per 1,000 infantry, and at Wagram, Borodino, and Waterloo he had concentrated grand batteries of over 100 guns to be used in smashing opposing infantry to mush. In 1863, the Army of Northern Virginia brought 283 cannon with it on the Gettysburg campaign, and would have brought more but for lack of horses (and the fodder they required) to haul them; the rebels would capture 26 more guns along the way. The Federal artillery at Gettysburg comprised 372 guns (including horse artillery batteries and an artillery reserve of 118 pieces to be deployed in any emergency), so that the Army of the Potomac actually had a field ratio of artillery to infantry that exceeded European patterns (the ratio of the Prussian 3rd Army at Sedan was approximately 4 pieces per 1,000 infantry).[20]

Not only had the artillery grown in numbers, it had grown in organizational capacity, as both Joseph Hooker and Robert E. Lee reorganized their artillery arms into quasi-independent commands, with clusters of batteries attached to different corps commands and a large artillery reserve to be deployed at the discretion of a reserve chief. And like their European counterparts, American artillerists tended to behave as though they owed nothing to anyone. "Gunners are a race apart," ran the British doggerel, "hard of head and hard of heart." At Waterloo, it was all senior British officers could do to prevent independent-souled artillerymen from throwing away their energy and their ammunition on counterbattery duels with opposing artillery batteries. "Do not direct your fire on the enemy's artillery," sternly advised a British artillery handbook, "unless your troops suffer more from his fire than his do from yours." The same was true among American artillerists. "The captain of a battery has a very independent position," wrote an officer in the 13th New York Battery, "and it lies with him almost entirely whether his battery is a good and serviceable one or not"—or what targets he would choose. (The Army of the Potomac's chief of artillery, Henry J. Hunt, would actually impose a rule of firing no more than "one round from each gun in two minutes; and that rate should only be reached at critical moments"; otherwise, "one round in four to six minutes is as rapid as should be permitted.") And it was a rule of thumb among gunners that a concentration of eighteen guns, like the Russian battery at Borodino or the eighteen guns with which Auguste de Marmont saved the day at Marengo for Napoleon, could shake whole regiments apart and break up any infantry assault.[21]

Controlling the artilleryman's instinct to let loose was vital, and never less so in the Civil War than at Gettysburg. The chief responsibility of artillery was (according to the U.S. Army's *Instruction for Field Artillery*) "to break an enemy's line or prevent him from forming." This could be done in three ways, beginning with the use of the long-range *shell* (timed by fuse to explode over the heads of oncoming infantry and spraying white-hot shards of shell or small lead shot over the heads of the enemy). If this did not disperse the attackers, mid-range *solid shot* would. Gunners would aim to "graze" solid shot at 400 yards so that it would ricochet at just the right level and smash the maximum amount of human flesh and bone in its path. Like some brutal nemesis, or "like a rock skipped upon the surface of the ocean by the powerful arm of a giant," solid shot could be watched "bounding like rubber balls," landing "with a heavy thud" and coming "right at the line with the sound of a huge circular saw ripping a log." "A dozen at a time" could come "bounding along like footballs," hitting "the ground once or twice" and caroming off at unpredictable and lethal angles into an oncoming infantry formation. William Wheeler, in Oliver Otis Howard's 11th Corps, "saw an infantry man's leg taken off by a shot, and whirled like a stone through the air, until it came against a caisson with a loud whack." Another officer in the 11th Corps on

July 1st noticed how "many officers dismounted or bent low whenever they felt the pressure of the air created by the shot," except for "one unfortunate officer [who] was nailed by a six-pounder against a big tree. I got hold of his bushy hair and pulled him down, as he presented a ghastly appearance." If neither shell nor shot stopped attackers, the cannoneers' last resort was close-range *canister*—a tin can filled with lead balls that could be blasted directly from the muzzle of an artillery piece in a thirty-two-foot-wide spread at 100 yards, like so many pumpkin slugs.[22]

When it was well laid, artillery could cause destruction of absolutely hellish proportions, physically and emotionally. Explosive shells used at long distances multiplied the stress experienced by enemy infantry because under shell fire neither flight nor aggression are possible. "Spherical case shot"— the kind of explosive shell filled with "scores of cast-iron bullets"—was particularly dreaded by Henry Nichols Blake in the 11th Massachusetts because it "could not be avoided . . . and was very destructive." Solid shot was, if anything, even more horrible, since the low muzzle velocities of nineteenth-century artillery guaranteed that attacking infantry at anything less than 1,000 yards could actually see solid shot flying at them from the muzzles of aimed guns. But artillery also had its limitations. Gunners who opened fire at enemy infantry too early in the process of the attack would exhaust themselves from sponging and loading, and the heat from overextended periods of fire could cause bronze or brass gun barrels to droop or to burst, especially in high temperatures.[23]

On May 26th, Robert E. Lee presided at a "grand review" of Dick Ewell's corps, starting with Jubal Early's division, then proceeding on the 29th to Robert Rodes' division, which "marched three miles to the reviewing grounds, and stood for several hours before getting properly aligned." Longstreet's corps would follow on June 1st, with the corps artillery firing a thirteen-gun salute to Lee, bands playing at the head of each brigade, every company "bringing their pieces from 'right shoulder' to 'carry' . . . and from 'carry' to 'present arms' when stationary." Each regiment passed by in column of companies, "music in front of each brigade, in front of the old hero, who saluted each flag as it passed by taking off his hat, and exhibiting his cotton scalp to the admiring throng around him." (The cotton surprised a soldier in the 53rd North Carolina, who remembered how, one year before, when Lee took command, "his hair was black [and] now he is a gray-headed old man.") Rumors of a new campaign were already flying up and down the review columns, and George Campbell Brown, Ewell's stepson and staffer, noticed that "they are all for [invading] Maryland & Pennsylvania." And perhaps, when they did, it would all come to an end. A great battle would be fought, and through the smoke and fire, the way home would finally be open, and there would be peace, independence, and plenty—but especially peace.

Oddly, across the Rappahannock River, soldiers in the Army of the Potomac had come to the same conclusion. A gunner in Battery B, 4th U.S. Artillery, decided that, "If we are whipped here, and I pull through it alive, I'm going to make tracks for home, and the provost-guard may be damned." There had been enough fighting to no purpose. "I am inclined to think that this Campaign is going to end this show either one way or the other," wrote another artilleryman in the 1st Massachusetts Light Artillery, "for if Lee gets the best of us now we are gone up and its no use talking and I think if we get the best of him he is gone the same way."[24]

In the evening, the rebel brigade bands that had played so thumpingly through the reviews played again on the banks of the Rappahannock, with strains of "Dixie" and "The Bonnie Blue Flag" echoing in the still twilight. On the far side of the river, the bandsmen of the Army of the Potomac stirred themselves, and they, too, began to play, this time offering "Yankee Doodle" and "The Star-Spangled Banner." And then, remembered George Henry Mills of the 16th North Carolina, on some mysterious cue the bands on both riverbanks struck up "Home, Sweet Home." And there "was on both sides a universal shout, reverberating from one to the other, back and forth, showing that there was one tie held in common by these two grand armies."[25]

CHAPTER FOUR

A perfectly surplus body of men

IF THERE WAS ONLY one lesson to be learned from Robert E. Lee's first try at an invasion northward in 1862, it would be about Harpers Ferry. Lodged tightly between the confluence of the Shenandoah and the Potomac rivers, some fifty miles northwest of Washington, Harpers Ferry was ringed by the limestone ridges of Maryland Heights (on the north bank of the Potomac), Loudoun Heights (on the east, overlooking the Shenandoah River), and Bolivar Heights (west of the town). These tall ridges didn't make Harpers Ferry into some kind of natural fortress; rather, it became the deep center of a bowl that was too wide to be defended. On that assumption, Lee decided in 1862 to cross the Potomac into Maryland downstream from Harpers Ferry, where he could move the Army of Northern Virginia easily up to Frederick, and from there into the Cumberland Valley of Pennsylvania, and left Harpers Ferry in his rear to be snatched up by Stonewall Jackson. But it did not surrender as easily as Lee expected. The tiny Federal garrison put up just long enough of a fight that Stonewall Jackson only barely caught up with Lee in time to fend off the Army of the Potomac's fast descent at Antietam. Once Lee fell back into Virginia, Harpers Ferry was blithely reoccupied by Federal forces as though the Confederates had never passed that way.

Harpers Ferry was not enough of a prize to be worth a second risk of that sort. So in the summer of 1863, Lee's plan for another invasion of the North would point farther westward, bypassing Harpers Ferry entirely. He would pull away from the lines along the Rappahannock where the two armies had been glowering at each other since Chancellorsville, and shift north and west over the Blue Ridge, entering the great tunnel formed by the Shenandoah and Cumberland Valley, and crossing the Potomac at points between ten and twenty-five miles above Harpers Ferry. Once across the Potomac, Lee would make Hagerstown, in the Cumberland Valley, his first objective (instead of Frederick), and then begin a long curl north and east, down the valley, through Greencastle, Chambersburg, Shippensburg, Carlisle, and finally to Harrisburg and the banks of the Susquehanna. Along that entire line, there was only one Federal outpost of any size worth worrying about, and that was Winchester, at the lower end of the Shenandoah Valley and just twenty-five miles from the Potomac. But there were fewer than 7,000 Federal soldiers there, and the town had changed hands so often during this war that it was not likely to put up much resistance to changing hands again.

It seems odd to modern eyes that Lee wrote out none of these plans, gave no precise timetables, and specified no schedule of objectives. (If anything, Lee was still fiddling with the realignment of the army's artillery, and still haggling with Secretary of War Seddon for the addition of five more brigades of infantry from North Carolina and the defenses of Richmond.) Nothing of that nature seems to have survived apart from two operational orders issued to A. P. Hill on June 5th and June 16th, and even these are merely directives to move and occupy certain points, without any specifics about how or when.[1] But this was not unnatural in the mid-nineteenth century, when the movement and communication of armies were still surprisingly haphazard affairs, especially through the broad expanses of the American landscape. In 1863, twenty-five miles represented a full day's travel—the experiential equivalent of, say, a coast-to-coast flight—so that a trip from Philadelphia to Chicago in 1863 would feel like going halfway around the world. Within those limits, campaign plans were always going to be full of improvisation, with plenty of loose room left for unanticipated encounters, unforeseen obstacles, and raw happenstance.

In European warfare, the new technologies of the railroad and the telegraph were rapidly closing these distance gaps, and annihilating the delays in travel and information which had previously made mischance and make-it-up-as-you-go part of the normal play of war. The fifteen state-owned railroads and thirty-one private railroads in the kingdom of Prussia had been severely subordinated to a military railroad commission and a section of the Prussian general staff in the 1850s, and elaborate mobilization timetables had been developed to govern the concentration and movement of Prussian troops in any eventuality. In 1855, the British Army experimented with constructing a military railroad in the Crimea to supply the siege lines at Sevastopol, and in the North Italian War in 1859, Napoleon III moved 130,000 French troops at unprecedented speed into the war zone.[2]

But Robert E. Lee had nothing like these rail systems at his disposal. His

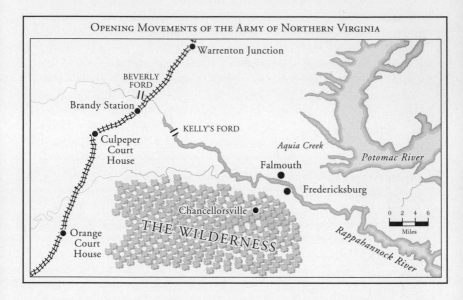

OPENING MOVEMENTS OF THE ARMY OF NORTHERN VIRGINIA

main railroad support consisted of a cluster of lines which came up from the Carolinas to Petersburg and Richmond, and even these were inadequate to the supply needs of the Army of Northern Virginia. From Richmond, only two major rail lines were strung northward to the Potomac—the Richmond, Fredericksburg & Potomac, which was controlled by the Federals north of the Rappahannock River, and the combined lines of the Virginia Central and Orange & Alexandria, which passed out of Confederate control north of Culpeper Court House. The only effective rail link between Lee and the Shenandoah Valley in 1863 ran westward through Charlottesville to Staunton, way at the upper head of the Shenandoah, and that was ninety miles from Harpers Ferry. Even if Lee had wanted to devise a tight plan of campaign operations, the tools needed for such a plan simply didn't exist for him or the Army of Northern Virginia.[3]

Once the parades and reviews of the three infantry corps of the Army of Northern Virginia were complete, Lee began the first stage of the long journey northward on June 3rd, with Lafayette McLaws' and John Bell Hood's divisions of Longstreet's corps discreetly packing up and marching south (in order to disappear from Federal sight) through the green groves of locusts and oaks toward Spotsylvania Court House and then turning westward, across the Rapidan River, to Culpeper Court House, on the Orange & Alexandria Railroad. (Longstreet's third division, under George Pickett, was waiting on two of the brigades Lee was struggling to shake loose from Secretary Seddon; those two units, under Micah Jenkins and Montgomery Corse, would finally stay put, north of Richmond, to protect the capital.)[4]

Turning to look back over the artillery battalion he commanded, Edward Porter Alexander felt a surge of "pride & confidence . . . in my splendid battalion, as it filed out of the field into the road, with every chest & ammunition wagon filled, & every horse in fair order, & every detail fit for a campaign." Few of these Confederate soldiers, however, stayed splendid for long. The weather was "beautiful" and "bright" on the 3rd, but the next day, when it became the turn of Dick Ewell's corps to begin slipping away toward Spotsylvania, it became "very warm & we were in a cloud of dust most of the time." The marching was kept easy—ten-minute rest breaks every hour, and camp by 3:30 in the afternoon. Ewell's corps followed Longstreet's across the Rapidan at noon on June 7th and camped by four o'clock near Culpeper. Neither of them entirely evaded Union observation. The Army of the Potomac began experimenting in late 1861 with hydrogen-filled observation balloons supplied by the ingenuity of Thaddeus Sobieski Coulincourt Lowe. A number of the balloons were still operational, and on June 5th Ewell's corps noticed the ascent of "the Yankee balloon" over Banks' Ford on the Rappahannock.[5]

Lee kept A. P. Hill's corps in position on the Rappahannock and thinned it along the south bank, "making such disposition as will be best calculated to deceive the enemy, and keep him in ignorance of any change in the disposition of the army." But thanks to the balloon, Hooker was already notifying Lincoln that the Army of Northern Virginia was on the road and that Lee must be intending "to move up the [Rappahannock] river, with a view to the execution of a movement similar to Lee's of last year." That would mean either a move "to cross the Upper Potomac" above Harpers Ferry "or to throw his army between mine and Washington" by lunging around Hooker's flank and reoccupying the old Bull Run battlefield.

Only a few months before, Hooker had been riding a tide of success so neatly that he was allowed to report directly to Lincoln, and would hardly have needed to signal Lincoln at all in order to deal with a Confederate movement. But Hooker's stock had fallen so flat after Chancellorsville that when he suggested a countermove across the Rappahannock, he met with the president's stony disapproval: "It does not appear probable to me that you can gain any thing by an early renewal of the attempt to cross the Rappahannock." The more Hooker persisted in asking for authorization to respond, the more irritable Lincoln became, and on June 5th, he curtly notified Hooker that henceforward he would report to Major General Henry Wager Halleck, the general in chief of all the Union armies. This was bad news for Hooker, since

Halleck had rarely ever used his role as general in chief to do more than act as a glorified liaison officer, and because Halleck and Hooker had known each other before the war, and on the worst possible terms.[6]

Hooker pressed Halleck to allow him to cross the Rappahannock in force, overwhelming whatever rebel force had been left at Fredericksburg, and then lunging down the line of the Virginia Central toward an almost undefended Richmond. "Will it not promote the true interest of the cause," Hooker was reduced to pleading, "for me to march to Richmond at once?" And Hooker went so far as to push across the Rappahannock at Franklin's Crossing (three miles below Fredericksburg) with a division of John Sedgwick's 6th Corps while the Army of the Potomac's engineers hurriedly built a pontoon bridge. The Yankee division cleared about a mile of the far bank of the Rappahannock, with skirmishers keeping up "a sharp firing all day," and the other two divisions of the 6th Corps took turns over the next few days occupying the newly conquered pocket around the crossing. As he had suspected, a great many of the rebels were gone.[7]

Establishing this little bridgehead was Hooker's way of demonstrating that the road to Richmond was demonstrably open, but it merely drew from Halleck and from Lincoln the immediate and frosty reminder that a move toward Richmond would leave the field open for Lee to trade queens by attacking an almost undefended Washington. Besides, those generals animated by "the true interest of the cause" would be seeking out a decisive confrontation with the Confederate Army, not Richmond. Hooker had been selected for command by Lincoln because he was supposed to be "Fighting Joe," the perfect anti-McClellan who would wade in and land the jaw-crushing blow to the Army of Northern Virginia that the McClellan lovers refused to throw. But not only had Hooker allowed his own jaw to be crushed at Chancellorsville, he was now bleating for permission to betake himself to Richmond while the rebel army held the entire Potomac River to ransom. "I think Lee's army, and not Richmond, is your sure objective point," Lincoln replied coolly on June 10th. "If he comes toward the Upper Potomac, follow on his flank and on his inside track." And that was that.[8]

Hooker must have known by this point that he had been weighed in the balances and found wanting by Lincoln, and that Halleck would welcome any opportunity to make the balances weigh even heavier against him. "I think & know that Hooker feels very bad," the army's excitably vigilant provost marshal, Marsena Patrick, wrote in his diary. Yet, there was also vanity enough in Hooker to make him hope that, somehow, he had the wherewithal to redeem himself from the irredeemable depths. On June 11th, Hooker's staff adjutant, Brigadier General Seth Williams, circulated orders to all corps commanders "for all civilians to leave the Army at once, all extra baggage to be sent to the rear, and the men's extra luggage reduced to the lowest possible amount."[9]

The 3rd Corps would jump off first, heading twenty-five miles north to Catlett's Station (on the Orange & Alexandria Railroad) and from there up the line to old familiar battlegrounds around Manassas Junction; John Reynolds' 1st Corps would follow, and behind Reynolds would come Otis Howard and the 11th Corps. The 6th Corps' bridgehead over the Rappahannock was quietly abandoned after darkness on June 12th, and the next day the remaining four infantry corps of the Army of the Potomac—Hancock's 2nd Corps, the 6th under Sedgwick, George Meade's 5th Corps, and Henry Slocum's 12th Corps—were on the roads, swinging slightly to the east of the others and headed for Fairfax Court House. It was "a terrible suffocating march." A sergeant in the 28th Pennsylvania counted only nine men present in his company when they reached Fairfax, and he "was completely faged out, almost sick." But at least this way, the Army of the Potomac would always be interposed between Lee and Washington. It was not the kind of campaign Joe Hooker really wanted to carry on, but by this point, as Marsena Patrick sadly wrote, "Halleck is running the marching and Hooker has the role of a subordinate."[10]

One notion which kept nagging at Joe Hooker was the possibility that Lee's mysterious departure for Culpeper might not be a serious movement at all, but instead a cover for a large-scale cavalry raid by the Army of Northern Virginia's cavalry and its flamboyant J.E.B. Stuart. "It may be that they have only intended a cavalry raid," Hooker wondered hopefully, "and moved their infantry in the vicinity of Culpeper to support it." That, at least, would seem to explain why Lee was leaving an entire corps' worth of his infantry—A. P. Hill's—still in place around Fredericksburg. If Hooker launched a preemptive strike of his own and broke up whatever cavalry raid might be in the offing, he could have something to offer Halleck and Lincoln which might justify a release from the tight leash they had buckled around his neck. On June 6th, Hooker casually informed Halleck that a "heavy rebel force of cavalry about Culpeper may mean mischief," and that he was taking steps to nip the "mischief" in "its incipiency." What he was actually planning to do was to take all three divisions of the Army of the Potomac's cavalry, "stiffened by about 3,000 infantry," lunge across the Rappahannock upriver at Kelly's Ford, and deliver a thumping surprise to the Confederate cavalry in its camps around Culpeper.[11]

This was not as easy an assignment as it seemed. The cavalry of the Army of the Potomac was suffered as the poor relation of the infantry, with the result that "this arm of our service has been of little account heretofore." Rebel cavalrymen laughed their Union counterparts to scorn: "Most of the Federal cavalry of the Army of the Potomac in 1861 was inefficient, awkward, uncouth horsemen," wrote a captain in the 1st Virginia Cavalry. "I have seen raw Dutchmen strapped on the horses by straps buckled around their waists and legs and fastened to the saddle." Old Winfield Scott had no use for cavalry units larger than a company or an ad hoc battalion. The cavalry McClellan had taken with him on his great campaign up the peninsula formed by the James River, to the doors of Richmond, in 1862 amounted to less than 4,000 out of 98,000 Union troops, and had been parceled out among the big infantry corps for escort and provost guard duties, except for a small two-brigade "reserve." McClellan eventually concentrated his cavalry into a single division before Antietam, and placed it under Brigadier General Alfred Pleasonton, a West Pointer of the class of 1844 with service in the 2nd Dragoons under Zachary Taylor in Mexico. But Pleasonton's and the division's actual contribution to McClellan's blandly managed battle at Antietam was minimal: while the rest of the Army of the Potomac submitted to the loss of 2,100 lives in that single day in September, the entire cavalry division reported 4 killed and 20 wounded—one of them being Pleasonton, who was deafened in the right ear by the concussion of artillery.[12]

It was really Joe Hooker who took the Yankee cavalry firmly in hand, reorganized it into a full-fledged corps of three divisions, and placed it all in the hands of George Stoneman. "I give you full power over your officers," Hooker warned, "arrest, cashier, shoot—whatever you will," but get them working as a useful unit. Hooker's principal mission for Stoneman was raiding "remote from the supporting army . . . in which the aim was not to encounter the enemy in force and fight him, but rather to avoid serious conflicts of arms and expend all possible energy in the destruction of lines of communication and depots of military supplies." In that expectation, George Stoneman turned out to be a colossal disappointment, riding his cavalry corps almost entirely out of contact with Hooker at Chancellorsville and only doing "easily repaired" damage along the Virginia Central Railroad between Richmond and the Rappahannock. The crestfallen Stoneman sheepishly removed himself from Hooker's wrath by taking medical leave for "the cavalryman's complaint"—hemorrhoids—and command of the cavalry fell back to Alfred Pleasonton, who had assiduously undermined Stoneman and positioned himself to replace him.[13]

Pleasonton was a kid-glove-wearing dandy, a ladies' man, a vivid talker, with a full, placid face, a sharp eye for the main chance, and an open door for reporters who might obligingly puff his name in the papers. Charles Francis

Adams, in the 1st Massachusetts Cavalry, moaned that Pleasonton was "a newspaper humbug . . . a bully and toady" who "does nothing save with a view to a newspaper paragraph," and that view was shared pretty broadly by the rest of the cavalry corps. But Pleasonton had seniority, and he had political pull—he was closely tied to John Franklin Farnsworth, a Radical Republican representative from Illinois' 2nd District, and Farnsworth's nephew, Elon, was one of Pleasonton's staff officers—and so the task of popping whatever bubble J.E.B. Stuart and the rebel cavalry were developing around Culpeper would go to Pleasonton.[14]

Stuart struck many people as a mirror image of Pleasonton. "There were few men produced by the war whose character was so mixed with gold and dross as Stuart," remembered an officer in the 4th Virginia Cavalry. He could be "brave as his sword," but "frivolous to the point of ridicule," as though he was always (in the words of one staffer) "on stage." Like Pleasonton again, he owed much of his rapid advancement to command of the cavalry of the Army of Northern Virginia to his assiduous cultivation of the powerful—in this case, of both Joseph Johnston and Robert E. Lee. He met Lee while still a cadet at West Point in the 1850s, and he had the exquisite good fortune to be in the secretary of war's office in October 1859 when the secretary called for a volunteer to take an urgent message about John Brown's raid on Harpers Ferry to Lee. Stuart took command of the 1st Virginia Cavalry at the outbreak of the war, and so impressed Joe Johnston as having "by nature . . . the qualities necessary for an officer of light cavalry" that he earned his brigadier general's stars that September. (That impression was strengthened by Stuart's considerable talent for flattery: "Johnston is in capacity head and shoulders above every general in the Southern Confederacy," Stuart announced, including Lee, with whom Stuart was now "disappointed.") But when Lee succeeded Johnston in command, Stuart at once reintroduced himself and proposed a cavalry raid which would ride a circle around George McClellan and the Army of the Potomac. Lee was dubious. But Stuart pulled it off by sheer audacity, and from that moment his reputation as the Confederacy's— and Lee's—favorite cavalryman was sealed. Stuart returned the compliment by appointing Virginians to command four of his division's five brigades, including a son and a nephew of Robert E. Lee.[15]

There would always be some question about the real value of Stuart's raid. Porter Alexander groused that the raid only "alarmed McClellan for his rear" and thwarted Lee's larger goal of cutting off McClellan's retreat. It was so bloodless (the great raid cost Stuart's 1,200 troopers exactly 1 dead and 4 wounded) and so limited that it never quite proved to the infantry's satisfaction that cavalry had a job worth doing. "I call them a perfectly surplus body of men," snorted a Georgia infantryman. "The real fighting must be and is done by our foot cavalry." In a fight, sneered another Georgian, "the bravery of one man is rarely sufficient to overcome the running propensities of six legs." There was, however, one singular lesson which Stuart took away from the raid, and that was raiding would easily garner headlines in the Richmond papers.[16]

Raiding was, therefore, what both the newspapers and Joe Hooker expected Stuart to do, sooner or later. Hooker gave Alf Pleasonton unusually explicit instructions about blighting any cavalry raid while it was still in the bud: move up to Warrenton Junction on June 7th, scout the area, and then in the early hours of June 9th cross the Rappahannock at Kelly's and Beverly fords "and march directly on Culpeper." There, Pleasonton should "disperse and destroy the rebel force assembled in the vicinity of Culpeper, and . . . destroy his trains and supplies of all description to the utmost of your ability." Even if Pleasonton did no more than give the Confederate cavalry a good running off, Joe Hooker would be satisfied and Washington would be impressed. One of Hooker's aides, Captain Ulric Dahlgren, would act as Pleasonton's overall guide and (since Pleasonton seems to have had no more fixed notion of where Culpeper was than he did Mecca) Dahlgren would "hand you some maps of the direction in which you are operating."[17]

What actually happened on the 9th held surprises for both Pleasonton and J.E.B. Stuart. The day before, Stuart scheduled the last of the Army of Northern Virginia's great campaign reviews for Robert E. Lee on the broad 2,200-acre plantation of the unhappy Virginia Unionist John Minor Botts. A captain in the 6th Virginia Cavalry remembered how "Gen. Lee, with his staff, first rode rapidly along the front of the line, around the left flank, then along the rear, around the right flank to his position on the hill in the front," and then "at the sound of the bugle, taken up and repeated along the line, the corps of horsemen broke by right wheel into columns of squadron, and moving south for a short distance, the head of the column was turned to the left, and again to the left, moving in this new direction, whence it passed immediately in front of the commanding general . . . ten thousand sabres flashing in the sun light . . . before the greatest soldier of modern times." The most dour of Stuart's five brigade commanders, the aptly nicknamed William "Grumble" Jones, was heard muttering about Stuart's "horse show and sham fight," and predicted that Stuart would soon enough "have a fight without the sham." But Robert E. Lee was well pleased with Stuart's review: "It was a splendid sight," he wrote to Mary Custis Lee. "Stuart was in all his glory."[18]

Lee and Stuart might have done better to have listened more carefully to Grumble Jones, because at five o'clock on the morning of the 9th, an entire division of Federal cavalry forded the three-and-a-half-foot-deep waters of the Rappahannock at Beverly Ford, emerging out of early morning river mists and quickly pouring along the road toward Beverly Ford and Culpeper, ten miles away. Two regiments of Grumble Jones' rebel cavalry who had been posted along the road turned hastily and bleary-eyed out of their blankets, recovering horses turned out to graze and sometimes only mounting bareback, and struggled to fight a series of delaying actions along the road. But what surprised the Federal troopers was that they were there at all, since the reports Alfred Pleasonton had collected the day before had no Confederate cavalry located between the river and Culpeper. But Stuart, after the review of June 8th, had camped most of his wearied cavalry east of Culpeper, nearer the river, and set up his own headquarters tent on a low ridge known locally as Fleetwood Hill, and by the time the Federal cavalry had worked its way along the Beverly Ford road toward Fleetwood Hill, more than enough Confederate cavalry, along with sixteen guns from Stuart's collection of light artillery, had collected itself at a small crossroads two miles west of Beverly Ford. There, by 7:30, the Federal advance slowed to a stop, and a headlong attempt by the 6th Pennsylvania Cavalry to overrun the rebel artillery collapsed into a melee of Union and Confederate horsemen, popping away with revolvers or hacking futilely at each other with sabers.[19]

Alf Pleasonton had another surprise in waiting. His two other divisions of cavalry crossed the Rappahannock eight miles below Beverly Ford that morning, also moving west and with the understanding that they would link up with the first division somewhere near Brandy Station before pushing on to Culpeper. This second arm of Pleasonton's attack then divided itself, with one division under David Gregg angling northward toward the rendezvous at Brandy Station and the other, smaller division under a nervous French émigré (and Crimean War veteran) gloriously named Alfred Napoleon Duffié moving straight west to the crossroads of Stevensburg to shield the main body of Pleasonton's force from any possible interference from Confederate infantry away to the south. The appearance of yet more uninvited Yankee visitors perversely delighted Grumble Jones, who seemed pleased that Stuart would "damned soon see for himself" the folly of his ways.[20]

Gregg's division heard the booming of Stuart's horse artillery, and swung up toward the southern spur of Fleetwood Hill to hit the rebel horsemen from behind. After noon, a breathless Confederate courier spurred up to Stuart with a warning that Gregg's troopers were already heading up the lower rise of the hill. Stuart at first refused to believe him. But a second courier with the same message finally got Stuart's attention, and Stuart pulled an entire brigade of rebel cavalry back at an angle to fend off Gregg's attack. The result was an even bigger melee in the open fields below Fleetwood Hill and east of Brandy Station, full of regiments and companies fighting with no particular direction amid dust clouds, "terrific, grand, and ludicrous" by one observer's reckoning, "acres and acres of horsemen sparkling with sabers, and dotted with brilliant bits of color where their flags danced above them." Horses, "wild beyond the control of their riders," carried men in and out of their opponents' reach, and in one Federal unit several troopers "escaped because their clothes were so covered with dust that they looked like graybacks." One of them was captured and recaptured three times, while another was so coated with grime that he "played secesh orderly to a secesh colonel for a while, and then escaped."[21]

By the middle of the afternoon, it was obvious to Pleasonton that this was going nowhere. Robert E. Lee himself arrived "as calm and unconcerned as if he were inspecting the land with a view of a purchase," and with him came an entire division of rebel infantry which Lee had detached from Dick Ewell's corps around Culpeper. Pleasonton pulled his three divisions back across the Rappahannock, confident that he had done as much as either Joe Hooker or the circumstances had warranted. "I did what you wanted, crippled Stuart so that he can not go on a raid," Pleasonton chirped to Hooker in a note written that evening, which was putting as good a face on a frustrated plan as possible. Lee bestowed accolades on Stuart for his "judicious and well planned" handling of his troopers—which could not quite disguise the fact that Stuart had not only been caught by surprise, but had been given the fight of his life. "The cavalry fight at Brandy Station can hardly be called a victory," one of Longstreet's staff officers wrote to his wife. "Stuart was certainly surprised and but for the supreme gallantry of his subordinate officers and the men in his command it would have been a day of disaster and disgrace."[22]

The fight around Brandy Station was a reasonably good example of what happened when large numbers of light cavalry pitched into one another at full tilt—which was to say, not very much, apart from killing eighty-one of Pleasonton's officers and troopers and leaving fifty-one dead among the Confederates. For what was otherwise the largest cavalry-on-cavalry battle of the entire war, this amounted to less than one percent of all those in action. Although numerous stories of hand-to-hand fighting emerged out of Brandy Station—including a joust of sorts between Capt. Wesley Merritt of the 2nd U.S. Cavalry and Robert E. Lee's son "Rooney" Lee—there were also less well-publicized stories about cavalry units who displayed a noticeable reluctance to come to close bloodletting quarters. A lieutenant in the 6th U.S. Cavalry wrote in irritation three days after Brandy Station about urging his squadron to charge with the sabre "but [I] could not get those cowboys to come on." The 2nd South Carolina and the 4th Virginia Cavalry broke and ran "like sheep," and in his official report, the colonel of the 4th Virginia, unable to evade what he frankly termed the regiment's "disgraceful" conduct, added humbly that he was ready for "any inquiry" Stuart "may see fit to institute." But Stuart had problems of his own after Brandy Station. The first reports in the Richmond newspapers announced in stinging terms that "All seemed to concur in the opinion . . . that our forces were surprised, and did not know of the presence of the enemy until reports of his artillery were heard." Elsewhere, the newspaper criticisms were even more severe: "a disastrous fight," a "needless slaughter." Even within Lee's staff, the best that could be said was that "It was nearly an even fight . . . neither can be said to have made a great dent."[23]

What was bad news for J.E.B. Stuart, though, did not necessarily become good news for Joe Hooker. Hooker wired Lincoln the following afternoon to announce that Pleasonton's "affair with the rebel cavalry yesterday near Brandy Station" had clearly forced Stuart to abandon "his contemplated raid into Maryland," and would the president now finally authorize him to take the offensive and cross the Rappahannock with the Army of the Potomac to attack Richmond?

The answer came back as a flat *no* that evening, accompanied the next morning by a terse *amen* from Halleck. The fact was that, even though Lincoln remained "partial to Hooker," Lincoln, Halleck, and War Secretary Edwin Stanton were already preparing to replace him. But only preparing: firing Hooker outright would be politically perilous because of Hooker's connections with the antislavery Radical Republicans in Congress. Inducing Hooker to turn in a resignation himself was preferable but would require some very adroit painting into a corner. In the meantime, Lincoln had begun quietly interviewing the corps commanders of the Army of the Potomac as a replacement for Hooker, beginning with Darius Couch on May 22nd, then Henry Slocum of the 12th Corps, Winfield Scott Hancock of the 2nd Corps, and John Sedgwick of the 6th Corps, and finally John Reynolds of the 1st Corps on June 2nd.[24]

Nothing had as yet emerged from this, first because Hooker turned a blind eye to any signals that a resignation would be welcomed, and then because command of the army had by now become such a bull's-eye for political combat that none of the army's senior major generals wanted the job. The Radical Republicans in Congress had already shown their mistrust of the prevailing McClellanism in the army in 1861 by creating the Joint House-Senate Committee on the Conduct of the War with full powers to investigate the decisions and the politics of the army's commanders, and no officers with Democratic or McClellanite leanings were eager to put their necks into the Joint Committee's noose. Hancock, in particular, had rebuffed the idea of succeeding Hooker precisely because "I do not belong to that class of generals whom the Republicans care to bolster up. I should be sacrificed," the same way McClellan had been. So for the moment, Hooker would remain in command, but only by default, and any notions of galloping wildly off toward Richmond would stay firmly collared by Lincoln and Halleck.[25]

It was Robert E. Lee who really made the question of Hooker's movements moot. Every indication he had from Ambrose Powell Hill's corps, still at Fredericksburg, confirmed in Lee's mind that the bulk of the Army of the Potomac was sitting inertly on the Rappahannock and not devoting serious resources to tracking Lee's movement to Culpeper. The way was now clear for Lee's great invasion plans to unfold. On June 11th, the day George Pickett's division finally caught up with the rest of Longstreet's corps at Culpeper, Dick Ewell's corps began the first leg of its march north. His lead division under Robert Rodes swiftly passed over sixteen miles to Flint Hill, arriving the next day at Chester Gap in the Blue Ridge Mountains and entering the Shenandoah Valley at Front Royal, where, as one North Carolina soldier in Rodes' division wrote, "the ladies treated us very good." The rest of Ewell's corps was hard on Rodes' heels—Jubal Early's division arrived at Front Royal on the 12th, followed by Edward Johnson's division, and by the 13th all of Ewell's corps was in the Shenandoah. Longstreet's corps, with Lafayette McLaws' division in the van, took up the march parallel to Ewell, on the east side of the Blue Ridge, covering the other passes into the Shenandoah—Manassas Gap, Ashby's Gap, Snicker's Gap—from any potential interference.[26]

Lee was already anticipating that his invasion plans were likely to have far more than just a military impact. "Recent political movements in the United States . . . have attracted my attention," Lee wrote to Jefferson Davis even as he was preparing for this next movement northward. In the first half of June, the Northern newspapers that Lee regularly gleaned for information were full of uproar over the arrest and imprisonment of Clement Vallandigham, an uproar that included a gigantic antiwar meeting in Albany and a peace rally at New York City's Cooper Institute. Vallandigham's arrest was promptly followed by the sensational shutdown by Federal troops under the disastrously impulsive Ambrose Burnside of the anti-administration *Chicago Times* (followed by a protest assembly of 20,000 people in Chicago). "Under these circumstances," Lee urged, "we should neglect no honorable means of dividing and weakening our enemies," even if it meant stretching the truth a little by offering to negotiate a restoration of the Union. Once the negotiating began, "the war would no longer be supported" in the North, and at that point "the desire of our people for a distinct and independent national existence" could be put forward without much fear that the negotiations would be suspended or the war resumed. The final straw for Lincoln-weary Northerners would be a successful invasion of the North.[27]

With Lee's urging in mind, Davis wired Alexander Stephens, the Confederate vice president, to come to Richmond for a briefing on a special mission. Stephens, curiously, had also written Davis, on June 12th, urging the opening of some kind of discussions in Washington about a "general adjustment"

MOVEMENTS OF THE ARMY OF NORTHERN VIRGINIA
TO WINCHESTER AND THE POTOMAC

based on "recognition of the Sovereignty of the States." Whether Stephens was prepared to insist on Confederate independence was uncertain, but he was willing to try, and Davis was willing to authorize him. Stephens arrived in Richmond on June 26th, where Davis handed him a letter he was to present under a flag of truce to Abraham Lincoln. Ostensibly, Stephens' mission was "to arrange and settle all differences and disputes which may have arisen or may arise in the execution of the cartel for exchange of prisoners of war." But if the circumstances provided an opening for a more freewheeling discussion of issues of reconciliation, Stephens had the latitude to proceed. And the circumstances would in large measure be shaped by what Robert E. Lee would accomplish somewhere north of the Potomac.[28]

The Shenandoah Valley, not Harpers Ferry, would be the route to the

Potomac in 1863, and the Army of Northern Virginia would cross the river at Boteler's Ford (near Shepherdstown) and at Williamsport. To get there, the Federal garrison in Winchester would have to be evicted, and that would mean tackling the three brigades stationed there and the fortifications they occupied under the command of Robert Milroy. These 6,900 Union soldiers—mostly Ohio and West Virginia recruits—had done little since their enlistments but guard duty on the Baltimore & Ohio Railroad and their fortifications were badly sited to resist a determined attack. Above all, Brigadier General Milroy was a man of big mouth and small talent as a soldier. An Indiana lawyer, an unbuttoned abolitionist, and (perhaps most to his advantage) a political ally of Lincoln's secretary of the interior, John P. Usher, Milroy won his brigadier general's star in September 1861, and did some minor but undistinguished campaigning in the western Virginia mountains and the Shenandoah Valley.[29] Apart from that, Milroy's energies had been turned toward nominating himself to be emancipation's missionary to the Shenandoah. This did little beyond antagonizing a populace already ill-disposed to Union occupation, and painting a large target on Milroy's back. "Everywhere we hear the same talk of [the] oppression and cowardly cruelty of Milroy," wrote one of Longstreet's staff officers. "The reign of Milroy," proclaimed the Richmond papers, was a lesson in "brutality and robbery," and the "one prayer in Winchester . . . is 'Oh, God, how long, how long!'" The Virginia legislature branded Milroy an "outlaw" and it was rumored in Winchester that "the Confederacy (some people in the Confederacy)" had put a price of $100,000 on Milroy's gray-bearded head. Even Robert E. Lee, in a rare moment of vindictiveness, branded Milroy "atrocious" and suggested to Secretary of War Seddon in January 1863 that "prisoners from his command captured by our forces be not exchanged but that they be held as hostages for the protection of our people against the outrages which he is reported to be committing."[30]

Dick Ewell drew the ticket to carry the torch to Milroy. This only seemed appropriate, given that the sixty-four infantry regiments of Ewell's corps included twenty-five who had fought under Stonewall Jackson and won Jackson's most spectacular victories at Front Royal and Winchester in 1862. And if the unusual concentration of eccentric division and brigade commanders in the corps was any proof, the stamp of Stonewall Jackson was still very deep on Ewell's command. His senior division commander, Jubal Early, was the army's most caustic and opinionated curmudgeon. Edward Johnson (who ranked just behind Early) commanded the next division, and "always carried a big hickory club or cane" which he preferred as a weapon to a saber or revolver. (Johnson, known affectionately as "Allegheny Ed" and "Old Allegheny," had the distinction of crossing swords with Milroy in western Virginia back in 1861 and again in 1862.) Early's senior brigade commander, Harry Thompson

Hays, commanded five Louisiana regiments who had collectively borrowed the "Louisiana Tigers" label from its original owners in 1862. Early's second brigade was commanded by William Smith, who won the sobriquet "Extra Billy" from the surcharges he had skimmed for carrying government mail on his stagecoach line during the presidency of Andrew Jackson. Although Extra Billy would be sixty-six in September and candidly admitted that he was "wholly ignorant of drill and tactics," he had just been elected (for the second time) governor of Virginia, and for that reason alone no one in this Virginia-besotted army was eager to dispute his place at the head of a brigade.[31]

The confidence Lee put behind Ewell's corps was richly rewarded. Ewell hurried his corps for twenty-three miles, fording the Shenandoah without giving the men "time to stop & take off shoes & socks," and arrived within three miles of Winchester before noon on the 13th. He then split his divisions, with three brigades of Jubal Early's division swinging away to the west of Winchester, Early's remaining brigade and Allegheny Johnson's division deploying beside the turnpike south of the town, and Robert Rodes' remaining division out to the east (where they cleared one of Milroy's brigades out of an advanced post at Berryville).[32]

Startled at the sudden appearance of masses of Confederate infantry, Milroy hastily manned Winchester's defensive lines and spent most of the afternoon hours of the 13th looping shells at the rebel infantry he could see south of the town. Neither he nor anyone else in the defenses caught sight of Jubal Early's three brigades as they moved quietly into position west of the town "by a blind and circuitous road" and "spent the night in a drenching rain." On the morning of the 14th, Harry Hays and his adjutant were able to creep up "to the edge of the woods" near one of Milroy's outlying artillery emplacements and "discovered several men lying on the ground under the shade of a tree" while "sentinels lazily paced their rounds, and everything betokened a total ignorance of our proximity." That was enough to persuade Jubal to attack, and at 6:00 p.m. Early's artillery battalion (plus one battery from Allegheny Johnson's division) began firing shells at the Federal emplacements and trenches on the west side of Winchester. After forty-five minutes, the brigades of Hays and Extra Billy Smith, and the North Carolina brigade of Isaac Avery, burst from the treelines that had concealed them, and "in a few minutes they were over the breastworks, driving the enemy out in great haste and confusion." Only the fall of night kept the Confederates from swarming into the streets of Winchester itself.[33]

Robert Milroy, who had a great deal more to answer for than most Union soldiers if he was captured, convened a hasty conference at nine o'clock with his three brigade commanders, and decided to make a run for it. It was too late. Dick Ewell guessed that the Federals would bolt down the turnpike toward Martinsburg or Harpers Ferry, and in the night he directed Allegheny Johnson to march three of his brigades around Winchester and position themselves athwart the turnpike at Stephenson's Depot, where a railroad embankment for the Winchester & Potomac Railroad cut across the pike. Milroy's would-be escapees barged into Johnson's brigades in the predawn light, and tried to run over them. But after three attempts "to storm and capture their batteries," Milroy gave every regiment leave to look out for itself, and what had once been Milroy's command broke up in desperately fleeing fragments. Some made it to safety in Martinsburg, others—including the hapless Milroy—to Harpers Ferry. But 2,500 fell prisoner to Johnson, and another 1,500 were taken in Winchester by Jubal Early when his brigades entered Winchester that morning and tore down the huge garrison flag which had waved over Milroy's main fort. If Ewell had had more than just one company of cavalry with his corps, he might have bagged still more of the running Yankees; as it was, the few horsemen he had at his disposal spent "two days after the defeat of Milroy . . . actively engaged in pursuing and harassing the enemy" and running down bands of fugitives "who were retreating in great disorder."[34]

It was one of the most swift, total, and bloodless Confederate victories of the war. Only 42 out of the 23,000 men of Ewell's corps had been killed; in return, Ewell had surprised and obliterated 3 Union brigades (which would, in fact, never be reconstituted), captured 23 pieces of Union artillery, and gobbled up "ammunition and a large number of wagons and teams." A "gentleman from the Valley" estimated that Ewell had acquired between 6,000 and 7,000 Union prisoners, 2,800 horses, 400 to 500 wagons, and stores worth $1.5 to $2 million. There was enough captured material for "the Qr. Master" to reequip Early's division with "all necessaries . . . from this post, and everybody is now completely equipped for the campaign." The artillery officer detailed to inventory the captured Union guns did a little gobbling of his own "among the plunder" and "found myself possessed of a nice pair of oil cloth pants and writing materials sufficient to stand a 12 mos siege," while Sam Pickens in the 5th Alabama supplied himself with "a good Havre sack, almost new & . . . an abundance of good soap & some nice toilet soap."[35]

For the moment, it appeared that any concerns Robert E. Lee had nursed about Ewell's fitness for independent action—and especially for filling Stonewall Jackson's boots—had been triumphantly erased. The egg-headed Ewell now became "our glorious Ewell" in the *Richmond Daily Dispatch,* which announced that Jackson's former division commander "has indeed caught the mantle of the ascended Jackson. Brilliantly has he re-enacted the scenes of the spring of '62, on the same theatre." When the news reached Longstreet's corps on the other side of the Blue Ridge, they were inclined to cheer the same way. "Ewell won his right to Jackson's game on Jackson's ground," Charles Blackford, one of Jackson's veteran officers, wrote to his wife, Susan, on June 16th. "This success will give the corps more confidence in Ewell." Or, *almost* more confidence. The shadow of Jackson did not dissipate quite so easily. A Virginian who had served in Stonewall's old brigade in the Shenandoah in 1862 acknowledged that Ewell "did well in routing Milroy from Winchester." But if Jackson had been in command on June 14th, he added, Jackson "would have had his line of battle around Winchester, and captured the whole command"—especially Robert Milroy. "If he had been captured by some of our men he would have fared badly."[36]

CHAPTER FIVE

Victory will inevitably attend our arms

MILROY DID NOT, in fact, fare badly at all, despite the dissolution of his command. He admitted that he had been surprised by the speed with which the Confederates had reached Winchester from the Rappahannock. "I believed that Lee could not move his large army, with its immense artillery and baggage trains, and perform a six days' march in my direction, unless I received timely notice of that important fact." But that, in Milroy's mind, only thrust the real blame onto his superiors—onto Henry Halleck as general in chief and onto Robert Schenck as his department commander—who, presumably, had access to the latest news on Lee's movements and should have given him more than the ambiguous directives he had received from Washington and Baltimore. Halleck was infuriated, and on June 20th he ordered Milroy's arrest. But a court of inquiry that fall cleared Milroy of responsibility for the Winchester debacle, and he went on to take command of another backwater railroad district in Tennessee, where he once again set the civilian population's teeth on edge and invited another price on his head.[1]

One person who might have derived some bleak satisfaction from seeing Halleck tagged with blame for the Winchester debacle was Joseph Hooker. The day before Winchester was attacked, Hooker warned Halleck that "my sources of information" indicated that "Longstreet's and Ewell's corps" were on the march "toward the Valley." The next day he coyly wired Lincoln to ask whether "anything further" had been "heard from Winchester." Lincoln, of course, had lost all communication with Winchester, and anxiously asked Hooker whether, "if they could hold out a few days, could you help them." Surely, Lincoln reasoned uneasily, "if the head of Lee's army is at Martinsburg

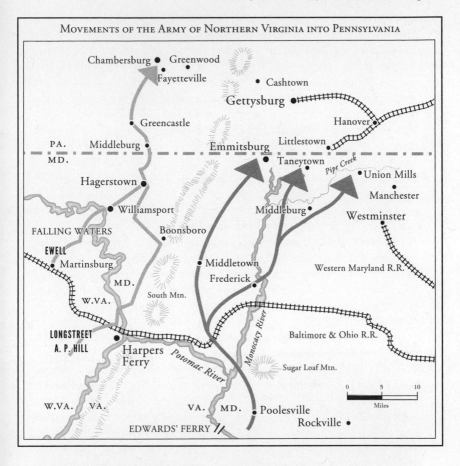

MOVEMENTS OF THE ARMY OF NORTHERN VIRGINIA INTO PENNSYLVANIA

and the tail of it on the Plank road between Fredericksburg and Chancellors-ville, the animal must be very slim somewhere. Could you not break him?" But the slim part would lie in the Shenandoah Valley, and the valley lay in someone else's military department, and after Chancellorsville, Halleck and Lincoln had limited any discretion Hooker had to give orders anywhere outside the Army of the Potomac. So it pleased Hooker only too well to be able to say—and to say directly to Halleck—that "the instructions of the President, approved by yourself, and your original letter of instructions, compel me" to stick close to the line of the Orange & Alexandria Railroad in order to protect Washington, not Winchester.[2]

But Hooker now had more to do than snicker darkly at his nemesis in Washington. The fall of Winchester removed the one serious obstacle in Robert E. Lee's path down the valley to the Potomac, and with that gate open, there was no longer any need to conceal his intentions so closely. Powell Hill's corps, which had kept the Army of the Potomac pinned uncertainly to the Rappahannock, was on the march for Culpeper by the afternoon of the 14th, and by the 19th, they, too, were in the Shenandoah. Ahead of them, Longstreet abandoned his shielding position east of the Blue Ridge gaps and concentrated his three divisions at Winchester on the 15th, while Ewell sent Robert Rodes' untried division, which Ewell had kept in reserve at Winchester, to clear out Martinsburg and secure the upriver Potomac ferry at Williamsport. Fanning out on the other side of the Potomac were two cavalry brigades, one under John Imboden and the other under Albert Gallatin Jenkins. These cavalrymen were little better than local rangers, but for the purpose of setting off a confusing cloud of alarms in south-central Pennsylvania they would do very nicely. Jenkins, in particular, would start across the Potomac on June 15th, heading for Chambersburg, Pennsylvania, the first major town on the valley route into Pennsylvania. There, he would spend three days, torching bridges, wrecking railroad equipment, burning warehouses, cutting telegraph wires in Chambersburg and throughout the nearby towns of McConnellsburg, Mercersburg, and Greencastle—and diverting attention from Lee's crossing of the Potomac.[3]

Lee still preferred to keep any discussion of ultimate objectives under wraps. "From orders read out at dress parade this evening," one Virginia private in Longstreet's corps guessed that "there is some great move on hand, but I do not know what it is, or where we are going." The adjutant of Joseph Kershaw's South Carolina brigade "came around with orders" and relayed the headquarters gossip that "we were on our way to Hagerstown, Md." Another new division commander in Hill's corps, the North Carolinian Dorsey Pender, wrote to his wife that "tomorrow morning we start as I suppose for Penn[sylvani]a," something he had long believed "the large majority of the Army would like to" do. But that gave no joy to his wife, Fanny Pender, who was convinced that any kind of war which was not strictly a defense of North Carolina's hearths and homes was unjust and illegitimate, and tempted God. She was not alone. In the 26th North Carolina, nine men deserted on June 16th, and five more three days afterward. "Our men are deserting fast," wrote a private in the 26th, "and a great many more talks of leaving." What kept more of them from deserting was the prospect that this would be the last campaign—that "the South is going to gain her independence during this campaign," as one soldier in the 8th Virginia wrote, with another adding, "So far Gen. Lee's campaign has been very successful and I hope that a few weeks may bring the war to a happy conclusion."[4]

Having moved so swiftly from Culpeper to Winchester, Ewell's corps was already showing "unmistakable signs of exhaustion." The Confederates now slowed their pace to the Potomac, spending three days covering the forty miles between Winchester and the river. Once again, Ewell's corps took the lead, with the 14th North Carolina being the first of Ewell's regiments to cross. The two divisions of Allegheny Johnson and Jubal Early used Boteler's Ford, just below Shepherdstown, to cross the Potomac between June 18th and 22nd. The river there "was very high," which forced the men to strip, sling "their clothing and accoutrements" over their rifles, and carry everything "above their heads to keep them dry." One Louisiana Tiger thought it made for no end of comedy "to see the long lines of naked men" fording the river; the chill of the water added to the amusement, since it made "the men as they entered it . . . scream and shout most boisterously." A Virginian saw the soldiers' spirits lift as they crossed into Maryland: "The health of the troops was never better and above all the *morale* of the army was never more favorable for offensive or defensive operations. . . . Victory will inevitably attend our arms in any collision with the enemy."[5]

The same skylarking spirit appeared when Robert Rodes' division from Ewell's corps waded the Potomac on June 19th, fifteen miles upriver near the ferry at Williamsport. From there, Ewell's and Rodes' troops marched the ten miles up to Hagerstown, Maryland, where the regimental colors were uncased and the bands blared "The Bonnie Blue Flag" through the streets. Longstreet's corps caught up to the Potomac at Williamsport on June 25th, crossing as though it was a holiday, with bands playing "Maryland, My Maryland," and men singing the dirgelike popular song "All Quiet Along the Potomac To-night." Lee was traveling with Longstreet, and out of deference to the commander and "the ladies who came down to see the sight," Longstreet's divisions "waded into the water without stopping to roll up their pantaloons." But they "came over in good order as if on review, cheering at every step" and took up the parade through Hagerstown "in columns of companies."[6]

Few things puzzled these rebels more than the indifferent response they received from Marylanders along their routes, given that Marylanders were, after all, Southerners and denizens of a slave state. Robert Emory Park, a private in the 12th Alabama, thought that "a majority of the people" were "unionists." Or at least the males seemed to be: in Hagerstown, one of Ewell's North Carolinians thought that "here the men greeted us very shabby, but the ladies quite the reverse." It was "the ladies" whom the 5th Alabama noticed "wav[ing] handkerchiefs & some Confederate flags," and young Park was delighted the next evening to be invited to a party, where he heard "young ladies just from a Pennsylvania female college . . . play and sing Southern songs." The weather posed disappointments of another sort, since it began raining on June 19th, and then turned into full-blown thunderstorms till the

22nd, drenching the men in Longstreet's corps "in the hardest rains I ever saw, pouring down during the entire night." The "disagreeable" rain started again on June 24th, and Powell Hill's corps had to march through Hagerstown in the downpour, the bands of the North Carolina regiments "playing lively tunes" but *sans* ladies' handkerchiefs.[7]

The next day brought a more sobering event. A deserter from the 18th Virginia, John Riley, had been recaptured, tried, and sentenced to death, and on the evening of the 25th the men of his brigade (in Pickett's division) were paraded in a three-sided square near Hagerstown to witness a twelve-man firing squad execute "the poor unfortunate." Charles Blackford noted in a letter to his wife that "there were four like executions, I was told, in Rodes' division," and another in Longstreet's corps, in the 56th Virginia on June 26th. The effect on any others contemplating an unplanned flight homeward, as one observer wrote dryly, "was beneficial." In Longstreet's other divisions and in Hill's corps, the execution news was anesthetized with a liberal "quantity of whiskey," and "about one-third got pretty tight." In Carnot Posey's brigade of Mississippians, "nearly all the brigade" was "more or less inebriated and boisterous," while a captain in the 17th Georgia estimated that it took only "thirty minutes" before "Hood's division presented the liveliest spectacle I ever saw."[8]

Morale in an army is a compound of attitudes—satisfaction with food, clothing, equipment, assigned duties; confidence in the competence and empathy of officers; a fairly enforced code of behavior; and a level of training, individually and as a group, that imparts a sense of the reliability of others in a tight place. With so many parts, morale in an army quivers like the needle of a delicate compass, and any failure to keep the needle steady, especially in democratically minded armies of short-term volunteers in the nineteenth century, could be fatal to the army's survival. Robert E. Lee, like other professional soldiers of his generation, feared the ease with which morale could disintegrate in an American army, and how little could be done by officers to restrain it—in fact, how little restrained the officers were from becoming the cause of disintegration themselves. If the soldiers were ill-fed and ill-clothed, or if their officers were characterless clowns, or if their training had never succeeded in making them think of themselves as a unit rather than as freebooting individuals, then the evaporation of morale would only be quicker. Lee had nearly come to disaster at Antietam largely because so much of the Army of Northern Virginia had evaporated into wholesale straggling and left him with perilously reduced numbers to face the Yankees; he could not afford to let that happen this time.

The problem was that freebooting was going to be difficult to resist. As

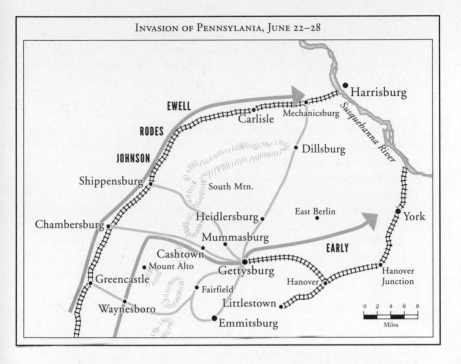

INVASION OF PENNSYLANIA, JUNE 22–28

the Army of Northern Virginia crossed the Potomac, it was putting itself beyond "the last point where we will be in railroad communication with Richmond." The Confederates would be fed and clothed only by what they carried in their wagons—and by what they could take from the countryside. "Beef we can drive with us," Lee warned Dick Ewell, "but bread we cannot carry, and must secure it in the country." If that taking was not carefully controlled, it would encourage the taking of everything, and soon the army would become so lawless that it would be unable to fight.[9]

For the moment, however, the morale of the army, as it crossed the Potomac and headed for Pennsylvania, seemed to soar. Rodes' division, still in the lead of Dick Ewell's corps, crossed the Maryland-Pennsylvania state line on June 22nd, marched through Middleburg, and occupied Greencastle without any opposition. Longstreet and Hill closed up behind Ewell, and as they crossed the state line, too, a triumphant sense of hilarity broke out. In John Bell Hood's division, the stone boundary marker beside the road set off waves of rebel yells. In the Texas brigade, one extrovert staged a little pantomime, pivoting out of column to hail his captain, William Martin: "Captain, I have fallen back for reinforcements. I want you to help me capture the State of Pennsylvania." Martin laughed indulgently. "All right, sonny. Show me the Keystone and we'll smash her into smithereens." Linking arms, they stepped over the state line and "invaded the United States." In Powell Hill's corps, three men of the 9th Alabama stopped at the state line, straddled it "with one foot in Maryland and the other in Pennsylvania," and drank a toast from their canteens.[10]

They might well drink a toast to Pennsylvania, although they did not mean this as a compliment to its people. "Such long head men I never saw," wrote a Georgian in Hood's division, "and the features of the women would have made vinegar ashamed of itself for sourness." Another Georgian thought "the Girls of Pennsylvania are the ugliest set of mortals I ever saw—longfaced, barefooted, big nosed, and everything else that it takes to constitute an ugly woman." Even the "well-dressed ones . . . showed unmistakable signs of lowness and vulgarity." But the richness and beauty of the countryside offered such a contrast to the overworked and war-ravaged farmlands of the South that nearly every Confederate who wrote about the Gettysburg campaign felt compelled to mention it. "Country fine, houses & barns good. The crops look well," scribbled a soldier in the 2nd Mississippi. One man in the 4th Texas wrote more expansively that this was "the most beautiful country I ever beheld . . . the entire landscape covered with the most magnificent farms, orchards and gardens, for miles along the road." "We saw the finest kind of wheat all along the road, & some fields of Oats, rye & barley," wrote Samuel Pickens of the 5th Alabama. "Also the richest fields of Clover & hay grasses. This is a great country for small grain & stock."

One feature in particular took Southerners' notice, and that was the comparative smallness of the landholdings, as defined by the endless interweaving of miles and miles of wooden fences. In Virginia, the 500-acre plantation was the rule, making up by acreage what the thin soils of the South could not produce by their own strength; in Pennsylvania, wrote Charles Blackford, the soil supported "small farms divided into fields no larger than our garden and barns much larger than their houses." All of it—"orchards, meadows, fields of grain"—was surrounded by "substantial fences" and "above all the mighty barns, which are the glory of the Pennsylvania farmer." These Southerners scarcely reflected upon a larger reason for the miniature checkerboard of Pennsylvania's farmland. The state had mandated the gradual emancipation of its slaves in 1780, which drove downward the size of farmholdings that could be managed by a single owner or tenant. Lee's soldiers also missed the significance of the multitude of "substantial fences" needed to enclose those small free-soil farms; these fences would play a role of their own in defeating slaveholding's bid for independence on a hot July afternoon not much more than a week away.[11]

What delighted the eye of an invading army might also destroy it, if the men in that army enjoyed plundering those delights enough to lure them from the march, from roll call, from fatigue duty, from the commands of officers, from the soldiers' communion with one another. On June 21st (while Longstreet's and Hill's corps were still waiting to cross the Potomac), Robert E. Lee issued the first of two general orders, demanding that "no private property shall be injured or destroyed by any person belonging to or connected with the army." Only authorized staff personnel, whether commissary, quartermaster's, or medical staff, would "make requisitions . . . for the necessary supplies" on local authorities or inhabitants for "necessary supplies," and they were to pay "the market price for the articles furnished," with receipts issued in duplicate.

In years to come, this order would be the source of limitless satisfaction to Lee's veterans, who would point to it as evidence of the South's gentlemanly and civilized restraint in the making of war. What was forgotten was that Lee's restraining order only offered Confederate paper money for the requisitions; that those who were disinclined to take Confederate paper would be offered receipts and the supplies taken anyway; and that anyone trying to "remove or conceal property necessary for the use of the army" would have it confiscated outright. This did not provide as much security as it seemed for the farmers and shopkeepers whose inventories were thus rendered fair game. But as the order was passed down from corps to division headquarters throughout the army, it did create a disciplined process which would keep the ordinary Confederate soldier from deputizing himself as his own chief provider. It was not plundering that was undesirable, but uncontrolled plundering that led to uncontrollable soldiers sprawled across the countryside. After all, Lee had already given orders to strip the Baltimore & Ohio workshops at Martinsburg of "tools, machinery, and materials much needed by the railroads of the Confederacy," and one of his principal rationales for coming north was to feed his army on the vast buffet of Pennsylvania farming. Plunder could be good—provided it was regulated.[12]

Keeping up that caveat seems to have been harder than anyone expected. "General Lee has issued orders prohibiting all misconduct or lawlessness and urging the utmost forebearance and kindness to all," wrote an Alabamian. But no sooner had the army crossed the state line than the march descended dangerously close to a free-for-all. After all, "the rebel officers and men" declared to anyone along the way who would listen that "they had been fighting this war long enough in the South, and they were going to Pennsylvania to make it the battle-ground"—which included "taking what they pleased without paying for it." An apprehensive Dorsey Pender wrote to his disapproving wife on June 28th, "Until we crossed the Md. Line our men behaved as well as troops could," but now "they have an idea that they are to indulge in unlicensed plunder." Once encamped, rebel soldiers dispersed to "forage after chickens, eggs, butter, vegetables, apple butter, honey, etc." Lee might issue "orders against . . . unauthorized taking," admitted one artillery lieutenant, but "our boys lay waste the land on the sly." Jeremiah Tate marveled in a letter to his wife that "when we first arrived in Pennsylvania we saw a fine time we got evry thing to eat that hart cood wish, such as milk and butter apple butter chickens honey molases sugar coffee tea chease and Whiskey wines of all kindes, everything was cheap all it cost us was to go after it." Soldiers could get away with this because all too many officers preferred to invent excuses for ignoring Lee's order rather than invite outright disobedience. In Evander McIvor Law's Alabama brigade, "there were ninety-five sheep skins in Law's camp." When "someone spoke to" Law about the suspicious skins, "he said that no man's sheep could bite his men without getting hurt." John Bell Hood was even more indulgent: "Boys, you are now on the enemy's soil, stack your arms and do pretty much as you please."[13]

Once Ewell's corps reached the town of Chambersburg, the pillaging became even easier, given the concentration of stores and warehouses in a town of 5,000 inhabitants. At nine o'clock on the morning of June 24th, Robert Rodes' division pulled itself together sufficiently to parade into Chambersburg, with a band tooting a reprise of "The Bonnie Blue Flag." Dick Ewell, who had been traveling in a carriage with his crutches and prosthesis, set up command at the town bank, where he presented his formal requisition for supplies: 5,000 jackets and trousers, 50,000 pounds of bread, 500 barrels of flour, 5,000 bushels of grain, and so forth. A hastily assembled civilian committee tried to bargain with Ewell, but to no avail. Squads of Confederate soldiers began breaking open locked-up stores, and Chambersburg's "grocery, drug, hardware, book and stationery, clothing, boot and shoe stores were all relieved of most of their remaining contents." Ewell's stepson, Campbell Brown, and another veteran staffer did some private foraging of their own in Chambersburg's shops, since Brown's mother had sent him off with a list of goods to pick up in Pennsylvania. Ewell's chief engineer also had a list thoughtfully provided by his wife, which included "about $100 worth of calico, wool delaine, bleached cotton, hoops, gloves, bread, gingham, pins &c &c" to be piled onto empty wagons heading south for resupply.[14]

Confiscation soon degenerated into robbery. "A group of 'Louisiana Tigers'" stopped men on the streets and demanded their hats and boots; the pastor of the German Reformed Church, Benjamin Schneck, "one of the best citizens of the place," was stripped of his gold watch and $50 in cash. Soon enough, the robberies turned into simple vandalism. Several Confederates broke into the Odd Fellows Hall and "cut to pieces and destroyed a greater portion" of the lodge's regalia, "broke open several of the desks and drawers, and mutilated everything they could lay their hands on." A "respectable" soldier in the 15th Georgia said "the streets of Chambersburg are strewn with gloves and fragments of goods."[15]

From there, the vandalism veered into kidnapping of a very specific and lucrative sort. In 1860, some 1,700 free black people lived in and around Chambersburg, Mercersburg, and Greencastle. A few were fugitives from slavery, and "free" only in fact, and for them the descent of the Army of Northern Virginia on south-central Pennsylvania was the beginning of "a regular slave hunt." But not even those blacks whose families had been free for generations in Pennsylvania expected the Confederate armies to spend any time distinguishing between who was legitimately free and who was not. Free black civilians working under Union Army contracts, as well as "contrabands" who found refuge within Union Army camps, were all alike to the rebels, and when Harpers Ferry was overrun by Confederates in 1862, black fugitives "who thought . . . the hour of freedom" had come, and who "had gathered under the flag which to them was its starry symbol," were roughly lined up along with the garrison's black teamsters, cooks, grooms, and ostlers, while Confederate soldiers and officers strolled down the lines, free to claim any of them as "their property."[16]

A year later, the same opportunity presented itself in Chambersburg. When Albert Jenkins' rough-hewn cavalrymen made their initial foray into the Cumberland Valley in mid-June, "they took up all [the people of color] they could find, even little children, whom they had to carry on horseback before them" to be claimed or sold in the slave markets in Richmond. One prosperous Chambersburg farmer, William Heyser, was shocked to discover that the Confederates had taken with them "250 colored people again into bondage." The infantry of Ewell's corps who followed on June 24th were even less fastidious about sweeping up any black people they could lay their hands upon. George Steuart's Maryland brigade, looping westward to Mercersburg and McConnellsburg, threatened to "burn down every house which harbored a fugitive slave, and did not deliver him up within twenty minutes," and in Mercersburg twenty-one blacks were rounded up and driven south, including "two or three" who "were born and raised in this neighborhood." A local magistrate who protested taking "free negroes" was abruptly told, "Yes, and we will take you, too, if you do not shut up!" This might, in the larger scheme of the campaign, have seemed a waste of military time, but slaves were a valuable commodity. As one farmer was told by Confederates who were escorting "four wagon loads of women & children between Chambersburg & the Maryland line," even the children "will bring something." This was, after all, an army whose cause was inextricably bound up with the defense of

black enslavement. To have left Pennsylvania's blacks in undisturbed freedom
would have been tantamount to denying the validity of the whole Confederate enterprise.[17]

Robert E. Lee was not amused by this boys-out-of-school behavior. It belied
his own self-cultivated image of the dispassionate master-general, not to mention indulging precisely the crimes for which he had long indicted his Federal
opponents in Virginia. When he arrived in Chambersburg with Longstreet's
corps on June 27th, Lee issued a second general order, chiding the army for
"instances of forgetfulness, on the part of some," of his first directive against
looting. His principal concern, however, remained the discipline of the troops,
not the offense of pillaging or kidnapping. He was perfectly happy to see John
Imboden's horsemen round up "the cattle and sheep you have sent to the
Valley," even while Imboden continued to tear up the Baltimore & Ohio
Railroad, and urged Imboden to "make every exertion to collect all the supplies you can." Undirected thievery was what worried Lee. "It is absolutely
necessary . . . to our salvation that our army not become demoralized," wrote
Longstreet's senior division commander, Lafayette McLaws, "which would be
the case should our men be permitted to rob and take at pleasure." It would
bring down "disgrace" on the army, and become "subversive of the discipline
and efficiency of our army, and destructive of the ends of our present movement." But even wanton looting sometimes passed without Lee's rebuke. Tal-
iferro Simpson of the 3rd South Carolina (in Longstreet's corps) remembered
that "Lee seemed to disregard entirely the soldiers' open acts of disobedience."
Simpson saw the henhouses of a roadside farm being emptied by "a party of
some thirty or forty men" when the "old lady" of the house caught sight of
Lee and "bawled out in a loud voice, 'Genl Lee, Genl Lee, I wish to speak to
you sir.'" But Simpson saw Lee only raise his hand and say, "Good morning
madam," and ride on.[18]

But even if Lee had wanted to intervene, he simply did not have the
staff needed to review and regulate every infraction of his anti-plundering
orders. "Our staff organizations were never sufficiently extensive and perfect
to enable the Commanding General to be practically present every where,"
complained Porter Alexander years after the war. On the Peninsula, Lee complained angrily that McClellan "will get away because I cannot have my orders
carried out." And once again, the proof was in the numbers. Partly because
of the statutory restraints invented by the Confederate Congress and partly as
a matter of his own personal taste, Robert E. Lee functioned on a daily basis
with only six personal staffers—his chief of staff, Robert Chilton (who wrote
out the fatal "lost orders" before Antietam); his adjutant and principal aide,

Walter H. Taylor; his two military secretaries, Armistead Lindsay Long and Charles Marshall; the army's inspector general, Charles Venable; and Thomas Talcott, Lee's aide and later engineer.[19]

There was also a somewhat larger general staff—Lee's personal spiritual friend, the elderly William Nelson Pendleton, who served as chief of artillery; James Lawrence Corley, the army's quartermaster general; Col. Robert G. Cole, the army's commissary general; the chief medical officer, Lafayette Guild; Col. Briscoe Baldwin, Lee's chief ordnance officer; and his engineers, Col. William Proctor Smith and Capt. Samuel R. Johnston. But that, together with two companies of escort cavalry and the clerks who assisted the staff, was all that Lee relied upon to administer the Army of Northern Virginia. Their average age was only thirty, and their burdens were not light. "I am harassed by an accumulation of miserable paper calling for my attention," wailed Walter Taylor. No one in those circumstances had time to chase after hat stealers and watch stealers, leaving Lafayette McLaws to reflect years later that "The great defect in our army was in staff organization & its practices."[20]

Lee and his shorthanded staff had larger matters to occupy them in Pennsylvania. Thus far, Lee's invasion had moved almost effortlessly across two major rivers, through two small battles, and through three states, and he was pleased enough with this remarkable degree of success to authorize the next stage of the invasion *and* to renew his pleas to Jefferson Davis to release the two brigades around Richmond, under Micah Jenkins and Montgomery Corse. Just as he had predicted in May, Federal "apprehension for the safety of Washington and their own territory" had caused the Army of the Potomac to fall back from the Rappahannock riverline, while other Federal invaders were being evacuated from coastal North Carolina and from Kentucky. This was the moment, Lee politely suggested, for Joe Johnston to take the Confederate armies in the West on the offensive, and magnify the pressure on the Lincoln government by invading Kentucky, perhaps even Ohio. In fact, it might not be a bad idea if Davis called up the Confederate forces Pierre Beauregard was sitting upon down in the Carolinas and bring them up to Culpeper, "even in effigy," to distract the Army of the Potomac still further. (Both Beauregard and the skeptical Secretary Seddon at once began stuffing Davis' incoming mail with notices of renewed Federal activity in the Carolinas and on the James River peninsula.)[21]

Lee's most immediate concern was the next phase of the Pennsylvania invasion, and on June 22nd he was satisfied enough with the Army of Northern Virginia's progress to instruct Dick Ewell to begin moving his corps north in a great right-turning arc, up through the Cumberland Valley and along the line of the Cumberland Valley Railroad, until by June 28th he would be poised on the western bank of the Susquehanna, opposite Harrisburg. Longstreet and Hill would continue to move up behind him, but it would be up to Ewell to determine the exact "progress and direction" of his forces, just as it had been at Winchester. And like Winchester, "If Harrisburg comes within your means, capture it."[22]

Using Albert Jenkins' cavalry brigade as his forward screen, Ewell decided to duplicate the Winchester strategy—as well as lighten the traffic burden of his corps on just one road—by splitting his corps. Rodes' and Allegheny Johnson's divisions, together with the corps wagon trains, would move north and east through Shippensburg and Carlisle toward Harrisburg. Jubal Early's division, however, would split sharply to the east, passing through the cover of South Mountain at the Cashtown Gap and following on a straight line from there to York and the Susquehanna, where he could then cross the Susquehanna, turn north, "levy a contribution on the rich town of Lancaster, cut the [Northern] Central Railroad, and threaten Harrisburg from behind and below while General Ewell was advancing against that city from the other side."[23]

This time, there was no Federal cavalry and no Brandy Station to threaten the Confederate line of march. Apart from the out-of-reach wig-wagging of Union signalers on the peaks of South Mountain and small parties of mounted observers, "there were no indications of any enemy near us and the march was entirely without molestation." There had been a brief skirmish with a detachment of New York cavalry just north of Greencastle on June 22nd (which resulted in the death of one New Yorker, the first fatality of the invasion in Pennsylvania, Corporal William H. Rihl), and some minor bushwhacking by cleaned-out farmers determined to revenge themselves on Confederate stragglers. Otherwise, Ewell's path to Carlisle was largely unobstructed, and having covered nearly fifty miles in two days, Rodes' division marched in late on the afternoon of June 27th, with the band at the head of the division column thundering "Dixie."[24]

Carlisle happened to be a minor homecoming for Dick Ewell: the town had been a military settlement even before the American Revolution, and the U.S. Army had maintained a barracks, a depot, and a cavalry training school, where Ewell, as a newly coined second lieutenant, had his first posting. (James Longstreet had also been assigned there in 1848; so had Robert E. Lee's nephew Fitzhugh Lee, whom the Carlisle newspapers would shortly be denouncing as an "incarnate fiend.") The citizens of Carlisle, represented by two members of the town council, William N. Penrose and Robert Allison, went out of their way to assure Ewell that there would be no resistance.[25]

The Carlisle Barracks consisted of thirteen buildings, including five two-story, wide-verandaed barracks, an enormous U-shaped stable, and a post hospital. But since its main purpose had for years been to provide training for recruits, it was protected only by an eight-foot-high wooden fence, and the Barracks' commandant, Capt. Daniel H. Hastings, had already evacuated the entire establishment of 268 men across the Susquehanna to Harrisburg two days before. Ewell, with three of Rodes' brigades, camped in the Barracks, while George P. Doles' Georgia brigade took possession of Carlisle's other major institution, Dickinson College, and Rodes' last brigade camped two miles outside the town.[26]

Carlisle was, by all accounts, the most comfortable billet the Confederates would enjoy in the entire campaign. "This city is certainly a beautiful place," marveled one North Carolinian, "we were treated very good by the ladies." The next day, a Sunday, the Reverend Beverly Tucker Lacy, the fierce-faced Presbyterian clergyman who served as Stonewall Jackson's unofficial chaplain-at-large, conducted services at the Barracks and preached "an excellent sermon" for the troops, while the Methodist chaplain of the 30th North Carolina, Alexander Davis Betts, preached in the afternoon and "baptize[d] five by pouring." The invaders "were bountifully supplied with provisions and forage by the citizens," who surprised the men of Rodes' division by looting the abandoned barracks themselves of "a sofa . . . chairs, tables &c" and "plunder of all sorts." One Virginia artilleryman strolled into Carlisle, "had ice cream," and stopped to visit "a residence near the barracks," where he had seen "some nice girls." But there were also holdouts. An Alabamian took himself into town and found dinner at the National Hotel, where "an unfriendly and scowling crowd of rough-looking men" looked on silently. "The dinner was quite a poor one," Robert Emory Park wrote, "and was rather ungraciously served by a plump, Dutchy looking young waitress." He paid her "in Confederate money."[27]

So much of this invasion had gone so well that even Robert E. Lee was becoming more relaxed and talkative about his plans. To Jefferson Davis, he hinted that if "I can throw General Hooker's army across the Potomac and draw [Federal] troops from the south," it might prove the saving of the western Confederacy. Once he had forced the Yankees to relax their grip on Vicksburg and Tennessee he could then "return" to Virginia at his leisure. "Our true policy is, as far as we can, so to employ our own forces as to give occupation to his at points of our selection." That much, Lee knew, would satisfy Davis and Seddon. But if Harrisburg should turn out to be as ill-defended as Winchester had been (and Ewell's scouting reports on June 29th all confirmed that it was), then Ewell was to ford the Susquehanna; Longstreet would move up behind Ewell; and A. P. Hill would follow Jubal Early's division through York and cross the Susquehanna to cut "the communications of Harrisburg with Philadelphia, and to co-operate with General Ewell, acting as circumstances might require." The weeping and anxiety this would induce across the North would have vast political consequences in the fall elections in Ohio and Pennsylvania, and if those states moved into the Democratic column, their governors would have the leverage to demand that Lincoln open negotiations.

This was the message which trickled down to staffers and junior officers who were now convinced that "Harrisburg was Lee's objective point." Line officers in John Bell Hood's division were assured "that General Lee was going to [Pennsylvania] to subsist his army [and] that he would probably remain there two months." Or maybe longer: one North Carolinian assured a Maryland family that "we have no idea of taking a back track across the Potomac; we have come to stay." Nor would the Confederates necessarily stay put in Harrisburg, since it appeared to one Texas captain that "the way will be clear to Baltimore Philadelphia Washington and so on." Another North Carolinian even "felt like going on to New York."[28]

But always at the back of Lee's mind had been the possibility of the so-far-elusive Napoleonic battle, the winner-take-all, annihilating victory which would shut the entire war down at once. Everything had gone so providentially well thus far. They had given Hooker the slip, overrun Winchester, gotten across the Potomac without opposition, and were now within reaching distance of Harrisburg. Assuming that this would "draw Hooker" in pursuit, Hooker would then be so late in starting and in such a hurry to catch up that the Army of the Potomac would soon find itself strung out and panting on the roads into Maryland. That might give Lee the chance to turn on the disjointed and jaded Federals somewhere "on the Monocacy" River and deliver the war's knockout blow. "We have again out-maneoeuvred the enemy, who even now don't know where we are or what are our designs," Lee confided to old Isaac Trimble, in an expansive moment on June 24th. The Union Army would be "obliged to follow us by forced marches" and wear themselves into exhaustion and disorganization, and that might allow the Confederates to "crush them, beat them in detail, and in a few hours throw the whole army into disorder."[29]

Three days later, he was still more confident, and more specific. Distracted by "hunger and hard marching," the Army of the Potomac's seven infantry corps would allow themselves to become "strung out on a long line and much demoralized." And when they did, Lee would turn and pounce with every man he had on the isolated lead corps, "crush it, follow up the success, drive one corps back on another, and by successive repulses and surprises . . . create a panic and virtually destroy the army." And where would this likely occur? Trimble testified that Lee traced his map of south-central Pennsylvania to a crossroads town which at that moment was the center point of the vast arc which the Army of Northern Virginia was occupying in the Cumberland Valley. "He laid his hand on the map, over Gettysburg, and said hereabout we shall probably meet the enemy and fight a great battle, and if God gives us the victory, the war will be over and we shall achieve the recognition of our independence."

He offered a glimpse of the same plan to Dorsey Pender: "Hooker has a small army and that very much demoralized," Pender wrote on June 23rd. "The General says he wants to meet him as soon as possible and crush him and then . . . our prospects for peace are very fine." The mapmaker Jedediah Hotchkiss had it directly from Dick Ewell that "the battle would come off near Frederick City or Gettysburg," which suited Hotchkiss nicely, since "the land is full of everything, and we have an abundance."[30] There were, however, two problems, and not just about foraging. The first was, *Where is Joe Hooker?* The second was more plaintive: *Where is Jeb Stuart?*

CHAPTER SIX

A goggle-eyed old snapping turtle

I T WAS NOT UNTIL Milroy's garrison at Winchester was on the point of erasure that Joseph Hooker finally awoke to the dimensions of the march Lee and the Army of Northern Virginia had stolen on him. "I now feel that invasion is his settled purpose," Hooker concluded—although almost at once he guessed wrongly about Lee's probable direction. "He will be more likely to go north, and to incline to the west." Hooker was, even at that moment, concerned less about Lee than about his quarrel with Halleck. "I do not know that my opinion . . . is wanted," he sniffed, but he was still hoping that it might turn out to be a "cavalry raid" intended only to divert attention from the West. In that event, Hooker still dreamed that he might be able to seize the chance to launch a strike at Richmond. He could, for instance, slip behind the rear of Lee's invasion in order to "threaten and cut their communications," while the Federal garrison based at Fortress Monroe could take advantage of the chaos to make yet another move, up the James River peninsula, to Richmond.[1]

What Hooker also wanted was restoration to complete control over Federal troops everywhere in Virginia and Maryland, and that was not what Halleck or Lincoln were going to give him. "You have long been aware, Mr. President, that I have not enjoyed the confidence of the major-general commanding the army," Hooker pleaded with Lincoln on June 16th, "and I can assure you so long as this continues we may look in vain for success." In particular, Hooker wanted control over the military department of Washington (which covered all the artillerymen manning the fortifications of the capital, plus two divisions of infantry and one of cavalry commanded by Samuel

Heintzelman) and the four infantry divisions of Robert Schenck's Middle Department (which was responsible for defending Baltimore, Annapolis, Harpers Ferry, and the Potomac riverline). This was not an unreasonable request, and in fact Halleck grudgingly granted Hooker some limited call on Heintzelman's and Schenck's troops, if needed. And on June 20th, Treasury Secretary Salmon Chase, the patron saint of the army's abolitionists, wrote privately to Hooker to assure him that "you will want nothing which can contribute to your success." But Hooker quickly learned how little slack there was on this leash. Halleck only intended to place "the troops outside of Washington and Baltimore under your orders"—in other words, any stray units not already assigned to some duty within Heintzelman's or Schenck's departments—and when Hooker reached for the control he thought he had, he was frankly told that he would not be obeyed.[2]

As far as Halleck and Lincoln were concerned, Hooker's one responsibility was to ensure that, wherever Lee was going (and the speculation in the War Department included Pittsburgh and Wheeling), the Army of the Potomac shielded Washington. Daniel Butterfield, Hooker's loyal chief of staff, groused that "since we were not allowed to cross [the Rappahannock] and whip A. P. Hill," and then march on Richmond "while Longstreet and Ewell were moving off through Culpeper," the army had "lost the opportunity of doing a thing which we knew we could accomplish with a certainty." But as Lee had foreseen, Lincoln was more anxious about protecting Washington than capturing Richmond, and so on June 16th, a day after the fall of Winchester, Hooker issued orders to pull his seven infantry corps away from the Rappahannock and northward to Dumfries and Manassas Junction for resupply by rail. Signal stations were to be established along the crests of South Mountain to report on Lee's movements, Pleasonton's cavalry were to begin poking at the gaps in the mountains to see whether any view of the Confederates could be snatched, and Maj. George Sharpe's intelligence service was to activate its network of agents and scouts, borrowing "ten good scouts" from Schenck to watch central Maryland.[3]

The army itself would move in three groups to ease the flow of traffic on the roads of northern Virginia—the 1st, 3rd, and 11th Corps (in other words, John Reynolds, Dan Sickles, and Otis Howard) would aim directly for Manassas and then proceed to Leesburg on the Potomac and the crossing at Edwards' Ferry. The 5th Corps (under George Meade) would be routed through Manassas Junction and follow the others to Leesburg via the old battlefields around Centreville and Bull Run; and the rear would be brought up by the 2nd, 6th, and 12th Corps (under Winfield Hancock, John Sedgwick, and Henry Slocum), coming through Dumfries and Fairfax Court House in order to cover the evacuation of the army's supply base at Aquia Creek. Halleck did at last release to Hooker some spare units from Baltimore and Washington—a brigade of Vermonters under George Stannard, who had actually only signed up for nine months' duty and were now approaching the expiration of their enlistment, a brigade of Maryland home guards under Henry H. Lockwood, and the so-called Pennsylvania Reserve Division under Samuel Wylie Crawford. But this barely replaced the veteran two-year units whose time had expired in May and early June, and who had by now headed home and forced Hooker to do some last-minute rejuggling of officers and regiments whose brigades had been reduced to single regiments. And it did nothing to help Hooker's equanimity that in at least two regiments—the 2nd Maine and the 36th New York—two-year men whose enlistments had expired mutinied when they discovered that they would be held in service "till the expiration of the full two years of the last company of their regiment mustered into the United States service." In the 2nd Corps, "an immense crowd" rioted over "three wagon loads of stuff" brought into camp by a sutler from Washington, and officers only managed to restore order "with drawn revolver."[4]

Unlike the Confederate Army, this march would not be remembered fondly by the Army of the Potomac. Hooker had a great deal of fast marching to do, with no time for planning and most of it during alternating intervals of baking dry heat and heavy rains. The officers of the 11th Massachusetts had been "playing a game of base ball, when the adjutant arrived with marching orders" that had them all in motion by one in the afternoon, ready or not. The 6th Corps was marched all day on June 14th to Stafford Court House, made camp, but then was tumbled back into the line of march at ten o'clock that night. "What a march was made that Sunday night; wagons, heavy guns, and soldiers, all contending for the road, such whipping and swearing, such pulling and hauling, such starting and halting." The army's provost marshal, Marsena Patrick, raged in his diary at the poor planning and the worse results: "a badly managed march . . . the [supply] Train had a bad time in getting under way—I found the road blocked, with all sorts of obstacles— miserable Officers in charge of Artillery. . . . This made very great delays and I had to turn in several times to get Waggons out of the way." The next day was even worse. "We had a most horrible march. 8000 men fell out from this Corps in sheer exhaustion," wrote a soldier in the 3rd Corps. "This is the most of a scorcher we have had yet."[5]

If the heat was sickening, so were some parts of the line of march. The 1st Corps passed "directly through the field of the first Battle of Bull Run" and saw "hundreds of skeletons lying about," washed out of "shallow graves." Horse and mule carcasses gave off "a foul odor," and even the trees and fences were still scarred by bullets and shell fragments. "The men were evidently affected and depressed at the sight," wrote the colonel of the 116th Pennsylvania, and "murmurings of discontent arose from the ranks." In the 13th New Jersey, the situation might have turned bleaker still had not one "soldier with a penchant for absurd remarks" noticed a half-buried corpse with its arm sticking up toward the sky and turned it all to black laughter by shouting "Say, boys, see the soldier putting out his hand for back pay."[6]

And then, on June 18th, the rains came down. *Oh! How it rains!* wailed a soldier in the 29th Ohio. In the 17th Maine, a soldier remembered that as night fell and the march kept on, "it was with the greatest difficulty that we could distinguish even a faint outline of each other marching side by side; and it was only by continually shouting to our comrades that we were enabled to keep our places in the ranks." Virginia seemed to have been converted overnight into "one vast expanse of mud" in which "the heavily loaded wagons, and the ponderous wheels of the gun carriages sink," while "the drivers whip and scream and swear—principally the latter—and infrequently the pressing infantry come in for a share of the maledictions." If the adjacent fields were level enough, the infantry columns would "take to the fields" and bypass the mired wagons and artillery. But in the gloomy woodlands, "horses and drivers and tugging artillerists . . . occupy all the available room, and only now and then a common soldier can dodge past." So when they were not cursing the teamsters and drivers, or being cursed by them, the sodden soldiers cursed their commander. "The boys here damn Hooker and wish for little Mac and any one that says Hooker is as popular as Mac is a damn liar."[7]

In case there were any inclinations to desertion, the Army of the Potomac resorted to the same lesson plan as its Confederate counterpart. The 1st Corps had to do its firing squad duty as soon as the orders to march had been received, although the firing party only managed to wound their target, a private in the 19th Indiana who deserted because he "had a wife at home, back in Indiana, who was lying desperately ill." One member of the detail, deliberately and with every eye riveted on him, reloaded and shot the deserter through the head to end the misery. On June 19th, a pause in the downpours gave the 12th Corps time to stop and "witness the shooting of three deserters," two from the 46th Pennsylvania and one from the 13th New Jersey. "There were the usual terrible formalities," wrote a soldier from the 20th Connecticut, "the ready excavated graves, the coffins at their brink, with the wretched prisoners and condemned seated thereon . . . and the word 'fire!' from the lips of the commanding officer and, perforated each with eight bullets, somebody's son, or brother, or father, tumbles over into his box, and the tragedy is ended."[8]

One thing the Army of the Potomac had in its favor was a bridge train it could call up from Washington and stretch across the Potomac over a string of sixty or more pontoon boats. The crossing occupied the better part of three days, from June 25th to June 27th, and in the meantime Hooker was planning one last gambit to retrieve his reputation, inspired in part by the comment Lincoln made a week earlier about "Lee's army" covering so much distance that "the animal must be very slim somewhere." It occurred to Hooker that if the three corps which made up his left wing could quickly move up to Frederick, they could veer west, unite with the Harpers Ferry garrison, cross the Catoctin Mountains, and hit the thinned-out Confederate columns somewhere near the old Antietam battlefield. Harpers Ferry, now swollen by escapees from Winchester and Martinsburg, contained 10,000 men, the equivalent of a small-sized infantry corps. The Harpers Ferry troops would be combined "with General Slocum's corps . . . the two making about 25,000 men." Hooker would then "throw them rapidly in rear of General Lee's army, cut his communications . . . and capture his trains, and then reunite with the main army for the battle. . . . If the enemy turned back to attack this force in their rear, the corps at Middletown holding the mountain passes could fall on their flank."[9]

Lincoln could hardly tell him not to take Lincoln's own advice, telegraphing Hooker that "it gives you back the chance that I thought McClellan lost last fall." Hooker snatched at this encouragement, and on June 24th was ready to launch an operation which would "paralyze" the Army of Northern Virginia's "movements by threatening its flank and rear if it advances." But the key component here was Hooker's demand to have the Harpers Ferry garrison released to his control, and Halleck interpreted that demand as Hooker's real object, not attacking Lee. When Halleck objected to Hooker's demand, Lincoln refused to intervene. Hooker rode into Harpers Ferry himself on June 27th, and when he discovered that Halleck had vetoed his commandeering of Harpers Ferry ("Pay no attention to Hooker's orders" was Halleck's directive to the commandant at Harpers Ferry), Hooker played his last card and wired Halleck that afternoon that he would appeal directly to Lincoln for confirmation, or else resign as commander of the Army of the Potomac.[10]

Hooker returned to Frederick, knowing in all likelihood what the result would be. He unburdened himself to his chief of staff, Dan Butterfield, explaining "that if every available man could not be concentrated and used against Lee" and if "Halleck did not give him that cordial assistance and cooperation which he had a right to expect," then it "was his duty to withdraw from the command." In any case, "he would rather go into the ranks as a private soldier than to hold the position he then held." He would soon enough get his chance. Halleck tersely acknowledged Hooker's telegram at eight o'clock that night. Half an hour later, Lincoln even more tersely directed Halleck: "Accept his resignation." Before midnight, War Secretary Edwin Stanton's own chief of staff, James Hardie, was on his way by train from Washington with Lincoln's order removing Hooker from command. (He found a seat on the train beside no one less than Dan Sickles, returning from leave to command of the 3rd Corps, and managed to chat with him "all the way, without revealing a word of his mission.")[11]

Ridding himself of Hooker was a major triumph for Halleck; but replacing him would pose a greater challenge, with the army in mid-stride, but even more particularly because so many voices were ready at once to clamor for the return of George McClellan. At the army's headquarters, Marsena Patrick grudgingly acknowledged that "the feeling is strong" in the army "that McClellan must resume his position"—which was putting it very mildly, since a staff officer who announced to the 118th Pennsylvania that "McClellan had been restored to the command of the army" was met with "shout and yell and cheer, and as they echoed and re-echoed from battery to battalion and battalion back to battery, the woods and fields were resonant with the enthusiastic demonstration."[12]

Lincoln would probably have preferred to cut off his right hand rather than put McClellan back in charge of the Army of the Potomac, not the least because it was no secret by the summer of 1863 that McClellan was ogling the possibility of the Democratic presidential nomination for 1864, and was in fact taking his first steps in that direction by publicly endorsing the Democratic candidate for Pennsylvania's governorship, George Woodward. Having been pleasantly but firmly turned down by every other corps commander in the Army of the Potomac, Lincoln turned, almost by default, to the one corps commander in the Army of the Potomac he had not bothered before to interview, and that was the commander of the 5th Corps, George Gordon Meade. This time, Lincoln did not consult, request, or beg; he simply ordered Meade to take command.[13]

George Meade was forty-seven years old on the morning that command of the Army of the Potomac was unceremoniously dumped into his lap by James Hardie, and there is no reason to doubt Meade's protest that this rendered him the most surprised man in the army. Meade had never wanted to be a soldier in the first place, much less take over direction of an army which, at that moment, was facing its ultimate wartime challenge. His father was a second-generation Philadelphia merchant whose investments turned horribly sour and led to his premature death in 1828. West Point was the one place where the young Meade could obtain a free college education, and there he went, never intending "to remain in the army after his graduation, but merely to serve in it sufficiently long to warrant his resigning, as having afforded an equivalent for his education." He graduated nineteenth in a class of fifty-six in 1835, put in a year as a second lieutenant in the 3rd Artillery, and then resigned his commission to become a civil engineer.

Four years later, he made up the lost social distance caused by the bankruptcy and death of his father by marrying into Philadelphia's Whig ascendancy—his bride, Margaretta Sergeant, was the daughter of Henry Clay's running mate in Clay's failed Whig Party presidential bid against Andrew Jackson in 1832. But Meade does not seem to have prospered in civil employment, and in 1842 he took the unusual step of reentering the army, as a second lieutenant in the Corps of Engineers. He served as a staff officer during the Mexican War, with neither too much risk nor too much distinction, and by the time he made captain in 1856, George Meade's principal achievements were a series of lighthouses on the New Jersey and Florida shores, and a survey of the Great Lakes. He was still on duty in Detroit when, on August 31st, 1861, he received a summons to report to Major General George B. McClellan and take up a command in the Pennsylvania Reserve Division as a brigadier general of volunteers.[14]

The figure of George McClellan looms large behind George G. Meade, a fact Meade's later biographers were not always eager to admit. Both were from socially prominent Philadelphia families that had been conservative Whigs until the mid-1850s, when the disappearance of the Whig Party drove them into the arms of the Stephen Douglas Democrats. Meade's brigadier general's commission "was due to him [McClellan], and almost entirely to him," and Meade reciprocated McClellan's endorsement. "I have great confidence personally in McClellan," Meade wrote shortly before coming east in 1861, "know him well—know he is one of the best men we have to handle large armies." Meade also had great confidence in McClellan's politics, since McClellan stood for the idea of limiting the war strictly to the goal of national reunion, leaving the slavery question out of the picture entirely. "Duty required I should disregard all political questions & obey orders," but that did not keep him from wishing that "the rulers on both sides" would "terminate this unnatural contest." He frankly hoped that "the *ultras* on *both* sides" would somehow "be repudiated, & the masses of conservative & moderate men may compromise & settle the difficulty." In the eyes of a Boston-born staffer in the 1st Corps, Stephen Minot Weld, "all the soldiers are still strong McClellanites, and General Meade among the number."

If anything, Meade had an even greater stake in compromise than McClellan: Virginia governor Henry Wise was one of Meade's brothers-in-law on the Sergeant side, and two of his sisters had married Southerners, one of whom lost two of her sons fighting for the Confederacy. If Meade desired victory, it was a limited victory which would either convince the South that "it is useless to contend any longer," or one which induced "the people of the North . . . to yield the independency of the South on the ground that it does not pay to resist them." It was not clear whether George Meade had a particularly well-defined preference either way.[15]

Meade performed well as a brigade commander on the Peninsula, and then as a division commander in the 1st Corps at Antietam. As he rose in rank, he also rose in notice, although not quite in the ways he might have wanted. A soldier in the 19th Maine described Meade as "a tall, spare man with grayish whiskers and a large nose" who "always wore spectacles." One officer spoke of Meade's "elegant manners" and "patrician aspect," and his "large, bulging, brilliant eyes and a hawk nose." The war correspondent Charles Coffin was pleased that Meade was "thoughtful and silent" and "cared but little for the pomp and parade of war." The problem, wrote Charles Francis Adams (the son of the American minister to Great Britain and an officer in the 1st Massachusetts Cavalry) was that although everyone granted that Meade was "a man of high character," he frequently spoiled that impression by being "irritable, petulant and dyspeptic." Theodore Lyman, one of Meade's staffers, put it as diplomatically as he could when he said that Meade "is a man full of sense or responsibility"—in other words, he feared being in over his head—and these attacks of anxiety gave Meade "the most singular patches of gunpowder in his disposition." One soldier thought "he might have been taken for a Presbyterian clergyman, unless one approached him when he was mad," and then the unhappy messenger was liable to be hosed down with a livid stream of fury, impatience, and arrogance. Behind his back, he was called "a damned old goggle-eyed snapping turtle," and an officer in the 118th Pennsylvania, who called him "Old Four Eye," thought that Meade "certainly cares very little for the rank and file" and "appears to be a man universally despised."[16]

The critics, unhappily, were not exaggerating. He had no good opinion at all of the volunteer service. "They do not any of them officers or men seem to have the least idea of the solemn duty they have imposed upon themselves in becoming soldiers. Soldiers they are not in any sense of the word." He relented enough to admit that the men in the ranks "are good material," but "the officers, as a rule with but few exceptions are ignorant, inefficient & worthless." Meade had seen in his own family how precarious success could be, and after only a year of service in the Civil War, he did not want to be sunk by others' failures. That included George McClellan. After the Peninsula debacle, Meade began cautiously distancing himself from McClellan, who "has lost the greatest chance any man ever had on this continent," and who now displayed to Meade the "vice" of "always waiting [to] have every thing just as he wanted before he would attack." Meade was frankly jealous of his fellow Pennsylvanian John Fulton Reynolds for standing in the way of promotion.

When Reynolds was detailed to Pennsylvania during the Maryland Campaign of 1862 to organize the Pennsylvania militia, Meade hoped Reynolds would stay in Pennsylvania permanently and leave him free to move up to corps command. Instead, Reynolds returned to assume command of the 1st Corps, leaving Meade to complain, "I do wish Reynolds had staid away, and that I could have had a chance to command a corps in action."

But he could not shake off the suspicion of Radical Republicans in Congress that he was just another politically unreliable McClellan Democrat, an impression Meade had unwisely made in the spring of 1861 when he refused Radical Michigan senator Zachariah Chandler's invitation to participate in a mass Union meeting in Detroit. In retaliation, Chandler tried to block Meade's initial appointment as a brigadier general under the assumption that Meade must have been born a Southerner, and "they would not trust the chicken hatched from an egg laid in that region." William Lloyd Garrison's abolitionist newspaper, *The Liberator,* weighed Meade and found him wanting in zeal for the destruction of slavery. "There seems to be a marked deficiency of benevolence, and a dainty, aristocratic look, which . . . reveals a character that never yet efficiently and consistently served a liberal cause." He was, in *The Liberator*'s caustic opinion, an example of how "McClellan's spirit is still in the army. Is some of it in Gen. Meade, and in some of the Major Generals under him?"[17]

None of this prevented Meade from finally winning corps command after leading the only near-successful Union attack at Fredericksburg in December 1862, and he continued to serve as commander of the 5th Corps throughout the Chancellorsville Campaign. But the decision to appoint Meade as Hooker's successor was anything but a foregone conclusion. It was four in the morning when Hardie (disguised in civilian dress in case Confederate guerrillas ambushed his train to Frederick) arrived at Meade's tent, carrying the orders. He startled Meade by woefully announcing, "General, I am the bearer of sad news." This induced Meade to think for a moment that he was being put under arrest, since he and Hooker had been at violent loggerheads over the blame for Chancellorsville to the point where Alexander S. Webb (who would shortly have a brigade in the 2nd Corps thrust into his hands to command) feared that "a court martial might ensue." The orders, when Meade tore them open, told an entirely different tale, and his first instinct was to wire Halleck and decline. His next impulse was to protest that he was being vaulted over the heads of three other senior major generals in the Army of the Potomac, Reynolds, Sedgwick, and Slocum, and that would create an unholy amount of resentment on the part of career professionals who might not enjoy taking orders from their junior. Above all, he balked at Hardie's proposition to walk over to Hooker's tent and inform Hooker face-to-face of his deposition. Protocol dictated that Meade should first be recalled to Washington and commissioned directly by the president or Halleck. Hardie had to tell him that each of these objections had been anticipated, and the answer was, in each case, *no*.[18]

Meade finally relented, mounted up, and rode with Hardie to break the news to Hooker. Fighting Joe had been puzzled by the abrupt response Halleck gave his ultimatum of the previous afternoon, and by the time he went to bed he had convinced himself that the ensuing silence meant that he had beaten Halleck. "It was a bitter moment" to be awakened by Hardie and Meade to learn the opposite, and Hooker "could not wholly mask the revulsion of feeling." Neither could Hooker's allies in the army, chief of whom was Dan Sickles of the 3rd Corps. Sickles "knew [Meade] was hostile, dating from several incidents in the Chancellorsville campaign," and Sickles' own staff recommended he resign on the spot. Meade's first concern, however, had to be for the army, since as one corps commander out of seven, he had hardly the faintest idea of where to find the rest of the army which was now presumably his to direct. Hooker called in Dan Butterfield (who had his own reasons for disliking Meade), and Meade characteristically said the first thing that came to his mind, which was that "he was shocked at the scattered condition of the army."

Once the conference was over, Meade drew up a quick note to Halleck, stating with a certain woodenness that "the order placing me in command of this army" had been received and that "as a soldier, I obey it"—as though he regarded his appointment as an ambush and he was being sent on a suicide charge. The only thing he would say for sure about his intentions was that he would at once break off Hooker's plan to send Reynolds, Sickles, and Howard across South Mountain to attack Lee. "I can only now say that it appears to me I must move toward the Susquehanna, keeping Washington and Baltimore well covered, and if the enemy is checked in his attempt to cross the Susquehanna, or if he turns toward Baltimore, to give him battle." Until he could get himself properly and comfortably in the seat of command, he would play a game of observation and defense.[19]

Meade had good reason for caution. He was the fourth commanding general the Army of the Potomac had seen in less than a year, and word of his appointment did not set off spontaneous demonstrations of joy in the army. Beyond Meade's own 5th Corps, "the army knew but very little about Meade," and his "appointment . . . in place of Hooker, just on the eve of battle, was any thing but a pleasant surprise to the whole army." But a larger reason for caution was Meade's political self-consciousness: he was clearly not Lincoln's first choice, something which was surely traceable to his identification with George McClellan. If he was successful in protecting Washington and Baltimore or if he somehow defeated Lee and drove the Confederates back across the Potomac, he would receive precious little credit from the Lincoln admin- istration; if he failed, even for the most plainly military reasons, he expected to be pilloried without mercy as a halfheart and a traitor. No Democratic officer in the Army of the Potomac could forget the fates of Charles Stone or Fitz-John Porter—court-martialed, cashiered, and disgraced—and it was not difficult for Meade to conclude that if this was the way Lincoln wanted to run the war, then he would have no one to thank but himself when his generals played the safest hand they could.

In a confirmation of precisely how personal and petty Halleck's quarrel with Joe Hooker had been, Halleck went out of his way to inform Meade, in a covering letter with Lincoln's order placing him in command, that as of that date, "Harper's Ferry and its garrison are under your direct orders," and that "your army is free to act as you may deem proper under the circumstances." But the safest thing Meade could imagine doing now was to recall the army's moving parts to Frederick, and then find a defensible position beneath the arc of Lee's invasion into Pennsylvania which would allow him to shield Bal- timore and Washington and keep the Army of the Potomac from losing any more battles. Fifteen miles north of Frederick was Pipe Creek, a tributary of the Monocacy River, which in turn flowed down into the Potomac. The ravines and bluffs of the stream offered the kinds of defensive opportunities dear to an engineer's heart, and less than ten miles behind Pipe Creek was the railhead town of Westminster, where he would have a direct supply link over the Western Maryland Railroad to Baltimore and Washington. That would be the place to plant the Army of the Potomac—on the defensive, protective of the capital, and demanding of no sort of risk, at least until some other plan became clear in Meade's mind.[20]

Until the Pipe Creek line was laid out and marked by his engineers, Meade wanted the army to stay within at least observation distance of Lee's army in the Cumberland Valley. To keep contact, Reynolds, as the senior major general of the 1st, 3rd, and 11th Corps, would move up from Frederick to Emmitsburg, using the cavalry division which had been riding with him well out to the north and west, near Fairfield and Gettysburg, to track Lee's movements on the other side of South Mountain. Henry Slocum's 12th Corps would also move northward to the east of Reynolds, across Pipe Creek and into Pennsylvania through Littlestown and Two Taverns. The 2nd, 5th, and 6th Corps would begin securing the Pipe Creek line, while Meade planted his headquarters at Taneytown, Maryland. With a little cooperation from Robert E. Lee, Reynolds and Slocum would bait the hook and lure the Army of Northern Virginia down to its destruction along the banks of Pipe Creek. Or perhaps not: but in that event, Meade would still have at least saved Wash- ington. Lincoln should be satisfied with that.[21]

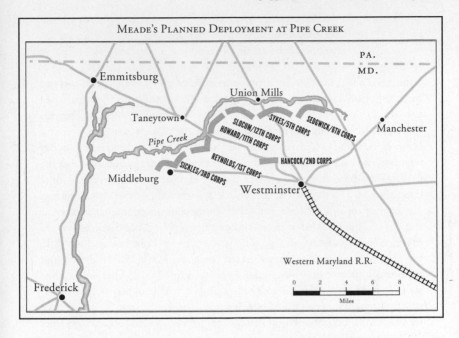

MEADE'S PLANNED DEPLOYMENT AT PIPE CREEK

This would still require a great deal of hard marching by the Army of the Potomac. John Reynolds and the 1st Corps crossed the Potomac on the pontoon bridge at Edwards' Ferry on June 25th at five in the morning, and marched up to Poolesville, Maryland, and on to Barnesville. The 11th Corps also crossed the Potomac at Edwards' Ferry on June 25th and marched eighteen miles that day; by June 28th, it had reached Frederick and "marched straight through to Emmettsburg, making a distance of thirty-seven miles in twenty-four hours," even in pouring rain. Equipment wore out; uniforms were snagged into tatters. "Men who had left the Rappahannock twelve days before with new shoes on their feet were now practically bare-footed," wrote a soldier in the 1st Minnesota, "and there were quite a number with feet so badly bruised or blistered that they walked like foundered horses."[22]

But for all the pounding of the march, the men's spirit rose by steady notches as the columns forged northward through Maryland. As the first company of the 157th New York stepped off the pontoon bridge onto Maryland soil, the men began to cheer and sing an old Sunday School hymn:

> We go the way that leads to God,
> The way that saints have ever trod;
> So let us leave this sinful shore,

For realms where we shall die no more.
We're going home, we're going home,
We're going home to die no more.

Which was about what one in six of them would be doing in approximately one week. But that was veiled by the newly felt roll of the hills, the familiar lay of the farms, the evidence of a world that approached *normal*, untouched by war. They joked, they sang, swinging along at an Olympic pace of "five miles an hour, as indicated by the milestones we passed." They had been defeated, but they had risen anew, and it helped to have a sympathetic populace to line the roads. "One thing that is noticeable since our entrance into Maryland"—or at least Maryland on the eastern side of South Mountain—"and that is the loyalty of the people. . . . There is not that sourness in the countenance of every passers-by which greeted us in our wanderings over the 'sacred soil' of the 'old Dominion.'" When the 3rd Corps marched through Frederick on June 28th, the "enthusiastic reception they received" prompted David Bell Birney to put his division in neat marching order, "preceded first by orderlies with drawn sabers, a band playing *John Brown's Body,* and then he marched with his staff." One "pretty child" was pushed out in front of one of Birney's brigadiers, the transplanted Frenchman Philippe Régis de Trobriand, and held up a bouquet "full of flowers" with the cry, "Good luck to you, general!"[23]

"Our new commander is determined not to let the grass grow under his feet," wrote Charles Wainwright in the 1st Corps, "and his dispositions would indicate that he has some pretty certain ideas as to where Lee is, and what he ought to do himself." At the beginning of the campaign, a number of these ideas came from Professor Lowe's balloons. But Lowe was in the process of shutting down his balloon operation, and the army had hardly left the Rappahannock before Lowe's "aerial ship was folded up and stowed away" and "that was the last we saw of ballooning in the army of the Potomac." Another, less direct, source of information on Confederate movements would be Alfred Pleasonton and the army's three cavalry divisions. Pleasonton's principal task, after Brandy Station, was to penetrate the screen of mountains behind which the Confederate army was moving and report on Lee's progress northward. This was, however, easier said than done. Pleasonton tried repeatedly to force a passage through the principal gaps in the Blue Ridge. But Stuart's cavalry were harboring a slow burn of resentment after their embarrassment at Brandy Station, and the Confederate horsemen stymied three attempts by Pleasonton—at Aldie on June 17th–18th, at Middleburg on June 18th, and at

Upperville on June 21st–22nd—to force his way through the gaps for a look-around after the Confederate infantry.[24]

In the end, Lee, Hooker, and Meade alike would rely far more on civilian informants and scouting detachments to pierce the fog of war than their cavalry. George Sharpe's Bureau of Military Information deployed at least fifteen enlisted operatives who faded in and out of Confederate lines in civilian clothes to garner stray pieces of information, as well as a larger weir of deputized civilians who could furtively watch (and count) the passing of Confederate troops and report themselves or through Sharpe's professionals. "Nine thousand men and sixteen pieces of artillery passed through Greencastle yesterday," reported John Babcock, Sharpe's chief assistant, on June 24th; two "gentlemen of undoubted veracity" counted Early's division "with twelve regiments of infantry and two of cavalry and sixteen pieces of artillery" as it passed through "Smithsburg toward Greencastle and Chambersburg" later that day. An informal detachment of volunteer scouts under a lawyer named David McConaughy operated out of Gettysburg and reported on the movements of Albert Jenkins' Confederate cavalry around Hagerstown and Greencastle. "Contrabands," prisoners, and deserters—all of them turned over to Sharpe's bureau for interrogation—provided still more sources of intelligence.[25]

The Army of Northern Virginia ran the same sorts of agents, although in a much less coordinated fashion. The Confederacy's primary intelligence bureau was headquartered in Richmond and relied on resident agents and couriers in Northern cities to collect strategic information which might have little or nothing to do with Lee's immediate tactical situation on the ground. There was no chief signals officer among Lee's general staff, so that Lee often turned to his staff engineers for reconnaissance. But Lee's corps commanders—particularly Longstreet—maintained scouts for their own staffs, and they proved remarkably adept at slipping in and around the covert corridor that lay between Washington and Richmond, eavesdropping in Washington saloons and clipping volumes of reports from Northern newspapers whose correspondents cheerfully announced every move of every Union unit. Sometimes, even ordinary Confederate soldiers could pick up all they needed to know about Union troop movements from captured newspapers. For all that the cavalry was spoken of as "the eyes and ears" of the armies, their real task was to seal off the incursions of enemy scouts and spies—sometimes with a drumhead court-martial and a rope, as Federal cavalrymen did at Frederick on June 27th when they captured a Confederate spy named Will Talbot—and to *prevent* the gathering of intelligence, rather than do that work themselves.[26]

All of this throws a curious light on what was now to become the single most controversial decision of the invasion. Still smarting from the criticism that had fallen upon him after Brandy Station, J.E.B. Stuart began casting about "for some other point at which to deliver an effective blow." According to his official report in August 1863, he proposed that, instead of routinely screening the army's movement northward across the Potomac, he should loop eastward, gallop around the tail of the Army of the Potomac as it moved after the Confederates, and give a presumably underdefended Washington the scare of its life. Stuart had what he counted upon as "accurate and reliable" information from "the fearless and indefatigable" ranger, John Mosby, about Union movements, and once he had sown confusion between Washington and the Army of the Potomac, he could circle north and rejoin "our army north of the Potomac." Stuart would leave two brigades behind to guard the Blue Ridge gaps; but otherwise he would let the mountains do the screening, and launch his third great cavalry raid of the war.[27]

Since Stuart's first outline of this plan has not survived, it is difficult to pinpoint exactly when the idea was first conceived and when it was first brought to Lee's notice. John Mosby recalled that Stuart first raised the possibility of a raid on June 19th, and Lee's military secretary, Charles Marshall, referred vaguely to a "conversation" Lee had with Stuart and Longstreet at Paris, Virginia (near Ashby's Gap), which could only have occurred on June 20th. Lee's first recorded comment, on June 22nd, was an answer to a written plan Stuart had submitted first to Longstreet. It is important to notice, even at this stage of the invasion, that Lee was already annoyed at having to deal with a certain intelligence deficit, since he began his letter by asking Stuart if he knew where Hooker was "and what he is doing? I fear he will steal a march on us and get across the Potomac before we are aware." Nevertheless, Lee authorized Stuart to carry out his plan, provided he left enough cavalry to guard the gaps, and move "into Maryland, and take position on General Ewell's right . . . guard his flank, keep him informed of the enemy's movements, and collect all the supplies you can for the use of the army."[28]

This is an oddly worded letter, since it does not appear to be answering the question Stuart claims in his August report to have put before Lee—whether he could launch a raid around the Army of the Potomac toward Washington. If anything, it reads like a response to a far simpler suggestion that Stuart's cavalry quit guarding the Blue Ridge gaps and move north across the Potomac with Dick Ewell's corps, at the head of the invasion. If we remember that the Army of the Potomac's infantry was still dribbled out on the roads between Fairfax, Manassas Junction, and Leesburg, then giving up the gaps was actually a serious proposition, since Hooker might then turn abruptly westward, overrun the gaps, and move into the Shenandoah Valley behind Lee. Certainly, Lee still nursed some anxiety that the cavalry collisions at Aldie, Upperville, and Middleburg might signal "a real advance toward the valley" by Hooker. But Ewell's corps was already at Greencastle on the 22nd; that same day Lee authorized him to strike north and east through the Cumberland Valley to Harrisburg, and by that point Lee may have regarded the gaps as superfluous. Stuart, then, could go and join Ewell on the Susquehanna—where, presumably, the action would be—and Lee advised Ewell that he should expect Stuart "to march with three brigades across the Potomac" and screen Ewell's right, while John Imboden's independent cavalry brigade would "perform the same offices on your left."[29]

Lee routed this authorization through Longstreet, so that Longstreet would be aware that his right flank would have only a two-brigade screen in the gaps. Stuart's headquarters was at that moment at Rector's Crossroads, just ten miles east of Ashby's Gap and the road northwest to Winchester, and it would have cost Stuart little in the way of time or trouble to have pivoted north, keeping the Blue Ridge on his left, and cross the Potomac just below Harpers Ferry. But Longstreet forwarded the authorization to Stuart on the evening of the 22nd with a "suggestion" that Stuart "pass by the enemy's rear if he thinks that he may get through." That was an entirely different proposition, since getting anywhere near "the enemy's rear" would have forced Stuart to turn east rather than north, swinging below Manassas Junction and coming up to cross the Potomac somewhere between Washington and the Union Army at Edwards' Ferry. Longstreet had evidently had some conversation with Lee about this, since he added for Stuart's benefit that Lee spoke "of your leaving via Hopewell Gap"—just north of Thoroughfare Gap, in the diminutive Bull Run mountain range, and southeast of Rector's Crossroads— "and passing by the rear of the enemy." Almost as an afterthought, Longstreet explained that if Stuart followed strictly in the path of the Army of Northern Virginia, it would surely send to Hooker the message that Lee had completely abandoned the Shenandoah, whereas a movement eastward would be "less likely to indicate what our plans are." After all, Longstreet was still operating under the assumption that Lee was not looking for anything more than a defensive battle north of the Potomac, and there was no point in poking Hooker into motion by a gesture as dramatic as the disappearance of the last sizable Confederate forces south of the Potomac.[30]

If Lee had indeed been worried that Stuart might give his game away, by the next day he had changed his mind. On June 23rd, Lee sent a supplementary order to Stuart, directing him that, "if General Hooker's army remains inactive," he could make his move eastward. But if Hooker should "now appear to be moving northward," then the game was afoot and Stuart need not worry about tipping the Army of Northern Virginia's hand. In that case, Stuart should pull his cavalry back into the Shenandoah Valley, and cross the Potomac at Shepherdstown after Longstreet and Hill. Only then should he turn east, to Frederick, and then make a straight beeline north to catch up to Ewell so that he could begin screening "the right of Ewell's troops." But Lee then added this fatal liberty: if "you can pass around their army without hinderance," Stuart should consider himself the best judge and instead "cross the river east of the mountains." A good deal of what happened afterward hung on the exact meaning of the words *east of the mountains*. (Charles Marshall believed that Lee meant that Stuart was to cross the Potomac "immediately east of the mountains, so as to be close to the right flank of the army.") Stuart could, if he thought best, use the *east of the mountains* option for crossing the Potomac. But it was Lee's opinion that "you had better withdraw this side of the mountain to-morrow night" and "cross at Shepherdstown next day."[31]

This is far cry from a grant of full discretion; there is nothing which implies that Lee intended *pass around their army* to mean a joyride around the entire Army of the Potomac or even just the three Federal corps which formed the westernmost wing of Hooker's pell-mell rush to the Potomac. Both Stuart and, years later, Stuart's aide Major Henry B. McClellan argued that Lee followed this June 23rd order with a third order that night, explaining "at considerable length . . . that, as the roads leading northward from Shepherdstown and Williamsport were already encumbered by the infantry, the artillery, and the transportation of the army," Stuart should not only ride eastward, but far enough eastward that when he turned north, he would rendezvous with Jubal Early on the Susquehanna, rather than with "Ewell at Harrisburg." But even if the "third order" was actually a confusion introduced by Stuart's report, as Charles Marshall claimed, or an invention of Henry McClellan's postwar imagination, Lee had still given Stuart an opening; and given how badly Stuart wanted what Longstreet half-apologetically called "something better than the drudgery of a march along our flank," even a tea-cup crack would have sufficed. *East of the mountains* thus became any point on the Potomac between Harpers Ferry and Washington.[32]

After spending June 24th organizing and preparing, Stuart and three brigades of Confederate cavalry, 4,900 men in all, set out in the predawn darkness of June 25th. And from that moment, nearly every part of Stuart's grand design began to go awry. Moving through Glasscock's (rather than Hopewell) Gap to Haymarket, the head of Stuart's column bumped unexpectedly into "an immense wagon train," which turned out to be the tail end of Winfield Hancock's 2nd Corps, blocking the roads north in exactly the fashion Lee had described as a "hinderance." Stuart had been assured by Mosby's scouts that there were no Federals nearer than Manassas Junction, but here was a dauntingly large number of them, and he dared do nothing more than unlimber a battery of light horse artillery and lob a few annoying shells their way. [33]

Stuart might have read the signs for what they were, and doubled back to

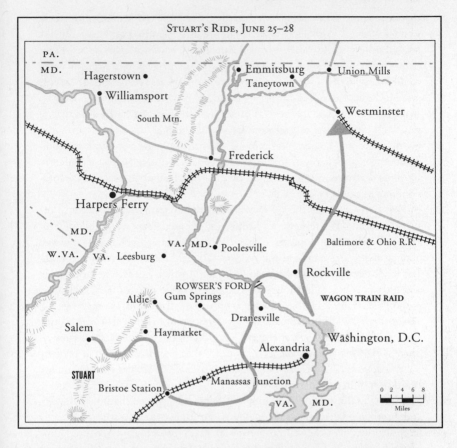

STUART'S RIDE, JUNE 25–28

PA.
MD.
Hagerstown •
• Williamsport
South Mtn.
Harpers Ferry
MD.
W.VA.   VA.   Leesburg •
VA. MD. • Poolesville
Aldie • Gum Springs
ROWSER'S FORD
Salem   • Haymarket
•
STUART
Bristoe Station   • Manassas Junction
• Emmitsburg
Taneytown
• Union Mills
• Westminster
• Frederick
Baltimore & Ohio R.R.
• Rockville
WAGON TRAIN RAID
Dranesville
Washington, D.C.
Alexandria
VA.   MD.
0 2 4 6 8
Miles

the Shenandoah toward Shepherdstown. Instead, he took this as the encouraging omen he wanted, and rode eastward, barging into Fairfax Court House on June 27th just as the Federals had left it behind, and heading for Rowser's Ford, only ten miles above Washington, to cross the Potomac. A few miles more, and Stuart's horsemen struck the National Road west of Washington, where to their delight they bagged an eight-mile-long Federal wagon train with 140 wagons and mule teams. The train's cavalry escort tried to turn the head of the train around, but as soon as "the rebels . . . saw the turning wagons," they descended "with lightning speed." Wagons trying to turn out of the road collided with wagons already in flight, "taking off wheels, breaking the tongues, and . . . becoming a total wreck." Only "about fifteen or twenty" of the wagons managed to escape; the rest, along with 600 mules, "swapped hands in an hour." The last wagon in the train was so close to Washington that "the dome of the capitol was distinctly visible" and Stuart sat down to wonder whether it might be worth "our entering Washington City." But the heavy artillery in the Washington fortifications would offer more resistance than unarmed teamsters, and since "most of the drivers were negroes," who could be converted into high-value slave property in Richmond, there was more to be accomplished in sorting out these new prizes. (One trooper even "recognized and claimed" several of his relatives' runaways.) Besides that, it was finally beginning to dawn on Stuart that he had "lost much time from my march to join General Lee," and it was time to rendezvous with his commander. The problem was that, although Stuart had made a few perfunctory attempts to communicate with Lee, by June 28th he had no idea of Lee's location, much less Early's or Ewell's.[34]

In the years after the Civil War, Stuart's dilemma would become the shackles around his reputation. Embittered Confederates would blame Stuart's "wild ride" (as Longstreet called it) for blinding Lee's eyes, failing to obtain intelligence on the numbers, direction, and leadership of the Federals, and forcing him to fight a battle at Gettysburg which Lee had never planned and did not want. "The failure to crush the Federal army in 1863," solemnly pronounced Harry Heth, "can be expressed in five words—*the absence of our cavalry.*" Lee himself started to grow restive in Stuart's absence on June 27th, and began sending out scouts "inquiring of the whereabouts of General Stuart." By June 28th he was complaining "that he was much disturbed" by Stuart's absence. "I cannot think what has become of Stuart. I ought to have heard from him long before now."[35]

Stuart's raid was, indeed, an act of folly—ill-planned, badly conducted, and (until the very end) executed with an almost total disregard for any interest other than the self-promotion of J.E.B. Stuart. And yet, one crime which Lee should not have hung on Stuart's shoulders was that of depriving the Army of Northern Virginia of the intelligence the cavalry owed it. John Mosby insisted, in Stuart's defense, that "nobody can show that General Lee did, or omitted to do, anything on account of his ignorance of the situation of the Northern army." Nor was Lee as ignorant of Stuart's position as was later portrayed. Lee told Campbell Brown that he knew "Gen'l Stuart had not complied with his instructions" but instead had "gone off clear around" the Federal army, because "I see by a (Balto or N.Y.?) paper that he is near Washington." It was not the absence of information that Stuart ought to have supplied, "as that of Stuart himself, that so disturbed General Lee."[36]

The proof of that arrived at Lee's headquarters tent near Chambersburg on the evening of June 28th, just as Stuart's whooping cavalrymen were corralling the great wagon train outside Washington. It came in the form of a scout, and his name was Harrison.

CHAPTER SEVEN

A universal panic prevails

T HE COLLAPSE OF WINCHESTER into Dick Ewell's hands on June 14th was the signal for Abraham Lincoln to issue a proclamation calling out 100,000 militia from Maryland, Pennsylvania, Ohio, and West Virginia "to serve for the period of six months." It was obviously not a good sign: "Such a call surely would not have been made except under the pressure of a grave emergency," speculated one Washington newspaper. Two new military departments were declared by the War Department, one to cover Pittsburgh and western Pennsylvania (known as the Department of the Monongahela) and the other the Department of the Susquehanna for central Pennsylvania, with its headquarters at Chambersburg—although by the time anyone was able to do anything about it, Chambersburg was already in the hands of the Confederates.[1]

The Confederate crossing of the Potomac also poured a violent flood of panic northward through the Cumberland Valley to Harrisburg and then spilling east and south to Baltimore, Washington, and Philadelphia. Anxious Northerners thought it made perfect sense for Lee to "make a bold push for Pittsburgh" and then to "strike across there and then to Cincinnati" while Union forces struggled to fortify the railroad lines Lee would surely destroy in his wake. Every bulletin of Confederate advance over the next ten days generated fresh swells of fear and flight across eastern Pennsylvania and Maryland. All through the Cumberland Valley to the Susquehanna, "inhabitants who had scarcely decided whether war had broken out or not" now were "aroused to a sense of danger" by the prospect of "their cattle and horses flying southward, urged on by southern bayonets." Pittsburghers began digging fortifications on Mount Washington and "on the outer side of the Allegheny" River, and summoned "Colored Men of the City" to "turn out en masse" to complete them. In Baltimore, "they were expecting Lee to come in a few days. Every street was barricaded with large hogsheads filled with sand—just room in the middle of the streets for one vehicle to pass through, and the streets were full of artillery, all double-shotted at these barricades." The Baltimore police impressed "about one thousand colored persons from different sections of the city" to shore up "the defensive works" of the city.

On the east side of the Susquehanna, "refugees from the seat of war . . . & other counties the other side of the river" choked the roads toward Philadelphia, camping "along the roads with horses, cattle & wagons loaded with grain and familys." In Lancaster, "all business is suspended. . . . Every negro has left or is leaving the place, and nearly every white person," while the roads between the river and Lancaster were "strewn with citizens and vehicles, trudging along to the north and east." The governor of New Jersey angrily warned Lincoln that "the people of New Jersey are apprehensive that the invasion of the enemy may extend to her soil," and the former Republican governor of New York beseeched Secretary of War Stanton to "take immediate measures for the defense of the harbor of New York." Everywhere, gloated Robert Kean, the chief of staff for the Confederate War Department in Richmond, "Yankeedom is in a great fright at the advance of Lee's army to the Potomac, and considers this part of Pennsylvania south of the Susquehanna as good as gone."[2]

Kean would have gloated still more had he been privy to the divided counsels that prevailed in Philadelphia, the second largest city in the country. As a commercial entrepôt with close economic ties to the South, Philadelphia had been "the great emporium of Southern commerce," recalled Alexander McClure. Although it had been the home of the earliest American antislavery society, in the election of 1860 Philadelphia gave Abraham Lincoln only a token majority of 2,039 votes out of over 76,000. If "the Union is to be divided," announced Pennsylvania Supreme Court justice George Woodward, "I want the line of separation to run north of Pennsylvania." To date, Philadelphia's most significant contribution to the war had been its favorite son, George B. McClellan.[3]

But after the fall of Winchester, the City Council "suddenly discovered that the city was without protection." Mayor Alexander Henry called in the "lieutenants of the several Police districts" and deputized them to "enroll . . . volunteers . . . for city defense." Stores were to be shut down "for the purpose of enabling their employees to drill," churches were opened for congregations to debate "the plan best to be pursued, and their duty in this, our darkest hour," and a city-wide patriotic rally convened on Independence

Square. But the recruiting details trudging through the near-empty streets "with drum & flag" were followed only by "a few ragged boys." When Major General Napoleon Dana arrived in the city on June 26th to take command of the Military District of Philadelphia, he found only 400 Union soldiers on hand to defend the city (with another 600 reinforcements available from the ambulatory patients in the city's military hospitals) and some rudimentary entrenchments. The money markets behaved accordingly: by June 12th, "the stock market was unsettled and irregular" and the price of an ounce of gold was pushing up from 141⅜ on June 13th to 147⅛ three days later. By the 30th of June, "a great depression of almost all securities" prevailed.[4]

Composure was also in short supply in Pennsylvania's capital city, Harrisburg. Governor Andrew Gregg Curtin was (like Lincoln) a lawyer and an old-line Whig who had gone over to the Republicans after the death of the Whig Party in 1856, and been nominated and elected as a Republican in February 1860. He was a handsome and talented administrator who had kept the Commonwealth firmly aligned with Lincoln's policies, and rallied to repeated calls on Pennsylvania for militia in 1861 and again in the fall of 1862. But Curtin was in political trouble now—one of the numerous political troubles Robert E. Lee was hoping to capitalize upon this summer—and even as the Confederates surged northward, Pennsylvania Democrats were in the process of nominating George Woodward as Curtin's challenger.

The prospect of a Confederate invasion only sharpened Curtin's anxieties. Even before the fall of Winchester, Curtin nervously issued a call of his own for a "corps" of "emergency militia" for "the defense of our own homes, firesides, and property from devastation." But, to Curtin's embarrassment, the response was negligible. Lincoln's militia proclamation on June 15th crossed wires with Curtin's emergency militia call, and potential recruits were suddenly uncertain whether they were being mustered into state service or Federal service, how long they would be expected to serve, and who would be paying them. On June 26th, Curtin had to issue a second proclamation for 60,000 emergency militia, specifying that they would only be in state service for ninety days and begging Pennsylvanians not to "undergo the disgrace of leaving your defense mainly to the citizens of other States." But by the 29th, there were only about 16,000 ill-sorted volunteers on hand to defend Harrisburg, and a "wearied and disappointed" Curtin seemed to a New York reporter to be "resigned to the fate that awaits the capital of the glorious old Commonwealth."[5]

The truth was that more people were trying to get out of Harrisburg as refugees than to get there as its defenders. "People of the Keystone State," exhorted the *Philadelphia Public Ledger,* with a deliciously satirical appeal to pure self-interest:

Hostile footsteps press your soil
Pause not now for cold debate
While your foemen seize the spoil.
See, they come, on plunder bent!
Haste the mischief to prevent:
Save the produce of your tillage,
Save your fields and farms from pillage.
Save your stores and dwelling-houses,
Comfort your affrighted spouses;
Plainly show those hungry sinners
You'll not furnish them with dinners . . .
Pennsylvania can't afford
These voracious gangs to board . . .

The American-born piano virtuoso Louis Moreau Gottschalk arrived in Harrisburg as part of a concert tour he was taking through the North that season, and though he drew a surprisingly "respectable audience" to his performance, he was more entertained himself by the frantic rage of most of Harrisburg's population to leave town. The scene "at the depots," gibbered the *Washington National Intelligencer,* "was indescribable if not disgraceful. A sweltering mass of humanity thronged the platform, all furious to escape the doomed city." The roads were packed with "carriages, carts, chariots . . . spring carts, trucks, buggies," and even "wheelbarrows" were trundling out of the city, piled high with "trunks, boxes, bundles of clothes, furniture, mattresses, kitchen utensils, and even pianos," a great deal of which soon ended up on the side of the road. In the state capitol, clerks "in their shirt-sleeves" hurriedly packed records, books from the state library, and portraits of former governors for shipment to safety.[6]

The solitary circle of calm in Harrisburg's circus of terror was Darius Nash Couch, who until May had been the commander of the 2nd Corps of the Army of the Potomac and the army's senior major general under Joe Hooker. A New Yorker by birth, Couch had been a classmate of McClellan's at West Point and had served in the Mexican War, but left the service in 1855 after a dispute with then–secretary of war Jefferson Davis. A moderate pro-war Democrat, Couch had put a uniform back on and risen from regimental command to senior corps command at Chancellorsville. But Hooker's erratic behavior at Chancellorsville convinced Couch that any further service under Hooker was futile, and on May 22nd he offered to resign in disgust. The president instead appointed Couch to take control of the newly created Department of the Susquehanna, effectively promoting Couch to Hooker's equal.[7]

Couch arrived in Harrisburg on June 11th, finding little more on hand than a hastily outfitted staff of worried civilian politicians and a temporary office in the state capitol. Unflappability was Couch's long suit, and he at once signed up 3,000 workers to dig entrenchments, including "priests, pastors, rectors, ministers of all denominations," who were soon "engaged in wheeling barrows full of earth and in digging pits for sharpshooters." Once Dick Ewell's corps occupied Carlisle on June 27th, Couch calmly confessed to Stanton that he fully expected the Confederates to "ford the river" either above or below Harrisburg.

He would not have to wait all that long to find out, either. On June 28th, Ewell's small cavalry brigade (under Albert Jenkins), exploring routes for Ewell's advance to the Susquehanna, brushed some of Couch's militia out of Mechanicsburg, only seven miles from the river; the 14th Virginia Cavalry actually closed to within sight of Harrisburg from "a dominating hill" and an accompanying battery of horse artillery fired a few rounds in the capital's general direction. Ewell was already preparing Rodes' division to move out from Carlisle toward the Harrisburg river crossings. "We are here and the Yankees can't run us away," a Confederate surgeon wrote on the 28th. "I . . . suppose we will go to Harrisburg." It might be fortified, and the militia "may make a stand there, but judging from the way they have been doing it is very doubtful."[8]

Twenty-two miles to the southwest, the town of Gettysburg lacked even fortifications, much less a river to protect it. The town James Gettys laid out seventy years before had grown into the county seat of Adams County, with some 2,390 residents in 1860, along with piped water, gas-lit streets, two banks, a college, seven churches, a Lutheran theological seminary, three newspapers, and (as the cash cow of the town) ten carriage manufacturers employing "probably 200 skilled workmen." The Gettysburg Railroad Company built a sixteen-and-a-half-mile railroad line to nearby Hanover in 1858, and (wrote one schoolgirl in an essay competition in 1860) "a new future was opened for our native village." To the more sophisticated eyes of the antislavery journalist and novelist John T. Trowbridge, however, Gettysburg "is but a fair sample of a large class of American towns, the builders of which seem never to have been conscious that there exists such a thing as beauty." The town "consists chiefly of two-story houses of wood and brick, in dull rows," with "no special natural advantages" apart from its location at the intersection of "several important roads."

The outlying farmers of Adams County were overwhelmingly German and Lutheran—Herbsts, Millers, Pitzers, Zeiglers, Leisters, Culps (or Kolbs), Benners, Houcks, Weikerts, Sherfys, and Klingels dotted the quilt of small-scale farm properties surrounding Gettysburg. Two of the town's churches were Lutheran (a third was German Reformed, with the Calvinist Heidelberg Catechism pushing against the Lutheran Augsburg Confession), as was the seminary and Pennsylvania College, with its whitewashed cupola-crowned "Old Main" building. But the actual levers of economic and political power in Gettysburg belonged to its first-settler Scots-Irish Presbyterian minority. The borough council (all of five members and a burgess in the role of mayor) was dominated by McPhersons, McConaugheys, and Harpers, while the weekly newspapers—the Democratic *Gettysburg Compiler,* the Republican *Sentinel* and *Star and Banner*—were owned and operated by John T. McIlhenny, Robert Goodloe Harper, and Henry J. Stahle.

The ascendency of the town lived along two of the principal streets radiating from the central diamond, on Chambersburg Street (running west), where the violent abolitionist Thaddeus Stevens had opened his first law office back in the 1830s, and on Baltimore Street (running south). The far southern end of Baltimore Street descended (physically and economically) into a working-class shanty village of tanning yards and a hostler's hotel, until the ground pitched up sharply to a broad, flat plateau where a new town graveyard, the Evergreen Cemetery, had been laid out in 1855. From Cemetery Hill, a ridgeline snaked southward to a pair of desolate, upthrust granite hills, where students from Pennsylvania College went in solitude to practice "an elocutionary gamut" and "gestures that would be some what more graceful than the handle of the town pump in action."[9]

Like much of the larger border region between slave and free states, Gettysburg leaned Democratic, and occasionally pro-Southern. The war "struck a blow at every manufacturing business in the county . . . because it cut off all Southern trade"—and it was for the sake of that trade that unhappy businesses in Gettysburg blamed Lincoln, not the rebels, for their trouble. At the beginning of the Civil War, the townspeople had rallied loyally to the Union, sending off the local militia company (the seventy-man "Gettysburg Blues") in response to Lincoln's first call for state militias in 1861. But the loyalties were not always uniform. Young Gettysburg men like Matthew Miller and Wesley Culp followed education and employers into Virginia and ended up serving in the Confederate Army, and frequent scares interrupted the first summer of the war in a town only seven miles from the Mason-Dixon line. The War Department had even considered establishing "cantonments" in Gettysburg and York, twenty-five miles to the east, and the 10th New York Cavalry had been garrisoned in Gettysburg in the winter of 1861–62 as a precaution.[10]

But nothing more than rumor came close to Gettysburg until the fall of 1862, when J.E.B. Stuart ran one of his notorious raids into the Cumberland Valley. Stuart actually came as close as Cashtown, eight miles west of Gettysburg in one of the principal gaps in South Mountain. But he had then turned away south and west to Fairfield, and galloped out of the ken of Gettysburg for what the town hoped would be forever. Apart from Stuart's raid, the closest the war impinged on Gettysburg was the deep rumbling of artillery that could be heard from the battle of Antietam, ten months before this newest invasion. "No one had ever seen a Confederate," wrote Leander Warren, a thirteen-year-old in 1863 living on Railroad Street, "and everyone imagined that they were wild men."[11]

To the black population of Gettysburg, wild men, and worse, were exactly what the Confederates were likely to be. One hundred and eighty-six free blacks appeared on the 1860 census in Gettysburg, with another 1,500 scattered through Adams County. Slavery was abolished as an institution in Pennsylvania in 1780, but emancipation in the Commonwealth was to be gradual—all slaves were to be free by July 4, 1827—and there were loopholes in the statute which meant that as late as 1840 there were sixty-four black Pennsylvanians who were still legally chattels of their owner. But it hardly mattered whether Pennsylvanians were slow or fast about bringing in freedom; once free, whites had no intention of regarding blacks as little better than the same low-caste laborers they had been in slavery. The Scots-Irish McAllisters, who operated a mill south of the town, sheltered fugitive slaves, and a small knot of students at Pennsylvania College organized a clandestine abolitionist fraternity, the Beta Deltas, or "Black Ducks." But abolition lecturers got cold receptions in Gettysburg, and even those Gettysburg whites who opposed slavery did so in the hope that emancipation would be at once followed by the colonization of all blacks to Africa.[12]

Gettysburg's blacks had no one to look out for their interests but themselves, although in a few cases those interests had prospered in a modest way. Jobs were plentiful in Gettysburg and schooling free, and the hope they proffered balanced the risk of living so close to the upper boundary of slavery. The light-skinned Owen Robinson, who served as the groundskeeper for the Presbyterian church on Baltimore Street, "kept a little restaurant" at the corner of Washington and High streets, "where he sold oysters in the winter and ice cream in the summer," and managed to become a "well-to-do Negro." Basil Biggs had been a free black teamster in Baltimore until he moved to Gettysburg in 1858 so that his children could take advantage of Pennsylvania's Free School Act. He farmed at first as a tenant and then bought a property south of Cemetery Hill in 1865. Abraham Bryan spent twenty years scrimping and saving as a "laborer" until he was finally able to buy a twelve-acre farm on the west side of Cemetery Hill. But the threat of the fugitive hunters always hovered over these small edges of ease. Owen Robinson always carried his free papers (dating from 1817, when he was emancipated in Maryland) around with him as legal insurance. Mag Palm, who rented a small house on Abraham Bryan's farm, had nearly been carried off in 1860 by "a group of men" who hoped to sell her for "quite a profit."

And as soon as Winchester fell and the Confederate invasion wave lapped up to the Pennsylvania border, Gettysburg's blacks concluded to take no chances, gathered up their handfuls of belongings, and fled north and east toward Harrisburg and York. Matilda (or, as she was called by her family, Tillie) Pierce, a white girl living on Baltimore Street, remembered seeing black women "with bundles as large as old-fashioned feather ticks slung across their backs" hurrying out the Bonneautown road on foot, "crowding, and running against each other in their confusion." One of George Arnold's bank clerks, Samuel Bushman, also noticed the pathetic parade of blacks "on foot, burdened with bundles containing a couple of quilts, some clothing and a few cooking utensils . . . trundling along their little belongings in a two-wheeled handcart" or "driving a single sheep or hog or a cow and a calf." Twelve-year-old Mary Montfort saw her mother's hired help, Rebecca Johnson, pack up and leave: *Yo ol' Aunt Beckie is goin' up into de hills. No rebel is gonna catch me and carry me back to be a slave again.* Even as far east as Lancaster, "every negro has left or is leaving the place."[13]

It soon enough became the turn of white Gettysburg to panic, too. "We had often heard that the rebels were about to make a raid," remembered Tillie Pierce, "but had always found it a false alarm." What, asked one Gettysburg woman, "would the rebels ever want to come to Gettysburg for?" That question stopped being asked after Winchester, and after Curtin's and Lincoln's emergency calls. A fire in Emmitsburg, eleven miles south, touched off a crying panic that "the Rebels are coming and burning as they go." The next day, eighty-three Gettysburg boys (including sixty-one students from Pennsylvania College) signed up as a company of "emergency militia" and took the train north to Harrisburg to be mustered in (as Company A of the 26th Pennsylvania Emergency Militia). A staffer from General Couch, Maj. Granville Haller, arrived a day later to call a public meeting at the courthouse on Middle Street and "take into consideration the subject of placing the county in a state of military organization."

A small company of horsemen more or less commanded by a thirty-three-year-old farmer, Robert Bell, was deputized to watch the roads around Gettysburg, reinforced by a company of the First City Troop from Philadelphia (a gorgeously uniformed team of what were otherwise purely ceremonial city militia). Day after day, there were repeated scares of the-rebels-are-coming. Major Haller became convinced that Confederate scouts were infiltrating the area, and on June 23rd, he wired Couch to ask for "a Regiment of Infantry" to "restore confidence and rally the people to arms." Couch had little enough in the way of infantry to spare from defending Harrisburg, so he sent the 26th Pennsylvania Emergency Militia, together with its Gettysburg company, off to Gettysburg. Six miles out, their train hit a cow and derailed.[14]

The cycle of alarm and reprieve soon began "to be an old story," and in the town people "tried to make ourselves believe that they would never come." But real danger was nearer than they expected. Dick Ewell's third division, under the irascible Jubal Early, split off from Ewell's advance up the Cumberland Valley on June 22nd. Early's division (accompanied by Col. William French's 17th Virginia Cavalry and Elijah White's 35th Virginia Battalion for screening) hugged the western slope of South Mountain through the hamlets of Waynesboro, Quincy, and Mount Alto and then turned due east, heading for York and the bridges crossing the lower Susquehanna at Wrightsville. There, unless Robert E. Lee issued a recall order, Early (followed at some distance by Powell Hill) would cross the river and join with Ewell in taking Harrisburg.[15]

Square in Jubal Early's path to York, however, was Gettysburg. The town's only defense on June 26th were the six-day soldiers of the 26th Pennsylvania (who finally made it to Gettysburg on a second train that morning, to be greeted with a lavish breakfast), the Philadelphia cavalry troopers, Robert Bell's home guard horsemen, and several of David McConaughy's civilian scouts. The home guards had already traded a few shots with Early's cavalry screen at Fairfield and the Monterey Gap, and Major Haller had set farmers to felling trees as obstructions on the road from Cashtown to Gettysburg. None of this was likely to do more than annoy Early's 6,500 hungry, confident veterans, but Major Haller was determined to make at least some sort of flourish, and although it had now begun to rain, the 26th Pennsylvania and the gaggle of scouts, home guards, and the finely dressed troopers from Philadelphia marched sullenly westward, out the Cashtown Pike.[16]

Jubal Early took no more notice of what was reported as "a large force of Pennsylvania militia" than he did of the weather. Between noon and two o'clock, he sent one of his three brigades, under a grandiloquent Georgian, John Brown Gordon, straight along the Cashtown Pike to where the 26th Pennsylvania was deployed behind Marsh Creek, three miles from the center of Gettysburg, and then hooked his two other brigades and William French's cavalry northward, to the left, along the Hilltown Road. The entire encounter could not have lasted more than twenty minutes. "The militia, who no doubt had previously resolved to die if need be in defense of their homes and friends," wrote a sardonic Confederate staff officer, "changed their minds when they caught a glimpse" of Gordon's infantry. The 26th Pennsylvania Emergency Militia broke and ran for their lives, some hoping to reach the train station in Gettysburg to make a quick exit eastward, others struggling north and east with French's cavalry regiment in pursuit. The home guards also bolted back to the town, where Captain Bell told them to disband and fade back to their homes. Major Haller, the author of this little affair, took off in the direction of York, accompanied by the First City Troop in all their finery. All told, Gordon and French scooped up 175 prisoners; one of Bell's home guards, George Washington Sandoe, was shot and killed by Confederate cavalry just south of Gettysburg, thus earning a fatal nomination as the first soldier (of sorts) to die at Gettysburg.[17]

The home guards were also the first to gallop through Gettysburg with the news that "the Rebels" were now indisputably coming. Miss Carrie Sheads' girls school on the Cashtown Pike was dismissed and the girls sent running and crying into town, where they sought refuge in the lobby of the Eagle Hotel on Chambersburg Street. Hugh Scott, who operated the town telegraph office out of his parents' home on Chambersburg Street, promptly disconnected the telegraph, strode out the door, and drove off frantically in the direction of York in a borrowed horse and buggy. Shelves in John L. Schick's clothing store on the diamond had advertised a "great variety" of gloves, glasses, parasols, umbrellas, and the best "dress trimmings" at "prices to defy competition," but on this afternoon the shelves had been swept clean and the stock sent off to Philadelphia.

Then, around four in the afternoon, Elijah White's battalion of "Comanches" galloped wildly into town from the west, along Chambersburg Street, "yelling most unearthly, cursing," noisily firing carbines and revolvers into the air "like so many savages from the Rocky Mountains" and "not caring whether they maimed man, woman or child; and rushing from stable to stable in pursuit of horses." Doors slammed shut, window shutters closed, horses were rounded up off the streets, heads peered nervously out of second-story windows. They stalked into George Arnold's Farmer's and Mechanics Savings Institution and demanded that Samuel Bushman, the clerk, clean out the vault, and when Bushman rapidly explained that everything had been sent to Philadelphia by train for safekeeping, one "Comanche" threatened to "send me and the treasurer to Richmond."[18]

Presently, along came Early's infantry into town, slopping through the mud and drizzle, in line with Jubal Early himself, "tall and well-looking . . . with the stars of a major general decorating his collar, and a capacious brown felt hat, looped up at the right side, resting easily on his head." Riding into the diamond, Early demanded to speak to "the mayor of your town," only to be told that the town burgess, Robert Martin, had beaten a prudent path out of Gettysburg. *Very well, what about the town council?* David Kendlehart, the council president, had stayed put at his boot shop on Baltimore Street, and was pulled out to negotiate with Early. The brusque Confederate snapped off a list of requisitions—flour, bacon, sugar, coffee, salt, onions, hats, and a thousand pair of shoes. This was impossible, Kendlehart pleaded. "The quantities required are far beyond that in our possession." *Fine,* replied Early, *then we will take whatever we can lay hands on ourselves.*

For the rest of the rainy afternoon, parties of Confederate soldiers ransacked "barns, stores and chicken coops" for everything from hatfuls of candy from Peter Winter's candy shop on Chambersburg Street to horseshoes from the blacksmith's shop behind Sarah Barrett King's house. Some simply demanded to be fed. Others "had a pile of hats on their heads, looking comical, strings of muslin and other goods trailing to the ground" and "blankets, quilts and shawls . . . piled up on their horses." John Wills, whose father ran the Globe Hotel, actually recognized one of Early's staffers as a spy who had been earlier scouting the region to supply Jedediah Hotchkiss with mapmaking data. They did not look the part of either cavaliers or devils. They were "clad almost in rags," wrote Tillie Pierce, and "covered with dust," and prim Michael Jacobs, one of the five regular members of the Pennsylvania College faculty, was almost nauseated from their smell. But at least they did not "molest the women," and the worst Jubal Early devised for a dispirited crowd of prisoners from the 26th Pennsylvania was a lecture on the folly of going so ill-prepared to war. "You boys ought to be home with your mothers," Early snarled, "and not out in the fields where it is dangerous and you might get hurt," and then paroled them.[19]

The carnival, punctuated by regimental bands thumping out "Dixie" "and other Confederate airs," lasted till eleven o'clock, when the last Confederates staggered off to their bivouac northeast of the town. Early had no more time to spend looting, and since "I had no opportunity of compelling a compliance with my demands," the next morning his division was up and on the road to York—although not before men of Gordon's brigade had chopped down the town flagpole, burned the modest wooden bridge on the east side of town, and boasted that they intended "to remain all summer" in Pennsylvania and meant "to go as far as Philadelphia." But most of them would have trouble just getting to York, since "the men having too free access to liquor, of which there were large quantities in Gettysburg, many of them were drunk," and caused Early's staffers "much trouble to make them keep up with the column."

Those who weren't drunk in Gettysburg soon had the opportunity elsewhere. Elijah White's "Comanches" passed through McSherrystown, on the Hanover Road, and emptied a dry goods store of $400 worth of clothing and ten gallons of whiskey, then torched "the railroad buildings" at Hanover Junction "and a bridge or two south of it on the Northern Central." As they continued eastward, the wide fan of looters and foragers discovered that advance parties of swindlers had been at work ahead of them. As soon as the Army of Northern Virginia crossed into Pennsylvania, "agents" of the shadowy underground Knights of the Golden Circle began circulating through Adams and York counties, offering "for von tollar" to induct farmers into the Knights, and show them the secret order's "signs and grips" to ward off Southern plunderers. These "agents" were, of course, con men, and when farmers tried out "de grip, de passwords and everytings" on mystified Confederate soldiers, the rebels fell all over themselves with laughter—and took everything they could lay hands on.[20]

Early's infantry struck eastward, John Gordon's brigade on the York Pike, and two other brigades (under Harry Hays and Extra Billy Smith) moving north of Gordon and parallel to the pike. So much had gone so easily that Early was growing apprehensive that the Yankees were concentrating their forces to defend York and finally pick a real fight. But by the time Early caught up with Gordon outside York, the latter was already able to report that "there was no force in York" to speak of. If so, Early said, then Gordon should move past York as quickly as possible and secure the great railroad bridge on the Susquehanna that linked Wrightsville on the west bank with Columbia on the east.[21]

It was no ordinary bridge. A mile and a quarter long and built on twenty-eight piers, the railroad bridge at Wrightsville was the longest roofed bridge in North America, and seizing it would give Early a vital lodgment on the east side of the Susquehanna. He could then "march upon Lancaster, lay that town under contribution, and then attack Harrisburg in the rear while it should be attacked in front by the rest of [Ewell's] corps." In Early's and Gordon's way, however, Darius Couch planted another hastily contrived militia regiment, the 27th Pennsylvania Emergency Militia. This regiment was commanded by the forty-five-year-old Jacob Gellert Frick, whom Couch also put in charge "of all bridges and fords on the line of the Susquehanna, in Lancaster County." Unlike his militiamen, Frick was not a stranger to war or politics. He had served in Mexico and in the 11th U.S. Infantry, and in 1860 had been a delegate to the Republican national convention, which had nominated Abraham Lincoln. In 1862, Frick took command of the 129th Pennsylvania, a nine-months' regiment raised for the Antietam emergency, and won distinction for leading his regiment, colors in hand, at Fredericksburg, and then saving the same colors when they nearly fell into rebel hands at Chancellorsville. Frick's problem was his prickly sense of rectitude about his own judgment. He had held one commission in the volunteer service already, in the 96th Pennsylvania, and resigned in 1862 because he couldn't get along with the regiment's colonel. Then, he was nearly booted from the army in January 1863 for "insubordination," stemming from his refusal to make a requisition for "frock coats" so that the 129th Pennsylvania could appear on parade in full dress. As a soldier, Frick was perfectly willing to fight; he simply couldn't distinguish friend from foe.[22]

No one, however, had ever put Frick's competence in dispute. He managed to enlist three companies of home guards to construct earthworks around the railroad bridgehead at Wrightsville (although the civilians quit when a fourth company of blacks was brought in) and reeled in a Maryland militia company, 187 ambulatory volunteers from the military hospital in York, and a few understrength companies of Philadelphia customshouse workers who formed the 20th Pennsylvania Emergency Militia—all told, about fifteen hundred men. (Their numbers were slightly increased, and morale correspondingly decreased, by the arrival of Major Haller and the gaudy troopers of the First City Troop in their flight from Gettysburg.) For the purposes of putting up a fight for York, this was a hopeless proposition, and the terror-stricken citizens of York knew it. A three-man Committee of Safety was designated to intercept Gordon's brigade as it moved to the outskirts of York on the morning of June 28th and abjectly offered to surrender the town.[23]

That suited Jubal Early handsomely. Isaac Avery's and Extra Billy Smith's brigades were ordered to occupy York; Harry Hays would bivouac two miles out of town at the county fairgrounds; and John Gordon would pass through, move the last ten miles down to "the Susquehanna and secure the Columbia Bridge, if possible." It was Sunday, and the churches were already filling up with "well-dressed . . . church-going men, women and children" when Gordon's brigade swung along Main Street, with bands playing and the colors flying. The 31st Georgia stopped in the town center to haul down a garrison-sized Stars and Stripes from a 100-foot-high flagstaff there (provoking one elderly attorney, John L. Evans, to burst out at his apathetic neighbors, *Is it possible to have lived to this day to see the flag torn down and trampled in the dirt?*; the minister of Christ Lutheran Church, hearing the naughty strains of "Dixie" during his sermon, could only bow his head on the pulpit and weep). Early made his headquarters in the York County Court House, and once again the division quartermaster published the requisitions: 165 barrels of flour or 28,000 pounds of baked bread . . . 3,500 pounds of sugar . . . 1,650 pounds of coffee . . . 300 gallons of molasses . . . 1,200 pounds of salt . . . 32,000 pounds of fresh beef or 21,000 pounds of bacon or pork . . . 2,000 pair of shoes or boots . . . 1,000 pairs of socks and 1,000 felt hats . . . and $100,000 in cash.[24]

Gordon pushed on to Wrightsville, topping a rise that allowed him to inspect "the blue line of soldiers guarding the approach" to the bridge from a distance. He could already imagine descending upon the shaky Pennsylvania militia, seizing the bridge, and launching on a march which would "pass rapidly through Lancaster in the direction of Philadelphia." So, at 6:30, with daylight beginning to slip away, Gordon's six regiments of Georgians shook out lines of skirmishers and began trading potshots with Jacob Frick's picket line, "and we had it quite lively for some time." Eventually, Gordon brought up two of the 20-pounder Parrott rifles captured at Winchester and began throwing shells in Frick's direction.

Frick actually had no intention of fighting. He knew he lacked the means to hold the bridge. But he certainly had the wherewithal to destroy it. Behind a barricade of coal cars drawn up at the bridge's mouth on the Wrightsville side, Frick's black laborers and white militiamen began taking up the plank flooring of the bridge, setting explosive "torpedoes," and sawing through archways and trusses. After a sprightly firefight of about an hour, Frick ordered everyone to scramble back along the bridge, and as soon as they had reached the fourth span of the bridge Frick ordered the first torpedo fired.[25]

The torpedo failed to blow the span completely, but Frick had torches at hand to set fires, and in forty-five minutes the entire bridge was burning luridly from the middle toward both ends. "The moon was bright" as the bridge burned, wrote a newspaper correspondent for the *York Gazette,* making it possible for "the red glare of the conflagration to be seen for many miles." Jubal Early, who was just then riding out from York to join Gordon, saw it first as an "immense" funnel of smoke "rising in the direction of the Susquehanna," and soon guessed what this would mean to his plans for crossing the river. The bridge burned all night, and "some of the timbers, as they fell into the stream, seemed to form themselves into rafts, which floated down like infernal ferry-boats of the region pictured by Dante." Flying embers from the fire lodged in roofs in Wrightsville, setting homes and stores ablaze, and shortly Gordon's Confederates had stacked their rifles and were passing buckets in long lines to save the town, as though all thought of the war which had brought them there had been forgotten.[26]

In military terms the burning of the bridge was only a reprieve. There were other bridges within marching distance of Early's division, and although the Susquehanna was wide, it also grew shallow as it descended toward the Chesapeake Bay, and it would not have taken Early too long to have found another way to cross over. As it was, he had more than enough on June 29th to occupy him in stockpiling the requisitioned supplies that York's merchants tremblingly hauled to the town's market for his troops. Yet, on the morning of the 30th, the rebels were gone. "Early, with 8,000, left York this morning," Darius Couch excitedly telegraphed Halleck that afternoon, bound either "westerly or northwesterly." Not only had Early disappeared from all "other points on the Susquehanna river," but so had Ewell from Carlisle. Lincoln was dumbfounded. "I judge by absence of news that the enemy is not crossing, or pressing up to the Susquehannah," he wired Couch. "Please tell me what you know of his movements." Couch could only confirm that the "Rebel infantry force left Carlisle early this morning." Why, and where they were going, neither Couch nor anyone else on the east side of the Susquehanna seemed to know. All that Couch could tell the president was that, from what he could learn, "Rebels at York and Carlisle yesterday [were] a good deal agitated about some news they had received."[27]

Even in the dark and disguised as a tramp, James Longstreet knew the man who came out of the dripping rain as his most "active, intelligent, enterprising scout"—which meant, "more properly, a *spy*." Longstreet eagerly reached out his hand: "Good Lord, I am glad to see you! I thought you were killed!"

The "ragged, weather-beaten" man was Henry Thomas Harrison, a Tennessean who had served briefly in a Mississippi regiment in the West, and early on demonstrated more than a little knack for "secret, perilous adventure." The Confederate War Department brought him east and assigned him to operations inside the occupied Federal zone in coastal North Carolina, and it was there, while Longstreet's corps was wintering around Suffolk in early 1863, that he came to Longstreet's attention. Since Robert E. Lee preferred to keep spies at sniffing distance, Longstreet and his staff became Harrison's controllers and paymasters (at the extravagant sum of $150 a month), and in June 1863 Harrison was armed with Confederate treasury gold and sent off to Washington, to slip into the capital and glean what he could from pliable or drunken Union officials, and scout the general path of Joe Hooker's pursuit. Longstreet gave him a long leash. He told Harrison that "I did not care to see him till he could bring information of importance." Now, on the night of June 28th, Harrison had the report he thought Longstreet needed to hear, and allowed himself to be "arrested" by Longstreet's pickets around Chambersburg and brought before Lee's "war-horse."[28]

"Truly," wrote Longstreet's chief of staff, Moxley Sorrel, Harrison's "report was long and valuable." The spy had a complete account of all of the Army of the Potomac's movements since leaving the Rappahannock line and up to the last forty-eight hours, and in particular he had even more recent news about the command of the Union army, "of the removal of Hooker and the appointment of George Meade to command of the Army of the Potomac." Longstreet was at once "on fire at such news," and sent Harrison with an aide to rouse Lee, who listened to Harrison's report with "great composure and minuteness." This confirmed what Lee already suspected: that the Army of the Potomac was shaking itself into pieces that Lee could turn upon and beat one by one, with all the odds in his favor. If he succeeded in "crushing Meade's army, Philadelphia will be at his mercy, or he may come down on Washington in its rear." Nor was he apprehensive about the Army of the Potomac's new commander. He appraised Meade with remarkable accuracy when he remarked that "General Meade will commit no blunder in my front, and if I commit one he will make haste to take advantage of it"—an elegant way of saying that George Meade would likely do nothing rather than run the risks of doing something.

So, rather than wait to be hunted by the Yankees (which is what Longstreet believed Lee had promised back in Virginia), Lee would go hunting himself for the climactic victory he had always wanted. "Ah! General, the enemy is a long time finding us," Lee remarked to John Bell Hood, when Longstreet's junior division commander stopped by to pay his respects. "If he does not succeed soon, we must go in search of him." And he now had a fairly good idea of where the searching should begin. "We will not move to Harrisburg, as we expected," Lee announced to his staff on the afternoon of the 29th, "but will go over to Gettysburg and see what General Meade is after."[29]

The only unhappy person in the Army of Northern Virginia seemed to be Dick Ewell, whose heart had been set on capturing Harrisburg, and his men, who "expected to go to Philadelphia or New York." Do not "destroy any of the barracks at Carlisle," Ewell ordered the commander of his rear guard, "as he hoped we would return there in a few days and would want to occupy them again."[30]

CHAPTER EIGHT

You will have to fight like the devil
to hold your own

G EORGE MEADE took up command of the Army of the Potomac on the morning of June 28th with only the dimmest idea of how its parts were spread over the surface of central Maryland. He and most of his subordinates were also unfamiliar with the topography facing the army as it moved toward Pennsylvania. "Maps, whenever possible, must be obtained from citizens," pleaded the army's chief of staff, Daniel Butterfield.[1] But within twenty-four hours, Meade had gotten a reasonably good fix on the locations of his seven infantry corps:

- The 1st, 3rd, and 11th Corps lay along a ten-mile-wide line, just north of Frederick, on either side of the Monocacy Creek and east of South Mountain, facing on a slight tilt to the northwest.
- The 2nd, 5th, and 12th Corps were positioned around Frederick.
- The 6th Corps, bringing up the rear, was ten miles south of Frederick.

Screening them to the west were two divisions of Pleasonton's cavalry, with the lead division under a veteran of Indian chasing on the Plains who was just this spring taking over his first field command in the war, John Buford.

Thanks to George Sharpe's intelligence network and the flurry of reports relayed to him from Darius Couch in Harrisburg, Meade also knew that Lee was moving north and east, with Longstreet's and Powell Hill's corps around Chambersburg, Ewell almost at the Susquehanna at Harrisburg, and Early in York. To keep the Army of the Potomac between them and Washington,

Meade redirected the 1st, 3rd, and 11th Corps north toward Emmitsburg and the Pennsylvania state line, and the 2nd, 5th, 6th, and 12th Corps to the northeast, toward Pipe Creek and Taneytown, where Meade would pitch his temporary headquarters.[2]

It had been raining off and on since the 24th and the endless kill-pace marches in the drizzle and mud wore the men down. "It does seem as though we were being marched to death," complained a lieutenant in the 5th Corps. But when his regiment reached Union Mills, on Pipe Creek, "we were met by the inhabitants with loud cheers, and a flag . . . was proudly waving on the principal house of the town," and the prospect of "approaching the border of a 'free state' " put more energy in the soldiers' step. The 1st Corps passed through a town whose "streets were lined with welcoming people, the colors were unfurled, the bands and drum-corps struck up, and, quickly taking the step, with muskets at a shoulder, the regiments treated the delighted citizens to an exhibition scarcely less stately and impressive than a grand review." Near Mechanicstown (just five miles below Emmitsburg), "coffee, tea, and milk were tendered to the men as they passed, and fresh bread, cakes and pies easily found their way into capacious haversacks." Farther along the route, "the farmers with their families came out to see us pass" and "brought to the roadside immense loaves of home-made bread . . . in pans as large as milk-pans, and with them crocks of sweet fresh butter." One soldier in the 80th New York marveled at how the women "with one broad sweep of a huge knife" could "spread the butter over the face of the mighty loaf," and with "a swift stroke" detach "a thick slice" and hand it off in time to cut off another fat slice for the next men in line. "Someone at the head of the column" of the 97th New York "struck up the John Brown chorus, which was quickly taken up along the whole line, and presently every man fell into a step in time with the cadence of this simple yet soul stirring hymn."[3]

Still, in other places, the civilians' reactions seemed as unsympathetic as the weather. An officer commanding a battery of light artillery with Plea-sonton's cavalry ordered a rail fence taken down to get his guns and horses across a field, only to be accosted by "one old fellow" who pleaded, "For God's sake, gentlemen, don't go into that field. Don't you see my wheat is only three days up?" Even the roads seemed uncooperative. On the days when the rain stopped and the sun baked the mud, the 5th Corps found itself punching up "a fine white powder" as it marched, "making an unspeakable dust that covered the fields on either side with a white cloud, as far as we could see." John Sedgwick was pushing the men of the 6th Corps so hard that his own horse gave out from fatigue, sparking raillery from passing soldiers: "Get another horse and come on; we'll wait for you, Uncle John; we're in no hurry, Uncle John." In the 2nd Corps, men grumbled that they were being overmarched because their commander, Winfield Hancock, had "a wager of 1500" dollars with George Sykes of the 5th Corps "that the old Second could outmarch the Fifth." Along the roads, men began to straggle, and brigades leaked clots of exhausted soldiers, who in turn obstructed the path of other units struggling to maintain their places on the roads. George Stannard's nine months' brigade of Vermonters had spent most of their time in the safety of Washington's fortification, until they were ordered forward to bulk up Hancock's 2nd Corps. They had little experience of long marches, and so "the men fell out badly, in consequence of exhaustion." In the 3rd Corps, the 141st Pennsylvania drew the job of picking "up all stragglers . . . a task both difficult and unpleasant" since any number of the laggards had somehow managed to get "their canteens filled with whisky, became intoxicated" and "were too drunk to travel." Alexander Webb, who had just inherited command of the 2nd Corps' Philadelphia Brigade, had his brigade bugler signal officer's call and furiously told them to "arrest any of the men found straggling and to bring them to him and he would shoot them like dogs."[4]

This would have been small thanks for what was, by any measure, an extraordinary job of marching. Even under the most favorable conditions, armies moved slowly in the nineteenth century. In the Prussian Army, a single infantry regiment with "light baggage" was expected to occupy 1,350 yards, or three-quarters of a mile of road; an entire division "in column of march" would occupy "nearly 10 miles." The trains alone might "extend over seventy miles." The best marching speed that could be expected of the Prussian Army was about three miles an hour, "but when the terrane loses the character of a parade, it is entirely different." If bottlenecks—the sort created by pontoon bridges requiring wagons to be widely spaced to prevent knocking the bridge apart, or by crossroads that brought two marching columns into gridlock, or simply by incorrect deployment of units in the march column—then traffic could immobilize an army for hours. On those terms, Napoleon's soldiers, marching from Boulogne to Austerlitz in 1803, thought it was extraordinary to have covered an average of just over eight miles a day. By contrast, the Army of Northern Virginia covered the 120-mile line from the Rappahannock through the Shenandoah to Williamsport and Shepherdstown in only ten days, while pausing to fight at Brandy Station and to besiege Winchester. The Army of the Potomac covered the sixty miles between Fredericksburg and Edwards' Ferry in four days, and then covered the next fifty miles to the Pennsylvania state line in three. The 5th Corps managed twenty miles on the road from Monocacy Junction (below Frederick) to Union Mills on Pipe Creek on June 30th; the 6th Corps logged thirty-four. Whatever American volunteers lacked in discipline, they more than made up for in mobility.[5]

There were no concessions to fatigue, weather, and equipment on this march. "No interval was allowed between any two units of the corps, whether artillery or infantry," wrote an officer in the 20th Massachusetts. "It was the closest marching column that we had ever experienced." By the time the 6th Corps reached the Pipe Creek line, "many were marching in their drawers." The soldiers themselves marched as comfortably, or as sloppily, as they dared. "Here comes a man," wrote the chronicler of the 19th Massachusetts, whose "cap is turned around with the visor covering one ear and half of one eye. . . . His blouse is hitched up in a roll above the belt . . . his cartridge box is around on his hip, the belt loose, while his haversack and canteen are dangling in front of him." The everlasting road dust "settled upon us, and adhering to the moist skin, gave one uniform color of dirty brown to caps, coats, faces, hands, trousers, and shoes." And always there was "the monotonous clatter of tin dippers against bayonets and canteens." Men might be "noisy with conversation" in the early hours of the march, but by late afternoon they "have no stomach or spare wind for words, and scarcely anything is heard but the groan of some sufferer from blistered feet, or the steady clink of the bayonet swinging at the left side against its neighbor the canteen."[6]

On June 29th and again on the 30th, Meade sent out fresh sets of orders to his corps commanders, instructing the 1st and 11th Corps to cross the state line and move toward Gettysburg and the 3rd to stay behind them in support at Emmitsburg; the 5th Corps would move up, in parallel ten miles east, to Hanover, with the 6th Corps in reserve behind them at Manchester; the 2nd and 12th Corps would plant themselves midway between the others, at Taneytown (just below the state line) and Two Taverns (just beyond it). As long as Lee continued to move northward, Meade could keep his army hovering between the Confederates and Baltimore or Washington. But if Lee suddenly turned, like some coiled snake, to strike, Meade already had his engineers at work behind Pipe Creek. He assured Halleck that he was prepared, if necessary, to move over the Pennsylvania line "in the direction of Hanover Junction and Hanover" after the rebels. But shortly before noon on June 30th, he received an urgent wire from Secretary Stanton in the War Department, alerting him that "Lee is falling back suddenly from the vicinity of Harrisburg. . . . York has been evacuated. Carlisle is being evacuated." All of it looked like "a sudden movement against Meade," intending "to fall upon the several corps and crush them, in detail." That was precisely what Meade wanted to hear. His task was "to compel [Lee] to loose his hold on the Susquehanna." Having thus "relieved Harrisburg and Philadelphia," it was now time "to look to his own army, and assume position for offensive or defensive, as occasion requires, or rest to the troops." And that meant "the collecting of our troops behind Pipe Creek."[7]

Meade's most advanced—and therefore most vulnerable—units were the three infantry corps around Emmitsburg: John Reynolds' 1st Corps, Otis Howard's 11th Corps, and the 3rd Corps, whose commander, Dan Sickles, had only just caught up with his men after returning from leave. Meade had no love for either Sickles, the renegade Democrat, or Howard, the evangelical abolitionist. His first two communications to Sickles had been nasty little reprimands for "the very slow movement of your corps yesterday," and he pushed the lot of them to the edge of his thinking by placing all three corps under the temporary "wing" command of John Reynolds. But when Meade learned that Reynolds had in fact moved the 1st Corps up and over the Pennsylvania line to Marsh Creek, just below Gettysburg, Meade warned him (at midday on June 30th) to beat a retreat to Emmitsburg "without further orders" if any Confederates showed their heads. He had "made up his mind to fight a battle on what was known as Pipe Creek," and in the meantime he would draw up a general circular, recalling all units north of Pipe Creek to "form line of battle with the left resting in the neighborhood of Middleburg, and the right at Manchester."[8]

This withdrawal, despite Meade's wishes, was precisely what John Reynolds had no inclination whatsoever to perform.

"To those who knew little of" John Fulton Reynolds, "he may at times have appeared stern and unnecessarily exacting," even "cold and somewhat haughty," wrote one of his regimental officers in the 1st Corps. In an army of volunteers, almost any Regular officer might have been seen that way, although John Reynolds really was by temperament a taciturn and private man. On the 30th of June 1863, Reynolds' moods were fluctuating by the hour, by turns "inflamed" and "depressed." South-central Pennsylvania was, after all, his home. Born in Lancaster in 1820 and descended from Huguenot and Protestant Irish forebears who had accumulated some of the largest landholdings in Lancaster County, John Reynolds grew up in a household where national politics was the stuff of everyday acquaintance. His father owned the Democratic *Lancaster Journal,* sat in the Pennsylvania legislature as a Democrat, and was a political ally of President James Buchanan's. The Reynolds' family political connections made it easy to secure an appointment for the young Reynolds at West Point in 1837, although he only managed to graduate twenty-sixth out of a class of fifty-two. He was commissioned into the 3rd Artillery, fought at Monterrey and Buena Vista in the Mexican War, and in 1859 went back briefly to West Point as commandant of cadets. At the outbreak of the Civil War, the Reynolds name translated into a brigadier general's commission to command one of the volunteer brigades making up the Pennsylvania Reserve Division, and in 1862, when Robert E. Lee's first thrust northward threatened Pennsylvania, Governor Curtin begged to have Reynolds returned to Pennsylvania to take charge of the militia. After the Maryland Campaign, Reynolds came back to the Army of the Potomac as a major general of volunteers to command the 1st Corps at Fredericksburg and Chancellorsville. In the eyes of the soldiers of the 1st Corps, he was "alertness personified."[9]

One individual who was not happy at Reynolds' return to the army in the fall of 1862 was George Gordon Meade. Like Reynolds, Meade had also first obtained brigade command in 1861 in the Pennsylvania Reserves—just one step beneath Reynolds in seniority. When Meade moved up to division command in the 1st Corps before Antietam, he was set to succeed to command of that corps after its commander was wounded, especially with Reynolds out of the way in Pennsylvania. But when Reynolds returned to the Army of the Potomac, the 1st Corps command Meade hungered for went to Reynolds. And it was Reynolds, not Meade, to whom Lincoln had first turned as a possible replacement for Joe Hooker. Meade remained cordial and polite with Reynolds, but privately his letters curdle with envy, even when corps command finally came Meade's way after Fredericksburg.[10]

Meade's opinion of Reynolds would have turned darker still if he had had any inkling on June 30th that Reynolds was seriously planning to upset his calculations for a retreat to Pipe Creek. Reynolds complained to Abner Doubleday, who commanded one of the three divisions in the 1st Corps, that if Meade gave the rebels "time by dilatory measures or by taking up defensive positions they would strip" Pennsylvania "of everything." For days, since crossing the Potomac, Reynolds had been impatient "to attack the enemy at once, to prevent his plundering the whole State," and Chapman Biddle, the colonel of the 1st Corps' 121st Pennsylvania, heard Reynolds urge "striking them as soon as possible. He was really eager to get at them." Meade's June 30th order, directing the 1st Corps toward Gettysburg, might bring him close enough to engage; the follow-up dispatch at midday which told him that if "it is your judgment that you would be in a better position at Emmitsburg than where you are, you can fall back," seemed to offer Reynolds the option to do as he pleased. Or at least, it told him that he could fall back to Emmitsburg if he wanted. Nothing was said that forbade him to advance on Gettysburg—although it did puzzle Meade that Reynolds' acknowledgments of his communiqués seemed "to be given more with a view to an advance on Gettysburg, than a defensive position."[11]

Thanks to John Buford's cavalry screen, Reynolds may have known more about the precise location of the Army of Northern Virginia than the Union commanding general did. Buford "resembles Reynolds very much in his manners," wrote Charles Wainwright of the 1st Corps artillery, "reserved and

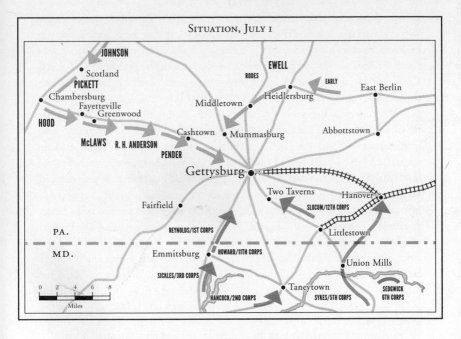

SITUATION, JULY 1

somewhat rough." He was also, like Reynolds, a Regular, born in Versailles, Kentucky, in 1826 (but raised in Illinois), from a long line of Bufords who had fought in the Revolution and the War of 1812. And he was a West Pointer, class of 1848, and was commissioned into the dragoons. Entering the army just months too late for Mexican War service, Buford had instead spent most of the 1850s tracking and fighting Indians on the Plains. The outbreak of the Civil War brought him a militia commission from the governor of Kentucky to serve in what was then a still undeclared border slave state. Buford refused: "I sent him word I was a Captain in the United States Army and I intend to remain one." Still, for a solid year, Buford twiddled away his time behind a desk in the army inspector general's office. He finally broke out of the paper ghetto when the ill-starred John Pope, who had known Buford in Illinois and could vouch unreservedly for his loyalty, wangled him command of a brigade of cavalry. After Pope's debacle at Second Bull Run in August 1862, Buford was returned to staff duties. But in January 1863, he was once more put in charge of a cavalry brigade in the field, and in June he was promoted to major general and distinguished himself by his handling of one of Pleasonton's divisions at Brandy Station. "He is a man of middle height with a yellow mustache," wrote one of Meade's staff, "and a small triangular eye," as though he were capable of reading someone's mind.[12]

Once Meade took command of the Army of the Potomac, Buford's cavalry division was posted well to the west of the Army of the Potomac, so that his two brigades would provide a screen for John Reynolds and the three-corps "wing." Buford's brigades moved on June 29th to spread out and check the South Mountain gaps between Boonsboro and Monterey, and then cross the state line on up to Fairfield (where Buford would be, north and west of the head of Reynolds' infantry at Marsh Creek). As his troopers slumped wearily into Fairfield that evening, Buford was met by two scouting reports, one from David McConaughy in Gettysburg "giving the locality of Confederate troops" and the other from a Maryland Unionist who reported "a rebel camp one mile above Cashtown." Buford and several of his officers rode to the top of Jack's Mountain and saw in the distance an unwelcome sight: a multitude of campfires along the roads west from Fairfield, which could only mean Confederate infantry, and lots of it. Early the next morning, Buford decided to feel them out, "exchanging a few shots" and brushing up against what he described as "two Mississippi regiments of infantry and two guns." Buford had no desire to try consequences with what were, in all likelihood, elements of Powell Hill's corps, and instead sent off a galloper to Reynolds at 5:30 on the morning of June 30th to warn him that Confederate infantry was as close to him as Cashtown.[13]

Staying across the head of Reynolds' column, Buford then took his brigades into Gettysburg, and an hour and a half later reported driving off some of Hill's infantry outside the town. The people in the town were ecstatic to see Buford's troopers, especially after Jubal Early's whirlwind clean-out of the town three days before. Two regiments of Federal cavalry had passed through Gettysburg on the 28th, but they were bound for service with Couch and the defense of Harrisburg, and they only stayed through the night outside town. Buford, on the 30th, was bringing two entire brigades, and he seemed determined to stay. A captain in the 8th Illinois Cavalry was amazed at how "men, women and children crowded the side walks and vied with each other in demonstrations of joyous welcome. Hands were reached up eagerly to clasp the hands of our bronzed and dusty troopers. Cake, milk, water and beer were passed up to the moving column."[14]

That afternoon, Buford himself rode four miles south to Reynolds' camp on Marsh Creek, then that night sent another galloper back to Reynolds, warning that "A.P. Hill's corps is massed just back of Cashtown, about 9 miles from this place," with Confederate infantry pickets planted for the night only four miles west of Gettysburg, on the Cashtown Pike. Reynolds was "convinced that the enemy would attempt to interpose between Gettysburg . . . and the main part of the army by way of Fairfield," and "seeing the importance of Gettysburg as a position . . . ordered Buford to hold onto it to the last." If Buford could buy enough time, he might be able to get his infantry into line "before the enemy should seize the point." Ten minutes later, Buford sent another courier off to find the chief of cavalry, Alfred Pleasonton, so Pleasonton could report these encounters to Meade.[15]

One of Buford's brigade commanders, a former carriage-maker-turned-soldier from New York named Thomas Devin, tried to deflect any unease by suggesting that whatever the Confederates were likely to send in the direction of Gettysburg on the next day could be handled quite easily by the Yankee cavalry. "No you won't," growled Buford. "They will attack you in the morning and they will come booming—skirmishers three deep. You will have to fight like the devil to hold your own." And why? Because, Buford continued, "the enemy must know the importance of this position and will strain every nerve to secure it, and if we are able to hold it, we will do well." Two signals officers had been detached for service with each corps, and Aaron Jerome, an Alabama-born signals lieutenant who had originally signed up with a New Jersey infantry regiment and then transferred to the Signal Corps, had been assigned to Buford's division. Buford told him "to look out for campfires, and in the morning for dust."[16]

Both Robert E. Lee and John Reynolds had particular reason to want to secure control over Gettysburg. "Gettysburg was of considerable importance to General Lee," wrote one Union veteran, "as it was the first point he could reach after crossing the South Mountain." If Lee wanted to concentrate his three corps, Gettysburg would be the easiest place to do it, since ten roads radiated from the town diamond, drawing in traffic from all points of the compass. In addition, the undulating waves of ridgelines which swam eastward from South Mountain to the Susquehanna created a series of lovely defensible lines for infantry to seize and hold against any attacker coming from the west, through the Cashtown Gap. Alfred Pleasonton was one of the few senior Union officers who knew the Gettysburg area reasonably well, since the year before he had been selected by George McClellan to survey the area against the possibility of Lee getting loose in Pennsylvania, and he was "satisfied . . . that there was but one position in which for us to have a fight, and that was Gettysburg." But in addition to the topography and road network, Gettysburg possessed one other advantage, and that was Cemetery Hill, the gentle 505-foot height just south of the town that accommodated the town's Evergreen Cemetery and the farms of Thomas Miller and David Zeigler.[17]

Those undulating ridges whose names have become the staple of Gettysburg lore—Herr Ridge, McPherson's Ridge, Seminary Ridge—may have

been valuable as defensive positions for infantry, but their crests lack the elevation required by nineteenth-century artillery (which was, ideally, one percent
of the distance to the target and never greater than 7 percent of the distance).
Likewise, their spines were almost all too narrow to support batteries of artillery with any ease, since artillery (unlike infantry) used a substantial back
space to accommodate limber chests, caissons, horse teams, and battery wagons.[18] The chief exception to this geographical conundrum is Cemetery Hill.
Although modern visitors standing there can get no idea of this because of
the foliage that has grown up since 1863, a four-negative panorama taken from
Cemetery Hill in 1869 by the local Gettysburg photographers William Tipton
and Robert Myers shows a dramatically uncluttered viewshed to the west and
south. And since the hill is actually a broad flat plateau, Cemetery Hill constituted an artillerists' ideal: a gun platform with plenty of room to accommodate at least three batteries of artillery plus their teams and chests, and
at an elevation which would allow either an unobstructed arc to rifled guns
firing shell to the north or west; or, at 105 feet above the surrounding terrain,
just the elevation prescribed to "graze" (or ricochet) solid shot into oncoming
attackers at 600 yards distance. It was "a battlefield to make an artilleryman
grow enthusiastic," wrote one Pennsylvania officer. "This high ground which
dominated the town and the fields in all directions, save one" (to the east)
gave to an artillerist's eye "an unobstructed view of the rolling country open
and accessible to the fire of our guns." Even Confederate observers admitted
that Cemetery Hill was "made, one might say, for artillery."[19]

John Reynolds was nothing if not "a most accomplished artilleryman,"
and he could fully translate the meaning of Cemetery Hill for cannoneers.
Even more, in the fall of 1862, Reynolds had been in command of the Pennsylvania militia, headquartered at Carlisle, and, "therefore, knew the importance of the Gettysburg pass." It was Reynolds, agreed his adjutant, Joseph
Rosengarten, "who first appreciated the strength and value of Cemetery Hill."

That made George Meade's notion of pulling back to Pipe Creek, seventeen miles south, all the more agonizing. On the evening of June 30th, Reynolds summoned the nearest of the other two corps commanders in his "wing,"
Oliver Otis Howard, to his temporary headquarters at the Moritz Tavern, on
Marsh Creek. Howard presented an almost complete contrast to John Reynolds. Born in Maine in 1830, he was ten years Reynolds' junior (although he
was only two notches below Reynolds in seniority on the volunteers' service
list), graduated from Bowdoin College at age nineteen, then went on to West
Point, where he graduated fourth in his class. It was there that Otis Howard
met Reynolds, and it was there that the voluble Howard and the taciturn
Reynolds somehow became "warm friends." Howard, like Reynolds, had been
commissioned into the artillery. But in 1857, he experienced a profound spiri-

tual conversion to evangelical Protestantism and seriously considered leaving the army "to preach the Gospel of Peace." The cascade of events that led to the Civil War arrested that decision. "It is," Howard concluded, "no time for a man who loves his country and has been educated by it, to desert her." The question was whether his country, or at least the army, wanted Howard. As the Duke of Wellington had once remarked, an army was no place for "a man who has nice notions about religion." The U.S. Army was not much different. Regular officers were a tight-lipped, unemotional club; praying soldiers were at best the butt of jokes, and at worst the victims of social shunning. The prewar army employed only thirty post chaplains, and not until August 1861 did Congress enact provisions for chaplains in each regiment, Regular and volunteer.[20]

Otis Howard had experienced both the jokes and the shunning. Meade's staff rolled their eyes when Howard, invited to "quite an elaborate 'spread'" at Meade's headquarters, "asked grace, with the true New England style." None of it deterred him. "It is not how people see me," he explained to an inquirer, "but I wonder *how God sees me*." But Howard was not the stereotypical Holy Joe. He had been given command of a brigade of raw New Englanders at First Bull Run, and managed to extricate them in remarkably good order from the jaws of a three-way trap on Chinn Ridge. He had lost his right arm to a nasty wound on the Peninsula, where "he won the name of an excellent officer and brave man," and returned to command the Philadelphia Brigade (in the 2nd Corps) at Antietam and a division at Fredericksburg. He might be "the only religious man of high rank . . . in this army," but no one could fault Otis Howard for courage. Charles Wainwright, who had no very high opinion of the pious, thought Howard was "the most polished gentleman I have met."

Howard was, in fact, a sign of how thoroughly evangelical religion had permeated Anglo-American society in the nineteenth century, and even begun to acquire a grudging respect in the profane culture of the military profession. The 1850s were witness to the rise of the model "Christian soldier," whose outlines were drawn in the best-selling *Memorials of Captain Hedley Vicars, 97th Regiment,* an evangelical British officer killed during the siege of Sevastopol, and in the life of Major General Henry Havelock, the victor of battle after battle against forbidding odds during the Indian Mutiny. In the Army of Northern Virginia, the martial piety of Stonewall Jackson shut the mouths of more than a few scoffers. Howard's problem was that he was not only an evangelical; he was an abolitionist and a Republican, and his blending of political and religious moralism in one skin—holding prayer meetings that condemned slavery, admitting the army's black teamsters and cooks to these meetings as equals—covered him with contempt. Hostility to abolition in the army was, as Howard learned, "bitter and unmeasured."[21]

When Joseph Hooker appointed him to command the 11th Corps in April 1863, the Germans who made up half of the 11th Corps' units "made very long faces," and mocked Howard with taunts of "Boys, let us pray!" "Tracts now, instead of sauerkraut!" When the 11th Corps broke and ran under the blows of Stonewall Jackson's attack at Chancellorsville, the army as a whole cursed the "flying Dutchmen" in the 11th Corps. "Every man" of them, raged a captain in the 2nd Corps, "ought to be hauled off the face of the Earth." The "Dutchmen," in turn, cursed Howard, and all the more vigorously when Howard banned the issue of lager. As Howard learned later, even "several officers high in command, some aspiring" to take his place, "went to Mr. Lincoln at the White House and besought my removal."[22]

Not Reynolds, though. He and Howard "were together at Centreville, Va., at Middletown, Md., and at Frederick and Emmetsburg" on the march up to Maryland, and when Reynolds and the 1st Corps continued on to the Pennsylvania line on June 29th, Howard and the 11th Corps stopped and pitched their tents at Emmitsburg, followed in turn by Dan Sickles and the 3rd Corps on the afternoon of the 30th. Late that afternoon, a rider from Reynolds brought a note asking Howard to "ride up to Marsh Creek and see him" at "his Hd. Qrs, near *Marsh Run*." Howard arrived in time to eat dinner with Reynolds and his staff in the front room of the Moritz Tavern. After the meal had been cleared away, Reynolds took Howard into the back room of the tavern, which he had converted into a command post. There, Reynolds had piled up "a bundle of dispatches," "the maps of the country," and a collection of reports "from Buford at Gettysburg, from scouts, from alarmed citizens, from all directions." And from that moment until eleven o'clock, "we looked over the different maps, discussed the probabilities of a great battle, and talked of the part our wing would be likely to play in the conflict." It struck Howard that Reynolds "seemed depressed, almost as if he had a presentiment of his death."[23]

Meade's plans for Pipe Creek notwithstanding, Reynolds intended to move up to Gettysburg with the 1st Corps in the morning, and he wanted Howard and the 11th Corps in support, followed as fast as possible by the 3rd Corps. It was Howard's understanding that Reynolds planned to "have reserved a portion of my Corps" and "placed me at once on the Cemetery heights, and then brought his own thither as soon as he found the enemy in a large force." He would, in other words, use the 1st Corps to measure how much Confederate strength was moving toward Gettysburg; and if that strength was more than the 1st Corps could handle, he would fall back to Cemetery Hill, where Howard and the 11th Corps were waiting. This would, without saying it, also force George Meade's hand, and the other corps of the Army of the Potomac would have to be marched to Gettysburg to fight the "great battle" there, not in Maryland. To expedite Howard's move up to Gettysburg, Reynolds specified that one of Howard's divisions would move up the main road from the south into Gettysburg, the Emmitsburg Road, while his other two divisions would split off to the east at a crossroads known as Horner's Mill and use a parallel road into town that linked Gettysburg to Taneytown.[24]

Howard rode back to Emmitsburg in the dark. "It was general talk at headquarters" that Reynolds was going to provoke an action at Gettysburg—that "there would certainly be a contest." The 17th Maine's Charles Mattocks, bedded down "upon a nice bed of straw in my shelter," was convinced from the thick cloud of flying rumors that "we are now close upon the enemy, and I somewhere think there will be a few guns fired July 1st." Forty miles distant, a Baltimore newspaper managed to come to the same conclusion. "There is a probability," the *Baltimore American* solemnly speculated, "that a great battle will be fought in the course of the present week in the neighborhood probably of Hanover or Gettysburg."[25]

Robert E. Lee cultivated an image of serene and unruffled detachment. A civilian, watching him in camp, noted that although "he has a grey beard and moustache, and presents quite an elderly appearance," he was dressed simply, "in a neat looking grey coat and light colored felt" hat without "any indication of rank." The operations of his mind, however, were more complicated than this impression, and his recall orders involved at least five movements by the Army of Northern Virginia:

- Dick Ewell was to return his corps from its advanced position at Carlisle, march down to Heidlersburg, on the east side of South Mountain, and "proceed to Cashtown or Gettysburg, as circumstances might dictate," sending his trains on the long route back through Shippensburg to Chambersburg so as not to bottle up the roads to Heidlersburg.
- Powell Hill's corps was to pack up on June 29th and move eastward from its bivouac east of Chambersburg to Cashtown, and keep moving "in the direction of York . . . and to co-operate with General Ewell, acting as circumstances might require."
- Longstreet's corps was to close up to Chambersburg, and then turn east toward Greenwood (on the Cashtown Pike) to follow Hill.
- Jubal Early's division was to turn back westward, this time marching through East Berlin, to meet the rest of Ewell's corps somewhere between Heidlersburg and Middletown.

- And the cavalry brigades of John Imboden and Beverly Robertson, which had been posted to screen the western approaches of the army's advance and the army's communication lines back through the Shenandoah Valley, were ordered to catch up to the main army concentration as swiftly as possible.

"There can be no other conclusion than they and the rest of the Confederate army had been moving toward one common centre . . . like a huge machine."[26]

It would take at least two days—the 29th and the 30th of June—and perhaps more for that machine to complete its concentration, especially since the rains had made "the roads very muddy," forcing "the infantry" to march off the roads "in the fields along side where they would trample broad paths in the wheat, nearly ripe" while the artillery edged gingerly around the sodden roads. This was the sort of incidental damage in wartime that these veterans had long since removed to the category of routine, but among the "Dutch in that section of the country," it was an apocalypse. It amused Longstreet's men to have an "old farmer" announce in dismay over his trodden-down wheat, "I have heardt and I have readt of de horrors of warfare, but my utmost conceptions did not equal dis." By June 30th, as the rain began to taper off, one of Powell Hill's divisions (Harry Heth's) had passed Cashtown, with the other two (Richard Heron Anderson's and Dorsey Pender's) six miles behind. Two of Longstreet's three divisions were just behind Anderson's, with the third (George Pickett's) left at Chambersburg. Dick Ewell, riding in his carriage along with Robert Rodes' division, made twenty-two miles on the road to Heidlersburg, nine miles north of Gettysburg, by the end of the same day; at the same moment, Jubal Early's division was closing in, just three miles east of Heidlersburg. Allegheny Johnson's division took the outer route, following the corps trains back to Scotland, where he would then turn east to rejoin Ewell. The last details of Ewell's cavalry brigade did not quit Carlisle until the afternoon of the 30th.[27]

Hill's divisions, however, could not stay at Cashtown. So long as the Confederates relied heavily on foraging to feed themselves, each division would (by the reckoning of nineteenth-century armies) require a circle of twelve and a half miles around its encampments to forage (for water, firewood, and feed for men and horses); one single regiment could denude an acre of woodland just for firewood every three days. The Cashtown area did not afford nearly enough of such space to support three of Hill's divisions plus two of Longstreet's. Hill would have to make room for Longstreet's advance, and the only room that would keep Hill within hailing distance of both Longstreet and

Ewell was eastward to Gettysburg. In the overall scheme of Lee's concentration, the next day—July 1st—should see two of Hill's divisions move there and camp on the eastern side of the town (toward York), while Richard Anderson's division and the two lead divisions of Ewell's corps occupied the bivouac Hill had just vacated around Cashtown. "Lee's plan had long been formed to concentrate his own army somewhere between Cashtown and Gettysburg," wrote Porter Alexander, "in a strong position where it would threaten at once Washington, Baltimore, and Philadelphia." By sundown on the 1st of July, Hill would have occupied Gettysburg in strength, with Ewell situated just behind him, and Longstreet closing in from the west. "When General A.P. Hill started his column across the mountain on the 29th," wrote one of his staffers, "his orders were to proceed through Gettysburg towards York."[28]

And it was at this moment, and not on June 28th, that Lee began to feel most keenly the absence of J.E.B. Stuart—not because Stuart was failing to provide intelligence, but because Stuart was unavailable to provide screening to ward off Federal interference with the convergence at Gettysburg. Ideally, Stuart should have been picketing to the south and east of Gettysburg, in a long line from Fairfield on the west to Littlestown on the east, to allow the concentration of Lee's three corps to take place without observation. His absence left Ewell relying on the 1,600 or so horsemen of Albert Jenkins' cavalry brigade to screen his corps on its way southward, and Early relying on the wild boys of Elijah White's solitary cavalry battalion, who probably could not have formed a worthwhile screen even if all of their mothers had asked. Powell Hill lacked even that much cavalry—which is why, on June 29th, Hill fell back on the clumsy expedient of sending two regiments of infantry out to his right as a screen, down to Fairfield, where they collided with John Buford's Yankee cavalry. And it was the same reason why, on June 30th, Hill sent an entire infantry brigade down the Cashtown Pike to Gettysburg to do the screening in Stuart's place.

It was not, at first, a difficult assignment. Harry Heth's division was Hill's lead division in the line of march, and Heth detailed James Johnston Pettigrew's North Carolina brigade to push on ahead into Gettysburg and report back. Pettigrew was an intelligent choice for the job: he was a cultivated *litterateur,* had traveled through Europe and written a travelogue, *Notes on Spain and the Spaniards,* and had even spent time in Italy as a volunteer aide with the French and Italian forces against the Austrians in 1859.[29] In his after-action report in September 1863, Heth would mention in passing that Pettigrew's brigade was also to "search the town for army supplies (shoes especially)," and a *New York Herald* reporter who got himself captured along the Cashtown Pike passed Confederates "loaded with chickens, butter, eggs and vegetables of every description." (Harry Heth himself claimed a fine felt hat from a store in Cashtown, and although it was a size too large, an enterprising staffer rolled up "a dozen or more sheets of foolscap paper" and stuck them into the sweatband of the hat to make it fit.) If he discovered Yankees prowling around, he was to report back at once.[30]

The most significant witness to Pettigrew's mission was a physician, John William Crapster O'Neal. Born in Virginia, O'Neal was educated at Pennsylvania College, and then trained as a physician at the University of Maryland. He practiced medicine in nearby Hanover in the 1840s, and then moved his practice to Baltimore until 1863, when he returned to Gettysburg as Adams County's medical director (supervising the county almshouse north of town and the county jail on High Street). Late in the morning of June 30th, O'Neal was riding out to a sick call on the Cashtown Pike when he met "a body of men coming down the pike from [the] direction of Cashtown" at "the old Herr tavern," a mile west of the town. The body of men turned out to be three regiments of North Carolinians. They stopped him, and Pettigrew proceeded briefly to interrogate O'Neal on the road, and then let him go on.

O'Neal did not get very far. A rebel orderly came pelting after him and pulled him back to Pettigrew, who "reexamined me, asking whether there were any Yankees in town, when I left town and whether I had any newspapers." O'Neal knew nothing about Yankees in Gettysburg, and so a second time Pettigrew released him. But this time, Pettigrew demanded that O'Neal ride with him into Gettysburg and go no farther out along the pike. They jogged only a short distance farther when, perched upon a steep ridgeline between them and the town, Pettigrew saw "about a half-dozen mounted men"—Union cavalry. "I understood you to say there were no Yankees in [the] town," Pettigrew said irritably. "There are mounted men!" O'Neal was as surprised as Pettigrew, since there had been no Federal cavalrymen in Gettysburg when he left on his rounds that morning. More bad news soon came back to Pettigrew. Two Confederates—Heth's division surgeon, E. B. Spence, and Longstreet's spy, Henry Harrison—had taken themselves ahead of Pettigrew that morning into town, Surgeon Spence to "procure some medical supplies" at "the first drug-store" he could find, and Harrison to look around the general area. Both of them were there when Buford's troopers came riding up from below town, and both bolted back to warn Pettigrew "that a superior force of the enemy were moving on Gettysburg." A few of Pettigrew's officers claimed they could hear "drums beating on the farther side of town." That meant infantry, and infantry very likely could mean the Army of the Potomac.[31]

Bearing in mind Heth's warning "not to bring on an engagement," Pettigrew ordered a pullback for four miles, beyond Marsh Creek, and went to report to Heth, whom he found at Cashtown together with Powell Hill. According to Heth's account in 1877, Hill dismissed any concerns about Union forces in or around Gettysburg. "The only force at Gettysburg is cavalry, probably a detachment of observation." Hill had just come from Lee's temporary headquarters up the road at Greenwood, and Lee had assured him that "the information he has from his scouts" indicated that "the enemy are still at Middleburg, and have not yet struck their tents." (Although there were four Middleburgs or Middletowns along the general path of Lee's invasion, Hill probably meant Middleburg, *Maryland,* just behind Pipe Creek.)[32]

This assurance was all that Harry Heth needed to hear, and he promptly asked Hill if he might take his entire division back into Gettysburg the next day, July 1st, to "get those shoes!" Did Hill have any objection? "None in the world," Hill replied. Pettigrew was aghast at Hill's nonchalant attitude, and he tried to get one of his staffers, Lt. Louis Young, who knew Hill, to "tell General Hill what I had seen while re-connoitering." The Union cavalry's "movements were undoubtedly those of well-trained troops and not those of a home guard," and Pettigrew was not sure that there might not be Yankee infantry somewhere close behind them. But Hill scoffed at Young's intervention: he "still could not believe that any portion of the Army of the Potomac was up; and in emphatic words, expressed the hope that it was, as this was the place he wanted it to be." No wonder that, thirty-three years later, an accusing John Mosby believed on these grounds that Hill sent Heth "to Gettysburg just for an adventure."[33]

But Hill may not have been as unconcerned as Mosby and Heth believed. Rumors flickered through Hill's corps that "the enemy [are] reported in front," with "a fight expected tomorrow." Hill, in fact, sent off a courier to Lee to apprise "the general commanding" that "Pettigrew had encountered the enemy at Gettysburg (principally cavalry), but in what force he could not determine." He also took care to order Richard Anderson's division to close up on Cashtown in the morning, and sent a courier to Ewell, warning him not to move down on Gettysburg until Hill could "discover what was in my front." In the larger scheme of Lee's recall order, Hill was going to have to move on Gettysburg anyway on July 1st, if only to vacate the area around Cashtown for Longstreet, and to secure the Gettysburg crossroads to allow Ewell to move within connecting distance of Longstreet and Hill. And since Harry Heth's division was first on the line of march, with its pickets already at Marsh Creek, his job would be what Stuart's normally was: "to ascertain what force was at Gettysburg, and if he found infantry opposed to him, to report the fact immediately, without forcing an engagement."[34]

It was the role of pickets to act as a trip wire, alerting the rest of a command in camp or at rest to the probing presence of an enemy. For that reason, infantry units whose officers liked going by the book would post two or three "concentric lines" of pickets, "disposed in *a fan-shaped order.*" The outermost line could be posted as much as three miles in advance of an encampment, with each outpost composed of four men not "farther apart than 600 paces," or farther in advance of the next line than "300 paces." The third line would be sited another "200 paces" behind the second, so that a reasonably thick curtain of pickets could snare and contain any but the most large-scale attack. An officer in overall charge of the pickets was responsible for keeping small patrols moving along the outpost lines (if only to keep the pickets awake and alert).[35]

Cavalry pickets (or, to use their own term, *videttes*) had more flexibility in setting distances, and John Buford would need to push that flexibility to the limit. Only two of the three brigades of his cavalry division were with him when he rode into Gettysburg at midday on June 30th (the division's Reserve Brigade was lagging behind with the division's supply train at Mechanicsburg, Maryland, four miles south of Emmitsburg), so he was compelled to spread his vidette posts—about 700 men—very thinly. They prescribed a wide arc reaching from the Black Horse Tavern, south and west of Gettysburg on the Fairfield Road, then along Knoxlyn Ridge to the west, then across the Mummasburg and Carlisle Roads to the north, and finally ending east of the town on the York road. Buford used the point where the Cashtown Pike crossed the Knoxlyn Ridge as a rough dividing line, posting details from the 8th New York Cavalry and the 8th Illinois Cavalry along the line that ran from Black Horse Tavern to the Cashtown Pike, and then squads of the 12th Illinois Cavalry, 6th New York Cavalry, 17th Pennsylvania Cavalry, and the 9th New York Cavalry along the outpost lines running back to the north and east of Gettysburg. Buford put William Sackett, the colonel of the 9th New York, in overall charge of the outposts for the night, and set up his own headquarters in the Eagle Hotel in Gettysburg. The rest of his two brigades made up camp on the west side of the town, just beyond the fields surrounding Pennsylvania College.[36]

It was a jumpy night, and the lowering clouds "poured down a drenching rain." Buford's videttes were "in sight" of the Confederate outposts Pettigrew had left along Marsh Creek, and he was certain that he would be facing all of "A.P. Hill's corps, composed of Anderson, Heth, and Pender." W. C. Hazleton, a captain in the 8th Illinois Cavalry, "having charge of a reserve picket-post out on a turnpike near a farmer's house," was invited (with his pickets) to dinner, but had to refuse, being "on duty." The old farmer offered to stand watch for them while they ate, and when Hazelton apologized and turned that offer down, too, the amiable farmer "came out and chatted with us till late at night." Before darkness fell, a patrol from the 9th New York collided with a squad of Confederate cavalry on the northeast-running Hunterstown road, and captured one of them before the rest took off. The prisoner turned out to be one of Ewell's corps, which hinted at yet another problem brewing to the north. Later, a farmer was passed through the videttes of the 17th Pennsylvania, north of Gettysburg, in order to warn the 17th's colonel that the rebel Ewell's corps was somewhere just to the north and intended marching on Gettysburg the next day.[37]

If it really was rebel infantry coming his way, there was no point for Buford to even think of a mounted action like Brandy Station. William Gamble's brigade had only "about 1,600" men for any fight Buford was contemplating; Devin may have had another 1,600 men available. Besides, massed infantry fire would riddle a light cavalry charge before any horseman even came close. At best, he could dismount his cavalry and fight them as infantry with their carbines. But the vast mix of carbines his troopers were armed with—top-loading Merrills, lever-action Sharps, Burnsides, and Gallaghers, and break-open Smiths—lacked both the punch and range of infantry rifles, and the need to detail horse holders while the men were dismounted would take one out of every four of his available men off the firing line. Even worse, both "men and horses" were "fagged out" by the time they arrived in Gettysburg; he could get no fodder for the horses and "Early's people seized every shoe and nail," so he had neither materials nor facilities for reshoeing them. Buford could screen for Reynolds; and if Reynolds wanted to secure Gettysburg before the rebels could, he could even fight a small-scale delaying action to give Reynolds some time. But if John Reynolds wanted Gettysburg, he needed to get the 1st Corps and whatever other infantry was at hand up from Marsh Creek the next morning to do the work himself.[38]

The one advantage Buford held was that he knew what was likely coming against him in the morning. Powell Hill and Harry Heth did not; or at least, Hill was unsure enough to warn Heth not to get tangled in a fight with Union forces from which he could not extricate himself safely, and decided to authorize what would have otherwise been a signal of serious action ahead—a tot of whiskey to any man in the corps who wanted one. Orders went out from Heth to have the division ready to march at five the next morning, and given that Pettigrew's brigade had done the hard work the previous day, the lead brigades on the march would be a newly organized brigade of Mississippians (plus one North Carolina regiment) under President Davis' stuffy and ambitious nephew, Joseph Robert Davis, and James J. Archer's mixed brigade of Tennesseans and Alabamians. Archer was a Marylander, a Princeton graduate and a lawyer, but one who abandoned law for a second career in the old

Army. In battle, he was a "little gamecock" who "had no sense of fear," and at Fredericksburg Archer led the 5th Alabama Battalion in a counterattack that saved the Confederate hold on Prospect Hill. But his officers found him an "enigmatical man . . . very noncommunicative, and . . . for a time, one of the most intensely-hated of men." He was neither "a politician or aristocrat," which went some way toward explaining why Harry Heth, an intellectual lightweight but a pet of Lee's, had been promoted over Archer's head to division command.

Pettigrew's brigade would fall in behind Archer and Davis, followed by Heth's least reliable brigade, John Mercer Brockenbrough's four Virginia regiments. Brockenbrough had begun the war as the colonel of one of these regiments, and inherited command of the brigade when its commander, Charles W. Field, was taken out of action in 1862. A wealthy but rough-looking Virginia planter, Brockenbrough had never managed the brigade well, especially at Fredericksburg, and Lee briefly returned him to regimental command and promoted Harry Heth to put some spirit back into the brigade. But when Heth went up to division command in the post-Chancellorsville reshuffle, Brockenbrough, by default, resumed command of the brigade (although without any recommendation from Lee about promotion to brigadier general). The four regiments that made up Brockenbrough's brigade had been "sadly reduced in numbers" and in morale, and one man in the 47th Virginia wrote fearfully that "we know not what will befall us for some of our soldiers have done mity bad."[39]

Joseph Davis' brigade suffered from a similar crisis of confidence. The 2nd and 11th Mississippi had been organized in 1861 under a galaxy of local worthies (one of whom was William C. Falkner, the great-grandfather of novelist William Faulkner) and had gone through blood and fire together from the Peninsula through Antietam. But after Antietam, they were spliced together with two newly raised regiments, topped with an inexperienced brigadier general in the form of Joe Davis, and sent off to the backwater of North Carolina until after Chancellorsville. Davis had been a lawyer before the war, and briefly colonel of the 10th Mississippi. Most of his service had been as an aide on the staff of his president-uncle, and the principal force behind his promotion to brigade command was simon-pure nepotism. The Confederate Senate had actually rejected President Davis' nomination of his nephew for promotion; the president bought off a few objectors with promises of patronage, and Joe Davis got his star. It was harder, though, to buy the affections of a brigade where two of the regiments mistrusted not only the commander, but the reliability of two of its as yet untested units. What was worse for Joe Davis was that, as his brigade shuffled out into the Cashtown Pike to follow Archer's brigade, they were minus one of their two veteran outfits—the 11th

Mississippi had been detailed to guard the corps supply train, still parked at Cashtown.[40]

The "misty rain" continued till dawn, but as Heth's division fell regiment by regiment into the Cashtown Pike, the rain stopped, leaving a fleecy, light cloud cover and temperatures already in the 70s. The "rains during the night had laid the dust," recalled one of the officers Pettigrew had left on the Confederate picket line. "I never saw troops in better spirits, everybody seemed lively." A brigade at the head of a column of march would usually have a small advance party of skirmishers and axemen (or "pioneers") to clear obstructions, fanning out in open order and about "a thousand paces" ahead, accompanied by skirmishers along the flanks of the advancing column, and led by a mounted staff officer. Most of the division assumed that this morning's movement was simply one more part in the army's overall concentration of forces, and John Brockenbrough told one of his colonels, William Christian of the 55th Virginia, that "we probably might meet some of Ewells command or Stuarts." But Heth sent a staffer down the column to the brigade and regimental commanders, warning them that there might be a fight up the road and convincing Brockenbrough that they were all surely in for fireworks. The colonel of the 13th Alabama "rode back to the colorbearer" of the regiment "and ordered him to uncase the colors, the first intimation that we had that we were about to engage the enemy." Otherwise, as one of the crew of the four-gun Fredericksburg Artillery remembered, "we moved forward leisurely smoking and chatting as we rode along."[41]

The advance party, followed by the head of Archer's brigade, crested the last ridge before dipping down to Marsh Creek between 7:00 and 7:30, moving through the pickets left by Pettigrew the previous evening. Across the creek, the road rose to Knoxlyn Ridge, where the home of a blacksmith, Ephraim Wisler, was perched. There, watching the long Confederate column cross the creek and begin its ascent of the road, was one of Buford's outlying videttes—four troopers of the 8th Illinois Cavalry. The four cavalrymen hallooed for their sergeant, and when they could not find him, one of the troopers, Thomas Kelley, mounted up and galloped the 200 yards back to the reserve post to find Lt. Marcellus Jones. Kelley and Jones came up in a hurry, and the four troopers pointed to the moving column and "the old Rebel flag" up ahead. When their sergeant, Levi Shafer, also showed up, Lieutenant Jones asked him for his carbine, steadied and aimed it "in a crotch" of a rail fence, and squeezed off a shot. Pettigrew's outpost officer "was watering my horse" in Marsh Creek while Heth's "troops were passing" when he was startled by a shot in the thick morning air, some 400 yards ahead. His first thought was that it was some slovenly soldier's "accidental discharge." It was, instead, the first shot of the battle of Gettysburg.[42]

PART 2

The First Day

CHAPTER NINE

The devil's to pay

THE NEWS of the Confederate contact set the chain of picket lines into motion: Lieutenant Jones sent a trooper back to his captain, Daniel W. Buck, at a "wayside inn about a mile and a half from camp," and Buck in turn sent a galloper to find Major John Beveridge of the 8th Illinois, and then on again to find William Gamble and Buford at the Eagle Hotel. Buford's signal officer, Aaron Jerome, caught the message as the courier hurried past, and took his "glass" with him up into the cupola of the Lutheran seminary. Beveridge ordered boots-and-saddles, and by the time Gamble and Buford rode up the Cashtown Pike to Gamble's bivouac, "the brigade stood to horse, prepared to mount," and off they went, moving a long dismounted skirmish line along the next ridge, where the Cashtown Pike crossed the farm property of Edward McPherson, a protégé of Thaddeus Stevens' and a former Republican congressman. Buford sent Gamble off with his brigade and ordered Tom Devin to extend Gamble's line on the ridge northward on the other side of the pike. A knot of boys from the town had come out to poke around Devin's encampment and rub shoulders with real soldiers, but the call for boots-and-saddles quickly scattered them.[1]

Buford climbed up into the Lutheran seminary's cupola (it was a small flat affair, open on all sides, with a wooden canopy, and accessed by a ladder and hatch) to have a look westward with Lieutenant Jerome's heavy signal telescope, and what he saw did not please him. "He seemed anxious," Jerome noticed, "even more so than I ever saw him." He kept climbing up and down from the cupola, spitting orders, riding out along the line of McPherson's Ridge to supervise the placement of Gamble's and Devin's brigades, then rid-

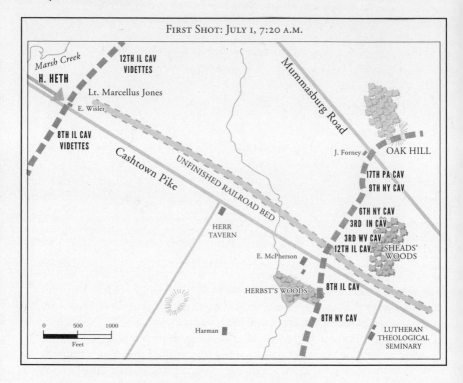

FIRST SHOT: JULY 1, 7:20 A.M.

Marsh Creek
H. HETH

12TH IL CAV
VIDETTES

Lt. Marcellus Jones

E. Wisler

8TH IL CAV
VIDETTES

Cashtown Pike

UNFINISHED RAILROAD BED

HERR
TAVERN

E. McPherson

HERBST'S WOODS

Harman

Mummasburg Road

J. Forney   OAK HILL

17TH PA CAV
9TH NY CAV

6TH NY CAV
3RD IN CAV

3RD WV CAV
12TH IL CAV   SHEADS'
WOODS

8TH IL CAV

8TH NY CAV

LUTHERAN
THEOLOGICAL
SEMINARY

0   500   1000
Feet

ing back to the seminary and climbing up to the cupola again. A slow-witted staffer whom Reynolds had sent up to Gettysburg to act as a messenger for Buford asked dully, "Why, what is the matter general." At that moment, a dull boom revealed that someone in the distance had unlimbered artillery and was trying the range. "That," Buford snarled, "is the matter." Only three miles separated Lieutenant Jones from the diamond at the center of town, and if Reynolds did not get his infantry athwart the Cashtown Pike in the next two hours, he might as well stay at Moritz Tavern.[2]

Buford's troopers might, however, buy Reynolds at least some extra innings. He had a battery of long-range 3-inch Ordnance Rifles under Lt. John Calef which might force a little hesitation on the rebels' part, and he also had Harry Heth's uncertainty about what might lie behind Buford's pickets to add to the delay. And sure enough, Harry Heth's first reaction was to stop the line of march, unlimber a battery "in the road," and shake out skirmishers from Archer's brigade to clear the ground in front of them. As Archer's skirmishers deployed, a company of the 8th Illinois under Capt. Amasa Dana conveniently showed up, and this allowed Jones and Dana to set up a skirmish line of their own on the next ridge. "Scattering my men to the right and left, at intervals of thirty feet, and behind post and rail fences," Dana "directed them to throw up their carbine sights to 800 yards, then taking rest on the top rail we gave the enemy the benefit of long range practice."[3]

It is not clear how many times the 8th Illinois played cat and mouse with Archer's skirmishers, backing up the Cashtown Pike toward Gettysburg. (They probably inflicted the first Confederate casualty of the battle, too, a skirmisher named Henry Raison of the 7th Tennessee.) But every time the Confederate column stopped to swat at the Yankee cavalry, formations at the rear of the advance slackened, men fell out to boil coffee, and tempers frayed. And the clock ticked: the Confederates, just to be certain that it was *only* cavalry in front of them, would need to move from marching column into line of battle, and orders from a division commander in Heth's position to his brigade commanders would require at least twenty minutes for transmission (including writing them out, and sending them by courier), and another fifteen to get verbal orders from brigade commanders down to the colonels of the brigade's regiments. To preserve the unity of companies in a regiment, a column could not simply be turned off the road and allowed to convert column files into battle lines; it required a complicated process, starting with the regimental lieutenant colonel (or adjutant) galloping off to mark where the far flank of the regiment was to rest, and the junior major of the regiment marking the other flank. Company sergeants had to mark out the points along the line which would be filled by companies, always ensuring that the regimental colors were front and center. Whatever artillery was on hand would also need to be galloped into place, unlimbered, and readied for action. And this was likely to consume yet another forty-five minutes to an hour.[4]

Which is just what it did. From his vantage point with Brockenbrough's brigade, the brigade chaplain could see Archer's lead regiments reach the crest of Herr Ridge, and then begin to "file to the right off the road and march by column of fours, or marching order, at right angles to the road," and then begin forming battle lines. And in "a few moments," orders came down the road for Brockenbrough's brigade to begin doing likewise. As Archer's brigade turned off the Cashtown Pike to its right on Herr Ridge, Joe Davis' brigade turned off to the left, so that they could present one long, two-rank line of battle, stretched on either side of the Cashtown Pike. The two artillery batteries Heth brought with him also rolled up into positions on the ridge, and regimental officers began dressing the lines, holding impromptu weapons inspections, and trying to make little speeches of encouragement before going into action against the Yankee cavalrymen on the next ridge. "Men, clean out your guns, load and be ready," repeated Col. John Stone, as he walked up and down the line of the 2nd Mississippi. "We are going to have it." The

Confederate cannon—in this case, Edward Marye's Fredericksburg Artillery, with their two Ordnance Rifles and two 12-pounder Napoleons—let off the first shells at McPherson's Ridge.[5]

This teasing, jolting retreat gave Buford at least an hour and a half to concentrate most of his two brigades along the line of McPherson's Ridge in dismounted order. It was now close to ten o'clock, and Buford had done almost everything that his horse soldiers could be expected to do. Calef's battery could trade shots with the Confederate guns for as long as anyone liked, but once the rebel infantry started forward, his men would be knocked out of the way like snakes by a stick. It would be only a matter of a few volleys of carbine fire before his troopers would have to mount up and bolt south or east through the town. Heth was putting out skirmishers, and a splutter of small-arms fire was igniting along the thin line of dismounted cavalrymen. Buford dashed off a quick message to Meade, warning him that "the enemy's force (A. P. Hill's) are advancing on me at this point, and driving my pickets and skirmishers very rapidly." This might have been the curtain call for Buford had not Lieutenant Jerome, still in the cupola of the Lutheran seminary, caught sight to the south, along the Emmitsburg Road, of "the corps-flag of General Reynolds."

Shortly Reynolds himself "and staff came up on a gallop," leaving the lead elements of his 1st Corps behind on the road. It was the first of a series of heart-stopping moments at Gettysburg when the entire battle would come down to a scramble of minutes getting to one place or another. "Now we can hold the place," Buford said, and added to a note to Alf Pleasonton, "General Reynolds is advancing, and is within 3 miles of this point with his leading division."[6]

John Reynolds was up early on the morning of July 1st. He had been waiting to the last minute to see which way Meade would jump—to move forward and support the 1st Corps and 11th Corps, or issue a final, inalterable order to withdraw to Pipe Creek—and at six o'clock called for his senior division commander, Abner Doubleday. No more waiting: "He then instructed me," said Doubleday, "to draw in my pickets, assemble the artillery and the remainder of the corps, and join him as soon as possible."[7]

The sun soon came up, a dim blood-red disk behind the clouds on the eastern horizon, and some morning drizzle briefly pelted the rousing soldiers. Reynolds did not stay with Doubleday, but rode on ahead with an escort, meeting couriers from Buford on the way. Once on the move, the men's spirits lifted, and in one German company, recruited from Milwaukee, the soldiers struck up a "soul-stirring song" in the *Männerchor* fashion "such as only the

Germans can sing." But the enthusiasm did not last long. First, they began passing melancholy knots of refugees, stumbling southward, in the opposite direction. "Citizens were met driving cattle and horses before them in search of a safe retreat," and one Pennsylvania officer was particularly melted when he passed by "two children—a boy and a girl . . . on one horse, crying as if their little hearts would break." Alongside the 76th New York rushed "gray-haired old men . . . women carrying their children, and children leading each other, while on the faces of all were depicted the indices of . . . terror and despair." Then they heard the first, faint crump of artillery. One soldier in the 6th Wisconsin, unwilling to let the high spirits of the morning dissipate, tried to joke that "the Pennsylvanians have made a mistake and are celebrating the 4th [of July] three days ahead of time." But there could be no mistaking what artillery meant—up ahead, someone was fighting, hard enough and in sufficient numbers to make it worth their while to unlimber artillery and commit it to the fight.[8]

If anyone needed further convincing, they had it when, less than a mile south of the town, Reynolds himself reappeared. Pounding ahead of the blue column, Reynolds and a cluster of aides had ridden into Gettysburg, got quick directions from Union cavalrymen still milling around the Eagle Hotel, then turned west to the seminary and the ridge it sat upon. "Seeing Buford in the cupola," Reynolds shouted up, "What's the matter, John?" "The devil's to pay," cracked Buford. And when he came down, Buford tersely explained, "Reynolds, I have run upon some regiments of infantry"—or, in reality, they had run upon him—"they are in the woods," somewhere on the other side of McPherson's Ridge, "and I am unable to dislodge them."[9]

That settled matters in Reynolds' mind, and he delivered to his aides a short volley of orders and messages which put the final seal on the battle. First, to Meade at Taneytown, a verbal notice to be carried by Capt. Stephen Weld: "Ride at once at your utmost speed"—even if it killed his horse—"to General Meade; tell him the enemy are advancing in strong force and that I fear they will get to the heights beyond the town before I can. I will fight them inch by inch and if driven into town, I will barricade the streets and hold them back as long as possible." He then added for Meade, almost as an afterthought, *While I am aware that it is not your desire to force an engagement at that point, still I feel at liberty to advance and develop the strength of the enemy.* Then, to Abner Doubleday: "I will hold onto the Chambersburg Road," while "you must hold on to the Millersville Road." Third, to Otis Howard: "he had encountered the enemy apparently in force" and Howard was "to bring your corps forward as rapidly as possible." And finally, to Dan Sickles and the 3rd Corps, even more concisely: "Tell General Sickles *I think* he had better come up." This would leave Meade with no choice. Once Reynolds had committed three of Meade's seven infantry corps to Gettysburg, Meade could not refuse to support him with the other four.[10]

But if he was going to trigger a stand-up fight, Reynolds would need to do it quickly, before the Confederates on Herr Ridge could deploy and advance, and for that he would need to bring up whatever pieces of the 1st Corps he could lay hands upon. The 1st Corps, with James Wadsworth's division in the lead, had come abreast of the red farmhouse and barn of Nicholas Codori, whose property generously straddled the Emmitsburg Road just south of Gettysburg, and as they had done in so many towns on this march, the colonel of the 6th Wisconsin ordered the regimental colors uncased, and the fifes and drums to strike up a tune to march by. (The regimental drum major chose "The Campbells Are Coming.") "Here we were met by General Reynolds," a soldier at the head of the column remembered, and Reynolds pulled Wadsworth off the road for a rapid consultation. Reynolds "looked careworn, and we thought, very sad, but the high purpose of his patriotic soul was stamped upon every lineament." In the distance, the men could see a long cloud of smoke rolling up from Buford's artillery and "hanging about . . . in clouds."[11]

Wadsworth had a map that one of his staffers had scrounged from "some friendly farm-house" which he now unfolded, looking for the best route through the town. But Reynolds told him to forget marching through Gettysburg, and cut across farmer Codori's fields to the left of the road, skirt the southwest edge of town, and come up over Seminary Ridge, and do it on the double-quick. Like the Confederates two miles distant, a Union division would have an advance guard on the road at the very front for quick deployment, followed by a brigade of infantry and a battery of artillery, and then the main body of the division's infantry and the rest of its artillery, with wagons and ambulances and a small rear guard. In James Wadsworth's division that morning, the lead brigade was composed of four New York regiments and a Pennsylvania one, with the snappiest-looking unit of the five being the 14th Brooklyn, kitted out in French chasseur uniforms with red caps and red trousers and taking an unholy satisfaction in being called "the red-legged devils." (Officially, they were the 84th New York Volunteer Infantry; but they were originally recruited from Brooklyn, and they had constituted the old 14th New York State Militia before the war. The regiment had more or less unanimously enlisted as a three-year volunteer regiment in 1861, but insisted on being known by their militia moniker as the 14th Brooklyn.) They were commanded by a frowning fifty-six-year-old New Englander named Lysander Cutler, who was one of the army's tougher customers. In his first job, as a schoolteacher, he had imposed a fair sense of order on his pupils by beating the starch out of any bullies who tried to intimidate him; he went on to become an agent for a mining company in Wisconsin, facing down a variety of outlaws and Indians, and in 1861, he was handed a commission as colonel of the 6th Wisconsin. His schoolmaster manner did not endear him to the 6th, but his performance under fire at Second Bull Run wiped away whatever disgruntlement his regiment felt, and in due time he was promoted to brigadier general and given command of a brigade in James Wadsworth's division.

Cutler's brigade would move up the Emmitsburg Road to a farm lane that angled off toward the Lutheran seminary, followed by the six guns of Battery B, 2nd Maine Artillery, under Lt. James Hall. Behind them marched one of the most famous brigades in the entire Army of the Potomac, the five regiments commanded by the unwieldy six-foot, seven-inch Solomon Meredith. Three of these regiments were from Wisconsin—one of them, the 6th, was Lysander Cutler's old regiment—and the other two from Michigan and Indiana. They were absurdly proud of being an all-Western brigade in an Eastern army, prouder still of sticking to the prewar army's outfit of tall-crowned black hats, thigh-length frock coats, and gaiters, and proudest of all at being known as the Iron Brigade, a nickname they had won at the battle of South Mountain in 1862. Meredith's Westerners would turn directly into the fields, and move up to the Lutheran seminary on a line parallel with Cutler's brigade. The "call for 'pioneers to the front'" went up, followed by "a swinging of axes at all the posts on the left side of the road," and then it was "oblique" through the breaks in the fences, along the lanes, and across the fields in two large columns.[12]

This was no light jog. On a straight line, Wadsworth's two brigades would have to double-quick for a mile and a quarter in the thick humidity just to reach the seminary. From a small widow's walk on the top of his store at Baltimore and Middle streets, Henry J. Fahnestock could watch Wadsworth's brigade columns "passing . . . along the base of Seminary Hill," knocking down more fences along the Fairfield Road, and finally flowing up onto Seminary Ridge. The Iron Brigade stopped for breath and direction "to the left of the Seminary" while Wadsworth pointed Cutler's brigade beyond the seminary and the Cashtown Pike. Coming up even with the seminary, these men could see for the first time the battle they had only been hearing at a distance.[13]

Six hundred yards away, along the line of McPherson's Ridge, Buford's dismounted cavalrymen were already backing out of a parklike woodlot (owned by a local farmer, John Herbst) to reclaim their horses and shout, "They are coming, give it to them." To the right of the woodlot was the McPherson farm, and to the right of that, the Cashtown Pike, where John Calef's horse artillery was banging away at the Confederates visible to the west on Herr Ridge. On the other side of the pike, a deep cut for an unfinished railroad bed ran parallel to the pike, and beyond that, stretching north, was another somewhat parallel road (leading to Mummasburg) and the emi-

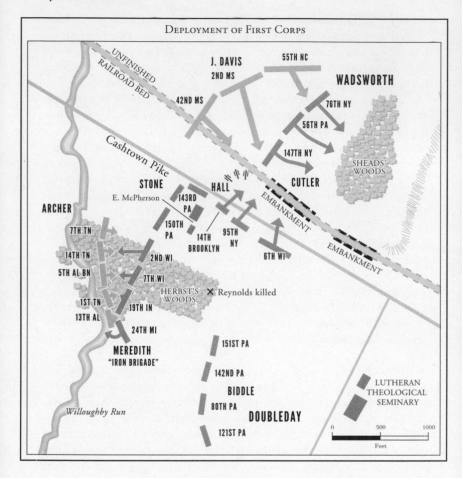

Deployment of First Corps

nence known locally as Oak Hill. Reynolds wanted Wadsworth's division to secure the ridgeline as far northward as they dared, so Wadsworth placed three of Cutler's regiments north of the pike and deployed them into line; Cutler's remaining two regiments would cover the McPherson farm on the south side of the pike. Meredith's Iron Brigade would push forward on the left of Cutler's two regiments in the farm buildings and clear farmer Herbst's woodlot.

They would not have much time to do it, either, since lines of Confederate skirmishers could easily be seen moving down the face of Herr Ridge toward the woods and the McPherson farm. The last of the Iron Brigade's regiments had barely reached the crest of Seminary Ridge when a staffer—

whether from Sol Meredith or from James Wadsworth, it was never clear—
"came on a gallop" with orders to move out of column into line of battle, send
back musicians and other noncombatants, throw out skirmishers, and rush
for the woods on McPherson's Ridge. There wasn't time to form a proper
brigade line, so each regiment, starting with the 2nd Wisconsin, went in as
soon as it was ready, loading and fixing bayonets as best they could on the
way. In fact, there wasn't even time to find out what, exactly, they were going
to meet in those woods. Lucius Fairchild, the colonel of the 2nd Wisconsin,
was simply told "that he would find the enemy in his immediate front as soon
as he could form."[14]

John Reynolds was up on Seminary Ridge as Wadsworth's brigades
arrived, and took personal care in replacing John Calef's overmatched rifled
guns with Hall's 2nd Maine battery. He wanted the battery on the north
side of the Cashtown Pike, where they would cover the westward approaches
of the pike and become the center of a continuous line formed by Cutler's
and Meredith's brigades along McPherson's Ridge. Hall's task would be "to
damage the [enemy] Artillery to the greatest possible extent, and keep their
fire from our infantry until they are deployed." If these units could be gotten
into position on the ridge, then Abner Doubleday's division could be used to
extend the line on the left of the Iron Brigade. If Reynolds then moved John
Cleveland Robinson's division up to the ridge, they could extend the line
northward; and if Otis Howard and the 11th Corps were following, then both
corps could hold the line from the Fairfield Road on the left all the way up to
Oak Hill on the right. Doubleday, in fact, had ridden ahead of his division
and caught up with the tail end of the Iron Brigade "just as it was going into
action." From McPherson's Ridge, and certainly from Seminary Ridge, Reynolds could stymie quite a good deal of Confederate infantry for a number of
hours—long enough, at least, to keep the rebels piled up on the west side of
Gettysburg while Meade came up with the rest of the Army of the Potomac
and secured Cemetery Hill.[15]

But he would need those woods. At about 10:15, Reynolds rode across the
swale between the seminary and Herbst's Woods, trailed by two aides and his
orderly, urging the 2nd Wisconsin and the following regiments of the Iron
Brigade to move forward. "Forward, men! Forward for God's sake, and drive
those fellows out of the woods." As he saw the 2nd plunge into the woods,
Confederate skirmishers let off a "hot fire," and when Reynolds "turned to
come out again" from the woods, a bullet from the rebel skirmishers in the
trees drilled into his head behind the right ear. He slumped forward, falling
facedown from his saddle, but catching one boot in the stirrup, so that his
agitated horse dragged him for several feet. The orderly, Sgt. Charles Veil, was
the first to reach Reynolds on the ground; he turned Reynolds over and tried

to raise his head. Veil could see "no wound or blood," and hoping against hope that Reynolds had only been knocked unconscious, the two aides, Robert Mitchell and Edward Baird, tried to wake him up, asking, "General are you in pain?" Baird got a canteen and tried to pour a drink through his lips. It was useless. John Reynolds was dead, and it was all that Sergeant Veil could do to round up a few winded stragglers from Cutler's brigade to help him carry Reynolds' body to safety on an army blanket. Mitchell and Baird galloped off to find Abner Doubleday and inform him that he was now in command; even more important, someone needed to find Oliver Otis Howard and the 11th Corps.[16]

By the usual standards, Harry Heth had every reason to feel confident. In later years, Heth would even deny that the stand-and-run tactics of the Yankee horsemen amounted to "so much as a skirmish" that morning, and the colonel of the 13th Alabama (which Heth had deployed on the skirmish line to roll the cavalry back) agreed that "our advance was not retarded, and that the cavalry did us no damage." Still, it was unnerving to have to fight on unfamiliar ground, and as he remained "ignorant what force was at or near Gettysburg," it seemed to Heth like no time to take chances on what might be concealed behind McPherson's Ridge. So he ordered Archer's and Joe Davis' brigades to deploy into line of battle along Herr Ridge, Archer to the right of the Cashtown Pike, Davis on the left. Behind them, more Confederate artillery under Willie Pegram "were unlimbered in front of a brick building which looked like an old Virginia county courthouse tavern" (this was Herr Tavern) and opened fire on "a squad of cavalry" that could be seen in the distance. As soon as the lines were dressed and skirmishers sent ahead, both brigades would clear McPherson's Ridge and open the road into Gettysburg.[17]

Like so many of the ridges they had crossed that morning, Herr Ridge fell away from the newly forming Confederate battle line into a shallow ravine and a meandering watercourse known as Willow Run, or Willoughby Run. Once formed up, Archer and Davis would sweep down into the ravine, cross the run, and mount the rise to McPherson's Ridge to drive off the dismounted Union troopers and their artillery. Farmer Herbst's woodlot grew down to the banks of the run, so Archer's men would be briefly advancing blind up the slope of McPherson's Ridge, and the run and the woods would both conspire to slow Archer's two Alabama and three Tennessee regiments as they moved forward. But these were regiments with considerable fighting experience, and in no especial hurry. They "continued to advance, but in a walk," with the skirmishers up ahead "loading and firing as we went."[18]

Yet this advance did not quite play according to script. Even in the racket of artillery and skirmishers trading shots with the dismounted cavalry up ahead, James Archer, tramping along with his rebel brigade, sensed that something was wrong. In the distance, one of his captains noticed troops in motion that he did not think were cavalry, and Archer "suggested" in a message to Heth that his 1,200-man brigade "was too light to risk so far in advance of support." Heth waved away Archer's uncertainty and ordered him to get his brigade moving and "ascertain the 'strength and line of battle of the enemy.'" But as the rebels moved forward 200 yards, crossed the run, and penetrated the willow thickets on its banks, the firing in the brigade's front suddenly roared to a new volume. Through the trees, Archer's skirmishers could be seen lying down, "waiting for the line of battle to come to their relief." Beyond them bobbed the tall black hats of the Iron Brigade's 2nd Wisconsin. Without time to reflect on where these apparitions had come from, Archer's two left regiments, the 7th and 14th Tennessee, whipped up their rifles and let off a volley that hit the Wisconsin regiment full in the face, forcing them to veer slightly to the Tennesseans' left. But before Archer and his men could recover themselves, a new avalanche of black-hats rolled down the ravine onto them—the 7th Wisconsin, coming head-on with fixed bayonets (they had had no time to load their weapons). Beside them appeared their fellow Westerners of the 19th Indiana and, slightly behind them, the 24th Michigan. A confused murmur went up along Archer's line: *Thar comes them old black-hats! It's the Army of the Potomac, sure!* and *We are deceived, 'tis the Army of the Potomac* and *There are those damned black-hatted fellows again! 'Taint no militia. It's the Army of the Potomac.*[19]

In a few minutes, the Indiana and Michigan regiments were curling around the unguarded right flank of Archer's brigade, where the surprised men of the 1st Tennessee and 13th Alabama tried to pull back across the run and bend their line "to the right and formed at nearly right angles to the original line." But the Iron Brigade had the momentum, and all along Archer's line, fragments and detachments turned and bolted back toward Herr Ridge. "We went down at them pretty lively," remembered a soldier in the 19th Indiana. There were other Federal units coming up near the McPherson barn, beyond the woods' edge, and they, too, were opening fire on Archer's men. "The engagement, which seemed to be raging along the whole of the brigade line, soon eased," reported the lieutenant colonel of the 19th Indiana, "and we found the rebel brigade in our front in full retreat."[20]

Chief of these prizes was James Archer. The temperamental Marylander, "very much exhausted with fatigue," did not believe in losing gracefully. Seeing himself surrounded, he tried to break "his sword in the ground" rather than surrender it to an opposing brother officer, according to the traditional cursus honorum of military chivalry. But the "beautiful steel-scabbard sword" wouldn't break, and while Archer stamped and pushed on it, a private in Company G of the 2nd Wisconsin, Patrick Maloney, nudged him to surrender. Archer was not about to turn over his uncooperative sword to a mere ranker; not until he spied the captain of Maloney's company, Charles C. Dow, did he stiffly proffer the weapon. But Dow generously refused: "Keep your sword, General, and go to the rear; one sword is all I need on this line." Archer trudged off, but any mollification he felt at being allowed to keep the sword was destroyed when a brigade staffer, Lt. Dennis Dailey, caught up with the Confederate general and demanded Archer surrender it to him. By the time the disgruntled Archer came in sight of Abner Doubleday, it was all he could do keep from exploding. Doubleday, who seems to have had some acquaintance with Archer going back to the Mexican War, greeted him chirpily, "Good morning, Archer, how are you? I am glad to see you." "Well," growled Archer, "I am not glad to see you by a damn sight." And off he went to the provost marshal's hastily improvised prisoner pen, and from there to a prison camp in Ohio, where his never-robust health was so undermined that, even though he would be exchanged in August 1864, he would live for only two more months.[21]

The repulse of Archer's brigade was success enough for the moment, and lacking any further orders, Solomon Meredith pulled his black-hats back to the eastern side of Willoughby Run, and began sorting them out, switching the 2nd and 7th Wisconsin so that the 7th was now the right flank regiment of the brigade, and doing likewise with the 19th Indiana and 24th Michigan, so that the 19th was on the brigade's left. Company sergeants began calling the roll to get a count of casualties (the 2nd Wisconsin lost 116 men in their hectic charge; the 19th Indiana had only 6 wounded and 1 man unaccounted for), and Samuel Williams, the colonel of the 19th Indiana, personally went from company to company, congratulating his Hoosiers on their good show.[22]

Matters went no more easily for the other part of Harry Heth's division on the north side of the Cashtown Pike, where Joe Davis' brigade was also supposed to sweep off the Union cavalrymen with no difficulty. Davis had three big regiments in hand—the 2nd and 42nd Mississippi and the 55th North Carolina, totaling around 1,700 men—and started them forward at more or less the same time as Archer's brigade, expecting nothing more in the way of resistance than the ribbon of dismounted Union cavalry on the north extension of McPherson's Ridge. What they did not see until much too late were the sprinting files of Lysander Cutler's brigade, moving into line through a series of wheat fields, behind the cavalrymen. And in accordance with John Reynolds' directive to extend a line on the ridge northward from the Iron Brigade in Herbst's Woods, Cutler peeled off two of his five regiments—the

95th New York and the red-legged 14th Brooklyn—to link up with the Iron Brigade's right and fill in the space between the woods and the Cashtown Pike. Hall's battery had unlimbered just on the other side of the pike, where the west end of the railroad cut flattened out; and beyond Hall's guns, Cutler rushed into place his remaining three regiments—the 147th New York, 56th Pennsylvania, and 76th New York. That gave Cutler fewer than 1,000 men to put in the path of Davis' brigade. But they scrambled, panting, into place, laid down in line to allow Tom Devin's retreating troopers to file to the rear, and in five minutes "they encountered the enemy and the fight commenced."[23]

In their hurry, neither Wadsworth nor Cutler had ordered out skirmishers, and there was enough powder smoke from the artillery firing, in the undulating depressions between the ridgelines, to make the identity of Davis' Confederates appear uncertain. A lieutenant in the 147th New York could see "innumerable heads of rebels bobbing up and down" as they felt their way forward toward McPherson's Ridge, but farther to the right the colonel of the 56th Pennsylvania, William J. Hoffmann, hesitated, turned back to one of his captains and asked, "Is that the enemy?" *Yes it was*, the captain replied, and Hoffmann quickly barked out, "Ready—Right oblique—Aim—Fire." That became the signal for a general firefight to erupt between Cutler's 56th Pennsylvania and 76th New York, and Davis' 42nd Mississippi and 55th North Carolina. Very quickly, the larger Confederate regiments began to sidle to the left and lap around the exposed right flank of the 76th. The colonel of the 55th North Carolina, John K. Connally, called for fixed bayonets and a charge, picking up the 55th's four-foot-by-four-foot regimental flag and starting forward. The North Carolinians lurched forward, only to see Connally go down almost at once with wounds to the arm and hip. The regiment's senior major, Alfred Belo, bent over Connally to catch some last words, only to have Connally splutter, *Pay no attention to me. Take the colors and keep ahead of the Mississippians*, as though this was a footrace rather than a live shooting gallery. The 76th New York was beginning to wilt under its losses, starting with its commanding officer, Andrew Grover, and after thirty minutes of mounting pressure, it collapsed, dragging the 56th Pennsylvania back with it toward a long woodlot of oak trees along Seminary Ridge.[24]

This left the 147th New York and Hall's battery dangling without a connection to other units, and with the 2nd and 42nd Mississippi in front and the North Carolinians moving somewhere around to their rear. Pummeled from two sides, the 147th flattened themselves in the knee-high wheat. "The fire of the enemy . . . cut the grain completely covering the men, who would reach over the ridge, take deliberate aim, fire and then slide under their canopy of covering of straw, reload and continue their firing." Cutler sent an order to withdraw for the lieutenant colonel of the 147th, Francis C. Miller, but Miller was "wounded on top of the head just at the time the order was delivered to him." Command fell to Maj. George Harney, who unknowingly "kept [the 147th] on the line" until men in the regiment began to notice "the colors of the 56th and 76th N.Y. away back to the rear of the woods." Finally, one of Wadsworth's staffers "with his coal-black hair pressing his horse's mane" rode down to Harney, gesturing to the rear with his sword over the noise of the firing, "and we then broke for the rear ourselves." Wadsworth himself told Hall to "lose no time in getting your guns" out, and Hall coolly pulled his battery back, section by section, keeping the hungry skirmishers of the 42nd Mississippi at bay with canister. Even so, one of his precious Ordnance Rifles was overrun by the rebels. The color sergeant of the 147th, John Hinchcliff, had been shot dead just as the New Yorkers turned to run, and the regiment's colors would probably have been captured had not another sergeant "retraced his steps . . . under a severe fire, rolled from off the flag the dead color sergt. and brought it off." The 147th, a regiment of "plowboys" from Oswego County, left forty-four dead behind.[25]

Fifty of the New Yorkers on the left of the regiment made their escape down the railroad cut, whose four-foot depth offered some shelter from Confederate fire from the north. It did nothing, though, to keep the 2nd Mississippi from following them into the cut and firing into the backs of the fleeing Yankees. One New Yorker actually clambered up the side of the cut to get out again, and as "I grasped hold of shrubs and sticks to assist me," the near-misses of Mississippi bullets "threw dirt in my face . . . passed between my hands and body, around my head, between my legs . . . and sounded like a lot of angry bees." As the 2nd Mississippi packed into the cut to pursue the remnants of the New York regiment, the collapse of Cutler's front attracted the attention of three Union regiments on the south side of the pike. Two of them, the 14th Brooklyn and 95th New York, had been posted by Cutler around the McPherson farm buildings; the third was the 6th Wisconsin, the reserve regiment of the Iron Brigade. Seeing the other regiments in Cutler's brigade falling back, Maj. Edward Pye (of the 95th New York) assumed that he should do likewise and "retired a short distance."[26]

The lieutenant colonel of the 6th Wisconsin, Rufus Dawes, had other ideas. Dawes (whose great-grandfather William rode with Paul Revere to warn Lexington and Concord in 1775) entered the 6th Wisconsin as a captain in 1861, and worked his way up to command of the regiment in time for the Chancellorsville battle. Ordered to form in column in the swale between the Lutheran seminary and Herbst's Woods, he had a clear view of "the men of Cutler's brigade . . . falling back," pursued by "an apparently strong but scattered line of rebels pushing slowly" over McPherson's Ridge. One of Abner Doubleday's staffers came pelting over with orders for Dawes to move up the pike and get into line of battle. "Go like hell!" he directed, with a fine disregard for language. "It looks as though they are driving Cutler." (There was a nice irony in this: Lysander Cutler had been the 6th Wisconsin's first colonel, and now they were going to the rescue of Cutler's brigade.) Once there, Dawes opened a long-range "fire by file," rifles "resting on the fence rails" that lined both sides of the pike. This "took the enemy *enfilade,* and checked his advance immediately and mixed up his line considerably." But the 2nd Mississippi found, as they pursued Cutler's beleaguered men, that the railroad cut offered them as much protection from Union bullets as the 147th New York hoped it would offer them from Confederate ones, and the Mississippians "ran into the railroad cut" and proceeded to "pour . . . a heavy fire . . . upon us from their cover in the cut."[27]

Without any further prompting from Doubleday, Dawes ordered his men to dress up and charge the fifty or so yards separating them from the lip of the railroad cut. As he did so, Dawes noticed that Major Pye of the 95th New York had likewise taken it upon himself to line up the 95th New York and 14th Brooklyn on the left of the 6th Wisconsin, and Dawes ran over to Pye to explain, "We must charge." "Charge it is," Pye answered, and forward they went, pulling down the fences or clambering over them, "with the colors at the advance point." The 2nd Mississippi waited too long. The three Union regiments got over the fences and rushed the cut with "yells enough to almost awaken the dead." The Mississippians fired off a terrific volley that knocked down Dawes' horse and bowled over what seemed to one sergeant like "half our men." But the momentum of the Yankee charge carried the rest up to the cut, where Dawes' men now pointed their rifles down at the frantically reloading rebels, demanding their surrender, and a savage little hand-to-hand fight broke out over the 2nd Mississippi's flag. Dawes came up on foot to the edge of the cut and bluffed them: "Where is the colonel of this regiment?" Dawes shouted. "Who are you?" a voice from the milling rebels replied. "I am the commander of this regiment," Dawes shouted back. "Surrender, or I will fire on you." The owner of the rebel voice was Maj. John Blair, who "replied not a word" further, "but promptly handed me his sword, and all his men, who still held them, threw down their muskets."[28]

In all, Dawes' little moment of inspiration netted him more than 200 prisoners, a rebel battle flag, and six or seven officers' swords which Dawes had to hand awkwardly over in a bundle to his adjutant. It also took the edge off the advance of the rest of Joe Davis' brigade. No one had told Davis, any more than they had told James Archer, to expect Union infantry on McPherson's Ridge. Davis was wholly unprepared for the resistance he had encountered, and Dawes' counterattack on the railroad cut convinced him that "a heavy force was . . . moving rapidly toward our right." Davis signaled a pullback to his first position on Herr Ridge, Cutler's battered brigade moved back out to "occupy the crest of the ridge," and in the scramble James Hall's gunners were able to recover their lost piece.[29]

It was now between eleven o'clock and noon, and Harry Heth had quite an unlooked-for mess on his hands. The easy saunter into Gettysburg he had anticipated that morning started with frustration and slow-ups, risen to a full-scale deployment of two of his brigades, and now culminated in a humiliating repulse by Federal infantry which shouldn't have been there at all. Should he break off? Should he go back in with his next two brigades, under Pettigrew and Brockenbrough? Should he wait for instructions from Powell Hill? If he waited, would more Federal infantry appear to threaten him? The last of these questions was about to become the most urgent, because (although Heth could not know it) another Federal corps was arriving in Gettysburg from the south, and its commander, Oliver Otis Howard, was at that moment climbing up to the widow's walk on Henry Fahnestock's store to have a look around.

CHAPTER TEN

You stand alone, between the Rebel Army and your homes!

G EORGE GORDON MEADE arrived with his staff at Taneytown, Maryland, at midday on June 30th, to be greeted by "the stars and stripes
floating from a Liberty-pole and a signal flag from the cupola of a meeting-
house." He had now been in command of the Army of the Potomac for all of
three days and he was still struggling to sort out his priorities. His orders on
the morning of the 30th had been for continued movement northward on a
broad front—the 1st Corps and 11th Corps to move up toward Gettysburg,
the 3rd Corps to Emmitsburg, the 5th Corps to Hanover, the 12th Corps to
Two Taverns, and the 6th Corps in reserve at Manchester, behind Pipe Creek.
But beyond that, he admitted that "he had not had time to give the subject as
much reflection as he ought to give it, having been so pressed with the duties
incident upon taking command." When Buford's warning arrived at headquarters that "the enemy are advancing, probably in strong force, on Gettysburg" Meade sent out a second circular, instructing his corps commanders "to
hold this army pretty nearly in the position it now occupies until the plans
of the enemy shall have been more fully developed"—all of which meant, in
practical terms, that Reynolds was to halt at Emmitsburg, Slocum was to stop
at Littlestown, and the others were to stand down while Meade made up his
mind what to do next.

Between noon and one o'clock, Meade sent a plea to Pleasanton for "reliable information of the presence of the enemy, his forces and his movements,"
and especially whether Lee looked like he was trying to slip around Meade's

right flank "in the vicinity of York" or around his left, "toward Hagerstown and the passes below Cashtown." But at one o'clock, he redirected Winfield Hancock and the 2nd Corps to move through Taneytown and prepare to support George Sykes and the 5th Corps at Union Mills on Pipe Creek "in case of a superior force of the enemy there." A bit later, Meade received a curious note from Dan Sickles, just below Emmitsburg, where he was steaming over Meade's criticism of "the very slow movement of your corps." Informing Meade that Reynolds had ordered him to move up toward Gettysburg, Sickles almost insolently reminded Meade that his orders were to plant the 3rd Corps at Emmitsburg—which order was he to obey? "Shall I move forward?" Sickles asked.[1]

Sometime that evening, Meade settled on the plan he had been nursing all along for a pullback to Pipe Creek, and in the morning he composed yet another circular, directing the Army of the Potomac to "withdraw . . . from its present position, and form line of battle with the left resting in the neighborhood of Middleburg, and the right at Manchester, the general direction being that of Pipe Creek." Reynolds was to abandon any movement on Gettysburg and pull the 1st, 3rd, and 11th Corps "direct to Middleburg." Once in position, Reynolds would command the left of the Pipe Creek line, Slocum would take charge of both the 12th and 5th Corps to form the center, and Sedgwick would hold down the right flank at Manchester with the 6th Corps. Hancock and the 2nd Corps would "be held in reserve . . . to be thrown to the point of strongest attack." Meade left open the possibility that "developments may cause the commanding general to assume the offensive from his present positions," but that was only one sentence in a circular of 866 words, the balance of which was devoted entirely to "withdrawal." For good measure, Meade sent the army's chief of artillery, Henry Hunt, to scout "the country behind Pipe Creek for a battle-ground."[2]

By noon on July 1st, however, the plan was dead. First, Meade received Couch's warning "of the enemy's withdrawal from Harrisburg," which stoked his eagerness to concentrate the army "to the rear . . . on Pike Creek, between Middleburg and Manchester, covering my depot at Westminster." When the 2nd Corps arrived at Taneytown around 11 a.m., Winfield Hancock rode over to pay the honors to his new commander and found Meade ready "to fight on Pipe Creek; that he had not examined the ground, but, judging from his maps, it was the strongest position he could find; that the engineers were examining and mapping it, and that he had made an order for the movement to occupy that line." (He would have had the order printed and distributed before this, he claimed, except that the army's chief of staff, Dan Butterfield, whom he "roundly damned" for his "slowness in getting out orders," was only then in the process of having it copied.) Half an hour later came Capt. Ste-

phen Weld with the alarming news from John Reynolds that he had taken the
1st Corps into a stand-up fight at Gettysburg. Meade's first inclination was to
treat Reynolds' move as a covering action for the Pipe Creek withdrawal, and
he sent Sedgwick and Slocum a note informing them that Reynolds would
probably "hold the enemy in check, and fall slowly back." In that case, "the
line indicated in the circular of to-day will be occupied to-night." But then
came word from Buford with the same dire news of a collision at Gettysburg, followed by yet another note from Buford, via his chief, Alfred Pleasanton, announcing that "General Reynolds was killed this morning" and that
"there seems to be no directing person" in charge. *We need help now,* pleaded
Buford.[3]

This was not the battle that Meade wanted, nor was it in the place he
had wanted. But the 1st Corps was in serious trouble, and perhaps the 11th
Corps as well. The unpredictable Sickles sent another dispatch, energetically
informing Meade that Otis Howard had called on the 3rd Corps "to support
him," and Sickles was now on the road to Gettysburg, so for all Meade knew,
almost half of his army was heading into some unknown maw sixteen miles
to the north. Moreover, John Reynolds was dead, and that made the Pipe
Creek plan look like a run for cover. On the other hand, the information from
Gettysburg was so fragmentary that Meade could not be sure what he would
be ordering the rest of the army into if they went there—would the 1st Corps
still be holding its ground? If they were overrun and scattered by the time
Meade could get troops there, would each of his corps be smashed in similar
fashion as they arrived?[4]

He improvised. The Pipe Creek Circular would go off to the 3rd, 5th, 6th,
and 12th Corps, so that at least half the army was on its way to the new defensive line; he would need more information about the 1st and 11th Corps, and
he had the 2nd Corps near at hand if he needed to cover any possible retreat
by Doubleday and Howard. Meade himself would stay put at Taneytown so
that Sickles, Sykes, Sedgwick, and Slocum would know where to find him.
Butterfield promptly recommended that Meade "send me as his representative" to Gettysburg. But Meade, who privately detested Butterfield as one
of Hooker's toadies and would soon enough look up a replacement for him,
cringed at the idea of putting Butterfield in charge of anything, much less a
battle. Butterfield then suggested that Meade send Hancock, and before Butterfield could write up the orders Meade had ridden off to find Hancock and
send him to Gettysburg to discover what was happening and recommend the
best response.[5]

In the report Meade submitted in October, he described his directive
to Hancock as simply "to represent me on the field" and act "in conjunction with Major-General Howard." But years later, that was not how Han-

cock remembered it. "General Meade came immediately to my headquarters and told me to transfer command of the Second Corps to [Brigadier General John] Gibbon, and proceed at once to the front," Hancock recalled, "and in the event of the truth of the report of General Reynolds's death or disability, to assume command of the corps on that field." Hancock was startled, partly from the news that "General Reynolds has been killed, or badly wounded," and partly because, whether he realized it or not, Meade was disregarding the cardinal rule of army seniority. Hancock had only been in corps command for little more than a month, and was four steps below Otis Howard in seniority in the volunteer service, while John Gibbon was actually junior to another of Hancock's division commanders, John Caldwell. Meade paid no attention to Hancock's scruples. He "must have a man who he knew and could trust," someone who could make a politically reliable estimate of the situation, and not some wild-eyed call to an abolitionist suicide ride. Hancock was as steady a McClellanite as Meade himself, while Gibbon was, if anything, even more contemptuous of the Republican crusaders. Besides, Lincoln and Stanton had given Meade the blanket authority, denied to Joe Hooker, to override seniority and delegate authority to whomever he wished: *You are authorized to remove from command, and to send from your army, any officer or other person you may deem proper, and to appoint to command as you may deem expedient.*[6]

That was good enough for Hancock. "The moment these instructions were given me, I turned over command of the Second Corps to General Gibbon, and then started, with my personal staff at a very rapid pace for the battlefield." Hancock and his chief of staff, Charles Morgan, commandeered an ambulance so that they could sit and study a "poor little map that had been furnished" by Meade as they took to the Taneytown Road, while Hancock's aide-de-camp, William Mitchell, pelted on ahead to notify Howard. There was not much to be learned from Meade's map, and Hancock finally lost patience with the pace of the ambulance, ordered up the horses, and took off "galloping to the front." He and his staff were still four miles from Gettysburg when they passed another ambulance, headed in the other direction and escorted by a single officer. It contained the body of John Reynolds, laid out in a crude coffin. "A deep silence fell upon the staff, and not a word was spoken till . . . the panorama of Gettysburg lay unrolled before them."[7]

It was not clear to Hancock, at that moment, whether Meade intended him to take charge of a fight or arrange for a retreat, "extricating from peril the two corps at the front." But even as Hancock was on his way, dispatches and wig-wags from the signalers continued to come in to Taneytown, and Meade's mind slowly began revolving toward a decision to redirect the army toward Gettysburg. By three o'clock, the 2nd Corps was on the road to Gettysburg; the Pipe Creek Circular was canceled, and at 4:30 Meade began issuing orders to Sykes, Slocum, and Sedgwick to turn their corps around and "move up to Gettysburg at once."[8]

This would come as a jolt to Slocum and Sykes. Through most of July 1st, Slocum and the 12th Corps "sauntered slowly" from Littlestown to Two Taverns, just five miles below Gettysburg, where the corps fell out for a "leisurely" lunch. Still, even before Meade's orders reached them, the 12th Corps was already seeing disturbing signs of something gone seriously wrong up ahead. "Groups of frightened women and children, on their way to safe shelter, met us with imploring eyes; men hurrying away with their household goods in carts reported disaster to our army." George Sykes' 5th Corps had been on the march all day, crossing the Pennsylvania state line around noon. The colonel of the 118th Pennsylvania marked the crossing by ordering the regimental colors unfurled, and riding "down the column," calling for "3 cheers for Penn., which were given with a will." Col. Strong Vincent, a Pennsylvanian from Erie, who had been boosted to brigade command in the 5th Corps only on May 20th, also ordered his brigade's flags uncased when they approached Hanover "about dusk." Vincent "reverently bared his head" and announced to his adjutant, "What death more glorious can any man desire than to die on the soil of old Pennsylvania fighting for that flag?" Sykes had sent his staffers ahead to mark out bivouac sites around Hanover for the thirty-five regiments in the 5th Corps, and the men were "in the act of issuing fresh meat, inspection of arms etc." when a general officers' call was sounded. Brigade and division commanders soon came back with the news that "the enemy had been met that day by our advanced corps, at Gettysburg, and that tomorrow would probably be fought the decisive battle of the war." That meant down with shelter tents and coffee boilers, and "we took up the line of march" again, this time "sharply to the left," toward Gettysburg. Sykes pushed them on until, by two in the morning, "all human endurance was on the verge of utter collapse."[9]

Based on the pay and muster reports recorded on June 30th, Meade should have had an army of approximately 112,000 men on hand, either for Pipe Creek or for Gettysburg. Determining the manpower of Civil War armies is a tricky business, compounded by lost or unsubmitted reports and differing definitions of what counted as "present" (which usually meant everyone who was issued rations) or "present for duty" (subtracting the sick but not the noncombatants) or "present for duty equipped" (those actually armed for the line of battle). In the 69th Pennsylvania, for example, the present and accounted for tallies on May 30th listed 389 men; but 52 of these were actually absent in hospital. Other men leaked away through desertion, and by the time they reached Gettysburg, the 69th could only count 292 on hand. In the 18th Massachusetts, the present-for-duty report listed 314 men, but the sergeant who "kept the company accounts" knew that only 108 "were found at the front" at Gettysburg. Meade himself believed that he had "about 95,000 . . . including all arms of service," but in terms of troops ready to engage in combat, the Army of the Potomac was probably ready to furnish somewhere between 83,000 and 85,000 men.

The army's real strength may have been more fragile even than that, since the expiration of many two-year enlistments from 1861 and emergency nine-monthers from 1862 had reduced the Army of the Potomac, after Chancellorsville, to as few as 40,000, and it was only by drawing some 37,000 troops from Schenck's and Heintzelman's garrisons in Baltimore and Washington that Meade was able to pull together a force worth challenging Lee. Units like George Stannard's Vermont brigade, George Willard's New York brigade (newly exchanged after being captured at Harpers Ferry in 1862 and cruelly mocked as the "Harper's Ferry Cowards"), and Samuel Wylie Crawford's Pennsylvania Reserve Division all increased the raw numbers of the army, but it remained to be seen how well they would fit with the rest of the army, or even if they would fight at all. Meanwhile the best estimate Meade had of Lee's strength pegged the Army of Northern Virginia at 109,000—"about 90,000 infantry, from 4,000 to 5,000 artillery, and about 10,000 cavalry." Chief of staff Butterfield seconded Meade: based on scouting and citizen reports "at different points," Butterfield estimated that "Lee had 91,000 infantry, 12,000 cavalry, and 275 pieces of artillery."[10]

The Confederates had a humbler view of their numbers: Augustus Dickert in the 3rd South Carolina reckoned that "by the non-extension of all furloughs and the return of the slightly wounded," Lee could count on "sixty-eight thousand," and Lee's adjutant, Walter Taylor, calculated that Lee had only 67,000, counting infantry, cavalry, and artillery. In fact, Lee is likely to have had as many as 80,000 men in all three arms. Like their Union counterpart, these numbers included the addition of untested regiments and brigades, not to mention two new corps commanders. But the Army of Northern Virginia enjoyed invisible assets denied to the Army of the Potomac. "There were no employees in the Confederate army," wrote William Allan, one of Stonewall Jackson's old staffers, in 1877, assessing the strength of the Army of Northern Virginia. Instead, as the British military observer Lt. Col. Arthur James Lyon Fremantle of the Coldstream Guards noticed, "in rear of each regiment were from twenty to thirty negro slaves." From the beginning of the war, Confederate armies had annexed large contingents of slaves—between 12,000 and 20,000 at Manassas Junction in 1861, and "fifteen or twenty thousand" on the Peninsula in 1862. By the time of the Gettysburg Campaign,

Thomas Caffey, an English-born Confederate artilleryman, estimated that "in our whole army there must be at least thirty thousand colored servants who do nothing but cook and wash." In his battalion alone, Caffey counted "a cooking and washing corps of negroes at least one hundred and fifty strong!"

Add, then, to the 80,000 white soldiers Lee commanded, the unnumbered corps of 10,000 to 30,000 black slaves who marched with the Army of Northern Virginia (and performed many of the noncombatant duties that, in the Army of the Potomac, were performed by those "present for duty"), and George Meade may not have been at all unjustified in believing "that General Lee was, as far as I could tell, about 10,000 or 15,000 my superior." It made Meade all the more conscious that one wrong move on his part, and not only the Army of the Potomac, but the entire Union cause, could be lost in the next twenty-four hours, and he would join that long gallery of American failures that included Horatio Gates in the Revolution, William Hull in the War of 1812, and, inevitably, Meade's own bankrupt father.[11]

It was after 10:45 when the firing died down along McPherson's Ridge, and a lull settled over the flattened wheat fields and now railless fences held by James Wadsworth's battered Union division. The division's ammunition train had arrived, and the wagon handlers worked down the line, spilling big wooden boxes of cartridges off the backs of the wagons for the men to break open and distribute. With the death of Reynolds, overall command of the 1st Corps fell to Abner Doubleday, as the senior division commander. Only that morning, Doubleday had been complaining that, with Meade's promotion just four days before, command of Meade's 5th Corps ought to have gone to him, by seniority. Now Doubleday had his corps command, only it was the 1st Corps, and it came to him by the death of Reynolds rather than by the mechanics of rank. His own division was arriving at the seminary, although it really contained only two small brigades under Tom Rowley and Roy Stone, and somewhere behind them was the last of the 1st Corps' divisions, with two big brigades under John Cleveland Robinson. Doubleday had received no direction from Reynolds about what steps to take next, but his instinct was "to hold on to the position until ordered to leave it," and an officer in the 149th Pennsylvania heard Doubleday say that "all he could do was fight until he got sufficient information to form his own plan."[12]

Doubleday planted Roy Stone's three Pennsylvania regiments (the 143rd, 149th, and 150th) on the right of the Iron Brigade, so that they could occupy the McPherson house and barn, which had been vacated when the 95th New York and 14th Brooklyn charged the railroad cut. Stone was only twenty-six years old, but he had risen to the rank of major in the old 42nd Pennsylvania, which touted itself as a regiment of marksmen by tacking a buck's tail to their caps, and in 1862 Stone was commissioned to raise an entire brigade of "Bucktails." The original 42nd Pennsylvania disdained them as "Bogus Bucktails," and Gettysburg would offer them their first opportunity to live that sneer down. Tom Rowley was a Pittsburgh Republican alderman and contractor who had served with the 1st Pennsylvania Volunteers in the Mexican War, but who brought to the war in 1861 little more than good political intentions. He had commanded the 102nd Pennsylvania on the Peninsula, survived a head wound that fractured his skull, and gone up to brigadier general in the 6th Corps after Antietam, only to be bumped out of place by a brigadier with seniority. Rowley was instead assigned to the 1st Corps, commanding (like Roy Stone) a newly confected brigade of Pennsylvanians (the 121st, 142nd, and 151st Pennsylvania) and the 80th New York, and his job would be to hold down the left flank of the Iron Brigade, extending the 1st Corps line down toward the Fairfield Road.[13] John Cleveland Robinson's division arrived on the heels of Stone and Rowley, and Doubleday held it at the Lutheran seminary as a reserve. Robinson was a burly, undemonstrative New Yorker, yet another abolitionist in this corps teeming with abolitionist officers. Like Doubleday he had paid for his opposition to slavery by slow promotion and even slower recognition.

Meanwhile, the unemployed cavalry of William Gamble's brigade, who had put up the fight that enabled the 1st Corps to throw its shield between Gettysburg and Harry Heth's Confederates, were being redeployed by John Buford. The 8th Illinois Cavalry was posted "out to the south-west," beyond the dangling left flank of the 1st Corps, and the other dismounted cavalrymen and the men of Robinson's division were set to work building a hasty "crescent-shaped" barricade of fence rails and fieldstone on the seminary's west side.[14]

Doubleday fully expected that Meade "would ride to the front to see for himself what was going on, and issue definite orders of some kind." But just before eleven o'clock, it was not Meade who showed up, but Oliver Otis Howard. As soon as Reynolds' summons of the 11th Corps had come into Howard's hands at Emmitsburg, he put his three divisions into motion. The division of Francis Barlow would take the main road between Emmitsburg and Gettysburg (the same one Reynolds was at that time using from Marsh Creek). He sent the other two divisions, under Carl Schurz and Adolf Steinwehr (who was actually Baron Adolph Wilhelm August Friedrich von Steinwehr, a onetime officer in the army of the Duke of Brunswick-Wolfenbüttel) on the parallel Taneytown road, so as to avoid traffic snarls. (Barlow's division was on the shorter of the two routes, but he ran into Reynolds' "trains

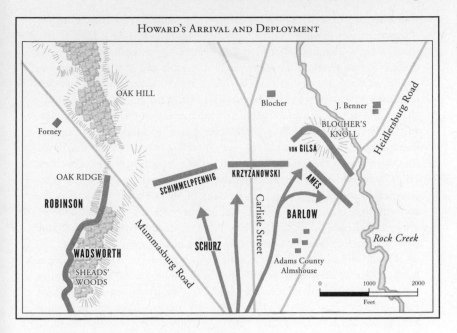

HOWARD'S ARRIVAL AND DEPLOYMENT

OAK HILL

Blocher

J. Benner

Heidlersburg Road

Forney

BLOCHER'S KNOLL

VON GILSA

OAK RIDGE

SCHIMMELPFENNIG

KRZYZANOWSKI

AMES

ROBINSON

Carlisle Street

BARLOW

Mummasburg Road

SCHURZ

Rock Creek

WADSWORTH

SHEADS' WOODS

Adams County Almshouse

0   1000   2000

Feet

and artillery carriages" on the Emmitsburg Road and ended up arriving later than both Schurz and Steinwehr.) Howard himself took off ahead, meeting yet another messenger from Reynolds at about 10:30, begging Howard to "Come quite up to Gettysburg," then another: "I am hardly pressed; have your troops come up at the double-quick." By way of relay, Howard sent off staffers to Sickles, back at Emmitsburg, to Slocum and the 12th Corps, and to Meade at Taneytown, repeating Reynolds' plea. "Where does he want my divisions placed," Howard asked. The aide—the hard-riding Maj. William Riddle—shrugged his shoulders impatiently: "Choose your ground anywhere near here." Heading the other way were the inevitable crowds of civilian refugees, followed by wounded cavalrymen and mounted couriers. "Within six or seven miles of Gettysburg . . . the distant boom of cannon could be heard."[15]

Howard was long ahead of his men by that time. He got his first glimpse of the town on a small rise in the road, beside a peach orchard owned by Joseph Sherfy, a deacon in the Marsh Creek Church of the Brethren and "a pioneer in the peach business." Around eleven o'clock, he arrived on Cemetery Hill. "Here was a broad view which embraced the town, the seminary, the college, and all the undulating valley of open country spread out between the ridges." Howard turned to his adjutant, Theodore Meysenberg, and noted,

"This seems to be a *good position,* colonel." Meysenberg looked around. "It is the *only* position, general."[16]

The head of Steinwehr's division arrived soon after, hard on the heels of the last wagons of the 1st Corps trains, and even in the "dull, vapory atmosphere" of an overcast summer's day, "the magnificent panorama" almost took the soldiers' collective breath away. "As far as the eye could reach, until the earth touched the heavens in their convergence, was one expanse of ever-varying field and wood, hill and dale, interspersed here and there with farmhouses, while from over the hills in every direction roads came trailing down into the village of Gettysburg." Howard at once turned them onto Cemetery Hill. There was an elaborate brick gatehouse on the eastern flank of the cemetery, and Howard spread the two brigades of Steinwehr's division, plus the corps artillery under Maj. Thomas Osborn, between the gatehouse and the Taneytown Road, facing north. Schurz's division would arrive by the same path an hour later, and then Barlow on the Emmitsburg Road.

Hoping to link up with Reynolds, Howard sent off his aide (and younger brother) Charles Howard to find Buford or Reynolds, and then rode up into the town, along Baltimore Street, looking for a useful eminence from which to take his bearings. His first notion was to use the steeple of the county courthouse; but that steeple turned out to be a closed box, with only slits to see through, and anyway, no one could find a ladder. Looking up from the street, one of Howard's staffers noticed Henry Fahnestock's wife and two teenaged boys on the widow's walk above the Fahnestock store. One of the boys, Daniel Skelly, went down to let Howard into the store by the side entrance on Middle Street, and guided Howard and "a staff officer, who seemed to be a Captain and a German . . . with a large field-glass" up to the "observatory."[17]

The "General with only one arm . . . took the glass and swept the field long and anxiously." Howard could see the network of roads radiating outward from Gettysburg toward "Bonnaughtown, York, Harrisburg, Carlisle, Shippensburg, Chambersburg, and Hagerstown." But closer at hand, he could also see "Wadsworth's division of infantry, fighting near the Oak Ridge railroad cut" and "Doubleday's division beyond the Lutheran seminary, filing out of sight beyond the Oak Ridge to the south of west, a mile away." He would have no time to reflect on these observations, because "as I stood there" an officer clattered up Middle Street, saluted, and shouted something to Howard: "General Reynolds is wounded, sir." Howard did not, at first, want to believe this. "I am very sorry," Howard shouted back. "I hope he will be able to keep the field." Any hope of that was soon banished when another rider followed, this time the ubiquitous Major Riddle: "General Reynolds is dead, and you are the senior officer of the field."

A sense of cold misery crept over Howard. "Is it confessing weakness," he asked years later, "to say that when the responsibility of my position flashed upon me I was penetrated with an emotion never experienced before or since?" He had walked into a battle begun by someone else, in the presence of an enemy whose numbers he could not estimate, and with help far enough away that "it seemed almost hopeless that Meade could gather his scattered forces in time for any considerable success to attend our arms"—and he, of course, would be held to account for it all.[18]

And then the iron entered into him: "God helping us, we will stay here till the army comes." He had already sent off requests to Slocum and Sickles, so there was nothing more he could do, until they arrived, to shore up the 1st Corps apart from getting his own corps into action. His first order was to make sure that Steinwehr and the corps artillery brigade stayed put on Cemetery Hill, then "rode slowly" back to the gatehouse, where he met Schurz, coming in ahead of his own division. They would have half a chance, Howard decided, if he could get Schurz's and Barlow's divisions through the town and up onto Oak Hill, on Wadsworth's right flank, and thus present a stable line of defense for over a mile against whatever the Confederates might choose to send at them during the afternoon. If the 1st Corps and 11th Corps together could hug that long ridgeline, with the McPherson farm at its center, then Meade and the others would have time to collect the rest of the Army of the Potomac and stride to their rescue; if not, there was always Cemetery Hill (and Steinwehr's division) as the fallback. "I directed Schurz to move forward and seize a woody height in front of his left, on the prolongation of Oak Ridge." As soon as Barlow came up, Howard would send Barlow's division in support. By the clock in the courthouse tower, it was 11:15.[19]

Carl Schurz "briskly" hurried through the town with his division, its two big brigades under Alexander Schimmelpfennig, a liberal Prussian Army captain from Posen who had fled Germany with Schurz after the failure of the 1848 Revolution, and the sinister-faced Wladimir Krzyzanowski, a cousin of Frederic Chopin's and yet another refugee from the '48 who had signed up to crush the "terrible trade in human flesh." The morose and small-statured Schimmelpfennig's name sounded faintly ludicrous in American ears—as frizzy-sounding as the stereotypical German was supposed to be frizzy-minded—and Lincoln had quipped that commissioning someone named Schimmelpfennig would probably win him the German vote even if Schimmelpfennig knew nothing about soldiering. "His name will make up for any difference there may be, and I'll take the risk of his coming out all right."

Schimmelpfennig actually had more military experience than almost any-one else in the Army of the Potomac, and it took him aback to discover that American-born generals "have no maps, no knowledge of the country, no eyes to see where help is needed." Unlike Moltke's Prussian general staff, the Americans select staff officers from among their "relations, sons of old friends, or men recommended by Congressmen" who then "lose their heads and are unable to control, assist or manoeuvre their corps" in combat. He told one of his fellow Prussian aides, the continent-hopping Baron Otto Friedrich von Fritsch, that Lincoln was a "great President," but he lacked "a commander who possesses some of Naploeon's or Moltke's genius," and if they ever got into a fight, "let us look out for ourselves, and never expect outside help."[20]

In the lead of Schimmelpfennig's brigade were Georg von Amsberg's 45th New York (organized back in 1861 as the 5th German Rifles) and Battery I of the 1st Ohio Light Artillery, commanded "at a trot" by yet another German, Captain Hubert A. C. Dilger, an adventure-seeking officer in the Duchy of Baden's horse artillery. Once beyond the railroad north of town, the Germans angled north and east, past the buildings of Pennsylvania College, heading up the Mummasburg Road to connect with Wadsworth's division. Far to the rear, on Cemetery Hill, Howard was anxiously waiting for Barlow's division to arrive on the Emmitsburg Road, so that they could be put in alongside Schurz's Germans. Barlow sent ahead an aide, Lt. Edward Culp, when the division was only four miles away, and when Howard finally saw the head of Barlow's column come into view, he trotted off with "a couple of orderlies" to meet him. "The air was lively with bursting shells" from artillery over beyond the town, and that left Barlow with little to ask in the way of questions except "Where now, General?" Howard was just as direct: "Straight through the town, on to the right." Barlow slackened pace only to allow two batteries of artillery to pass to the front of his column, and from there, he and Howard rode together up Baltimore Street and through the diamond as Howard hast-ily briefed him on what had happened so far.[21]

But neither Schurz nor Barlow were ever to make their linkup with Rob-inson and the dangling right flank of the 1st Corps. As Schurz's division moved "outside the town and north and east of the Pennsylvania College," artillery began speaking from beyond the distant knob at the north end of Oak Ridge, and Dilger's battery stopped and unlimbered to reply. Amsberg threw out four companies of the 45th New York as skirmishers to feel ahead. But by the time they reached the base of the knob, where Moses McLean's T-shaped farmhouse and red barn sat beside the Mummasburg Road, it was plain for all to see that Confederate artillery was unlimbering and perch-ing on the knob, and Confederate skirmishers were swarming down the hill toward them. They were Georgians and Alabamians from George Doles' and

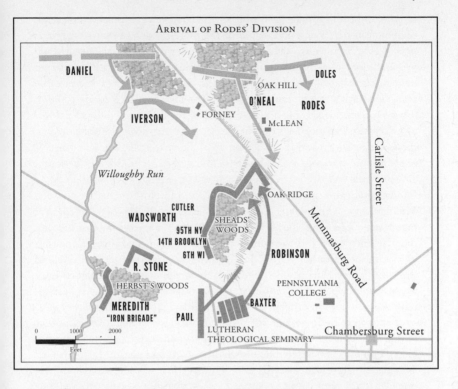

ARRIVAL OF RODES' DIVISION

DANIEL

DOLES

OAK HILL

O'NEAL   RODES

IVERSON   FORNEY

McLEAN

Carlisle Street

Willoughby Run

OAK RIDGE

CUTLER

WADSWORTH   SHEADS'
WOODS

95TH NY
14TH BROOKLYN
6TH WI

Mummasburg Road

ROBINSON

R. STONE

HERBST'S WOODS

PENNSYLVANIA
COLLEGE

BAXTER

MEREDITH
"IRON BRIGADE"   PAUL

0   1000   2000

Feet

LUTHERAN
THEOLOGICAL SEMINARY   Chambersburg Street

Edward O'Neal's brigades and they were the announcement that Richard S. Ewell's corps had arrived on the scene.[22]

One division of Dick Ewell's corps, under Robert Rodes, reached Heidlersburg on the evening of June 30th after a thumping-hard march of twenty-two miles through rain, and camped there with Jubal Early's division, fresh from the occupation of York, just three miles to the east. (Ewell's other division, under Allegheny Johnson, was off to the west, escorting the corps trains through the village of Scotland.) Ewell, who was still traveling with Rodes, fully expected to arrive within supporting distance of Powell Hill's corps somewhere between Cashtown and Gettysburg on the next day, although it annoyed Ewell that the orders Lee had issued for this concentration failed to specify whether he was to move on Cashtown *or* Gettysburg, and he wondered out loud (for all to hear) why someone on Lee's headquarters staff couldn't learn to write understandable orders. He assumed that Cashtown was the desired point. With Hill heading for Gettysburg, it would be logical for Ewell to take over Hill's bivouac at Cashtown as part of Lee's concentration plan. In the morning, Rodes' division, with the one-legged Ewell in his carriage, headed for Cashtown by way of Middletown. Early's division would be ready to move along after them through Heidlersburg. But Rodes and Ewell had only gotten as far as Middletown at around ten o'clock when a courier came panting up with "word from General Lee or Hill to march to Gettysburg, to which point the latter had moved." The Newville Road led directly down to Gettysburg, so all that Ewell had to do was turn Rodes' division left at the Middletown crossroads, and then order Early to make the same turn at Heidlersburg; the roads would bring them together, eight miles to the south, at Gettysburg.[23]

It was not an easy eight miles for Rodes and Ewell. The country between Middletown and Gettysburg rolls and pitches deeply, and short as the line of march may be, it is all sharply up hill and down dale, with the first hard on the men and the second hard on the horses. "We marched thirteen miles in quick time that morning . . . without resting," complained Jeremiah Tate of the 5th Alabama, "many was broke down before going in to the fight." Even worse, Ewell had no good information on what Hill's situation at Gettysburg was, and he sent off couriers to Hill and to Lee. But by 11:30, they were close enough to begin hearing the rumble of artillery, so that it was clear that Powell Hill's people had run into something troublesome. Two miles short of Gettysburg, Rodes sent an aide to explore the ground ahead, then deployed Thomas H. Carter's artillery battalion and the first of the division's five big brigades into line of battle (followed by the other four in column) and gingerly pressed his skirmishers forward.[24]

Neither Ewell nor Rodes seem to have realized it, but they could not have arrived at a better place or at a better time for the Army of Northern Virginia. The 1st Corps was still panting from its exertions on McPherson's Ridge over the last two hours, and on the corps' right flank Lysander Cutler's battered brigade stuck straight north along the ridge without any cover. Schurz's 11th Corps division was on its way through the town to join that exposed flank and extend it along the ridge and over the knob of Oak Hill, but it wasn't there yet, and it had no inkling that a large body of Confederate infantry was moving toward them from the north with plans of its own for Oak Hill. Ewell had it within his power to roll over the knob of Oak Hill, driving into the gap between the 1st Corps and the 11th Corps like a maul, and send both Union corps fleeing in disarray.[25]

The first people to discover that an entirely new set of players was about to arrive were Union cavalry. While John Buford had been spending his morning arranging William Gamble's cavalry brigade as obstacles in the path of Harry Heth's division on the Cashtown Pike, Buford's other brigade, under

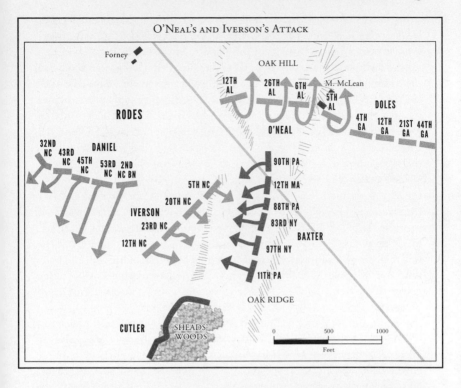

Tom Devin, had been maintaining its picket lines in their semicircle north of Gettysburg. Even as Gamble's troopers were staging their slow pullback to McPherson's Ridge, Devin ordered his regiments to saddle up and move out to thicken his pickets, as a precaution. Sure enough, by eleven o'clock, Devin's outposts to the northwest reported that "long and strong" lines of skirmishers, backed by "heavy columns of infantry," were now visible "over the hills and across the fields." One of those outposts, belonging to the 9th New York Cavalry, let the new arrivals come close enough to confirm that they were indeed Confederates, then let off a few shots from their carbines and wheeled their horses around for a fast getaway. Soon, Devin had more notice: the 17th Pennsylvania Cavalry, posted on the Carlisle Road straight north, had traded shots with another sizable force of Confederate infantry, moving toward them from that direction as well.[26]

James Wadsworth seems to have been the first senior officer in the 1st Corps to awake to this peril. "I am not sure that they are not moving around on our right flank," Wadsworth wrote suspiciously in a note he dashed off to Doubleday just past noon, "though I do not see any indication of it." As a precaution, he pulled Cutler's brigade back from the northern extension of McPherson's Ridge into Sheads' Woods "to take such position as [Cutler] deemed proper," and begged from Doubleday a brigade from John Robinson's reserve division at the seminary to plant on Cutler's flank, barely reaching to the Mummasburg Road. As the rebel skirmishers gradually pushed the Yankee cavalrymen backward toward the town, Rodes and Ewell finally mounted the knob of Oak Hill, and there they could see that they "could strike the force of the enemy with which General Hill's troops were engaged upon the flank." But they could also see the head of Schurz's division moving up from the town onto the broad plain below Oak Hill, so if they were to move, it would have to be done quickly. Doles' Georgians were swung well out to the left, to warn off Schurz's oncoming Germans and pin them in place on the plain, and O'Neal's Alabamians and Junius Daniel's five North Carolina regiments deployed on either side of Alfred Iverson's leading brigade, poised to roll up the 1st Corps' unprotected right flank. "It was the only time in the war that we were in position to get such a view of contending forces," marveled one of O'Neal's Alabamians, and what Rodes saw convinced him (as he wrote in a hasty note to Jubal Early) that "I can burst through the enemy in an hour."[27]

But it was not quite as comprehensive a view as he thought. In his haste to "push the attack vigorously," Rodes now proceeded to make one overeager mistake after another. Once Hubert Dilger's Ohio battery rolled into position on the plain north of Pennsylvania College, they began splintering Rodes' artillery battalions, sitting in the open on the slopes of Oak Hill. "They blew up two or three caissons and entirely disabled one or two of the guns." The battalion commander, Thomas Carter, accosted Rodes and asked, "General, what fool put that battery yonder?" only to realize after an "awkward pause and a queer expression on the faces of all" Rodes' staffers that Rodes himself had placed it there. Nor did Rodes take the usual precautions: none of the three brigades poised to roll down on the 1st Corps flank bothered to put out skirmishers, and none of the three brigade commanders was sure what the signal for an advance would be. These were three cavaliers to whom it was not wise to give too much of their own lead. Edward O'Neal was quarrelsome and unhappy under Rodes, still mired at the rank of colonel and convinced that Rodes was planning to replace him; Alfred Iverson was a Richmond political pet whose promotion was deeply resented in his North Carolina brigade as a vote of no confidence in their political loyalties; and Junius Daniel hadn't been in action with the Army of Northern Virginia since the Peninsula Campaign. Moreover, the majority of the North Carolinians in both Daniel's and Iverson's brigades had never yet been in a major battle. "Although we had been

Major General George Gordon Meade
(1815–1872). Put hastily and unexpectedly
in command of the Army of the
Potomac, Meade preferred to conduct
a cautious, defensive campaign against
the 1863 Confederate invasion. He was
"cownservative and cautious to the last
degree, good qualities in a defensive battle,
but liable to degenerate into timidity when
an aggressive or bold offensive becomes
imperative."

General Robert Edward Lee (1807–1870)
was convinced that only by risking an
invasion of the North in 1863 could he
save the Confederacy from the defeat
he was certain would otherwise occur.
"He is a strongly built man, about five-feet-
eleven in height, and apparently not more
than fifty years of age," wrote a British
admirer. "His hair and beard are nearly
white; but his dark brown eyes still shine
with all the brightness of youth, and beam
with a most pleasing expression. Indeed,
his whole face is kindly and benevolent in
the highest degree."

TOP, LEFT James Longstreet (1821–1904) was the senior corps commander of the Army of Northern Virginia. Lee regarded him as his "warhorse," even though Longstreet questioned the wisdom of a Pennsylvania invasion in general and fighting an offensive battle at Gettysburg in particular. In the years after the war, he would be mercilessly (and unjustly) pilloried by Lee's partisans as the principal bearer of blame for Confederate defeat.

TOP, RIGHT Major General John Fulton Reynolds (1820–1863), commander of the 1st Corps of the Army of the Potomac. His determination not to leave Pennsylvania open to Lee's invasion helped trigger the battle at Gettysburg.

RIGHT Andrew Gregg Curtin (1817–1894). Republican governor of Pennsylvania, Curtin struggled to rouse the surprisingly sluggish response of his state to the Confederate invasion. "Five counties of our State are invaded and in the hands of rebels, five counties are overrun, and the soil of Pennsylvania is poisoned by the tread of rebel hordes. My God! Can Pennsylvanians sleep when Pennsylvanians are driven from their homes?" After the battle, Curtin authorized David Wills to take oversight of the creation of the Soldiers' National Cemetery at Gettysburg.

TOP, LEFT Major General Oliver Otis Howard (1830–1909), commander of the 11th Corps of the Army of the Potomac. Together with Reynolds, Howard was responsible for forcing a fight at Gettysburg, instead of waiting passively at Pipe Creek. "He is the only religious man of high rank that I know of in the army," wrote Charles Wainwright in his diary, "and, in the little intercourse I have had with him, shewed himself the most polished gentleman I have met."

TOP, RIGHT Major General James S. Wadsworth (1807–1864). A wealthy lawyer and committed abolitionist from upstate New York, Wadsworth commanded the first of the Army of the Potomac's infantry divisions to reach Gettysburg on July 1, 1863.

RIGHT Lieutenant General Richard Stoddert Ewell (1817–1872), who inherited command of "Stonewall" Jackson's corps in the Army of Northern Virginia after Jackson's death. He won accolades for his perfectly executed capture of Winchester in the first stages of the Gettysburg campaign, but was widely blamed for not pushing his corps to finish the rout of the Union forces on July 1, 1863. After the war, Ewell was supposed to have admitted that it took many mistakes to cause the Confederate loss at Gettysburg, "and I made most of them."

ABOVE Major General Winfield Scott Hancock (1824–1886), commander of the 2nd Corps of the Army of the Potomac. Colorful, profane, and combative, Hancock played the lead role in holding off Confederate attackers on both July 2nd and 3rd.

RIGHT Major General Daniel Edgar Sickles (1819–1914) was the prime example of everything that was wrong with the practice of putting politicians in command of troops in the Civil War. Commander of the 3rd Corps, he nearly lost the battle singlehandedly for the Army of the Potomac on July 2nd. "He is, perhaps, loved more sincerely, and hated more heartily, than any man of his day. To serve his friends he will do anything which is tolerated by the license of modern politics: when he resolves upon the overthrow of a political enemy the strongest man finds him formidable."

ABOVE The Cashtown Pike, looking westward from Gettysburg; Oak Ridge is visible on the horizon, with a cut through the ridge to accommodate an as-yet-unfinished railroad. It was the first of three such cuttings through the ridges west of Gettysburg. Retreating Union soldiers followed this road into the town on July 1st.

(Levi Mumper) Courtesy of William A. Frassanito, Gettysburg Then and Now: Touring the Battlefield with Old Photos, 1865–1889 *(1996)*

LEFT The colors of the 14th Brooklyn. Regimental flags were carried into battle in the Civil War to serve as markers and rallying points in the midst of battlefield noise that overpowered officers' voice commands and thick banks of powder smoke that sharply limited visibility. The 14th Brooklyn was actually the 84th New York Volunteer Infantry, but most of the regiment had originally been members of the 14th New York State Militia, based in Brooklyn, and they insisted on identifying themselves by their old militia designation. They were uniformed in the pattern of French-style chasseurs (light attack infantry) in baggy red trousers and red kepis.

14th Brooklyn.

GHT The charge of the h Wisconsin Volunteers the middle railroad tting west of Gettysburg July 1st. This drawing ces west, with the ashtown Pike and the cPherson farm buildings sible to the left, the ilway line on the right, d South Mountain in e distance.

evi Mumper) Courtesy of William Frassanito, Gettysburg Then d Now: Touring the Battlefield th Old Photos, 1865–1889 *(1996)*

Pennsylvania College in 1862, looking northward along Washington Street. From left to right, the buildings are the house of President Henry L. Baugher, Linnaean Hall, and Pennsylvania Hall; Oak Hill can be seen in the distance, rising behind Linnaean Hall. Classes met on the morning of July 1st, but most of the college's 116 students had already scattered, and when the fighting began, the classes were dismissed. "Amid repeated failures on the part of the class, our professor remarked 'We will close and see what is going on, for you know nothing about the lesson anyhow.'"

The view from the college cupola, looking west and slightly south toward the Lutheran Theological Seminary (faintly visible to the left). The structure in the foreground is the college's Linnaean Hall. The railroad bed and the Cashtown Pike run upward to the right across the photograph.

"Defending the Colors at Gettysburg, July 1, 1863." The 24th Michigan lost thirteen color-bearers during the fighting retreat that brought the regiment to its last stand around the Lutheran Theological Seminary on July 1, 186 "When its flag was presented to the regiment in Detroit, solemn vow was taken, never to allow it to trail before the enemy or fall into his hands. That flag, pierced by twenty three fresh bullets from the enemy's guns, aside from tho that splintered its staff in this engagement, spoke more forcibly than any words could, with what sacredness the vow was kept."

ABOVE The Lutheran Theological
Seminary and Seminary Ridge,
looking southwestward from the
Cashtown Pike.

ABOVE The Evergreen Cemetery's gatehouse, looking west from
the crest of East Cemetery Hill. This photograph was taken in
mid-July 1863, when the 1st Corps' artillery emplacements were still
untouched. The ninety-foot poplar tree on the right was a Cemetery
Hill landmark until it was struck by lightning in 1876 and finally
removed in 1886. The tree is faintly visible in this book's jacket
photograph of three Confederate prisoners, spiking the distant
horizon.

RIGHT John Burns (1793–1872). Former town constable and
veteran of the War of 1812, Burns became celebrated as "the Hero of
Gettysburg" for attaching himself, even though a civilian, to the 1st
Corps and fighting alongside the Iron Brigade.

Barlow's (or Blocher's) Knoll, looking south from Rock Creek toward the position of Leopold von Gilsa's 11th Corps brigade on July 1st. Jubal Early's division of the Army of Northern Virginia arrived at this point after marching south from Heidlersburg that morning, and successfully attacked von Gilsa's men, who had only briefly planted themselves on the crest of the hill.

Francis Channing Barlow (1834–1896), the gentleman ranker who commanded the first division of the 11th Corps. Severely wounded and left behind by the retreat of his corps, he was carried to the Josiah Benner farmhouse, where he recovered sufficiently to return to command in the Army of the Potomac the following year.

Lee's headquarters at Mrs. Mary Thompson's house on the north side of the Cashtown Pike.

in the field nearly sixteen months," admitted a soldier in one of Daniel's regiments, "it was our first regular battle."[28]

O'Neal and Iverson promptly justified those doubts. Three of O'Neal's five Alabama regiments bolted forward prematurely and collided at the Mummasburg Road with Union infantry that wasn't supposed to have been there. These were the six regiments of Henry Baxter's brigade—two New York, three Pennsylvania, and one Massachusetts—that Wadsworth had planted at the last minute on Lysander Cutler's unprotected right flank. Henry Baxter was a blunt, rumple-bearded miller from Hillsdale County in south-central Michigan who seemed to rise conveniently in the rifle sights of every Confederate he encountered, sustaining a bad wound to the midsection on the Peninsula, a wound to the leg at Antietam, and another to the shoulder at Fredericksburg. From each, he bounced back, his feistiness undiminished, and he was steadily promoted until reaching brigadier general by March 1863. As a convinced abolitionist, he was happily parked in John Cleveland Robinson's division of the 1st Corps on the road to Gettysburg. All six of the regiments in Baxter's brigade had seen action before, but the brigade itself had only been cobbled together in late May, and Gettysburg would be their first fight together.[29]

Rodes saw Wadsworth bend Cutler's brigade back "so as to occupy" Sheads' Woods on Seminary Ridge; what he missed was Baxter's stealthy tiptoe behind Cutler and out along Cutler's flank. Anything Rodes sent to attack Cutler would either be flung back by Baxter, or (depending on the axis of attack) be hit from the flank by fire from Baxter—in the event, both happened. Baxter placed two of his regiments—the 11th Pennsylvania and the 97th New York—beside Cutler's brigade, then faced the remaining four northward along the Mummasburg Road. Some berserk "Union horseman . . . charged wildly" past the 97th, shouting, "There are no troops behind you! You stand alone, between the Rebel Army and your homes! Fight like hell!"—although there was no report afterward whether this encouraged or depressed the New Yorkers. Someone in the 88th Pennsylvania struck up the John Brown song, and soon everyone was bawling out "Glory, glory, hallelujah" until Confederate infantry could be seen gathering in front. While Baxter was busy shifting his regiments into position, he heard a racket of complaint from the brigade's rear, where the provost's detail was loudly demanding to be put into the line with the rest of their regiments; Baxter grinned at their enthusiasm, and told them, "Well, if that is the case, you are just the men I want there. Go to your regiments!" Baxter was just in time to stop O'Neal's Alabamians. Baxter's men quickly put them "under a heavy fire from the front" while Schurz's skirmishers from the 11th Corps, poking along the fence line of the McLean farm, peppered them with "a cross fire" from a distance, and in short order

O'Neal's men "had to fall back to a fence where the Brig. was rallied by Col. O'Neal & Genl Rodes."[30]

Then, Iverson's brigade started forward, *sans* Iverson, who preferred to remain behind and watch—and watch he did, as his brigade swept grandly over the Mummasburg Road "in magnificent order, with perfect alignment, guns at right shoulder and colors to the front," in a three-rank column of divisions (six companies in each division), wading into lushly fragrant and utterly unprotected fields of wheat and "a rank crop of timothy." With exquisite timing, Baxter barked out the order for the 11th Pennsylvania and 97th New York to rise from behind the shelter of a low fieldstone wall, where they had waited with "rifles cocked and fingers on the triggers," and hurl a deadly and unsuspected volley into the unprepared North Carolinians. "At the command," wrote a Pennsylvanian, "a sheet of flame and smoke burst from the wall . . . flaring full in the face of the advancing troops." Men in the North Carolina lines were toppled over like rag dolls, "falling like leaves in a storm." As Baxter's men now began firing at will, the colonel of the 23rd North Carolina, Daniel Christie, tried to rally his disintegrating command, only to be shot through both lungs. Entire companies broke or dove for the ground, while thickening banks of powder smoke became "so dense you could not perceive an object ten feet from you." Trying to pile surprise on surprise, Henry Baxter roared out over the cracking of rifle fire, "Up boys, and give them steel," and groups of men from the 11th Pennsylvania and 97th New York scampered forward with fixed bayonets as isolated bunches of numbed North Carolinians "rose singly and in groups" to "show the white flag." (A captain in the 88th Pennsylvania actually had a fistfight with the color-bearer of the 23rd North Carolina for possession of the flag.) Out of the 1,520 men Iverson had started with at Middletown that morning, 233 were rounded up as prisoners (along with the flag of the 20th North Carolina); another 170 were dead (or nearly dead, with ghastly wounds), 79 of them lying "in a straight line . . . perfectly dressed."[31]

The repulse of O'Neal's Alabama brigade and the destruction of Iverson's North Carolinians left Junius Daniel's brigade moving ahead on its own, "uncovered." Two of Daniel's regiments angled off to face Cutler's brigade while the remainder bore down blindly on the railroad cut. They walked into a blazing volley from Union soldiers occupying the railroad cut and "close enough . . . to cut all three ranks down at one firing." The 45th North Carolina and the 2nd North Carolina Battalion actually pushed some of their tormentors out of the railroad cut, and "the men in their ardor slid down the almost precipitous bank and attempted to scale the opposite" before it became clear that, without any other support, they (like Joe Davis' Mississippians a few hours before) were actually in "a most deadly trap." Junius Daniel, "in his stentorian tones, audible in command a quarter of a mile or more away," ordered his brigade back "without regard to company or regimental formation," and Robert Rodes' plan to "burst through the enemy" with his division evaporated.[32]

It was the regiment, more than anything else, that gave the soldier of these armies his primary identity, and in the regiment "the colonel, as a father, should have a personal acquaintance with every officer and man." On the battlefield, however, the basic tactical unit was the brigade, and brigadier generals (or senior colonels who happened to be in temporary command of a brigade or awaiting confirmation of promotion) were expected to lead, if not from the front, then certainly alongside their brigades, if only in the interest of coordinating the movement of their regiments. The survivors of Iverson's brigade, who already thought of him as a sort of secessionist policeman, would never forgive Iverson for violating that rule, and he was accused of everything from drunkenness to cowardice. "I was left alone without any orders," the colonel of the 12th North Carolina bitterly complained, "our general [being] in the rear, and never coming up." Daniel Christie, the badly wounded colonel of the 23rd North Carolina, swore that he would have "the imbecile Iverson" cashiered if it was the last thing he did (which, in fact, it was, since Christie died in Winchester on July 17th). Iverson was "relieved from the Command of his Brigade" by Robert E. Lee ten days later "for misconduct at Gettysburg."[33]

But Iverson's failure was only one facet of a larger problem experienced by the Army of Northern Virginia on July 1st. The collective bloody nose suffered by Harry Heth's division that morning could, after all, be blamed on Heth's inexperience in division command. Not so Robert Rodes, a Virginia Military Institute graduate and the man whom Stonewall Jackson had put at the head of the attack that collapsed the Union Army at Chancellorsville. Yet, he had botched his division's attack as surely as Heth had. The figure who seems curiously absent from much of this action is Dick Ewell, although there is some evidence that Ewell, who had switched to horseback to oversee operations despite his wooden leg, was put temporarily hors de combat when a Federal shell knocked the corps commander and his horse down. Ewell, who had performed so smoothly as a corps commander at Winchester that he seemed like the resurrection of Jackson, now displayed a propensity for looking over his shoulder, as though he was reverting mentally to his old role as a division commander "without responsiveness and without suggestiveness."[34]

The man Ewell was particularly looking for—as though the one-legged Ewell had forgotten he was in command of a corps rather than a division— was Robert E. Lee. That morning, however, Lee was still on the other side of South Mountain, and still issuing orders to coordinate the concentration of the Army of Northern Virginia between Cashtown and Gettysburg. His plan was to move his headquarters "for the present" to Cashtown, "east of the mountains," and that morning he set off eastward on the Cashtown Pike, with James Longstreet in tow and Longstreet's lead division under Lafayette McLaws on the road behind. If all went well, by the end of the day Lee would have most (if not all) of Hill's corps in Gettysburg, two of Ewell's divisions at Cashtown (and maybe three, if Allegheny Johnson could move Ewell's wagon trains down from Scotland fast enough), and Longstreet between Chambersburg and Cashtown; all three corps would again be within easy supporting distance of one another, and ready to strike on Lee's command at the disjointed march of the Army of the Potomac on July 2nd or 3rd.

Longstreet found Lee "in his usual cheerful spirits on the morning of the 1st, and called me to ride with him," which he did until they encountered the head of Johnson's division at an intersection, "cutting in on our front, with all of Ewell's reserve and supply trains." Johnson had indeed moved swiftly, and since Lee wanted Ewell's corps kept together, he instructed Longstreet to give Johnson right-of-way to move ahead, and hold his own corps at the crossroads until Johnson passed. But Ewell's trains alone turned out to be "fourteen miles" in length, and "after a little time General Lee proposed that we should ride on." It was when they emerged through a rain squall on the eastern side of the Cashtown Gap and passed the division of Richard H. Anderson on the road that Lee, for the first time, began to hear "reports of cannon" in the distance. "General Lee passes, going toward the front," noted a Mississippian in his diary, even as "the cannonading . . . keeps up briskly." The firing "seemed to be beyond Cashtown, and as it increased" Lee left Longstreet behind and spurred into Cashtown to find Powell Hill and discover what the trouble was.[35]

Hill heard the thumping, too, and so did Anderson's division in the line of march. "Some one hears a boom in front," recalled one Virginian, but the rest shrug it off as "some-one tapping the bass drum." Then more, and more, and soon "we know that someone is fighting ahead." When Lee caught up with Hill in front of the Cashtown inn, "Little Powell" could not offer Lee much enlightenment: he had sent Harry Heth forward that morning with only the expectation of sweeping some odds and ends of Yankee cavalry out of the way and a warning not to start any sort of sizable fight by himself. But what they were hearing was plainly artillery, and presently a courier from Heth arrived with the highly unwelcome news that he had collided with the 1st Corps of the Army of the Potomac and would Hill please send up supports. Hill was not about to do anything until he had seen matters for himself, and so off he rode toward Gettysburg, leaving Lee at Cashtown "very much disturbed and depressed." When Richard Anderson's division stopped at mid-day at Cashtown, Lee poured out his irritation to Anderson, beginning with the missing Stuart. "I cannot think what has become of Stuart; I ought to have heard from him long before now." Lee had not planned on meeting the Federals for at least another twenty-four hours, yet here they were in Gettysburg, and Lee had no idea whether "it may be the whole Federal army, or . . . only a detachment."

Soon enough, "orders were received from General Hill" for Anderson to "move forward to Gettysburg," and just after noon Lee and his staff "quickly followed." A courier from Ewell caught up with them at a crossroads beyond Cashtown, informing Lee that Ewell was turning down toward Gettysburg. This only brought on a new round of irritation from Lee: he had been repeating to all of his corps commanders that "a general engagement was to be avoided until the arrival of the rest of the army," and yet here was not only Hill, but Ewell as well, about to leap blindly into the mess up ahead. Lee's vehemence surprised the courier (who happened to be Ewell's stepson, George Campbell Brown), knowing "Lee's habitual reserve." But Lee's reddest wrath was reserved for Stuart, who—from what Lee had gleaned from the newspapers—was on the other side of Meade's army and coming to no good end.[36]

It took Lee about two hours to work his way up the Cashtown Pike, through the thick backward-flowing stream of wounded, stragglers, couriers, and teamsters, until, around two o'clock, he caught up with Powell Hill on Herr Ridge, and was joined by Harry Heth. "Turning into a grass field on his left he sat on his well-bred iron gray, Traveller, and looked across the fields eastward, through the smoke rising in puffs and long rolls," wrote a staff officer. "He held his glasses in his hand and looked down the long slope by the Seminary, over the town to the rugged heights beyond." Rodes' division was just breaking off its mangled attempt to dislodge the 1st Corps, and Heth begged Lee for permission "to go in . . . as Rodes appeared to be heavily engaged." This proposal did not enchant Lee at all. "On arriving at the scene of battle," Walter Taylor wrote, "General Lee ascertained that the enemy's infantry and artillery were present in considerable force." That led him to an immediate conclusion: "I do not wish to bring on a general engagement today," he declared. "Longstreet is not up." And without all of his infantry within close reach, Lee wanted to run no risk of clamping down on the 1st Corps, only to discover that it was connected to the rest of the Army of the Potomac.[37]

That, at least, was Lee's initial assessment. But the longer he pondered the situation, and the more he and Hill received reports from prisoner interrogations, the more it began to seem that—perhaps—the coveted opportunity to pinch off pieces of the Federal army and crush them one by one might be exactly what was happening after all. All that was in front of him was the 1st Corps; the 11th Corps was deploying north of the town. But apart from that, there was no word from the prisoners of any other Union infantry within striking distance. If he broke off the action, it would be a bad sign to his own men, that in fact they had been defeated. And while Lee could see that the Yankees were holding their ground pretty stoutly, Harry Heth's pestering for a second chance was an indication that the two repulses the Confederates had sustained had done nothing to dampen rebel self-confidence. At least for this afternoon, there were also far more Confederates soldiers within easy call than Yankees. Dorsey Pender's division of Hill's corps, 6,000 strong, was moving up behind Heth; and Heth still had Pettigrew's and Brockenbrough's brigades (another 3,700 or so) unbloodied. Rodes, likewise, still had Stephen Dodson Ramseur's brigade in reserve, and both Daniel's and Doles' brigades had plenty of fight in them. And there was still the entirety of Jubal Early's division, closing in somewhere along the road from Heidlersburg. Was this not what he had prayed for? *Had not God delivered the Philistines into his hands?* Who was he, then, to pull back? "It had not been intended to fight a general battle" on July 1st, Lee explained afterward, but a battle began anyway, and it "became a matter of difficulty to withdraw." When Heth came up a second time asking for permission to attack, Lee had a different answer: "Wait awhile and I will send you word when to go in."[38]

He would not have to wait long.

CHAPTER ELEVEN

The dutch run and leave us to fight

ABNER DOUBLEDAY was well aware that the 1st Corps had only survived two serious Confederate attacks because of extremely bad Confederate management. They were not likely to give Doubleday such gifts again, nor had they actually left him in a particularly enviable position. The corps had been pulled like taffy along a line that had to protect the Fairfield Road on the left, the Cashtown Pike in the middle, and the Mummasburg Road on the right. Starting at the Fairfield Road, one brigade of Doubleday's original division was strung thinly across the Herbst farm, barely managing to link hands with the Iron Brigade in Herbst's Woods. On the other side of the Iron Brigade, Doubleday's other brigade (under Roy Stone) formed an elbow around the McPherson house and barn, with the 149th and 143rd Pennsylvania bent backward along the Cashtown Pike. Cutler's brigade, which had been rejoined by the 95th New York and 14th Brooklyn after their fight over the railroad cut, permanently abandoned any attempt at holding on to the north extension of McPherson's Ridge and were backed up against Sheads' Woods, where they connected with Henry Baxter's brigade at the Mummasburg Road. Doubleday had only one brigade left in reserve, and Buford's cavalry brigades, one posted to the north and east of the town and the other below the Fairfield Road, and neither would be able to offer much in the way of assistance if the rebels looked like they would overrun Doubleday's positions. There was clearly no hope that the 11th Corps could move up on the other side of the Mummasburg Road, because Rodes' rebels, however unsuccessful they had been on the attack, held the knob of Oak Hill in greater strength than the 11th Corps could bring up to drive them from it. At least

Doubleday had plenty of artillery. All six batteries of the 1st Corps' artillery were now up and in place, evenly balanced between 3-inch Ordnance Rifles for distance and 12-pounder Napoleons for short-range work.[1]

Doubleday sent off an aide, followed by his adjutant, Eminel Halstead, to beg reinforcements from Howard, but there were none to spare. "Tell General Doubleday that I have no reinforcements to send him." At two o'clock, Howard came up to the seminary to see Doubleday's position for himself, and he frankly advised that if the two big Confederate forces that had attacked earlier came back again in strength, Doubleday would have to "fall back to Cemetery Hill" and make a final stand there. Sickles and the 3rd Corps were somewhere on their way up from Emmitsburg, and Howard dispatched one of his staff captains to find Sickles and hurry him up. But he was pinning his real hopes on the next nearest Union corps—Henry Slocum's 12th Corps—which had started north from Littlestown and was now at Two Taverns, only five miles to the southeast. If Slocum could make Gettysburg in the next hour and a half, Howard could post the 12th Corps on the right flank of his own corps and firm up the defensive arc that now stretched west and north of Gettysburg. Almost as an afterthought, he sent another courier to Meade with "a report of the state of things as then existing."[2]

In lieu of reinforcements, Doubleday's regiments picked up some strange volunteers. The 9th New York Cavalry was approached by "a young man in citizens' clothes who said his name was James Watson" and "expressed a desire to go into the fight." The troopers of Company A found him a blue sack coat, and "he rode with that company." The 12th Massachusetts (in Baxter's brigade) absorbed an enthusiastic local sixteen-year-old named Charles Weakley on the march up from Emmitsburg, and equipped him with a borrowed "cap, blouse, musket and roundabout . . . together with a supply of ammunition." A twenty-three-year-old "photographist" named Phineas Branson "went out to meet the Rebels," as did a "gray-haired man, sixty years of age," who turned out to fight alongside the 56th Pennsylvania in Cutler's brigade "and fought with that Regiment all day." Another "stranger to the regiment" took up a position "about fifteen paces to the rear" of the 16th Maine (in Gabriel Paul's brigade) and began "loading and firing independently," until a lieutenant in Company G, convinced that the "stranger" would end up shooting his men in the back, "kicked him rapidly to the rear."[3]

The strangest of all these impromptu fighters was John Burns, a cantankerous sixty-nine-year-old shoemaker, former town constable, and veteran of the War of 1812, who showed up behind the 150th Pennsylvania at the McPherson farm in "a bell-crowned hat, a swallow-tailed coat with rolling collar and brass buttons and a buff vest," and an 1812-vintage flintlock musket "on his shoulder." Burns served with the Union Army as a teamster in 1861, so it was not at all out of character for him to assume that this was an opportunity to impress both the neighborhood and the Army of the Potomac with his martial skill. He had showed up earlier behind Lysander Cutler's brigade, but Cutler, who wondered what on earth had dropped this apparition on them, shooed him off. Burns wandered over the Cashtown Pike and made straightaway for an officer of the 150th Pennsylvania, demanding to "fight with our regiment." The officer pointed Burns to the 150th's colonel, who wickedly suggested that Burns might find things more interesting if he "went into the wood" and tendered his services to the Iron Brigade (and became *their* problem). Relentlessly, Burns tracked down the lieutenant colonel of the 7th Wisconsin, John Callis, who advised this village Don Quixote to "go to the rear or you'll get hurt." Up came all of Burns' mock-offended bravado: "No, sir, if you won't let me fight in your regiment I will fight alone. . . . There are three hundred cowards back in that town who ought to come out of their cellars and fight, and I will show you that there is one man in Gettysburg who is not afraid." Finally, Callis shrugged: if that was what Burns wanted, the lieutenant colonel of the 7th Wisconsin had better things to do than argue with garrulous old shoemakers. A sergeant found a rifle captured from Archer's brigade to replace Burns' flintlock, and put Burns on the line, "as cool as any veteran among us."[4]

It is difficult to piece together Robert E. Lee's activities once he arrived from Cashtown that afternoon, but his injunction to Harry Heth to "wait awhile" makes sense if Lee's mind was moving toward a massive, coordinated assault which would begin with the arrival of Early's division on the Heidlersburg Road, and then add Doles' brigade and the rest of Rodes' division, and finally Dorsey Pender's division on the Cashtown Pike. Early, however, was taking his time. He had more miles to cover than Rodes had that morning, and while Lee waited, he inspected Ewell's deployment, all the way over to where Doles' skirmishers were popping away at the 11th Corps, "observing that the men were very much wearied . . . ordered the band of the 4th Georgia to play for the men."[5]

Finally, by 2:30, Early's column arrived at a small intersection a mile north of Gettysburg, where the neatly tended farms offered "an open undulating" view straight down to where "we could see the battle raging on our right." A courier from Ewell carried Lee's directions to "attack at once," and the sharp-tongued Early rode up "towards the front." John Gordon's Georgia brigade was in the lead that afternoon, and Early turned Gordon off to the right to link up with Doles (whom Lee now shifted eastward, to cement the link) and start skirmishing in earnest. Early then posted Harry Hays' Louisiana brigade astride the Heidlersburg Road, and split Isaac Avery's North Carolina brigade out to the left beyond Hays (keeping Extra Billy Smith's Virginians

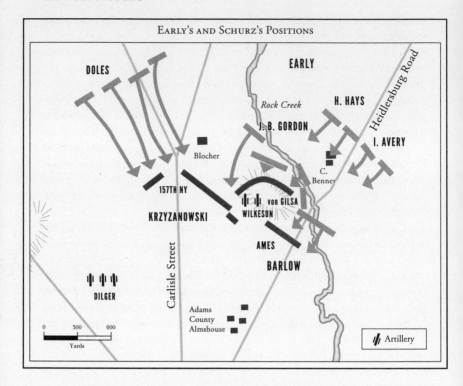

EARLY'S AND SCHURZ'S POSITIONS

DOLES

EARLY

Rock Creek

H. HAYS

J. B. GORDON

I. AVERY

Blocher

C. Benner

157TH NY

von GILSA

KRZYANOWSKI

WILKESON

AMES

Carlisle Street

BARLOW

DILGER

Adams County Almshouse

Heidlersburg Road

0   300   600

Yards

Artillery

in column on the road as a reserve). Lastly, he directed the sixteen guns in his division artillery battalion into place, and "in quick sharp tones" ordered them to unlimber and open up. The guns, in turn, were the signal for Gordon and Hays to attack "at the double-quick." Watching from Oak Hill, Campbell Brown remembered it as "one of the most warlike & animated spectacles I ever looked on—Gordon & Hays . . . sweeping everything before them . . . towards the Seminary [Pennsylvania College] & the town."[6]

For the previous two hours, the Yankees they were about to fall upon had been struggling to make sense of their situation. Carl Schurz brought his two brigades north of the town limits after noon in the expectation of extending Wadsworth's flank over Oak Hill. Rodes' Confederates had beaten him to that knob, and though the rebels had been roughly handled by Baxter's brigade when they tried to move farther, they were still up there on the knob, and Schurz had no prospect of doing anything about it. He shook out Schimmelpfennig's brigade into a long line, more or less at right angles to Baxter up on his ridge, between the Mummasburg Road and the Carlisle Road, and put the entire 45th New York out as skirmishers. But he kept Krzyzanowski's four regiments in a closed column (by companies) behind Schimmelpfennig's, ready to jump whatever way the rebels themselves jumped next. "Either the enemy was before us in small force," Schurz wrote, "or he had the principal part of his army there, and then we had to establish ourselves in a position which would enable us to maintain ourselves until the arrival of reinforcements" in the form of the 12th Corps. As Rodes' attack on the other side of the ridge petered out, Schurz contented himself with pushing "forward only a strong force of skirmishers" to keep track of any movement by Doles' Georgians up in front. Shortly after one o'clock, Francis Barlow and his two-brigade division came swinging up from the town on Washington Street. Schurz was by right of seniority temporarily in command of his own and Barlow's divisions, and he expected Barlow to "refuse his right wing"—in other words, to turn his lead brigade under Leopold von Gilsa to the right of the Carlisle Road and extend Schimmelpfennig's front facing north. Schurz wanted Barlow's remaining brigade, under Adelbert Ames, kept in "the right rear . . . in order to use it against a possible flanking movement by the enemy."[7]

Barlow had ideas of his own. He had never had a very high opinion of Schurz in particular or Germans in general. As the only non-German division commander in the 11th Corps—in fact, one of only two general-rank officers who were *not* Germans—Francis Channing Barlow was a Brahmin of the Brahmins. Son of a Boston Unitarian minister, his family had close ties to the intellectual circles of the Transcendentalists and even participated in the short-lived Brook Farm community. The teenaged Barlow entered Harvard in 1851, breezing through at the top of his class, and went into partnership practicing law in New York City and writing for Horace Greeley's *New-York Tribune* until the outbreak of the war. His promotion to brigadier general after Antietam carried endorsements from Ralph Waldo Emerson, Oliver Wendell Holmes, and Nathaniel Hawthorne.

Snobbishness lay too close to the skin for Barlow to conceal—he found army life "very tedious living so many months with men who are so little companions for me as our officers are"—and he quickly developed a reputation as a "Billy Barlow," the boorish martinet who (as Schurz delicately put it) carried "his virtues to excess." But not even Otis Howard had better polished abolitionist and anti-McClellan credentials than Francis Barlow, and it was those credentials that led Howard to "seduce" Barlow into taking command of a division in the 11th Corps after Chancellorsville. He soon regretted it. Barlow disliked the beery and impenetrable Germans in his division as much as he disliked Democrats. He had, he admitted, "always been down on the 'Dutch' & I do not abate my contempt now." That spring, he pulled his family's many wires to "take command" of a more suitably Brahmin project—a "Negro brigade"—but to no avail. The correspondence about the "Negro brigade" was still in his pocket as his division marched out of the town along the Heidlersburg Road.[8]

Howard came out to inspect Schurz's handiwork around two o'clock, as Barlow's division was still deploying, and it was not until Schurz commandeered "the roof of a house behind my skirmish line" and glanced over in Barlow's direction that he saw that Barlow had not done at all what Schurz had ordered. Instead of marching his brigades over to the Carlisle Road, stopping there and bending them backward from Schimmelpfennig's brigade, Barlow had "advanced his whole line" all the way eastward to a small eminence beside the Heidlersburg Road known simply as Blocher's Knoll, leaving a sizable gap between himself and Schimmelpfennig. On the knoll, Barlow had placed 900 men of Leopold von Gilsa's brigade, with two sections of Lt. Bayard Wilkeson's Battery B, 4th U.S. Artillery as stiffening, and then drew up Ames' brigade in column behind. "These troops marched in perfect order," observed an almost admiring Isaac Trimble from Ewell's command perch on Oak Hill, "but they had not sent out scouts." Barlow, with typical insouciance, regarded the knoll as "an admirable position," and may have assumed that Schurz ought to fill the gap with Krzyzanowski's reserve brigade. Neither Schurz nor Barlow ever got the time to discuss the fine points, because at 2:45, Jubal Early's carefully sited artillery sent their first brace of shells winging Barlow's way, and the rebel infantry of Gordon, Hays, and Doles lurched forward into full view.[9]

There had been intimations that morning, gleaned from the last few detachments of Buford's cavalry on picket north of the town, that there was "a large force at Heidlersburg that is driving . . . from that direction." Midway between noon and one o'clock, Buford sent Howard "word that the enemy was massing between the York and Harrisburg roads, to the north of Gettysburg, some 3 or 4 miles from the town," and half an hour later, Howard sent out another plea to Slocum and the 12th Corps to come up, because Early "is advancing from York." He could have saved himself the trouble. Slocum stopped at Two Taverns, only to be overtaken there by the tardy delivery of Meade's Pipe Creek Circular. Caught between Howard's cry in extremis and Meade's order, Slocum decided to stop and wait for clarification. The 12th Corps would not begin moving again until 3:35 (by Slocum's watch). Howard was not going to get any relief from Sickles, either. The staffer who had been sent off to prod Sickles forward to Gettysburg managed to get himself lost, and wouldn't actually find Sickles until after three o'clock. Howard and the 11th Corps—along with Doubleday and the 1st Corps—were on their own. The only reserves were the two diminutive brigades Howard posted back on Cemetery Hill, who were to hold on to that particularly valuable piece of ground rather than to be sent off to the rescue of anyone else. If these two corps—one already hollowed with battle shock, the other with the depressing onus of Chancellorsville still hanging over its head—failed to stop an attack, or failed at the last gasp to slow it down enough for darkness to fall, then the hill would be gone, a quarter of the Army of the Potomac would be gone, and maybe the whole war, too.[10]

Howard may not have been surprised, but Barlow certainly was when the scream of Early's artillery broke on Yankee ears, followed by the deadly trill of the rebel yell. The blue-blooded ex-lawyer had just arranged von Gilsa's brigade and Bayard Wilkeson's battery across Blocher's Knoll and sent a heavy line of skirmishers down the front of the knoll toward the rambling brick farmhouse of Josiah Benner, when a sudden violent upsurge of popping and banging broke out. The Union skirmishers came hurrying back, followed by rebel skirmishers and by John Gordon's Georgians in "three lines of battle." Early's artillery zeroed in on the four guns of Lieutenant Wilkeson, knocking down Wilkeson and severing a leg, smashing one of his guns, and making the knoll so hot that the lieutenant who took over from Wilkeson hurriedly shifted position around the knoll, and finally dragged the guns backward with *prolonge* ropes to escape the deluge of vicious shell shards.

Two months before, von Gilsa's brigade was the first to shatter and run before Stonewall Jackson's flank attack. Now, with Gordon's yipping Georgians rushing up to them "with a resolution and spirit . . . rarely excelled," they once again began to disintegrate. One private was almost knocked over by another soldier beside him, falling dead "with his face towards me," and it unnerved him so much that he almost could not finish ramming a cartridge down his rifle's muzzle; then the man on his left fell over and "the thought occurred that I might be the next." Von Gilsa's "line was broken in the left and our right was attacked in flank," and after only fifteen minutes there was nothing for it but "to retire or surrender." Behind them, von Gilsa's men left "a regular swath of blue coats . . . piled up in every shape, some on their backs, some on their faces, and others turned and twisted in every imaginable shape."[11]

Barlow was beside himself at the collapse of von Gilsa's brigade: "We ought to have held the place easily for I had my entire force at the very point where the attack was made. . . . But the enemies skirmishers had hardly attacked us before my men began to run." Nor was Barlow the only one unable to contain his disgust. "The dutch run and leave us to fight," complained Oscar D. Ladley, a lieutenant in the 75th Ohio who was drawn up behind the knoll in Ames' brigade, "My sword was out and if I didn't welt them with it my name ain't O.D.L." Barlow tried to head the fleeing Germans off and "rally

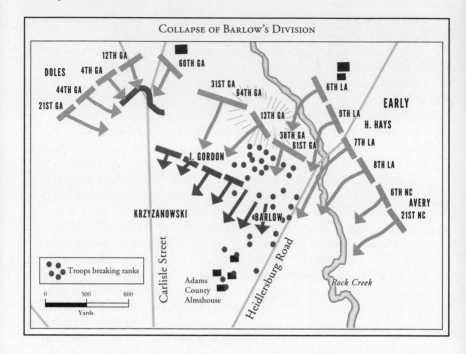

COLLAPSE OF BARLOW'S DIVISION

them." But one of Early's batteries, attracted by "one of the large white flags which I think they used to designate a Corps commander," got the range perfectly, dropped a shell over them, and "dispersed the party, killing at least one, whom I saw them carry off." Barlow was hit in the left side. He was not dead, but he was badly hurt, and since Adelbert Ames ranked von Gilsa, Ames now took charge and sent in his own brigade to push the rebels back.

Ames was Maine-born and the son of a Yankee clipper captain, and graduated fifth in the early crop of West Point's class of 1861. He had been an artillery officer at Bull Run and the Peninsula, was tagged to command the new 20th Maine Volunteers in 1862, and had just been promoted to brigadier general six weeks before. But he had no better time of it than Barlow. He spread four companies of the 17th Connecticut on the east side of the road to guard his flank and ordered up his three Ohio regiments—the 25th, 75th, and 107th—to "check the advance of the enemy" over Blocher's Knoll. Ames took his brigade in "on foot" and "in front," and they actually cleared the knoll itself and moved down to "the thin woods in front"—until Gordon's Georgians began pushing them back, then lapping around their flanks. "Trees were felled everywhere by the cannon balls," wrote Otto von Fritsch, and "without orders" the 75th Ohio's colonel, Andrew Harris, "began to fall back . . . in skirmish line."[12]

And no wonder, because by now Ames was bearing the brunt not only of Gordon's Georgia brigade in front, but the weight of Harry Hays' Louisianans sweeping away the thin line of the 17th Connecticut's skirmishers on one side, and the onslaught of George Doles' brigade of Georgians to the left of the knoll. "The Confederates approached slowly, and in magnificent order . . . screaming savagely," Fritsch remembered. Not so among the Federals: "No order was preserved or thought of," and though some knots of men "began to retreat in fine order, shooting at us as they retreated," most of them "in their flight . . . threw away their knapsacks to accelerate their escape." Part of the 25th Ohio stood its ground long enough for the color-bearer of one of Gordon's regiments to get into a personal fight with the 25th's color-bearer, so that "the flag-bearers struck each other with their flag-staffs." Carl Schurz, watching the entire right flank of the 11th Corps begin to break up, called up his own reserve brigade, Wladimir Krzyzanowski's, and threw them against the oncoming wave of Doles and Gordon. And he might have stood half a chance if he had been able to fold Krzyzanowski's regiments behind the Carlisle Road and force Gordon to wheel to the right to attack him. Krzyzanowski's men had been quietly watching the to-and-fro of Barlow's division and their mates in Schimmelpfennig's brigade, resting "in line." One of his colonels, John Thomas Lockman of the 119th New York, sat with his adjutant "under an apple tree." As the fury of the fight on Blocher's Knoll developed, Thomas predicted that "we are going to have some hot work shortly," and as an "upright, conscientious" Episcopalian, Thomas and his adjutant "knelt down under the tree, and uttered, each in his own heart, a prayer to the God of Hosts." Presently, "three or four of the cracking rifles ahead sufficed to tell us" that "a great crisis had come," and the brigade moved forward "in line of double columns."[13]

But Krzyzanowski's brigade was able only to push back Doles' right-flank regiment, the 21st Georgia; the 4th and 44th Georgia, which had been occupied in outflanking Blocher's Knoll, now turned their unencumbered attention to Krzyzanowski and flung the Polish émigré's brigade back like broken toys. A shell fragment knocked down Albert Walber, a lieutenant in the 26th Wisconsin, and the rush of the Confederates was so quick that none of the rebel officers even stopped to take him prisoner. Officers in the 82nd Ohio tried to steady their men with an "order . . . to call the rolls." (This little piece of defiance struck Capt. Alfred Lee "as being sublime, so firm and decided were the answers of the men.") It was "almost a hand-to-hand struggle" alongside the Carlisle Road, with Schurz everywhere trying to hold back the collapsing front of Krzyzanowski's regiments. Theodore Dodge, in the 119th New York, saw one "brave boy" go down with a leg wound, but insist on "loading and firing" from a sitting position "with as much regularity and coolness as if untouched, now and then shouting to some comrade in front of him to make room for his shot."[14]

It did no good. Dodge estimated that they might have held on for as much as half an hour, until Doles' Georgians began moving forward again. It was "not a charge on the double-quick, but a simple advance, firing as they came on." Schurz's horse took a bullet "clean through the fatty ridge of the neck just under the mane," as did Krzyzanowski's, but his other officers did much worse. The 26th Wisconsin lost its colonel to a shell splinter, then the senior major, and soon command of the regiment was in the hands of the Prussian-born captain of Company A; every member of the color guard was down, and by the end of the day only thirty-two of the 26th's men were left— although "this gallant squad" still had the regimental flags. Francis Mahler, the colonel of the 75th Pennsylvania, had been an old "revolutionary comrade" of Schurz's in Baden in the '48 uprising. Mahler went down with a fatal wound, and "with death on his face" he reached out for Schurz's hand "to bid me a last farewell."

First, Barlow's division, now Krzyzanowski's brigade. It was, said Krzyzanowski, "a portrait of hell." All that was left of the 11th Corps north of the town was Schimmelpfennig's brigade, dangling perilously from its handhold with the 1st Corps up on Oak Ridge. Even as they watched, a new danger materialized from over the knob of Oak Hill—Robert Rodes' reserve brigade under Stephen Dodson Ramseur, a thousand strong and untouched, and ready to stride forward in support of Doles' Georgians. To face them all, Schimmelpfennig had exactly one regiment in reserve, the 157th New York, commanded by a school principal and less than a year old as a unit, but they would have to do.[15]

Even in a corps full of abolitionists, the 157th may have had the most impeccable abolitionist credentials of them all, since they had been sent off to war in 1862 with the assistance of no one less than Gerrit Smith, the wealthy philanthropist who had also funded John Brown's raid in 1859, and unlike other parts of the army, the Emancipation Proclamation met with "the hearty concurrence of the regiment." But they had only seen their first battle in May, at Chancellorsville, and with only 350 men they had been held in position in a "field east of the Mummasberg road and just opposite the Pennsylvania College," and then moved up behind Dilger's battery astride the Carlisle Road. Now, however, their colonel, Philip Brown, was ordered by Schimmelpfennig "to move over some distance to the right and attack the enemy." Brown must have known that he was being sent in as an expendable distraction to give the remnant of Krzyzanowski's brigade the chance to escape from Doles' advance, but in they went all the same, starting "forward in double-column on the center." This indeed got the attention of "the Rebel Commander who immediately changed his front toward the regt. and poured in such a tremendous fire of balls, that many fell to breathe no more." Colonel Brown tried to get them to charge right into "the line of rebel heads." But instead, the 157th stopped, exchanging "8 or 10 volleys" while "the boys were falling in all shapes," until they finally began ducking down into the wheat and "the fighting continued in indian fashion." After twenty minutes, one of Schurz's staffers rode up under fire to recall them. The staffer's horse went down, but the man got to his feet, "waved his hand to Col. Brown" as though he were calling in recess at a grade school, "then unfastened his saddle and with it started for the rear." Less than fifty of the 157th were able to rise out of the wheat and follow.[16]

Schurz's recall to the 157th was the signal that he had given up hope of holding any part of the 11th Corps' line north of town. "An order was received" by Adelbert Ames "from General Schurz, or one of his staff" to fall back "through . . . the outskirts of the town," and so the two broken divisions turned and flowed backward through the banks of gunpowder smoke. Barlow's division had the head start, though it gave the appearance to a Confederate onlooker of being "shriveled up as a scroll." With Barlow down, Ames struggled to pull his brigade back as deliberately as he could, "in line order, shooting at us as they retreated," so that one private in the 8th Louisiana had the impression that "the Yanks . . . rather walked off." This would not be the 11th Corps' second Chancellorsville if they could help it.

Ames and Leopold von Gilsa tried to gather enough men together around a cluster of buildings on the west side of the Heidlersburg Road which served as the Adams County almshouse—an all-purpose poorhouse, insane asylum, and hospice—von Gilsa all the while riding "through a regular storm of lead" and swearing his men into standing still with "the German epithets so common to him." But as they did, Harry Hays' Louisiana brigade wheeled and slapped them on the flank even as Gordon's brigade continued to press them from in front. "This line, too, was driven back in the greatest confusion," wrote Gordon, "and with immense loss in killed, wounded, and prisoners." Ames' brigade broke completely, abandoning in the process the severely wounded Francis Barlow. "The smoke lifting from the field" as the firing died away and "revealed to our sight the defeated Federals in disorderly flight, hotly pursued by the gallant Georgians." Schurz's division followed, "vanishing as a mist" and leaving "the golden wheat-fields . . . covered with the dead and wounded in blue."[17]

Left behind in the retreat was Theodore Dodge, the adjutant of the 119th

New York, who had been praying with his colonel only a short while before. "A Minie ball had gone through my ankle-joint," and he was able to do nothing more than sit until "a rebel straggler, unkempt and powder-begrimed," ambled suspiciously up to Dodge and demanded that he surrender his sword and revolver. Dodge told him to go to hell, not least because Dodge had no intention of waiving the unspoken protocol which allowed only an officer to demand another officer's surrender. The rebel "raised his gun, as if to club me," but one of John Gordon's staff officers rode over and shooed away the "would-be immolator," took Dodge's weapons, and called over "a Confederate tatterdemalion" to help Dodge limp off to find a surgeon.

Capt. Alfred Lee of the 82nd Ohio met the same unexpected kindness of enemies. Bowled over by a bullet and "benumbed with pain," Lee found himself alone in a "field . . . alive with hooting rebels." But the soldier in "the usual coarse gray homespun" who found Lee propped him up with a canteen and regretted that "you ones were all out here against us this way." He tried to find a surgeon or an ambulance, but returning with neither, "he now directed some negroes to go and gather from the debris of battle such articles as might improve our comfort." John Gordon himself found Francis Barlow and ordered one of Jubal Early's staffers to have Barlow carried to the shade of the Benner farmhouse. In the years after the war, Gordon would spin an enormously embellished story of chivalry and reconciliation out of the encounter. But in fact the kind of story Gordon embroidered was happening spontaneously all over the fields where men had been, a few minutes before, trying to kill one another.[18]

At 3:20, Schurz sent Otis Howard one last plea for reinforcements, even for just a brigade to post temporarily as a screen across the north end of the town that would allow his division and Barlow's to reach Cemetery Hill unharassed. Howard was still reluctant to "spare any troops" from Cemetery Hill. He kept looking southeastward for Slocum and the 12th Corps. Surely, Slocum must be near; if they could hold on a little longer, Slocum would come piling in on the Confederates' flank like Blücher at Waterloo, and the day would be saved. "Hold out, if possible, awhile longer, for I am expecting General Slocum every moment."[19]

But the roar and the smoke billows he could see above the roofs and spires of Gettysburg told Howard that the relief the 11th Corps needed was now, and north of the town. He relented. At four o'clock, he sent orders to Schurz and Doubleday to fall back to Cemetery Hill, and then sent one of the last of the 11th Corps' brigades, under Charles Coster, "beyond the town, to cover the retreat." Coster, the son of a wealthy New York merchant, may have had, at most, 800 men in his four regiments, but he called in the skirmishers he had posted around Cemetery Hill and off the brigade trotted through the

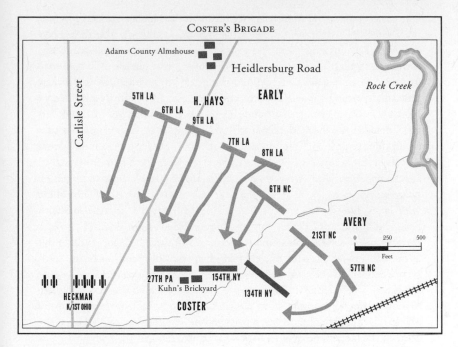

town, toward the 11th Corps' inferno. Coster met Schurz along the way, "who ordered him to take a position north and east of Gettysburg," and rode out with him to guide the brigade past fat trickles of wounded men and stragglers from the "confusion and disaster" up ahead, "dripping with blood . . . limping slowly and painfully to the rear in search of field hospitals." As Coster's brigade "uncovered from the town," rebel shells "came shrieking closer to their heads, and every shot a little closer." Schurz left one of Coster's regiments (the 73rd Pennsylvania) in reserve at the railroad station on Carlisle Street, and strung out the other three thinly in front of a brickyard, in the path of Early's Confederates. With Lewis Heckman's Ohio battery drawn up on their left on the west side astride the Carlisle Road, this position looked as though it would allow them to cover the two main streets leading in and through the town, Carlisle and Stratton. It was, actually, a terrible position. A small rise north of the brickyard masked any of the approaches to Coster's line, so that "we were scarcely in position" before the first elements of Early's division were on top of them.[20]

Jubal Early had used up Gordon's Georgia brigade in overrunning the almshouse, so he now turned to Harry Hays' Louisianans and Isaac Avery's brigade of North Carolinians to keep up the momentum. Once the almshouse was cleared, Hays and Avery rolled down the Heidlersburg Road, until the road branched into Stratton Street and the brickyard. Together, Hays and Avery had eight big regiments to face Coster's three small ones, and they assaulted Coster's line without even bothering to shift out of "solid column." Lined up behind a rail fence beyond the brick kilns, "our men stood their ground, returning the enemy's fire with interest." But, effortlessly, Avery's North Carolinians wrapped around the uncovered right flank of Coster's brigade, doubling up the 134th New York, and closing like a set of enormous jaws on all three regiments. "The enemy was gradually closing in upon us," wrote an officer in Coster's center regiment, the 154th New York, and if they stayed any longer, Hays and Avery would gobble them up en masse as prisoners. Large numbers of Coster's men bolted back up Stratton Street, only to collide with Hays' Louisianans, "and a fierce hand to hand conflict ensued," with both Union and Confederate "mingled in promiscous confusion." Heckman's battery got off (by their reckoning) 113 rounds of canister before pulling out at the last moment, leaving one of their guns behind. Handfuls of the 154th New York fought their way clear with bayonets, but most of the rest—some 148 men—were captured. The collapse had happened so quickly that there had been time for no more than 7 of the 154th to be killed. Colonel Coster also survived, although how he escaped was never clear; he resigned from the army in the fall and never filed an official report.[21]

The men of the 11th Corps were not the only ones in trouble that afternoon. Up on Oak Ridge, the men of Henry Baxter's brigade could look uneasily over their right shoulders and see, down on the plain behind them, the gradual collapse and disintegration of the 11th Corps. "The fields northwest, west and south of Gettysburg were covered over with shattered lines[,] retreating in companies, squads and singly towards the town into which they were pursued," wrote a gleeful Confederate officer.[22]

Both Otis Howard and Abner Doubleday could see this, too, and all that it meant for the now unprotected northern flank of the 1st Corps. Howard sent off couriers with "positive orders" for Doubleday "to fall back to the cemetery as slowly as possible." (Doubleday claimed never to have received the orders; one of Howard's staffers believed that the order had, indeed, been conveyed to Doubleday, but the "German" courier spoke in broken English, and made a retreat to the *cemetery* sound like a retreat to the *seminary*.) Doubleday still had one brigade of John Cleveland Robinson's division back at the Lutheran seminary as a last-hope reserve, and he now decided to put it to work, extending and protecting Baxter's flank.

This was Gabriel Paul's brigade, another mixed multitude of six regi-

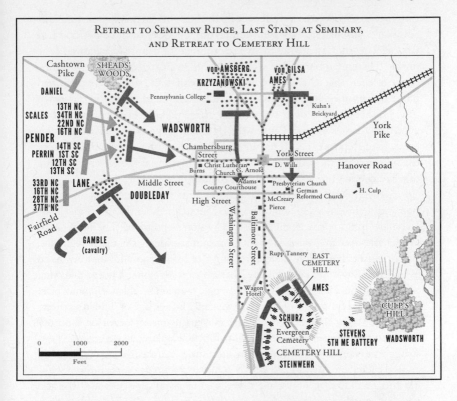

RETREAT TO SEMINARY RIDGE, LAST STAND AT SEMINARY,
AND RETREAT TO CEMETERY HILL

ments from Maine, Massachusetts, New York, and Pennsylvania, numbering between 1,300 and 1,500 men. They had been busy erecting the "crescent-shaped barricade" of "rails" around the seminary building begun by Baxter's brigade earlier in the day. Paul's working parties were called in, and the brigade was moved up to Oak Hill, relieving Baxter's regiments, which were shoved down the line to create a stronger link with Cutler's brigade, still guarding Sheads' Woods and the line north of the railroad bed. They drove off some Confederate skirmishers who had crept along their front from the knob of Oak Hill, but they were hardly in position before it was clear that considerable Confederate forces were massing on the knob for another lunge at the Oak Ridge position—Dodson Ramseur's full, fresh brigade of North Carolinians, bulked up with the one reasonably unscathed regiment of Alfred Iverson's massacred brigade and pieces of Edward O'Neal's Alabamians. In contrast to Iverson, Dodson Ramseur spurred up to the front of his brigade, "and, waving his hat, cried out for us to follow him."[23]

Ramseur's was the smallest of the five brigades in Rodes' division, and they may have been attacking Baxter's and Paul's brigades at a numerical disadvantage. No matter: they had momentum, and Baxter and Paul soon had Confederates moving behind them and cutting off their path back toward the town. "The fire on our right," wrote a soldier in Baxter's 88th Pennsylvania, "came so near" that it "became evident to the exhausted soldiers that they had no further business being there." It was too late for a pullback directly down the Mummasburg Road, so after a short, fierce firefight (in which a Confederate bullet struck Gabriel Paul in the right temple and blew out both of his eyes), John Robinson began retiring his division southward along the line of the ridge toward the railroad cut, hoping to turn left at the rail line and use that as a conduit into the town and beyond.

"General Robinson, evidently feeling a little nervous over his own position," left behind one regiment, the 16th Maine, to "hold the hill at any cost" and allow him to "save as much of the division as possible." The 16th's colonel, Charles Tilden, protested that this meant sacrificing the entire regiment. But Robinson, noticeably irked and rising "in his stirrups and with his hand extended towards Colonel Tilden," barked out, "Colonel Tilden, take that position and hold it as long as there is a single man left." Tilden had no choice: "All right, General; we'll do the best we can." But as one of Tilden's officers lamented, "every man knew that the movement meant death or capture." The 16th spread itself out and "fought like hell as long as we could." They struggled to fall back fighting, but in short order Ramseur's brigade closed in around them, and finally "every man commenced to look after himself without further orders." Only 84 men managed to avoid capture out of the 300 who had marched up from Marsh Creek that morning. In the last moments, Colonel Tilden plunged his sword into the ground and tried to break it, and ordered the regiment's colors torn from the staffs and cut up into patches the men could hide "about the persons of the survivors," before finally surrendering. The Confederates of the 45th North Carolina were only able to seize a "very fine flag-staff and tassels" and some scraps of "a fine Yankee flag . . . lying in different places."[24]

Robinson's retreat startled his fellow division commander, James Wadsworth, who pulled Cutler's brigade back to the railroad cut (as though it were a large-size trench) in order to cover the flight of Baxter's and Paul's brigades down the railroad tracks toward the town. Backing Cutler's regiments at the railroad were two batteries of artillery, Battery B, 4th U.S. Artillery under James Stewart, and (on the south side of the pike) Greenleaf T. Stevens' Battery E, 5th Maine Artillery. They would not tarry there long, because coming down on the right flank of Ramseur's attack was Junius Daniel's North Carolina brigade, striding in line more or less parallel to the railroad cut and the Cashtown Pike, and ready for a second try at capturing the pike and the railroad. Directly in their path on the south side of the Cashtown Pike were the three Pennsylvania regiments of Roy Stone's brigade, who had been positioned there around noon and had thrown back Daniel's first attack. Two of Stone's regiments—the 149th and 143rd Pennsylvania—were lined up behind the pike, with skirmishers out front along the railroad embankment; the third regiment, the 150th Pennsylvania, was bent back to face westward across the McPherson farm and link hands with the Iron Brigade, still in Herbst's Woods.

This time, Junius Daniel was not going to be surprised. "A converging fire from the rebel batteries west, northwest and north" made the corner formed by Stone's brigade "most uncomfortable," and the major of the 150th could see "projectiles . . . plainly visible in the air" (although he had the satisfaction of noticing that the rebel shells frequently "struck the ground and ricocheted without exploding"). In spite of the artillery duds, Daniel's North Carolina regiments rolled relentlessly over the Union skirmishers, and when the 149th Pennsylvania tried to blunt the rebel onslaught by launching a spoiling attack of their own at Daniel's brigade, they did little more than give the Confederate onslaught a momentary pause. Roy Stone went down with a wound to the hip which splintered his pelvis, and a Confederate battery boldly rode up and unlimbered to take the 149th in flank with canister. After a few minutes, the 149th was knocked back to its starting position, considerably worse for the wear. The senior colonel of the brigade, Langhorne Wister of the 150th Pennsylvania, tried to stiffen the resistance of the other two regiments along the pike by pivoting half of his own regiment into line along the pike with them, and staging yet another little countercharge. It was to no avail. The colonel of the 149th went down with a wound to the thigh, Wister was hit in the jaw by a bullet and spun backward, spurting blood, and the last two senior officers of the 150th were felled by wounds to the chest and the upper arm.[25]

With so many officers gone, "it seemed to me that every man fought his own hook," wrote a sergeant in the 150th, and at least one company of the 150th swung back to the left and attached itself to the Iron Brigade, with sergeants and little knots of men "retreating in that direction." Slowly the weight of Daniel's advance pressed the three Pennsylvania regiments back at right angles to the pike, and then kept pressing them down the pike in the direction of the town. The Pennsylvanians took "advantage of every favorable spot to make a defensive stand . . . firing as we went." But the color detail of the 149th had not received any order to fall back, and both the state and national flags were overrun in a flurry of hand-to-hand fighting. The 149th's color sergeant, Henry Brehm, was jumped by a Confederate who grabbed the Stars and Stripes, shouting, *This is mine.* The two locked around each other's throats and rolled around on the ground, until Brehm got loose and tried to make off with the flag "at the top of his speed"—only to be shot down in the pike. The color sergeant of the 143rd Pennsylvania, Benjamin Crippen, made off with both of his regiment's flags, but when he turned to shake his fist (or make some similar but less virtuous gesture) in contempt at Daniel's pursuing rebels, Confederate fire cut him down. (The 143rd's colors, at least, were saved.) Now, a second stream of Union refugees was heading for the town.[26]

Like a fall of dominoes, the unhinging of each Union brigade along Oak Ridge or McPherson's Ridge caused its left-hand neighbor to give way in succession. The next in order was the Iron Brigade in Herbst's Woods, which received an extra shove backward from the two brigades Harry Heth had *not* thrown away that morning, under Johnston Pettigrew and John Brockenbrough. Behind them came Dorsey Pender's entirely new division of Powell Hill's corps, which, along with Powell Hill, had at last arrived from Cashtown. Linked to the left of the Iron Brigade was the last of the 1st Corps brigades, Chapman Biddle's four regiments, backed up by the last two of the 1st Corps artillery batteries, parked 600 yards to the rear near the Lutheran seminary. This was not a formidable array: there were 1,300 men in the brigade, but three of Biddle's regiments had barely been in action before, and one of them (the 151st Pennsylvania) was actually just a nine-months' regiment which Biddle wisely planted behind the others. What was worse, the officer who should have been in charge of this end of the fighting, the "short, fat and hearty" Thomas Rowley, had clearly been bucking himself up to his task with too much drink, and by now was nearly incoherent. He rode up to James Wadsworth and loudly asked why the cavalry wasn't charging. As Wadsworth's staffers gawked in disbelief, Rowley announced with slurred bravado, "By God, I shall order them to charge," and rode off to give the orders—only to fall off his horse. Eventually, Rowley's own staff had to lead him miserably away toward the town. (He would be court-martialed and forced to resign before the end of the war.)[27]

With Biddle succeeding to command of the brigade, the men had little to do except post skirmishers at Willoughby Run and try to guess what the Confederates would do next. They had the luxury of occupying "a line" in the "broad meadows" between the Willoughby Run and the seminary "a few hundred yards behind us," and without much more than an errant shell from Oak Hill scattering splinters around them. Across the run was a small farm owned by Emmanuel Harman, a Baltimore merchant, but operated by his sister, Susan Harman Castle. The two-story brick farmhouse was occupied by Confederate skirmishers who used its elevation to take potshots at Biddle's men and whizz long-range fire at James Cooper's 1st Pennsylvania battery near the seminary. This annoyed Biddle and Wadsworth sufficiently that they ordered up a company of the 80th New York to clear the rebels out of their little fortress. Beyond that small clash, it was not until after three o'clock, as the rumbling from the far side of the ridgelines quickened in volume, that Biddle's brigade understood that its hour had come. "A heavy reinforced line of the enemy" could be seen massing in the woods on the other side of Willoughby Run "for a grand charge." They appeared first on the Cashtown Pike as "a long column of rebels," but then "filed off to our left . . . a mile so in our front," followed by another ominous column which also "faced into line" behind them. Charles Wainwright, the 1st Corps' artillery chief, sat among the four batteries he had placed on Seminary Ridge and could see that "when they advanced they outflanked us at least half a mile on our left."[28]

This "long column" was Pender's division, with its four big brigades under James Henry Lane, Edward Thomas, Alfred M. Scales, and Abner Perrin. Of these four, Scales, Lane, and Perrin—an avalanche of 5,000 men—would face off against Biddle's untempered brigade. Despite their size, many of these Confederate units were actually not much more acclimatized to war than their opposite numbers. A captain in the 16th North Carolina "was struck" by a shell splinter "and his head was cut and scratched in several places," making him jump up and run for the rear, screaming, "I'm dead, I'm dead." (The colonel of the 16th dryly told two stretcher-bearers to chase after him and "go and take that dead man off—if you can catch him.") The 26th North Carolina, in Pettigrew's brigade, had been under serious fire only once before, at Malvern Hill, and its colonel was a twenty-one-year-old named Henry King Burgwyn.[29]

Pettigrew's plan was to send his men in by "echelon by battalion," so that they would cross Willoughby Run and hit the Iron Brigade in staggered order, starting on the Federals' right. This maneuver would drain troops out of the Iron Brigade's left flank and weaken it to the point that it would collapse easily when Pettigrew's last unit went over the run against it. "Attention! Every man was up and ready and every officer at his post," wrote the bandmaster of the 26th North Carolina, and in they went, wading the run and fumbling through the "briars and underbrush" on the far side. Abner Perrin had his men up in line as well, and gave them a little speech and instructions not to fire their rifles but "give them the bayonet." Perrin, "his horse, his uniform, and his flashing sword," would be leading from the front.

The Westerners in their black Hardee hats were not unready for them— *Come on, Johnny! Come on!* was what Rufus Dawes remembered the men in his 6th Wisconsin crying—and "as the Confederates crossed the run," the men in the 2nd Wisconsin "tried to make it lively for them." The 26th North Carolina, as the first of Pettigrew's echelon, took the Iron Brigade's fire full in the face. The color sergeant was killed "quite early in the advance"; a private from Company F picked up the flag, was shot once, stumbled, stood back up, and cried, *Come on, boys* until another bullet knocked him down for good. A captain picked up the colors, only to be "killed a moment or two later," and then Henry Burgwyn, the "Boy Colonel," picked up the flag and called out to the regiment to "dress on the colors." He turned to hand the colors to a private, only to be hit in the left side, puncturing both lungs; the impact of the shot twisted him around and entangled Burgwyn in the flag. His lieutenant colonel took the colors in hand, and shouting, *Twenty-Sixth, follow me!* managed to lead them unscathed until they had almost cleared Herbst's Woods, when a bullet hit him "in the back of the neck, just below the brain" and "crashed through the jaw and mouth."[30]

All told, the 26th North Carolina lost 549 out of the 843 men it had lined up that afternoon; its regimental flag went through thirteen sets of hands. But as bloodied as the 26th North Carolina was in Herbst's Woods, the rest of Pettigrew's brigade crossed the run and wrapped itself pythonlike around the 19th Indiana and 24th Michigan, and began pushing the entire Iron Brigade backward. Henry Morrow, the colonel of the 24th, told his men to "withhold their fire until the enemy should come within short range of our guns," but "their advance was not checked, and they came on with rapid strides, yelling like demons." This produced "the bloodiest and most stubbornly contested point in all the fighting of that day," wrote a captain in the 24th Michigan; in front of the 19th Indiana, the 11th North Carolina lost its colonel and senior major, and (by at least one calculation) was suffering five or six men shot every sixty seconds as they advanced.

To avoid being cut off in the woods, the sergeant major of the 19th Indiana, Asa Blanchard, was sent off to find Wadsworth and see if anything could be done to relieve the pressure. But Wadsworth had no reserves; the best he could do was order the nine-months' men of the 151st Pennsylvania out of their protected pocket between the seminary and the woods and send them in a desperate, headlong charge at Pettigrew's right-flank regiments. The colonel of the 151st, George McFarland, hadn't even gotten the regiment properly deployed before "the enemy greeted me with a volley which brought several of my men down," and in short order the 151st broke and scampered for "the temporary breastwork" near the Lutheran seminary. The unprotected Iron Brigade began backing out of Herbst's Woods "by echelon of alternate battalions," turning and stopping six times to beat back the Confederate pressure. At one point, the 24th Michigan's colonel, Henry Morrow, "took the flag to rally the remnant of his devoted band" until a private from Company E grabbed it from Morrow's hands, saying, "The Colonel of the Twenty-fourth Michigan shall not carry the colors while I am alive." The words were hardly out of his mouth before a bullet killed him.[31]

The 24th Michigan made its last stand at the barricade of "rails, stumps, etc." that Paul's and Baxter's brigades had thrown up earlier that day on the west side of the seminary; their fellow Westerners in the 2nd Wisconsin groped their way back to a brick house next to the seminary building owned by one of the seminary professors. The Western men were joined there by the fragments of Chapman Biddle's brigade, whose skirmish outpost at the Harman farmstead was easily overrun. Biddle, down to three regiments, wasted no time pulling back to the ridge, although in the process he was "hit in the head" by a stray bullet. "The sound of the blow was distinctly heard" by Theodore Gates, the colonel of the 80th New York, who was "conversing" with Biddle "in rear of the line," and at first "both gentlemen thought the injury of a serious character." It turned out to be only a scalp wound, although it was "very painful" and Biddle had to submit to having his "head bandaged." His men would join the Federal stand on Seminary Ridge, and if they failed there, "the whole thing would turn into a perfect rout."[32]

CHAPTER TWELVE

Go in, South Carolina!

T HE EIGHTEEN GUNS of the 1st Corps assembled near the seminary gave
the retreating Federals a brief respite. Eleven of the guns—James Cooper's battery, Greenleaf Stevens' 5th Maine, and a two-gun section of the 1st
New York, had been bunched tightly on the south side of the seminary building, with barely five yards (instead of the regulation fourteen) between their
hubs. "This line of artillery opened" fire "as if every lanyard was pulled by the
same hand . . . and Seminary Ridge blazed with a solid sheet of flame." The
artillery stopped Pettigrew's onrushing brigade short of the "little rough rail
intrenchment" around the seminary building and bought the battered Federal survivors one last breathing spell to establish a line "curved slightly back
on either side" of the seminary building, with the "rail entrenchment" on the
west side forming a slight bulge at the center.

The pause also gave any novice who wanted to know what a battlefield
looked like a good opportunity to judge. From the seminary, George McFarland of the 151st Pennsylvania could see an orchard where "the trees . . . had
been cut off or rather splintered and shivered from the roots up at least ten
feet, as the lightning splinters tough young trees," littering the ground with a
carpet of tree limbs. A veteran in the 150th New York remembered "trees cut
and marred by bullets and shells, broken branches hanging down; wounded
men walking and limping towards the rear, some sitting or lying on the
ground; dead men here and there; straggling members of defeated and scattered regiments wandering to the rear." William Peel, a lieutenant in the 11th
Mississippi, belatedly catching up to the rest of Joe Davis' brigade later that
day, saw "implements of war . . . scattered in every direction," and "here and

there lay horses in every conceivable degree of mutilation." Occurring in the path of the war tornado were moments of almost Romantic innocence. A soldier in the 53rd North Carolina, dipping his tin cup in "a puddle of muddy water," was about to drink "and just as I raised it to my lips, I discovered a wounded Yank a few feet from me." The North Carolinian "gave him the cup," reflecting afterward that "five minutes before I would have shot him, but instead of an enemy he was only a helpless man."[1]

> *Not hate, but glory made their chiefs contend,*
> *And each brave foe was in his soul a friend.*

The helpers, however, were not always motivated by benevolence. John Cabell Early noticed two Confederate stretcher-bearers who were "lagging behind" with more of a mind to dodging the front lines than helping the wounded. The fifteen-year-old Early, who was acting as a volunteer aide on the staff of his uncle, Jubal Early, "insisted that they should go at once to the front with me." The surly stretcher-bearers told him what he could do with himself, some "lively words were used on both sides," and finally they told the boy to get off his horse and try consequences with them. He promptly dismounted and tore off his jacket preparatory to a fistfight, but at that moment another officer came by, "gave all three of us a severe scolding," and all of them went back to their original business.[2]

Those moments of help were balanced by visions of an inferno, populated by ghouls. Lieutenant Peel remembered seeing one wounded man who "must have been lying down when he was struck, for a Minnie ball had struck him near the top of his head & appeared to go directly in." The man's brains were lying out—"quite a quantity," as Peel recalled—but he was still alive, "perfectly unconscious" but "breathing freely." William Cheek of the 26th North Carolina, who had helped carry his dying Boy Colonel, Henry King Burgwyn, to the rear, was helped by "some South Carolina lieutenant"— who then proceeded to filch Burgwyn's pocket watch. Cheek indignantly "demanded the watch . . . of my colonel," and "cocking my rifle and taking aim," Cheek threatened "that I would kill him as sure as powder would burn." The pickpocket gingerly replaced the watch. The temperamental John Cabell Early found a dead Federal officer "with his pockets turned out" near the almshouse; anything of value had been removed, but scattered beside the body were papers granting the man a furlough to go home and be married and a letter from his bride-to-be "expressing her happiness at the approaching event." Sometimes, random cruelty mixed itself with the mercies. In front of the 14th Brooklyn, a corporal from Company C, "who had been wounded in the advance earlier in the day" around the railroad cut, was lying dead some distance in front. "Four of his comrades" decided to retrieve the body, and dashed out with a tent canvas, rolled the body onto the shelter-half, and carried it toward the 14th's position, with each man holding a corner. They never made it back. A Confederate shell "exploded right among them," killing three of the rescuers, and tearing off the leg of the fourth. "His scream of agony was heard even above the vast, pulsating roar of the battle."[3]

The 1st Corps' respite did not last long. Both Doubleday and Wadsworth gamely rode among the jumbled-up knots of men, bracing them for the next attack, and "mingled groups" from the 149th and 150th Pennsylvania joined the Iron Brigade at the seminary rampart. Doubleday put his own forty-man headquarters escort "around and into the [seminary] building," and even lent a hand at "sighting the artillery." The captain of Robert Beecham's company of the 2nd Wisconsin called together the "handful of men" who had survived the fallback to the seminary, gathered them "around the old regimental flag . . . riddled and rent," and took the occasion to pop open his pocket watch and announce, "It is four o'clock." The "crippled lines of General Pettigrew's Brigade" had halted and been made to lie down, but this only allowed the brigades of Abner Perrin and Alfred Scales to march over and through them, and angle up the last 200 yards toward the seminary barricade. (Perrin remembered that Pettigrew's "poor fellows could scarcely raise a cheer for us as we passed," although one of his sergeants remembered that some of them managed to hoot, *Go in, South Carolina! Go in, South Carolina!*) With Perrin "dashing through the lines of the brigade" on horseback, his South Carolina brigade "threw itself . . . with all its fury" against the barricade. Scales was also moving forward, creeping toward the Stevens and Stewart batteries on either side of the Cashtown Pike in hope of a chance to cut them off.[4]

"For a mile up and down the open fields before us the splendid lines of the veterans of the army of Northern Virginia swept down upon us," remembered Rufus Dawes, from the 6th Wisconsin's perilous seat athwart the railroad. The Union artillery took its time getting the range: "Every shot was fired with care, and Stewart's men . . . worked their guns upon the enemy . . . with the regularity of a machine." (Stevens later calculated that his battery fired off "about fifty-seven rounds of canister" on that spot.) The Iron Brigade—or what was left of it—also waited until the rebels were close enough that they could hear Scales' officers shouting to encourage their men. And then, at "about two hundred yards," the combined weight of the artillery and rifles opened up, and in front of the 7th Wisconsin, "their ranks went down like grass before the scythe." George McFarland of the 151st Pennsylvania stooped down to catch a glimpse under the rolling bank of powder smoke and thought he saw "their lines breaking to the rear." Albert Scales himself went down with a ripping wound to his leg from a shell splinter. But Perrin's brigade swarmed up to Chapman Biddle's fast melting line "with a yell & without firing a gun," the rebels "throwing away their knapsacks and blankets to keep up." The 1st and 14th South Carolina slipped around the flanks of the rail barricade, while the 12th and 13th South Carolina struck Biddle's brigade through "a furious storm, of musketry and shells," forcing Biddle's thinned-out regiments to fall back behind the seminary.[5]

It was (by George McFarland's reckoning) "20 minutes after 4 o'clock," and it was now plainly time to go. Doubleday ordered James Wadsworth to pull out the last of his division. Too late for McFarland: as his 151st Pennsylvania fell back around the north end of the seminary a "great [volley] knocked both legs from under me," and "one of my boys" carried him into one end of the seminary. Too late also for old John Burns. The gouty old constable had limped back toward the seminary along with the Iron Brigade, and there he was wounded three times and left behind for the Confederates to pick up and carry back to his house on Chambersburg Street. (They imagined that they had merely rescued an unarmed old man who had wandered into the line of fire, instead of a civilian belligerent whom they would have been perfectly justified under the conventions of nineteenth-century warfare in shooting out of hand.) Some of the South Carolinians, meanwhile, barged into the seminary from the other end and "captured some ten or more of the panic-stricken enemy who had sought shelter in one of the rooms of the Seminary building."

Other isolated Federals died harder. The last glimpse a captain in the 24th Michigan had as he turned to run was the torn shreds of the regiment's flag, held for the last time by a "wounded soldier," unable to move and lying "on his right side," but still clutching the colors. Beside him was a wounded sergeant, unable to load a rifle but still gamely tearing cartridges with his teeth, and handing the opened cartridges to the few men still around him. A soldier in the 143rd Pennsylvania saw a Southern skirmisher get close enough to Stevens' Maine battery to lay a hand on one of the pieces and cry triumphantly, "This gun is mine." The Union gunner, with his friction tube and lanyard at the breech, snarled back, *Damn you, take it then,* pulled the lanyard, and blew the overeager rebel to fragments. A rebel officer, also too eager to get at the guns in Stewart's battery, had his head cracked by one of the gunners, wielding a rammer like a club. That was enough to make the artillerymen take thought for their precious guns, and Stewart's and Stevens' batteries were hastily "limbered up & passed through the town." Two of Stewart's guns had been smashed by rebel artillery fire, and rebel skirmishers were able to bring down the wheel horse of one of the 1st New York Light Artillery's pieces, stalling the gun in the middle of the Cashtown Pike and forcing its abandonment.[6]

Now there was another stream of Union fugitives, pouring off Seminary Ridge into the Cashtown Pike, and heading into the town in tandem with the remains of Baxter's, Paul's, and Stone's brigades. Some of Biddle's brigade and the Iron Brigade made off southward from the seminary, where they were protected by covering fire from cavalry squads posted by John Buford, and could skirt entirely around the west and south sides of the town. (Lane's North Carolina brigade might have cut them off at the Fairfield Road, but Buford staged a small-scale bluffing attack, and, for the only time under fire in the Civil War, Lane formed his brigade into a Waterloo-style hollow square to repel cavalry.) But the rest were piling on top of one another into a town whose layout none of them knew, and where they were bound to collide at right angles with the disorganized and desperate refugees of the 11th Corps. Unless someone figured out how to organize an escape path for approximately 8,000 frightened and demoralized men, none of them might ever make it to the refuge of Cemetery Hill in a better condition than the one for which the hill had been originally designed.[7]

"From the time that Lee's army had crossed the Potomac we knew there was trouble ahead for us," wrote Harriet Bayley, who lived on a farm just north of Gettysburg. But for most of Gettysburg, that "trouble" had already come and gone, in the form of Jubal Early's brief passage through the town a week before. "The funds of the bank and the goods of the merchants had been removed to places promising more security," recalled Henry Eyster Jacobs, the nineteen-year-old son of Pennsylvania College mathematics professor Michael Jacobs, but "as to the position of the two armies there was much speculation but no information." Harriet Bayley had no "thought that a battle would be fought"; the worst she could imagine might come from "reckless raiders and their foraging expeditions." Charles Tyson, who operated a photographic studio on Chambersburg Street, opened his gallery for business that morning, since the other stores were "all open and doing business." Classes in both the college and the seminary were ready, despite noticeable absenteeism, to begin "prayers and recitations as usual." The town boys who had gathered curiously around the main encampment of Yankee cavalrymen behind the seminary were disappointed when the horse soldiers were bugled to boots-and-saddles and trotted off westward, and a number of them were so oblivious to what was happening that several of them—including young Daniel Skelly and Albertus McCreary—tried to follow them, finally settling on climbing the trees on Oak Ridge to keep their newfound heroes in view. They were soon joined by "men and boys from town . . . not having the slightest conception of the proximity of the two armies." A few tried to tease information out of "a number of mounted pickets standing by the roadside" about the cavalry's movement beyond the town.[8]

The answer came first in the form of "skirmish fire . . . about three miles" from Daniel Skelly's leafy perch on Oak Ridge. The sound of firing "seemed to be coming nearer and nearer," until presently shells "began to plow" up the ground around them. Daniel Skelly heard something pass "dangerously near the top of the tree I was on," and when Albertus McCreary saw a shell fall "only a short distance from us" and explode, he concluded "that I had better make for home." Up in his tree, Skelly saw the civilians make "a general stampede toward town," and he made haste to slide down from the tree and join the retreat. From the rear balcony of her home in the town, Catharine Foster was almost amused at the spectacle of seminary students taking an unauthorized dismissal from class and "running down the hill faster than 'Double Quick.'" Over at the college, Martin Colver was on his way to prepare for the eleven o'clock recitation he would face. As he walked the short space between Pennsylvania Hall and Linnaean Hall with "book in hand," another student, Horatio James Watkins, called to him from a third-floor window in Pennsylvania Hall and asked whether Colver could hear "shooting." Colver was about to answer no, when for the first time he noticed "the ominous sounds."

Colver wanted a good look, and he and a few other students clambered hurriedly up the steps that led to the rooftop cupola of Pennsylvania Hall. There, "not far distant from us," they could see skirmishers "of both armies exchanging bullets—saw the first batteries planted on our side . . . heard a shell from the first rebel battery pass in close proximity to our ears." The shell failed to explode, but that was enough to send the college boys clattering back down the cupola steps—passing on the way down the mathematics professor, Michael Jacobs, guiding a party of blue-coated signalmen with flags and telescopes on the way up "to make observations from the tower." Down in the classrooms, the college president, Henry L. Baugher, was struggling to hold the attention of his class of seniors through all the stair clumping inside and the growing military rumbling outside. "Amid repeated failures on the part of the class," Baugher wearily gave up. "We will close and see what is going on," he said, "for you know nothing about the lesson anyhow." Another "solid shot went through the roof of the College" and lodged in the cupola.[9]

Just as no one in the town had been ready for a battle, no one in the 1st Corps or the 11th Corps seems to have given much thought to how they were to get through the town. Otis Howard had waited so optimistically for the arrival of Henry Slocum and the 12th Corps that he had failed to make any plan for conducting a fallback to Cemetery Hill—no directions for moving the ammunition wagons and their teams, no plan for reserving certain routes through the town for the artillery, no staff officers posted at critical intersections to direct the reflux of two Federal infantry corps. (Almost the only instructions anyone thought to give them were orders to clear civilians off the streets and into their cellars, anticipating that "the rebels will shell the town.") Even in the last few minutes of the stand at the seminary, word was still being passed along, "Hold a little longer, the Twelfth Corps is coming." A staff officer whose path crossed Abner Doubleday's assured Doubleday that he "had passed Slocum's (Twelfth) Corps only a little ways out." *Where is he?* Doubleday lit up. *When did you see him?* And then, "turning to me with a savage expression," Doubleday lapsed back into skepticism and growled, "Get out of my way, son, we all know where Slocum was this morning. Where is he now? Who in hell are you, anyhow?"[10]

On a map, the town of Gettysburg presents a neat grid of small streets, intersecting at clear right angles, and grouped around the diamond. But Gettysburg is also a town of alleys running behind the streets, crisscrossing in an internal labyrinth, sometimes ending abruptly, frequently turning off into unlooked-for dead ends. Into these streets, from the north and west, poured the dislocated crumblings of the 1st and 11th Corps, knowing only that escape meant a hill somewhere south of the town. "The streets . . . were soon filled with a confused mass of troops, artillery, and ambulances," with no one visibly in charge. Both Carl Schurz and Abner Doubleday would swear afterward that "there was no element of dissolution in it," that their men even "walked leisurely from the Seminary to the town, and did not run." In one sense, this is true: regiments, or what was left of them, managed to stay more or less together, grouped around their colors or behind a junior officer who thought he knew where to go. But even Schurz conceded that "the retreat through the town was of course more or less disorderly, the streets being crowded with vehicles of every description, which offered to the passing troops exceedingly troublesome obstructions." Someone, or some officers, tried to rise above the chaos, and at one intersection shouts of "First Corps this way" and "Eleventh Corps this way" went up; but no one could tell who was giving the orders or what street or alley was meant by *this way*.[11]

As the pursuing rebel infantry pressed into the streets, fear sparkled viciously through the tangled masses of Federal soldiers. Men began breaking away down alleys that ran, like the one used by the 82nd Illinois, "into a cul-de-sac," and together the men had to "have a heavy, tight board fence knocked down to make it possible to proceed." An officer in the 80th New York saw "an opening like an alley leading through to the next street parallel to the one I was on . . . to regain the road to the right which I should have taken" in the first place. The streets now "became a battleground," and the crowds of soldiers "overflowed into yards and alleys," struggling to escape capture. Men from the 150th Pennsylvania were "leaping fences, crossing gardens, or passing through shops and dwellings in order to reach streets to which the pursuing forces had not yet penetrated." Henry Morrow, the colonel of the 24th Michigan, staggered into Gettysburg, bleeding from a wound to the head; he was taken in by Mary McAllister, "a lady of Gettysburg," who bandaged his wound, but he refused her offer to hide him or give him a civilian coat, and was gobbled up by pursuing Confederates as soon as he ventured out into the streets again. The adventurous Prussian Otto von Fritsch was stopped by an "excited fellow" who grabbed the bridle of Fritsch's horse. The rebel failed to see the heavy Saxon cavalry saber Fritsch carried. "You be damned," Fritsch snarled, "and cut off his hand." Fritsch spurred his horse down the street, but lost himself in the maze of alleys, "surrounded by high fence rails." With rebels closing in from behind, he put the horse to the fence "with an enormous effort" and jumped it clear "and made off towards Cemetery Hill."[12]

Many others had less happy prospects. Alexander Schimmelpfennig turned into an alley off Washington Street, only to face a dead end, with Confederates in hot haste behind him. He vaulted over the Garlach family's back fence (the Garlach house faced onto Baltimore Street), and frantically squeezed himself into "a wooden culvert" over "an old water course in our yard," where the exasperated Prussian would hide for three more days. Corporal Leander Wilcox of the 151st Pennsylvania burst in the back door of Catharine Foster's house on Washington Street, and was hidden in Foster's potato bin. The chaplain of the 90th Pennsylvania, Horatio Howells, was tending wounded men in a makeshift hospital in Christ Lutheran Church. Staggering from the church after a shell hit the roof, Howells only appeared to jubilant South Carolinians as another Federal officer, and they shot him down on the church steps.[13]

As the overcast sky began its first fading, clumps of raggedly battered men from the 1st and 11th Corps began toiling up from the town toward the gatehouse on Cemetery Hill. There, with fat whitish-gray columns of smoke and the erratic staccato of rifle fire ascending behind them, the survivors of the day's fighting came into view, some in reasonably good order, some in companies, some in dribbles, some (mostly 1st Corps men) picking their way around the edge of the town to find the Emmitsburg Road, all drooping in dejection and exhaustion. They found, on arrival, that Oliver Otis Howard had prepared a crisscrossing pattern of 12-pounder Napoleons and 3-inch Ordnance Rifles from the two 11th Corps batteries he had held in reserve, plus the three 11th

Corps batteries that made it back to the hill through the town. Together with the six 1st Corps batteries, there were forty-five guns atop Cemetery Hill—enough to blow any would-be Confederate attackers in the other direction.[14]

The infantry was another matter. After sending off Charles Coster's brigade to its untimely demise, Otis Howard had only the four regiments of Orland Smith's brigade on Cemetery Hill, and it was a good question in Howard's mind whether "the broken regiments . . . emerging from Gettysburg" could be rallied to stand there, much less to fight. "When the very first of the troops came up the pike there was a little reluctance manifested to face about, march back and form a new line of battle." The Iron Brigade had come up the road to Gettysburg that morning with between 1,800 and 1,900 men in the ranks; of that number, 1,212 were either dead, prisoners, wounded and hors de combat, or simply wandering somewhere in the opaque gloom of the smoking battlefield. Even under the most favorable conditions, units which lost 36 percent of their number in action were virtually incapacitated; a loss of 60 percent would would invite a rout. Too many pieces in the vital communication chain of officers, noncoms, and privates would be gone, and the result would be ill-sorted muddles of soldiers who had no idea who was giving direction, and no idea whether the strangers on either side of them would stay or run. By that standard, the Iron Brigade, which had lost 65 percent of its strength, was a military derelict; the 24th Michigan, which set the Iron Brigade's record with an 80 percent casualty rate, had been pounded into a bloody wreck. The 1st Corps as a whole was in even worse straits: of the 8,300 men who had followed John Reynolds' call to come up to Gettysburg, 69 percent had been killed, wounded, captured, or simply gone missing at the end of the day. The 11th Corps was only marginally healthier. Otis Howard had started July 1st with 6,000 men under his command; he was ending it without 53 percent of them.[15]

If these men were going to be rallied, Otis Howard would have to do it personally. The first 11th Corps regiment to work its way up to the gatehouse was the 45th New York. At its head was the disheartened Georg von Amsberg, who muttered something to Howard "in German—his English was not at his command just then." Howard may not have understood the words, but he caught the meaning clearly enough, and standing at a "stone wall, near the edge of the city," Howard called out to the regiment's color sergeant, "Sergeant, plant your flag down there in that stone wall." The sergeant looked at him dumbly, then collected his wits and said, "All right, if you will go with me, I will!" And so the one-armed Howard grasped the flag with his remaining hand, tucking the staff under his stump, and "the regiment seeing the General with difficulty carrying their colors under his one arm, raised a hearty shout and followed upon the double quick" to set the flag in the wall.

Adelbert Ames, whose brigade had been crushed on Blocher's Knoll, came up next, and remarked almost as woefully that Barlow was probably dead and Barlow's division was "all cut to pieces." *That's no way to talk,* Howard curtly reined him in: "Do what you can, Ames, to gather the fragments and extend the line to the right." A colonel with "a very wilted and drooping appearance" ignored Howard's order; Howard "promptly put him under arrest and put another officer in charge of the regiment." Gradually, as they came dribbling in, Howard posted the remains of the 11th Corps to the right of Orland Smith's brigade, so that they all formed a north-facing crescent around Cemetery Hill, backed up by the artillery and protected in front by what was left of the 25th Ohio—some sixty men—as skirmishers "in the outskirts of the town."

Otis Howard had made as many mistakes as anyone else that day, but he did two things which were incontestably right: he fixed on Cemetery Hill as the point to hold from his first moment at Gettysburg and he made the wrecked debris of two infantry corps, who should have been reduced to nervelessness, stop and dig in. There was "no hurry, no confusion in his mind," wrote one admiring veteran of the 25th Ohio. And no more Chancellorsvilles, either. It was Otis Howard's finest hour, and he was taking the first steps on the path that would make him (in William Tecumseh Sherman's estimate) a corps commander of "the utmost skill, nicety, and precision" by the end of the war. "I have seen many men in action," wrote a journalist afterward, "but never so imperturbably cool as this General of the Eleventh Corps."[16]

Otis Howard's hour, however, would prove, almost literally, to be not much more than an hour. Winfield Scott Hancock, bearing George Meade's directive "to assume command," arrived on Cemetery Hill sometime in the late afternoon, although the estimates of exactly *when* he showed up vary to the point of suspicion. Thirteen years after the battle, Hancock insisted that he rode up to the cemetery gatehouse "by 3:30 P.M., having had over two hours in which to travel the thirteen miles" between Gettysburg and Taneytown. What Hancock wanted, in the years after the battle, was the credit for having taken command and organized Union resistance on Cemetery Hill all by himself, and saving the Army of the Potomac from having the insult of rout added to the injury of defeat. But an arrival this early would have put Hancock on Cemetery Hill even before Early's attack on Blocher's Knoll, and Hancock undermined his own claim by describing how he found "our troops retreating in disorder and confusion from the town" and "General Howard . . . endeavoring to stop the retreat of his troops, many of whom were passing over the hill and down the Baltimore pike." Hancock's own first dispatch back to Meade is timed at 5:25, and refers to Hancock's having "arrived here an hour since." Organizing "a position in the cemetery" had been well under way, Hancock added, which could not have been so if Hancock had arrived any earlier than five o'clock. Howard actually noted Hancock's arrival time as "4 p.m.," and Charles Howard, likewise, fixed Hancock's arrival "at about 4:25," so that Hancock found Charles Howard's one-armed brother "already occupying Cemetery Ridge." But even an arrival time of 4:25 may be too early, since the last of the 1st Corps refugees do not seem to have reached Cemetery Hill until sometime between five and six o'clock.[17]

Whatever the exact timing of Hancock's arrival, Howard was looking for Slocum, not Hancock, at that moment, and he was even more surprised when Hancock proceeded to announce that "he had been ordered to assume command." *Command?* Hancock later insisted that Howard "acquiesced in my assumption of command" and from that point "gave no orders save to the troops of his own corps." Hancock's chief of staff even added that Howard "was pleased that Hancock had come," and declined Hancock's offer to show him the written directive from Meade. But this was not how Howard remembered the moment. Very much to the contrary, he was "deeply mortified," principally because Howard enjoyed a healthy amount of seniority over Hancock in the Volunteer service, and as far as Howard was concerned, Meade's orders only designated Hancock "to represent Meade as Butterfield, the chief of staff, would have done on the field of battle."

But there was more behind Howard's mortification at Meade "superseding me in command of the field by a junior in rank" than just the technicalities of seniority: it would be missed by no one that an order to Hancock to supersede Howard was a gesture of political contempt for the army's senior Republican. In the ranks of the 11th Corps, Hancock's appearance was interpreted as something even more ominous: that Hancock had been sent by Meade "to withdraw his forces, and not attempt to hold the position he had chosen." (This, said an officer in the 25th Ohio, "was talked about and believed by nearly all the officers in the corps.")[18]

Rather than happily surrendering responsibility to Hancock on Cemetery Hill, Abner Doubleday remembered that Howard immediately burst out in protest: "Why, Hancock, you cannot give any orders here! I am in command and rank you!" Hancock had evidently anticipated that this would not be easy, and replied, "I am aware of that, General, but I have written orders in my pocket from General Meade which I will show you if you wish to see them." Howard would not budge: "No. I do not doubt your word, General Hancock, but you can give no orders while I am here." By now, the silliness of arguing over precedence while two badly mauled infantry corps were struggling to dig themselves into Cemetery Hill began to dawn on both Howard and Hancock, although it is not clear which one was the first to offer a face-saving compromise. Abner Doubleday's chief of staff later claimed that Hancock (who had nothing but his own staffers around him to enforce his authority) gave in first, saying, "Very well, General Howard, I will second any order that you have to give," as if duplicating orders was sufficient to preserve the authority of each general. But he also added a comment which must have chilled Howard. "General Meade has also directed me to select a field on which to fight this battle in rear of Pipe Creek"—something which appeared nowhere in Meade's orders to Hancock and which no one afterward would admit having heard Meade say. What pulled the stinger on that warning was Hancock's hasty assurance that he was willing to endorse Howard's stand on Cemetery Hill as "the strongest position by nature upon which to fight a battle that I ever saw, and if it meets your approbation I will select this as the battlefield."[19]

Less than half a mile to the east, Hancock could see the thickly wooded eminence of another hill, named for the farmer, Henry Culp, whose house and barns lay at its north foot. Howard had no opinion that Culp's Hill could be turned into a second artillery platform to match Cemetery Hill. But Culp's Hill did overlook the Baltimore Pike, which linked Gettysburg to the railhead at Westminster, Maryland. If he was indeed going to make a fight of it here, he would need that pike secured. So Hancock took it upon himself to order the woozy remnants of the 1st Corps over to Culp's Hill, with Stevens' 5th Maine battery posted to cover the saddle between Culp's Hill and Cemetery Hill. Hancock sent his report back to Meade with William Mitchell, "informing him that I could hold the position until nightfall, and that I thought that the place to fight our battle."[20]

Otis Howard was writing to Meade, too, although his message was a complaint about Hancock's usurpation of his seniority, the opening gun in an ongoing war of words between Howard and Hancock which lasted for the rest of their lives. "I believe I have handled these two corps to-day from a little past 11 until 4," Howard complained, and all that Hancock did after that was to assist "in carrying out orders which I had already issued." Hancock's assertion that he had been sent to rescue the 1st and 11th Corps from disaster "has mortified me and will disgrace me." In an army with a heavy McClellanite tilt at the top, and stacked against a corps commander with as enviable a reputation as Hancock's, this was a debate the overstigmatized Howard was doomed to lose. But looked at closely, it was Howard, and not Hancock, who saved Cemetery Hill as the Army of the Potomac's redoubt, and who (in all likelihood) carried out John Reynolds' determination to compel George Meade to fight at Gettysburg.[21]

In the gray twilight, Henry Slocum's 12th Corps finally swung into view on the Baltimore Pike, "arriving there in the evening." Slocum would never adequately explain why he had waited for three hours at Two Taverns, within earshot of what could have been heard as a major battle, before coming up to Gettysburg. "In the morning, or very soon afterwards, we heard rumblings of artillery," wrote one man in the 27th Indiana, and the "firing early became so distinct and rapid that many were apprehensive that the decisive battle . . . might be on." If Slocum had pressed on, "the distance . . . might have been traversed by noon." But Slocum was operating under the Pipe Creek Circular. As Abner Doubleday put it, Slocum was anxious not to "antagonize the plans of the General-in-Chief," and he would not take the chance of irritating Meade by leaving Two Taverns until Meade's countermand arrived around four o'clock. But once on the road, Slocum pounded ahead till "men fell out of the ranks in squads by the roadside for a brief rest." The advance guard of the 12th Corps finally reached Cemetery Hill around six o'clock, to the "notes of the bugle and the inspiring strains of bands." One of Slocum's divisions (under the onetime territorial governor of "Bleeding Kansas," the six-foot, six-inch John White Geary) was posted on the left of Cemetery Hill, where a gentle ridgeline dangled southward, and the other alongside the gnarled bits of the 1st Corps who had been sent to Culp's Hill. In the process, Slocum's provost guard spread out across the Baltimore Pike to begin snagging nearly 1,500 stragglers and returning them to the ranks, while George Stannard's nine-months' Vermont brigade and the 7th Indiana (on detached duty guarding the 1st Corps ammunition train) showed up to put some modest weight back into the 1st Corps.[22]

The arrival of Henry Slocum and the 12th Corps put a practical end to the jostling between Howard and Hancock, since Slocum outranked them both. Moreover, Meade had instructed Hancock to defer to Slocum when the 12th Corps finally arrived—although, even then, Hancock could not resist trying to take charge of Slocum's lead division before Slocum himself galloped up to the gatehouse in the darkening twilight. (In his after-action report, a tight-lipped Slocum was at pains to claim that his first division was actually deployed "agreeably to suggestion from General Howard.") Hancock had briefly worried that "the enemy will mass in town and make an effort to take this position," and Doubleday was frantic that "there was nothing to prevent the enemy from encircling and capturing us all, for every division of the Confederate forces . . . was either in line of battle or very near the town." But as the last light died away, "no very serious demonstrations were made against our new position." Otto von Fritsch remembered that "everything remained quiet," while "plenty of cartridges were distributed, and, now and then, a box of crackers was carried to a starved regiment."[23]

In the twilight, Confederate skirmishers began peppering the Union positions on Cemetery Hill with sporadic fire. Union soldiers began knock-

ing down "headstones and iron fence" in the cemetery to clear fields of fire
and make room for the artillery. But even that died away after dark, and in
"a lower room of the gate house of the Gettysburg Cemetery . . . six or seven
generals" gathered around a barrel with a "burning tallow candle stuck in
the neck of a bottle on top of it." They listened "to the accounts of those
who had been in the battle of the day . . . discussing what might have been
and finally all agreeing in the hope that General Meade . . . would decide to
fight the battle of the morrow on the ground on which we then were." This
impromptu debriefing broke up, and the commanders wandered back to their
units to "lay down, wrapt in our cloaks, with the troops among the gravestones." None of them afterward remembered commenting on the irony of
their position—whether the Army of the Potomac had been digging its own
grave on that hill. There was nothing but "profound stillness in the graveyard,
broken by no sound" but the snoring of the exhausted men, the nervous paw-
ing of the artillery horses, "and sudden rumblings mysteriously floating on the
air from a distance all around."[24]

CHAPTER THIRTEEN

If the enemy is there to-morrow, we must attack him

FOR AN EVENT which has been the subject of so much relentless historical study, professional and amateur alike, there remain surprisingly large
gaps in the record of the Gettysburg battle, and none of them is more peculiar at this juncture than the invisibility of Robert E. Lee on the afternoon
of July 1st. Once Lee joined Harry Heth on Herr Ridge around two o'clock,
almost all mention of Lee evaporates. George Henry Mills of the 16th North
Carolina (in Dorsey Pender's division) saw "Gens. Lee, A.P. Hill, Longstreet
and others watching the fighting with their glasses" near the Cashtown Pike.
Just as Pettigrew launched his attack on the Iron Brigade in Herbst's Woods,
a soldier in the 52nd North Carolina crossed Willoughby Run and saw "General Lee . . . sitting on his horse just across the Run, and we boys cheered
him. He raised his hat. It was about 3:15 in the afternoon." Willie Pegram,
who commanded an artillery battalion in Hill's corps, was rewarded with a
compliment from Lee, which also locates Lee on the west side of the fighting.
Coleman Anderson, acting as a courier for Ewell, found Lee around "4:30
o'clock that afternoon . . . standing alone on an eminence in an open field,
some distance to the right of Heth's division, with the bridle rein of Traveller
thrown over his right arm and looking anxiously through his field glasses
at . . . Cemetery Ridge."[1]

Still, even in the absence of a trail of witnesses, it is hard to survey the
resounding success and coordination of the late afternoon attack that swept
the 1st and 11th Corps off their feet without seeing the hand of Robert E. Lee
at work. The first set of attacks that day, by Heth and then by Rodes, had been

thoughtless impulses, embarrassingly uncoordinated, and easily rebuffed by hastily deployed Union forces. Three hours later, after Lee's arrival, a second series of attacks (beginning with the arrival of Jubal Early's division) steps off in perfectly timed harmony and support, and rolls over two Union corps with almost no hindrance. If this does not bear Lee's thumbprint, there is no knowing what does. Once having driven the Federal infantry off Seminary Ridge, Lee seems to have expected Powell Hill to keep moving, and to drive the broken refugees through the town and off the flat-topped eminence Lee could see on the horizon. He even sent one of his staffers, Lindsay Long, "to make a reconnaissance of the Federal position," and we know that at least one order Lee gave was to the chief of his artillery reserve to find "positions on the right" along Seminary Ridge which could "enfilade the valley between our position and the town and the enemy's batteries next the town" and begin "a flank movement against the enemy in his new position."

But this was not, after all, the way Lee liked to do business. Instead of allowing his corps commanders to take charge on the field, Lee had been required to take charge *of* them and get them moving properly, and this was not his preferred modus operandi. Hill, who had started the day being surprised by the presence of Federal troops in his path, was now wary of making any more such unanticipated discoveries, and his notion of pressing the fleeing enemy was to allow Abner Perrin's brigade to move into the town, "taking position after position of the enemy" until Hill was satisfied they had gone as far forward as they could go with safety. "The want of cavalry had been and was again seriously felt," Hill later explained. But what he really meant was that he was determined not to make that morning's mistake a second time in the afternoon, with Lee watching: "Prudence led me to be content with what had been gained." And after adding that the two divisions of his corps that had borne the brunt of the fighting—Heth's and Dorsey Pender's—were "exhausted and necessarily disordered," Hill allowed the momentum which had carried him over Seminary Ridge to leak away. That Hill had an entire, unengaged division under Richard Heron Anderson and two uncommitted brigades from Pender's division, halted back at Herr Ridge, went unnoticed in Hill's battle report that fall.[2]

Not unnoticed, however, by officers in his command. David McIntosh, who commanded an artillery battalion in Hill's corps, thought it was "almost incomprehensible" that "the Seminary Ridge should not then have been occupied with Confederate artillery to play upon the opposing heights" and give it enough pounding to "have led to an abandonment" of Cemetery Hill. A surgeon in the 13th South Carolina, writing home to his wife, was sure that "If 'Old Stonewall' had been alive and there, it no doubt would have been done." Dorsey Pender begged Hill to bring up Anderson's division, "but neither Anderson nor his Division were anywhere to be found." Abner Perrin was unsure whether this was "Gen Hill's fault" or whether "it may have been the fault of Anderson himself," but either way, it gave "the enemy during this eventful time" the opportunity to gain "their new position at the Cemetery Hill." If Hill had added Anderson to the pursuit, "it is more than probable that the whole Yankee force would have been captured." And so, almost spontaneously, the tongues in Hill's corps began to wag in criticism. "Hill was a good division commander," the wise heads were already concluding before the campfires had even been lit, "but he is not a superior corps commander. He lacks the mind and sagacity of Jackson."[3]

It has to be said, however, that it was not just "prudence" that led Hill to balk at rushing after the shattered Federal infantry. Between 4:30 and 6:00, the streets and alleys of Gettysburg were filled with a paralyzing accumulation of small gun battles. As the French had learned to their sorrow at Magenta in 1859, the tacticians of the nineteenth century had no workable doctrine that governed street fighting, which is why both attackers and defenders in the Civil War did their best to avoid it. No Confederates moving through Gettysburg were eager to pass by potential knots of Union soldiers hiding in cellars and garrets, lest they find enough courage again to start sniping at Confederates from behind, and so still more rebel soldiers had to be detailed to clear Gettysburg's houses and shops of concealed Federals. Albertus McCreary's family had finally taken refuge in their cellar as the fighting moved down Baltimore Street, and the cloud had hardly passed over before "the outer cellar doors were pulled open and five Confederate soldiers jumped down among us," announcing that "we are looking for Union soldiers." Sure enough, the rebels found "thirteen of our men" in the upper floors of the McCreary house, "some under beds, and one under the piano, and others in closets." A lieutenant in the 6th Louisiana wrote his brother to describe how "we shot them, bayonetted them, & captured more prisoners than we had men in the brigade." Three Union officers (one of them from the Iron Brigade) tried to hide in the pile of store goods and firewood in the Stoever family's home on the town diamond, only to be rousted out "after a diligent search." Even if the Federals surrendered, time was required to round up and disarm them, and then men were needed to escort them to temporary holding pens. As much as Dorsey Pender might have wanted to keep moving through the town, even he had to order the 1st South Carolina "to halt, and go back and take the prisoners out." Chaplain J. Marshall Meredith, in Brockenbrough's Virginia brigade, could hardly move forward into Gettysburg because of the "long and large force of Federal prisoners marching back on the Cashtown road westward."[4]

Confederates who could not find hidden Yankees soon turned their attention to other prizes of war. Liberty Hollinger, on the east side of Gettysburg, remembered that rebels who had satisfied themselves that no Union soldiers were hiding in the Hollinger home proceeded to help "themselves to anything they could find," and "forced the locks" on her father's storehouse "and took what they wanted and then ruined everything else." Nellie Auginbaugh, who was twenty years old and living with her parents on Carlisle Street near the railroad station, saw a "Union soldier . . . shot down right in front of Mother's home." In a few minutes, "a Confederate came along, and he searched the dead man's clothes," only to find "nothing of value" but a "small picture of the dead man and apparently his wife and two little children." Auginbaugh's grandfather carefully slipped out the door and rolled the body up in a blanket—only to have another Confederate come along a few minutes later, unroll the blanket, and go "through the pockets, as the other had done."[5]

Whether it was prisoners or loot, the constant stopping and starting of Confederate regiments and individuals through the town made the possibility of a concerted advance by Hill's corps vanish into the dusk. Like their commander, many of Hill's men were inclined to believe that quite enough of a victory had already been obtained. "We thought the battle of Gettysburg was over," wrote one soldier in the 16th North Carolina, and on the town diamond a Confederate band set up to play "Dixie."

And that, at the end of the day, may also have been Robert E. Lee's conclusion. Thus far, a day which had begun so badly for the Army of Northern Virginia had ended miraculously close to what Lee was hoping for—two entire infantry corps of the Union Army had been wrecked, probably beyond repair, beginning the process whereby Lee hoped to defeat the strung-out Federal pursuers in isolated pieces. Plus, the overcast day really was losing light, and many of his men had marched and fought to the point of exhaustion. If the well-pummeled Yankees were still up on Cemetery Hill tomorrow morning, he had plenty of fresh troops to move in behind them and finish them off, then turn to face the next dribble of Union infantry who would be laid hurriedly and sacrificially in his path on the road to Baltimore or Washington. He would be sorry that Hill had not gone in for a final smash-up, and irked that he had needed to take so much charge of the fighting into his own hands, and he would also tell James Longstreet, when Longstreet rode up later in the afternoon, that he was disappointed that Longstreet's corps was still "three or four miles in our rear." But he would not press the matter now, when the conclusion could be grasped tomorrow anyway. Perhaps, in the end, it was the great mistake of Robert E. Lee at Gettysburg that, having had to reach past his corps commanders to direct operations that afternoon, he did not keep reaching past them. Whatever blame attaches to Ambrose Powell Hill in the twilight of July 1st also attaches to Robert E. Lee for not overriding him.[6]

Lee would not press Dick Ewell, either, in what would soon become famous as the most sensational Confederate misjudgment of the war, and the next great controversy of the battle after Stuart's ride, Meade and the Pipe Creek Circular, and Howard's argument with Hancock. Unlike Hill, Dick Ewell closely followed his two victorious divisions into the town, and by five o'clock Ewell "sat in his saddle under the shade" of a large elm tree outside McClellan's Tavern on "the town square of Gettysburg," chatting "amiably" with the milling throng of jubilant Confederate soldiers in the diamond, and even with "the Federal prisoners gathered about him." There was still some desultory sniping going on in the town, and "General Ewell was fired on from the houses." But Jubal Early then joined Ewell and urged him to go forward and have a look at "the enemy's position" on Cemetery Hill "while the troops were reformed & halted on the right & left of the town." One more all-or-nothing attack against the hill seemed feasible to Ewell, and he ordered Early and Robert Rodes to prepare whatever parts of their divisions they could get sorted out for an attack.

Two considerations pulled Ewell back. First, Extra Billy Smith, commanding Early's reserve brigade, sent over an aide to tell Ewell that his pickets out to the east of Gettysburg were reporting that "a heavy force was . . . moving up in their rear," and until Ewell could be sure of what this meant, he would be foolish to launch the bulk of his two divisions in the other direction. "I don't much believe in this," Ewell added, but he would "suspend [his] movements until I can send & inquire into it." Ewell's other second thought was about Powell Hill. Jubal Early reminded him that an attack on Cemetery Hill by his division would have to be funneled through the streets "by flank or in columns so narrow as to have been subjected to a destructive fire from the batteries on the crest of the hill," and nothing was more fearsome in prospect than infantry, moving in column, heading straight into artillery fire. Perhaps it would be better if Ewell could "communicate with Hill" and see if Hill was also moving to the attack "on the right," rather than trying to deal with the Federals on the hill all by himself, and he sent off an aide, James Power Smith, to find Lee and ask whether he "could go forward and take Cemetery hill." In the meantime, Ewell and Early moved down Baltimore Street, then over to Stratton Street near the German Reformed Church, where Ewell could survey the milling Union forces on Cemetery Hill. He became less and less convinced as he moved about the wisdom of an attack on Cemetery Hill. But he did have Allegheny Johnson's fresh division finally moving within reach,

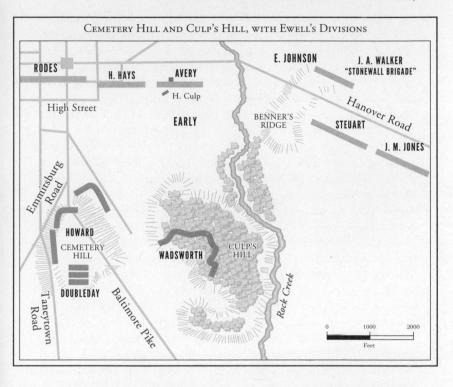

CEMETERY HILL AND CULP'S HILL, WITH EWELL'S DIVISIONS

and even if he did nothing with Early's and Rodes' divisions, he could send Johnson's division to "seize & hold the high peak"—Culp's Hill—which he could see "to our left of Cemetery Hill."[7]

James Power Smith crossed paths with Lee's adjutant, Walter Taylor. The report Lee had from Lindsay Long was that "an attack at that time by the troops then at hand would have been hazardous." If a movement by Powell Hill was "of very doubtful success," then perhaps Ewell could "secure possession of the heights," since Lee "could see the enemy retreating over those hills, without organization and in great confusion. *Press the enemy,* Lee instructed Taylor to tell Ewell, *and secure the heights if possible.* No written order to this effect has survived, if it was ever written at all. But Lee referred to more or less the same directive in his official report when he described sending instructions to Ewell "to carry the hill occupied by the enemy, if he found it practicable," but to "avoid a general engagement until the arrival of the other divisions of the army." *Practicable.* This was an odd word to use (if indeed Lee actually used it). It resembles *practical,* and so it carries some sense of describing a course of action which is useful, direct, or down-to-earth.

But *practicable* is actually more specific. It has the connotation of looking for the most economical way of accomplishing what is (presumably) a practical end—the method easiest to put in play or most likely to achieve the result in mind. *If practicable.* If there is an easy or efficient way of doing this, you may do it; if Ewell is sure this will not entangle him with Federal forces he has not anticipated, and thus will not bring on a "general engagement" from which the rest of the Army of Northern Virginia would have to extricate him, then let the attack proceed.

Once James Power Smith "found General Lee quite well to the right, in an open field, with General Longstreet, dismounted, and with glasses inspecting the position of the south of Cemetery Hill," Lee agreed that "the elevated position in front was . . . the commanding position" of the field. But Hill was not ready to help, nor was Longstreet within striking distance, and so "he had no force on the field with which to take that position." He only "wished him to take Cemetery hill if it were possible," and he was just as interested to know whether Ewell could "send out a party to open communications with Stuart." That was enough for Dick Ewell. Without any distraction provided by Powell Hill, Early was right about the suicidal results of an attack on Cemetery Hill through the town. And since Lee seemed in no urgent hurry, and had left the matter, apparently, "to Gen'l Ewell's discretion," that was the end of that.[8]

This was not the conclusion Jubal Early had been hoping for, or at least not the one he would promote years later. "Unless we go up the hills to night the Yankees will be down upon us in the morning," Early objected. He had already bolted ahead and sent a reconnoitering party up to Culp's Hill, and found it safely deserted. If not an attack on Cemetery Hill, would Ewell at least authorize the occupation of Culp's Hill? But Robert Rodes chose this moment to correct Early: "the men were tired & footsore & he did not think it would do any thing 'one way or the other' " to occupy Culp's Hill. Early turned away in irked disbelief. "If you do not go up there to-night," he warned, "it will cost you ten thousand to get up there to-morrow." Isaac Trimble, who had been tagging along with Ewell as a sort of supernumerary general, also chimed in: "Well, General, we have had a grand success; are you not going to follow it up and push our advantage." Ewell demurred. "General Lee had instructed him not to bring on a general engagement without orders." Trimble noticed that Ewell "was far from composure" in saying this, and the Marylander unwisely assumed that what Ewell was hoping for was a polite nudge from a subordinate in the direction of what Ewell wanted to do anyway.

Trimble was wrong. When he volunteered to lead "a division" to "take that hill," Ewell ignored him. Give me a brigade, Trimble begged, even "a good regiment and I will engage to take that hill!" At that moment, Ewell turned on Trimble and snapped, "When I need advice from a junior officer, I generally ask it." Trimble was just as rude. "Gen'l Ewell I am sorry you don't appreciate my suggestions, you will regret it as long as you live." Ewell might indeed have been suffering from "indecision" (as Trimble thought), but if Lee was not going to commit Hill to an attack on Cemetery Hill, then Ewell would "make no direct attack" of his own. As an afterthought, he conceded that, if Allegheny Johnson got into position in time, Johnson could occupy Culp's Hill. But by the time Johnson sent out his own scouting party to Culp's Hill, Winfield Scott Hancock had finally planted Wadsworth's thinned-out 1st Corps division to the hill, and night was upon them.[9]

This decision may have appeared reasonable to Dick Ewell, but not to the ordinary men in his corps. "It was very difficult to restrain the men from just pitching forward . . . without waiting for orders." So, once again, critical tongues began to flap. "There was not an officer, not even a man, who did not expect that the war would be closed upon that hill that evening," raged an officer in the 57th North Carolina. Winchester vanished from their memory, and the old veterans of Jackson's corps now decided that "If Stonewall had been there he would not have waited for orders, nor until the morrow." William Seymour spoke for his Louisiana Tigers when he said that "Here we all felt the loss of Gen. Jackson most sensibly; had he been alive and in command when we charged through the town, I am sure that he would have given his usual orders . . . 'push on the infantry.'"[10]

But was this really Ewell's fault? In some ways, *yes:* at Winchester, Ewell had been on his own, and he had acted in precisely the independent fashion a corps commander should. On July 1st, with Robert E. Lee nearby, Ewell reverted to the habits of a division commander—waiting, alert and ready, for specific orders which would send him in specific directions—which was exactly what Lee had been most concerned about when appointing Ewell to corps command. And Ewell (and Powell Hill) had a point, too, about exhaustion: these men had been on the march and in the fight since sunup, and there were limits to the endurance of even the Army of Northern Virginia. "It was an excessively hot day & we were going through wheat fields & ploughed ground & over fences, it almost killed us," complained a soldier in the 5th Alabama. "I was perfectly exhausted & never suffered so much from heat & fatigue in my life."[11]

Press the attack, and in the oncoming darkness the result might indeed resemble Chancellorsville—not the shattering of the Federal infantry under Stonewall Jackson's relentless hammer, but the confusion and disarray in the darkness which had cost Jackson his life and left his corps too disorganized to act the next morning. Stop now, sang the voice of reason, smarten things up in the twilight, and an early morning jump-off would be far more likely to succeed. Ultimately, though, the decision was neither Hill's nor Ewell's—if

Robert E. Lee had thirsted to drive the Yankees off Cemetery Hill or Culp's Hill, he certainly knew how to give the orders for it. But this day, which had started so poorly, had ended with almost all the results for which Lee had been hoping. He would finish the job on the morrow, just as he had done at Second Bull Run and Chancellorsville, and he would do no more than suggest to Ewell that if the circumstances seemed favorable, the victor of Winchester could move ahead and occupy the hills.

The legion of postwar Lee worshippers would, in the decades to come, try to shield Lee from the consequences of this decision, arguing that he was too much of a Virginia gentleman to issue thunderbolt instructions to his subordinates. But neither Lee nor Ewell really misunderstood each other that night, nor did the situation at nightfall on July 1st seem to require much in the way of urgency. The chances that the other Union corps were closer than a full day's march were unlikely, and even if two or three of them did make it up to Gettysburg in the night, the 1st and 11th Corps would be in no shape to help them, while Lee would have added Longstreet's corps to his own striking power. *God had been gracious.* He had moved in a mysterious way his wonders to perform, and the enemy had been delivered up. "If the enemy is there tomorrow, we must attack him," Lee announced. Tomorrow, "he intended to make the Yankees that day (Thursday) dance."[12]

The commander rode over to the college, which had been transformed from a seat of learning into a bedlam of wounded and dying men, and climbed up to the cupola and "surveyed the surroundings . . . a little before sunset." Satisfied that nothing more could be done in the fading light, Lee rode to Ewell's improvised headquarters in the superintendent's home at the almshouse, arriving around nine o'clock. He rebuffed one more effort by Isaac Trimble to get some sort of movement on Culp's Hill authorized, but he did inform Ewell, Robert Rodes, and Jubal Early that he was planning to attack somewhere "on the enemy's left" the next day if Longstreet's corps "could be got up." In any case, Ewell should make whatever preparations he needed to launch a diversionary attack of his own "upon Cemetery Hill when a favorable opportunity should offer."[13]

Lee rode back over to his headquarters, in a half-dozen tents pitched for him and his staff on the Cashtown Pike, near the one-and-a-half-story stone cottage owned by the Widow Thompson. "All night long ossifers was comin' and goin', getting ready to fight in the mornin'," complained the widow. The men in Rodes' division spread out and camped in a long straight line in Middle Street, extending all the way out from the town along the Cashtown Pike and the railroad embankment, while Early's brigades sidled out to the east beyond the Hanover Road, and "struck camp in a deep ravine" facing Cemetery Hill. By ten o'clock, an uneasy quiet settled over the embattled town. "At every corner, and dotted all along the streets, could be seen little groups of 'Johnnies,'" remembered one Confederate staff officer, "freely conversing and disputing with the citizens, male and female, on the merits of their respective armies, and especially of their officers," as though a political convention instead of an army had taken up residence in the town. Professor Jacobs ventured out of his house at Washington and Middle streets to chat with the rebels there, who were boiling coffee, going out on picket, trying to sleep, a few "plundering the houses and cellars of citizens." They told the curious mathematician that "the Yankees have a *good position*," but "to-morrow, Longstreet, who just arrived this evening, and has not yet been in the fight, will give the Yankees something to do." On the east side of town, Early's division could hear "the Federals . . . chopping away and working like beavers" up on Culp's Hill "all that night."[14]

George Gordon Meade was not having a quiet evening, either. Sending off Hancock to observe effectively immobilized Meade at Taneytown. It was not until "shortly after six o'clock" that Hancock's first report arrived, a brief verbal description of "the situation of affairs" carried by William Mitchell and advising Meade that they could certainly "hold the ground until dark." A second (and written) report followed in less than an hour, assuring Meade that "we will be all right till night," but still holding off on a final recommendation until Slocum arrived and "it can be told better what had best be done." Meade's mind, however, had evidently been inclining more and more in the Gettysburg direction anyway. He dismissed Mitchell with the decisive comment, "I will send up the troops." And even before Hancock's written assessment was brought in, Meade had dashed off a note to Hancock and Doubleday that "it seems that we have so concentrated that a battle at Gettysburg is now forced on us." Hancock departed Gettysburg "about dark," leaving Slocum in overall charge, and when he finally arrived back in Taneytown, he found that Meade "had already given orders . . . to advance at once to Gettysburg, and was about proceeding there in person."[15]

Every energy now was turned "to advance his converging corps," and Meade proceeded to fire off orders to Sykes and the 5th Corps (at seven o'clock) and the reserve brigades of the 3rd Corps at Emmitsburg to get to Gettysburg "with the greatest dispatch." He also needed to compose a report on his decisions for Henry Wager Halleck in Washington, and since the nearest reliable telegraph station was in Frederick, there would be considerable delay in the delivery, not to mention the receipt of any helpful directive from Halleck. Meade wanted the ever-reliable John Sedgwick to "report here in person" in Taneytown with the 6th Corps, and Meade had to give him time to do this. He waited, while all the sprawling equipage of a headquarters was taken down (and all this took till ten o'clock), and then when he could delay no longer, Meade sent Sedgwick one more set of orders to meet him instead in Gettysburg, and "proceeded to the field."[16]

The clouds which had overcast the entire day at Gettysburg now dissipated, giving Meade the unlooked-for aid of a brilliant full moon to light the long road between Taneytown and Gettysburg. This was no jubilant cavalcade: the army's intelligence chief, George Sharpe, recalled "with distinctness the solemnity of our reflections and discussions." Throughout the day—only his fourth full day in command of the Army of the Potomac—Meade had been going without intermission since early in the morning, and when he cantered up the slope of Cemetery Hill around one in the morning, Carl Schurz was taken aback to see that "his long-bearded, haggard face, shaded by a black military felt hat the rim of which was turned down, looked careworn and tried, as if he had not slept the night." He showed up accompanied by only a single staff officer and an orderly, and without the sort of whoop-ti-do fanfare that McClellan and Hooker liked to indulge. Meade had "nothing in his appearance or his bearing—not a smile not a sympathetic word addressed to those around him—that might have made the hearts of the soldiers warm up to him."[17]

Someone went off to rouse Howard and Slocum from their hasty slumber, and the little knot of generals was soon joined by Dan Sickles, who had also just arrived in advance of his 3rd Corps. Howard launched into a briefing of the situation and "told Meade at once what I thought of the cemetery position," especially with Sickles and Slocum at hand. "I am confident we can hold this position," Howard concluded. Slocum chimed in, "It is good for defense," and even Sickles thrust in his endorsement: "It is a good place to fight from, general." To Howard's relief, Meade agreed, although with something less than his generals' bounce. "I am glad to hear you say so, gentlemen, for it is too late to leave it." Carl Schurz quizzed Meade about how many men they could expect to fight with. "In the course of the day I expect to have about 95,000," Meade replied, although again without enthusiasm. "Enough, I guess for this business."[18]

And then, with the generals trailing behind him, Meade rode off to reconnoiter the two hills and the ridgeline behind Cemetery Hill for himself. Overall, the Union position that night resembled a shallow half-circle, with the center curved around Cemetery Hill and facing north, held largely by the remains of the 11th Corps and the artillery batteries Howard and Hancock had bunched there. To the right, Cemetery Hill fell off sharply into a deep swale whose lower end was covered by Stevens' 5th Maine battery, and then sloped up steeply again to form the tree-studded crest of Culp's Hill,

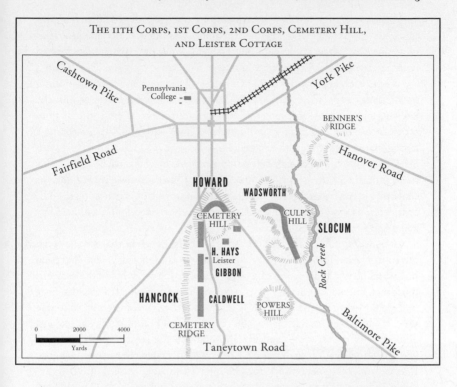

THE 11TH CORPS, 1ST CORPS, 2ND CORPS, CEMETERY HILL,
AND LEISTER COTTAGE

where the 1st Corps and one division of the 12th Corps now rested. Off to the left, where Cemetery Hill tapered gently down to the low ridge known simply as Cemetery Ridge, Slocum's other 12th Corps division was posted, and they would soon be joined by the 3rd Corps as Sickles' men arrived in the night along the Emmitsburg Road. Meade "rode around the lines through the cemetery . . . taking a full survey of the natural features of the position." He stopped to quiz Charles Wainwright about the "dispositions" of his 1st Corps artillery, and at one point "as they rode along the line towards the left," a few of the light sleepers among the men "sprang up and cheered"—not for Meade, but for McClellan, having mistaken Meade for Little Mac. They rode as far down the ridgeline as a pair of rocky, conelike hills, then circled back to Culp's Hill, and finally back to Cemetery Hill, with Meade's staff topographer, Capt. William Paine, busily sketching the terrain as best he could in the milky white moonlight.

As they completed this circuit, the silver of the full moon was already beginning to yield noiselessly to the dawn. Meade "sat upon his horse as the sun was rising," once more surveyed "Cemetery Hill and its environments," and began ordering adjustments. Slocum's two divisions would be concentrated on Culp's Hill, which (as it turned out) was not actually one peak, but two; the 11th Corps would continue to hug Cemetery Hill and the massed batteries around the Evergreen Cemetery. The 3rd Corps was to take up a remote position at the lower end of Cemetery Ridge; when Hancock brought up the 2nd Corps, they would fill in the space on the ridge between Sickles and Cemetery Hill. Meade took for a headquarters the tiny one-and-half-story farm cottage of Lydia Leister, an illiterate widow "with a German face and a strong German accent" who had prudently fled the scene the day before with her four children. But Meade was still uninspired by the battlefield Reynolds and Howard had thrust on him. It was what Abner Doubleday described as "an open secret" that Meade privately "disapproved of the battle-ground." Still, Meade shrugged and said to Carl Schurz, "we may fight it out here just as well as anywhere else."[19]

Meade made several other decisions at the same time that wear a more puzzling aspect. The first of these concerned poor Doubleday, who had been in command of the 1st Corps since the death of John Reynolds the previous morning. The written update Hancock sent back to Meade from Gettysburg included a brief statement—"Howard says that Doubleday's command gave way"—which became fixed in Meade's mind as proof that Doubleday had lost all control of the 1st Corps and somehow caused the collapse of both the 1st and the 11th Corps. It is difficult to believe that either Howard or Hancock intended any judgment this dire, although Doubleday would never forgive either of them. But in the polarized political atmosphere of the Army of the Potomac, it suited Meade to believe that this constituted a very good reason to yank backward one of the better-known Republican abolitionists in the army. And so, in the same orders that authorized Hancock to "take command" over Howard's head, Meade canceled Doubleday's takeover of the 1st Corps, returning him to command of his division, and inserting in Reynolds' place one of John Sedgwick's division commanders in the 6th Corps, John Newton.[20]

Doubleday was aghast. Not only was John Newton some twenty heads behind Doubleday in seniority, he had been a fixture of the McClellanite regime in the 6th Corps and played a direct role in undermining Ambrose Burnside after Fredericksburg. In Washington, the Joint Committee on the Conduct of the War zeroed in on Newton as one of its chief offenders and balked at approving his promotion to major general until March 1863. To Meade, who had served at Fredericksburg alongside Newton under the arch-McClellanite William Buel Franklin, Newton was the only other major general he could trust politically. To the ordinary soldiers, however, Newton was simply an unknown who had "rather ungraciously" usurped Doubleday. "I

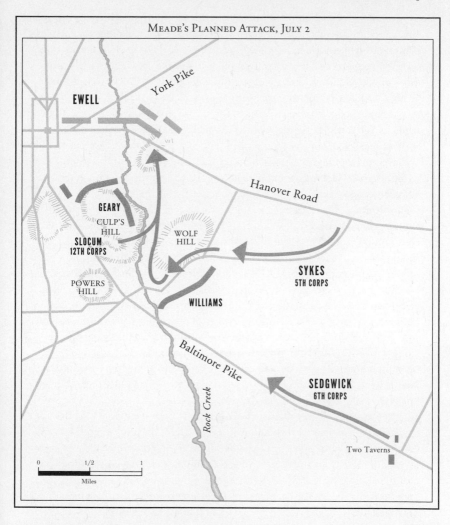

MEADE'S PLANNED ATTACK, JULY 2

EWELL

York Pike

Hanover Road

GEARY

CULP'S
HILL

SLOCUM
12TH CORPS

WOLF
HILL

SYKES
5TH CORPS

POWERS
HILL

WILLIAMS

Baltimore Pike

Rock Creek

SEDGWICK
6TH CORPS

Two Taverns

0   1/2   1

Miles

know nothing as to what sort of a general he is," wrote Charles Wainwright when he learned of Newton's appointment. Nevertheless, it was Newton who "was sent for by General Meade to take command of the 1st corps, because it was said the officer left in command was wounded, or was not satisfactory, or something of that kind."[21]

Doubleday could guess in exactly what way he was "not satisfactory" to Meade. He was furious at what he interpreted as a barefaced humiliation, but there was also little he could do about it. Meade had been given a blank check to promote, dismiss, or retain as he wished. And anyway, Meade did not have much in the way of plans for the battered 1st Corps, no matter who was commanding it. In the pearly dawn's light, Meade was scanning the territory north of Cemetery Hill and Culp's Hill and wondering whether the 5th and 6th Corps could arrive quickly enough to combine with Slocum's 12th Corps "with a view to descend into the plain and attack Lee's left."

When Slocum arrived at Gettysburg, he pointed his first division, under Alpheus Williams, to the right of the Union line and posted them as far east as Wolf's Hill, just beyond Culp's Hill. Slocum scouted the area personally and eventually pulled Williams' division back toward Culp's Hill. "Hence we withdrew from Wolf's Hill and the Hanover Road," wrote a captain in the 2nd Massachusetts. But if the 5th Corps was already on the way from Hanover, then it would still be relatively simple to turn them off the Hanover Road at Wolf's Hill and effect a juncture with the 12th Corps. If the 6th Corps was coming along somewhere behind the 5th Corps, then by mid-morning Meade should have a sufficiently critical mass of infantry to launch a heavy blow east of Wolf's Hill at the overextended flank of Dick Ewell's Confederates.[22]

But where, exactly, were George Sykes and the 5th Corps, and where were John Sedgwick and the 6th Corps? Sykes pulled down his bivouac near Hanover as soon as Meade's orders to move on Gettysburg arrived at dusk on July 1st. Baggage wagons were sent south to Westminster, while Sykes' infantry, along with "the ammunition wagons and ambulances, were pushed forward" on the Hanover Road. The column stopped briefly at two in the morning, "when we laid down in an open woods" near the village of Bonaughtown, but after an hour's respite, "the drums beat reveille, and soon after we were again in motion." The 5th Corps had marched "over sixty miles" in the last three days, twenty-six of them alone since 7:00 a.m. on July 1st, and so many "shoeless and hatless" men "dropped out of the ranks" that roll calls were "not averaging more than thirty men to each company." It was only on the road that men in the 5th Corps "were informed of the trouble at Gettysburg" and "the close presence of the enemy," and as the sun rose over the thick crowns of oak trees ahead the old rumor ignited up and down the columns: "McClellan is to command us to-morrow." By seven o'clock, the 5th Corps had reached "outriders of Slocum's corps," who wheeled them off the Hanover Road and massed them behind Wolf's Hill. Bringing up the rear was Samuel Wylie Crawford's division of Pennsylvania Reserves, one of whose regiments contained a company recruited from Gettysburg. As they turned off the Hanover Road "the members of the company" could "see their homes, in the village before them," and "all of them within the enemy's lines."[23]

The 6th Corps, however, was having a harder time reaching Gettysburg. "After five days' severe marching," John Sedgwick had stopped at Manchester, Maryland, twelve miles east of Meade's headquarters at Taneytown and twenty-three miles from Gettysburg if he went by way of Hanover. The 6th Corps, however, had no plans to go anywhere, since Manchester sat at the eastern end of Pipe Creek, and the men of the 6th spent most of July 1st "devoted to rest, to cleaning arms, and repairing clothing." Then came a galloper from Meade "just after sunset," ordering the entire corps onto the road to Taneytown at once. "Immediately came the verbal order . . . to 'pack up and fall in immediately,'" wrote a soldier in the 10th Massachusetts, and "in an amazing short space of time . . . the column filed into the road." Two hours later, one of Sedgwick's own staffers, Thomas Hyde, found him with new orders from Meade "to make a forward march to Gettysburg" and to detach John Newton for service with the 1st Corps.

Sedgwick angled the line of march northeast, toward Littlestown. Something in Meade's orders had set the alarms ringing in the usually easygoing Sedgwick. He got up one of the bands to play "Old John Brown"—*John Brown's body lies a-mouldering in the grave*—and in short order "a score of voices joined throats to the music, then a hundred, then a thousand, and soon ten thousand voices rolled out the battle song: 'Glory, Glory, Hallelujah, His soul is marching on.'" Sedgwick kept the musicians going all through the night to speed up the pace, but the men had more than music animating them: the simple solidarity of the soldiers themselves. "Every man in the Corps knew," wrote the colonel of the 37th Massachusetts, "that our comrades of the Army of the Potomac were expecting us." All night long, added a brigade staffer, "we marched eagerly forward to take our places beside our comrades."[24]

By dawn, the 6th Corps had reached Littlestown, where they first began to meet walking wounded on the road or "citizens bringing the wounded from the field in their carriages," and "with scarcely an exception the tale they told was one of disaster to the Federal army." *You fellows will catch it; the whole army is smashed to pieces!* In the distance they caught the "booming artillery" and could see "through an opening between the hills what looks like a white bank of fog." Closer on, and the fog could be seen full of "white puffs of bursting shells . . . flashing forked lighting," making the hills seem to a veteran in the 61st Pennsylvania to be "sending up fire and smoke like a volcano in active eruption."[25]

For all of Sedgwick's pushing, however, the 6th Corps had no chance of reaching Gettysburg before two o'clock in the afternoon—in truth, they would not be there until closer to five o'clock—undermining Meade's plan to mass the 5th, 6th, and 12th Corps for a counterblow at the Confederates east of Gettysburg. Henry Slocum was also having second thoughts about the wisdom of such an attack. "At my request," wrote Slocum, "Gen. Meade sent

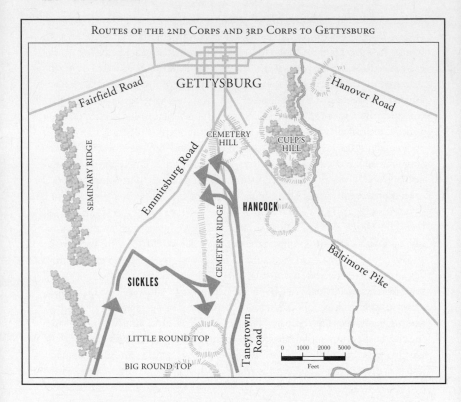

ROUTES OF THE 2ND CORPS AND 3RD CORPS TO GETTYSBURG

GETTYSBURG

Fairfield Road

Hanover Road

SEMINARY RIDGE

Emmitsburg Road

CEMETERY HILL

CULP'S HILL

CEMETERY RIDGE

HANCOCK

SICKLES

Baltimore Pike

Taneytown Road

LITTLE ROUND TOP

BIG ROUND TOP

0   1000   2000   3000
Feet

Gen. [Gouverneur] Warren to examine our position and the ground in our front." When Warren, Meade's own chief engineer, added his doubts about the feasibility of attacking across ground that was gullied and uneven, "the order was countermanded." The 12th Corps would be "detailed for the construction of breastworks and abatis" on the peaks of Culp's Hill, and the 5th Corps would be moved into a reserve position around the small knoll of Powers Hill, behind Cemetery Hill along the Baltimore Pike.[26]

The attention Meade lavished on the planned morning attack around Wolf's Hill stands in puzzling contrast to the offhand decision he made that morning to park Dan Sickles' 3rd Corps far out of range of his attention, near the conical hills at the end of Cemetery Ridge. In response to Reynolds' early-morning instruction that "he had better come up," Daniel Sickles already had most of the 3rd Corps on the road to Gettysburg by midday on July 1st, with the band of the 26th Pennsylvania cheerfully playing "Home, Sweet Home" as they crossed the Pennsylvania state line. Already in his short tenure as commander of the Army of the Potomac, Meade had been cuttingly abrupt with

Sickles, and if there was any corps commander he would gladly have cashiered on the spot, the self-important New York solon was it. So, although Slocum had originally sent orders for Sickles to move up and link with the left flank of the 11th Corps on Cemetery Hill, Meade issued different instructions when he arrived on the scene. Hancock and the 2nd Corps, who were expected to arrive by six o'clock on the morning of July 2nd, would be slotted into the position beside the 11th Corps; Sickles and the 3rd Corps could content themselves with a more distant perch at the tail of Cemetery Ridge.[27]

The less George Meade saw of Sickles, the happier he was, and he was more than content to place Sickles out of sight and out of mind on the far left. Meade would discover too late that in getting Sickles out of his own way, he had put him directly in the way of Robert E. Lee.

The commander of the Army of Northern Virginia never aspired to be an innovator (unlike the man to whom he would eventually surrender, Ulysses S. Grant, who understood that "War is progressive, because all the instruments and elements of war are progressive"). Whenever Robert E. Lee found a tactical trick that worked, he liked to keep using it until it broke. This was a pattern he had established on the Peninsula in 1862, when he had used headlong frontal assaults to win the day at Gaines' Mill, only to find out at Malvern Hill how costly and fruitless they could be. He then learned at Second Bull Run how frighteningly effective it was to clinch one part of an enemy's army, even at unfavorable odds, while gathering and landing an overwhelming blow on the enemy's flank. This had worked to even more devastating effect at Chancellorsville, when Stonewall Jackson's lengthy loop to the west concluded with a descent on Joe Hooker's flank that splintered everything in its path. This, therefore, would be the trick he would play on George Meade at Gettysburg. Dally and fool with Meade on his right around Cemetery Hill and Culp's Hill, while launching a stealthy but massive blow on the other side of Cemetery Hill. It might well be a costly attack, and he no longer had Jackson to carry this through. But he did have the man who had first shown him how it worked at Second Bull Run, and that was James Longstreet.[28]

Longstreet had had a busy day on July 1st, accompanying Lee that morning as far as Cashtown, then turning back to nudge his two stalled divisions to tread on Allegheny Johnson's heels and move toward Gettysburg. When he rejoined Lee at Gettysburg around five that afternoon, it was only to report that these two lead divisions—John Bell Hood's and Lafayette McLaws'—had been "completely blocked up" on the Cashtown Pike by Johnson's division in its struggle to rejoin the rest of Ewell's corps. As the daylight expired, McLaws' division had only made it as far as Marsh Creek, and Hood would not make it even that far until midnight. When Lee quizzed Longstreet on how close his corps was, Longstreet had to point backward and admit, "General, there comes the head of my column where you see that dust rising," some "three or four miles in our rear." Longstreet offered to push up his two lead brigades, if that would help, but Lee declined. It was "too late . . . to go on this evening." Lee's mind was already turning on how he could use Longstreet's corps the next day, and Longstreet sent a courier back to Chambersburg to summon the last of his divisions, George Pickett's, to Gettysburg.[29]

This became the moment on which the next great controversy of the battle would hang, as the postwar keepers of Lee's memorial flame shifted the artillery of blame from Stuart's ride and Dick Ewell at Cemetery Hill to Longstreet. In 1866, William Swinton, the Scottish-born correspondent for the *New York Times*, wrote a bulky survey, *Campaigns of the Army of the Potomac,* with material from interviews he conducted with a number of the commanders, including Longstreet. The burly Longstreet did not mind telling Swinton that "General Lee expressly promised his corps-commanders that *he would not assume a tactical offensive,* but force his antagonist to attack him." But as they approached Gettysburg, Lee abandoned his promise and went on attack. This, Longstreet added, was "a grave error," but "having . . . gotten a taste of blood in the considerable success of the first day," Longstreet believed that Lee had "lost that equipoise in which his faculties commonly moved, and he determined to give battle."

Longstreet's comments were lost in one of Swinton's footnotes until 1872, when Jubal Early sketched the outlines of an accusation which would help sink Longstreet's reputation even lower than Ewell's—that after the evening conference at the almshouse, "Lee left us for the purpose of ordering up Longstreet's corps in time to begin the attack at dawn next morning." Longstreet, however, dallied. His "corps was not in readiness to make the attack until four o'clock in the afternoon of the next day," and by that time all hope of success had evaporated. Early was seconded a few months later by Lee's old artillery chief, William Nelson Pendleton, who also insisted that Lee had ordered Longstreet "to make an attack at daylight the next morning," which Longstreet failed to do "but sat on his horse until about 4 p.m." on July 2nd.[30]

A good many of Lee's and Longstreet's subordinates, including Lafayette McLaws, Charles Venable, and Charles Marshall, scoffed at Early's claim. But stung by Early's charges, Longstreet wrote two self-justifying articles, "put together rapidly," for the *Philadelphia Weekly Times* in 1876. In 1887, Longstreet contributed yet another article, "Lee's Invasion of Pennsylvania," to *The Century*'s "Battles and Leaders of the Civil War" series, frankly laying out his disagreement with Lee about attacking the Federal army. According to

Longstreet, Lee demurred: "No, the enemy is there, and I am going to attack him there. . . . I am going to whip them or they are going to whip me."[31]

The host of Lee's admirers assumed that Longstreet's self-confessed lack of a "spirit of confidence" was all the evidence required to believe that he really had dragged his heels about "an attack at daylight." Early delightedly recruited a coterie of Lee defenders to load the pages of the *Southern Historical Society Papers* with denunciations of Longstreet in a special issue in 1877, and they were joined in the years that followed by still more Lee acolytes who now "remembered" orders for a dawn attack on July 2nd, or who recalled Lee mysteriously anticipating Longstreet's slow-footed handling of his troops. Longstreet inadvertently helped them pin the tail of defeat to his coat by turning Republican after the war and counseling Southerners to collaborate with the Reconstruction governments lest they get something worse in their place. But most of the accusations of Longstreet's "delay" on July 2nd came from people who could have had only the most indirect sort of knowledge of any order from Lee for a dawn attack. Certainly, no written order to this effect has ever surfaced. Cadmus Wilcox, who commanded a brigade in Powell Hill's corps, informed Early that he was "inclined to believe that he [Longstreet] was so ordered" but admitted that "of this I have no knowledge personally." The further in time from July 2nd, the more suspiciously precise the recollections of Lee's "order" become: "Longstreet was slow—unaccountably slow," complained William Goldsborough, a staff officer in Ewell's corps. "Had he attacked in the early morning, as he was expected to do, the enemy would have been driven from his strong position." But this was what Goldborough remembered in 1900, thirty-five years after the war.[32]

And yet, Longstreet was also guilty in the postwar years of exaggerating the doubts he expressed in 1863; he might question Lee's judgment, but at Gettysburg, Longstreet never suggested that the outcome of Lee's plan would be anything but "a certainty." So, he turned back from Gettysburg to rejoin McLaws' division at Marsh Creek for the night, and roused them at four o'clock to begin moving forward. "We were called to arms," wrote a soldier in the 17th Mississippi, "and a detail of ten men from each company drew twenty rounds of extra cartridges for the bloody fray."[33]

PART 3

The Second Day

CHAPTER FOURTEEN

One of the bigger bubbles of the scum

L EE "BREAKFASTED and was in the saddle before it was fairly light." The sun would be up at 4:12 the morning of July 2nd, but it would be hard to mark it at first because of a "considerable fog" that would not entirely burn off until 10:00 a.m. By midday, Lee would enjoy "a cloudless day." The temperatures, which were already at 74 degrees at seven o'clock, would climb into the 80s, so that the "heat was intense." Curiously, if what Lee expected was a dawn attack by Longstreet, he displayed suspiciously little anxiety about it. Nor should he have, since any decision about an attack somewhere on the right had to wait on someone to go and look at what was there. The two stony hills in the distance might conceal the unwanted approach of other Federal infantry, and Lee wanted to be sure that nothing of that nature had arrived under cover of darkness. He turned to Capt. Samuel Johnston, his staff "topographical engineer" and a former civil engineer in Virginia, and told him "to reconnoiter along the enemy's left and return as soon as possible."[1]

Johnston took along one of Longstreet's staff, Maj. John Clarke, and a small mounted escort, and together they swung south and west in a wide arc that would curl downward toward the stony hills. (Significantly, Johnston would write years later that nothing was said about a dawn attack by Longstreet: "I cannot see how Genl Lee's friends can contend that . . . Lee gave order to . . . Longstreet to make an attack on the morning of the second.") They picked their way along the Fairfield Road, crossed a bridge over Willoughby Run, and worked along a road which brought them to a farm owned by James Warfield, a black farmer who ran a blacksmith's shop alongside his "excellent" fruit trees. The Warfield farm stood on a rise which was actually the continuation of Seminary Ridge, and from there, Johnston could turn east toward the Emmitsburg Road, past the peach orchard of Joseph Sherfy, which John Reynolds had passed only a day before, and follow the farm lanes to the rocky knobs that thrust up against the lightening sky—two hills which would only after the battle become known as Big and Little Round Top.[2]

Lee had other scouting parties out that morning, too. He directed Lindsay Long to take the chief of Powell Hill's artillery, Reuben Walker, and identify a location with good elevation somewhere along Seminary Ridge which would allow Hill's artillery to support an attack; he ordered William Nelson Pendleton, the chief of the army's artillery reserve, to scout another useful position. While waiting for Longstreet, Lee paid a quick visit to Ewell at the almshouse, and by the time he had returned to his own headquarters at the Thompson house, the sun was up and the head of McLaws' and Hood's column could be seen, tramping down the Cashtown Pike toward Herr Ridge, preceded by Longstreet and his staff.[3]

A generals' call brought Longstreet, Hood, McLaws, Lee, and Powell Hill together, along with their staffs. This included Harry Heth, who had been hit in the head by a bullet late the previous day and saved by the rolled-up newspapers stuffed into the band of his purloined hat; he was unconscious for an anxiously long time, and would turn command of his division over to Johnston Pettigrew. (The gathering also featured a trio of foreign military observers: the Coldstream officer Fremantle, the Prussian Justus Scheibert, and Edward Fitzgerald Ross, English-born but German-educated and serving as a captain in an Austrian cavalry regiment.) Hood's and McLaws' men were "allowed to stack arms and rest until further orders." To his gathered officers, Lee began laying out the plan he had devised—as soon as Longstreet's two divisions were in hand, they would turn to their right and march south, following a route that Captain Johnston would provide upon his return.

This would place them south and west of Cemetery Hill, and there they would wheel left and, facing north and into the rear of Cemetery Hill, "attack up the Emmettsburg road." From there they would drive into whatever forces were guarding the left flank of the hill, and overrun the Union artillery and infantry posted there. Ewell would attack from the opposite side of the hill as soon as he heard Longstreet's artillery go into action, and would provide the anvil against which Longstreet's hammer would smash whatever was left of the 1st and 11th Corps, or any other Union reinforcements which might have arrived overnight. After that, Lee would be free to turn the entirety of the victorious Army of Northern Virginia either south or east to meet and crush in similar fashion the next batch of Union infantry to come blundering into his path. Long before the last Union regiment had been destroyed, he would

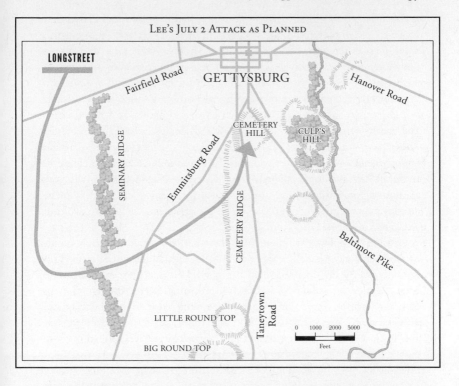

be in either Philadelphia or Washington, and the cries for negotiation would inundate the Lincoln administration.[4]

Lee seemed to John Bell Hood "full of hope, yet, at times, buried in deep thought." In spite of the heat, he was primly dressed as if on parade, "coat buttoned to the throat, sabre-belt buckled around the waist, field glasses pending at his side," as though already prepared to accept some Union general's surrender. Longstreet had a new objection. He did not like the idea of launching a major attack with only two of his three divisions available, since George Pickett's division had to come all the way from Chambersburg and probably wouldn't arrive until late in the day. "I never like to go into battle with one boot off," Longstreet remarked to Hood as he sat down on a tree trunk. As it was, one of Hood's brigades (under Evander McIvor Law) had been "left by Hood on picket" below the pike stretching back to Chambersburg, and was far behind the others.

Lee assured Longstreet that he could make up the deficit in numbers by borrowing Richard Heron Anderson's division from Powell Hill. Anderson had five brigades behind Herr Ridge which hadn't gotten into action at all on July 1st, and they could take Pickett's place in this attack. "The enemy is here," he said, repeating his sentiment from the evening before, "and if we do not whip him, he will whip us." Hill and Longstreet peeled away and sat down to discuss the intricacies of temporarily transferring command of Anderson's division, while Longstreet sent off Edward Porter Alexander to "get an idea of the ground," bring up the corps artillery, "and choose my own positions and means of reaching them." If this was to be a second Chancellorsville, Longstreet wanted no risk of his march being spotted en route—that had happened at Chancellorsville, and only the unwillingness of Federal observers to see Jackson's columns for what they were saved Jackson from having his trap sprung prematurely. Longstreet "specially cautioned" Alexander "to keep all movements carefully out of view of a signal station whose flags we could see wig-wagging on Little Round Top."[5]

Lafayette McLaws wondered out loud whether it wouldn't be a good idea to send someone out along that path to scout the field, and Lee replied that not only had he done so, but that his scout was at that moment just arriving back. Captain Johnston returned from his reconnaissance between seven and eight o'clock, and found the "Generals Lee, Longstreet, and A. P. Hill sitting on a log near the seminary." Lee wanted a report at once, and Johnston was able to trace on a map Lee was holding "the route over which I had made the reconnaissance." It would require marching about five miles to get troops into position for the kind of attack Lee had in mind—maybe two hours at most. Lee pointed at the smaller of the two stony hills. "Did you get there?" Yes, Johnston replied. His party had even trotted up to the top, "where I had a commanding view." And he had the very best news Lee could have desired: there were no Federal troops anywhere south of Cemetery Hill. Johnston had crossed paths with "three or four" Union cavalrymen, and trying to stay out of their sight had delayed his return. But otherwise, nothing. That was all that Lee needed to hear. The back door to Cemetery Hill was open.[6]

Lee turned to Longstreet and said, "I think you had better move," and Longstreet called over Hood and McLaws to give them directions. Porter Alexander did not "get the impression that General Lee thought there was any unnecessary delay going on," and when Longstreet asked Lee for permission to wait the arrival of McIvor Law's trailing brigade, Lee patiently gave it. But Law took even longer than Longstreet had expected. Estimates put their arrival at anywhere between ten o'clock and two, while Law himself remembered his brigade "arrived there shortly before noon." Once Law's Alabamians arrived, "we were allowed but a few minutes' rest" before the "divisions of McLaws and Hood were moved in line by the right flank" (i.e., in column) and Longstreet's flank march began. Captain Johnston and

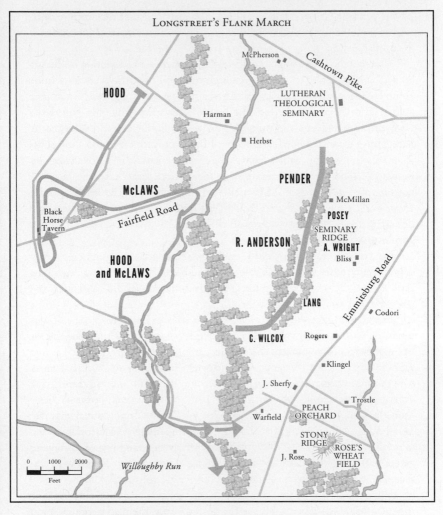

LONGSTREET'S FLANK MARCH

McLaws' own engineer officer Lt. Thomas Moncure would ride ahead with the advance guard, so that Johnston could retrace his early morning scouting path. Richard Heron Anderson's division had already been moved up into position along Seminary Ridge by Powell Hill by ten o'clock; McLaws and Hood (with Joseph Kershaw's South Carolina brigade in the van of McLaws' division) filed southward on Herr Ridge, twisting west on the Fairfield Road to the Black Horse Tavern, and then doubling to the south and east. The showers of the previous days had wetted the track sufficiently to keep down most of the dust, and the thick stands of woods would conceal them from the

Union signalers on the ridges and hills to the east. To make certainty certain, "orders had been issued not to display the colors as we were supposed to be in ambush."

"We marched at a slow and halting gait," remembered a captain in the 3rd South Carolina, slow and halting enough to tempt bored soldiers to hijinks. Some men in the 8th Georgia, jerking to a halt beside a deserted farmhouse, took it into their heads to loot the house. They came out, not with loot, but wearing a collection of women's gowns and bonnets, and proceeded to ham things up to the howls and roars of their comrades. But most of Longstreet's men were unusually silent on the march "save the tread of thousands in motion"—not from "any want of confidence or doubt of ultimate success," but because "each felt within himself that this was to be the decisive battle of the war." Longstreet shared their mood. One South Carolina officer saw Longstreet pass "once or twice," and each time "he had his eyes cast to the ground, as if in a deep study."[7]

Robert E. Lee was also quiet. He took the opportunity of Longstreet's departure to ride over to Ewell, where he could be sure of prodding Ewell into action when the noise of Longstreet's attack commenced. But as the quarter-hours clicked away, nothing was heard.[8]

Just beyond Black Horse Tavern, the road turned sharply to the east and mounted to a small rise about twenty or thirty feet higher than the rest of the roadbed. There, Longstreet's column stopped. Longstreet moved up to see what had caused the stoppage, and when he caught up with McLaws, Moncure, and Captain Johnston at the head of the column, Longstreet found exactly the problem he had warned Porter Alexander against—from the rise, Johnston and McLaws "were in full view of Round Top, from which the signal flags of the enemy were rapidly wavering." Any column of infantry marching over that rise would give themselves away as surely as if they were giants on stilts. "What is the matter?" Longstreet asked, puzzled, when he met McLaws on the reverse slope of the hill. "Ride with me," McLaws irritably replied, "and I will show you that we can't go on this route, according to instructions, without being seen by the enemy." Longstreet and McLaws rode "to the top of the hill," and that ended all argument from Longstreet. "Why this won't do. Is there no way to avoid it?" No, there wasn't, and McLaws was foaming with irritation at Johnston, who was supposed to have known all about the route they were taking. "He seems to have forgotten that he was the guide conducting troops over ground," McLaws fumed, "he alone of all of them had reconnoitered, and that every step taken was under his direction, of course." And from there, McLaws descended to "saying things" which one member of Kershaw's brigade "would not like my grandson to repeat."[9]

There was nothing for it but to turn around, countermarch the entire huge column back to the last crossroads, and find an alternate route, out of sight. In the tactics books, a countermarch required something more complicated than just to "cause the column to face about"—it meant peeling the heads of a column to the right and the left and pivoting them around to the rear, company by company, regiment by regiment, with the colonel of each regiment superintending the process. It was, in other words, tedious and time-consuming; but it was necessary if the regiments and brigades were to retain the march order which would, later on, allow them to deploy in the pattern to which they had been drilled. Executing the order was not helped by the fact that some of Hood's units had "lapped" the rear of McLaws', so that it took "some little time" to get the mess sorted out and the men moved back. The countermarch pulled the advance back to the tavern and back up the Fairfield Road for a half a mile, until the entire column (with McLaws still in the lead) found a farm lane that led to the right and allowed the Confederates to regain their original route on the far side of the all too revealing hill. Two miles farther on, they passed a schoolhouse and turned eastward on the Millerstown Road until they reached the west-facing slope of Seminary Ridge, a little more than 600 yards from the Emmitsburg Road.[10]

What Longstreet and McLaws expected to see from this point was a broad and unoccupied vista, with the Emmitsburg Road stretched out parallel to the battle lines they would shortly deploy into. Ahead and to the right, there was a studding of farmhouses and barns—directly ahead, the deserted Warfield farm and Joseph Sherfy's house and barn, with his peach orchard just on the other side of the Emmitsburg Road, and then, as the ground dipped down on the far side of the road, a stone farmhouse and barn belonging to George Rose, and another, owned by John Slyder, still farther to the right. Beyond the farmhouses, there was another low, stony ridge, carpeted with trees; but behind that loomed the Round Tops, reminding one of the officers in Anderson's division of "a volcano." To the left, a mile northward, was the flank brigade of Richard Anderson's division, waiting for McLaws and Hood to deploy and create one vast attack line behind Seminary Ridge. Longstreet overhauled McLaws to ask how he planned to deploy his division. "That will be determined when I can see what is in my front," McLaws replied. No worry, Longstreet answered, "There is nothing in your front; you will be entirely on the flank of the enemy."[11]

McLaws rode forward, and when he "reached the edge of the woods" on Seminary Ridge, "one rapid glance" showed him that Captain Johnston had made more than one mistake that morning. Instead of an unobstructed path along which they could wheel north, bracket the Emmitsburg Road, and move up to crush the Union forces on Cemetery Hill, McLaws was looking at lines of Union soldiers, arrayed on the east side of the road, clenching

Sherfy's peach orchard with artillery, and "in force much greater than I had, and extending considerably beyond my right." As Longstreet rode up "to see the cause of the delay," he and his staff had the same disappointing epiphany. "Just as we rode from the timber into the open," wrote one of Longstreet's couriers, they were "brought face to face with the Union army," which was settling into a long line along the length of the Emmitsburg Road as far south as Sherfy's peach orchard, and then bent eastward at a right angle until it disappeared out of sight over the stony ridge. "The Union army . . . had piled rails and whatever else they could get that would aid in making a breastworks, and were lying behind these rails awaiting our attack."

At some point, John Bell Hood joined the perplexed knot of Confederate observers and "found that in making the attack according to orders"—in other words, according to Lee's plan of wheeling left and driving up the Emmitsburg Road—"I should have first to encounter and drive off this advanced line of battle." Hood's first reflex was to send a six-man scouting team from his old 4th Texas to find out exactly what force was out in front of them, while Longstreet's was to start positioning McLaws' division to the left and Hood's to the right. Even as they did so, "puffs of smoke" began to rise "at intervals . . . as the Federal batteries fired upon such portions of our line as became exposed to view."[12]

This, as Lafayette McLaws dryly remarked sixteen years later, "presented a state of affairs which was certainly not contemplated when the original plan or order of battle was given, and certainly not known to General Longstreet a half hour previous." According to Captain Johnston's morning report, there should have been *no* Union forces of any substance anywhere south of Cemetery Hill, all of which raises the very peculiar question of what, exactly, Captain Johnston saw, or did not see, that morning. By every Union account, the area south of Cemetery Hill had been swarming with Federal activity from sundown on July 1st straight through to noon of the 2nd—John Geary's division of the 12th Corps had been the first to be posted along Cemetery Ridge on the night of July 1st; Geary moved over to Culp's Hill early in the morning of July 2nd, as the 3rd Corps arrived piece by piece from Emmitsburg to replace him; and Winfield Scott Hancock's 2nd Corps moved up the Taneytown Road behind the Round Tops and finished getting into position between the 3rd Corps and Cemetery Hill as Geary's division was pulling out.[13]

Taken together, these Federal troop movements make Johnston's claim to have ridden straight up to the summit of Little Round Top unopposed and with nothing to observe simply incredible—unless, of course, Johnston had not been anywhere near the Round Tops in the first place. The broad undulating plain between South Mountain and the Susquehanna is punctuated with any number of cones, drumlins, moraines, and hillocks, and on the morning of July 2nd, it was also blanketed with "a heavy fog" which "hung over the field." Samuel Johnston was certainly no novice at reconnaissance. But he was, as a Virginian, on entirely new and unmarked ground in south-central Pennsylvania, with a dearth of existing maps to help him (Johnston mentions Lee possessing a map of the general area, but never mentions carrying one himself on his early morning expedition). The gentlest conclusion to draw is that Johnston climbed *some other hill*, and thought it was the Round Tops (which may, in turn, account for his surprise at leading McLaws and Moncure along a road and up a rise which, without warning, revealed them to Federal signalmen), and thus completely overlooking the mass of Union troops between Cemetery Hill and the Round Tops that morning. It was a harmless enough error, taken by itself. But it was not by itself; it joined forces with the oversized and overheated imagination of Daniel Edgar Sickles to create a catastrophe of carnage.[14]

Dan Sickles belonged in a novel rather than an army. Corrupt and confident, he coruscated political charm, talked in the grandest of hotel manners, and oozed sleaze and dissimulation from every pore. He was born in 1819—although Sickles persistently gave out alternative birth dates—in New York City, where his father's fortune in real estate speculation guaranteed him the finest of tutors (including Lorenzo Da Ponte, who taught Italian literature at Columbia and had, in his long-ago youth, written libretti for Wolfgang Amadeus Mozart) and an unceasing bankroll of funding for lascivious escapades. Sickles was, from the beginning, a spoiled brat, and he matured from there into a suave, charming, and pathological liar, not unlike certain characters in Mozart operas. He studied law, but his real passion quickly became politics, which in New York City meant Democratic politics. He made his maiden speech at the tender age of sixteen on behalf of Martin Van Buren, and from there he rose to editing a campaign newspaper for James Knox Polk, sitting in the New York state assembly, wangling an honorific commission in the state militia, tagging along with James Buchanan as an assistant during Buchanan's four years as American minister in London, and getting himself elected to Congress in 1856. His fellow New York lawyer, George Templeton Strong, recoiled from Sickles as "belonging to the filthy sediment of the profession," or at least "one of the bigger bubbles of the scum."

Scum or not, Sickles sailed regally on the sea of his father's money, dispensed patronage to loyal allies, and married a "ravishing" sixteen-year-old Italian beauty named Teresa Bagioli—whom he had probably seduced. Any eyebrows raised by this mésalliance were raised still further in 1859, when, after renting a lavish home on Lafayette Square in Washington, he caught the seducible Teresa being seduced by Philip Barton Key, the U.S. attorney for the District of Columbia and the son of Francis Scott Key. An enraged Sickles pursued Key across Lafayette Square and then shot him to death after an energetic scuffle on the curbside across from the White House.[15]

The murder thrust Sickles luridly into national headlines, but the high-priced legal team he assembled succeeded in convincing the jury that Sickles' discovery of his wife's infidelity had induced an attack of "mental unsoundness"—temporary insanity—and after a seventy-minute delibera-tion the jury found Sickles not guilty. Sickles reconciled three months later with Teresa, an accomplishment he fully expected to be "fatal to my profes-sional, political, and social standing." He was right. Congressman Sickles was shunned even on the floor of Congress, where he "was left to himself as if he had smallpox." He wisely decided not to tempt fate by running for reelec-tion, and he might otherwise have dropped soundlessly into the footnotes of American political history had not the Civil War broken out.

As a rakehell Democrat, Sickles was expected to fall in with the abun-dant fellowship of New York City's Democratic Lincoln haters, and at first, Sickles actually defended "the recognized right of secession" as "a conservative safeguard." But he balked when the Southern states turned secession into a reality, and instead Sickles bound himself to the Union cause. "I did not vote for" Lincoln, Sickles proclaimed, "but I will fight under his orders and I will trust him everywhere." He set about recruiting a five-regiment brigade which he named for the New York state motto, the "Excelsior Brigade." The govern-ment was happy to have the men, but paused at commissioning the likes of Sickles as a brigadier general to command them. In 1861, however, Lincoln needed to rally all the bipartisan support he could muster, and the following spring the Senate very reluctantly confirmed Sickles as a brigadier general.[16]

Dan Sickles may have been the epitome of the confidence man. But he was also "a Bowery boy," an indisputable genius of the glad hand, and an organ-grinder of boodle. "Through his whole life, he has been distinguished by the strength and devotion of his friendships, and the consequent inten-sity of his partisanships," which made him (as *Harper's Weekly* said in its struggle to understand Sickles' baffling appeal) "loved more sincerely, and hated more heartily, than any man of his day." Even George Templeton Strong had to admit, against his will, that "there are judicious men who rate Sickles very high." One such man—although not necessarily one of the more judicious—was Joe Hooker, who thought Sickles a "gallant leader" and an "intrepid chief" and "one of the greatest soldiers of the day." Sickles' Excel-sior Brigade was attached to Hooker's division in the 3rd Corps during the Peninsula Campaign, and when Hooker moved to take command of the 1st Corps before Antietam, Sickles took over his slot. In tandem, when Hooker was given command of the Army of the Potomac, Sickles was rewarded with command of the 3rd Corps and a major general's commission, as well as the adoration of the men of the 3rd Corps who saw Sickles as "an ideal soldier of volunteers."[17]

Among those who *were* judicious but loathed Sickles was George Gordon Meade, who believed that Sickles, "being intellectually more clever than Hooker," had obtained "an injurious ascendency over him." Meade had little love for the 3rd Corps as it was, since from its earliest organization under Samuel Heintzelman in 1862 it had been stoutly anti-McClellanite. Sickles' senior division commander, David Bell Birney, was a raspy "pale, Puritanical figure, with a demeanor of immovable coldness," who would only "smile politely when you spoke to him." Birney and Meade had been breathing out flames at each other ever since Fredericksburg, when Meade had galloped up to Birney's brigade and demanded support in terms so profane it "almost makes the stones creep." After that, Meade was "especially disliked by General Birney." So, as the lead elements of the 3rd Corps came up the Emmitsburg Road in the twilight, the only task Meade had in mind for them was to turn off the road to the east and shuffle into place on Cemetery Ridge, alongside John White Geary's 12th Corps division; in the morning, Meade would move Geary's men over to Culp's Hill, where he expected the real action to take place. The 3rd Corps would not only be left way off to his left flank and out of sight, but Meade would detach Buford's cavalry division (which had been picketing the ground west of Cemetery Ridge) and send them back to Emmitsburg to refit, as though the 3rd Corps had no need of cavalry screening.[18]

The last of the troops Sickles put on the road to Gettysburg on the afternoon of July 1st did not catch up to him on the low end of Cemetery Ridge until 1:00 a.m; an ad hoc brigade Sickles left in Emmitsburg (under an old political flunky of his from New York named Charles K. Graham) did not finish their march until nine o'clock on the morning of the 2nd. By then, Geary had pulled out his division to join the rest of the 12th Corps over near Culp's Hill, and the gap between Sickles' corps and Cemetery Hill was being filled by Hancock's 2nd Corps. Meade left Sickles with no particular direction about how to deploy his two divisions, despite Sickles sending his chief of staff, Henry Tremain, to Meade's headquarters "several times in the morning of that day, for the purpose of reporting the situation and of obtaining such instructions as might be necessary." Meade had no such instructions; any battle worth fighting was going to take place over on Meade's right, and Tremain afterward thought that "the actual situation never seemed to have been fully appreciated by General Meade."[19]

Sickles, however, was becoming convinced that Meade had some darker motive in shunting the 3rd Corps away from the glory of combat. As a man with long experience in the art of the setup, and with plenty of reason to believe that Meade might be happy to have the 3rd Corps end up like the hapless 11th Corps at Chancellorsville, Sickles began grasping at phantoms. When Charles Graham arrived that morning, he jangled Sickles' anxieties by reporting a brush-up against Confederate pickets not far from the peach orchard, where he had turned to join Sickles. "The pickets and skirmishers were uneasy and kept up a desultory fire, little puffs of thin blue smoke dotting the plain before us." Two months before, Sickles had seen signs of Stonewall Jackson's great flank column in motion far in the distance, only to have Joe Hooker dismiss the reports as evidence that Jackson was beginning a retreat. Determined not to be lulled into passivity a second time, Sickles and Birney called up Hiram Berdan, who commanded the only genuinely specialized skirmish troops in the entire Army of the Potomac, the 1st and 2nd U.S. Sharpshooters, and ordered Berdan to "send forward a detachment of 100 sharpshooters" to the west side of the Emmitsburg Road to investigate. Berdan found nothing. But Birney and Sickles were convinced that something had to be happening, and around noon Birney ordered another company of the U.S. Sharpshooters "farther to the left of our lines," with an entire regiment—the 3rd Maine—as supports, "with directions to feel the enemy."[20]

Sickles actually had no hard evidence beyond his own jumpy intuition that the 3rd Corps was in the line of danger. But when Berdan's Sharpshooters plunged into the oak and chestnut woods beyond the Warfield farm, "they met a small boy who warned them . . . 'Look out! There are lots of rebels in there, in rows.'" And they did indeed collide with Confederate skirmishers—Alabamians from Cadmus Wilcox's brigade who were moving into position as part of Powell Hill's contribution to the great flank attack. The firefight which erupted probably lasted no more than twenty minutes, but it was long enough for Berdan to glimpse "three columns in motion in rear of the wood, changing direction . . . by the right flank." He sent off Capt. Joseph Briscoe to report to Birney, and then slowly disengaged, gradually pulling back across the Emmitsburg Road until, by two o'clock, he was able to report to Birney in person on "the result of our operations."[21]

Sickles was now certain that Meade had deliberately left him alone in the path of a Confederate landslide, with no cavalry screen and no supports within easy distance. Major Tremain's repeated visits to headquarters had been met first with indifference, and then by a visit from one of Meade's staffers (who happened to be George Meade junior) "to inquire of [Sickles] if his troops were yet in position, and to ask what he had to report." Young Meade hadn't even taken the trouble to find Sickles himself, but left the message with the chief of the 3rd Corps' artillery, George Randolph. Meade came back an hour later with an irritated order from his father for Sickles to get into position, and at eleven o'clock, a troubled Sickles took himself directly up to the Widow Leister's cottage to see Meade personally. "Observing, from the enemy's movements on our left, what I thought to be conclusive indications of a design on their part to attack there," Sickles later testified, "I went in person to headquarters and reported the facts and circumstances which led me to believe that an attack would be made there, and asked for orders." He got nothing but a dismissive instruction to tie his right flank to the 2nd Corps and his left flank to the Round Tops. "I found that my impression as to the intention of the enemy to attack in that direction was not concurred in at headquarters," and when Sickles asked Meade to at least come over and have a look for himself, Meade replied that "his engagements did not permit him to do that." If not Meade himself, would Meade at least send his chief engineer, Gouverneur K. Warren? The answer was even more curt: *no*.[22]

If Meade had not been convinced that the main attack "would be made upon his right," he might have noticed that the signalers up on the Round Tops had (notwithstanding the best efforts at concealment by Longstreet, McLaws, and Porter Alexander) been sending messages to headquarters as early as noon about the movement of the "enemy's skirmishers . . . from the west, 1 mile from here," and how "the rebels are in force," and describing Berdan's firefight. More warnings followed about the approach of "a heavy column of enemy's infantry . . . opposite our extreme left," and then two more just after two o'clock. Instead, Meade snorted loftily at Sickles' worries: "Generals are all apt to look for the attack to be made where they are." Sickles countered the rebuff with a request: if Meade had no plans to intervene, could Sickles at least move his men around to suit his own judgment? Yes, Meade snapped impatiently, within reasonable limits, "any ground . . . you choose to occupy I leave to you." Sickles also wrested assent from Meade to take the army's artillery chief, Henry Hunt, back to the 3rd Corps position. Meade told Hunt, who had just returned from inspecting Union artillery positions, that Sickles "wished me to examine a new line" so that Sickles could make better use of his artillery.[23]

That was all Sickles needed to hear. At Chancellorsville, Joe Hooker had compounded the mistake of indolence in the path of Stonewall Jackson by evacuating, a day later, an ideal artillery plateau at Hazel Grove, and allowing Confederate artillery to plant themselves there and pound the hapless Hooker and his cinched-in lines around the Chancellor house. The Federal troops whom Hooker pulled away from Hazel Grove had been, not surprisingly, those of the 3rd Corps, and from that Sickles had learned a lesson about holding on to high ground which he swore never to forget. As Sickles explained matters to Hunt, Cemetery Ridge declined imperceptibly by almost fifty feet as it snaked south from Cemetery Hill, so that at the point where the 3rd Corps was bivouacked, his troops were actually sitting, not on a ridge, but in "a low marshy swale." Not only was it in "a hole" compared to Cemetery Hill, it was actually sixty feet lower than Sherfy's peach orchard out at the Emmitsburg Road. And in between his "swale" and the road stretched three-quarters of a mile, bisected by a stony ridge which would be "unfit for artillery & [a] bad front for infantry." The solution would be to move his two divisions up to the Emmitsburg Road and Sherfy's peach orchard, where they would have the advantage of "the commanding ground."[24]

Hunt shifted uneasily. Examining the proposed Emmitsburg Road line with Sickles, Hunt pointed out what should have been obvious to Sickles: the Emmitsburg Road might well be "commanding ground," but to get there Sickles would have to unhook himself from Hancock's 2nd Corps, and leave a 600-yard gap yawning between Hancock's left flank and Sickles' right. At the other end, if Sickles lined up his divisions behind the Emmitsburg Road, the subtle angle of the road to the southwest would swing his other flank far out into the air, leaving the Round Tops completely uncovered. If Sickles was right, and the rebels were moving in force on the other side of the Emmitsburg Road, then he was presenting them with a target, begging to be bowled over. "The right of his proposed line was out where it would not be connected with the 2nd Corps," Hunt gingerly explained, and "it would have to be connected, perhaps, by throwing out the left wing of the 2nd corps, and that could not well be done" unless the stony ridge "was under our control."

Sickles, who had already authorized David Birney to get his division in motion, offered a compromise. He would post his junior division commander, Andrew Atkinson Humphreys, along the Emmitsburg Road to secure the "commanding ground" down to Sherfy's peach orchard, but then angle the line back severely—almost 90 degrees—and use Birney's division to trace a line down toward the Round Tops. Could he do that? Hunt hesitated: this idea would "so greatly lengthen our line—which in any case must rest on Round Top, and connect with the left of the Second Corps—as to require a larger force than the Third Corps alone to hold it." Hunt was an artilleryman, not an infantry officer, and he did not relish being caught between a corps commander whom everyone knew carried terrific clout with the politicians and George Meade, who had not yet confirmed Hunt's position as chief of the army's artillery. "So far as it was a line for troops to occupy," Hunt diplomatically replied, "it was a very good line." But, Hunt warned, Sickles "should wait orders from General Meade" before making such a dramatic move. And with that, Hunt rode off to report, "very briefly, to General Meade."[25]

Not for the first or last time would Sickles hear a *no* and pretend he had heard a *yes*. He took Hunt's careful attempt to refer the decision to Meade

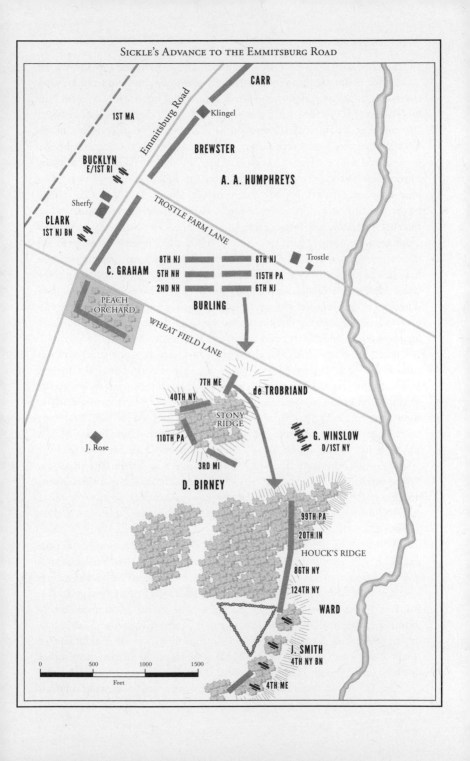

SICKLE'S ADVANCE TO THE EMMITSBURG ROAD

CARR

1ST MA

Klingel

Emmitsburg Road

BREWSTER

BUCKLYN
E/1ST RI

A. A. HUMPHREYS

TROSTLE FARM LANE

Sherfy

CLARK
1ST NJ BN

C. GRAHAM

8TH NJ   8TH NJ   Trostle
5TH NH   115TH PA
2ND NH   6TH NJ

PEACH
ORCHARD

BURLING

WHEAT FIELD LANE

7TH ME   de TROBRIAND

40TH NY

STONY
RIDGE

G. WINSLOW
D/1ST NY

110TH PA

J. Rose

3RD MI

D. BIRNEY

99TH PA

20TH IN

HOUCK'S RIDGE

86TH NY

124TH NY

WARD

0   500   1000   1500

J. SMITH
4TH NY BN

Feet

4TH ME

as "the approval of his own judgment," which, when Hunt explained it all to Meade, would doubtless be endorsed by the army commander as coming from a less offending source than Daniel E. Sickles. So, the orders went out, and "our line was advanced to the new position." A slightly bewildered and "uncomfortable" Humphreys "sent out working parties" to take down "all the fences" along the road "in my front," and along the road he pieced out one of his three brigades, under Joseph B. Carr, "in line of battle." Behind Carr, Humphreys placed the old Excelsior Brigade (commanded these days by William Brewster), drawn up in a close-interval column, "in line of battalions in mass." Humphreys' last brigade was "massed in column of regiments," at intervals of 200 yards. Birney's division, which Sickles originally wanted to commit in toto to the Emmitsburg Road line, had its three brigades parceled out to cover the road only as far as Sherfy's peach orchard (which would be held by Charles Graham's all-Pennsylvania brigade), back to the stony ridge (where Philippe Régis de Trobriand would deploy his brigade), and then down to a massively forbidding rock outcropping known locally as Devil's Den, where John Henry Hobart Ward's brigade (which included Berdan's Sharpshooters) would screen any approach to the Round Tops.

If the 3rd Corps had brought with it to Gettysburg its third division (which had instead been sent to bulk up the garrison of Harpers Ferry), Sickles might just barely have been able to defend this ground. As it was, his 10,000 would have to cover a line that stretched more than 2,700 yards— three men for every yard, if you counted every non-combatant, and kept no reserves—and which still did not connect with the 2nd Corps or put a single soldier on the Round Tops. There were so few men available to cover all the necessary yardage that Sickles, as an afterthought, sent off an appeal to the artillery reserve for any extra batteries they could spare (they sent him three six-gun batteries—the old eighteen-gun rule), so that he could stuff them into the gap behind the peach orchard between Graham and de Trobriand.[26]

Fully in character for Dan Sickles' corps, the divisions "advanced in a brilliant line." The 63rd Pennsylvania (from Birney's division) and the 1st Massachusetts (from Humphreys' division) were thrown out as skirmishers for the advance, and the fifteen-piece brass band of the 114th Pennsylvania ("Collis' Zouaves") thumped away to mark the time. (The regiment was unreservedly proud of its band: they had played on the field at Fredericksburg, although in a fit of oversight someone had forgotten to notify them when the Army of the Potomac retreated, and left the whole ensemble to be bagged as prisoners by the Confederates.) "The eye beheld," wrote an officer in Carr's brigade, "battery and brigade extended from point to point," full of "moving columns and gay banners." It was "a grand sight to witness this little corps of two divisions gallantly move on the advance," and despite taking place on what was, after all, a battlefield, it all "appeared to be a peaceful review," with a "herd of thirteen or fourteen cows . . . quietly grazing upon the field."[27]

Over to the right, John Gibbon, "standing on [Cemetery] hill" with the 2nd Corps, turned a puzzled eye on the show unfolding "out to our left and front." One staffer gaped at Sickles' "incomprehensible movements," while "both officers and men" of the 2nd Corps stood up to offer commentary "as [to] the comparative merits of the line" Sickles was acquiring. Hancock saw it, too: "I recollect looking on and admiring the spectacle, but I did not know the object of it." He "quietly" remarked to his staff, "Gentlemen, that is a splendid advance" and "beautiful to look at." But he could not imagine that Meade had sanctioned this parade, and he predicted that "those troops will be coming back again very soon."[28]

George Meade was actually one of the last people on Cemetery Hill to learn about Sickles' maneuver, and this was largely because his impromptu headquarters at the Widow Leister's ramshackle cottage sat on the reverse slope of a hill and was out of sight of anything to the south. At three o'clock, he received the happy tidings that, at last, John Sedgwick and the 6th Corps were supposed to be closing in, and Meade was finally ready to call for a council of his corps commanders to deliberate on what the now concentrated Army of the Potomac was going to do next. He also dashed off a quick message to Halleck, informing the general in chief that he had put any plans for an attack on hold until the 6th Corps had arrived, but might also "fall back to my supplies at Westminster"—which was to say, to Pipe Creek—"if I find it hazardous to do so." Gouverneur Warren, who had been informed by an aide of what Sickles was up to, strolled into Meade's headquarters at the Widow Leister's cottage and asked casually whether Meade was aware that Sickles had redeployed the entire 3rd Corps out to the Emmitsburg Road. Startled by Warren's news, Meade erupted in Vesuvian proportions, and demanded that Sickles report to him for an explanation.

Sickles at first refused. He "sat upon his white horse, received the papers," and told the courier, "Say to General Meade that it will be impossible for me to report at his Hd Quarters at this time as this battle will be precipitated upon us before I could reach his Hd Quarters." Meade furiously sent off a second demand, and this time Sickles obeyed, although the reason had less to do with deference to his commander's wishes and more with the fact that Charles Graham had glimpsed from his new position in the peach orchard large clumps of Confederate infantry in the woods to the west. Sickles "had not gone 60 ft. before a shell passed over our heads, bursting in air far beyond," wrote one soldier in Sickles' old Excelsior Brigade, and "in a few minutes the battle had Commenced." When Sickles arrived, lathered and dusty, Meade stopped him from dismounting, and told him to turn around back to his corps, and he would follow. He ordered George Sykes to get his 5th Corps men, who were sitting comfortably down by Powers Hill on the Baltimore Pike, up and hurrying to Sickles' aid, and then he was off himself, outracing his hastily mounted staffers toward the peach orchard, where Sickles had ridden out, dismounted, and was trying to glimpse a "column of infantry" which was "then moving rapidly towards . . . our left."[29]

Amid the shells arching over their heads, Meade surveyed the Emmitsburg Road. He could see Humphreys' division, drawn up along the road. *Where was the rest of the 3rd Corps?* Sickles described the long, attenuated deployment of Birney's division from the Emmitsburg Road down to Devil's Den. Meade, "turning and pointing to the rear," angrily told Sickles where his corps *ought* to have been—"between the left of the Second Corps and Little Round Top"—and that he had "advanced his line beyond supporting distance of the army." *And what was the artillery banging away at?* David Birney now leaned-in on Sickles' behalf, explaining "the position and movements of the enemy; that they were moving in order to turn our left, and we had opened upon them." The question that blossomed in Meade's mind was whether Sickles could hold this ground long enough for Meade to get more troops up behind Sickles. "Are you not too much extended, General," Meade demanded. "Can you hold this front?" Yes, Sickles lied handsomely, but "I shall need support." He then shifted to what would turn out to be the first in a half-century's worth of defenses, justifications, excuses, half-truths, and rationalizations. "I have made these dispositions to the best of my judgment." And he *had* occupied the high ground. But, Sickles quickly added, he *could* pull his men back to where they had started, if that was what Meade wanted. "General Sickles," Meade sliced in, slamming all the weight of his sarcasm on Sickles' fingers, "this *is* in some respects higher ground than that to the rear; but there is still higher ground in front of you, and if you keep on advancing you will find constantly higher ground all the way to the mountains."

Very well, Sickles stiffly agreed, he would "be happy to modify" his position "according to your views." Meade considered this, then rejected it. It was too late for that, he retorted. Artillery was the overture to infantry, and Confederate infantry would be on Sickles' doorstep before any orders to fall back could be distributed. "No," Meade said, "I will send you the Fifth Corps, and you may send for support from the Second Corps." Then Meade rode off in "a heavy shower of shells." He was riding a borrowed horse, and the shelling drove the beast "into an uncontrollable frenzy." From the woodline in the distance, long lines of Confederate infantry were stepping out and dressing their ranks.[30]

Robert E. Lee wanted Dick Ewell to get moving as soon as the sound of Longstreet's engagement began, and it was not a good sign that he felt the need to be on Ewell's coattails. But as the afternoon began to drag onward past two o'clock with no whisper of combat from Longstreet's direction, Lee's anxieties attached themselves to Longstreet instead. "Perceiving the great value of time, General Lee's impatience became so urgent that he proceeded in person to hasten the movement of Longstreet," and set off once again, trailing aides, escorts, and observers, to find out what had gone wrong. He arrived to find that skirmishers from Anderson's division had captured "a Federal sergeant . . . who was found, on examination, to belong to a division" in the 3rd Corps, which wasn't even supposed to be in Gettysburg yet. When Longstreet joined Lee "at about three o'clock in the afternoon," he was as perplexed at the developing situation as Lee was, for now there were clearly large formations of Federal infantry and artillery lining up at the Emmitsburg Road and in the peach orchard. Lee and Longstreet "held a conference on horseback," and then Longstreet took off "up the line and down again, occasionally dismounting, and going forward to get a better view of the enemy's position."[31]

McLaws' division was drawn up "in column of companies," waiting for an order to move forward, seize the Emmitsburg Road, "and when well on the enemy's flank to face or form to the left" and drive up to Cemetery Hill. But the enemy was now clearly *on* the Emmitsburg Road itself. John Bell Hood's scouts came back, breathlessly reporting that while there were obviously Federal troops occupying the peach orchard and the line of the Emmitsburg Road above the orchard, the rest of these Federals were thinly stretched along two stony ridges about a mile directly ahead, and no Federals were posted on the Round Tops, which loomed behind them. Best of all, the scouts had found a major Union wagon park behind the Round Tops, and if Hood was allowed to "march around the base of Round Top to the right," he could roll up the unanchored Union flank and overrun the wagon park. Hood had already "placed one or two batteries in position and opened fire," and he was ready to send his division forward in a long curl around the rough outlines of the Round Tops.[32]

But this would place a terrible burden on soldiers who had been on the march for almost twelve hours without intermission. In Kershaw's South Carolina brigade, "the soldiers fell down . . . as soon as the halt was made . . . and soon most of them were fast asleep." And anyway, Lee and Longstreet

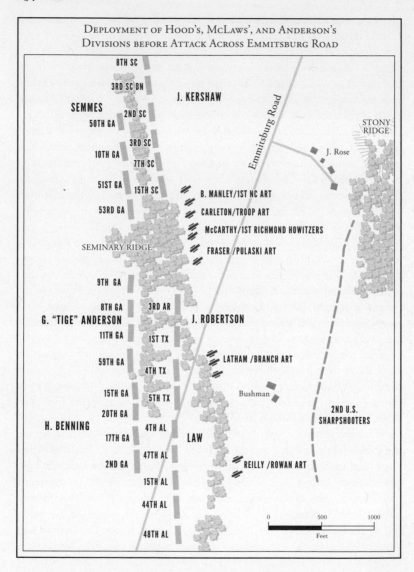

DEPLOYMENT OF HOOD'S, McLAWS', AND ANDERSON'S
DIVISIONS BEFORE ATTACK ACROSS EMMITSBURG ROAD

were working on a different plan. "Gen. Lee was already fretting over the delay which had occurred," and even if it was no longer possible to launch an attack that wheeled up the Emmitsburg Road, he was certainly not going to call the whole thing off. Taking the situation as it was, Lee proposed to attack the Federals in the road head-on, drive them out of the way, and *then* execute a long curve toward Cemetery Hill. Both an offhand inspection and Hood's report were evidence that the position could not be very strongly held, and in any case it would be easier to crush these Yankees in the open than if they were backed up against Cemetery Hill; in fact, it was a mercy that they had moved out and revealed themselves in this fashion, because if they had been concealed from view farther to their rear, Longstreet's original wheel up the Emmitsburg Road would have offered a disastrously vulnerable flank for them to counterattack. *Had not God delivered the Philistines into his hands?* The attack would go forward, but this time heading straight eastward, rolling over the weak Federal positions and cutting off all the Federal troops posted on Cemetery Hill from behind, while Ewell attacked them from the front. Longstreet's artillery "should open along the front for ten minutes, then a pause, a signal of three guns from the right battery, in rapid succession, and the attack was to commence without further order." Hood's division would jump off first, heading for one of the stony ridges (the property of an elderly farmer named John Houck; after the battle, it would become known as Houck's Ridge) and the Round Tops. McLaws would follow at a decent interval, overwhelming the other, nearer stony ridge and crushing the peach orchard position, "with a view of gaining a line resting upon Little Round Top on the right and the Peach Orchard on the left." Richard H. Anderson's borrowed division would go in last of all.[33]

This was what, in technical terms, could be called an *echelon* attack, or what Porter Alexander described as the "progressive type, as distinguished from the simultaneous" assault. The genius of the echelon was the way it forced an enemy to use his own instincts against himself. Attacked on one flank, a defending enemy would shore up that flank by pulling units out of unthreatened parts of the line and sending them in as reinforcements; as the next stage in the echelon threatened the next part of the line, the defenders would drain still more troops away from the unthreatened parts; by the time the final part of the echelon was launched, the remaining sector of the defenders' line would have been bled so dry of troops that it would break and collapse, and the entire position would come unhinged. On the other hand, the echelon had its risks, too, since it required exquisite planning and timing, and a certain amount of cold blood in the veins while the first elements of the echelon were chewed to pieces. In this situation, Lee and Longstreet were hurriedly trying to impose a complicated tactical form on a situation they had not anticipated—and they would just as hurriedly fail to communicate the full shape of this plan down through the ladder of staffers and subordinates.[34]

None of this sat well with John Bell Hood, who continued to pester Longstreet with entreaties "to turn Round Top." Longstreet was sufficiently uncertain about these last-minute overhauls of the attack plan that his only advice to Hood was the less than hearty endorsement, "We must obey the orders of General Lee." Longstreet himself dismounted "and held his reins over his arms," sending off "staff officers and couriers along the line of battle to watch the movements and report to him," while "General Lee left us." The artillery whose voice would be the signal to Ewell for his own action to begin three miles away was wheeled into position, and Porter Alexander hoped that "with my 54 guns & close range," he could also "overwhelm & crush" the Federal artillery he saw rolling up to Sherfy's peach orchard. Alexander's own battalion opened fire from "the edge" of the woods "next the Peach Orchard" at about "500 yards distance." Hood's division sprang up "as if at a game of ball," McIvor Law's Alabama brigade and Jerome Robertson (a dark, beetle-browed Kentuckian who had been a hatter, a doctor, a volunteer in the Texas revolution of 1836, and a Texas state senator) with Hood's old Texas brigade in front, and Benning's and "Tige" Anderson's Georgia brigades drawn up in back of them. "Fix bayonets, my brave Texans," Hood shouted as he galloped across the front of Robertson's brigade, "forward and take those heights." And they cheered him in response: "Follow the Lone Star Flag to the top of the mountain!" cried the lieutenant colonel of the 1st Texas, and there "arose such a wild indescribable battle yell that no one having heard ever forgot."[35]

CHAPTER FIFTEEN

You are to hold this ground at all costs

UNTIL FIVE DAYS BEFORE, the 11,000 men who made up the 5th Corps had been George Meade's own corps, and his promotion to top command had boosted his senior division commander, George Sykes, to his place. Sykes was a West Pointer's West Pointer—thirty-ninth in a class of fifty-six in 1842, a Regular Army lifer who had seen action in the Seminole War and the Mexican War, and as doggedly average a soldier as the army could offer. At West Point, they had called him "Tardy George" and "Slow Trot," and unthinking, methodical, and deliberate adherence to by-the-book plodding was Sykes' trademark. Until Sedgwick arrived, the 5th Corps formed the army's reserve, and Meade positioned them around Powers Hill, a small knob that rose about 100 feet above the track of the Baltimore Pike, a mile north and east of the Round Tops. But under these new circumstances, George Meade's first priority became getting Sykes and his 5th Corps moving to Sickles' support, and it would be vital for "Slow Trot" Sykes to abandon his tardiness for once.

The backbone of the 5th Corps was Romeyn Ayres' three-brigade division—two of the brigades (under Hannibal Day and Sidney Burbank) were composed of ten regiments of the Regular U.S. Army. A second three-brigade division was commanded by James Barnes, filled with a medley of Massachusetts, Michigan, Pennsylvania, and New York regiments, along with one from Maine. The last division had only been attached to the 5th Corps on June 28th: they were Samuel Wylie Crawford's two brigades' worth of Pennsylvania Reserves, marching from the defenses of Washington to the rescue of their native state. Crawford had quite an unusual personal history with this war. His father was a Reformed Presbyterian minister (which is to say, exclusively psalm-singing Calvinist and militant abolitionist, too) who doggedly insisted on remaining in his pulpit in Chambersburg during the rebel occupation; Crawford himself had been the post surgeon at Fort Sumter in 1861, so that the war assumed for him the dimensions of a personal feud, "a conspiracy against God and humanity." Ayres and Barnes were cut more along the model of Sykes. Romeyn Ayres was a tall, indolent New Yorker who managed to graduate solidly in the middle of the West Point class of 1847, while James Barnes, a West Point classmate of Robert E. Lee's, had spent the previous twenty-two years before the war as an undistinguished railroad executive. Solemn, smiling, slightly puzzled, he was only in command of the division because its regular commander, Charles Griffin, was still recovering from Chancellorsville.[1]

With little more to do than wait for Sedgwick and the 6th Corps to arrive and take over the role of army reserve, the 5th Corps sprawled out comfortably around Powers Hill, more or less in battalion columns, "to rest and make up for the loss of sleep" that had been experienced on the swift march from Hanover the night before. If they had any prospect of action, it would be as a support for the 12th Corps, to the east. Then, in midafternoon, the sporadic rifle fire that they had heard through the day "increased to a roar" and "shells, shot wild of their intended destination, passed over the closely crowded reserve and exploded harmlessly far beyond." The lounging formations were roused by *Fall in, attention, load at will, load,* "harsh, stern, determined, in quick succession." Meade wanted to "personally superintend the posting of his old corps on the left of the Third," but he had to be content with sending "several staff officers to hurry up the column under Major General Sykes." Nor did he propose waiting for Sykes to gather the entire corps: "Send a brigade to report to Sickles" was Meade's directive, and the rest of Sykes' command could follow. This turned out to be wise. Sykes would take the better part of an hour, between four o'clock and five, to pull the 5th Corps together and get his first available brigade moving at the head of his first available division in Sickles' direction. That division turned out to be James Barnes' with just over 3,400 men; its lead brigade belonged to Strong Vincent, who had only the day before speculated grandiloquently on how glorious a death in defense of the soil of old Pennsylvania would be. As it turned out, he would never reach Sickles at all.[2]

The reason was Gouverneur K. Warren. This slightly built, droopy-mustached New Yorker looked more like an Italian chef than a soldier, and he invited people who judged only by appearances to discount him as yet another colorless military hack. Quite the opposite: he graduated second in his class at West Point in 1850, began the war as the lieutenant colonel of the snappy

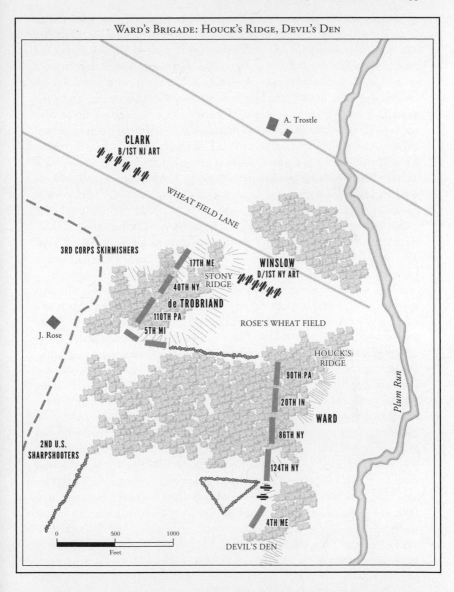

WARD'S BRIGADE: HOUCK'S RIDGE, DEVIL'S DEN

A. Trostle

CLARK
B/1ST NJ ART

WHEAT FIELD LANE

3RD CORPS SKIRMISHERS

17TH ME

WINSLOW
D/1ST NY ART

40TH NY   STONY
RIDGE

de TROBRIAND

110TH PA

J. Rose

5TH MI

ROSE'S WHEAT FIELD

HOUCK'S
RIDGE

90TH PA

20TH IN

WARD

86TH NY

2ND U.S.
SHARPSHOOTERS

124TH NY

Plum Run

0   500   1000

Feet

4TH ME

DEVIL'S DEN

5th New York ("Duryea's Zouaves"), commanded a brigade under Meade in the 5th Corps, and was tapped by the watchful Joe Hooker to become his staff topographical engineer, and then chief engineer of the Army of the Potomac. This was in spite of Warren's personal suspicions of Hooker and his deep allegiance and admiration for Meade. When Hooker's head fell, Meade's first inclination had been to send Daniel Butterfield packing after Hooker, and put Warren in Butterfield's place as the Army of the Potomac's chief of staff. But in the midst of a campaign, Warren advised Meade not to make more changes at the top than he absolutely needed to; Warren would stay on as chief engineer for now, and allow Meade to use him as the de facto chief of staff. It was Warren who counseled Meade not to try consequences with Ewell's corps at Wolf's Hill that morning; it was also Warren who had alerted Meade to Dan Sickles' advance to the Emmitsburg Road. Now, after having accompanied Meade to the commanding general's infuriating interview with Sickles, Warren looked around and suggested to Meade that it might be a good idea if he went up to the signal station on Little Round Top and see if the rocky hill gave him any direct sight of the Confederates massing in the woods west of the Emmitsburg Road. "I felt so worried at the outlook," Warren later wrote, "that I requested General Meade to let me go to Little Round Top. . . . He directed me to do so, and I did not see him again till the attack had spent its force."[3]

The Round Tops were really one, large natural tumulus with two pronounced peaks—the larger peak, Big Round Top, was the taller one, at 660 feet, but it was heavily wrapped in old-growth forest and offered little in the way of a vista despite its height. The lower peak was really a narrow spine, running north–south for about 250 yards, and heavily littered with granitelike boulders. Its east face was, like Big Round Top, thickly forested. But the west face had been conveniently cleared by logging operations, and from the spiny peak anyone with a horse nimble enough to clamber up the logging trails would emerge into a spectacular view across a rock-littered ravine, and see the granite undulations of ridgelines running in parallels to the mountains on the horizon. The nearest of these unsmiling ridges was Houck's Ridge, where Sickles had planted the far left of his 3rd Corps line—John Henry Hobart Ward's five regiments, with James Smith's 4th New York Independent Battery set up amid the enormous rock outcroppings of Devil's Den. To their right was an open expanse of wheat field, and then another smattering of blue regiments spiked with flags and artillery batteries—de Trobriand's brigade, strung out along the other stony ridge. In the far distance was the Sherfy peach orchard and the Emmitsburg Road, and Andrew Humphreys' division, with its right flank hanging awkwardly unhinged from the larger formations of Union troops gathered on Cemetery Hill.[4]

What made Warren's blood pool when he gained the peak of Little Round Top was the spectacle unfolding beyond the Emmitsburg Road: "From that point I could see the enemy's lines of battle," fixed bayonets glinting in the sun. Four big Confederate brigades were coming out of the woods like a pack of ravenous wolves, then four more on their left flank, and then still more, on and on up the line, with enough weight of numbers to crash through Sickles' corps as though it was a dead hedge. "The whole Confederate line was sweeping from out the woods in which it had formed," wrote a junior officer in the 5th Corps, "far outflanking the left of the Third Corps line, where Smith's battery, in air and almost unsupported on the rocks of the Devil's Den, gallantly waited their doom." And not only theirs. The rebels farthest to Warren's left were moving first; they would have to cover almost a mile of ground to reach Devil's Den and Ward's pitiful little brigade, but once they did, they would flatten everything in their path, spill over the stony ridge, and either swarm unopposed up the west face of the Round Tops, or plow right into the rear of the 3rd Corps.[5]

The signals detachment on Little Round Top had seen all of this for themselves, and had been trying in vain to awaken "General Sickles and . . . the general commanding" to their peril since first catching sight of Longstreet's column that morning. Now they were packing up their equipment and getting ready to remove themselves from the threat no one else seemed interested in paying attention to. Warren's first job was to tell them in reasonably blunt language to stay put and keep their flags wagging, if only to suggest to the oncoming Confederates that something was happening up there. His second was to get the help the signalers had been unsuccessful in attracting. Warren had two aides with him. He turned to one of them, Lt. Ranald Mackenzie—"a fine, well-trained mind, a quick appreciation of every thing, and a brain always at work"—and sent him off down the rocky hillside to find Sickles and warn him to get some troops up on Little Round Top without delay, then find Meade and tell him "that we would at once have to occupy that place very strongly." Meade was already trying to regain control of the situation by dispatching one of his own staffers to pull Andrew Humphreys' division off the Emmitsburg Road and send it down to Little Round Top. But not even Humphreys thought this was a good idea, and Meade quickly countermanded it. Sickles, who got Warren's message through Mackenzie, flatly refused to send anyone to Little Round Top: he had not a regiment to spare, but if Mackenzie could find the 5th Corps, Sickles had been assured that George Sykes' troops could be used where they were needed. Off Mackenzie sped again, this time to find Sykes, who had ridden ahead of the 5th Corps to lay out lines of deployment. Sykes heard him out, then sent off an aide, twenty-one-year-old Capt. William Jay, to intercept Barnes' division and send a brigade up to Warren. Jay spied the head of the column, expecting to find Barnes there as well; what he found instead was Strong Vincent.[6]

Vincent was a native of Erie, in the far northwest corner of Pennsylvania, a Harvard graduate (class of 1859), handsome, popular, sporting a flamboyant set of side-whiskers. He volunteered with a local company at the outbreak of the war, and ended up as lieutenant colonel of the 83rd Pennsylvania. First impressions of Vincent were of a stuffed shirt. Oliver Wilcox Norton, who would serve as Vincent's orderly, "thought him a dude and an upstart." But nobody in the 83rd had much to say about Vincent's hauteur after Fredericksburg, where, "with sword in hand," he "stood erect in full view of the enemy's artillery, and though the shot fell fast on all sides, he never wavered nor once changed his position." As Amos Judson of the 83rd remarked afterward, "a high and chivalrous sense of duty" could make a lot of other defects pale in the estimate of the privates in the ranks. Vincent inherited command of the brigade the 83rd served in, though not a brigadier general's star to go with it, and he was ambitiously frank in hoping that the orders to march to Sickles' succor "will either bring me my stars, or finish my career as a soldier."[7]

As Captain Jay approached, Vincent "left the head of his brigade and rode forward" and asked what he wanted. Jay replied that he had a message for General Barnes from General Sykes. That gave Vincent pause, since Vincent was aware that Barnes, like Thomas Rowley the day before, had been medicating his pre-battle anxieties "out of a black commissary quart bottle" and was already "hollow from skull to boots." What was the message, Vincent demanded. Captain Jay must have hesitated, because Vincent, already sure that Barnes was lost in his alcoholic fog, interjected, "What are your orders? Give me your orders." The orders, said Jay, were for Barnes to "send one of his brigades to occupy that hill yonder," pointing to Little Round Top. Very well, Vincent replied, he would take his own brigade, and also the responsibility for finding a way up to the crest of the hill. The column turned to the left, searching along the base of Little Round Top for a usable track, and finding none until they located a lane running up the south face of the hill. Vincent's brigade sprinted up the hill, and it was from there, at around 4:30, that Strong Vincent could look down on a scene of pure disaster.[8]

Devil's Den

The attack began to go awry with the first step Hood's division took. Longstreet placed McLaws' division "about parallel to the Emmitsburg Road," and because the Emmitsburg Road ran at a northeast–southwest angle, "Gen. Hood was deployed at an angle of about forty-five degrees to northward across it and leaning towards Round Top." This was awkward, but Hood was going to make it worse, because he was unreconciled to Lee's directive to cross the road and then curl left. He grumbled to Philip Work, the colonel of the 1st Texas, that once "we get under fire, I will have a digression" (or maybe it was *discretion*) to make the move he wanted to make around Little Round Top. In order to speed up their approach, his lead brigades—McIvor Law's Alabamians and Jerome Robertson's Texans, numbering around 1,850 men— were to move forward in column and get over Devil's Den and its stony ridge as fast as possible. But Gouverneur Warren had scribbled off a warning to James Smith's 4th New York Independent Battery, perched on Devil's Den with long-range 10-pounder Parrott rifles that could punish Hood's rebels as soon as they made an appearance. The boulder-thick ground limited Smith to using just four of his guns, with the remaining two and the battery's cais- sons parked below and behind Devil's Den. But four Parrotts were more than enough to do the sort of damage for which Warren was hoping. Smith had been trading fire with "a battery of six Light 12-pounders" in the distance for almost two hours, but with the appearance of the infantry, Smith was deter- mined "to oppose and cripple this attack and check it as much as possible."[9]

At four o'clock, Hood's men came out into the open "in heavy columns of battalion," and there they stopped, wrote a soldier in the 4th Texas, "dur- ing which the batteries commenced to play on us." Smith's Parrotts straddled the Texas brigade, the first salvo falling short, and the second screaming over their heads. But the third, of solid shot, "hit our line about eight feet in front" then bouncing up and "knocking off one soldier's head and cutting another in two, bespattering us with blood." While the division's pioneers were sent forward to tear down obstructions in front, Hood moved his bri- gades out of column, where their bunched masses were horribly vulnerable to the carom of solid shot, into line, which presented less of a packed target but which would be slowed to a crawl by the need to dress and redress the lines as they moved over the uneven ground in front of them. Even the temperatures were "extremely hot," recalled another member of the 4th Texas, and "knap- sacks, blankets, and other cumbersome non-essential battle equipment" was discarded.[10]

Law's and Robertson's brigades had hardly moved beyond the line of their own artillery supports when the next wheel came off. John Bell Hood was determined to go forward with this attack in person "on the left of a line" from the Texas brigade. The massed brigades had crossed the Emmitsburg Road, rifles at right-shoulder-shift or at trail-arms, heading downslope toward the stone farmhouse of Michael Bushman, when John Cheves Haskell (one of Hood's division artillery officers) brought up two batteries Hood wanted to position more closely in support of his attack. Haskell had just reported when Hood "turned, apparently to give me orders." Instead, one of James Smith's Parrott shells exploded over the group of mounted officers and aides around Hood and a shell splinter sliced through Hood's left arm, from above the elbow to the hand, breaking the bone. "I saw a spiracle [spherical] case shot explode twenty feet over Hood's head," wrote Colonel Work of the 1st Texas, "saw him sway to and fro in the saddle." Hood slid into the arms of his staffers, "utterly prostrated and almost fainting." It was not actually as dramatic a wound as it looked, but Haskell could see that "it evidently gave him intense pain and utterly unnerved him, so that I could get no orders from him" about where to place the batteries. Neither would anyone else be getting orders from Hood that afternoon. A stretcher party lifted the wounded general and carried him to an ambulance, where a dazed and shocked Hood sat "in front with the driver, his arm in a bloody bandage." From that moment, his division would be "without a leader and ignorant of where the enemy is."[11]

Parked on the crest formed by Devil's Den and Houck's Ridge, the five Union regiments in John Ward's brigade "saw the enemy's Infantry coming out of the woods . . . marching as if on parade, across the open field." Ward threw out a line of skirmishers to a stone wall 175 yards in front of Round Top composed of the 2nd U.S. Sharpshooters, and as Hood's division opened out from "columns of regiments" and bore down on the Sharpshooters, Smith's four Parrott rifles let loose at them with "a heavy and destructive fire of canister, grape, and shell." The bewildering variety of ordnance was no exaggeration: Smith was firing anything he had on hand, as his crews struggled to bring up ammunition from the caissons parked behind Devil's Den. "The guns were worked to their utmost," remembered a nearby infantryman in the 124th New York. "I heard the gunners directed to use five and six second fuse, and when the gunners reported that the case shot and shrapnel were all gone, I heard the order, 'Give them shell! Give them solid shot! Damn them, give them anything.'" And at long distance, the Parrotts could do their work extremely well. "The battery," wrote one sergeant in the 124th New York, "working as I never saw gunners work before or since, tore gap after gap through the ranks of the advancing foe."[12]

They not only put John Bell Hood out of commission, but flattened "many of [the] gallant officers and men" in the division's long lines; the unwieldy battle lines themselves "became broken and confused and the men exhausted." The ground was rocky and formed "defiles" which forced men in the lines to bunch up in groups of "3 or 4" to pass, tripping, stumbling, "breaking up our alignment and rendering its reformation impossible." Jerome Robertson understood Hood's last orders to have been for him to keep his left flank on the Emmitsburg Road and his right tied to Law's Alabama brigade. But this began to unravel almost at once. Regiments pulled apart from one another: the 1st Texas and 3rd Arkansas (in Robertson's brigade) stopped and started, then began to stray to their left, while their companion

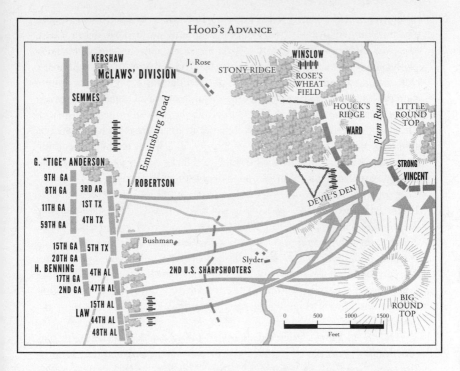

HOOD'S ADVANCE

KERSHAW
McLAWS' DIVISION
J. Rose
STONY RIDGE
WINSLOW
ROSE'S
WHEAT
FIELD

SEMMES
HOUCK'S
RIDGE
LITTLE
ROUND
TOP
Plum Run
WARD

Emmitsburg Road

G. "TIGE" ANDERSON
9TH GA
8TH GA   3RD AR
11TH GA   1ST TX
59TH GA   4TH TX
J. ROBERTSON
DEVIL'S DEN
STRONG
VINCENT

15TH GA   5TH TX
20TH GA
H. BENNING
17TH GA   4TH AL
2ND GA   47TH AL
Bushman
Slyder
2ND U.S. SHARPSHOOTERS

15TH AL
LAW   44TH AL
48TH AL
BIG
ROUND
TOP

0   500   1000   1500
Feet

regiments—the 4th and 5th Texas—wobbled rightward and attached themselves to McIvor Law's Alabama brigade. But then Law's brigade began to
separate: the 4th Alabama obligingly hitched itself to the 4th and 5th Texas
and began heading unsteadily around the southern edge of Devil's Den; the
47th and 15th Alabama also began wandering rightward and eventually slid in
behind the mixed-together Texans and Alabamians; the remaining two regiments of Law's brigade, the 44th and 48th Alabama, stumbled even farther
rightward, toward Big Round Top. Behind Robertson's and Law's brigades,
the backup brigades of George Anderson and Henry Benning were also moving forward, but they were skewing to the left, instead of following in the
tracks of Robertson and Law, heading toward the farmstead of John Rose and
the nearer stony ridge which pointed toward the Sherfy peach orchard. Some
of Benning's Georgians became so entangled with Robertson's Texans that
"after several ineffectual efforts . . . to separate the men," the officers just gave
up and the mass went forward "thus commingled."[13]

But the closer the Confederate lines approached, the more difficult it was
for Smith to avoid overshooting, until "we could hear the charges of canister

passing over us with the noise of partridges in flight." The Confederate infantry, "marching in line of battle at a brisk gait," easily pushed back Hiram Berdan's U.S. Sharpshooters, the 4th Alabama edging ahead and driving them "with the bayonet." The ground now turned sharply upward toward Devil's Den, and after pausing near the base of the ridge for a few minutes to reform the line, the Confederates began swarming over the "rough and rugged" ground toward the crest of Houck's Ridge and Devil's Den. "A stake-and-rider fence" stood in the path of the 5th Texas, and one captain called out, "Ten dollars to the first man who gets over that fence." Two of them climbed over it together, but there was no record afterward "whether they got" the reward "or not," especially since Ward's brigade now stood up and opened fire and a "sheet of flame burst from the rocks less than a hundred yards away." The 1st Texas and 3rd Arkansas were temporarily halted in their tracks, which gave Ward's regiments a chance to reload and get off another volley. But George Branard, the color-bearer of the 1st Texas, "called upon his color guard to follow him, and, mounting the rocks, dashed toward the Yankee lines." A shell from one of Smith's guns blew off the top of Branard's flagstaff and laid him "unconscious on the ground," but the rest of the Texans scrambled up the ridge behind him, working up the rough incline "very slowly, only a few feet at a time."[14]

Drawn up along Houck's Ridge were John Ward's 99th Pennsylvania, 20th Indiana, and the 86th and 124th New York (nicknamed the "Orange Blossoms," from upstate Orange County). This line butted against Smith's battery on Devil's Den, and a fifth regiment, the 4th Maine, was posted on the other side of the battery, where Devil's Den fell away amid the boulders and monoliths. They did not have many illusions about holding their position. Ward's regiments had "but a single line of battle unsupported." In the ravine behind them which led up to Little Round Top, there was (as far as any of them knew) nothing but "a herd of horned cattle," while in front of them they could see "four distinct lines of battle" whose "superiority in numbers, seen at a glance, seemed overwhelming." The colonel of the Orange Blossoms, Augustus Van Horne Ellis, tried to launch a spoiling attack of his own, downhill at the 1st Texas. The major of the regiment, twenty-three-year-old James Cromwell, led the charge, mounted and whirling "his sword twice above his head." But all Cromwell achieved for his efforts was to get himself shot out of the saddle, and in short order the 124th was brutally hurled back.

The 1st Texas now began to overrun Smith's battery, while Smith pled for the milling Union infantrymen to save his guns. The gunners fought off the Texans with anything they could use for a weapon, including their rammers. The 4th Maine and 99th Pennsylvania quickly evicted the attackers (the colonel of the 4th Maine said he would "never forget" the deadly metallic *click* made by the locking ring of his men's bayonets as they were fixed for the attack). But there was not much more of this they could take. Smith's gunners were down to using "canister without sponging" out the gun barrels to extinguish lingering sparks. The color sergeant of the 99th, who survived despite thirteen bullet holes in his clothing and losing every other member of the color guard, remembered being "frightened almost to death," and he "prayed as I never prayed before or since."[15]

David Birney now began to obey the logic Lee and Longstreet imposed by their method of attack: Birney peeled off the 40th New York (a regiment from de Trobriand's brigade), and begged the 6th New Jersey from Humphreys' division out at the Emmitsburg Road, both moving down through the ravine toward Devil's Den. They never made it. Before Ward could find them a position in which to shore up his line, "a heavy battle line" of Confederate infantry appeared at the other end of the ravine—the 44th and 48th Alabama, along with Henry Benning's Georgia brigade. "Give them hell," roared Benning, a former Georgia Supreme Court justice and secession hotspur in 1861, "give them hell"—which it afforded the 17th Georgia "the utmost pleasure" to do. Confederate officers, in the frenzy, threw aside their swords and picked up rifles. Even Longstreet's artillery chief, James Walton, "got a gun from a fallen Confederate and went into the fight," his "face powder-stained from biting off the cartridges." Ward saw the end coming, and dragged his bloodied regiments northward along Houck's Ridge, the 4th Maine bringing up the rear. But there was not much left after this battering: Smith's four guns atop Devil's Den were lost and the 124th New York had "hardly more than a skirmish-line left" on its feet. The howling Confederates, "leaping to and fro from boulder to boulder," rushed over the abandoned ridge, prodding away "between 140 and 200 prisoners" and sending up the "music of the unmistakable Confederate yell."[16]

The too-late 40th New York and 6th New Jersey tried to hold the ground down in the ravine alongside the two remaining Parrotts that James Smith had parked there before the fighting began. "The Alabamians' battle flag drops three different times from the effect of our canister," Smith wrote. "Thrice their line wavers and seeks shelter in the woods." But once Benning's Georgia brigade had secured the top of Devil's Den, Smith's remaining gunners were caught in a crossfire from in front and from above, and they, too, joined the pullback "through the woods." The left flank of Dan Sickles' ill-starred 3rd Corps line was gone, and the jubilant rebels could at last execute their pivot northward and begin the steady roll-up of the Army of the Potomac, straight toward Cemetery Hill. It was then that they noticed, for the first time, the appearance of Union infantry above them, on the lip of Little Round Top.[17]

Little Round Top

While he waited for troops to show up on Little Round Top, Gouverneur Warren was joined there by a trickle of the curious and the constrained. Daniel Klingel, who fled his log house on the Emmitsburg Road when the 3rd Corps took up positions around it, was waylaid by one of Warren's staffers, who took him up on Little Round Top to identify the "names of roads, distances" for Warren. A correspondent for the *New York Herald* mounted the hill to watch as Hood's division "came out . . . and silently but swiftly moved down upon us." As the fighting erupted, the lines were enveloped in a "canopy of smoke" and the declining sun on the western horizon "gleamed . . . like a fiery furnace." Thomas Hyde, who had been sent ahead by John Sedgwick to confirm the route of the 6th Corps, rode up to "a little rocky crest" on Little Round Top, and "borrowing a glass from the signal officer," was "able to distinguish much moving about of troops and artillery." Descending to the rear of the hill, Hyde was surprised to encounter one of the 6th Corps' sutlers, staggering drunk, who was nearly blown to perdition by a shell that "shrieked . . . with more than usually fiendish noise." The inebriated sutler grinned lopsidedly at Hyde, put "his hand up to his ear," and croaked, *Listen to the mocking-bird*.[18]

Warren appeared to the *Herald* reporter to be "cool and undisturbed, watching with his glass the distant woods, and anxiously scanning the forests at our left." He had good reason, since at least two of McIvor Law's Alabama regiments had disappeared into the woods at the base of Big Round Top, and if they wheeled and came up the south slope of Little Round Top, there would be nothing to prevent them from going straight over the hill and into the rear of the 3rd Corps. But the only Federal troops who showed up were artillerymen—Lt. Charles Edward Hazlett's Battery D, 5th U.S. Artillery, which was attached to the 5th Corps, and had been following in the rear of Barnes' division as they lumbered out of their bivouac around Powers Hill to Sickles' rescue. At some point, the 5th Corps artillery chief, Augustus Martin, suggested to Hazlett that "there might be a good position for a battery on the summit of the hill if we could reach it, though it seemed somewhat doubtful from the rough and rocky appearance of the westerly slope." So, accompanied by "an officer" who "rode up and said, 'Battery D, this way,'" Hazlett's horses, caissons, and six big 10-pounder Parrott rifles peeled out of the division column and headed for Little Round Top.[19]

How they would get to the crest was even more of a problem for artillery than for infantry. The logging trails up the east face of the hill offered one possibility, but it meant "whips and spurs vigorously applied" to the horses

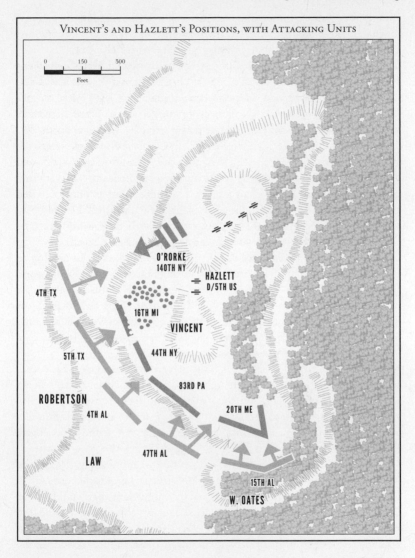

VINCENT'S AND HAZLETT'S POSITIONS, WITH ATTACKING UNITS

in front, and rounding up "stragglers from the Third Corps" to push and lift from behind. The usual procedure for getting guns up a steep incline like this was to "fox-wedge" them—cutting posts and jamming them into rocks, and looping cables around the guns for "a company of infantry" to haul them forward, pulley-wise. But Hazlett had neither time nor men for by-the-book procedures. The battery's caissons were parked at the foot of Little

Round Top, and one by one the pieces were driven, manhandled, and shoved "by hand and handspike" through the trees and up the slope. Once the first gun got to the top, two more problems presented themselves: first, the crest of Little Round Top was only a rocky spine which would let Hazlett's guns train in only one direction, westward. Woe betide them if the rebels came up the hill on the left. Second, Hazlett's Parrott rifles were (like James Smith's New York battery on Devil's Den) lovely for long-distance purposes, but they would be nearly useless if Confederate infantry came swarming up the hill at close range, under the barrels of his guns. Warren was glad enough to see Hazlett, but frank enough to tell him that this "was no place for efficient artillery fire—both of us knew that." Hazlett waved him away. " 'Never mind that,' he replied, 'the sound of my guns will be encouraging to our troops and disheartening to the others, and my battery's no use if this hill is lost.' "[20]

Sitting "on his horse on the summit of the hill," wearing a white straw hat and "pointing with his sword towards the enemy," Hazlett seemed to Warren "the impersonation of valor and heroic beauty." But if he was to hold on to Little Round Top, Warren needed infantry and not just valor and beauty, and finally losing what was left of his patience, Warren took himself and the last of his staffers down the hill to find them himself. He missed, by what must have been minutes, precisely the infantry he had been praying for—Strong Vincent's brigade, bolting up the paths on the far side of Little Round Top. What Vincent saw when he reached the lower end of the crest was far from comforting: "Devil's Den was a smoking crater," and the ravine which separated Devil's Den from Little Round Top "was a whirling maelstrom." Ward's men along the stony ridge, some 500 yards beyond them, "formed again and went to the ridge among the bowlders, disappeared into the woods, stayed a few minutes, and then, like a shattered wreck upon the foaming sea, came drifting to the rear."

Of Vincent's four regiments, the 44th New York led the way, followed by Vincent's own 83rd Pennsylvania, the 20th Maine, and finally the 16th Michigan. Vincent placed the 16th Michigan on the right, where they would line up below the first of Charles Hazlett's guns, as they were rolled one by one into position; beside the Michiganders, "in a semi-circle formation" that curled around the south face of Little Round Top, were the 44th New York, then the 83rd Pennsylvania; on the very end of the brigade and facing south toward Big Round Top was the 20th Maine, commanded by a man who, up till a year before, had been a professor of rhetoric at Bowdoin College, Joshua Lawrence Chamberlain. Vincent, who had been in such a hurry that he didn't bother unstrapping his sword from his saddle, but went into action armed with nothing more threatening than a riding crop, dressed the lines of the 20th Maine and solemnly warned, "I place you here! This is the left of the Union line. You understand. You are to hold this ground at all costs." *You,* at this moment, included everyone who could stand up: "Pioneers and provost guard" were "sent . . . to their companies," drummer boys "seized the musket," and "the cooks and servants not liable to such service asked to go in." Even Vincent's brigade bugler dismounted, took up a rifle, and found a place on the line.[21]

They did not have long to wait. "The brigade had scarcely formed line of battle and pushed forward its skirmishers" when the *pop-pop* of Confederate skirmishers could be heard from the woods at the base of Big Round Top, and quickly "three columns"—two regiments each of McIvor Law's Alabamians and the third composed of the 4th and 5th Texas—"approached." The 47th Alabama pressed to "within fifteen yards" of the 83rd Pennsylvania, before going to ground "behind the rocks" and keeping up "a deadly fire upon our troops." Over on the left of the line, Chamberlain and the 20th Maine could see the rebels filtering through the woods "in rear of their line engaged," trying to curl around the end of his last company. Chamberlain "stretched my regiment to left," the men opening intervals of "3 to 5 paces" between themselves and bending their line back so that the left of the 20th Maine "was nearly at right angles with my right." The Alabamians came up "in three lines on a double-quick . . . with bayonets fixed," with the heaviest weight of the attack hitting the 83rd Pennsylvania and 44th New York in the center. There was one coordinated volley—"most destructive to our line," wrote a soldier in the 5th Texas—and "for the first time in the history of the war," the Texans began to "waver."

In front of Chamberlain's 20th Maine, the Alabamians caught their wind, and "pushed up to within a dozen yards of us before the terrible effectiveness of our fire compelled them to break and take shelter." A soldier in the 44th New York saw a Confederate officer take off "his coat, and swinging it over his head . . . ran directly in the rear of the line as fast as he could go from one end of it to the other, pushing and urging his men right up to . . . the very face and teeth of our men on the slope of the hill." The powder smoke became so thick in the woods that the major of the 20th Maine could at first only see the legs of the Confederates. Theodore Gerrish remembered "how rapidly the cartridges were torn from the boxes and stuffed in the smoking muzzles of the guns; how the steel rammers clashed and clanged in the heated barrels; how the men's hands and faces grew grim and black with burning powder," all of it joining in "a terrible medley of . . . shouts, cheers, groans, prayers, curses, bursting shells, whizzing rifle-bullets, and clanging steel."[22]

The Alabamians came again, breaking into Chamberlain's lines and making the fight "literally hand-to-hand." The Alabamians were pushed back again, and the Maine men pounced on ammunition and weapons from any "disabled friend or foe on the field." At last, the Alabamians gathered themselves "in two lines in *echelon* by the right" for a fourth try, and "came on as if they meant to sweep everything before them," shrieking the rebel yell. Chamberlain beat them to the punch. Fixing bayonets, Chamberlain launched a spoiling attack of his own (like that of the 124th New York at Devil's Den) with the bayonet, "and with one yell of anguish wrung from its tortured heart, the regiment charged." The surprise of it rocked the Alabamians back on their heels. "In this charge the bayonet only was used on our part," wrote Chamberlain four days later, "& the rebels seemed so petrified with astonishment that their front line scarcely offered to run or to fire." The company Chamberlain had detached to cover his left now swung around and added their fire into the fleeing Alabamians, and that "cleared the front" so completely that Chamberlain had to restrain his jubilant men from pursuing the rebels "to Richmond."[23]

Things did not go nearly so well along the rest of Vincent's brigade line. "Repeated charges were made on the center of the brigade" and at moments the fighting degenerated into "a terrible, close bayonet fight." It reminded a man in the 4th Texas of "Indian fighting" more "than anything I experienced during the war." John Stevens, in the 5th Texas, remembered that "the enemy in front . . . were not over 25 or 30 paces from us," and the Texans ended up firing off some "10 or 12" volleys, one after another. Waving his riding crop in the air, Strong Vincent was shouting, "Don't yield an inch now men or all is lost," when a bullet ripped into his groin. (He was done for this battle and all other battles, and would die five days later in Lewis Bushman's farmhouse.) But they *were* yielding. The 48th Alabama and the 4th Texas began edging around the right flank of the 16th Michigan, and finally the Michiganders began to crack. The lieutenant colonel, Norval Welch, and the color party of the 16th Michigan drifted backward, and then stumbled down the reverse slope of Little Round Top. The Texans had lost all order climbing up the rock-strewn slope, "occasionally pulling each other up on account of the rocks." But at that moment the way was open for the Texans to "overlap, and turn" the entire length of Vincent's line and Little Round Top with it.[24]

And then, over the crest of the hill, led by a sword-waving officer in muttonchop whiskers, ran Union soldiers, companies A and G of the 140th New York, piling into the unprepared Texans from the north end of Little Round Top. They were the men Gouverneur Warren had gone looking for.

A year earlier, Warren had been busy commanding a brigade in the 5th Corps, in the days when George McClellan's closest friend, Fitz-John Porter, had been the corps commander. And when Warren came madly loping down the north face of Little Round Top on that late July afternoon, it was his old brigade, now under the acting command of Stephen Weed, which he met on the road at the base of Little Round Top, heading to the relief of Dan Sickles. Directly in his path was the rear regiment of the brigade, the 140th New York, commanded by Patrick O'Rorke. "Paddy" O'Rorke was born in County Cavan, Ireland, but in 1836 his parents brought him to Canada with them as a small child, finally emigrating again to Rochester, New York, in the 1840s. When his father died in 1850, O'Rorke was left the principal breadwinner of his family. But he won a city-wide college scholarship competition in 1855, and then a place at West Point in 1857. Less than 2 percent of the ranks of West Point's cadets were foreign-born. But O'Rorke placed at or near the top in every department but languages, and was commissioned into the Corps of Engineers in 1861. He circulated through a variety of staff duties until being named colonel of the 140th New York in the fall of 1862, and now his old brigade commander was bearing down on him, shouting something that startled O'Rorke.[25]

Warren "called out to O'Rorke, beginning to speak while still some eight or ten rods from us," and he did not mince words: *Paddy, Give me a regiment.* Startled, O'Rorke protested that "General Weed is ahead and expects me to follow him." "Never mind that," Warren cut him off. "Bring your regiment up here and I will take the responsibility." And so O'Rorke turned his regiment around, and got them moving up the north face of Little Round Top in column of fours. Warren gave him a parting warning—at the top, don't bother to pause for dressing the regiment's line. "No time now Paddy, for alignments. Take your men immediately into action." And then Warren was off, looking for Stephen Weed in hope of persuading Weed to send the rest of the brigade as well. Meanwhile, O'Rorke and the 140th (guided by Warren's aide, Lt. Washington Roebling) went up the slope of Little Round Top at the double-quick, and at the crest O'Rorke dismounted, threw his reins to his regimental sergeant major, and shouted, "Down this way, boys!"

The first two companies went headlong into the milling and astonished Texans without even pausing to load. "Here they are, men," O'Rorke shouted. "Commence firing." The Texans succeeded in getting off only one ragged volley, but it was close enough that a bullet sliced through O'Rorke's neck and spine, killing him instantly, along with two other officers and twenty-five of O'Rorke's New Yorkers. Then the 140th New York was all through them, taking prisoners and driving the shattered Texans off the hill "in disorder." It was 5:30, and O'Rorke was dead, and Vincent was down, but they had held Little Round Top—even if it had been by the skin of their teeth.[26]

This did not guarantee that Little Round Top had been rendered permanently safe for the Army of the Potomac. Warren found Weed, got the rest of Weed's brigade turned around and headed for Little Round Top, and eventually they came trotting up the same path blazed by the 140th New York. (The last of Hazlett's guns was being hauled up, and the crew "plunged directly through our ranks, the horses being urged to frantic efforts by the whips of their drivers and the cannoneers assisting at the wheels.") But the Confederates showed little taste for another grand assault: Robertson's Texas brigade, like the rest of Hood's division, had been on its feet since first light, had attacked and carried a bitterly defended position on Houck's Ridge and Devil's Den, and, by the time Robertson led them toward Little Round Top, three of the four regimental commanders in the brigade were down. The Alabamians "were fainting and falling, overcome with heat and weariness, and in spite of exhortations from their officers." William Oates, commanding the 15th Alabama, would later claim that he had ordered the 15th and 47th Alabama to retreat *before* Chamberlain launched his bayonet charge, and with good reason: W. F. Perry, the colonel of the 44th Alabama, had been "prostrated by heat and excessive exertion"; the colonel of the 47th Alabama, Michael Bulger, had taken a bullet through his left lung (he would, marvelously, survive); and three of Oates' company captains in the 15th Alabama were missing. Of 2,000 Alabamians who started the day in Law's brigade, 27 percent were casualties; of the 1,700 or so in Robertson's brigade, over 30 percent were out of action. Both brigades were only inches away from organizational breakdown.[27]

Nevertheless, Confederate skirmishers across the ravine in Devil's Den kept up a steady sore-loser fire from behind the boulders in the Den and along Houck's Ridge, and in short order "the bullets were flattening themselves against the rocks all about." Among their victims was Stephen Weed, who had just ordered his brigade bugler to blow officer's call to get his regimental commanders around him. He was felled by a "shot through the lungs," which left him paralyzed and dying. Charles Hazlett, in the act of dismounting after hearing of Weed's wounding, was himself "shot in the left side of his head," lost consciousness at once, and died after midnight. (Both Weed and Hazlett had been officers in the 5th U.S. Artillery at the start of the war, and were supposed to have been such "dear friends" that Hazlett was killed while bending over Weed to catch his words.)[28]

In the decades after Gettysburg—and especially from the 1890s onward—the fight for Little Round Top assumed a stature almost equal to the entire balance of battle at Gettysburg. Gouverneur Warren would pay himself the handsome compliment of having seen "that this was the key of the whole position," and Warren had at least some confirmation for this claim when McIvor Law conceded that Little Round Top was "really the key to the whole position of Gettysburg." Union veterans, and battlefield tour "delineators," unfailingly pointed to Little Round Top as "the key of the field in front beyond a doubt," and popular historians upped the ante to the point where Joshua Chamberlain and the 20th Maine "saved the Union at Little Round Top."[29]

It takes nothing away from the tenacity of the fighting—the last-minute arrivals, the desperate and sometimes hand-to-hand combat, the just-in-time swing and flow of the action—to say that the drama of Little Round Top has been allowed to run away with the reality. Credit for defending it belongs primarily to Gouverneur Warren, Strong Vincent, and Patrick O'Rorke, and only after them to Chamberlain. But the others faded from view for reasons that left the stage open to the former Bowdoin professor. O'Rorke died there, and Vincent followed him after five days of suffering, which removed the two principal nominees for celebration; and Warren (who would be pilloried by Philip Sheridan for misconduct at Five Forks in 1865) was far from looking like the laurel-wearing type. Chamberlain, however, would survive three wounds in 1864 (one of them near-fatal), win the Congressional Medal of Honor, and end the war as a major general. Between Appomattox and his death in 1914, Chamberlain would serve four terms as governor of Maine and as president of Bowdoin College, and in the process he would have the time to publish at least seven accounts of Gettysburg, giving himself the starring role on Little Round Top, and Little Round Top the starring role in the battle as the last extension of the Union left flank. Other veterans of Vincent's brigade were not impressed: "Chamberlain," complained Porter Farley of the 140th New York, "is a professional talker and I am told rather imaginative withal." Chamberlain's charge was indeed a beau geste, but it was only one of several such spoiling attacks that day, and Little Round Top was more of an outpost than the real flank of the Union line. Mortality, and the ex-professor's considerable flair for self-promotion, vaulted him ahead of the others.[30]

The puffing of Joshua Chamberlain and the 20th Maine is a subset of the larger problem of glamorizing Little Round Top itself. As Charles Hazlett had warned Warren, Little Round Top's narrow spine offered very little in the way of a gun platform, and certainly not on the order of Cemetery Hill's broad plateau. What is even more important to realize is what defending Little Round Top took away from other vulnerable places. When Warren spontaneously began pulling away elements of the 5th Corps—two entire brigades—he subtracted from the defense of Sickles' line at the Emmitsburg Road, and made it all the easier for Longstreet to land the real blow of the afternoon, on the lopsided angle around Joseph Sherfy's peach orchard. In his eagerness to fend off Hood's attack, Warren set up Sickles for the blow which would clear the Emmitsburg Road and bring the Army of the Potomac to its knees. Which is why Gouverneur Warren, who saw this unfolding, now galloped off to "rejoin General Meade near the center of the field, where a new crisis was at hand."[31]

CHAPTER SIXTEEN

I have never been in a hotter place

T HE SOLDIER sees very little of the general engagement," wrote one veteran of the 52nd Virginia thirty-five years after Gettysburg, and he warned people who thirsted for reminiscences and retellings of the great battle from its survivors that the old soldier tends to "describe the field" mostly on "other people's information, not his own knowledge." Confusion, and not orderliness, was what the soldier actually saw and felt, especially when "orders are sent by messengers, but the messenger is killed or captured before he can give them," and a regiment or an individual is left to "act on his own judgment." Even a major general like Abner Doubleday admitted that "it is difficult in the excitement of a battle to see every thing going on around us, for each has his own part to play and that absorbs his attention to the exclusion of every thing else." The billows of smoke expelled by the massed thousands of firearms, just by themselves, "shut the combatants from sight," admitted a soldier in the 1st Minnesota on July 2nd, "and we could only judge of the direction of the fight by the sound . . . to tell who were retreating and who advancing." Entire brigades easily "lost their way in the blinding sulphurous canopy," and from a distance, cavalry pickets on higher ground around Gettysburg could only see "smoke in the valley beyond."[1] What the soldier mostly experienced in battle was "the booming thunder of the musketry" and "the smoke-cloud" that "rolls up above the trees." Only afterward, when "each man tells his neighbor what he saw," does an entire narrative began to take shape. "We tell the whole story—thus picked up and patched together—until some of us, after a while, swear to being an eye witness to every scene and movement of that battle."

A battlefield is "the lonesomest place which men share together," and once the shooting begins, the individual soldier's experience in battle becomes "utterly abnormal" and tightly concentrated into an immediate semicircle in front and beside him. Isolated from sight by one another, as well as by fear for survival, it was the other senses which became the nineteenth-century soldiers' chief inlets of information, beginning with the variety of bizarre sounds which dominated the nineteenth-century battlefield—the weird harmonic ring of bullets striking fixed bayonets, the clicking of the locking ring on the bayonet when fixed on the rifle's muzzle, the deceptively harmless sound of rifle volleys (Wilbur Fisk of the 2nd Vermont compared it to the results of holding "a large popper full of pop-corn over a good fire"), the thud of rounds striking flesh or the metallic clink when they struck bone or the dropped-china crack when they hit teeth. Thomas Livermore, a sergeant in the 1st New Hampshire, remembered that the "thundering roll of musketry" was so deafening that "shouts and loud commands . . . were drowned in that awful noise." But individual rounds zipping close by could be heard all too well "over our heads in piping tones," and sometimes even closer, "like a very small circular saw cutting through thin strips of wood." Other explosive noises acquired familiar musical associations: "The different calibers, metals, shapes, and distances of the guns" all gave different artillery batteries distinctly different pitches, like "the chimes of old Rome when all her bells rang out."[2]

Soldiers generated other kinds of noise themselves. As pulse rates spiked, the mechanisms of personal self-control crumbled, producing loss of bladder and bowel control, along with other ordinary cultural inhibitions. Profanity turned out to be a surprisingly easy way for even the most mild-mannered soldiers to release their tensions. A young enlistee in the Pennsylvania Reserves, Benjamin Urban, "knew the very best and consistent Christian men of my company to swear in the frenzy of battle and be utterly oblivious of it afterward." One Methodist officer was rebuked by a private for foul language under fire, and when the infuriated officer denied doing so, the soldier merely referred him to another officer who confirmed that, indeed, he had never heard anyone swear so much in his life. "In the excitement of battle . . . the Captain was absolutely unconscious that he had acted thus."

Others lapsed into gallows humor, providing a certain measure of self-protecting bravado. "Men standing in line got in paroxysms of laughter and shouted 'Say, boys, isn't this the mos'est fun for the leastest money?' Tears from laughter made lines on powder-grimed faces, and a general spirit of hilarity prevailed." Others would compensate for their tension simply by shouting. Rufus Dawes was surprised how combat induced men to behave with "demoniacal fury and shouting and laughing hysterically" while "the whole field before us is covered with rebels fleeing for life, into the woods." The deadliest sound of all was the gasp of the wounded man, although by comparison with the other contributions to pandemonium all around, it seemed almost the gentlest. In a particularly sharp firefight, a soldier hit by a bullet would "throw up his arms with an 'Ugh!' and drop," or fall "by your side with the awful groan and agony of death"; anyone killed outright "would drop flat on his face, or on his back, without a sound."[3]

There were other senses that came into play in combat, not the least of which was—in this age of close-order formations—touch. Men sought the "touch of elbow" with the men on either side in line of battle, to serve as a reassurance that they were not being left behind or overly exposed to enemy fire. Taste also made a mark on the soldier, mostly in the form of gunpowder from cartridges ripped open with the teeth. "We bit off the end of the cartridge with our teeth," related one Union soldier, and "always got a few grains of powder in our mouth, and as the taste was not unpleasantly peculiar, we chewed the paper which we had bitten off, and by the time we had fired a few times we had a good wad of paper in our mouths which we would chew as a school-girl would chew gum." Even the weapons in the soldiers' hands had tactile messages: in the 1st Minnesota, a soldier noticed how "as the shells from our own and the enemy's guns passed over us," there would be a "wiggling vibration of the line of muskets."

As with sounds, it was the impact of wounds which were liable to be felt most cruelly, although not nearly so painfully as might have been imagined. "The first sensation of a gunshot wound is not one of pain," wrote a Michigan veteran. "The feeling is simply one of shock, without discomfort, accompanied by a peculiar tingling, as though a slight electric current was playing about the site of injury," and followed by "a marked sense of numbness, involving a considerable area around the wounded part." For most, the impact of a bullet "was as though someone had struck them sharply with a stick" and men often "turned to accuse a comrade of the act" until they discovered "from the flow of blood, that they had been wounded." But even if the immediate sensation was not one of agony, the results might be. Overall, 90 percent of all wounds in Civil War battles were caused by gunshot, "and the remainder by shell fragments and other large projectiles." Of these, wounds to the abdomen were fatal in 87 percent of the cases; gunshot wounds to the chest achieved a level of 65 percent fatality.[4]

And yet, the staggering mortality inflicted by Civil War combat remained more a product of the sheer volume of fire delivered in motionless line-to-line slugfests, rather than any extraordinary lethality in the weapons technology. None of the rifle's much-vaunted improvements was sufficient to trump the volunteer soldier's mediocre training, his amateur officers, the cumbersome nine-step loading sequence, or the inevitable palls of powder smoke. "What precision of aim or direction can be expected," asked one British officer, when "one man is priming; another coming to the present; a third taking, what is called, aim; a fourth ramming down his cartridge," and all the while "the whole body are closely enveloped in smoke, and the enemy totally invisible." The answer, of course, was *not much*. At the battle of Stone's River, six months before Gettysburg, Union major general William S. Rosecrans worked out a general estimate of how many shots needed to be fired to inflict one hit on the enemy, and came up with the astounding calculation that 20,000 rounds of artillery fired during that battle managed to hit exactly 728 men; even more amazing, his troops had fired off 2 million cartridges and inflicted 13,832 hits on the rebels, all of which meant that it required 27 cannon shots to inflict 1 artillery hit and 145 rifle shots to score 1 infantry hit.

This was, to be sure, a great improvement over the smoothbore musket, which could require "3,000 to 10,000 cartridges as the proportion to one man killed or wounded." But it was still worse than the Crimean War, where British and French troops at the Alma scored 1 hit for every 125 shots—as if even that came close to annihilating an opposing enemy line. "In actual service, not more than one shot in six hundred takes effect," estimated a Federal officer in early 1862, "and, except for the moral effect of the roar of the musketry and whistling of the balls, the remaining five hundred and ninety-nine might better have been kept in the cartridge boxes." A modest-sized regiment, letting off a volley at an oncoming enemy, might be doing very well to hit one or two of them; an entire brigade, firing simultaneously, might be able to hit four or five of its enemies at any single opportunity. Given how attacking infantry, moving over 1,700 yards, could cover that ground in approximately sixteen minutes, then the most each rifleman in massed brigade on the defensive could hope to deliver during the attack were ten reasonably aimed shots.[5]

It was not the technical improvements of the rifle musket or antiquated tactical theories which sent men charging in suicidal rushes to their deaths which caused the staggering length of the casualty lists of the American Civil War. They were, instead, the result of the inexperience or simple terrified unwillingness of both volunteer officers and soldiers to make those charges swiftly with the bayonet and the consequent bogging down of lines of battle in prolonged and motionless exchanges of fire. Well might old-line generals like Edwin Sumner urge his officers, "If they come out here, give 'em the bayonet; give 'em the bayonet, they can't stand that." But in practice, as Langhorne Wister of the 150th Pennsylvania informed his curious Philadelphia friend Sidney George Fisher, the reality of bayonet combat "was so shocking that it very rarely happened that bayonets are crossed."[6]

This requires taking the constant assertion in soldier memoirs and reminiscences that *the air was filled with the most destructive fire,* or that *a constant hail of bullets fell around us,* with a long measure of caution. By the experience of most American volunteers who had never been under lethal fire before, the Civil War battlefield certainly was an amphitheater of fear and anxiety. "A person has not much time to think of danger while in action," Oscar Ladley of the 75th Ohio wrote home after Chancellorsville, "but still a person has a vague idea that he is in considerable danger," especially after "a shell passes near you like lightning" and "you have a faint idea it is not far off and that the next one will take your head off." But there was no constant, unremitting hail of fire at all moments, and men could actually stand upright on a Civil War battlefield with at least a certain space of safety, and soldiers on the firing line could indulge in antics that seem more appropriate to the scrimmage line. "You yell, you swing your cap, you load and fire as long as the battle goes your way," wrote one officer, "it is a supreme minute to you; you are in ecstasies." John Cook of the 80th New York had "one reckless fellow" in his regiment rest "the muzzle of his gun on my left shoulder and banged away." The crack of the rifle "not six inches from my ear, made me jump." But instead of apology or regret, "I was overwhelmed by the laughter of the men at the start it had given me." A month after Gettysburg, a Union artillery officer could write in perfect candor that "somehow or other I felt a joyous exaltation, a perfect indifference to circumstances, through the whole of that three days' fight, and have seldom enjoyed three days more in my life." Charles Edward Benton, a soldier in the 150th New York, expressed "a feeling of disappointment in my first and each succeeding experience of battle scenes." But even Benton was incredulous when, under artillery fire, a "member of another regiment" with whom he had been swapping stories "casually remarked" that being under sustained artillery fire "always makes me sleepy," and despite "the fact that shells were dropping and exploding here and there . . . he was soon sleeping soundly on the grass" (this was probably the result of a stress-related spike in heartbeat, since a pulse rate which reaches 175 beats per minute will constrict blood vessels and induce sleep).[7]

The overall looseness of discipline in the Civil War armies, combined with the relative impunity with which the Civil War battlefield could be negotiated, made maneuver and combat appear surprisingly slow, like the choreographed movement of a large but clumsy ballet company. And it gave manifest opportunities for the less than heroic to remove themselves from danger simply by walking away. "There is a certain percentage in every marching column and battle line that are looking for an opportunity to get away from it before matters get too serious," commented James Wright in the 1st Minnesota, "and opportunity is seldom lacking." A wounded man would be assisted by one or two others to the rear, who would then stay there. "A large number of skulkers concealed themselves in the forests," complained Henry Nichols Blake of the 11th Massachusetts, "and feigned wounds by binding up their heads and arms in blood-stained bandages." In spite of every exasperated effort by the Army of the Potomac's provost marshal, Marsena Patrick, and the 2,000 men assigned to military policing duties, "several thousand men" dribbled away from the Gettysburg battle "on a grand straggle" from "Frederick to Westminster, to Hanover, to Gettysburg, and back again to Frederick." The battlefield also created opportunities for looting as an alternative to fighting. "The army thieves," added Nichols, "plundered the slain," and "grasped with their remorseless hands the valuables, clothing and rations of the unwary, wounded soldiers." Frank Holsinger thought it was "sacreligious" to see "a cluster of men . . . engaged in cutting the buttons from the coat" of a fallen rebel colonel, but there was nothing he could do to stop them.[8]

And yet these were men who could forget almost at once that they were soldiers and revert to being horrified and sympathetic Samaritans. Young Henry Eyster Jacobs looked out on the morning of July 2nd at the Georgians who had camped in front of the Jacobs house on Middle Street and was amazed to see men who had "breathed fire and fury at their foes" the day before, and "were full of what they were going to do to the hated north," quietly "reading from their pocket testaments" after breakfast. Amos Judson never lost his surprise at how the men of his 83rd Pennsylvania "never had any compunction of conscience in their treatment of an attacking foe"—which was, of course, to kill them—"yet the moment the foe were prostrate and helpless at their feet, they would throw away their guns and everything else to render them assistance." A private in the 20th Georgia went down near Devil's Den; a captured sergeant from the 4th Maine was being prodded rearward, and the Georgian "called out to him for help." The Yankee told him to "put your arm around my neck. . . . Don't be afraid of me. Hurry up, this is a dangerous place." And as they hobbled off, the incongruity of mercy in the middle of battle struck the Yankee, and he said, "If you and I had this matter to settle, we would soon settle it, wouldn't we?" (A half-century later, the Georgian would publish an account of Gettysburg that included a plaintive inquiry about the sergeant: "If he is living, I would be glad to hear from him.")

Robert Carter of the 22nd Massachusetts found a fatally wounded captain of the 5th Texas who had been left behind after the fight for Devil's Den and the Round Tops, and Carter gave him "water in which we had soaked coffee and sugar. . . . He expressed his gratitude and gave us a partial history of this attack," as though they had all been gathered around a convivial saloon table. What galled Carter was not the Texan's easy assumption that Carter meant him no harm; it was the persistence of rebel skirmishers in firing on "a sergeant and others" who were attempting to rescue other downed men, despite Carter's efforts to hail the skirmishers, "explaining our object." A man in Amos Judson's 83rd Pennsylvania made repeated trips under fire to bring in wounded Confederates. He was finally "shot dead by the comrades of the men he was attempting to succor." But Judson proclaimed it the "most sublime instance of courage and humanity" he had ever seen "upon the battlefield."[9]

The Stony Ridge

Joseph Brevard Kershaw was probably the most popular brigade commander in the entire Army of Northern Virginia. His South Carolinians—the 2,100 men of the 2nd, 3rd, 7th, 8th, and 15th South Carolina, along with the seven companies which made up the 3rd South Carolina Battalion—adored him as "a very fine man and a good officer" who is "liked by everyone." Actually, this forty-one-year-old lawyer from Camden (whose only military experience had been as a lieutenant of volunteers in the Mexican War) was a chronic depressive, unhappily married, and "intensely lonely." But in Camden, he was "our favorite citizen," and in the fellowship of his brigade he was renowned for "how he prayed, got up, dusted his knees, and led his men on to victory with a dash and courage equal to any Old Testament mighty man of war." There was, said a sergeant in the 2nd South Carolina, "not a man . . . who would not follow him to the death." Judging by what Kershaw had seen happening to John Bell Hood's division that afternoon, it was entirely possible that Kershaw's men would get exactly that chance.[10]

Once Hood's four brigades jumped off on their attack on the right, it would be the turn of Lafayette McLaws' division to go in. Drawn up in the woodline on the left of Hood's division, Kershaw's South Carolinians and William Barksdale's Mississippians were in front, with the two Georgia brigades of Paul J. Semmes and William Wofford directly behind them. Kershaw's brigade would go first; but the problem he saw in front of him was *go where?* Longstreet's instructions were to "advance my brigade and attack the enemy," then "turn his flank" and pivot to the left to attack the peach orchard. (Hood's division—presumably—would be executing its own larger pivot, and end up somewhere on Kershaw's right flank, facing north.) But if he did so, Union soldiers whom he could see posted on a stony ridge 900 yards away, behind the Emmitsburg Road, would fire into his flank as the brigade pivoted; if he shifted the direction of his attack to the stony ridge, he would have to maneuver around the stone farmhouse and barn of farmer John Rose. (John Rose was only a tenant; the 230-acre farm was actually owned by his brother, George.) This would leave Kershaw's left-hand regiments open to the unobstructed fire of four or five Union batteries he could see unlimbering near the peach orchard.

Kershaw did not have much time to dither: the guns of Longstreet's

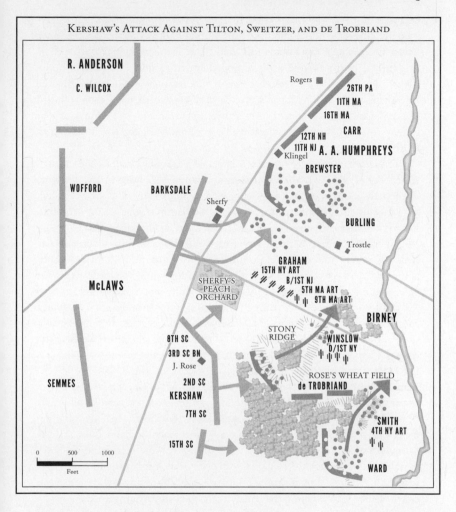

KERSHAW'S ATTACK AGAINST TILTON, SWEITZER, AND DE TROBRIAND

corps artillery would give him ten minutes' worth of softening-up fire on the new Union positions, and then a three-gun signal that meant *move*. "I determined to move upon the stony hill with my center," formed by the 3rd, 7th, and 15th South Carolina. But he would divert his three left units, the 2nd and 8th South Carolina and 3rd South Carolina Battalion, toward the peach orchard, assuming that they could act together with Barksdale's Mississippians in distracting the attention of the Federal batteries. Once he had seized the stony ridge, Kershaw could wheel to rejoin the others and push northward. "I had each regimental officer instructed in these orders, with instructions to communicate them to company commanders." The artillery-men actually gave him a good thirty minutes' worth of firing, then (shortly before five o'clock) "the signal guns fired, "and at the word *march!* the whole line (of the brigade) went off." Joining them at the last minute was Long-street himself, "who accompanied me in this advance on foot, as far as the Emmitsburg Road." It was only after he had started forward that he heard in the distance Barksdale's drummers beating Assembly—which meant that they were only just starting to get ready. Kershaw's brigade would have it all to do themselves.[11]

It might have given Kershaw some solace to have seen his brigade through the eyes of the Union soldiers who were at that moment lying under the shade of the trees along the stony ridge. Earlier that afternoon, when the ebullient Dan Sickles paraded his 3rd Corps out to the Emmitsburg Road, he posted David Bell Birney's division to cover the long, open flank that ran from Joseph Sherfy's peach orchard down to Devil's Den. The unhappy Birney had only two brigades—the 3,500 men of John Ward's and Régis de Trobri-and's brigades—to cover nearly a mile of upfolded moraines, thick clumps of alder and oak, and a wheat field with stone fences just high enough to keep livestock from meandering through the crops. By the time Kershaw's attack surged forward, Ward's brigade had been battered senseless by Hood's divi-sion, and was drifting piecemeal in the direction of Cemetery Hill. That left only the five small regiments of de Trobriand's brigade to enforce what was left of Sickles' chicken-brained plan, and even then the expatriate French-man peeled off his largest regiment to send to Ward's aid; posted another, the 17th Maine, to hold off the tide of Georgians and Texans spilling over Houck's Ridge; and spread still another, the 3rd Michigan, in skirmish order to link up with the other Federal troops in the peach orchard. Even after he borrowed two understrength regiments—the 8th New Jersey and the 115th Pennsylvania—from the 3rd Corps' other division, de Trobriand had only a little more than 900 men thinned out along the stony ridge when Kershaw's skirmishers began hopping the fences along the Emmitsburg Road.[12]

De Trobriand's one hope was the same hope Sickles, Meade, and Warren were appealing to, and that was George Sykes' 5th Corps. Sykes was indeed on the way, but his lead division under James Barnes had already seen one of its three brigades siphoned off to Little Round Top. That left Barnes with two brigades still in hand, one belonging to Col. William Tilton and the other to Col. Jacob Sweitzer. Tilton was a thirty-five-year-old businessman from Newburyport, Massachusetts, and only in temporary command of his bri-gade since May 5th; Sweitzer was a lawyer from Cannonsburg, Pennsylvania, "a gentleman in the noblest sense of the word," but he, too, had been in bri-gade command only since the previous December. Nevertheless, they brought de Trobriand another 2,000 men, who were posted on the upper end of the stony ridge. If Sweitzer and Tilton could buck up de Trobriand's jittery regiments on the stony ridge, and the 17th Maine could keep the overflow from Hood's Confederates from spilling into the wheat field behind the ridge, they all might be able to hang on to this ground until the balance of the 5th Corps arrived on the scene.[13]

Which they almost did. De Trobriand had only one battery, George Winslow's Battery D, 1st New York Light Artillery, but he planted Winslow's six 12-pounder Napoleons on a small rise in Rose's wheat field that gave the gunners a clear line of sight to plaster anything which overran either the stony ridge or the Maine men's stone wall. For almost an hour, the 17th Maine held the back door to Rose's wheat field and the stony ridge shut. Battering them from in front were the frustrated hordes of Tige Anderson's Georgia brigade, and they pressed the Maine men so hard that "one third of the regiment" was bent backward "at nearly a right angle." The fighting became "a desperate struggle at close quarters," frequently "hand-to-hand." For a moment, a Georgia regiment's flag "was planted upon the very wall behind which we lay," but the color-bearer was shot down. Bodies piled up "within three feet of our line" and other Georgians were speared by bayonets "in endeavoring to scale the wall."

Some of the 17th's men divided labor: Charles Mattocks "had three men loading for me, and I blazed away at the Rebs." Eventually, the 17th Maine's "ammunition was exhausted, and "we had used nearly all we could get from the dead and dying or wounded." As the 17th Maine began to creep slowly backward, de Trobriand galloped up and pleaded with them to make one more stand, even if it was only "with the bayonet." But on the other side of the stone wall Anderson's Georgia brigade finally scented weakness. "The Confeds came right over the wall undaunted," recalled one Maine private, "and we had to go." David Birney now came up "with several of his staff" and begged the Maine men "to move forward," but to no avail.[14]

The collapse of the 17th Maine could not have come at a worse moment for de Trobriand and Birney. Winslow's New York battery continued to spray Tige Anderson's triumphant Georgians, first with solid shot angled over the heads of the disappearing 17th Maine, then firing off "shell and case shot at about one degree of elevation" with a perilously short "one to one-half second fuse." Winslow kept the Georgians at bay long enough for the 17th Maine—as well as stragglers from Ward's brigade and the two orphaned Parrott rifles of Smith's battery—to scramble out of range in the direction of Cemetery Hill. But this would only work until the Georgians began sliding around to Winslow's left. Winslow slewed one section of the battery around to beat the Georgians' heads down with canister, and then galloped off to find David Birney and get the division commander's approval to pull out. Yes, Birney agreed: "Be careful not to get cut off." By the time Winslow returned, rebel bullets were "clipping the heads of wheat from the stalks as they whistled past . . . cutting down my men and horses" with skirmish fire. After a few last rounds—and "impressing into service some of the horses" from Smith's battery which had been tethered behind the New Yorkers—Winslow began limbering up his bronze 12-pounders, one by one, from the left and got them out of danger.[15]

At that point, de Trobriand's regiments at the southern end of the stony ridge—the 110th Pennsylvania and the 5th Michigan, plus the two borrowed units, the 8th New Jersey and 115th Pennsylvania—began looking nervously over their shoulders. They, too, had sustained a series of short, brutal rushes by Anderson's Georgians, and were "holding on only in fragments." With the fallback of the 17th Maine, de Trobriand became desperate to pull them out of harm's way. "Riding onto the line unattended by staff or orderly," de Trobriand gave (in his thicky accented English) "ze order tree or four times" to "Change quick, or you all be gobbled up; don't you see you are flanked? Ze whole rebel army is in your rear." Once de Trobriand's men began inching to the rear, Tilton's and Sweitzer's brigades suffered their own tremor of isolation on the ridge. And their fears for what was happening to their left and behind them were compounded by the appearance of Kershaw's South Carolinians, "plainly seen as his regiments gained the Rose [farm] building," all along their front. The Union "skirmishers came in hurriedly," recalled by the regimental sergeant-majors "with sword drawn." Right on their heels, the South Carolinians "appeared through the smoke" like a malevolent fury, "moving with shout, shriek, curse and yell . . . loading the firing with deliberation as they advanced, begrimed and dirty-looking fellows in all sorts of garb, some without hats, some without coats, none apparently in the real dress or uniform of a soldier."

Tilton's and Sweitzer's marooned brigades put up a brief but determined fight along their end of the stony ridge. "A shot—one—two—three—and then with a perfectly startling rattle and roar, the line blazed forth, followed by an incessant cheer that seemed to thrill one's very marrow," and in the 22nd Massachusetts, men were "placing a heap of cartridges and caps on the ground in front of them" to speed up "loading and firing as rapidly as possible." One Massachusetts man noticed the odd "tremulous, wavering movement" along the line "when a shell burst" overhead; but the oddest sound of all—a sound which could be heard even over a battle racket that drowned out bugles and drums—was the repeated dinging of John Rose's farm bell as errant bullets ricocheted off it. Neither Yankee brigade had enough men to hold the stony ridge, and with Anderson's Georgians spilling across the wheat field behind them and the ridge itself "nearly surrounded," both brigades retrieved their caps and cartridges, hefted their wounded on unrolled blankets, and abandoned the ridge to Kershaw. There were now no Union troops, from Sherfy's peach orchard down to Little Round Top, left to stand in the Confederates' path, and the remaining brigades of the 3rd Corps along the Emmitsburg Road were ready to be rolled up at leisure.[16]

Little of this looked leisurely to Kershaw's South Carolina regiments. Until Kershaw's brigade reached the Emmitsburg Road, "little damage was done us," apart from Union skirmishers who "injured us while climbing the two fences that line the pike." One rebel skirmish company, striding through "a large patch of ripe blackberries," actually slowed down long enough to scoop up "the ripe fruit" and were "eating berries" until they bumped into the Federal skirmish line. But once the six South Carolina regiments cleared the road and moved on to the Rose farm, they found themselves hit, as Kershaw had feared, not only from in front by the rifle fire of Tilton's and Sweitzer's men, but from their left flank, where Union batteries could bowl solid shot and canister their way with obscene ease. "We saw plainly that their artillerists were loading their guns to meet our assault, while their mounted officers were dashing wildly from gun to gun, to be sure that all were ready," recalled one soldier in the 2nd South Carolina, and when they opened fire, "every Federal cannon let fly at us" with solid shot and canister. "O the awful deathly surging sounds of those little black balls as they flew by us, through us, between our legs, and over us!" Hearing the canister balls "clatter . . . against walls and houses" of Rose's farm, Kershaw boiled with resentment that Barksdale's Mississippians had not moved forward with him—they should have been on Kershaw's left, giving the Yankee batteries all the distraction they required. "I have never been in a *hotter* place," he claimed years afterward.[17]

Kershaw's three left regiments turned north to face the Yankee cannon fire, and as they did they took a terrific pounding. "We were in ten minutes or less time, terribly butchered," wrote Franklin Gaillard, the lieutenant colonel of the 2nd South Carolina (and one of three brothers in the regiment). "I saw half a dozen at a time knocked up and flung to the ground like trifles," including "familiar forms and faces with parts of their heads shot away, legs shattered, arms tore off." Kershaw took his other three regiments forward toward the stony ridge "on foot . . . looking cool, composed and grand," while "men fell here and there from the deadly Minnie-balls." In their confusion, the 7th South Carolina moved to the left of the Rose farmhouse, got too far ahead, and overlapped the line of its neighbor, the 3rd South Carolina, as the 3rd came around the other side of the house; the 15th South Carolina lost touch and drifted far off to the right. But then, to Kershaw's surprise, "the troops we first engaged seemed to melt away." These were Tilton's and Sweitzer's brigades, and as they scrambled down the rear of the stony ridge, Kershaw's men swept victoriously to the crest, where they could look down from its "copse of woods, covered with granite boulders," into the wheat field.

What they saw at the apex of the ridge froze them, and sent Kershaw running as fast to the rear as he could in search of his supporting brigade, Paul Semmes' Georgians. Kershaw had seen "a heavy column" of infantry, moving "in two lines of battle across the wheat-field," aiming to "attack my position" and take back the ridge. It was the 2nd Corps of the Army of the Potomac, and, as the clocks moved toward six o'clock, it was also the beginning of the best evening of Winfield Scott Hancock's life.[18]

John Rose's Wheat Field

After his brief stint as George Meade's majordomo on Cemetery Hill on the evening of July 1st, Winfield Hancock rode back toward Taneytown to report to Meade and to locate his 2nd Corps, which he had left under John Gibbon's command. He did not have to go far. Gibbon marched the 2nd Corps pretty vigorously through the evening, and Hancock had only ridden three miles out of Gettysburg before encountering them. One of his brigade commanders, Samuel Carroll, asked him point-blank what he intended to recommend to Meade, and Hancock confidently assured him that "If Lee does not attack before all our forces are up, we can hold the position . . . against the whole Confederacy." Hancock reported to Meade at his Taneytown headquarters around nine o'clock, lay down to sleep for a few hours, and then was back in the saddle before two o'clock to rejoin the 2nd Corps. In the process, grumbled Hancock's chief of staff, Charles Morgan, Hancock had managed to kill "nearly every horse belonging to the General or his staff" with "hard riding." At four o'clock, Hancock had the 2nd Corps back on its feet and on the Taneytown Road to Gettysburg, and by seven he was positioning them "by brigade in mass" along the shallow ridgeline that tailed southward from Cemetery Hill.[19]

The 2nd Corps contained three of the smaller-sized infantry divisions in the Army of the Potomac, with an average of about 3,500 men apiece. This had once been old Edwin "Bull" Sumner's corps, and it had fought with enviable energy on the Peninsula, at Antietam, and at Fredericksburg. Two of its brigades, the Philadelphia Brigade and the Irish Brigade, were among the rare brigades in the Army of the Potomac to earn a brigade nickname. The 2nd Corps had also suffered some stupefying punishment—one-third of the corps had been struck down, dead or wounded, at Antietam, and three of the Irish Brigade's regiments were so understrength that they had actually been consolidated into a single six-company battalion. Above all, the 2nd Corps was bitterly unhappy over the dismissal of McClellan and the release of the Emancipation Proclamation. "It was nothing but the nigar lovers of the North who took [McClellan] from us," lamented a corporal in the Philadelphia Brigade. As they took up their positions on the ridge below Cemetery Hill, it was "given out that McClellan had taken command," a piece of unlikely news which nevertheless made the men "perfectly wild with joy. . . . Each battalion as it moved past stepped to the encouraging shouts of thousands of voices in one grand chorus for 'little Mac.'" In the Irish Brigade, there was a lingering resentment at the way they had been "driven to mere slaughter" for the sake of "cursed Yankees" and "savage blacks."[20]

The 2nd Corps was not made happier when the reinforcements detailed to join the corps on the march to Pennsylvania turned out to be the "Harpers Ferry Cowards"—Col. George Willard's disgraced brigade of the 39th, 111th, 125th, and 126th New York, who had been surrendered en masse when Harpers Ferry was captured by Stonewall Jackson during the Antietam Campaign. The surrender was no fault of their own, but the official report branded their conduct "disgraceful" and they had languished in a parole camp, smarting under "the lasting shame of the surrender." Once exchanged under the official prisoner of war cartel, they were herded dismally into the defenses of Washington, digging ditches and doing maintenance on the capital's chain of forts. The new uniforms they had been issued and the unseemly number of tenderfoots who fell out of the brutal route marches to Gettysburg only made them better targets for mockery by the rest of the corps.[21]

But whatever the 2nd Corps had lost in numbers or integrity by 1863, it still had Hancock, and despite Hancock's reputation for dark tempers and even darker profanity, no other corps commander was so admired for his dash (the Louis Napoleon whiskers, the spic-and-span military outfitting) or for his sheer physical courage. "General Hancock is in his element and at his best in the midst of a fight, which cannot be said of some of the general officers," wrote a 2nd Corps staff officer, Josiah Favill. At Chancellorsville two month before, Favill had been astonished to see "General Hancock ride along amidst this rain of shells utterly indifferent, not even ducking his head when one came close to him, which is a difficult thing to do, for one seems to do it involuntarily." The corps also had two enormously effective division commanders in John Gibbon and the sarcastically combative Alex Hays. It was the third (and ironically most senior) of the 2nd Corps' division heads, John Curtis Caldwell, who was the big question mark. Caldwell had been a private high school principal before the war, and there were whispers that he had been an "infurnal cowardly soul" at Antietam and Fredericksburg. But Caldwell had powerful political friends. (He had been recommended for his

brigadier general's star by Maine Republican congressman Israel Washburn.)
And so he had taken over Hancock's original brigade when Hancock went up
to division, and then ascended automatically to command of Hancock's division when Hancock took over the 2nd Corps after Chancellorsville.[22]

Unlike Dan Sickles, Winfield Scott Hancock displayed no special anxiety about his position on the left of the Army of the Potomac. Caldwell's
division, the farthest to the left of the three divisions, "was massed in brigade
columns," but otherwise the men "were allowed to sit or lay down in their
ranks, while the officers gathered in groups and discussed the probable outlook for the day." In the Irish Brigade, "arms were stacked and the colors lay
folded on the upturned bayonets." There was the usual random skirmish-line
firing, but no intimation that very much was in store for Hancock's men until
Sickles staged his grand movement forward around two o'clock. Watching in
mingled admiration and disbelief, John Gibbon muttered something about
it being magnificent "but it is not war" to Charles Morgan—just what the
French had said about the Charge of the Light Brigade at Balaklava. Soon
enough, the Confederate onslaught began. Now it was clear "that a general
engagement would follow," and the 2nd Corps "stood to arms."[23]

It was just as well that Hancock had his men ready for whatever might be
afoot, because once George Meade had gotten Sykes and the 5th Corps moving and satisfied himself that Sedgwick and the 6th Corps were within hailing distance on the Taneytown Road, Meade crossed back toward Cemetery
Hill and found Hancock and Gibbon, "just to the left" of a small woodlot of
trees (which in another twenty-four hours would achieve a sort of immortal-
ity of its own). "Something must be done," Meade barked out; Sykes was not
going to be able to shore up Sickles' paper-thin line in time. At least, "send a
couple of regiments out in support of Humphrey[s]" to fill in the gap between
Humphreys' right flank on the Emmitsburg Road and the 2nd Corps.

At some point, Meade decided to peel one of Hancock's divisions away,
too; he was getting impatient for Tardy George to move up, and if Sykes
couldn't hop to it, one of Hancock's divisions would have to do. Since
Caldwell's division would have the least distance to cover, Hancock cantered
over to Caldwell and ordered him to "get your division ready" and move
down to Sickles' rescue. Then "a column of the Fifth Corps"—Tilton's and
Sweitzer's brigades—swung into view, and Hancock recalled the order. Not
for long, though. Around 5:15, as the Federal positions in the wheat field and
on the stony ridge began to fall in, Hancock got Caldwell on his feet again,
with orders to report to Sykes. Caldwell "moved rapidly, a portion of the time
at the double-quick," his lead brigade commanded by the irascible and colorful Col. Edward Cross. "Boys, you know what's before you," announced the
ever-belligerent Cross, "give 'em hell!" and with a shout his brigade echoed,

"We will, Colonel!" (Cross was not as optimistic as he sounded; it was always his habit to lead his men into a fight wearing a red bandanna to make himself easier to find in the smoke and confusion of a battle, but today he tied a black scarf around his head, somehow certain that "this is my last battle.") Cross' brigade was followed by the Irish Brigade, then Samuel Zook's brigade of three New York and one Pennsylvania regiments, and last by John Brooke's mixed-bag brigade of New Yorkers, Pennsylvanians, the 27th Connecticut, and the 2nd Delaware.[24]

Caldwell moved his division along in column—"in a chunk," as one lieutenant recalled—stopping at the farm lane that bordered the north side of the wheat field and deploying them into line along the lane, starting with Cross' brigade. "We stood in line of battle, officers and sergeants in front," and then "scaled the fence" along the lane and lined up in the wheat field. Guidons went up to correct the brigade's alignment, and then "the officers and file closers passed through the ranks and got in rear of the men." Behind them, the Irish Brigade was still in column, waiting its turn to deploy along the wheat field lane, when the Catholic chaplain of the 88th New York, Father William Corby, took the halt as the opportunity to put some last-minute fire into the worn-down ranks. Corby was a priest of the Congregation of the Holy Cross, the "most priestly of priests" and "scholastic, gentle, refined, cultured." He had only been ordained on Christmas Day in 1860, but, along with seven other Holy Cross priests, he was directed by his superiors to volunteer for war service to demonstrate that Catholics could be as patriotic as their nativist despisers.

Scrambling onto a "large rock," Corby proposed to offer absolution to every Catholic "on condition that they make a sincere act of contrition" and that none "turns his back upon the foe or deserts his flag." Caps flew off heads "and the entire brigade"—including the smattering of Protestants in the ranks—"knelt from 'Parade rest' . . . on the right knee with musket erect in the right hand." (Out of the corner of his eye, Corby could see that even the luxuriantly profane Hancock had "removed his hat" and "bowed in reverential devotion.") *Dominus noster Jesus Christus vos absolvat,* Corby intoned, and even before he could finish, "the order came to move." The watch of the adjutant of the 140th Pennsylvania read "just six o'clock."[25]

Caldwell did not have an easy time getting the division deployed properly ("some of the officers alleged that the troops were not put into action very handsomely by the division commander," and the color company of the 148th Pennsylvania found itself "far out of place" on the flank of the regiment"). Caldwell could not find Sykes, and had to rely on one of Sykes' staffers to learn "where to place" the division so as not to blunder into the path of the 5th Corps. Still more disruptive, refugees from the 3rd Corps were stream-

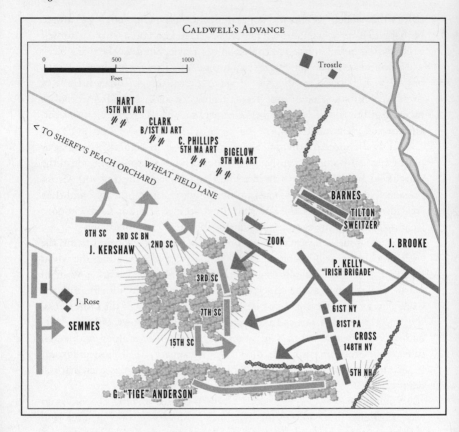

CALDWELL'S ADVANCE

0   500   1000
Feet

HART
15TH NY ART

CLARK
B/1ST NJ ART

C. PHILLIPS
5TH MA ART

BIGELOW
9TH MA ART

< TO SHERFY'S PEACH ORCHARD

WHEAT FIELD LANE

Trostle

BARNES
TILTON
SWEITZER

8TH SC   3RD SC BN
J. KERSHAW   2ND SC

ZOOK

J. BROOKE

P. KELLY
"IRISH BRIGADE"

3RD SC

7TH SC

61ST NY
81ST PA

J. Rose

CROSS
148TH NY

SEMMES

15TH SC

5TH NH

G. "TIGE" ANDERSON

ing over the wheat field lane and "were almost inextricably mixed up with" Caldwell's men even as Caldwell was trying to use the road to form a line of battle. Then Dan Sickles put his oar in. From his temporary command post at Abraham Trostle's farm, Sickles could see Caldwell's division heading for the wheat field, and impulsively dispatched Henry Tremain to tear loose a brigade and send them to stanch the ebb of Tilton's and Sweitzer's men from the stony ridge.[26]

The first brigade commander Tremain found was Samuel Zook. The forty-two-year-old Zook was a Pennsylvanian, born and raised near Valley Forge and infatuated from his boyhood with stories of the Revolution (Zook took Kosciusko as his middle name, and his sister married into the family of the Revolutionary general Mad Anthony Wayne). But soldiering was not his profession. He built a youthful interest in the electrical telegraph into the presidency of the Washington & New York Telegraph Company, and moved to New York City. He finagled a commission in the New York state militia, and with the outbreak of war in 1861, Zook took command of the 57th New York and was promoted to brigadier general just before Fredericksburg.

Zook was not the most approachable of men; he was rumored to be the only general in the Army of the Potomac who could outproduce Hancock in picturesque blasphemy. But Tremain took his staff rank in his hands, and begged Zook to pivot to his right and retake the stony ridge. "With soldierly mien," Zook told him he would do nothing of the sort; he belonged to Caldwell's division, and no underling from another corps had the authority to give him orders—unless, of course, this was a direct order from Sickles as a major general. Very well, Tremain replied, if that was what Zook required, "I do give General Sickles's orders." That satisfied Zook, and he turned his four regiments and swung around toward the ridge where Kershaw's South Carolinians had paused in triumph.[27]

For the second time that day, the nineteen acres of Rose's wheat field became an arena of confrontation, the slow-moving blocks of infantry moving to within deadly range and blazing away until one or the other began to wilt and fold. Edward Cross' brigade was the first into the wheat field, with Cross' old regiment, the 5th New Hampshire, on the left and in front. The Georgians of Anderson's brigade who had just swept de Trobriand's regiments out of the wheat field stopped and waited for the New Hampshire men, then stunned them with a volley that felled almost half of the regiment's 177 men. That included Cross, who was hit in the abdomen by a bullet which tore all the way through him and exited near his spine. But behind them came the 148th and 81st Pennsylvania and the 61st New York, who let off a volley and waded through the "breast-high wheat" to the stone wall at the south end of the field.

"Here the battle was desperate and sanguinary"—and, true to form, here the Pennsylvanians and Georgians stood with "unyielding tenacity" and shot each other to ribbons. Charles Augustus Fuller, a lieutenant in the 61st New York, described it simply as "a case of give and take," with his regiment's line shrinking "into clumps" as the volleying went on. Still, Fuller saw "no flinching or dodging," except for a single lieutenant who was bending behind the firing line "so as to bring his head below the line of the heads of the men." An irritated captain saw this as a fall from masculinity, and whacked the doubled-up lieutenant with his sword, growling, "Stand up like a man."[28]

To the left and out of sight of the 61st New York, the 530 men of the Irish Brigade rolled through the wheat field and, angling slightly toward the stony ridge, headed for Kershaw's South Carolinians. Catching his first glimpse of the lines of the Irish Brigade emerging from the smoke banks below the ridge, Elbert Bland (the lieutenant colonel of the 7th South Carolina) instinctively remarked to the colonel of the 7th, "Is that not a magnificent sight?" It did not feel particularly magnificent to the Irish Brigade: "The ground was exceedingly uneven . . . which made a regular line of battle impossible," wrote John Noyes, an Irish Brigade lieutenant, and the awkward angle at which they were approaching the stony ridge allowed the South Carolinians at the north end of the ridge to fire straight down along the front of the brigade, "decimating the front line, whose gaps were promptly filled by each file-closer stepping to the front as his file leader fell." As the Irish Brigade scrambled up the ridge, they were hit from in front with a volley from the 3rd and 7th South Carolina. But the rebels "became too excited and fired too quickly, resulting in the volley passing overhead," and for a few minutes the Irish Brigade and Kershaw's men were fighting face-to-face, at revolver and bayonet distance. "The enemy's infantry came up and stood within thirty steps of each other," wrote another officer in the 7th South Carolina. "I was so desperate I took two shots with my pistol."[29]

The South Carolinians had an additional distraction: out of the smoke appeared Samuel Zook's brigade on the north end of the ridge, followed some distance behind by the reappearance of the wayward brigades of Tilton and Sweitzer. Caldwell himself rode up to Sweitzer "in great haste," jubilantly announcing that his division "was driving the enemy like Hell over yonder in the woods . . . and asked if I would give him the support of my brigade." Most of these Yankees could hardly see where they were going: a soldier in the 32nd Massachusetts found "the powder smoke . . . so thick in front of the rebel ranks as to make them invisible to us," and sergeants who were supposed to be guiding their advance from the flank had to navigate "by the jets of smoke and flame just where the muzzles of their guns were."[30] Then, with exquisite timing, the 800 men of John Brooke's brigade, whom Caldwell had kept back as his reserve, also swarmed into the wheat field, through a gap between the 61st New York and the Irish Brigade. They pressed down upon the remaining pieces of Kershaw's rebels on the ridge (as well as mingled bits of Georgians and the errant 15th South Carolina), although like Tilton's and Sweitzer's men, Brooke's brigade had only the dimmest idea of where they were going, because "a dense pall of smoke, from the heavy fire of musketry, hung so close to the ground . . . that nothing could be seen 15 yards away." The 140th Pennsylvania had to grope forward "until we saw a blaze of light in front" that betrayed the firing line. By 6:30, Brooke, the Irish Brigade, and Zook were "rapidly and irresistibly pushing back the enemy, driving them entirely" off the ridge and back to the Rose farm buildings; now the Federal troops could once more see the Emmitsburg Road in the distance.[31]

This vision of recovered ground did not last for long—perhaps only twenty minutes, by John Brooke's reckoning, a half-hour by Kershaw's—and the price Caldwell's division paid for it was steep. In retaking the Rose wheat field and the stony ridge, the division lost not only Edward Cross, but Samuel Zook as well. Zook shook out his brigade—the big 140th Pennsylvania in front in two lines and Zook's old 57th New York, with the 52nd and 66th New York behind—and was leading them from the front line when "a minie ball entered the left side of the stomach, perforating his sword belt, and lodging in the spine." A soldier in the 76th New York saw "the General lean back in his saddle pale as death and . . . they knew he was badly hurt as he never gave up for triffles." Zook slipped slowly forward, caught in the arms of his adjutant, groaning, "It's all up with me." It was all up with a deadly percentage of Zook's brigade, too. The 140th Pennsylvania marked down 263 casualties out of the 515 men with which it went into action; its colonel was dead, and "many of the companies . . . came out under the command of a sergeant." Even more disorienting, "men from every regiment in the division were intermingled with ours in one confused mass."

It was no better in Brooke's brigade, and for some, a good deal worse. The diminutive 27th Connecticut started the day with only two companies' worth of men; in the wheat field they lost their commander, Henry Merwin, and their senior captain, Jedediah Chapman. "Our number by this time was reduced to less than half that started in the fray," wrote a grimly proud Connecticut private, "but we had the flags with us." Brooke, who had led his brigade with the colors of the 53rd Pennsylvania in his hands, found himself on the crest of the stony ridge with "my ammunition . . . nearly gone."[32]

Still, Brooke was convinced that "I could have held the place" with more ammunition, and Caldwell was relieved to see the heads of the next division of the 5th Corps—Romeyn Ayres' division, with its two brigades of U.S. Regulars—coming up the wheat field lane from the east. But Brooke was far away from the 2nd Corps ordnance supplies, and every man in his brigade could see, a lot closer and in front of them, "the indistinct forms of masses of men, presenting the usual dirty, greyish, irregular line . . . dimly visible and moving up with defiant yells, while here and there the cross-barred Confederate battle-flags were plainly to be seen." This was not just Kershaw's South Carolinians on the rebound. Brooke spied "a heavy column of the enemy . . . coming upon my left," while at almost the same moment the lieutenant colonel of the 140th Pennsylvania noticed "rebels, apparently fresh troops, in large numbers and in good order marching to outflank us on the right." They had come at the summons of Joseph Kershaw, who had "hurried in person . . . 150 yards in my right rear" to find Paul Semmes and the brigade of Georgians which had been lined up behind Kershaw to follow the South Carolina bri-

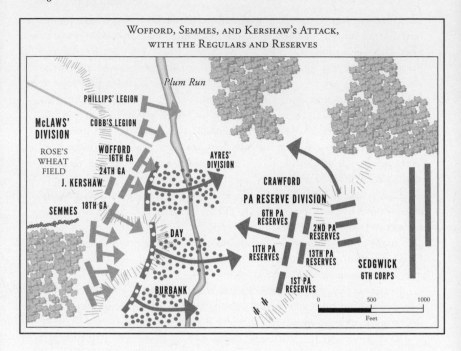

WOFFORD, SEMMES, AND KERSHAW'S ATTACK,
WITH THE REGULARS AND RESERVES

Plum Run

PHILLIPS' LEGION

McLAWS'
DIVISION

COBB'S LEGION

ROSE'S
WHEAT
FIELD

WOFFORD
16TH GA

AYRES'
DIVISION

24TH GA

J. KERSHAW

CRAWFORD
PA RESERVE DIVISION

18TH GA

SEMMES

6TH PA
RESERVES

2ND PA
RESERVES

DAY

11TH PA
RESERVES

13TH PA
RESERVES

SEDGWICK
6TH CORPS

1ST PA
RESERVES

BURBANK

0   500   1000

Feet

gade into the attack. Semmes "promptly responded to my call." But "when I got to open ground" at the Rose farm buildings, Kershaw's greatest delight was to see, sometime after seven o'clock, "Wofford coming in in splendid style."[33]

William Tatum Wofford was once described by James Seddon, the Confederate war secretary, as a "representative man"—a northern Georgia lawyer, a newspaper owner, of "high moral bearing . . . of the strictest sobriety, and, indeed, of irreproachable moral character." A veteran of the Mexican War who had done a good deal more fighting than most of the Army Regulars, Wofford was also "very ambitious of military fame and one of the most daring of men," not to mention possessing an uncanny resemblance to Robert E. Lee. He was also a painful example of the way secessionist politics had laid its snares in the Army of Northern Virginia. Wofford had been a delegate to the Democratic National Convention in 1860, and then to the Georgia state secession convention in January 1861, and in both venues Wofford set his face resolutely against secession. He "took the field as an anti-secession candidate to the secession convention," and even after the war began, "he was a decided union man from first to last during the whole war." Wofford saw "with exceptional prescience . . . the certain fatality" of secession, but once the deed was done, he closed ranks and was elected colonel of the first Georgia regiment to volunteer for the war. Nevertheless, he languished at regimental command of the 18th Georgia until 1863, always playing second fiddle to the more glamorous and favored John Bell Hood, and remained a brigadier till the end of the war.[34]

But in the glorious late afternoon of July 2nd, Wofford drew everyone's attention to himself. "Oh, he was a grand sight," enthused a Confederate artillery officer as he watched Wofford's Georgia Brigade—three full regiments and three battalions, over 1,600 men in all—move down the wheat field lane to strike the stony ridge, "and my heart is full now while I write of it." The onlooking Yankees gaped in reluctant admiration: "They were marching steadily, with colors flying as though on dress parade, and guns at right-shoulder-shift." Even Longstreet was exhilarated by the spectacle. "General Longstreet went forward some distance with Wofford's brigade, urging them on by voice and his personal example." (This horrified the British observer Arthur Fremantle, who was appalled that "Longstreet will expose himself in such a reckless manner . . . hat in hand, in front of everybody.") Add to Wofford's men the 1,300 Georgians in Paul Semmes' brigade, plus what must have been at least 1,600 of Kershaw's original 2,100 men, and the Union reoccupation of the stony ridge began at once to look very, very short-lived. "Coming on at a double quick the whole line as it advanced became heavily engaged . . . but Wofford's brilliant advance struck the attacking force in their flank," and "in a few minutes the blue whelps were tooling away."[35]

Kershaw's left-wing regiments—the 2nd and 8th South Carolina and 3rd South Carolina Battalion—"met Gen'l. Wofford who pointed to his fresh troops and"—with a wave of his hat—"called upon them to go . . . with him, which they did." Kershaw, leaving those regiments to Wofford's direction, turned and rallied the two regiments which had retired to the Rose farm buildings—the 3rd and 7th South Carolina—and led them forward again against the stony ridge, while the wandering 15th South Carolina and Paul Semmes' Georgia brigade came up behind them and lapped around the southern edge of the ridge.

To his dismay, St. Clair Mulholland, in the Irish Brigade, also saw Wofford's brigade "coming in on the right" in column "in battalion front." In the directionless murk, several of the Federal officers were somehow "under the impression" that Wofford's men "were Union troops." Caldwell was also deceived: he had gone looking for Romeyn Ayres, and when he found him, one of Ayres' staffers noticed an unseemly commotion up ahead in Caldwell's division. "General, you had better look out, the line in front is giving way," warned Ayres' aide-de-camp, William Powell. Caldwell, annoyed at an interruption from a staff lieutenant, brushed him off, saying sharply, "That's not so, sir, those are my troops being relieved." Powell shut up for the moment, but he "continued to watch the line in front," and in a few minutes he interrupted again, this time addressing Ayres: "You will have to look out for your command. I don't care what any one says, those troops in front are running away." Four hundred yards away, Ayres and Caldwell could now plainly see "our troops . . . retiring with their colors drooped," and Ayres burst out, "Those regiments are being driven back. . . . A regiment does not shut up like a jack-knife and hide its colors without it is retreating." Abashed at the rebuke, Caldwell "put spurs to his horse and rode off."[36]

Crushed between the jaws of Wofford, Kershaw, and Semmes, the Irish Brigade, the dying Zook's brigade, and then Brooke's brigade, followed by Tilton's, all began to collapse, streaming down off the stony ridge and back the way they had come through the wheat field. A lieutenant in the Irish Brigade noticed that Brooke's brigade had "precipitately retired," and "feeling deserted by the men on our left," the Irish Brigade concluded that "nothing was left but to retire." Sweitzer's brigade had never actually made it all the way to the ridge, and it now stood in the wheat field as the boiling mass of refugees from Caldwell's division foamed around it, struggling to provide cover against yet another Confederate onslaught from Anderson's brigade. Tige Anderson himself had been wounded and his brigade was now being directed by the lieutenant colonel of the 11th Georgia. But the sheer weight of Southern numbers pushing on the south and west perimeter of the wheat field carried their own authority with them, and so for the third time that day, John Rose's wheat field became a hellhole of combat.[37]

This time, however, no one was making any pretence to it being deliberate or orderly. Hancock's chief of staff, Charles Morgan, was returning from an errand to the 6th Corps when he was engulfed by "Caldwell's division, or the remnants of it, flying to the rear, with no shadow of an organization." On the flank of the Irish Brigade, St. Clair Mulholland and the 116th Pennsylvania were ready to "go forward and attack, if necessary a whole brigade of the enemy," but presently "a staff officer" ran up and "in a very excited manner" shouted that "we were surrounded and to fall back and save as many of our men as possible." Mulholland had the colors cased up, told his regiment that it was every man for himself, and with a party of "some thirty men," darted down into the wheat field. Zook's 140th Pennsylvania dissolved into "shattered fragments" and was "seen to fly" without any notion of "where our line would rally," while the rest of Zook's brigade "gave way . . . in considerable disorder."

As they fled, the remnants of the three 2nd Corps brigades barged into Jacob Sweitzer's brigade, which was "greatly embarrassed by squads of men and parts of regiments, who, hurrying from the front, broke into and through my line." One 5th Corps officer was a little less scathing: Caldwell's division was not so much running as it was "moving sullenly to the rear at a walk." But "very few of our men were firing—a man now and then would stop and take a shot," and the "great mass" of "retreating soldiers" filled the entire wheat field in "no organized force, a mere mass of men, officers and men, inextricably mixed." That included dead men—one Irish Brigade officer remembered keenly how "that plain as I came over it close to the colors of our regiment was rapidly becoming encumbered with the bodies of dead & wounded men."[38]

Caught in the open in the wheat field, Sweitzer's brigade tried to slow down the Confederate pursuit, but it swiftly came down to a close-order melee of rushes and counterrushes, none with the slightest hope of doing more than buying a little time. "It was give-and-take with them," wrote a 2nd Corps staff officer, "no quarter being shown on either side." One of Sweitzer's colonels, a twenty-nine-year-old lawyer named Harrison Jeffords of the 4th Michigan, saw the regiment's flag fall, to be picked up by a Confederate. Jeffords and two fellow officers, Michael Vreeland and Watson Seage, impulsively rushed forward to retrieve the colors. Jeffords grabbed the staff, Seage slashed the neck of the rebel with his sword, "killing him instantly," and a lethal brawl broke out in which the flag was "torn to shreds." But numbers overwhelmed valor, and Jeffords was mortally wounded "by bayonet thrust through the body," while his two friends were shot down, "side by side."[39]

"Gallantly our men swept the enemy before them," wrote Lafayette McLaws to his wife five days later, chasing them toward Houck's Ridge "with great slaughter" and with "the enemy in crowds running to our lines" as prisoners. There was still Romeyn Ayres' two brigades of Regulars to deal with, and they moved across Houck's Ridge and the southern edge of Rose's wheat field "in column of battalions, closed en masse, but marching as steadily as though on parade." The Regulars "cheered and broke into a run towards the enemy." But the cheers "were in the nature of shrieks." They knew what they were running into. "Any of you who have had the nightmare and attempted to scream and could not," wrote one survivor, "can imagine the reason we could not give forth good lusty hurrahs instead of shrieks."

Ayres' plan had been "to move forward and sweep through and occupy the woods in my front." But he had no sooner given the orders when Wofford's relentless column appeared, "coming down on my rear from the right." After a spectacularly sharp firefight with Wofford's brigade along Houck's Ridge, the Regulars, too, joined the general drift "in as good an order as the nature of the ground would admit," across the wheat field lane and toward Cemetery Hill. *As good an order,* according to Romeyn Ayres: to an onlooker, it looked more like Ayres' Regulars had been reduced to "fragments of regiments . . . running back without arms, and behind them in solid column over the wheat field and through the woods came the masses of the enemy." To another onlooker, it seemed as though "the late afternoon sun" had become "a red ball of fire . . . through the sulphurous canopy that overhung the valley."[40] *Sulphurous canopy*—how often these soldiers came back to that phrase. But it was not theirs alone; it was a snatch from a popular war poem written six decades before, and it reveals something of the hyperliteracy of mid-nineteenth-century Americans that their almost-unconscious frame of reference for describing battle was poetry.

> *. . . but scarce yon level sun*
> *Can pierce the war-cloud rolling dun,*
> *Where furious Frank and fiery Hun*
> *Shout, mid' their sulphurous canopy.*
>
> THOMAS CAMPBELL,
> *"On the Battle of Hohelinden" (July 1803)*

If ever there was a moment for Longstreet's corps to have begun the long-planned for pivot to the left which would finally bring it astride the Emmitsburg Road and make the straight path to Cemetery Hill plain, this was it. A gigantic wheel executed now would allow Wofford to swing from column into line, backed up by Kershaw and Semmes, and by whatever of Henry Benning's and Tige Anderson's brigades were in sufficiently good shape to join them, all pointed northward at last on the east side of the Emmitsburg Road. But the Army of the Potomac—and George Sykes' 5th Corps—had one more ace to play, and that was the last of Sykes' divisions, the newly attached Pennsylvania Reserves, under the muttonchopped doctor and Sumter veteran Samuel Wylie Crawford.[41]

Actually, Crawford had only one brigade of Reserves to fight with—the other, under Joseph Fisher, was held back as the 5th Corps' last resort—and part of the reason it had taken them so long to come over from Powers Hill was the mounting numbers of 3rd Corps and 5th Corps "wounded walking to the rear and ambulances going the same way." (Among those wounded was the dying Stephen Weed, being carried by "a party of officers and men," followed by another detail with the body of Charles Hazlett.) Crawford had about 1,500 men, and he was now backed up by two 5th Corps batteries, Lt. Aaron Walcott's Battery C, 3rd Massachusetts, with six deadly short-range Napoleons, and Capt. Frank Gibbs' Battery L, 1st Ohio, with another six Napoleons.

As the Reserves cleared the north base of Little Round Top near eight o'clock, Crawford formed them up in two big lines, with the 6th and 1st

Reserves in the front and the 13th and 2nd Reserves "massed on the first" (a stray regiment from Fisher's brigade, the 11th Reserves, "united itself to and fought with" the front line). Gibbs' Ohio battery had been ordered by Sykes "to cover the valley" between Houck's Ridge and Little Round Top, and to get the most out of his guns, Gibbs split the battery into three sections, two guns low on the north slope of Little Round Top (which the crews had to "place . . . in position by hand") and the other two astride the wheat field lane. "We had hardly placed our guns in position when the Fifth Corps was forced back by a terrific charge of Longstreet's corps." They had to wait until the "confused masses" of fugitives had cleared past them to see skirmishers lapping up to the foot of Little Round Top, and behind them, "the irregular, yelling line of the enemy." Then the gunners got to work "with double charges of canister," fired so rapidly that the bronze Napoleons "became too hot to lay a hand on."[42]

Now it was the turn of Crawford's Reserves. "The enemy in masses were coming . . . across the low ground towards the hills upon which we stood," Crawford recalled, while the broken shards of the Regulars "were flying . . . in every direction." Crawford ordered the Reserves forward until only fifty yards separated the Reserves from the Confederate skirmish line. "The first line delivered two volleys," and then Crawford—like Ellis and the 124th New York, and Chamberlain and the 20th Maine—called for yet another last-hope spoiling charge. "With the peculiar shout of the Reserves," Crawford led his Pennsylvanians forward "in the name of Pennsylvania," shaking them out into a single double line of five regiments. Mounted on a "spirited" bay, Crawford reached theatrically for the colors of the 1st Reserves, intending to carry them himself. The corporal of the color guard unceremoniously yanked the flag back, which should have been enough to settle Crawford's mind. Instead, the floridly bewhiskered general demanded the flag with injured authority: "Don't you know me? I am your General. Give me your colors." The corporal reluctantly surrendered the flag, but he grabbed Crawford's pants leg and stayed with him, as though waiting for the general to issue a receipt. While this little drama was being played out, the surprised Confederates "endeavored for a moment to stand, but soon broke beneath the impetuous charge, and fled in disorder" back over Houck's Ridge and into the wheat field.[43]

This moment was the beginning of an orgy of self-congratulation among the Pennsylvania Reserves which lasted through the life of every survivor and beyond. "No foe could withstand a charge impelled by hearts thus nerved to the combat," boasted the first historian of the Reserves in 1865. But part of the ease of their success in stopping what had otherwise looked like a tidal wave must surely be, as one Maine officer objected, that "Wofford's Georgians and Kershaw's brigade had spent the force of their charge, were not an organized line, but were captured in squads representing many parts of regiments." One of Tige Anderson's captains testified that his "little band" had been "thinned and exhausted by three and a half hours' constant fighting" and were too "worn out with fatigue" to continue their advance. Farther away, Longstreet's staff believed that "Wofford's men had seen that they were not protected or supported on the left, and had begun to retreat," and that Longstreet's and Wofford's "personal appearance on the field" was all that prevented a panic among the Georgians.

The other factor was, as Wofford ever afterward insisted, Longstreet's orders. Lafayette McLaws had gone forward to keep track of the brigades of Semmes and Kershaw and "to correct some irregularities," when he saw Wofford's brigade—"General W. on his horse in rear of it"—coming back "from the woods, through which it had charged, and I halted it and asked what was the matter." Wofford explained that "he had driven everything in his front" when "he was ordered back by General Longstreet." Goode Bryan, a colonel of one of Wofford's regiments, would "most positively assert that I received the order to fall back from a courier of General Longstreet." There had been some discussion about "an effort . . . to get enough men together to charge Little Round Top," but Longstreet's orders put an end to it. The recall made Wofford "not only very much excited about it, but exceedingly angry." [44]

Longstreet never offered much in the way of an explanation for these orders. In his official report, he merely indicated that he "thought it prudent not to push farther." He was more blunt thirteen years later, when he was under attack from Robert E. Lee's paladins for the outcome of the battle, calling it "madness . . . to urge my men forward under these circumstances . . . and I withdrew them in good order." He was at his most expansive in his posthumous autobiography in 1908, explaining that, as far as he could see and hear, "Meade's lines were growing" while "the weight against us was too heavy to carry." What was worse, he had heard nothing of the attack Dick Ewell was supposed to be launching little more than a mile away. And finally, time was running out. It was after eight o'clock and "the sun was down." So, "I ordered recall of the troops . . . leaving picket lines near the foot of the Round Tops."

But Longstreet actually had a better reason than any of these for breaking off the attack of Wofford's brigade, and that was, quite simply, that they had done all that they needed to do. The great swing up the Emmitsburg Road was being performed by the last of McLaws' brigades and by the crushing weight of the division Longstreet had been lent by Powell Hill, and the battle should, before the passage of another hour and a half and the fall of darkness, have been over. [45]

No one was more grateful for Longstreet's order than the Pennsylvania Reserves. They had recaptured Houck's Ridge with remarkably few

casualties—20 men killed in the charge, out of 2,800 in the entire division—
and they could afford to feel satisfied. As the fighting died down and the sun
sank, one rebel who had been separated from his regiment and never got the
word to pull back, came wandering, "unattended," up into the lines of the
18th Massachusetts, one of William Tilton's regiments from the 5th Corps.
The 18th Massachusetts was composed mostly of volunteers from Wrentham
and its surrounding towns. They had lost one out every five men in the regiment that afternoon—stabbing, shooting, breaking rifle butts over heads—
and they could not have been in a good humor. But the situation of this
solitary rebel, walking headlong at a whole regiment, was so ludicrous that
they began falling down in laughter. "Hello, Johnnie," someone cried. "You
aren't going to capture us all alone, are you?"[46]

CHAPTER SEVENTEEN

The supreme moment of the war had come

Joseph Sherfy's Peach Orchard

Among the many questions which might have been asked between seven and eight o'clock in the evening of July 2nd: *Why was William Wofford's brigade where it was?* Wofford had been designated as the follow-up to Barksdale's Mississippi brigade, supporting the Mississippians' assault on Joseph Sherfy's peach orchard and wheeling around behind them to follow the Emmitsburg Road toward Cemetery Hill. Yet Wofford's brigade had appeared, rolling majestically past the peach orchard and down the wheat field lane, where only an hour before three of Kershaw's regiments had been pounded to pieces by Federal artillery.

The answer was simple enough: the peach orchard, as an outpost of Dan Sickles' 3rd Corps, had ceased to exist.

Deacon Sherfy owned two small-sized parcels of land, the larger of which straddled the Emmitsburg Road and wrapped around the intersection of the lane leading down to Rose's wheat field. At this corner, Sherfy had built a highly successful operation in "canned and dried fruits," which made the peach orchard he planted on the southeast corner of the intersection a landmark of sorts on Adams County's 1858 survey map. The stumpy, thick-branched peach trees were arranged in rows on a seven-and-a-half-acre rectangle, and sat on a slight knob that gave an unobstructed view of the ground to the north (to Cemetery Hill) and to the southeast (to the stony ridge and the Rose farm). The knob was originally supposed to serve as the pivot point for the great wheel Longstreet's corps would make up the Emmitsburg Road,

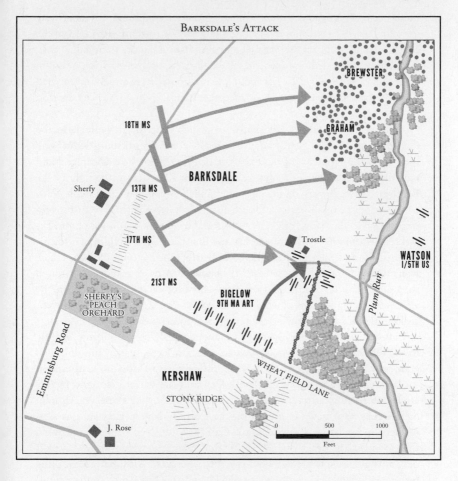

BARKSDALE'S ATTACK

and provide an extra bonus in the form of a platform for his artillery to cover them, since (as Lee afterward wrote) "our artillery could be used to advantage in assailing the more elevated ground beyond."[1]

Or would have, but for Dan Sickles. There were only six brigades in the 3rd Corps, and two of them (from David Birney's division) were already broken beyond repair along the slanting line which ran from the stony ridge down to Devil's Den. Birney's third brigade, under Sickles' old New York political crony Charles Graham, had been assigned to the peach orchard, two of its six Pennsylvania regiments on the south edge of the orchard, three more bent back northward at a right angle along the Emmitsburg Road, and the final one out on the skirmish line to the west of the Emmitsburg Road. But the other three brigades, which formed Andrew Humphreys' division, were stretched out like thin rubber in a line along the Emmitsburg Road, from the peach orchard and past the Sherfy house and barn for more than half a mile, until their line ended, abruptly, just beyond the tiny one-story log house of Peter and Susan Rodgers. There could be no Confederate attack up the road until the peach orchard was in Confederate hands and that Yankee division on the road was destroyed.

Not that Humphreys' division posed much more of an obstacle to the Confederates than Birney's had. Stacked along the Emmitsburg Road were the New York regiments of the Excelsior Brigade, Sickles' old command and now directed by a Sickles acolyte, Col. William Brewster; to the right of the Excelsiors were the six regiments commanded by Brig. Gen. Joseph Carr, whose principal qualifications for a brigadier's star lay entirely with his pre-war service in the New York state militia and his political cultivation of Dan Sickles. (A captain in his brigade snorted that Carr was "well known for his cowardice," and men in the ranks chuckled behind Carr's back that "there won't be any fighting while he leads the brigade." A nasty rumor ran through the brigade that he "had taught dancing schools of a low character before the war," which tempted the clowns to "call off" dance steps—"Eight and left," "All promenade to the bar"—whenever Carr "rode by them.")

Humphreys kept his last brigade, under Col. George Burling, slightly to the rear of the other two as a reserve. But not even that would do much good now. Humphreys had been paring off regiments through the afternoon to shore up pressure points at Devil's Den and the wheat field, and by late afternoon there were only three regiments left in Burling's reserve. All told, Sickles may have had 5,000 men on the road (and farther forward as skirmishers) in Graham's, Brewster's, and Carr's brigades, but they had to cover a frontage from the peach orchard to the Rodgers house which would have left only a single rank of men to hold the entire position. And that did nothing for the gap which yawned between Sickles and the 2nd Corps (on the right) or between the peach orchard and the stony ridge, which one of Régis de Trobriand's regiments occupied thinly as a skirmish line.[2]

Sickles tried to stiffen these paper-thin brigades with artillery borrowed from the Army of the Potomac's artillery reserve. The 3rd Corps had only five batteries in its artillery brigade, so the army's chief of artillery, Henry Hunt, gave Sickles a blank check to draw on the nineteen batteries of reserve artillery parked between Powers Hill and Little Round Top. One battery, Nelson Ames' Battery G, 1st New York Light Artillery, with six 12-pounder Napoleons, was already on its way, and was making for the south side of the peach orchard. It was followed by an entire artillery brigade under a one-time sea captain, Freeman McGilvery, who brought up two batteries each of

Napoleons and 3-inch Ordnance Rifles. One of McGilvery's batteries joined Nelson Ames in the peach orchard; the others were spaced along the wheat field lane, facing south. It would be their job to hold the road down to the stony ridge by themselves.[3]

It was these guns along the wheat field lane which kept three of Joseph Kershaw's regiments of South Carolinians pinned down while the first attack on the stony ridge took place, and which fired a shell whose shrapnel ripped a gash in the leg of Paul Semmes when his Georgia brigade came up to support Kershaw. The batteries took Kershaw's infantry very much in stride. One of them "opened with shell and case shot, firing slowly, first by gun, next by section, then by half battery, and once or twice by battery." But as the afternoon stretched on, and Hood's division, and then Kershaw's and Semmes' brigades, slowly crushed Birney's division, the ammunition in the batteries' limber chests began running low, starting in the peach orchard with Nelson Ames' New York battery, whom Ames ordered "to shelter themselves until the enemy advanced to within canister range." When Kershaw's regiments tried to creep closer, the New Yorkers returned to their guns (and their canister) and "threw them into great confusion." After that, their ammunition was completely gone, and they prepared to limber up the guns and head for the rear. "Some staff officer of General Sickles" found a battery belonging to the 5th Corps (Lt. Malbone Watson's Battery I, 5th U.S.) to put in its place, but before they could move up, the "enemy commenced moving down our front and right in heavy columns, from 600 to 800 yards distant." It was the Mississippi brigade of William Barksdale, and it was now about to flatten everything in its path.[4]

Barksdale's four Mississippi regiments contained just over 1,600 men, but their most colorful asset was William Barksdale himself. A big, fleshy caricature of a Southern politico, Barksdale had been one of the most violent secessionist fire-eaters in Congress in the 1850s. In 1858, he was involved in a full-scale brawl on the floor of the House of Representatives which featured "Congressman Barksdale's wig" being "torn from his head." Barksdale had no trouble obtaining a commission as colonel of the 13th Mississippi, and rose to command an all-Mississippi brigade in late 1862. But he did not have a particularly lengthy combat record; his best moment had been at Fredericksburg, contesting the Rappahannock river crossings. He had been slow getting his brigade deployed to move with Kershaw toward the stony ridge, and by the time he was ready, Longstreet was having second thoughts, and instead he allowed Wofford (who had originally been formed up behind Barksdale) to bring his men up to the line "on Barksdale's right."[5]

This only made Barksdale more eager to get moving. "I wish you would let me go in, General," he pleaded with Longstreet, pointing to one of the Federal batteries in the peach orchard, 600 yards away. "I would take that battery in five minutes." Longstreet refused. "Wait a little," he said, "we are all going in presently." Getting nowhere with Longstreet, Barksdale appealed to McLaws "two or three times" for permission to attack, begging almost like a child, "General, let me go; General, let me charge!" Finally, at 6:30, Longstreet gave the go-ahead, and a jubilant Barksdale, "radiant with joy," brought his four regiments out of the treeline and took them forward. Wigless and hatless, Barksdale rode "fifty yards in front of his brave boys," and his bald pate and long white hair, streaming behind him, reminded one of McLaws' staffers of lines from Macaulay's *Ivry*.

> *And if my standard-bearer fall, as fall full well he may,*
> *For never saw I promise yet of such a bloody fray,*
> *Press where ye see my white plume shine, amidst the*
> *   ranks of war,*
> *And be your oriflamme to-day, the helmet of Navarre.*[6]

The Mississippi brigade drove forward at the double-quick and "literally rushed the goal," yipping the rebel yell "with the savage courage of baited bulls." They struck the peach orchard squarely on its angle, the 21st Mississippi wrapping around to crush the south side of the orchard, and the remaining three regiments rolling straight for Graham's brigade. Three of Graham's regiments moved to the east side of the road to support one of the 3rd Corps artillery batteries beside the Sherfy barn, but they did not stay there long. As the Mississippians advanced "to within 40 yds," the 68th Pennsylvania, which "formed an angle fronting on the pike," was first to fold. Hit from two sides, the 68th crumbled "retiring slowly and contesting the ground inch by inch." Next to go was the 114th Pennsylvania, whose gaudy Zouave uniforms promptly began littering the yard around the Sherfy barn, windmill, and canning house. "Every door, window and sash of the Sherfy house was shivered to atoms" and the barn was "riddled like a sieve from base to roof." George Gerald, the major of the 18th Mississippi, led a surge up to the barn, kicked in the barn door, "and within less than two minutes we had killed, wounded or captured every man in the barn."

The battery the Zouaves had tried to save—Battery E, 1st Rhode Island Light Artillery—had a long association with the regiment, but there was nothing to do for them now. The battery's commander, Lt. John Bucklyn, lost "nearly one-half of our horses and one third of our men were either killed or wounded," and Bucklyn was reduced to hauling off his guns by their *prolonge* ropes. As they pulled back, a domino effect overcame Graham's last two regiments on the Emmitsburg Road—the 57th Pennsylvania and 105th Pennsylvania—who only "checked the advancing rebels for a few minutes" and then came unstitched and ran like the rest. (At the last moment, an offi-cer in the 57th Pennsylvania remembered that he had posted a fifteen-man detail inside the Sherfy buildings; anxious not to leave them behind, he bolted into the Sherfy house, up the stairs, and "ran from one room to another" to get them out before the Confederates closed in.)[7]

In the peach orchard itself, "showers of branches fell from the peach trees" and made pulp of the near-ripe fruit. Three Union regiments—Graham's 141st Pennsylvania, the 2nd New Hampshire from George Burling's reserve, and the orphaned 3rd Maine—were holding the south-facing boundary of the orchard, and, since "the foliage of the peach orchard screened" the infantry, occasionally, "an officer would . . . saunter out . . . to take in the situation." But the confidence of these mismatched regiments could not have been very high. It was not that they lacked for numbers: together, they probably had about 1,000 men, whereas Barksdale may have had not more than 1,600, which should have made for a fairly even fight. But numbers are rarely the deciding consideration. The French veteran of the Crimea Ardant du Picq learned from experience that "four brave men who do not know each other will not dare to attack a lion," but "four less brave, but knowing each other well, sure of their reliability and consequently of mutual aid, will attack reso-lutely. There is the science of the organization of armies in a nutshell." And what told fatally against Graham's regiment in the peach orchard was that none of them had ever fought side by side before.

Standing in the line of battle, the Civil War soldier needed to know one thing above all others—that the men on either side of him would not run. "There is a profound and mysterious gratification to the reciprocal agreement to protect another person with your life," writes Sebastian Junger, the modern journalist, "and combat is virtually the only situation in which that happens regularly." A soldier sandwiched between two strangers will be constantly checking to the right and the left to make sure he is not left alone, and if he senses weakening and hesitation, the soldier will at once begin to look to his own safety. Men begin to waver, drop back by ones and twos, then turn and walk away or bolt at high speed, and in short order an entire brigade can go to pieces.[8]

That was the price now paid by Graham and his men. The 2nd New Hampshire watched the Mississippians approach in "a compact mass of humanity" to "within point-blank range," where they fired a staggering vol-ley. Thirty men out of the 209 in the 141st Pennsylvania went down, and as they pulled back from the perimeter of the orchard, the colonel, Henry J. Madill, "takes up the rent, shot-pierced flag and bears it from the field." The

3rd Maine collapsed next, caught between Barksdale's Mississippians on their front and flank. "It literally melted away," wrote a survivor. "Every man of the color-guard was either killed or wounded" and "in a short time, measured by minutes, a third at least of the one hundred and fifty men" in the regiment were down. The 2nd New Hampshire went last, under "a perfect hail of metal." The remaining artillery in the peach orchard—James Thompson's Pennsylvania battery of 3-inch Ordnance Rifles—"were pounced upon, and half of them taken in a trice, whilst the others limbered up and made off."[9]

Trying to stem the collapse by his own personal example, Charles Graham rode into the morass of Federal soldiers, had one horse shot dead underneath him, mounted his adjutant's horse, lost his bearings, and then mistook "a line of men . . . seen approaching from the flank" for reinforcements. They were actually Mississippians, and when they called on him to stop, Graham wheeled around and defiantly shouted, "I won't surrender. I'm a Brigadier General, and I won't surrender." The Mississippians, unimpressed, shot Graham's mount from under him a second time, "which in falling rolled upon the General, holding him as in a vise, in which condition he was captured by the enemy." Nor was Graham the only one. "As our onrushing line sped down the slope from the Peach Orchard . . . many of the enemy were outstripped and left behind as prisoners." One of them, curiously, took the moment to shake his captors' hands and compliment them on "the most splendid charge of the war."[10]

Nervously, the New Yorkers in William Brewster's brigade along the Emmitsburg Road looked to their left and saw Graham's brigade "melting away through the smoke, and our wounded in hundreds . . . streaming back over the Emmitsburg Road, and riderless horses went dashing among them in bewilderment and fright." Andrew Humphreys could also see how easily the disintegration of Graham's brigade would expose his own division, and he hurriedly rallied the last regiment of George Burling's reserve brigade and tried to lay down a new line perpendicular to the Emmitsburg Road before the Mississippians swung leftward to grasp the flank of his division. Humphreys might have stood a chance if Barksdale had listened to the advice of two of his colonels who, "covered with dust and blackened from the smoke of battle," tried to talk the fiery Mississippian into stopping to reorganize. But Barksdale was having none of it: "No! Crowd them—we have them on the run. Move your regiments."

To add more punch to Barksdale, Longstreet seized this moment to order Porter Alexander, who had been directing the artillery firing on Sherfy's peach orchard, to take forward a full battalion of artillery—six batteries' worth, including the four 24-pounder howitzers of George Moody's Madison Artillery—to the newly captured peach orchard and set up shop. This was the sort of order Alexander lived for, and forward they all went, "some cannon-eers mounted, some running by the sides," all of them "in a general race and scramble to get there first" and begin pummeling Humphreys' division along the Emmitsburg Road. The only obstacles were the omnipresent fence lines, but one of the battalion officers corralled "several hundred" Yankee prisoners and ordered them "with an oath" to pull down the fences. "The frightened prisoners rushed at them, and, each man grabbing a rail, the fences literally flew into the air."[11]

At that moment, it seemed to both Barksdale and Humphreys that the entire Federal left flank was caving in, that the road to Cemetery Hill was yawning open, and that the most complete victory of the war was beckoning to them. For the first time that afternoon, a Confederate brigade was obeying the original directive to wheel left at the Emmitsburg Road and drive north-ward, as Barksdale's troops slowly shifted direction. "Brave Mississippians, one more charge and the day is ours," bawled the exuberant Barksdale, with his sword upraised "at an angle of forty-five degrees," as though striking the perfect military tableau. "When I saw their line broken & in retreat," wrote Porter Alexander, "I thought the battle was ours," and he exultantly waved his artillerymen into position on the north side of the peach orchard with the promise that "we would 'finish the whole war this afternoon.' "[12]

Just 600 yards north, Andrew Atkinson Humphreys' spirits sank in direct proportion as Alexander's and Barksdale's rose. "For the moment, I thought the day was lost," and with it, Humphreys' own career. Humphreys was a West Pointer, graduating two years after Robert E. Lee, and perhaps the best engineer officer in the prewar army. (He was elected to membership in the American Philosophical Society in 1857 and to the American Academy of Arts and Sciences in 1863.) Humphreys had been a devoted member of McClellan's staff on the Peninsula, and rose meteorically to division command in the fervently McClellanite 5th Corps in September 1862. (His "special aide," Carswell McClellan, was George McClellan's nephew.) After Chancellors-ville, Humphreys was put in charge of a division in Sickles' 3rd Corps, where he had not been at all happy with the mincing bootlickers with which Sickles liked to surround himself. David Birney he loathed above all the others, and now the destruction of Birney's division looked like it was about to drag him down with it.[13]

Humphreys' improvised line could not have lasted long. The regimental chaplain of the 120th New York declared that they stood up to the Missis-sippians for "an hour or more," but George Burling thought that "all the troops were forced back, in a few moments." The likeliest guess is that Bur-ling, along with help from Brewster's Excelsiors, held on to their improvised line until 7:30, or about twenty minutes. All the while, stragglers from Graham's brigade "passed through our lines" without stopping, gabbling all kinds of demoralizing predictions: *It's all up with us, boys* and *We are overpowered* and *My regiment is all gone* and *We did the best we could, but we could not whip the world*. Rounds from Porter Alexander's newly unlimbered artillery in the peach orchard were slicing into Brewster's Excelsiors without much hindrance. A captain in the 120th New York was narrowly missed by a solid shot that tore away his haversack; and when he turned to make small talk of it, a second shot "came along and killed him." Both Humphreys and Brewster "took positions personally in the rear of our lines, Humphreys, being mounted and Brewster on foot," Humphreys "walking his horse up and down our line" and Brewster acting "as a file closer with our own line officers." The colonel of the 120th New York tried to find out from Humphreys, "as we were pacing up and down the line behind," if there was any help on the way, but "neither he nor Brewster" were "opening their mouths during that tedious combat."[14]

The Excelsiors might have made a longer fight of it, but new troubles were already descending on them. At seven o'clock, the officer in charge of Joseph Carr's skirmishers warned Andrew Humphreys that two more Confederate brigades were "deploying from the wood" in front of the Emmitsburg Road, and were coming across the fields in "three heavy lines of battle."[15]

The destruction of Charles Graham's brigade at the peach orchard and around the Sherfy house opened up the vulnerable flank of Humphreys' division along the Emmitsburg Road. It also opened up the even more vulnerable line of artillery batteries which Sickles hoped would cover the open space to the left of the peach orchard, along the wheat field road. Ever since wheeling into line, these four batteries—Clark's New Jersey battery, plus the three batteries from the artillery reserve under John Bigelow (9th Massachusetts), Charles Phillips (5th Massachusetts), and Patrick Hart (15th New York Light Artillery), had been having the day to themselves, keeping down the heads of Kershaw's South Carolinians around the Rose farmhouse. Clark's New Jersey battery estimated roughly that "in our front were over 120 dead from three South Carolina regiments." No wonder: Clark's battery alone had fired off 1,342 rounds that afternoon. But the pressure had been slowly mounting, and by 6:30 Clark's gunners were firing three tins of canister at a time to clear the ground on the other side of the wheat field lane. These four batteries were, in fact, "so intent upon our work that we noticed not" until Charles Phillips "happened to see our infantry falling back in the Peach orchard," and Bigelow "saw that the Confederates (Barksdale's Brigade) had come through and were forming a line 200 yards distant."[16]

Freeman McGilvery, who had brought these batteries up from the artil-

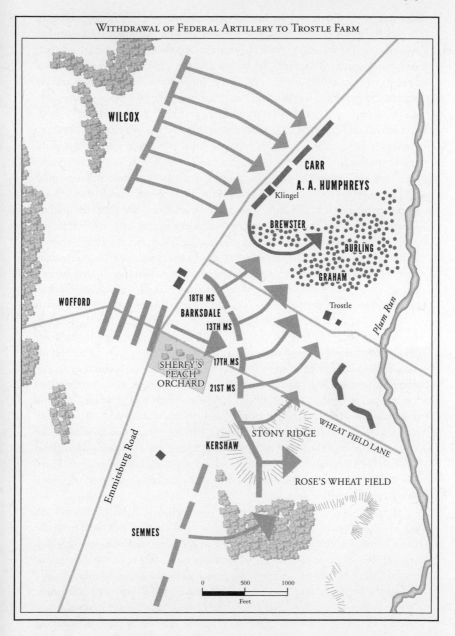

WITHDRAWAL OF FEDERAL ARTILLERY TO TROSTLE FARM

WILCOX

CARR

A. A. HUMPHREYS

Klingel

BREWSTER

BURLING

GRAHAM

WOFFORD

Trostle

18TH MS

BARKSDALE

13TH MS

SHERFY'S
PEACH
ORCHARD

17TH MS

21ST MS

Plum Run

WHEAT FIELD LANE

STONY RIDGE

KERSHAW

ROSE'S WHEAT FIELD

Emmitsburg Road

SEMMES

0   500   1000
Feet

lery reserve, saw the peach orchard collapse, too, and coolly began arranging to pull the guns out of danger. Clark's New Jersey battery was the first to go, followed by Patrick Hart's four 12-pounder Napoleons. The retreating artillery teams careened through the last of George Burling's reserve regiments, the 7th New Jersey, "causing . . . the right four companies" of the regiment "to separate from the line . . . to avoid being crushed to death by the reckless drivers of the battery." McGilvery wanted Clark and Hart, followed by the others, to turn around 250 yards to the rear at another farm road that ran down to Abraham Trostle's barn and set up again. But the drivers kept going for a full mile and completely out of the fight.[17]

That left Bigelow and Phillips. Phillips ordered the limbers of his center and left sections reversed in preparation for hitching up, while the other section kept the rebels at bay, hoping to leap-frog backward until they all reached "Trostle's house and go in battery there." But "the enemy had by this time got through the Peach orchard" and shot down the horses and drivers of the right section, forcing Phillips to fix *prolonge* ropes to the guns and start them to the rear by hand. Now it was John Bigelow and the 9th Massachusetts battery alone on the wheat field road, and by the time McGilvery ordered Bigelow to "limber up and get out," there was no time to do the first and not much chance of the second apart from imitating Phillips and dragging off the guns by *prolonge*. Still, Bigelow managed to get all six of his guns back to the Trostle farm. All that he found there, however, was a desperate Freeman McGilvery, his horse bleeding from four bullet wounds. "Major McGilvery came to me," Bigelow recalled, "and said that for 4 or 500 yards in my rear there were no troops." What was left of the 3rd Corps was fighting for its life up along the Emmitsburg Road, the 5th Corps had been mangled division by division, and Caldwell's division of the 2nd Corps had long since disappeared in the smoky chamber of the wheat field, with only clumps of disorganized survivors drifting back out. "For heavens sake hold that line," McGilvery begged, "until he could get some other batteries in position" behind them and patch together one last-ditch artillery line.[18]

Bigelow never seems to have questioned what was clearly a sacrificial, even suicidal, order. He wheeled his guns into a line across the lane from the Trostle house, facing one section slightly to the southwest and the other two sections directly into the path of the oncoming Confederates (which at this moment was the 21st Mississippi). Bigelow had barely gotten his guns loaded before the Mississippians were running for them. He started with solid shot, "for a ricochet" right into their ranks, then switched to double loads of canister, which the Massachusetts gunners emptied into the faces of the charging rebels "not six feet from the muzzles of our guns." A German-born gunner named Augustus Hesse thought that "we mowed them down like grass, but they were thick and rushed up." Men and horses went down, "the horses . . . plunging and laying about all around."¹ There was no time to run back to the limbers for reloads; Bigelow had the ammunition taken out of the limbers "and laid beside the pieces," where a stray spark could easily blow them all to Tophet. This was calculating survival by the minute, and Bigelow decided to use his remaining horses to save at least the two guns in his left section. (The drivers faced a stone wall in their path, and resorted to jumping the horses and limbers over the wall, so that they came down with a "crash of rocks and wheels"—but still upright.)

In the last rush, the Mississippians began filtering out around Bigelow's flanks, climbing up on the abandoned limber chests, "and shooting down cannoneers that were handling the pieces." But "glancing anxiously to the rear," Bigelow could see McGilvery, some 500 yards away, bringing fresh artillery batteries into position. The 9th Massachusetts had given their mite, and Bigelow shouted "orders for the small remnant of the four gun detachments" to leave the guns and run for their lives. Bigelow himself was knocked out of his saddle by two bullets, and could hear "the officers of the 21st Miss. order their men not to fire at me" so that he could be captured. But Bigelow's orderly, Charles Reed, lifted his captain onto his own horse and, "taking the reins of both horses in his left hand, with his right supporting me in the saddle," walked Bigelow to safety.[19]

Not everyone got off as miraculously as Bigelow. Malbone Watson had been slated to relieve Nelson Ames' New York battery in the peach orchard with Battery I of the 5th U.S., but it was commandeered "by some unknown officer of the Third Corps," and positioned a short distance east of the Trostle house, without any infantry support. When the 21st Mississippi overran Bigelow's guns, Watson's four 3-inch Ordnance Rifles were directly in their path. Without pausing, the Mississippians bowled ahead, capturing Watson's four guns "before they fired," and putting Watson down with a wound to his right leg that ended in amputation and permanent disability.[20]

The Trostle farm claimed a far more sensational casualty, and that was no one less than wild Dan Sickles himself. Once Sickles moved the 3rd Corps to the Emmitsburg Road that afternoon, he had little to do afterward except wrest pieces of the 5th Corps and 2nd Corps away to succor the parts of his own hapless position which were splintering under the weight of Longstreet's attack. It could not have taken him long to realize that he had handed George Meade all his grim commander needed to take his head off, and it must have, in a bleak sort of way, provided him with a better exit than Meade would have designed when a flying piece of Confederate ordnance cracked the bones of his right leg just below the knee.[21]

It is not certain exactly what Sickles was hit *by*: witnesses' accounts varied from a rifle slug to a shell splinter. George Randolph, who as an artilleryman might be presumed to know, thought Sickles had fallen victim to a solid shot, but another staffer was certain that the wound had come from "a terrific explosion" which "shook the very earth," and could only have been a shell. Even Sickles was not sure what had struck him. "I never knew I was hit," he insisted in 1882, and only knew something was wrong when he became "conscious of dampness along the lower part of my right leg," and after pulling his leg out of his "high-top boots . . . was surprised to see it dripping with blood." He guessed that the work had been done by "a piece of shell," but twenty-seven years later he compromised: it might have been "a bullet or a shell-fragment." What is certain is that Sickles, who was mounted, "standing under a small tree . . . close by the" Trostle farmhouse, was in the process of yielding to Randolph's entreaties to get under better cover when "the shot struck him." As the dizziness of shock began to set in, Sickles slowly slid off the left side of his horse and hobbled painfully to the side of the Trostle barn, calling, "Quick, quick! Get something and tie it up before I bleed to death." Most of Sickles' "staff were absent," but Randolph and "a couple of orderlies" rushed over with kerchiefs and saddle straps, and a musician on stretcher duty rushed in with a "Turnkey" to cut off the bleeding. Henry Tremain arrived a few moments later. "Throwing myself from the saddle," Tremain asked what may have been the most pointless question of the afternoon: *General, are you hurt?* Sickles was struggling to keep from passing out, and only replied, "Tell General Birney he must take command," and when Birney galloped up in a lather, Sickles repeated his order. Apart from that, Sickles' principal concern was "fear of being taken prisoner."[22]

The musician, William Bullard of the 70th New York, thought Sickles had sustained "a compound fracture of the leg." But it looked much worse— "mangled" and "almost severed," according to Tremain; "so badly shattered that it hung merely by a shred," according to Thomas Cook of the *New York Herald*—and to George Randolph "it was a very long time (seemingly) before the ambulance and surgeon arrived." Private Bullard, noticing "how white the Gen. was," poured some medicinal brandy for Sickles, which seemed to revive him a little, and as Sickles was eased onto a stretcher he had the presence of mind to ask Bullard, "Won't you be kind enough to light a cigar for me?" Bullard fumbled around "in his Inside pocket," found a cigar case, bit off the end of a "small" cigar, then lit it up and "placed it in the Gen. mouth." Tremain and the others got Sickles into an ambulance, and they all set off for the 3rd Corps' field hospital. Sickles was by now fading in and out of consciousness, at one point insisting that 3rd Corps stragglers be allowed to see him and be assured "that I am allright and will be with you in a short time." The ambulance stopped at a two-story brick house on the Baltimore

Pike instead, and on an improvised surgical table the 3rd Corps chief medical director, Thomas Simms, chloroformed Sickles and amputated the butchered leg. "How much missed is his clear-sighted direction and his all-pervading energy," wept the adoring *New York Times*. Those who did *not* adore Sickles had a different interpretation: that Sickles had been only slightly wounded, but ordered the amputation to engender sympathy and "save him from the mess he got in." Given what had befallen the 3rd Corps so far, this might have been ungenerous, but not surprising; given what was about to happen to Andrew Humphreys and his division, now under the overall command of a man Humphreys frankly despised, it might even have been plausible.[23]

Richard Heron Anderson had been a classmate of James Longstreet's and Lafayette McLaws' at West Point, and under almost any circumstances would have been happier serving under Longstreet than mired as he was, commanding a division under the erratic Ambrose Powell Hill. For that matter, he would have probably preferred not to have been in the Confederate Army at all. Although Anderson was born and raised in South Carolina, he had courted and married a Pennsylvanian—the daughter of the chief justice of Pennsylvania—in 1850 during a posting to the Carlisle Barracks. Shy and laconic by temperament, he was notably unenthusiastic about both slavery and secession, and joined the Confederate Army only after being browbeaten by his father into a sense of obligation to follow "the old Palmetto State." He was jumped to brigadier general in May 1861, then to major general after the Peninsula (where he became a protégé of Longstreet's). But there, like William Wofford and so many others who lacked the requisite egotism, secessionism, or Virginia-ism, Anderson stalled. He was assigned to division command in Powell Hill's corps, where he did not hesitate to make his displeasure with Hill known to a sympathetic James Longstreet. Anderson's division had come up at the tail end of Hill's corps on the Cashtown Pike on July 1st, and when Lee authorized Longstreet to substitute Anderson for George Pickett's division, he could not have made Longstreet or Anderson a more mutually agreeable gift.[24]

"Shortly after the line had been formed," Anderson wrote, "I received notice that Lieutenant-General Longstreet would occupy the ground on the right" and that Anderson was to "put the troops of my division into action by brigades as soon as those of General Longstreet's corps had progressed so far in their assault as to be connected with my right flank." Those brigades were five in number, and Anderson had positioned them so that Cadmus Wilcox's brigade of Alabamians would be the first to go in, followed by a diminutive Florida brigade under the temporary command of David Lang, yet another

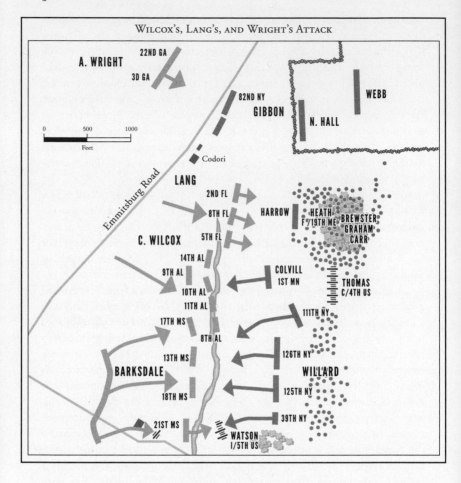

WILCOX'S, LANG'S, AND WRIGHT'S ATTACK

A. WRIGHT
22ND GA
3D GA

82ND NY
GIBBON
WEBB
N. HALL

0   500   1000
Feet

Codori

LANG
2ND FL
8TH FL
HARROW
HEATH
F/19TH ME
BREWSTER
GRAHAM
CARR

C. WILCOX
5TH FL
14TH AL
9TH AL
COLVILL
1ST MN
THOMAS
C/4TH US
10TH AL
11TH AL
111TH NY
17TH MS
8TH AL
126TH NY
13TH MS
WILLARD
BARKSDALE
18TH MS
125TH NY
21ST MS
39TH NY
WATSON
I/5TH US

brigade of Georgians under a highly flammable lawyer and politician named Ambrose Ransom Wright, and Carnot Posey's Mississippians (the last brigade, of Virginians under William Mahone, would act as Anderson's reserve). This amounted to over 7,000 men, with the single biggest concentration in the 1,700 soldiers of Wilcox's five Alabama regiments.[25]

Like Anderson, Cadmus Marcellus Wilcox suffered from being a non-Virginian. Born in North Carolina, he had grown up in Tennessee, and gone from the University of Nashville to West Point and the same graduating class in 1846 that produced George McClellan. He resigned from the army after the secession of Tennessee, but was put in command of the 9th Alabama, where he caught the eye of James Longstreet. He made brigade command, but there he languished, despite being what one of his Alabamians described as "one the best . . . in our army." As the lead brigade of Anderson's division, Wilcox had been instructed to "advance when the troops on my right [Hood, then McLaws] should advance" and "report this to the division commander" so that Anderson could start the other brigades forward himself.

The firing over by Little Round Top had died away by now, but Caldwell's and Kershaw's men were grappling for control of the wheat field and the Massachusetts artillery's final stand at the Trostle farm was reaching its crescendo. In order to avoid crowding in on Barksdale's Mississippi regiments, Wilcox formed his Alabamians in column and started forward toward the Emmitsburg Road. Unlike Hood and McLaws, Anderson did not stack his brigades in pairs; he had a long front to cover and the sun was dipping toward South Mountain, and Anderson wanted every brigade except Mahone's Virginians at the front. David Lang's three Florida regiments would move up alongside Wilcox, and Wright's Georgians would hitch their right flank to the Floridians—so that, for once, Virginians in the Army of Northern Virginia would be compelled to take a backseat to other parts of the Confederacy.[26]

Unlike Hood and McLaws, they would be able to get over the ground quickly. From the oak groves on Seminary Ridge, Wilcox had less than half a mile to cover to Emmitsburg Road, and moving in column would make that passage even faster. Humphreys' skirmishers—nine companies of the 1st Massachusetts—saw "the enemy's advancing columns," and decided that the "tornado of whizzing missiles" made them "a little tremulous." They scampered back to the road, forming up in front of the 26th Pennsylvania, in Joseph Carr's brigade. The "lively popping" of the skirmishers reminded one of Humphreys' staffers of the beginning of a rain squall, an odd association until it was connected with "the heavy sulphurous" smoke clouds drifting in from farther down the road. Being hit in column by the Massachusetts skirmishers brought the 11th Alabama to an unplanned halt, so Wilcox moved them into line and picked the pace up again.

"The first line of the enemy in front gave way precipitately," wrote a soldier in the 11th Alabama, and the 8th Alabama (Wilcox's right-hand regiment) "swept like a hurricane over cannon and caissons." The Floridians, likewise, "charged splendidly," and made it a "grand sight to see." Not quite all of it was grand, though. Hilary Herbert, the colonel of the 8th Alabama, remembered years afterward "one little boy in blue, apparently not more than fifteen years old," mounted "on the lead front horse" of a limber but unable to get his own horse to pull away because the two horses behind him were dead in their traces. "I was near enough to have touched him with my sword," remembered Herbert, wincing with the thought. And then "the dust flew from his jacket just under his shoulder blade, and he fell forward dead."[27]

Even as Joseph Carr's brigade struggled to fend off Wilcox's and Lang's assault, William Brewster's Excelsior Brigade, which Humphreys had drawn back at a right angle to Carr, gave way before the relentless pounding of Barksdale's 13th, 17th, and 18th Mississippi. Capt. Henry Blake, drawn up with his 11th Massachusetts along the road, saw "the batteries and infantry which were posted on the extreme left" bend and break "before the yells and bullets of the enemy." Carr tried to stem the tide and protect his own line by whipping back one of his regiments, the 11th New Jersey, to act as a breakwater. In later years, the survivors of Brewster's and Carr's brigades would announce that not "a single man" in any of their regiments had shown "the least cowardice under . . . the fierce charge which we met." But the painful truth was that Brewster's brigade—Sickles' own favorites—simply disintegrated, and trying to get Carr's regiments to change front while being hit from two sides was an impossibility which only "a veteran can possibly understand." To a watcher in the 2nd Corps, "the Excelsior Brig. and the men were running back before the enemy as if they were but a line of skirmishers." Andrew Humphreys "could not hold his men, for as soon as they found themselves assailed both in front and flank they broke and retreated." Joseph Carr was blown off his horse by an exploding shell, and the dead horse "fell on him and crushed his leg."

Like so many others, Humphreys afterward claimed that the collapse was all calm and orderliness, thanks to him: "Twenty times did I [bring] my men to a halt & face about, myself & . . . others of my staff forcing the men to do it." But at the moment, Humphreys, whose "indignation often flamed up" under stress, seems to have lost all self-control. Francis Seeley, who was desperately trying to move his battery from the Emmitsburg Road, glimpsed Humphreys, "bareheaded, and unattended" and "endeavoring to rally (with only partial success, I judge) the retreating infantry of the 3rd Corps." Every time Humphreys looked to the rear, "no other guns or a solitary soldier could be seen. . . . The Fed. Army" had been sliced "in twain."[28]

Humphreys could not repair a disaster this serious singlehanded. Some of the 71st New York, on their own hook, "would fire at the enemy, walk to the rear, loading as they went, then turn, take deliberate aim and fire again." But for the rest of Brewster's Excelsiors, "there was no commanding officer to collect them and form a second line; nor use them to cover the long gap in the lines." As one officer in the 73rd New York admitted, "the shattered line was retreating in separated streams . . . leaving their dead and dying under their feet." A 2nd Corps regiment had to open up and allow "many of them, to the number of thousands," pass "between our files" to the rear. Their officers "undertook to stop and put them in line, but found it impossible," and several Confederates stopped to watch in horrified fascination as desperate Union officers, "standing in the rear of their line of battle," were seen to "slash" their fleeing men "across their faces, pull them by the collars, and kick them back to their positions."[29]

The worst of these offenders was Humphreys. Fumbling through the confused mob of retreating soldiers, he washed up against the 19th Maine, another 2nd Corps regiment Winfield Hancock had sent to cover, as best they could, the gap between the 2nd Corps at the rear of Cemetery Hill and the 3rd Corps out at the Emmitsburg Road. Humphreys "rode back to the Nineteenth" and, in manic rage, ordered the colonel of the 19th Maine, Francis Heath, to fix bayonets "and stop with the bayonet the soldiers of his command." Francis Heath was a fair-haired twenty-five-year-old who had left his father's law office in 1861 to become a lieutenant in the 19th. He was aghast at Humphreys' order, and refused to obey, offering instead that if Humphreys would get out of the way, Heath's Maine regiment would stop the avalanche to the rear by example. But Humphreys was past reasoning with. He hysterically ordered Heath "to the rear," and "rode down the line of the Nineteenth, giving the order himself." Heath indignantly took after Humphreys, "closely countermanding his orders" and telling the men to ignore the general. Heath had not come to make war on his own people, and he was certainly not taking orders from some madman from another corps. Soon enough, Humphreys and his broken-down division disappeared "in the smoke and confusion."[30]

What was despair for Humphreys was joy to Wilcox's Alabama brigade. "Never perhaps in all its history did the men of the 8th Alabama feel the thrill of victory so vividly," wrote Hilary Herbert. Like Porter Alexander, Herbert "felt that the supreme moment of the war had come—that victory was with our army and we ourselves were the victors."[31] All that remained was for Ambrose Wright and Carnot Posey to trample down the last Federal regiments behind Cemetery Hill, and they could snap the Army of the Potomac's spinal cord at the nape of its neck. It would be the end of the battle, and of the war.

CHAPTER EIGHTEEN

Remember Harper's Ferry!

A NDREW HUMPHREYS once swore that he would never, under any circumstances, serve under David Birney, and George Meade was fully determined, after he had been informed of Dan Sickles' disablement, that Humphreys would not have to. Rather than allow Birney to succeed Sickles, Meade ordered Winfield Scott Hancock (in a reprise of his designation of Hancock as his authority on Cemetery Hill the night before) to take charge of whatever was left of the 3rd Corps and somehow stave off a complete collapse until the coming of darkness could bring the fighting to a standstill.

How, exactly, Hancock was to accomplish this was anyone's guess. He was having more than enough problems in the 2nd Corps without adding Sickles' mess to his responsibilities. Of the three divisions the 2nd Corps began the day with, one (Caldwell's) was already gone past recall. That left John Gibbon's division, and then Alex Hays' wobbly-legged division, which was butting up against the left flank of what remained of the 11th Corps on Cemetery Hill. As it was, Hancock had already begun handing out regiments from other 2nd Corps brigades to hold up the forlorn ends of Humphreys' division—first the 15th Maine and 82nd New York, then the 19th Maine—and in fairly short order Hancock realized that he had sent away an entire brigade from Gibbon's division. Barksdale had wheeled and was driving up the Emmitsburg Road; Wofford was roaring down the wheat field lane in pursuit of Ayres' Regulars. And now, coming against what was left of Humphreys' division along the Emmitsburg Road, were Wilcox's Alabama and Lang's Florida brigades, bent on delivering the coup de grâce to Humphreys. And it was while that last gray cloud was rolling toward Humphreys that "General

Meade informed me that General Sickles had been wounded, and directed me to assume command of the Third Corps in addition to that of my own."[1]

John Gibbon heard Hancock growl "some expressions of discontent." But discontent or not, Hancock wasted no time in taking charge. He wanted artillery, and sent an aide off to the artillery reserve to get some; he wanted infantry, and more aides were sent off to find Otis Howard and Henry Slocum and beg troops from their corps; he rode into Humphreys' "depleted command" (and the distracted Humphreys, unable to get Francis Heath's Maine men to obey him, had no more than what was "scarcely equal to an ordinary battalion" standing with him) and told him "that I was commanding that front, including the 3rd Corps." Hancock even managed to find David Birney. "General, you are nearly surrounded by the enemy," Hancock announced, as though this was news to Birney. "I know it," Birney irritably shot back; wasn't Hancock aware that "we have been contending against a superior force all the afternoon"? No matter, replied Hancock, "I have seen this," and he was there to save the day.[2]

The first priority was to string together some sort of fallback line between the loose end of the 2nd Corps and the artillery line Freeman McGilvery was struggling to amass east of the Trostle farm. In addition to the three regiments he had already posted in that gap, Hancock got a small dribbling of help from the depleted artillery reserve. The help consisted of only two batteries, the six Napoleons of Evan Thomas' Battery C, 4th U.S., and another half-dozen Napoleons in the form of Gulian Weir's Battery C, 5th U.S. Artillery, but they would have to do. Hancock personally situated them to anchor the three regiments, Weir in the middle and Thomas on the left flank of the 19th Maine—and then, for good measure, he pulled in yet another regiment, the 1st Minnesota, to cover Thomas' battery.

These guns would do little more than make up the loss of Humphreys' last two batteries on the Emmitsburg Road, which were at that moment making a singularly disorganized exit. Careening toward the 19th Maine, they forced Francis Heath to order "files broken to the rear to let the guns & horses pass." They also triggered a crack of profane thunder from Hancock, who roared, "If I commanded this regt. I'd be God Damned if I would not charge bayonets on you"—which, considering that Heath had refused an order from Humphreys to do just that, might have had interesting consequences. But neither Weir nor Thomas, or the 1st Minnesota, were enough to cover the toothless gap of 400 yards that the flight of the 3rd Corps had opened up, much less to protect McGilvery from the still oncoming crush of Barksdale's yowling, triumphant Mississippians. Hancock looked to his right, to Alex Hays' division, and sent off an aide to Hays, at the far north end of the 2nd Corps line. "General Hancock sends his compliments," the staffer reported, "and wishes you to send one of your best Brigades over there," pointing to the Trostle farm, where the Mississippians had just overrun Malbone Watson's battery.[3]

At that moment, Alexander Hays, who was the rare man in this army who loved fighting and brawling more than anything else in life, had been chatting with Col. George Willard. Hays turned a cocked eye on Willard and snorted: "Take your Brigade over there and knock Hell out of the rebs." Hardly anyone would have regarded George Willard's brigade as Hays' "best." These were the notorious "Harpers Ferry Cowards"—the 39th, 111th, 125th, and 126th New York. But the supercharged Hays had adopted the New Yorkers as his pet rehabilitation project and by mid-May 1863, he was able to boast that "the Harper's Ferry boys have turned out trumps, and when we do get a chance look out for blood." It was nearly eight o'clock, and the sun was "declining behind the hills in the west." But to Willard, who had been a captain in the Regulars until taking over the 125th as its colonel, it was high noon, and he was about to lead them to the reclamation of their honor.[4]

Willard took them forward with fixed bayonets in "close column by division," waiting until he had reached "the rear of a bushy swale" which ran across the front of the Mississippians. Through the swale ran a meandering little stream, hardly more than a drainage ditch, known as Plum Run, and there Willard deployed his regiments out into a line, the 125th New York on the left, the 126th in the center, and the 111th on the right. (Willard wanted to leave the 111th behind as a reserve, but Hancock, who rode part of the way with Willard, had no patience with observing the niceties of reserves at a time like this and "in great haste" ordered the 111th to close up on the others.) Barksdale's Mississippians, who could see little in front of them "because of the smoke covering the field," had barely enough time to collect themselves and get off one "deadly volley at less than ten paces" before the "Cowards" were on top of them, shouting deliriously *Remember Harper's Ferry! Remember Harper's Ferry!* "A short but terrible contest ensued in the bushes in the swale," and then the Mississippians' "fire slackened and they began to give back." As they did, "large numbers" of them, staring at "the very points of our bayonets," surrendered and "lay down in ranks." The 126th New York was "scarcely able to step without treading on them."[5]

The last of Willard's regiments, the 39th New York, had been consolidated into only four companies, and was posted on Willard's left flank as a guard against unlooked-for flanking movements by any other lurking Confederates. But the 39th had scores of their own to settle. An artillery lieutenant, Samuel Peeples, who had been knocked loose from Watson's battery when the 21st Mississippi captured it, appealed to the 39th's four companies to retake the battery. "If those Confederates are able to serve my guns, those troops you have just been forming . . . won't stay there a minute," Peeples added as a warning. So, "without drum or bugle, but with a single Hurrah," the 39th surged forward, with the forlorn lieutenant picking up a rifle to join the charge. In minutes, they were "driving the enemy from the guns" and "the battery was ours." The whooping New Yorkers promptly began "hauling the guns off the field by hand" toward McGilvery's gun line.[6]

Still in the van of his Mississippians, William Barksdale, in his gold-braided roundabout jacket, was "almost frantic with rage" at the repulse of his brigade, and "was riding in front of his troops" and "trying to make his fleeing men stand." *They are whipped!* Barksdale pleaded. *We will drive them beyond the Susquehanna!* This only made him a prominent target, and after "numerous shots" were fired at him from both the 125th and 126th New York, Barksdale dropped from his saddle with "a ball hole through the breast." With Barksdale down, the colonel of the 21st Mississippi, Benjamin Humphreys, concluded that "we had advanced too far to the front for safety." To the right, he could see "Kershaw give way and Wofford retiring toward the Peach Orchard," so it was clearly time for "a hurried retreat." (With a curious sort of detachment, the Mississippian retrieved a horse from the broken fragments of Bigelow's battery at the Trostle farm, and an officer's "satchel" containing "photographs of 2 very fine-looking boys about 12 or 14 yrs. old, I suppose his children.")

Barksdale was left, half-alive, to be picked up later that evening and brought back to a field hospital on the Taneytown Road by a detail from the 14th Vermont. He died that night, conscious to the end, and alternately asking that his minders "tell my wife I fought like a man and will die like one" and threatening them that "Gen. Lee will clean out this place to-morrow" or that "before we knew it Ewell would be thundering in our rear." The next morning, a Vermont lieutenant who remembered seeing Barksdale in action "on the floor of Congress," recognized the cantankerous Mississippian's body, lying in the sunshine "with open and unblinking eyes" but "without the wig which Speaker [Galusha] Grow once knocked off in the Hall of Representatives."[7]

The repulse of Barksdale's Mississippians did not give Hancock much respite, for as he turned to look backward, he saw a large body of troops with flags coming out of the battle fog. Hancock at first thought that they were supports from the 12th Corps, arriving from Culp's Hill at just the moment he needed them to seal off the breach between Willard and McGilvery at one end and the 2nd Corps at the other. He was wrong. They were Cadmus Wilcox's Alabamians, and they "opened fire" and "twice wounded" Hancock's only remaining aide, William DeWitt Miller, "whom I immediately told to ride away." This would be Hancock's defining moment at Gettysburg, for as he twisted around to look for troops to throw into the path of the Alabamians, he saw absolutely no one—except for one regiment, lying down beside Evan Thomas' battery where they had been posted a short time earlier. "My God! Are these all the men we have here?" Hancock profanely erupted. But there was no time for careful deductions of risk. The Alabamians, supported on their left by David Lang's three Florida regiments, were looming up clearly now, in what looked like "three long lines." Hancock "spurred to where" the regiment lay, calling out, "What regiment is this." *First Minnesota,* replied the regiment's colonel, William Colvill.[8]

Hancock, pointing toward the Alabamians, wasted no time in instructing Colvill, "Charge those lines!" (In a slightly different version, Hancock tells Colvill, "Do you see those colors? Take them!") *With what?* Colvill might have replied. (The actual head count of the 1st Minnesota, like so many other numerical reckonings at Gettysburg, is a mystery: the regiment's payrolls indicated that it had 399 officers and men present on June 30th; but 10 of these were noncombatant musicians, 37 were on detached service, 33 members of Company F were on a skirmish line, and another company had been detailed for provost guard duties.) In all, Colvill could probably lead just over 230 men into action, against two entire Confederate brigades with more than ten times that strength. This was, in other words, yet another forlorn hope, for no other purpose than to buy time for the gallopers Hancock had sent off to Cemetery Hill and Culp's Hill to come back with reinforcements to stop the collapse. "I had no alternative but to order that regiment in," Hancock later explained. "I saw that in some way five minutes must be gained or we were lost."[9]

"Every man realized in an instant what that order meant," but Colvill, without the slightest protest, called the 1st Minnesota to its feet, rifles at right-shoulder-shift, and down into the swale they went, toward the meager margins of Plum Run, where Wilcox and Lang had paused for a moment to reorder their lines. (Fence climbing had "disordered" the Alabama regiments, and by the time the Mississippians, Alabamians, and Floridians had reached Plum Run, they "were in marked confusion, mixed up indiscriminately, officers apart from their men, men without officers.") Of all the moments of deliberate self-immolation that the Army of the Potomac performed that afternoon—whether it was the 124th New York in Devil's Den, or Chamberlain and O'Rorke on Little Round Top—nothing quite hit the bell of the sublime as deeply as the charge of the 1st Minnesota. With "no hesitation, no stopping to fire," Colvill led them in a fast trot, breaking into a full-scale run as he shouted, "Charge!"

They were briefly concealed by a thick bank of smoke which "had settled into the ravine" formed by Plum Run, so that the Alabamians had no warning of their approach until the Minnesotans burst on top of them. Hilary

Herbert's 8th Alabama looked up to see "in front of us" what "seemed to be . . . two compact lines, probably regiments, and here and there were groups of [Union] fugitives endeavoring to rally." The front rank of the Alabamians took one look at the "leveled bayonets coming with such momentum and evident desperation" and promptly broke, stumbling and tripping over their rear rank. Colvill pulled the Minnesotans up at the line of Plum Run and "we then poured in our first fire." It was as though "the ferocity of our onset seemed to paralyze them." Worse than paralyze, it convinced David Lang that "a heavy force had advanced upon General Wilcox's brigade, and was forcing it back." Lang at once concluded that they had walked into a massive Federal trap, and Lang "immediately ordered my men back to the [Emmitsburg] road, some 300 yards to the rear."[10]

Overall, the clash between the 1st Minnesota and the two Confederate brigades lasted for no more than fifteen or twenty minutes. "We had not fired but a few shots," wrote a soldier in Company D, "before we were ordered to fall back." The Minnesotans came limping back out of the smoke with only handfuls of the regiment which had gone in—35 dead, 180 wounded, Colvill twice wounded and lying stunned in the ditch water of Plum Run, and only 47 men able to answer roll call. But their long-shot charge had worked. Barksdale's brigade had been stopped and thrown back by Willard's "Cowards"; now Wilcox and Lang had been scattered back to the Emmitsburg Road (and in fact they "continued to fall back, rallying and reforming upon the line from which we started").[11]

Or had it really worked? Hancock, like Sykes, Caldwell, and every other Union general that afternoon, managed to shore up Dan Sickles' misbegotten line along the Emmitsburg Road by robbing divisions and brigades from anyone not under immediate pressure and sending them to suffocate the emergencies breaking out in place after place from Devil's Den to Plum Run. But there was going to come a moment when some part of the Union defenses was going to find itself so denuded by emergencies elsewhere that it would have nothing left for its own defense and nowhere to borrow more. Hancock had bled his own corps—ten infantry brigades when the day began—down to exactly three, with only about 1,400 men. They would have to face over 4,200 Confederates, because the last brigades of Richard Heron Anderson's division were stepping out into the lengthening shadows and moving forward, on a line pointed straight at a small woodlot where the last bits of the 2nd Corps readied themselves for what was already looking like the Army of the Potomac's Götterdämmerung.[12]

As early as noon on July 2nd, Anderson notified Ambrose Ransom Wright that his Georgia brigade (the 3rd, 22nd, and 48th Georgia, with the four companies that made up the 2nd Georgia Battalion) would be going in to the attack as soon as Wilcox and Lang had started forward, and that he could look for Carnot Posey's Mississippi brigade to "move forward upon my advance."

Wright was "a very gifted man, a powerful writer, an effective orator, and a rare lawyer." He was notorious for possessing a bullwhip temper which made him "self-willed and combative." Like his division commander, Wright had been less than enthusiastic about secession. His brother-in-law was Herschel Johnson, the vice presidential running mate of Stephen Douglas, whose nomination as the Democratic presidential candidate in 1860 impelled the secessionist fire-eaters to split the party, and Wright himself had strayed even further from secession orthodoxy by endorsing the centrist Constitutional Union candidates, John Bell and Edward Everett. Proud, intensely self-concerned, and with an innate sense of personal superiority, Wright did not endear himself to the Virginia elite in the Army of Northern Virginia. And he had narrowly missed a bushwhacker's bullet near Hagerstown that "cut off some of his long, black, curly hair."[13]

Wright's temper was improved neither by a "severe indisposition" that made him "very sick" the day before nor by the lay of the land he now had before him. Wright's brigade, along with Posey's and then William Mahone's reserve brigade, were "placed in line of battle behind a small grove of large oaks . . . along the line of a stone fence that over-looked the open field between the hostile lines." The Emmitsburg Road lay parallel to the treeline and 800 yards away, across gently dipping and rising fields, broken only by a solitary stone barn and "double log and frame" farmhouse owned by an elderly New Englander named William Bliss (the Bliss family had prudently decamped from the property the day before). The road itself sank unevenly through the dips and rises, creating in some places a substantial embankment, and both sides were lined by heavy "rail and plank fences." Beyond the road, the ground swelled gently upward for another hundred yards to form the modest spur of Cemetery Ridge, and there Wright saw the lines of the 2nd Corps—in this case, the divisions of Alex Hays and John Gibbon—and the thick concentration of Federal artillery on Cemetery Hill. And it led Wright to growl to one of his staff that "if we were required to charge it, the sacrifice of life would necessarily be great."[14]

But charge they would, and Wright would lead them himself, sickness or not. He wanted to move fast. With so much Federal artillery clustered within easy range on Cemetery Hill, he dared not put his regiments in column for the easy target they would make. But Wright took them forward so quickly that the skirmish line formed by the 2nd Georgia Battalion had no time to "form all its companies on the left of the brigade," and some of them had to fall "into line with other regiments of the command." The Federal artillery leapt into action at once, sending "shot and shell . . . screaming through the air in every direction." But so long as they stayed in line and kept moving at the "double quick step," the Union guns could not fix any solid targets, and even though Wright's Georgians were constantly having to stop and tear down "numerous post and rail fences," they moved swiftly through William Bliss's fields of "oats, wheat and young corn" and shouldered past a clump of Federal skirmishers who had barricaded themselves in the Bliss barn, "a rambling structure seventy-five feet long and thirty-five feet wide," built of stone and brick and "plentifully supplied with doors and windows." Federal skirmishers along the Emmitsburg Road were caught so much by surprise that instead of falling back by twos and fours, hand-to-hand fighting broke out along the roadbed; pioneers from the 106th Pennsylvania who had been chopping down some of the fences had no time but to use their axes to defend themselves. One captain in the 3rd Georgia "with his sword stood on top of a pile of rails, thrusting at a burly Federal who tried to jab the captain with his bayonet."[15]

The Federal skirmishers dropped back toward the ridgeline, and then it was up and out of the roadbed for the Georgians, notwithstanding the stout fences that lined both sides of the road. Two of the regiments Hancock had posted earlier in the afternoon to cover Andrew Humphreys' division, the 15th Massachusetts and 82nd New York, saw the wave coming at them too late and were overrun by "the yelling exultant Georgians." The 15th Massachusetts scampered away "in some disorder, being pressed so closely that we lost quite a number of prisoners," and their flight, in turn, allowed Wright's Georgians to pounce on Battery B, 1st Rhode Island Artillery. The Rhode Island battery was attached to John Gibbon's 2nd Corps division, but earlier that afternoon it was moved up by Gibbon toward a large red farmhouse and barn on the east side of the Emmitsburg Road belonging to Nicholas Codori. (Codori actually lived in the town and used the farm as a rental property.)

The artillerymen were caught napping. Wright closed the gap so quickly that the Rhode Islanders mistook the men running toward them for the 15th Massachusetts being somehow recalled to Gibbon's original line on the ridge. "But when we commenced to receive their fire and heard that well known 'rebel yell,' as they charged for our battery, we were in doubt no longer." The battery's commander, Fred Brown, managed to get off a few rounds of shell with fuses "cut at three, two, and one second, and then canister at point blank range." But the Georgians were "advancing so rapidly" that all order disappeared in a welter of calls to *Limber to the rear* and *Get out of that, you will all be killed* and the gunners' last resort, *Don't give up the guns.* It did them no good. "Men and horses were wounded before we could retire behind our line of support," and in short order the Georgians were swarming over four of Brown's guns.[16]

Beyond them lay a low stone wall at the crest of Cemetery Ridge, anchored on its left by the small woodlot, and for that moment only John Gibbon's last two brigades, the Philadelphia Brigade and Norman J. Hall's mixed brigade of New Yorkers, Michiganders, and New Englanders, stood in the way of a complete and disastrous breakthrough, worse than Devil's Den or the wheat field, right in the rear of Cemetery Hill. Hancock was already in the midst of the Philadelphia Brigade, trying to sort out what action they should take. The hubbub along Cemetery Ridge forced "Gen. Meade . . . to abandon his own Head Quarters" a hundred yards below at the Leister cottage, and "for a few minutes affairs seem critical in the extreme." Wright was exultant: "We had now accomplished our task—we had stormed the enemy's strong position, had drove off his infantry, had captured all his guns in our front, except a few which he succeeded in running off, and had up to this moment suffered but comparatively small loss." So were Wright's men. The 3rd and 22nd Georgia pushed through an opening on the flank of the Philadelphia Brigade and reached the crest of the ridge. "Seizing artillery horses, shooting down the riders and cutting the traces from the casons," they pressed "on over these guns up to the crest of the hill, where thirteen other pieces of artillery are captured—thus cutting entirely in twain the army of Mead," one of the captains in the 3rd Georgia would remember years later. Gibbon's line, "heavily engaged along his whole front," began to bow and break. George Meade straightened up in his stirrups and drew his sword, as if he was ready to go down swinging right there rather than live with the consequences of the catastrophe staring at him.[17]

And then, for what must have seemed like the umpteenth time that afternoon, the cry went up, *There they come, general!* It was, to Ambrose Wright's dismay, "a heavy column of Yankee infantry on our right flank." Abner Doubleday, still smarting from his demotion back to division command in the 1st Corps, sent over two regiments and a battalion from his one unbattered brigade, George Stannard's nine-month Vermonters, with the 14th Vermont leading the way across the Taneytown Road "in close column by division, at a sharp double quick" and "forming in line of battle." (Stannard himself was left behind on Culp's Hill; Doubleday had been in such a hurry to respond to Hancock that he forgot to inform Stannard that he had gone over his head, and that evening Stannard furiously "rebuked" the Vermonters "for wandering off without his orders.") Hancock whooped upon seeing them, and pointed in the direction of Brown's captured Napoleons: *Could they retake that battery?* "We can," shouted the Vermonters. "Forward boys!"

ABOVE The town center of Gettysburg, looking southward from the diamond, down Baltimore Street.

(Levi Mumper) Courtesy of William A. Frassanito, Gettysburg Then and Now: Touring the Battlefield with Old Photos, 1865–1889 *(1996)*

ABOVE Professor Michael Jacobs (1808–1871) of Pennsylvania College. A mathematician, Jacobs made meticulous weather observations and later wrote the first history of the battle, *Notes on the Rebel Invasion of Maryland and Pennsylvania* (1863).

RIGHT Major General Lafayette McLaws (1821–1897). A Georgian, McLaws commanded one of the three divisions employed by James Longstreet in his overwhelming attack on the Union left flank on July 2nd. Named for the Revolutionary War hero, he nevertheless disliked the tendency of Southerners to collapse it into two syllables: *Lafet*. Although a mediocre student at West Point, he "has always been distinguished for his talents and sound judgment."

TOP On the spine of Little Round Top, looking southward toward Big Round Top, from approximately the position occupied by the right flank of Strong Vincent's brigade. "The ground occupied by the brigade in line of battle was . . . composed mostly of high rocks and cliffs in the center and becoming more wooded and less rugged as you approached to the left. The right was thrown forward somewhat to the front of the ledge of rocks, and was much more exposed than other parts of the line."

LEFT Looking northwest from the spine of Little Round Top, toward Houck's Ridge and, beyond it, John Rose's wheat field.

Colonel Strong Vincent (1837–1863). "If Vincent had not taken upon himself the responsibility of taking his brigade" to Little Round Top on the afternoon of July 2nd, "the arrival of his brigade would have found the enemy in possession of the ground, from which in all probability it could not have been dislodged."

Joseph Sherfy's
peach orchard, at
the intersection of
the Wheat Field
Lane (left) and the
Emmitsburg Road;
to the east, Little
Round Top and
Big Round Top are
clearly visible in
the distance.

*(Levi Mumper) Courtesy
of William A. Frassanito,
Gettysburg Then and
Now: Touring the
Battlefield with Old
Photos, 1865–1889 (1996)*

The Joseph Sherfy house, looking
northward. William Barksdale's
Mississippi brigade stormed through
this yard on July 2nd.

The Emmitsburg
Road, looking
north toward
Gettysburg and
Cemetery Hill; the
Rogers house and
the Codori barn
can be seen on the
left and the right of
the road.

*(Levi Mumper) Courtesy
of William A. Frassanito,
Gettysburg Then and
Now: Touring the
Battlefield with Old
Photos, 1865–1889 (1996)*

LEFT The Wheat Field Lane looking east from the stony ridge across the wheat field and Houck's Ridge toward Little Round Top; the monument in the center marks the place where Brigadier General Samuel Zook was mortally wounded on July 2, 1863.

RIGHT Confederate dead, probably of Paul Semmes' brigade, on the Rose Farm, looking north toward the Wheat Field Lane; the stony ridge rises to the right.

LEFT Colonel Francis Edward Heath (1838–1897), 19th Maine Volunteers, who refused Andrew A. Humphreys' frenzied order to have his regiment turn their bayonets on Humphreys' own men.

RIGHT Union skirmishers in houses at the base of Cemetery Hill, looking north up Baltimore Street, at the intersection with the Emmitsburg Road.

LEFT The wreckage of John Bigelow's 9th Massachusetts Artillery in the Abraham Trostle farmyard, as it appeared on July 6th or 7th, 1863.

BELOW Officers and staff of the 69th Pennsylvania, Philadelphia Brigade.

LEFT Brigadier General Cadmus Marcellus Wilcox (1824–1890) graduated from West Point in 1846, in the same class as George B. McClellan and "Stonewall" Jackson, and commanded an Alabama brigade in R. H. Anderson's division. Wilcox's attack on July 2nd delivered the final knockdown to the 3rd Corps of the Army of the Potomac, but was eventually stopped by the suicidal charge of the 1st Minnesota.

RIGHT A prewar image of William Barksdale (1821–1863), with his wig. A congressman from Mississippi before the war, he had served in McLaws' division of Longstreet's corps for a year before Gettysburg. He was mortally wounded on July 2nd when his brigade was finally halted by George Willard's "Harpers Ferry Cowards," and he died in Union hands that night.

LEFT Edward Porter Alexander (1835–1910), Longstreet's liaison with Pickett's Division. Like so many of the officers clustered around Longstreet, Porter Alexander was a non-Virginian (he was born in Georgia). His postwar memoirs are among the most valuable observations of the commanders of the Army of Northern Virginia.

RIGHT Meade's headquarters at the Widow Leister's cottage, looking north to Cemetery Hill; the Taneytown Road is visible to the right. It was (according to John Trowbridge) a "little square box of a house . . . scarcely more than a hut, having but two little rooms on the ground-floor, and I know not what narrow, low-roofed chambers above . . . whitewashed outside and in, except the floor and ceilings and inside doors, which were neatly scoured."

The angle where Richard Garnett's and Lewis Armistead's brigades fought with the Philadelphia Brigade at the apex of Pickett's Charge; from a stereo view made in 1882, looking south toward the Round Tops.

Albertus McCreary beats a hasty retreat from his rooftop perch. "From this trap-door we saw Pickett's charge . . . While we were watching this charge, a neighbor was watching it also, from his trap-door. He was peeping around the chimney, when a bullet struck just above his head and knocked off a piece of brick. He disappeared so quickly that we both laughed. Almost immediately two bullets struck within a foot of my head in the shingles of the roof, and we followed our neighbor's example and dropped out of sight also."

David Emmons Johnston, 7th Virginia Infantry, Pickett's division; he was wounded in the bombardment that preceded Pickett's Charge, and so lived to write his memoirs of service in the Army of Northern Virginia. "I had raised my head up to get, if possible, a breath of fresh air . . . when the shell exploded, which for a few moments deprived me of my breath and sensibility; I found myself lying off from the position I was in when struck, gasping for breath. My ribs on left side were broken, some fractured, left lung badly contused, and left limbs and side paralyzed."

The house of Abraham Bryan, where James Johnston Pettigrew's division reached its final limit of advance; taken mid-July 1863.

Brigadier General Alexander Stewart Webb (1835–1911), who commanded the Philadelphia Brigade at the angle. "Gettysburg," he said in 1883, "was, and is now throughout the world known to be the Waterloo of the Rebellion."

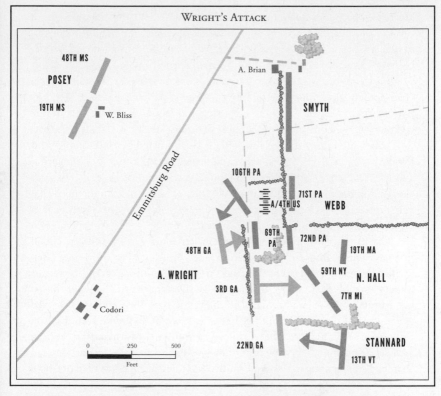

WRIGHT'S ATTACK

48TH MS

POSEY

19TH MS

W. Bliss

A. Brian

SMYTH

Emmitsburg Road

106TH PA

71ST PA

A/4TH US

WEBB

69TH PA

72ND PA

48TH GA

19TH MA

A. WRIGHT

59TH NY

N. HALL

3RD GA

7TH MI

Codori

22ND GA

STANNARD

13TH VT

0   250   500

Feet

At the same time, up came the 150th New York and the 1st Maryland Home Brigade Regiment, the first wave of five brigades of 12th Corps troops that Henry Slocum had pulled off Culp's Hill and sent to the rescue. At their head was Slocum's senior division commander, Alpheus Williams, who "had no precise instructions as to the point I was to support" but simply "followed the sound of the heaviest firing." (Taking bearings by sound was trickier than it seems: it led Williams from pillar to post, around Powers Hill and behind Freeman McGilvery's artillery, but he got there anyway.) Meade gushed as politely as he could with relief. "Come on, gentlemen," he said, doffing his hat to Williams' skirmish line, and repeating, half to himself, "Yes, but it is all right now, it is all right now."[18]

Ambrose Wright, squatting precariously on Cemetery Ridge, was ready to roll down the reverse slope and carry Meade, his headquarters, and the rear of Cemetery Hill with him. "The brave Georgians gained the crest of the ridge and drove the enemy down the opposite side," wrote an admiring onlooker in the 61st Virginia. Expectantly, Wright looked to his left "through the smoke," to where Carnot Posey's brigade was supposed to be coming up, in perfect position to knock back the oncoming Union reinforcements.[19]

But there was no one there. Posey, to Ambrose Wright's Herculean rage, "had not advanced on our left," leaving Wright "perfectly isolated from any portion of our army, a mile in its advance," and "about to be sacrificed to the bad management and cowardly conduct of others." In the weeks after the battle, Posey would insist that he had actually been ordered by Anderson to send forward only "two of my regiments, and deploy them closely as skirmishers," and use his other two regiments to eliminate the knot of Federal resistance clustered in the Bliss farm buildings. Whether or not Anderson intended that Posey treat the Bliss buildings as though they were Gettysburg's equivalent of Hougoumont, Posey proceeded to behave that way.

The Bliss farm buildings provided shelter for five companies of Union infantry sent out beyond the skirmish lines by Alex Hays, who had been annoyed when Confederate skirmishers used the buildings earlier in the day to take potshots at him on Cemetery Ridge. Despite the small size of this ad hoc battalion, Posey had been just as annoyed to have the buildings occupied by Yankees taking potshots, and he had even brought up several rifled cannon to knock the place loose of them. Posey, handsome, commanding, and an arch-secessionist and onetime subordinate of Jefferson Davis in the Mexican War, had a certain reputation for timidity, not to mention bouts of depression, so when Posey received his orders to move forward with Wright, and secure the Bliss farm in the process, the Mississippian cautiously pushed his 12th and 16th Mississippi around the Bliss farm and concentrated on squeezing it into surrender. The Yankees put up a brief resistance, and then began legging it for the safety of Cemetery Ridge (where an infuriated Hancock put the senior officer "under arrest for cowardice in the face of the enemy"). But Posey had wasted enough time in forcing them out that only one of his regiments, the 48th Mississippi, ever managed to keep up with Wright.[20]

And then there was William Mahone. A graduate of Virginia Military Institute and a highly successful railroad engineer in Virginia before the war, "Little Billy" Mahone commanded the only Virginia brigade in Richard Anderson's division—one of only two Virginia brigades in Powell Hill's entire corps. Mahone was an ardent secessionist, filling out a profile which should have guaranteed easy promotion. Except that, like his fellow Virginian John Brockenbrough, he was a singularly odd number. Rail-thin to the point of emaciation and "not weighing over a hundred pounds," Mahone was an eccentric of the Stonewall Jackson school. Daniel Harvey Hill, in whose division Mahone served during the Peninsula Campaign, would have court-martialed Mahone for withdrawing "his brigade without any orders" in the face of a "furious attack" at the battle of Seven Pines in 1862; as it was, Mahone tried to challenge Hill to a duel, and had to be talked out of it. Mahone had "failed to distinguish himself in any of the major battles from Manassas to Gettysburg," and was, as one critic put it, "a little too careful in looking after his men" and preferred to keep them "out of the fighting."

Richard Anderson had designated Mahone's brigade as his division reserve, which Mahone interpreted literally as an inert reservoir of manpower. "The brigade took no special or active part in the actions . . . during the days and nights of July 2 and 3," Mahone wrote in his official report a week after the battle, and he was not exaggerating. So when Anderson sent a staffer to summon Mahone to the support of Wilcox and Wright, Mahone (with a Bartleby-like insouciance) told him that his orders were to stay put as Anderson's reserve. But, argued Anderson's aide, Samuel Shannon, "I am just from General Anderson and he orders you to advance." No, responded Little Billy, "I have my orders from General Anderson to remain here." And he did not budge.[21]

Without Posey and Mahone, there was nothing for Wright to do but extricate his brigade as fast as he could from what was beginning to look like a noose. In addition to the Vermonters and the 12th Corps men, the reserve regiment of the Philadelphia Brigade "was moved forward from behind the crest and ordered to attack" with "bayonets fixed"; in Norman Hall's brigade, the 59th New York leapt to attack the 48th Georgia. "With painful hearts we abandoned our captured guns, and prepared to cut our way through the closing lines in our rear." This was the "dreadful part of the whole matter," since nothing makes soldiers more vulnerable to being wounded or killed than a pell-mell retreat. One Georgian "unbuckled his cartridge box, canteen and other such things that might impede his race for the rear. . . . Down went my gun, up went my heels." Others in the 48th Georgia and 2nd Georgia Battalion, "thinking the command would hold their works, delayed in obeying the order," and ended up being captured. The colonel of the 22nd Georgia went down, the colonel of the 48th Georgia was wounded and captured, the major commanding the 2nd Georgia Battalion was "seriously and dangerously wounded" (and "has since died," Wright added in his official report). Wright himself, with "several balls passing through his hat," found the 2nd Georgia Battalion "without a single officer" standing and "took charge of it in person."[22]

Overall, the Georgians did a good deal of "halting and reforming" to keep things from turning into a rout, but fully half of Wright's brigade were casualties. In the 22nd Georgia, one company began the attack with forty-five men, "and got out with twenty-two, and every man of the twenty-two was hit somewhere with a bullet but one"; in the 48th Georgia, a corporal discovered that only three of the seventy-three men in Company I "escaped without a bullet piercing their bodies."[23]

Neither Wright nor his surviving officers ever forgave Posey. "If the same advance had been made on our left," lamented a captain in the 3rd Georgia, "a different history might have been written wherein Gettysburg . . . would have been the Salamis and Marathon of our independence." Four days after the battle, Wright composed an incendiary letter for the *Augusta Constitutionalist* which frankly alleged that both Posey and Mahone had disobeyed orders from Anderson to join him on Cemetery Ridge. Anderson was forced to file charges against Wright for "matters connected with publications which appeared in the Augusta Constitutionalist." The court-martial acquitted him, but Wright had made himself too hot to handle in the Army of Northern Virginia. He served through the Overland Campaign of 1864, but in the end, he was transferred to Georgia to take command of the state militia and feud with Georgia's individualistic and cocksure governor, Joe Brown.

None of this, of course, gave Hancock and Meade all that much to celebrate. For them, it had been another close call, staving off another Chancellorsville through unscripted decisions and split-hair timing. If Posey and Mahone had joined Wright, "it is doubtful whether the Union line, disorganized and broken as it was . . . would have been able to stand the shock."[24] And in fact, there was yet one more shock in store.

We are the Louisiana Tigers!

IF JAMES LONGSTREET'S CORPS was to serve as the hammer on July 2nd, Dick Ewell's corps was intended to provide the anvil, and maybe provide enough of a distraction over on the east side of Cemetery Hill to drain still more Union troops away from the Emmitsburg Road. But any action by Ewell was "to be a feint & converted into a real attack only if an apparently favorable opening appeared." And if actions are any explanation, Lee showed no expectation that Ewell would provide more than a "feint." Once Lee left Ewell around two o'clock to play catch-up with Longstreet, he gave Ewell little attention. He "joined Hill" around four o'clock and "remained there nearly all the time, looking through his field-glass—sometimes talking to Hill and sometimes to Colonel Long of his Staff." What was more, the Britisher Fremantle noticed that "during the whole time the firing continued, he only sent one message, and only received one report." Fremantle added that he supposed it was Lee's "system to arrange the plan thoroughly with the three corps commanders, and then leave to them the duty of modifying and carrying it out to the best of their abilities," and in that respect Fremantle could not have been more correct.[1]

The only specific direction Ewell was given was to wait "until I heard General Longstreet's guns open on the right." But almost as though he was determined to wipe away any grousing about his inertia the evening before, Ewell "spent the morning in examining all parts of his position & decided to attack along his whole line." A wounded Union officer, sheltered in the crowded sanctuary of Christ Lutheran Church on Chambersburg Street, saw "Gen. Ewell and several of his staff officers" enter the church "for observation from the cupola of the church." Ewell's wooden leg kept him from ascending the ladder to the roof and his staffers had to call down bearings to him. He also tried the cupola of St. Francis Xavier Church on High Street, again sending staffers to shout down reports while he remained in the street below. At the same time, Ewell took the precaution of deploying his three divisions in a long arc around Cemetery Hill, with Allegheny Ed Johnson's division shuffling into line opposite Culp's Hill, Jubal Early's division on the left of the town and facing the east slope of Cemetery Hill, and Robert Rodes' division "on the right of the main street of the town . . . extending out on the Fairfield road."[2]

From first light, Confederate skirmishers in the town, and Union skirmishers adventuring down Cemetery Hill, began thickening the air with "quick and sharp musketry firing, with an occasional sound of artillery." Oliver Otis Howard, sleeping "inside of a family lot in the cemetery . . . with a grave mound for a pillow," was awakened by the shooting at five o'clock. "It began like the pattering of rain on a flat roof . . . till it attained a continuous roar." Ranged around the perimeter of the hill were the misshapen remnants of the 11th Corps. The one untouched brigade, Orland Smith's brigade of Ohioans, New Yorkers, and Massachusetts men, held the vulnerable west face of Cemetery Hill, and linked hands with Alex Hays' 2nd Corps division; the north face of the hill was held by the bundled splinters of Coster's brigade and Carl Schurz's division; and the east face by what had been Francis Barlow's division (now directed by Adelbert Ames, since Barlow was missing and presumed dead). At most, Howard could not have had more than 5,000 men left from the 9,200 with which he began the day before; in practical terms, he may have had as few as 2,500. What he did have, though, was artillery—the five batteries of his own corps artillery, plus another six belonging to the 1st Corps, carefully positioned to cover every possible line of approach to the hill.[3]

That could not prevent rebel skirmishers concealed in trees and houses from constantly peppering Yankee artillerymen and infantry. The buildings on the south end of Gettysburg were "filled with rebel sharp-shooters," and from time to time parties of Yankee skirmishers had to be sent down the hill to clear away nests of rebel riflemen who had crept too close. In the 55th Ohio, at the north apex of Cemetery Hill, Capt. Frederick Boalt called out for volunteers to clean out a house at the foot of Baltimore Street which had become an annoying little post for rebel riflemen. With "twenty or twenty-five" men," Boalt "crawled along the Taneytown road . . . keeping under cover as much as possible" until his storming party was close enough to rush the house, kick in the doors, and capture the rebels inside. At the same time, it amused the colonel of the 82nd Illinois to draw Otis Howard's attention to a sign posted in the Evergreen Cemetery: DRIVING, RIDING AND SHOOTING ON THESE GROUNDS STRICTLY PROHIBITED. ANY PERSON VIOLATING THIS ORDINANCE WILL BE PUNISHED BY FINE AND IMPRISONMENT. The colonel solemnly warned Howard that "he would get into trouble after the battle for violating this order." But a wayward Confederate shell wobbled over and "knocked it into a thousand pieces." Howard remarked that it seemed to him that the ordinance had been pretty effectively rescinded.[4]

This was less amusing for the wounded men who by now had begun to crowd the brick gatehouse of the cemetery, since the "arched brick building" made an ideal guide for Confederate fire. And it made the infantry lines in front of the batteries "one of the hottest places" an officer of the 153rd Pennsylvania thought he had been in. Occasionally, the Yankees gave as good as they got: Dick Ewell sent off Albert Jenkins' diminutive cavalry brigade to "reconnoiter," only to have Federal shell explode among Jenkins and his staff, "wounding the General and his horse." One Yankee gunner grew so "annoyed by a sharp-shooter in one of the church steeples" that he "bade his men run around the cannon and turn somersaults" to induce the sniper to peer out "to see what the queer action meant." He did, and the gunner let loose. "The shell struck only a foot above" the sniper's head, and "he came down out of the steeple swearing he could not stand such shooting as that."[5]

Once the rumble of Longstreet's artillery could be heard, Ewell got his corps moving—Allegheny Johnson's 6,400-man division moved up behind a small ridge on the farm of Daniel Benner and prepared to face Culp's Hill; Jubal Early put his two least-damaged brigades from the day before (Isaac Avery's North Carolina brigade and Harry Hays' wild Louisianans) in line to strike the eastern face of Cemetery Hill; and Rodes' division filed out of the town to position themselves to hit Cemetery Hill directly on the west. First, Ewell needed to suppress the deadly array of Federal artillery on Cemetery Hill, and for that he turned to Johnson's division artillery battalion, fourteen guns under a fresh-faced nineteen-year-old Virginia Military Institute graduate named Joseph White Latimer.

On paper, this battalion was supposed to be under the command of Lt. Col. Richard Snowden Andrews, a highly unmilitary Baltimore architect but a brother-in-law of Robert E. Lee's military secretary. However, Andrews had an unusual penchant for getting in the way of nasty wounds, and he had taken one of them at Winchester. That left Latimer, who would ordinarily have been little more than an apprentice, as the battalion's ranking officer. Not that he was undeserving: Latimer won plaudits at Fredericksburg as "one of the coolest and bravest boys I have ever met with," and Dorsey Pender thought he was "as brave a soldier as I ever saw." Latimer had "an unusual readiness and precision in the details of instruction" and a "solid, imperturbable earnestness with which he gave all his orders." Under any other circumstances, the gunners and crews would have "considered it humiliating to be placed under the tuition of such a child." Instead, Latimer won them over as a sort of novelty—a "Boy Major," like J.E.B. Stuart's now dead protégé John Pelham—and soon enough they "spoke of him as 'our little Latimer.'"[6]

"Little Latimer" had done some preliminary scouting of the area for good artillery locations, but Benner's Ridge seemed to be about the only eminence that satisfied him. A thousand yards distant from Culp's Hill and 1,300 yards west of Cemetery Hill, it was barely close enough to hit either hill accurately; unhappily, it was also fifty feet shy of the elevation of either Culp's Hill or Cemetery Hill, and as a spiny ridge like so many other spiny ridges east of South Mountain, it had only limited space for deployment and recoil, and none for caissons and horses, not to mention "no covering of any kind to guns and men." In the absence of any worthwhile alternatives, however, it was Benner's Ridge or nothing. It took an hour to gather the battalion and guide it up onto the ridge, but once in position their opening fire was remarkably true. Charles Wainwright thought "their fire was the most accurate I have ever seen on the part of their artillery," and James Stewart was surprised to see three of his battery's limber chests blown up into thin-looking smoke-stalks. The battery horses started to bolt down the Baltimore Pike; some of the drivers and gun crews actually ran out into the road to bring them back in, and found that "every hair was burnt off the tails and manes of the wheel horses."[7]

Despite its accuracy, the Confederate artillery fire was not particularly effective. In Adelbert Ames' division, a Connecticut officer admitted that "we hugged the ground pretty close," but none of "our brigade were either killed or wounded." And Latimer's gunners had no sooner opened their first fire on Cemetery Hill when the enormous weight of the Federal artillery there swiveled around and slowly proceeded to pound the Confederate batteries into flames and dust—"guns dismounted and disabled, carriages splintered and crushed, ammunition chests exploded, limbers upset, wounded horses plunging and kicking, dashing out the brains of men tangled in the harness; while cannoneers with pistols were crawling around through the wreck shooting the struggling horses to save the lives of the wounded men."

After an hour and a half, Latimer's battalion had been "hurled backward, as it were, by the very weight and impact of the metal, from the position it had occupied on the crest," and Latimer himself sent off his sergeant major to ask Ed Johnson for permission to withdraw, "owing to the exhausted state of his men and ammunition and the severe fire of the enemy." He kept the last four guns in place to cover the pullback, but as he did so, "a shell presently explodes over him and down go horse and rider, the first dead and the other wounded." The shell had "shattered completely" Latimer's right arm, and though the arm was amputated, he would die of gangrene a month later, one of twenty-two dead and twenty-nine wounded in the battalion.[8]

It now fell to the infantry to keep up the "distraction," and the fate of Latimer's battalion on Benner's Ridge gave everyone in Early's division a perfect view of what might be in store for them. This may be why it took Ewell's three divisions an unusually long time to dress their ranks, inspect weapons, and move into position—Latimer's cannonade probably ended around 5:30, and Ed Johnson does not seem to have finally readied his division for an attack until well after 6:00, as the struggle for the wheat field was reaching its peak, as though they were hoping they would not be required to offer more than a demonstration. Ewell had other ideas, and, as the late afternoon shadows lengthened, "old Gen. Early is seen emerging from one of the streets of the town, and, riding slowly across the field in the direction of our position." Harry Hays paid particular attention to his Louisiana brigade, riding "along our line of battle" and exhorting them with the challenge that "Genl Early" had specifically ordered "the Louisianans and . . . North Carolinians to take the guns on the hill," and that Gordon's brigade would then "come up" to relieve them "and hold the works."[9]

Up on Cemetery Hill, Charles Wainwright caught sight "of the head of their column" as Early's Louisianans and North Carolinians deployed into line and "rushed for the hill." A sergeant in the 5th Maine Artillery "suddenly . . . shouted, 'Look! look at those men,' and he pointed to . . . where, in line of battle extending nearly to Rock Creek at the base of Benner's Hill, the enemy could be seen climbing the walls and fences and forming for the assault." In the lull following Latimer's abandonment of Benner's Ridge, the Federals had gradually assumed that their fighting for the day was done. "We did not expect any assault," and "could not have been more surprised if the moving column had raised up out of the ground amid the waving timothy grass of the meadow." Some of the men in the 73rd Ohio had actually begun "to wrap our blankets around us and think of snatching a little rest." And as the sunlight shortened, it was also harder for the artillery batteries to pick their targets. Even though both the Maine gunners and the batteries up on the hill opened up with a roar as soon as the Confederates came into view, they were not hitting very much. There was "an awful roar of big guns and . . . the enemy's batteries kept up a terrific fire," wrote a soldier in the 6th North Carolina, "but most of the shells . . . passed over our heads." What made the situation even more awkward for the Federal defenders of the hill was that the east side of Cemetery Hill fell off into a steep ravine, with a small lane at the base; the steepness of the hillside offered a sick discouragement to any direct infantry attack, but it also made it impossible for the gunners up on the hill to depress the muzzles of their pieces if the attackers ever got under the lip of the ravine.[10]

Which is what they now did. Adelbert Ames' two brigades were strung out in a thin line along the lane at the base of east Cemetery Hill, probably amounting to no more than 1,000 men to face the 4,000 rebel attackers. Andrew Harris, the colonel of the 75th Ohio who inherited Ames' brigade command, was sure his brigade "did not exceed 500 men," and even after every possible man was prodded up to the stone wall that ran along the lane, each of them had "all the elbow room he wanted." Together, they got off at least one volley, but the momentum of the Confederates carried them straight over the wall and Hays' Louisiana brigade was "not delayed by this impediment more than [a] minute." The Louisianans "came on us . . . yelling like demons with fixed bayonets," and "their officers & colors in advance." The Prussian captain von Fritsch heard them screaming *We are the Louisiana Tigers!* A Pennsylvania officer farther down the lane saw Hays' rebels pour over the dam of the stone wall, "muskets being handled as clubs; rocks torn from the wall in front and thrown, fist and bayonet. A captain in the 107th Ohio, at point-blank range, shot with his revolver a "rebel Color bearer (8th La. Tiger Regt. as it proved by the inscription on the vile rag)." Another rebel color-bearer mounted the wall, "his musket in one hand and a Rebel color in the other," shouting *Surrender, you damned Yankees*—only to have a Yankee ram a bayonet into his chest and simultaneously discharge the rifle it was fixed to, "blowing into shreds" the back of the rebel's shirt.[11]

Within minutes, Ames' brigades were dissolving into an uncontrollable spray of fugitives or inconsequential knots of resistance in the lane, as the rebel tide flowed beyond them, and then began mounting the hillside toward the Federal artillery. Otis Howard thought it took not more than "three minutes" before the Louisianans had scaled the grassy slope and "were upon our batteries." There were four of these batteries perched on the east side of the hill—Michael Weidrich's Battery I, 1st New York Light Artillery, from the 11th Corps; twelve 3-inch Ordnance Rifles in James Stewart's Battery B, 4th U.S. Artillery and Gilbert Reynolds' Battery L, 1st New York Light Artillery, from the 1st Corps—and six more Ordnance Rifles of the combined batteries F and G of the 1st Pennsylvania Light Artillery, under Bruce Ricketts, from the artillery reserve. At any other place, these would have been more than enough to keep any assortment of rebel infantry at a respectful distance. But the speed with which the Confederates moved to the attack, and the sharp incline of the hill, limited how much damage the Union batteries were able

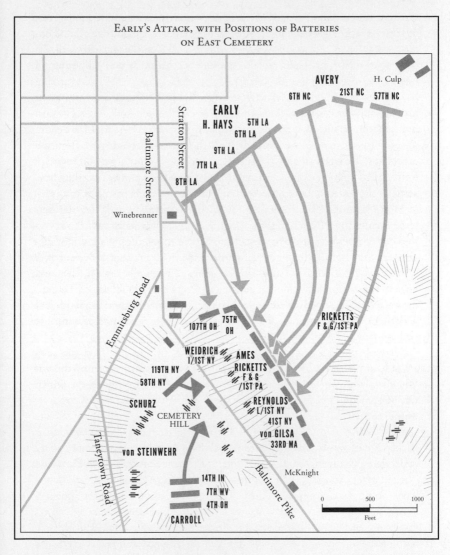

EARLY'S ATTACK, WITH POSITIONS OF BATTERIES
ON EAST CEMETERY

AVERY

H. Culp

6TH NC   21ST NC   57TH NC

EARLY
H. HAYS   5TH LA
6TH LA
9TH LA
7TH LA
8TH LA

Stratton Street

Baltimore Street

Winebrenner

107TH OH   75TH OH

RICKETTS
F & G/1ST PA

WEIDRICH
I/1ST NY

AMES
RICKETTS
F & G
/1ST PA

Emmitsburg Road

119TH NY
58TH NY

SCHURZ

CEMETERY
HILL

REYNOLDS
L/1ST NY
41ST NY

von GILSA
33RD MA

von STEINWEHR

Taneytown Road

McKnight

14TH IN
7TH WV
4TH OH

CARROLL

Baltimore Pike

0   500   1000

Feet

to do, and as the rebels came bounding up the hill there was no time to get off more than one or two rounds of canister before the rebels were dancing among the guns in whooping delight.[12]

There was no question about limbering up and removing the guns. The gunners and drivers would have to fight for their guns, and do it with "hand-spikes and rammers"—anything, in fact, "calculated to inflict pain or death was now resorted to." Michael Weidrich's gunners were Germans, and as one of Harry Hays' Tigers confidently threw himself onto the muzzle of a Napoleon, he shouted, *I take command of this gun!* A German gunner with the piece's lanyard in his hand replied, *Du sollst sie haben* (it was a line from a German birthday song—*you can have it*) and blew the rebel into smoking bits. A lieutenant in Ricketts' battery forgot that he had his officer's sword on his belt, and "picked up a stone" to knock another rebel down. Otis Howard himself took up his stand among the guns, sending off orders for Carl Schurz to bring up whatever other parts of the 11th Corps he could spare from the other side of Cemetery Hill. This time, Howard could not get the fugitives from Ames' division to stop and stand, and "the rushing crowd of stragglers" actually prevented Schurz from bringing "the two regiments nearest to me" to Howard's aid. (The drivers and crews from Stewart's U.S. Regular battery actually spread out along the Baltimore Pike with fence rails "to try to stop the runaways, but could do nothing.") When Charles Wainwright disgustedly asked Howard why he didn't have their officers shot for cowardice, Howard's faith in his 11th Corps finally broke, and he sadly replied, "I should have to shoot all the way down" to the privates; "they are all alike." Perhaps he was asking too much of men who had been hit too often and too hard, and with too few of the familiar elbow-to-elbow cues to keep them from running; perhaps he was asking too much of himself.[13]

It was now dusk, almost dark. Among the milling mobs on the eastern side of Cemetery Hill, Weidrich's battery was finally overrun by the 9th Louisiana, and Bruce Ricketts, in a last desperate effort, ordered the 3-inch Ordnance Rifles in his battery to fire shells without fuses, so that the rounds would actually detonate in the barrels and spray out shell splinters like canister—that is, if the guns didn't blow up in the crews' faces. And then Ricketts, too, was submerged in the rebel flood, and "every piece of artillery which had been firing upon us was silenced." Far to the rear, Jubal Early had "several rebel batteries . . . in readiness to gallop on to Cemetery Hill," while rebels on the crest struggled to turn "some of the guns on the enemy and tried to fire them."[14]

And then, in yet another of those miracle moments which had by now become the routine of the Army of the Potomac at Gettysburg, Federal troops appeared out of the darkness and bore down on the jubilant Confederates and their newly acquired prizes. Four hundred yards to the west, on the other side of Cemetery Hill, Winfield Scott Hancock and George Meade had only just finished clearing the last of Ambrose Wright's prisoners and wounded from the front of the 2nd Corps when the rising racket of infantry fire to the east caught Hancock's ear. "At last this fire became so heavy and so threatening" that Hancock, who had been peeling off regiments, brigades, and divisions to send someplace else all afternoon, gave no second thought to peeling off some more. His first impulse was to send a regiment apiece toward Culp's Hill (where he dispatched the 71st Pennsylvania) and the Evergreen Cemetery gatehouse (where the 106th Pennsylvania was sent). But as the roar swelled, he turned to John Gibbon and said, "Send a brigade, send Carroll."[15]

Carroll meant Samuel Spring Carroll, a luxuriantly sideburned colonel of the 8th Ohio who had taken over command in March 1863 of what turned out to be the only other all-"Western" brigade in the Army of the Potomac (in this case, "Western" meant the 4th and 8th Ohio, the 14th Indiana, and the 7th West Virginia). Carroll, with his brick-red hair, often reminded people of his manic-aggressive division commander, Alex Hays, and this occasion was no exception. Carroll wheeled his brigade around from where it had been stacked in column of regiments and, with the 14th Indiana in the lead, sprinted "headlong" across the hill, across the Taneytown Road, past "gravestones" in the Evergreen Cemetery "struck by the spiteful Minnie ball," and emerged onto the Baltimore Pike just as the last of the "maddened gunners" were "striking the rebels with fist, rammer, ammunition and stones." Carroll had no guide except for the muzzle flashes ahead, and no time to deploy the brigade except to feed each regiment from column into line as they crossed the road. Even that meager order was quickly lost in the melee: "Bayonets and butts of guns at once joined the efforts of the heroic gunners, with flanks of regiments overlapping" and everyone colliding in an "every-man-in-as-you-can sort of way."[16]

Harry Hays and his Louisianans had no idea who these Yankees were (at first, he had not even been sure they were Yankees, since Robert Rodes' division was supposed to have attacked the west side of Cemetery Hill, and this might be the tip of Rodes' breakthrough), or how many of them there were. Hays had already taken enough casualties to call it a day, and the North Carolinians had lost Isaac Avery to a bullet in the neck in the first few minutes of the attack. Hays decided to pull back, first retreating down the hill to the lane, and then toward his original starting point. A captain in the 14th Indiana was less measured in his description: "They ran pell mell . . . in thirty minutes the attack was repulsed and the battery saved."[17]

No one was angrier at the results of the attack on Cemetery Hill than Jubal Early, who could not understand why Robert Rodes' division, on the west side of Cemetery Hill, had never put in an appearance. The difficulty facing Rodes was that by the time he had moved his 5,000-man division out of Middle Street and into line opposite Cemetery Hill, the moon had come up, and his brigade commanders had become dicey about "the idea of charging strong fortifications in the night time." Rodes yielded to a plea from Stephen Ramseur to reconnoiter the ground in front of them, and Ramseur came back with the depressing report that the western face of Cemetery Hill was defended by "two lines of infantry behind stone walls," with artillery backing them." The nerveless Alfred Iverson claimed that "we were advancing to certain destruction." And so Rodes called it off. In his diary, William Seymour described Harry Hays on Cemetery Hill, waiting "anxiously . . . to hear Rodes' guns co-operating with us on the right; but unfortunately, no such assistance came to us."[18]

Robert Rodes did not survive the war, and so had nothing he could say in his own defense. But Jubal Early had good reason to gnash his teeth in disappointment. Of all the nearly-so moments that litter the record of July 2nd, Early's attack on east Cemetery Hill scattered a Federal division, captured at least two batteries of artillery, and, for a moment, stood in possession of enough ground on Cemetery Hill to have compelled an immediate Federal evacuation. Subtract Carroll's brigade (and Hancock's intuition in sending it), and add even a token assault by Rodes, and Jubal Early would have been within inches and minutes of pulling down the center pole of the Army of the Potomac. That it did not happen speaks volumes instead about the uncoordinated command style that had become Robert E. Lee's habit, and for the paralyzing evaporation of initiative that crept over the senior generals of the Army of Northern Virginia the longer and deeper they remained in the unfamiliar environment of Pennsylvania.

Even after the misfire on Cemetery Hill, there was still Allegheny Ed Johnson's division, and for once in this long day of Confederate misfires, something in Robert E. Lee's plans actually looked as though it was going to work. Since the morning of July 2nd, Culp's Hill had been the property of Henry Slocum's 12th Corps, aided by the fragments of the 1st Corps. The low spur that connected the west face of Culp's Hill with Cemetery Hill was defended by the fragile survivors of James Wadsworth's 1st Corps division, which by this point amounted to little more than an ordinary brigade; from there Culp's Hill actually developed into two peaks, north and south, and Slocum delegated one of his divisions to the higher north peak and the other to the south.

Culp's Hill had little military significance of its own—unlike Cemetery Hill and Little Round Top, it was blanketed with a thick canopy of trees which made observation difficult and serving artillery nearly impossible unless Slocum wanted to exhaust the entire corps with lumberjack duties. But livestock grazing had kept the area almost entirely clear of underbrush, so the hill could be attacked by troops if they maintained at least minimal order in line. Culp's Hill also screened the Baltimore Pike as it headed south from

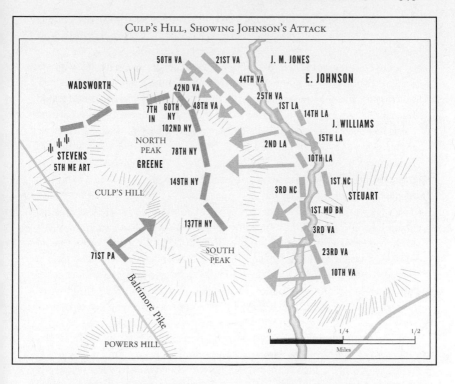

CULP'S HILL, SHOWING JOHNSON'S ATTACK

50TH VA   21ST VA   J. M. JONES

44TH VA   E. JOHNSON

WADSWORTH   42ND VA   25TH VA

7TH   60TH   48TH VA   1ST LA   14TH LA
IN   NY   J. WILLIAMS
       102ND NY   15TH LA

NORTH   2ND LA
PEAK   78TH NY   10TH LA
STEVENS
5TH ME ART   GREENE

149TH NY   3RD NC   1ST NC
CULP'S   STEUART
HILL   1ST MD BN

137TH NY   3RD VA

71ST PA   SOUTH   23RD VA
           PEAK
                    10TH VA

Baltimore pike

POWERS HILL

0   1/4   1/2
Miles

Gettysburg and Cemetery Hill, and if Meade was to keep open a supply line, or a line of retreat to Pipe Creek, he would need to hold Culp's Hill simply to prevent the Confederates from curling around behind his army and snipping the pike. So the 12th Corps would spread itself out not only to occupy the twin peaks, but also planted two brigades beyond the south peak to cover the open ground between the peak and the pike. Across from the point where Slocum's men touched the pike loomed Powers Hill; there Meade positioned three batteries of artillery to create a last redoubt along the pike if the Confederates ever overran Cemetery Hill.[19]

At first, few people in the 12th Corps seem to have had much apprehension that the Confederates would attempt a head-on attack on Culp's Hill. "The first formation" of John White Geary's division on the north peak "was in line of battalions in mass with diminished intervals between battalions," and neither Geary nor Thomas Ruger (who was in temporary command of the division holding the south peak) was troubled enough by the likelihood of rebel movements to give any orders to improve their hillside positions by digging trenches or chopping down enough trees to form rough protective walls.

"No orders were given to entrench," although at one point Geary got so much nagging from one of his brigade commanders that he gave him "permission" to do so.

This particular brigade commander was George Sears Greene, who was a member of the West Point class of 1823 and also the Army of the Potomac's oldest general officer (at age sixty-two) at Gettysburg. Born in Rhode Island, Greene had endured enough reverses in his career to develop a remarkably thick hide: his first wife and their three children had all died within seven months of one another . . . he served thirteen years in the U.S. Army with only a single promotion, to first lieutenant . . . he re-married, fathered six more children and left the Army for private engineering practice . . . and then in 1861, volunteered for service and mustered-in as colonel of the 60th New York. He was short and stocky, with a sharply pointed Vandyke beard which gave him something of the appearance of a gnome out of a German fairy tale, and his men delighted in calling him "Pap" or "Old Pappy." He rose to command a division in the 12th Corps at Antietam, only to get bumped back to brigade command for—without any shade of irony—lack of seniority in the volunteer service. He was "a most remarkable man," said Oliver Otis Howard, "a man whose reputation will grow; a man who was not appreciated during his lifetime."[20]

Uncomplaining, Greene had saved his brigade at Chancellorsville by having them clear a 200-foot-wide space in front of their position and digging in with bayonets, tin cups, and canteen-halves. Greene's instincts warned him that it would be a good idea to do the same here, and Geary relented. "Right and left," Greene's five New York regiments "felled the trees, and blocked them up into a close fence." A line of trees was felled down the slope with "branches sharpened in regular order," to form a ready-made abatis, and serve as a primitive forerunner of barbed wire fencing. Stacks of cordwood left from logging operations were piled up "against the outer surface of the logs," and any pioneer details "which had spades and picks" set to work piling up a battening of earth over the felled logs. They were finished by noon, and "a very fair work" it was. But then, at mid-afternoon, came the erupting roar in the distance that signaled Longstreet's attack, followed by the artillery duel between the "Boy Major" Latimer's battalion on Benner's Ridge and the Federal artillery on Cemetery Hill, and as Greene "walked along the lines with care, giving personal direction to the measurements and the angles" of the earthworks, both Slocum and Geary began feeling prickles of anxiety over reports of large-scale rebel troop movements in the woods to the east.[21]

Prickles, however, are not proof against orders. At 7:30, as Ambrose Wright's Georgians curled toward the crest of Cemetery Ridge, Meade summoned Slocum and the 12th Corps to the rescue of the staggering 2nd Corps.

Much as he required Culp's Hill, Meade needed to save Cemetery Hill even more. But the summons could not have come at a worse moment for Slocum, who was growing convinced that Culp's Hill was about to receive its own attack. Slocum sent his adjutant back to Meade, asking to be permitted to keep "General Geary's division to cover the works of the corps, and not to leave them deserted." Slocum's reply must have seemed as pedantic to Meade as Meade's order seemed risky to Slocum, but in the end Slocum was "permitted to retain one brigade, and I retained Greene's." As the rest of the 12th Corps hurried away, Greene's brigade resigned itself to stretching out to cover, as best it could, the lines vacated along both peaks of Culp's Hill. Given that Greene had less than 1,400 men and one battery of artillery to count on, there was more stretching than cover. Greene "formed his brigade in a single line, with spaces between the men, the regiments moving to the right as the line lengthened," and the smallest of the regiments (the 78th New York) forming a loose line of skirmishers in front. They had "scarcely accomplished this extended formation when a sharp crackling fire announced" that both Old Pappy and Henry Slocum had been right to worry.[22]

Allegheny Ed Johnson sheltered the three big Confederate brigades he would throw against Culp's Hill behind Benner's Ridge and on the north side of the Hanover Road for most of the afternoon. ("One of our staff" prudently "conducted religious services . . . the men gladly joining in the solemn exercises.") Once the blackened remains of Latimer's artillery battalion had pulled themselves to safety, "aides were seen dashing furiously down the long line of infantry on our right, who spring to their feet as they pass." Johnson's would actually be the first element of Dick Ewell's corps to begin the "distraction," and "as soon as Johnson was heard engaged," Early's division would move to its attack on east Cemetery Hill. Johnson moved his brigades stealthily along the face of Culp's Hill until they faced almost due west of the two peaks, then shook out into line of battle and waded Rock Creek ("waist-deep in some places") to begin ascending the slope. One of Greene's officers could make out Johnson's advance in the gathering dusk, "and counting battle flags and intervals in the front line, I calculated that there were eight regiments, and of probably about 400 to 500 muskets in each," with "two smaller lines of infantry" formed up behind them and "two or more regiments" in column on their left flank.

This was a remarkably good estimate. Johnson had indeed arranged his division so that the Virginia brigade of the newly promoted brigadier John Marshall Jones (to the incalculable confusion of nearly everyone, he replaced John *Robert* Jones, who was not only no relation, but had been charged repeatedly with cowardice under fire), the five Louisiana regiments commanded by Jesse Williams, and half of George "Maryland" Steuart's brigade would form a front of eight regiments. They were backed up by a line of six more regiments, while the remaining half of Steuart's brigade was kept back beyond Rock Creek on the left. (Johnson's fourth brigade, the old "Stonewall" Brigade which had originally been commanded by Stonewall Jackson, was held in reserve.) In all, Johnson was sending in about 4,700 men, which would usually have been more than enough to sweep Pap Greene's brigade out of their path like dead leaves.

That, certainly, was what many of Greene's men expected. "It seemed to me that something like two hours must have elapsed," wrote a New Yorker as the slow-motion ballet of deployment played out beneath their gaze. They waited for their skirmishers to begin firing and falling back, "moments . . . which were years of agony" as the soldiers' "pale faces, staring eye-balls, and nervous hands grasping loaded muskets told how terrible were those moments of suspense." From behind their log walls, they saw an officer ride along the front of the Confederate battle line who "must have made some remarks to the men," and then with "a flutter of battle flags and hats waving in the air," the rebels started forward "with arms at right-shoulder-shift, their movement in perfect alignment . . . at a slow measured tread," with a skirmish line and a line of pioneers "clearing the way" through fallen trees and other obstructions.[23]

Greene's skirmishers, the 78th New York, fell back "slowly up the hill," trying "to hold the enemy at bay to the last notch" and using "the heavy timber" to make "every tree and rock a veritable battlefield." Johnson was evidently concerned about the disrupting effect of the terrain on his advance, because "the Confederate infantry halted from time to time, waiting for its advance to clear the way." And no wonder, since "we found the ground here very uneven, and covered with immense rocks, which necessitated the dismounting of field & staff officers." But on they pressed, "up the steep acclivity through the darkness," cracking dead branches underfoot, slipping and skidding, drawing with each breath the dankness of woods still saturated from a week's worth of heavy rain, guided forward in some places "only by the flashes of the muskets" of the Yankee skirmishers as they fell back. Greene took the precaution of ordering his men "closely concealed . . . behind the works," and even had the regimental flags kept below the barricades to disguise his regiments' positions. He waited, in fact, until the Confederate advance had struggled its way through the abatis and had stopped "to dress up the line"—in other words, "within pistol shot range"—before ordering a general open fire "like chain-lightning" from his brigade.[24]

The volley in front and the abatis behind trapped John Marshall Jones' Virginia brigade "scarcely thirty yards from the enemy's breastworks," and the Virginians promptly went to ground while their officers figured out what to do next. "We held this point with the briskest fire we could concentrate," and in George Steuart's regiments on the left, "we could distinctly see the Federals rise and fire at us from the works in front." Paralyzed in this position for "probably fifteen minutes," the Confederates were finally gotten to their feet and rushed Greene's feebly manned emplacements. "They succeeded this time in getting up to the works," and then another of Gettysburg's savage rifle-butt and bayonet-thrust fights broke out. "They reached the works and sought to climb over, and in several places their dead fell within our line." One lieutenant in the 60th New York counted "four separate and distinct charges"; a sergeant in the 102nd New York counted three. In the 149th New York, the regimental flag had eighty-one bullet holes in it, and its staff was hit so often that the regimental color sergeant, William Lilley, had to keep splicing it together and replanting it on the log walls. But Jones' Virginians could not punch their way through Old Pappy's cleverly laid-out revetments, and Marshall Jones himself went down and out of action with a wound in the thigh.[25]

Greene, meanwhile, was finally getting some reinforcement. He sent off pleas to Geary, to Otis Howard on Cemetery Hill, and even to Winfield Hancock, and though Geary had no choice but to ignore him, Hancock sent one regiment, the 71st Pennsylvania. They did not do much on Greene's behalf. The colonel blundered around the south peak of Culp's Hill, let loose a scattering fire at some Confederates, then decided that it was no part of their job to "have his men murdered" in the dark, and walked back to Cemetery Ridge. But James Wadsworth sent over a small ad hoc brigade—the 6th Wisconsin, the red-legged chasseurs of the 14th Brooklyn, and the stubborn survivors of the 147th New York; and Otis Howard dispatched four regiments from the brigade of the still missing Alexander Schimmelpfennig. Together, this amounted to little more than 700 men. But at that moment, as they charged "with all their might . . . without regard to alignment and in silence," they "tumbled the rebels out" of any breaks in Greene's line. Their brief rush gave Greene's own men time to step back, swab out their powder-fouled rifle barrels, and scavenge for spare ammunition. Finally, between 9:30 and 11:00, darkness and disappointment quieted the last of the Confederate attacks. If a former professor of rhetoric had saved Little Round Top, Old Pappy Greene had saved Culp's Hill.[26]

What Old Pappy could not do, however, was to prevent Maryland Steuart's brigade from wrapping around the overstretched Federal grip on the south peak. The 6th Wisconsin and 14th Brooklyn, which were detailed by Greene to cover the south peak alongside Greene's own 137th New York, found Steuart's Confederates already swarming over the lower part of the peak's slopes and the positions occupied only a few hours before by the rest of the 12th Corps—including the vital back door to the Baltimore Pike. An officer in one of Steuart's regiments, William Goldsborough, "having acquired some knowledge of the country in my youth," was sure that the pike lay only a few hundred yards away. With another officer and "one of his most reliable men," Goldsborough conducted an impromptu reconnaissance in the dark until he was "so close to the turnpike that he was able to see the wagons in motion." There were no Yankees between Steuart and the pike, and if Steuart took the three regiments of his brigade sitting in reserve beyond Rock Creek, or if Johnson could summon up the Stonewall Brigade, they could be planted securely across the Army of the Potomac's lifeline.

Goldsborough, however, could not get Steuart to pay attention to this news, nor (when he tried) could he make much of an impression on Allegheny Ed Johnson. "He could easily have flanked it," wrote Goldsborough in despair. "But, then, General Johnson was not a Stonewall Jackson, and the opportunity was allowed to pass unimproved." If Johnson had listened and acted, there was, as one of Greene's staffers later admitted, nothing Greene could have done about it. "Had Lee succeeded in . . . placing himself square across the Baltimore pike in rear of the center and right wing of the entire army," wrote an officer in the 60th New York, the results could have been nothing less than "disastrous"; Greene's brigade was already too overextended to spare a company to defend the pike. But "the Rebels . . . apparently fearing a trap, hesitated to press their advantage . . . though their skirmishers advanced without opposition to the Baltimore Pike." It was becoming symptomatic of the Army of Northern Virginia—advantages not pressed, initiative not taken, and passivity and uncertainty in charge.[27]

But this time, the opportunity had not been completely missed. Johnson's division had obtained a critical lodgment on the lower peak of Culp's Hill and if Slocum did not find a way to retrieve that ground, then daylight could easily bring the refocused Confederates howling down on the pike—and the rear of the Army of the Potomac—without any significant obstruction except Powers Hill. It had taken all of July 2nd, but finally, by the light of a rising full moon, Robert E. Lee had finally forced Meade, by withdrawing the 12th Corps from Culp's Hill, to remove a piece from the board whose place he could not fill.

So much of the fighting ended in agonizingly near misses for the Army of Northern Virginia—the within-an-inch failure to capture Little Round Top . . . the last-minute blunting of Barksdale and Wilcox by George Willard's "Cowards" and the charge of the 1st Minnesota . . . Ambrose Wright's bitter moment of abandonment, just shy of Cemetery Ridge . . . Harry Hays'

Tigers having victory (not to mention captured Federal artillery) snatched from their hands by Samuel Carroll's helter-skelter counterattack by the Evergreen Cemetery gatehouse and left without support by Rodes' inertia . . . and finally the failure to overrun just one Union brigade on Culp's Hill—that it has become almost a matter of habit to speak of Longstreet's attack or Early's assault on east Cemetery Hill purely in the mordant tones of failure. This is not really true. In the first place, although James Longstreet's corps failed to turn Dan Sickles' collapse into a complete rout, this was no more of a failure than Stonewall Jackson's famous flank attack at Chancellorsville on May 2nd. Jackson, like Longstreet, achieved a great initial success; but Jackson's attack, also like Longstreet's, fell far short of dislodging the entire Federal army (that work had to be completed by Lee on May 3rd). Jackson, again like Longstreet, had begun his attack so late that darkness forced him to halt substantially short of that goal. Yet no one has ever suggested that Jackson's descent on the Union right flank at Chancellorsville was a failure—or at least not in the way Longstreet's descent on the Union left at Gettysburg would be described.

No one that night seemed much dismayed over the results, either. James Risque Hutter of the 11th Virginia found his old friend Lindsay Long "making some disposition of the Prisoners captured from Genl Reynold's command." Long, as one of Lee's personal staff, assured Hutter that "all we had to do was to follow them up the next day." Henry Morrow, the captured colonel of the 24th Michigan, thought his rebel captors "very sanguine of their ability to dislodge the Army of the Potomac from its position, and the capture of Washington and Baltimore was considered a thing almost accomplished." When William Swallow rode through the town that night to report to Lee's headquarters, he found Gettysburg "filled with Confederates, who, soldier like, were busy preparing their meals all along the streets. They appeared to be in the highest spirits." And at Lee's headquarters at the Widow Thompson's, "All seemed gratified with the results of the day; certainly nobody looked gloomy or desponding."[28]

The Army of Northern Virginia had dealt its Union counterpart a series of blows which, purely in terms of casualties and human destruction, had the unhappy Army of the Potomac as thoroughly on the ropes as it had ever been. The 1st Corps and 11th Corps had been crushed down to the nubs on July 1st; on July 2nd, the 3rd Corps and 5th Corps, along with an entire division of the 2nd Corps, had been ground into oblivion. By moonrise on the night of July 2nd, George Meade had only the 12th Corps and the 6th Corps in any sort of fighting shape, along with four brigades in Hancock's 2nd Corps which had managed to escape mauling with the others. Meade would need to put the two divisions of the 12th Corps back on Culp's Hill in the morning; he would need the 6th Corps as his last-option reserve, and he would post them near

Powers Hill; after that, he would have only those four brigades of Hancock's and the sweepings of the 1st and 11th Corps to hold Cemetery Hill. David Birney muttered, in "a moment of despondency," to de Trobriand that "he had had a horse killed under him, and . . . wished he had shared the fate of his horse. He believed the day lost; he counted up his friends dead and wounded; he saw his command half-destroyed, and, thinking of the Republic, he trembled for it." Lee, by contrast, would have an entire division of Longstreet's corps ready to put into action anywhere he might choose, along with several lightly dented portions of Powell Hill's corps, and at least one of Dick Ewell's brigades, plus that lodgement on Culp's Hill.[29]

It must have occurred to George Meade that perhaps the stand at Gettysburg had been a big mistake, after all. Perhaps the retreat to Pipe Creek which had been so unthinkable that morning was now worth contemplating, especially since Meade would have a very obvious, and deliciously appropriate, scapegoat to absorb the president's disappointment in Dan Sickles. Perhaps it was time to bring his surviving corps commanders together for a face-saving consultation which would authorize Meade to do what he had all along been convinced he should do.

The call to the generals went out.

CHAPTER TWENTY

Let us have no more retreats

O N THE 5TH OF MARCH, 1864, George Gordon Meade sat down before Senator Benjamin Franklin Wade to contribute his testimony to what he had been disingenuously advised was the desire of the Joint Congressional Committee on the Conduct of the War to create "a sort of history of the war." Meade was not fooled by this, or by the smiling assurance of "Bluff Ben" Wade that this was not an inquisition and that there were no "charges against me." Three days before, on the floor of the Senate, Wade's Radical Republican colleague Morton Wilkinson accused Meade of ordering "a retreat" from Gettysburg, and Meade was only too well aware that "Generals Sickles and Doubleday" had been whispering to the committee about a directive Meade had composed for a withdrawal to Pipe Creek on July 2nd.

For three hours, Meade "gave . . . a full history of all the circumstances attending the battle of Gettysburgh, and also of his subsequent conduct." A week later, Meade appeared again before committee—in this case, Wade alone—with copies of the orders he had issued for the Army of the Potomac's concentration at Gettysburg, and a month later he submitted a written statement unequivocally denying that he had ever issued or authorized such an order; then came a procession of witnesses to contradict him. Meade was then directed to return to the committee for a third round of testimony. This time, Meade's fiery temper was only barely in restraint: "I utterly deny, under the full solemnity and sanctity of my oath, and in the firm conviction that the day will come when the secrets of all men shall be made known—I utterly deny ever having intended or thought, for one instant, to withdraw that army, unless the military contingencies which the future should develop during the course of the day might render it a matter of necessity that the army should be withdrawn."[1]

And this, in large measure, is where the matter has been allowed to rest for a century and a half. "The charge of a desire to retreat," insisted Meade's friends and defenders, consisted of nothing but "groundless aspersions," ginned up by envious bitter-enders like Sickles and Doubleday, who either wanted cover for their own sins or revenge for imagined slights. The most indubitable confirmation of Meade's innocence came from his own senior officers—John Sedgwick, John Newton, George Sykes, John Gibbon—in response to a circular from Meade on March 10, 1864, requesting confirmation from them "regarding his intention of retreating from Gettysburg." *At no time in my presence did the General Commanding insist or advise a withdrawal of the army,* they repeated one after another, and that, as far as Meade was concerned, "put to rest the injurious statements made" about a retreat on July 2nd.

What no one noticed at the time were the subtle equivocations buried inside a number of the generals' endorsement letters: *At no time in my presence,* wrote Sedgwick, which did not exclude Meade having said otherwise to others . . . *nothing that I heard him say,* wrote John Newton . . . *never received or heard of any order directing a retreat,* added George Sykes, which also fell somewhat short of asserting that no such "order" had actually been contemplated. Nor did anyone remark on the peculiar fact that all of the respondents to the circular were hard-core McClellanites. No response was received from Otis Howard or Henry Slocum, or even Winfield Scott Hancock, and in fact, none may have been solicited.[2]

One thing beyond contest is that "soon after all firing had ceased" on the evening of July 2nd, "a staff officer from army headquarters" was sent off to all the senior commanders, summoning them to Meade's headquarters in the Leister cottage. There was evidently some confusion over what constituted a senior commander. John Newton was invited, rather than Doubleday, to represent the 1st Corps; David Birney showed up for the 3rd Corps, even though Winfield Hancock understood that he was in command of that corps, and brought John Gibbon with him as titular commander of the 2nd Corps. Sykes, Sedgwick, and Howard were there for the 5th, 6th, and 11th Corps; but Slocum, under the impression that he was still some sort of wing commander, brought Alpheus Williams with him as commander of record for the 12th Corps. Gouverneur Warren was also there, as Meade's chief engineer, and Daniel Butterfield, chief of staff. "These twelve men were all assembled in a little room not more than ten or twelve feet square, with a bed in one corner, a small table on one side, and a chair or two."[3]

Under any circumstances, calling a council would not be a good sign.

There was a well-known maxim of Horatio Nelson's: "If a man consults whether he is to fight, when he has the power in his own hands, it is certain that his opinion is against fighting," and Joe Hooker had borne that wisdom out all too well at Chancellorsville. At least Meade had scattered a few preparatory hints about the discussion. He warned Henry Hunt, the Army of the Potomac's artillery chief, that he was worried that "some corps had left behind parts of their ammunition trains" and that "he would not have enough amn." to "carry us through the battle." And in a midday report to Henry Halleck, Meade had proposed that, despite occupying "a strong position for defensive" operations, if he found the Confederates "endeavouring to move to my rear and interpose between me and Washington, I shall fall back to my supplies at Westminster"—which was, of course, behind Pipe Creek.[4]

With that possibility in mind, at some point before the attack on the 3rd Corps, Meade had quietly asked Dan Butterfield, as chief of staff, to draw up a contingency plan for a withdrawal to Pipe Creek, even making "a rough sketch showing the position of the corps" and how he wanted them detached from contact with the Confederates. Butterfield drew up the order, and showed it to John Gibbon, who happened to be at Meade's headquarters behind the 2nd Corps. Gibbon was alarmed that the order even spelled out "the movement of army corps on specified roads to points in the rear." *Good God*, Gibbon exclaimed, *Gen. Meade is not going to retreat, is he?*

Once the 3rd Corps disintegrated and took the 5th Corps with it that afternoon, Alfred Pleasonton found Meade in a state of "so little assurance . . . in the strength of his position," that he "directed me to gather what cavalry I could, and prepare to cover the retreat of the army." When the summons to the council arrived at 6th Corps headquarters, John Sedgwick, despite his testimony before the Joint Committee eight months later, drew precisely the same conclusion as Gibbon. "Gen. Sedgwick called" his chief of staff, Lt. Col. Martin McMahon, "about nine [o'clock], saying that he had been called to a Council" and "that General Meade was thinking of a retreat." Sedgwick's own aide-de-camp whispered to Thomas Hyde that "the general was going to the headquarters to a council of war" and that "we were going to march back twenty miles that night."[5]

But if Meade was looking for an affirmation for a fallback to Pipe Creek after this disastrous day, he did not get it. "The discussion was at first very informal," with Meade asking the tightly packed room of generals for an estimate of their losses that day, and then a reckoning of the available troops in each corps. The numbers could not have been reassuring. At best, the generals guessed that the Army of the Potomac could muster 58,000 men, and as the tension of the meeting was occasionally interrupted by eruptions of volleying and artillery fire from the direction of Culp's Hill, the generals were reminded that those numbers were suffering further subtractions through more casualties even as they spoke.

John Newton loyally supplied the table-setting observation that Gettysburg was "a bad position" and that Cemetery Hill "was no place to fight a battle in." Picking up that cue, Meade then asked everyone "whether our army should remain on that field and continue the battle, or whether we should change to some other position," like Pipe Creek, "which was impregnable." The answers came bounding back in exactly the opposite direction. "By the custom of war," John Gibbon wrote, "the junior member votes first as on courts-martial," and so Gibbon chimed in with a polite but vigorous demurrer: "Correct the position of the army," Gibbon advised, but do "not retreat." Alpheus Williams was next: "Stay," and he was seconded by David Birney and George Sykes. Newton entered the weak plea that "if we wait, it will give them a chance to cut our line," but he could see which way the wind was blowing, and finally agreed with Gibbon's "not retreat." On it went: Howard voted to remain, and even urged an attack if the Confederates stayed their hand. Hancock confirmed Gibbon's advice, and added with a touch of anger, "Let us have no more retreats. The Army of the Potomac has had too many retreats. . . . Let this be our last retreat." Sedgwick also voted to "remain" and "await attack"; Slocum went last and uttered only three determined words: *Stay and fight.*

This was not the conclusion Meade had wanted; if Sickles' misbehavior had given him the excuse he needed for retreating, his corps commanders had just stripped it away. "General Meade arose" from where he had been sitting at Lydia Leister's table, and grumpily reinforced Newton's objection: "Have it your way, gentlemen, but Gettysburg is no place to fight a battle." He had taken the poll and it had not gone his way, and he would have to live with it. No one doubted Meade's personal courage, but there was a general sense that this was not the moment to revert to McClellan-style risk-aversion. "He thought it better to retreat with what we had, than run the risk of losing all," and there was no doubt in Henry Slocum's mind that "but for the decision of his corps commanders," Meade and the Army of the Potomac "would have been in full retreat . . . on the third of July."[6]

The council broke up near midnight, just as Henry Hunt rode up to the Leister cottage. He quickly learned that "the question had been spoken of as to what they should do . . . about falling back," but "there was no person at all in favor of leaving the ground we had then."[7]

Robert E. Lee may also have been anticipating a meeting on July 2nd, albeit a private one, and the atmosphere was, if anything, more likely to be charged

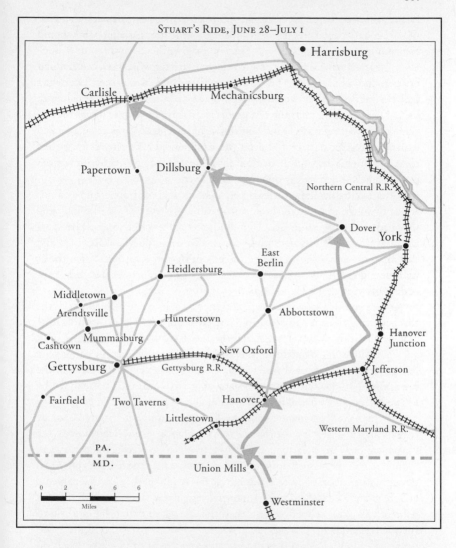

with greater disappointment and unhappiness than Meade's with his generals. After eight days of invisibility, James Ewell Brown Stuart was finally reporting.

By the time Stuart and his cavalry descended on the last wagons in the Rockville supply train on June 28th, his anxieties about finding the rest of the Army of Northern Virginia began to crowd out whatever plans he might have entertained for prolonging his raid around the Federal army, capturing Joe Hooker, or making a sensational dash on Washington. "It was important for me," Stuart realized, "to reach our column with as little delay as possible." He paroled the 400 prisoners taken with the train, and probably should have dumped the wagons as well, since managing them had become a "serious embarrassment." His men pulled down telegraph wires, burned railroad bridges, and tore up track, but the overriding problem was that Stuart had only the vaguest idea of where Lee and the rest of the army might be found. He could only guess from the newspapers and from interrogating his prisoners that "the enemy was . . . moving through Frederick City northward," and make a rough calculation of how far the army should have progressed by this time. Although Stuart would be roundly blamed for having left Lee to wander in the dark, Lee had hardly done less to Stuart.[8]

Stuart actually guessed remarkably well. He had his troopers up and riding early on the morning of June 29th, heading north, and by mid-morning they had reached Westminster, Maryland, pointed toward Hanover, Pennsylvania. Westminster was a terminus for the Western Maryland Railroad and the rail yards at Westminster were staked out by two companies from the as yet untested 1st Delaware Cavalry. To them, nothing much seemed to be happening between there, Hanover, or Gettysburg.[9]

Proof of how wrong they were appeared at 3:30 on the afternoon of the 29th, when a civilian came tearing into Westminster with a warning that Confederate cavalry was approaching from the south. Capt. Charles Corbit got his two cavalry companies into their saddles, calling at the same time for the streets to be cleared. As soon as Corbit's horsemen emerged from the town, they ran into the advanced guard of Stuart's column, commanded by Fitzhugh Lee. In an act of almost suicidal audacity, Corbit ordered a charge directly into the Confederate column. This struck the 4th Virginia Cavalry entirely by surprise, and Corbit's seventy-odd troopers actually forced the Confederates back, and fended off two poorly organized countercharges. "The charge was of such impetuosity that we drove them back some distance," wrote one satisfied Delaware trooper—until Fitz Lee himself came up to take charge. Lee sorted out his tangled regiments, threw out the 4th Virginia in a flanking maneuver, and then closed back in on Corbit in a "short, sharp, decisive" fight. Corbit's horse was shot down, and Corbit himself captured, "standing astride of his dead horse" and trying to fight the rebels off with his revolver. Lee's enraged troopers chased Corbit's men back into the town, hunting them down one by one, and by the end of the day, sixty-seven of the Delaware contingent were killed, wounded, or prisoners.[10]

Stuart's cavalry had already been showing serious signs of fatigue before arriving at Westminster, and this little escapade did not help. "After a series of exciting combats and night marches," Stuart lamented, "whole regiments slept in the saddle, their faithful animals keeping the road unguided." The interruption posed by Corbit's charge was all the persuasion Stuart needed to call a halt, authorize some local foraging, and assemble a hasty meeting of his three brigade commanders. "Straddling a chair on the sidewalk," Stuart then nodded off into an exhausted sleep for a few hours. He was up and going again with his men by five o'clock on the morning of the 30th, but in the process he had lost "from ten to twelve hours" because of the Westminster skirmish, and he was going to pay dearly for them.[11]

Stuart's column crossed Pipe Creek at Union Mills, then turned northward into Pennsylvania. Stuart learned from scouts that a considerable body of Federal cavalry was just to the west, at Littlestown, so he pushed on toward Hanover, hoping to find Ewell's infantry. He almost did, as Jubal Early's division was at that moment on the road from his point of farthest advance at York and at noon on June 30th was probably less than twenty miles northeast of Stuart's position. Stuart did not know that, and what was worse, he did not know that the Yankee cavalry the scouts had reported was actually a full Federal cavalry division of 3,500 men, under the newly promoted Judson Kilpatrick.

A raffish, red-haired, and highly overrated womanizer with a damningly selfish willingness to throw away his troopers' lives in battle (which earned him the unflattering nickname "Kill-cavalry"), Kilpatrick was nevertheless a favorite of Alfred Pleasonton's. And even though Kilpatrick had spent three months under military arrest for a host of infractions that included pocketing money from the sale of government property, Pleasonton was so eager to purge foreign-born officers from the cavalry corps of the Army of the Potomac that he handed command of Julius Stahel's division to Kilpatrick and sent him off to screen the center of Meade's pursuit of Lee into Pennsylvania. Kilpatrick had for brigadiers two officers who had just as dramatically jumped the seniority queue from captain to brigadier general, Elon Farnsworth and the "incorrigible" George Armstrong Custer, a former McClellan aide-de-camp. Both were cut from nearly the same cloth as Kilpatrick in their passion for action and display, for their mischievousness and recklessness.[12]

Kilpatrick set off for Hanover early on the morning of the 30th, slouching easily through the town square before noon. He had already sent Custer's brigade through the town, to the accompaniment of bell ringing and schoolchildren singing patriotic songs, when skirmish fire broke out to the southwest. At the moment, Kilpatrick had indulgently permitted the troopers of Farnsworth's brigade a time-out to enjoy the hospitality of Hanover. As the staccato ricketing of carbine fire was joined by the deeper thud of artillery, he sent off a galloper to bring back Custer, and then, standing up in his stirrups, said for all to hear: "Boys, look at me. I am General Kilpatrick. I want you to know me, and where I go I want you to follow. Stuart is making a call on us, and we are going to whip him." And together they went pelting back through the town in search of trouble.[13]

While Kilpatrick had been leisurely walking his division through Hanover, moving east, the head of Stuart's cavalry had appeared, coming north on the Westminster road, and barged into Farnsworth's rear guard. The skirmishing quickly took on serious dimensions, spilling into the streets of the town. (Unlike Gettysburg, a substantial number of Hanoverians grabbed firearms to take aim at the Confederate cavalrymen in the streets, and an ad hoc detail of mounted civilians, armed with shotguns, tried to offer their services to Kilpatrick.) Farnsworth's brigade thundered into the rebels, evicting the Confederate skirmishers and "driving the rebels in confusion along the road and through the fields." Stuart had neither wanted nor anticipated a fight at Hanover, but by the time he came up to the head of his column he could already see his lead brigade—John R. Chambliss' three Virginia and one North Carolina cavalry regiments—falling back in disorder from the town. "As General Stuart saw them rushing out of the place," he rode up and began trying to rally them. No success: "The long charge *in*, the repulse *out* . . . had thrown them into utter confusion."[14]

Instead of rallying, Stuart and his staff had to hightail for it themselves, jumping a high fence and drainage ditch like Saturday-morning fox hunters. Custer came blazing back down the road and, leaving Farnsworth to mop up in the town, the Boy General wheeled his brigade into the open ground just south of the town. But Stuart had more cavalry coming up the road, and this made Custer decide to limit himself to little more than threatening gestures. At sundown, Stuart quietly disengaged, and filed his brigades to the east, where they would have a clear route toward York and—he hoped— Dick Ewell. Kilpatrick made no effort to pursue him. Reports of Confederate infantry to the north (this was Jubal Early's division, heading toward their rendezvous with Ewell and Rodes at Heidlersburg) convinced Kilpatrick that he was too exposed for comfort, and Stuart was allowed to slip away in the night.[15]

Jubal Early was actually close enough to hear the distant rumble of artillery from the Hanover fight. Getting up from lunch in a tavern in the hamlet of Davidsburg, Early and his staff "heard the booming of cannon toward the southwest." Casually, Harry Hays remarked, "I suppose a battle has begun." And not only Harry Hays, but "the whole command distinctly heard Stuart's guns." But Early proved to be more curious about paying the bill, handing the proprietor twenty dollars in Confederate notes to cover the meals for his staff and senior officers, and moved off to his rendezvous with Ewell. When Fitz Lee's advance guard reached the York Pike that night, they found that Early's division had passed through some twelve hours before.

By now, Stuart's troopers were "broken down & in no condition to fight." A lieutenant in the 9th Virginia Cavalry saw men slumped in saddles, "so tired and stupid as almost to be ignorant of what was taking place around them. Couriers in attempting to deliver orders to officers would be compelled to give them a shake and call before they could make them understand." Even the drivers of the captured wagon train were falling asleep on their seats and causing fits of stop-and-start that further slowed Stuart's column. Yankee prisoners from the Hanover fight had to be pressed into duty as drivers "and it required the utmost exertions of every officer on Stuart's staff to keep the train in motion."[16]

Stuart's bleary-eyed brigades stumbled into the village of Dover in the wee hours of July 1st. The only information he could glean about Early's possible direction was some local rumor about him marching toward Carlisle or Shippensburg. "I still believed that most of our army was before Harrisburg," Stuart wrote, "and justly regarded a march to Carlisle as the most likely to place me in communication with the main army." But when Stuart reached Carlisle early that evening with Fitz Lee's brigade, not only had two divisions of Dick Ewell's corps left Carlisle the day before, but Federal infantry were now in possession of the town. Upon closer inspection, it turned out that the infantry amounted to just over 2,500 Pennsylvania emergency militia, with two guns manned by thirty of the U.S. Regulars who had been forced so incontinently to abandon the Carlisle Barracks a few days before. The prospect of administering a convenient whipping to some open-jawed militia roused Stuart's men as a compensation for their long frustration. "We were preparing to have the time of our lives with the Pennsylvania Militia," wrote one of Stuart's artillerymen. But Stuart preferred to waste as little in the way of lives or strength as possible, and sent in a courier under a flag of truce—"a third of an ordinary bed sheet" in size—warning that Stuart would bombard the town if it was not surrendered to him at once.[17]

The Yankees may have been militia, but their commander was not. He was William Farrar Smith, known more colloquially as "Baldy" Smith, West Point class of 1845, colonel of the 3rd Vermont at First Bull Run, a division commander in the Army of the Potomac on the Peninsula and then of the 6th Corps at Fredericksburg. "Shell away," he snarled to Stuart's messenger, "and be damned." For three and a half hours, Fitz Lee's artillery flung shells and solid shot on the hapless town, striking houses and the county courthouse, but doing "no particular damage." It was not a task Fitz Lee enjoyed: "My first military service after graduating from West Point was there" and he had "received the hospitalities of most of its citizens"—whom his artillery were now very likely to kill. "It was with much regret that I proceeded."[18]

When the bombardment produced no further response from Baldy

Smith, the increasingly testy Stuart ordered the 4th Virginia Cavalry to torch the Carlisle Barracks, and for a grand finale Stuart's gunners shelled the town gas works, which blew up in a spectacular red cloud of flame. Stuart sent one last courier to Smith at midnight, but the Confederate shelling had done nothing to make Baldy more pliable. He asked "that the bearer inform General [Fitzhugh] Lee that he would see him in a hotter climate first." Stuart's gunners had fired over 135 rounds into the town to no useful effect, and after a little more desultory firing, they gave up. Whatever pleasure the shelling gave Stuart, it gave little to his men. "I could not but reflect as I looked back on the burning town, on the wickedness, the horrors of this felt war," wrote one of Stuart's weary junior officers. "I was made to feel very unhappy indeed, and to pray, 'God grant that terrible war may lead to an early peace.'"[19]

Stuart's irritation faded before the fires he had set burned out, because "about midnight," one of Stuart's couriers "returned with the first information we had received from our army and with orders from Gen. R.E. Lee for Stuart to march to Gettysburg at once." Stuart's column swayed perilously southward toward Gettysburg until they had passed through the village of Hunterstown, just five miles north of the town. Sometime between two and four o'clock in the afternoon, as the rear guard under Wade Hampton cleared Hunterstown, Federal cavalry skirmishers began nipping at the heels of the column. But Dick Ewell sent a pair of 10-pounder Parrott rifles to back Hampton up—the first direct involvement of the army with Stuart's cavalry since the campaign began—and by dusk the skirmishing finally petered out. After eight days of almost ceaseless riding and fighting, Stuart's cavalry had been forced to ride and fight right up to the end.[20]

However late Stuart was in arriving, the Army of Northern Virginia was still glad to see him. As he rode along the York Pike into Gettysburg, "such joyful shouts as rent the air I never heard" and "the cavalry for once was well received." Lee, however, had grown increasingly "uneasy & irritated by Stuart's conduct," recalled George Campbell Brown and "had no objection to [Brown] hearing of it," which was surprising for "a man of Lee's habitual reserve." In time, descriptions of an epic confrontation between Lee and Stuart surfaced, mostly for the purpose of showing that Robert E. Lee himself pointedly held Stuart responsible for the Gettysburg battle. But there is no contemporary description of such a meeting, despite its inflation in subsequent retellings to a level with the return of the Prodigal Son. Although it is safe to say that Stuart *may* have reported directly to Lee after his arrival in the late afternoon of July 2nd, the few descriptions we have of Stuart that evening place him "at the vidette-post nearest" the "Infantry" or Ewell's corps, near Rock Creek. As for Henry McClellan, Stuart's chief of staff, his only comment on Stuart's arrival in Gettysburg (in his 1893 biography of Stuart) was to describe, laconically, how "for eight days and nights, the troops had been marching incessantly," and "on the ninth night they rested within the shelter of the army, and with a grateful sense of relief which words cannot express."[21]

There were other voices beside those of the generals to be heard at Gettysburg that night. Some came from sergeants calling company rolls to find out who was still available to answer. In the 19th Massachusetts, roll calls were the cue for the battle's first laments: *John was killed before we fired a shot* or *I saw Frank throw up his arms and fall just after we fired the first volley* or *Jim was shot through the head* or *George was killed by a piece of shell, while we were firing.* The names went on into the empty air, and "strong men sobbed."[22]

Much louder and more numerous were the sounds that came from the throats of thousands of mangled and dying men left to lie, immobilized with smashed legs, internal hemorrhages so massive that they had scarcely more than the strength to wail, or so crazed with shock that they took to stumbling about in the dark. "You would hear some poor friend or foe crying for water, or for 'God's sake' to kill him," remembered Louis Léon of the 53rd North Carolina, or "some of your comrades, shot through the leg, lying between the lines, asking his friends to take him out, but no one could get to his relief, and you would have to leave him there, perhaps to die." Henry Blake in the 11th Massachusetts bitterly condemned "the chief portion of the ambulance corps" for sticking to "safe positions" through the night; it was the ordinary soldiers who made up small details from each regiment to gather up canteens to "succor their wounded comrades" and who "bore the suffering to the hospitals in blankets and upon muskets, and rails." Occasionally, "squads of rebels . . . upon a similar mission" would wander into Union picket lines, but they were usually released, as if some kind of unspoken contract had come to prevail. One Confederate who was stopped by Blake's pickets said, "I am your prisoner, if you say so; but I am giving water to all that ask for it." They let him go.[23]

All across the darkened ridges, and especially across Devil's Den, the peach orchard, and the Emmitsburg Road, men with "lighted lanterns . . . passed to the front and scattered over the valley, seeking out the wounded," and as the Confederates did likewise, the "space between the two armies" became filled with "wandering jets of light." Over on the other side of Culp's Hill, William Swallow found "both banks of Rock Creek lined with wounded Confederates washing and tying up their wounds," while others were compelled to fight off the unwanted attentions of local livestock who had been turned loose to wander by the fighting. A lieutenant in the 118th Pennsylvania was surrounded by "a number of stray hogs" who "commenced rooting and tearing at the dead men around me," and when "one hog of enormous size . . . attempted to poke me," the lieutenant had the presence of mind to jam "my sword into his belly, which made him set up a prolonged, sharp cry."[24]

The miserable condition of the wounded and dying in Civil War battles has always been one of the first of the war's horrors to demand both recoil and reproach. In an age without any knowledge of sepsis, and only the crudest of surgical tools and techniques, any wound could be a ticket to death from infection alone. "We had no clinical thermometers; our only means of estimating fever was by touch," admitted Philadelphia surgeon William W. Keen. "We had no hypodermatic syringes" and so "the mouth and the bowel were the only avenues for the administration of remedies." The wounds themselves were made all the more horrible by the weaponry that inflicted them, for while the rifle musket might fall considerably short of its reputation for accuracy, the weight of the unjacketed lead rounds it fired (between .45 and .69 caliber) were heavy enough that when they did strike a human target, the damage would almost always be life-threatening. *A little powder and a lot of lead,* was the rule in the British Army, *shoot them once and shoot them dead.* One Union soldier remembered "a soldier named Scottie who received as severe a wound as I have ever known"—a slug struck "him at the base of the jaw, broke those bones and drove the fragments and his teeth out of his mouth" and "as he breathed his cheeks seemed to meet, as there was not anything to keep them apart."

Wounds to the arms and legs could be treated by amputation, as a preemptive strategy to head off the onset of gangrene and blood poisoning. But men with wounds to the chest, and especially to the abdomen, were often simply set aside, to be made as comfortable as possible as they slowly died. As a result, nearly 15 percent of the wounded *would* die, which was more or less equivalent to what the British Army endured in the Crimean War. "Wounds of the abdomen involving the viscera were almost uniformly fatal," wrote Surgeon Keen. "Opium was practically our only remedy and death the usual result." He could not remember "more than one incontestable example of recovery from a gunshot wound of the stomach and not a single incontestable case of recovery from wounds of the small intestines."[25]

None of this was helped by the sketchy field hospital arrangements. The Crimean War had brought the first great revulsion against the inadequacies of military medical services; five years later, Henri Dunant was so unhinged by the spectacle of the battlefield of Solferino in the North Italian War of 1859 that he set in motion the creation of the first Red Cross organization. No news of this arrived in time to prepare the American armies for the Civil War. There were little over a hundred surgeons in the U.S. Army in 1861, presided over by a geriatric veteran of the War of 1812, and not until 1862 was a military ambulance corps authorized for the Army of the Potomac.

But even if they had paid better attention to the improvements in care developed as a result of the Crimean and North Italian wars, there was still the lead ceiling formed by the limitations on medical knowledge, and by the improvised conditions of medicine on a battlefield. It was the first task of regimental, brigade, division, and corps medical staff to select likely sites for field hospitals; their best choices were often an old stone barn or a grove of shade trees.[26] Overall, some 160 different places in Gettysburg and across the surrounding landscape were pressed into service as "hospitals," some of them churches, still others houses, many of them farmhouses and barns, but some just "out-of-doors, where . . . surgeons have placed themselves to receive the wounded." The 11th Corps fixed its corps hospital at the Adams County almshouse on July 1st, only to have to abandon it almost as soon as it was set up; eventually, the 11th Corps settled on a farm owned by George Spangler near Powers Hill, with a large stone-and-timber bank-barn. Four crude operating tables were put up, and during the day between 700 and 1,000 wounded men arrived, propped up against stalls and cribs, or carried out when dead to make room for more. Still more "were lying with but feeble, or in most cases no shelter . . . against the sides of the barn, and in an orchard adjoining the sheds." A Confederate hospital, set up for the wounded of Rodes' division in the barn of David Shriver's 150-acre farm on the Mummasburg Road, overflowed with "the wounded and mangled," having only "a couple of impromptu tables for operating purposes," and only three surgeons to treat 760 wounded men.[27]

Hospitals set up in the town had better cover, but because they lay between the two armies, they were also more likely to be hit by stray shells. The Washington Hotel, which had been taken over by the medical officers of the 1st Corps, was seized by the Confederates on July 1st, but being filled with Union wounded gave it no exemption from friendly fire. "Two shells struck it, pieces of one taking off the thumb of one of Dr. [James L.] Farley's attendants" and the other perforating the rear wall of the hotel and exploding, but "without doing any personal damage." Nor were the conditions any less haphazard than those in the barns. A soldier from the 12th Massachusetts was carried into the house of Pennsylvania College president Henry Baugher (along with "twenty or more of us lying in the hallway and lower rooms") where "shells were frequently bursting around the grounds, the fragments crashing against the walls of the building and tearing the limbs from the trees in the yard."[28]

The great enemy of the surgeon was time. Joe Hooker's original campaign orders had cut down the size of the trains accompanying the Army of the Potomac to two wagons per brigade—over the protests of the Army of the

Potomac's chief medical officer, Jonathan Letterman, who could see that this would require limiting precious medical supplies. And sure enough, the battle began with only barely sufficient supplies of "dressings, chloroform, and such articles," and for "several days . . . we were obliged to skirmish around the country to get something for the wounded to eat." The surgeons of James Barnes' 5th Corps division had to place the wounded "in long rows, with no reference to the nature or gravity of their injuries, nor condition or rank," and in the dark, "opiates were administered to alleviate pain, and water supplied to appease their thirst" until daylight would enable them to begin inspecting, sorting, operating.

Others tried to labor by whatever meager light they could find: an artilleryman in Clark's 1st New Jersey Artillery remembered his bivouac near a stone barn where "a dozen or more surgeons were at work at the amputating tables by candlelight, and all night." The Confederate medical officers were just as shorthanded, and caught just as much off guard. In their hurry, the surgeons in Powell Hill's corps "had hardly opened our battlefield supplies" before the wounded began to arrive, and there was no alternative but to improvise with nearly anything as an operating table—"doors laid on barrels," wrote one Confederate surgeon, "or any box we could lay hold of." The 800 or so Confederate wounded who crowded into the Lutheran seminary and the white-pillared main "edifice" of Pennsylvania College took up space "in the Library, and in the halls of the Societies, as well as in the recitation rooms, chapel, and student rooms," where they used "volumes of old German theologians" as pillows.[29]

Dealing with other people's wounds could be nearly as traumatic as receiving them oneself. Shell can blow parts of a body to hanging shreds or rupture internal organs; solid shot can mangle or sever body parts; lead rifle bullets could smash and splatter, trailing ooze; and wounded men can lose control over bodily functions and even over their sanity. The amputations came off the tables in a gruesome tumble, as "the red, human blood ran in streams from under the operating tables, and huge piles of arms and legs, withered and horrible to behold" dropped off onto the ground and were, at intervals, carried away. A Vermont officer saw "by the door" of one field hospital "a ghastly pile of amputated arms and legs, and around each of them lay multitudes of wounded men, covering the ground by the acre, wrapped in their blankets and awaiting their turns under the knife." Carl Schurz was unnerved to see "the surgeons, their sleeves rolled up to the elbows, their bare arms as well as their linen aprons smeared with blood, their knives not seldom held between their teeth, while . . . around them pools of blood and amputated arms or legs in heaps," were collecting sometimes "more than man-high."

One 3rd Corps surgeon "performed at the least calculation fifty amputations," fourteen of them at one stretch "without leaving the table."

The surgeons sometimes developed a protective layer of professionally bleak humor to cope with this, although even then some of them cracked under the strain. (Schurz had seen how a "surgeon, having been long at work, would put down his knife, exclaiming that his hand had grown unsteady, and that this was too much for human endurance—not seldom hysterical tears streaming down his face.") A soldier's comrades, or the musicians and ordinary soldiers dragooned into duty as bearers and nurses, could often be more undone by the sight of wounded men than dead men. An officer in the 3rd Corps who volunteered on the night of July 2nd to assist with the wounded was "appalled" by the "prostrate men, their groans, and piteous appeals for help." Men screamed "in a state of delirium . . . as if upon the battlefield." But what finally drove him to run away was "a man I was about stepping over," who "sprang to his feet, shook in front of me a bloody bandage he had just torn from a dreadful gaping wound in his breast, and uttered a hideous laughing shriek which sent the hot blood spurting from his wound into my very face." A Pennsylvania College student, Horatio Watkins, was brushed back by "a rebel soldier" with a bandaged head, "insane from his wound," who "raised his hands, tore wide open his eyes, and turned towards me."

> *Eyes of men thinking, hoping, waiting*
> *Eyes of men loving, cursing, hating*
> *The eyes of the wounded sodden in red*
> *The eyes of the dying and those of the dead.*[30]

For those civilians left in the town, the experience of Confederate occupation followed no consistent or predictable theme. The rebel soldiers were not shy about helping themselves to the stockrooms of Gettysburg's stores, although (unlike Jubal Early's earlier foray on June 26th) the looting was as much about asserting a sense of power as it was from a prescribed agenda of occupation. Joseph Polley of the 4th Texas let himself into a store "on the main street of the little town" and discovered "a lot of . . . cloth gaiters such as ladies wear." Even though he had "as little idea what I wanted them for" as he might for a "grindstone," he "selected a pair of No. 3's and brought them away." If they served no other purpose, they could be sold to the sutlers for spot cash. Deserted houses and stores were considered fair game for breaking and entering, and several members of the 33rd Virginia's pioneer detail helped themselves to a "large farmhouse," where they found "several barrels of flour, a smokehouse full of bacon, a springhouse full of milk and butter," and even a table set "with the dishes on it. . . . If we did not live well for two days," one of the detail smirked, "I don't know a good thing when I see it." Army bureaucracy also asserted itself: the press of the Republican *Star and Banner* was used to print a fresh supply of blank army forms. At least Daniel Klingel had the acid satisfaction of returning to his farm and finding the rebels who had broken into his house to make off with a pan and some flour all dead, sitting around what had been their fire. "They had a pan, with a portion of cake remaining in the pan, showing that the explosion of a shell had killed the four men while they were enjoying their meal."[31]

But not even houses whose occupants had stubbornly decided to stay and hold on to their property were free from threats and theft. From their cellar, Leander Warren and his mother heard "several Confederates in our kitchen going through the cupboard. They took everything there was to eat, leaving us with almost nothing." Confederates "stole everything eatable" around Alexander Cobean's farm, "took all the cured meat and killed the cattle in the fields for fresh meat." Horatio Watkins, who had taken shelter with several fellow students in the cellar of a house, heard "some of the wandering rebels" try to break into the cellar. When he tried to persuade them that there was nothing there worth their effort, "one of the band" popped out with the old pickpocket's ploy, *What time is it?* Watkins knew what he wanted: *Four o'clock.* No, the rebel replied, *What time of your watch? It's broken,* Watkins countered again. *Let me see it,* the rebel demanded, and finally Watkins had to bring out his watch, which the rebel promptly appropriated. One part of the population in which the rebels showed an entirely different interest was the handful of Gettysburg's blacks who had stayed in the town. The McCrearys' "old washerwoman," Elizabeth Butler, was flushed out of hiding in the town, along with several others who were marched out Chambersburg Street, "going back to slavery." At least for the McCrearys' "Old Liz," the story had a happier ending; she slipped away into Christ Lutheran Church, "climbed up into the belfry," and hid there for two days.[32]

Houses on the south side of the town offered other attractions than looting. "The Rebs occupied the whole part of the town out as far as the back end of my house," complained John Rupp, who owned the tannery at the foot of Baltimore Street. After building a barricade across the street, the rebels "occupied my porch" and used that nook to keep up a spray of fire on the Union soldiers on Cemetery Hill. Other houses allowed rebel riflemen to mix business and pleasure. Harry Handerson was amused to find "the majority of my company" sitting down to "a generous meal" in a house facing Cemetery Hill, while "at each of the front windows a couple of men were occasionally exchanging shots with the enemy." After a while, the shooters came downstairs, "being relieved at intervals by their comrades and retiring to join in the feast until their turn once more came around."

In these houses, the Confederates usually had a blunt ultimatum to deliver to any stay-behinds: get out, or get to the cellar. Catharine Sweney's house on the west side of Baltimore Street had a convenient line of sight from its garret window to Cemetery Hill, and in short order Sweney and her daughter were packed off "to seek refuge" back in the town. Albertus McCreary, who had already gotten into enough trouble for one boy, got into still more when he and his brother used a trapdoor in the roof of their house on Baltimore Street to get "a good view of Cemetery Hill and of the fields near the Emmetsburg Road." They noticed a neighbor do likewise, until a bullet struck the brickwork of his chimney "just above his head." The neighbor dropped so quickly back down his trap door "that we both laughed"—until two bullets stripped off shingles within a foot of McCreary's head, and he and his brother sought the refuge of the cellar without any further laughter.[33]

The cellars might be safe, but they also sealed the townspeople into a bubble just as unnerving as the law of the bullets in the street, apart from "the reports given us by the Confederate soldiers." Those reports, as Albertus McCreary quickly learned, were more in the nature of mockery than information. "They said their men had taken Harrisburg, Philadelphia, Baltimore, and were nearing Washington, and that all was up with us." The experience of the cellar was a kind of deafness added to blindness. In fact, one of McCreary's neighbors who shared the McCreary cellar "was a deaf and dumb man, who, though he could not hear the firing, plainly felt the vibrations." If a shell burst heavily and closely, "he would spell out on his fingers, 'That was a heavy one.'" For the twenty-two people who sought shelter in David Troxel's house, the blankness of the cellar eased their anxiety, because it shut out everything in the external world. When a shell struck the upper floor of the Troxel house, "no one mentioned the fact though . . . a number of men heard it enter [the] house while they were in [the] cellar. They were afraid it would excite the women and children to talk about it." John Schick coped with his exile to the cellar of his store by smoking "21 cigars in one day."[34]

Perhaps the cigars worked some peculiar safeguard, because the most unusual aspect of the Gettysburg battle was how little damage was done to civilians or their property. Only one documented civilian fatality occurred, on the morning of July 3rd, when Mary Virginia Wade incautiously left the cellar of her sister's house on Baltimore Street, on the north slope of Cemetery Hill, to bake bread in the kitchen. A bullet drilled through two doors, striking her "in the back of her neck" and killing her instantly. In addition to John Burns, six civilians were wounded—Jacob Gilbert, Georgianna Stauffer, Duncan Carson, the dry goods merchant Robert F. McIlhenny, and two students, Amos Whetstone and Frederick Lehman (who would survive being shot below the knee but would walk with a limp for the rest of his life)—none of them seriously.

Apart from the "seventeen bullet holes" Matilda Pierce was able to count in the upper balcony of her home, and bullets that chipped brickwork and broke windowpanes in other south-side houses, there was little real physical damage done to the town. Part of this may have been simply due to lack of opportunity; the town was contested territory for all three days of the battle, and the Confederate occupiers had relatively little time for systematic destruction of the sort they would visit a year later in nearby Chambersburg. But another is linked to what cannot be said often enough about the technology of Civil War combat—that the weapons of the armies were neither sufficiently accurate nor sufficiently destructive to wreak the kind of obliteration which Krupp guns and aerial bombings would visit on European cities and towns in the twentieth century. The number of Gettysburg buildings which survive to this day with nothing more serious than bullet scrapes and the odd solid shot wedged into a rafter are a reminder not to rush too quickly to descriptions of the Civil War as a *modern,* or *total,* war. Even had the armies possessed the malevolence equal to such destructiveness, they did not possess the means.

And, in the end, they lacked the malevolence, too. During the night, George Hillyer of the 9th Georgia heard someone in McLaws' division begin singing, and loudly enough to be heard over both exhausted lines:

> *Come, ye disconsolate, where e'er ye languish*
> *Come to the mercy seat, fervently kneel;*
> *Here bring your wounded hearts,*
> *Here tell your anguish;*
> *Earth has no sorrow that heaven cannot heal.*

Hillyer wrote years later that he had "heard [Alice] Neils[e]n and [Adelina] Patti and much that the world applauds in the way of high grade music, but . . . I have never heard music like that." The voice quavered through hymns and songs, and finally finished its impromptu serenade with "When This Cruel War Is Over." Across the now silent battlefield, "thousands of soldiers on both sides clapped and cheered."[35]

PART 4

The Third Day

The general plan of attack was unchanged

THE SUN ROSE ON JULY 3RD behind a thin layer of "cumulo-stratus clouds" (according to Professor Michael Jacobs' relentless meterological record keeping) which eventually burned off or blew away by noon. Temperatures outside the shade of the oak trees were already in the mid-70s by seven o'clock, and the atmosphere was charging with the edgy promise of a thunderstorm in the afternoon. On Cemetery Hill, "monuments and headstones" in the Evergreen Cemetery "lie here and there overturned." Graves "have been trampled by horses' feet" and the "neat and well-trained shrubbery" had vanished. One soldier in the 20th Massachusetts, near the little woodlot on Cemetery Ridge which Ambrose Wright's Georgians had come so close to holding the evening before, looked down the 2nd Corps line as the dawn painted color onto the deadly landscape, and thought that it "appeared like a country fair on a colossal scale." Turning around and looking to his rear, he could see Powers Hill and Culp's Hill, and the road running up to the rear of Cemetery Hill, "covered over with ambulances, wagons, reserve artillery." There were "thousands of horses with saddles on, mules in harness, hitched to fences, trees, wagon wheels" while they munched "the hay and grain that had been fed out to them. But the most striking sight was that of "seventy thousand muskets, with bayonets fixed" and "stacked in a row four miles long," marking the line he and his fellows would defend "when the battle note should be sounded."

Men also began stirring on the skirmish lines between the two armies, "making the most economical use of any little depression, or a fence-rail or two from the fences thrown down during the night," and beginning the familiar crackle of skirmish firing. Four-man skirmish teams "acted together, firing by volley into any puff of smoke that would be thrust out by the enemy." It did not take long for the firing to begin taking its toll, and even though skirmish fire was going to do little or nothing to determine the overall outcome of the battle, the men it killed would be just as dead as if they had been heroically leading the last brave charge of the war. Skirmishers who were too successful violated an unspoken rule of fairness, and when several Confederates "were able to reckon their game with every shot," their Federal opponents shouted "the wildest imprecations" at them "and threats were made that if taken they would get no quarter."

But for all the threats, the skirmishers of the 14th Connecticut actually felt "relief and gladness" when a wounded Confederate, "trying, by a series of flops, to drag his body up the slope to the shelter of his own lines," finally succeeded in getting out of range. Later, a solitary rebel "was seen to rise . . . and advance toward the Federals with his hand raised." The Union fire slackened, and the word was passed down the skirmish line, *Wait till we see what he wants.* The rebel skirmisher "suddenly dropped upon the grass and for an instant was lost to the sight." But in a moment, the Federal skirmishers cheered "as hearty as if given in a charge." The Confederate had heard a wounded Yankee "lying helpless on the ground between the lines . . . begging in his agonizing thirst for a drink" and "had gone forward to give some comfort to his distressed enemy." Once he had "performed his act of mercy," he sprinted back to his own skirmish line, and the cry went up from the Confederates, *Down, Yanks; we're going to fire,* and the soldiers returned to the business at hand of killing one another.[1]

By mid-morning, the skirmish fire had grown especially annoying for Alex Hays, commanding the other 2nd Corps division on Cemetery Ridge. Confederate skirmishers had once more set up in the William Bliss barn, where they could carry on sniping from less than 600 yards away. Hays called up four companies of the 14th Connecticut to clean out the Bliss barn and farmhouse, and when it became obvious that they could not hold the buildings against a serious Confederate counterattack, Hays ordered both burned. Details from the 12th New Jersey, 1st Delaware, and 111th New York trundled out and began setting fire to the barn with "burning wisps of hay or straw." They did their work well, and by the time they scrambled back to the Federal skirmish line along the Emmitsburg Road, "both buildings were in flames."[2]

Long before this, Robert E. Lee had made up his mind what course to follow. The men in Kershaw's South Carolina brigade were certain "that Lee would not yield to a drawn battle without, at least, another attempt to break Meade's

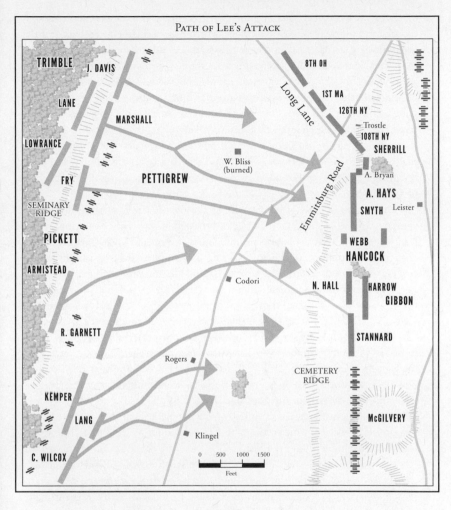

PATH OF LEE'S ATTACK

front," and most expected that "Lee would undertake the accomplishment of the work of the day before." They were right. Climbing up to the open cupola of Pennsylvania College, Lee saw nothing which suggested that he shouldn't hit the Federals again in the same fashion. The "partial successes" of July 2nd "determined me to continue the assault the next day." Moreover, Dick Ewell's foothold on the south peak of Culp's Hill "was such as to lead to the belief that he would ultimately be able to dislodge the enemy," and so "the general plan of attack was unchanged."

Longstreet would resume the attack with the one remaining division of his corps which was only just reaching the battlefield, that of George E. Pickett, plus "two brigades of Hill's corps" which had had time to recover from the fighting on July 1st. (On second thought, Lee added four more brigades from Hill's corps, just to make certainty certain.) The overall effect would be a renewal of the attack of July 2nd, and its goal would be the Union line— what was left of it—on Cemetery Ridge. If Ewell could extend his grip on Culp's Hill, the Baltimore Pike artery could be severed; if Longstreet could crush the remaining Federals on Cemetery Ridge, the Yankee artillery on the cemetery plateau would be pinched off and forced to surrender. Stuart and the cavalry would screen Ewell's flank and rear, but otherwise this was to be the infantry's show, with some preliminary assistance from a "grand battery" of the army's artillery.[3]

Dick Ewell got his orders for the attack on the night of the July 2nd, apprising him that "an attack would be renewed at daylight of the third, by Longstreet. We were to cooperate, as before, by opening with artillery & engaging the attention of the enemy as far as possible. Also to push out success on the left if practicable." (Again, that maddening phrase, *if practicable*.) Lee followed with a personal visit to Longstreet early "on the morning of the 3d," just "after sunrise," directing Longstreet to "renew the attack against Cemetery Hill. For that purpose he had already ordered up Pickett's division." This did not completely surprise Longstreet, who suspected that Lee "was still in his disposition to attack." But Longstreet assumed that the idea of attacking Cemetery Hill "had been fully tested the day before," and that Lee would now be in a more agreeable frame of mind to hear about skirting the entire left flank of the Army of the Potomac and slicing the Baltimore Pike below Powers Hill. Longstreet had even had "scouting parties out during the night in search of a way by which we might strike the enemy's left," and "found a way that gave some promise of results."[4]

Lee was not interested. Pointing "with his fist" toward Cemetery Hill, Lee replied just as he had the morning before, *The enemy is there, I am going to strike him.* Pickett's division would move up to Seminary Ridge, using the thick forestation for cover, and after a softening-up bombardment, they would follow more or less the same track as Cadmus Wilcox and Ambrose Wright had followed the afternoon before, hitting the 2nd Corps of the Army of the Potomac along Cemetery Ridge between the west side of Cemetery Hill and the woodlot—"a clump of trees," or, as others described it in less flattering terms, a "clump of bushes" or "a clump of dwarfed trees"—visible on the ridge. Longstreet was taken aback at the bluntness of the plan. He argued that the kind of attack Lee had in mind would require 30,000 men. Pickett's division had only about 10,500; the other units he would borrow from Powell

Hill would only bring that to about 13,000, and even then they "would have to march a mile under concentrating battery fire, and a thousand yards under long-range musketry."

Lee disagreed. The distance they would have to cover was, at most, 1,400 yards, and he would reinforce Pickett to bring the "strength of the column" up to 15,000. Longstreet was ready to throw his hands in the air. "General," Longstreet pleaded, "I have been a soldier all my life. I have been engaged in fights by couples, by squads, companies, regiments, divisions and armies, and . . . it is my opinion that no fifteen thousand men ever arrayed for battle can take that position." It was no use. Lee "was impatient of listening, and tired of talking, and nothing was left but to proceed." As soon as Pickett's division was in place, two divisions of Powell Hill's corps would be "arranged along his left. . . . We were to open with our batteries, and Pickett was to move out as soon as we silenced the Federal batteries. The artillery combat was to begin with the rapid discharge of two field-pieces as our signal."[5]

That left, of course, Powell Hill, and Lee now rode over to Hill's head-quarters near the seminary to brief him. "I was directed," wrote Hill, "to hold my line with Anderson's division . . . and to order Heth's division"—now commanded by Johnston Pettigrew as a result of Heth's head wound on July 1st—"and [James H.] Lane's and [Alfred] Scales' brigades of Pender's division, to report to Lieutenant General Longstreet as a support to his corps in the assault on the enemy's lines." Hill impulsively offered Lee "my whole Army corps," but Lee declined, since "what remains of your corps will be my only reserve." Hill would probably have been more content if he could have actually sent Dorsey Pender to join Pickett, but Pender had been wounded by an errant shell on the evening of July 2nd, and a ragged splinter "about two inches square" had cut into Pender's left thigh. It did not seem life-threatening at the moment (in fact, once Pender was evacuated to Staunton after the battle his femoral artery burst; the surgeons tried to eliminate the threat by amputating the leg on July 18th, but Pender died). Still, Pender was certainly in no shape to direct an attack, so his division was given a new commander in the shape of the voluble—and conveniently available—Isaac Trimble.[6]

And then there were arrangements for the artillery to be made, which Lee left in Longstreet's hands as the officer responsible for directing the attack. Longstreet, in turn, called in his artillery chief, James Walton, and his favorite, Porter Alexander, and told them "that we would renew the attack early in the morning." Walton would continue to oversee the corps artillery, but Alexander was "an officer of unusual promptness, sagacity, and intelligence," and Longstreet would use Alexander in a special staff role, not unlike the one Meade had devised for Hancock on July 1st. Alexander had already guessed that the morning of July 3rd would bring some renewal of the fighting, and he had been requisitioning ammunition and positioning portions of Longstreet's corps artillery reserve since midnight. In addition to the thirty-four guns of the corps reserve, he would be able to call on the division artillery battalions of Pickett and Lafayette McLaws for another thirty-eight guns, and could expect support for the attack from Powell Hill's batteries as well, including two deadly Whitworth rifles which had been run through the blockade from England, and which were the proud property of Powell Hill's artillery reserve. Counting every gun which Alexander and the other corps artillery chiefs could bring to bear, there may have been as many as 171 muzzles pointed at Cemetery Ridge.[7]

But bringing these forces to bear on Cemetery Ridge would take time. Lee's word to Ewell was to expect an attack "at daylight of the third, by Longstreet," and Porter Alexander likewise had the impression that Longstreet would have everything ready to begin by eight o'clock, "perhaps earlier." But action by Longstreet depended on Pickett, and if there was one thing George Pickett could be relied upon for, it was unreliability. Born in 1825, Pickett was charming, talkative, self-confident—and indolent. He was the embodiment of Henry Adams' estimate of the Virginia ruling class: "He had . . . the Virginian habit of command and took leadership as his natural habit," and could be, for a while, "the most popular and prominent young man in his class." The problem was that "no one knew enough to know how ignorant he was; how childlike. . . . He was simply beyond analysis; so simple that even the simple New England student could not realize him." Exasperated with their son's lack of spark, Pickett's parents wangled an appointment for him to West Point, where he graduated dead last in the class of 1846, and only five behavioral demerits shy of expulsion.

As a lieutenant in the Mexican War, Pickett distinguished himself leading the charge that breached the defenses of Churubusco, and snatched up the colors of the 8th U.S. Infantry (from the hands of no less than a wounded James Longstreet) and planted them on the ramparts of Chapultepec. Apart from those moments, Pickett's career was a blank. His wife died in childbirth in 1851, along with the child, and when he was posted to the Washington Territory he married a Yakima woman, fathered a son, triggered an international incident over an island in Puget Sound, and in 1861 abandoned them all to take up a commission as a captain of infantry in the new provisional army of the Confederacy. He proposed to a Virginia girl, LaSalle Corbell, who was eighteen years his junior (he married her in September 1863), and spent more time trying to play the part of "a Virginia slave-baron . . . proud in bearing, head lifted in arrogance" than in actual combat. Whatever moments he could spare from self-adornment were devoted to the neglect of his duties, and he was so little good as an officer that Longstreet had to assign staffers to Pickett to explain things "very fully; indeed sometimes stay with him to make sure he did not get astray." Longstreet, however, was also Pickett's indulgent angel, and was "exceedingly fond" of him. Pickett (according to LaSalle Pickett) had stepped up to supervise the funeral arrangements for Longstreet's children after their deaths in 1862, and generosity of that order, even if accompanied by a certain dimness of the intellect, is enough to cover a multitude of mediocrity. The only officer on record as praising Pickett as "the best infantry soldier developed on either side" seems to have been George McClellan.[8]

Robert E. Lee was not nearly so indulgent, even if Pickett was a Virginian. When Pickett took over command of Longstreet's old division in the fall of 1862, his performance made so little impression on Lee that Pickett was soon packed off (with his division) to fend off a Federal threat to Richmond from south of the James River "and there await further orders." He unpleasantly impressed one of his colonels, Eppa Hunton, who thought "his example to his soldiers was exceedingly bad." The two brigades of the Army of Northern Virginia which Lee grudgingly allowed Secretary of War Seddon to keep near Richmond during the invasion of Pennsylvania—Micah Jenkins' and Montgomery Corse's—were peeled away from Pickett's division. This left Pickett with only three brigades—under Lewis Armistead, James L. Kemper, and Richard Garnett—none of which had ever fought alongside one another.

Each of the brigade commanders, in turn, had a question mark over their heads. Although all three were Virginians, Kemper was a politician, not a soldier; Garnett had been humiliated by accusations of cowardice by Stonewall Jackson in 1862; and Armistead may have been the weakest reed of all. Although raised in a military family (his father and four uncles fought in the War of 1812), Armistead was bounced out of West Point, not once but twice, and it took some political strong-arming to get him a commission as a second lieutenant in the 6th U.S. Infantry in 1839. His service in the Mexican War was undistinguished, and his parting from the army in 1861 to join the Confederacy was marred by the pain of having to bid farewell to his longtime friend Winfield Scott Hancock. "Hancock, good-bye," Armistead lamented, "you can never know what this has cost me." Armistead took command of the 57th Virginia, and rose to brigade command in time for the fighting on the Peninsula in 1862. But his performance was lackluster, and soldiers complained that he preferred "saying 'Go on boys' but has never said 'come on' when we are going into a fight." During the Maryland Campaign in 1862, he was relegated to provost marshal duties, and missed both Fredericksburg and Chancellorsville.[9]

When Longstreet's corps marched east from Chambersburg on July 1st, Pickett's division was left behind to complete the humdrum task of "the destruction of a railroad near Chambersburg by piling up the wooden ties and kindling them into huge fires, on which the iron rails were heated and bent." All of this changed when Longstreet sent off orders to Pickett to "move up to Gettysburg as rapidly as possible" late in the afternoon of July 1st. The orders did not reach Pickett until one in the morning of July 2nd, and though Longstreet's courier believed that "there was not ten minutes' time consumed" by Pickett in rousing his staff and mounting up, the entire division could not have been in motion much before three o'clock. The distance to be covered between Chambersburg and Gettysburg was, unlike on July 1st, choked by backward-moving wagons, ambulances, and the general backwash of wounded men, supply clerks, prisoner details, and sutlers, and all under "a burning July sun." But Pickett's men were in fine fettle. "Officers and men were alike inspired with the greatest confidence in our ability to defeat the enemy anywhere . . . and never . . . in better fighting trim and spirit." And the news from up ahead was exciting: a quartermaster passing Pickett's men whooped, "Been fighting for two days—driving the Yankees all the time—got 6000 prisoners already—hurrah for Lee!"[10]

The question was, *How soon could they get there?* "On the march over South Mountain" and "passing through the small hamlets of Cashtown and Seven Stars," men in the 7th Virginia could "plainly" hear "the roar of Long-street's battle of that evening"—which meant that, since these Virginians were in the lead brigade of Pickett's column, it is unlikely that the van of the division could have reached Gettysburg before darkness. Pickett himself may have ridden ahead and arrived at Gettysburg as early as three in the afternoon on July 2nd, but by nightfall the bulk of his division was still strung out for miles to the west. Lee might have believed, when he met Longstreet "at sunrise" that morning, "that General Pickett would soon report to me." But portions of Pickett's division were still arriving at Gettysburg "about sunrise morning of the 3rd." Fitzgerald Ross, the Anglo-Austrian hussar and observer, had been up and "riding over the battlefield of yesterday . . . when Pickett's division of three brigades . . . passed us," which would put Pickett's arrival much later than "sunrise." Pickett himself did not report to Longstreet until "about seven o'clock," with the as yet unfulfilled promise "that his troops would soon be upon the field."[11]

None of this prevented the postwar hyenas from asserting that Longstreet had once again indulged in self-centered foot-dragging, delaying another attack which would otherwise have succeeded, and sabotaging the possibilities for Confederate victory at Gettysburg. The first witness was Lee himself, in his official report, which noted obliquely that "General Longstreet's disposition were not complete as early as expected." Jubal Early was the next on the witness stand in 1872, just as obliquely suggesting that Longstreet had been fully as tardy in launching his attack on July 3rd as he had been on July

2nd, while John Brown Gordon was more explicit: "It now seems certain that impartial military critics, after thorough investigation, will consider . . . as established . . . that General Lee ordered Longstreet to attack at daybreak on the morning of the third day, and that he did not attack until two or three o'clock in the afternoon, the artillery opening at one." In time, even men who made the attack would point their fingers at Longstreet. Eppa Hunton, the colonel of the 8th Virginia, thought "it is pretty well established that President Davis wanted to court-martial Longstreet" after Gettysburg, but was dissuaded by Lee because of the dissension which would be raised by the "large number of friends in the army" Longstreet had. "Pickett's men could have gone into battle on the previous evening, when they reached Gettysburg," reasoned a veteran of the 1st Virginia; but, added one of Pettigrew's staffers, since Longstreet "had little heart for the second day's fight," it was not surprising that "he had none at all for the third day's; and to this cause, without seeking any other, may be traced its failure."[12]

Longstreet only fouled his own nest when he tried to defend his disagreement with Lee. "Never was I so depressed as upon that day," he wrote in 1876. "I felt that my men were to be sacrificed, and that I should have to order them to make a hopeless charge." People who were happy to take him at his word converted that admission into prima facie evidence that Longstreet had delayed the attack as long as he dared, somehow hoping that it could be canceled. Hence, by failing to move on Lee's schedule, and coordinate his attack with a renewed assault on Culp's Hill, Longstreet had thrown away the best chance for its success.

But if Longstreet was somehow in violation of Lee's wishes, Lee certainly showed no evidence of it at the time. Men up and down the line saw "Gens. Lee and Longstreet on foot, no aids, orderlies or couriers, fifteen or twenty steps apart, field glasses in hand . . . stopping now and then to take observations . . . arranging, as we soon found out, for the famous charge of Pickett's division"—and all without any sign of impatience or bad feeling. Others saw "Gen'l Lee and Col. W. H. Taylor" ride "near our lines" and "spread out a map on a stump and were looking over it when Gen'l Longstreet joined them and . . . appeared to be holding a council of war as they had sentinels thrown around the group of officers."

Longstreet might have been reluctant to initiate an attack on July 3rd, but that is far from being the same thing as deliberately refusing to implement it. "It is all wrong," he told the chief of Hood's division artillery, "but we will have [to do] it." Longstreet frankly told Lee that "his command would do what any body of men on earth dared do," even if it was still true that "no troops could dislodge the enemy from their strong position." In fact, what impressed Porter Alexander was the care with which Longstreet gave orders for the preliminary artillery bombardment. "It was not meant simply to make a noise, but to try & cripple" the opposing Federal artillery, "to tear him limbless, as it were." And only if we fly in the face of repeated testimony which puts the arrival of Pickett's division well after sunup on the 3rd can we imagine that it was James Longstreet who made an early morning attack out of the question.[13]

This does not necessarily mean that Longstreet's objections were correct, or that some kind of extended flanking movement would necessarily have succeeded. In retrospect, the kind of head-down, full-in-front attack which became Pickett's Charge wears all the appearance of folly that over-the-top assaults acquired on the Western Front half a century later. But 1863 was closer on the clock of war technology to Waterloo than the Somme, and even though Robert E. Lee was not a man to offer arcane precedents from military history to justify the straight-on frontal infantry attack, he had several lying easily to hand over the previous decade. At the Alma in September 1854, Lord Raglan sent forward four divisions of infantry, numbering about 20,000 men, in an enormous double line of battle two miles long. They were compelled to attack across 4,000 yards of uneven terrain, including the knee-deep moat formed by the sluggish river Alma, ascend the steep slopes of Kourgan Hill and Telegraph Hill, drive off 14,000 Russian infantry on the top, and capture a series of "earthwork batteries, containing 24 and 32-pounders . . . supported by field-pieces and howitzers." It cost Raglan 353 dead and 1,612 wounded out of his attacking force, but the Russians were not only driven back, but driven away in "such a confusion as no person ever saw." The same tactics had won the day for the French at Magenta and Solferino in 1859, to the point where the defeated Austrians dropped rifle training from their drill regimen and concentrated on *stosstaktik*—storming forward with the bayonet. If Lee needed a rationale for the attack on July 3rd, he did not have far to look for it, Longstreet's objections notwithstanding.[14]

The one significant difference from the Alma and Solferino was the artillery bombardment Lee wished to hurl as the overture to the attack. The purpose of a preliminary artillery bombardment, at Gettysburg as it had been at Waterloo, was to silence enemy artillery, to "try & cripple" it. Silencing the enemy's artillery was so important at Waterloo because Napoleon proposed to make his final grand attack there in column, and needed to close down the British artillery so that they would not make havoc of the large blocks of French attackers. His nephew, Napoleon III, proposed doing much the same thing at Solferino in 1859 when he used a concentrated grand battery to soften up the Austrian center, prior to a headlong infantry assault. "No column could withstand a well-directed fire of shrapnel shells for twenty minutes," was the dictum born of British experience. "It would have to deploy." The only alternative was to smother the defenders' artillery.[15]

But Raglan's attack at the Alma dispensed with any artillery bombardment, for the simple reason that he intended to advance in line of battle from the start. Just as an advance in line was slower than a swiftly moving column, it also presented a much thinner and more modest target for artillery to disrupt at long range (with shell) or medium range (with solid shot). There is no surviving evidence whether Lee expressed a tactical preference for the shape of Longstreet's attack, and it would have been unlike him in any event to have reached that far down into what were, after all, Longstreet's prerogatives as a corps commander. But Lee's insistence on a bombardment massive enough to tear the Yankee artillery "limbless" does raise the interesting question of whether Lee intended not only to make an attack in *stosstaktic* style, but in column. For why else would such a bombardment be necessary, especially when (as Alexander was already beginning to realize) the ammunition supplies for the artillery were dangerously low after two days of battle? This may not be the image of Pickett's Charge which finally emerged on the pages of many of the histories of Gettysburg, but it would place Robert E. Lee in some very good nineteenth-century company.

It was only when Henry Slocum and Alpheus Williams returned to Culp's Hill after Meade's war council that they learned how much advantage the Confederates had taken of the 12th Corps' absence. "We had heard none of the tumult of Ewell's attack," wrote a captain in Slocum's command; when they began fumbling their way back to their "old position on the right," many of them found their positions on the south peak of Culp's Hill occupied by Confederates from Allegheny Johnson's division. In the darkness, Slocum's men imagined that these occupiers were somehow Pap Greene's men. "They mistook each other for friends" and "mingled and talked freely," until some remark revealed that they were not among friends at all. A Connecticut soldier thought he was conveying welcome information when he shouted to a shadowy figure, "The Rebs have caught Hail Columbia on the left." The figure erupted, "Hell! These are Yanks!" and "a general mêlée took place." There was a spring at the base of the south peak of Culp's Hill known as Spangler's Spring, from the farmer on whose property it sat, and a detail was sent out from the 46th Pennsylvania to fill up canteens. They collided with Confederates "also there filling their canteens," but the captain in charge of the detail could not convince the colonel of the regiment that these were really Confederates. The 123rd New York was ready to shuffle back into its place between the two peaks of Culp's Hill when it was greeted with a who-goes-there. "Come on, it's all right," called out a lieutenant on the skirmish line, and walked right into the arms of the rebels.

This surprise was aggravated by a smarting sense of resentment, especially in units which had spent some time and effort imitating Pap Greene and building up little entrenchments. "It was exasperating to see them benefiting by our labors," although the men of the 3rd Wisconsin "were somewhat consoled by the capture of a picket of twenty Confederates." Little firefights broke out as other 12th Corps regiments blundered into Confederate squatters, and presently "orders were at once issued for" Geary to get his division back up to the north peak of Culp's Hill, while Slocum's other division, under Williams and Thomas Ruger, was readied for "an attack at daybreak" to take back control of the south peak.[16]

By first light, Slocum and Williams had not only repositioned Greene's brigade and Geary's division, and gotten three brigades drawn up in the open fields between the Baltimore Pike and the lower peak, but had planted two of the 12th Corps' batteries on a small rise beside the Baltimore Pike, "within 600 to 800 yards of the woods" on the lower peak that the men of Steuart and Allegheny Johnson occupied. Together with the last-ditch batteries planted on Powers Hill, Williams could hit the Confederates with twenty-six guns, and he confidently predicted that "from these hills back of us we will shell hell out of them." The light strengthened in the east, accompanied by "the jostle of soldiers, followed by the clatter of canteens and other utensils . . . in addition to that of their arms as these clashed together in the efforts of the men to get into ranks." Pap Greene's brigade, "now pretty well exhausted with constant fighting," and their rifles "foul from constant use," were relieved by Geary's brigades and other portions of the 1st Corps sent over by James Wadsworth from the saddle joining Culp's Hill and east Cemetery Hill. Greene's grateful New Yorkers fell back "to the foot of the hill, replenished their [cartridge] boxes, cleaned their guns and got their coffee."[17]

Finally, the sun rose, dull and indifferent behind the translucent clouds, and the artillery Alpheus Williams had so carefully assembled broke out in a chorus of crashes, aimed at "Johnson's troops, who were within the cover of the woods." Skirmish fire on both sides spurted, and after fifteen minutes of shelling, the six regiments of Archibald MacDougall's brigade "pressed forward" to clear the Confederates out of their precarious lodgment on the south peak. For their part, the Confederates had not exactly been inert during the night. Dick Ewell was convinced that Robert Rodes had mishandled his role in what was supposed to be a joint attack on Cemetery Hill with Jubal Early, an attack which "had it been otherwise, I have every reason to believe . . . that the enemy's lines would have been carried." If Rodes did not know how to use his division properly, Ewell did, and under cover of darkness he transferred two of Rodes' brigades around the semicircle of Cemetery Hill and planted them on the right of Allegheny Johnson's division. For good measure, Ewell added Jubal Early's reserve brigade under Extra Billy Smith. "At daylight Friday morning," Ewell received orders from Lee "to renew my attack." But "before the time fixed for General Johnson to advance," Ewell wrote, "the enemy attacked him, to regain the works captured by [Maryland] Steuart the evening before." Or, as Johnson himself snorted, "the enemy had saved him the trouble of deciding whether to attack."[18]

The Confederates slowly worked their way up the rock-pitted slopes of both peaks, the firing becoming "close and deadly, while the echoing of the woods increased the appalling roar." It was "almost continuous, at times tremendous," and even in the town the family of Michael Jacobs, huddled in their cellar on Middle Street, thought "the noise of the musketry fire from that point as it reached the house was actually deafening." Louis Léon found himself firing his rifle so often that "my gun became so hot that the ramrod would not come out, so I shot it at the Yankees." He wondered afterward "if it hit a yankee; if so, I pity him." Up on the north peak, a soldier in the 28th Pennsylvania had a similar experience: "We were in action 3 hours, during which time I fired 65 rounds of Amunition . . . more than I have used in any battle. I often had to wait for my rifel to cool, ramming home the ball with a stone." The rain of bullets was so heavy that trees were "shot off about breast high" and "came tumbling down," and a soldier in the 78th New York was startled to find "hundreds of small birds" landing "among the men in the firing line, as if for protection, often lighting upon their shoulders."[19]

But Pappy Greene and John Geary ("dressed in an old blouse, with few of the outward appearances of a general") calmly cycled regiments in and out of the earthworks Greene had dug the day before, giving their men time "to secure ammunition, clean pieces, etc." Altogether, Johnson launched four attacks at Culp's Hill that morning; each time, they were beaten back, only to "retire a short distance to form again." At 10:25, a third wave of attackers came up the slope against Geary's division, charging in "with the usual yell in closed column in mass" in a solid block of companies only "a pace apart." This accomplished no more than the first two attacks, and a single volley, delivered "within seventy paces," shook "the entire column," and it broke to the rear.[20]

On the left of the 5th Ohio, a sergeant noticed something he had not expected: "An American citizen of African descent had taken position, and with a gun and cartridge box, which he took from one of our dead men, was more than piling hot lead into the Graybacks." There is no way of knowing whether this solitary black fighter was a civilian teamster who decided to join the Ohioans or a refugee from the town who had come out of hiding to do his bit (or even a member of the Adams County company that had tried, unsuccessfully, to volunteer itself to the new all-black 54th Massachusetts). He was certainly not a soldier, since none of the new black regiments recruited since the issue of the Emancipation Proclamation were attached to the Army of the Potomac. Whoever he was, he is the only African American on record as a combatant fighting at Gettysburg. "His coolness and bravery was noticed and commented upon by all who saw him," and the Ohio sergeant who described him thought that "if the negro regiments fight like he did, I don't wonder that the Rebs . . . hate them so."[21]

The odds were mounting against Allegheny Johnson. By eleven o'clock, Slocum was getting reinforcements from a new source. John Sedgwick's 6th Corps finally arrived in force during the evening of July 2nd, and though George Meade's original notion had been to put them into the line along Cemetery Ridge, the position Dan Sickles was originally supposed to occupy, Sedgwick peeled off two brigades to help Slocum. They arrived in time for the fourth and last attack to come boiling up out of the woods at Geary and Pap Greene, with "two of Johnson's brigades . . . formed in column by regiments," and Maryland Steuart's brigade "started forward to meet death and defeat" against the south peak. Steuart's men did not get far; overtaxed by eight hours of fighting, men "threw themselves upon the ground, and despite the pleadings and curses of their officers refused to go forward." On the north peak, the Confederates actually made it "fairly into our lines." But Pappy Greene's regiments drained the attackers of strength, and "in this last charge" some of them actually "rushed forward with white flags to surrender." Enraged and embarrassed at the surrenders, Allegheny Johnson's adjutant and chief-of-staff, Benjamin Leigh, spurred forward "to prevent this surrender, but was shot down when very near our lines." The 12th Corps was once more "in full possession of its original line," and "Johnson's troops withdrew to Rock Creek, leaving a strong picket line in their front." If Robert E. Lee had expected Ewell to be the other horn on which the Army of the Potomac would be gored on July 3rd, that horn had now been broken off. And once again, the mysterious genie of coordination had eluded him. "We accomplished nothing," wrote a captain in the 53rd Virginia.[22]

As the Confederates faded away into the woods, the one thing which a Union soldier noticed above all others was "the lifeless body of Adjt. Gen. Leigh of Gen. Johnson's staff, as stark in death he had fallen by the side of a dead horse close up to our works." Pappy Greene had the body searched for "papers indicating the troops engaged to our front," and then ordered him given "a soldier's burial in rear of our line, and near the graves of our own officers and men." The trees were stripped of leaves and bark, and the trunks "looked like target boards, and many of them had not space upon them where a man could put his hand and not cover a bullet hole." Even "the ground was covered with flattened bullets, and the rocks were pitted with lead marks."

All through the woods was a littering of over 1,800 rifles, and 500 corpses, "piled up on each other four and five deep." But at least the fighting had "practically ceased," remembered one Union officer, followed by a "period of perfect quiet." Then, breaking the stillness, there came the distant boom of two artillery pieces.[23]

Are you going to do your duty today?

GEORGE GORDON MEADE did not get to sleep much before midnight, but he took the time after his war council broke up to send off a message to be telegraphed to Halleck, confirming that "I shall remain in my present position to-morrow." But exactly what he would do in that position was unclear, even to him. "I am not prepared to say, until better advised of the condition of the army, whether my operations will be of an offensive or defensive character." When he awoke on the morning of the 3rd, Meade dictated an order to William French at Frederick (where French had removed the Harpers Ferry garrison), warning him that the day might end in "our discomfiture and withdrawal," and in that case French should "look to Washington, and throw your force there for its protection." Meade rode toward Culp's Hill, then went on "to various parts of the field, reforming the troops and strengthening their positions." Just before nine o'clock, he dashed off another note to be telegraphed, this time to Margaretta in Philadelphia, assuring her "all well and going on well with this Army" but admitting that "both armies [are] shattered." The Army of the Potomac was in "fine spirits & every one determined to do or die," but the "result remains to be seen." He distributed orders to round up stragglers, collect discarded weapons and equipment, and have everyone equipped "to move at a moment's notice."

But where he might move them to was a mystery. The night before, as the council broke up, Meade warned John Gibbon that any rebel attack the next day would probably fall on his 2nd Corps division, on Cemetery Ridge. "If Lee attacks tomorrow, it will be *in your front*." This puzzled Gibbon, and Meade explained: "Because he has made attacks on both our flanks and failed and if he concludes to try it again, it will be on our centre." But by noon of the 3rd, Meade had changed his mind. He predicted to Winfield Hancock that "the next attack would be made on his right," and he pinpointed the locus of the attack by telling John Cleveland Robinson "that he anticipated an attack on the cemetery by the enemy's forces massed in the town."[1]

Winfield Hancock was up early, too, ordering up shovels, picks, and axes for details to begin creating some crude trenches and "rifle pits." Hancock had the primary responsibility for defending 1,600 yards of territory along the crest of Cemetery Ridge, running from the western face of Cemetery Hill down to the edge of the sprawling farm property of Nicholas Codori. At that moment, he could count on only four brigades of infantry to keep watch. Lined up from right to left, this included the "Harpers Ferry Cowards" (who had spent July 2nd redeeming themselves) and Thomas Smyth's brigade, which had undertaken the burning of the Bliss farm buildings—both brigades comprising what was left of Alex Hays' division. Hays, "persistently riding along his line," ordered his men "to hunt up all abandoned small arms, clean and load them, ready for use." With this added firepower, Hays' two brigades were posted around the small white cottage and barn owned by the black farmer Abraham Bryan.

The other two brigades were the Philadelphia Brigade, commanded by Alexander Webb, and Norman Hall's mixed brigade of two New York regiments (the 42nd and 59th), two Massachusetts (the 19th and 20th), and one Michigan regiment (the 7th). Their position was broken up by a two-and-a-half-foot-high stone boundary wall which jutted far enough ahead of Abraham Bryan's property line to create a hundred-yard-deep angle, protruding westward toward the Emmitsburg Road. One of the Philadelphia regiments—the 71st Pennsylvania—had to be posted half by half along Bryan's line and then along the angle. The Philadelphians had their hands full clearing brush and saplings along the stone wall at the angle in their line; the wall still had wooden rails crossed over the stone to prevent cattle straying, and that, together with the piled-up undergrowth, would provide some added measure of cover. With some thought for what might happen later on, they also collected the scattering of rifles and cartridge boxes left behind by Wright's Georgians. "Almost every man had two to five guns," many of them .69 caliber smoothbore muskets, which the 69th Pennsylvania reloaded as buckshot "putting 12 to the load."[2]

There were also some fragments of William Harrow's brigade (which also belonged to Gibbon) on the line—the 19th Maine, the 15th Massachusetts, the 1st Minnesota—but they had been so badly chewed up the day before that any roll call made them look more like companies than regiments. Hancock could also call on George Stannard and his brigade of Vermonters, who had been moved into position on Hancock's left after stopping Ambrose Wright the evening before. The Vermonters energetically "built such slight breast-works as we could on the crest of the ridge," using "old rails and logs." But they were nine months' volunteers and their enlistments were about to expire, and Hancock did not expect much from them.[3]

Not that the others were in reliable shape. The "Harpers Ferry Brigade" had taken some rough handling from Barksdale's Mississippians, and they lost their commander, George Willard, when an errant shell decapitated him the evening before at the height of his brigade's newfound glory. They were now commanded by Eliakim Sherrill of the 111th New York, and Sherrill had managed to irritate Hancock sufficiently for the short-fused Hancock to put him under arrest. The 20th Massachusetts lost its colonel, Paul Joseph Revere, to a shell fragment on July 2nd; so had the 72nd Pennsylvania in the Philadelphia Brigade. The 69th Pennsylvania was down to 258 men; the 59th New York could count only 137 men. All told, Hancock's four brigades may have had no more than 3,500 infantry in their crooked line. Apart from Stan-nard's Vermonters and the provost guard, there was no other reserve between themselves and the rear of Cemetery Hill or the Baltimore Pike.[4]

As temperatures rose into the upper 80s, "many of the men" created "improvised shelters by inverting their muskets, with the bayonets stuck in the ground . . . to which, by means of the hammers, pieces of shelter tents or blankets were fastened." Then they "lolled, sweltered, and waited under the tropical sun." Samuel Robert, the major of the 72nd Pennsylvania, sat on "one end of a fence-rail . . . passively listening to some jesting remarks about some girls in Philadelphia, made by a sergeant, who was sitting upon the other end of the rails." In the 82nd New York, "the men rested idly in line as they lis-tened to the incessant roll of musketry at Culp's Hill." In the 1st Minnesota, men went "one or two at a time back to the rear, where they were allowed fires and cooking," to get coffee. Once the skirmishing over the Bliss farm was over and the columns of black smoke from its burning billowed skyward, a peculiar quiet settled over the ridge. Out at the Emmitsburg Road, details of skirmishers from the 72nd, 69th, and 106th Pennsylvania formed a skirmish line in the roadbed. The booming to the east, from the struggle for Culp's Hill, petered out around noon, and "a strange hush fell on the battle-field."[5]

John Gibbon was feeling the pangs of hunger. Somewhere, his division staffers had "picked up . . . an old and tough rooster which was prepared for the pot and made into a stew." He invited Hancock over to share whatever the rooster might yield in the way of sustenance, setting up "an old mess chest for a table." Then George Meade, accompanied by John Newton of the 1st Corps and Alf Pleasonton, cantered past, headed toward his headquarters behind the ridge at the Leister cottage. Gibbon may have been overestimating what one rooster could provide, but he urged Meade and the others to join him. Meade at first refused; he had reports coming in and paperwork to oversee. But Gibbon cajoled him, arguing that the makeshift mess table was "in plain sight, that he would be absent but a few minutes." So Meade, who had eaten no breakfast and looked "worn and haggard," relented. "An old cracker box was found which served as a seat for the commander of the Army of the Potomac," and for once the "general feeling was hopeful." Meade stayed only long enough to share "our coffee and stewed rooster," and then rode back to the cottage. But the others stayed "on the ground chatting over the probable events of the day," lighting up cigars, "while the opposing armies waited in deep suspense under the oppressive heat of the July sun."

The men in the ranks were just as hungry as the officers, but without any equivalent access to roosters. What they did have access to was whiskey. Alcohol was, in fact, being ladled out pretty freely in both armies; Richard Garnett and Cadmus Wilcox sat down to a lunch in the shadow of Joseph Sherfy's house with cold mutton and a bottle of whiskey. Porter Alexander was puzzled to find "two lieutenants, of a Miss. Regt.," apparently rifling through the pockets of a dead Confederate officer, only to discover that the officer was the regimental surgeon who was drunk and passed out. Lewis Armistead could be seen "taking out a small flask" before the advance, and a Union prisoner "lying on the ground near General Pickett's headquarters" could not help noticing that Pickett had been fortifying himself with more than encouraging reflections. "In looking at his cheeks and nose, we divined that their color was not caused by drinking sodawater only."[6]

And then, at "about one o'clock," there was a loud bang from what Charles Bane, the adjutant of the Philadelphia Brigade, thought sounded like "a single Whitworth gun . . . fired from the extreme left of Seminary Ridge." Professor Michael Jacobs checked his watch (or was it a mantel clock?) and saw its hands had moved to 1:07 p.m. A soldier in the 82nd New York happened to be looking down toward the peach orchard, and "saw a puff of white smoke . . . darting across the meadow," and shouted, *There she goes!* even before the "sound of the discharge could reach the eager spectators on the Union side." The shell landed a little to Bane's left, among the 19th Massachusetts, where it blew apart a lieutenant who "had leaped to his feet at the sound." Then there was "another stream of thick, white smoke, streaked with flame," and another round which also flew into the midst of the 19th Massachusetts, "striking among the gun stacks of the Nineteenth." And then Adjutant Bane heard "at intervals along the entire line solitary shots were fired" like an engine coughing to life, "and in a few moments there burst forth from the whole Confederate line a most terrific fire of artillery." Michael Jacobs turned to his son, Henry, and could only think of a verse from St. John's apocalypse: *Seven thunders uttered their voices.*[7]

Around noon, James Walton and Porter Alexander reported to Longstreet that "all [was] ready" with the artillery. But all was not ready with Longstreet's infantry. After marching "about 25 miles on the 2d," Pickett's division "bivouacked about four miles from Gettysburg on the Chambersburg turnpike" for the night, and even when they got moving again "at 3 o'clock A. m. to take our position in line of Battle," the entire maneuver was not finished until at least "11 o'clock A. M"—if even by then. (Alexander remembered that as late as noon, he was still waiting to hear whether "Pickett was ready.") In the meanwhile, Longstreet wanted Alexander "to take a position where I could see the field well & take one of Picketts couriers with me, & that I must send Pickett word when to charge." Once the infantry was finally in place, Longstreet would signal Walton to open fire with "all the guns on the line . . . simultaneously," and Walton's own signal to the artillery would be "two guns [fired] in quick succession by the Washington Artillery" at the peach orchard. Alexander's job would be to observe the effect of the artillery bombardment, and once it was clear the batteries of Federal guns on Cemetery Ridge had been silenced, he would send off Pickett's galloper with the signal for the infantry to advance.[8]

Pickett's three brigades moved down the Cashtown Pike, filed off to the southwest on the Knoxlyn Road, and then worked their way across the Fairfield Road—behind the Lutheran seminary, behind the divisions from Hill's corps which would go into action with them—until by eight o'clock they moved into position in a hollow "four hundred yards or so from the top, under the crest" of Seminary Ridge. It was a "shady quiet march," ending under the grateful cover of Henry Spangler's woods, almost due west from Hancock and the 2nd Corps. There, "arms were stacked" and the men fell out "with the understanding that when two signal guns were fired" they would "take arms and lie flat on the ground." Kemper's brigade had the lead on the march in, so the three brigades, when they finally deployed for the attack, would create a front rank of Kemper's and then Garnett's brigade, with Armistead's drawn up a hundred yards behind.

Guiding off Pickett would be Harry Heth's division, "formed in line of battle" and now commanded by Johnston Pettigrew; the four brigades of the division would be lined up with James Archer's thinned brigade (directed by Birkett Fry, since Archer's capture two days before), James Marshall's North Carolina brigade (Marshall having stepped in for Pettigrew as brigade commander), Joe Davis' North Carolinians, and John Mercer Brockenbrough's woebegone Virginia brigade. Drawn up behind them would be two of Dorsey Pender's North Carolina brigades, forming a sort of semi-division, marching (for the time being) under the garrulous Isaac Trimble. Several of these brigades were not in good form: Birkett Fry's brigade was down by 250 men from the 1,200 who had marched so confidently down the Cashtown Pike on July 1st; Joe Davis' 2nd Mississippi had come out of the railroad cut with only 118 men; Pettigrew's own brigade was, likewise, down by almost a thousand from July 1st, and with all the internal administrative disruption this could imply.[9]

Added up on paper, Pettigrew and Trimble would be, at best, able to provide 6,200 men to support Pickett. Pickett himself would be able to count just over 5,000. Almost as an afterthought, Lee decided to let Longstreet use Cadmus Wilcox's well-used brigade, along with Lang's Florida brigade. But after their battering the day before, they would add only another 1,700 men to the attack. There would be around 13,000 men in the attack—if all of them could be gotten to move.[10]

And many of them did not like the prospect of moving once they had seen where they would be going. Cadmus Wilcox formed his brigade just forty yards behind the crest of Seminary Ridge, giving his men a far better vantage point than Pickett's to see ahead, and what they saw set them to "ominous shakes of the head . . . as to the wisdom of such a move." Wilcox rode over to Richard Garnett and muttered "in the hearing of" several officers "that he considered Cemetery Ridge" impossible to take, that he "had lost between 4[00] and 500 men there the day before in some 15 or 20 minutes, without making the slightest impression." Porter Alexander found the observer's perch he needed near Ambrose Wright, and the disgruntled Georgian lost no time in telling Alexander "that the difficulty was not so much in *reaching* Cemetery Hill, or taking it—that his brigade had carried it the afternoon before—but that the trouble was to hold it." In Pettigrew's division, a sergeant in the 14th Tennessee, Junius Kimble, strolled forward to take a look. He saw "an open plain, with a slight incline to the front of Cemetery Ridge . . . with no obstructions . . . except three fences, two worm or rail fences and one slab fence, nearest to the enemy's front." He shivered, and asked "aloud the question, 'June Kimble, are you going to do your duty today?'" Kimble summoned up the resolve to say, "I'll do it, so help me God." But when he returned to the lines of the 14th Tennessee and was asked how things looked, he could only mumble, "Boys, if we have to go, it will be hot for us."[11]

And yet, few of them seem to have seen the task as outright suicide. "Come on, boys," cried one of the 11th Virginia's privates, "let's go and drive away those infernal Yankees." It was plain to Wilcox's Alabamians that "many, very many, would go down under the storm of shot and shell . . . but it never occurred to them that disaster would come" on Cemetery Ridge. James Crocker, a lieutenant in the 9th Virginia and, oddly enough, a graduate of Pennsylvania College, thought that "all fully saw and appreciated the cost and the fearful magnitude of the assault, yet all were firmly resolved, if possible, to pluck victory from the very jaws of death itself." George Pickett, in particular, saw nothing but victory and glory ahead (although privately, he urged Richard Garnett to get his brigade "across those fields as quick as you can, for in my opinion you are going to catch hell"). At least for the benefit of his division, Pickett appeared "entirely sanguine of success, and was doing nothing but congratulating himself on the opportunity."[12]

There were a few last-minute arrangements. Isaac Trimble rode up and down the lines of his two brigades, "halted at different regiments and made us little speeches, saying he was a stranger to us and had been sent to command us in the absence of our wounded general, and would lead us upon Cemetery Hill." Lee, Longstreet, and Powell Hill met in front of Pettigrew's division for a final consultation, and the men in the ranks "voluntarily arose and lifted in reverent adoration their caps to their beloved commander." In the 14th Virginia, one captain marked out three or four men who were "habitual play-outs" and advised the sergeants who would be forming the rear line of file closers "to take them into that fight or kill them" if they had to, and "he would be responsible." Staff officers and couriers "began to move about briskly," wrote Birkett Fry. "General Pettigrew rode up and informed me that after a heavy cannonade we would assault the position in our front," and Fry in turn met with Pickett and then Richard Garnett, who "agreed that he would dress on my command" as "the directing brigade of the line of battle."[13]

Finally, it was done. Longstreet sent off a courier with a handwritten order for James Walton:

Headquarters, in the Field, July 3d, 1863.

Colonel: Let the batteries open. Order great care and precision in firing. If the batteries at the peach orchard cannot be used against the point we intend attacking, let them open upon the rocky hill. Most respectfully,

> *J. Longstreet*, Lieutenant-General Commanding.
> To Colonel *Walton*.

But to Porter Alexander, Longstreet sent a more ambiguous message:

Hd. Qrs., July 3rd, 1863.

Colonel. If the artillery fire does not have the effect to drive off the enemy, or greatly demoralize him, so as to make our efforts pretty certain, I would prefer that you not advise Gen. Pickett to make the charge. I shall rely a great deal on your good judgment to determine the matter & shall expect you to let Gen. Pickett know when the moment offers. Respectfully,

> *J. Longstreet*, Lieutenant-General Commanding.
> To Colonel *Alexander*.

Alexander at once recoiled from this message—not just because it suggested that Longstreet still had enough reservations about the attack to contemplate canceling it, but because it seemed as though Longstreet was saddling *him* with the responsibility for making the call. This was not quite the case: Longstreet was in the habit of giving staffers wide latitude for decision making, and even more so than Robert E. Lee. (Longstreet would do this to extremely good effect a year later in the Wilderness, when he allowed his chief of staff, Moxley Sorrel, to direct the attack that crushed Hancock's 2nd Corps along the Orange Plank Road.) And given Alexander's expertise in artillery matters, this was not an imprudent—much less evasive—delegation. Longstreet would later admit that he had been "unwilling to trust myself with the entire responsibility." But this was less a matter of sloughing the burden onto other shoulders as it was a calculation that Alexander was better fitted "to carefully observe the effect of the fire upon the enemy."

Alexander did not read the message that way. He wrote back, "I will only be able to judge of the effect of our fire on the enemy by his return fire . . . and the smoke will obscure the whole field. If . . . there is any alternative to this attack, it should be carefully considered." But instead of seizing on Alexander's caution, Longstreet brushed hesitation away. "The intention is to advance the infantry if the artillery has the desired effect. . . . When the moment arrives advise General Pickett, and of course advance such artillery as you can use in aiding the attack." That settled the question, and Alexander determined in his own mind that once the artillery barrage began, Pickett would go forward at any hazard. "My mind was fully made up that *if the artillery opened Pickett must charge*." And so he replied to Longstreet, "General: When our artillery fire is doing its best, I shall advise General Pickett to advance."[14]

All of the machinery of the great attack was now in motion. Down at Sherfy's peach orchard, James Walton turned to Benjamin Franklin Eschleman, the major commanding the ten-gun Washington Artillery battalion, and ordered the firing of the two signal guns. The first one, a Napoleon (and not a Whitworth, as the soldier in the 82nd New York thought) from the Washington Artillery's No. 2 Company, "rang out upon the still summer air"; then there was a clumsy pause. The friction primer inserted in the touchhole of the other gun was a dud, and there had to be some fumbling around to pull it out and replace it with one that worked. The second gun was "immediately followed by all the battalions along the line." Over on the other side of the town, a captain in the 14th Virginia Cavalry "heard the big gun—way in the distance—miles to our right." And then, after only a momentary pause, "we heard the firing grow nearer and nearer," as batteries chimed in, one after another, rippling from right to left around the crescent of artillery aimed at Cemetery Hill, "till the whole line was firing." The hill itself became shrouded in "dense smoke . . . which was cleared every now and then, for a Small space, by the explosion of a Caisson that circled through the cloud of smoke."[15]

When the formidable Henry Knox first recommended to George Washington the organization of an artillery arm for the Continental Army in 1776, his notion involved the supply of just 120 pieces for the entire American service (including fortifications), most of which ended up being shipped to America by the French. The battle of Buena Vista was won by Zachary Taylor with the support of only two batteries of artillery, as opposed to the seventeen guns deployed by his Mexican opponent, Santa Anna. Not until the Civil War did American armies begin to make use of large-scale Napoleonic-style artillery forces on the battlefield—the 100 guns used by Napoleon at Wagram, the 94 deployed by the Russians at Inkerman. Even then, at Malvern Hill, the most famous artillery-dominated battle in the war thus far, only 37 Union guns had faced down 16 Confederate ones. Nevertheless, the impact was beyond anything American soldiers had seen before. "The fire from the enemy's artillery was truly terrific," wrote one awed Confederate general. Two and half months later, at Antietam, Stonewall Jackson held off the Federal attack on the West Woods with 40 guns, and Harvey Hill held back Federal attacks in the center with 50, earning Antietam the nickname "Artillery Hell."[16]

But in all of this, there was nothing to match the stupendous concentration of artillery which James Walton and Porter Alexander had arranged for Longstreet on July 3rd. It would be, in fact, the single loudest sound ever heard on the North American continent. "The noise and din were so furious and overwhelming as well as continuous that one had to scream to his neighbor lying beside him to be heard at all," wrote one of Wilcox's Alabamians. "Men could be seen, especially among the artillery, bleeding at both ears from concussion." Ten miles to the southwest, at Jack's Mountain, a signal officer could see "hundreds of shells" bursting, and even as far away as Hagerstown, "we could distinctly hear the cannonading." In York, "the roar of artillery" was "heard distinctly . . . at times rapid and heavy." In Lancaster, "persons who had arrived there from McCall's Ferry, Peach Bottom and Safe Harbor" on the Susquehanna "report a continuous cannonade audible at all these points . . . from the direction of Gettysburg." One hundred and twenty miles away, farmers in Cecil County, Maryland, and Chester County, near Philadelphia, "looked up to the sky in puzzlement for the source of thunder on a cloudless day."[17]

The sheer noise of the first ripple of fire along the massed line of Confederate batteries, followed by the unremitting blasts of fire from two miles' worth of artillery, beggared description. Hidden in his family's cellar on Baltimore Street, "the vibrations could be felt" by young Albertus McCreary, "and the atmosphere was so full of smoke that we could taste the saltpeter." Behind the Confederate lines, teamsters parked "two or three miles away, declared that the sashes in the windows of buildings where they were shook and chattered as if shaken by a violent wind." At the far end of the Confederate line, a Texan in Hood's division thought it was like being "an eagle in the very midst of a tremendous thunderstorm," and compared it to "Milton's account of the great battle between the combined forces of good and evil."

> *Now storming fury rose,*
> *And clamour such as heard in Heaven till now*
> *Was never; . . .*
>   *. . . dire was the noise*
> *Of conflict; over head the dismal hiss*
> *Of fiery darts in flaming vollies flew,*
> *And flying vaulted either host with fire.*
> [Paradise Lost, Book VI]

Both the detonations of the guns and the crack of exploding shell overhead "joined in one demonic chorus" composed of "the crash of the bursting spherical case, the howl of the [rifle]-shell" and the "wicked hiss of the solid Whitworth." Charles Bane in the Philadelphia Brigade also noticed the bazaar of sounds. He could distinguish "the shrieking of shells or the heavy thud of round shot . . . from the rotary whizzing of the Whitworth bolt." George Benedict, in Stannard's Vermont brigade, listened as "spherical case exploded over our heads and rained iron bullets upon us; the Whitworth solid shot, easily distinguished by their clear musical ring, flew singing by . . . and round shot ploughed up the ground."[18]

Or if it was not the noise, it was the incessant concussions and the damage that rippled outward from them. "It seemed an earthquake would not have caused the foundations to tremble as did the fire of those . . . pieces of artillery," marveled one Confederate. A soldier in the 1st Minnesota felt solid shot "strike the ground in front of us and . . . go on their way growling in an anger too terrible for conception." So unnerving was the shaking of the ground that "loose grass, leaves and twigs arose from six to eight inches above the ground." Soldiers anywhere near trees saw "the iron tempest" sheer off "branches large and small" and "strewed the ground with fragments, and placed us in great danger even from falling limbs." One Federal artillery officer described it as a "deluge of limbs falling from tree tops."

Abraham Bryan had planted shade trees around his whitewashed cottage on Cemetery Hill, and Bryan's neighbor, David Zeigler, had planted an orchard on the west side of Cemetery Hill, beside Bryan's property. But now the Confederate artillery tore "large limbs . . . from the trunks . . . and precipitated [them] down upon our heads. . . . Small trees were cut down and large ones shattered almost to pieces." Or if not tree limbs, then pieces of fence or housing. A solid shot struck Bryan's barn and whirled a board through the air, hitting a captain in the 111th New York. A Federal artilleryman on Cemetery Ridge even caught a glimpse of the wheat fields beyond the Emmitsburg Road moving in waves as the unending blasts of the artillery blew it "like gusts of wind."[19]

Given the low muzzle velocities of Civil War artillery, some Union soldiers discovered that "if you rolled on your back and looked up into the heavens," it was possible to pick out solid shot and shell as they sailed overhead, and in the 12th New Jersey several men kept track of multiple lines of flying projectiles. "We turn on our backs, look up and trace the course of the shells; we could see a dark line flit across overhead and others cross this towards every point of the compass." Or else, also flying through the air, men could see their rifle stacks being knocked into carousels. "So thick did the missiles fly that in a few moments nearly all the inverted muskets were knocked down or shot off," and "pieces of shell were plainly visible as they hissed by."[20]

Near the Leister cottage, "two shells in every second fell around" George Meade's headquarters. Shells blew off the doorsteps, knocked down the front door, cut off "the legs of a chair in which a staff officer was seated," and crashed into the loft under the roof. The line of staffers' horses tied up to the fence palings outside was particularly hard hit. "A dozen of the frightened animals fell by rebel projectiles, and others broke away and fled in the wildest fright towards the rear." They were joined in an undignified stampede by "hospital attaches, camp followers" and even a few "citizens" who had evaded army picket lines to catch a glimpse of the commanding general. "In a few minutes the Taneytown Road in our rear was filled" with them, as "shells were screaming and bursting everywhere."[21]

Meade took it all with stoic indifference; people may not have liked

Meade's brimstone manner, but no one could gainsay the man's marvelous contempt for physical danger. Noticing in passing that his staffers "were gradually, and probably unconsciously, edging around to the lee side of the house," Meade was withering: "Gentlemen," he asked, "are you trying to find a safe place?" They reminded him, he said, of the teamster on "the field of Palo Alto" who hid under an ammunition wagon, and when old Zachary Taylor upbraided him for sheltering under cover that was more dangerous than the enemy's fire, the man pleaded that he knew it wasn't safer, "but it kind o' feels so." Nevertheless, in short order, both Meade and chief of staff Dan Butterfield were grazed by pieces of flying ordnance, and Meade ordered the cottage abandoned. He took himself first, with only one aide, to Cemetery Hill, where he had told John Robinson to expect a Confederate attack to come, and went from battery to battery to emphasize "to our officers that this point must be held at all hazards." He then took off down the Baltimore Pike toward Powers Hill. There, of course, was where he had parked the artillery he would use if he had to cover a retreat. If this bombardment indeed presaged Robert E. Lee's final hammer blow, Meade wanted to be in a position to supervise the evacuation of as much of his army as possible.[22]

The soldiers along the line of Cemetery Ridge had no similar options. They instinctively dove to earth, "hugging the ground very closely," ground that "we would like to get into it if we could." A few men in the 108th New York, "shook up by the explosion of the shells," tried to bolt to the rear, only to be hunted down and prodded back into line by vigilant lieutenants. When one of the 3-inch Ordnance Rifles in Alonzo Cushing's battery had a wheel damaged, Cushing saw a sergeant head to the rear, explaining that he meant to retrieve the spare wheel usually carried on the gun's caisson. Cushing drew his revolver. "Sergeant Whetstone, come back to your post. The first man who leaves his post again, I'll blow his brains out!" Even George Meade pushed men back. Riding along the Baltimore Pike, Meade was passed by an Ohio battery, and when Meade asked "the capt what he was leaving for," he was told that the battery was "out of Ammunition." All you need to do to replenish your ammunition, Meade glowered back, was to send your caissons back "as there was plenty in the Train." Meade treated him to "some little advice . . . giving him to understand that he would look into his case another time."[23]

Some men tried to brass it out. Alexander Webb of the Philadelphia Brigade stood "in the most conspicuous and exposed place, leaning on his sword and smoking a cigar, when all around the air was pierced by screeching shot and shell," standing "like a statue watching the movement of the enemy." John Gibbon also decided to put a little insouciance up for show, walking down the line of his division as if he was unaware of any danger, asking the men how they were holding up, and getting snarky answers: "O, this is bully," "We are getting to like it," "O, we don't mind this." Alex Hays, who "always seemed happiest when in the thickest of the fight," never dismounted, and rode through his division without the Confederate artillery seeming "to intimidate him in the least." (At the other extreme, Wheelock Veazey, the colonel of the 16th Vermont, was puzzled to see men fall into the peculiar narcolepsy caused by artillery bombardment, as "I think a majority, fell asleep.") Somewhere, a band struck up "The Star-Spangled Banner," and Winfield Hancock decided to one-up both Hays and Gibbon by riding, mounted on a borrowed light bay and accompanied only by three staffers and an orderly, John Wells, from left to right across the front of the 2nd Corps.[24]

But bravado was not insurance. Otis Howard remembered "a young artilleryman" who managed to sing and whistle, while keeping his battery's horses from shying or bolting under the bombardment. "Just as I was remarking him for his heartiness and lovely conduct, a solid shot struck him on his thigh; he gave one sharp cry and was no more." Up on Cemetery Hill, "there was plenty of dead men and horses strewing the ground," along with "guns and caissons knocked into a cocked hat." Theodore Gates saw a solid shot kill a man who "flopped over like a pancake and never moved a muscle—was stone dead." The bombardment caught a 6th Corps regiment, the 37th Massachusetts, while it was in column, shifting to a new position, and "tore terrible, bleeding gaps" through the close-packed men, killing and wounding thirty-one. One shell burst so near James Barnes, at the head of his 5th Corps division, that Barnes was wounded in the leg and one of his staffers "had his face filled with powder."[25]

Still, anyone who had the presence of mind to notice could see that the number of infantry casualties being inflicted by the bombardment was surprisingly small. (The British had discovered this same thing at the Alma: "Our young soldiers found themselves, as they imagined, in a thick storm of shot and cannon-balls; but it seems that missiles of war fly crashing so audibly through foliage that they sound more dangerous than they are.") The 69th Pennsylvania suffered one killed and sixteen wounded; their comrades in the rest of the Philadelphia Brigade lost another thirty. One of the Vermont regiments reported a loss of "about sixty men while lying there"; the 7th Michigan, in Norman Hall's brigade, simply noted that "not as much damage was done us as would naturally be expected from such a storm of missiles."

On the other hand, it was not the infantry which was Walton's and Alexander's target. "Their fire was directed at our batteries," observed an infantryman in the 1st Minnesota; "not a single shell dropped in this regiment." And the batteries, as Gibbon's aide Frank Haskell could see, "had been handled much more severely." Horses were killed, "in some batteries more than half of all." In front of Norman Hall's brigade, five horses and their drivers in

James Rorty's New York battery went down, caissons burst, and soon the battery was reduced to two guns, then one. To the right, Hall could see three of Cushing's limbers blown up, while "horses, men and [gun] carriages were piled together" and the battery was reduced to two serviceable guns. Within an hour, four of the five batteries along the 2nd Corps line were completely, or almost completely, out of action. And if the Confederates had shifted their targets to include the batteries on Cemetery Hill, "there would not have been a live thing on that hill fifteen minutes after they opened fire."[26]

The instinct of every gunner was to return fire, and after fifteen minutes, as the Federal batteries cleared for action, "we . . . worked our guns on the enemy as lively as we could." On Cemetery Hill, guns were slewed around "by hand to the front" to face westward toward Seminary Ridge, and as soon as one barrel became too hot to "use it any longer . . . we run and got another gun and rolled it up in position and fired that until it was impossible to bear our hand on it." They certainly gave as good as they had gotten. After a few ranging shots "flew harmlessly over our heads," one of the Confederate gunners in the peach orchard saw "the entire front of Cemetery Ridge . . . light up in a blaze. . . . The tops of the trees near us were cut off, limbs broken, and the leaves fairly covered us." A Confederate limber was struck by a shell, and shot "a thick, hot, white ring . . . straight up into the air," so that "shapeless fragments of wood and iron were hurled high above the trees and fell on all sides in an irregular shower."[27]

In Pickett's division, the major of the 8th Virginia saw a shell take "off the head of Sergt. Morris of my brother tom's Co. & plaistered his brains over my hat." Another shell wounded the colonel of the 53rd Virginia, William Aylett, and the colonel of the 3rd Virginia was struck by a "handful of earth mixed with blood and brains" which had, a moment before, belonged to "two poor fellows," and seriously wounded the sergeant major of the neighboring 7th Virginia. That sergeant major, David Johnston, survived fractured ribs, a "badly contused" left lung, and paralysis down his left side, and years later described Pickett's division as sort of a grotesque shooting gallery in which "at almost every moment muskets, swords, haversacks, human flesh and bones flying and dangling in the air or bouncing above the earth, which now trembled as if shaken by an earthquake." The incessant discharging, blasting, cracking, and pounding created its own miniature weather system, and a soldier in the 16th Mississippi was amazed to see that "birds, attempting to fly, tumbled and fell to the ground."[28]

Still, sangfroid was the rule on the Confederate side as much as on the Union one. One of the artillerymen heard a voice, "when the artillery fire was at its height," singing a parody of Elizabeth Allen's sentimental "Rock Me to Sleep" from the summer of 1860:

> *Backward, roll backward, O Time in thy flight:*
> *Make me a child again, just for this fight!*

Another voice irreverently interrupted: "Yes; and a *gal* child at that." James Kemper was astonished to see Longstreet nonchalantly riding down the front of Pickett's division, "slowly and majestically, with an inspiring confidence, composure, self-possession and repressed power." In the 56th Virginia, however, the men in the regiment were less impressed by Longstreet's bravado and more concerned about the likelihood that he would attract the unwelcome attention of Federal gunners to their position. "You'll get your old fool head knocked off," they shouted unceremoniously. "We'll fight without you leading us."[29]

And yet, like the Confederate artillery, the sound and fury of the Union guns signified comparatively little, once the dust settled. In Joe Davis' North Carolina brigade, "the fire was heavy and incessant," but at the end, the final bill was "2 men killed and 21 wounded." In Pickett's division, the 8th Virginia's colonel, Eppa Hunton, counted 5 dead out the 205 men he had ready for the attack; Randolph Shotwell, also from the 8th Virginia, estimated that in the entire division Pickett may have lost between 350 and 500 men killed and wounded, certainly not nearly enough to prevent Pickett's division from making its attack. And there might not have even been that many, if Henry Hunt, Meade's chief of artillery, had been able to get his way.[30]

The opening of the Confederate bombardment at one o'clock caught Hunt on Little Round Top, in the midst of "an inspection of the whole line." Hunt guessed with cool accuracy what the Confederates were up to. From Cemetery Ridge, he could see "batteries already in line or going into position" from Sherfy's peach orchard all the way up to the outskirts of Gettysburg itself. At each point, Hunt had "instructed the chiefs of artillery and battery commanders" to wait for the Confederates to act first, and if they had to open fire at all, to "concentrate . . . with all possible accuracy on those batteries which were most destructive to us." By one o'clock, Hunt had worked his way down to Benjamin Rittenhouse, who had succeeded to command of Hazlett's battery of 10-pounder Parrotts on Little Round Top. There, Hunt remarked that he had been observing a lot of Confederate artillery activity "opposite our centre and left," along Seminary Ridge, and that he was sure they "were getting ready for a charge on our centre."

That attack, however, would begin "with their artillery," and Hunt wanted Rittenhouse to understand that he would not tolerate any yielding to the usual artilleryman's temptation to fire back and turn things into a useless artillery duel. Hunt repeated for Rittenhouse the same orders he had given the others: "not to return their fire, but to reserve my ammunition for the charge." If they must return fire, do it "deliberately and slowly as at target practice," and that would save "at least half our ammunition . . . to meet the assault when it came." Once the "furious cannonade" opened up, Hunt estimated that he was seeing "one hundred to one hundred and twenty guns . . . bearing on our west front," and he took himself off to what was left of the by-now-depleted artillery reserve, and ordered the reserve chief, Robert Tyler, to get the four remaining batteries of the reserve limbered up and moving to the front.[31]

Convinced that the barrage would certainly be followed by an infantry assault, Hunt rode up behind Freeman McGilvery's gun line, still parked across the gap made by the collapse of the 3rd Corps the day before, and kept urging them to reply slowly, "so that when the enemy's ammunition was exhausted, we should have sufficient left to meet the assault." He worked northward, up the ridgeline, noticing the "infantry . . . lying down on its reverse slope, near the crest, in open ranks." He was pleased to find the 2nd Corps batteries obeying his advice to keep their fire "deliberate." But a quick check of the limbers showed Hunt that "the ammunition was running low," and since Meade had left the Leister cottage for parts unknown to Hunt, the schoolmasterish artilleryman "rode back along the ridge, ordering the fire to cease." A half-hour after leaving Little Round Top, Hunt returned to McGilvery's batteries with the same orders.

However much satisfaction this gave to Henry Hunt, it gave none whatever to Winfield Hancock. Infantry can, with training and experience, put up with a great many things whirling dangerously around them in battle, but one thing most likely to break the patience, and worse, of the infantryman is to sit or lie, cowering in trenches or rifle pits, under the dropping fire of artillery, and with no effective way of responding. "The inward prayer of every one of us," wrote a soldier in the 43rd Massachusetts, "would have been, 'For God's sake give us something to do!' The suspense of such moments is terrible, and each moment seems an age." It was still worse for the nineteenth-century infantryman, whose artillery was often within a pebble's throw of his own position; no infantryman pretended to understand if his own guns were making little or no attempt to return fire. The odds of an artillery duel actually doing anything to relieve the pressure of the enemy's bombardment were nugatory, but at least it gave the sense of someone striking back on their behalf.[32]

Oddly, it was usually infantry *officers* who wanted the guns to keep quiet, in hope of offering enemy artillery less incentive for heaving explosives at their heads, and artillery officers who were the most eager to have them speak. Hunt and Hancock now reversed those roles, as Hancock noticed that "the batteries of his own corps did not reply." This touched off an immediate fury in Hancock, who ordered his corps artillery chief, Capt. John Hazard, to get to work. The confused Hazard replied that he had only just been ordered by General Hunt to slack off firing, but Hancock was hearing nothing of it and "compelled a rapid reply to the enemy." It galled Hancock even more to notice that, just a few hundred yards to the left, Freeman McGilvery's gun line had fallen silent. Hancock "came riding up to him in hot haste" and demanded to know "why in hell do you not open fire with those Batteries." His men were taking a pounding in silence, and "unless our Batteries opened fire his troops would not stand it much longer."

Hancock might be able to order his own corps artillery around as he pleased, but McGilvery's eight batteries belonged to the artillery reserve, and McGilvery had just received orders to stand down from the army's chief of artillery. He felt no obligation to listen to "some general commanding." This brought a red-hot stream of "language . . . profane and blasphemous such as a drunken Ruffian would use" from Hancock. But McGilvery, the "cool, clear-headed old sailor," was probably not the best choice for profanity practice. He tartly informed Hancock that "he was not under Gen. Hancock's orders, and . . . I could not see why the Second Corps could not stand the fire as well as the other troops, or as well as my gunners." Hancock, he added with an impudent twist, "seemed unnecessarily excited, was unduly emphatic and . . . his orders would result in a most dangerous and irreplaceable waste of ammunition."[33]

A great deal of Hancock's impatience, unlike Hunt's, grew from uncertainty over just what the Confederate bombardment meant. George Meade was still expecting an attack "from the town" on Cemetery Hill, and along the line of the Philadelphia Brigade, Alexander Webb became convinced that the barrage meant that "the Confederate infantry will not advance and attack our position." Even Henry Hunt at first mistook the Confederate artillery deployment as a ruse "to replace infantry sent to Ewell's assistance, or perhaps simply to strengthen their line against a counter attack from us." At one point during the barrage, Hancock dispatched his aide William Mitchell to John Gibbon to ask "what I thought the meaning of this terrific fire" might be. Gibbon himself was not sure. "I replied I thought it was the prelude either to a retreat or an assault." Neither of them, however, remained long in doubt. Gibbon walked back from the front of his division line at the angle of the stone wall, "the men peering at us curiously from behind the stone wall as we passed along," and then behind the crest of Cemetery Ridge. Suddenly, "the fire on both sides . . . considerably slackened," and a division staffer and an orderly, leading Gibbon's horse, "met me with the information that the enemy was coming in force."[34]

The shadow of a cloud across a sunny field

U SUALLY A CANNONADE against an infantry line can be but for one purpose only—to disturb and rattle the infantry so that their lines may be the easier penetrated," wrote Union veteran Robert Beecham. But in the case of the Confederate bombardment that afternoon, Robert E. Lee's specific purpose for "Longstreet and his batteries" was to "silence those of the enemy." In particular, James Walton had targeted the batteries he had seen grouped behind Hancock's four brigades between Cemetery Hill and the "clump of trees" on the ridge. The trees were pointed out "as the proposed point" of Pickett's attack and the damage Walton's guns caused among the Union batteries around those trees was considerable: four of Alonzo Cushing's guns "had been struck by solid shot and dismounted"; Fred Brown's Rhode Island battery had already lost two pieces the day before, and now lost another and had to be pulled off the line. George Woodruff's battery had exhausted all its shell and shrapnel, and was wheeled back into an orchard on the western face of Cemetery Hill owned by David Zeigler to present less of a target. It was the task of Porter Alexander to observe the effect, judge the right moment to begin the infantry attack, and send the go-ahead word to Pickett; and from Alexander's perspective, the artillery had accomplished almost exactly what Longstreet had asked of it.[1]

But it still took much longer than Alexander had anticipated. "I had not the ammunition to make it a long business," Alexander wrote years afterward, and he calculated that the Confederate artillery could hit the Federals pretty hard for about twenty minutes. That would see each of the Confederate guns firing about ten times if managed "carefully," and would do no serious harm to the remaining supply of ammunition; at worst, if the gunners got too hurried, they might fire off as much as thirty rounds, "& ammunition burns up very fast in an affair like that." The minutes ticked by, and Alexander saw that the Confederate batteries weren't silencing much of anything along the Union line, and that "it seemed madness to launch infantry into that fire . . . at midday under a July sun." Pickett began sending couriers, demanding to know when he could advance, and Alexander kept putting them off, until, in exasperation, he wrote an irritated note to Pickett: "If you are coming at all, you must come at once, or I cannot give you proper support; but the enemy's fire has not slackened at all; at least eighteen guns are still firing from the cemetery itself." Which was as much as saying, *Don't.*[2]

And then, to Alexander's amazement, "the enemy's fire suddenly began to slacken," and, what was more, he could see Federal batteries along the ridge limbering up and disappearing. "We Confederates often did such things as that to save our ammunition," Alexander wrote, "but I had never before seen the federals withdraw their guns simply to save them up for the infantry's fight." He waited another five minutes to be sure, thinking that if the Yankees do "not run fresh batteries in there in five minutes, this is our fight." Then he decided: "For God's sake, come quick," he scribbled in a note to Pickett. "The eighteen guns are gone; come quickly, or my ammunition won't let me support you properly."[3]

What Alexander did not realize was that the slacking off of the Federal artillery fire was only partly due to the suppressing fire of the Confederate batteries; it was also Henry Hunt's device to "save up" his artillery elsewhere along the Union line "for the infantry's fight." Nor did Alexander realize that the batteries he had seen being pulled away were to be replaced at once by a pair of batteries from the artillery reserve—Andrew Cowan's 1st New York Independent Battery and Gulian Weir's Battery C, 5th U.S.—which were already waiting on the reverse slope of Cemetery Ridge to be waved into position. But Pickett was relieved at last to have something to do, and showed Alexander's note to Longstreet, whom he presumed would be similarly pleased. He wasn't. Without meeting Pickett's gaze, Longstreet merely nodded his head. Unsure how to interpret Longstreet's glum silence, Pickett fell back on the orders he had been given earlier. "I am going to move forward, sir," and off he galloped.

Longstreet, still nursing doubts, "mounted and spurred to Alexander's post" to ask if he was certain. Not entirely, Alexander replied: the bombardment had gone on far longer than he had expected, about forty-five minutes, and that had surely drained the ammunition reserve. Longstreet seized on that caveat: "Stop Pickett immediately and replenish your ammunition." No,

Alexander, replied, that would take too long and give the Federals a chance to reinforce the line Alexander believed had been shattered by the bombardment. Alexander had the sense that "a word of concurrence from me would have stopped the charge then & there," and he was probably right. Longstreet said, "very emphatically," that "I don't [want] to make this attack. It can't possibly succeed. I would not make it now but that Gen. Lee has ordered it & expects it." And then the moment was gone: "Pickett's division swept out of the wood and showed the full length of its gray ranks and shining bayonets, as grand a sight as ever a man looked on."

Out to Pickett's left, Pettigrew's division also moved out into the sunshine, stretching beyond Alexander's sight, "farther than I could see." Way off to the right, Lafayette McLaws joined a little knot of his brigade commanders "and saw the advancing Confederates moving to the charge." It was "magnificent," McLaws remembered sixteen years later, "it stirred all the highest and deepest emotion of our nature, of admiration for the splendid bearing and courage of our Southern men." Even for a Union officer like Philippe Régis de Trobriand, who had seen a good deal of warfare in Europe, "it was a splendid sight." As the artillery fire petered out, Hancock's men along Cemetery Ridge shook themselves, stood up to stretch, hoping that the sudden silence meant that the battle was over. But then they saw "a long line of men coming out of the woods," and the word fluttered nervously up and down the line, *They are coming.* "The regimental flags and guidons were plainly visible along the whole line," wrote an officer with the 126th New York's skirmish line, "the guns and bayonets in the sunlight shone like silver." *Here they come! Here they come!* the warning raced around the 19th Massachusetts. *Here comes the infantry.*[4]

Arthur Fremantle and Fitzgerald Ross hoped to make it into the town to view the attack from "some commanding position," but failed to get there before the Federal bombardment made it impossible. They were forced to turn back, unwillingly accompanied by a local "urchin" who "took a diabolical interest in the bursting of the shells, and screamed with delight when he saw them take effect." Fremantle might have saved himself trouble if he had known that the cupolas, steeples, and roofs of the town were already crowded with gaping spectators, from civilians to Union prisoners. Even the methodical mathematician, Michael Jacobs, called his eighteen-year-old son, Henry, up to the garret of their house on Middle Street to look through his "small but powerful" telescope. "Quick," Jacobs called to his son, "Come, Come! You can see now what in all your life you will never see again." Ten miles south, at the Federal signal station on the Indian lookout above Emmitsburg, crowds of people brought "glasses, viz. telescopes, spy, and opera glasses," each vying with the others for "a clear view of the field" and "the men in their lines, attending cannon, the cannon themselves, making charges, officers riding along about their lines. . . . In a word the whole scene was spread out to our view."[5]

Pickett's Division

Almost every account of any importance describes the jump-off of Pickett's Charge as "a long gray line" emerging from "the dark fringe of timber on Seminary Ridge," or "the long gray line of infantry . . . in nearly perfect alignment," or a "force . . . in two lines . . . their formations opened to sift through the momentarily quiet batteries." But the closer to the actual event, the less certain the testimony becomes. A survivor of the 27th Connecticut remembered in 1866 that Pickett's attack developed in "two heavy lines of troops," and Theodore Gates, whose 80th New York was part of a contingent of 1st Corps survivors posted on Hancock's left, wrote in his diary on July 3rd that "the enemys Infantry advanced directly upon us in two lines on his right & one on his left." But Abner Doubleday spoke of the Confederates coming on in *three* lines, while John Gibbon counted *four* lines—"a heavy line of skirmishers," said Gibbon, "then a line of infantry, then another line behind that, and, I believe, a third behind that."[6]

Whatever the formation, Pickett and all of the division's officers took the moment to dress and align their troops, and give little speeches. Pickett sent staffers to his brigadiers to convey directions; Capt. Robert Bright was sent to Kemper and told to instruct him "to go in dismounted; dress on Garnett and take the red barn," the big barn belonging to Nicholas Codori, on the far side of the Emmitsburg Road. Kemper, in turn, briefed his staff "as to the character of the movement, the points to be watched and particulars reported." Lee accompanied Pickett's division down to the point where Pickett's left flank was to join Pettigrew's right, but, true to form, he allowed Pickett and the others to do the talking. At each brigade, Pickett paused, swinging and shouting his cap, "Remember Old Virginia!" (as he passed Garnett's brigade) or "Up, men, and to your posts! Don't forget today that you are from Old Virginia!" (to Kemper's brigade).

Lewis Armistead, in the rear of Kemper's and Garnett's brigades, brought his men up with "Attention, battalion!" and then proceeded to perform a small tableau of his own. Addressing Leander Blackburn, the color sergeant of the 53rd Virginia, Armistead asked theatrically, "Sergeant, are you going to put those colors on the enemy's works to-day?" On cue, the sergeant replied, "I will try, sir, and if mortal man can do it, it shall be done." There were last orders—keep "common time," do not break ranks, do not cheer, carry rifles "at will"—and then the color-bearers, and the corporals and sergeants who made up the color guard, took their mandated four steps forward, and the orders began to leap from "the stentorian lungs" of the regimental colonels: *Attention, battalion! . . . Dress in line, men! . . . Steady, in the centre! . . . Guide upon your right, Men! . . . Forward! . . . March! . . . Advance slowly with arms at will . . . No cheering . . . No firing . . . No breaking from common to quick step . . . Dress on the center.* They maneuvered past the long lines of Confederate artillery, whose crews "sat astride their smoking guns" and cheered the infantry as they passed: *Give it to 'em, boys; we've got 'em demoralized; and you 'uns can make 'em gut up an' dust out'n them dirt piles!* Far to the right, a band began to play "in the same manner that it would, had the division been passing in review."[7]

At some point, the brigades which had been stacked in column moved out into line of battle, and "when their line of battle was formed," men as far away as Little Round Top could see the Confederate officers dismount and walk forward "with sword in hand" to lead their men. Not all of them, however: the thin, pale Garnett had been kicked viciously by a "fiery steed," and could barely walk. He was determined to make the charge; however, he would do it mounted on his thoroughbred bay, Red Eye, and dressed in a "fine, new gray uniform," with a brigadier's star on the collar, and top boots. Lewis Williams, the colonel of the 1st Virginia, in the center of Kemper's brigade, argued, "I am sick to-day . . . will you let me ride," and so he did; Eppa Hunton, also "being unable to walk," also remained mounted. It was still early enough for men to joke. Thomas Lewis, a captain in Joseph Mayo's 3rd Virginia, "carrying his sword point foremost over his shoulder," was already warning his men, "Don't crowd, boys; don't crowd," when Mayo remarked, "Pretty hot, Captain." The captain only replied, "It's redicklopus, Colonel; perfectly redickloous." Some of Pickett's men took the ridiculous aspect of the charge more seriously. In the 1st Virginia, a number of men, "in whom there is not sufficient courage," refused to get to their feet, and Joseph Mayo saw "a disorderly crowd of men" attempt to bolt for the rear, only to be stopped by Pickett and several of his staff. But to the Union soldiers across the fields, they looked compact, orderly, irresistible. "No one who saw them could help admiring the steadiness with which they came on," wrote John Cook, a captain in the 80th New York. They were like "the shadow of a cloud seen from a distance as it sweeps across a sunny field."[8]

Not for long, though. Each regiment in Pickett's division told off a detail of skirmishers who spread out in a cautious shield, 200 yards ahead of the main body of infantry; they were followed by details of pioneers, whose job it was to knock down the annoying crisscross of "stake-and-rider fences which obstructed the path of the division" up to the Emmitsburg Road. A Confederate picket line had earlier been posted several hundred yards in front (whose men had spent the bombardment digging holes with "bayonets, pieces of board, any thing to get out of sight"), and as the skirmishers quick-timed through the pickets, they discovered that "with the exception of an orchard covering one tenth of the distance, and one small house, we had no protection whatever." They also discovered that Union skirmishers were drawn up behind the heavy post-and-board fences lining the Emmitsburg Road and in a small embankment through which the road cut like a natural trench. These skirmishers had proven unusually aggressive about sniping at the Confederate artillery batteries, and now they showed no inclination to yield. "I was surprised . . . that our skirmishers had been brought to a stand by those of the enemy," wrote a captain in the 11th Virginia. And no wonder, since the Federal skirmishers were using the top rail of the Emmitsburg Road fence to steady their aim, making their fire "so accurate and severe" that the Yankees could not be forced back. "The latter only gave ground when our line of battle had closed up well inside of a hundred yards of our own skirmishers." (The captain of one of the Federal skirmish details described it as "the hottest skirmish I was ever in.") Only then did the Union skirmishers retire "in perfect order" toward Cemetery Ridge, "firing as they fell back."

This posed an unanticipated problem for Pickett: the single most important factor in the success of any infantry attack is momentum, not firepower. The impulse for poorly disciplined or inexperienced soldiers when encountering fire was to stop and return the fire, and then prove almost impossible to get moving again. "Men charging," said Alexander Webb, "are apt to seek any shelter that may offer itself unless forced to move on by their officers. . . . Some would drop behind the irregularities of the ground and stay there as men will do under heavy fire." A stubborn line of enemy skirmishers would induce precisely that kind of stopping and firing. That, in turn, would give no time for the pioneers to break down the fences along the road; the infantry would have to climb one fence, cross the road, then climb the other, form up, dress ranks, and check alignments, and that would take off still more momentum. Confederate officers had to increase the amount of prodding and shoving: *Steady boys . . . Don't fire . . . Close up . . . Never mind the skirmish line.*[9]

Pickett's brigades were not going to be allowed to do this at leisure, either, because after covering only 300 to 500 yards (about a third to a fourth of the distance Pickett's division would have to travel), the Federal artillery that Hunt had so peevishly commanded to keep quiet now opened with repressed vengeance on the Confederates. Freeman McGilvery had his batteries pulled out of the earthen lunettes their crews had built up that morning and, "by training the whole line of guns obliquely to the right, we had a raking fire through" Pickett's entire division. They "fired shell and shrapnel until the right" of Pickett's division "came within 500 yards," when they switched to canister, "which took good effect." Up on Little Round Top, several of the 10-pounder Parrott rifles which had been precariously seated there the day before finally came into their own, scorching the 56th Virginia in Garnett's brigade, and one Federal officer noticed the rebel stretcher-bearers scurry for cover. Andrew Cowan had just brought his battery of six 3-inch Ordnance Rifles into line near the little stand of trees on the ridge when "I saw a body of Confederates appear. . . . They dressed their lines before advancing," and "we opened at once and continued pouring shell upon them till they came within canister range." As they did, Cowan could see "gaps opened in their lines," and behind the gaps a "stream of wounded men" heading to the rear turned from a "rivulet" to become "a river." But "no sooner had one company of the Confederate column been scattered by the bursting shells than its place was taken promptly and in good order by others." Cowan watched them close up and maintain "a splendid front," and it occurred to him that most of these Confederates seemed to be "marching to this copse of trees."[10]

At the right of the 2nd Corps line, Alex Hays was his usual exhilarated self, beaming with the glow of anticipated violence. "Now, boys, look out," he shouted as the Confederate infantry began rolling forward, "you will see some fun!" Nearby, George Woodruff's battery was rolled back from its cover under David Zeigler's orchard with help from men of the 108th New York, and all along his division front Hays was furiously exhorting the men of Smyth's brigade and the "Harpers Ferry Cowards" to "stand fast and fight like men." *Boys, don't let 'em touch these pieces,* he shouted, and as the Union artillery started shredding the oncoming infantry, Hays began laughing and singing at the top of his voice, *Hurrah, boys, we're giving them hell.* Alongside Hays, Eliakim Sherrill also remained mounted "on a *white horse,* against the entreaties of all his officers," as if to single-handedly finish wiping out the name of "Harpers Ferry Cowards" from his brigade.[11]

To James Crocker, in the 9th Virginia, it seemed as though "men fell like ten-pins in a ten-strike." The thickening banks of powder smoke darkened the air "with sulphurous clouds," and even the sun, "lately so glaring, is itself obscured." Garnett's brigade "had to climb three high post-and-rail fences," or else crowd through "at the openings where the fences had been thrown down," temporarily making superb targets for Union cannoneers. In the 53rd Virginia, "every man of Company F" was "thrown flat to the earth by the explosion of a shell from Round Top," and the 19th Virginia was struck end-on by shells "which enfiladed nearly our entire line with fearful effect, sometimes as many as 10 men being killed and wounded by the bursting of a single shell." A soldier in the 14th Virginia could see "now & then a man's head or arm or leg . . . fly like feathers before the wind." A chaplain in Pickett's division was following on the heels of his regiment with a party of stretcher-bearers when a shell "fell within 6 feet of my brave 20 men and myself and made a hole in the earth large enough to put two horses in." It killed six of the men with him, and "a fragment of shell blew off my cap and . . . tore off all the hair from the top of my head."[12]

And yet, "every man who was not killed or desperately wounded sprang to his feet, collected himself and moved forward to close the gap in the regimental front." On they came, officers with swords outthrust straight from the shoulder, men with the sun dazzling on rifle barrels, and on bayonets brighter than the barrels. In Armistead's brigade, "our line was steady and unshaken, except the gaps made by the enemy's fire, which were speedily closed and all necessary maneuvers were performed with the same promptitude and precision as when on Battalion drill." They could do this because the Federal artillery was not, even with these targets, proving to be all that effective. Little Round Top was not the impressive artillery asset people might have supposed, and the preliminary bombardment had wrought more havoc among the Union batteries than even Porter Alexander had realized. "The volume of their fire did not seem great & certainly it failed entirely to check or break up Pickett's advance" was the estimate of Porter Alexander. "Up to this time we had suffered but little from the enemy's batteries," because a number of the guns in the surviving Federal batteries—especially in Cushing's battery at the angle of the stone walls occupied by the Philadelphia Brigade—really had been "much crippled." Those that were still ready for action, especially Woodruff's battery, had only short-range canister left to fire. Above all, the distance being covered by Pickett's division kept the Virginia division under long-range fire for no longer than fifteen minutes, and the Federal artillery was trying to hit wafer-thin lines of battle rather than stout blocks of column.

Of course, to the thirty-five hundred infantry of Hancock's corps on the ridge, Pickett's division appeared as "acres of soldiers in solid mass," and a tremor of apprehension replaced the curiosity with which the sight had first been greeted. A few, in the 108th New York, "mounted some stones and waved the colors towards the enemy and shouted to them to come on," and some of the New Yorkers even opened a premature and undisciplined fire until their colonel "ordered them to reserve their fire until the enemy came closer." But for others, "it was a terrible sight to us" as the Confederate lines grew relentlessly closer to the Emmitsburg Road, and the skirmishers began falling back. "I looked on our small force" as being "not one tenth of theirs," wrote a lieutenant in the 126th New York, "I almost felt that we were gone." To William Davis, in the 69th Pennsylvania, it looked as though "no power could hold them in check." Even Alex Hays decided to take no chances, and sent off his division provost marshal to find Meade and tell him, "We must have reinforcements or we cannot hold our position."[13]

George Pickett was having apprehensions of his own as his division approached the Emmitsburg Road. Pickett went forward with the division, taking up a position "one hundred yards behind" so that he could keep a clear eye to his left, where he needed to dress on Pettigrew's right-flank brigade. But his first concern was with his own division's right flank, where he noticed that Cadmus Wilcox's two brigades were missing. Pickett sent three couriers off to find Wilcox. Robert Bright, Pickett's aide-de-camp, finally located him. He had been waiting for orders before moving, and he greeted Bright "with both hands raised waving and saying to me, 'I know, I know.'" Few of his men were, by now, eager to come to Pickett's support. "Knowing what we had to encounter," wrote a lieutenant in the Florida brigade, the order "was not obeyed with the same alacrity as was the case yesterday." When they did finally jolt forward, they crossed directly into the path of Freeman McGilvery's batteries, and a lieutenant in the 5th Florida found himself in a bewildering storm of "men falling all around me with brains blown out, arms off, and wounded in every direction."

Then Pickett had to cope with a second problem, posed by geography. Neither the Emmitsburg Road nor Seminary Ridge was exactly parallel to the Union position on Cemetery Ridge; instead, both ran at a slight southwestward tilt away from the ridgeline. This meant that any of Pickett's brigades which lined up along Seminary Ridge would actually be advancing off target, inclining ever so gradually away from Hancock's position and in the direction of Little Round Top. This odd conformation of the ground was not easy to discern at eye level, but it meant that at some point Pickett's lead brigades—Kemper's and Garnett's—were going to have to shift their line of attack to the left. Pickett sent a courier, Thomas Friend, to instruct Richard Garnett to close to his left, and then passed the order to Kemper, who tried to make the adjustment in mid-stride, shifting to his left either by moving into close column (which made a brigade easier to navigate) or by "obliqueing" to the left. This gave Kemper's brigade the look of zigzagging a little drunkenly as it made its approach, crowding men into Garnett's brigade and crushing Kemper's own regiments into one another. "Can you do nothing with your men," cursed an irate Lewis Williams, the colonel of the 1st Virginia, in the direction of his neighbor officers in the 11th Virginia, "they are crowding me out of line." Williams got little sympathy: "If you will go & attend to that damned little squad of yours," one of the 11th Virginia's officers shot back, "and let my Regiment alone, we will get along better."[14]

But the most difficult moment occurred when Garnett and Kemper

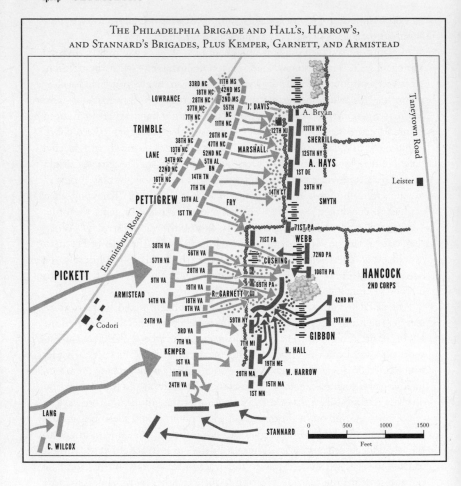

THE PHILADELPHIA BRIGADE AND HALL'S, HARROW'S,
AND STANNARD'S BRIGADES, PLUS KEMPER, GARNETT, AND ARMISTEAD

finally reached the Emmitsburg Road. Not only did the rebels have to stop and clamber over the "slab," or "plank," fence and pour down into "the sunken bed of the Emmittsburg road," but there was a parallel fence on the other side of the road to mount as well, and obstacles of that nature made it all too easy for men to halt, and to "prevail on a number of others to halt, and open fire." William Swallow saw men climb to the top of the fence and then tumble "flat into the bed of the road," a good many of whom "remained in the road and never crossed the second fence." Those who did manage to climb back out of the roadbed emerged "somewhat disordered," which "caused a confusion . . . not easily repaired by the officers in command."

Although they had been able to see "nothing but smoke and flame . . . while we were advancing on the heights," Pickett's men now were close enough to Cemetery Ridge to have a full view of "a dense blue line rising from behind" the stone wall along the crest, a hundred yards away, and it took every ounce of exhortation from Richard Garnett to get his brigade moving again: *Faster men, faster, we're almost there.* There was no time for precision anymore. "They came forward, sticking it up to our front and in no line-of-battle, but a mob," gradually merging "into one crowding, pushing line, many ranks deep." All "organization ceased," and the rebels became "merely a mass of struggling men." It had taken them, in all, "just nineteen minutes" to make it from Seminary Ridge to their place on the Union side of the Emmitsburg Road.[15]

This was the moment Hancock's men behind the stone wall had been dreading. Alonzo Cushing, who had been "slightly wounded in the thigh," limped over to Alexander Webb to ask whether he should pull out and make room for Andrew Cowan's battery. No, Webb replied, "We've all got to stay. Not a man can leave the front." In that case, Cushing begged, could Webb spare him some infantrymen to help roll the last two Ordnance Rifles of his battery down to the stone wall, where they would have a clear line to fire into the rebels instead of having to shoot over the heads of the 69th Pennsylvania. Webb agreed, and a detail from the 71st Pennsylvania wheeled the guns between companies of the 69th and hurriedly loaded them with whatever came to hand—"pieces of broken shell, small stones, bayonets, etc."—and let fly. The "artillery . . . opened on us with canister," wrote the lieutenant colonel of the 53th Virginia, "and twice I saw the color-bearer stagger and the next man seize the staff and go ahead," until the "third time the colors struck the ground . . . the adjutant of the regiment, rushed to them and seized them, and, I think, carried them into the enemy's works."[16]

Then it was the turn of the Union infantry. Garnett's brigade was creeping menacingly toward the stone boundary wall held by the Philadelphia Brigade, with the 69th Pennsylvania and two companies of the 71st Pennsylvania at the wall, and the 72nd Pennsylvania (plus two companies of the 106th Pennsylvania which had been out on the skirmish line) and the balance of the 71st behind where Cushing's battery had sat—and where the remains of most of that battery remained. The colonel of the 69th Pennsylvania, Dennis O'Kane, had been warning his men, Bunker Hill–style, to "hold your fire until you see the whites of their eyes." Alexander Webb, likewise, was walking among the other regiments of the Philadelphia Brigade, "speaking encouragement." They waited until the shapeless cloud of Garnett's brigade, "fifteen to thirty deep," began to move slowly up from the road—perhaps "halfway across"—when a voice shrilled, *Stick it to them!* Whether it was O'Kane or someone else, the 69th Pennsylvania and the companies of the 71st stood up, almost as a unit, hard brass rifle butts to the shoulder, and let off a volley "with deliberation and simultaneously." At this range, the effects were hideous, and they were made more so as the men of the 69th picked up the spare rifles they had stockpiled and began firing over and over again into the staggering mass of Confederates for another fifteen or twenty seconds. ("A few weeks" afterward, William Swallow would see the planks in the fence at the road "so completely perforated with bullet holes that you could scarcely place a half inch between them"; one sixteen-foot-by-fourteen-inch "slab" was "perforated with eight hundred and thirty-six musket balls.")[17]

Richard Garnett made it, still mounted, nearly to the wall, "gallantly waving his hat and cheering the men on to renewed efforts," before he was knocked off his horse, "shot through the brain" and the abdomen. Every colonel in Garnett's brigade was hit—one of them killed, another mortally wounded, the other three wounded; in the 8th Virginia, the colonel (Eppa Hunton), lieutenant colonel, major, and six of his company captains were either dead or wounded; in the 18th Virginia, seven of the eleven company captains were casualties. Of the 1,400 men Garnett had started out with, perhaps 800 were still on their feet, scattered between the road and the stone wall. To the right, passing to the other side of Nicholas Codori's "red barn," James Kemper's five medium-sized Virginia regiments lunged up from the Emmitsburg Road toward the line south of the trees held by Norman Hall's brigade. Hall was ready for them, and when Kemper's men were "within 3 or 4 rods of us . . . the regiment rose up and delivered two or three volleys" at Hall's command. But Hall's front-rank regiments—the 59th New York, 20th Massachusetts, and 7th Michigan—began to waver and leak men to the rear, leaving the 59th New York "to contend" with the rebels "alone." Andrew Cowan, standing behind his New York battery, was disgusted to see Michigan and Massachusetts "officers among them . . . and cursed them." Standing up in his stirrups, Kemper called out, "There are the guns, boys, go for them!" A "young officer" of the 14th Virginia leapt over the wall, "followed by a number of men," and Cowan heard him shout, *Take the gun!* But as Kemper's men surged forward to exploit the breach, Cowan was waiting for them, and at just thirty feet, five of his six Ordnance Rifles blew canister directly into the jumbled mass.[18]

Cowan's guns were not Kemper's only problem. Cadmus Wilcox had started off late to catch up with Kemper's flank, had lagged a good twenty minutes behind it thereafter, and totally lost connection with Kemper's weird zigzagging toward the Emmitsburg Road. That left Kemper's right flank uncovered as his brigade surged up to the wall, and in one more of those moments of spontaneous epiphany which had saved the Army of the Potomac over and over again in this battle, George Stannard, the commander of the Vermont brigade, saw what looked to him like a perfectly low-risk opportunity to do serious damage to Kemper's brigade. While two of his three oversize greenhorn regiments were keeping up a lively fire at Kemper's men, Stannard "ordered Colonel [Francis] Randall [of the 13th Vermont] to change front forward and form again on the flank" of the rebels. They were new men, and they executed the wheel to their right so clumsily that Stannard was afraid that "his order had been misunderstood" and they would blunder half-formed into the crowd of Confederates. "There was danger . . . that the hesitation and disorder might extend down the line," until a quick-witted staff officer sorted them out, faced them "promptly into line," and let fly "ten or fifteen" volleys into Kemper's right-flank regiment, the 24th Virginia, "at half pistol shot range."

The 24th and the 11th Virginia struggled to bend their line backward to present a firing line to the Vermonters, but between Cowan's battery and Stannard's flankers, "the effect upon the rebel lines was instantaneous" and "their progress ceased close upon the low breastworks of the 2d Corps." Which meant, in plainer terms, that "the rebels began to run, scattering individually back across the field." Those who *could* run: of Kemper's five colonels, only Joseph Mayo was unhurt. Lewis Williams of the 1st Virginia "was knocked out of the saddle by a ball in the shoulder near the brick-house, and in falling was killed by his sword," mourned Mayo. "His little bay mare kept on with the men in the charge. I can see her now as she came limping and sadly crippled down the hill." Mayo himself barely escaped when "a hissing sound, like the hooded cobra's whisper of death," followed by "a deafening explosion," momentarily blacked him out. "When I got on my feet again there were splinters of bone and lumps of flesh sticking to my clothes." The 11th Virginia lost seven company captains; the 1st Virginia lost six and the regiment's major, plus the entire color guard. Insensibly, Kemper and his battered brigade began to drift to the left, and Kemper himself was knocked "from my horse" with a bullet "through the breast, the ball lodging in his back."[19]

But the Union soldiers paid an equally dear price. Alonzo Cushing went down with a bullet in the face. His thumb, on the vent of the last of his Ordnance Rifles, was burned to the bone; his collapse was broken by the arms of his German-born battery sergeant, Frederick Fuger. Dennis O'Kane went down also, with a bullet in the groin, followed by the major and the lieutenant colonel of the 69th Pennsylvania. And now they had to face a fresh wave of Confederates—Armistead and his brigade, coming up, behind and through Garnett's stalled survivors, with Armistead in front, "thirty or forty paces in advance of his brigade with his hat off, which he carried on the point of his sword raised high above his head," as if it were a personal guidon. The hat "slipped down to the hilt" as Armistead reached the rear of Garnett's stalled brigade, but by that time he no longer needed it. They knew where he was going. "Boys, we must use the cold steel, who will follow me?" Armistead turned and shouted.

Andrew Cowan thought that "a hundred or two hundred of his bravest men" followed him, the 53rd Virginia leading the surge. Their major roared as he followed Armistead, "Look at your General! Follow him," and a corporal of the 53rd—Robert Tyler Jones, no less, a grandson of a U.S. president, John Tyler—planted the regiment's colors on the stones. Next came the 56th Virginia, rallying from its initial repulse with the rest of Garnett's brigade and splitting open the seam which joined the 69th Pennsylvania to the companies of the 71st Pennsylvania on its right. The Philadelphia regiments peeled back to each side, and Armistead and his men bowled through the gap, heading straight for the crest.[20]

As the 69th Pennsylvania leaned back to its left, the men collided with the clump of trees which sat a few yards behind the stone wall. It was, observed one officer, the habit "of the men to fall back a pace or two, each time to load," which "gave the line a retiring direction." But the trees—whether they were really "dwarfs" or "bushes" or a poor man's woodlot—acted to brake the retreat of the Philadelphians. "Even a single tree, in the centre of a small square of infantry," wrote the British tactician George Twemlow, would enable "two hundred infantry to hold firm, and resist successive charges." The same peculiar charm worked here. The 69th stiffened; the Virginians pushed up against them; and a wild melee broke out. "Men fire into each other's faces not five feet apart," wrote Jacob Hoke. "There are bayonet thrusts, sabre strokes, pistol shots, cool deliberative movements on the part of some; hot passionate, desperate efforts on the part of others; recklessness of life, tenacity of purpose, fiery determination, oaths, yells, curses, hurrahs, shoutings." Frederick Fuger "saw General Armistead leap over the stone wall with a number of his troops," and Fuger rallied what was left of his cannoneers and drivers "to stand their ground, fighting hand to hand with hand spikes, pistols, sabers, ramrods." An officer in the 69th Pennsylvania saw both Union and Confederate men crushed so closely together that they could not work their rifles free to use as clubs, but "struck at each other with the barrels of their rifles."[21]

But Lewis Armistead was not interested in bogging down into a slugging match around the trees. Directly ahead he saw the ruined guns of Cushing's battery, and behind them Alexander Webb's last reserve regiment of the Philadelphia Brigade, the "Fire Zouaves" of the 72nd Pennsylvania, and beyond them . . . *nothing*. Nothing but the provost guard and the dead horses and overturned wagons in the Taneytown Road, nothing but daylight and victory and the destruction of the Army of the Potomac and the end of the war and independence and peace, and so he lowered his sword and called, *The day is ours, men, come turn this artillery on them.* And for a moment, the balances shivered and teetered, unsure which future world to bless.[22]

Alexander Webb watched his Philadelphia Brigade, his new command, crack open before his eyes. "The Army of the Potomac was never nearer being whipped than it was here," Webb would later write, and like David Birney, he "almost wished to get killed." He went down "the whole line during the melée," using his sword alternately to point out targets and, in one case, to "put it into a man . . . one of my own men" who tried to flee. A "charge of buckshot" winged him in the right leg, and he could see a rebel officer pointing at him to get someone to take another shot. He and his aide, Frank Haskell, stopped the pullback of the 71st Pennsylvania, and then, "as the damned red flags of the rebellion began to thicken and flaunt along the wall," Webb turned to his last hope, the 72nd Pennsylvania.

The "Fire Zouaves" began trading fire from the crest with the Virginians in the angle, and together with the fire from the 69th Pennsylvania they hit Armistead. "He swerved . . . as though he was struck in the stomach," dropped his sword and hat, staggered for "two or three . . . steps," then collapsed with his left hand on the muzzle of one of Cushing's silent guns. Two or three of Armistead's men clustered around their fallen chief, but the others now began to pause, drift backward, drop to the ground, or turn and run back the way they had come. The sight of Armistead's fall enthused Webb, and he began waving his sword over his head, calling on the 72nd to charge: "Yes, boys, the enemy is running, come up, come up."

But more than a few men in the 72nd had no idea that Webb was their new brigadier, and when he got no response, he rode up to the color sergeant of the 72nd, William Finecy, ordered him forward, and then tried to seize the colors himself. Webb had almost given up and turned back toward the mass of rebels when Finecy bolted forward, flourishing the colors and crying, "Will you see your color storm the wall alone?" That was enough of a signal. Finecy went down, hit thirteen times, but the line of the 72nd sprang forward, surged around Armistead and the remains of Cushing's guns, and rolled, pell-mell, all the way down to the stone wall "without any special formation," more a "melée than a line of battle."[23]

This one regiment alone (even if they were backed up by the two companies of the 106th Pennsylvania who stood at the rear with them) would not have been enough to clean the Virginians out of the angle without the unlooked for assistance of Norman Hall's brigade. As the pressure from Kemper's attack eased, Hall's men could look to their right and easily see Armistead's

Confederates breaking into the angle, and normally this would have been an open invitation to find the first path to the rear. Instead, "a strange, resistless impulse seemed to seize the whole Union line," and company officers called out, "To our right and front," pointing toward the trees. One of Hall's colonels caught sight of Winfield Hancock and appealed directly to Hancock for permission to plunge into the gap where the rebel "colors are coming over the stone wall." *Go in there pretty God-damned quick,* Hancock shouted in response, and Hall's brigade swung backward in a rough wheel, then plunged straight for the clump of trees and into the angle. (Hancock later remarked that "it was not done in the way he wanted, but still it was splendidly done.") No one could remember whether "the command 'Charge!' was given by any general officer"; if anything, "it seemed . . . to come in a spontaneous yell from the men, and instantly our line precipitated itself on the enemy."

And not only Hall's brigade. The handfuls of survivors from Harrow's brigade—the 1st Minnesota, the 15th Massachusetts, Francis Heath's 19th Maine, the 82nd New York, regiments which had sustained the highest casualty rates of any brigade in the 2nd Corps—"hurried to the right and joined the troops in front of Pickett's men." Jammed together "five and six deep," these undirected men formed a crescent with the 69th Pennsylvania along the south end of the angle, standing and firing in a loose mob "until all appearance of formation was lost." Even Henry Hunt, who had ridden up to Freeman McGilvery's batteries when the infantry attack started, now galloped into the writhing tangle of smoke and fire, firing his revolver and shouting crazily, "See 'em! See 'em!" until his horse was shot down and some of Cowan's cannoneers had to extricate him. (A few yards away, Alexander Webb noticed that Hunt "had ridden up," and in the strange stress of combat Webb "had to laugh" because Hunt "looked so funny, up there on his horse, popping at them.")[24]

For "perhaps five minutes," the men were simply a motionless mass of shooters. "Every time a man stops to load, others crowd in ahead of him so that he will have to elbow his way through in order to get another chance to fire." The smoke rolled in so thickly that men had to shoot at their enemies' feet, "which was about all we could see of them at the time." This served "to prevent" any further advance by the Confederates, but otherwise "our shots affected them little," and the masses of humanity in the angle foamed together in a bloody equipoise. Then, over top of the mayhem, the voice of a soldier in the 15th Massachusetts, George Cunningham of Company B, roared: *For God's sake let us charge, they'll kill us all if we stand here.* "The men sprang forward like a thunderbolt." The color-bearer of the 19th Massachusetts knocked down the color-bearer of the 14th Virginia "with his color staff," while all around him men "just rushed in like wild beasts . . . and struggled and fought, grappled in hand-to-hand fight, threw stones, clubbed muskets, kicked and yelled and hurrahed." With Armistead down and the Federals closing in, the dwindling mass of Virginians "started on the run towards the Emmitsburg Road." The Federals kept up firing "until they got out of range," and then it was over.[25]

A small knot of Union soldiers from the 72nd Pennsylvania gathered around Armistead, some of them imagining that he was actually James Longstreet. The judge advocate of the 2nd Corps, Henry Bingham, had been "on the right and alongside of Webb's brigade," and he stopped "several privates" who were carrying Armistead rearward. Bingham himself had just sustained a nasty wound to his scalp, but almost as though he were helping the victim of a road accident, Bingham halted the little group, and introduced himself to Armistead as a member of General Hancock's staff. Hancock? Armistead gasped. Winfield Scott Hancock? Yes, replied Bingham. Hancock is "an old and valued friend," Armistead said. Tell him, Armistead continued, "that I have done him and you all an injury which I shall repent the longest day of my life."[26]

It would have sharpened his repentence immeasurably if Armistead had known that, only a few minutes before, Hancock had joined the wounded himself. Riding down to rally Hall's and Stannard's brigades, Hancock was hit in the right thigh by a bullet that drilled through the pommel of his saddle and drove itself, several splinters of wood, and a bent ten-penny nail four inches up into his groin. These deadly fragments barely missed an artery, and the 2nd Corps' chief medical officer, Alexander Dougherty, was able to extract the nail and contain the bleeding sufficiently that Hancock could, even "lying down," continue to "observe the operation of the enemy and give direction accordingly." But by this point, there was not much left to direct. Hancock dictated a quick message to Meade—"Tell General Meade that the troops under my command have repulsed the enemy's assault and that we have gained a great victory"—and sent it off with his aide William Mitchell. Meanwhile, the wrecked pieces of Pickett's three brigades "fled to the rear over dead and wounded, mangled, groaning, dying men, scattered thick, far and wide" and "officers and privates side by side, pushed, poured and rushed in a continuous stream, throwing away guns, blankets and haversacks as they hurried on in confusion toward the rear."[27]

Pettigrew's Division

Johnston Pettigrew may not have been the best choice to take over command of Harry Heth's division—he had only seen serious action in this war on the Peninsula, where a bullet damaged his windpipe and should have killed him—but he was a better choice than either of Heth's other brigade commanders, Joe Davis and John Brockenbrough, in addition to having seniority over both. The same was true of the decision to give command of the two brigades borrowed from Pender's division to Isaac Trimble (who was also senior on the Confederate Army list to both Heth and Pender).

All of these men belonged to Powell Hill's corps, and Hill proposed to Lee putting in everything he had left, which would have added Pender's remaining two brigades (Thomas' Georgians and Abner Perrin's South Carolinians) and perhaps the underused brigades of Mahone and Posey from Richard Heron Anderson's division. Lee disagreed. He needed some form of reserve for the rest of the army, and besides, Pettigrew's role was more in the nature of support for Pickett. (Longstreet's first design had, in fact, been to place Pettigrew in the *rear* of Pickett.) This was small comfort to the men Pettigrew would be commanding, who spent "about four hours or more" while George Pickett's division was getting into position looking glumly over the cheerless fields they would shortly have to cross, "every veteran . . . counting the probable results."

As soon as he saw Pickett's division emerge from the woods and pause to deploy into line, Pettigrew had his men up, too, putting the four brigades of his newly acquired division in a first line (with the regiments in columns formed by five-company battalions), and then Trimble's two brigades in a second. Birkett Fry, who was now in charge of Archer's depleted brigade, occupied the right-hand slot in the front line, and would serve as the brigade of direction for the charge, trying to keep an eye out for the movements of Pickett's division, 400 yards farther to the right. Of the twenty-seven regiments Pettigrew would lead, only four (Brockenbrough's brigade) were Virginians; fifteen were North Carolina regiments, and so it seemed only natural that Pettigrew would ride across their front, exhorting them, "For the honor of the good old North State, forward." But it was from the throats of the Tennesseans in Fry's brigade that the shrill yipping of the rebel yell went up, and the whole line went forward.[28]

The impetus began to slow almost at once. For one thing, Pettigrew was following Pickett by three or four hundred yards, and the temptation to let Pickett attract as much Federal attention as possible was irresistible. There were also the interminable fences to be climbed, making alignments "so imperfect and so drooping" that it looked like Pettigrew was leading a wedge rather than a line. Pettigrew stopped them once they reached the smoldering ruins of the Bliss farm, trying to adjust and dress the lines, but as he did so he found that John Brockenbrough's always unreliable brigade had disappeared—parts of it may actually have failed to move at all—and Joe Davis was lagging far behind. Then, "halfway over the plain," the Federal artillery on Cemetery Hill opened up on Pettigrew's division. Pettigrew's line was "at once enveloped in a dense cloud of smoke and dust," from which "arms, heads, blankets, guns, and knapsacks were thrown and tossed in the clear air."[29]

The principal advantage Pettigrew had was the lay of the land: the slant of Seminary Ridge and the Emmitsburg Road meant that his division had a far shorter distance to cover than Pickett's. "From the top of Seminary Ridge," it took Pettigrew only "about eight minutes" to reach the Emmitsburg Road. But the pounding of the artillery was already cracking the steadiness of Joe Davis' brigade. Isaac Trimble was alarmed to see "Pettigrew's troops" stopping and "firing against orders," and soldiers from the 11th and 26th North Carolina "'Turkeyed' in fine style." They were slowed down still further by a Union regiment which materialized on the left flank of Pettigrew's line; this was the 8th Ohio, the only regiment of Samuel Carroll's brigade which was left behind the evening before when Carroll went off to push Jubal Early's division down east Cemetery Hill. A large portion of the 8th Ohio had been out on the skirmish line at noon, but rather than recalling them at the beginning of the Confederate attack, their colonel, Franklin Sawyer, instead "by a still further advance and left wheel" (just as George Stannard was doing several hundred yards away) flung the regiment out on a line perpendicular to Pettigrew's advance. "Facing the left flank of the advancing column of rebels, the men were ordered to fire into their flank at will."

Then the rebels hit the big fences on either side of the road. "The Confederates did not mind the stone wall" in front of them or the "picket fences" behind them, claimed a member of the 14th Tennessee, "but this mortised post and rail fence checked the charge and confused the whole command." It did not help their confusion that the Emmitsburg Road, at this point, sank into an even deeper embankment than the one encountered by Garnett and Kemper. "The time it took to climb to the top of the fence seemed to the men an age of suspense," and then they spilled over the immovable fence into the deep roadbed. There, an embarrassingly large number of them stayed, "and no orders, threats or entreaties could induce them to again face the iron storm."[30]

The Union soldiers forty yards away at the crest had stored up a good deal of malice for these rebels. Alex Hays sited both of his remaining brigades behind a low stone wall, one of them where it could connect to the two rear companies of the 71st Pennsylvania, and the other—the "Harpers Ferry Cowards"—on the right, around the Bryan barn, with George Woodruff's battery on their flank as an anchor. They thought the advance of Pettigrew's division "was a splendid sight to see," and it was intimidating enough that several hopped up to "start for the rear," while an officer of the 111th New York buried his face in the ground and tried to hide ridiculously behind an empty box of hardtack. But in the 12th New Jersey, a regiment which had stuck stubbornly with its old .69 caliber "buck-and-ball" smoothbore muskets, the men were busy repackaging their paper cartridges with multiple rounds, like buckshot, while the 1st Delaware and 14th Connecticut "collected all the spare guns . . . and laid them in rows beside them." Alex Hays, riding up and down the line behind them, was brief and to the point: "They are coming, boys; we must whip them," and to the 12th New Jersey, "You men with buck and ball, don't fire until they get to that fence." And they did wait, until "the Confederates began to climb the hither fence" and Alex Hays could shout, *Show them your colors and give them hell, boys.* When they did, "the storm of lead was beyond description." After that, the rebels "melted away like wax." Many of those in Pettigrew's first line went no farther forward than "about five yards," then "returned to and laid down in the pike." Isaac Trimble had the impression that Fry's brigade crossed the road, but this may have been no more than "some fifty or seventy five of the most reckless."[31]

Pettigrew lost his horse to shell fire in the march over the fields, but he scaled both fences along with "broken squads" and tried to organize an attack aimed at the Bryan barn. Birkett Fry went down with a bullet "through the thigh" but kept on urging his Tennesseans onward as though all it would require was one determined push and the Army of the Potomac would disintegrate before their eyes: "Go on; it will not last five minutes longer!" Fry and Pettigrew had the help of Trimble's two brigades, who reached the fence, plowed on through, and "passed over . . . and went forward." But even then, "only half" of Trimble's North Carolinians "managed to cross the road." Together, there may have been as many as three separate rushes past the Bryan barn and at the stone wall behind it, but none of them had any realistic chance. Behind the wall, soldiers in the 126th New York taunted the rebels, *Come on; Come on; come to death!*

Men from Joe Davis's 11th and 42nd Mississippi also made it to the barn, clustered around it, and exchanged fire with the 39th and 111th New York. One of the 42nd's captains, Henry Davenport, ran forward to plant the regiment's flag on the wall, only to be shot down; the colonel of the 42nd, Hugh Miller, was "mortally wounded through the left lung . . . some twenty-five yards from their line of stone fences." On the other side of the barn, a small party from Trimble's 37th North Carolina actually got over the wall before they were quickly rounded up and captured; one of their lieutenants, with the incongruous name of Iowa Michigan Royster, ran forward "in his new uniform . . . waving his sword" and "singing Dixie," only to be cut down, struck in the chest and thigh. The 37th's right-hand neighbors, the 7th North Carolina, never got closer than forty yards to the wall. Fry's brigade (the same brigade which had begun the battle on July 1st, under James Archer's command) probably made the most serious push up to the wall, where they fought with the 12th New Jersey, the 14th Connecticut, and the 1st Delaware, using stones, bayonets, rifle butts—even, as Birkett Fry noticed, the "spear on the end of my regimental colors." But already, a captain in Fry's brigade could see that "to the left of the First Tennessee our lines had entirely given way." An aide told Trimble, who had "been wounded and taken from my horse," that his brigades were starting to fall back. Should he try to "rally them" for another try? No, said Trimble, who was becoming "faint with loss of blood," there was no point. "No Charley the best these brave fellows can do is to get out of this," so "let them get out of this, it's all over."[32]

Pettigrew's division "gave way, not in sullen retreat, but in disordered flight," and unlike their counterparts in the Philadelphia Brigade, Alex Hays' men were up and eager for the pursuit. The 1st Delaware "sprang over the stone wall *en masse* and charged with the bayonet upon the rebel fugitives," led by their color sergeant "with the national flag," as did the color sergeant of the 125th New York, while the 111th New York carefully cleared out the Bryan barn of any remaining Confederates. Alex Hays was in raptures. As a captured rebel officer was being prodded past him, the rebel asked contemptuously if this was all the men Hays had been able to summon: "If I had known that this is all you have, I would not have surrendered." Well, snarled Hays happily, *Go back and try it again.*

A captain in the 126th New York picked up a North Carolina regimental flag which had, among the battle honors painted on its bars, HARPERS FERRY. Hays wanted this flag, and he wanted to flaunt it for the benefit of the "Harpers Ferry Cowards," who had finally evened up their scores with the Confederacy on this afternoon. "Gen. Hays took this flag in his hand and rode the length of the brigade in his front, trailing the flag on the ground amid the continuous and deafening cheers of the men," followed by his two surviving staffers, trailing captured rebel banners in the same fashion. At the angle, he encountered Alexander Webb, "with his hat off, very much excited," picking through the bodies of the 72nd Pennsylvania in their "dark blue zouave uniforms." Webb was looking for some encouraging Victorian sentiment from Hays, saying with a sigh, "Hays, they got through my line." Alex Hays was the wrong man to expect sentimentality from. He shot back wickedly, "I'll be damned if they got through mine."[33]

It seems to have occurred to neither Webb nor Hays nor anyone else at that moment how ironic it was that the Army of Northern Virginia's last hope for a victorious breakthrough expired in bleeding flight from the property of Abraham Bryan, a free black man, a species of humanity which was, by most Confederate understandings, not even supposed to exist. Lee and his men had given what Porter Alexander later called "the best we had in the shop," right down to handsome young lieutenants, moving bravely and impossibly to the attack, singing "Dixie" under waving swords and snapping flags, and they had, in the end, not been able to roll the stone to the top of the mountain after all. There was already a faint sense in the minds of these soldiers on Cemetery Ridge, standing there as the sun—and the hopes of the Confederacy— together sank toward South Mountain, that something unutterably vital had just happened, something to be engraved in bronze books and on pedestals of gray granite, something that would make every man who had been there and survived raise a toast, like Harry the King's happy few, on every anniversary of the battle, something which would make this place a name everyone would recognize without explanation. But the greatest achievement of the great battle would turn out to be its humblest, as well. For Abraham Bryan would return to his twelve acres, and his whitewashed cottage and barn, and he and his family would live there until he sold the property in 1869. *And no one would make them afraid, for the mouth of the Lord of hosts has spoken it.*

As clear a defeat as our army ever met with

GENERAL ROBERT E. LEE stayed at the point of Pickett's jump-off throughout the charge, sitting first on an oak stump (which an aide had thoughtfully spread with Lee's all-weather oilcloth coat) and then "on a camp chair under a hastily-rigged tent-fly" (which his staff had even more thoughtfully contrived). Lee was "outwardly calm," the only nervousness shown being his habit of "twirling his spectacles in his hand." Once the Union artillery opened up, the curtains of smoke closed in and there was little to see, but after Pettigrew's division went in, "a loud cheering arose in the enemy's lines." Lee sent a staffer, Frederick Colston, to "ride forward and see what that cheering means." Colston met only ghastly streams of wounded men, staggering rearward, and by the time he was close enough to catch any glimpse worth reporting, all he was able to see was "a Union general galloping down his line," which was probably Alex Hays in triumph. The fields which Pettigrew's division had crossed were now "dotted with our soldiers, singly and in small groups, coming back from the charge, many of them wounded, and the enemy were firing at them as you would a herd of game." Colston himself had bullets cut off one bridle rein and bore holes through the brim of his new hat.[1]

Longstreet divined what had happened before Lee, probably because he was expecting it. Arthur Fremantle arrived at where Longstreet had settled himself, "at the top of a snake fence at the edge of the wood," and unwisely bubbled with enthusiasm, "I wouldn't have missed this for anything." Longstreet rounded angrily on the Guards officer: "The devil you wouldn't! I would like to have missed it very much; we've attacked and been repulsed: look there!" Fremantle cast his eye over the "open space between the two positions, and saw it covered with Confederates slowly and sulkily returning towards us in small broken parties." They moved no "faster than a walk . . . in irregular and small groups, trailing their arms," limping in "bleeding swarms." Staffers who had gone forward with Pickett now came dribbling back in disarray— one "on foot, carrying his saddle, having just had his horse killed," another "in the same predicament." Then there was Pickett, "his dark dusty begrimed face bowed almost to his saddle and his horse at a walk . . . motioning men towards the rear with his hand" and howling to the first of Longstreet's staff he met, *Where, oh! Where is my division?* He found Longstreet and poured out his heart "in terrible agony": *General, I am ruined; my division is gone—it is destroyed.* Then it was the turn of Pettigrew, "his arm shattered," to make the same dismal report, and apologize for being "unable to bring his men up again." Never mind, Longstreet replied, "just let them remain where they are: the enemy's going to advance and will spare you the trouble."[2]

Powell Hill, who was observing the attack with Lee, "burst into tears . . . when the charging column was repulsed and streamed back from the enemy's works." Eventually, he collected himself sufficiently to walk down to Porter Alexander's batteries, where he seemed to one of Alexander's artillerymen "as if he were dazed, if not confounded at the scene before him." Hill moved over to Carnot Posey's skirmish line, ordering Posey's Mississippians "to stop the retreating men and make them form." But neither Posey nor Hill could make them rally, and beaten rebels continued back into the woods and beyond. Joe Davis came up "with his sword in his hand" and was stopped by one of Posey's men: "General Davis, where is your brigade?" Davis looked up at him, then "pointed his sword at the skies," and wordlessly "walked on."[3]

Robert E. Lee had spent most of the attack with "the light of battle . . . in his eyes, and it was plain he longed to be with the charging column." If Raglan had been right at the Alma, and Napoleon III had been right at Solferino, then Lee had every expectation of being right in sending Pickett and Pettigrew into this great attack. And then, in the manner of some Southern Agave come suddenly to a realization of what he had done, Lee "ordered his horse and rode forward to meet the retreating divisions." He met Pickett and took him "by the hand," saying as apologetically as he could, "General, your men have done all that men could do, the fault is entirely my own." Pickett should place his division "in rear of this hill, and be ready to repel the advance of the enemy should they follow up their advantage." Pickett angrily interrupted him: *General Lee, I have no division now.* But Lee missed the point of Pickett's anguish completely. "General Pickett," he struggled soothingly, "you and your men have covered yourselves with glory." Glory, Pickett replied, was not going to have the weight in the balances of loss that victory might have had. "Not all the glory in the world, General Lee, can atone for the widows and orphans this day has made." Nor was Pickett the only one refusing to be consoled. Cadmus Wilcox stumbled up to Lee, complaining that he "came into Pennsylvania with one of the finest brigades in the Army of Northern Virginia and now my people are all gone." *It is all my fault, General,* Lee repeated, and when Johnston Pettigrew found Lee, he received the same assurance, *General Pettigrew, it is all my fault.*[4]

Yet the battle was not, strictly speaking, over. Early on the morning of July 3rd, J.E.B. Stuart's cavalry, now reinforced by Albert Jenkins' brigade (which had remained attached to Ewell's corps throughout the invasion) moved east along the York Pike, "pursuant to instructions from the commanding general." Just what those instructions might be never was spelled out; Stuart implied in his official report that he "hoped to effect a surprise upon the enemy's rear" while Longstreet's great attack was under way. Stuart's loyal aide Henry B. McClellan insisted two decades later that Stuart intended "to make a diversion which might aid the Confederate infantry to carry the heights held by the Federal army," and perhaps even launch an attack on "the enemy's rear." How Stuart was to accomplish this with the 4,800 weary troopers he had brought into Gettysburg the afternoon before, plus Jenkins' 1,100, is still anyone's guess. Lee, a cavalry officer himself in the 1850s, had never used light cavalry for anything beyond the customary duties of scouting and screening, so it is far from likely that Lee was ready to sanction the use of Stuart's horsemen for an infantry-cracking juggernaut-task in the spirit of Joachim Murat or the Prussian uhlans. It is remotely possible that Lee—or Stuart—might have had some notion of looping the cavalry far out to the east and then turning south to cut the Baltimore Pike somewhere east or south of Gettysburg. But the idea that Stuart meant to commit his small cavalry force to an attack on infantry belies every tactical lesson the Civil War afforded.[5]

Still, if Stuart was looking for a fight, or merely to renew the brushfire encounter of the afternoon before at Hunterstown, he did not have to go far to find it. Three miles east of Gettysburg, Stuart's four brigades brushed up against George Armstrong Custer's Michigan cavalry brigade and a battery of artillery, and a spattering of artillery fire was traded back and forth along yet another undulating rise known as Cress Ridge, between the York Pike and the Hanover Road. In short order, a second Federal cavalry brigade, under John McIntosh, came up to reinforce Custer, followed by yet another brigade, this one belonging to John Irvin Gregg, followed by the overall division commander, John Gregg's brother, David McMurtrie Gregg. McIntosh's brigade was supposed to be Custer's relief (Custer belonged to Judson Kilpatrick's division, and Kilpatrick had moved the bulk of his division to the south end of the battlefield), but David Gregg easily persuaded Custer, who "conjectured" that some rough play was in the offing, to stay and the fight was on.

For almost an hour, from 12:30 to 1:30, both sides jockeyed for advantage in a long-range duel between dismounted cavalry, fighting with carbines, and artillery. Stuart tried to dislodge the stalemate with an aggressive mounted attack across the farm of John Rummel, which in turn was met by a furious saber-swinging mounted counterattack by Custer and his Michigan cavalry, Custer at their head crying, "Come on, you Wolverines!" For an hour, the Rummel farm was turned into a smaller-scale version of the cavalry scrum at Brandy Station a month before. In the end, both sides drew off with little to show for it except for some minor casualties—less than 5 percent for Stuart, and half that for David Gregg, except for Custer's brigade (where 32 men were killed and 147 wounded, a pattern of heedless bloodletting which Custer would carry to a more famous spot on a dusty hillside in Montana thirteen years later).[6]

There was another cavalry action, this one involving a poorly calcu-lated mounted attack on some of John Bell Hood's infantry down by Big Round Top. As battered as Hood's men had been by the fighting on July 2nd, they illustrated how little hope there was of light cavalry doing anything even remotely harmful to infantry by shooting the Union brigade apart. "We called out for them to throw down their sabres and get off their horses," wrote an infantryman in the 1st Texas, "but they still kept on until shot." The entire business got the brigade's commander and twenty of his men killed, and on the whole it has to be said that the battle of Gettysburg would not have ended five minutes sooner or later if either affair had never happened.[7]

Lee did have one other use for the cavalry, however. That night, he sum-moned John Imboden, whose rough-edged Virginia cavalry brigade had only just arrived the night before from Chambersburg. Imboden knew that "the day had gone against us," but he assumed "that with to-morrow's dawn would come a renewal of the struggle." Lee, "who betrayed so much physical exhaus-tion" that Imboden "stepped forward to assist him," knew that he had noth-ing left to fight with. The Army of Northern Virginia had fought enough in three days to equal three separate battles, where Lee had only been prepared, at most, to fight one, and if he asked any more of it, the entire army might fall apart. "The unsuccessful issue of our final attack" determined Lee's mind to withdraw "to the west side of the mountains." If the Federals attempted to follow him, he did not mind taking the chance of a strictly defensive fight, "if the enemy offers it." But once on the far side of South Mountain, he would continue his retreat until the Confederates were once again on the south side of the Potomac.[8]

The notion of "active operation" Lee now had in mind for Imboden was for the unstylish cavalryman (whom J.E.B. Stuart had deemed "inefficient") to take immediate charge of the logistics of the retreat. "We must return to Virginia," Lee began. "I have sent for you because your men are fresh, to guard the trains back to Virginia." There were two routes open: the Cashtown Pike, leading back the way they had come, to Greenwood and thence south to Maryland and Williamsport on the Potomac, and the Fairfield Road, which led through the village of Fairfield and crossed South Mountain at Monterey Pass, and reached Waynesboro before also turning down toward Williamsport. The Fairfield route was twenty miles shorter, but the Chambersburg route had better roads, and so rather than risk piling the entire army onto just one thoroughfare, Lee wanted Imboden to take all the army's ammunition, supply, and ambulance wagons by the more northerly Cashtown-to-Greenwood route. The infantry would use the Fairfield-to-Waynesboro route, with Powell Hill's corps in the lead, followed by Longstreet's, and then Ewell's. Screening would be provided by Stuart and the cavalry, Fitz Lee's brigade accompanying Imboden, and the rest covering the infantry's tail.[9]

This was not going to be an ordinary chore. "The wagons and ambulances and the wounded could not be ready to move till late in the afternoon," Imboden wrote. Maps would have to be drawn up and distributed; orders would have to be written and sent off as far as Winchester to have empty wagons brought to meet the trains at the Potomac crossing; lists of names would have to be compiled and a rough triage would have to be performed by the surgeons, separating the wounded who could be accommodated by the existing transport from those who would have to be left behind for the Yankees to pick up. But Imboden did better than Lee could have hoped, and the head of his hastily organized train began rolling westward fifteen hours later. "The wagons and ambulances were loaded with all the wounded that could be moved," wrote one of Fitz Lee's troopers, "but we had to leave many of our poor fellows that we never saw again."[10]

It began to rain that night, "in blinding sheets," and horses and mules "were blinded and maddened by the wind and water." Longstreet's men found "the roads muddy, wagon ruts deep, the night awful," and Longstreet's chief of staff, Moxley Sorrel, remembered a night of "rain in torrents, howling winds, and road almost impassable." The gloom of the weather was matched by the slumping spirits of the army. "The battle of Gettysburg was . . . as clear a defeat as our army ever met with," admitted Franklin Gaillard, the lieutenant colonel of the 2nd South Carolina. In the North Carolina and Georgia regiments, the misery fanned dissent. "The men from North Carolina . . . believe they will go back in the Union," warned a soldier in the 53rd Georgia, while "the men from Georgia say that if the [Union] army invades Georgia they are going home. I don't believe our army will fight much longer." Even Lewis Armistead's parting comment to Henry Bingham before Armistead was carried off—about doing an injury to "you all" which he would "repent"—sounded to Bingham like an admission that "the sentiment" of repentance now prevails "among some of the leading men of the South."[11]

There was more bad news the next morning. On July 4th, the 29,000 Confederate soldiers who formed the garrison of Vicksburg "marched out of their works, and formed line in front, stacked arms"—and surrendered. Bobbing in the waters of Chesapeake Bay, Alexander Stephens' truce boat waited in Hampton Roads for permission to proceed up the Potomac, but with the news that "Lee is on the retreat," Stephens' request to come to Washington was deemed by Lincoln and his cabinet to be "inadmissible." In Pittsburgh, the newspapers exulted that "the peace-at-any-price leaders . . . are trimming their sails to the fresh gale of success favoring the Union cause." In New York City, "soon after daylight," church bells "began clanging, and cannon firing . . . in Union Square," and New York's Democratic governor was persuaded to omit from a scheduled speech "a fierce attack upon the war management of the Government and its generals and a eulogy of McClellan." Everything Robert E. Lee had hoped to gain by coming north had been lost.[12]

At first, George Gordon Meade had no idea that Pickett's final attack had been repulsed. Having taken himself, in a worst-case scenario, down to the artillery redoubt on Powers Hill, Meade had "only a few orderlies" with him and it was only after "the enemy's artillery fire ceasing, heavy musketry firing being heard, and . . . meeting many men moving to the rear," that it occurred to Meade that defeat had not descended upon him after all. He started off for the Taneytown Road, meeting his son, Capt. George G. Meade, Jr., and telling young George to join him "at his Head Qrs. or on the line." Meade came up behind the right flank of the 2nd Corps, and gradually worked his way up the line, looking for Alex Hays or anyone who could tell him what had happened. (Meade was, for a moment, surrounded by "a large body of prisoners" who recognized that "he was someone in authority" and began asking *him* "where they should go.")

Finally, John Gibbon's aide Frank Haskell came up and Meade began pummeling him with questions. "How is it going here?" Meade asked, "earnest and full of care." Haskell replied, "I believe, General, the enemy's attack is repulsed." Meade was astonished: "What! Is the assault already repulsed." "It is, sir," Haskell delightedly answered. *Thank God,* Meade marveled. Meade pushed on farther to find Hays, and instead found an officer commanding Woodruff's battery who also assured Meade that the rebels had just turned and fled. Meade sat himself down "on a great bowlder" as reports began to stream in—he was particularly curious about the rumor "that General Longstreet had been killed . . . at the head of the charge"—and a band struck up "Hail to the Chief" and "Yankee Doodle." Major Mitchell, Winfield Hancock's aide, finally found Meade with Hancock's message about "a great victory gained," and he dictated a reply, thanking Hancock "for the service he has rendered the Country and me this day."[13]

It eventually occurred to Meade that he needed to find out if anything was in the offing elsewhere, and so he rode first up to Cemetery Hill, and then down to Little Round Top. From the ambulance which carried him from the field, Hancock sent Meade a follow-up message, explaining to Meade as delicately as a subordinate dared that "nothing is wanting" in the victory they had won but "to make it decisive," which Meade could easily do if "the Sixth and Fifth Corps" are "pressed up." Alf Pleasonton, who joined Meade at "the top of the mountain," also begged Meade "to order a general advance of his whole army in pursuit of the enemy." This was, Pleasonton argued, Meade's once-in-a-lifetime chance "to show yourself a great general" and destroy Lee's army the same way Wellington had Napoleon's at Waterloo. (The Federal officers were not the only ones expecting Meade to attack; Longstreet, for one, shuddered at the possibility of seeing "Meade ride to the front and lead his forces to a tremendous counter-charge," and so did Lee, who "expected Meade to follow the fugitives of Pickett's division.") But Meade only had the 6th Corps as his reserve, and only Crawford's Pennsylvania Reserves from the 5th Corps were in any kind of useful shape, and though he ordered George Sykes to have Crawford and the Reserves "clear the woods" in front of Little Round Top where Hood's and McLaws' depleted divisions lay, he added that if Crawford "found too strong a force I was not to engage them." Crawford's Reserves actually gained a good deal of ground, pushing disheartened rebel skirmishers past the wheat field and the stony ridge and bagging "over two hundred prisoners" before enough resistance forced Crawford to call it off. Otherwise, Meade was not in a mood to jeopardize what he was now beginning to realize was the first clear-cut victory the Army of the Potomac had enjoyed. And so although "Meade ordered demonstrations in front of our line," a sighing Gouverneur Warren said, "they were very feebly made."[14]

When the morning of the 4th came, the rain was still plunging down in torrents, "but all was quiet," and to the relief of the Confederates, "no enemy was in sight." That afternoon, David Birney summoned the band of the 114th Pennsylvania "to play in honor of the National Anniversary" up on the "line of battle." They played the usual "national airs, finishing up with 'The Star Spangled Banner.' At that moment, the rebels sent a shell over our lines." It was the last shot of the battle of Gettysburg.[15]

That night, Meade called another council of war. Despite the weather, Union signalers had spotted the movement of Lee's wagons on the Fairfield and Cashtown roads, and on the strength of those reports Meade issued a congratulatory order to the Army of the Potomac, announcing that the enemy "has now withdrawn from the contest . . . utterly baffled and defeated." On the other hand, he had word from Francis Barlow, who turned out to be quite alive after his ordeal on July 1st and was convalescing at the Josiah Benner farmhouse, warning that "the movement of the enemy" was "a mere feint." So, Meade added to his order, "our task is not yet accomplished," and he looked to "the army for greater efforts to drive from our soil every vestige . . . of the invader." He followed the order with a circular to the corps commanders that no "present move" would be made by the Army of the Potomac, "but to refit and rest" and "get the commands well in hand."[16]

The council met that night in a temporary headquarters Meade borrowed from one of the 6th Corps division commanders, and for all the congratulations he had issued earlier in the day Meade's tone was still apprehensive. He opened the meeting by suggesting "that the enemy were making a flank movement, and would probably try to interpose between us and Washington." He sternly reminded everyone that his primary responsibility was to protect the capital, and having stated the situation, he asked "the corps commanders for their advice as to what course he should pursue"—follow on Lee's heels . . . shadow him at a distance, moving parallel to Lee down the eastern side of South Mountain into Maryland . . . . or (according to John Sedgwick), "move back to Westminster." Because "so little" was "definitely known as to the position and designs of the enemy," the consensus quickly favored waiting until they "could find out something." This satisfied Meade quite nicely. The succession of heavy rains had made the Potomac unfordable, so it was not likely that Lee could go far, and besides, "My army requires a few days rest, and cannot move at present."

But this conclusion did not satisfy Otis Howard, Alf Pleasonton, or David Birney (who had been jumped back into command of what was left of the 3rd Corps by Hancock's wounding), nor did it satisfy Gouverneur Warren (as chief engineer), who already thought he could see forming the same constellation of attitudes which had allowed Lee to escape from McClellan after Antietam. "Give me command of a division," Warren excitedly interrupted, and "by 8 o'clock the next morning I would tell them whether the enemy was retreating or not." The offer received only a stiff acknowledgment. "There was a tone amongst most of the prominent officers that we had quite saved the country for the time, and that we had done enough; that we might jeopardy all that we had won by trying to do too much." So in the end, by a vote of five to three, it was agreed "to remain twenty-four hours longer in our position, and that General Sedgwick . . . should be sent with his corps to find out" where the rebels were headed. Later that night, Meade remembered Darius Couch and Baldy Smith, and sent off an order to Couch to gather his little odds-and-ends army of militia and start poking southward through the Cumberland Valley.[17]

The Confederates expected more from Meade, and were relieved not to get it. They had come into Pennsylvania, "beginning to look for peace before a great while," but now their primary fear was "defeat in the enemy's country." Their temper was darkened still further by the miseries of having "to stand & wait for an hour or more" on roads "blocked up with troops," and by the unearthly screaming, shrieking, weeping, moaning, "oaths, and execrations" which arose from the army's ambulances as the "wagons kept the road" and the uninjured survivors "marched through the fields & woods on each side." Occasionally, there would be "a brass band on the side of the road . . . playing 'Dixie' & 'Maryland,'" but this did not do much to drown out the cries heard by John Imboden from thousands of voices in the backs of jolting wagons and ambulances: *O God! Why can't I die? . . . My God! Will no one have mercy and kill me and end my misery? . . . Oh! stop one minute and take me out and leave me to die on the roadside. . . . I am dying! I am dying! My poor wife, my dear children! What will become of you?* Meade's hesitation gave both parts of Lee's army a full day's grace, but since the wagon trains alone occupied anywhere from fifteen to twenty miles of road, the likelihood of Lee putting any great distance between himself and pursuit was dim. Jubal Early's division, bringing up the rear of the enormous infantry column on the Fairfield Road, didn't get moving in the direction of South Mountain until two o'clock on the morning of July 5th, all the while "halting now and then to see if the Yankee Army would come out and give us battle."[18]

They needn't have worried. John Sedgwick's 6th Corps played a very slow game of catch-up, covering only three very cautious miles along the Fairfield Road by noon on July 5th. Three more miles brought them up to Jubal Early's skirmish lines outside Fairfield, and Sedgwick sent little more than some random shelling in their direction. The next day, Sedgwick "showed no disposition to push this rear guard." His skirmishers crept into "the somewhat dilapidated village" of Fairfield, but after throwing "a few shells down the street" in the morning fog, Sedgwick informed Meade that "the enemy have a very strong rear guard and will hold the gaps strongly." Meade ordered them all back to Gettysburg, apart from one brigade which would content itself with shadowing the rebel column.

Caution was Meade's compass. There was no need to fall back to West-minster, he concluded, but also no sense in a hot pursuit of Lee's infantry. "I am not able to say what Lee is going to do," Meade wrote to Baldy Smith, "but expect he is off for the Potomac or the lower end of the Valley; he may, however, remain behind the mountains." The one thing he knew he could not do was what McClellan usually did, which was to stay put and lick his wounds. But if he must get up and chase after Lee, he was determined to do so with all antennae quivering. He would move down the east side of South Mountain, keeping the mountains between himself and Lee, and keeping the Army of the Potomac between Lee and the capital. At Frederick, he would meet the 6,000 wagons which made up the army's quartermaster and com-missary trains, and then he would judge whether "I may have an opportunity of attacking." For now, he would leave it to his cavalry to harass and delay Lee's movements.[19]

This was live bait to Pleasonton, Judson Kilpatrick, and John Buford. On July 4th, Kilpatrick swung around the flanks of Lee's infantry on the Fairfield Road and struck seven miles west of Fairfield, at Monterey Pass, slashing and hacking at Dick Ewell's column. A few hours later, troopers from one of Buford's brigades ambushed Imboden's seventeen-mile-long train at Greencastle, making off with "130 wagons . . . two iron guns, and 200 pris-oners"; late that same day, another ambush sliced off 134 wagons and 645 prisoners. A day after, on July 6th, Buford's cavalry raided Williamsport itself ahead of Lee's arrival. On July 6th, Stuart fended off an attempt by Kilpat-rick's horsemen to seize Hagerstown; the same day, he parried Buford's blow at Williamsport, keeping the line of Lee's retreat to the Potomac open, and on July 8th he fought a successful delaying action behind Lee's infantry at Boonsboro. Despite "rain and mud, rough mountains, and difficult roads," and despite harassment from emboldened civilians in Greencastle who jeered at "ye lousy Revelscallims," stole rebel horses, and stove in the spokes of "ten or a dozen wheels and dropping the wagons in the streets," Imboden made Williamsport with "nearly the whole of the immense train" on July 6th. Lee and the rest of the Army of Northern Virginia made it on the 7th, ready to cross over into Virginia.[20]

Williamsport, however, quickly took on the shape of a trap rather than a haven. The cross-river traffic there was usually served by a ferry, punted across on a wire cable strung between the Maryland and Virginia shores; there were also numerous shallow fords around the ferry, and the Confederates had made easy use of them in June when they first crossed the Potomac. Four miles downstream at Falling Waters, Confederate engineers had also built a pontoon bridge in June for the army's use. But the on-again, off-again rains had swollen the Potomac "to an almost unprecedented height," well "beyond fording stage," and the pontoon bridge at Falling Waters had been destroyed by a Federal raiding party on July 4th. Barred by the high water, Lee cast around quickly for alternatives, and wanted Imboden to name for him "all fords as high up as Cumberland [Maryland], and describe minutely their character, and the roads and surrounding country on both sides of the river."

But the situation was no better at any of those alternatives and Lee did not have the luxury of waiting for the river to fall. "There was neither rations or ammunition for the troops and prisoners, nor food for the starving animals, who could scarcely drag themselves through the mud." So, Lee improvised a long defensive line along a ridge that covered both Williamsport and Falling Waters, and set his engineers to tearing down everything in the neighborhood made of wood and stripping every sawmill along the river of "boards and crossbeams" to construct makeshift pontoons. If he could bluff his pursuers, he might be able to buy the time he needed to build an escape route; if not, then Lee would be facing a second Antietam, only this time with his back to a Potomac that offered him no "hope of long resistance." Porter Alexander was amazed to see how much serenity Lee was able to summon, but one of Alexander's officers admitted that "every one feels how disastrous to us our defeat at Gettysburg was . . . and the retreat has been almost as bad for us as the defeat."[21]

None of this made Meade move any faster. The Army of the Potomac swung into pursuit on the evening of the 5th, "moving in the direction of Emmitsburgh . . . feeling their way at every step" in the rain and gloom. They crossed the Monocacy River on the 6th, where regiments formed square to hear Meade's congratulations order; in Frederick, on July 8th, "mail was distributed" for the first time since the beginning of the campaign. One landmark which almost everyone in the Army of the Potomac seems to have noticed as they passed through Frederick was "the body of a spy that had been hung by Gen. Buford." The man was one of Stuart's scouts, and he had been "tried by a drum-head court-martial" and "hanged upon a locust tree" with a tent cord. Soldiers passing by "had stripped the bark from the trunk of the tree," and then gone to work on the spy's clothes "until the body was entirely nude."[22]

Then, they turned west to the mountain gaps—Fox's, Turner's, Crampton's. Getting over the mountains turned out to be a slower business than anyone anticipated. "The animals," Meade reported to Halleck, were "completely exhausted, many falling on the road." It took until July 11th for the Army of the Potomac to descend the far side and begin crossing the Antietam Creek. All the while, still more rainstorms and flash floods soaked the Federals. A soldier in the 18th Massachusetts complained that "nothing could be kept dry, and if a battle had occurred only bayonets could be used," because the cartridges were so damp that not "one musket in ten could have been discharged."[23]

If the pouring rains mired Meade's progress, so did "anxiety & responsibility." Meade complained that he "can get no reliable information of the enemy, and have to grope my way in the dark." On went the litany: "I have not changed my clothes, have not had a regular night's rest and many nights not a wink of sleep, and for several days did not wash my face & hands—no regular food, and all this time in a great state of mental anxiety." He was, in truth, worried sick about his own inadequacy. He had been in command of the Army of the Potomac for exactly ten days, he wrote to Margaretta, and everyone—"the people & the Govt."—now believed that "I must always be victorious" and that Lee must be "demoralized & disorganized." Did they not realize, he continued in the same vein, that "battles are often decided by accidents"? He possessed no genius, no magic formula, and as for tactic and strategy, "no man of sense will say in advance what their result will be." He was almost ready to admit that his great triumph at Gettysburg had been as much a surprise to him as to the rebels, that he had really directed nothing, and that the fine laurel that Gettysburg had planted upon his brow had arrived so mysteriously that it might disappear just as easily. He must be cautious, leaving nothing vulnerable, doing nothing headlong. This, in turn, put Meade in a particularly testy mood when Henry Halleck began needling him to get on with things. "There is reliable information that the enemy is crossing at Williamsport," Halleck officiously wired him on July 8th. "The opportunity to attack his divided forces should not be lost" and Meade "should move against him by forced marches." Meade's temper, not surprisingly, detonated even more grandly than usual. "My army is and has been making forced marches, short of rations and barefooted," Meade fired back. If Halleck would just back off, "I will use my utmost effort to push forward this army."[24]

But Lee was not going to wait for him. Ammunition was brought up from Winchester and punted across to Williamsport on the ferry, and ambulances and prisoners were ferried back on the return trip. Confederate engineers, sometimes with only one axe or one saw to each squad, managed to cobble together sixteen pontoons, and together with ten pontoons recovered from the wreck of the previous bridge, they strung an 800-foot-long floating causeway across the Potomac at Falling Waters. "It was built in two sections," wrote one of the engineers, "the first starting on the Maryland side and extending to an island about a hundred yards wide, and then from the south side of the island to the Virginia shore." Three ferries were now in operation at Williamsport, and, even better, the rains stopped, and the river began to fall—a foot and a half by July 12th. The next afternoon, Lee issued orders to cross the river under cover of darkness: Hill's and Longstreet's corps would cross on the bridge at Falling Waters; Ewell's corps, Stuart's cavalry, and whatever else was still in Williamsport would use the fords or the punts.[25]

Meade promised Halleck on July 10th that he would have the Army of the Potomac within four miles of Lee's defenses that evening. But by July 12th, Meade had only just crossed the Antietam Creek and advanced a mile beyond it in Lee's direction, and although he promised Halleck again that he "would attack them to-morrow," that evening ("about 8 or 9 o'clock"), Meade called for yet another council of war. This time, he had a very different audience than the one he had greeted in Gettysburg: Howard, Slocum, Sykes, and Sedgwick were still in command of their corps, but Meade had dumped Birney from the 3rd Corps again and replaced him with William French, and in Hancock's place, Meade had appointed a nonentity named William Hayes, over the heads of both Alex Hays and John Caldwell. Above all, he sloughed off the wounded Dan Butterfield as chief of staff and appointed Andrew Humphreys, which gave Meade an altogether different choir to conduct. In the years to come, this council would be portrayed as the moment when a suddenly offensive-minded Meade was restrained by his timid corps commanders. Meade "stated briefly the condition of our forces." But when he put to them the question—*Shall we, without further knowledge of the position of the enemy, make an attack?*—they all with one consent began to make excuses. He reported to Halleck the next day that his proposal for an attack had been overruled, "five out of six" of the corps commanders" being "unqualifiedly opposed to it."[26]

But a faint suspicion of things not being quite what met the eye hangs over this council. For one thing, Meade changed his story about the council nine months later, testifying before the Joint Committee on the Conduct of the War that he "cannot state positively what each individual vote was," but thought that an attack had been favored by *two* corps commanders, Otis Howard and James Wadsworth (who was temporarily in command of the 1st Corps). Howard remembered *three* dissenters—himself, Wadsworth, and Pleasonton—as did Wadsworth. And then there was the question itself, whose "peculiar phraseology" convinced Slocum that it "indicated the decision the commanding general anticipated" so that the council's conclusion would be "precisely what he desired and anticipated it would be when he framed the question." Meade, in other words, wanted to be on record as favoring an attack, but he also wanted it on the record that he had been talked out of it, which he "at once used to sustain himself at the expense of his brother officers." Wadsworth was certainly incensed by the decision. He came storming back to the 1st Corps artillery chief, Charles Wainwright, talking "very freely on the subject, and loudly against the decision." Howard, however, was merely resigned. Although he believed that at a word, he could attack Lee and "double him up," it was apparent that Meade would not. "I fear that Lee is getting away."[27]

Halleck read through the same lines: "You are strong enough to attack and defeat the enemy before he can effect a crossing," he frantically wired Meade late on July 13th. "Act upon your own judgment and make your generals execute your orders. Call no council of war." Above all, "do not let the enemy escape." But by the time Meade received Halleck's telegram, the escape was already in progress. Although still more rain began to fall and Longstreet darkly warned that it might be better to wait for the next day, Lee's "anxiety was intense" to get away, and so the evacuation proceeded. "And a crazy affair it was, too," remembered Moxley Sorrel. The rain came down in "blinding sheets," and wagons stalled in mud on the approaches to the pontoon bridge, and Lee's men could only risk keeping "three or four torches alight, and those were dimmed at times when heavy rains came." But "our father, Lee, was scarcely ever out of sight," and by morning, only the last of Harry Heth's division was still crossing at Falling Waters. The last regiment to pass was the ghostly 26th North Carolina, without its colonel, its colors, and without almost three-quarters of the men who had crossed the river so happily less than a month before. And then the ropes sustaining the jury-rigged bridge were cut and the retaining cables were pulled to bring the pontoon boats over to the Virginia shore. Except for some 1,500 stragglers and the skirmishers of the 4th Alabama (who had to swim for it), the Army of Northern Virginia was safe.[28]

There is bad faith somewhere

THE ARMY ROBERT E. LEE brought back to Virginia had been hideously, cruelly damaged. "You have all heard all the particulars of the terrible battles around Gettysburg," wrote a demoralized lieutenant in the 10th Virginia. "It had all the bad results of a defeat." George Pickett, to begin with, was only slightly exaggerating when he claimed that his division had been destroyed at Gettysburg. As in any Civil War military numerations, there are different sets of numbers claiming to be the official calculation, so the most important of them for Pickett's division might as well be spelled out here:

	KILLED	WOUNDED	MISSING AND/OR CAPTURED	TOTAL
Earl J. Hess, *Pickett's Charge—The Last Attack at Gettysburg* (2001), 333–34	498	833 "wounded and captured" 681 "captured" 643 "wounded"		2,655
John Busey & David Martin, *Regimental Strengths and Losses at Gettysburg* (2005), 271	626	1,296	840	2,762
Robert Krick, *The Gettysburg Death Roster: The Confederate Dead at Gettysburg* (2004), 7	232	1,157	1,499	2,888
Kathy Georg Harrison, *Nothing but Glory: Pickett's Division at Gettysburg* (1986), 138				"over 2,600 casualties"

George R. Stewart, *Pickett's Charge: A Microhistory of the Final Attack at Gettysburg, July 3, 1863* (1959), 263	500	2007	375	2,882
O.R., series one, 27 (pt. 2):339	301	537	1,817	2,655
Walter Harrison, *Pickett's Men: A Fragment of War History* (1870), 102				3,393

Within Pickett's command, Richard Garnett's brigade was particularly hard hit. Of the more than 1,400 men who marched with him down the Cashtown Pike to join the battle, about 950 of them never came back. Within each regiment, the impact was even greater: the regiment was the soldier's home neighborhood, and the numbers have a keener edge. The 18th Virginia lost at least 50 dead, 77 wounded, and 104 otherwise unaccounted for; only 50 men returned from the great charge unharmed. The 8th Virginia went into action with anywhere from 205 men (according to its colonel, Eppa Hunton) to 189 men (according to a private, Randolph Shotwell), but in the overall effect, it hardly mattered. Hunton counted only 10 men after the charge, Shotwell 15. The returns of the other two brigades in Pickett's division are only a little less dreary: Armistead's approximately 2,000 men left just over half of their numbers behind; of Kemper's 1,600, 700 or so were missing by the time they returned to Seminary Ridge. Put it all in rough but denatured percentages, and Pickett's division hemorrhaged two-thirds of its listed strength in that one afternoon.[1]

Johnston Pettigrew's division hardly fared better. "Our troops are badly cut up," wrote an officer in the 55th North Carolina. "Brigades now are not larger than Regts were befor[e] the fight." Pettigrew's old brigade lost 1,573 men out of the 2,584 who were ready for duty on July 1st. On the regimental level, it hurt even more. The 26th North Carolina sustained 172 dead, 443 wounded, 72 missing; by the end of the battle, the 800 or so men who had been on the regiment's rolls had been reduced to nothing more than "a very good skirmish line" of 67 enlisted men and 3 officers (not counting "cooks and extra duty men," who were probably slaves). In the 11th Mississippi, 32 men were killed and 170 wounded. This translated, within separate companies, to wholesale decimation. Company K "took thirty-eight into the charge" and "at roll call that evening seven answered"; Company D had 10 survivors out of 50; Company E "took in thirty-eight men, of whom fifteen were killed and twenty-one wounded," including its captain and all three lieutenants; Company A, the "University Grays" (which had back in 1861 numbered 135 and comprised almost the entire student body of the University of Mississippi), had the unwelcome distinction of being wiped out.[2]

But numbers, no matter how added or multiplied, are still anodyne. "The reality of war is largely obscured by descriptions that tell of movements and maneuvers of armies, of the attack and repulse, of victory and defeat, and then pass on to new operations," complained Charles Augustus Fuller of the 61st New York. "All this leaves out of sight the fellows, stretched out with holes through them, or with legs and arms off." It was not merely that men were dead or wounded or captured; it was who they were and what they meant to one another and to their homes. John Oates, the brother of the William Oates who had led the Alabamians up the slopes of Little Round Top, was shot seven times on July 2nd, and lingered till July 23rd, dying slowly from blood poisoning. The battered 26th North Carolina lost a pair of twin brothers, Joseph and W. E. Phillips, in Company F on July 1st; two of the four Kirkman brothers in Company G also were killed on July 1st, and the other two died in Union captivity. Others defiantly dodged the neat categories. Thomas Jolly of the Phillips Georgia Legion was shot, bayoneted, and reported dead at Gettysburg, and his wife filed a death claim on August 14th; but a year later he turned up at his Dalton, Georgia, home, having managed to recover from his wounds and be released from the Union prison at Point Lookout. William Gaskins of the 8th Virginia survived wounding and capture at Pickett's Charge, only to die in captivity four months later of "obstinate" diarrhea. (On the other hand, a sergeant in the 3rd South Carolina, Young Pope, was hit three times, in the thigh, hip, and arm, but survived to become a lawyer, state attorney general, and chief justice of the South Carolina Supreme Court.)[3]

The casualty numbers also fail to explain the damage done to the command infrastructure of the army. In the 18th Virginia, twenty-nine of the regiment's thirty-one officers were killed or wounded; in the 8th Virginia, the colonel, lieutenant colonel, and major were all wounded, and three company captains killed, and two captured. John Bell Hood's division also lost the colonels of the 2nd, 9th, and 20th Georgia, while in Joseph Kershaw's South Carolina brigade two more regimental commanders were killed. Jubal Early's division lost a brigade commander, Isaac Avery, who was mortally wounded and died in the farmhouse of Henry Culp, plus the colonels of the 8th Louisiana and 38th Georgia. Robert Rodes' hapless division saw three colonels killed and seven wounded (two of whom were also captured). Powell Hill's corps reeled from the worst hits to its regimental commanders: four of the five colonels in Cadmus Wilcox's Alabama brigade were wounded, alongside two in the angry Ambrose Wright's brigade. And worst of all, every one of Johnston Pettigrew's colonels was killed, wounded, or captured, as were all of Joe Davis'.

Nor were general officers exempt, beginning at the top with Hood. Of Lee's fifty-two generals at Gettysburg, a third of them were casualties of some sort, starting with the wounding of Alfred Scales and the capture of James Archer (and two of his colonels) on July 1st. Lafayette McLaws lost two of his brigadiers, the ebullient William Barksdale but also Paul Semmes, who was wounded by a shell fragment in the leg on July 2nd and was expected to recover, but died on July 10th. Dick Ewell lost only one brigadier to wounding, John Marshall Jones, but Pickett lost Armistead and Garnett (though not James Kemper, despite nearly everyone's prediction that his wound was fatal). Old Isaac Trimble was also wounded during Pickett's Charge, and at age sixty-one managed to survive both the amputation of his leg *and* Union imprisonment, and lived for twenty-five more cantankerous years. Keenest of all were the two losses no one expected. The first was Dorsey Pender. The other was Johnston Pettigrew, who survived both the battle for Herbst's Woods on July 1st and the great charge on July 3rd, only to be shot in the abdomen by a Federal cavalryman while covering the tail end of Hill's corps as it crossed the pontoon bridge at Williamsport. "The noble Pettigrew" was carried across the bridge and died three days later in Martinsburg. All of these casualties reduced or eliminated months and years of experience, familiarity, networking, and confidence which could not be replaced merely by promotion of the next in line.[4]

Surveying the army's survivors, Lee reported 2,592 killed, 12,700 wounded and 4,150 "captured or missing" after Gettysburg—20,451 casualties in all, based on data collected by the army's chief medical officer, Lafayette Guild. Each of these numbers has a blurred boundary, since those *missing* might have been killed without leaving any record, or be deserters who might, or might not, at some point rejoin the army. *Wounded* included anything from a minor gunshot wound (like Harry Heth's) to a blast to the head which caused the victim to linger for days or weeks before succumbing. In the 2nd South Carolina, James Casson, a twenty-three-year-old private, "had a portion of his skull shot away above one eye" by an artillery round from Federal artillery in the peach orchard on July 2nd; he lived for five days, but "was out of his mind instantly." Would Casson, or would William Gaskins, who survived his wound but then died of disease in a Union prison, be best defined as merely *wounded*? Any way the numbers are piled, though, the results were equivalent to a historic catastrophe. Even if one takes the lowest mark, the Army of Northern Virginia suffered something comparable to two sinkings of the *Titanic,* the 2001 attacks on the World Trade Center and the Pentagon, ten repetitions of the Great Blizzard of 1888, and two Pearl Harbors. Or, if percentages provide more clarity, the Confederates at Gettysburg sustained two and a half times the losses taken by the Allied armies in Normandy from D-Day through August 1944. And anyone who had any doubts about the impact needed only to consult the officer who wrote to his sister on July 17th, "The campaign is a failure and the worst failure that the South has ever made . . . and no blow since the fall of New Orleans has been so telling against us."[5]

The Army of the Potomac was in scarcely better shape. George Meade himself had a rough tally ready for his July 4th council which came up with 56,138 infantry and artillery ready for action. That would mean that he had lost nearly 22,000 men. Meade's first report to Halleck on August 3rd was more specific, and cited 2,834 killed, 13,713 wounded, and 6,643 missing; two months later, he adjusted those numbers slightly, and then submitted final figures which set the totals at 3,155 killed, 14,529 wounded, and 5,365 "captured or missing." In his testimony before the Joint Committee on the Conduct of the War the following spring, Meade simply rounded the figures up to "24,000 men killed, wounded and missing," and these numbers have become the generally received calculation of Union casualties. And yet, there is almost as much uncertainty about these numbers as about Lee's. Michael Jacobs, the Pennsylvania College mathematician, estimated that there were "9,000 dead" and "20,000 wounded" in Gettysburg after the armies left, which would require pegging Union deaths at more than 4,000; St. Clair Mulholland, colonel of the 116th Pennsylvania, also estimated the number of Union dead at closer to 4,400; and in 1900, Thomas Livermore, a veteran of the battle, painstakingly recalculated unit reports and put the reckoning at 3,903 dead, 18,735 wounded, and 5,425 "missing," so that the entire butcher's bill edged up to 28,063. (Most of these casualties, Meade added in his congressional testimony, occurred on July 2nd—"over 20,000 of them"—so that the second day of the battle alone came nearly equal with the horrendous single-day losses at Antietam the year before.)

Officer grades in the Army of the Potomac had suffered even more severely than their Confederate peers. One corps commander (John Reynolds) had been killed and two others (Dan Sickles and Winfield Hancock) were wounded and put hors de combat. Reynolds' 1st Corps lost four of its seven brigade commanders to wounds on July 1st. In the 2nd Corps, John Gibbon was wounded and lost ten of his division's thirteen colonels; John Caldwell's heroic charge into the wheat field cost his division three of its four brigade commanders; and Alex Hays lost three. Each of the 3rd Corps divisions lost a brigadier; the 5th Corps and the 11th Corps each lost a division commander, but the 5th Corps had more to mourn in the death of Strong Vincent (on July 7th, after finally receiving his brigadier's star). Some individual units had almost ceased to exist. The Philadelphia Brigade was down to 660 men (the 69th Pennsylvania could only count 115 after the battle);

the fabled Iron Brigade was left with less than 700 of the 1,829 who followed Reynolds into action on July 1st.[6]

But unlike the Confederates, the men of the Army of the Potomac were, for once, brimming with eagerness to come to grips with the rebels. "What do the people of the North think now of the Old Army of the Potomac," exulted a soldier in the 28th Pennsylvania. John White Geary wrote to his wife that his division was "now refitting the clothing and equipments of the command. . . . The result of the war seems no longer doubtful, and . . . the beginning of the end appears." John Chase, in the 1st Massachusetts Light Artillery, saw the men take the burdens of the miserable weather and even more miserable roads after Gettysburg "like Martyrs saying if only we can get at them again before they get out of Maryland and get as good a Ration of Rebs as we did at Gettysburg." It was a rare day, wrote Henry Nichols Blake, when the "veterans are anxious to fight," but "animated by the glorious triumphs of Gettysburg" they "wished with a united voice to be led to the work of carnage" at Williamsport.

The pace of the march, however, struck the first note of suspicion. "We thought our corps commander displayed little energy in finding the enemy," complained a Pennsylvania colonel in the 5th Corps about the listlessness of George Sykes' pursuit, and what was being said about Sykes gradually repeated itself throughout the army. "It began to look as though it were intended that Lee should be allowed to cross the Potomac without another fight, if he wished." When they awoke on the morning of July 14th, there was a great deal of head wagging and I-told-you-so-ing about Meade. The 77th New York was "more incensed than surprised," and "for a long time the most awful curses were uttered in connection with the names of Meade and certain generals who opposed the assault." John Chase was confident that "we could [have] just cleaned them from the word go," but "I suppose that is the last thing a good many of our damn poor apologys for officers want to see is this war ended." In the 118th Pennsylvania, the men refused the call of their colonel for three cheers for Meade. "Not a man moved in response, not a voice was heard, all stood still."[7]

The soldiers were not the only ones infuriated at the escape. The *Washington Sunday Morning Chronicle* released the first news of the Gettysburg victory on July 5th, trumpeting its certainty "that Lee's army is already seriously interfered with, and his escape from our army will be a matter of great difficulty." A week later, the *Chronicle* was ever more ebullient: "That there will be another battle . . . is highly probably. . . . It will probably be a bloody conflict but we do not hesitate to predict that it will be a great, if not, indeed, a decisive victory over the insurgents." Both Senator Henry Wilson, the chair of the Senate's Committee on Military Affairs, and Vice President Hannibal

Hamlin came up from Washington to be present at the finish, and no one was more eager to see the Army of the Potomac go in for a funeral than Abraham Lincoln. The president released an announcement of the Gettysburg victory on the morning of July 4th, praising the army for "news . . . such as to cover that Army with the highest honor" and "to promise a great success to the cause of the Union." In the first flush of good news, he was "more than satisfied with what has happened North of the Potomac so far," and on July 11th, he seemed to his secretary John Hay to be "in a specially good humor, as he had pretty good evidence that . . . Meade had announced his intention of attacking them." But it did not take long before Lincoln's anxieties began to rise. He was disturbed by "Meade's slow movements since Gettysburg," and he was particularly irritated at the phrase in Meade's congratulatory order to the army on July 4th and its call to "drive the invaders from our soil." *Drive the invaders from our soil!* Lincoln burst out in unrestrained dismay, *My God! Is that all?* He grumbled to Hay, "Will our Generals never get that idea out of their heads? The whole country is *our* soil." And he added ominously, "This is a dreadful reminiscence of McClellan."[8]

McClellan was not the name Meade should have wanted his own to conjure up in Lincoln's mind. The president had never shaken off the sense that McClellan deliberately pulled his military punches on the Peninsula and after Antietam so that the war could be drawn out further and further toward the mutual exhaustion of both sides, and some form of negotiated settlement. "They did not mean to gain any decisive victory," he confided to Hay, "but to keep things running on so that they, the army, might manage things to suit themselves." By July 13th, Lincoln worried that no one has "yet heard of Meade's expected attack," and Lincoln took the desperate step of sending Meade a plea which did everything but sink down on bended knee: "You will follow up and attack Genl. Lee as soon as possible before he can cross the river. If you fail this dispatch will clear you from all responsibility and if you succeed you may destroy it." (This message may have been hand-carried to Meade by Hannibal Hamlin, as the real mission of the Hamlin-Wilson visit to Williamsport.) But at noon on the 14th, Meade sent the news Lincoln wanted least to hear. "On advancing my army this morning," Meade reported, "I found, on reaching his lines, that they were evacuated."[9]

Lincoln was not a man often given to displays of emotion, but that afternoon, he was—as Hay put it—"deeply grieved." Lincoln's son Robert was home from Harvard, and walked into his father's office to find him "in much distress, his head leaning upon the desk in front of him, and when he raised his head there were evidences of tears upon his face." *We had them in our grasp,* Lincoln wailed. *We had only to stretch forth our hands & they were ours.* That image of Meade and his war council holding "the war in the hollow of their hand & they would not close it" kept coming back to Lincoln, and he began to wonder whether "if I had gone up there I could have whipped them myself." Hamlin, likewise, met the journalist Noah Brooks at Meade's headquarters, "raised his hands and turned away his face with a gesture of despair." When Lincoln encountered Gideon Welles, his secretary of the navy, on "the lawn" between the War and Navy department buildings, his mind was already turning toward the possibility that "Meade, Couch, Smith and all" had some McClellan-like plot up their sleeves. "He said, with a voice and countenance which I shall never forget, that he had dreaded yet expected this. . . . There is bad faith somewhere. . . . What does it mean, Mr. Welles? Great God! what does it mean?"[10]

Meade really had no such grandiose schemes. But far from feeling any embarrassment, when Meade learned through Halleck that "the escape of Lee's army without another battle has created great dissatisfaction in the mind of the President," Meade considered himself the injured party. He replied to Halleck's telegram as immediately as the wires permitted, indignantly requesting that he be given the martyr treatment. "The censure of the President conveyed in your dispatch . . . is, in my judgment, so undeserved that I feel compelled most respectfully to ask to be immediately relieved from the command of this army." But he must have known that neither Halleck nor Lincoln would actually dare to cashier him. The Northern newspapers were full of jubilation over Gettysburg, and full of praise for a commanding general whom they could praise, and Lincoln was not about to throw things into a cocked hat by replacing Meade for not winning more. Halleck tamely damped Meade's indignation: "My telegram, stating the disappointment of the President at the escape of Lee's army, was not intended as a censure but as a stimulus to an active pursuit." And Lincoln himself wrote a soothing letter, insisting on how "very—*very*—grateful" he was "to you for the magnificent success you gave the cause of the country at Gettysburg." But even as he assured Meade that he was "sorry now to be the author of the slightest pain to you," the bitterness still seeped back in. "I do not believe you appreciate the magnitude of the misfortune involved in Lee's escape." Again, the image of the unclosed hand came to him. "He was within your easy grasp, and to have closed upon him would, in connection with our other late successes, have ended the war." And then, realizing the futility of it, he filed the letter away, scribbling on the envelope, *To Gen. Meade, never sent, or signed.*[11]

George Meade, for his part, never saw the slightest fault in himself. "This is exactly what I expected," he wrote to Margaretta after Halleck's no-censure telegram arrived. "Unless I did impracticable things, fault would be found with me." He certainly had the backing of the other McClellanites. "You will wonder . . . why we did not crush the enemy," John Sedgwick wrote to his sister on July 17th; she should know that "the enemy crossed the river at Williamsport" with "forces . . . far superior in numbers to our own." McClellan himself put his imprimatur on Meade's decision by assuring him that "you have done all that could be done and the Army of the Potomac has supported you nobly. . . . I feel very proud of you and my old Army." Meade would surely "have another severe battle to fight, but I am confident that you will win." So there was no need for Meade to hang his head. "I have ignored the senseless adulation of the public and press," Meade congratulated himself, "and I am now just as indifferent to the censure bestowed without just cause." He had dodged both disgrace and disaster, which was more than his own father had done, and there must have been at least one small part of George Gordon Meade which would actually have welcomed retirement at that moment so that he could preserve his Gettysburg laurels intact for the rest of his life.[12]

McClellan was right about the "severe battle" to be fought, but it would not be fought with the Army of Northern Virginia. Meade did not cross the Potomac until July 18th, his bands playing "Carry Me Back to Old Virginny," and by that time the Confederates were well out of his grasp. There was some menacing checkerboarding across northern Virginia for several weeks, but by mid-August the two armies were pretty much back where they had been at the beginning of June on the Rappahannock. Another burst of tactical energy that fall nearly produced a serious confrontation at Bristoe Station, and again at Mine Run, and Lincoln once again offered to take all the blame and let Meade have all the credit if only Meade would act. But at the last minute Meade pulled back, and the two armies went into winter quarters and the war in 1863 ended in Virginia as unresolved as It had been when the year started.

This did not mean that Meade lacked for enemies to fight, but they were all within his own army, starting with Dan Sickles. The abundantly confident New Yorker survived the amputation of his leg surprisingly well, convalescing exuberantly in Washington and filling the ears of any politicians, all the way up to the president, with tales of how the 3rd Corps had saved the Army of the Potomac from sure destruction on July 2nd and prevented Meade from packing up for a retreat to Pipe Creek. Word of this came back to a stony-faced Meade, and when Sickles returned to the army on October 18th, expecting restoration to command, Meade made it bluntly clear that under no imaginable circumstances would he ever agree to having Sickles in charge of anything in the Army of the Potomac. In fact, Meade wanted to be rid of the entire 3rd Corps, not to mention the troublesome spirits in the 1st Corps, and in the spring he ordered the breakup of both corps and the redistribution of their divisions among the much more reliable 2nd and 5th Corps.[13]

Other heads rolled, as well. Abner Doubleday protested Meade's promotion of John Newton to command of the 1st Corps, and was flatly dismissed on July 5th, never to return to command in the Army of the Potomac. In November, when a massive Federal defeat in the west (at Chickamauga) impelled Lincoln and Stanton to pull troops away from the East to send to the rescue of a besieged Federal army in Chattanooga, Meade was only too happy to send Otis Howard and Henry Slocum and most of their corps as his contribution to the rescue. (Once free from the onus of the Army of the Potomac's politics, Otis Howard developed into one of the finest corps commanders in the Union Army; he marched with Sherman through Georgia, and though the profane Sherman could not have occupied a more different mental world than the pious Howard, Sherman picked him to succeed his own protégé, James B. McPherson, as commander of the Army of the Tennessee.) It may be too much to call this a *purge* of abolitionists and Republicans, but by the end of the year, the Army of the Potomac had no one of either description in command at corps level.[14]

In the end, however, Meade found himself outflanked by the politicos. Sickles turned in fury from his dismissal by Meade, gained the ear of Lincoln and his old friends in Congress, and began assiduously poisoning as many minds as he could reach with the message that "General Howard and perhaps himself" had been the ones who determined to fight at Gettysburg, and that Meade was on the verge of abandoning the position on July 2nd when Sickles forced the issue by moving forward to the Emmitsburg Road. Some refused to listen. "Allowance must always be made for Sickles," sighed Gideon Welles. After all, Sickles' move amounted to something very close to outright disobedience of orders, which put him in more trouble than he had been since the murder of Philip Barton Key. Diverting attention to George Meade's failures was Sickles' best strategy for concealing his own.[15]

But there was more evidence than Meade liked to admit that he had been strangely negligent about the threat to his left flank on July 2nd until it was too late, and that he really had favored a pullout for Pipe Creek at his council of war that night. "There is no doubt," Henry Slocum insisted, "but for the decision of his corps commanders, the army on the third of July would have been in full retreat," and the Independence Day which followed it would have been "the darkest day ever known to our country." Slocum teasingly insisted that "I have in my possession a small scrap of paper three or four inches long . . . that would throw a flood of light on the battle of Gettysburg," and which "would appear after his death"; instead, Slocum's papers were destroyed. Samuel Wylie Crawford assured Sickles in 1886 that "a staff officer of Gen. Meade . . . goes far to establish your assertions in regard to Meade's determination to leave Gettysb[urg]," but the officer feared for his career, and nothing was ever made public.

Even Welles was persuaded that Meade "can obey orders and carry out orders better than he can originate and give them, hesitates, defers to others, has not strength, will, and self-reliance." In December, when the first session of the new 38th Congress assembled, Henry Wilson introduced a resolution of thanks for Gettysburg that, to Meade's fury, singled out for praise "Maj. Gen. Joseph Hooker, Maj. Gen. George G. Meade, Maj. Gen. Oliver O. Howard"—as though Hooker and Howard deserved an equal share with Meade in securing the Gettysburg victory. Lincoln signed the resolution anyway on January 28th, and in February the Joint Committee on the Conduct of the War (with some behind-closed-door-urging from Dan Sickles) opened its hearings into the Confederate escape. The first witness was Sickles, insisting that the destruction of the Confederate army at Williamsport "was the great aim and object of our army and . . . I do not think there was any military difficulty to prevent a decisive attack upon General Lee."[16]

Sickles gave his knife one more valedictory twist on March 12, 1864—a week after Meade himself had been hauled before the committee—with a sensational 4,370-word article in the *New York Herald* which made Sickles the hero of the battle and accused Meade of ignoring "the repeated warnings of that sagacious officer, General Sickles." It was signed only HISTORICUS, but few people had much doubt that it emanated from Sickles' staff, or perhaps from the pen of Dan himself. Meade certainly believed that Sickles was the author, and he was ready to demand a court of inquiry "to ascertain whether Major-General Sickles has authorized or indorses this communication." Halleck advised against it, and after the Historicus feud went through several back-and-forths in the *Herald,* and as Meade's old 5th Corps officers rose in his defense, the controversy finally burned itself out.[17]

A more serious threat to Meade's standing came in a more subtle fashion during that same session of Congress, when Illinois congressman Elihu Washburne proposed a bill "to revive the grade of general in the United States Army"—meaning the rank of lieutenant general, once held by George Washington and Winfield Scott. Washburne had long been the principal congressional cheerleader for Ulysses S. Grant, and it was obvious that this was intended as Grant's promotion to the top of the army; even though the final bill made no mention of Grant, it was Grant to whom Lincoln offered the post. Grant came east in early March to receive his commission, and Lincoln made it clear to Grant that he hoped Grant would use his new rank to take direct control of the Army of the Potomac. In the end, a reluctant Grant compromised: he would stay in the East as senior officer of the entire Union Army and retain Meade in local command of the Army of the Potomac, but he would travel with Meade and give as much supervision as the situation seemed to warrant. Meade understood all too well that this could very likely include the appointment of "some one else whom he knows better in command of this army."[18]

To their mutual surprise, Grant and Meade seemed at first to be quite content with each other. Grant "has expressed himself and acted towards me in the most friendly manner." But once the campaigning season began again in May 1864, a frost between the two set in. By June, Meade was complaining that Grant "has greatly disappointed me, and since this campaign I really begin to think that I am something of a general," and he began foaming at every "real or imaginary slight . . . in regard to which he appeared to think sufficient importance had not been given to his opinion as Commander of the Army of the Potomac." Grant soon began to understand why Lincoln had such a jaundiced view of Meade. "Meade and I got on perfectly well together," Grant insisted long after the war, but he admitted that Meade's "fits of despondency, or temper . . . were trying." Despondency led to tantrums, and tantrums led to threats of resignation, and eventually Grant "resolved, should he repeat the offer of his resignation, to accept it." He kept Meade in titular command of the Army of the Potomac through the end of the war, but Meade was increasingly reduced to the level of a glorified adjutant, executing orders for the Army of the Potomac which were spelled out by Grant.

Meade, for his part, never admitted that he had been mistaken at Williamsport: "If I had attacked [Lee] on the 13th [of July] . . . it is believed by several of my officers who subsequently inspected his lines . . . that it would have been a failure." Although he protested that he was "nothing of a copperhead," he never shook off the suspicions that he had been "in correspondence with McClellan" all through the campaign. Privately, Meade continued to hope that Lincoln would "make terms of some kind or other with the South," and in January 1865, when Confederate commissioners headed by Alexander Stephens came through the Union lines to hold one last-minute round of negotiations with Lincoln at Hampton Roads, Meade "talked very freely with them" and offered them talking points to use in the negotiations. "I told them very plainly what I thought was the basis on which the people of the North would be glad to have peace," which might not have been all that unusual apart from being proffered by a major general of the Union Army. What was needed, Meade claimed, was simply "the emphatic restoration of the Union." As for slavery, dealing with this issue was "not insurmountable," and as though he had never heard of the Emancipation Proclamation, Meade "thought some system could be found accommodating both interests, which would not be as obnoxious as slavery."[19]

———————

The Confederacy got the news of Gettysburg slowly. "The enemy has been completely routed," rejoiced the *Charleston Mercury*. "Forty thousand prisoners were taken on Sunday." Except, of course, that they hadn't. Robert E. Lee sent off his first dispatch to Jefferson Davis on July 4th, delicately apprising the Confederate president that after two days of success at Gettysburg, "our troops were compelled to relinquish their advantage and retire." He was less opaque in a second dispatch on July 7th about "the unsuccessful issue of our final attack on the enemy in the rear of Gettysburg," and on the 12th he admitted to his wife that "our success at Gettysburg was not as great as reported. In fact, we failed to drive the enemy from his position & that our army withdrew to the Potomac." But on July 15th, he once again labored to put as good a face as he could on the invasion. His "return is rather sooner than I had originally contemplated, but having accomplished what I proposed on leaving the Rappahannock, viz., relieving the Valley of the presence of the enemy & drawing his army north of the Potomac, I determined to re-cross the latter river"—as though the battle had been purely incidental.

Lee was not alone in soft-pedaling the consequences of Gettysburg. The traveling Georgia correspondent Peter Wellington Alexander described the battle in a July 4th report as "the bloodiest and most desperate battle of this bloody and desperate war," and managed to conclude that "the Confederates have had the best of the terrible conflict." Three days later, Alexander accounted for the "apparent retrograde movement" of the Army of Northern Virginia as an attempt to reopen "communications." For at least a week, the only word most Southerners had of the battle was that "Gen. Lee has given the Yanks a sound threshing at Gettysburg Pa." and that the battle had resulted "in the substantial destruction of the Northern 'Army of the Potomac,' and the unheard-of capture of 40,000 men." Only on the 14th, safely across the Potomac, did Alexander admit that he had not been able "to tell the whole truth, lest . . . important information [be] communicated to the Federal commander." Readers should brace themselves for the term *unfortunate* "as applies to the operation of the army in Maryland." Not until the 19th did the *Charleston Mercury* finally admit that Gettysburg was a defeat in every detail.[20]

The soldiers, however, knew all too well what had happened. Randolph McKim, who had watched the failure of Allegheny Johnson's brief occupation of Culp's Hill, wrote dazedly in his diary on July 11th, "I went into the last battle feeling that victory must be ours—that such an army could not be foiled, and that God would certainly declare himself on our side. Now I feel than unless He sees fit to bless our arms, our valor will not avail." A soldier in the 11th Georgia, a regiment which had fought its way over the rocky slopes of Devil's Den, wrote his mother that "the Armey is Broken harted" and "don't Care which Way the War Closes, for we have Suffered very much," and one of the survivors of Ewell's corps mourned how he began the campaign "in good hopes that the war would soon be over," but "it don't look much like it at this time."[21]

By July 12th, well-placed civilians were also beginning to understand the dimensions of what had happened. "It turns out that the battle of Gettysburg was a virtual if not an actual defeat," Robert Kean in the Confederate War Department wrote in his diary, "the success" of the first two days of the battle "went for nothing." A week later, Kean was so despondent over both Gettysburg and Vicksburg that "in the present state of affairs it would seem to be worthy of consideration whether it would not be well to obtain the assistance of some powerful foreign state, even at the expense of some pride and independence" in a "sort of protectorate." The Richmond papers were now full of the tidings of defeat. The *Richmond Enquirer* was willing to concede on July 10th that "after three days' fighting in Pennsylvania, with we know not what success, Gen. Lee has fallen back, withdrawn his forces backward from Gettysburg," and on July 13th the *Richmond Examiner* admitted that "the Confederates did not gain a victory," although it was quick to add, "neither did the enemy." By the 24th, however, the *Enquirer* had shifted down to admitting that "it cannot be denied that the invasion has been a failure." By September, there was "great depression . . . in all parts of the country . . . and in many States positive disaffection."[22]

Almost at once, there had to be a reason why. After all, Lee had enjoyed what was acknowledged on all sides as success on the first two days; Pickett's Charge ought to have finished the matter in the same way Raglan's attack at the Alma had chased off the Russians. The blame was deposited on a number of doorsteps, some of it before the battle was even finished. Dick Ewell's failure to strike for Culp's Hill and Cemetery Hill on the evening of July 1st produced many pursed lips even then, and men in Ewell's corps who had served under Stonewall Jackson were not reluctant to repeat over and over "that if we had had Jackson with us at the battle of Gettysburg he would have flanked the enemy off those heights with his corps, if he had to take one day's rations and go around by Washington City to get there." The *Charleston Mercury* took up the cry against Ewell in mid-August, declaring that "we lost the golden opportunity in not keeping up the attack that evening. . . . Timidity in the commander (Ewell) that stepped into the shoes of the fearless Jackson prompted delay." Ewell never replied in print, but he was conscious that "I have been blamed by many for not having pressed my advantage the first day at Gettysburg." Still, he could not understand why he was being condemned when the responsibility really lay with Lee. "General Lee came upon the ground before I could have possibly done anything, and after surveying the enemy's position, he did not deem it advisable to attack." Others blamed

John Bell Hood for allowing himself to be distracted by Devil's Den and Little Round Top, and failing to "envelop the enemy's left," although others contended that it was "the wounding of General Hood early in the action" which "was the real misfortune of the day."

Pickett's survivors were pointing fingers at Pettigrew's division even as they walked back in defeat, and Jedediah Hotchkiss wrote this accusation in his diary before the guns had cooled: Pickett's men, he said, "drove the enemy from their works . . . but Pettigrew failed to sustain him." (This was all the easier to believe because "the troops in the movement were mostly North Carolinians.") But among Pettigrew's survivors, it was "the failure of [Isaac] Trimble to support Pettigrew" which "resulted in disaster" on July 3rd. Alternately, claimed the *Richmond Enquirer,* it was the failure of "Brig. Gen. Posey, commanding a Mississippi brigade, and Brig. Gen. Mahone, commanding a Virginia brigade . . . to advance" in support of Wright's Georgians on July 2nd which cost the Confederacy its victory. All of these units belonged to Powell Hill's corps, and so Hill also came in for a share of brickbats.[23]

None of the Army of Northern Virginia's leaders received more concentrated abuse than J.E.B. Stuart and James Longstreet. Charles Marshall, Lee's military secretary, played the principal role in condemning Stuart, bringing down on the would-be cavalier's head the charge that Stuart had disobeyed Lee's orders "to move . . . into Maryland, and take position on General Ewell's right, place himself in communication with him, guard his flank, and keep him informed of the enemy's movements." Longstreet was denounced, not only for deliberately dragging out the launch of his flank march early on the morning of July 2nd, but for dragging out the launch of Pickett's Charge as well, and then failing to commit Hood's and McLaws' divisions to Pickett's support. This *j'accuse* was launched by Jubal Early and William Nelson Pendleton, but it was joined by Lafayette McLaws, who announced that "if the corps had moved boldly into position by eight or nine o'clock in the morning [on July 2nd], as it could have done beyond question . . . Round Top could have been occupied without any considerable degree of difficulty." Of course, McLaws was writing long after he had quarreled with Longstreet over promotion and seniority; but even as early as July 7th, McLaws had concluded that Longstreet was "a humbug—a man of small capacity, very obstinate, not at all chivalrous, exceedingly conceited, and totally selfish." Eventually, the catalog of Longstreet's condemners expanded internationally, to include no one less than the model of a modern major general, Sir Garnet Wolseley.[24]

The ultimate arbiter of blame for Gettysburg would be Robert E. Lee, and Lee's original impulse was to blame himself, beginning with that moment of agonized realization that dawned on him as Pickett's division was covered in defeat. "Our failure is to be charged to me," he told one of Longstreet's staffers as they crossed the pontoon bridge at Falling Waters, and during the retreat to the Potomac, Lee spoke at length to the Anglo-Austrian hussar Fitzgerald Ross with unusual candor about his responsibility. "Had he been aware that Meade had been able to concentrate his whole army . . . he certainly should not have attacked him," but he had been "led away, partly by the success of the first day," into the belief that "Meade had only a portion of his army in front of him, and seeing the enthusiasm of his own troops, he had thought that a successful battle would cut the knot so easily and satisfactorily, that he had determined to risk it." His initial reports to Jefferson Davis mentioned no other culprits, and he sharply criticized the *Charleston Mercury* at the end of July for heaping "censure upon the operations of the army" and singling out Harry Heth for "the failure of the battle." He had, he explained, "no complaints to make of any one but myself." In August, Lee attempted to offer Davis his resignation, but Davis waved it away. "To ask me to substitute you with someone more fit to command," said Davis, "is to demand an impossibility."[25]

But even during the retreat, Lee was already starting to shift that blame to other shoulders. He began with Stuart, since Lee's "want of knowledge of the enemy's movements" was "attributed to Stuart having got too far away from him with his cavalry." In his first official report on July 31st (which was not published in the *Richmond Enquirer* until October 3rd), Lee began to hint that "the absence of the cavalry rendered it impossible to obtain accurate information" about Meade's army and thus forced "the march toward Gettysburg" to be "conducted more slowly than it would have been had the movements of the Federal Army been known." When Lee submitted a longer, more detailed report of operations in January 1864, there was a keener edge to the criticism of Stuart. "It was expected that as soon as the Federal Army should cross the Potomac, General Stuart would give notice of its movements," Lee now decided and it was "absence of the cavalry" which forced him "to concentrate the army east of the mountains." (It was not missed that, when Lee mandated the reorganization of his cavalry divisions as a single corps, he did not recommend that Stuart be promoted, like his other corps commanders, to the rank of lieutenant general.) Five years later, Lee had grown even more prickly about Stuart. "Stuart's failure to carry out his instructions *forced the battle of Gettysburg*," he informed William Allan, a onetime staffer for Stonewall Jackson.[26]

Over time, Lee extended blame to a variety of targets within the Army of Northern Virginia. Some of them were benign: Harry Heth maintained that Lee told him the real cause of the failure to take Cemetery Hill was the shell splinter that wounded Dorsey Pender on July 2nd. "I shall ever believe if General Pender had remained on his horse half an hour longer we would have carried the enemy's position." Some of them were not: "If I had had Stone-wall Jackson with me"—and not Dick Ewell—"I should have won the battle of Gettysburg." He did not doubt that Ewell was "a fine officer," but Ewell "would never take the responsibility of exceeding his orders, and having been ordered to Gettysburg, he would not go farther and hold the heights beyond the town." He also confided to John Imboden that he believed that Johnston Pettigrew had failed Pickett on July 3rd, "and if they had been supported as they were to have been . . . we would have held the position and the day would have been ours." Even Longstreet had to endure some fault-finding from Lee for "dispositions" which "were not completed as early as was expected." And he grew increasingly reluctant to speak of Gettysburg as a mistake, much less "all my fault." He told Jefferson Davis that "I do not know what better course I could have pursued," and he continued that line of thought with Heth in the spring of 1864, explaining that if he could "cross the Potomac and invade Pennsylvania" yet again, he would do it, because he believed that "an invasion of the enemy's country" must be "our true policy." In the largest sense—and perhaps the most shameless one, too—Lee blamed his men. The problem in 1863 was not poor planning or defective execution, but that "more may have been required of them than they were able to perform." He had expected "too much" of his army's "prowess and valour." This allowed him to admit a mistake, but also to lay the origin of the mistake on others. After Appomattox, he would shift blame in the same direction, only this time he would characterize his soldiers' resistance as "feeble."[27]

Others were not so sure that Lee could evade responsibility so ambiguously. The *Richmond Enquirer* was the first to ask, on July 21st, how "Gen. Lee was led to this by overweening confidence in his troops." Lee's unthinking overestimation of the Confederate soldier and the equally unthinking underestimation of his Yankee counterpart had been noticed by the British observer Fremantle, who was bothered by "the universal feeling in the army . . . of profound contempt for an enemy whom they had beaten so constantly, and under so many disadvantages." This was a contempt which, according to both John Esten Cooke (who was an aide to Stuart) and James Dabney McCabe (a VMI graduate who interviewed Lee for a biography in 1866), Lee shared to the point where it impaired his judgment. "General Lee, it is said, shared the general confidence of his troops, and was carried away by it." That hubris, in turn, played into a sensational letter Longstreet wrote on July 24th, claiming that Lee had been too full of himself to listen to Longstreet's advice, and thus lost the great opportunity to "have destroyed the Federal army, marched into Washington, and dictated our terms; or, at least, held Washington, and marched over as much of Pennsylvania as we cared to." But no one burned with more resentment over Lee's cavalier assumption that the Confederate soldier could be asked to win it all without any consideration of cost than George Pickett. In 1870, John Mosby met Pickett in Richmond and persuaded him to "call and pay respects" to Lee, who was visiting the former Confederate capital with his daughter. "The interview was cold and formal," Mosby remembered, "and evidently embarrassing to both." And when they left, Pickett spoke "very bitterly of General Lee, calling him 'that old man'" who "had my division massacred at Gettysburg."[28]

This means that, by a strange coincidence, both Meade the victor and Lee the vanquished spent a substantial amount of effort disclaiming personal responsibility for the outcome of what a member of the 24th Michigan called "the bloody water-mark of the rebellion." So who was responsible for Gettysburg? And what difference did assigning responsibility make?

Comparatively few people understood that the principal figure in making the Gettysburg battle happen in the way it did was a man who wasn't even there for most of the three days, and that was John Reynolds. The Army of Northern Virginia went into Pennsylvania in 1863 for approximately the same reasons it had tried to do so in the late summer of 1862. For Robert E. Lee there was an additional incentive imposed by the threat of Jefferson Davis and James Seddon to detach parts of the army and send them to prop up the Confederacy's fortunes in the West. But Lee's principal motivation remained logistical—mid-nineteenth century armies consumed such vast amounts of food and provender that the threadbare soils of northern Virginia were approaching a point of no return. If the opportunity permitted, Lee would engage the Army of the Potomac in battle. But he was not deceiving James Longstreet when he said that this would be a purely secondary aim. Lee would fight only if the Army of the Potomac obligingly proffered the right circumstances. What Lee allowed Longstreet to believe was that the only right circumstances would be those in which the Union army threw itself at a well-dug-in Confederate army. What Lee told Isaac Trimble was something different: that he would actually take the offensive if the Army of the Potomac could be enticed to pursue him, and in pursuing, string itself out into disconnected little pieces that Lee could turn on and rend one by one.

Lee never specified what might happen after the Army of Northern Virginia won such an engagement, but the possibilities did not require too much imagination. One alternative would be the simple military collapse of the Army of the Potomac. "I do not hesitate to express the conviction," wrote Augustus Buell (who was not at Gettysburg, but passed himself off as a soldier so effectively in the pages of the Union veterans' newspaper, *National Tribune,* that one officer was sure Buell had been in his command), "that, had the Army of the Potomac been whipped at Gettysburg . . . it would have dissolved." Doubtless "some of the other volunteer regiments would have held together and made some sort of retreat toward the Susquehanna," but the others would simply have deserted en masse in much the same way Napoleon's army disintegrated after Waterloo, leaving "the rebel chieftain . . . at liberty to go where and do what he pleased." The other alternative scenario would be political collapse—the victory of a Clement Vallandigham or George Woodward in the fall 1863 gubernatorial elections, and a successful demand by them for the opening of peace talks. Or, had Lee seized Cemetery Hill and driven the Army of the Potomac off in disarray, he might have been witness to both kinds of collapse. "The Northern sympathizers with secession," speculated one Union officer, "now taking their cue from the success of the rebel army, would have established mob rule over the whole chain of Atlantic cities . . . and thus paralyzed the whole machinery of our Government." Almost at a signal, the New York City draft riots broke out on the day Lee crossed the Potomac at Williamsport. If Lee had been crossing the Susquehanna on that day instead, it might have been the Army of Northern Virginia which was called in to restore order, rather than units from Henry Slocum's 12th Corps.[29]

All of this was spoiled, however, by John Reynolds. By swinging well north into the Cumberland Valley and bypassing Harpers Ferry, Lee fooled Joe Hooker into staying too long at the Rappahannock, and then induced Hooker to rush headlong into pursuit in just the fashion Lee hoped for. Although George Meade planned to recall the Union army from its strung-out pursuit and concentrate it behind Pipe Creek, it is not likely that either Halleck or Lincoln would have permitted him to remain there for long. By that time Lee would have already turned and begun laying his trap along the Cashtown–Gettysburg line, so that any move Meade (or any other successor) made from Pipe Creek northward would fall straight into Lee's embrace. Reynolds, however, disagreed with Meade's defensive shrinking back into Maryland; instead, with the connivance of Oliver Otis Howard, Reynolds pushed ahead and sprang Lee's trap prematurely, something which was made all the easier by the absence of Stuart and a cavalry screen. It cannot be repeated too often: Lee did not lack for intelligence—for *strategic* information about the location, strength, and movement of the enemy; what he lacked was screening—*tactical* concealment of his own movements from observation and contact by the enemy. The result for Lee was that, rather than having the luxury of concentrating all three of his infantry corps between Cashtown and Gettysburg, two of those corps stumbled into contact with Reynolds' advance detachments on July 1st. They then wasted enough of their own leaderless momentum on Reynolds and Howard that even after Lee arrived and coordinated the drive that eviscerated the 1st and 11th Corps on the afternoon of

July 1st, they fell just short of seizing the single most dominant feature of the landscape, the artillery plateau formed by Cemetery Hill.

Lee should have obeyed his first instinct—*avoid a general engagement*. At the end of the day on July 1st, an entire third of the Army of Northern Virginia was still in transit from Chambersburg, and at least a third of that would not be within easy call for another thirty-six hours. But how does a hunter repair a bent trap? Especially when some of his prey is already snared there? And what explanation does he give his fellow hunters? It was here that Lee felt most keenly the absence of screening and scouting, because those functions would have warned Powell Hill's corps away from Gettysburg on July 1st, and would have signaled to Lee on July 2nd that the other pieces of the Army of the Potomac were a lot closer to Gettysburg than he supposed. By the time the 12th Corps, then the 3rd Corps, and then the 2nd and 5th Corps arrived on July 2nd, any real hope that Lee's destroy-them-by-pieces plan would work was mostly gone.

Lee did not know that, and the routine intelligence-gathering mission on which he sent Captain Johnston on the morning of the 2nd gave him the false confidence that the Army of Northern Virginia would, in fact, only be facing the ruined remnants of the 1st and 11th Corps on Cemetery Hill. Johnston's staggeringly inaccurate assessment worked far more damage to the Army of Northern Virginia than Stuart's vacancy, even though, once Johnston's error became apparent, the great flanking arc Lee planned for James Longstreet came marvelously close to success. Johnston's mistake notwithstanding, Longstreet immolated both the 3rd and 5th Corps, plus a substantial amount of the 2nd Corps, all of which was, by any standard, a greater achievement than Stonewall Jackson's more famous flank march at Chancellorsville two months before.

Longstreet's attack fell so narrowly short of its goal that it gave Lee hope that he had regained control of his trap. Unfortunately, that regained control was an illusion. To the contrary, Lee experienced an unusually difficult time prodding his staff and other corps commanders to act. This was not because Powell Hill or Dick Ewell were incompetents—Ewell had certainly demonstrated an unusual amount of tactical skill in the Valley Campaign of 1862 and in capturing Winchester—but because they were too new at corps command to have shaken the smaller-scale habits of brigade and division command, and no longer operating on ground that gave them the confidence to act aggressively. (Powell Hill, in particular, is the mystery man of Gettysburg, a famously vigorous fighter who makes only the most infrequent and pallid appearances at Gettysburg.) For them, Pennsylvania's endless barns and wheat fields, the tiny cross-check of farm boundaries, the everlasting and immovable fences created a landscape of uncertainty. "Our men are better satisfied on this side of the Potomac," wrote Lee's adjutant, Walter Taylor, on July 17th. "They are not accustomed to operating in a country where the people are inimical to them." Even for those like Ewell, who had briefly been stationed in Pennsylvania, the unfamiliar expanse of a free state induced paralysis. Only a few of Lee's subordinates *acted* at Gettysburg, and when they did so it was often (as in the case of Stuart) in erratic and uncontrollable fashion.[30]

It can be said, then, that Lee lost a battle he should have won, and lost it because (a) he began the battle without completely concentrating his forces, (b) he proved unable to coordinate the attacks of the forces he did have available, and (c) he failed to reckon with how tenaciously the Army of the Potomac, in contrast to the Russians in 1854 and the Austrians in 1859, would hold its ground under direct infantry attack on July 3rd. Perhaps, if a cavalry screen could have brushed away Buford from outside Gettysburg on June 30th, or cushioned Hill from walking into a "general engagement" until that concentration had taken place . . . perhaps, if Dick Ewell had asked just a little more from his corps or taken greater care in getting them into place so that they could move together . . . perhaps, if Powell Hill had done likewise, and brought Wright, Posey, and Mahone banging with their full weight against Cemetery Ridge that evening of July 2nd . . . perhaps, if those fences had not been the way small-scale farmers kept their livestock from wandering into the Emmitsburg Road . . . it might all have been different. But Stuart's presence would only have averted an unscheduled contact; it would not have guaranteed victory in some subsequent, larger collision. As for Ewell and Hill, no one could have known from their brief time in corps command how far short of Stonewall Jackson's mark they were going to fall, or how cruelly inadequate Lee's minuscule staff would prove in directing them. And the fences were merely the mute resistance of free men and free soil to the invasion of slavery, which few people would heed until it was too late. "I noticed after the battle," recalled one Virginian, that "there were more dead and wounded by the fences than elsewhere," probably because "the men came more directly in the range of the enemy's guns while on the fence."[31]

George Meade's problem was the exact opposite of Lee's—Meade's difficulty was restraining his subordinates from acting as though he didn't exist. Corps commanders like Slocum and Reynolds were accustomed to seeing George Meade as an equal, or even a junior; they certainly did not see him as their superior. To the extent that the Republican major generals also saw Meade as an acolyte of McClellanism, they had all the more reason to do what was right in their own eyes. This attitude was not ameliorated in the slightest by Meade's ferociously molten temper and his willingness to let political identities cloud his military judgment, especially in the treatment he dealt out to Abner Doubleday and David Birney, and the dismissive fashion in which he planted Sickles and the 3rd Corps as far out of sight as he could.

Meade has had his admirers over the years, but much of the admiration is dutiful rather than enthusiastic, almost forced. Apart from his single impulse to organize some sort of strike on the morning of July 2nd, Meade's behavior at Gettysburg was entirely reactive, a matter of responding to critical situations as they were thrust upon him. He missed the first day's fighting completely, and began the battle of Gettysburg off balance. Granted: he was in top command for only three days, with staff he didn't know and didn't have time to replace, on a battlefield he hadn't chosen and wasn't even noddingly familiar with. But he also stayed reactive to the very end, even down to missing Pickett's Charge. "Having suddenly and unexpectedly thrust upon him a problem with which he was utterly unprepared to grapple, without plans or time to prepare them, and with the certainty that within a few days . . . he would be compelled to meet a victorious and exultant enemy," wrote Thomas Rafferty (who commanded the 71st New York at Gettysburg), Meade could be forgiven for failing to rule the Army of the Potomac with a rod of iron, "to employ it to its fullest extent and annihilate Lee's army." But that only meant that winning the battle had less to do with Meade than it did with a bevy of otherwise minor characters—Pap Greene, Joshua Chamberlain, Samuel Carroll, Alexander Webb, Francis Heath, Patrick O'Rorke, Strong Vincent, Gouverneur Warren, Norman Hall, George Stannard—who stepped out of themselves for a moment and turned a corner at some inexpressibly right instant. These self-starting performances became almost routine for Union officers at Gettysburg; by contrast, they are achingly absent from the Army of Northern Virginia.[32]

It is possible to say, in that light, that Robert E. Lee lost the battle of Gettysburg much more than George Meade won it. "He escaped complete defeat," as one officer in the Vermont brigade ungenerously put it, "through the want of proper co-operation among his assailants." But this does not mean that Lee's decisions were foolish. When he concluded not to press Ewell into an attack on Cemetery Hill or Culp's Hill unless it was practicable, Lee was not being prissy or ill-informed. Ewell's corps was exhausted; it had had a long, debilitating march, sustained some unexpectedly fierce resistance, and there was no reason to suppose that much in the tactical picture as it appeared on the night of July 1st would change all that much by the morning of July 2nd. Based on what Lee knew of the scattering of the Army of the Potomac across the Maryland landscape, he should have had no difficulty wiping Cemetery Hill clean and then converting it into a club to beat the hapless Federals with whenever the rest of them finally arrived.

Longstreet's attack, likewise, was an unobjectionably logical approach to the situation as Lee found it on the morning of July 2nd. He would stage a repeat of Chancellorsville; Longstreet would circle onto the Federal flank and knock it silly; and if Longstreet did not actually send the Federals completely over the moon by nightfall, all that Lee would need to do the next day was follow matters up the way he had at Hazel Grove and Fairview Cemetery at Chancellorsville. Only this time, the Army of the Potomac would not be retreating across the Rappahannock; it would be streaming in despair for the Susquehanna crossings, and the Keystone State would be ready to go up in flames. "Between the repulse of McClellan . . . and the Battle of Gettysburg, most of the adherents of the North were consciously hoping against hope," wrote William Michael Rossetti, one of the founders of the Pre-Raphaelite Brotherhood and Walt Whitman's British editor. "By "the time of . . . the Northern invasion by Lee in 1863," the Union's British sympathizers "were almost ready to confess the case desperate." The ultras in the Army of the Potomac, like Henry Nichols Blake, would never let Meade forget that he deserved only "a very small degree of the honor for this decisive triumph." But considering what happened at Chancellorsville, and how easily it might have happened all over again at Gettysburg, that was a well enough earned honor, after all.[33]

Many people assumed that the battle of Gettysburg was, as Blake said, "a decisive triumph," and given the forces involved, the length of time elapsed, and the casualties afterward, perhaps it should have been. But not in 1863. "An army of 60,000 or 80,000 men is not to be knocked in pieces by any such battle as we have fought yet," Andrew Atkinson Humphreys reminded the Joint Committee on the Conduct of the War when he testified before them in March 1864. If by decisive, people meant a single knockout round which ended matters on one battlefield, Humphreys was right, and Lincoln was wrong—those kinds of decisive battles, where an army closed its hands and eliminated the enemy, were no longer tactical possibilities, as they had been in the days of Napoleon. Even with the horrendous losses Lee sustained, and even with the Army of Northern Virginia's back to the Potomac, "it is a rare thing to read of an army being completely broken in pieces, so that it cannot be collected together again." And it is probably wise not to assume that the Gettysburg Campaign would have yielded such an end.

As it was, Gettysburg did not end the war; even the powerful combination of Gettysburg *and* Vicksburg did not end the war. It would go on for almost two more years, because two more years would be required to grind the latent resistance of the Southern Confederacy down to the nub. The Army of Northern Virginia's morale, which sank so low in the weeks after Gettysburg, proved how elastic a factor like morale could be, rebounding through the fall and winter of 1863 to the point where Confederates could open a new campaigning season in 1864 "in fine spirits and anxious for a fight." Even Stuart's cavalry shook off the pall of blame and "is now generally considered to be in better spirits & health, also better armed and equipped &c, than at any previus [*sic*] time during the war." Nor did Gettysburg write a blank check for the Union forces. Little more than a year after Gettysburg, two Federal armies (in Virginia and in Georgia) would appear to be hopelessly mired in sieges of Atlanta and Petersburg which had no visible ending point, and Abraham Lincoln would be so close to losing the White House to George McClellan (as the Democrats' presidential nominee in 1864) that he felt the need to obtain a pledge from his cabinet to fight the war down to his last day in office, because after McClellan would take the presidential oath, everything would go straight to the negotiating table.

But Gettysburg *was* record setting for its sheer carnage: in a war which began with one-day set-piece battles over a field two or three miles square, Gettysburg had been drenched in three days of unremitting slugging, cast over fifteen square miles, like some gigantic boxing tournament gone wildly into three-digit extra rounds. Gettysburg also put an end to a certain set of expectations—that the South really could carry the war into the North, that the Army of Northern Virginia could triumph on valor alone, that Robert E. Lee was so magisterially wise that only an act of God (like the Lost Orders before Antietam) could frustrate him. Even as he led his Alabamians up the slopes of Little Round Top to grapple with Strong Vincent, William Oates knew that the long-term odds were against the Confederacy, even if "none of us were ready to admit it." After Gettysburg, they could stave it off no longer. Oates and his fellows would recover their fighting spirits and continue "to fight manfully for the cause and win victories." But when contemplating their long-term prospects, even the optimists "began to despair when Lee turned back from Gettysburg." And when Lincoln won reelection, and with it the support of the North for pressing the war to its last bitter drop, it would become possible to look back at Gettysburg and really see it as a sort of turning point in the war. "The battle of Gettysburg," declared Michael Jacobs, "must be regarded as the great and decisive battle of this wicked war. Although treason has been met in many a bloody field . . . at Gettysburg it received a blow, from which it will never recover."[34]

In the final accounting, Gettysburg was a victory, for George Meade, for the Army of the Potomac, and for the Union. "Public feeling has been wonderfully improved and buoyed up by our recent successes at Gettysburg and Vicksburg," John Nicolay, one of Lincoln's secretaries, rejoiced. It was not decisive enough to bring the Confederacy to its knees, but it was decisive enough for the Union that, as even Jefferson Davis conceded, "the drooping spirit of the North was revived."

Writing more than a year later, Richard Henry Dana believed that Gettysburg "was the turning-point in our history," not so much for winning a victory as for avoiding a defeat that would have proved the Army of the Potomac's—and the Union's—last defeat. "Had Lee gained that battle, the Democrats would have risen and stopped the war. With the city of New York and Governor [Horatio] Seymour, and Governor [Joel] Parker in New Jersey, and a majority in Pennsylvania, as they then would have had, they would so have crippled us as to end the contest. That they would have attempted it we at home know." So even if Gettysburg was less than decisive in strictly military terms, it was decisive enough to restore the sinking morale of the Union, decisive enough to keep at bay the forces which hoped Lincoln could be persuaded to revoke emancipation, decisive enough to make people look back and understand that the Confederacy would never be able to mount a serious invasion again, decisive enough that the momentum of the war would from now on belong solely to the Union, decisive enough that after Gettysburg, the sun never shone for the South again.[35]

To Sweep & plunder the battle grounds

DANIEL SKELLY was awakened "about midnight" on July 4th "by a commotion" near his home on Middle Street in Gettysburg. It was made by "Confederate officers passing through the lines of Confederate soldiers bivouacked on the pavement below, telling them to get up quietly and fall back. Very soon the whole line disappeared." Mary McAllister was nudged out of sleep in her home on Chambersburg Street by the rumble of wagons and a man who "came running down the street," announcing, "Get up, get up, we are retreating." Federal skirmishers and pickets also noticed the laconic stillness and odd lack of activity in the town. At first light, James Wadsworth sent out details from the 56th Pennsylvania and 7th Indiana to investigate, and so did Adelbert Ames, who ordered "out a skirmish-line consisting of 10 men under a Lieutenant and Sergeant." Unwary men could still get themselves shot—a sergeant in the 2nd U.S. Sharpshooters "was killed by a shot in his fore-head" as his company probed slowly out to the Emmitsburg Road—so they moved cautiously through the fog and drizzle, communicating "by signs of the hand." Early-rising farmers along the Fairfield Road galloped into town by side roads, seeking out Federal cavalry pickets to describe the enormous Confederate trains, and Federal signalers also caught sight of the long, withdrawing column.[1]

As civilians and soldiers alike poked around in ever increasing circles, what they found across the battlefield made words fail on the lips. In the town, the streets were littered with "coffee and groceries of all kinds, boxes and barrels, wagons and guns." The photographer Charles Tyson returned to his home on Chambersburg Street to find that his desk "had been ransacked and the contents scattered over the room," and in the parlor he "found a small heap of ashes, the residue of burned letters and papers. Tyson's "cellar and pantry" had been "pretty well cleaned out," but at least his gallery was "undisturbed." Along the York Pike, east of town, were "exploded caissons . . . abandoned wagons, leveled fences, dwellings in whose yards were bloody clouts." The "shutters and walls look like a target at a shooting match." The open fields were thickly stippled with "everything belonging to soldiers afoot or on horseback, such as caps, hats, shoes, coats, guns, cartridge and cap boxes, belts, canteens, haversacks, blankets, tin cups, horses, saddles, and swords." Along the Emmitsburg Road, details of Union soldiers from Alex Hays' division began retrieving some 2,500 rifles from where Pickett's men had thrown them away, thrusting them bayonet-down into the ground so that they were "standing as thick as trees in a nursery."[2]

In Joseph Sherfy's peach orchard, "only skeletons of trees" were "left; there was scarcely a leaf remaining," and Sherfy's house had been ransacked, "turning everything in drawers etc. out and clothes, bonnets, towels, linen etc. were found tramped in indistinguishable piles and filth of every description was strewn over the house." At least Sherfy still had the house; the Sherfy barn had caught fire and burned to the ground, and William Bliss' house and barn had been deliberately torched. (All that was left were the stone walls of the barn; on July 29th, Bliss filed a claim for compensation to the tune of $1,256.08, but he never received a cent, and finally sold the farm for half of what it had cost him in 1857.) Overall, the town and the surrounding farmlands suffered over half a million dollars in damages, including 800 confiscated horses and 1,000 head of cattle. But few in Adams County ever saw a penny in compensation; in York County, claims for the depredations of Jubal Early's division amounted to a quarter-million dollars, but even fewer saw anything in the way of recompense. There were even a few missing persons: the Confederates may have missed John Burns, but they arrested nine other Gettysburg civilians on suspicion of bushwhacking, and carried them off to Richmond, where they remained imprisoned for the rest of the war.[3] And there is no record of anyone ever learning the fate of Gettysburg's kidnapped blacks.

The Confederates left stragglers and prisoners of their own in Gettysburg, a number of whom were rousted from cellars and houses in the town where they had overslept their leave, or else simply decided they had done enough fighting. Harriet Bayly found a "woebegone little 'Reb'" of "about 17 years of age" on her doorstep north of Gettysburg in the wee hours of July 5th, "who said . . . he belonged to the North Carolina service" and "never intended doing any more fighting for the Confederacy." Bayly found him "a suit of citizen's clothes" and hid him on her farm, and in the end he "remained with the family," married and acquired a farm in Adams County, and "has been more successful in peaceful pursuit than those of war." Other rebels were more resigned, or more defiant. Details of Federal soldiers went through the town, "going up to the barn doors and pounding on them with the butts of our muskets . . . and commanding the Johnnies to come out at once, and to leave their guns behind." But civilians also began rounding up stray Confederates, posse-style. Robert McLean and his younger brother "assisted in hunting them up," and found "one in our stable loft fast asleep. I called a couple of soldiers and he was a prisoner before he knew it." (A few people had scores to settle with their own neighbors: Henry Stahle, the editor of Gettysburg's Democratic newspaper, the *Compiler,* was denounced by local Republicans for "pointing out the refuge of Union Soldiers to Rebel Officers," and briefly imprisoned at Fort McHenry.) Eventually, the provost guard got prisoners moving down to Westminster as soon as possible, where they were herded into "a vacant lot" to await transportation to the Federal prisoner of war camp on Johnson's Island, near Sandusky, Ohio.[4]

"Generally speaking," the rebels appeared to be "ragged, torn, bruised, mutilated, dirty . . . many of them . . . miserably ignorant and unable to read or write" and dressed in "every style and color, butternut cloth, half uniforms, no uniforms, full of mud from heavy rains." But not all of them, and no one less so than Lt. James Crocker of the 9th Virginia, the Pennsylvania College alumnus. Captured at the end of the great charge, Crocker was only slightly hurt, and in that remarkably relaxed view toward prisoners of war that still prevailed in the mid-nineteenth century, he obtained a pass and walked off into his old college town "alone, unattended." Even Crocker could appreciate that it was "a queer, incongruous sight to see a rebel lieutenant in gray mingling in the crowd." But Crocker soon enough "met . . . my dear old professor of mathematics," Michael Jacobs (who "whispered to me in the kindest, gentlest way not to talk about the war"), and strolling over toward the college itself on Washington Street he crossed paths with the son of the college president, Henry Baugher, who extended "a cordial invitation to dine with him and his father." Given that "old Dr. Baugher" had buried another son in the Evergreen Cemetery who died of wounds at Shiloh, the unannounced appearance of an unrepentant Confederate might have made for a highly indigestible meal. But "the venerable Doctor saw before him only his old student, recalled only the old days, and their dear memories."[5]

Crocker's peculiar college cheerio sat incongruously beside the rows upon rows of wounded men who crammed "the town churches and public offices" and "many of the private houses in town," as well as the corps hospitals which had been set up "two to four miles out." Albertus McCreary remembered "four churches (within a block of us) which had been converted to hospitals" with the "pews in the churches covered with boards . . . to make beds for the wounded," plus "two school-houses" on High Street "and the court-house . . . and many private residences." The McCreary house was one of those "private residences" and in it "all of our beds were occupied." The McCrearys could hardly feed themselves, much less convalescent soldiers, and they had to be rescued by the arrival, beginning on July 5th, of a small army of civilian volunteers—a wagonful of nuns from the Sisters of Charity in Emmitsburg, the Patriot Daughters of Lancaster, the U.S. Christian Commission, and the U.S. Sanitary Commission. But even with the assistance of citizen volunteers, there were 21,000 sick and wounded men in a town that usually numbered no more than 2,500, and the suffering easily broke over the thin boundaries of help that surgeons and volunteers tried to build around them. There were "wounds of every imaginable description, and upon all parts of the person . . . wounds in the head, the breast, the abdomen, the legs, the feet, the hands," faces "partly shot away, leaving, perhaps, only a single eye or row of teeth." Over half of the amputations performed in these hospitals resulted in death; by the fall, 14 percent of all the wounded would be dead.[6]

The Confederate wounded were the lowest in the priorities of the 106 Federal medical officers who stayed behind the Army of the Potomac to supervise the care of the wounded and dying. A number of Confederate medical personnel remained with their wounded after the withdrawal: Dr. Simon Baruch (the father of the famed financier Bernard Baruch) was ordered, along with two other Confederate surgeons, "to remain behind at the Black Horse Tavern field hospital" with 222 "seriously wounded men" and 10 orderlies, and spent six weeks working hand in hand with the Christian Commission and the Sanitary Commission. Baruch's patients were the happy ones, by contrast with the wounded cluttering the halls and classrooms of Pennsylvania College. "All the rooms, halls and hallways were occupied with the poor deluded sons of the South," and "the moans prayers, and shrieks of the wounded and dying were heard everywhere." Between 500 and 700 wounded Confederates were jammed in with "five of our surgeons" and "no nurses, no medicines, no kinds of food proper for men in our condition, our supply being two or three hard crackers a day with a small piece of fat pork, with now and then a cup of poor coffee." Amputations took place on the college portico because the air inside had become "impregnated with the peculiar and sickening odor of blood and wounds." Not until July 16th was a temporary general hospital on the York Pike, next to the railroad line, laid out under the supervision of Dr. Henry Janes (a Vermont regimental surgeon who had been in charge of post-Antietam hospital organization), and not until July 22nd were Union and Confederate wounded finally moved there.[7]

Camp Letterman, as Janes named it, developed into a hundred-acre village of cots and tents, with its own morgue and cemetery, and served more than 3,000 wounded men before it was finally closed in November. But even at their best, the hospitals and the medical knowledge of the day could only provide the most painfully basic services; in some cases, they could not even keep adequate track of who the wounded were. James J. Melton, a private in the 7th Ohio, was wounded "in the head . . . and afterward taken to a hospital." But being "unable to give any account himself . . . he is supposed to have become deranged and wandered away . . . since which his friends have heard nothing from him."[8]

Gettysburg attracted far greater numbers of a less useful breed of visitor. As early as July 5th, "hundreds from the country around . . . came down in their wagons to see the sights." By the beginning of August, people were coming to visit the Evergreen Cemetery and picnic on Little Round Top, despite the "dead horses, shallow graves, cartridge boxes etc." Others "wanted relics," although the line between relic hunting and outright looting quickly disappeared. John Mumma Young, a student at the college, was approached by two local boys who had dug up a Confederate officer's body to cut "the buttons and lace" from his uniform, and then sell them. The Army of the Potomac's provost marshal general, Marsena Patrick, was infuriated at how intent the locals were "to Sweep & plunder the battle grounds" for things they could sell back to the army. Since abandoned equipment and weapons on the battlefield were, abandoned or not, still government property, Patrick and his officers warned "citizens visiting the battle-field . . . against carrying away" blankets, rifles, swords, wagons, horses, or what-not. Finally, by July 11th, Patrick was forced to ask for reinforcements in the form of Pennsylvania militia to cope with the scavengers, and he commissioned his assistant quartermaster, the aptly named Henry Boyden Blood, to begin scouring the countryside "in search of Govt property." Blood quickly made himself more hated than the rebels had ever been. Nathaniel Lightner, who lived on the Baltimore Pike, called him "the meanest man in the world," especially after Blood arrested Lightner for selling "two or three dollars' worth of things" to a relic hunter from New York. Blood's diary is full of glee at arresting "one or two citizens" a day "for taking govt. property," at uncovering "two Wagon loads" of purloined equipment "in One small hut," searching "several houses" on the Mummasburg Road and finding "about 50 guns, one horse, one wagon and other property."[9]

The idea that the battle offered commercial possibilities took particularly quick root among farmers whose properties had been trampled over, crops and orchards destroyed, and who were now staring ruin in the face. The solution: to charge exorbitant prices for every possible service that could be rendered to the soldiers and the tourists. "The people of Gettysburg came sneaking back and expressed their gratitude for the saving of their homes from destruction by charging wounded officers five dollars each for carrying them back two miles to the . . . hospital," railed a soldier in the 20th Connecticut, "and five cents a glass for cool water for the parched and fevered lips of wounded soldiers." Much as they might explain that this was "to compensate for what an enemy has stolen from you," it made no good impression on soldiers—or newspaper reporters—to be charged "from $.60 to $1.00 a loaf for bread, and $.25 a quart for milk, and all things in such proportion." It did no good, either, to be told that at least "the Gettysburg women were kind and faithful to the wounded and their friends," because there were all too many voices raised to identify the women as the "lineal descendent of some original Hessian" or as "dumpy" and "lukewarm" for wanting "a dollar for a gallon of milk, and half dollar for a cruet of vinegar." And it did not take long for the Army of the Potomac to become convinced that "these Dutch farmers" are nothing but "tight-fisted miscreants" who "turned to with all their souls to make money out of their defenders."[10]

The deepest cut came from Lorenzo Crounse, the *New York Times'* correspondent in Gettysburg. On July 9th, the *Times* ran an article by Crounse that accused Gettysburg's people of being "so sordidly mean and unpatriotic, as to engender the belief that they were indifferent as to which party was whipped,"

> *In the first place the male citizens mostly ran away, and left the women and children to the mercy of their enemies. On their return, instead of lending a helping hand to our wounded, and opening their houses to our famished officers and soldiers, they have only manifested indecent haste to present their bills to the military authorities for payment of losses inflicted by both armies. . . . Their charges, too, were exorbitant—hotels, $2.50 per day; milk, 10 and 15 cents per quart; bread, $1 and even $1.50 per loaf; twenty cents for a bandage for a wounded soldier! And these are only a few specimens of the sordid meanness and unpatriotic spirit manifested by these people, from whose doors our noble army had driven a hated enemy.*

Twenty Adams County clergy signed a riposte to Crounse which appeared in the *Adams County Sentinel* on July 11th. But that only gave Crounse another opportunity to flog "the unpatriotic and illiberal conduct of many citizens of Gettysburgh" in the pages of the *Times*. Maybe, added one Massachusetts soldier, the good Dutch farmers of Gettysburg could find less opprobrious employment "in burying the rebel dead, which they will be obliged to do, or go visiting for a year or two."[11]

The dead did indeed present a problem—the single biggest problem of all for post-battle Gettysburg. The armies had lingered only long enough to perform the most perfunctory burials, and that meant that the fields in and around the town remained encumbered with corpses, many of which had been decomposing rapidly for three or four days in the humid July heat, "swollen to twice their original size." Men sickened and vomited. "I have been over the battlefield," Thomas Bradbury of the 17th Maine wrote in his diary on July 6th. "I never saw such a sight . . . thousands upon thousands lying dead and wounded and piled on top of another." Artillery casualties were the worst in appearance, since, as a weary soldier in the 150th New York saw, "canister showed the human form torn and disfigured beyond description."

> In one case I noticed the hand, now stiffened in death, still clasped against the protruding entrails where the jagged fragment of a shell had torn open the abdominal cavity. In another instance I remember the whole front of the chest of a large man had been literally torn away, exposing to view its interior, including the heart and lungs. . . . All were bloating and blackening in the July heat.

These images could not be blotted out simply by averting the eyes. The stench of decay was inescapable and, wrote John White Geary, "horrible and beyond description. . . . My very clothes smell of death." In the town, people found the "stench from the battle-field . . . so bad that every one went about with a bottle of pennyroyal or peppermint oil," and "every window . . . was fastened down tight, all the doors kept shut; so it was stifling." Nor were the corpses exclusively human: one correspondent "counted twenty-eight dead artillery horses" where John Bigelow and the 9th Massachusetts Artillery had made their last stand in the Trostle farmyard. Jenny Jacob "counted seventeen dead horses that had been killed by the storm of shells . . . around Gen Meade's headquarters," and there were "thirty dead horses" around Woodruff's battery beside the Bryan house. The effort to bury dead horses was beyond the time or patience of the burial details, so the carcasses were piled together and burned. "Here and there, great girdles of fire blazoned the slopes, telling of slaughtered animals slowly consuming." As "awfull" as Antietam was, wrote John Chase to his father, "it was not a circumstance to this one."[12]

What made this worse was that those whom the armies actually had buried kept coming back. Franklin Sawyer, the colonel of the 8th Ohio, wrote on July 5th that "large details of our corps are made up to bury the dead," but all that the dead got was "a trench about seven or eight feet wide and about three feet deep—for there is no time for digging deeper." So many "were buried . . . so near the surface that their clothing came through the earth." And not only clothing. Henry Eyster Jacobs remembered that "the Union dead on the field of the first day's battle were covered with only a few inches of soil," so that "as the rain washed away the soil . . . portions of the body protruded." One Presbyterian minister whom Jacobs obligingly guided over the battlefield was so overwrought by the shallow trenches in which the Confederate dead had been thrown that he came back the next week "with a shovel, and covered one of these trenches that was most repulsive." Piles of amputated arms and legs were tripped over by the unwary. "In consequence of the earth washing away by rains, the dead bodies, bones, skulls &c. are protruding and look offensive," complained the *Philadelphia Inquirer,* and by the end of summer, "the arms legs and skulls of those buried project from the ground," and "in many instances hands & feet are sticking through."[13]

Just as New York and Pennsylvania sent their state militias into the Gettysburg Campaign, they also sent their state agents with the armies to look after the welfare of state volunteer regiments. In the summer of 1863, the role of New York's state agent fell to John Seymour and his deputy, Theodore Dimon. One of Dimon's principal responsibilities was administering "pecuniary aid in the expense attending the exhumation, disinfecting, coffining and transportation of" New York's battle fatalities "to their former homes." Given the staggering number of New York dead at Gettysburg—over a quarter of the dead were New Yorkers—Dimon wanted neither to shoulder the expense of transporting a thousand bodies nor leave them "buried like a dead horse, when in another year all marks . . . would be obliterated by the owner of the soil." Dimon's alternative was the creation of a *national* cemetery for all the Union dead—created jointly by the states whose soldiers fought in the battle—and to do it *at Gettysburg.* The key component would be obtaining the sponsorship of Pennsylvania, and for that, they turned to the Gettysburg native son who seemed to have the fastest connections to Pennsylvania's governor, Andrew Gregg Curtin, and that was David Wills.[14]

Wills was a graduate of Pennsylvania College in 1851, a protégé of Thaddeus Stevens', and above all other things the son-in-law of the powerful Pennsylvania Republican Alexander McClure. He had already been designated by Curtin as Pennsylvania's representative for supervising the exhumation "of the bodies of Pennsylvanians killed in the late battle," and so it was logical for Seymour and Dimon to request a meeting with Wills and unload their plan. Wills evidently liked it, because on July 24th Wills wrote to Curtin, turning on all of his persuasive power to convince the governor. "Our dead are lying on the field unburied," Wills declared. "In many instances arms and legs and sometimes heads protrude and my attention has been directed to several places where the hogs were actually rooting out the bodies and devouring them. . . . [H]umanity calls on us to take measures to remedy this." Together with Seymour and Dimon, Wills "suggested . . . the propriety and actual necessity of the purchase of a common burial ground for the dead, now only partially buried over miles of country around Gettysburg." He already had the perfect location in mind: on Cemetery Hill, between the Taneytown Road and the Baltimore Pike, on the western boundary of the Evergreen Cemetery. "There is one spot very desirable for this purpose. It is the elevated piece of ground on the Baltimore Turnpike opposite the Cemetery." Curtin, who saw nothing in the plan but roses for his reelection campaign, bestowed upon Wills "full power to act upon the suggestions in his letter, and to correspond with the governors of all the States that had been represented by troops in the battle."[15]

It took Wills less than a month to obtain assents from the eighteen Northern states whose troops had fought at Gettysburg, and by mid-August Wills had purchased seventeen acres for the modest sum of $2,475.87, signed agreements with a noted landscape gardener, William Saunders, for the layout of the new cemetery, and with a local contractor, Franklin Biesecker, for the exhumation, identification, and reburial of over 3,300 bodies. The reburial work did not actually begin until October 27th (and would not be finished until the following March). But by then, Wills already had his plans for a grand dedication ceremony well in hand. He recruited, as the marshal for the ceremonies, Ward Hill Lamon, the marshal of the District of Columbia, and extended invitations to governors, members of the presidential cabinet, Henry Wadsworth Longfellow, and the diplomatic corps. Above all, in September, he invited Edward Everett, the former Massachusetts governor and congressman, president of Harvard, and secretary of state, to give the formal oration. Everett wrote back with regrets, but the date Wills had set—October 23rd— was simply not enough time to prepare an address equal to the occasion. Wills, however, was determined to recruit Everett, and at Everett's prompting, Wills rescheduled the entire affair for November 19th.

He also invited Abraham Lincoln, and it is likely that some suggestion was informally communicated to the president about participating in the ceremonies; it was not until November 2nd, just seventeen days before the ceremony was scheduled to take place, that Wills formalized the idea that, "after the oration," Lincoln should, "as Chief Executive of the nation," perform the actual dedication of "these grounds to their sacred use by a few appropriate remarks."[16]

Epilogue

THE MIND OF THE TALL MAN in the White House had been weighing what the battle signified ever since the news of Gettysburg first came sparking over the telegraph wires to the War Department on July 4th. Three days later, at his morning cabinet meeting, he wore "a countenance indicating sadness and despondency" over George Meade's perplexing tardiness in pursuing the Army of Northern Virginia, but Navy Secretary Welles had cheered him out of his dour mood with the official dispatch from Admiral David Dixon Porter, "communicating the fall of Vicksburg on the fourth of July." At once, he was "beaming with joy." *What can we do for the Secretary of the Navy for this glorious intelligence?* He exulted, *It is great, Mr. Welles, it is great!* That night, the capital joined in reveling over the twin victories. "The news immediately spread throughout the city, creating intense and joyous excitement," and "flags were displayed from all the Departments, and crowds assembled with cheers." A large throng marched up Pennsylvania Avenue with the Marine Band at their head, milling in front of the White House and calling on him for a speech.[1]

The tall man did not like speaking unrehearsed, but he appeared at a second-floor window on the north side of the executive mansion and allowed his speculations to ramble. *How long ago is it?* he asked rhetorically, *eighty odd years—since on the Fourth of July for the first time in the history of the world a nation by its representatives, assembled and declared as a self-evident truth that "all men are created equal."* The victories of Gettysburg and Vicksburg, coming on the anniversary of that *self-evident truth,* had now put "the cohorts of those who opposed the declaration that all men are created equal" on the run. This was, he continued, "a glorious theme," but "I am not prepared" to make a speech "worthy of the occasion." *Bring up the music,* he said, and off they went to the War Department to call for Stanton.[2]

He was not prepared to speak on the "glorious theme," but in fact he had been preparing for such a speech all of his adult life. "I have never had a feeling politically that did not spring from the sentiments embodied in the Declaration of Independence," he said in 1861. Those sentiments sprang from one single, animating idea: that the most ordinary of people had been created with the same set of natural rights as the most extraordinary, that no one was born either with crowns upon their heads or saddles upon their backs. "Most governments," he wrote in a brief sketch in 1854, "have been based, practically, on the denial of equal rights of men." The founders of the American republic had taken a different route; they made what he called "an experiment," to see whether in fact democratic self-government was really a possibility.

More than they had any reason to expect, this "undecided experiment" had now emerged as a "successful one." Of course, that depended on how one defined *success.* The cynical and the self-interested sneered that this success was only temporary, only waiting for the first real test, at which point all of those ordinary people with their equal say in government would begin quarreling obscenely with one another, and on the basis of possessing their precious rights would stalk out of the chambers of government and proceed to do whatever they wanted. "When you have governed men for several years," Otto von Bismarck declared, "you will become a Monarchist. Believe me, one cannot lead or bring to prosperity a great nation without the principle of authority—that is, the Monarchy." Let an issue arise which posed real challenges, and the "experiment" would be revealed as a fraud.

Precisely such an issue was buried deep in the foundations of the American republic itself. The founders of the republic tolerated the existence of chattel slavery in the new "experiment," despite its obvious contradiction of the principle that everyone was, by natural right, authorized to govern themselves. The founders also expected that this was a problem already dying of its own failures, a disease which could be left to cure itself. But it did not. Instead, it grew and prospered, and in time it brought into question the integrity of the whole "experiment" in popular government, because if one entire segment of the people were to be excluded from pursuing their own self-government, then why wasn't this proof of Bismarck's dictum, that government from the top down was the natural order of things? By the 1850s, the tall man was asking himself and others whether the resurgent economic power of slavery was threatening the very premises upon which the American democracy was built. "I should like to know if taking this old Declaration of Independence, which declares that all men are equal upon principle, and making exceptions to it—where will it stop?"[3]

His election as president was a sign to the nation that a stop had indeed been called to the metastasization of slavery. But now came the moment when the evil eye of the aristocrats began to gleam, since the people of the slaveholding states proclaimed a predictably democratic unwillingness to be disagreed with, and used that unwillingness to pull down the entire house. The tall man had insisted over and over again that Southern secession was not really a free exercise of equal rights to do as democratic equals pleased, but a refusal to abide by the rules of democracy and an aboveboard national election. It was not *rights* or *liberty* the Southern Confederacy was asserting, but anarchy, and anarchy could lead nowhere but into the hands of the despots, who would promise the restoration of order.

The tall man had once hoped that the secession problem could be resolved without dealing too harshly with the seceders, that appeals to "the mystic chords of memory" would draw them back. But appeals to the bonds of fraternity were met with defiance and civil war, and this man who once confessed that he could barely bring himself to pull a trigger on wild game now found himself directing armies numbering nearly two million men. And far from the people of the democracy rallying to the cause in noble ranks and undivided loyalty, there had been lethal levels of dissension over how the war should be conducted and whether the aims of the war should include the destruction of slavery as the original burr under the saddle. His energy sapped, he wrestled with the daily dreariness of the war's news, and even though he was not an explicitly religious men, he increasingly was tempted to wonder if "God was against us in our view of the subject of slavery in this country, and our method of dealing with it."[4]

And then came Gettysburg. It was not merely that Gettysburg finally delivered a victory, or that it administered a bloody reverse to Southern fortunes at the point and in the place where they might otherwise have scored their greatest triumph, or that it had come at such a stupendous cost in lives. It was that the monumental scale of that bloodletting was its own refutation to the old lie, that a democracy enervates the virtue of its people to the point where they are unwilling to do more than blinkingly look to their personal self-interest. That the news of Gettysburg came in conjunction with the fall of Vicksburg, and came together on the anniversary of the Declaration he held so dear, seemed like a sign written in the clouds, and that was the first meaning he attached to Gettysburg in his impromptu speech on the night of July 7th. But the idea continued to mature. By September, he had become convinced that Gettysburg had not only made "peace . . . not appear so distant as it did," but that it would demonstrate that "there can be no successful appeal from a fair election, but to the next election." The new national cemetery added the final stone in the arch of his thinking, because the cemetery was the city of the battle's dead, and the size of that city was its own mute testimony that the citizens of a democracy were not merely a population of bovine shopkeepers and blank-stare farmers, but citizens who had seen something transcendental after all in the rainbow promise of democracy, something worth dying to protect, something worth communicating to the living.[5]

As was his wont, the tall man began committing his ideas to paper piecemeal, telling the journalist Noah Brooks on November 15th that the "remarks" he would deliver at the cemetery's dedication were "written, but not finished," and his soon-to-be attorney general James Speed, that it was "nearly done."[6] He left Washington just after noon on Wednesday, the 18th of November, accompanied by three of his cabinet secretaries (William Seward, John P. Usher, and Montgomery Blair), plus his two White House staffers, John Nicolay and John Hay, the Marine Band, and assorted generals, admirals, and the French and Italian ministers, Henri Mercier and Joseph Bertinetti, and their military attachés, all accommodated in three passenger cars and a baggage car. In Baltimore (where two years before he had been threatened with assassination), he came out onto "the platform of the car" to acknowledge the cheering crowds who surrounded him. He arrived in Gettysburg "about sundown" to be greeted by the local eminentos, including David Wills and the college president, Henry Baugher. The others would be put up at Gettysburg's brimming hotels; Wills claimed the right to play host to the president.[7]

Thursday the 19th dawned as a "beautiful Indian summer day," bright but hazy, the air filled with a kind of golden smoke. The tall man was still dickering with the wording of his "remarks," rewriting sentences, crossing out words, careting in new ones. The parade to the cemetery began forming up in the town diamond at nine o'clock, with "officers and soldiers of the Army of the Potomac" in the van, followed by the tall man, "mounted upon a young and beautiful chestnut bay horse" and dressed in "a black frock coat . . . his towering figure surmounted by a high silk hat." It took them an hour to get organized, and another hour to traverse the closely packed, cheering length of Baltimore Street and move up the slope of Cemetery Hill to the new cemetery's entrance, while artillery salutes were fired every minute. "The crowd was so dense that the air was rendered so close even on that day in the late fall that more than one lady and even men fainted."

The program began as Birgfield's Band, which had been brought in from Philadelphia, struck up a special commission by their director, Adolph Birgfield, his "Homage d'un Heros"; the chaplain of the House of Representatives,

Thomas Stockton, followed with a prayer, and the Marine Band (under the baton of its enterprising director, Francis Scala) played a dolorous version of the Doxology—*Praise God from whom all blessings flow.* Finally it was the turn of the orator Edward Everett: *Standing beneath this serene sky, overlooking these broad fields . . .* The tall man had once appraised Everett as one of the most overrated public speakers in America, and he could be forgiven if his mind wandered at points during the 13,000 words which poured forth from Everett in one Latinate period after another.[8]

He told Noah Brooks that he would keep his own remarks "short, short, short," planning to say much the same thing as he had said in July. He did not propose to trespass on Everett's territory; he would leave to the eloquent New Englander the review of the war and the battle and the question of how much the battle had cost and its significance in the overall course of things. Instead, he would look for the meaning of this battle and its dead in the larger historical scheme of the American "experiment." What would be military history in Everett's hands would become metaphor and symbol in his. He would begin (as he had back in July) by connecting the battle with the republic's founding, although now he would drop the preoccupation with one Independence Day leading to a second one. He would also drop the pedestrian opening he employed in July—*How long ago is it?—eighty odd years?*—and replace it with a poetic flourish reminiscent of the Psalmist's calculation of the life span of humanity: *Four-score and seven years ago . . .* Mary Todd Lincoln remembered in 1866 that her husband "felt religious More than Ever about the time he went to Gettysburg," and it showed in his "remarks." (It was also an echo of an earlier Independence Day speech, by Galusha Grow, after Grow had been elected Speaker of the House in the special session of Congress called for July 4, 1861: "Fourscore years ago, fifty-six bold merchants, farmers, lawyers, and mechanics, the representatives of a few feeble colonists, scattered along the Atlantic sea-board, met in convention to found a new empire, based on the inalienable rights of man." Grow's speech had been widely reprinted, from Frank Moore's *Rebellion Record* to *Beadle's Dime Patriotic Speaker,* and Lincoln had few scruples about adopting and bettering other people's locutions.) From there, biblical images would abound: . . . *our fathers brought forth upon this continent a new nation* (as though it was the Mother of God bringing forth her firstborn and wrapping him in swaddling clothes) *conceived in liberty, and dedicated to the proposition that "all men are created equal."*[9]

It was a matter of ridicule in the eyes of both the kings and the commoners alike that a nation could be dedicated to anything as rationalistic as a *proposition,* fully as much as it had seemed ridiculous ages before that a heavenly King could be born in a stable. Nations, they scoffed, are not *dedicated;* they simply are. And *propositions* are not the building stuff of a people's identity; nations are made by time, by collective memory, by racial and religious solidarity, by histories of loyalty and submission to a select race of leaders, warriors, and rulers. *Propositions* are fit for debates, disputations, and tutorials, but not for nation building. But this was just what the American founders had done. It might take twelve centuries to make a Frenchman, but it would take only twenty minutes of reasoning to make an American.[10]

Now we are engaged in a great civil war. And not merely a war, but a *testing,* a kind of pass/fail examination to determine once and for all whether the American founding had indeed been misbegotten—whether a democracy built solely out of the fragile reeds of constitutional propositions was merely a fuzzy pipe dream or whether people really could survive without crowns and saddles—*whether that nation, or any nation so conceived, and so dedicated, can long endure.* Gettysburg proved that democracy had not in fact enervated and debased the American people, but had instead made them stronger and more determined to resist any backsliding from the integrity of the proposition to which they had been dedicated in 1776.

The tall man did not speak of the war as a crusade of liberation from slavery, which doubtless surprised people then and surprises people now. But the destruction of slavery was actually a subset of the larger contest over democracy. If democracy failed, and the South triumphed, there would be no point in talking about emancipation; if democracy did survive and the republic was reunited, then slavery was doomed just by the fact of that successful reuniting. Emancipation, however great a righting of a historic wrong, would be meaningless unless it was set within the larger question of democracy's survival. "The central idea pervading this struggle," he told his secretary John Hay back at the beginning of the war, "is the necessity . . . of proving that popular government is not an absurdity," for "if we fail it will go far to prove the incapability of the people to govern themselves."[11]

We are met on a great battle field of that war, which is a reminder that those very ordinary people whom the cultured despisers of democracy hold in such contempt have been willing to mount some very extraordinary efforts to preserve it. Especially, *we have come to dedicate a portion of it, as a final resting place for those who died here, that the nation might live.* Live, and be reminded that those who died here did so because they saw in democracy something more than opportunities for self-interest and self-aggrandizement, something that spoke to the fundamental nature of human beings itself, something which arched like a comet in the political sky. *This we may, in all propriety do.* (This was clumsy; he dropped it and replaced it with *It is altogether fitting and proper that we should do this . . .*)

On this hinge, he turned from what had been done to what was being done, and what yet remained to do. *In a larger sense, we cannot dedicate—we cannot consecrate—we cannot hallow, this ground. The brave men, living and dead, who struggled here, have hallowed it, far above our poor power to add or detract.* For all the planning, foresight, and expenditure which had gone into the creation of the Gettysburg cemetery, the real focus of attention would always be, and deserved to be, on the soldiers who had fought and won the greatest battle, not so much of a war, but of the age-old struggle of commoners and kings. *The world will little note, nor long remember what we say here; while it can never forget what they did here.*

Any dedication to be done that day would have to be performed in the hearts of the people standing all around, by the 15,000 spectators who crammed into Gettysburg for the ceremonies, by the dignitaries and generals and politicians who would sit stiffly on the twelve-by-twenty-foot platform William Saunders had erected on the cemetery grounds, dedicating themselves in a peculiar form of baptism to the true loftiness of the democratic faith. *It is for us, the living, rather, to be dedicated here to the unfinished work which they who fought here, have, thus far, so nobly advanced.* Because dedication is not only an end, as it was for the soldiers who died at Gettysburg; it is also a beginning, the first step in pouring new wine into the old wineskins, of extolling the virtues of democracy and preaching its worth as the one true and natural system of human society. *It is rather for us to be here dedicated to the great task remaining before us,* the great task of winning the war (*that cause for which they here gave the last full measure of devotion*), but also the task of reaffirming and reappropriating the spirit of the founders.

If he was wrong about democracy, if the war went on in the resultless way the half heart generals had managed things, if the people took counsel of their weariness and grief and installed someone like McClellan in the presidency who would negotiate everything away—if these dead had *died in vain*—then he and every other American were surely of all men most miserable. What Gettysburg must become, then, was the occasion of something which bordered on a national revival, a new birth of freedom (and though he had not planned to do so, he would reinforce this point by inserting *under God* to reinforce the tent-meeting urgency of that renewal)—so that *government of the people, by the people, for the people, shall not perish from the earth. . . .*

Everett was almost finished: *. . . in the glorious annals of our common country there will be no brighter page than that which relates the battles of Gettysburg.* There was then a "Consecration Hymn" to be sung by the National Union Musical Association, five stanzas' worth of "holy ground" and "widow's tears." Ward Hill Lamon was ready to make the next introduction, and as he did, the tall man leaned over and thanked Everett.

"Ladies and gentlemen, the President of the United States," announced Lamon. In the distance, South Mountain slumbered in a soft blue haze. The platform faced westward, and from there, the cupola of the college, where Lee stood on the morning of Pickett's Charge, and the smaller cupola of the Lutheran seminary which John Buford used to direct his early morning stand on July 1st, were plainly visible. The tall man stood up, unfolded his wire-rim spectacles, produced two or three sheets of paper from his inside pocket, and grasped, as was his habit, his left coat lapel.

He spoke slowly, and with that penetrating clarity which made him heard even at the far edges of the crowd. Altogether, he delivered his dedication address "in a firm free way, with more grace than is his wont," wrote John Hay in his diary, and in little more than two and a half minutes.

Then he was done. A photographer on an elevated platform at the edge of the crowd cursed the brevity of the tall man's speech because he could not get his sticky, wet glass plate ready in time to capture an image. There was a patter of applause from the crowd, unsure whether this was the end or merely the introduction to something longer, although it quickly swelled to full volume once it was clear that the tall man was indeed finished. "And the music wailed and we went home through crowded and cheering streets." And, added Hay, "all the particulars are in the daily papers."

The last invasion was finally over.[12]

Notes

PROLOGUE

1. Andrew Brown, *Geology and the Gettysburg Campaign* (1962; Harrisburg: Commonwealth of Pennsylvania, 2006), 8–10; Stephanie J. Perles et al., *Vegetation Classification and Mapping at Gettysburg National Military Park and Eisenhower National Historic Site* (Philadelphia: National Park Service Northeast Region, 2006), 5–7; James T. Lemon, *The Best Poor Man's County: A Geographical Study of Early Southeastern Pennsylvania* (New York: W. W. Norton, 1972), 89–91, 108–9; Garry E. Adelman and Timothy H. Smith, *Devil's Den: A History and Guide* (Gettysburg: Thomas Publications, 1997), 1–3; "First Settlers on the Manor of Maske," *Historical Register: Notes and Queries, Biographical and Genealogical Relating to Interior Pennsylvania for the Year 1884*, ed. William Henry Egle (Harrisburg: Lane S. Hart, 1884), 2:153–55; "An Act to release all claims, on the part of the Commonwealth, to certain lands within the Manor, or reputed Manor, of Maske," in *Laws of the Commonwealth of Pennsylvania* (Philadelphia: J. Bioren, 1803), 5:229–30.
2. Israel Daniel Rupp, *The History and Topography of Dauphin, Cumberland, Franklin, Bedford, Adams, and Perry Counties* (Lancaster: Gilbert Hills, 1846), 526–47, 541; John T. Riley, *History and Directory of the Boroughs of Gettysburg, Oxford, Littlestown, York Springs, Berwick, and East Berlin* (Gettysburg: J. E. Wible, 1880), 12–13; John Badger Bachelder, *Bachelder's Illustrated Tourist's Guide of the United States* (Boston: Lee, Shephard & Dillingham, 1873), 7; George Sheldon, *When the Smoke Cleared at Gettysburg: The Tragic Aftermath of the Bloodiest Battle of the Civil War* (Nashville: Cumberland House, 2003), 22–23.

CHAPTER ONE *People who will not give in*

1. Howard, *Autobiography* (New York: Baker & Taylor, 1907), 1:440.
2. Theodore Ropp, *War in the Modern World* (New York: Collier, 1962, 175, 178–79; Robert Cole, in R. E. L. Krick, " 'The Great Tycoon' Forges a Staff System," in *Audacity Personified: The Generalship of Robert E. Lee*, ed. Peter Carmichael (Baton Rouge: Louisiana State University Press, 2004), 98; Richard Taylor, *Destruction and Reconstruction: Personal Experiences of the Late War in the United States* (Edinburgh: Wm. Blackwood & Sons, 1879), 38.

3. Abraham Oakley Hall, *Horace Greeley Decently Dissected: In a Letter on Horace Greeley Addressed to A. Oakley Hall by Joseph Hoxie, Esq.* (New York: Ross & Tousey, 1862), 32.

4. *The American Almanac and Repository of Useful Knowledge for the Year 1859* (Boston: Crosby, Nichols, 1859), 114, 151–54; Halleck, *Elements of Military Art and Science; or, Course of Instruction in Strategy, Fortification, and the Tactics of Battles* (New York: D. Appleton, 1846), 145–46; Carol Reardon, *With a Sword in One Hand and Jomini in the Other: The Problem of Military Thought in the Civil War North* (Chapel Hill: University of North Carolina Press, 2012), 55; Alexander McKay, *The Western World; or, Travels in the United States in 1846–47* (London: Richard Bentley, 1850), 3:210–13.

5. Paul R. Van Riper and Keith A. Sutherland, "The Northern Civil Service: 1861–1865," *Civil War History* 11 (December 1965), 351; Edward McPherson, ed., *The Political History of the United States During the Great Rebellion* (Washington: Philp & Solomons, 1864), 115; Wayne Wei-siang Hsieh, *West Pointers and the Civil War: The Old Army in War and Peace* (Chapel Hill: University of North Carolina Press, 2009), 75–76; Phillip Howes, *The Catalytic Wars: A Study of the Development of Warfare, 1860–1870* (London: Minerva Press, 1998), 177.

6. John S. Robson, *How a One-Legged Rebel Lives: Reminiscences of the Civil War* (Durham, NC: The Educator Co., 1898), 8; Carlton McCarthy, *Detailed Minutiae of Soldier Life in the Army of Northern Virginia, 1861–1865* (Richmond: Carleton McCarthy, 1882), 29–30, 39, 115; Benjamin H. Trask, *9th Virginia Infantry* (Lynchburg,VA: H. E. Howard, 1984), 45, 47–48; Ervin L. Jordan and Herbert A. Thomas, *19th Virginia Infantry* (Lynchburg, VA: H. E. Howard, 1987), 2–3, 39–41; James I. Robertson, *Soldiers Blue and Gray* (Columbia: University of South Carolina Press, 1988), 25; Earl J. Hess, *The Union Soldier in Battle: Enduring the Ordeal of Combat* (Lawrence: University Press of Kansas, 1997), 134; Randall C. Jimerson, *The Private Civil War: Popular Thought During the Sectional Conflict* (Baton Rouge: Louisiana State University Press, 1988), 201; "An Army: Its Organization and Movements," *Continental Monthly* 6 (September 1864), 332.

7. William Henry Morgan, *Personal Reminiscences of the War of 1861–5; In camp—in bivouac—on the march—on picket—on the skirmish line—on the battlefield—and in prison* (Lynchburg, VA: J. P. Bell, 1911), 24–25; Mosby, *The Memoirs of Colonel John S. Mosby* (1917; Nashville: J. S. Sanders & Co., 1995), 102; Mark H. Dunkelman, *Brothers One and All: Esprit de Corps in a Civil War Regiment* (Baton Rouge: Louisiana State University Press, 2004), 189, 211, 217; Hsieh, *West Pointers and the Civil War*, 144; Hyde, *Following the Greek Cross; or, Memories of the Sixth Army Corps* (Boston: Houghton Mifflin, 1894), 16, 37; Robertson, *Soldiers Blue and Gray*, 127.

8. Christian B. Keller, "Flying Dutchmen and Drunken Irishmen: The Myths and Realities of Ethnic Civil War Soldiers," *Journal of Military History* 73 (January 2009), 120–22, 126–27; Martin Oefele, "German-Americans and the War up to Gettysburg," in David L. Valuska and Christian B. Keller, eds., *Damn Dutch: Pennsylvania Germans at Gettysburg* (Mechanicsburg, PA: Stackpole Books, 2004), 18, 20, 21, 25; Christian B. Keller, *Chancellorsville and the Germans: Nativism, Ethnicity, and Civil War Memory* (New York: Fordham University Press, 2007), 10, 31–32; Michael Bacarella, *Lincoln's Foreign Legion: The 39th New York Infantry, the Garibaldi Guard* (Shippensburg, PA: White Mane Press, 1996), 117, 121, 129; Robert B. Edgerton, *Death or Glory: The Legacy of the Crimean War* (Boulder, CO: Westview Press, 1999), 49, 87; C. V. Tevis and D. R. Marquis, *The History of the Fighting Fourteenth, Published in commemoration of the fiftieth anniversary of the muster of the regiment into the United States service, May 23, 1861* (Brooklyn: Eagle Press, 1911), 213; Trevor Royle, *Crimea: The Great Crimean War, 1854–1856* (New York: St. Martin's Press, 2000), 107; George Norton Galloway, *The Ninety-fifth Pennsylvania Volunteers (Gosline's Pennsylvania Zouaves) in the Sixth Corps* (Philadelphia: Collins, 1884), 6, 8.

9. Scott, in Jason Mann Frawley, "Marching Through Pennsylvania: The Story of Soldiers and Civilians During the Gettysburg Campaign," Ph.D. dissertation, Texas Christian University (2008), 45; Spencer Glasgow Welch to Cordelia Strother Welch (August 18, 1862), in *A Confederate Surgeon's Letters to His Wife* (New York: Neale Publishing, 1911), 20.

10. Elizabeth Brown Pryor, *Reading the Man: A Portrait of Robert E. Lee Through His Private Letters* (New York: Viking, 2007), 540; J. Boone Bartholomees, *Buff Facings and Gilt Buttons: Staff and Headquarters Operations in the Army of Northern Virginia, 1861–1865* (Columbia: University of South Carolina Press, 1998), 27, 34, 35–36, 39, 105, 107, 108, 144–45, 202–3, 277–78; Edward Hagerman, "Field Transportation and Strategic Mobility in the Union Armies," *Civil War History* 34 (June 1988), 143, 144–45, 147–48, and *The American Civil War and the Origins of Modern Warfare: Ideas, Organization, and Field Command* (Bloomington: Indiana University Press, 1988), 62, 66; Arden Bucholz, *Moltke and the German Wars, 1864–1871* (Houndsmills, U.K.: Palgrave, 2001), 20, 21, 32–34; Taylor, *Destruction and Reconstuction*, 106–8; Frederick G. Burnaby, "The Practical Instruction of Staff Officers in Foreign Armies," *Journal of the Royal United Services Institution* 16 (January 1872), 638; C. W. Tolles, "An Army: Its Organization and Movements," *Continental Monthly* 6 (June 1864), 713; Scott Bowden and Bill Ward, *Last Chance for Victory: Robert E. Lee and the Gettysburg Campaign* (Cambridge, MA: Da Capo Press, 2001), 24; R. L. DiNardo, "Longstreet and Jackson Compared: Corps Staff and the Exercise of Command in the Army of Northern Virginia," in *James Longstreet: The Man, the Soldier, the Controversy*, eds. R. L. DiNardo and Albert A. Nofi (Conshohocken, PA: Combined Books, 1998), 167, 170–71; Joseph Orton Kirby, "A Boy Spy in Dixie," *National Tribune* (July 5, 1888); "The Union Cavalry Service" (July 15, 1863), in *Rebellion Record* (1864), 7:185.

11. Morgan, *Personal Reminiscences*, 24–25; E. J. Allen, *Under the Maltese Cross, Antietam to Appomattox: The Loyal Uprising in Western Pennsylvania, 1861–1865* (Pittsburgh: Werner Co., 1910), 184; Augustus Horstmann (June 16, 1862), in Walter D. Kamphoefner and Wolfgang Johannes Helbich, eds., *Germans in the Civil War: The Letters They Wrote Home* (Chapel Hill: University of North Carolina Press, 2006), 122; Andrew Elmer Ford, *The Story of the Fifteenth Regiment Massachusetts Volunteer Infantry in the Civil War, 1861–1864* (Clinton, MA: J. Coulter, 1898), 278; Alfred Seelye Roe, *The Tenth Regiment, Massachusetts Volunteer Infantry, 1861–1864: A Western Massachusetts Regiment* (Springfield, MA: 10th Regiment Veterans Assoc., 1909), 56–58; Theodore B. Gates, diary entry for January 9, 1863, in *The Civil War Diaries of Col. Theodore B. Gates, 20th New York State Militia* (Hightstown, NJ: Longstreet House, 1991), 60.

12. John Hamilton SeCheverell, *Journal History of the Twenty-Ninth Ohio Veteran Volunteers, 1861–1865: Its Victories and Its Reverses* (Cleveland, OH: n.p., 1883), 73–74; Hyde, *Following the Greek Cross*, 136; Torrance to Sarah Torrance (September 9, 1861), in "The Road to Gettysburg: The Diary and Letters of Leonidas Torrance of the Gaston Guards," *North Carolina Historical Review* 36 (October 1959), 483.

13. "An English View of our Civil War," *National Intelligencer* (May 28, 1863); Varina Davis Brown, *A Colonel at Gettysburg and Spotsylvania: The Life of Colonel Joseph Newton Brown and the Battles of Gettysburg and Spotsylvania* (Columbia, SC: State Co., 1931), 12; Handerson, *Yankee in Gray: The Civil War Memoirs of Henry E. Handerson*, ed. C. L. Cummer (Cleveland: Western Reserve University Press, 1962), 28; Ruth Hairstone Early, *Lieutenant General Jubal Anderson Early, C.S.A.: Autobiographical Sketch and Narrative of the War Between the States* (Philadelphia: J. B. Lippincott, 1912), ix–x; Joseph T. Glatthaar, *General Lee's Army: From Victory to Collapse* (New York: Free Press, 2008), 18–22; Elisabeth Lauterbach Laskin, "Good Old Rebels: Soldiering in the Army of Northern Virginia, 1862–1865," Ph.D. dissertation, Harvard University (2003), 4–5, 22–27, 117, 421–30; Kent Masterson Brown, *Retreat from Gettysburg: Lee, Logistics, and the Pennsylvania Campaign* (Chapel

Hill: University of North Carolina Press, 2005), 31, 49–50; Richard Rollins, "Black Confederates at Gettysburg—1863," *Gettysburg Magazine* 6 (January 1992), 94–97; Alexis de Tocqueville, *Democracy in America*, ed. Harvey Mansfield and Delba Winthrop (Chicago: University of Chicago Press, 2000), 360.

14.   Gary W. Gallagher, *The Confederate War* (Cambridge, MA: Harvard University Press, 1999), 140; Gallagher, "'Our Hearts Are Full of Hope': The Army of Northern Virginia in the Spring of 1864," in *The Wilderness Campaign* (Chapel Hill: University of North Carolina Press, 1997), 49–50; J. B. Turney, "The First Tennessee at Gettysburg," *Confederate Veteran* (December 1900), 537.

CHAPTER TWO   *There were never such men in an army before*

1.   Peter W. Alexander, "Confederate Chieftains," *Southern Literary Messenger* 37 (January 1863), 34; Winey, *Confederate Uniforms at Gettysburg*, 20; Michael Fellman, *The Making of Robert E. Lee* (New York: Random House, 2000), 90.

2.   Alexander, *Fighting for the Confederacy: The Personal Recollections of General Edward Porter Alexander*, ed. Gary W. Gallagher (Chapel Hill: University of North Carolina Press, 1989), 90; Pryor, *Reading the Man*, 34; Fellman, *The Making of Robert E. Lee*, 10, 11, 13.

3.   Pryor, *Reading the Man*, 56; Chesnut, diary entry for July 24, 1861, in *Mary Chesnut's Civil War*, ed. C. Vann Woodward (New Haven: Yale University Press, 1981), 116.

4.   J. William Jones, *Personal Reminiscences, Anecdotes, and Letters of Gen. Robert E. Lee* (New York: D. Appleton, 1875), 60, 482; Pryor, *Reading the Man*, 67–68, 187; Fellman, *The Making of Robert E. Lee*, 60.

5.   Pryor, *Reading the Man*, 125, 144–45, 278; Douglas Southall Freeman, *R. E. Lee: A Biography* (New York: Scribners, 1936), 1:372; Armistead L. Long, *Memoirs of Robert E. Lee: His Military and Personal History*, ed. M. J. Wright (Philadelphia: J. M. Stoddart, 1887), 83; Mosby, "A Rejoinder to General Robertson," *The Century* 35 (December 1887), 323; *My Life in the Old Army: The Reminiscences of Abner Doubleday from the Collections of the New-York Historical Society*, ed. Joseph E. Chance (Fort Worth: Texas Christian University Press, 1998), 214–15; Roy Blount, *Robert E. Lee: A Life* (New York: Penguin, 2003), 62, 63; Thomas Connelly and Barbara Bellows, *God and General Longstreet* (Baton Rouge: Louisiana State University Press, 1982), 98–99.

6.   Emory M. Thomas, *Robert E. Lee: A Biography* (New York: W. W. Norton, 1995), 173; Alan Nolan, *Lee Considered: General Robert E. Lee and Civil War History* (Chapel Hill: University of North Carolina Press, 1991), 112–13; Lee to Jefferson Davis (July 6, 1864), in *Lee's Despatches: Unpublished Letters of General Robert E. Lee, CSA, to Jefferson Davis*, eds. D. S. Freeman and G. McWhiney (New York: G. P. Putnam's, 1957), 368; Lee to G. W. C. Lee (February 28, 1863), in *The Wartime Papers of Robert E. Lee*, eds. Clifford Dowdey and L. H. Manarin (Boston: Little, Brown, 1961), 411; Peter S. Carmichael, "Lee's Search for the Battle of Annihilation," in *Audacity Personified: The Generalship of Robert E. Lee* (Baton Rouge: Louisiana State University Press, 2004), 17.

7.   Stephens, "My Impression of General R. E. Lee," *Southern Bivouac* 1 (February 1886), 538; *Memoirs of Colonel John S. Mosby*, 375.

8.   Pryor, *Reading the Man*, 125, 144–45; Freeman, *R. E. Lee*, 1:372; Long, *Memoirs of Robert E. Lee*, 83; Mosby, "A Rejoinder to General Robertson," *The Century* 35 (December 1887), 323; *My Life in the Old Army: The Reminiscences of Abner Doubleday from the Collections of the New-York Historical Society*, ed. Chance, 214–15; Blount, *Robert E. Lee*, 62, 63; Alexander, in *Fighting for the Confederacy*, 91; Davis, "Robert E. Lee," *North American Review* 150 (January 1890), 65; Thomas Connelly, *The Marble Man: Robert E. Lee and His Image*

in American Society (New York: Alfred A. Knopf, 1977), 208; *Memoirs of Colonel John S. Mosby,* 374.

9. Davis, "Robert E. Lee," 62; Clifford Dowdey, *The Seven Days: The Emergence of Lee* (Boston: Little, Brown, 1964), 139–42; Stephen W. Sears, *To the Gates of Richmond: The Peninsula Campaign* (New York: Ticknor & Fields, 1992), 155–56; "Special Orders No. 22" (June 1, 1862), in *The War of the Rebellion: A Compilation of the Official Records of the Union and Confederate Armies* (Washington, DC: Government Printing Office, 1890–1901), series one, 11 (pt. 3):569 (hereafter abbreviated as *O.R.*); Nofi, "Introduction: History, Politics and James Longstreet," in *James Longstreet,* 13; Robert M. Epstein, "The Creation and Evolution of the Army Corps in the American Civil War," *Journal of Military History* 55 (January 1991), 22, 25, 26.

10. A. R. Boteler, "Stonewall Jackson in the Campaign of 1862," *Southern Historical Society Papers* 40 (September 1915), 165 (hereafter abbreviated as *SHSP*); Henry Kyd Douglas, *I Rode With Stonewall, Being Chiefly the War Experiences of the Youngest Member of Jackson's Staff* (Chapel Hill: University of North Carolina Press, 1968), 113; Lee to Jefferson Davis (June 5, 1862, and September 4, 1862), in *Wartime Papers of Robert E. Lee,* 183–84, 288; "Letter From Major General Heth, of A.P. Hill's Corps, A.N.V.," *SHSP* 4 (October 1877), 153–54; Glatthaar, *General Lee's Army,* 174–82, 223; Brian Steel Wills, *The War Hits Home: The Civil War in Southeastern Virginia* (Charlottesville: University Press of Virginia, 2001), 74; Lee to Milledge L. Bonham (May 22, 1861), in *O.R.,* series one, 2:865; Fellman, *The Making of Robert E. Lee,* 126, 127–28; Schiebert, *Seven Months in the Rebel States During the North American War,* W. M. S. Hoole, ed. (1958; Tuscaloosa: University of Alabama Press, 2009), 75.

11. Lee to James A. Seddon (June 8, 1863) and Jefferson Davis (June 10, 1863), in *O.R.,* series one, 27 (pt. 3):869, 882; Thomas, *R. E. Lee,* 287.

12. Lee to Jefferson Davis (March 21, 1863), in *Lee's Despatches,* 81; Carmichael, "Lee's Search for the Battle of Annihilation," 15–16; Schiebert, *Seven Months in the Rebel States,* 75; Epstein, "Creation and Evolution of the Army Corps," 24–26; Douglas Southall Freeman, *Lee's Lieutenants: A Study in Command* (New York: Scribner's, 1943), 2:467–94; Russell F. Weigley, *The American Way of War: A History of United States Military Strategy and Policy* (New York: Macmillan, 1973), 108.

13. Lee to Jefferson Davis (May 20, 1863), in *Wartime Papers of Robert E. Lee,* 488; "Special Orders No. 146" (May 30, 1863), in *O.R.,* series one, 25 (pt. 2):840; Ethan S. Rafuse, *Robert E. Lee and the Fall of the Confederacy, 1863–1865* (Lanham, MD: Rowman & Littlefield, 2008), 42.

14. Lee to John Bell Hood (May 21, 1863), in *Wartime Papers of Robert E. Lee,* 490; Alexander, "Confederate Chieftains," 37–38; William Garrett Piston, *Lee's Tarnished Lieutenant: James Longstreet and His Place in Southern History* (Athens: University of Georgia Press, 1987), 4–6, 21–22, 26–27, 33, 97; William Garrett Piston, "Petticoats, Promotions, and Military Assignments: Favoritism and the Antebellum Career of James Longstreet," in *James Longstreet,* eds. DiNardo and Nofi, 57–61; Daniel Harvey Hill, "McClellan's Change of Base and Malvern Hill," in *Battles and Leaders of the Civil War,* eds. R. U. Johnson and C. C. Buel (1884–1888; New York: Thomas Yoseleff, 1956), 2:391; Fitzgerald Ross, *A Visit to the Cities and Camps of the Confederate States* (Edinburgh: Wm. Blackwood & Sons, 1865), 146; Thomas Goree to Sarah Williams Kittrellm Goree (December 14, 1861), in *Longstreet's Aide: The Civil War Letters of Major Thomas J. Goree* (Charlottesville: University Press of Virginia, 1995), 60; Bela Estvàn, *War Pictures from the South* (London: Routledge, Warne & Routledge, 1863), 308; Lafayette McLaws to Isaac Pennypacker (August 28, 1888), Lafayette McLaws Letters, Wofford College

15. James I. Robertson, *Stonewall Jackson: The Man, the Soldier, the Legend* (New York: Mac-

millan, 1997), 585, 590, 595, 627, 639, 679–80, 693; Lee to Jefferson Davis (May 20, 1863), in *Wartime Papers of Robert E. Lee*, 488; James I. Robertson, *General A. P. Hill: The Story of a Confederate Warrior* (New York: Random House, 1987), 192, 193; William J. Miller, *Mapping for Stonewall: The Civil War Service of Jed Hotchkiss* (Washington, DC: Elliott & Clark, 1993), 167.

16. Donald C. Pfanz, *Richard S. Ewell: A Soldier's Life* (Chapel Hill: University of North Carolina Press, 1998), 135, 268, 273, 277; Thomas H. Carter, "General Richard S. Ewell," *SHSP* 39 (April 1914), 7; Taylor, *Destruction and Reconstruction*, 39; Paul D. Casdorph, *Confederate General R. S. Ewell: Robert E. Lee's Hesitant Commander* (Lexington: University Press of Kentucky, 2004), 23–24, 27, 81, 85, 204; Robert G. Tanner, *Stonewall in the Valley: Thomas J. "Stonewall" Jackson's Shenandoah Valley Campaign, 1862* (Garden City, NY: Doubleday, 1976), 52; Peter Cozzens, *Shenandoah 1862: Stonewall Jackson's Valley Campaign* (Chapel Hill: University of North Carolina Press, 2009), 329; *Campbell Brown's Civil War: With Ewell and the Army of Northern Virginia*, ed. Terry L. Jones (Baton Rouge: Louisiana State University Press, 2001), 157–58.

17. Gary W. Gallagher, "Confederate Corps Leadership on the First Day at Gettysburg: A. P. Hill and Richard S. Ewell in a Difficult Debut," in *Three Days at Gettysburg: Essays on Confederate and Union Leadership* (Kent, OH: Kent State University Press, 1999), 37–38; Larry B. Maier, *Gateway to Gettysburg: The Second Battle of Winchester* (Shippensburg, PA: Burd Street Press, 2002), 284; Hunter McGuire, "Clinical Remarks on Gun-shot Wounds of Joints" (January 10, 1866), *Richmond Medical Journal* 1 (March 1866), 262; John Warwick Daniel, "General Jubal A. Early" (December 13, 1894), *SHSP* 22 (January–December 1894), 328; R. H. Early, *Lieutenant General Jubal Anderson Early*, xxiv–xxv.

18. Jefferson Davis to Robert E. Lee (May 26, 1863), in *The Papers of Jefferson Davis: January–September 1863*, eds. L. L. Crist et al. (Baton Rouge: Louisiana State University Press, 1997), 191; Robert K. Krick, "The Unfulfilled Promise of Robert E. Lee's Favorite Officer," *America's Civil War* 20 (January 2008), 43–44; Bartholomees, *Buff Facings and Gilt Buttons*, 40; Robertson, *A. P. Hill*, 177–78; Lee to Jefferson Davis (May 28, 1863), in *Lee's Despatches*, 96; Jedediah Hotchkiss, "Virginia," in Clement A. Evans, ed., *Confederate Military History: A Library of Confederate States History* (Atlanta: Confederate Publishing, 1899) 3:392; *One of Lee's Best Men: The Civil War Letters of General William Dorsey Pender*, ed. W. W. Hassler (Chapel Hill: University of North Carolina Press, 1965), 4–5; Frank A. O'Reilly, *"Stonewall" Jackson at Fredericksburg: The Battle of Prospect Hill, December 13, 1862* (Lynchburg, VA: H. E. Howard, 1993), 28.

19. Longstreet, *Manassas to Appomattox: Memoirs of the Civil War in America* (Philadelphia: J. B. Lippincott, 1908), 332; Piston, *Lee's Tarnished Lieutenant*, 40.

20. Bartholomees, *Buff Facings and Gilt Buttons*, 206–7; Henry G. Wayne to Joseph E. Brown (August 12, 1863), in *Americana Catalog 157* (December 2005), Abraham Lincoln Bookshop, Chicago, IL; Alexander McNeil (August 16, 1863), in Don Ernsberger, *Also for Glory Muster: The Story of the Pettigrew-Trimble Charge* (LaVergne, TX: Xlibris Corp., 2008), 184; Robert J. Wynstra, *"The Rashness of That Hour": Politics, Gettysburg, and the Downfall of Confederate Brigadier-General Alfred Iverson* (El Dorado Hills, CA: Savas Beatie, 2010), 327; R. H. G. Kean, diary entries for May 3 and 20, 1863, in *Inside the Confederate Government: The Diary of Robert Garlick Hill Kean*, ed. Edward Younger (New York: Oxford University Press, 1957), 55, 64.

21. Torrence to Sarah Ann Torrence (March 28, 1863), in "Diary and Letters and Leonidas Torrence," 504; Vance to James A. Seddon (January 5, 1863) and L. S. Fash to Vance (June 1, 1863), in *Papers of Zebulon Baird Vance*, ed. Joe A. Mobley (Raleigh: North Carolina Division of Archives and History, 1995), 2:5, 180; Ruffin Barnes to Mary Bryant Barnes (June 8, 1863), in Hugh Buckner Johnston, ed., "The Confederate Letters of Ruffin Barnes

of Wilson County," *North Carolina Historical Magazine* 31 (January 1954), 81; Vance to Jefferson Davis (March 9, 1864), in *O.R.*, series one, 51 (pt. 2):831–32.

22.   Horace Greeley, *The American Conflict: A History of the Great Rebellion in the United States of America, 1860–'65* (Hartford: O. D. Case, 1866), 2:484; John W. Chase to Samuel S. Chase (January 11, 1863), in *Yours for the union: The Civil War Letters of John W. Chase, First Massachusetts Light Artillery*, ed. J. S. and B. B. Collier (New York: Fordham University Press, 2004), 189; Henry Wilson Hubbell [40th New York] to mother (January 15, 1863), in Henry W. Hubbell Papers, New-York Historical Society.

23.   Browning, diary entry for January 12 and 19, 1863, in *The Diary of Orville Hickman Browning*, ed. T. C. Pease and J. G. Randall (Springfield: Illinois State Historical Library, 1925), 1:613, 616; Strong, diary entry for November 5, 1862, in *Diary of the Civil War*, ed. Allan Nevins (New York: Macmillan, 1962), 271–72; John Torrey Morse, *Abraham Lincoln* (Boston: Houghton Mifflin, 1899), 2:121–25; "Illinois Legislature Prorogued," *Washington National Intelligencer* (June 12, 1863); "Speech of Richard Yates," *Illinois State Journal* (July 13, 1863); Arnold Shankman, "Draft Resistance in Civil War Pennsylvania," *Pennsylvania Magazine of History & Biography* 101 (April 1977), 191, 192, 195, 196; "The Enrollment in Pennsylvania," *Washington National Intelligencer* (June 11, 1863); Franklin Boyts to brother John (May 21, 1863), in Franklin Boyts Papers, Historical Society of Pennsylvania.

24.   McClure, *Colonel Alexander K. McClure's Recollections of Half a Century* (Salem, MA: Salem Press, 1902), 474–75; Tevis and Marquis, *History of the Fighting Fourteenth*, 238; Asa W. Bartlett, *History of the Twelfth Regiment, New Hampshire Volunteers in the War of the Rebellion* (Concord, NH: Ira C. Evans, 1897), 36; Nelson V. Hutchinson, *History of the Seventh Massachusetts Volunteer Infantry in the War of the Rebellion of the Southern States Against Constitutional Authority* (Taunton, MA: Authority of the Regimental Association, 1890), 158–59.

25.   Richard Margerum to William Margerum (November 11, 1863) in Corp. Richard Margerum Letters (1861–1864), Historical Society of Pennsylvania; McClellan to Mary Ellen McClellan (August 16, October 31, and November 17, 1861), in *The Civil War Papers of George McClellan: Selected Correspondence, 1860–1865*, ed. Stephen W. Sears (New York: Ticknor & Fields, 1989), 85, 114, 135; Erasmus Keyes to Chase (June 17, 1862), in *The Salmon P. Chase Papers*, ed. John Niven et al. (Kent, OH: Kent State University Press, 1996), 3:212–13; Edwin M. Stanton to Ulysses S. Grant (March 3, 1865), in *O.R.*, series one, 46 (pt. 2):802; Stephen R. Taaffe, *Commanding the Army of the Potomac* (Lawrence: University Press of Kansas, 2006), 9–13.

26.   "The Doomed Army," *Wilkes' Spirit of the Times* (December 12, 1863); George Sewall Boutwell, *Reminiscences of Sixty Years in Public Affairs* (New York: McClure, Phillips & Co., 1902), 1:309; Walter H. Hebert, *Fighting Joe Hooker* (New York: Bobbs-Merrill, 1944), 147–48; O. R. Howard and William H. Rauch, *History of the "Bucktails": Kane Rifle Regiment of the Pennsylvania Reserve Corps* (Philadelphia: Electric Printing Co., 1906), 223; Robert K. Beecham, *Gettysburg, the Pivotal Battle of the Civil War* (Chicago: A. C. McClurg, 1911), 23.

27.   "General Orders No. 47" (April 30, 1863), in *O.R.*, series one, 25 (pt. 1):171; Régis de Trobriand, *Four Years with the Army of the Potomac* (Boston: Ticknor & Co., 1889), 414; "To Joseph Hooker" (May 14, 1863), in *The Collected Works of Abraham Lincoln*, ed. R. P. Basler et al. (New Brunswick: Rutgers University Press, 1953), 6:217; Robert Grandchamp, "The 2nd Rhode Island Volunteers in the Gettysburg Campaign," *Gettysburg Magazine* 42 (July 2010), 73.

28.   Epstein, "Creation and Evolution of the Army Corps," 29, 30, 31, 33–34; Frederick Elizur Goodrich, *Life of Winfield Scott Hancock, Major-General, U.S.A.* (Boston: B. B. Russell, 1886), 332; Sedgwick to his sister (April 14, 1862) and to William French (September 1, 1863), in *Correspondence of John Sedgwick, Major-General* (Norfolk, CT: Carl Stoeckel,

1903), 2:43–44, 155; Meade to "Dear Doct" (August 5, 1861), Meade to John Sergeant Meade (March 29, 1862, October 23, 1862, and March 31, 1863), and Meade to Margaretta Meade (November 24, 1861, August 9, 1863, and January 20, 1865), in George G. Meade Papers (box 1, folders 3 and 4, and box 2, folder 10), Historical Society of Pennsylvania; Ethan S. Rafuse, *George Gordon Meade and the War in the East* (Abilene, TX: McWhiney Foundation Press, 2003), 22–23; Abner Doubleday and William Newton, in William B. Styple, ed., *Generals in Bronze: Interviewing the Commanders of the Civil War* (Kearny, NJ: Belle Grove Publishing, 2005), 47, 167; Almira Hancock, *Reminiscences of Winfield Scott Hancock* (New York: Charles L. Webster, 1887), 90, 94–95; Cross to Henry Kent (December 17, 1861) and to Franklin Pierce (April 14, 1863), in *Stand Firm and Fire Low: The Civil War Writings of Colonel Edward E. Cross*, Walter Holden, W. E. Ross, and Elizabeth Slomba, eds. (Hanover: University of New Hampshire Press, 2003), 97, 137; George Alfred Townsend, in William B. Styple, *McClellan's Other Story: The Political Intrigue of Colonel Thomas M. Key, Confidential Aide to General George B. McClellan* (Kearny, NJ: Belle Grove Publishing, 2012), 204.

29.   Thomas A. Desjardin, *These Honored Dead: How the Story of Gettysburg Shaped American Memory* (New York: Da Capo Press, 2003), 78–79; Sickles, "Address at The Cooper Union for the Advancement of Science and Art" (November 1863), in Gilder-Lehrman Collection, New-York Historical Society; Sickles to Adam Badeau (August 26, 1887), Seth Kaller, Inc. Historic Documents Catalog #20340.1 at www.sethkaller.net/catalogs /abraham-lincoln/34-abraham-lincoln/150-general-sickles-lincoln-dictator-dispute; Charles Elihu Slocum, *The Life and Services of Major-General Henry Warner Slocum* (Toledo, OH: Slocum Pubs., 1913), 9; Thomas E. Hilton, ed., "To the Memory of Henry Slocum: A Eulogy by Oliver O. Howard," *Civil War Times Illustrated* (March 1982), 40; Carlos Martyn, "Introduction," in Howard, *Fighting for Humanity; or, Camp and Quarter-Deck* (New York: F. Tennyson Neely, 1898), vii; "Testimony of Major General Abner Doubleday" (March 1, 1864), in *Report of the Joint Committee on the Conduct of the War*, 4:311; Strong, diary entry for September 13, 1862, in *Diary of the Civil War*, 256.

30.   Richard Slotkin, *The Long Road to Antietam: How the Civil War Became a Revolution* (New York: Liveright/W. W. Norton, 2012), 381; "Oration of Henry S. Huidekoper" (1899), in *Pennsylvania at Gettysburg: Ceremonies at the Dedication of the Monuments Erected by the Commonwealth of Pennsylvania*, ed. John P. Nicholson (Harrisburg: Wm. Stanley Ray, 1914), 2:991–92, and "Address of Mr. J. G. Rosengarten" (March 8, 1880), in *Reynolds Memorial: Addresses delivered before the Historical Society of Pennsylvania upon the occasion of the Presentation of a Portrait of Maj.-Gen. John F. Reynolds, March 8, 1880* (Philadelphia: J. B. Lippincott, 1880), 16, 19.

31.   W. E. Doubleday to Chandler (July 5, 1861), in Zachariah Chandler Papers, Bentley Historical Library, University of Michigan; Abner Doubleday, *Reminiscences of Forts Sumter and Moultrie in 1860–'61* (New York: Harper & Bros., 1876), 137; Wayne Mahood, *General Wadsworth: The Life and Times of Brevet Major General James S. Wadsworth* (Cambridge, MA: Da Capo Press, 2003), 80, 111; Henry Clay Christiancy to Charlotte Elizabeth Christiancy, in Christiancy & Pickett Family Papers (box 1, file 1), Library of Congress; George L. Wood, *The Seventh Regiment: A Record* (New York: James Miller, 1865), 161; Noah Brooks, "Too Many Generals" (July 23, 1863), in *Lincoln Observed: Civil War Dispatches of Noah Brooks*, ed. Michael Burlingame (Baltimore: Johns Hopkins University Press, 1998), 60; *Inside Lincoln's Army: The Diary of Marsena Rudolph Patrick, Provost Marshal General, Army of the Potomac*, ed. Daniel S. Sparks (New York, 1964), 209.

32.   Sears, *Chancellorsville*, 18; Sears, *Controversies and Commanders: Dispatches from the Army of the Potomac* (New York: Houghton Mifflin, 1999), 185; Wright, *No More Gallant a Deed*, 268; George A. Custer to I. P. Christiancy (May 17, 1863), Special Collections, University

of Virginia; Oliver Otis Howard, "Campaign and Battle of Gettysburg, June and July, 1863," *Atlantic Monthly* 38 (July 1876), 48; Orson Blair Curtis, *History of the Twenty-fourth Michigan of the Iron Brigade* (Detroit: Winn Hammond, 1891), 141–42; Alan T. Nolan, *The Iron Brigade* (Madison: State Historical Society of Wisconsin, 1975), 223–24; James Lorenzo Brown, *History of the Thirty-Seventh Regiment, Mass. Volunteers, in the Civil War of 1861–1865* (Holyoke, MA: Clark W. Bryan & Co., 1884), 167–68.

33. Wood, *The Seventh Regiment*, 162; Richard Margerum to William Margerum (November 11, 1863), in Margerum Letters, HSP; Marshall Phillips to Diana Phillips (June 2, 1863), in *Yankee Correspondence: Civil War Letters Between New England Soldiers and the Home Front*, eds. N. Silber and M. B. Sievans (Charlottesville: University of Virginia Press, 1996), 39; Oliver Edwards to Eunice Lombard Edwards (January 13, 1863), Gilder-Lehrman Collection, New-York Historical Society.

CHAPTER THREE *This Campaign is going to end this show*

1. Pender to Fanny Sheppard Pender (June 28, 1863), in *One of Lee's Best Men: The Civil War Letters of General William Dorsey Pender*, 254; Rafuse, *Robert E. Lee and the Fall of the Confederacy*, 35–37; Johnston to Davis (December 22, 1862), in *O.R.*, series one, 27 (pt. 2):801; "Fears in the North of General Lee's Army," *Charleston Mercury* (June 12, 1863).

2. Davis to Johnston (March 16, 1863), in *O.R.*, series one, 23 (pt. 2):712; Rafuse, *Robert E. Lee and the Fall of the Confederacy*, 35–37; Lee to Davis (April 2, 1863) and Seddon to Lee (April 6, 1863), in *O.R.*, series one, 25 (pt. 2):700, 709; Archer Jones, "The Gettysburg Decision," *Virginia Magazine of History & Biography* 68 (July 1968), 332–35.

3. Lee to Anne Lee Marshall (April 20, 1861), in *Wartime Papers of Robert E. Lee*, 10; James Dabney McCabe, *Life and Campaigns of General Robert E. Lee* (Philadelphia: National Publishing, 1866), 31; Vincent A. Welsher to John Warwick Daniel (March 15, 1906), John Warwick Daniel Papers, Special Collections, University of Virginia; Wilbur Sturtevant Nye, *Here Come the Rebels!* (Baton Rouge: Louisiana State University Press, 1965), 8; William Swallow, "From Fredericksburg to Gettysburg," *Southern Bivouac* 4 (November 1885), 352–53; Donald J. Stoker, *The Grand Design: Strategy and the U.S. Civil War* (New York: Oxford University Press, 2010), 281; Long, *Memoirs of Robert E. Lee*, 269.

4. William J. Cooper, *Jefferson Davis, American* (New York: Alfred A. Knopf, 2000), 468; Thomas, *Robert E. Lee: A Biography*, 288, 290; Rembert W. Patrick, *Jefferson Davis and His Cabinet* (Baton Rouge: Louisiana State University Press, 1944), 137; John H. Reagan, *Memoirs, with Special Reference to Secession and the Civil War*, ed. W. F. McCaleb (New York: Neale Publishing, 1906), 151; Jones, "The Gettysburg Decision," 338; Longstreet, *Manassas to Appomattox*, 327; Longstreet, "Lee in Pennsylvania," in *Annals of the War Written by Leading Participants North and South* (Philadelphia: Times Publishing, 1879), 417; Jeffrey D. Wert, "No Fifteen Thousand Men Can Take That Position: Longstreet at Gettysburg," in *James Longstreet*, eds. DiNardo and Nofi, 82; Krick, *The Smoothbore Volley That Doomed the Confederacy*, 62–63; Alexander, *Fighting for the Confederacy*, 220.

5. Thomas Arnold, *Introductory Lectures on Modern History* (London: Longmans, Green, 1874), 153; Col. George Twemlow, *Considerations on Tactics and Strategy* (London: Simpson, Marshall & Co., 1865), 187.

6. Bruce Catton, *A Stillness at Appomattox* (Garden City, NY: Doubleday, 1953), 154–55. For a modern repetition of this view, see David White, "Born in the USA: A New World of War," *History Today* 60 (June 2010), 12.

7. Peter Smithurst, *The Pattern 1853 Enfield Rifle* (Oxford: Osprey Publishing, 2011), 8–12, 26, 34; Cadmus Marcellus Wilcox, *Rifles and Rifle Practice: An Elementary Treatise upon the*

Theory of Rifle Firing (New York: D. Van Nostrand, 1859), and George L. Willard, *Manual of Target Practice for the United States Army* (Philadelphia: J. B. Lippincott, 1862). It's worth adding that the U.S. armory system had been itself producing rifled weapons for general use (although with patched ball) for twenty years before the Civil War; and that no one less than Jefferson Davis had outfitted his Mississippi Volunteers in Mexico with rifles (he later made rifled weapons the standard for all infantry and, as secretary of war, approved J. G. Benton and Benjamin Huger's *Reports of Experiments With Small Arms for the Military Service* [1856], attesting to their practicality). My thanks to John M. Rudy of Harpers Ferry NHP for bringing this to my attention.

8. Colston, "Modern Tactics," *Southern Literary Messenger* (January 1858), 10; Lt. Col. John Mitchell, *Thoughts on Tactics and Military Organization* (London: Longman, 1838), 164; Richard Brooks, *Solferino 1859: The Battle for Italy's Freedom* (Oxford: Osprey Publishing, 2009), 84; Saul David, *The Indian Mutiny: 1857* (New York: Penguin, 2002), 248, 250; Bucholtz, *Moltke and the German Wars*, 106.

9. Andrew Steinmetz, "Military Gymnastics of the French," *Journal of the Royal United Services Institute for Defence Studies* 5 (1861), 390; Charles Carleton Coffin, "Memories of Gettysburg," in *Stories of Our Soldiers: War Reminiscences by "Carleton," and by Soldiers of New England* (Boston: Journal Newspaper, 1893), 109; Andrew Cowan to J. B. Bachelder (August 26, 1866), in *The Bachelder Papers: Gettysburg in Their Own Words*, eds. D. and A. Ladd (Dayton, OH: Morningside House, 1994), 1:281; Earl J. Hess, *Pickett's Charge: The Last Attack at Gettysburg* (Chapel Hill: University of North Carolina Press, 2001), 197; Earl J. Hess, *The Rifle Musket in Civil War Combat: Reality and Myth* (Lawrence: University Press of Kansas, 2008), 17–18, 58; Gerald J. Prokopowicz, "Tactical Stalemate: The Battle of Stones River," *North & South* 2 (September 1999), 16; O'Reilly, *"Stonewall" Jackson at Fredericksburg*, 59.

10. See Philip M. Cole, *Command and Communications Frictions in the Gettysburg Campaign* (Orrtanna, PA: Colecraft Industries, 2006), 80; Ethan S. Rafuse, *The American Civil War* (Ashgate, 2005), 230; Richard Holmes, *Sahib: The British Soldier in India, 1750–1914* (London: HarperCollins, 2005), 344; Earl J. Hess, *The Union Soldier in Battle: Enduring the Ordeal of Combat* (Lawrence: University Press of Kansas, 1997), 80–81; Brooks, *Solferino*, 84.

11. Cross, in *Stand Firm and Fire Low*, 51; Wright, *No More Gallant a Deed*, 22; William Payne, "Notes on War and Men—Summer 1865," *North & South* (September 1999), 83; Hess, *The Rifle Musket in Civil War Combat*, 30, 198, 201–2; Hsieh, *West Pointers and the Civil War*, 150, 152; Philip Haythornthwaite, *British Napoleonic Infantry Tactics, 1792–1815* (Oxford: Osprey Publishing, 2008), 10; Bell I. Wiley, *The Life of Billy Yank*, 51; Nosworthy, *The Bloody Crucible of Courage*, 144–45; "Report of Col. William B. Franklin" (July 28, 1861), in *O.R.*, series one, 2:407; William Valmore Izlar, *A Sketch of the War Record of the Edisto Rifles, 1861–1865* (Columbia, SC: August Cohn, 1914), 55–57; George F. Noyes, *The Bivouac and the Battlefield; or, Campaign Sketches in Virginia and Maryland* (New York: Harper & Bros., 1864), 333; Robertson, *Soldiers Blue and Gray*, 55, 56–57.

12. Twemlow, *Considerations on Tactics and Strategy*, 1–2; Richard Holmes, *Redcoat: The British Soldier in the Age of Horse and Musket* (New York: W. W. Norton, 2001), 216, 218–19. Sir Evelyn Wood, in his retrospective *The Crimea in 1854, and 1894* (London: Chapman & Hall, 1895), 38, noted that at the Alma one of Lord Raglan's infantry divisions extended "nearly a mile" when deployed out into line, "and it became difficult for the General officer commanding it to supervise its advance."

13. "The Column of Attack," *Colburn's United Service Magazine and Military Journal* 70 (1852), 196; Paddy Griffith, *French Napoleonic Infantry Tactics, 1792–1815* (Oxford: Osprey

Publishing, 2007), 6–8, 22–2; Hew Strachan, *From Waterloo to Balaclava: Tactics, Technology, and the British Army, 1815–1854* (Cambridge: Cambridge University Press, 1985), 20–21, 25–26.

14. William Jesse, *Russia and the War* (London: Longman, Brown, Green & Longman, 1854), 34; Brent Nosworthy, *The Bloody Crucible of Courage: Fighting Methods and Combat Experience of the Civil War* (New York: Carroll & Graf, 2003), 44; Greenlief T. Stevens, "Stevens' Fifth Maine Battery," in *Maine at Gettysburg: Report of the Maine Commissioners Prepared by the Executive Committee* (Portland: Lakeside Press, 1989), 90; Timothy J. Orr, "'Sharpshooters Made a Grand Record This Day': Combat on a Skirmish Line at Gettysburg on July 3," in *The Third Day: The Fate of a Nation, July 3, 1863* (Gettysburg: Gettysburg National Military Park, 2010), 57; Walker, *History of the Second Army Corps in the Army of the Potomac* (New York: Scribners, 1886), 450–51; Brian Holden Reid, *The Civil War and the Wars of the Nineteenth Century* (New York: Smithsonian Books, 1999), 29.

15. Giles St. Aubyn, *The Royal George: The Life of H. R. H. Prince George, Duke of Cambridge* (New York: Knopf, 1963), 78; Fletcher and Ishchenko, *The Battle of the Alma*, 140; Patrick Mercer, *Give Them a Volley and Charge: The Battle of Inkerman, 1854* (Stroud: Spellmount, 1998), 8, 98; Capt. R. Hodasevich, *A Voice from Within the Walls of Sevastopol: A Narrative of the Campaign in the Crimea and of the Events of the Siege* (London: John Murray, 1856), 67–71; Brooks, *Solferino*, 12–13; Philip Haythornthwaite, *British Napoleonic Infantry Tactics, 1792–1815* (Oxford: Osprey Publishing, 2008), 13; Eric Dorn Brose, *The Kaiser's Army: The Politics of Military Technology in Germany During the Machine Age, 1870–1918* (New York: Oxford University Press, 2001), 17; Steven D. Jackman, "Shoulder to Shoulder: Close Control and 'Old Prussian Drill' in German Offensive Infantry Tactics, 1871–1914," *Journal of Military History* 68 (January 2004), 87–89; Jennifer M. Murray, "'And so the murderous work went on': Pickett's Charge and Other Civil War Frontal Assaults," in D. Scott Hartwig, ed., *The Third Day: The Fate of a Nation, July 3, 1863* (Gettysburg: Gettysburg National Military Park, 2010), 152–53.

16. Francis J. Lippett, *Treatise on the Tactical Use of the Three Arms: Infantry, Artillery, and Cavalry* (New York: D. Van Nostrand, 1865), 134; John Keegan, *The American Civil War: A Military History* (New York: Alfred A. Knopf, 2009), 339–40; Hseih, *West Pointers and the Civil War*, 51–52; Weigley, *The American Way of War*, 15–16, 71; Howes, *The Catalytic Wars*, 47, 381, Epstein, "The Creation and Evolution of the Army Corps in the American Civil War," 45–46.

17. William W. Averell, "With the Cavalry on the Peninsula," in *Battles & Leaders*, 2:429; Michael Asher, *Khartoum: The Ultimate Imperial Adventure* (New York: Penguin, 2005), 112; Holmes, *Redcoat*, 228–29; Bartolomees, *Buff Facings and Gilt Buttons*, 62–63.

18. Eric J. Wittenberg, "'A Dash of Conspicuous Gallantry': The 6th Pennsylvania Cavalry at Brandy Station, June 9, 1863," *Gettysburg Magazine* 41 (July 2009), 13–14; "Letter from V.A.S.P." (June 10, 1863), in *Writing and Fighting from the Army of Northern Virginia: A Collection of Confederate Solider Correspondence*, ed. William B. Styple (Kearny, NJ: Belle Grove Publishing, 2003), 228; Alessandro Barbero, *The Battle: A New History of Waterloo*, trans. John Cullen (New York: Walker & Co., 2003), 60; Michael Barthorp, *The British Army on Campaign, 1816–1902: The Crimea, 1854–1856* (Oxford: Osprey Publishing, 1987), 3; Douglas Fermer, *Sedan 1870: The Eclipse of France* (London: Pen & Sword, 2008); Strachan, *From Waterloo to Balaclava*, 75, 77.

19. Charles Jean Jacques Joseph Ardant du Picq, *Battle Studies*, trans. J. N. Greely and R. C. Cotton (New York: Macmillan, 1921), 85; Sears, *Chancellorsville*, 233–35; James Robbins Jewell, "Theodore Garnett Recalls Cavalry Service with General Stuart, June 16–28, 1863," *Gettysburg Magazine* 20 (June 1999), 48; Bowen and Ward, *Last Chance for Victory*, 45; Lip-

pett, *Treatise on the Tactical Use of the Three Arms*, 128; Bartholomees, *Buff Facings and Gilt Buttons*, 256; Kirby, "A Boy Spy in Dixie," *National Tribune* (June 28, 1888); Edward C. Browne, "Col. George H. Sharpe's 'Soda Water' Scouts," *Gettysburg Magazine* 44 (January 2011), 29, 34–35; Toombs, *New Jersey Troops in the Gettysburg Campaign*, 107.

20. Griffith, *French Napoleonic Infantry Tactics*, 52–53; Bartolomees, *Buff Facings and Gilt Buttons*, 81, 83, 85, 87, 89; John C. Ropes, "The War As We See It Now," *Scribner's Magazine* 9 (June 1891), 776, 784; "Reports of Henry J. Hunt, Chief of Artillery, Army of the Potomac" (September 27, 1863), in *O.R.*, series one, 27 (pt. 1):241; John H. Rhodes, *The History of Battery B, First Regiment Rhode Island Light Artillery, in the War to Preserve the Union* (Providenc, RI: Snow & Farnham, 1894), 176–77; Bradley Gottfried, *The Artillery of Gettysburg* (Nashville: Cumberland House, 2008), 12; George W. Newton, *Silent Sentinels: A Reference Guide to the Artillery at Gettysburg* (El Dorado, CA: Savas Beatie, 2005), 4.

21. J. Morton Spearman, *The British Gunner* (London: Parker, Furnivall & Parker, 1844), unpaginated; William Allan, "Reminiscences of Field Ordnance Service with the Army of Northern Virginia—1863–'5," *SHSP* 14 (January–December 1886), 140–41; L. Van Loan Naiswald, *Grape and Canister: The Story of the Field Artillery of the Army of the Potomac, 1861–1865* (Mechanicsburg, PA: Stackpole Books, 1999), 260; R. L. Murray, *Artillery Tactics of the Civil War: A Study of the Tactical Use of Artillery Based on the First Day's Battle at Gettysburg* (Wolcott, NY: Benedum Books, 1998), 9–10, 11–12, 25; Hunt (December 4, 1862), in *O.R.*, series one, 21:827; R. D. Osborn, "The Siege of Delhi," *North American Review* 107 (October 1868), 598; Twemlow, *Considerations on Tactics and Strategy*, 27; John Strawson, *Beggars in Red: The British Army, 1789–1889* (1991; Barnsley, S. Yorks: Pen & Sword, 2003), 43.

22. William Wheeler to "Dear Grandfather and Aunt" (July 26, 1863), in *In Memoriam: Letters of William Wheeler of the Class of 1855, Y.C.* (Cambridge, MA: H. O. Houghton, 1875), 409–11; Robert Dale Mitchell, "The Rise and Survival of Private Mesnard, Part II," *Civil War Times Illustrated* 24 (February 1986), 14; *A Gallant Captain of the Civil War: Being the Record of the Extraordinary Adventures of Frederick Otto Baron von Fritsch*, ed. Joseph Tyler Butts (New York: F. Tennyson Neely, 1902), 75.

23. *Instruction for Field Artillery* (J. B. Lippincott, 1860), 2; Richard Rollins, "Lee's Artillery Prepares for Pickett's Charge," *North & South* 2 (September 1999), 47; Capt. Tyler, "The Rifle and the Spade; or, The Future of Field Operations," *Journal of the United Service Institution* 3 (1860), 173–74; R. L. Murray, *E. P. Alexander and the Artillery Action in the Peach Orchard: A Tactical Overview of the Artillery Action near the Peach Orchard at Gettysburg on July 2, 1863* (Wolcott, NY: Benedum Books, 2000), 8; Strachan, *From Waterloo to Balaclava*, 115, 116; Holmes, *Sahib: The British Soldier in India*, 339, 340, 343, 345; Maj. Alfred Mordecai, *Military Commission to Europe, in 1855 and 1856* (Washington: George W. Bowman, 1861), 141; Jay Luvaas, "A Prussian Observer with Lee," *Military Affairs* 21 (Fall 1957), 109–10; William W. Strong, *History of the 121st Regiment Pennsylvania Volunteers: "An Account from the Ranks"* (Philadelphia: Catholic Standard & Times, 1906), 31; Blake, *Three Years in the Army of the Potomac* (Boston: Lee & Shepard, 1866), 206–7, 216–17. There was actually only one 6-pounder gun in the artillery of the Army of Northern Virginia.

24. Robert Emory Park, "Sketch of the Twelfth Alabama Infantry," *SHSP* 33 (January–December 1905), 241; Samuel Pickens, in *Voices from Company D: Diaries by the Greensboro Guards, Fifth Alabama Infantry Regiment, Army of Northern Virginia*, ed. G. W. Hubbs (Athens: University of Georgia Press, 2003), 172; "From the 4th North Carolina, Camp near Fredericksburg, May 27th, 1863," in *Confederate Correspondent: The Civil War Reports of Jacob Nathaniel Raymer, Fourth North Carolina*, ed. E. B. Munson (Jefferson, NC: McFarland, 2009), 77; John Camden West, *A Texan in Search of a Fight: Being the Diary*

and Letters of a Private in Hood's Texas Brigade (Waco, TX: J. S. Hill, 1901), 54–55; Louis Léon, diary entry for May 29, 1863, in *Diary of a Tar Heel Confederate Soldier* (Charlotte, NC: Stone Pubs., 1913), 28; George Campbell Brown to Lizinka Brown (May 31, 1863), in *Campbell Brown's Civil War*, 105; D. Augustus Dickert, *History of Kershaw's Brigade* (Newberry, SC: Elbert Aull, 1899), 227–28; Naiswald, *Grape and Canister*, 263; John W. Chase (July 1, 1863), in *Yours for the Union*, 255.

25. Mills, *History of the 16th North Carolina Regiment in the Civil War* (1897; Hamilton, NY: Edmonston Publishing, 1992), 33–34.

CHAPTER FOUR *A perfectly surplus body of men*

1. Lee to A. P. Hill (June 5 and 16), in *O.R.*, series one, 27 (pt. 3):859, 896; Bowden and Ward, *Last Chance for Victory*, 36; Alexander, *Fighting for the Confederacy*, 104–5; Murray, *E. P. Alexander*, 22. John Imboden, who commanded a cavalry brigade in the Shenandoah, recalled receiving "a long confidential letter from General Lee, informing me of his purpose to cross the Blue Ridge . . . to capture Winchester, and cross the Potomac," but if this letter was a "lost" operational plan, no copy seems to have survived. See Imboden, "Lee at Gettysburg," *The Galaxy* 11 (April 1871), 508–9.

2. Bucholz, *Moltke and the German Wars, 1864–1871* (New York: Palgrave, 2001), 146–47, 162; Reid, *The Civil War and the Wars of the Nineteenth Century*, 32, 187.

3. Charles W. Turner, "The Virginia Central Railroad at War, 1861–1865," *Journal of Southern History* 12 (February–November 1942), 517, 530.

4. Bowden and Ward, *Last Chance for Victory*, 48–49; James K. Swisher, *Prince of Edisto: Brigadier General Micah Jenkins, C.S.A.* (Berryville, VA: Rockbridge Publishing, 1996), 92–93.

5. Lafayette McLaws, "Gettysburg," *SHSP* 7 (February 1879), 65–66; Charles Marshall, "Events Leading Up to the Battle of Gettysburg" (January 1896), *SHSP* 24 (January–December 1896), 210–11; Nye, *Here Come the Rebels!*, 43; Bowden and Ward, *Last Chance for Victory*, 50; Samuel Pickens, diary entry for June 4, 1863, in G. W. Hubbs, ed., *Voices from Company D*, 173–74; Alexander, *Fighting for the Confederacy*, 221; John Camden West, *A Texan in Search of a Fight*, 57–58, 58–59; Gary W. Gallagher, *Stephen Dodson Ramseur: Lee's Gallant General* (Chapel Hill: University of North Carolina Press, 1985), 68; "The Diary of Bartlett Yancey Malone," ed. W. W. Pierson, in *James Sprunt Historical Publications* (Chapel Hill: University of North Carolina Press, 1919), 16:34; George B. Davis, "The Strategy of the Gettysburg Campaign" (1898), *Papers of the Military Historical Society of Massachusetts* (Wilmington, NC: Broadfoot Publishing, 1989), 3:422–23; William Seymour, diary entry for June 5, 1863, in Gettysburg National Military Park Vertical Files [#7-LABrigade—B6, folder 1]; Daniel Butterfield to George Meade (June 4, 1863), in *O.R.*, series one, 27 (pt. 3):5.

6. Lee to Hill (June 5, 1863) and Hooker to Lincoln (June 5, 1863), in *O.R.*, series one, 27 (pt. 1):30 and (pt. 3):859; Lincoln, "To Joseph Hooker" (May 14 and June 5, 1863), in *Collected Works*, 6:217, 249.

7. Samuel Toombs, *New Jersey Troops in the Gettysburg Campaign from June 5 to July 31, 1863* (Orange, NJ: Evening Mail Publishing, 1888), 19, 20, 21–22, 25; Andrew J. Bennett, *The Story of the First Massachusetts Light Battery, attached to the Sixth Army Corps* (Boston: Deland & Barta, 1886), 113; Andrew J. Boies, *Record of the Thirty-third Massachusetts Volunteer Infantry: From Aug. 1862 to Aug. 1865* (Fitchburg, MA: Sentinel Publishing, 1880), 29; Joseph Keith Newell, *"Ours": Annals of the 10th Regiment, Massachusetts Volunteers in*

the Rebellion (Springfield, MA: C. A. Nichols, 1875), 214–15; Hooker to Lincoln (June 10, 1863) and "Reports of Col. Lewis A. Grant, Fifth Vermont Infantry, commanding Second Brigade" (June 6, 1863), in *O.R.*, series one, 27 (pt. 1):34, 676–78.

8.   Halleck to Hooker (June 5, 10 and 11, 1863), 31, 34, 35, in *O.R.*, series one, 27 (pt. 1): 31–32, 35; Lincoln, "To Joseph Hooker" (June 10, 1863), in *Collected Works*, 6:257.

9.   "Circular" (June 11, 1863), David Birney to J. H. H. Ward (June 11, 1863), Hooker to Howard (June 12, 1863), Daniel Butterfield to "Commanding Officer, Sixth Corps" (June 12, 1863), in *O.R.*, series one, 27 (pt. 3):58, 59, 67, 69.

10.   John H. Rhodes, *The History of Battery B, First Regiment Rhode Island Light Artillery, in the War to Preserve the Union* (Providence, RI: Snow & Farnham, 1894), 187; Michael Hanifen, *History of Battery B: First New Jersey Artillery* (1905; Hightstown, NJ: Longstreet House, 1991), 65; Ambrose Hayward to "Dear Father" (June 16, 1863), in *Last to Leave the Field: The Life and Letters of First Sergeant Ambrose Henry Heyward, 28th Pennsylvania Infantry*, ed. Timothy J. Orr (Knoxville: University of Tennessee Press, 2010), 155; Charles S. Wainwright, diary entry for June 7, 1863, in *A Diary of Battle: The Personal Journals of Charles S. Wainwright*, ed. Allan Nevins (1962; Cambridge, MA: Da Capo Press, 1998), 217; Rafuse, *Robert E. Lee and the Fall of the Confederacy*, 48; Patrick, diary entry for June 17, 1863, in *Inside Lincoln's Army*, 260.

11.   Daniel Butterfield to George G. Meade (June 13, 1863) and Hooker to Halleck (June 6, 1863), in *O.R.,* series one, 27 (pt. 1):33 and (pt. 3):86–87.

12.   Noah Brooks, "A Presidential Visit to the Army" (April 12, 1863), in *Lincoln Observed*, 39; William A. Morgan to J. B. Bachelder (April 1886), in *The Bachelder Papers: Gettysburg In Their Own Words*, eds. D. and A. Ladd (Dayton, OH: Morningside House, 1994), 2:1274–75; Russel H. Beatie, *Army of the Potomac: McClellan Takes Command, September 1861–February 1862* (Cambridge, MA: Da Capo Press, 2004), 264; Joseph E. Johnston, "Opposing Forces at Seven Pines," "Opposing Forces in the Maryland Campaign," and William W. Averell, "With the Cavalry on the Peninsula," in *Battles & Leaders*, 2:219, 314, 429, 600; Jack D. Welsh, *Medical Histories of Union Generals* (Kent, OH: Kent State University Press, 1996), 260.

13.   Sears, *Chancellorsville*, 67–68, 83–90; Bigelow, *The Campaign of Chancellorsville* (1910; New York: Smithmark, 1995), 136, 458–59; Edward G. Longacre, *Lincoln's Cavalrymen: A History of the Mounted Forces of the Army of the Potomac* (Mechanicsburg, PA: Stackpole Books, 2000), 127–28, 133, 147; Brooks, "A Presidential Visit to the Army" (April 12, 1863), in *Lincoln Observed*, 39; John D. Imboden, "Cavalry Raiding in 1863," in *New Annals of the Civil War*, 307.

14.   Edward G. Longacre, *The Cavalry at Gettysburg: A Tactical Study of Mounted Operations During the Civil War's Pivotal Campaign, 9 June–14 July, 1863* (Rutherford, NJ: Farleigh Dickinson University Press, 1986), 48; Longacre, *Lincoln's Cavalrymen*, 97, 150; Joseph W. McKinney, *Brandy Station, Virginia, June 9, 1863: The Largest Cavalry Battle of the Civil War* (Jefferson, NC: McFarland, 2006),58; Durwood Ball, *Army Regulars on the Western Frontier, 1848–1861* (Norman: University of Oklahoma Press, 2001),8; George Rollie Adams, *General William S. Harney: Prince of Dragoons* (Lincoln: University of Nebraska Press, 2001),212; *One of Custer's Wolverines: The Civil War Letters of Brevet Brigadier General James H. Kidd, 6th Michigan Cavalry*, ed. Eric J. Wittenberg (Kent, OH: Kent State University Press, 1999), 40.

15.   William H. Payne, "Notes on War and Men—Summer 1865," 85; John Esten Cooke, "General Stuart in Camp and Field," in *Annals of the War*, 665; John Camden West, *A Texan in Search of a Fight*, 52; Pryor, *Reading the Man*, 253; Emory Thomas, *Bold Dragoon: The Life of J.E.B. Stuart* (1986; Norman: University of Oklahoma Press, 1999), 29–30, 31, 54, 233; Robert J. Trout, *They Followed the Plume: The Story of J.E.B. Stuart and His Staff*

(Mechanicsburg, PA: Stackpole Books, 1993), 202–3; John Williamson Thomason, *Jeb Stuart* (1929; Lincoln: University of Nebraska Press, 1994), 138; Freeman, *Lee's Lieutenants*, 1:276–300.

16. Alexander, *Military Memoirs of a Confederate: A Critical Narrative* (New York: Scribner's, 1907), 114; John C. Ropes, "General Stuart" (1886), in *Critical Sketches of Some of the Federal and Confederate Commanders: Papers of the Military Historical Society of Massachusetts*, ed. Theodore F. Dwight (Boston: Houghton Mifflin, 1895), 10:158; Warren Wilkinson and Steven E. Woodworth, *A Scythe of Fire: A Civil War Story of the Eighth Georgia Infantry* (New York: William Morrow, 2002), 216; Warren C. Robinson, *Jeb Stuart and the Confederate Defeat at Gettysburg* (Lincoln: University of Nebraska Press, 2007), 37.

17. Pleasonton to Seth Williams (June 7, 1863) and Daniel Butterfield to Pleasonton (June 7, 1863), in *O.R.*, series one, 27 (pt. 3):25, 27–28.

18. Botts, *The Great Rebellion: Its Secret History, Rise, Progress, and Disastrous Failure* (New York: Harper & Bros., 1866), 194; Daniel A. Grimsley, "Culpeper as a Battle Ground in the War Between the States," in *Battles in Culpeper County, Virginia, 1861–1865: And Other Articles* (Culpeper, VA: Raleigh Travers Green, 1900), 8; William L. Wilson, diary entry for June 8, 1863, in *A Borderland Confederate*, ed. Festus P. Summers (Pittsburgh: University of Pittsburgh Press, 1962), 71; Daniel P. Oates, *Hanging Rock Rebel: Lt. John Blue's War in West Virginia and the Shenandoah Valley* (Shippensburg, PA: Burd Street Press, 1994), 198; R. E. Lee to Mary Custis Lee (June 9, 1863), in *Wartime Papers of Robert E. Lee*, 507; Stephen Z. Starr, *The Union Cavalry in the Civil War: From Fort Sumter to Gettysburg, 1861–1863* (Baton Rouge: Louisiana State University Press, 1979), 374–76.

19. Alfred Pleasonton, "The Campaign of Gettysburg," in *Annals of the War*, 448–49; M. C. Butler to O. G. Thompson (August 17, 1907), in U. R. Brooks, *Butler and His Cavalry in the War of Secession, 1861–1865* (Columbia, SC: State Co., 1909), 151; Eric J. Wittenberg, *The Battle of Brandy Station: North America's Largest Cavalry Battle* (Charleston: History Press, 2010), 75–91; Clark B. Hall, "The Battle of Brandy Station," *Civil War Times Illustrated* (June 1990), 33–34; Roger H. Harrell, *The 2nd North Carolina Cavalry* (Jefferson, NC: McFarland, 2004), 118; Neil Hunter Raiford, *The 4th North Carolina Cavalry in the Civil War: A History and Roster* (Jefferson, NC: McFarland, 2003), 42; Bennett Young, *Confederate Wizards of the Saddle: Being Reminiscences and Observations of One Who Rode with Morgan* (Boston: Chapple Publishing, 1914), 516; Thomas, *Bold Dragoon*, 221; Eric J. Wittenberg, "'A Dash of Conspicuous Gallantry': The 6th Pennsylvania Cavalry at Brandy Station," *Gettysburg Magazine* 41 (July 2009), 7.

20. Eric J. Wittenberg, "The Fight at Stevensburg, June 9, 1863: Saving Jeb Stuart from Defeat at Brandy Station," *Gettysburg Magazine* 44 (January 2011), 7–10; Scott Patchan, *The Battle of Piedmont and Hunter's Raid on Staunton: The 1864 Shenandoah Campaign* (Charleston: The History Press, 2011), 33.

21. Harriet Bey Mesic, *Cobb's Legion Cavalry: A History and Roster of the Ninth Georgia Volunteers* (Jefferson, NC: McFarland, 2009), 64; "Fight at Brandy Station, Va" (June 10, 1863), in *The Rebellion Record: A Diary of American Events*, ed. Frank Moore (New York: D. Van Nostrand, 1864), 7:288–89; Thomas, *Bold Dragoon*, 222; Fairfax Downey, *Clash of Cavalry: The Battle of Brandy Station, June 9, 1863* (New York: D. McKay, 1959), 139; "Sketches of Hampton's Cavalry," in *Stories of the Confederacy*, ed. U. R. Brooks (Columbia, SC: State Co., 1912), 150; "The Great Cavalry Fight—The Fight at Stevensburgh," *New York Times* (June 16, 1863).

22. Paul D. Casdorph, *Confederate General R. S. Ewell: Robert E. Lee's Hesitant Commander* (Lexington: University Press of Kentucky, 2004), 232; Luther W. Hopkins, *From Bull Run to Appomattox: A Boy's View* (Baltimore: Fleet-McGinley, 1908), 92; Wittenberg, *Battle of Brandy Station*, 183, 185; Lee to Stuart (June 16, 1863), in *O.R.*, series one, 27 (pt. 2): 687;

Nye, *Here Come the Rebels!*, 57–58; Charles M. Blackford to Susan Blackford (June 12, 1863), in *Letters from Lee's Army; or, Memoirs of Life in and Out of the Army in Virginia During the War Between the States*, ed. C. M. Blackford III (1947; Lincoln: University of Nebraska Press, 1998), 175; "Cavalry Fight of Tuesday," *Washington National Intelligencer* (June 11, 1863).

23.   "Return of Casualties in the Union Forces at Brandy Station," "Tabular Statement of Casualties in Cavalry Division, Army of Northern Virginia," and "Reports of Col. William C. Wickham, Fourth Virginia Cavalry," in *O.R.*, series one, 27 (pt. 1):168–70 and (pt. 2):719, 745; Wittenberg, *Brandy Station*, 153–54, 160; "The Cavalry Fight in Culpeper—Further Particulars," *Richmond Daily Dispatch* (June 11, 1863); Thomas, *Bold Dragoon*, 227; Walter H. Taylor to Bettie Saunders (June 11, 1863), *in Lee's Adjutant: The Wartime Letters of Colonel Walter Herron Taylor, 1862–1865*, ed. R. L. Tower (Columbia: University of South Carolina Press, 1995), 56.

24.   Hooker to Lincoln (June 10, 1863), Halleck to Hooker (June 11, 1863), in *O.R.*, series one, 27 (pt. 1):34–35; Lincoln, "To Joseph Hooker" (June 10, 1863), in *Collected Works*, 6:257; Gideon Welles, diary entry for June 28, 1863, in *Diary of Gideon Welles*, ed. John T. Morse (Boston: Houghton Mifflin, 1911), 1:349; Charles F. Benjamin, "Hooker's Appointment and Removal," in *Battles & Leaders*, 3:241; A. M. Gambone, *Hancock at Gettysburg . . . and Beyond* (Baltimore: Butternut and Blue, 2002), 2; Oliver J. Keller, "Soldier-General of the Army: John Fulton Reynolds," *Civil War History* 4 (June 1958), 123–24.

25.   Almira Hancock, *Reminiscences of Winfield Scott Hancock* (New York: Charles L. Webster, 1887), 94–95; Sears, *Controversies and Commanders*, 161–62.

26.   "Report of Lieut. Gen. James Longstreet, C.S. Army" (July 27, 1863), in *O.R.*, series one, 27 (pt. 2):357; Casdorph, *R. S. Ewell*, 233; Frank E. Fields, *28th Virginia Infantry* (Lynchburg, VA: H. E. Howard, 1985), 23–24; Louis Léon, *Diary of a Tar Heel Confederate Soldier*, 30–31.

27.   Richard Junger, *Becoming the Second City: Chicago's Mass News Media, 1833–1898* (Urbana: University of Illinois Press, 2010), 51–52; Lee to Davis (June 10, 1863), in *O.R.*, series one, 27 (pt. 3):880–82.

28.   Davis to Lincoln, *O.R.* series two, 6:76; Thomas E. Schott, *Alexander H. Stephens of Georgia: A Biography* (Baton Rouge: Louisiana State University Press, 1988), 376–80; Varina Davis, *Jefferson Davis: Ex-President of the Confederate States of America: A Memoir* (New York: Belford, 1809), 400–11; "The Mission of A. H. Stephens," in *Rebellion Record*, ed. Moore (1864), 4:199–200.

29.   Pfanz, *Richard S. Ewell*, 281–82; Larry B. Maier, *Gateway to Gettysburg: The Second Battle of Winchester* (Shippensburg, PA: Burd Street Press, 2002), 3, 9, 35–36, 37, 55–56, 115; Nye, *Here Come the Rebels!*, 70–71, 73.

30.   Richard R. Duncan, *Beleaguered Winchester: A Virginia Community at War, 1861–1865* (Baton Rouge: Louisiana State University Press, 2007), 135–56; Jerry W. Holsworth, *Civil War Winchester* (Charleston, SC: History Press, 2011), 83–90; Maier, *Gateway to Gettysburg*, 57–58, 63–64, 126–27; Jonathan A. Noyalas, *"My Will Is Absolute Law": A Biography of Union General Robert H. Milroy* (Jefferson, NC: McFarland, 2006), 79–80, 84; David S. Reynolds, *John Brown, Abolitionist: The Man Who Killed Slavery, Sparked the Civil War and Seeded Civil Rights* (New York: Random House, 2005), 3; Charles Blackford to Susan Blackford (June 19, 1863), in *Letters from Lee's Army*, 179; "Milroy's Reign in Winchester," *Richmond Daily Dispatch* (June 18, 1863); Lee to Seddon (January 10, 1863), in *O.R.*, series two, 5:806–7.

31.   Lee to Jefferson Davis (June 15, 1863), in *O.R.*, series one, 27 (pt. 2):295; Darrell L. Collins, *Major General Robert E. Rodes of the Army of Northern Virginia: A Biography* (El Dorado Hills, CA: Savas Beatie, 2008), 240–42; "General Lee and the Officer," in *The Grayjackets:*

And How They Lived, Fought and Died, for Dixie (Richmond, VA: Jones Bros., 1867), 103; Eddie Woodward, "An Affair of Outposts: Edward Johnson, the Army of the Northwest, and the Battle of Allegheny Mountain," *West Virginia History* 59 (2001–2003), 1–35; John Overton Casler, *Four Years in the Stonewall Brigade* (Girard, KS: Appeal Publishing, 1906), 163; Gary Shreckengost, *The First Louisiana Special Battalion: Wheat's Tigers in the Civil War* (Jefferson, NC: McFarland, 2008), 36; J. W. Minnich, "Picturesque Soldiery," *Confederate Veteran* 31 (August 1923), 295; Furgurson, *Chancellorsville*, 291; Thomas Hughes, *A Boy's Experience in the Civil War, 1860–1865* (Washington, DC: n.p., 1904), 14–17.

32. Samuel Pickens, diary entry for June 12, 1863, in *Voices from Company D*, 176; Pfanz, *Richard S. Ewell*, 282–83; William Seymour, diary entry for June 12, 1863, in *The Civil War Memoirs of William J. Seymour*, 58–60; "Diary of Bartlett Yancey Malone," 34–35; Samuel Pendleton, diary entry for June 12, 1863, in Diary of Samuel H. Pendleton, Special Collections, University of Virginia; Gary W. Gallagher, *Stephen Dodson Ramseur: Lee's Gallant General* (Chapel Hill: University of North Carolina Press, 1985), 68–69; Louis Léon, diary entry for June 13, 1863, in *Diary of a Tar Heel Confederate*, 30–31; Maier, *Gateway to Gettysburg*, 158, 164.

33. "Report of Maj. Gen. Jubal Early, C.S. Army" (August 22, 1863), in *O.R.*, series one, 27 (pt. 2):462–63; Maier, *Gateway to Gettysburg*, 143, 146–47, 178–179, 180, 181–82, 188, 189, 195, 198; Charles S. Grunder and Brandon Beck, *The Second Battle of Winchester, June 12–15, 1863* (Lynchburg, VA: H. E. Howard, 1989), 34; William Seymour, diary entry for June 14, 1863, in Isaac Seymour File, Gettysburg National Military Park Vertical Files; Pfanz, *Richard S. Ewell*, 284, 286; William Seymour, diary entry for June 14, 1863, in *Civil War Memoirs of William J. Seymour*, 61, 62; Casdorph, *R. S. Ewell*, 235–36; Thomas Benton Reed, *A Private in Gray* (Camden, AR: T. B. Reed, 1905), 36–37; W. G. Loyd, "Second Louisiana at Gettysburg," *Confederate Veteran* (September 1898), 417; Randolph H. McKim, *A Soldier's Recollections: Leaves from the Diary of a Young Confederate Soldier, with an Oration on the Motives and Aims of the Soldiers of the South* (New York: Longmans, Green, 1910), 145–47.

34. "Return of Casualties in the Union Forces at Winchester, Va., June 13–15, 1863," "Report of Lieut. Gen. Richard S. Ewell, C.S. Army," and "Reports of Maj. Gen. Edward Johnson, C.S. Army" (August 18, 1863), in *O.R.*, series one, 27 (pt. 2):53, 441, 501–2; Maier, *Gateway to Gettysburg*, 214, 216–17, 221, 238, 254, 263, 264, 266; Pfanz, *Richard S. Ewell*, 287–88; William Seymour, diary entry for June 15, 1863, in *Civil War Memoirs of William J. Seymour*, 62–63; Nye, *Here Come the Rebels!*, 104–5; "Recent Battles in Virginia," *Brooklyn Daily Eagle* (June 18, 1863); Bowden and Ward, *Last Chance for Victory*, 98; Frank A. Bond, "Company A—First Maryland Cavalry," *Confederate Veteran* (February 1898), 78.

35. Allan, "Reminiscences of Field Ordnance Service with the Army of Northern Virginia—1863–'5," *SHSP* 14 (January–December 1886), 142–43; Wiley Sword, "Confederate Maj. John W. Daniel Describes the 2nd Battle of Winchester at the Beginning of the Gettysburg Campaign," *Gettysburg Magazine* 35 (July 2006), 9; "The Victory at Winchester," *Charleston Mercury* (June 22, 1863); Nye, *Here Come the Rebels!*, 122–23; Samuel Pendleton, diary entry for June 15, 1863, in Diary of Samuel H. Pendleton, Special Collections, University of Virginia; Pickens, diary entry for June 13, in *Voices from Company D*, 177.

36. "The News from the Potomac—Our Forces Reported to Be in Maryland—Reported Capture of Milroy," *Richmond Daily Dispatch* (June 18, 1863); "Good News from Winchester," *Macon Daily Telegraph* (June 18, 1863); "General Orders No. 44" (June 15, 1863), in *O.R.*, series one, 27 (pt. 3):895; Blackford to Susan Blackford, June 16, 1863, in *Letters from Lee's Army*, 177; Casler, *Four Years in the Stonewall Brigade*, 167; William A. and Patricia C. Young, *56th Virginia Infantry* (Lynchburg, VA: H. E. Howard, 1990), 77.

CHAPTER FIVE   *Victory will inevitably attend our arms*

1. "Report of Maj. Gen. Robert H. Milroy, U.S. Army" (June 30, 1863), in *O.R.*, series one, 27 (pt. 2):51; Halleck to Schenck (June 15, 1863), "Special Orders No. 162" (June 17, 1863), and Halleck to Schenck (June 20, 1863), in *O.R.*, series one, 27 (pt. 3):124, 180, 190, 237; "Shenandoah Valley News," *Washington National Intelligencer* (June 17, 1863); Noyalas, *"My Will Is Absolute Law,"* 119; Lincoln, "To Robert H. Milroy" (June 29, 1863), in *Collected Works*, 6:308–9

2. Hooker to Halleck (June 13, 1863), Hooker to Lincoln (June 14, 1863), in *O.R.*, series one, 27 (pt. 1):38–41.

3. "Report of Maj. Gen. Richard H. Anderson, C.S. Army" (August 7, 1863), Longstreet to John Bell Hood, George Pickett and Lafayette McLaws (June 14, 1863), in *O.R.*, series one, 27 (pt. 3):613, 887–88; Léon, *Diary of a Tar Heel Confederate Soldier*, 31–32; Rafuse, *Robert E. Lee and the Fall of the Confederacy*, 48–49; Robertson, *General A. P. Hill*, 200; Lt. Herman Schuricht, "Jenkins' Brigade in the Gettysburg Campaign," *SHSP* 24 (January–December 1896), 340–41; Frawley, "Marching Through Pennsylvania," 34, 36–37, 38, 39, 40, 50–51.

4. W. A. and P. C. Young, *56th Virginia Infantry*, 77; D. Augustus Dickert, *History of Kershaw's Brigade* (Newberry, SC: Elbert Aull, 1899), 226–27; Pender to Fanny Pender (April 19 and June 15, 1863), in *One of Lee's Best Men*, 226, 247–48; Earl J. Hess, *Lee's Tar Heels: The Pettigrew-Kirkland-MacRae Brigade* (Chapel Hill: University of North Carolina Press, 2002), 113; James A. Wright, in Rod Gragg, *Covered with Glory: The 26th North Carolina Infantry at the Battle of Gettysburg* (New York: HarperCollins, 2000), 49; John E. Devine, *8th Virginia Infantry* (Lynchburg, VA: H. E. Howard, 1983), 19–20.

5. "Report of Maj. Gen. R. E. Rodes, C.S. Army," in *O.R.*, series one, 27 (pt. 2):550; James Johnson Kirkpatrick, diary entry for June 24, 1863, in *The 16th Mississippi Infantry*, 172–73; Casler, *Four Years in the Stonewall Brigade*, 180–81; Loyd, "Second Louisiana at Gettysburg," 417; Casdorph, *R. S. Ewell*, 237–38; William W. Chamberlaine, *Memoirs of the Civil War Between the Northern and Southern Sections of the United States of America, 1861 to 1865* (Washington: Byron S. Adams, 1912), 63–64; William Seymour, diary entry for June 23, 1863, in *The Civil War Memoirs of William J. Seymour*, 64–65; LeRoy S. Edwards, in Gary W. Gallagher, "'If the Enemy Is There, We Must Attack Him': R. E. Lee and the Second Day at Gettysburg," in *Three Days at Gettysburg: Essays on Confederate and Union Leadership* (Kent, OH: Kent State University Press, 1999), 109; Collins, *Major General Robert E. Rodes*, 246.

6. Samuel Pickens, diary entry for June 19, 1863, in *Voices from Company D*, 178–79; Robert Emory Park, "Sketch of the Twelfth Alabama Infantry," *SHSP* 33 (January–December 1905), 242; William Swallow, "From Fredericksburg to Gettysburg," in *Southern Bivouac* 4 (November 1885), 356–57; Dickert, *History of Kershaw's Brigade*, 229; Benjamin Trask, *9th Virginia Infantry* (Lynchburg, VA: H. E. Howard, 1984), 24–26; Charles Blackford to Susan Blackford (June 25, 1863), in *Letters from Lee's Army*, 182; West, *A Texan in Search of a Fight*, 91–92; Léon, *Diary of a Tar Heel Confederate Soldier*, 31–32; Lee A. Wallace, *3rd Virginia Infantry* (Lynchburg, VA: H. E. Howard, 1986), 35.

7. Park, "Sketch of the Twelfth Alabama Infantry," 242; Samuel Pickens, diary entry for June 19, 1863, in *Voices from Company D*, 179; Don Ernsberger, *Also for Glory Muster: The Story of the Pettigrew-Trimble Charge* (LaVergne, TX: Xlibris, 2008), 18; Robertson, *General A. P. Hill*, 203.

8. W. A. Young and P. C. Young, *56th Virginia Infantry*, 78; Robertson, *18th Virginia Infantry*, 20; Blackford to Susan Blackford (June 25, 1863), in *Letters from Lee's Army*, 182; West, *A Texan in Search of a Fight*, 91; Mills, *History of the 16th North Carolina Regiment in the Civil*

War, 36; James Johnson Kirkpatrick, diary entry for June 26, 1863, in *The 16th Mississippi Infantry*, 173; John E. Divine, *8th Virginia Infantry* (Lynchburg, VA: H. E. Howard, 1983), 20; "Letter from V.A.S.P., in Pennsylvania" (June 26, 1863), in Styple, *Writing and Fighting from the Army of Northern Virginia*, 239.

9. Lee to A. P. Hill (June 16, 1863) and Lee to Ewell (June 22, 1863), in *O.R.*, series one, 27 (pt. 3):896, 914.

10. Frawley, "Marching Through Pennsylvania," 42, 48, 54; Wilkinson and Woodworth, *Scythe of Fire*, 219–21.

11. "Letter from Tout le Monde in Pennsylvania" (June 29, 1863) and "Letter from Lee's Army" (July 18, 1863), in Styple, *Writing and Fighting from the Army of Northern Virginia*, 240, 254; John Alexander Barry to "Dear Sister" (July 26, 1863), in Barry Papers, Southern Historical Collection, University of North Carolina; Robert T. Hubard, Jr., to R. T. Hubard (July 20, 1863), in *The Civil War Memoirs of a Virginia Cavalryman*, ed. T. P. Nanzig (Tuscaloosa: University of Alabama Press, 2007), 121; Ernsberger, *Also for Glory Muster*, 19; Pickens, diary entry for June 24, 1863, in *Voices from Company D*, 180; George Anson Bruce, *The Twentieth Regiment of Massachusetts Volunteer Infantry, 1861–1865* (Boston: Houghton Mifflin, 1906), 267; Blackford to Susan Blackford (June 28, 1863), in *Letters from Lee's Army*, 184–85; Cook, "Reminiscences of Gettysburg," in *Gettysburg Sources*, 2:125.

12. "General Orders No. 72" (June 21, 1863), Col. J. F. Gilmore to Capt. T. B. Lee (June 17, 1863), in *O.R.*, series one, 27 (pt. 3):902, 912; "Report of Maj. Gen. Robert E. Rodes, C.S. Army," in *O.R.*, series one, 27 (pt. 2):551.

13. "Reports from Frederick," *New York Times* (June 30, 1863); Pender to Fanny Pender (June 28, 1863), in *One of Lee's Best Men*, 253; Ernsberger, *Also for Glory Muster*, 19; Walter, diary entry for June 28, 1863, in *Norfolk Blues: The Civil War Diary of the Norfolk Light Artillery Blues*, Kenneth Wiley, ed. (Shippensburg, PA.: Burd Street Press, 1997), 73; Collins, *Major General Robert E. Rodes*, 247; Jeremiah Tate to Mary Tate (July 19, 1863), in Gilder-Lehrman Collection, New-York Historical Society; William Izard Clopton, in Robert H. Moore, *The Richmond Fayette, Hampden, Thomas and Blount's Lynchburg Artillery* (Lynchburg, VA: H. E. Howard, 1991), 77; John W. Stevens, *Reminiscences of the Civil War* (Hillsboro, TX: Hillsboro Mirror Print, 1902), 106–7, 108–9.

14. Jacob Hoke, *The Great Invasion of 1863; or, General Lee in Pennsylvania* (Dayton, OH: W. J. Shuey, 1887), 135–36, 139; *Campbell Brown's Civil War*, 198; Frawley, "Marching Through Pennsylvania," 53, 60; Rachel Cormany, diary entries for June 25 and 28, 1863, in *The Cormany Diaries: A Northern Family in the Civil War*, ed. James C. Mohr (Pittsburgh: University of Pittsburgh Press, 1982), 335, 337.

15. "Rev. Benjamin S. Schneck, D.D.," in *The Fathers of the German Reformed Church in Europe and America*, eds., Henry Harbaugh and D. Y. Heisler (Reading, PA: Daniel Miller, 1881), 5:127; Edward L. Ayers, *In the Presence of Mine Enemies: War in the Heart of America, 1859–1863* (New York: W. W. Norton, 2003), 402; "Letter from V.A.S.P., in Pennsylvania" (June 26, 1863), in Styple, *Writing and Fighting from the Army of Northern Virginia*, 240.

16. Arabella Willson, *Disaster, Struggle, Triumph: The Adventures of 1000 "Boys in Blue," from August, 1862, to June, 1865* (Albany, NY: Argus Co., 1870), 88.

17. "The Invasion—The Army of the Potomac—Visit Inside the Rebel Lines," *New York Herald* (July 2, 1863); William S. Christian [55th Virginia], in Donald J. Frey, *Longstreet's Assault—Pickett's Charge: The Lost Record of Pickett's Wounded* (Shippensburg, PA: White Mane Books, 2000), 18–19; Jacob Hoke, *Historical Reminiscences of the War; or, Incidents Which Transpired in and About Chambersburg, During the War of the Rebellion* (Chambersburg, PA: M. A. Foltz, 1884), 38; Schaff, "The Gettysburg Week," *Scribner's Magazine* 16 (July 1894), 24, 26; Thaddeus Stevens, "Speech on State Elections (September 17, 1863), in *The Selected Papers of Thaddeus Stevens*, ed. B. W. Palmer (Pittsburgh: University of Pitts-

burgh Press, 1997), 1:407–08; Frawley, "Marching Through Pennsylvania," 38–39, 66–67; Ted Alexander, "'A Regular Slave Hunt': The Army of Northern Virginia and Black Civilians in the Gettysburg Campaign," *North & South* 7 (September 2001), 84–89, Rafuse, *Robert E. Lee and the Fall of the Confederacy*, 54–55.

18. McLaws to Emily McLaws (June 15, 1863), in *A Soldier's General: The Civil War Letters of Major General Lafayette McLaws*, ed. John C. Oeffinger (Chapel Hill: University of North Carolina Press, 2002), 190; "General Orders No. 73" (June 27, 1863) and Lee to Imboden (June 23, 1863), in *O.R.*, series one, 27 (pt. 3):924, 943; Simpson to Anna Tallulah Simpson (July 27, 1863), in *Far, Far from Home: The Wartime Letters of Dick and Tally Simpson, 3rd South Carolina*, eds. G. R. Everson and E. H. Simpson (New York: Oxford University Press, 1994), 262.

19. Alexander, "Causes of the Confederate Defeat at Gettysburg," *SHSP* 4 (September 1877), 110; Earl J. Hess, *Trench Warfare Under Grant and Lee: Field Fortifications in the Overland Campaign* (Chapel Hill: University of North Carolina Press, 2007), 15; Thomas, *R. E. Lee*, 241–42; Robert E. L. Krick, "'The Great Tycoon' Forges a Staff System," 87–89, 100–101.

20. Epstein, "Creation and Evolution of the Army Corps," 35–37; Krick, *Staff Officers in Gray: A Biographical Register of the Staff Officers in the Army of Northern Virginia* (Chapel Hill: University of North Carolina Press, 2003), 14; Taylor to Bettie Saunders (August 8 and 21, 1863), in *Lee's Adjutant*, 68, 71.

21. Lee to Davis (June 23 and 25, 1863) and Seddon to Daniel Harvey Hill (June 25, 1863), in *O.R.*, series one, 27 (pt. 3):925, 931–32.

22. Lee to Ewell (June 22, 1863), in *O.R.*, series one, 27 (pt. 3):914.

23. Pfanz, *Richard S. Ewell*, 294–95; Rafuse, *Robert E. Lee and the Fall of the Confederacy*, 50–51; R. H. Early, *Lieutenant General Jubal Anderson Early*, 254, 261; William J. Seymour, diary entry for June 28–29, 1863, in *Civil War Memoirs*, 67, 68.

24. Herman Schuricht, "Jenkins' Brigade in the Gettysburg Campaign," *SHSP* 24 (1896), 342; R. H. Early, *Lieutenant General Jubal Anderson Early*, 254; Hoke, *The Great Invasion*, 125; W. P. Conrad and Ted Alexander, *When War Passed This Way* (Shippensburg, PA: White Mane Books, 1982), 136–38; Benjamin Matthias Nead, *Waynesboro: The History of a Settlement in the County formerly called Cumberland but later Franklin* (Harrisburg, PA: Harrisburg Pubs., 1900), 224.

25. Casdorph, *Confederate General R. S. Ewell*, 240–41; Jeffrey D. Wert, *General James Longstreet: The Confederacy's Most Controversial Soldier: A Biography* (New York: Simon & Schuster, 1993), 46; "Fitzhugh Lee," *Carlisle American* (July 22, 1863).

26. Roger S. Durham, *Carlisle Barracks* (Charleston, SC: Arcadia, 2009), 22; Horatio C. King, *History of Dickinson College* (New York: American University Magazine Publishing Co., 1897), 33; Pfanz, *Richard S. Ewell*, 298–99; Collins, *Major General Robert E Rodes*, 254.

27. Louis Léon, diary entry for June 25, 1863, in *Diary of a Tar-Heel Confederate Soldier*, 33–34; *Campbell Brown's Civil War*, 202; Betts, *Experience of a Confederate Chaplain, 1861–1864* (N.C. Conference Methodist Episcopal Church, South, 1900), 38; Casdorph, *Confederate General R. S. Ewell*, 240–41, 242; Wharton Jackson Green, *Recollections and Reflections: An Auto*[biography] *of Half a Century and More* (Raleigh, NC: Edwards & Broughton, 1906), 174; James K. Swisher, *Warrior in Gray: General Robert Rodes of Lee's Army* (Shippensburg, PA: White Mane Books, 2000), 119; *Campbell Brown's Civil War*, 201–2; Samuel Pendleton, diary entry for June 29, 1863, in Diary of Samuel H. Pendleton, Special Collections, University of Virginia; Park, "Sketch of the Twelfth Alabama Infantry," 243.

28. Rafuse, *Robert E. Lee and the Fall of the Confederacy, 1863–1865*, 53; "Report of Lieut. Gen. Ambrose P. Hill, C.S. Army" (November, 1863), in *O.R.*, series one, 27 (pt. 2):606; Green, *Recollections and Reflections*, 173; William Swallow, "From Fredericksburg to Gettysburg,"

353; Kent Masterson Brown, *Retreat from Gettysburg: Lee, Logistics, and the Pennsylvania Campaign* (Chapel Hill: University of North Carolina Press, 2005), 16; Anthony J. Milano, "A Call of Leadership: Lt. Col. Charles Redington Mudge, U.S.V., and the Second Massachusetts Infantry at Gettysburg," *Gettysburg Magazine* 6 (January 1992), 71; *The Civil War Memoirs of William J. Seymour*, 58; Collins, *Major General Robert E. Rodes*, 258.

29. R. G. H. Kean, diary entry for June 29, in *Inside the Confederate Government*, 77; Trimble, "The Battle and Campaign of Gettysburg," *SHSP* 26 (January–December 1898), 117–19; Trimble to J. B. Bachelder (February 8, 1883), in *Bachelder Papers*, 2:925–26.

30. Trimble, "The Battle and Campaign of Gettysburg," 120–21; Trimble to John C. Bachelder (February 8, 1883), in *Bachelder Papers*, 2:925–26; Bowden and Ward, *Last Chance for Victory*, 138; Rafuse, *Robert E. Lee and the Fall of the Confederacy, 1863–1865*, 56; Pender to Fanny Pender (June 23, 1863), in *One of Lee's Best Men*, 251; Hotchkiss, diary entry for June 26, 1863, in *Make Me a Map of the Valley*, 155. In 1891, Daniel Butterfield, Joe Hooker's chief of staff, claimed that Hooker had done likewise "early in June," predicting that Lee would cross the Potomac at Williamsport, cross over South Mountain toward Gettysburg, "and we will fight the battle here." See Butterfield, "Further Recollections of Gettysburg," *North American Review* 152 (March 1891), 279–80.

CHAPTER SIX *A goggle-eyed old snapping turtle*

1. Hooker to Lincoln (June 15, 1863), Halleck to W. T. H. Brooks (June 14, 1863), and Hooker to Halleck (June 17, 1863), in *O.R.*, series one, 27 (pt. 1):43–44, 50, and (pt. 3):113.

2. Hooker to Lincoln (June 16, 1863), Hooker to Halleck (June 13, 1863), and Daniel Butterfield to Hooker (June 24, 1863), in *O.R.*, series one, 27 (pt. 1):38, 45, and (pt. 3):287; J. W. Schuckers, *The Life and Public Services of Salmon Portland Chase* (New York: D. Appleton, 1874), 468; Hebert, *Fighting Joe Hooker*, 241.

3. Butterfield to Rufus Ingalls (June 17, 1863), John G. Reynolds to George G. Meade (June 16, 1863), Schenck to Halleck (June 16, 1863), Hooker to Halleck (June 18, 1863), and "Report of Capt. Lemuel B. Norton, Chief Signal Officer" (September 18, 1863), in *O.R.*, series one, 27 (pt. 1):51, and (pt. 3):146, 151–52, 157, 201; Rafuse, *Robert E. Lee and the Fall of the Confederacy, 1863–1865*, 48–49.

4. "Circular" (June 16, 1863), in *O.R.*, series one, 27 (pt. 3):175; Samuel Toombs, *New Jersey Troops in the Gettysburg Campaign from June 5 to July 31, 1863* (Orange, NJ: Evening Mail Publishing, 1888), 111–12; Amos M. Judson, *History of the Eighty-Third Regiment, Pennsylvania Volunteers* (Erie, PA, 1865), 114, 115; W. A. Croffut and John M. Morris, *The Military and Civil History of Connecticut During the War of 1861–65* (New York: Ledyard Bill, 1869), 378, 379–80; James Lorenzo Brown, *History of the Thirty-Seventh Regiment, Mass. Volunteers, in the Civil War of 1861–1865* (Holyoke, MA: Clark W. Bryan & Co., 1884), 165; Charles W. Reed to "Dear Mother" (June 20, 1863), in *"A Grand Terrible Dramma": From Gettysburg to Petersburg—The Civil War Letters of Charles Wellington Reed*, ed. Eric A. Campbell (New York: Fordham University Press, 2000), 111–12; Karlton D. Smith, "Alexander Hays and 'the Blue Birds': Brig. Gen. Alexander Hays and the Third Division, Second Corps, During Longstreet's Assault," in *The Third Day: The Fate of a Nation, July 3, 1863* (Gettysburg: Gettysburg National Military Park, 2010), 171.

5. Newell, *"Ours": Annals of the 10th Regiment, Massachusetts Volunteers in the Rebellion*, 217; Edward G. Longacre, *To Gettysburg and Beyond: The Twelfth New Jersey Volunteer Infantry, II Corps, Army of the Potomac, 1862–1865* (Hightstown, NJ: Longstreet House, 1988), 112; Blake, *Three Years in the Army of the Potomac*, 191; Patrick, diary entry for June 14, 1863,

in *Inside Lincoln's Army*, 258–59; John H. Rhodes, *The History of Battery B, First Regiment, Rhode Island Light Artillery, in the War to Preserve the Union* (Providence: Snow & Farnham, 1894), 189.

6. Charles Mattocks, diary entry for June 15, 1863, in *"Unspoiled Heart": The Journal of Charles Mattocks of the 17th Maine*, ed. Philip N. Racine (Knoxville: University of Tennessee Press, 1994), 38; St. Clair A. Mulholland, *The Story of the 116th Regiment, Pennsylvania Infantry* (1903; Gaithersburg, MD: Olde Soldier Books, n.d.), 127; Tevis and Marquis, *History of the Fighting Fourteenth*, 77; Toombs, *New Jersey Troops in the Gettysburg Campaign*, 93.

7. SeCheverell, *Journal History of the Twenty-Ninth Ohio*, 67–68; Edwin B. Houghton, *The Campaigns of the Seventeenth Maine* (Portland: Short & Loring, 1866), 74–75; Brown, *History of the Thirty-Seventh Mass.*, 162–63; John W. Chase to Samuel S. Chase (June 19, 1863), in *Yours for the Union*, 251–52.

8. Lance J. Herdegen and William J. K. Beaudot, *In the Bloody Railroad Cut at Gettysburg* (Dayton, OH: Morningside House, 1990), 142; Orson Curtis Blair, *History of the Twenty-fourth Michigan of the Iron Brigade* (Detroit: Winn & Hammond, 1891), 144, 146; Tevis and Marquis, *History of the Fighting Fourteenth*, 76; John Whiting Storrs, *The "Twentieth Connecticut": A Regimental History* (Ansonia, CT: Naugatuck Valley Sentinel, 1886), 70–71; John Richards Boyle, *Soldiers True: The Story of the One Hundred and Eleventh Regiment, Pennsylvania Veteran Volunteers* (New York: Eaton & Mains, 1903), 107–8; Henry C. Morhous, *Reminiscences of the 123rd Regiment, N.Y.S.V.: Giving a Complete History of Its Three Years of Service in the War* (Greenwich, NY: People's Journal Book and Job Office, 1879), 43–44; Ambrose Hayward to "Dear Father" (June 21, 1863), in *Last to Leave the Field*, 157; "Bivouac Near the Potomac" (June 23, 1863), in William B. Styple, ed., *Writing and Fighting the Civil War: Soldier Correspondence to the New York Sunday Mercury* (Kearny, NJ: Belle Grove Publishing, 2004), 196.

9. Philip M. Cole, *Command and Communication Frictions in the Gettysburg Campaign* (Orrtanna, PA: Colecraft Industries, 2006), 6–7; Boies, *Record of the Thirty-third Massachusetts*, 30; Andrew J. Bennett, *The Story of the First Massachusetts Light Battery, Attached to the Sixth Army Corps* (Boston: Deland & Barta, 1886), 118; Lincoln to Hooker (June 14 and June 16, 1863), in *Collected Works*, 6:273, 280, 281; Daniel Tyler to Hooker (June 23, 1863), H. Winchester to Halleck (June 24, 1863), G. K. Warren to Hooker (June 24, 1863), and Hooker to Halleck (June 27, 1863), in *O.R.*, series one, 27 (pt. 1):60, (pt. 2):27, and (pt. 3):289, 292; "Testimony of Major General Daniel Butterfield" (March 25, 1864), in *Report of the Joint Committee on the Conduct of the War, at the Second Session, Thirty-Eighth Congress* (Washington, DC: Government Printing Office, 1865), 418; William P. Fox, "Slocum and His Men: A History of the Twelfth and Twentieth Army Corps," in *In Memoriam: Henry Warner Slocum, 1826–1894* (Albany, NY: J. B. Lyon, 1904), 173–74; Howard, *Autobiography*, 1:387, 395; Davis, "The Strategy of the Gettysburg Campaign" (1898), 400.

10. John Singleton Mosby, *Stuart's Cavalry in the Gettysburg Campaign* (New York: Moffat, Yard & Co., 1908), 103; Welles, diary entries for June 14 and 26, 1863, in *Diary of Gideon Welles*, 1:329, 344; Hebert, *Fighting Joe Hooker*, 241–42.

11. "Testimony of Major General Daniel Butterfield" (March 25, 1864), in *Report of the Joint Committee on the Conduct of the War* (1865; Wilmington, NC: Broadfoot Publishing, 1999), 4:418; Benjamin P. Thomas and Harold M. Hyman, *Stanton: The Life and Times of Lincoln's Secretary of War* (New York: Alfred A. Knopf, 1962), 273; George Boutwell, in *Reminiscences of Abraham Lincoln by Distinguished Men of His Time*, ed. A. T. Rice (New York: North American Publishing Co., 1886), 128; Sickles, "Further Recollections of Gettysburg," *North American Review* 152 (March 1891), 259.

12. John L. Smith, *History of the 118th Pennsylvania Volunteers, Corn Exchange Regiment, from*

Their First Engagement at Antietam to Appomattox (Philadelphia: J. L. Smith, 1905), 237; Patrick, diary entry for June 23, 1863, in *Inside Lincoln's Army*, 263; Gideon Welles, diary entry for June 26, 1863, in *Diary of Gideon Welles*, 1:345; McClure to Lincoln (June 30, 1863), in *O.R.*, series one, 27 (pt. 3):436; Wainwright, diary entry for June 21, 1863, in *A Diary of Battle*, 223; "The Rebel Invasion—Our Harrisburg Correspondence," *New York Herald* (June 18, 1863); "A Calm Appeal," *Washington National Intelligencer* (June 18, 1863); John C. G. Kennedy to Horatio Seymour (June 26, 1863), in *A Catalog of Lincolniana*, ed. Thomas F. Madigan (Cedar Rapids, IA: Torch Press, n.d.), #137.

13. William J. Wray, *History of the Twenty-Third Pennsylvania Volunteer Infantry, Birney's Zouaves* (privately published, 1903), 93; Smith, *History of the 118th Pennsylvania Volunteers*, 237; John J. Pullen, *The Twentieth Maine: A Volunteer Regiment in the Civil War* (Philadelphia: J. B. Lippincott, 1957), 95–96; Meade to Margaretta Meade (February 27, 1863), in *Life and Letters*, 1:355–56, 388; Meade to Margaretta Meade (June 22, 1863), in Meade Papers, HSP; Peter S. Michie, *General McClellan* (New York: D. Appleton, 1901), 445–46.

14. Richard Meade Bache, *Life of General George Gordon Meade: Commander of the Army of the Potomac* (Philadelphia: Henry T. Coates, 1897), 9; George G. Meade, Jr., *The Life and Letters of George Gordon Meade: Major-General, United States Army* (New York: Scribner's, 1913), 1:16–17; Ethan S. Rafuse, *George Gordon Meade and the War in the East* (Abilene, TX: McWhiney Foundation Press, 2003), 17–20.

15. Meade to Margaretta Meade (May 5, 1862), in *Life and Letters*, 1:263; Meade to "Dear Doct" (August 5, 1861), to Joshua Barney (September 7, 1861), to Margaretta Meade (November 24, 1861), and to John Sergeant Meade (March 29, 1862), in George G. Meade Papers, Historical Society of Pennsylvania; Weld to "Father" (June 28, 1863), in *War Diary and Letters of Stephen Minot Weld, 1861–1865*, ed. H. W. Montague (1912; Boston: Massachusetts Historical Society, 1979), 228; Joseph E. Persico, *My Enemy, My Brother: Men and Days of Gettysburg* (New York: Collier, 1977), 75; Stephen R. Taaffe, *Commanding the Army of the Potomac* (Lawrence: University Press of Kansas, 2006), 110–11, 112.

16. John Day Smith, *The History of the Nineteenth Regiment of Maine Volunteer Infantry, 1862–1865* (Minneapolis: Great Western Printing, 1909), 77–78; Joseph Hayes interview with Alexander Kelly, In *Generals in Bronze*, 136; Charles Carleton Coffin, *The Boys of '61; or, Four Years of Fighting; Personal Observation with the Army and the Navy* (Boston: Dana Estes & Co., 1901), 283; John J. Hennessy, "I Dread the Spring: The Army of the Potomac Prepares for the Overland Campaign," in *The Wilderness Campaign*, ed. Gary W. Gallagher (Chapel Hill: University of North Carolina Press, 1997), 68–69; Lyman, diary entries for October 13, 16, and 17, in *Meade's Army: The Private Notebooks of Lt. Col. Theodore Lyman*, ed. D. W. Lowe (Kent, OH: Kent State University Press, 2007), 49, 53; Horace Porter, *Campaigning with Grant* (New York: Century Co., 1897), 248; James Hessler, "Sickles and Meade Prior to Gettysburg," *Gettysburg Magazine* 41 (July 2009), 55; Capt. Francis Donaldson to "Dear Auntie" (June 28, 1863), in *Inside the Army of the Potomac: The Civil War Experience of Captain Francis Adams Donaldson*, ed. J. Gregory Acken (Mechanicsburg, PA: Stackpole Books, 1998), 289.

17. Meade to Margaretta Meade (October 12, 1861, November 24, 1861, August 16, 1862, September 29, 1862, and January 2, 1863), in Meade Papers, HSP; Rafuse, *George Gordon Meade*, 22–23, 45–46; William Henry Powell, *The Fifth Army Corps (Army of the Potomac): A Record of Operations During the Civil War in the United States of America, 1861–1865* (New York: G. P. Putnam's, 1896), 13; "Gen. George Gordon Meade," *The Liberator* (August 14, 1863).

18. Michael E. Hennessy, "Gen. Hooker's Resignation: An Unpublished Incident of the Battle of Gettysburg," *Donahoe's Magazine* 35 (January 1896), 37; Charles S. Wainwright,

diary entry for June 28, 1863, in *A Diary of Battle,* 219; Gouverneur K. Warren interview with Alexander Kelly, in *Generals in Bronze,* 87; Benjamin, "Hooker's Appointment and Removal," in *Battles & Leaders,* 3:243.

19.   Meade to Halleck (June 27, 1863), in *O.R.,* series one, 27 (pt. 1):61; Benjamin, "Hooker's Appointment and Removal," in *Battles & Leaders,* 3:243; Freeman Cleaves, *Meade of Gettysburg* (1960; Dayton, OH: Morningside House, 1980), 124–26; Sickles, "Further Recollections of Gettysburg," *North American Review* 152 (March 1891), 259.

20.   Capt. Robert K. Beecham, *Gettysburg: The Pivotal Battle of the Civil War* (Chicago: A. C. McClurg, 1911), 118–19, 128–29; Henry Wilson Hubbell to mother (July 1, 1863), in Henry W. Hubbell Papers, New-York Historical Society; Halleck to Meade (June 27, 1863), in *O.R.,* series one, 27 (pt. 1):61; Curt Anders, *Henry Halleck's War: A Fresh Look at Lincoln's Controversial General-in-Chief* (Carmel, IN: Guild Press, 1999), 447; *Life and Letters of George Gordon Meade,* 2:3–4; Mahood, *General Wadsworth,* 149.

21.   Régis de Trobriand, *Four Years with the Army of the Potomac* (Boston: Ticknor & Co., 1889), 483–84; Peter C. Vermilyea,"The Pipe Creek Effect: How Meade's Pipe Creek Circular Affected the Battle of Gettysburg," *Gettysburg Magazine* 42 (July 2010), 24, 26; Abner Doubleday, *Chancellorsville and Gettysburg* (New York: Charles Scribners, 1882), 114–15.

22.   Hartwell Osborn, *Trials and Triumphs: The Record of the Fifty-fifth Ohio Volunteer Infantry* (Chicago: A. C. McClurg, 1904), 89; Franklin Boyts, diary entry for June 25, 1863, in Franklin Boyts Papers, Historical Society of Pennsylvania; Isaac Hall, *History of the Ninety-Seventh Regiment, New York Volunteers* (1890; Baltimore: Butternut and Blue, 1991), 130–31; William B. Jordan, *Red Diamond Regiment: The 17th Maine Infantry, 1862–1865* (Shippensburg, PA: White Mane Books, 1996), 65, 66; Julian Wisner Hinkley, *A Narrative of Service with the Third Wisconsin Infantry* (Madison: Wisconsin History Commission, 1912), 81; Wright, *No More Gallant a Deed,* 280; Ernest Linden Waitt, *History of the Nineteenth Regiment, Massachusetts Volunteer Infantry, 1861–1865* (Salem, MA: Salem Press Co., 1906), 217.

23.   Isaac O. Best, *History of the 121st New York State Infantry* (Chicago: Jas. H. Smith, 1921), 86–87; Albert Rowe Barlow, *Company G: A Record of the Services of One Company of the 157th N.Y. Vols. in the War of the Rebellion* (Syracuse, NY: A. W. Hall, 1899), 118; Gilbert Adams Hays, *Under the Red Patch: Story of the Sixty-Third Regiment, Pennsylvania Volunteers, 1861–1864* (Pittsburgh: Sixty-Third Pennsylvania Volunteers Regimental Assoc., 1908), 190; Nelson V. Hutchinson, *History of the Seventh Massachusetts Volunteer Infantry in the War of the Rebellion of the Southern States Against Constitutional Authority* (Taunton, MA: Authority of the Regimental Association, 1890), 149–50; de Trobriand, *Four Years with the Army of the Potomac,* 478–80; Edwin B. Houghton, *The Campaigns of the Seventeenth Maine* (Portland, ME: Short & Loring, 1866), 84

24.   Wainwright, diary entry for June 29, 1863, in *A Diary of Battle,* 228; George H. Washburn, *A Complete Military History and Record of the 108th Regiment N.Y. Vols., from 1862 to 1864* (Rochester, NY: E. R. Andrews, 1894), 47; Edward G. Longacre, *General John Buford* (Conshohocken, PA: Combined Books, 1995), 172–73, 175; Thomas, *Bold Dragoon* , 234–39; Nye, *Here Come the Rebels!,* 172, 187; Robinson, *Jeb Stuart and the Confederate Defeat at Gettysburg,* 21, 23, 24; Robert Grandchamp, " 'Our Regiment Has Just Been Cleaned Up': The 1st Rhode Island Cavalry at Middleburg," *Gettysburg Magazine* 37 (January 2008), 10–11, 13.

25.   Darius Couch to Edwin M. Stanton (June 16, 1863), Babcock to Hooker (June 24, 1863), H. Winchester to Halleck (June 24, 1863), and Meade to Halleck (June 28, 1863), in *O.R.,* series one, 27 (pt. 3):162, 285, 289, and (pt. 1):65; Edward C. Browne, "Col. George H. Sharpe's 'Soda Water' Scouts," *Gettysburg Magazine* 44 (January 2011), 28–40.

26.   Edmund H. Cummins, "The Signal Corps in the Confederate States Army," *SHSP* 16 (January–December 1888), 98–99; Krick, *Staff Officers in Gray,* 27; Bartholomees, *Buff*

Facings and Gilt Buttons, 248–57; Pickens, in *Voices from Company D*, 180; "The Frederick Spy," *National Tribune* (April 3, 1884); Sheldon, *When the Smoke Cleared at Gettysburg*, 51.

27. "Report of the Operations of the Cavalry Division, Army of Northern Virginia" (August 20, 1863), in *O.R.*, series one, 27 (pt. 3):692.

28. Charles Marshall, *An Aide-de-Camp of Lee*, ed. Frederick Maurice (Boston: Little, Brown, 1927), 201; Robinson, *Jeb Stuart and the Confederate Defeat at Gettysburg*, 52, 53; Swallow, "From Fredericksburg to Gettysburg," 355; Lee to Stuart (June 22, 1863), in *O.R.*, series one, 27 (pt. 3):913.

29. Lee to Ewell (June 22, 1863), in *O.R.*, series one, 27 (pt. 3):914–15.

30. Longstreet to Stuart (June 22, 1863), in *O.R.*, series one, 27 (pt. 3):915.

31. Lee to Stuart (June 23, 1863), in *O.R.*, series one, 27 (pt. 3):923; Marshall, *An Aide-de-Camp to Lee*, 211; Robinson, *Jeb Stuart and the Confederate Defeat at Gettysburg*, 56, 58, 60–61, 72, 84–85.

32. Bowden and Ward, *Last Chance for Victory*, 111–12; Stuart, "Report of the Operations of the Cavalry Division, Army of Northern Virginia" (August 20, 1863), in *O.R.*, series one, 27 (pt. 2):692; Henry B. McClellan, *The Life and Campaigns of Major-General J. E. B. Stuart: Commander of the Cavalry of the Army of Northern Virginia* (Boston: Houghton Mifflin, 1885), 317; Longstreet, "Lee in Pennsylvania," *The Annals of the War Written by Leading Participants, North and South*, ed. A. K. McClure (Philadelphia: Times Publishing, 1879), 435; Marshall, "Events Leading Up to the Battle of Gettysburg," *SHSP* 23 (January–December 1895), 220–21; Mark Nesbitt, *Saber and Scapegoat: J.E.B. Stuart and the Gettysburg Controversy* (Mechanicsburg, PA: Stackpole Books, 1994), 66–68.

33. Eric J. Wittenberg and J. David Petruzzi, *Plenty of Blame to Go Around: Jeb Stuart's Controversial Ride to Gettysburg* (El Dorado Hills, CA: Savas Beatie, 2006), 19, 26–27; Thomas, *Bold Dragoon*, 241; Bowden and Ward, *Last Chance for Victory*, 115; Gary G. Lash, *"Duty Well Done": The History of Edward Baker's California Regiment* (Baltimore, MD: Butternut and Blue, 2001), 326; Stuart, "Report of the Operations of the Cavalry Division, Army of Northern Virginia" (August 20, 1863), in *O.R.*, series one, 27 (pt. 2):692–94; David Powell, "Stuart's Ride: Lee, Stuart, and the Confederate Cavalry in the Gettysburg Campaign," *Gettysburg Magazine* 20 (January 1999), 32–33.

34. Jewell, "Theodore Garnett," 50; Wittenberg and Petruzzi, *Plenty of Blame*, 32–37; John W. Stevens, *Reminiscences of the Civil War* (Hillsboro, TX: Hillsboro Mirror Print, 1902), 111; "A Bold Rebel Raid," *Chicago Tribune* (June 28, 1863); George W. Beale, "A Soldier's Account of the Gettysburg Campaign," *SHSP* 11 (July 1883), 320–322; William Willis Blackford, *War Years with Jeb Stuart* (New York: Charles Scribners, 1945), 224.

35. Longstreet, "Lee's Invasion of Pennsylvania," in *Battles & Leaders*, 3:251; Heth, "Why Lee Lost at Gettysburg," in *Battles and Leaders of the Civil War*, ed. Peter Cozzens (Urbana: University of Illinois Press, 2002), 5:367; James Power Smith, "General Lee at Gettysburg," *SHSP* 33 (January–February 1905), 138–39; "Reports of General Robert E. Lee, C.S. Army" (July 31, 1863), in *O.R.*, series one, 27 (pt. 2):307; Mosby, "Stuart in the Gettysburg Campaign," *SHSP* 38 (January–December 1910), 192–93; Douglas Craig Haines, "Confederate Command Failure at the Blue Ridge," *Gettysburg Magazine* 35 (July 2006), 19.

36. *Campbell Brown's Civil War*, 204–5; Luther S. Trowbridge, "The Operations of the Cavalry in the Gettysburg Campaign" (October 6, 1886), in *War Papers Read Before the Commandery of the State of Michigan, Military Order of the Loyal Legion of the United States* (Detroit: Winn & Hammond, 1893), 1:4–6.

CHAPTER SEVEN *A universal panic prevails*

1. Lincoln, "Proclamation Calling for 100,000 Militia" (June 15, 1863), in *Collected Works*, 6:277–78; "Untimely Exultation," *Washington National Intelligencer* (June 18, 1863); W. J. Tenney, *The Military and Naval History of the Rebellion in the United States* (New York: D. Appleton, 1866), 385; William A. Blair, "'A Source of Amusement': Pennsylvania Versus Lee, 1863," *Pennsylvania Magazine of History and Biography* 125 (July 1991), 321–22.

2. Willson, *Disaster, Struggle, Triumph*, 146–47; "Rally, Colored Men," *Pittsburg Daily Dispatch* (July 3, 1863); "The Situation," *New York Herald* (June 16, 1863); "The Invasion—Our Lancaster Correspondence," *New York Herald* (June 30, 1863); "The Defense of Baltimore," *Washington National Intelligencer* (June 23, 1863); John W. Stevens, *Reminiscences of the Civil War*, 119; Harper, *"If Thee Must Fight,"* 223–24; E. D. Morgan to Stanton (June 24, 1863) and Joel Parker to Lincoln (June 29, 1863), in *O.R.*, series one, 27 (pt. 3):299, 409; Tenney, *Military and Naval History of the Rebellion*, 394; "Our Special Washington Dispatches," *New York Times* (June 28, 1863); Kean, diary entry for June 21, 1863, in *Inside the Confederate Government*, 75–76; "Our Harrisburg Letter," *Philadelphia Inquirer* (June 22, 1863); Earl J. Hess, *Field Armies and Fortifications in the Civil War: The Eastern Campaigns, 1861–1864* (Chapel Hill: University of North Carolina Press, 2005), 219–21.

3. McClure, *Old Time Notes of Pennsylvania* (Philadelphia: John C. Winston, 1905), 1:467–68; Nicholas Wainwright, "The Loyal Opposition in Civil War Philadelphia," *PMHB* 88 (July 1964), 297–98.

4. *Life of David Bell Birney, Major-General, United States Volunteers* (Philadelphia: King & Baird, 1867), 163–65; "The Invasion—Preparations for the Defence of Philadelphia," *Philadelphia Press* (June 29, 1863); "Office of the Mayor of the City of Philadelphia," *Philadelphia Inquirer* (June 29, 1863); "Response to the Proclamations of Gen. Dana and His Honor the Mayor," *Philadelphia Press* (June 30, 1863); "The City—Preparations for the Defence of Philadelphia," *Philadelphia Press* (July 1, 1863); "The Money Market," *Philadelphia Public Ledger & Transcript* (June 13, 16, and 30, 1863).

5. *Andrew Gregg Curtin: His Life and Services*, ed. William H. Egle (Philadelphia: Anvil Printing, 1895), 29–35; A. K. McClure, *The Life and Services of Andrew G. Curtin: An Address* (Harrisburg, PA: State Printer, 1895), 17–18; Tenney, 386; Nye, *Here Come the Rebels!*, 60–61, 153–54, 157, 216; Curtin (June 16 and 26, 1863) and Darius Couch to Stanton (June 29, 1863), in *O.R.*, series one, 27 (pt. 3):169, 347, 407; Frawley, "Marching Through Pennsylvania," 29–30; "The Rebel Invasion—Our Harrisburg Correspondence," *New York Herald* (June 18, 1863).

6. "The Rebel Raid," *Philadelphia Public Ledger & Transcript* (June 24, 1863); Gottschalk, *Notes of a Pianist* (Philadelphia: J. B. Lippincott, 1881), 200–203, 217–18; "The Panic at Harrisburg," *Washington National Intelligencer* (June 18, 1863); Charles Carleton Coffin, *The Boys of '61; or, Four Years of Fighting: Personal Observation with the Army and Navy* (Boston: Dana Estes & Co., 1901), 281; "The Rebel Invasion—Our Harrisburg Correspondence," *New York Herald* (June 18, 1863).

7. "Major General Couch," *The Portrait Monthly of the New York Illustrated News* 1 (July 1863), 16; Sears, "The Revolt of the Generals," in *Controversies and Commanders*, 161–62; Bradley Gottfried, *Roads to Gettysburg: Lee's Invasion of the North, 1863* (Shippensburg, PA: White Mane Books, 2001), 34.

8. Couch to Stanton (June 15, June 18, June 22, and June 29, 1863), in *O.R.*, series one, 27 (pt. 3):129, 203, 264, 407; Crist, "Highwater 1863: The Confederate Approach to Gettysburg," 173–74, 178; A. E. McGarity to wife (June 28, 1863), in "Letters of a Confederate Surgeon: Dr. Abner Embry McGarity, 1862–1865, Part II," *Georgia Historical Quarterly* 29 (September 1945), 160.

9. Trowbridge, "The Field of Gettysburg," *Atlantic Monthly* 16 (November 1865), 617; William Frassanito, *Early Photography at Gettysburg* (Gettysburg: Thomas Publications, 1995), 2; Robert L. Bloom, *A History of Adams County, Pennsylvania, 1700–1900* (Gettysburg, Adams County Historical Society, 1992), 71, 73, 87, 102, 103, 107; H. C. Bradby et al., *History of Cumberland and Adams Counties, Pennsylvania* (Chicago: Warner, Beers & Co., 1886), 3:191, 144, 147, 181; Sheldon, *When the Smoke Cleared at Gettysburg*, 25–27; Charles H. Gladfelter, "George Arnold (1799–1879) and a Town Immortalized," *Adams County History* 12 (2006), 6–9, 17; Lizzie J. Beller, "Gettysburg—As the Historic Town Appeared Before and After the Battle," *National Tribune* (March 17, 1892); David Culp, "Gettysburg's Culp Family Experience: Freedom, Civil War, and the Battle of Gettysburg," *Gettysburg Magazine* 25 (July 2001), 95, 99, 101, 103.

10. *History of Cumberland and Adams Counties*, 168; Trowbridge, "The Field of Gettysburg," 617; Bloom, *History of Adams County*, 87, 186, 193; "Capt. M. A. Miller," *Confederate Veteran* 13 (April 1905), 175; Gerald R. Bennett, *Days of "Uncertainty and Dread": The Ordeal Endured by the Citizens at Gettysburg* (Gettysburg: Gettysburg Foundation, 1994), 4–5; "Details of Eastern News," *San Francisco Daily Bulletin* (June 3, 1861); Warren W. Irish, "Before the Battle—A New York Trooper Tells How He and His Comrades Went to Gettysburg," *National Tribune* (March 31, 1898).

11. "Gen. Stuart's Expedition into Pennsylvania—Official Reports," *Baltimore Sun* (October 30, 1862); "A Woman's Story: Three Days of Rebel Rule, and William Hamilton Bayly's Story of the Battle," *Gettysburg Magazine* 41 (July 2009), 115–16; "Stories of the Battle by William Hamilton Bayley," Gettysburg National Military Park Library Vertical Files; Warren, "My Recollections of What I Saw Before, During and After the Battle of Gettysburg," in *Gettysburg Sources*, eds. J. and J. McLean (Baltimore: Butternut and Blue, 1990), 3:197.

12. Bloom, *History of Adams County*, 172, 177; Peter C. Vermilyea, "Jack Hopkins' Civil War," *Adams County History* 11 (2005), 11; Margaret S. Creighton, *The Colors of Courage: Gettysburg's Forgotten History; Immigrants, Women, and African Americans in the Civil War's Defining Battle* (New York: Perseus Books, 2005), 56–58; G. Craig Caba, ed., *Episodes of Gettysburg and the Underground Railroad as Witnessed and Recorded by Professor J. Howard Wert* (Gettysburg: Caba Antiques, 1998), 15, 53–55, 78–79.

13. Peter C. Vermilyea, "The Effect of the Confederate Invasion of Pennsylvania on Gettysburg's African American Community," *Gettysburg Magazine* 24 (July 2001), 1113–19; Timothy H. Smith, *Farms at Gettysburg: The Fields of Battle* (Gettysburg: Thomas Publications, 2007), 37; Creighton, *Colors of Courage*, 62–63, 74, 75; Tillie Pierce Alleman, *At Gettysburg; or, What a Girl Saw and Heard of the Battle* (New York: W. Lake Borland, 1889), 18–20; Sheldon, *When the Smoke Cleared at Gettysburg*, 39; Bushman, "The Bank Clerk," in *Battleground Adventures: The Stories of Dwellers on the Scenes of Conflict in Some of the Most Notable Battles of the Civil War*, ed. Clifton Johnson (Boston: Houghton Mifflin, 1915), 193; Bennett, *Days of "Uncertainty and Dread,"* 16, 17; Larry C. Bolin, "Slaveholders and Slaves of Adams County," *Adams County History* 9 (2003), 17; "The Invasion—Our Lancaster Correspondence," *New York Herald* (June 30, 1863); Alexander, " 'A Regular Slave Hunt': The Army of Northern Virginia and Black Civilians in the Gettysburg Campaign," 88.

14. Bennett, *Days of "Uncertainty and Dread,"* 7–8; Bloom, *History of Adams County*, 195; Creighton, *Colors of Courage*, 77; Alleman, *At Gettysburg*, 18; Sheldon, *When the Smoke Cleared at Gettysburg*, 20–21, 33–34; Peter C. Vermilyea, "The Professor and the Major: A Gettysburg Controversy," *Gettysburg Magazine* 37 (January 2008), 17–19

15. Swallow, "From Fredericksburg to Gettysburg," 356–57; Chapman Biddle, *The First Day of the Battle of Gettysburg: An Address Delivered Before the Historical Society of Pennsylvania,*

March 8, 1880 (Philadelphia: J. B. Lippincott, 1880), 14; Nye, *Here Come the Rebels!*, 267–68; "Report of Maj. Gen. Jubal A. Early, C.S. Army," in *O.R.*, series one, 27 (pt. 2):464.

16. Early, *Lieutenant General Jubal Anderson Early*, 256–57; Michael Jacobs, *Notes on the Rebel Invasion of Maryland, Pennsylvania, and the Battle of Gettysburg* (Philadelphia: J. B. Lippincott, 1863), 11; Samuel Pennypacker to J. B. Bachelder (August 26, 1881), in *Bachelder Papers*, 2:758; Nye, *Here Come the Rebels!*, 271–72.

17. "Report of Maj. Gen. Jubal A. Early, C.S. Army," in *O.R.*, series one, 27 (pt. 2):465; J. David Perruzzi and Steven Stanley, "They Came with Barbarian Yells and Smoking Pistols," *Hallowed Ground* 10 (Spring 2009), 22–25; Nye, *Here Come the Rebels!*, 273, 275, 276–77; William J. Seymour, diary entry for June 26–27, 1863, in *Civil War Memoirs of William J. Seymour*, 65; David L. Valuska, "The Pennsylvania Dutch as First Defenders," in *Damn Dutch: Pennsylvania Germans at Gettysburg*, D. L. Valuska and Christian Keller, eds. (Mechanicsburg, PA: Stackpole Books, 2004), 51, 52.

18. Bennett, *Days of "Uncertainty and Dread,"* 7, 10; "The Rebel Invasion—Our Harrisburg Correspondence," *New York Herald* (June 18, 1863); Bradsby, *History of Cumberland and Adams Counties*, 3:154; Jacobs, *Notes on the Rebel Invasion*, 15; Slade and Alexander, *Firestorm at Gettysburg*, 25; John M. Rudy, "A Time to Rend, and a Time to Sew": Martin Luther Stoever's Civil War," manuscript chapter from "Pennsylvania College in the Civil War"; 1–2; Bushman, "The Bank Clerk," 193; Alleman, *At Gettysburg*, 21–23; Christina Ericson, "'The World Will Little Note Nor Long Remember': Gender Analysis of Civilian Responses to the Battle of Gettysburg," in *Making and Remaking: Pennsylvania's Civil War*, eds. W. A. Blair and W. Pencak (University Park: Penn State University Press, 2001), 86; William McSherry, *History of the Bank of Gettysburg, 1814–1864, The Gettysburg National Bank, 1864–1914* (Gettysburg: Gettysburg National Bank, 1914), 43.

19. Hoke, *The Great Invasion*, 171–72; Emmy E. Werner, *Reluctant Witnesses: Children's Voices from the Civil War* (Boulder, CO: Westview Press, 1998), 61; "Battle Days in 1863," *Gettysburg Compiler* (July 4, 1906); Creighton, *Colors of Courage*, 80–82; Early, *Lieutenant General Jubal Anderson Early*, 257–58; *History of Cumberland and Adams Counties*, 2:153.

20. "A Swindled German," *Yankee Notions* (October 1, 1863); R. H. Early, *Lieutenant General Jubal Anderson Early, C.S.A.: Autobiographical Sketch*, 265; Frawley, "Marching Through Pennsylvania," 164; "The Invasion—The Army of the Potomac—Visit Inside the Rebel Lines," *New York Herald* (July 2, 1863); Albertus McCreary, "Gettysburg: A Boy's Experience of the Battle," *McClure's Magazine* 33 (July 1909), 243; "Report of Maj. Gen. Jubal A. Early, C.S. Army," in *O.R.*, series one, 27 (pt. 2):465, 466; Petruzzi and Stanley, "They Came with Barbarian Yells," 25; Charles J. Tyson to Noble D. Preston (January 16, 1884), in William McKenna, ed. "A Refugee from Gettysburg," *Civil War Times Illustrated* 27 (November–December 1989), 17; Leander Warren, "My Recollections," 198–99; William J. Seymour, diary entry for June 26–27, 1863, in *Civil War Memoirs*, 65; Scott L. Mingus, "White's Comanches on the Warpath at Hanover Junction," *Gettysburg Magazine* 42 (July 2010), 11, 12.

21. Early, *Lieutenant General Jubal Anderson Early*, 257–58.

22. Roger D. Hunt, *Colonels in Blue: Union Army Colonels of the Civil War, the Mid-Atlantic States: Pennsylvania, New Jersey, Maryland, Delaware and the District of Columbia* (Mechanicsburg, PA: Stackpole Books, 2007), 67; Samuel P. Bates, *Martial Deeds of Pennsylvania* (Philadelphia: T. H. Davis, 1876), 833–34; Francis B. Wallace, *Memorial of the Patriotism of Schuylkill County in the American Slaveholder's Rebellion* (Pottsville, PA: Benjamin Bannan, 1865), 244–47; W. F. Beyer and Oscar F. Keydal, *Deeds of Valor: How America's Heroes Won the Medal of Honor* (Detroit: Perrien-Keydal, 1901), 1:117–18.

23. "Special Orders No. 14" (June 24, 1863), in *O.R.*, series one, 27 (pt. 3):297; William J. Wray, *History of the Twenty-Third Pennsylvania Volunteer Infantry*, 151–52; Scott L. Mingus,

"Jubal Early Takes York," *Gettysburg Magazine* 37 (January 2008), 25; Frawley, "Marching Through Pennsylvania," 82–83; "The Occupation of York, Pa." (June 29, 1863), in *Rebellion Record*, ed. Moore, 7:321; Anthony Waskie, *Philadelphia and the Civil War: Arsenal of the Union* (Charleston, SC: History Press, 2011), 133.

24. Early, *Lieutenant General Jubal Anderson Early*, 259–60; "The Occupation of York, Pa." (June 29, 1863), in *Rebellion Record*, ed. Moore, 7:321–22; John B. Gordon, *Reminiscences of the Civil War* (New York: Charles Scribner's, 1903), 42; Richard Sauers, *Advance the Colors: Pennsylvania Civil War Battle Flags* (Harrisburg: Capitol Preservation Committee, 1991), 2:406–7. My thanks to Scott Mingus for a tentative identification of Christ Lutheran as the church in question.

25. Gordon, *Reminiscences*, 147; Wray, *History of the Twenty-Third Pennsylvania*, 152; Russell F. Weigley, "Emergency Troops in the Gettysburg Campaign," *Pennsylvania History* 25 (January 1958), 49–50; "Report of Col. Jacob G. Frick, Twenty-Seventh Pennsylvania Militia" (July 1, 1863), in *O.R.*, series one, 27 (pt. 2):278; "The Invasion of Pennsylvania—Fight at Columbia Bridge," *Philadelphia Public Ledger & Transcript* (June 30, 1863); "The Invasion—Our Columbia Correspondence—The Black Troops," *New York Herald* (July 2, 1863).

26. "Fight at Wrightsville" (June 29, 1863), in *Rebellion Record*, ed. Moore, 7:322; Scott L. Mingus, *Flames Beyond Gettysburg: The Confederate Expedition to the Susquehanna River, June 1863* (El Dorado, CA: Savas Beatie, 2011), 260–65; "Report of Maj. Gen. Jubal A. Early, C.S. Army", in *O.R.*, series one, 27 (pt. 2):467; E. J. H., "Burning of the Columbia Bridge," *Harper's Weekly* (July 18, 1863), 459; "The Burning of Wrightsville, Pa.," in *Under the Southern Cross: Soldier Life with Gordon Bradwell and the Army of Northern Virginia*, ed. P. D. Johnson (Macon, GA: Mercer University Press, 1999), 127–28; "Telegram from Lancaster," *New York Times* (June 29, 1863).

27. Scott L. Mingus, *The Louisiana Tigers in the Gettysburg Campaign, June–July 1863* (Baton Rouge: Louisiana State University Press, 2009), 84–85; Couch to Stanton (June 30, 1863) and Couch to Lincoln (June 30, 1863) in *O.R.*, series one, 27 (pt. 3):434; Lincoln, "To Darius N. Couch," *Collected Works*, 6:310; Stephen S. Raab, "A Midnight Ride: A Young Telegrapher Carries an Urgent Message," *Civil War Times Illustrated* 33 (March–April 1994), 24; Charles H. Howard, "First Day at Gettysburg" (October 1, 1903), in *Military Essays and Recollections: Papers Read Before the Commandery of the State of Illinois, Military Order of the Loyal Legion of the United States* (Chicago: A. C. McClurg, 1895), 4:245.

28. Swallow, "From Fredericksburg to Gettysburg," 360; James O. Hall, "A Modern Hunt for a Fabled Agent: The Spy Harrison," *Civil War Times Illustrated* (February 1986), 20–24; Bernie Becker, "A Man Called Harrison," *America's Civil War* 17 (November 2004), 46–52; Kirby, "A Boy Spy in Dixie," *National Tribune* (July 5, 1888); Longstreet, *Manassas to Appomattox*, 333; John Bakeless, *Spies of the Confederacy* (1970; New York: Dover, 1997), 327–28; G. Moxley Sorrel, *Recollections of a Confederate Staff Officer* (New York: Neale, 1905), 156–57; Tony Trimble, "Harrison: Spying for Longstreet at Gettysburg," *Gettysburg Magazine* 17 (January 1998), 17–19.

29. Trimble, "The Campaign and Battle of Gettysburg," *Confederate Veteran* 25 (May 1917), 211; George Cary Eggleston, *A Rebel's Recollections* (New York: G. P. Putnam's, 1878), 145–46; Bowden and Ward, *Last Chance for Victory*, 163; "The Situation in Pennsylvania," *Charleston Mercury* (July 7, 1863); Hood, *Advance and Retreat: Personal Experiences in the United States and Confederate Armies* (New Orleans: Hood Orphan Memorial Fund, 1880), 55; Dr. J. S. D. Cullen to James Longstreet (May 18, 1875), in Longstreet, "Lee in Pennsylvania," *Annals of the War*, 439; Freeman, *R. E. Lee*, 3:64; Thomas, *Robert E. Lee*, 293.

30. Maj. Benjamin F. Eakle to Henry B. McClellan (April 7, 1886), in *Bachelder Papers*, 2:1294–95; Thomas Daniel Gold, *History of Clarke County, Virginia, and Its Connection with the War Between the States* (Berryville, VA: n.p., 1914), 183–84; Pfanz, *Ewell*, 302.

CHAPTER EIGHT   *You will have to fight like the devil to hold your own*

1. Angie Lurz, "A Secret War for Gettysburg," *Hallowed Ground* 10 (Spring 2009), 30; "Dedication of Monument, 41st Regiment Infantry (Twelfth Reserves)—Address by Brig. Gen. M. D. Hardin," in *Pennsylvania at Gettysburg: Ceremonies at the Dedication of the Monuments Erected by the Commonwealth of Pennsylvania*, ed. John P. Nicholson, 266; "Testimony of Major General Daniel Butterfield" (March 25, 1864), in *Report of the Joint Committee on the Conduct of the War* (Washington, DC: Government Printing Office, 1865), 4:421.
2. Robinson, *Jeb Stuart and the Confederate Defeat*, 32, 124.
3. Ziba Graham, "On to Gettysburg: Ten Days from My Diary of 1863" (1889), in *War Papers Read Before the Commandery of the State of Michigan*, 1:6; Thomas Chamberlin, *History of the One Hundred and Fiftieth Regiment, Pennsylvania Volunteers, Second Regiment, Bucktail Brigade* (Philadelphia: F. McManus, 1905), 115; Capt. John D. S. Cook, "Personal Reminiscences of Gettysburg" (December 12, 1903), in *War Talks in Kansas: A Series of Papers Read Before the Kansas Commandery of the Military Order of the Loyal Legion of the United States* (Kansas City, MO: Franklin Hudson, 1906), 321–23; Isaac Hall, *History of the Ninety-Seventh Regiment, New York Volunteers* (New York: L. C. Childs & Son), 133.
4. Alexander Pennington, in *Generals in Bronze*, 258; George William Curtis, in Dwight C. Kilbourn, "Historical Address," *Dedication of the Equestrian Statue of Major-General John Sedgwick on the Battlefield of Gettysburg* (Hartford, CT: n.p., 1913), 56; George H. Washburn, *A Complete Military History and Record of the 108th Regiment, N.Y. Vols., from 1862 to 1894* (Rochester: E. R. Andrews, 1894), 47–48; Second Vermont Brigade, Extract from General Stannard's Diary, in *Bachelder Papers*, 1:52–53; David Craft, *History of the One Hundred Forty-first Regiment, Pennsylvania Volunteers, 1862–1865* (Towanda, PA: Reporter-Journal Printing, 1885), 111–12; Gary D. Lash, *"Duty Well Done": The History of Edward Baker's California Regiment (71st Pennsylvania)* (Baltimore, MD: Butternut and Blue, 2001), 329.
5. J. von Verdy du Vernois, *Studies in the Leading of Troops*, trans. William Gerlach (Kansas City, MO: Hudson Press, 1906), 1:45–46, 87–88; J. Morton Spearman, *The British Gunner* (London: Parker, Furnival & Parker, 1844), unpaginated; George Thomas Stevens, *Three Years in the Sixth Corps: A Concise Narrative of Events in the Army of the Potomac from 1861 to the Close of the Rebellion, April, 1865* (Albany, NY: S. R. Gray, 1866), 223–24; Howes, *The Catalytic Wars*, 59, 64, 493; Evan M. Woodward, *Our Campaigns; or, The Marches, Bivouacs, Battles, Incidents of Camp Life and History of Our Regiment* (Philadelphia: John E. Potter, 1865), 262; Holmes, *Acts of War*, 116; Strawson, *Beggars in Red*, 60; Grandchamp, "The 2nd Rhode Island Volunteers," 77; Robert Tilney, *My Life in the Army: Three Years and a Half with the Fifth Corps, Army of the Potomac* (Philadelphia: Ferris & Leach, 1912), 45–46.
6. George Anson Bruce, *The Twentieth Regiment of Massachusetts Volunteer Infantry, 1861–1865* (Boston: Houghton Mifflin, 1906), 269–70; Capt. Robert G. Carter, "Reminiscences of the Campaign and Battle of Gettysburg," in *War Papers: Read Before the Commandery of the State of Maine, Military Order of the Loyal Legion of the United States* (Portland, ME: Lefavor-Tower, 1902), 158, 159; Charles D. Page, *History of the Fourteenth Regiment, Connecticut Vol. Infantry* (Meriden, CT: Horton Printing, 1906), 130–31; Martin A. Haynes, *History of the Second Regiment, New Hampshire Volunteers: Its Camps, Marches and Battles* (Manchester, NH: P. Livingston, 1865), 132–33; Ernest Linden Waitt, *History of the Nineteenth Regiment, Massachusetts Volunteer Infantry, 1861–1865* (Salem, MA: Salem Press Co., 1906), 219–20; Capt. Charles W. Cowtan, *Services of the Tenth New York Volunteers (National Zouaves) in the War of the Rebellion* (New York: Chas. H. Ludwig, 1882), 199.
7. "Testimony of Major General George G. Meade" (March 5, 1864) and "Testimony of Gen-

eral Henry J. Hunt" (April 4, 1864), in *Report of the Joint Committee on the Conduct of the War*, 4:329–30, 452; "Circular" (June 29, 1863), "Orders" (June 30, 1863), Meade to Halleck (June 30, 1863), and Stanton to Meade (June 30, 1863), in *O.R.*, series one, 27 (pt. 1):68–69, and (pt. 3):402, 416; Herman Haupt, "The Crisis of the Civil War," *Century Magazine* 44 (September 1892), 795; Seth Williams to O. O. Howard (June 30, 1863), in *O.R.*, series one, 27 (pt. 3):415.

8. Seth Williams to John Reynolds (June 30, 1863), Reynolds to Daniel Butterfield (June 30, 1863), "Circular" (July 1, 1863), and Meade to Reynolds, in *O.R.*, series one, 27 (pt. 3):414–15, 419–20, 458; "Testimony of Major General W. S. Hancock" and "Testimony of Major General Daniel E. Sickles" (February 26 and March 22, 1864), *Report of the Joint Committee*, 4:295, 403–4; Rafuse, *George Gordon Meade*, 73–74; Richard S. Shue, *Morning at Willoughby Run: The Opening Battle at Gettysburg, July 1, 1863* (Gettysburg: Thomas Publications, 1998), 50–51.

9. Thomas Chamberlin, *History of the One Hundred and Fiftieth Regiment*, 111; "Mr. Rosengarten's Address," in *Reynolds Memorial: Addresses Delivered Before the Historical Society of Pennsylvania upon the Occasion of the Presentation of a Portrait of Maj.-Gen. John F. Reynolds, March 8, 1880* (Philadelphia: J. B. Lippincott, 1880), 7–8, 12, 15; Edward J. Nichols, *Toward Gettysburg: A Biography of General John F. Reynolds* (New York, 1958), 4, 13; Kalina Ingam Hintz, " 'My Life as a Cadet Here . . .': The West Point Years of Maj. Gen. John F. Reynolds," *Gettysburg Magazine* 25 (July 2001), 23, 28; Abner R. Small, *The Road to Richmond: Civil War Memoirs of Major Abner R. Small of the Sixteenth Maine Volunteers*, ed. H. A. Small (Berkeley: University of California Press, 1939), 51.

10. Meade to Margaretta Meade (September 29, 1862), in Meade Papers [box 1, folder 14], HSP; "Oration of Colonel Henry S. Huidekoper" (1899), in *Pennsylvania at Gettysburg*, 2:995; Rafuse, *George Gordon Meade*, 38–39.

11. "Address of Colonel Chapman Biddle," in *Reynolds Memorial*, 59, 63; Abner Doubleday, *Chancellorsville and Gettysburg* (New York: Charles Scribners, 1882), 122; Doubleday, "Gettysburg Thirty Years After," *North American Review* 152 (February 1891), 143; Meade to Reynolds (June 30, 1863), in *O.R.*, series one, 27 (pt. 3):420; Alanson Henry Nelson [57th Pennsylvania], *The Battles of Chancellorsville and Gettysburg* (Minneapolis, 1899), 128.

12. Wainwright, diary entry for July 8, 1863, in *A Diary of Battle*, 258; Michael Phipps and John S. Peterson, *"The Devil's To Pay": Gen. John Buford, USA* (Gettysburg: Farnsworth Military Impressions, 1995), 19; Theodore Lyman, diary entry for September 13, 1864, in *Meade's Army*, 34–35.

13. "Reports of Brig. Gen. John Buford" (August 27, 1863), in *O.R.*, series one, 27 (pt. 1):922, 923, 924, 926; Shue, *Morning at Willoughby Run*, 30, 42–43; Edward G. Longacre, *General John Buford* (Conshohocken, PA: Combined Books, 1995), 180–81; "Mr. Rosengarten's Address," in *Reynolds Memorial*, 21; Lt. Walter Kempster, "The Cavalry at Gettysburg" (October 1, 1913), in *War Papers Read Before the Commandery of the State of Wisconsin, Military Order of the Loyal Legion of the United States* (Milwaukee: Burdick & Allen, 1914), 4:399, Toombs, *New Jersey Troops in the Gettysburg Campaign*, 146, 148; Michael Phipps, "Walking Point: John Buford on the Road to Gettysburg," in Scott Hartwig, ed., *"This Has Been a Terrible Ordeal": The Gettysburg Campaign & First Day of Battle* (Gettysburg: Gettysburg National Military Park, 2005), 132–33.

14. Charles Elihu Slocum, *The Life and Services of Major-General Henry Warner Slocum* (Toledo, OH: Slocum Pubs., 1913), 96; Shue, *Morning at Willoughby Run*, 45–46; Hassler, *Crisis at the Crossroads*, 16.

15. "Oration of Colonel Henry S. Huidekoper" (1899), in *Pennsylvania at Gettysburg*, 2:993–94; Kempster, "The Cavalry at Gettysburg," 400–401.

16. *New York Monuments Commission for the Battlefields of Gettysburg and Chattanooga, Final*

Notes to Pages 123–126

Report on the Battlefield of Gettysburg (Albany, NY: J. B. Lyon, 1900), 1:9; H. A. Hall, W. B. Besley, G. G. Wood, *History of the Sixth New York Cavalry, Second Ira Harris Guard* (Worcester, MA: Blanchard Press, 1908), 133–34; "Report of Capt. Lemuel B. Norton, Chief Signal Officer" (September 18, 1863), in *O.R.*, series one, 27 (pt. 1):200–201; Bennett, *Days of "Uncertainty and Dread,"* 17–19; on Jerome, see Guy V. Henry, *Military Record of Civilian Appointments in the United States Army* (New York: D. Van Nostrand, 1873), 162.

17. Theodore Gerrish and John S. Hutchinson, *The Blue and the Gray: A Graphic History of the Army of the Potomac and that of Northern Virginia, Including the Brilliant Engagements of These Forces from 1861 to 1865* (Bangor, ME: Brady, Mace, 1884), 345; "Testimony of Major General Alfred Pleasonton" (March 7, 1864), in *Report of the Joint Committee on the Conduct of the War*, 4:359; Kirby, "A Boy Spy in Dixie," *National Tribune* (July 19, 1888).

18. On July 3rd, Lt. B. F. Rittenhouse of Battery D, 5th U.S. Artillery, could only bring two of his six 10-pounder Parrott rifles on Little Round Top to bear on Pickett's Charge, "as the others could not be run out far enough to point them to the right." See Rittenhouse, "The Battle of Gettysburg as Seen from Little Round Top" (May 4, 1887), in *War Papers: Being Papers Read Before the Commandery of the District of Columbia*, 1:43.

19. Nosworthy, *The Bloody Crucible of Courage*, 421, 422; William A. Frassanito, *Early Photography at Gettysburg* (Gettysburg: Thomas Publications, 1995), 175–90, and Frassanito, *The Gettysburg Then & Now Companion* (Gettysburg: Thomas Publications, 1997), 45; Capt. Tyler, "The Rifle and the Spade; or, The Future of Field Operations," *Journal of the United Service Institutions* 3 (1860), 173–74; Ralph Willett Adye, *The Bombardier and Pocket Gunner* (London: T. Edgerton, 1827), 16; Whittier, "The Left Attack (Ewell's), Gettysburg" (1891), in *Papers of the Military Historical Society of Massachusetts: Campaigns in Virginia, Maryland and Pennsylvania, 1862–1863* (1903; Wilmington, NC: Broadfoot Publishing, 1989), 315; Martin D. Hardin, "Gettysburg Not a Surprise to the Union Commander" (March 10, 1892), in *Military Essays and Recollections: Papers Read Before the Commandery of the State of Illinois*, 4:268; Martin D. Hardin, *History of the Twelfth Regiment, Pennsylvania Reserve Volunteer Corps*, 146; John Esten Cooke, "The Battles of Virginia, Including Sharpsburg and Gettysburg," *The Old Guard* 5 (September 1867), 660; Rosengarten, "General Reynolds' Last Battle," in *Annals of the War*, 62. On the eighteen-gun rule, see Twemlow, *Considerations on Tactics and Strategy*, 27.

20. Olive Anderson, "The Growth of Christian Militarism in Mid-Victorian Britain," *English Historical Review* 86 (January 1971), 48–52, 61; Warren B. Armstrong, *For Courageous Fighting and Confident Dying: Union Chaplains in the Civil War* (Lawrence: University Press of Kansas, 1998), 1–3; Howard, *Autobiography* (New York: Baker & Taylor, 1907), 1:348–49; Howard, *Major-General Howard's Address at the Second Anniversary of the U.S. Christian Commission* (Philadelphia: C. Sherman, 1864), 10–11.

21. Wainwright, diary entry for May 24, 1863, in *A Diary of Battle*, 210; Theodore Lyman, diary entry for September 5, 1864, in *Meade's Army*, 28; Creighton, *Colors of Courage*, 16–19, 30, 179; *A Gallant Captain of the Civil War: Being the Record of the Extraordinary Adventures of Frederick Otto, Baron von Fritsch*, ed. Joseph Tyler Butts (New York: F. Tennyson Neely, 1902), 32; Howard, "Campaign and Battle of Gettysburg, June and July, 1863," *Atlantic Monthly* 38 (July 1876), 51; Howard interview with Alexander Kelly, in *Generals in Bronze*, 184.

22. Kreider, *Defeating Lee*, 103; Keller, *Chancellorsville and the Germans*, 93–94; Howard, "Reminiscences of Lincoln" (February 12, 1896) and "Some Reminiscences of A. Lincoln," Oliver Otis Howard Papers, Special Collections & Archives, Bowdoin College Library.

23. James Stewart, "Battery B, 4th United States Artillery at Gettysburg," in W. H. Chamberlin, ed., *Sketches of War History, 1861–1865: Papers Read Before the Ohio Commandery of*

the *Military Order of the Loyal Legion of the United States, 1890–1896* (Cincinnati: Robert Clarke, 1896), 4:182–83; W. P. Shreve [H/2nd U.S. Sharpshooters], in *Bachelder Papers*, 1:382–84; de Trobriand, *Four Years with the Army of the Potomac*, 485–86; Helen M. Sweeney, "Emmitsburgh—The Vestibule of Heaven," *Catholic World* 58 (December 1893), 335; Howard to Michael Jacobs (March 23, 1864), Oliver Otis Howard Papers, Special Collections & Archives, Bowdoin College Library; Howard, "Personal Reminiscences of the War of the Rebellion," *National Tribune* (November 20, 1884).

24. Howard to Henry Coppee (March 4, 1864), Oliver Otis Howard Papers, Special Collections & Archives, Bowdoin College Library; "Reports of Maj. Gen. Oliver O. Howard, U.S. Army, Commanding Eleventh Corps" (August 31, 1863), in *O.R.*, series one, 27 (pt. 1):701; Howard, "Campaign and Battle of Gettysburg," 52; Howard, *Autobiography*, 1:399, 402, 404; Charles H. Howard, "First Day at Gettysburg" (October 1, 1903), in *Military Essays and Recollections: Papers Read Before the Commandery of the State of Illinois*, 4:241–42;

25. Hardin, "Gettysburg Not a Surprise to the Union Commander," 267–68; *"Unspoiled Heart": The Journal of Charles Mattocks*, 46; "Speculations on the Rebel Invasion," *Baltimore American* (June 30, 1863).

26. "Rebel Invasion of Pennsylvania," *Pittsburg Daily Dispatch* (July 3, 1863); Swallow, "From Fredericksburg to Gettysburg," 361; J. H. Imboden, "Lee at Gettysburg," *The Galaxy* 11 (April 1871), 508; William J. Seymour, diary entry for June 30, 1863, in *Civil War Memoirs*, 69; Leslie J. Perry, "General Lee and the Battle of Gettysburg," *SHSP* 23 (January–December 1895), 255, 258–59; Nye, *Here Come the Rebels!*, 344–45; "Report of Lieut. Gen. Richard S. Ewell, C.S. Army," and "Report of Lieut. Gen. Ambrose P. Hill, C.S. Army," in *O.R.*, series one, 27 (pt. 2):444, 606.

27. Porter Alexander, *Fighting for the Confederacy*, 229–30; Capt. F. M. Colston, "Gettysburg As I Saw It," *Confederate Veteran* 5 (November 1897), 552; Capt. Frank A. Bond, "Company A—First Maryland Cavalry," *Confederate Veteran* (February 1898), 78; Pfanz, *Richard S. Ewell*, 304; Casdorph, *Confederate General R. S. Ewell*, 244; "Report of Maj. Gen. Jubal A. Early, C.S. Army" (August 22, 1863), "Report of Maj. Gen. R. E. Rodes, C.S. Army," and Johnson to A. S. Pendleton (September 30, 1863), in *O.R.*, series one, 27 (pt. 2):468, 503, 552; Vincent A. Witcher to John W. Daniel (March 1, 1906), John Warwick Daniel Papers, Special Collections, University of Virginia.

28. "An Army: Its Organization and Movements," *Continental Monthly* 6 (December 1864), 604; Howes, *The Catalytic Wars*, 65; William W. Chamberlaine, *Memoirs of the Civil War Between the Northern and Southern Sections of the United States of America, 1861 to 1865* (Washington: Byron S. Adams, 1912), 66; Alexander, *Military Memoirs of a Confederate*, 379.

29. Clyde N. Wilson, *The Most Promising Young Man of the South: James Johnston Pettigrew and His Men at Gettysburg* (Abilene, TX: McWhiney Foundation Press, 1998), 18–21; Michael O'Brien, *Conjectures of Order: Intellectual Life and the American South, 1810–1860* (Chapel Hill: University of North Carolina Press, 2004), 1:160–61.

30. By 1877, Heth would inflate the shoe-pinching aspect of this undertaking to claim that he had somehow learned that there were "plenty of shoes in the stores in Gettysburg" and that he had been principally interested in sending Pettigrew after shoes. By the time Heth wrote his memoirs, his men would become "sadly in want of shoes" and he would remember hearing of "a large supply of shoes . . . stored in Gettysburg." Before his death, he would inflate his justification still further by claiming that Lee himself had ordered Heth "to get the shoes even if I encountered some resistance." How he could have learned about a "large supply" of shoes in Gettysburg, apart from store advertisements in the local newspapers for shoes and boots, is a mystery. Gettysburg's best-known manufactured

commodity was carriages, not shoes (although there were three tannery operations in the town). And if it was just shoe pinching Heth intended, it is not clear why he needed three regiments of infantry plus three pieces of artillery to do this. And it is peculiar that no other officer's report from Heth's division (including the surviving report of the quartermaster of the 26th North Carolina) mentions shoes. See Porter Alexander, *Fighting for the Confederacy*, 231; Heth to J. W. Jones, "Letter from Major General Heth, of A.P. Hill's Corps, A.N.V.," *SHSP* 4 (October 1877), 157–58; Kempster, "The Cavalry at Gettysburg," 402; "The Invasion—The Army of the Potomac—Visit Inside the Rebel Lines," *New York Herald* (July 2, 1863); "The Memoirs of Henry Heth, Part II," ed. James L. Morrison, *Civil War History* 8 (September 1962), 303–4; Persico, *My Enemy, My Brother*, 80; Mark Acres, "Harry Heth and the First Morning at Gettysburg," *Gettysburg Magazine* 46 (January 2012), 29.

31.   Dr. J. W. C. O'Neal Account, Gettysburg NMP Vertical Files [#8–14], and *Gettysburg Complier* (July 5, 1905); J. Marshall Meredith, "The First Day at Gettysburg," *SHSP* 24 (January–December 1896), 183; Julius Leinbach, "Regimental Band of the Twenty-Sixth North Carolina," ed. Douglas McCorkle, *Civil War History* 4 (September 1958), 226; J. Timothy Cole and Bradley R. Foley, *Collett Leventhorpe, The English Confederate: The Life of a Civil War General, 1819–1885* (Jefferson, NC: McFarland, 2007), 109–10; Gragg, *Covered with Glory*, 82–83; Louis G. Young, "Pettigrew's Brigade at Gettysburg," in *Histories of the Several Regiments and Battalions from North Carolina in the Great War, 1861–'65*, ed. Walter Clark (Goldsboro, NC: Nash Brothers, 1901), 5:115.

32.   "Letter from Major General Heth," 157–58; "Report of Maj. J. Jones, Twenty-Sixth North Carolina Infantry, Commanding Pettigrew's Brigade" (August 9, 1863), in *O.R.*, series one, 27 (pt. 2):642; Capt. William H. Harries, "The Iron Brigade in the First Day's Battle at Gettysburg (October 8, 1895), in *Glimpses of the Nation's Struggle*, 342–43; Shue, *Morning at Willoughby Run*, 48; Thomas Desjardin, *These Honored Dead: How the Story of Gettysburg Shaped American Memory* (Cambridge: Da Capo Press, 2003), 56–57; Rafuse, *Robert E. Lee and the Fall of the Confederacy*, 70; Gary W. Gallagher, "Confederate Corps Leadership on the First Day at Gettysburg: A. P. Hill and Richard S. Ewell in a Difficult Debut," in *The First Day at Gettysburg: Essays on Confederate and Union Leadership* (Kent, OH: Kent State University Press, 1992), 42–44.

33.   "The Memoirs of Henry Heth, Part II," ed. James L. Morrison, *Civil War History* 8 (September 1962), 303–4; "Letter from Major General Heth," 157–58; Young, "Pettigrew's Brigade at Gettysburg," 116–17; Mosby, "Stuart and Gettysburg," *SHSP* 24 (January–December 1896), 352–53; Hess, *Lee's Tar-Heels*, 116–17; Robertson, *General A .P. Hill*, 205–6.

34.   Diary entry for June 30, 1863, in William D. Alexander Diary, Southern Historical Collection, University of North Carolina; "Report of Lieut. Gen. Ambrose P. Hill, C.S. Army" (November 1863), in *O.R.*, series one, 27 (pt. 2):607; David G. Martin, *Gettysburg, July 1* (Conshohocken, PA: Combined Books, 1999), 29; Kempster, "The Cavalry at Gettysburg," 402; Walter H. Taylor, "The Campaign in Pennsylvania," in *Annals of the War*, 307; Bowden and Ward, *Last Chance for Victory*, 148–49, 151.

35.   "West Point's Prolific Professor," *Civil War Times* 48 (August 2009), 22–23; Denis Hart Mahan, *An Elementary Treatise in Advanced-Guard, Outpost and Detachment Service of Troops* (New York: John Wiley, 1862), 83–92; Henry Wager Halleck, *Elements of Military Art and Science* (New York: D. Appleton, 1861), 109–10.

36.   Newel Cheney, *History of the Ninth Regiment, New York Volunteer Cavalry: War of 1861–1865* (Jamestown, NY: Martin Merz & Son, 1901), 105–7; Hassler, *Crisis at the Crossroads*, 30; Col. George Chapman (March 30, 1864), in *Bachelder Papers*, 1:130; John L. Beveridge, "The First Gun at Gettysburg" (February 8, 1885), in *Military Essays and Recollections:*

Papers Read Before the Commandery of the State of Illinois, 2:89–90; Shue, *Morning at Willoughby Run,* 54.

37. Hazelton, "People of Gettysburg—How They Inspired the Cavalry to do Their Effective Work," *National Tribune* (March 24, 1892); "Reports of Col. William Gamble, Eighth Illinois Cavalry" (August 24, 1863), *O.R.,* series one, 27 (pt. 1):934; Cheney, *History of the Ninth Regiment, New York Volunteer Cavalry,* 105–6; J. David Petruzzi, "John Buford by the Book," *America's Civil War* 18 (July 2005), 25.

38. Buford to Pleasonton (June 30, 1863), in *O.R.,* series one, 27 (pt. 1):923–24; Valuska and Keller, *Damn Dutch,* 118; "Lee's Army in Pennsylvania—Battle of Gettysburg," *The Land We Love* 2 (November 1866), 42; Joseph G. Bilby, *Small Arms at Gettysburg: Infantry and Cavalry Weapons in America's Greatest Battle* (Yardley, PA: Westholme Publishing, 2007), 26–28.

39. F. S. Harris, "Gen. Jas. J. Archer," *Confederate Veteran* 3 (January 1895), 18; Larry Tagg, *The Generals of Gettysburg: The Leaders of America's Greatest Battle* (Dayton, OH: Morningside House, 1998), 347; Jeffrey Wert, *Gettysburg, Day Three* (New York: Simon & Schuster, 2001), 116; Robert K. Krick, "Three Confederate Disasters on Oak Ridge: Failures of Brigade Leadership on the First Day at Gettysburg," in *The First Day at Gettysburg,* ed. Gallagher, 96–98; Bradley M. Gottfried, "To Fail Twice: Brockenbrough's Brigade at Gettysburg," *Gettysburg Magazine* 23 (January 2001), 66; O'Reilly, *"Stonewall" Jackson at Fredericksburg,* 62, 111.

40. "Second Regiment—Infantry" and "Forty-Second Regiment—Infantry," in *The Official and Statistical Register of the State of Mississippi, 1908,* ed. Dunbar Rowland (Nashville: Brandon Printing, 1908), 2:433, 510; "Major-Generals and Brigadier-Generals, Provisional Army of the Confederate States, Accredited to Mississippi," in *Confederate Military History,* ed. Evans, 7:249; "General Joseph R. Davis," *Confederate Veteran* 5 (February 1897), 63; Robertson, *General A. P. Hill,* 206–7.

41. "Lee's Army in Pennsylvania—Battle of Gettysburg," 42; J. Marshall Meredith, "The First Day at Gettysburg," *SHSP* 24 (January–December 1896), 184–85; Gottfried, "To Fail Twice: Brockenbrough's Brigade at Gettysburg," 66; E. T. Boland, "Beginning of the Battle of Gettysburg," *Confederate Veteran* 14 (July 1906), 308–9; John L. Marye, "The First Gun at Gettysburg: 'With the Confederate Advance Guard,'" *American Historical Register and Monthly Gazette of the Patriotic-Hereditary Societies of the United States of America, March–August 1895,* ed. Charles H. Browning (Philadelphia: Historical Register Publishing, 1895), 1228; Robertson, *General A. P. Hill,* 207; Hassler, *Crisis at the Crossroads,* 29.

42. "Lee's Army in Pennsylvania—Battle of Gettysburg," 42; John Beveridge, "First Shot at Gettysburg," *National Tribune* (July 31, 1902); Beveridge, "The First Gun at Gettysburg," 91–92; J. David Petruzzi, "Opening the Ball at Gettysburg: The Shot That Rang for 50 Years," *America's Civil War* 19 (July 2006), 30–35; Marshall Krolik, "Marcellus Jones' Proudest Moment," *Blue & Gray Magazine* 5 (November 1987), 27–29; Phipps, "Walking Point," 137–38; "First Shot Fired at Gettysburg—Gov. Beveridge's Statement Corroborated by an Ex-Confederate Officer," *Chicago Tribune* (September 5, 1891).

CHAPTER NINE *The devil's to pay*

1. Beveridge, "The First Gun at Gettysburg"; Howard, "First Day at Gettysburg," 246; Jerome to J. B. Bachelder (October 18, 1865), in *Bachelder Papers,* 1:201; Bennett, *Days of "Uncertainty and Dread,"* 20–24; James J. Dougherty, *Stone's Brigade and the Fight for the McPherson Farm: Battle of Gettysburg, July 1, 1863* (Conshohocken, PA: Combined Books, 2001), 30, 31, 32.

2. Longacre, *General John Buford,* 189–91; Doubleday, *Chancellorsville and Gettysburg,* 126; Wittenberg, "An Analysis of the Buford Manuscripts," *Gettysburg Magazine* 15 (January 1996), 10.

3. "Report of Capt. E.B. Brunson, C.S. Artillery" (July 31, 1863), in *O.R.,* series one, 27 (pt. 2):677; L. Van Loan Naiswald, *Grape and Canister: The Story of the Field Artillery of the Army of the Potomac, 1861–1865* (Mechanicsburg, PA: Stackpole Books, 1999), 267; Dana, in Theodore F. Rodenbough, "Cavalry War Lessons," *Journal of the United States Cavalry Association* 2 (June 1889), 112; Shue, *Morning at Willoughby Run,* 71–72; James Stewart, "Battery B, 4th United States Artillery at Gettysburg," 183–84

4. Beveridge, *Illinois Monuments at Gettysburg* (Springfield, IL: H. W. Rokker, 1892), 19; Swallow, "The First Day at Gettysburg," *Southern Bivouac* 1 (December 1885), 437; Samuel W. Hankins, "Simple Story of a Soldier," *Confederate Veteran* 20 (September 1912 and May 1913), 20; Boland, "Beginning of the Battle of Gettysburg," 308–9; Halleck, *Elements of Military Art and Science,* 123; Brig.-Gen. Silas Casey, *Infantry Tactics: For the Instruction, Exercise, and Manœuvres of the Soldier, a Company, Line of Skirmishers, Battalion, Brigade, Corps d'Armee* (New York: D. Van Nostrand, 1862), 3:49–50; Capt. William Dawes Malton, *Duties of Officers and Markers in Company and Battalion Drill* (London: William Clowes & Sons, 1876), 124–25; Sir Daniel Lysons, *The Crimean War from First to Last* (London: John Murray, 1895), 101–2; R. L. Murray, *Artillery Tactics of the Civil War,* 15–17; Philip M. Cole, *Command and Communication Frictions in the Gettysburg Campaign* (Orrtanna, PA: Colecraft Industries, 2006), 80; Bucholz, *Moltke and the German Wars, 1864–1871,* 55, 58.

5. Meredith, "The First Day at Gettysburg," 184–85; Ernsberger, *Also for Glory Muster,* 25–27; Murray, *Artillery Tactics of the Civil War,* 15–17; Hassler, *Crisis at the Crossroads,* 33.

6. Jerome to J. B. Bachelder (October 18, 1865), in *Bachelder Papers,* 1:201; Wittenberg, "Analysis of the Buford Manuscripts," 10; Buford to Meade (July 1, 1863), in *O.R.,* series one, 27 (pt. 1):924; "Oration of Colonel Henry S. Huidekoper" (1899) in *Pennsylvania at Gettysburg: Ceremonies at the Dedication of the Monuments Erected by the Commonwealth of Pennsylvania,* ed. John P. Nicholson (Harrisburg, PA: Wm. Stanley Ray, 1914), 2:993–94.

7. Doubleday, interview with Alexander Kelly, in *Generals in Bronze,* 46–47; "Reports of Maj. Gen. Abner Doubleday, U.S. Army, Commanding Third Division of, and First Army Corps" (December 14, 1863), in *O.R.,* series one, 27 (pt. 1):244; Doubleday, *Chancellorsville and Gettysburg,* 124–25; Henry Greenleaf Pearson, *James S. Wadsworth of Geneseo: Brevet Major-General of United States Volunteers* (New York: Charles Scribners, 1913), 203.

8. Lt. Sidney G. Cooke, "The First Day at Gettysburg" (November 4, 1897), in *War Talks in Kansas,* 278; Lt. Col. Thomas Chamberlin, *History of the One Hundred and Fiftieth Regiment, Pennsylvania Volunteers, Second Regiment Bucktail Brigade* (Philadelphia: F. McManus, 1905), 117–18; Tevis and Marquis, *History of the Fighting Fourteenth,* 81–82; Lance J. Herdegen and W. J. K. Beaudot, *In the Bloody Railroad Cut at Gettysburg* (Dayton, OH: Morningside House, 1990), 162–63; Abram P. Smith, *History of the Seventy-Sixth New York Volunteers* (Cortland, NY: Truaie, Smith & Miles, 1867), 236; Wayne Mahood, *General Wadsworth: The Life and Times of Brevet Major General James S. Wadsworth* (Cambridge, MA: Da Capo Press, 2003), 154, 156; Gary G. Lash, "Brig. Gen. Henry Baxter's Brigade at Gettysburg, July 1," *Gettysburg Magazine* 10 (January 1994), 11.

9. Wittenberg, "Analysis of the Buford Manuscripts," 10; Longacre, *General John Buford,* 192–93; James A. Hall, in *Reynolds Memorial,* 30; Cheney, *History of the Ninth Regiment, New York Volunteer Cavalry,* 109; Hall, Besley, and Wood, *History of the Sixth New York Cavalry,* 138–39

10. Weld, diary entry for July 2, 1863, in *War Diary and Letters of Stephen Minot Weld, 1861–1865,* 231–32; Harries, "The Iron Brigade in the First Day's Battle at Gettysburg," 341;

Biddle, *The First Day of the Battle of Gettysburg*, 23–24; "Mr. Rosengarten's Address," in *Reynolds Memorial*, 26; Howard, *Autobiography*, 1:411; Henry Edwin Tremain, *Two Days of War: A Gettysburg Narrative and Other Excursions* (New York: Bonnell, Silver & Bowers, 1905), 14; Tremain (June 28, 1880), in *Bachelder Papers*, 1:669; Doubleday, *Chancellorsville and Gettysburg*, 126–27; Doubleday, "Gettysburg Thirty Years After," *North American Review* 152 (February 1891), 144.

11. Beecham, *Gettysburg*, 61–62; Pearson, *James S. Wadsworth*, 202, 203, 207; Rufus R. Dawes, "With the Sixth Wisconsin at Gettysburg," *Sketches of War History, 1861–1865: Papers Read Before the Ohio Commandery of the Military Order of the Loyal Legion of the United States, 1888–1890*, ed. Robert Hunter (Cincinnati: Robert Clarke & Co., 1890), 3:364–65; Martin D. Hardin, "Dedication of Monument, 41st Regiment of Infantry," in *Pennsylvania at Gettysburg*, 1:268; Charles Carleton Coffin, "Memories of Gettysburg," in *Stories of Our Soldiers: War Reminiscences by "Careleton," and by Soldiers of New England* (Boston: Journal Newspaper, 1893), 109; *New York Monuments Commission for the Battlefields of Gettysburg and Chattanooga—Final Report on the Battlefield of Gettysburg* (Albany, NY: J. B. Lyon, 1900), 1:11.

12. "An Army: Its Organization and Movements," *Continental Monthly* 6 (September 1864), 333; Herdegen and Beaudot, *In the Bloody Railroad Cut at Gettysburg*, 163–64, 166–67; Sgt. C. W. Cook, "Who Opened Gettysburg—Another Comrade Says the Iron Brigade had Nothing To Do With It," *National Tribune* (November 24, 1892); Hall, *History of the Ninety-Seventh Regiment, New York Volunteers*, 134; I. N. Dubboraw, "The Big Battle—A Comrade Sends Reminiscences of a Citizen at Gettysburg," *National Tribune* (December 8, 1892); J. V. Pierce, "Gettysburg—Last Words as to What Regiment Opened the Battle," *National Tribune* (April 3, 1884); Dawes to J. B. Bachelder (March 18, 1868), in *Bachelder Papers*, 1:322–23; E. P. Halstead, "The First Day at the Battle of Gettysburg" (March 2, 1887), in *War Papers, Being Papers Read Before the Commandery of the District of Columbia*, 1:4.

13. Chamberlin, *History of the One Hundred and Fiftieth Regiment, Pennsylvania Volunteers*, 118; Lt. Cornelius Wheeler, "Reminiscences of the Battle of Gettysburg" (April 5, 1893), in *War Papers Read Before the Commandery of the State of Wisconsin, Military Order of the Loyal Legion of the United States* (Milwaukee: Burdick, Armitage & Allen, 1896), 219–20.

14. James Hall to J. B. Bachelder (December 29, 1869), "Report of Lt. Col. William W. Dudley" and "Notes from Conversation with Col. Lucius Fairchild, 2nd Wisconsin," in *Bachelder Papers*, 1:335–36, 385, and 2:940–41; Marc and Beth Storch, "'What a Deadly Trap We Were In': Archer's Brigade on July 1, 1863," *Gettysburg Magazine* 6 (January 1992), 21; Dawes, "With the Sixth Wisconsin at Gettysburg," 3:364–65; Tevis and Marquis, *History of the Fighting Fourteenth*, 82; Beecham, *Gettysburg*, 61–62; Nolan, *Iron Brigade*, 236; Steven H. Newton, *McPherson's Ridge: The First Battle for the High Ground, July 1, 1863* (Cambridge, MA: Da Capo Press, 2002), 41–42.

15. Hassler, *Crisis at the Crossroads*, 39–40; Capt. James Hall to J. B. Bachelder (December 29, 1869), in *Bachelder Papers*, 1:386; Bradley M. Gottfried, *The Artillery of Gettysburg* (Nashville: Cumberland House, 2008), 29; Doubleday, *Chancellorsville and Gettysburg*, 128; Halstead, "The First Day of the Battle of Gettysburg," 1:4; John F. Krumwiede, *Old Waddy's Coming!: The Military Career of Brigadier General James S. Wadsworth* (Baltimore: Butternut and Blue, 2002), 44; Naiswald, *Grape and Canister*, 269, 270; R. L. Murray, *Artillery Tactics of the Civil War*, 19–20.

16. Bates, *Martial Deeds of Pennsylvania*, 212; Joseph G. Rosengarten to Michael Jacobs (October 15, 1863), Franklin & Marshall College Archives; Wheeler, "Reminiscences of the Battle of Gettysburg," 217; "Sgt. Charles Veil's Memoir on the Death of Reynolds," ed. Robert Hoffsommer, *Civil War Times Illustrated* 21 (June 1982), 18–19, 22–23; Martin, *Gettysburg*,

July 1, 1863, 141–43; Rosengarten, "General Reynolds' Last Battle," in *Annals of the War*, 65; M. S. Persing to J. B. Bachelder (August 25, 1885), in *Bachelder Papers*, 2:1120; A. H. Huber, "At Gettysburg—Cutler's Brigade First and the Iron Brigade Next on the Field," *National Tribune* (December 8, 1892). One of the earliest reports from Gettysburg had Reynolds saying, "For God's sake! forward, my brave boys—forward!," and then, after being hit, murmuring to Capt. William H. Wilcox of the 95th New York, "Good God, Wilcox, I am killed." See "The Battle of Wednesday," *New York Herald* (July 4, 1863), "The Three Days' Battles," *Washington Daily Intelligencer* (July 6, 1863), and Derek Smith, *The Gallant Dead: Union and Confederate Generals Killed in the Civil War* (Mechanicsburg, PA: Stackpole Books, 2005), 156–57.

17.   Heth, in D. Scott Hartwig, "'I Have Never Seen the Like Before': Herbst Woods, July 1, 1863," in *This Has Been a Terrible Ordeal*, 191; Birkett D. Fry to J. B. Bachelder (February 10, 1878), in *Bachelder Papers*, 3:1932; W. F. Fulton, "The Fifth Alabama Battalion at Gettysburg," *Confederate Veteran* 31 (October 1923), 379; Bert Barnett, "'The Batteries Fired with Very Decided Effect': Confederate Artillery Operations on the First Day at Gettysburg," in *This Has Been a Terrible Ordeal*, 163, 203; Edward Marye, "The Fredericksburg Artillery," *SHSP* 32 (1905), 240; "Reports of Maj. Gen. Henry Heth, C.S. Army" (September 13, 1863), in *O.R.*, series one, 27 (pt. 2):637.

18.   Storch, "What a Deadly Trap We Were In," *Gettysburg Magazine* 6 (January 1992), 14; W. H. Moon, "Beginning of the Battle of Gettysburg," *Confederate Veteran* 33 (December 1925), 449.

19.   J. B. Turney, "The First Tennessee at Gettysburg," *Confederate Veteran* 8 (December 1900), 535–36; Carlton McCarthy, *Detailed Minutiae of Soldier Life in the Army of Northern Virginia, 1861–1865* (Richmond, VA: Carleton McCarthy, 1882), 98; Hartwig, "'I Have Never Seen the Like Before': Herbst Woods, July 1, 1863," 165; Beecham, *Gettysburg*, 66; Doubleday, *Chancellorsville and Gettysburg*, 132; Hassler, *Crisis at the Crossroads*, 52; "Report of Col. William W. Robinson, Seventh Wisconsin Infantry" (November 18, 1863), *O.R.*, series one, 27 (pt. 1):279; Orson Blair Curtis, *History of the Twenty-Fourth Michigan of the Iron Brigade* (Detroit: Winn & Hammond, 1891), 152, 156–57; Lt. Col. John Callis, in *Bachelder Papers*, 1:140; Mahood, *General Wadsworth*, 163; R. H. Spencer, "From the 147th Regiment," *Oswego Commercial Times* (July 13, 1863).

20.   June Kimble, "Tennesseans at Gettysburg—The Retreat," *Confederate Veteran* (October 1910), 460–62; R. E. McCullough, "Fourteenth Tennessee Infantry," in John Berrien Lindsley, *The Military Annals of Tennessee, First Series: Embracing a Review of Military Operations, with Regimental Histories and Memorial Rolls* (Nashville: J. M. Lindsley, 1886), 327; Paul C. Cooksey, "The Heroes of Chancellorsville: Archer's Brigade at Gettysburg," *Gettysburg Magazine* 36 (July 2007), 23, 25; M. C. Barnes to J. B. Bachelder (March 28, 1883), in *Bachelder Papers*, 2:937–38.

21.   "Report of Lieut. Col. S. G. Shepard, Seventh Tennessee Infantry," in *O.R.*, series one, 27 (pt. 2):646; "Report of Maj. John Mansfield, Second Wisconsin infantry" (November 15, 1863), in *O.R.*, series one, 27 (pt. 1):272; W. A. Castleberry, "Thirteenth Alabama—Archer's Brigade," *Confederate Veteran* (July 1911), 338; on Dailey, Dow, and Maloney, see *Wisconsin Volunteers: War of the Rebellion, 1861–1865* (Madison, WI: Democrat Printing, 1914), 225, 264, 625; Doubleday, "Gettysburg Thirty Years After," *North American Review* 152 (February 1891), 145; Thomas Barthel, *Abner Doubleday: A Civil War Biography* (Jefferson, NC: McFarland, 2010), 144; Harries, "The Iron Brigade in the First Day's Battle at Gettysburg," 340–41, and "The Sword of General James J. Archer," *Confederate Veteran* (September 1911), 419–20; Beecham, *Gettysburg*, 66.

22.   Callis, in *Bachelder Papers*, 1:140–41; Curtis, *History of the Twenty-fourth Michigan*, 157, 159; William Thomas Venner, *The 19th Indiana Infantry at Gettysburg: Hoosiers' Courage*

(Shippensburg, PA: Burd Street Press, 1998), 60; Beecham, *Gettysburg*, 69–70; Hassler, *Crisis at the Crossroads*, 53; Scott A. Richardson, "Col. Henry A. Morrow, 24th Michigan," *Gettysburg Magazine* 38 (January 2008), 34.

23. Winfield Scott, *Infantry Tactics; or, Rules for the Exercise and Manoeuvers of the United States Infantry* (New York: Harper & Bros., 1861), 2:144; John Sinnott, *Sinnott's Military Catechism, Adapted to the Revised System of the "Field Exercise & Evolutions of Infantry"* (London: W. Clowes & Sons, 1860), 3; Malton, *Company and Battalion Drill Illustrated*, 69, 85; McCarthy, *Detailed Minutiae of Soldier Life*, 98–99; Harrison, *Nothing but Glory*, 136; Busey and Martin, *Regimental Strengths and Losses*, 125, 298; Henry Lyman to J. B. Bachelder, in *Bachelder Papers*, 1:330–31; Hassler, *Crisis at the Crossroads*, 43; Bradley M. Gottfried, *Brigades of Gettysburg: The Union and Confederate Brigades at the Battle of Gettysburg* (Cambridge, MA: Da Capo Press, 2002), 49–52.

24. Cooke, "The First Day at Gettysburg," in *War-Talks in Kansas*, 279–80; Mahood, *General Wadsworth*, 161, 164; D. J. Dickson, "The 56th Pa.," *National Tribune* (November 19, 1891); "Report of Brig. Gen. Lysander Cutler, U.S. Army, Commanding Second Brigade" (July 9, 1863), in *O.R.*, series one, 27 (pt. 1):281–82; John A. Kellogg to J. B. Bachelder (November 1, 1865), and J. Volnay Pierce to J. B. Bachelder (November 1, 1882), in *Bachelder Papers*, 1:205–6 and 2:910–12; Glenn Dedmondt, *The Flags of Civil War North Carolina* (Gretna, LA: Pelican, 2003), 168; M. M. Whitney, "The 76th New York—How It Opened the Fight on the First Day at Gettysburg," *National Tribune* (July 21, 1887); J. B. Bachelder, "Address by Col. John B. Bachelder" (July 1, 1888) and J. V[olnay] Pierce, "Dedication of Monument—147th Regiment of Infantry" (July 1, 1888), in *New York Monuments Commission for the Battlefields of Gettysburg and Chattanooga—Final Report on the Battlefield of Gettysburg*, 2:616 and 3:991; Smith, *History of the Seventy-sixth Regiment, New York Volunteers*, 353–54; C. W. Cook, "The 76th N.Y. at Gettysburg," *National Tribune* (May 19, 1887); M. M. Whitney, "The 76th New York—How It Opened the Fight on the First Day at Gettysburg," *National Tribune* (July 21, 1887).

25. Shue, *Morning at Willoughby Run*, 122–23, 154–56; Henry Lyman, in *Bachelder Papers*, 1:331–32; Cooke, "The First Day at Gettysburg," in *War-Talks in Kansas*, 279–80; Crisfield Johnson, *History of Oswego County, New York: With Illustrations and Biographical Sketches of Some of its Prominent Men and Pioneers* (Philadelphia: L. H. Everts, 1877), 91; Capt. James Hall to J. B. Bachelder (December 29, 1869), in *Bachelder Papers*, 1:387–88; Michael A. Dreese, *Torn Families: Death and Kinship at the Battle of Gettysburg* (Jefferson, NC: McFarland, 2007), 43–44; "The Killed, Wounded and Missing of the 147th Regiment," *Oswego Commercial Times* (July 20, 1863); James Coey, "Cutler's Brigade: The 147th N.Y.'s Magnificent Fight on the First Day of Gettysburg," *National Tribune* (June 15, 1910).

26. "From The 147th Regiment," *Oswego Commercial Times* (July 28, 1863); J. Volnay Pierce to J. B. Bachelder (November 1, 1882), in *Bachelder Papers*, 2:912; Tevis and Marquis, *History of the Fighting Fourteenth*, 83.

27. Herdegen and Beaudot, *In the Bloody Railroad Cut*, 179; Dawes to J. B. Bachelder (March 18, 1868), in *Bachelder Papers*, 1:324; Dawes, "With the Sixth Wisconsin at Gettysburg," *Sketches of War History, 1861–1865*, 3:367–68; Doubleday, *Chancellorsville and Gettysburg*, 132–33.

28. Dawes to J. B. Bachelder (March 18, 1868), in *Bachelder Papers*, 1:323–25; Dawes, "With the Sixth Wisconsin at Gettysburg," *Sketches of War History, 1861–1865*, 3:366–70; Herdegen and Beaudot, *In the Bloody Railroad Cut*, 176–79, 182–86, 193–94, 196, 198; Herdegen, "For the Truth of History: July 1, 1863: The Charge on the Railroad Cut," *Gettysburg Magazine* 20 (January 1999), 87.

29. "Reports of Brig. Gen. Joseph R. Davis, C.S. Army" (August 26, 1863), in *O.R.*, series one, 27 (pt. 2):649; Terence J. Winschel, "The Colors Are Shrouded in Mystery," *Gettysburg*

Magazine 6 (January 1992), 80–82; Dawes, "With the Sixth Wisconsin at Gettysburg," *Sketches of War History, 1861–1865*, 3:371; Abram P. Smith, *History of the Sixty-Seventh Regiment, New York Volunteers* (Cortland, NY: Truaie, Smith & Miles, 1867), 239; Naiswald, *Grape and Canister*, 271, 272, 274; Shue, *Morning at Willoughby Run*, 165–66; Lyman, in *Bachelder Papers*, 1:331.

CHAPTER TEN   *You stand alone, between the Rebel Army and your homes!*

1. "Copied from the diary of Patrick H. Taylor," in *Bachelder Papers*, 2:960; "Orders" and "Circular" (June 30, 1863), Meade to Pleasonton (June 30, 1863), Seth Williams to Hancock (June 30, 1863), Sickles to Seth Williams (June 30, 1863), and Hancock to Seth Williams (June 30, 1863), in *O.R.*, series one, 27 (pt. 3):416–17, 421, 422–23, 424, 425; "Testimony of Major General Daniel Butterfield" (March 25, 1864), in *Report of the Joint Committee on the Conduct of the War*, 4:418–19; Meade, *Life and Letters of George Gordon Meade*, 2:16–17.

2. Meade, *Life and Letters of George Gordon Meade*, 2:29; "Circular" (July 1, 1863), in *O.R.*, series one, 27 (pt. 3):458–59; Hunt, "The Second Day at Gettysburg," *Battles & Leaders*, 3:291; Peter C. Vermilyea, "The Pipe Creek Effect: How Meade's Pipe Creek Circular Affected the Battle of Gettysburg," *Gettysburg Magazine* 42 (July 2010), 24.

3. Meade to Reynolds (July 1, 1863) Meade to Halleck (July 1, 1863), Buford to Meade and Buford to Pleasanton (July 1, 1863), Seth Williams to Sedgwick (July 1, 1863), Daniel Butterfield to Slocum (July 1, 1863), in *O.R.*, series one, 27 (pt. 3):461, 462, and (pt. 1):70–71, 924–25; Weld, diary entry for July 2, 1863, in *War Diary and Letters*, 230; Hancock, "Gettysburg: A Reply to General Howard," in *Battles & Leaders*, ed. Cozzens, 5:349; Alfred Pleasanton, "The Campaign of Gettysburg," in *Annals of the War*, 454; Rafuse, *George Gordon Meade and the War in the East*, 76; Meade, *Life and Letters of George Gordon Meade*, 2:36; Robert Himmer, "A Matter of Time: The Issuance of the Pipe Creek Circular," *Gettysburg Magazine* 46 (January 2012),11, 13, 15–16.

4. Sickles to Seth Williams (July 1, 1863), in *O.R.*, series one, 27 (pt. 3):464; Sickles, "Further Recollections of Gettysburg," *North American Review* 152 (March 1891), 262.

5. "Testimony of Major General Daniel Butterfield" (March 25, 1864), in *Report of the Joint Committee on the Conduct of the War*, 4:422; A. H. Nickerson, "Personal Recollections of Two Visits to Gettysburg," *Scribner's Magazine* 14 (July 1893), 19.

6. "Reports of Maj. Gen. George G. Meade, U.S. Army" (October 1, 1863), in *O.R.*, series one, 27 (pt. 1):115; Hancock, "Gettysburg: A Reply to General Howard," 350; Meade to Sedgwick (4:30 p.m.) and Sykes (7 p.m.), Halleck to Meade (June 27, 1863) in *O.R.*, series one, 27 (pt. 3):465, 467–68, and (pt. 1):61; Francis Amasa Walker, *General Hancock* (New York: D. Appleton, 1894), 108; Glenn Tucker, *Hancock the Superb* (Indianapolis: Bobbs-Merrill, 1960), 130–31; Pleasanton, "Campaign of Gettysburg," 454; Meade, *Life and Letters of George Gordon Meade*, 37–38; David M. Jordan, *Winfield Scott Hancock: A Soldier's Life* (Bloomington: Indiana University Press, 1988), 81.

7. Hancock, "Gettysburg: A Reply to General Howard," 351; Francis Amasa Walker, *History of the Second Army Corps in the Army of the Potomac* (New York: Charles Scribners, 1886), 265–66; Frederick Elizur Goodrich, *Life of Winfield Scott Hancock, Major-General, U.S.A.* (Boston: B. B. Russell, 1886), 135.

8. Hancock, "Gettysburg: Reply to General Howard," *Galaxy* 22 (December 1876), 821; Walker, *General Hancock*, 108; "Copied from the diary of Patrick H. Taylor," in *Bachelder Papers*, 2:961; Meade to Sedgwick (4:30 p.m.) and Sykes (7 p.m.), *O.R.*, series one, 27 (pt. 3):465, 467–68; "Testimony of General John Gibbon" (April 1, 1864), in *Report of the Joint Committee on the Conduct of the War*, 4:440.

9. John Whiting Storrs, *The "Twentieth Connecticut": A Regimental History* (Ansonia, CT: Naugatuck Valley Sentinel, 1886), 76–77; George Thayer, *Gettysburg, As We Men on the Right Saw It: A Paper Read before the Ohio Commandery of the Military Order of the Loyal Legion of the United States* (Cincinnati: H. C. Sherrick & Co., 1886), 10–11; Benjamin F. W. Urban, "The Story of Gettysburg: A Great Battle as Seen by a Lancaster Boy," *Gettysburg Magazine* 37 (January 2008), 88–90; Capt. Joseph Leeper to J. B. Bachelder, in *Bachelder Papers*, 2:895; Judson, *History of the Eighty-Third Regiment, Pennsylvania Volunteers*, 123; Oliver Wilcox Norton, *The Attack and Defense of Little Round Top, Gettysburg, July 2, 1863* (New York: Neale Publishing, 1913), 285; John J. Pullen, *The Twentieth Maine: A Volunteer Regiment in the Civil War* (Philadelphia: J. B. Lippincott, 1957), 94–95; Gottfried, *Roads to Gettysburg*, 216–17; James H. Nevins and William B. Styple, *What Death More Glorious: A Biography of Gen. Strong Vincent* (Kearny, NJ: Belle Grove Publishing, 1997), 67–68; Lt. Ziba Graham, "On to Gettysburg: Ten Days from My Diary of 1863" (1889), in *War Papers Read Before the Commandery of the State of Michigan*, 1:6–8.

10. "Abstract from Returns of the Army of the Potomac, June 10–July 31, 1863," in *O.R.*, series one, 27 (pt. 1):151; Samuel P. Bates, *The Battle of Gettysburg* (Philadelphia: T. H. Davis, 1875), 196–98; "Testimony of Major General George G. Meade" (March 5, 1864) and "Testimony of Major General Daniel Butterfield" (March 25, 1864), in *Report of the Joint Committee on the Conduct of the War*, 4:337, 419–20; Don Ernsberger, *Paddy Owen's Regulars: A History of the 69th Pennsylvania "Irish Volunteers"* (LaVergne, TX: Xlibris, 2004), 493–95, 531; Hardin, "Gettysburg Not a Surprise to the Union Commander," in *Military Essays and Recollections: Papers Read Before the Commandery of the State of Illinois*, 4:265; Biddle, "The First Day of the Battle of Gettysburg," in *Reynolds Memorial*, 60; C. W. Cook, "A Day at Gettysburg," *National Tribune* (April 7, 1898); David G. Martin, "Union Regimental Strengths," in Busey and Martin, *Regimental Strengths and Losses at Gettysburg*, 3–17; Thomas Livermore, *Numbers and Losses in the Civil War in America, 1861–1865* (Boston: Houghton Mifflin, 1900),102–3; *Fighting with the Eighteenth Massachusetts: The Civil War Memoir of Thomas H. Mann*, ed. John J. Hennessy (Baton Rouge: Louisiana State University Press, 2000), 181.

11. Dickert, *History of Kershaw's Brigade*, 222–23; Taylor, "Numerical Strengths of the Armies at Gettysburg," *SHSP* 5 (May 1878), 240, 245; John D. Busey, "Confederate Regimental Strengths," in Busey and Martin, *Regimental Strengths and Losses at Gettysburg*, 159–69; "Testimony of Major General George G. Meade" (March 5, 1864), in *Report of the Joint Committee on the Conduct of the War*, 4:420; Allan, "General Lee's Strength And Losses At Gettysburg," *SHSP* 1 (July 1877), 40; Fremantle, *Three Months in the Southern States, April–June 1863* (Edinburgh, U.K.: William Blackwood, 1863), 238; Caffey, *Battle-fields of the South: from Bull Run to Fredericksburgh* (New York: John Bradburn, 1864), 278; Glenn David Brasher, *The Peninsula Campaign and the Necessity of Emancipation: African Americans and the Fight for Freedom* (Chapel Hill: University of North Carolina Press, 2012), 52, 72, 118.

12. Lance J. Herdegen, "The Mule Train Charge at Gettysburg," *Gettysburg Magazine* 25 (July 2001), 43–45; Wainwright, diary entry for July 1, 1863, in *A Diary of Battle*, 232–33; Jacob F. Slagle, in Dougherty, *Stone's Brigade and the Fight for the McPherson Farm*, 35; Doubleday, *Chancellorsville and Gettysburg*, 134.

13. Dougherty, *Stone's Brigade and the Fight for the McPherson Farm*, 11–13; John F. Krumweide, *Disgrace at Gettysburg: The Arrest and Court-Martial of Brigadier General Thomas A. Rowley, U.S.A.* (Jefferson, NC: McFarland, 2006), 1–3; Tagg, *The Generals of Gettysburg*, 27–28; Col. Theodore B. Gates to J. B. Bachelder, in *Bachelder Papers*, 1:81–82; Gates, *"The "Ulster Guard" (20th N.Y. State Militia) and the War of the Rebellion* (New York: Benjamin H. Tyrrel, 1879), 432–33; Biddle, *The First Day of the Battle of Gettysburg*, 30–31.

14. "Major-General John Cleveland Robinson," in *Second Annual Report of the State Historian of the State of New York* (Albany, NY: Wynkoop, Hallenbeck, Crawford, 1897), 45–48; "John C. Robinson," in *Life Sketches of Executive Officers and Members of the Legislature of the State of New York for 1873* (Albany, NY: Weed, Parsons & Co., 1873), 21–24; "Testimony of Major General Abner Doubleday" (March 1, 1864), in *Report of the Joint Committee on the Conduct of the War*, 4:306–7; "Report of Lieut. Col. Augustus B. Farnham, Sixteenth Maine Infantry" (August 19, 1863), in *O.R.*, series one, 27 (pt. 1):295; "Sixteenth Maine Regiment," in *Maine at Gettysburg: Report of Maine Commissioners Prepared by the Executive Committee* (Portland, ME: Lakeside Press, 1898), 39; Abner Ralph Small, *The Sixteenth Maine Regiment in the War of the Rebellion, 1861–1865* (Portland, ME: B. Thurston, 1886), 116–18; Lash, "Brig. Gen. Henry Baxter's Brigade at Gettysburg, July 1," 11.

15. Howard, "Campaign and Battle of Gettysburg, June and July, 1863," *Atlantic Monthly* 38 (July 1876), 53; *The Reminiscences of Carl Schurz*, eds. F. Bancroft and W. A. Dunning (New York: Doubleday, Page & Co., 1917), 3:4–5; Howard, *Autobiography*, 1:408–9; "At Gettysburg—First Day's Work of the Eleventh Corps," *National Tribune* (December 12, 1889); James S. Pula, "The Fifth German Rifles at Gettysburg," *Gettysburg Magazine* 37 (January 2008), 51; Shue, *Morning at Willoughby Run*, 192–93; A. Wilson Greene, "From Chancellorsville to Cemetery Hill: O. O. Howard and Eleventh Corps Leadership," in *The First Day at Gettysburg*, ed. Gallagher, 63.

16. Timothy H. Smith, *Farms at Gettysburg: The Fields of Battle* (Gettysburg: Thomas Publications, 2007), 20; Howard, "Campaign and Battle of Gettysburg," 53–54; Howard, *Autobiography*, 1:408–10, 410–11; John A. Carpenter, "General O. O. Howard at Gettysburg," *Civil War History* 9 (September 1963), 273.

17. Alfred Lee, "Reminiscences of Gettysburg," *The Ladies' Repository: A Monthly Periodical, Devoted to Literature, Arts and Religion* 25 (September 1865), 550; L. A. Smith, "Recollections of Gettysburg" (1894) in *War Papers Read Before the Commandery of the State of Michigan, Military Order of the Loyal Legion of the United States* (Detroit: James H. Stone, 1898), 2:299; Howard, "Campaign and Battle of Gettysburg," 53–54; W. A. Bentley, "Howard at Gettysburg," *National Tribune* (February 12, 1885).

18. Howard, "Campaign and Battle of Gettysburg," 53–54, and *Autobiography*, 1:413; William Kiefer, *History of the One Hundred and Fifty-third Regiment, Pennsylvania Volunteers* (Easton, PA: Chemical Pubs., 1909), 74–75; Charles Howard, "First Day at Gettysburg," 242, 244; Kiefer, *History of the One Hundred and Fifty-third Regiment, Pennsylvania Volunteers*, 80.

19. Howard, "Campaign and Battle of Gettysburg," 54–55, and *Autobiography*, 1:414; Shue, *Morning at Willoughby Run*, 195–96; "Report of Capt. Lemuel B. Norton, Chief Signal Officer" (September 18, 1863), in *O.R.*, series one, 27 (pt. 1):201; "Historical Sketch by Regimental Committee," in *New York at Gettysburg*, 1:378; James S. Pula, "The Fifth German Rifles at Gettysburg," *Gettysburg Magazine* 37 (January 2008), 53–54.

20. Lincoln, in Fehrenbacher, *Recollected Words*, 165; *A Gallant Captain of the Civil War*, 28–29.

21. James Pula, "Fighting for Time: Carl Schurz on the First Day at Gettysburg," *Gettysburg Magazine* 35 (July 2006), 30; Howard, "Campaign and Battle of Gettysburg," 55–56, and *Autobiography*, 1:414; Creighton, *The Colors of Courage*, 14–15; Edward C. Culp, *The 25th Ohio Vet Vol. Infantry in the War for the Union* (Topeka, KS: Geo. W. Crane, 1885), 76–77, and "Gettysburg—Reminiscences of the Great Fight," *National Tribune* (March 19, 1885); "Memories of Gettysburg Recalled by Maj.-Gen. O. O. Howard Before His Death," *Gettysburg Compiler* (March 23, 1910).

22. Hassler, *Crisis at the Crossroads*, 66–67; Charles H. Howard, "First Day at Gettysburg," 251–52; Albert Rowe Barlow, *Company G: A Record of the Services of One Company of the 157th N.Y. Vols. in the War of the Rebellion* (Syracuse, NY: A. W. Hall, 1899), 126.

23. John Cabell Early, "A Southern Boy's Experience at Gettysburg," *Journal of the Military Service Institution of the United States* 48 (May 1911), 417; Douglas Craig Haines, "'Lights Mingled with Shadows': Lt. Gen. Richard S. Ewell," *Gettysburg Magazine* 45 (July 2011), 40; "Report of Lieut. Gen. Richard S. Ewell," "Report of Maj. Gen. Jubal A. Early" (August 22, 1863), and "Report of Lieut. Gen. Ambrose P. Hill" (November 1863), in *O.R.*, series one, 27 (pt. 2):444, 468, 607; Early, *Lieutenant General Jubal Anderson Early, C.S.A.: Autobiographical Sketch*, 266; Pfanz, *Richard S. Ewell*, 303; Isaac Trimble, "The Battle and Campaign of Gettysburg," *SHSP* 26 (January–December 1898), 122, and Trimble to J. B. Bachelder (February 8, 1883), in *Bachelder Papers*, 2:928.

24. Jeremiah Tate to Mary Tate (August 6, 1863), in Gilder-Lehrman Collection, New-York Historical Society; James K. Swisher, *Warrior in Gray: General Robert Rodes of Lee's Army* (Shippensburg, PA: White Mane Books, 2000), 123; J. Coleman Alderson, "Lee and Longstreet at Gettysburg," *Confederate Veteran* 12 (October 1904), 488; *Campbell Brown's Civil War*, 205.

25. Luther W. Minnigh, *Gettysburg: "What They Did Here"* (Gettysburg: Minnigh, 1892), 23.

26. Charles H. Howard, "First Day at Gettysburg," 253; Joel B. Swett, "The 8th New York Cavalry at Gettysburg," *National Tribune* (April 4, 1884); *New York at Gettysburg*, 1:9–10; H. A. Hall, W. B. Besley, and G. G. Wood, *History of the Sixth New York Cavalry, Second Ira Harris Guard* (Worcester, MA: Blanchard Press, 1908), 136–37; Hassler, *Crisis at the Crossroads*, 31, 139–40; Newal Cheney, *History of the Ninth Regiment, New York Volunteer Cavalry: War of 1861 to 1865* (Jamestown, NY: Martin Merz & Son, 1901), 106–8, 110–11; Henry J. Hunt, "The First Day at Gettysburg," *Battles & Leaders*, 3:274–75.

27. Wadsworth to Doubleday (July 1, 1863), in *O.R.*, series one, 27 (pt. 3):463; Pearson, *James S. Wadsworth of Geneseo*, 215–16; Smith, *History of the Seventy-sixth Regiment New York Volunteers*, 239; "Reports of Maj. Gen. Abner Doubleday" (December 14, 1863) and "Report of Brig. Gen. James S. Wadsworth" (July 4, 1863), in *O.R.*, series one, 27 (pt. 1):248, 266; "Report of Maj. Gen. R. E. Rodes," in *O.R.*, series one, 27 (pt. 2):552; C. D. Grace, "Rodes's Division at Gettysburg," *Confederate Veteran* (December 1897), 614; James M. Thompson, *Reminiscences of Autauga Rifles* (Autaugaville, AL: J. M. Thompson, 1879), 7; Collins, *Major General Robert E. Rodes*, 266; Jonathan Neu, "'But Few of This Force Escaped Us': An Account of Doles' Brigade and Its Actions on July 1, 1863," *Gettysburg Magazine* 36 (January 2007), 41.

28. "Report of Lieut. Gen. Richard S. Ewell," in *O.R.*, series one, 27 (pt. 2):444; "At Gettysburg—First Day's Work of the Eleventh Corps," *National Tribune* (December 12, 1889); Bradley M. Gottfried, *The Artillery of Gettysburg* (Nashville: Cumberland House, 2008), 61; Robert K. Krick, "Three Confederate Disasters on Oak Ridge: Failures of Brigade Leadership on the First Day of Gettysburg," in *The First Day at Gettysburg: Essays on Confederate and Union Leadership*, ed. Gary W. Gallagher (Kent, OH: Kent State University Press, 1992), 120–22; A. T. Marsh [Co. I, 53rd North Carolina], "North Carolina Troops at Gettysburg," *Confederate Veteran* 16 (October 1908), 516–17

29. Paul Clark Cooksey, "They Died as If on Dress Parade: The Annihilation of Iverson's Brigade at Gettysburg and the Battle of Oak Ridge," *Gettysburg Magazine* 20 (June 1999), 90–91, 107; Tagg, *The Generals of Gettysburg*, 24; Lash, "Brig. Gen. Henry Baxter's Brigade at Gettysburg, July 1," 7–8, 13; Crisfield Johnson, *History of Hillsdale County, Michigan, with Illustrations and Biographical Sketches of Some of Its Prominent Men and Pioneers* (Philadelphia: Evarts & Abbott, 1879), 55; "Report of Brig. Gen. Henry Baxter" (July 17, 1863), in *O.R.*, series one, 27 (pt. 1):307; Vautier, *History of the 88th Pennsylvania Volunteers in the War for the Union, 1861–1865*, 106.

30. "Report of Maj. Gen. R. E. Rodes," in *O.R.*, series one, 27 (pt. 2):552; Samuel Pickens, diary entry for July 1, 1863, in *Voices from Company D*, 182–83; Isaac Hall, *History of the*

Ninety-Seventh Regiment, New York Volunteers ("Conkling Rifles") in the War for the Union (Utica, NY: L. C. Childs, 1890), 135, 339–40; George Kimball, "Gettysburg," in *Stories of our Soldiers: War Reminiscences*, ed. C. C. Coffin (Boston: Boston Journal, 1893), 2:109; Lash, "Brig. Gen. Henry Baxter's Brigade at Gettysburg, July 1," 13.

31. "Twelfth Regiment," in *Annual Report of the Adjutant-General of the Commonwealth of Massachusetts* (Boston: Wright & Potter, 1864), 604; Capt. George A. Hussey, "Historical Notes," in *New York at Gettysburg*, 2:678; John Wesley Jaques, *Three Years' Campaign of the Ninth, N.Y.S.M., During the Southern Rebellion* (New York: Hilton & Co., 1865), 155; Richard M. Rollins, "*The Damned Red Flags of the Rebellion": The Struggle over the Confederate Battle Flag at Gettysburg* (Redondo Beach, CA: Rank and File Publications, 1997), 103; Benjamin F. Cook, *History of the Twelfth Regiment, Massachusetts Volunteers* (Boston: Twelfth [Webster] Regiment Association, 1882), 100; Vautier, *History of the 88th Pennsylvania Volunteers*, 106–7; Lash, "Brig. Gen. Henry Baxter's Brigade at Gettysburg, July 1," 18–19; Isaac Hall to J. B. Bachelder (August 15, 1884), in *Bachelder Papers*, 2:1062 and *History of the Ninety-Seventh Regiment, New York Volunteers*, 137; Henry Robinson Berkeley, diary entry for July 2, 1863, in *Four Years in the Confederate Artillery: The Diary of Private Henry Robinson Berkeley*, ed. W. H. Runge (1961; Richmond: Virginia Historical Society, 1991), 50.

32. Cyrus B. Watson, "Forty-Fifth Regiment," in *Histories of the Several Regiments and Battalions from North Carolina in the Great War, 1861–'65*, ed. Walter Clark (Raleigh, NC: E. M. Uzzell, 1901), 2:41–42; Richard E. Matthews, *The 149th Pennsylvania Volunteer Infantry Unit in the Civil War* (Jefferson, NC: McFarland, 1994), 84–89; Green, *Recollections and Reflections*, 262.

33. William T. Sherman, *Memoirs of General William T. Sherman* (New York: D. Appleton, 1904), 2:385; Wynstra, *"The Rashness of That Hour,"* 231–42, 297, 321, 350–51; Walter A. Montgomery, "Twelfth Regiment," in *Histories of the Several Regiments and Battalions from North Carolina*, 1:637.

34. Francis A. Walker, "General Gibbon in the Second Corps" (1896), in *Personal Recollections of the War of the Rebellion: Addresses Delivered Before the Commandery of the State of New York, Military Order of the Loyal Legion of the United States* (New York: J. J. Little & Co., 1897), 2:303–4; "Letter from Maj. Scheibert, of the Prussian Royal Engineers" (November 21, 1877), *SHSP* 5 (January–February 1878), 90.

35. "To General John D. Imboden" (July 1, 1863), in *Wartime Papers of Robert E. Lee*, 536; Mosby, *Stuart's Cavalry in the Gettysburg Campaign*, 119; Longstreet, *From Manassas to Appomattox*, 351–52; La Salle Corbell Pickett, *Pickett and His Men* (Atlanta: Foote & Davies, 1899), 272–73; Swallow, "From Fredericksburg to Gettysburg," 361; "Richmond *Enquirer* Account: In Camp, Near Hagerstown, Md., July 8, 1863," in *Rebellion Record*, ed. Moore (1864), 7:109; James Johnson Kilpatrick, diary entry for July 1, 1863, in *The 16th Mississippi Infantry*, 175.

36. Gold, *History of Clarke County, Virginia, and Its Connection with the War Between the States*, 183–84; Longstreet, "Lee in Pennsylvania," 420; "Report of Maj. Gen. Richard H. Anderson" (August 7, 1863), in *O.R.*, series one, 27 (pt. 2):613; Long, *Memoirs of Robert E. Lee*, 275–76; Robertson, *General A. P. Hill*, 209; Brown, in *Campbell Brown's Civil War: With Ewell and the Army of Northern Virginia*, 331; Douglas Craig Haines, "Lee's Advance Along the Cashtown Road," *Gettysburg Magazine* 23 (January 2001), 28.

37. "The Memoirs of Henry Heth, Part II," 305; Walter Herron Taylor, *Four Years with General Lee: Being a Summary of the More Important Events Touching the Career of General Robert E. Lee, in the War Between the States* (New York: D. Appleton, 1877), 92–93; James Power Smith, "General Lee at Gettysburg" (April 4, 1905), in *SHSP* 33 (January–December 1905), 143.

38. "Reports of Gen. Robert E. Lee" (July 31, 1863, and January, 1864), in *O.R.*, series one, 27 (pt. 2):308, 317; "The Memoirs of Henry Heth, Part II," 305; Bowden and Ward, *Last Chance for Victory*, 160–68; William W. Chamberlaine, *Memoirs of the Civil War Between the Northern and Southern Sections of the United States of America, 1861–1865* (Washington: Byron S. Adams, 1912), 66–68.

CHAPTER ELEVEN *The dutch run and leave us to fight*

1. Edward Fowler, "Colonel Fowler's Recollections of Gettysburg," 134–35; Herdegen and Beaudot, *In the Bloody Railroad Cut*, 217; Howard, *Autobiography*, 1:429.

2. Doubleday, *Chancellorsville and Gettysburg*, 137–38, 146–47; Howard, "Campaign and Battle of Gettysburg, June and July, 1863," *Atlantic Monthly* 38 (July 1876), 60; Halstead, "The First Day of the Battle of Gettysburg" (March 2, 1887), in *War Papers: Being papers Read Before the Commandery of the District of Columbia*, 1:5–6; Charles H. Howard, "First Day at Gettysburg," 248–50; Hassler, *Crisis at the Crossroads*, 72–73; "Reports of Maj. Gen. Oliver O. Howard" (August 31, 1863), in *O.R.*, series one, 27 (pt. 1):702–3; Carpenter, "General O. O. Howard at Gettysburg," 266.

3. Cheney, *History of the Ninth Regiment, New York Volunteer Cavalry*, 111; Theodore W. Bean, "Who Fired the Opening Shots? General Buford at Gettysburg," *Philadelphia Weekly Times* (February 2, 1878); George Kimball, "A Young Hero of Gettysburg," *Century Magazine* 33 (November 1886), 133–34; Biddle, "The First Day of the Battle of Gettysburg," 29–30; Smith, *History of the Seventy-Sixth Regiment, New York Volunteers*, 243–44; Small, *Sixteenth Maine Regiment*, 119; Frassanito, *Early Photography at Gettysburg*, 90–91.

4. Bates, *History of Pennsylvania Volunteers*, 4:653; Dougherty, *Stone's Brigade*, 155–60; Edmund Jacob Wolf, "John Burns at Gettysburg," in *The Higher Rock: Sermons, Addresses, and Articles* (Philadelphia: Lutheran Publication Society, 1905), 372–73; Martin, "The Saga of John Burns," in *Gettysburg—July 1*, 371–74; Alfred E. Lee, *The Battle of Gettysburg* (Columbus, OH: A. H. Smythe, 1888), 114–15; Trowbridge, "The Field of Gettysburg," *Atlantic Monthly* 16 (November 1865), 621; Thomas Chamberlin, "150th Regiment Infantry" (September 11, 1889), in *Pennsylvania at Gettysburg: Ceremonies at the Dedication of the Monuments Erected by the Commonwealth of Pennsylvania*, ed. John P. Nicholson (Harrisburg, PA: Wm. Stanley Ray, 1914), 2:753; Timothy H. Smith, *John Burns: "The Hero of Gettysburg"* (Gettysburg, PA: Thomas Publications, 2000), 11, 19, 35, 50–61.

5. Early to J. B. Bachelder (March 23, 1876), in *Bachelder Papers*, 1:459; Thomas Benton Reed, *A Private in Gray* (Camden, AR: T. B. Reed, 1905), 42; *Campbell Brown's Civil War*, 208, 209; C. D. Grace, "Rodes's Division at Gettysburg," *Confederate Veteran* 5 (December 1897), 614.

6. *Campbell Brown's Civil War*, 206; James MacDowell Carrington, "First Day on Left at Gettysburg," *SHSP* 37 (January–December 1909), 329–32; Early, "A Southern Boy's Experience at Gettysburg," *Journal of the Military Service Institution of the United States* 48 (May 1911), 417; James P. Gannon, "The 6th Louisiana Infantry at Gettysburg," *Gettysburg Magazine* 21 (January 2000), 89.

7. Pula, "Fighting for Time: Carl Schurz on the First Day at Gettysburg," 30–31; "Reports of Maj. Gen. Carl Schurz" (August 20, 1863), "Report of Adolphus Dobke, Forty-Fifth New York Infantry" (August 21, 1863) in *O.R.*, series one, 27 (pt. 1):727, 734; *Reminiscences of Carl Schurz*, 3:8. Krzyzanowski's brigade normally had five regiments, but one of them, the 58th New York, had been on detached duty and did not arrive at Gettysburg until late on July 1st.

8. Richard F. Welch, *The Boy General: The Life and Careers of Francis Channing Barlow* (Mad-

ison, NJ: Fairleigh Dickinson University Press, 2003), 20–24, 27, 37, 83; Edwin H. Abbot, "Francis Channing Barlow," in *Sons of the Puritans: A Group of Brief Biographies* (Boston: American Unitarian Association, 1908), 122–26; Introduction, and Barlow to Almira Barlow (April 24, 1863), in *Fear Was Not in Him: The Civil War Letters of Major General Francis C. Barlow, U.S.A.*, ed. Christian Samito (New York: Fordham University Press, 2004), xv, xix, xxxi, xxxv, 127; *Reminiscences of Carl Schurz*, 3:7; Creighton, *Colors of Courage*, 90.

9. *Reminiscences of Carl Schurz*, 3:8; Capt. M. Browne to J. B. Bachelder (April 8, 1864) and Trimble to J. B. Bachelder (February 8, 1883), in *Bachelder Papers*, 1:148 and 2:929; "At Gettysburg—First Day's Work of the Eleventh Corps," *National Tribune* (December 12, 1889); Barlow to Almira Barlow (April 24, 1863), in *Fear Was Not in Him*, 162.

10. "Reports of Maj. Gen. Oliver O. Howard" (August 31, 1863), Buford to Meade (July 1, 1863), T. A. Meysenburg to Slocum (July 1, 1863), and Slocum to Howard (July 1, 1863), in *O.R.*, series one, 27 (pt. 1):702–3, 924, and (pt. 3):463, 464; Neu, "'But Few of This Force Escaped Us': An Account of Doles' Brigade," 41; Doubleday, *Chancellorsville and Gettysburg*, 138; Greene, "From Chancellorsville to Cemetery Hill," 73; Jubal Early to J. B. Bachelder (March 23, 1876), in *Bachelder Papers*, 1:459.

11. J. Clyde Miller [153rd PA] to J. B. Bachelder (March 2, 1883, and March 2, 1884), in *Bachelder Papers*, 2:1025, 1211; Butts, *A Gallant Captain of the Civil War*, 75, 75–76; "Report of Maj. Thomas W. Osborn" (July 29, 1863), "Report of Brig. Gen. J. B. Gordon" (August 10, 1863), and "Reports of Lieut. Col. H. P. Jones, C.S. Army" (August 18, 1863), in *O.R.*, series one, 27 (pt. 1):748, (pt. 2):492, 494; Kiefer, *History of the One Hundred and Fifty-Third Regiment, Pennsylvania Volunteers*, 210–13; Hassler, *Crisis at the Crossroads*, 78.

12. Barlow to Almira Barlow (July 7, 1863), in *Fear Was Not in Him*, 162; Oscar Ladley to "Mother & Sisters" (July 16, 1863), in *Hearth and Knapsack: The Ladley Letters, 1857–1880*, ed. C. M. Becker and R. Thomas (Athens, OH: Ohio University Press, 1988), 147; *Campbell Brown's Civil War*, 208; Capt. M. Browne to J. B. Bachelder (April 8, 1864) and Andrew L. Harris [75th OH] to J. B. Bachelder (March 14, 1881), in *Bachelder Papers*, 1:148 and 2:744; Culp, *25th Ohio Vet. Vol. Infantry*, 77–78.

13. Butts, *A Gallant Captain of the Civil War*, 76; J. Clyde Miller [153rd PA] to J. B. Bachelder (March 2, 1884) and Lt. Col. Jeremiah Williams [25th OH] to J. B. Bachelder (June 18, 1880), in *Bachelder Papers*, 1:668 and 2:1026; Swallow, "The First Day at Gettysburg," *Southern Bivouac* 4 (December 1885), 440; Greene, "From Chancellorsville to Cemetery Hill," 76–77, 78–79; Pula, "Fighting for Time: Carl Schurz on the First Day at Gettysburg," 34, 35; Theodore A. Dodge, "Left Wounded on the Field," *Putnam's Monthly Magazine* 14 (September 1869), 319.

14. Lee, "Reminiscences of Gettysburg," 551; Dodge, "Left Wounded on the Field," 321; Walber, "From Gettysburg to Libby Prison," in *War Papers Read Before the Commandery of the State of Wisconsin*, 4:192.

15. Neu, "But Few of This Force Escaped Us," 47; Dodge, "Left Wounded on the Field," 321; Lee, "Reminiscences of Gettysburg," 550; Schurz, *Reminiscences*, 3:11–12; Valuska and Keller, *Damn Dutch: Pennsylvania Germans at Gettysburg*, 143; James S. Pula, "The 26th Wisconsin Volunteer Infantry at Gettysburg," *Gettysburg Magazine* 23 (January 2001), 81–83; Pula, *For Liberty and Justice: The Life and Times of Wladimir Krzyżanowski* (Polish American Congress Charitable Foundation, 1978), 97; Kevin E. O'Brien, "'Bullets Came as Thick as Hail': Krzyzanowski's Brigade Defends the Union Right on July 1, 1963," *Gettysburg Magazine* 24 (July 2001), 66, 67; H. Nauchtigall, "Account of the Part Taken by the Seventy-Fifth Pennsylvania Infantry in the Battle of Gettysburg, July 1, 2, and 3, 1863," in *Pennsylvania at Gettysburg*, 1:434.

16. James C. Carmichael, "Dedication of Monument" (September 8, 1886), in *New York Monuments Commission for the Battlefields of Gettysburg and Chattanooga: Final Report on*

the Battlefield of Gettysburg, 3:1058; "Madison County Regiment," *Utica Morning Herald* (October 3, 1862); John Stilwell Applegate, *Reminiscences and Letters of George Arrowsmith of New Jersey* (Red Bank, NJ: John H. Cook, 1893), 216, 222; Albert Rowe Barlow, *Company G: A Record of the Services of One Company of the 157th N.Y. Vols. in the War of the Rebellion* (Syracuse, NY: A. W. Hall, 1899), 126–27, 127–29; "Letter from Capt. Van Slyke, Co. B, 157th Regiment," *Oneida Dispatch* (July 8, 1863); Col. Philip P. Browne to J. B. Bachelder (April 4, 1864), in *Bachelder Papers*, 1:136–37.

17. Chuck Teague, "Brutal Clash at Blocher's Knoll," *Gettysburg Magazine* 32 (July 2005), 69; C. D. Grace, "Rodes's Division at Gettysburg," *Confederate Veteran* 5 (December 1897), 614–15; "Adams County Almshouse," in *First Annual Report of the Board of Commissioners of Public Charities of the State of Pennsylvania* (Harrisburg, PA: B. Singerly, 1871), 1:234; Martin, *Gettysburg July 1*, 305; George Washington Nichols, *A Soldier's Story of His Regiment (61st Georgia) and Incidentally of the Lawton-Gordon-Evans Brigade, Army Northern Virginia* (Jesup, GA: privately printed, 1898), 116; Casdorph, *Confederate General R. S. Ewell*, 250–51; "Report of Brig. Gen. Adelbert Ames" (July 28, 1863) and "Report of Brig. Gen. J. B. Gordon, C.S. Army" (August 10, 1863), in *O.R.*, series one, 27 (pt. 1):713, and (pt. 2):492; "At Gettysburg—First Day's Work of the Eleventh Corps," *National Tribune* (December 12, 1889).

18. Lee, "Reminiscences of Gettysburg," 552–53; Dodge, "Left Wounded on the Field," 322; William F. Hanna, "A Gettysburg Myth Exploded," *Civil War Times Illustrated* 24 (May 1985), 43, 44, 47; Henry M. Field, *Blood Is Thicker Than Water: A Few Days Among Our Southern Brethren* (New York: George Munro, 1886), 34–35.

19. "Reports of Maj. Gen. Oliver O. Howard" (August 31, 1863), in *O.R.*, series one, 27 (pt. 1):703–4, Mark H. Dunkelman and Michael J. Winey, "The Hardtack Regiment in the Brickyard Fight," *Gettysburg Magazine* 8 (January 1993), 19.

20. Charles H. Howard, "First Day at Gettysburg," 255, 257–58; "Reports of Maj. Gen. Oliver O. Howard" (August 31, 1863), "Report of Brig. Gen. Adolph von Steinwehr" (August 30, 1863), and "Reports of Maj. Gen. Carl Schurz" (August 20, 1863), in *O.R.*, series one, 27 (pt. 1):703–4, 721, 729; *Reminiscences of Carl Schurz*, 3:10–11; Busey and Martin, *Regimental Strengths and Losses at Gettysburg*, 88; Martin, *Gettysburg July 1*, 308; Dunkelman and Winey, "The Hardtack Regiment in the Brickyard Fight," 19; Valuska and Keller, *Damn Dutch*, 146; *Reminiscences of Carl Schurz*, 3:11–12; Howard, "Campaign and Battle of Gettysburg, June and July, 1863," 58; Lash, "Brig. Gen. Henry Baxter's Brigade at Gettysburg, July 1," 11.

21. Dunkelman and Winey, "The Hardtack Regiment in the Brickyard Fight," 21–22; "Interesting Narrative of the Escape of Two Officers of the 154th Regt. N.Y.S. Vol. from the Hands of the Rebels," Randolph (NY) *Register Supplement* (April 10, 1877); "Letter from Maj. Warner—The 154th," *Cattaraugus Freeman* (July 10, 1863); "Address of Col. Daniel B. Allen" (July 1, 1890) and E. D. Northrup, "Historical Sketch," in *New York at Gettysburg*, 1050, 1055; Gottfried, *Brigades of Gettysburg*, 323–25; Hartwell Osborn, *Trials and Triumphs: The Record of the Fifty-Fifth Ohio Volunteer Infantry* (Chicago: A. C. McClurg, 1904), 97.

22. Pearson, *James S. Wadsworth of Geneseo*, 217; Trimble to J. B. Bachelder (February 8, 1883), in *Bachelder Papers*, 2:929.

23. "Testimony of Major General Abner Doubleday" (March 1, 1864), in *Report of the Joint Committee on the Conduct of the War*, 4:307; Howard, *Autobiography*, 1:417; Wainwright, diary entry for July 1, 1863, in *A Diary of Battle*, 235; Busey and Martin, *Regimental Strengths and Losses*, 25; "Report of Brig Gen. John C. Robinson" (July 18, 1863) and "Report of Lieut. Col. Augustus B. Farnham, Sixteenth Maine Infantry" (August 19, 1863), in *O.R.*, series one, 27 (pt. 1):289, 295; John C. Robinson, "The First Corps—Its Important Ser-

vices at the Battle of Gettysburg," *National Tribune* (April 21, 1887); Andy Ward, "The 16th Maine Infantry at Gettysburg," *Gettysburg Magazine* 37 (January 2008), 39; Small, *The Sixteenth Maine Regiment*, 116–18; Wynstra, *The Rashness of That Hour*, 251.

24. Martin, *Gettysburg, July 1*, 253–54; Lash, "Brig. Gen. Henry Baxter's Brigade at Gettysburg, July 1," 22; Small, *The Sixteenth Maine Regiment*, 118; Harold A. Small, ed., *The Road to Richmond: The Civil War Memoirs of Major Abner R. Small of the 16th Maine Volunteers* (New York: Fordham University Press, 2000), 238–39; "Report of Capt. A. J. Hopkins, Forty-Fifth North Carolina" (July 17, 1863) and "Reports of Col. Richard Coulter, Eleventh Pennsylvania Infantry" (July 9, 1863), in *O.R.*, series one, 27 (pt. 1):293, and (pt. 2):575; Francis Wiggin, "Sixteenth Maine Regiment" and Abner Small, "Incidents of the Battle and Remarks Thereon," in *Maine at Gettysburg: Report of Maine Commissioners Prepared by the Executive Committee* (Portland, ME: Lakeside Press, 1898), 43–44, 57; George D. Bisbee, "Three Years a Volunteer Soldier in the Civil War, Antietam to Appomattox," in *War Papers: Read Before the Commandery of the State of Maine*, 4:122–21.

25. Hassler, *Crisis at the Crossroads*, 99; James J. Dougherty, " 'We Have Come to Stay!' The 143rd Regiment Pennsylvania Volunteer Infantry and the Fight for McPherson's Ridge," *Gettysburg Magazine* 24 (July 2001), 49–50; Peter Tomasak, "The 143rd Pennsylvania Volunteer Regiment in Hell's Firestorm on July 1st at Gettysburg," *Gettysburg Magazine* 38 (January 2008), 44–45; Chamberlin, *History of the One Hundred and Fiftieth Regiment*, 124–25; Swisher, *Warrior in Gray*, 131–32; "Memoranda of Lt. Col. Huidekoper Concerning the 150th Regt. Pa.," in *Bachelder Papers*, 2:951, 953.

26. Chamberlin, *History of the One Hundred and Fiftieth Regiment*, 133; Dougherty, *Stone's Brigade*, 59, 65, 77–78, 85–86; Sgt. William R. Ramsey to J. B. Bachelder (April 16, 1883), H. H. Spayd, "The Colors of the 149th Pa. at Gettysburg," and Capt. John H. Bassler to J. B. Bachelder (December 7, 1881), in *Bachelder Papers*, 2:763, 765–66, 949; Bassler, "The Color Episode of the 149th Regiment, Pennsylvania Volunteers," *SHSP* 37 (January–December 1909), 275–76; Richard K. Sauers, *Advance the Colors: Pennsylvania Civil War Battle Flags* (Harrisburg, PA: Capitol Preservation Committee, 1991), 2:434; Bates, *History of Pennsylvania Volunteers*, 4:488–89; Fremantle, *Three Months in the Southern States*, 254–55; M. D. Roche, "143rd Regiment Infantry," in *Pennsylvania at Gettysburg*, 2:703.

27. "Reports of Brig. Gen. Henry J. Hunt, U.S. Army" (September 27, 1863), in *O.R.*, series one, 27 (pt. 1):230–31; Hess, *Lee's Tar Heels*, 122; Lt. Col. George F. McFarland, "Report of the 151st Regt. Pa. Vols." (March 16, 1864), in *Bachelder Papers*, 1:89–90; John F. Krumwiede, *Disgrace at Gettysburg: The Arrest and Court-Martial of Brigadier General Thomas A. Rowley, U.S.A.* (Jefferson, NC: McFarland, 2006), 9, 88, 126, 191; Shue, *Morning at Willoughby Run*, 230–31; Cole, *Command and Communications Frictions in the Gettysburg Campaign*, 36; Dougherty, *Stone's Brigade*, 73; Hassler, "The Color Episode of the 149th Regiment," 287; Cook, "Personal Reminiscences of Gettysburg" (December 12, 1903), in *War Talks in Kansas*, 325–26. Rowley was far from the only one: the colonel of the 149th Pennsylvania was also staggering under the weight of alcoholic comfort, something one soldier regretted was "well-known to the men of his regiment." And a lieutenant in the 80th New York walked unevenly along the line, "insensible to shot and shell whistling around him," and entertained the men with a rendition of a bawdy ballad until brought up short before his colonel. "Raising his cap and wiping his heated face," the lieutenant boldly informed him, "Colonel, it's damned hot out there."

28. Cook, "Personal Reminiscences of Gettysburg" (December 12, 1903), in *War Talks in Kansas*, 324; Shue, *Morning at Willoughby Run*, 185; Michael A. Dreese, *The One Hundred Fifty-First Pennsylvania Volunteers at Gettysburg: Like Ripe Apples in a Storm* (Jefferson, NC: McFarland, 2000), 41; Martin, *Gettysburg, July 1*, 181; Scott L. Mingus, *Gettysburg Glimpses: True Stories from the Battlefield* (LaVergne, TX: Xlibris, 2009), 45–46; Mahood,

General Wadsworth, 174; Nelson, *The Battles of Chancellorsville and Gettysburg*, 134; Wainwright, diary entry for July 1, 1863, in *A Diary of Battle*, 235; McFarland, "Report of the 151st Regt. Pa. Vols." (March 16, 1864), in *Bachelder Papers*, 1:89.

29. Brown, *A Colonel at Gettysburg and Spotsylvania*, 77; Ernsberger, *Also for Glory Muster*, 35–36, 38–39; Mills, *History of the 16th North Carolina Regiment in the Civil War*, 36; Gragg, *Covered with Glory*, 29–31; Clark, ed., *Histories of the Several Regiments and Battalions from North Carolina in the Great War, 1861–'65*, 2:368; Archie K. Davis, *Boy Colonel of the Confederacy: The Life and Times of Henry King Burgwyn, Jr.* (Chapel Hill: University of North Carolina Press, 1985), 327; Hassler, *Crisis at the Crossroads*, 111–12.

30. Clark, ed., *Histories of the Several Regiments and Battalions from North Carolina in the Great War, 1861–'65*, 2:343; Hess, *Lee's Tar Heels*, 120–21, 131–32; Julius Leinbach, "Regimental Band of the Twenty-Sixth North Carolina," ed. Douglas McCorkle, *Civil War History* 4 (September 1958), 227, 28–29; B. F. Brown, "McGowan's South Carolina Brigade in the Battle of Gettysburg," *Confederate Veteran* 31 (February 1923), 53; "Extract from Chapter 9 of Caldwell's History of Gregg's (McGowan's) Brigade, Battle of Gettysburg, July 1, 1863," in *Bachelder Papers*, 2:903; Herdegen and Beaudot, *In the Bloody Railroad Cut at Gettysburg*, 217; Beecham, *Gettysburg*, 72; William M. Cheek, "How Colonel Henry King Burgwyn Lost His Life," *SHSP* 36 (January–December 1908), 245–46.

31. Hess, *Lee's Tar Heels*, 132–33; "Report of Col. Henry A. Morrow, Twenty-fourth Michigan Infantry" (February 22, 1864), "Report of Col. William W. Robinson, Seventh Wisconsin Infantry" (November 18, 1863), and "Report of Lieut. Col. George F. McFarland, One hundred and fifty-first Pennsylvania Infantry" (March 15, 1864), in *O.R.*, series one, 27 (pt. 1):268, 280, 327; Lt. Col. George F. McFarland (March 16, 1864, and February 7, 1867) and Capt. Albert M. Edwards (May 27, 1878) to J. B. Bachelder, in *Bachelder Papers*, 1:300, 613–14; Venner, *The 19th Indiana Infantry at Gettysburg*, 64, 71, 72; Curtis, *History of the Twenty-fourth Michigan of the Iron Brigade*, 164–65; Chamberlin, *History of the One Hundred and Fiftieth Regiment*, 134; Nolan, *The Iron Brigade*, 246–47; George L. Kilmer, "Fighting for the Flag—A Brave Defense of Regimental Colors at Gettysburg," *Los Angeles Times* (July 8, 1894).

32. Hess, *Lee's Tar Heels*, 128; Theodore Burr Gates, *The "Ulster Guard" (20th N.Y. State Militia) and the War of the Rebellion* (New York: Benjamin H. Tyrrel, 1879), 442–43; J. B. Hardenburgh to Theodore B. Gates (October 9, 1878), in Theodore Gates Miscellaneous Manuscripts, folder 1, New-York Historical Society; Cook, "Personal Reminiscences of Gettysburg," 326–27; "Report of Lt. Col. William W. Dudley," in *Bachelder Papers*, 2:942.

CHAPTER TWELVE *Go in, South Carolina!*

1. Naiswald, *Grape and Canister*, 279; Murray, *Artillery Tactics of the Civil War: A Study of the Tactical Use of Artillery Based on the First Day's Battle at Gettysburg* (Wolcott, NY: Benedum Books, 1998), 51, 52, 53, 54; Beecham, *Gettysburg*, 77–81; McFarland to J. B. Bachelder (February 7, 1867), in *Bachelder Papers*, 1:302; Charles Edward Benton, *As Seen from the Ranks: A Boy in the Civil War* (New York: G. P. Putnam's, 1902), 26–27; A. T. Marsh, "North Carolina Troops at Gettysburg," *Confederate Veteran* 16 (October 1908), 516–17; Peel, in Ernsberger, *Also for Glory Muster*, 41.

2. Early, "A Southern Boy's Experience at Gettysburg," *Journal of the Military Service Institution of the United States* 48 (May 1911), 419.

3. Peel, in Ernsberger, *Also for Glory Muster*, 41; Cheek, "How Colonel Henry King Burgwyn Lost His Life," *SHSP* 36 (January–December 1908), 246; Tevis and Marquis, *History of the Fighting Fourteenth*, 84–85; Early, "A Southern Boy's Experience at Gettysburg," 419.

4. Thomas Chamberlin, "150th Regiment" (September 11, 1889), in *Pennsylvania at Gettysburg*, 2:758–59; Abram P. Smith, *History of the Seventy-Sixth Regiment, New York Volunteers* (Cortland, NY: Truaie, Smith & Miles, 1867), 240; "Testimony of Major General Abner Doubleday" (March 1, 1864), in *Report of the Joint Committee on the Conduct of the War*, 4:308; Doubleday, *Chancellorsville and Gettysburg*, 147–49; Perrin to Milledge L. Bonham (July 29, 1863), in Bonham, "A Little More Light on Gettysburg," *Mississippi Valley Historical Review* 24 (March 1938), 522; B. F. Brown, "Some Recollections of Gettysburg," *Confederate Veteran* 31 (February 1923), 53; Beecham, *Gettysburg*, 88–89; Brown, *A Colonel at Gettysburg and Spotsylvania*, 78–79; Bowden and Ward, *Last Chance for Victory*, 168–69, 173–75; Dougherty, *Stone's Brigade*, 95–96.

5. Dawes, "With the Sixth Wisconsin at Gettysburg," 378; Venner, *19th Indiana Infantry*, 85–86; Theodore Gates to J. B. Bachelder (January 30, 1864), McFarland to Bachelder (February 7, 1867), and John A. Leach to Bachelder (September 12, 1882) in *Bachelder Papers*, 1:83, 301; 2:904–5; G. T. Stevens, "Stevens' Fifth Maine Battery," in *Maine at Gettysburg*, 84–85; Bowden and Ward, *Last Chance for Victory*, 173; Donald J. Frey, *Longstreet's Assault—Pickett's Charge: The Lost Record of Pickett's Wounded* (Shippensburg, PA: White Mane Books, 2000), 45–46; Perrin to Bonham (July 29, 1863), in Bonham, "A Little More Light on Gettysburg," 522; "Report of Col. William W. Robinson, Seventh Wisconsin Infantry" (November 18, 1863), in *O.R.*, series one, 27 (pt. 1): 280; B. F. Brown, "McGowan's South Carolina Brigade in the Battle of Gettysburg," *Confederate Veteran* 31 (February 1923), 51.

6. Brown, "Some Recollections of Gettysburg," 53; George F. McFarland, "151st Regiment Infantry" (July 1, 1888), in *Pennsylvania at Gettysburg*, 2:770; Smith, *John Burns*, 63–71; "Extract from Chapter 9 of Caldwell's History of Gregg's (McGowan's) Brigade, Battle of Gettysburg, July 1, 1863," Edward N. Whittier to J. B. Bachelder (July 16, 1863), McFarland to Bachelder (March 16, 1864), and John A. Leach to Bachelder (September 12, 1882) in *Bachelder Papers*, 1:26–27, 83, 90–91, 301; 2:903; "Report of Col. Henry A. Morrow, Twenty-fourth Michigan Infantry" (February 22, 1864), and "Reports of Brig. Gen. Henry J. Hunt, U.S. Army" (September 27, 1863), in *O.R.*, series one, 27 (pt. 1):231, 268–69; Nolan, *The Iron Brigade*, 247; Tomasak, "The 143rd Pennsylvania Volunteer Regiment," 52; James Stewart, "Battery B, 4th United States Artillery at Gettysburg," in W. H. Chamberlin, ed., *Sketches of War History, 1861–1865: Papers Read Before the Ohio Commandery of the Military Order of the Loyal Legion of the United States, 1890–1896* (Cincinnati: Robert Clarke, 1896), 4:186–87; Smith, *History of the Seventy-Sixth Regiment, New York Volunteers*, 241; Hassler, *Crisis at the Crossroads*, 121–24; Mahood, *General Wadsworth*, 176; E. P. Halstead, "The First Day of the Battle of Gettysburg," 8–9.

7. Doubleday, *Chancellorsville and Gettysburg*, 147–48; Halstead, "The First Day of the Battle of Gettysburg," 7–8; Col. George H. Chapman [3rd Indiana Cavalry] to J. B. Bachelder (March 30, 1864), in *Bachelder Papers*, 1:130–31; Brown, *A Colonel at Gettysburg and Spotsylvania*, 214–15; Longacre, *General John Buford*, 198, 199.

8. "Mrs. Joseph [Harriet] Bayley's Story of the Battle," Gettysburg National Military Park (GNMP hereafter), Library Vertical Files; Tyson to Noble D. Preston (January 16, 1884), in "A Refugee from Gettysburg," ed. William McKenna, *Civil War Times Illustrated* 27 (November–December 1989), 73–74; E. S. Breidenbaugh, ed., *The Pennsylvania College Book, 1832–1882* (Philadelphia: Lutheran Publication Society, 1882), 270; Jacobs, *Lincoln's Gettysburg World-Message* (Philadelphia: United Lutheran Publication House, 1919), 31; Colver, "Reminiscences of the Battle of Gettysburg," *1902 Spectrum* (Gettysburg College Yearbook, Special Collections, Musselman Library, Gettysburg College), 179–80; Sheldon, *When the Smoke Cleared at Gettysburg*, 61; Frassanito, *Early Photography at Gettysburg*, 83; Skelly, *A Boy's Experiences During the Battle of Gettysburg* (Hershey, PA: Gary T. Hawbaker,

1932), 10; McCreary, "Gettysburg: A Boy's Experience of the Battle," *McClure's Magazine*
33 (July 1909), 244; Bennett, *Days of "Uncertainty and Dread,"* 20–24.

9. Sheldon, *When the Smoke Cleared at Gettysburg*, 61; Henry Eyster Jacobs, "Gettysburg
Fifty Years Ago," *The Lutheran* (July 24, 1913); Linda G. Black, "War Comes to Professor
Michael Jacobs," *Gettysburg Magazine* 6 (January 1992), 99, 101; Watkins, "Gettysburg
War Incidents," *1902 Spectrum*, 182; Samuel G. Hefelbower, *The History of Gettysburg
College, 1832–1932* (Gettysburg: Gettysburg College, 1932), 205; Michael A. Dreese, *The
Hospital on Seminary Ridge at the Battle of Gettysburg* (Jefferson, NC: McFarland, 2002),
67; "Henry Lewis Baugher, Sr., D.D.," in Jens Christian Jensson, *American Lutheran Biog-
raphies; or, Historical Notices of over Three Hundred and Fifty Leading Men of the American
Lutheran Church* (Milwaukee: A. Houtkamp & Son, 1890), 63–65; H. E. Jacobs, *Lincoln's
Gettysburg World-Message*, 36; Catherine Mary White Foster, "Battle of Gettysburg: A
Citizen's Eyewitness Account," Adams County Historical Society; M. Jacobs, *Notes on
the Rebel Invasion of Maryland and Pennsylvania*, 25; David Garber, in "Around College
During the Battle," *Pennsylvania College Monthly* 1 (December 1877), 297.

10. Salome Myers, in *The Ties of the Past: The Gettysburg Diaries of Salome Myers Stewart,
1854–1922*, ed. Sarah Sites Rodgers (Gettysburg: Thomas Publications, 1995), xxx; Kirby,
"A Boy Spy in Dixie," *National Tribune* (July 5, 1888); Sidney G. Cooke, "The First Day
at Gettysburg" (November 4, 1897), in *War Talks in Kansas*, 283–84; Cole, *Command and
Communication Frictions in the Gettysburg Campaign*, 55; Jacobs, *Notes on the Rebel Invasion
of Maryland and Pennsylvania*, 26.

11. Dawes, "With the Sixth Wisconsin at Gettysburg," 379–80; Hartwell Osborn, *Trials and
Triumphs: The Record of the Fifty-fifth Ohio Volunteer Infantry* (Chicago: A. C. McClurg,
1904), 97; *Reminiscences of Carl Schurz*, 3:12–13; Doubleday, *Chancellorsville and Gettys-
burg*, 150; Cheney, *History of the Ninth Regiment, New York Volunteer Cavalry*, 113; Lt. Col.
Edward S. Salmon, "Gettysburg" (January 17, 1912), in *Civil War Papers of the California
Commandery of the Military Order of the Loyal Legion of the United States*, 398–99; Kirby,
"A Boy Spy in Dixie," *National Tribune* (July 5, 1888); Albert Rowe Barlow, *Company G: A
Record of the Services of One Company of the 157th N.Y. Volunteers*, 129–30; Venner, *The 19th
Indiana Infantry at Gettysburg*, 89–90; Cook, "Personal Reminiscences of Gettysburg,"
328–29.

12. In the years following the battle, 1st Corps and 11th Corps veterans would freely accuse
each other of having been more demoralized and disorderly than the other. A surgeon in
the 6th Wisconsin, who had set up shop in the Adams County Court House at Baltimore
and High streets, declared that the 11th Corps "fled for dear life, forming a funnel-shaped
tail, extending to the town. . . . I did not see an officer attempt to rally them or check
them in their headlong retreat." Another Iron Brigade surgeon, Jacob Ebersole of the 19th
Indiana, opened David McConaughy's railroad sheds for use as a hospital, then stopped in
amazement to see the 11th Corps "falling back in utter confusion . . . the colors trailing in
the dust, and our men falling on every side." Men in "Robinson's division have a very vivid
remembrance of a division of the Eleventh Corps throwing away its guns and manifest-
ing intense anxiety to regain the charming shelter of Cemetery Hill." Officers in Schimmelpfennig's brigade as much as admitted that "the greatest confusion reigned" in the 11th
Corps, to the point where the "retreat became a rout" that reminded them all too keenly of
their Chancellorsville disgrace two months before. The Confederates, meanwhile, debated
which rebel regiment was the first to set foot in the town in pursuit. Officers in both the
1st and 14th South Carolina, from Hill's corps, claimed to have the honors of conquest.
Washington Shooter of the 1st South Carolina saw "the Yankees running in wild disorder
and everything went merry as a marriage bell"; they were just as insistently contradicted by

the 3rd Alabama in Rodes' division, claiming that they were "the first troops to enter the town," and by the 4th North Carolina in Ramseur's brigade, who asserted that "we were the first to enter the town of Gettysburg, and halted to rest on the road leading out toward the west." See Salmon, "Gettysburg," 399; Cook, "Personal Reminiscences of Gettysburg," 329; Cooke, "The First Day of Gettysburg," 284; Herdegen and Beaudot, *In the Bloody Railroad Cut at Gettysburg,* 221–23; Thomas Chamberlin, "150th Regiment Infantry" (September 11, 1889), *Pennsylvania at Gettysburg,* 2:759; Scott A. Richardson, "Col. Henry A. Morrow, 24th Michigan," *Gettysburg Magazine* 37 (January 2008), 36–37; Bennett, *Days of "Uncertainty and Dread,"* 30–31; Chamberlin, *History of the One Hundred and Fiftieth Regiment,* 136; Sgt. William Ramsey to J. B. Bachelder (May 7, 1883), in *Bachelder Papers,* 2:958; Butts, *A Gallant Captain of the Civil War,* 76–77; "United at Gettysburg," *New York Times* (July 3, 1888).

13. McCreary, "Gettysburg: A Boy's Experience of the Battle," 245; *Reminiscences of Carl Schurz,* 3:18–19; Slade and Alexander, *Firestorm at Gettysburg,* 64; Michael A. Dreese, "The 151st Pennsylvania Volunteers at Gettysburg: July 1, 1863," *Gettysburg Magazine* 23 (January 2001), 65; "At Gettysburg—First Day's Work of the Eleventh Corps," *National Tribune* (December 12, 1889); Pula, "The Fifth German Rifles at Gettysburg," *Gettysburg Magazine* 37 (January 2008), 56, 59; Brown, *A Colonel at Gettysburg and Spotsylvania,* 223–24; Sheldon, *When the Smoke Cleared at Gettysburg,* 66, 67, 70; Cook, "A Day at Gettysburg," *National Tribune* (April 7, 1898); Chaplain Charles M. Blake to J. B. Bachelder (June 14, 1882), in *Bachelder Papers,* 2:888; "Colonel Fowler's Recollections of Gettysburg" (July 28, 1863), in *History of the Fighting Fourteenth,* 136; Bennett, *Days of "Uncertainty and Dread,"* 31–33; "Report of Capt. John E. Cook, Seventy-sixth New York Infantry" (July 11, 1863), in *O.R.,* series one, 27 (pt. 1):286; Vautier, *History of the 88th Pennsylvania,* 149; John C. Robinson, "The First Corps—Its Important Services at the Battle of Gettysburg," *National Tribune* (April 21, 1887).

14. Coffin, *The Boys of '61,* 290; Kiefer, *History of the One Hundred and Fifty-third Regiment,* 79; Charles Wainwright, diary entry for July 1, 1863, in *A Diary of Battle,* 238; Harry E. Pfanz, *Gettysburg—The First Day* (Chapel Hill: University of North Carolina Press, 2001), 335.

15. Howard, *Autobiography,* 1:419; Bucholz, *Moltke and the German Wars,* 124; Charles A. L. Totten, *Strategos: A Series of American Games of War, Based upon Military Principles and Designed for the Assistance of Both Beginners and Advanced Students* (New York: D. Appleton, 188), 170–73; Nolan, *The Iron Brigade,* 256; Bowden and Ward, *Last Chance for Victory,* 195–96. There is as much uncertainty about the last Union soldier or regiment to clear the town as there is about the first Confederates to enter it. Edward Salmon of the 82nd Illinois declared in 1912 that "the regiment under my command was the last troops to ascend Cemetery Hill" on July 1st. Abner Doubleday is sometimes described as the last general officer out of the town, "as cool and, except for his flushed face and bad humor, as easy in his style that dreadful afternoon as I have seen him since on ordinary occasions." The honors for the last officer to bring up the rear have been claimed for Capt. James D. Wood, of the Iron Brigade staff, "making every effort to keep the ranks closed up in the different Columns, to prevent confusion." See Edward Salmon, "Gettysburg" (January 17, 1912), in *Civil War Papers of the California and the Oregon Commandery,* 399; Kirby, "A Boy Spy in Dixie," *National Tribune* (July 5, 1888); and Charles A. Stevens, *Berdan's United States Sharpshooters,* 295.

16. Howard, *Autobiography,* 1:419; Howard, "Campaign and Battle of Gettysburg, June and July, 1863," *Atlantic Monthly* 38 (July 1876), 58; Kirby, "A Boy Spy in Dixie," *National Tribune* (July 19, 1888); Charles H. Howard, "First Day at Gettysburg, 258–59; Howard, interview with Alexander Kelly (December 11, 1905), in *Generals in Bronze,* 181; Hart-

well Osborn, *Trials and Triumphs: The Record of the Fifty-Fifth Ohio Volunteer Infantry* (Chicago: A. C. McClurg, 1904), 98; "Thursday's Doubtful Issue—Friday's Victory" (July 4, 1863), in *A Radical View: The "Agate" Dispatches of Whitelaw Reid, 1861–1865*, ed. James G. Smart (Memphis, TN: Memphis State University Press, 1976), 2:51; E. C. Culp, "Gettysburg—Reminiscences of the Great Fight," *National Tribune* (March 19, 1885); Greene, "From Chancellorsville to Cemetery Hill: O. O. Howard and Eleventh Corps Leadership," in *The First Day at Gettysburg*, ed. Gallagher, 70.

17. Meade to Halleck (July 1, 1863) and Howard to Meade (July 1, 1863), in *O.R.*, series one, 27 (pt. 1):72, 696; Hancock, "Gettysburg: Reply to General Howard," *The Galaxy* 22 (December 1876), 822, 823; Charles Howard, "First Day at Gettysburg," 262–63; Carpenter, "General O. O. Howard at Gettysburg," *Civil War History*, 9 (September 1963), 269–70, 276; Dougherty, *Stone's Brigade and the Fight for the McPherson Farm*, 103.

18. Hancock, "Gettysburg: Reply to General Howard," 822–23, 829–30; Howard, "Campaign and Battle of Gettysburg," *Atlantic Monthly* 38 (July 1876), 59, 60–61; Pfanz, *Gettysburg—The First Day*, 338–39; Walker, *General Hancock*, 108; E. C. Culp, "Gettysburg—Reminiscences of the Great Fight," *National Tribune* (March 19, 1885); "Testimony of Major General W. S. Hancock" (March 22, 1864), in *Report of the Joint Committee on the Conduct of the War*, 4:405.

19. E. P. Halstead, "The First Day of the Battle of Gettysburg," 6–7; Greene, "From Chancellorsville to Cemetery Hill," in *The First Day at Gettysburg*, 85–86.

20. Walker, *General Hancock*, 111–12; Cooke, "The First Day at Gettysburg," 284–85; Smith, "Recollections of Gettysburg" (1894), in *War Papers Read Before the Commandery of the State of Michigan*, 2:300; "Reports of Maj. Gen. Abner Doubleday, U.S. Army" (December 14, 1863), in *O.R.*, series one, 27 (pt. 1):252; Mahood, *General Wadsworth*, 180; John Archer, *"The Hour Was One of Horror": East Cemetery Hill at Gettysburg* (Gettysburg: Thomas Publications, 1997), 9, 11; Carpenter, "General O. O. Howard at Gettysburg," 274–75. Hancock also gave direct orders, bypassing both Doubleday and Howard, to the 55th Ohio (which was already on Cemetery Hill, as part of Orland Smith's reserve brigade), to Michael Weidrich's 11th Corps battery, and to Stewart's 4th U.S. Artillery battery, from the 1st Corps; see Osborn, *Trials and Triumphs*, 97, Weidrich to J. B. Bachelder (January 20, 1886), in *Bachelder Papers*, 2:1182, and Stewart, "Battery B, 4th United States Artillery at Gettysburg," in *Sketches of War History*, 4:189–90; Hancock to Fitz Lee (January 17, 1878), in "Review of the First Two Days' Operations at Gettysburg," *SHSP* 5 (April 1878), 168, 169.

21. Winfield Scott Hancock, "Gettysburg: Reply to General Howard," *The Galaxy* 22 (December 1876), 830; Howard to Meade (July 1, 1863), in *O.R.*, series one, 27 (pt. 1):696–97.

22. Edmund R. Brown, *The Twenty-Seventh Indiana Volunteer Infantry in the War of the Rebellion, 1861 to 1865* (Monticello, IN: privately printed, 1899), 365; C. H. Slocum, *Life and Services of Major-General Henry Warner Slocum*, 102; Julian Wisner Hinkley, *A Narrative of Service with the Third Wisconsin Infantry* (Madison: Wisconsin History Commission, 1912), 82; Doubleday, *Chancellorsville and Gettysburg*, 137; George Thomas Stevens, *Three Years in the Sixth Corps: A Concise Narrative of Events in the Army of the Potomac from 1861 to the Close of the Rebellion, April, 1865* (Albany: S. R. Gray, 1866), 244; E. C. Culp, *The 25th Ohio Vet. Vol. Infantry in the War for the Union* (Topeka: Geo. W. Crane, 1885), 78–79; Venner, *The 19th Indiana Infantry at Gettysburg*, 93; "Report of Col. James L. Selfridge, Forty-Sixth Pennsylvania Infantry" (July 18, 1863), in *O.R.*, series one, 27 (pt. 1):803; Toombs, *New Jersey Troops in the Gettysburg Campaign*, 187; John Richards Boyle, *Soldiers True: The Story of the One Hundred and Eleventh Regiment, Pennsylvania Veteran Volunteers* (New York: Eaton & Mains, 1903), 117–18; Cooke, "The First Day at Gettysburg," 284–85, 286; Tevis and Marquis, *History of the Fighting Fourteenth*, 90; Frey, *Longstreet's Assault*, 48;

Reminiscences of Carl Schurz, 3:15; Matthew W. Hutchinson, "To Gettysburg and Beyond: A Vermont Captain's Letters to His Wife," *Gettysburg Magazine* 25 (July 2001), 88; J. N. Hubbard, "Gettysburg: Wadsworth's Division on Culp's Hill," *National Tribune* (March 15, 1915).

23.   Hancock, "Gettysburg: Reply to General Howard," 826; Gambone, *Hancock at Gettysburg*, 58, 59, 64, 65; "Testimony of Major General W. S. Hancock" (March 22, 1864), in *Report of the Joint Committee on the Conduct of the War*, 4:405; Stewart, "Battery B, 4th United States Artillery at Gettysburg," 189–90; Doubleday, in *Letters and Addresses Contributed at a General Meeting of the Military Service Institution . . . in Memory of Winfield Scott Hancock* (New York: G. P. Putnam's, 1886), 20; "Reports of Maj. Gen. Abner Doubleday, U.S. Army" (December 14, 1863) and "Reports of Maj. Gen. Henry W. Slocum" (August 23, 1863), in *O.R.*, series one, 27 (pt. 1):252, 758; Butts, *A Gallant Captain of the Civil War*, 83.

24.   Hancock to Fitz Lee, in "Review of the First Two Days' Operations at Gettysburg," 168, 169; *Reminiscences of Carl Schurz*, 3:19–20; Boyle, *Soldiers True: The Story of the One Hundred and Eleventh Regiment Pennsylvania Veteran Volunteers*, 117–18; Samuel H. Hurst, *Journal-History of the Seventy-third Ohio Volunteer Infantry* (Chillicothe, OH, 1866), 67–68.

CHAPTER THIRTEEN   *If the enemy is there to-morrow, we must attack him*

1.   Mills, *History of the 16th North Carolina Regiment*, 36–37; W. Gordon McCabe, "Annual Reunion of Pegram Battalion Association" (May 21, 1886), *SHSP* 14 (January–December 1886), 15; J. Coleman Alderson, "Lee and Longstreet at Gettysburg,' *Confederate Veteran* 10 (October 1904), 488; John C. McInnis, "Saw Gen. Lee on First Day at Gettysburg," *Confederate Veteran* 21 (May 1913), 203; John Purifoy, "The Battle of Gettysburg, July 2," *Confederate Veteran* 31 (July 1923), 252.

2.   "Reports of Brig. Gen. William N. Pendleton, C.S. Army" (September 12, 1863) and "Report of Lieut. Gen. Ambrose P. Hill, C.S. Army" (November, 1863), in *O.R.*, series one, 27 (pt. 2):349, 607; Long, *Memoirs of Robert E. Lee: His Military and Personal History*, 277; Bowden and Ward, *Last Chance for Victory*, 177–79, 180; David Callihan, "Elusive Victory: Robert E. Lee at Gettysburg," *Gettysburg Magazine* 28 (January 2003), 11–13; Robertson, *General A. P. Hill*, 213.

3.   McIntosh, "Review of the Gettysburg Campaign by One Who Participated Therein," *SHSP* 37 (January–December 1909), 119; Spencer Glasgow Welch, *A Confederate Surgeon's Letters to His Wife* (New York: Neale Publishing, 1911), 67; Perrin to Milledge L. Bonham (July 29, 1863), in Bonham, "A Little More Light on Gettysburg," 523; "Richmond Inquirer Account" (July 8, 1863), in *Rebellion Record*, ed. Moore (1864), 4:109; Gallagher, "Confederate Corps Leadership on the First Day," in *The First Day at Gettysburg*, 46; Bowden & Ward, *Last Chance for Victory*, 180, 192, 194.

4.   McCreary, "Gettysburg: A Boy's Experience of the Battle," *McClure's Magazine*, 245–46; J. Warren Jackson to R. Stark Jackson (July 20, 1863), in Merl E. Reed, ed., "The Gettysburg Campaign—A Louisiana Lieutenant's Eye-Witness Account," in *Pennsylvania History* 30 (April 1963), 188; Meredith, "The First Day at Gettysburg," *SHSP* 24 (January–December 1896), 185–86; Seymour, diary entry for July 1, 1863, in *Civil War Memoirs of William J. Seymour*, 71, 72; Louis Léon, *Diary of a Tar Heel Confederate Soldier*, 34–35; Sgt. J. A. Leach to J. B. Bachelder (June 2, 1884), in *Bachelder Papers*, 2:1047; Clark, *North Carolina Troops*, 1:171, 254, 276–77, 312.

5. Hollinger, "The Battle of Gettysburg," 168–69; Nellie E. Auginbaugh, *Personal Experiences of a Young Girl at the Battle of Gettysburg* (Washington, DC: L. D. Leeds, 1926), 7; Slade and Alexander, *Firestorm at Gettysburg*, 93.

6. Clark, *North Carolina Troops*, 2:312; Robert McLean, "A Boy in Gettysburg—1863," *Gettysburg Compiler* (June 30, 1909); Bennett, *Days of "Uncertainty and Dread,"* 29; J. Coleman Alderson, "Lee and Longstreet at Gettysburg," *Confederate Veteran* 10 (October 1904), 488.

7. Isaac Trimble, "The Battle and Campaign of Gettysburg," *SHSP* 26 (January–December, 1898), 123; *Campbell Brown's Civil War*, 211, 332–33; Gallagher, "Confederate Corps Leadership," 39–40, 50–51; R. H. Early, *Lieutenant General Jubal Anderson Early*, 269; Smith, "General Lee at Gettysburg," *SHSP* 33 (January–February 1905), 144–45; Douglas C. Haines, " 'Lights Mingled with Shadows': Lt. Gen. Richard S. Ewell—July 1, 1863," *Gettysburg Magazine* 45 (July 2011), 51–52.

8. Taylor, "Memorandum by Colonel Walter H. Taylor, of General Lee's Staff," in *SHSP* 4 (July 1877), 83; Taylor, *Four Years with General Lee*, 99; Thomas, *Robert E. Lee*, 295–96; Smith, "General Lee at Gettysburg," 144–45; Casdorph, *Confederate General R. S. Ewell*, 256–58; "Draft of Letter to Gen. Doubleday" (December 6, 1881), in *Campbell Brown's Civil War*, 332–33; Pfanz, *Richard S. Ewell*, 308; Haines, " 'Lights Mingled with Shadows': Lt. Gen. Richard S. Ewell—July 1, 1863," 49.

9. Maj. E. C. Gordon, "Controversy About Gettysburg," *Confederate Veteran* (October 1912), 465; Trimble, *The Battle and Campaign of Gettysburg*, 123–24; Casdorph, *Confederate General R. S. Ewell*, 257–58; "Copy of a Portion of Capt. Turner's Memoranda," in *Campbell Brown's Civil War*, 321; "Letter of Maj. Gen. Isaac R. Trimble" to J. B. Bachelder (February 8, 1883), in *Bachelder Papers*, 2:930–31; Trimble, diary entry for July 1, 1863, in "The Civil War Diary of General Isaac Ridgeway Trimble," ed. W. S. Myers, *Maryland Historical Magazine* 17 (March 1922), 11; Gallagher, "Confederate Corps Leadership," 39–40; Bowden and Ward, *Last Chance for Victory*, 191, 241–43, 244–45; Pfanz, *Richard S. Ewell*, 314.

10. Frank C. Wilson, "Blunder in Battle of Gettysburg," *Confederate Veteran* (September 1912), 417; Bowden and Ward, *Last Chance for Victory*, 182, 185–86; Lafayette McLaws, "The Second Day at Gettysburg," *Philadelphia Weekly Times* (August 4, 1886); Seymour, diary entry for July 1–2, 1863, in *Civil War Memoirs of William J. Seymour*, 72

11. Samuel Pickens, in *Voices from Company D*, 182–83.

12. Martin L. Stoever letter (September 30, 1863), in Timothy H. Smith, *The Story of Lee's Headquarters, Gettysburg, Pennsylvania* (Gettysburg: Thomas Publications, 1995), 42.

13. John C. McInnis, "Saw Gen. Lee on First Day at Gettysburg," *Confederate Veteran* 21 (May 1913), 203; Hollinger, "Some Personal Recollections of the Battle of Gettysburg," 7; Early, *Lieutenant General Jubal Anderson Early*, 268, 271; Early, *The Campaigns of Gen. Robert E. Lee: An Address* (Baltimore: John Murphy, 1872), 34; John Purifoy, "The Battle of Gettysburg, July 2," *Confederate Veteran* 31 (July 1923), 52; William C. Oates, *The War Between the Union and the Confederacy, and Its Lost Opportunities* (New York: Neale Publishing, 1905), 204; Walter Taylor, "The Campaign in Pennsylvania," in *Annals of the War*, 305–6; John Cabell Early, "A Southern Boy's Experience at Gettysburg," *Journal of the Military Service Institution of the United States* 48 (May–June 1911), 420–21; John Imboden, "Lee at Gettysburg" (1871), in Kathleen Diffley, ed., *To Live and Die: Collected Stories of the Civil War, 1861–1876* (Durham, NC: Duke University Press, 2002), 164; Piston, *Lee's Tarnished Lieutenant*, 52, 54; *Campbell Brown's Civil War*, 218.

14. "Domestic Items," *Christian Recorder* (September 26, 1863); "Gettysburg After Twenty Years," *National Tribune* (May 14, 1885); Collins, *Major General Robert E. Rodes*, 280;

Jacobs, *Notes on the Rebel Invasion*, 39; Thomas Espy Causby, "Storming the Stone Fence at Gettysburg," *SHSP* 29 (January–December 1901), 340; Jubal Early to J. B. Bachelder (March 23, 1876), in *Bachelder Papers*, 1:460; Swallow, "The First Day at Gettysburg," *Southern Bivouac* 4 (December 1885), 443; William J. Seymour, diary entry for July 1–2, 1863, in *Civil War Memoirs*, 73; Wilson, "Blunder in Battle of Gettysburg," 417.

15. Sharpe (June 25, 1889), in Chaplain Cornelius van Santvoord, *The 120th Regiment, New York State Volunteers: A Narrative of Its Service in the War for the Union* (Rondout, NY: Kingston Freeman, 1894), 223–24, and in "Dedication of Monument—120th Regiment of Infantry," in *New York at Gettysburg*, 2:816; Meade, *Life and Letters of George Gordon Meade*, 2:38; Hancock to Meade (July 1, 1863), Meade to Hancock and Doubleday (July 1, 1863), "Reports of Maj. Gen. Winfield S. Hancock" and "Reports of Maj. Gen. George G. Meade (October 1, 1863), in *O.R.*, series one, 27 (pt. 1):115, 366, 369, and (pt. 3):466; Jordan, *Winfield Scott Hancock*, 86; *Hancock the Superb*, 137–38; Cleaves, *Meade of Gettysburg*, 137–38; Gambone, *Hancock at Gettysburg*, 72.

16. Butterfield to Sedgwick (July 2, 1863), in *O.R.*, series one, 27 (pt. 3):484–85.

17. Sharpe (June 25, 1889), in van Santvoord, *The 120th Regiment*, 224; *Reminiscences of Carl Schurz*, 3:20–21.

18. Meade to Halleck (July 1, 1863), Daniel Butterfield to Commanding General at Emmitsburg (July 1, 1863), and Meade to Lorenzo Thomas (October 1, 1863), in *O.R.*, series one, 27 (pt. 1):71–72, and (pt. 3):467; O. O. Howard interview with Alexander Kelly (April 15, 1899), in *Generals in Bronze*, 176–77; Howard, *Autobiography*, 1:423–24.

19. Wainwright, diary entry for July 2, 1863, in *A Diary of Battle*, 241–42; Frey, *Longstreet's Assault—Pickett's Charge*, 55; C. H. Howard, "First Day at Gettysburg," 264; Howard, *Autobiography*, 1:424; Sauers, *A Caspian Sea of Ink*, 117; Doubleday, *Chancellorsville and Gettysburg*, 156; *Reminiscences of Carl Schurz*, 3:21; Trowbridge, "The Field of Gettysburg," *Atlantic Monthly* 16 (November 1865), 623.

20. Hancock to Meade (July 1, 1863) and Seth Williams to John Sedgwick (July 1, 1863), in *O.R.*, series one, 27 (pt. 1):366, and (pt. 3):465; Doubleday, *Chancellorsville and Gettysburg*, 134; Barthel, *Abner Doubleday*, 154.

21. Frank Augustin O'Reilly, *The Fredericksburg Campaign: Winter War on the Rappahannock* (Baton Rouge: Louisiana State University Press, 2003), 469–70, 489; Tagg, *The Generals of Gettysburg*, 12–13; Taaffe, *Commanding the Army of the Potomac*, 116; Wainwright, diary entry for July 2, 1863, in *a Day of Battle*, 247; John S. D. Cook, "Personal Reminiscences of Gettysburg" (December 12, 1903), in *War Talks in Kansas*, 332; "Testimony of General A. P. Howe" (March 3, 1864), in *Report of the Joint Committee on the Conduct of the War*, 1:313.

22. Gibbon, *Personal Recollections of the Civil War*, 144–45; John Michael Priest, *Into the Fight: Pickett's Charge at Gettysburg* (Shippensburg, PA: White Mane Books, 1998), 45; Doubleday, *Chancellorsville and Gettysburg*, 156; Seth Williams and Daniel Butterfield to Henry Slocum (July 2, 1863), in *O.R.*, series one, 27 (pt. 3):486–87; George A. Thayer, "On the Right at Gettysburg," *National Tribune* (July 24, 1902); Storrs, *The "Twentieth Connecticut": A Regimental History*, 78; Troy Harman, "The Gap: Meade's July 2 Offensive Plan," in *"The Most Shocking Battle I Have Ever Witnessed": The Second Day at Gettysburg* (Gettysburg: Gettysburg National Military Park, 2008), 84–85, 88; Fox, "Slocum and His Men: A History of the Twelfth and Twentieth Army Corps," 176; Peter C. Vermilyea, "The Pipe Creek Effect: How Meade's Pipe Creek Circular Affected the Battle of Gettysburg," *Gettysburg Magazine* 42 (July 2010), 36, 37; George Meade, Jr., *Did General Meade Desire a Retreat at the Battle of Gettysburg?* (Philadelphia: Porter & Coates, 1883), 4–5.

23. Woodward, *Our Campaigns; or, The Marches, Bivouacs, Battles, Incidents of Camp Life and History of Our Regiment*, 263; E. J. Allen, *Under the Maltese Cross, Antietam to Appomattox:*

The Loyal Uprising in Western Pennsylvania, 1861–1865 (Pittsburgh: Werner Co., 1912), 162, 165; Robert G. Carter, "Reminiscences of the Battle and Campaign of Gettysburg," in *War Papers Read Before the Commandery of the State of Maine*, 2:164; Tilney, *My Life in the Army,* 47; John L. Smith, *History of the 118th Pennsylvania Volunteers, Corn Exchange Regiment, from Their First Engagement at Antietam to Appomattox* (Philadelphia: J. L. Smith, 1905), 233, 236, 238; Mary Genevie Brainard, *Campaigns of the One Hundred and Forty-Sixth Regiment, New York State Volunteers* (New York: G. P. Putnam's Sons, 1915), 110–11; Theodore Gerrish, "The Battle of Gettysburg," *National Tribune* (November 23, 1882); Judson, *History of the Eighty-Third Regiment Pennsylvania Volunteers,* 124; Capt. Dudley H. Chase, "Gettysburg," in *War Papers Read Before the Indiana Commandery of the Military Order of the Loyal Legion of the United States* (Indianapolis: Indiana Commandery, 1898), 299; "Testimony of Brigadier General S. W. Crawford" (April 27, 1864), in *Report of the Joint Committee on the Conduct of the War*, 4:469; Harman, "The Gap: Meade's July 2 Offensive Plan," in *"The Most Shocking Battle I Have Ever Witnessed,"* 82; Capt. H. N. Minnigh, *History of Company K, 1st (Inft.) Penn'a Reserves* (Duncansville: Home Print Publisher, 1891), 23.

24. Joseph Keith Newell, *"Ours": Annals of the 10th Regiment, Massachusetts Volunteers in the Rebellion* (Springfield, MA: C. A. Nichols, 1875), 221–22; Hyde, "Recollections of the Battle of Gettysburg," in *War Papers Read Before the Commandery of the State of Maine*, 1:194; James S. Anderson, "The March of the Sixth Corps to Gettysburg," in *War Papers Read Before the Commandery of the State of Wisconsin*, 4:78, 80; Hyde, *Following the Greek Cross*, 143–44; David A. Ward, " 'Sedgwick's Foot Cavalry': The March of the Sixth Corps to Gettysburg," *Gettysburg Magazine* 22 (July 2000), 60.

25. Nelson V. Hutchinson, *History of the Seventh Massachusetts Volunteer infantry in the War of the Rebellion of the Southern States Against Constitutional Authority* (Taunton, MA: Authority of the Regimental Association, 1890), 152–53; James Lorenzo Bowen, *History of the Thirty-Seventh Regiment, Mass. Volunteers, in the Civil War of 1861–1865* (Holyoke, MA: Clark W. Bryan & Co., 1884), 171, 174–75; George William Curtis, in Dwight C. Kilbourn, "Historical Address," *Dedication of the Equestrian Statue of Major-General John Sedgwick on the Battlefield of Gettysburg* (Hartford, CT, 1913), 56–57; George Thomas Stevens, *Three Years in the Sixth Corps: A Concise Narrative of Events in the Army of the Potomac from 1861 to the Close of the Rebellion, April, 1865* (Albany, NY: S. R. Gray, 1866), 240, 246; Abraham T. Brewer, *History [of the] Sixty-First Regiment, Pennsylvania Volunteers, 1861–1865, Under Authority of the Regimental Association* (Pittsburgh: Art Engraving & Printing, 1911), 61.

26. "Reports of Maj. Gen. Henry W. Slocum" (August 23, 1863) and Slocum to Meade (July 2, 1863), in *O.R.*, series one, 27 (pt. 1):759, and (pt. 3):487; Slocum, in "United at Gettysburg," *New York Times* (July 3, 1888); Meade, *Did General Meade Desire a Retreat at the Battle of Gettysburg*, 4–5; Harman, "The Gap: Meade's July 2 Offensive Plan," in *"The Most Shocking Battle I Have Ever Witnessed,"* 87–93.

27. Toombs, *New Jersey Troops in the Gettysburg Campaign*, 180–81; Asa W. Bartlett, *History of the Twelfth Regiment, New Hampshire Volunteers in the War of the Rebellion* (Concord, NH: Ira C. Evans, 1897), 119, 120; William B. Jordan, *Red Diamond Regiment: The 17th Maine Infantry, 1862–1865* (Shippensburg, PA: White Mane Books, 1996), 68, 70; Col. Thomas Rafferty, "Gettysburg" (November 7, 1883), in *Personal Recollections of the War of the Rebellion: Addresses Delivered Before the New York Commandery of the Loyal Legion of the United States, 1883–1891*, eds. J. G. Wilson and T. M. Coan (New York: privately printed, 1891), 4–5, 8; Sickles, "Further Recollections of Gettysburg," *North American Review* 152 (March 1891), 262; George Winslow, "On Little Round Top: The Position and Achievements of the First New York Volunteer Artillery," in *Gettysburg Sources*, 3:151–52; William E. Loring,

"On the Second Day—the 141st Pa. in the Gettysburg Battle," *National Tribune* (July 5, 1894); Blake, *Three Years in the Army of the Potomac*, 204; George Lewis, *The History of Battery E, First Regiment Rhode Island Light Artillery, in the War of 1861 and 1865, to Preserve the Union* (Providence, RI: Snow & Farnham, 1892), 192; Sgt. Henri Lefevre Brown, *History of the Third Regiment, Excelsior Brigade, 73rd New York Volunteer Infantry, 1861–1865* (Jamestown, NY: Journal Printing, 1902), 104.

28. Grant, in John Russell Young, *Around the World with General Grant: A Narrative of the Visit of General U. S. Grant, Ex-President of the United States, to Various Countries in Europe, Asia, and Africa, in 1877, 1878, 1879* (New York: American News, 1879), 2:353; Hotchkiss, diary entry for July 2, 1863, in *Make Me a Map of the Valley*, 157; Gary W. Gallagher, "'If the Enemy Is There, We Must Attack Him': R. E. Lee and the Second Day at Gettysburg," *Three Days at Gettysburg: Essays on Confederate and Union Leadership*, ed. G. W. Gallagher (Kent, OH: Kent State University Press, 1999), 124, 125.

29. William Swallow, "The First Day at Gettysburg," 443–44; D. Augustus Dickert, *History of Kershaw's Brigade* (Newberry, SC: Elbert Aull, 1899), 231; William Youngblood, "Unwritten History of the Gettysburg Campaign," *SHSP* 38 (January–December 1910), 313; Youngblood, "Personal Observations at Gettysburg," *Confederate Veteran* 19 (June 1911), 286; J. Coleman Anderson, "Lee and Longstreet at Gettysburg," *Confederate Veteran* 12 (October 1904), 488; Smith, "General Lee at Gettysburg," *SHSP* 33 (January–February 1905), 145, 146; Roger J. Greezicki, "Humbugging the Historian: A Reappraisal of Longstreet at Gettysburg," *Gettysburg Magazine* 6 (January 1992), 63.

30. Swinton, *Campaigns of the Army of the Potomac: A Critical History of Operations in Virginia, Maryland and Pennsylvania, from the Commencement to the Close of the War, 1861–1865* (revised ed., New York: Charles Scribners, 1882), 340; Early, *The Campaigns of Gen. Robert E. Lee*, 34; Glenn Tucker, *Lee and Longstreet at Gettysburg*, 5–6, 12; David Blight, "The Lost Cause and Causes Not Lost," in Janice Radway et al., eds., *American Studies: An Anthology* (Malden, MA: Wiley/Blackwell, 2009), 531; "Reports of Brig. Gen. William N. Pendleton, C.S. Army" (September 12, 1863) and "Report of Maj. Gen. Jubal A. Early, C.S. Army" (August 22, 1863), in *O.R.*, series one, 27 (pt. 2):348–49, 471; Early, "A Review by General Early," *SHSP* 4 (December 1877), 268; Sears Wilson Cabell, *The "Bulldog" Longstreet at Gettysburg and Chickamauga* (Atlanta, GA: Ruralist Press, 1938), 6–7.

31. Longstreet, "Letter from General Longstreet," *SHSP* 5 (January–February 1878), 53; Longstreet, "Lee in Pennsylvania" and "The Mistakes of Gettysburg," in *Annals of the War*, 420–21, 619 (these were subsequently reprinted with some minor editorial additions by Longstreet in the *Southern Historical Society Papers*); Wert, *General James Longstreet*, 257; Longstreet, "Lee's Invasion of Pennsylvania," *The Century* 33 (February 1887), 626; Gallagher, *Lee and His Generals in War and Memory*, 49–50, 51, 55, 58–59; Jeffrey D. Wert, "James Longstreet and the Lost Cause," in *The Myth of the Lost Cause and Civil War History*, eds. Gary W. Gallagher and Alan Nolan (Bloomington: Indiana University Press, 130–32; John Newton interview with Alexander Kelly (October 31, 1879), in *Generals in Bronze*, 79.

32. "Letter from Gen. J. A. Early" (March 12, 1877), "Letter from General Fitz Lee" (March 7, 1877), and "Letter from General A. L. Long" (April 1877), in *SHSP* 4 (July–September 1877), 59–60, 63, 72, 123; Smith, "General Lee at Gettysburg," *SHSP* 33 (January–February 1905), 146; "Memoranda of Conversations Between General Robert E. Lee and William Preston Johnson," *Virginia Magazine of History and Biography* (*VMHB*, hereafter) 73 (October 1965), 478; Long, *Memoirs of Robert E. Lee*, 276–77; David Callihan, "Elusive Victory: Robert E. Lee at Gettysburg," *Gettysburg Magazine* 28 (January 2003), 15–16; Thomas Connelly and Barbara L. Bellows, *God and General Longstreet: The Lost Cause and the Southern Mind* (Baton Rouge: Louisiana State University Press, 1982), 32–36; Krick, *The Smoothbore Volley That Doomed the Confederacy*, 67–69; William W. Goldsborough,

"With Lee at Gettysburg," *Philadelphia Record* (July 10, 1900); A. L. Long, in "Causes of Lee's Defeat at Gettysburg" and "Letter from General C. M. Wilcox" (March 26, 1877), in *SHSP* 4 (August–September 1877), 67, 114.

33. Gilbert Moxley Sorrell, *Recollections of a Confederate Staff Officer* (New York: Neale Publishing, 1905),166–67; Fremantle, *Three Months in the Southern States,* 256; Piston, *Lee's Tarnished Lieutenant,* 52; Gallagher, "'If the Enemy Is There, We Must Attack Him': R. E. Lee and the Second Day at Gettysburg," in *Three Days at Gettysburg,* 122; J. W. Duke, "Mississippians at Gettysburg," *Confederate Veteran* 13 (May 1906), 217.

CHAPTER FOURTEEN *One of the bigger bubbles of the scum*

1. Thomas, *Robert E. Lee,* 297; James R. Johnson, in Zack C. Waters and James C. Edmonds, *A Small but Spartan Band: The Florida Brigade in Lee's Army of Northern Virginia* (Tuscaloosa: University of Alabama Press, 2010), 66; Thomas L. Elmore, "Torrid Heat and Blinding Rain: A Meteorological and Astronomical Chronology of the Gettysburg Campaign," *Gettysburg Magazine* 13 (July 1995), 12–13; "Report of Col. Robert McAllister, Eleventh New Jersey Infantry" (August 3, 1863), in *O.R.,* series one, 27 (pt. 1):552; Michael Jacobs, "Meterology of the Battle," *Gettysburg Magazine* 10 (January 1994), 121.

2. Samuel R. Johnston to Bishop George Peterkin, GNMP Vertical Files; David A. Powell, "A Reconnaissance Gone Awry: Capt. Samuel R. Johnston's Fateful Trip to Little Round Top," *Gettysburg Magazine* 23 (January 2001), 88–89.

3. LaFayette McLaws, "Gettysburg," *SHSP* 7 (February 1879), 67–68; Hood, *Advance and Retreat: Personal Experiences in the United States and Confederate Armies* (New Orleans: Hood Orphan Memorial Fund, 1880), 56–57; "Reports of Brig. Gen. William N. Pendleton, C.S. Army" (September 12, 1863), in *O.R.,* series one, 27 (pt. 2):349–50.

4. A. L. Long, in "Causes of Lee's Defeat at Gettysburg," in *SHSP* 4 (August 1877), 67; Doubleday, *Chancellorsville and Gettysburg,* 167; Hood, "Leading Confederates on the Battle of Gettysburg," *SHSP* 4 (October 1877), 147–48; William W. Chamberlaine, *Memoirs of the Civil War Between the Northern and Southern Sections of the United States of America, 1861–1865* (Washington, DC: Byron S. Adams, 1912), 68–69; Troy Harman, *Lee's Real Plan at Gettysburg* (Mechanicsburg, PA: Stackpole Books, 2003), 19.

5. Hood to Longstreet (June 28, 1875), in *Advance and Retreat,* 56–57; Bowden and Ward, *Last Chance for Victory,* 255; Robertson, *General A. P. Hill,* 216, 221–22; *From Huntsville to Appomattox: R. T. Coles's History of 4th Regiment, Alabama Volunteer Infantry, C.S.A., Army of Northern Virginia,* ed. Jeffrey Stocker (Knoxville: University of Tennessee Press, 1996), 224; Alexander, *Fighting for the Confederacy,* 235–36; "Letter from General E. P. Alexander" (March 17, 1877), *SHSP* 4 (September 1877), 101; "Report of Lieut. Gen. James Longstreet, C.S. Army" (July 27, 1863), in *O.R.,* series one, 27 (pt. 2):358.

6. Samuel R. Johnston to Bishop George Peterkin, Lafayette McLaws to James Longstreet (June 12, 1873), and Johnston to Lafayette McLaws (June 27, 1892), Participant Accounts [folder V5], GNMP Vertical Files; "Letter from General E. P. Alexander" (March 17, 1877), *SHSP* 4 (September 1877), 101; McLaws, "Gettysburg," *SHSP* 7 (February 1879), 68; James Power Smith, "General Lee at Gettysburg," 148; "Report of Lieut. Gen. James Longstreet, C.S. Army" (July 27, 1863), in *O.R.,* series one, 27 (pt. 2):358.

7. George T. Anderson to J. B. Bachelder (March 15, 1876), in *Bachelder Papers,* 1:449; "Report of Maj. Gen. Richard H. Anderson, C.S. Army" (August 7, 1863), in *O.R.,* series one, 27 (pt. 2):613; Brooks Simpson, "'If Properly Led': Command Relationships at Gettysburg," in *Civil War Generals in Defeat,* ed. Steven Woodworth (Lawrence: University Press of Kansas, 1999), 170, 171; Evander M. Law, "The Struggle for 'Round Top,'" in *Battles &*

Leaders, 3:319; Bowden and Ward, *Last Chance for Victory*, 372–73; D. Wyatt Aiken, "The Gettysburg Reunion: What Is Necessary and Proper for the South to Do" (June 21, 1882), in *Gettysburg Sources*, 2:173; Dickert, *History of Kershaw's Brigade*, 235–36; Warren Wilkinson and Steven E. Woodworth, *A Scythe of Fire: A Civil War Story of the Eighth Georgia Infantry Regiment* (New York: William Morrow, 2002), 230–31.

8. Alexander, *Military Memoirs of a Confederate*, 391.

9. McLaws, "The Second Day at Gettysburg" (August 4, 1886), in *Gettysburg Sources*, 3:140, and "Gettysburg," *SHSP* 7 (February 1879), 68–69; J. B. Kershaw to J. B. Bachelder (March 20, 1876), in *Bachelder Papers*, 1:454; "Report of Brig. Gen. J. B. Kershaw, C.S. Army" (October 1, 1863), in *O.R.*, series one, 27 (pt. 2):366–67; Kershaw, "Kershaw's Brigade at Gettysburg," and Longstreet, "Lee's Right Wing at Gettysburg," in *Battles & Leaders*, 3:331, 340; Max Wyckoff, *A History of the 3rd South Carolina Regiment: Lee's Reliables* (Wilmington, NC: Broadfoot Publishing, 2008), 168; Karlton D. Smith, " 'To Consider Every Contingency': Lt. Gen. James Longstreet, Capt. Samuel R. Johnston, and the Factors That Affected the Reconnaissance and Countermarch, July 2, 1863," in *The Second Day at Gettysburg* (Gettysburg, PA: GNMP, 2008), 109–11; Alexander, *Fighting for the Confederacy*, 236, and "Causes of the Confederate Defeat at Gettysburg," *SHSP* 4 (September 1877), 101.

10. William J. Hardee, *Rifle and Light Infantry Tactics: For the Exercise and Manoeuvres of Troops When Acting as Light Infantry or Riflemen* (Philadelphia: Lippincott, Grambo & Co., 1855), 2:48, 79–81; McLaws, "The Second Day at Gettysburg" (August 4, 1886), in *Gettysburg Sources*, 3:140–41; Longstreet, "Lee's Right Wing at Gettysburg," in *Battles & Leaders*, 3:340.

11. Gen. W. F. Perry, "The Devil's Den," *Confederate Veteran* 9 (April 1901), 161–62; James Johnson Kirkpatrick, diary entry for July 2, 1863, in *The 16th Mississippi*, 176; John H. Martin, "Accurate Historic Records," *Confederate Veteran* 12 (March 1904), 114; McLaws, "Gettysburg," *SHSP* 7 (February 1879), 49–50.

12. William Youngblood, "Unwritten History of the Gettysburg Campaign, *SHSP* 38 (January–December 1910), 315–16; Hood to Longstreet (June 28, 1875), in "Leading Confederates on the Battle of Gettysburg," *SHSP* 4 (October 1877), 149–50; Bowden and Ward, *Last Chance for Victory*, 257; Law, "The Struggle for 'Round Top,' " Longstreet, "Lee's Right Wing at Gettysburg," and Kershaw, "Kershaw's Brigade at Gettysburg," in *Battles & Leaders*, 3:320, 332, 340; Longstreet, "Lee in Pennsylvania," in *Annals of the War*, 423.

13. McLaws, "Gettysburg," *SHSP* 7 (February 1879), 70–71.

14. John Foster Young, *New Jersey and the Rebellion: A History of the Service of the Troops and People of New Jersey in Aid of the Union Cause* (Newark, NJ: Martin R. Dennis, 1868), 288.

15. Hessler, *Sickles at Gettysburg*, 1–3; Thomas Keneally, *American Scoundrel: The Life of the Notorious Civil War General Dan Sickles* (New York: Anchor Books, 2002), 127–28; G. W. D. Andrews to Sickles (August 13, 1858), in Daniel E. Sickles Papers, New-York Historical Society.

16. Hessler, *Sickles at Gettysburg*, 14, 17, 25, 27; "Speech of John Graham, Esq." (April 9, 1859), in *Trial of the Hon. Daniel E. Sickles for Shooting Philip Barton Key, Esq.* (New York: R. M. DeWitt, 1859), 31; Sears, *Controversies and Commanders*, 198–204; Sickles, "Service on Special Committee" (December 10, 1860), in *Congressional Globe*, 36th Congress, second session, 40.

17. W. A. Swanberg, *Sickles the Incredible* (New York: Scribners, 1956), 57; Henrik Hartog, "Lawyering, Husbands' Rights, and 'the Unwritten Law' in Nineteenth-Century America," *Journal of American History* 84 (June 1997), 70–71; Strong, diary entry for May 17, 1863, in *Diary of George Templeton Strong*, ed. Allan Nevins (New York: Macmillan, 1952),

3:323; Theodore Lyman, *Meade's Headquarters*, 60; "Biographical Sketch of Hon. D. E. Sickles," *Harper's Weekly* (April 9, 1859); "Report of Brig. Gen. Joseph Hooker, U.S. Army" (June 8, 1862), in *O.R.*, series one, 11 (pt. 1): 820; Kelly (June 30, 1879), in *Generals in Bronze*, 41; Steve Courtney, *Joseph Hopkins Twichell: The Life and Times of Mark Twain's Closest Friend* (Athens: University of Georgia Press, 2008), 62–63; Hanifen, *History of Battery B, First New Jersey Artillery*, 78.

18. Meade to Margaretta Meade (January 26, 1863), Meade Papers, HSP; Taaffe, *Commanding the Army of the Potomac*, 28; James Hessler, "Sickles and Meade Prior to Gettysburg," *Gettysburg Magazine* 41 (July 2009), 58; "Testimony of Major General Daniel Sickles" (February 26, 1864), in *Report of the Joint Committee on the Conduct of the War*, 4:295, 296–97; Eric Wittenberg, "The Truth About the Withdrawal of Brig. Gen. John Buford's Cavalry, July 2, 1863," *Gettysburg Magazine* 37 (January 2008), 73, 75; Howard, "Campaign and Battle of Gettysburg, June and July, 1863," *Atlantic Monthly* 38 (July 1876), 62; Edward J. Hagerty, *Collis' Zouaves: The 114th Pennsylvania Volunteers in the Civil War* (Baton Rouge: Louisiana State University Press, 1997), 238–39; Rable, *Fredericksburg! Fredericksburg!*, 216; Levi Bird Duff to Harriet Duff (June 29, 1863), in *To Petersburg with the Army of the Potomac: The Civil War Letters of Levi Bird Duff, 105th Pennsylvania Volunteers*, ed. Jonathan E. Helmreich (Jefferson, NC: McFarland, 2009), 128; Capt. Charles H. Weygant, *History of the One Hundred and Twenty-fourth Regiment, N.Y.S.M.* (Newburgh, NY: Journal Printing House, 1877), 161; Busey & Martin, *Regimental Strengths and Losses*, 16; O'Reilly, *"Stonewall" Jackson at Fredericksburg*, 126.

19. Toombs, *New Jersey Troops in the Gettysburg Campaign*, 176; Thomas Rafferty, "Gettysburg—The Third Corps' Great Battle on July 2," *National Tribune* (February 2, 1888); "Testimony of Major General Andrew A. Humphreys" (March 21, 1864), in *Report of the Joint Committee on the Conduct of the War*, 4:389–90; Cpl. John M. Vallean, "Rapid March to the Battlefield and Heroic Part Taken in That Action by the 109th Pa.," *National Tribune* (May 9, 1901); Callihan, "Elusive Victory: Robert E. Lee at Gettysburg," *Gettysburg Magazine* 28 (January 2003), 43, 44; Maj. Henry E. Tremain to Sickles (June 28, 1880), in *Bachelder Papers*, 1:670–71; Tremain, *Two Days of War: A Gettysburg Narrative, and Other Excursions*, 49–50.

20. Tagg, *The Generals of Gettysburg*, 65; Frederick Lyman Hitchcock, *War from the Inside; or, Personal Experiences, Impressions, and Reminiscences by One of the "Boys" in the War of the Rebellion* (Philadelphia: J. B. Lippincott, 1904), 134; Stevens, *Berdan's United States Sharpshooters in the Army of the Potomac, 1861–1865*, 302, 303, 304–5, 308, 317; James E. Smith, "The Fourth Battery at Gettysburg," in *New York at Gettysburg*, 3:1289; Elijah Walker to J. B. Bachelder (January 5, 1885), in *Bachelder Papers*, 2:1093–94; Thomas Rafferty, "Gettysburg—The Third Corps' Great Battle on July 2," *National Tribune* (February 2, 1888), and "Gettysburg" (November 7, 1883), in *Personal Recollections of the War of the Rebellion*, 8–9; "Report of Brig. Gen. Cadmus M. Wilcox, C.S. Army" (July 17, 1863), in *O.R.*, series one, 27 (pt. 2):617.

21. "Report of Maj. Gen. David B. Birney" (August 7, 1863) and "Report of Col. Hiram Berdan, First U.S. Sharpshooters, Commanding First and Second U.S. Sharpshooters" (July 29, 1863), in *O.R.*, series one, 27 (pt. 1):482, 515; "Third Maine Regiment," in Charles Hamlin et al., eds., *Maine at Gettysburg: Report of the Maine Commissioners* (Portland, ME: Lakeside Press, 1898), 128; Bowden and Ward, *Last Chance for Victory*, 256; Sauers, *A Caspian Sea of Ink*, 95–96, 99, 107, and "Gettysburg: The Meade-Sickles Controversy," *Civil War History* 26 (September 1980), 215–16; "Twenty-five Years After—Friend and Foe Tenting on the Old Camp Ground," *National Tribune* (July 12, 1888).

22. Hessler, *Sickles at Gettysburg*, 110; "Testimony of Major General Daniel E. Sickles" (February 26, 1864), in *Report of the Joint Committee on the Conduct of the War*, 4:297–98; Richard

Meade Bache, *The Life of George Gordon Meade, Commander of the Army of the Potomac* (Philadelphia: H. T. Coates, 1897), 320, 323; Jared Peatman, "General Sickles, President Lincoln, and the Aftermath of the Battle of Gettysburg," *Gettysburg Magazine* 28 (January 2003), 119; Sears, *Controversies and Commanders*, 212–13.

23. David Craft, *History of the One Hundred Forty-first Regiment, Pennsylvania Volunteers* (Towanda, PA: Reporter-Journal Printing Co., 1885), 119; Sickles, "The Meade-Sickles Controversy," in *Battles & Leaders*, 3:416; Henry J. Hunt, "The Second Day at Gettysburg," in *Battles & Leaders*, 3:301; Tremain, *Two Days of War: A Gettysburg Narrative, and Other Excursions*, 55; Historicus, "Battle of Gettysburg—Important Communication from an Eye-Witness," in *O.R.*, series one, 27 (pt. 1):130; "Battle of Gettysburg" (March 1, 1864), in *Rebellion Record*, ed. Moore (1865), 8:346; Aaron Jerome and James S. Hall to Butterfield (July 2, 1863), in *O.R.*, series one, 27 (pt. 3):487–88; Tremain to Sickles (June 28, 1880), in *Bachelder Papers*, 1:670, 672–73; Meade, *Life and Letters of George G. Meade*, 2:70; "Testimony of Major General Daniel Sickles" (February 26, 1864) and "Testimony of Major General George G. Meade" (March 5, 1864), in *Report of the Joint Committee on the Conduct of the War*, 4:299, 331–32.

24. DePeyster, "The Third Corps at Gettysburg, July 2, 1863," in Daniel E. Sickles Papers, New-York Historical Society; Sauers, *A Caspian Sea of Ink*, 147.

25. "Testimony of General Henry J. Hunt" (April 4, 1864) in *Report of the Joint Committee on the Conduct of the War*, 4:449, 450; Hessler, *Sickles at Gettysburg*, 116–17; Hunt, "The Second Day at Gettysburg," in *Battles & Leaders*, 3:301.

26. "Testimony of Major General Daniel Sickles" (February 26, 1864) and "Testimony of Major General Andrew A. Humphreys" (March 21, 1864), in *Report of the Joint Committee on the Conduct of the War*, 4:298, 390–91; Rafferty, "Gettysburg—The Third Corps' Great Battle on July 2," *National Tribune* (February 2, 1888); Bartlett, *History of the Twelfth Regiment, New Hampshire Volunteers*, 121; Callihan, "Elusive Victory: Robert E. Lee at Gettysburg," *Gettysburg Magazine* 28 (January 2003), 44; Hessler, *Sickles at Gettysburg*, 116–17; Frederick C. Floyd, *History of the Fortieth (Mozart) Regiment, New York Volunteers* (Boston: F. H. Gilson, 1909), 201; Garry E. Adelman and Timothy H. Smith, *Devil's Den: A History and Guide* (Gettysburg: Thomas Publications, 1997), 7; David Powell, "Advance to Disaster: Sickles, Longstreet, and July 2nd, 1863," *Gettysburg Magazine* 28 (January 2003), 40, 41.

27. Blake, *Three Years in the Army of the Potomac*, 205; Frank Rauscher, *Music on the March, 1862–'65, with the Army of the Potomac, 114th Regt. P.V., Collis' Zouaves* (Philadelphia: Wm. E. Fell, 1892), 90–91; Jesse Bowman Young, *What a Boy Saw in the Army: A Story of Sight-Seeing and Adventure in the War for the Union* (New York: Hunt & Eaton, 1894), 300; O'Reilly, *"Stonewall" Jackson at Fredericksburg*, 153, 155; Warren H. Cudworth, *History of the First Regiment (Massachusetts Infantry), from the 25th of May, 1861, to the 25th of May, 1864; including brief references to the operations of the Army of the Potomac* (Boston: Walker & Fuller, 1866), 393.

28. "Testimony of Major General W.S. Hancock" (March 22, 1864) and "Testimony of General John Gibbon" (April 1, 1864), in *Report of the Joint Committee on the Conduct of the War*, 4:405–6, 440; Josiah Favill, diary entry for July 2, 1863, in *The Diary of a Young Officer Serving with the Armies of the United States During the War of the Rebellion* (Chicago: R. R. Donnelly, 1909), 245; "Statement of Lt. William P. Wilson," in *Bachelder Papers*, 2:1194; Walker, *General Hancock*, 125.

29. Beecham, *Gettysburg, the Pivotal Battle of the Civil War*, 162; Tremain, *Two Days of War: A Gettysburg Narrative, and Other Excursions*, 55–56, 61–62; Meade to Halleck (July 2, 1863), in *O.R.*, series one, 27 (pt. 1):72; David M. Jordan, *"Happiness Is Not My Companion": The Life of General G. K. Warren* (Bloomington: Indiana University Press, 2001), 91–92;

Cleaves, *Meade of Gettysburg*, 148; "Testimony of Major General Daniel Sickles" (February 26, 1864) and "Testimony of General Henry J. Hunt" (April 4, 1864), in *Report of the Joint Committee on the Conduct of the War*, 4:298–99, 450; W. H. Bullard to Sickles (September 13, 1897), in Daniel E. Sickles Papers, New-York Historical Society; Frank E. Moran to Sickles (January 24, 1882), in *Bachelder Papers*, 2:772.

30. "The Battle of Gettysburg," in *O.R.*, series one, 27 (pt. 1):131–32; Coffin, *The Boys of '61*, 299–300; Meade, *Life and Letters of George G. Meade*, 2:78–79; Isaac Rusling Pennypacker, *General Meade* (New York: D. Appleton, 1901), 167–68; Meade, *Did General Meade Desire to Retreat at the Battle of Gettysburg?*, 6; William H. Powell, *The Fifth Army Corps (Army of the Potomac): A Record of Operations During the Civil War in the United States of America, 1861–1865* (New York: G. P. Putnam's, 1896), 520; Tremain, *Two Days of War: A Gettysburg Narrative, and Other Excursions*, 63; Sears, *Controversies and Commanders*, 213–14; Tremain to Sickles (June 28, 1880), in *Bachelder Papers*, 1:671–72; "Testimony of Major General George G. Meade" (March 5, 1864) and "Testimony of Major General David Birney" (March 7, 1864), in *Report of the Joint Committee on the Conduct of the War*, 4:332, 366.

31. A. L. Long to Jubal Early (April 5, 1876), in "Causes of Lee's Defeat at Gettysburg," in *SHSP* 4 (August 1877), 67; McLaws, "Gettysburg," *SHSP* 7 (February 1879), 70–71; William Youngblood, "Unwritten History of the Gettysburg Campaign," *SHSP* 38 (January–December 1910), 315–16; Fitzgerald Ross, *A Visit to the Cities and Camps of the Confederate States* (Edinburgh, U.K.: William Blackwood, 1865), 54–56.

32. Capt. James F. Hart (March 22, 1886) and Surgeon Horatio N. Howard to J. B. Bachelder (March 23, 1882), in *Bachelder Papers*, 2:842, 1245; Youngblood, "Unwritten History of the Gettysburg Campaign," *SHSP* 38 (January–December 1910), 314–15; E. P. Alexander, in *Fighting for the Confederacy*, 237, and "Causes of the Confederate Defeat at Gettysburg," *SHSP* 4 (September 1877), 101; Hood to Longstreet (June 28, 1875), in "Leading Confederates on the Battle of Gettysburg," *SHSP* 4 (October 1877), 148; "Hood's Charge at Gettysburg," in *Camp Fires of the Confederacy: A Volume of Humorous Anecdotes, Reminiscences*, ed. Benjamin LaBree (Louisville, KY: Courier-Journal Job Printing, 1898), 366; Philip Thomas Tucker, *Storming Little Round Top: The 15th Alabama and Their Fight for the High Ground, July 2, 1863* (Cambridge, MA: Da Capo Press, 2002), 110.

33. Dickert, *History of Kershaw's Brigade*, 235; Alexander, in *Fighting for the Confederacy*, 237; Joseph Kershaw to J. B. Bachelder (March 20, 1876), in *Bachelder Papers*, 1:454–55.

34. The difficulty in imposing the orderliness of a concept like the echelon on Longstreet's flank assault—and it has been done routinely since the publication of Porter Alexander's memoirs in 1907 and Jesse Bowman Young's *The Battle of Gettysburg* in 1913—is that no written orders for the attack have survived, and so it is difficult to say that Lee or Longstreet were planning anything so deliberate and thought out. Even Porter Alexander, who would be responsible for Longstreet's artillery, could not "remember hearing of any conference or discussions among our generals at this time as to the best formations & tactics in making our attacks, & our method on this occasion struck me as peculiar even then." Ambrose Powell Hill was actually the only officer to use the term *echelon* in his official report, and even then he seems to have been referring only to the three brigades of his own corps which participated. Longstreet, writing in the *Philadelphia Weekly Times* in 1876, spoke about "the brigades of Wilcox, Perry, Wright, Posey and Mahone moving *en echelon*," but it is not clear from the context whether Longstreet meant just these brigades from Hill's corps, or a larger movement. Other officers—Jerome Robertson, Cadmus Wilcox, David Lang—all believed that their brigades were supposed to go in together, with the movement of the brigade on the right being the signal to its companion to the left to begin moving as well. See Young, *The Battle of Gettysburg: A Comprehensive Narrative* (New York: Harper & Bros., 1913), 262; Alexander, *Fighting for the Confederacy*, 238, and

Military Memoirs of a Confederate, 391, 395; Longstreet, "Lee in Pennsylvania," in *Annals of the War*, 424; "Report of Brig. Gen. J. B. Robertson, C.S. Army" (July 17, 1863), "Report of Lieut. Gen. Ambrose P. Hill, C.S. Army" (November, 1863), "Report of Brig. Gen. Cadmus M. Wilcox, C.S. Army" (July 17, 1863), and "Report of Col. David Lang" (July 29, 1863), in *O.R.*, series one, 27 (pt. 2):404, 607, 618, 631; Sir Archibald Alison, *The Military Life of John, Duke of Marlborough* (New York: Harper & Bros., 1848), 232; Russell F. Weigley, *The Age of Battles: The Quest for Decisive Warfare from Breitenfeld to Waterloo* (Bloomington: Indiana University Press, 1991), 175.

35. Hood, *Advance and Retreat*, 58–59, and Hood to Longstreet (June 28, 1875), in "Leading Confederates on the Battle of Gettysburg," *SHSP* 4 (October 1877), 149–50; Alexander, in *Fighting for the Confederacy*, 239, and "Causes of the Confederate Defeat at Gettysburg," *SHSP* 4 (September 1877), 101–2; Youngblood, "Personal Observations at Gettysburg," *Confederate Veteran* (June 1911), 286; Brian Craig Miller, *John Bell Hood and the Fight for Civil War Memory* (Knoxville: University of Tennessee Press, 2010), 72–73; Alexander Mendoza, "Brig. Gen. Jerome Bonaparte Robertson," in *Kentuckians in Gray: Confederate Generals and Field Officers of the Bluegrass State*, ed. Bruce Allardice and Lawrence L. Hewitt (Lexington: University Press of Kentucky, 2008), 223–25; William C. Ward, "Incidents and Personal Experiences on the Battlefield at Gettysburg," *Confederate Veteran* (August 1900), 347; Daniel M. Laney, "Wasted Gallantry: Hood's Texas Brigade at Gettysburg," *Gettysburg Magazine* 16 (January 1997), 36.

CHAPTER FIFTEEN   *You are to hold this ground at all costs*

1. Porter, *Under the Maltese Cross*, 165; John H. and David J. Eicher, *Civil War High Commands* (Stanford, CA: Stanford University Press, 2001), 521; "The Battle-Field of Gettysburg," in *Anecdotes, Poetry, and Incidents of the War, North and South: 1860–1865*, ed. Frank Moore (1865; New York: Arundel Print, 1882), 210; *History of the Corn Exchange Regiment, 118th Pennsylvania Volunteers, from Their First Engagement at Antietam to Appomattox* (Philadelphia: J. L. Smith, 1905), 240; Crawford, *The Genesis of the Civil War: The Story of Sumter, 1860–1861* (New York: Charles L. Webster, 1887), 452–53; "Samuel Wylie Crawford, D.D., in Alfred Nevin, *Men of Mark of* [the] *Cumberland Valley, Pa., 1776–1876* (Philadelphia: Fulton Publishing 1876), 163; W. M. Glasgow, "Covenanters at Gettysburg," *The Reformed Presbyterian and Covenanter* 26 (October 1888), 347–48; Tagg, *Generals of Gettysburg*, 84, 91–92; Oliver Wilcox Norton, *The Attack and Defense of Little Round Top, Gettysburg, July 2, 1863* (Dayton, OH: Morningside House, 1983), 237–38.

2. Daniel George Macnamara, *The History of the Ninth Regiment, Massachusetts Volunteer Infantry* (Boston: E. B. Stillings, 1899), 322–23; *History of the Corn Exchange Regiment*, 240; Charles H. Weygant, *History of the One Hundred and Twenty-Fourth Regiment, N.Y.S.V.* (Newburgh, NY: Journal Printing House, 1877), 174; "Testimony of Major General George G. Meade" (March 5, 1864), in *Report of the Joint Committee on the Conduct of the War*, 4:332; Powell, *The Fifth Army Corps*, 523.

3. Jordan, *"Happiness Is Not My Companion": The Life of General G. K. Warren*, 90; Emerson Gifford Taylor, *Gouverneur Kemble Warren: The Life and Letters of an American Soldier, 1830–1882* (Boston: Houghton Mifflin, 1932), 105, 120, 122–23; Michael T. Kelly, *"I Will Have Justice Done": Gen. Gouverneur K. Warren, USA* (Gettysburg: Farnsworth Military Impressions, 1997), 28.

4. Murray, *E. P. Alexander and the Artillery Action in the Peach Orchard*, 56–57. Weygandt, *History of the One Hundred and Twenty-fourth Regiment, N.Y.S.V.*, 173.

5. Powell, *The Fifth Army Corps*, 523; "Testimony of General G. K. Warren" (March 9, 1864),

in *Report of the Joint Committee on the Conduct of the War*, 4:377; Warren to Porter Farley (July 13, 1872), in Brian A. Bennett, "Truth Without Exaggeration: Porter Farley's Life-Long Study of the Events on Little Round Top," *Gettysburg Magazine* 28 (January 2003), 54.

6. Taylor, *Gouverneur Kemble Warren*, 126–27; Warren interview with Alexander Kelly (1880), in *Generals in Bronze*, 87; Norton, *Attack and Defense of Little Round Top*, 131–32; "Report of Capt. Lemuel B. Norton, Chief Signal Officer" (September 18, 1863), in *O.R.*, series one, 27 (pt. 1):202; Clayton R. Newell and Charles R. Shrader, *Of Duty Well and Faithfully Done: A History of the Regular Army in the Civil War* (Lincoln: University of Nebraska Press, 2011), 296; J. M. Wright, "West Point Before the War," *Southern Bivouac* 4 (June 1885), 16; "Testimony of General G. K. Warren" (March 9, 1864), in *Report of the Joint Committee on the Conduct of the War*, 4:377; Nevins and Styple, *What Death More Glorious*, 71.

7. Benjamin Woodbridge Dwight, *The History of the Descendants of Elder John Strong of Northampton, Mass.* (Albany, NY: Joel Munsell, 1871), 1:163; James R. Wright, "'I Will Take the Responsibility': Strong Vincent Moves to Little Round Top: Fact or Fiction?," *Gettysburg Magazine* 25 (July 2001), 54; Norton, *Attack and Defense of Little Round Top*, 283; "Strong Vincent," in *Harvard Memorial Biographies* (Cambridge, MA: Sever & Francis, 1866), 2:66–68; Nevins and Styple, *What Death More Glorious*, 18, 28; Judson, *History of the 83rd Regiment, Pennsylvania Volunteers*, 102; O'Reilly, *The Fredericksburg Campaign*, 382; *History of Erie County, Pennsylvania* (Chicago: Warner, Beers & Co., 1884), 1:966.

8. Norton, *Strong Vincent and His Brigade at Gettysburg, July 2, 1863* (Chicago: privately printed, 1909), 6–7; Nevins and Styple, *What Death More Glorious*, 72; John J. Pullen, *The Twentieth Maine: A Volunteer Regiment in the Civil War* (Philadelphia: J. B. Lippincott, 1957), 109.

9. Longstreet to J. B. Bachelder (April 10, 1876), in *Bachelder Papers*, 1:476; Work, in Frank B. Chilton, *Unveiling and Dedication of Monument to Hood's Texas Brigade on the Capitol Grounds at Austin, Texas* (Houston, TX: Rein & Sons, 1911), 339; "Report of Capt. James E. Smith, Fourth New York Battery" (July 20, 1863), in *O.R.*, series one, 27 (pt. 1):588; Murray, *E. P. Alexander and the Artillery Action in the Peach Orchard*, 92–93; Laney, "Wasted Gallantry," 36; John C. West, "Letter no. IX" (July 9, 1863), in *A Texan in Search of a Fight*, 87.

10. Hood to Longstreet (June 28, 1875), in *Advance and Retreat*, 57–58; J. B. Kershaw to J. B. Bachelder (March 20, 1876), in *Bachelder Papers*, 1:453–54; "Report of Maj. John P. Bane, Fourth Texas Infantry" (July 9, 1863), in *O.R.*, series one, 27 (pt. 2):410; Homer R. Stoughton to J. B. Bachelder (December 29, 1881), in *Bachelder Papers*, 2:767–68; Weygant, *History of the One Hundred and Twenty-fourth Regiment*, 175; Warren to Porter Farley (October 23, 1877), in Norton, *Attack and Defense of Little Round Top*, 314; Polley, *Hood's Texas Brigade*, 176; Adelman and Smith, *Devil's Den*, 22; Garry E. Adelman, *The Myth of Little Round Top* (Gettysburg: Thomas Publications, 2003), 28; Harold B. Simpson, *Hood's Texas Brigade: Lee's Grenadier Guard* (1970; Gaithersburg, MD: Olde Soldier Books, 1994), 272.

11. John C. West to Charles S. West (July 27, 1863), in West, *A Texan in Search of a Fight*, 93–94; John Cheves Haskell, *The Haskell Memoirs*, eds. Gilbert E. Govan and James Weston Livingood (New York: Putnam's, 1960), 49; John W. Stevens, *Reminiscences of the Civil War* (Hillsboro, TX: Hillsboro Mirror Print, 1901), 113–14; Morris Penny and J. Gary Laine, *Struggle for the Round Tops: Law's Alabama Brigade at the Battle of Gettysburg* (Shippensburg, PA: Burd Street Press, 2000), 40; Richard M. McMurry, *John Bell Hood and the War for Southern Independence* (Lincoln: University of Nebraska Press, 1992), 75; Wilkinson and Woodworth, *A Scythe of Fire*, 234, 235; Bowden and Ward, *Last Chance for Victory*, 284; Capt. F. M. Colston, "Gettysburg as I Saw It," *Confederate Veteran* 5 (November 1897),

551–52; Charles Winder Squires manuscript autobiography, Library of Congress; Miller, *John Bell Hood*, 72–73.

12.   James E. Smith, *A Famous Battery and Its Campaigns, 1861–'64* (Washington: W. H. Low-dermilk, 1892), 137; Maj. Thomas W. Bradley, "At Gettysburg—The Splendid Work Done by Smith's Battery," *National Tribune* (February 4, 1886).

13.   Jerome B. Robertson (April 20, 1876), Homer Stoughton (December 29, 1881), and Francis M. Cummins to J. B. Bachelder (February 21, 1884), in *Bachelder Papers*, 1:477 and 2:767–68, 1024; "Report of Brig. Gen. J. B. Robertson, C.S. Army," "Report of Lieut. Col. P. A. Work, First Texas Infantry" (July 9, 1863), "Report of Lieut. Col. K. Bryan, Fifth Texas Infantry" (July 8, 1863), "Report of Col. W. W. White" (August 8, 1863), and "Report of Lieut. Col. William S. Sheperd" (July 27, 1863), in *O.R.*, series one, 27 (pt. 2):397, 404, 408–9, 412, 420; Penny and Laine, *Struggle for the Round Tops*, 53; Col. William C. Oates and Gen. Jerome B. Robertson to J. B. Bachelder (March 29 and April 20, 1876), in *Bachelder Papers*, 1:464, 477; Glenn W. LaFantasie, *Twilight at Little Round Top, July 2, 1863—The Tide Turns at Gettysburg* (New York: John Wiley & Sons, 2005), 96.

14.   "Report of Brig. Gen. J. H. Hobart Ward" (August 4, 1863), "Report of Lieut. Col. L. H. Scruggs, Fourth Alabama Infantry" (August 8, 1863), "Report of Col. James L. Sheffield, Forty-Eighth Alabama Infantry" (August 7, 1863), and "Report of Col. Van H. Manning, Third Arkansas Infantry" (July 8, 1863), in *O.R.*, series one, 27 (pt. 1):493, and (pt. 2):391, 395, 407; Col. A. H. Belo, "The Battle of Gettysburg" and Ward, "Incidents and Personal Experiences on the Battle Field of Gettysburg," *Confederate Veteran* 8 (April–August 1900), 167–68, 347; Gen. W. F. Perry, "The Devil's Den," *Confederate Veteran* 9 (April 1901), 161–62; "Hood's Charge at Gettysburg, in *Camp Fires of the Confederacy*, ed. LaBree, 366; Robert Campbell, *Lone Star Confederate: A Gallant and Good Soldier of the 5th Texas Infantry*, eds. George Skoch and Mark W. Perkins (College Station: Texas A&M University Press, 2003), 120; Polley, *A Soldier's Letters to Charming Nellie*, 133; Henry J. Hunt, "The Second Day at Gettysburg," in *Battles and Leaders*, 3:305; Weygant, *History of the One Hundred and Twenty-Fourth Regiment*, 175.

15.   A. W. Tucker, "'Orange Blossoms': Services of the 124th New York at Gettysburg," *National Tribune* (January 21, 1886); Maj. Thomas W. Bradley, "At Gettysburg—The Splendid Work Done by Smith's Battery," *National Tribune* (February 4, 1886); Henry J. Hunt, "The Second Day at Gettysburg," in *Battles and Leaders*, 3:305; Weygant, *History of the One Hundred and Twenty-fourth Regiment*, 175; Col. Elijah Walker to J. B. Bachelder (January 5, 1885), in *Bachelder Papers*, 2:1095; Smith and Adelman, *Devil's Den*, 38, 40; James E. Smith, "The Fourth Battery at Gettysburg," in *New York at Gettysburg*, 3:1290; Harvey Munsell, "With the Colors in War Time," in Theodore F. Rodenbough, *Uncle Sam's Medal of Honor: Some of the Noble Deeds for Which the Medal Has Been Awarded, Described by Those Who Have Won It, 1861–1886* (New York: G. P. Putnam's, 1886), 186, 187.

16.   Weygant, *History of the One Hundred and Twenty-Fourth Regiment*, 180; A. W. Tucker, "'Orange Blossoms': Services of the 124th New York at Gettysburg," *National Tribune* (January 21, 1886); Perry, "Devil's Den," *Confederate Veteran* 9 (April 1901), 161–62; "Report of Lieut. Col. P. A. Work" (July 9, 1863) and "Report of Col. Wesley C. Hodges, Seventeenth Georgia Infantry" (July 27, 1863), in *O.R.*, series one, 27 (pt. 2):410, 425; William Youngblood, "Personal Observations at Gettysburg," *Confederate Veteran* (June 1911), 287; Bowden and Ward, *Last Chance for Victory*, 290–91; Polley, *Hood's Texas Brigade*, 169–70; John H. Martin, "Accurate Historic Records," *Confederate Veteran* 12 (March 1904), 114; *From Huntsville to Appomattox: R. T. Coles's History of 4th Regiment, Alabama Volunteer Infantry*, 107; Garry E. Adelman, "Benning's Georgia Brigade at Gettysburg," *Gettysburg Magazine* 18 (January 1998), 61–65.

17.   James E. Smith, "The Fourth Battery at Gettysburg," in *New York at Gettysburg*, 3:1291;

Penny and Laine, *Struggle for the Round Tops*, 64–67; "Report of Col. James L. Sheffield, Forty-eighth Alabama Infantry" (August 7, 1863), in *O.R.*, series one, 27 (pt. 2):396.

18. I. N. Dubboraw, "The Big Battle—A Comrade Sends Reminiscences of a Citizen at Gettysburg," *National Tribune* (December 8, 1892); "A Great Victory—Three Days Battles—Mr. S. M. Carpenter's Despatch," *New York Herald* (July 6, 1863); Hyde, "Recollections of the Battle of Gettysburg," 200–201.

19. Thomas H. Scott, "On Little Round Top," *National Tribune* (August 2, 1894); Augustus Martin, "Little Round Top—Story of the Fight There During the Battle of Gettysburg," *Gettysburg Compiler* (October 24, 1899); Garry E. Adelman, "Hazlett's Battery at Gettysburg," *Gettysburg Magazine* 21 (July 1999), 66–67.

20. Warren to Porter Farley (July 24, 1872), in Norton, *Attack and Defense of Little Round Top*, 131–32, 312; Twemlow, *Considerations on Tactics and Strategy*, 48–49; Joshua Lawrence Chamberlain, "Through Blood and Fire at Gettysburg," *Gettysburg Magazine* 6 (January 1992), 51; B. F. Rittenhouse, "The Battle of Gettysburg as Seen from Little Round Top" (May 4, 1887), in *War Papers: Being Papers Read Before the Commandery of the District of Columbia*, 37–38; James Lorenzo Bowen, *History of the Thirty-Seventh Regiment, Mass. Volunteers, in the Civil War of 1861–1865* (Holyoke, MA: Clark W. Bryan & Co., 1884), 182–83; Callihan, "Elusive Victory," 54, 55.

21. Warren, in Taylor, *Gouverneur Kemble Warren*, 129; Rittenhouse, "The Battle of Gettysburg as Seen from Little Round Top," 40; Coffin, *The Boys of '61*, 307; Capt. Benjamin F. Partridge to J. B. Bachelder (March 31, 1866), in *Bachelder Papers*, 1:243–44; Wright, "I Will Take the Responsibility," *Gettysburg Magazine* 25 (July 2001), 57; Wilcox, *Strong Vincent and His Brigade at Gettysburg, July 2, 1863*, 8; Lt. Ziba Graham, "On to Gettysburg: Ten Days from My Diary of 1863" (1889), in *War Papers Read Before the Commandery of the State of Michigan*, 1:9–10; Judson, *History of the Eighty-third Regiment, Pennsylvania Volunteers*, 125, 127; Norton, *Attack and Defense of Little Round Top*, 243, 265–66; Chamberlain, "Through Blood and Fire at Gettysburg," 48, 50; Nevins and Styple, *What Death More Glorious*, 75, 110, 111.

22. "Report of Brig. Gen. James Barnes" (August 24, 1863), "Report of Col. James C. Rice, Forty-Fourth New York Infantry" (July 31, 1863), and "Report of Col. Joshua L. Chamberlain, Twentieth Maine Infantry" (July 6, 1863), in *O.R.*, series one, 27 (pt. 1):603, 617, 623–24; William H. Brown, "A View from Little Round Top During the Progress of the Battle," *Philadelphia Weekly Times* (March 17, 1882); Chamberlain to James Barnes, in *Through Blood and Fire: Selected Civil War Papers of Major General Joshua Chamberlain*, ed. Mark Nesbitt (Mechanicsburg, PA: Stackpole Books, 1995), 81; Ellis Spear, *The Civil War Recollections of General Ellis Spear*, ed. Abbott Spear (Orono: University of Maine Press, 1997), 33; Theodore Gerrish, "The Battle of Gettysburg," *National Tribune* (November 23, 1882).

23. Stevens, *Reminiscences of the Civil War*, 114; Judson, *History of the Eighty-third Regiment, Pennsylvania Volunteers*, 127; Kevin O'Brien, "Valley of the Shadow of Death: Col. Strong Vincent and the Eighty-Third Pennsylvania Infantry at Little Round Top," *Gettysburg Magazine* 7 (July 1992), 46; Pullen, *The Twentieth Maine*, 125; Tucker, *Storming Little Round Top*, 229; Alice Rains Trulock, *In the Hands of Providence: Joshua L. Chamberlain and the American Civil War* (Chapel Hill: University of North Carolina Press, 1992), 147–48; Chamberlain to James Barnes (July 6, 1863), in "Letters from Joshua L. Chamberlain," ed. Thomas Desjardins, in *Civil War Times* 50 (June 2012), 39.

24. "Report of Brig. Gen. James Barnes" (August 24, 1863), in *O.R.*, series one, 27 (pt. 1):603; Lt. Charles Salter, in Gottfried, *Brigades of Gettysburg*, 248; Stevens, *Reminscences of the Civil War*, 114–15; Penny and Laine, *Struggle for the Round Tops*, 91; "Strong Vincent," in *Harvard Memorial Biographies*, 78–79; Capt. Eugene Arus Nash, *A History of the Forty-*

fourth Regiment, New York Volunteer Infantry, in the Civil War (Chicago: R. R. Donnelly, 1914), 145; John Michael Gibney, "A Shadow Passing: The Tragic Story of Norval Welch and the Sixteenth Michigan at Gettysburg and Beyond," and Chamberlain, "Through Blood and Fire at Gettysburg," *Gettysburg Magazine* 6 (January 1992), 39–40, 52, 55; "Hood's Charge at Gettysburg," in *Camp Fires of the Confederacy,* 366–67.

25. Brian A. Bennett, *Sons of Old Monroe: A Regimental History of Patrick O'Rorke's 140th New York Volunteer Infantry* (Dayton, OH: Morningside House, 1999), 53–57; Donald M. Fisher, "Born in Ireland, Killed at Gettysburg: The Life, Death, and Legacy of Patrick Henry O'Rorke," *Civil War History* 39 (September 1993), 234–35; "Gen. Patrick Henry O'Rorke," in *Second Annual Report of the State Historian of the State of New York* (Albany: Wynkoop, Hallenback & Crawford, 1897), 63–64.

26. Norton, *Attack and Defense of Little Round Top,* 130, 134, 135, 268–69, 274, 299, 317; Capt. Joseph Leeper to J. B. Bachelder, in *Bachelder Papers,* 2:896, and "Gettysburg—The Part Taken in the Battle by the Fifth Corps," *National Tribune* (April 30, 1885); Susannah Ural Bruce, *The Harp and the Eagle: Irish-American Volunteers and the Union Army, 1861–1865* (New York: New York University Press, 2006), 160–63; Porter Farley, "Reminiscences of Gettysburg," *National Tribune* (January 1, 1878); Bennett, *Sons of Old Monroe,* 231, 233, 234, 235; Callihan, "Elusive Victory," 83–84; Brainard, *Campaigns of the One Hundred and Forty-Sixth Regiment,* 116–18; Allen, *Under the Maltese Cross,* 168; Lt. Azor S. Marvin to Warren (October 29, 1877), Porter Farley to J. B. Bachelder (May 8, 1878), and Col. Kenner Garrard to Warren (October 31, 1877), in *Bachelder Papers,* 1:511, 513, 548; LaFantasie, *Twilight at Little Round Top,* 153.

27. Powell, *The Fifth Army Corps,* 523; W. F. Perry, "Devil's Den," *Confederate Veteran* 9 (April 1901), 161–62; Col. A. H. Belo, "The Battle of Gettysburg," *Confederate Veteran* 8 (April 1900), 168; Warren, in *Second Annual Report of the State Historian of the State of New York,* 43–44; Hyde, "Recollections of the Battle of Gettysburg," 198; Brainard, *Campaigns of the One Hundred and Forty-Sixth Regiment,* 119; William C. Oates to J. B. Bachelder (March 29, 1876) and Lt. Edgar Warren to Bachelder (November 15, 1877), in *Bachelder Papers,* 1:465, 515–16; Tucker, *Storming Little Round Top,* 206; "Report of Brig. Gen. J. B. Robertson, C.S. Army" (July 17, 1863) and "Report of Col. William C. Oates, Fifteenth Alabama Infantry" (August 8, 1863), in *O.R.,* series one, 27 (pt. 2):393, 405; Oates, *The War Between the Union and the Confederacy, and Its Lost Opportunities with a History of the 15th Alabama Regiment and the Forty-Eight Battles in Which It Was Engaged* (New York: Neale Publishing, 1905), 220; Busey and Martin, *Regimental Strengths and Losses,* 260, 262; LaFantasie, *Twilight at Little Round Top,* 273.

28. Rittenhouse, "The Battle of Gettysburg as Seen from Little Round Top," 39–40; Farley, "Reminiscences of Gettysburg," *National Tribune* (January 1, 1878); Norton, *Attack and Defense of Little Round Top,* 133; Thomas Desjardin, *These Honored Dead: How the Story of Gettysburg Shaped American Memory* (Cambridge, MA: Da Capo Press, 2003), 37; Allen, *Under the Maltese Cross,* 170; "Heroes of Gettysburgh" (November 3, 1863), in *Rebellion Record,* ed. Moore (1864), 7:77; William F. Breakey [surgeon, 16th Michigan], "Recollections and Incidents of Medical Military Service" (February 4, 1897), in *War Papers Read Before the Michigan Commandery,* 2:144.

29. Jordan, *"Happiness Is Not My Companion": The Life of General G. K. Warren,* 92; Law, "The Struggle for 'Round Top,'" in *Battles & Leaders,* 3:319; Beecham, *Gettysburg,* 185; H. S. Melcher, "The 20th Maine at Little Round Top," in *Battles & Leaders,* 3:315; *Sparks from the Camp Fire; or, Tales of the Old Veterans,* ed. Joseph Morton (Philadelphia: Keeler & Kirkpatrick, 1899), 31; Capt. James T. Long, *Gettysburg, How the Battle Was Fought* (Harrisburg: Clarence Busch, 1890), 34; Ken Discofarno, *They Saved the Union at Little Round Top* (Gettysburg: Thomas Publications, 2002); Tucker, *Storming Little Round Top,*

175; George L. Kilmer, "Crisis on Round-Top: Battle Between the Twentieth Maine and Fifteenth Alabama," *Gettysburg Compiler* (September 15, 1896).

30. Porter Farley to Warren (October 26, 1877), in Bennett, "Truth Without Exaggeration: Porter Farley's Life-Long Study of the Events on Little Round Top," *Gettysburg Magazine* 28 (January 2003), 57; Adelman, *The Myth of Little Round Top* (Gettysburg: Thomas Publications, 2003), 37–56; Desjardins, *These Honored Dead: How the Story of Gettysburg Shaped American Memory*, 127–41.

31. Warren (July 13, 1872), in Henry J. Hunt, "The Second Day at Gettysburg," in *Battles & Leaders*, 3:309.

CHAPTER SIXTEEN *I have never been in a hotter place*

1. John S. Robson, *How a One-Legged Rebel Lives: Reminiscences of the Civil War* (Durham, NC: The Educator Co., 1898), 94, 99–100; Wright, *No More Gallant a Deed*, 183–84; Richard Moe, *The Last Full Measure: The Life and Death of the First Minnesota Volunteers* (1993; St. Paul: Minnesota Historical Society, 2001), 262–63; Charles D. Page, *History of the Fourteenth Regiment, Connecticut Volunteer Infantry* (Meriden, CT: Horton Printing, 1906), 149–50; Dr. George S. Osborne [1st Massachusetts Cavalry] and Doubleday to J. B. Bachelder (May 14 and January 22, 1885), in *Bachelder Papers*, 2:1042, 1096.

2. E. Polk Johnson, "'Were You Scared?'" *Southern Bivouac* 4 (November 1885), 374; Richard Holmes, *Acts of War: The Behavior of Men in Battle* (New York: Free Press, 1985), 149, 177–78; Fisk, *Hard Marching Every Day: The Civil War Letters of Private Wilbur Fisk, 1861–1865*, ed. Ruth and Emil Rosenblatt (Lawrence: University Press of Kansas, 1983), 350; Livermore, *Days and Events, 1860–1866* (Boston: Houghton Mifflin, 1920), 67; Earl Hess, *The Union Soldier in Battle: Enduring the Ordeal of Combat* (Lawrence: University Press of Kansas, 1997), 28; "Report of Brig. Gen. Napoleon B. Buford" (October 13, 1862), in *O.R.*, series one, 17 (pt. 1):217.

3. Dodge, "Left Wounded on the Field," 321; Capt. Frank Holsinger, "How Does One Feel Under Fire" (May 5, 1898), in *War Talks in Kansas*, 294; Urban, "The Story of Gettysburg—A Great Battle as Seen by a Lancaster Boy," *Gettysburg Magazine* 37 (July 2007), 98; C. M. Damon, *Sketches and Incidents; or, Reminiscences of Interest in the Life of the Author* (Chicago: Free Methodist Publishing House, 1900), 70; William Smith to John W. Daniel (October 17, 1905), in Gordon C. Rhea, *The Battle of the Wilderness, May 5–6, 1864* (Baton Rouge: Louisiana State University Press, 1994), 323; Hess, *Union Soldier in Battle*, 112, 114; Dawes, *Service with the Sixth Wisconsin Volunteers*, 91.

4. Eugene Fitch Ware, *The Lyon Campaign in Missouri: Being a History of the First Iowa Infantry* (Topeka, KS: Crane & Co., 1907), 136; Wright, *No More Gallant a Deed*, 165–66; A. B. Isham, "The Story of a Gunshot Wound," *in Sketches of War History*, 4:430; S. Weir Mitchell, *Gunshot Wounds and Other Injuries of Nerves* (Philadelphia: J. B. Lippincott, 1864), 14; Sir Thomas Longmore, *Gunshot Injuries: Their History, Characteristic Features, Complications, and General Treatment* (London: Longmans, Green, 1895), 198–99, 692; Frederic S. Dennis, "Surgery of the Chest," in *A Treatise on Surgery by American Authors for Students and Practitioners of Surgery and Medicine*, ed. Roswell Park (Philadelphia: Lee Bros., 1896), 2:265; C. E. B. Flagg, "A Plea for Immediate Celiotomy in Penetrating Gunshots Wounds of the Abdomen in War," *Proceedings of the Association of Military Surgeons of the United States at Its Tenth Annual Meeting at St. Paul, Minnesota* (Carlisle, PA: Association of Military Surgeons, 1901), 110.

5. Lieutenant Colonel John Mitchell, *Thoughts on Tactics and Military Organization* (London: Longman, Orme, Brown, Green & Longmans, 1838), 160; Andrew Steinmetz, "Mili-

tary Gymnastics of the French," *Journal of the Royal United Services Institute for Defence Studies* 5 (1861), 386, 392; William Fox, "The Chances of Being Hit in Battle: A Study of Regimental Losses in the Civil War," *Century Magazine* 36 (May 1888), 104; "Reports of Maj. Gen. William S. Rosecrans, U.S. Army" (February 12, 1863), in *O.R.*, series one, 20 (pt. 1):197; "The Use of the Rifle," *Atlantic Monthly* (March 1862), 301.

6. Arthur Walker, *The Rifle: Its Theory and Practice* (London: J. B. Nichols, 1864), 208; Livermore, *Days and Events*, 67; Fisher, diary entry for August 31, 1862, in *A Philadelphia Perspective: The Civil War Diary of Sidney George Fisher*, ed. Jonathan W. White (New York: Fordham University Press, 2007), 164; Strachan, *From Waterloo to Balaclava*, 117–18.

7. Holsinger, "How Does One Feel Under Fire," 294; Ladley to "Mother & Sisters" (May 19, 1863), in *Hearth and Knapsack: The Ladley Letters*, 129; Wheeler, diary entry for August 9, 1863, in *Letters of William Wheeler*, 418; Cook, "Personal Reminiscences of Gettysburg," 335; Benton, *As Seen from the Ranks: A Boy in the Civil War* (New York: G. P. Putnam's 1902), 39–40, 47; Reardon, *With a Sword in One Hand*, 115; O'Reilly, *"Stonewall" Jackson at Fredericksburg*, 48.

8. *Lancaster Daily Express* (July 10, 1863), in Charles Teague, "The U.S. Marshal at Gettysburg," in *Gettysburg: The End of the Campaign and Battle's Aftermath* (Gettysburg: Gettysburg National Military Park, 2012), 100; Wright, *No More Gallant a Deed*, 183–84; Holsinger, "How Does One Feel Under Fire," 293; Edwin Clark Bennett, *Musket and Sword; or, The Camp, March, and Firing Line in the Army of the Potomac* (Boston: Coburn Publishing, 1900), 141; Blake, *Three Years in the Army of the Potomac*, 292.

9. Jacobs, "How an Eye Witness Watched the Great Battle—A Vivid Story of the Mighty Conflict," *Baltimore Sunday American* (June 29, 1913); J. W. Lokey, "Wounded at Gettysburg," *Confederate Veteran* 22 (September 1914), 400; Judson, *History of the Eighty-Third Regiment Pennsylvania Volunteers*, 131, 134; Robert G. Carter, "The Campaign and Battle of Gettysburg," in *War Papers Read Before the Commandery of the State of Maine*, 2:172, 179; Carter, *Four Brothers in Blue; or, Sunshine and Shadows of the War of the Rebellion: A Story of the Great Civil War from Bull Run to Appomattox*, ed. J. M. Carroll (Austin: University of Texas Press, 1978), 323.

10. Wyckoff, *History of the Second South Carolina Infantry*, 10–11, 522; Busey and Martin, *Regimental Strengths and Losses*, 179; Dickert, *History of Kershaw's Brigade*, 86–89; U. R. Brooks, *South Carolina Bench and Bar* (Columbia, SC: State Co., 1908), 1:227; Elisabeth Muhlenfeld, *Mary Boykin Chesnut: A Biography* (Baton Rouge: Louisiana State University Press, 1981), 163; *Mary Chesnut's Civil War*, ed. C. Vann Woodward, 135; Kershaw to J. B. Bachelder (April 3, 1876), in *Bachelder Papers*, 1:473.

11. "Report of Brig. Gen. J. B. Kershaw, C.S. Army" (October 1, 1863, in *O.R.*, series one, 27 (pt. 2):367; Kershaw to J. B. Bachelder (March 20, 1876), in *Bachelder Papers*, 1:454–55; Kershaw, "Kershaw's Brigade at Gettysburg," *Battles & Leaders*, 3:334; D. Scott Hartwig, "'I Have Never Been in a Hotter Place': Brigade Command at Gettysburg," *Gettysburg Magazine* 25 (July 2001), 66–67; Wilkinson and Woodworth, *A Scythe of Fire*, 247–48.

12. "Report of Col. P. Régis de Trobriand, Fifty-Fifth New York Infantry, Commanding Third Brigade" (July 1863), in *O.R.*, series one, 27 (pt. 1):520; de Trobriand to J. B. Bachelder (August 24, 1869), in *Bachelder Papers*, 1:374; Capt. George Verrill, "Seventeenth Maine Regiment," in *Maine at Gettysburg*, 193; de Trobriand, *Four Years in the Army of the Potomac*, 495.

13. John and Robert Parker, *Henry Wilson's Regiment: History of the Twenty-second Massachusetts Infantry* (Boston: Rand Avery, 1887), 582; Tagg, *The Generals of Gettysburg*, 86; *The Biographical Encyclopaedia of Pennsylvania of the Nineteenth Century* (Philadelphia: Galaxy Publishing, 1874), 646–47; Bennett, *Musket and Sword*, 287; Bates, *Martial Deeds of Penn-*

sylvania, 913–14; George Sykes to Oliver W. Norton (August 5, 1872), in Norton, *Attack and Defense of Little Round Top*, 294–95.

14. Jordan, *Red Diamond Regiment,* 74–75; John Haley to J. B. Bachelder (February 6, 1884), in *Bachelder Papers*, 2:1004; Jorgensen, *Gettysburg's Bloody Wheatfield*, 84, 86; Verrill, "Seventeenth Maine Regiment,"195; Mattocks to "My dear Mother" (July 3, 1863), in *"Unspoiled Heart": The Journal of Charles Mattocks of the 17th Maine*, ed. Philip N. Racine (Knoxville: University of Tennessee Press, 1994), 47–48; Edwin B. Houghton, *The Campaigns of the Seventeenth Maine* (Portland: Short & Loring, 1866), 92; Thomas Bradbury, diary entry for July 2, 1863, in Special Collections, University of Virginia; Charles W. Roberts, "At Gettysburg in 1863 and 1888," in *War Papers Read Before the Commandery of the State of Maine*, 1:51–52.

15. de Trobriand, *Four Years with the Army of the Potomac*, 499; "Report of Capt. George B. Winslow, Battery D, First New York Light Artillery" (July 28, 1863), in *O.R.*, series one, 27 (pt. 1):587; Thomas W. Osborn, "Dedication of Monument—Battery D "Winslow's" First New York Light Artillery" (July 2, 1888), in *New York at Gettysburg*, 3:1206–7; Winslow to J. B. Bachelder (May 17, 1878), in *Bachelder Papers*, 1:590; Winslow, "On Little Round Top: The Position and Achievements of the First New York Volunteer Artillery," in *Gettysburg Sources*, 3:152–54.

16. William J. Patterson, "62nd Regiment of Infantry" (September 11, 1889) and Edmund Shaw, "110th Regiment of Infantry" (September 11, 1889), in *Pennsylvania at Gettysburg*, 1:387 and 2:595; "Address of A. S. Shattuck," in *Michigan at Gettysburg: July 1st. 2d. and 3rd. 1863—June 12, 1889—Proceedings Incident to the Dedication of the Michigan Monuments upon the Battlefield of Gettysburg* (Detroit: Winn & Hammond, 1889), 76; Verrill, "Seventeenth Maine Regiment," 196–97; John L. Smith, *History of the 118th Pennsylvania Volunteers, Corn Exchange Regiment, from their First Engagement at Antietam to Appomattox* (Philadelphia: J. L. Smith, 1905), 244–45; Robert G. Carter, "Reminiscences of the Battle and Campaign of Gettysburg," in *War Papers Read Before the Commandery of the State of Maine*, 2:165–66; Jordan, *Red Diamond Regiment*, 74–75; Jorgensen, *Gettysburg's Bloody Wheatfield*, 76, 78–79.

17. John Coxe, "The Battle of Gettysburg," *Confederate Veteran* 21 (September 1913), 434; Arthur Peronneau Ford, *Life in the Confederate Army: Being Personal Experiences of a Private Soldier in the Confederate Army* (New York: Neale Publishing, 1905), 51–52; "Report of Brig. Gen. J. B. Kershaw, C.S. Army" (October 1, 1863, in *O.R.,* series one, 27 (pt. 2):368; Kershaw to J. B. Bachelder (March 20 and April 3, 1876), in *Bachelder Papers*, 1:455–56, 472, 474; Aiken, "The Gettysburg Reunion: What Is Necessary and Proper for the South to Do," in *Gettysburg Sources*, 2:173–74; Murray, *E. P. Alexander and the Artillery Action in the Peach Orchard*, 95; Hartwig, "'I Have Never Been in a Hotter Place,'" 67, 69.

18. Dickert, *History of Kershaw's Brigade*, 238; Kershaw to J. B. Bachelder (March 20, 1876), in *Bachelder Papers*, 1:455–56; Wyckoff, *History of the Second South Carolina Infantry*, 191, and *History of the 3rd South Carolina Regiment*, 170–71; Kershaw, "Kershaw's Brigade at Gettysburg," in *Battles & Leaders*, 3:336; Hartwig, "'I Have Never Been in a Hotter Place,'" 70; Verrill, "Seventeenth Maine Regiment," 199.

19. Gottfried, *Brigades of Gettysburg*, 163; "Report of Lt. Col. Charles H. Morgan," in *Bachelder Papers*, 3:1353; Gambone, *Hancock at Gettysburg*, 72; "Reports of Maj. Leman W. Bradley, Sixty-fourth New York Infantry" (July 17, 1863), in *O.R.*, series one, 27 (pt. 1):407.

20. Marion L. Armstrong, *Unfurl Those Colors! McClellan, Sumner, and the Second Army Corps in the Antietam Campaign* (Tuscaloosa: University of Alabama Press, 2008), 295; Kreiser, *Defeating Lee*, 55, 65; diary entry for July 1, 1863, in *Inside the Army of the Potomac: The Civil War Experience of Captain Francis Donaldson*, 298; Daniel M. Callaghan, *Thomas*

Francis Meagher and the Irish Brigade in the Civil War (Jefferson, NC: McFarland, 2006), 143.

21. Gottfried, *Brigades of Gettysburg*, 177; Eric Campbell, " 'Remember Harper's Ferry': The Degradation, Humiliation, and Redemption of Col. George L. Willard's Brigade," *Gettysburg Magazine* 7 (July 1992), 57, 59.

22. Favill, *The Diary of a Young Officer*, 234–35; W. L. Montague, *Biographical Record of the Alumni of Amherst College During Its First Half Century, 1821–1871* (Amherst, MA: J. E. Williams, 1883), 287; Charles F. Johnson to Mary Johnson (September 10, 1862), in *The Civil War Letters of Colonel Charles F. Johnson, Invalid Corps*, ed. Fred Pelka (Amherst: University of Massachusetts Press, 2004), 123; George C. Bradley and Richard L. Dahlen, *From Conciliation to Conquest: The Sack of Athens and the Court-martial of Colonel John B. Turchin* (Tuscaloosa: University of Alabama Press, 2006), 129.

23. St. Clair A. Mulholland, *The Story of the 116th Regiment, Pennsylvania Infantry*, 134–35; "Report of Lt. Col. Charles H. Morgan," in *Bachelder Papers*, 3:1354; "Report of Capt. John W. Reynolds, One Hundred and Forty-Fifth Pennsylvania Infantry" (August 14, 1863) and "Reports of Brig. Gen. William Harrow" (July 16, 1863), in *O.R.*, series one, 27 (pt. 1):414, 419; Favill, *The Diary of a Young Officer*, 244–45.

24. Waitt, *History of the Nineteenth Regiment, Massachusetts Volunteer Infantry*, 229–30; Meade, *Life and Letters of General Meade*, 2:86; "Reports of Maj. Gen. Winfield S. Hancock" and "Report of Brig. Gen. John C. Caldwell" (September 5, 1863), in *O.R.*, series one, 27 (pt. 1):369, 379; Jordan, *Winfield Scott Hancock: A Soldier's Life*, 91; D. Scott Hartwig, " 'No Troops on the Field Had Done Better': John C. Caldwell's Division in the Wheatfield, July 2," in *Three Days at Gettysburg: Essays on Confederate and Union Leadership*, ed. Gary W. Gallagher (Kent, OH: Kent State University Press, 1999), 211; Mulholland, *The Story of the 116th Regiment, Pennsylvania Infantry*, 371; Charles Augustus Fuller, *Personal Recollections of the War of 1861* (Fairfield, Glos.: Echo Library, 2010), 62; Holden, *Stand Firm and Fire Low*, 154–55.

25. Fuller, *Personal Recollections of the War of 1861*, 63; James D. Brady, "Reminiscences of Fr. Corby," in *The Corby Memorial Committee* (Philadelphia: Allen, Lane & Scott, 1911), 3, 12; Joseph G. Bilby, *The Irish Brigade in the Civil War: The 69th New York and Other Irish* (Cambridge, MA: Da Capo Press, 1997), 87; "Notes of a Conversation with Col. Mulholland 116 Pa.V.," Col. John R. Brooke to J. B. Bachelder (November 14, 1885) and "Statement of Lt. William P. Wilson" in *Bachelder Papers*, 1:420–21 and 2:140, 1195–96; Mulholland, *The Story of the 116th Regiment, Pennsylvania Infantry*, 372; William Corby, *Memoirs of Chaplain Life* (Chicago: LaMont, O'Donnell & Co., 1893), 184; W. S. Shallenberger, "140th Regiment Infantry" (September 11, 1889), in *Pennsylvania at Gettysburg*, 2:689.

26. "Report of Lt. Col. Charles H. Morgan," in *Bachelder Papers*, 3:1356; "Report of Brig. Gen. John C. Caldwell" (September 5, 1863), in *O.R.*, series one, 27 (pt. 1):379; Rafferty, "Gettysburg," in *Personal Recollections of the War of the Rebellion*, 22–23; R. H. Forster, "148th Regiment Infantry" (September 11, 1889), in *Pennsylvania at Gettysburg*, 2:735; Mulholland, *The Story of the 116th Regiment, Pennsylvania Infantry*, 135–36.

27. Tremaine, *Two Days of War*, 84; Harper, *"If Thee Must Fight,"* 240; Sara Gould Walters, *Inscription at Gettysburg: In Memoriam to Captain David Acheson, Company C, 140th Pennsylvania Volunteers* (Gettysburg: Thomas Publications, 1991), 83.

28. Holden, *Stand Firm and Fire Low*, 154–55; Duane E. Shaffer, *Men of Granite: New Hampshire's Soldiers in the Civil War* (Columbia: University of South Carolina Press, 2008), 157; Forster, "148th Regiment Infantry" (September 11, 1889), in *Pennsylvania at Gettysburg*, 2:735; Fuller, *Personal Recollections of the War of 1861*, 63.

29. Aiken, "The Gettysburg Reunion," in *Gettysburg Sources*, 2:175; John Buttrick Noyes to "Dear Father" (July 5, 1863), in John Buttrick Noyes Civil War Letters (MS Am 2332),

Houghton Library, Harvard University; "Statement of Lt. William P. Wilson," in *Bachelder Papers*, 1:1196–97; Mulholland, *The Story of the 116th Regiment, Pennsylvania Infantry*, 136; Jorgensen, *Gettysburg's Bloody Wheatfield*, 96–98.

30. Hartwig, "'No Troops on the Field Had Done Better': Caldwell's Division in the Wheat Field," 223; Bowden and Ward, *Last Chance for Victory*, 298–99, Hartwig, "'I Have Never Been in a Hotter Place,'" 69, 70–71; Jorgensen, *Gettysburg's Bloody Wheatfield*, 99, and *The Wheatfield at Gettysburg: A Walking Tour* (Gettysburg: Thomas Publications, 2002), 15; Oscar W. West, "On Little Round Top—The Fifth Corps Fight at Gettysburg," *National Tribune* (November 22, 1906).

31. Wyckoff, *A History of the Third South Carolina Infantry*, 173, 175; Robert L. Stewart, *History of the One Hundred and Fortieth Regiment Pennsylvania Volunteers* (Philadelphia: Franklin Bindery, 1912), 104; Smith, *History of the 118th Pennsylvania Volunteers*, 252–53; William P. Wilson to J. B. Bachelder (March 23, 1884) and "General Zook's Brigade at Gettysburg," in *Bachelder Papers*, 1:417 and 2:1032; Wilkinson and Woodworth, *A Scythe of Fire*, 249; *Fighting with the Eighteenth Massachusetts: The Civil War Memoir of Thomas H. Mann*, 180.

32. John B. Linn, "Journal of My Trip to the Battlefield of Gettysburg, July, 1863," *Civil War Times Illustrated* 29 (September–October 1990), 64; "Brigadier General Samuel K. Zook—Sketch of His Life—Civic and Military Preparations for His Funeral," *New York Herald* (July 12, 1863); Theodore W. Bean, *History of Montgomery County, Pennsylvania* (Philadelphia: Everts & Peck, 1884), 288; John S. Hammell to J. B. Bachelder, Kershaw to J. B. Bachelder (March 20, 1876), Brooke to Francis A. Walker (March 18, 1886), and "Report of Lt. Col. Charles H. Morgan, in *Bachelder Papers*, 1:418, 423, 456, 2:1233–34, and 3:1355–56; "Report of Maj. Peter Nelson, Sixty-Sixth New York Infantry," in *O.R.*, series one, 27 (pt. 1):398; W. A. Croffutt and John M. Morris, *The Military and Civil History of Connecticut During the War of 1861–65* (New York: Ledyard Bill, 1869), 392; Winthrop Dudley Sheldon, *The "Twenty-Seventh": A Regimental History* (New Haven: Morris & Benham, 1866), 77; Charles P. Hamblen, *Connecticut Yankees at Gettysburg*, ed. Walter Powell (Kent, OH: Kent State University Press, 1993), 49.

33. Powell, *The Fifth Army Corps*, 534; Kershaw to J. B. Bachelder (April 3, 1876) and Brooke to Francis A. Walker (March 18, 1886), in *Bachelder Papers*, 1:470 and 2:1234; Carter, "The Campaign and Battle of Gettysburg," 167; "Report of Brig. Gen. J. B. Kershaw, C.S. Army" (October 1, 1863), "Reports of Col. John R. Brooke, Fifty-third Pennsylvania Infantry" (August 15, 1863), and "Reports of Lieut. Col. John Fraser, One Hundred and Fortieth Pennsylvania Infantry" (August 7–8, 1863), in *O.R.*, series one, 27 (pt. 1):395, 401, and (pt. 2):369; Kershaw, "Kershaw's Brigade at Gettysburg," in *Battles & Leaders*, 3:336; Alonzo Myers, "Kershaw's Brigade at Peach Orchard," *National Tribune* (January 21, 1926).

34. "William Tatum Wofford—The Memorial Read at the Reunion of His Regiment, the Eighteenth Georgia," *Cartersville* (GA) *Courant American* (September 8, 1887); Tagg, *The Generals of Gettysburg*, 221–22; Robert K. Krick, *Parker's Virginia Battery, C.S.A.* (Wilmington, NC: Broadfoot Publishing, 1989), 174; Gerald J. Smith, *"One of the Most Daring of Men": The Life of Confederate General William Tatum Wofford* (Murfreesboro, TN: Southern Heritage Press, 1997), 19–20, 23, 37, 137; Robert M. Powell, "With Hood at Gettysburg," in *Battles and Leaders of the Civil War*, ed. Cozzens, 6:243; David Wyatt Aiken, in Frassanito, *Early Photography at Gettysburg*, 325.

35. Gilbert Frederick, "57th Regiment Infantry" (October 6, 1889), in *New York at Gettysburg*, 1:420; Bowden and Ward, *Last Chance for Victory*, 298–99; McLaws, "Gettysburg," *SHSP* 7 (February 1879), 73–75; Smith, *"One of the Most Daring of Men,"* 85; Longstreet, *From Manassas to Appomattox*, 372; Fremantle, *Three Months in the Southern States*, 261.

36. Frederick, "57th Regiment Infantry" (October 6, 1889), in *New York at Gettysburg*, 1:420;

Wyckoff, *History of the 3rd South Carolina Infantry*, 175, 194; Kershaw to J. B. Bachelder (April 3, 1876) and "Notes of a Conversation with Col. Mulholland 116 Pa.V.," in *Bachelder Papers*, 1:422, 471–72; Powell, *History of the Fifth Army Corps*, 534–35.

37.   Bowden and Ward, *Last Chance for Victory*, 301–2; Jorgensen, *The Wheatfield at Gettysburg*, 17; "Statement of Lt. Wiliam P. Wilson," in *Bachelder Papers*, 2:1197; Wilkinson and Woodworth, *A Scythe of Fire*, 250–51; Noyes to "Dear Father" (July 5, 1863), in John Buttrick Noyes Civil War Letters, Houghton Library, Harvard University.

38.   "Report of Lt. Col. Charles H. Morgan," in *Bachelder Papers*, 2:1197 and 3:1355; Mulholland, *Story of the 116th Pennsylvania*, 375; Shallenberger, "140th Regiment Infantry," in *Pennsylvania at Gettysburg*, 2:689; Gilbert Frederick, "57th Regiment Infantry" (October 6, 1889), in *New York at Gettysburg*, 1:420; "Report of Lieut. Col. Alford B. Chapman, Fifty-seventh New York Infantry" (August 5, 1863) and "Report of Col. William S. Tilton, Twenty-second Massachusetts Infantry" (July 9, 1863), in *O.R.,* series one, 27 (pt. 1):397, 608; Noyes to "Dear Father" (July 5, 1863), in John Buttrick Noyes Civil War Letters, Houghton Library, Harvard University.

39.   Martin D. Hardin, "41st Regiment of Infantry," in *Pennsylvania at Gettysburg*, 1:297; Henry S. Seage to J. B. Bachelder (September 23, 1884), in *Bachelder Papers*, 2:1071; Richard Bak, *A Distant Thunder: Michigan in the Civil War* (Ann Arbor, MI: Huron River Press, 2004), 129; Robert Campbell, "Pioneer Memories of the War Days, 1861–65," in *Historical Collections: Collections and Research Made by the Michigan Pioneer and Historical Society* 30 (Lansing, MI: Wynkoop, Hallenbeck, Crawford, 1906), 570; Martin N. Bertera and Kim Crawford, *The 4th Michigan Infantry in the Civil War* (Lansing: Michigan State University Press, 2010), 167; "Address of Capt. L. H. Salsbury," in *Michigan at Gettysburg*, 86; diary entry for July 2, 1863, in *Inside the Army of the Potomac: The Civil War Experience of Captain Francis Donaldson*, 306; Orvey S. Barrett, *Reminiscences, Incidents, Battles, Marches and Camp Life of the Old 4th Michigan Infantry in the War of Rebellion, 1861 to 1864* (Detroit: W. S. Ostler, 1888), 22.

40.   McLaws to Emily McLaws (July 7, 1863), in *A Soldier's General*, 196; Carter, "Campaign and Battle of Gettysburg," 197; Dudley H. Chase, "Gettysburg," in *War Papers Read Before the Indiana Commandery*, 301; "Reports of Brig. Gen. Romeyn Ayres, U.S. Army" (July 28, 1863) and "Report of Col. Sidney Burbank, Second U.S. Infantry" (July 21, 1863), in *O.R.,* series one, 27 (pt. 1):634; James A. Leyden, "The Fourth Regiment of Infantry," in *The Army of the United States: Historical Sketches of Staff and Line*, eds. T. F. Rodenbough and W. L. Haskin (New York: Maynard, Merrill, 1896), 404; Jorgensen, *Gettysburg's Bloody Wheatfield*, 121–22; Joseph Gibbs, *Three Years in the Bloody Eleventh: The Campaigns of a Pennsylvania Reserves Regiment* (University Park, PA: Penn State University Press, 2002), 221; B. F. W. Urban, "The Story of Gettysburg," *Gettysburg Magazine* 37 (July 2007), 93.

41.   "Testimony of Brigadier-General S.W. Crawford" (April 27, 1864), in *Report of the Joint Committee on the Conduct of the War,* 4:469.

42.   Martin Hardin, *History of the Twelfth Regiment, Pennsylvania Reserve Volunteer Corps,* 152–53; Thomson and Rauch, *History of the "Bucktails": Kane Rifle Regiment of the Pennsylvania Reserve Corps* (Philadelphia: Electric Printing Co., 1906), 265–66; Norton, *Attack and Defense of Little Round Top,* 239; Oliver Ayer Roberts, *History of the Military Company of the Massachusetts, Now Called the Ancient and Honorable Artillery Company of Massachusetts, 1637–1888* (Boston: Alfred Mudge & Son, 1901), 12–13; Frank L. Beeby, "Colonel Fred. Taylor and His Bucktails," in *Fourteenth Annual Reunion of the Regimental Association of the Bucktails, or First Rifle Regiment of the FRVC* (Philadelphia: Furlong, Gannon, Coulter, 1901), n.p.; George W. Newton, *Silent Sentinels: A Reference Guide to the Artillery at Gettysburg* (New York: Savas Beatie, 2005), 177, 179; H. N. Minnigh, "Who Occupied It?—A Discussion of the Movements About the Round Tops," *National Tribune* (Novem-

ber 19, 1891); "Report of Capt. Frank C. Gibbs, Battery L, First Ohio Light Artillery" (July 4, 1863), in *O.R.*, series one, 27 (pt. 1):662; Matt Spruill, *Summer Thunder: A Battlefield Guide to the Artillery at Gettysburg* (Knoxville: University of Tennessee Press, 2010), 135.

43. Robert A. McCoy, "The First Brigade at Gettysburg" (September 2, 1809) and "The Reserves at Gettysburg," E. M. Woodward, "31st Regiment Infantry," and George W. McCracken, "39th Regiment Infantry" (September 2, 1890), in *Pennsylvania at Gettysburg*, 1:74, 112–13, 228, 271; Woodward, *Our Campaigns; or, The Marches, Bivouacs, Battles, Incidents of Camp Life and History of Our Regiment*, 268; LaFantasie, *Twilight at Little Round Top*, 197; Gibbs, *Three Years in the Bloody Eleventh*, 222, 224; B. F. W. Urban, "The Story of Gettysburg," 95.

44. J. R. Sypher, *History of the Pennsylvania Reserve Corps: A Complete Record of the Organization; and the Different Companies, Regiments, and Brigades* (Lancaster, PA: Elias Barr, 1865), 461, 464–65; R. G. Carter to J. B. Bachelder (November 6, 1889), in *Bachelder Papers*, 3:1673; Bowden and Ward, *Last Chance for Victory*, 305–6; "Testimony of Brigadier-General S. W. Crawford" (April 27, 1864), in *Report of the Joint Committee on the Conduct of the War*, 4:469; McLaws, "The Second Day at Gettysburg," in *Gettysburg Sources*, 3:133–34; "Report of Capt. George Hillyer, Ninth Georgia Infantry" (July 8, 1863), in *O.R.*, series one, 27 (pt. 1):400; Youngblood, "Unwritten History of the Gettysburg Campaign," *SHSP* 38 (January–December 1910), 316; Col. Goode Bryan in "Report of the Committee," in *Pennsylvania at Gettysburg*, 1:103.

45. "Report of Lieut. Gen. James Longstreet, C.S. Army," in *O.R.*, series one, 27 (pt. 2):359; Longstreet, "Lee in Pennsylvania," in *Annals of the War*, 425; Longstreet, *From Manassas to Appomattox*, 373.

46. Carter, "Campaign and Battle of Gettysburg," 171.

CHAPTER SEVENTEEN   *The supreme moment of the war had come*

1. Smith, *Farms at Gettysburg*, 20; "Reports of General Robert E. Lee, C.S. Army" (July 31, 1863), in *O.R.*, series one, 27 (pt. 2):308; Harman, *Lee's Real Plan at Gettysburg*, 53.

2. Blake, *Three Years in the Army of the Potomac*, 200; Eric A. Campbell, "Hell in a Peach Orchard," *America's Civil War* 16 (July 2003), 41, and " 'The Key to the Entire Situation': The Peach Orchard, July 2, 1863," in *The Second Day at Gettysburg*, 155; Edward L. Bailey to J. B. Bachelder (March 29, 1882), in *Bachelder Papers*, 2:844, 846.

3. "Testimony of General Henry J. Hunt" (April 4, 1864), in *Report of the Joint Committee on the Conduct of the War*, 4:450; "Reports of Brig. Gen. Robert O. Tyler," in *O.R.*, series one, 27 (pt. 1):872; R. L. Murray, "The Artillery Duel in the Peach Orchard," *Gettysburg Magazine* 36 (January 2007), 72–73, 78–79, and *E. P. Alexander and the Artillery Action in the Peach Orchard*, 48–49, 50; George Lewis, *The History of Battery E, First Regiment Rhode Island Light Artillery, in the War of 1861 and 1865, to Preserve the Union* (Providence, RI: Snow & Farnham, 1892), 192–94.

4. John Bigelow, *The Peach Orchard at Gettysburg, July 2, 1863* (Minneapolis: Kimball-Storer, 1910), 52–53; Hanifen, *History of Battery B, First New Jersey Artillery*, 68–69, 73; Luther E. Cowles, *History of the Fifth Massachusetts Battery* (Boston: Luther E. Cowles, 1902), 624; Murray, *E. P. Alexander and the Artillery Action in the Peach Orchard*, 96; "Reports of Brig. Gen. Henry J. Hunt" (September 27, 1863), in *O.R.*, series one, 27 (pt. 1):235.

5. J. S. McNeily, "Barksdale's Mississippi Brigade at Gettysburg," *Publications of the Mississippi Historical Society* (University: Mississippi Historical Society, 1914), 14:236; James W. McKee, "William Barksdale and the Congressional Election of 1853," *Journal of Mississippi History* 34 (May 1972), 129–58; "Galusha A. Grow," *Harper's Weekly* (March

3, 1894); Williamjames Hoffer, *The Caning of Charles Sumner: Honor, Idealism, and the Origins of the Civil War* (Baltimore: Johns Hopkins University Press, 2010), 13; James Dinkins, "Griffith-Barksdale-Humphrey Mississippi Brigade and Its Campaigns," *SHSP* 32 (January–December 1904), 259; W. G. Johnson, "Barksdale-Humphreys Mississippi Brigade," *Confederate Veteran* 1 (July 1893), 207; Youngblood, "Personal Observations at Gettysburg," *Confederate Veteran* 19 (June 1911), 286.

6. Ross, *A Visit to the Cities and Camps of the Confederate States*, 54–56; McLaws, "Gettysburg," *SHSP* 7 (February 1879), 71–72, 74; George Clark, "Wilcox's Alabama Brigade at Gettysburg," *Confederate Veteran* 17 (May 1909), 229–30; Terrence J. Winschel, "Their Supreme Moment: Barksdale's Brigade at Gettysburg," *Gettysburg Magazine* 1 (July 1989), 74; Longstreet, *Manassas to Appomattox*, 370.

7. Alfred Craighead, "68th Regiment Infantry" (July 2, 1889) and David Craft, "141st Regiment Infantry" (September 12, 1889), in *Pennsylvania at Gettysburg*, 1:397–98 and 2:691; McNeily, "Barksdale's Mississippi Brigade at Gettysburg," 237, 238; J. R. Bucklyn to J. B. Bachelder (December 31, 1863), in *Bachelder Papers*, 1:72–73; Frank Moran, "A Fire Zouave—Memoirs of the Excelsior Brigade," *National Tribune* (November 6, 1890); Hagerty, *Collis' Zouaves*, 241–43; "Report of Calvin A. Craig, One Hundred and Fifth Pennsylvania Infantry" (July 11, 1863), in *O.R.*, series one, 27 (pt. 1):501; Robert Fuhrman, "The 57th Pennsylvania Volunteer Infantry at Gettysburg," *Gettysburg Magazine* 17 (July 1997), 66–67; Alanson Nelson, *The Battles of Chancellorsville and Gettysburg*, 149–51.

8. Busey and Martin, *Regimental Strengths and Losses*, 49, 50, 55, 180; Du Picq, *Battle Studies: Ancient and Modern Battle*, eds. J. N. Greeley and R. C. Cotton, 110; Penrose G. Mark, *Red, White, and Blue Badge, Pennsylvania Veteran Volunteers: A History of the 93rd Regiment* (Harrisburg, PA: Auginbaugh Press, 1911), 219; Sebastian Junger, *War* (New York: Twelve, 2010), 234.

9. Martin A. Haynes, *A History of the Second Regiment, New Hampshire Volunteer Infantry, in the War of the Rebellion* (Lakeport, NH: Republican Press Association, 1896), 171, 173, 179; "Third Maine Regiment," in *Maine at Gettysburg*, 131–32; "Report of Col. Moses B. Lakeman, Third Maine Infantry" (July 27, 1863), in *O.R.*, series one, 27 (pt. 1):508; David Craft, *History of the One Hundred Forty-first Regiment, Pennsylvania Volunteers, 1862–1865* (Towanda, PA: Reporter-Journal Printing, 1885), 126–27, 137; William E. Loring, "Gettysburg—The 141st Pa. at the Battle," *National Tribune* (July 9, 1885); O'Reilly, *"Stonewall" Jackson at Fredericksburg*, 153; Bates, *Pennsylvania Volunteers*, 4:440; Edward L. Bailey to J. B. Bachelder (March 29, 1882), in *Bachelder Papers*, 2:846–47; Ross, *A Visit to the Cities and Camps of the Confederate States*, 56; Lewis, *History of Battery E, First Regiment Rhode Island Light Artillery*, 209; Gary G. Lash, "'A Pathetic Story': The 141st Pennsylvania (Graham's Brigade) at Gettysburg," *Gettysburg Magazine* 14 (January 1996), 95–96.

10. Loring, "On the Second Day—The 141st Pa. in the Gettysburg Battle," *National Tribune* (July 5, 1894); McNeily, "Barksdale's Mississippi Brigade at Gettysburg," 242; McLaws to Emily McLaws (July 7, 1863), in *A Soldier's General*, 196.

11. Frank Moran to Daniel Sickles (January 24, 1882), in *Bachelder Papers*, 2:773; McNeily, "Barksdale's Mississippi Brigade at Gettysburg," 243; F. M. Colston, "Gettysburg as I Saw It," *Confederate Veteran* 5 (November 1897), 551–52; Youngblood, "Unwritten History of the Gettysburg Campaign," *SHSP* 38 (January–December 1910), 316; Alexander, "The Great Charge and Artillery Fighting at Gettysburg," in *Battles & Leaders*, 3:359–60; Jay Jorgensen, "Confederate Artillery at Gettysburg," *Gettysburg Magazine* 24 (January 2001), 30.

12. William A. Love, "Mississippi at Gettysburg," in *Publications of the Mississippi Historical Society* (Oxford, MS: Mississippi Historical Society, 1906), 9:32; Alexander, *Fighting for the Confederacy*, 240.

13. "Testimony of Major General Andrew A. Humphreys" (March 21, 1864), in *Report of the*

Joint Committee on the Conduct of the War, 4:392; J. W. De Peyster, *Andrew Atkinson Humphreys, of Pennsylvania: Brigadier General and Brevet Major General, U.S.A.* (Lancaster, PA: Intelligencer Print, 1886), 15, and "Andrew Atkinson Humphreys," *Magazine of American History* 16 (July–December 1886), 347–48; "Andrew Atkinson Humphreys," in *Proceedings of the American Academy of Arts and Sciences* (Boston: John Wilson & Son, 1884), 19:529.

14. Van Santvoord, *The One Hundred and Twentieth Regiment New York State Volunteers*, 24, 75; George C. Burling to J. B. Bachelder (February 8, 1884), in *Bachelder Papers*, 2:1008; Henry Lefevre Brown, *History of the Third Regiment, Excelsior Brigade, 72d New York Volunteer Infantry, 1861–1865* (Jamestown, NY: Journal Printing, 1902), 104; William L. Stork, "Gettysburg—Why Was Not the Twelfth Corps in the First Day's Fight?," *National Tribune* (September 10, 1891); George H. Sharpe, "Dedication of Monument—120th Regiment of Infantry" (June 25, 1889), in *New York at Gettysburg*, 2:820; Cornelius D. Westbrook, "On the Firing Line—The 120th New York's Firm Stand on the Second Day at Gettysburg," *National Tribune* (September 20, 1900).

15. "Testimony of Major General Andrew A. Humphreys" (March 21, 1864), in *Report of the Joint Committee on the Conduct of the War*, 4:392; C. B. Baldwin to J. B. Bachelder (May 20, 1865) in *Bachelder Papers*, 1:193.

16. Bigelow, *The Peach Orchard at Gettysburg*, 54–55; Hanifen, *History of Battery B, First New Jersey Artillery*, 76, 77; "Report of Lieut. Col. Freeman McGilvery" and "Report of Capt. Patrick Hart, Fifteenth New York Battery" (August 2, 1863), in *O.R.*, series one, 27 (pt. 1):882, 887.

17. Toombs, *New Jersey Troops in the Gettysburg Campaign*, 222–23; David L. Callihan, "A Cool, Clear Headed Old Sailor: Freeman McGilvery at Gettysburg," *Gettysburg Magazine* 31 (July 2004), 47; Bradley M. Gottfried, *The Artillery of Gettysburg*, 127.

18. Phillips and Bigelow to J. B. Bachelder, in *Bachelder Papers*, 1:167–68, 173; Murray, *E. P. Alexander and the Artillery Action in the Peach Orchard*, 101–2; "Scott on the Fight of July 2d," in Cowles, *History of the Fifth Massachusetts Battery*, 631; Bigelow, *The Peach Orchard at Gettysburg*, 17–18; Campbell, " 'The Key to the Entire Situation': The Peach Orchard, July 2, 1863," in *The Second Day at Gettysburg*, 191; Levi W. Baker, *History of the Ninth Mass. Battery* (South Framingham, MA: Lakeview Press, 1888), 60–61; Van Naiswald, *Grape and Canister*, 316–17.

19. "Letter of Capt. John Bigelow," in *Bachelder Papers*, 1:173–75; Baker, *History of the Ninth Mass. Battery*, 61; Bigelow, *The Peach Orchard at Gettysburg*, 57; Bigelow to the Adjutant-General (June 19, 1895), in *"A Grand and Terrible Dramma": From Gettysburg to Petersburg—The Civil War Letters of Charles Wellington Reed*, ed. Eric A. Campbell (New York: Fordham University Press, 2000), 344–45; Hesse to Almira Hesse (July 4, 1863), in "We Have Here a Great Fight," ed. Eric Campbell, *Civil War Times* 48 (August 2009), 41.

20. "Reports of Augustus P. Martin, Third Massachusetts Battery" (July 31, 1863), in *O.R.*, series one, 27 (pt. 1):660; Van Naiswald, *Grape and Canister*, 312–13; Schultz and Wieck, *The Battle Between the Farm Lanes*, 146–47; Benjamin Humphreys to J. B. Bachelder (May 1, 1876), in *Bachelder Papers*, 1:481.

21. Rafferty, "Gettysburg," in *Personal Recollections of the War of the Rebellion*, 22–23; Craft, *History of the One Hundred Forty-first Regiment, Pennsylvania Volunteers*, 127; Randolph to J. B. Bachelder (March 1866), George Winslow to J. B. Bachelder (May 17, 1878), and George W. Bonnell to J. B. Bachelder (March 24, 1882), in *Bachelder Papers*, 1:239–40, 590–91, 2:843–44; Jim Hessler, "Blowing Smoke," *America's Civil War* 22 (July 2009), 49, 50; Tremain, *Two Days of War*, 88; "Reports of Maj. Gen. David B. Birney" (August 7, 1863), in *O.R.*, series one, 27 (pt. 1):483. It is uncertain precisely at what time Sickles' wound occurred. Thomas Rafferty, the lieutenant colonel of the 71st New York, placed the incident at "about" the same time Samuel Zook was mortally wounded in Rose's wheat

field, which would put Sickles' wound shortly after six o'clock; George Winslow, who was in the process of hauling his New York battery out of the wheat field as Zook was crossing into it with the rest of Caldwell's division, also put the wounding "some two or three minutes" after Winslow had left the wheat field and reported to Sickles. But Rafferty was probably not an eyewitness, and it may have taken Winslow far longer to get his battery "through the woods" on the north side of the wheat field than he remembered when he recounted his view of what happened fifteen years later. What is more likely is that Sickles was hit closer to seven o'clock, since Col. Henry Madill and his pathetic little band of survivors from the peach orchard had just met Sickles near the Trostle farm when "a moment after . . . the gallant Sickles" was struck "by a musket ball, his leg fractured." George Randolph, the chief of the 3rd Corps' artillery, was with Sickles when the wounding occurred, and placed it roughly "towards 5 or 6 o'clock." But since one of the gunners in Clark's New Jersey battery remembered Sickles being struck by a "shell . . . in the rear of our battery" (which implies that Clark's battery was still blazing away at the wheat field lane), and since Randolph also remembered that he had just urged Sickles to move to the rear of the Trostle barn because "the place became too hot for a corps headquarters," the hour was surely closer to seven, and perhaps even a little after. Henry Tremain, Sickles devoted aide, pegged the time at 6:30 in his 1902 memoir of Gettysburg, and in 1909 Sickles also decided that it had happened "about 6.30."

22. John Bigelow to J. B. Bachelder and Randolph to J. B. Bachelder (March 1866), in *Bachelder Papers*, 1:171–72, 239–40; "Sickles Recalls Fighting Battle of Gettysburg," *New York Evening Mail* (December 2, 1909); "Affairs at Gettysburgh," *New York Times* (July 18, 1863); Tremain, *Two Days of War*, 90; "Gettysburg," in *Campfire and Battlefield: An Illustrated History of the Campaigns and Conflicts of the Great Civil War*, ed. Rossiter Johnson (New York: Bryan, Taylor & Co., 1894), 266; Hessler, *Sickles at Gettysburg*, 204–5.

23. "A Great Victory—Three Day's Battles—Mr. T. M. Cook's Despatch," *New York Herald* (July 6, 1863); W. H. Bullard to Sickles (September 13, 1897), in Daniel E. Sickles Papers, New-York Historical Society; Hessler, *Sickles at Gettysburg*, 223; Brown, *History of the Third Regiment, Excelsior Brigade*, 105; Hays, *Under the Red Patch: Story of the Sixty-third Regiment, Pennsylvania Volunteers, 1861–1864*, 199; "Affairs at Gettysburgh," *New York Times* (July 18, 1863); Alexander Webb interview with Alexander Kelly (October 7, 1904), in *Generals in Bronze*, 152–53.

24. Cornelius Irvine Walker, *The Life of Lieutenant General Richard Heron Anderson of the Confederate States Army* (Charleston, SC: Art Publishing Co., 1917), 19, 25; Alexander, *Fighting for the Confederacy*, 365; Steven H. Newton, *The Battle of Seven Pines, May 31–June 1, 1862* (Lynchburg, VA: H. E. Howard, 1993), 29, 99; Don Walters, "In Defense of Maj. Gen. Richard H. Anderson and His Division at Gettysburg, July 2, 1863," *Blue & Gray Magazine* (Holiday 2003),16, 18.

25. "Report of Maj. Gen. Richard H. Anderson, C.S. Army" (August 7, 1863), in *O.R.*, series one, 27 (pt. 2):614; Longstreet, *Manassas to Appomattox*, 365; Busey and Martin, *Regimental Strengths and Losses*, 234, 308.

26. "Report of Maj. Gen. Richard H. Anderson, C.S. Army" (August 7, 1863) and "Report of Brig. Gen. Cadmus M. Wilcox, C.S. Army" (July 17, 1863), in *O.R.,* series one, 27 (pt. 2):614, 618; John C. Carter, *Welcome the Hour of Conflict: William Cowan McClellan and the 9th Alabama* (Tuscaloosa: University of Alabama Press, 2007), 250; Waters and Edmonds, *A Small but Spartan Band*, 67.

27. Clark B. Baldwin to J. B. Bachelder (May 20, 1865) and Hilary A. Herbert to J. B. Bachelder (July 9, 1884), in *Bachelder Papers*, 1:193, 2:1057; Clark, "Wilcox's Alabama Brigade at Gettysburg," *Confederate Veteran* 17 (May 1909), 229–30; Warren H. Cudworth, *History of the First Regiment, Massachusetts Infantry* (Boston: Walker, Fuller & Co., 1866), 397; Kevin

O'Brien, "'To Unflinchingly Face Danger and Death': Carr's Brigade Defends Emmitsburg Road," *Gettysburg Magazine* 12 (January 1995), 15; "Colonel Hilary A. Herbert's 'History of the Eighth Alabama Volunteer Regiment, C.S.A.,'" ed. M. S. Fortin, *Alabama Historical Quarterly* 39 (1977), 117; Bowden and Ward, *Last Chance for Victory*, 327.

28. Asa W. Barlett, *History of the Twelfth Regiment, New Hampshire Volunteers in the War of the Rebellion* (Concord: Ira C. Evans, 1897), 121, 123–24; Blake, *Three Years in the Army of the Potomac,* 207–8; Toombs, *New Jersey Troops in the Gettysburg Campaign,* 238; Carr interview with Alexander Kelly, in *Generals in Bronze,* 95; Brown, *History of the Third Regiment, Excelsior Brigade,* 104; Rafferty, "Gettysburg" (November 7, 1883), in *Personal Recollections of the War of the Rebellion,* 26–27; Humphreys to Rebecca Humphreys (July 4, 1863), in Andrew Atkinson Humphreys Papers, Historical Society of Pennsylvania; Seeley to J. B. Bachelder, in *Bachelder Papers,* 1:607–8; Humphreys to Lafayette McLaws (January 6, 1878), Southern Historical Collection.

29. William Colvill to J. B. Bachelder (June 9, 1866), and Charles Richardson to J. B. Bachelder (May 8, 1868), in *Bachelder Papers,* 1:256–57, 339; Bigelow, *The Peach Orchard at Gettysburg,* 12; Moran, "A Fire Zouave—Memoirs of a Member of the Excelsior Brigade," *National Tribune* (November 6, 1890); "College Hospital in Gettysburg," *The Land We Love: A Monthly Magazine Devoted to Literature, Military History and Agriculture* 2 (February 1867), 293.

30. "Nineteenth Maine Regiment," in *Maine at Gettysburg,* 292; Heath to J. B. Bachelder (October 12, 1889), in *Bachelder Papers,* 3:1651–52; Schultz and Wieck, *Battle Between the Farm Lanes,* 75, 158–59; R. Lee Hadden, "The Granite Glory: The 19th Maine at Gettysburg," in *Gettysburg Magazine* 13 (July 1995), 52, 54. Forty-six years later, the regimental historian of the 19th Maine tried to squelch the story that Humphreys had ordered Heath to turn his weapons on his own men, but even then, he conceded that "doubtless some officer did urge Colonel Heath to do what he claimed" (see Smith, *History of the Nineteenth Regiment of Maine Volunteer Infantry,* 76). One of the 19th's line officers, Silas Adams, specifically rebutted Smith's denial in "The Nineteenth Maine at Gettysburg," in *War Papers Read Before the Commandery of the State of Maine,* 4:253.

31. "Colonel Hilary A. Herbert's 'History of the Eighth Alabama Volunteer Regiment, C.S.A.,'" 117.

CHAPTER EIGHTEEN *Remember Harper's Ferry!*

1. "Reports of Maj. Gen. Winfield S. Hancock," in *O.R.*, series one, 27 (pt. 1):370.

2. Gibbon, *Personal Recollections,* 137; Schultz and Wieck, *Battle Between the Farm Lanes,* 54; Bowden and Ward, *Last Chance for Victory,* 321; Hancock to J. B. Bachelder (November 7, 1885), in *Bachelder Papers,* 2:1135; *Life of David Bell Birney,* 189.

3. Francis Heath to J. B. Bachelder (October 12, 1889), in *Bachelder Papers,* 3:1651; Gambone, *Hancock at Gettysburg,* 101; Schultz and Wieck, *Battle Between the Farm Lanes,* 62–64, 69–71, 80–82; Waitt, *History of the Nineteenth Regiment, Massachusetts Volunteer Infantry,* 230–31.

4. Wayne Mahood, *Alexander "Fighting Elleck" Hays: The Life of a Civil War General, from West Point to the Wilderness* (Jefferson, NC: McFarland Publishing, 2005), 98; Campbell, "'Remember Harper's Ferry,'" 64; Ezra D, Simons, "'What Mean These Stones?" in *New York at Gettysburg,* 2:888, and *A Regimental History: The One Hundred and Twenty-fifth New York State Volunteers* (New York: Ezra D. Simons, 1888), 105.

5. A. B. Williams, "War Correspondence," in Lewis H. Clark, *Military History of Wayne County N.Y. in the Civil War, 1861–1865* (Sodus, NY: Clark, Hulett & Gaylord, 1863),

Appendix B, 6; Gambone, *Hancock at Gettysburg,* 92; "Oration of Gen. Clinton D. Mac-Dougall" (June 26, 1891), in *New York at Gettysburg,* 2:800; "Report of Col. Clinton Mac-Dougall, One Hundred and Eleventh New York Infantry" (August 26, 1863), in *O.R.,* series one, 27 (pt. 1):474; Walter Walcott, "Colors of the 126th Regiment," in *The Military History of Yates County, N.Y., Comprising a Record of the Services Rendered by the Citizens of This County* (Penn Yan, NY: Express Book and Job Printing House, 1895), 75–76; Willson, *Disaster, Struggle, Triumph,* 169; Schultz and Wieck, *Battle Between the Farm Lanes,* 77, 79–80, 89, 90, 104, 105; Simons, *A Regimental History,* 111, 113–14; Martin W. Husk, *The 111th New York Volunteer Infantry: A Civil War History* (Jefferson, NC: McFarland Publishing, 2010), 61; Charles Richardson to J. B. Bachelder (May 8, 1868), in *Bachelder Papers,* 1:339–40.

6.   Henry Dietrich, "Unveiling of Monument" (July 2, 1895), and Charles A. Richardson, "Historical Sketch," in *New York at Gettysburg,* 1:281 and 2:905; Bacarella, *Lincoln's Foreign Legion,* 137–38; Bigelow, *The Peach Orchard at Gettysburg,* 24; Campbell, "Remember Harper's Ferry," 70; "Report of Capt. Augustus P. Martin, Third Massachusetts Battery" (July 31, 1863), in *O.R.,* series one, 27 (pt. 1):660.

7.   Daniel W. Barefoot, *Let Us Die Like Brave Men: Behind the Dying Words of Confederate Warriors* (Winston-Salem, NC: John F. Blair, 2011), 119; Winey, *Confederate Army Uniforms at Gettysburg,* 30; Wheelock Veazey to J. B. Bachelder, Charles A. Richardson to J. B. Bachelder (August 18, 1867) and Benjamin G. Humphreys to J. B. Bachelder (May 1, 1876), in *Bachelder Papers,* 1:59, 315–16, 340, 481; George G. Benedict, *Vermont at Gettysburgh: A Sketch of the Part Taken by the Vermont Troops, in the Battle of Gettysburgh* (Burlington, VT: Free Press, 1870), 8–9; Evan Rothera, "Forgotten Fire-Eater: William Barksdale in History and Memory," *Journal of Mississippi History* 72 (Winter 2010), 401–25; "Reports of Maj. Gen. Abner Doubleday" (December 14, 1863), in *O.R.,* series one, 27 (pt. 1):260; Blake, *Three Years in the Army of the Potomac,* 214–15; Gambone, *Hancock at Gettysburg,* 95, 97; Muffly, *History of the 148th Pennsylvania,* 173; J. N. Searles, "The First Minnesota Volunteer Infantry," in *Glimpses of the Nation's Struggle: A Series of Papers Read Before the Minnesota Commandery,* 2:105.

8.   Francis A. Walker, "Hancock at Gettysburg," *National Tribune* (October 28, 1886); William Colville to J. B. Bachelder (June 9, 1866) and Hancock to J. B. Bachelder (November 7, 1885), in *Bachelder Papers,* 1:256–57, 2:1135; Shultz and Wieck, *Battle Between the Farm Lanes,* 92, 93; William Lochren, "The First Minnesota at Gettysburg," in *Glimpses of the Nation's Struggle,* 1:48–50; "Reports of Maj. Gen. Winfield Scott Hancock," in *O.R.,* series one, 27 (pt. 1):371.

9.   Moe, *The Last Full Measure: The Life and Death of the First Minnesota Volunteers,* 278, 349; *History of the First Regiment Minnesota Volunteer Infantry, 1861–1864* (Stillwater, MN: Easton & Masterman, 1916), 350; Franklyn Curtiss-Wedge, *History of Goodhue County, Minnesota* (Chicago: H. C. Cooper, 1909), 507–8; Brian Leehan, *Pale Horse at Plum Run: The First Minnesota at Gettysburg* (St. Paul: Minnesota Historical Society, 2001), 44, 56, 173–74, 176, 179; Colvill to J. B. Bachelder (August 30, 1866), in *Bachelder Papers,* 1:285; Walker, "Hancock at Gettysburg," *National Tribune* (October 28, 1886); Tucker, *Hancock the Superb,* 144.

10.   "Colonel Hilary Herbert's 'History of the Eighth Alabama Volunteer Regiment, C.S.A.,' " ed. M. S. Fortin, *Alabama Historical Quarterly* 39 (1977), 116–18; Searles, "The First Minnesota Volunteer Infantry," 105; Lochren, "The First Minnesota at Gettysburg," 48–50; Clark, "Wilcox's Alabama Brigade at Gettysburg," *Confederate Veteran* 17 (May 1909), 229–30; Patrick Hill, Perry Tholl, and Greg Johnson, " 'On This Spot . . .': Locating the 1st Minnesota Monument at Gettysburg," *Gettysburg Magazine* 32 (January 2005), 97; Waters and Edmonds, *A Small but Spartan Band,* 70–71; "Report of Col. David Lang, Eighth

Florida Infantry" (July 29, 1863), in *O.R.,* series one, 27 (pt. 2):631–32; Smith, *History of the Nineteenth Regiment of Maine Volunteer Infantry,* 71.

11. *History of the First Regiment Minnesota Volunteer Infantry,* 349; Searles, "The First Minnesota Volunteer Infantry," 107; "Report of Brig. Gen. Cadmus M. Wilcox, C.S. Army" (July 17, 1863) and "Report of Col. David Lang, Eighth Florida Infantry" (July 29, 1863), in *O.R.,* series one, 27 (pt. 2):618, 631–32; Leehan, *Pale Horse at Plum Run,* 74–75, 218–19.

12. Shultz and Wieck, *Battle Between the Farm Lanes,* 30–31.

13. "Report of Brig. Gen. A. R. Wright, C.S. Army" (September 28, 1863), in *O.R.,* series one, 27 (pt. 2):622; Isaac W. Avery, *The History of the State of Georgia from 1850 to 1881, Embracing the Three Important Epochs: The Decade Before the War of 1861–5; the War; the Period of Reconstruction* (New York: Brown & Derby, 1881), 40; "Delegates to the Southern Convention" and "Georgia Convention," *Macon Daily Telegraph* (January 26 and March 21, 1861); Margaret Mitchell, "General Wright: Georgia's Hero at Gettysburg," *Atlanta Historical Bulletin* 9 (May 1950), 85; Eric A. Campbell, "So Much for Comrades in Arms," *America's Civil War* (July 2007), 56; Matt Atkinson, " 'We Were Now Completely Masters of the Field': Ambrose Wright's Attack on July 2," in *The Second Day at Gettysburg,* 212; Frank H. Foote, "Marching in Clover: A Confederate Brigade's Tramp from the Rappahannock to Gettysburg," in *New Annals of the Civil War,* 276.

14. William H. Stewart, *A Pair of Blankets: War-Time History in Letters to Young People of the South* (New York: Broadway Publishing, 1911), 96–97; "Report of Maj. Gen. Richard H. Anderson, C.S. Army" (August 7, 1863), in *O.R.,* series one, 27 (pt. 2):614; Rev'd Henry Stevens, *Souvenir of the Excursions to Battlefields by the Society of the 14th Connecticut* (Washington, DC: Gibson Brothers, 1893), 16; *Address by Col. Claiborne Snead at the Reunion of the Third Georgia Regiment, at Union Point on the 31st July, 1874: History of the Third Georgia Regiment and the Career of Its First Commander, Gen. Ambrose R. Wright* (Augusta, GA: Chronicle and Sentinel Job Printing Establishment, 1874), 9; Charles Teague, *Masters of the Field at Gettysburg: A Tactical Study of the Charge of Brigadier General Ambrose R. Wright's Georgia Brigade on July 2, 1863* (privately printed, 2012), 17–18; "Private Letters from Lieut. Anderson, of Gen. Wright's Staff," *Macon Daily Telegraph* (July 22, 1863).

15. "Report of Capt. Charles J. Moffett, Second Georgia Battalion" (July 18, 1863) and "Report of Brig. Gen. A. R. Wright, C.S. Army" (September 28, 1863), in *O.R.,* series one, 27 (pt. 2):623, 630; Teague, *Masters of the Field at Gettysburg,* 19–20; Thomas L. Elmore, "Casualty Analysis of the Gettysburg Battle," *Gettysburg Magazine* 35 (July 2006), 95–96; Atkinson, " 'We Were Now Completely Masters of the Field': Ambrose Wright's Attack on July 2," 215; Charles D. Page, *History of the Fourteenth Regiment, Connecticut Vol. Infantry* (Meriden, CT: Horton Printing, 1906), 144; Edward G. Longacre, *To Gettysburg and Beyond: The Twelfth New Jersey Volunteer Infantry, II Corps, Army of the Potomac, 1862–1865* (Hightstown, NJ: Longstreet House, 1988), 124–25; Richard S. Thompson, "A Scrap of Gettysburg" (1897), in *Military Essays and Recollections: Papers Read Before the Commandery of the State of Illinois, Military Order of the Loyal Legion of the United States* (Chicago: Dial Press, 1899), 98–99.

16. Emerson L. Bicknell to J. B. Bachelder (August 6, 1883), in *Bachelder Papers,* 2:963–64; "Dedication of Monument. 2d Regiment N.Y.S. Militia (82d Volunteers)," in *New York at Gettysburg,* 2:664; "Report of Lieut. Col. George C. Joslin, Fifteenth Massachusetts Infantry" (July 11, 1863), in *O.R.,* series one, 27 (pt. 1):423; Andrew Elmer Ford, *The Story of the Fifteenth Regiment Massachusetts Volunteer Infantry in the Civil War, 1861–1864* (Clinton, MA: J. Coulter, 1898), 280; John H. Rhodes, *The History of Battery B, First Regiment Rhode Island Light Artillery, in the War to Preserve the Union, 1861–1865* (Providence, RI: Snow & Farnham, 1894), 201, 203; "Address by Colonel Joseph R. C. Ward," in *In Memoriam: Alexander Stewart Webb,* 82; Bowden and Ward, *Last Chance for Victory,* 330, 332; Bradley

Gottfried, *Stopping Pickett: The History of the Philadelphia Brigade* (Shippensburg, PA: White Mane Books, 1999), 158–59; Robert Grandchamp, "Brown's Company B, 1st Rhode Island at the Battle of Gettysburg," *Gettysburg Magazine* 36 (January 2007), 87–88; Gary G. Lash, *"Duty Well Done": The History of Edward Baker's California Regiment, 71st Pennsylvania Infantry* (Baltimore: Butternut and Blue, 2001), 332.

17. Campbell, "So Much for Comrades in Arms," 58; "Address by Colonel Joseph R. C. Ward," 82; *Address by Col. Claiborne Snead*, 9; Marsena Patrick, diary entry for July 6, 1863, in *Inside Lincoln's Army*, 267; Meade, *Life and Letters of George Gordon Meade*, 2:89; Cleaves, *Meade of Gettysburg*, 152–53.

18. Benedict, *Vermont at Gettysburgh*, 6–7; Shultz and Wieck, *Battle Between the Farm Lanes*, 115–17, 122–24, 126–27, 129; George H. Scott, "Vermont at Gettysburg," *Proceedings of the Vermont Historical Society* (1930), 1:66; Williams to J. B. Bachelder (April 21, 1864, and November 10, 1865), in *Bachelder Papers*, 1:163–64, 215; Meade, *Life and Letters of George Gordon Meade*, 2:89; Gibbon, *Personal Recollections*, 138.

19. Stewart, *A Pair of Blankets*, 96–97; Campbell, "So Much for Comrades in Arms," 58; Cooper H. Wingert, "Masters of the Field: A New Interpretation of Wright's Brigade and Their Assault at Gettysburg," *Gettysburg Magazine* 47 (July 2012), 74–75.

20. "Report of Brig. Gen. Carnot Posey, C.S. Army" (July 29, 1863) and "Report of Col. N. H. Harris, Nineteenth Mississippi Infantry" (July 29, 1863), in *O.R.*, series one, 27 (pt. 2):633, 634; Tagg, *The Generals of Gettysburg*, 319; John L. Brady to J. B. Bachelder (May 24, 1886), in *Bachelder Papers*, 3:1389; Elwood W. Christ, *"Over a Wide, Hot . . . Crimson Plain": The Struggle for the Bliss Farm at Gettysburg, July 2nd and 3rd, 1863* (Baltimore: Butternut and Blue, 1994), 20–30.

21. "Report of Maj. Gen. Daniel H. Hill, C.S. Army," in *O.R.*, series one, 11 (pt. 1):945; Hal Bridges, *Lee's Maverick General: Daniel Harvey Hill* (Lincoln: University of Nebraska Press, 1991), 49–50; John W. De Peyster, "A Military Memoir of William Mahone, Major General in the Confederate Army," *The Historical Magazine* 10 (July 1871), 20; Kevin Levin, "William Mahone, the Lost Cause, and Civil War History," *VMHB* 113 (2005), 381; "Report of Brig. Gen. William Mahone" (July 10, 1863), in *O.R.*, series one, 27 (pt. 2):621; Gottfried, *Brigades of Gettysburg*, 583; Freeman, *Lee's Lieutenants*, 3:127–28.

22. Foote, "Marching in Clover," in *New Annals of the Civil War*, 281; "Letter from Lee's Army" (July 15, 1863), in *Writing and Fighting from the Army of Northern Virginia*, 252; Teague, *Masters of the Field at Gettysburg*, 63, 71, 73–74; Zachery A. Fry, "'Rally on Your Colors': The 59th New York Volunteer Infantry from Antietam to Gettysburg," unpublished honors thesis, Kent State University (December 2010), 153; Joseph Ripley Chandler Ward, *History of the One Hundred and Sixth Regiment, Pennsylvania Volunteers* (Philadelphia: F. McManus, 1906), 400; William B. Judkins, "Memoir," in 22nd Georgia Regiment, Gettysburg National Military Park Vertical Files [#7-GA22]; "Report of Brig. Gen. A. R. Wright, C.S. Army" (September 28, 1863), in *O.R.*, series one, 27 (pt. 2):624–25; C. H. Andrews, "Flag of the Third Georgia Regiment," *Confederate Veteran* 2 (July 1894), 201.

23. William Paul, "Severe Experiences at Gettysburg," *Confederate Veteran* 19 (February 1911), 85; Bradley M. Gottfried, "Wright's Charge on July 2, 1863: Piercing the Union Line or Inflated Glory?," *Gettysburg Magazine* 17 (July 1997), 76; "Casualties in the Macon Guards," *Macon Daily Telegraph* (July 13, 1863).

24. Campbell, "So Much for Comrades in Arms," 56; *Memoirs of Georgia: Containing Historical Accounts of the State's Civil, Military, Industrial and Professional Interests* (Atlanta: Southern Historical Association, 1895), 1:966; Bates, *The Battle of Gettysburg*, 131–32.

CHAPTER NINETEEN *We are the Louisiana Tigers!*

1. *Campbell Brown's Civil War*, 216; Fremantle, *Six Months*, 259–60.

2. Henry S. Huidekoper, in Winey, *Confederate Army Uniforms at Gettysburg*, 24; Bowden and Ward, *Last Chance for Victory*, 346; "Report of Lieut. Gen. Richard S. Ewell, C.S. Army," in *O.R.*, series one, 27 (pt. 2):446; *Campbell Brown's Civil War*, 216; Early, *Lieutenant General Jubal Anderson Early, C.S.A.*, 273–74.

3. Howard, "Campaign and Battle of Gettysburg, June and July, 1863," 66; Wainwright, diary entry for July 1, 1863, in *A Diary of Battle*, 238; Bert H. Barnett, "'Our Position Was Finely Adapted to Its Use': The Guns of Cemetery Hill," in *The Second Day at Gettysburg*, 232.

4. Hartwell Osborn, *Trials and Triumphs: The Record of the Fifty-fifth Ohio Volunteer Infantry* (Chicago: A. C. McClurg, 1904), 99–100; Hurst, *Journal-History of the Seventy-third Ohio Volunteer Infantry*, 67–68; John Archer, *"The Hour Was One of Horror": East Cemetery Hill at Gettysburg* (Gettysburg: Thomas Publications, 1997), 15, 17–18; Edward S. Salmon, "Gettysburg" (January 17, 1912), in *Civil War Papers of the California Commandery and the Oregon Commandery of the Military Order of the Loyal Legion of the United States* (Wilmington, NC: Broadfoot Publishing, 1995), 403–4, 405.

5. Andrew Harris to J. B. Bachelder (April 7, 1864), in *Bachelder Papers*, 1:138; Kiefer, *History of the One Hundred and Fifty-Third Pennsylvania Volunteers*, 97; Herman Schuricht, "Jenkins' Brigade in the Gettysburg Campaign," *SHSP* 24 (January–December 1896), 344; Paul M. Shevchuk, "The Wounding of Albert Jenkins, July 2, 1863," *Gettysburg Magazine* 3 (July 1990), 61; Linn, "Journal of My Trip to the Battlefield of Gettysburg, July 1863," *Civil War Times Illustrated* 29 (September–October 1990), 62–63.

6. Tunstall Smith, *Richard Snowden Andrews: Lieutenant-Colonel Commanding the First Maryland Artillery* (Baltimore: Sun Job Printing, 1910), 96; Charles D. Walker, *Biographical Sketches of the Graduates and Élèves of the Virginia Military Institute Who Fell During the War Between the States* (Philadelphia: J. B. Lippincott, 1875), 332; O'Reilly, *"Stonewall" Jackson at Fredericksburg*, 117; *Campbell Brown's Civil War*, 217.

7. Stewart, "Battery B, 4th United States Artillery at Gettysburg," in W. H. Chamberlin, ed., *Sketches of War History*, 4:190; Seymour, diary entry for July 2, 1863, in *The Civil War Memoirs of William J. Seymour*, 74; "Report of Lieut. Col. R. Snowden Anderson, C.S. Artillery" (August 5, 1863), in *O.R.*, series one, 27 (pt. 2):544; Wainwright, diary entry for July 2, 1863, in *A Diary of Battle*, 243.

8. Seymour, diary entry for July 2, 1863, in *The Civil War Memoirs of William J. Seymour*, 74; Archer, *"The Hour Was One of Horror,"* 29; Stiles, *Four Years Under Marse Robert*, 218; "Report of Lieut. Col. R. Snowden Anderson, C.S. Artillery" (August 5, 1863), in *O.R.*, series one, 27 (pt. 2):544; Jay Jorgensen, "Joseph W. Latimer, the 'Boy Major,' at Gettysburg," *Gettysburg Magazine* 9 (July 1993), 33; Gary Kross, "The 'Long Arm' of Lee on Benner's Hill," *Blue and Gray Magazine* 14 (June 1997), 7–10.

9. Seymour, diary entry for July 2, 1863, in *The Civil War Memoirs of William J. Seymour*, 74; R. J. Hancock to J. W. Daniel (April 4, 1905), in John Warwick Daniel Papers, Special Collections, University of Virginia.

10. Wainwright, diary entry for July 2, 1863, in *A Diary of Battle*, 245; "Stevens' Fifth Maine Battery at the Battle of Gettysburg," in *Maine at Gettysburg*, 94; Archer, *"The Hour Was One of Horror,"* 32–33; Hurst, *Journal-History of the Seventy-Third Ohio Volunteer Infantry*, 71; Andrew L. Harris to J. B. Bachelder (March 14, 1881), in *Bachelder Papers*, 2:745–46; Seymour, diary entry for July 2, 1863, in *The Civil War Memoirs of William J. Seymour*, 75–76; Thomas Causby, "Storming the Stone Fence at Gettysburg," *SHSP* 29 (January–December 1901), 340; "Gettysburg—The Part Taken by the Eleventh Corps," *National*

Tribune (December 12, 1889); "Reports of Brig. Gen. Harry T. Hays, C.S. Army" (August 4, 1863), in *O.R.*, series one, 27 (pt. 2):480.

11. Archer, *"The Hour Was One of Horror,"* 17; Peter F. Young to J. B. Bachelder (August 12, 1867) and Andrew L. Harris to J. B. Bachelder (March 14, 1881), in *Bachelder Papers*, 1:310–11, 312, 2:745; Oscar Ladley to "Mother & Sisters" (July 5, 1863), in *Hearth and Knapsack*, 142–43; Butts, *A Gallant Captain of the Civil War*, 84–85; Seymour, diary entry for July 2, 1863, in *The Civil War Memoirs of William J. Seymour*, 75–76; Scott L. Mingus, *The Louisiana Tigers in the Gettysburg Campaign, June–July 1863* (Baton Rouge: Louisiana State University Press, 2009), 168; Barnett, " 'Our Position Was Finely Adapted to Its Use': The Guns of Cemetery Hill," in *The Second Day at Gettysburg*, 252; F. Nussbaum, "Louisiana Tigers and the 107th Ohio," *National Tribune* (July 15, 1909).

12. Howard, "Campaign and Battle of Gettysburg, June and July, 1863," 65; James A. Woods, "The 17th Connecticut and 41st New York: A Revisionist History of the Defense of East Cemetery Hill," *Gettysburg Magazine* 28 (January 2003), 96–97.

13. Barnett, " 'Our Position Was Finely Adapted to Its Use': The Guns of Cemetery Hill," 253; Hurst, *Journal-History of the Seventy-Third Ohio Volunteer Infantry*, 72; Butts, *A Gallant Captain of the Civil War*, 84–85; Kiefer, *History of the One Hundred and Fifty-third Regiment Pennsylvania Volunteers*, 87; R. Bruce Ricketts to J. B. Bachelder (March 2, 1866), in *Bachelder Papers*, 1:237–38; Ricketts, "Sketch of the Services of Battery F and G," in *Pennsylvania at Gettysburg*, 2:932; Carpenter, "General O. O. Howard at Gettysburg," 271; Wainwright, diary entry for July 2, 1863, in *A Diary of Battle*, 245, 247; Valuska and Keller, *Damn Dutch: Pennsylvania Germans at Gettysburg*, 176–77.

14. Naiswald, *Grape and Canister*, 321–22; "Reports of Brig. Gen. Harry T. Hays, C.S. Army" (August 4, 1863), in *O.R.*, series one, 27 (pt. 2):480; Causby, "Storming the Stone Fence at Gettysburg," 340–41; *Reminiscences of Carl Schurz*, 3:25; A. H. Huber, "On the Right—The 33rd Mass. and 'Steven's Knoll' at Gettysburg," *National Tribune* (March 11, 1909).

15. Gibbon, *Personal Recollections*, 138; Gottfried, *Stopping Pickett*, 164; "Reports of Brig. Gen. Alexander S. Webb" (July 12, 1863) and "Report of Lieut. Col. William L. Curry, One Hundred and Sixth Pennsylvania Infantry" (July 11, 1863), in *O.R.*, series one, 27 (pt. 1):427, 434; Ward, *History of the One Hundred and Sixth Regiment, Pennsylvania Volunteers*, 401.

16. William Kepler, *History of the Three Months' and Three Years' Service from April 16th, 1861, to June 22d, 1864, of the Fourth Regiment Ohio Volunteer Infantry in the War for the Union* (Cleveland: Leader Printing Co., 1886), 128–29; Lash, *The Gibraltar Brigade on East Cemetery Hill*, 82–92; Gottfried, *Brigades of Gettysburg*, 165.

17. "Reports of Brig. Gen. Harry T. Hays, C.S. Army" (August 4, 1863), in *O.R.*, series one, 27 (pt. 2):480; Frey, *Longstreet's Assault—Pickett's Charge*, 98; Archer, *"The Hour Was One of Horror,"* 72–76; J. L. Dickelman, "Gen. Carroll's Gibraltar Brigade at Gettysburg," *National Tribune* (December 10, 1908); Pete Tomasak, "An Encounter with Battery Hell," *Gettysburg Magazine* 12 (January 1995), 38. For the next thirty years, the humiliated survivors of Adelbert Ames' division would do their best to insist that they had "with indomitable pluck fought the enemy hand-to-hand" in the lane, "and that when Carroll's Brigade arrived the fighting was practically finished and victory won." Samuel Carroll would greet this claim with contempt: "Our brigade . . . alone drove the enemy from Cemetery Hill." Otis Howard tried to smooth over the dispute in 1876 when he paid tribute to Carroll's brigade for "carrying everything before them" on Cemetery Hill, but that only turned the wrath of Carroll's veterans on Howard. 1st Corps officers like Bruce Ricketts and Charles Wainwright turned Cemetery Hill into an ethnic slur on the "division of dutchmen," who "as soon as the charge commenced," began "running in the greatest confusion to the rear." See W. S. Wickham, "Gettysburg—An Ohio Comrade Upholds the Credit of the Elev-

enth Corps," *National Tribune* (May 7, 1891); Lash, *The Gibraltar Brigade on East Cemetery Hill*, 104; and R. Bruce Ricketts to J. B. Bachelder (March 2, 1866), in *Bachelder Papers*, 1:235, 236, 237–38.

18. "Report of Maj. Gen. Jubal A. Early, C.S. Army" (August 22, 1863), in *O.R.*, series one, 27 (pt. 2):470; Early, "Leading Confederates on the Battle of Gettysburg," *SHSP* 4 (December 1877), 280; Collins, *Major General Robert E. Rodes*, 286–91; Longstreet, *Manassas to Appomattox*, 374–75; Gallagher, *Stephen Dodson Ramseur*, 74; Wynstra, *"The Rashness of That Hour,"* 279–80; Early, *Lieutenant General Jubal Anderson Early, C.S.A.*, 273–74; Bowden and Ward, *Last Chance for Victory*, 353–54, 356. Early politely stung Rodes in his post-battle report by complaining that "no attack was made on the immediate right, as was expected, and not meeting with support from that quarter, these brigades could not hold the position they had attained." And in his sensational "review of the battle of Gettysburg" in 1877, Early would describe "the failure of Rodes' division to go forward" as "the solitary instance of remissness" shown in Dick Ewell's corps at Gettysburg—which was a whopper in its own right. But it is true that, after unwisely bolting ahead to the attack the day before, Rodes displayed an unusual inertia on the evening of July 2nd. Longstreet, for his part, blamed Early for recklessly ignoring Rodes' signal that "the moment had come for the divisions to attack" (although Longstreet was by that time less interested in Rodes than in paying back Early, who became Longstreet's primary postwar tormentor over who was responsible for Gettysburg). Rodes struggled to explain that the orders he had received from Dick Ewell "during the afternoon" instructed him to "co-operate," not with Early, but with Longstreet; it was only when after Ambrose Wright's attack had clearly fizzled that Rodes insisted that he "immediately sought out General Early, with a view of making an attack in concert with him."

19. Alpheus Williams to J. B. Bachelder (November 10, 1865) in *Bachelder Papers*, 1:214; J. M. Hubbard, "Wadsworth's Division on Culp's Hill," *National Tribune* (March 15, 1915); Mahood, *General Wadsworth*, 184.

20. Wayne E. Motts, "To Gain a Second Star: The Forgotten George S. Greene," *Gettysburg Magazine* 3 (July 1990), 65–68; Howard interview with Alexander Kelly (April 15, 1899), in *Generals in Bronze*, 176; David W. Palmer, "King of the Hill," *America's Civil War* 20 (July 2007), 48–53.

21. Charles P. Horton to J. B. Bachelder (January 23, 1867), in *Bachelder Papers*, 1:292–93; *In Memoriam: George Sears Greene, Brevet Major-General, United States Volunteers, 1801–1899* (Albany, NY: J. B. Lyon, 1909), 41–42; Frank C. Wilson, "Blunder in Battle of Gettysburg," *Confederate Veteran* (September 1912), 417; Richard Eddy, *History of the 60th Regiment, New York State Volunteers* (Philadelphia: n.p., 1864), 262–63; Jesse H. Jones, "The Breastworks at Culp's Hill," in *Battles & Leaders*, 3:316; John D. Cox, *Culp's Hill: The Attack and Defense of the Union Flank, July 2, 1863* (Cambridge, MA: Da Capo Press, 2003), 61; Hess, *Field Armies and Fortifications in the Civil War: The Eastern Campaigns*, 226–27.

22. *In Memoriam: George Sears Greene*, 41; "Reports of Maj. Gen. Henry W. Slocum" (August 23, 1863), in *O.R.*, series one, 27 (pt. 1):759; John W. Peck, "78th Regiment Infantry" and Henry M. Maguire, "102nd Infantry Regiment," *New York at Gettysburg*, 2:629, 634; M. L. Olmsted, "Recitals and Reminiscences—Stories Eminently Worth Telling of Experiences and Adventures in the Great National Struggle," *National Tribune* (December 17, 1908); John Richards Boyle, *Soldiers True: The Story of the One Hundred and Eleventh Regiment Pennsylvania Veteran Volunteers* (New York: Eaton & Mains, 1903), 122–23; John M. Archer, *"The Mountain Trembled": Culp's Hill at Gettysburg* (Gettysburg: Thomas Publications, 2000), 23, 52–53.

23. Washington Hands Civil War Notebook, Special Collections, University of Virginia; Randolph H. McKim, "Steuert's Brigade at the Battle of Gettysburg," *SHSP* 5 (June 1978),

293; Early, *Lieutenant General Jubal Anderson Early, C.S.A.*, 274; Olmsted, "Recitals and Reminiscence," *National Tribune* (December 17, 1908); George K. Collins, *Memoirs of the 149th Regt. N. Y. Vol. Inft.* (1891; Hamilton, NY: Edmonston Pubs., 1996), 138.

24. Olmsted, "Recitals and Reminiscence," *National Tribune* (December 17, 1908); John W. Peck, "78th Regiment Infantry," *New York at Gettysburg*, 2:629; McKim, "Steuert's Brigade at the Battle of Gettysburg," 293; Washington Hands Civil War Notebook, Special Collections, University of Virginia; Charles P. Horton to J. B. Bachelder (January 23, 1867), in *Bachelder Papers*, 1:294; Wilson, "Blunder in Battle of Gettysburg," 417.

25. William P. Zollinger, "General George H. Steuert's Brigade at the Battle of Gettysburg," *SHSP* 2 (July 1876), 106; "Report of Lieut.-Col. John C. O. Redington, Sixtieth New York Infantry" (July 6, 1863), in *O.R.*, series one, 27 (pt. 1):862; Edwin Merritt, "60th Regiment of Infantry" (July 2, 1888), in *New York at Gettysburg*, 1:451; Olmsted, "Recitals and Reminiscence," *National Tribune* (December 17, 1908); Fox, "Slocum and His Men: A History of the Twelfth and Twentieth Army Corps," 180.

26. Lash, *"Duty Well Done": The History of Edward Baker's California Regiment*, 334; Gottfried, *Stopping Pickett*, 165; "Colonel Fowler's Recollections of Gettysburg," in *The History of the Fighting Fourteenth*, 138; Motts, "To Gain a Second Star: The Forgotten George S. Greene," 73; Charles P. Horton to J. B. Bachelder (January 23, 1867) and Rufus R. Dawes to J. B. Bachelder (March 18, 1868), in *Bachelder Papers*, 1:294–95, 326–27; Charles F. Morse, "The Twelfth Corps at Gettysburg" (March 6, 1917), in *Papers of the Military Historical Society of Massachusetts: Civil War and Miscellaneous Papers* (Wilmington, NC: Broadfoot Publishing, 1990), 14:28; "Report of Brig. Gen. George S. Greene" (July 12, 1863), in *O.R.*, series one, 27 (pt. 1): 857.

27. William Worthington Goldsborough, *The Maryland Line in the Confederate Army, 1861–1865* (Baltimore: Guggenhiem, Weil & Co. 1900), 104; Charles P. Horton to J. B. Bachelder (January 23, 1867), in *Bachelder Papers*, 1:295; Jones, "The Breastworks at Culp's Hill," in *Battles & Leaders*, 3:317; Fox, "Slocum and His Men," 180.

28. Hutter to J. W. Daniel (no date), in John Warwick Daniel Papers, Special Collections, University of Virginia; "Report of Col. Henry A. Morrow, Twenty-fourth Michigan Infantry" (February 22, 1864), in *O.R.*, series one, 27 (pt. 1):272; Swallow, "The Second Day at Gettysburg," *Southern Bivouac* 4 (January 1886), 498.

29. De Trobriand, *Four Years with the Army of the Potomac*, 505.

CHAPTER TWENTY   *Let us have no more retreats*

1. Tap, *Over Lincoln's Shoulder*, 183; "Army of the Potomac," *Congressional Globe*, 38th Congress, first session (March 2, 1864), 898; Meade to Margaretta Meade (March 6 and April 2, 1864), in *Life and Letters of George G. Meade*, 2:169–73, 177; "Testimony of Major-General George G. Meade" (April 4, 1864), in *Report of the Joint Committee on the Conduct of the War*, 4:436; "Gen. Meade and the Battle of Gettysburgh," *New York Times* (March 7 and April 4, 1864); Sauers, *A Caspian Sea of Ink*, 46.

2. Cleaves, *Meade of Gettysburg*, 156; Meade, *Did General Meade Desire to Retreat at the Battle of Gettysburg?*, 23–25; Bache, *General George Gordon Meade*, 315–16; Coddington, *The Gettysburg Campaign*, 451–53; Noah Andre Trudeau, *Gettysburg: A Testing of Courage* (New York: HarperCollins, 2002), 414–15; Stephen W. Sears, *Gettysburg* (New York: Houghton Mifflin, 2003), 343–45; Harry W. Pfanz, *Gettysburg: Culp's Hill and Cemetery Hill* (Chapel Hill: University of North Carolina Press, 1993), 199–200.

3. John Gibbon, "The Council of War on the Second Day," in *Battles & Leaders*, 3:313; Alpheus Williams to H. W. Slocum (December 1863), in *Bachelder Papers*, 1:69; "Testi-

mony of Major General W. S. Hancock" (March 22, 1864) and "Testimony of Henry J. Hunt" (April 4, 1864), in *Report of the Joint Committee on the Conduct of the War*, 4:407, 452.

4. Meade to Halleck (July 2, 1863), in *O.R.*, series one, 27 (pt. 1):72; *Letters and Despatches of Horatio, Viscount Nelson, K.B., Duke of Bronte, Vice Admiral of the White Squadron*, ed. J. K. Laughton (London: Longmans, Green, 1886), 291; Hunt to J. B. Bachelder (July 27, 1880), in *Bachelder Papers*, 1:675; Eric J. Wittenberg, "The Truth About the Withdrawal of Brig. Gen. John Buford's Cavalry, July 2, 1863," *Gettysburg Magazine* 37 (January 2008), 76–77, 82; Hunt, "The Second Day at Gettysburg," in *Battles & Leaders*, 3:297.

5. Francis A. Walker, "Meade at Gettysburg," in *Battles & Leaders*, 3:411–12; Sauers, *A Caspian Sea of Ink*, 54–55; "Testimony of Major General Daniel Butterfield" (March 25, 1864) and "Testimony of General John Gibbon" (April 1, 1864), in *Report of the Joint Committee on the Conduct of the War*, 4:424, 442; Gibbon, *Personal Recollections of the Civil War*, 139; "Report of Maj. Gen. A. Pleasonton, Late Commander of Cavalry Corps, Army of the Potomac" (October 15, 1865), in *Journal of the United States Cavalry Association* 1 (November 1888), 399; Martin McMahon, interview with Alexander Kelly (October 11, 1879), in *Generals in Bronze*, 84; Hyde, *Following the Greek Cross*, 150–51.

6. Gibbon, "The Council of War on the Second Day," *Battles & Leaders*, 3:313, and *Personal Recollections of the Civil War*, 140, 142–44; "Minutes of Council, July 2, 1863," in *O.R.*, series one, 27 (pt. 1):73; "Testimony of Major General W. S. Hancock" (March 22, 1864) and "Testimony of General John Gibbon" (April 1, 1864), in *Report of the Joint Committee on the Conduct of the War*, 4:407, 441–42; Winfield Scott Hancock, interview with Alexander Kelly (September 2, 1880), and Daniel Butterfield, interview with Alexander Kelly (September 18, 1879), in *Generals in Bronze*, 66, 68, 71; Doubleday, *Chancellorsville and Gettysburg*, 184; Gambone, *Hancock at Gettysburg*, 106–7; Slocum to L. H. Morgan (January 2, 1864), in Fox, "Life of General Slocum," in *In Memoriam: Henry Warner Slocum, 1826–1894*, 84–85.

7. "Testimony of General Henry J. Hunt" (April 4, 1864), in *Report of the Joint Committee on the Conduct of the War*, 4:452.

8. "Reports of Maj. Gen. J.E.B. Stuart, C.S. Army" (August 20, 1863), in *O.R.*, series one, 27 (pt. 2):694–95; Wittenberg and Petruzzi, *Plenty of Blame to Go Around*, 44–45; James H. Wilson, "Captain Charles Corbit's Charge at Westminster with a Squadron of the First Delaware Cavalry, June 29, 1863," *Journal of the United States Cavalry Association* 24 (May 1914), 980.

9. "Report of Maj. Napoleon B. Knight, First Delaware Cavalry" (June 30, 1863), in *O.R.*, series one, 27 (pt. 2):201; Wittenberg and Petruzzi, *Plenty of Blame to Go Around*, 47–52.

10. George A. Rummel, *Cavalry on the Roads to Gettysburg: Kilpatrick at Hanover and Hunterstown* (Shippensburg, PA: White Mane Books, 2000), 158–59; Eric J. Wittenberg and J. David Petruzzi, "Corbit's Charge: Jeb Stuart Clashes with the 1st Delaware Cavalry at Westminster, Maryland, June 29, 1863," *Gettysburg Magazine* 36 (January 2007), 11, 13, 17; Wilson, "Captain Charles Corbit's Charge," 982; Frederic Shriver Klein, "Westminster: Little Skirmish, Big Affair?," *Civil War Times Illustrated* 7 (August 1968), 32–38.

11. "Reports of Maj. Gen. J.E.B. Stuart, C.S. Army" (August 20, 1863), in *O.R.*, series one, 27 (pt. 2):696; Wilson, "Captain Charles Corbit's Charge," 982; Wittenberg and Petruzzi, *Plenty of Blame to Go Around*, 60; 209; Longacre, *Lee's Cavalrymen*, 209.

12. J. M. Wright, "West Point Before the War," *Southern Bivouac* 4 (June 1885), 17; Samuel J. Martin, *Kill-Cavalry: The Life of Hugh Judson Kilpatrick* (Mechanicsburg, PA: Stackpole Books, 2000), 57, 62, 103; Wittenberg and Petruzzi, *Plenty of Blame to Go Around*, 65.

13. *Anthony's History of the Battle of Hanover (York County, Pennsylvania) Tuesday, June 30, 1863* (Hanover, PA: Anthony, 1945), 40–43; Samuel L. Gillespie, *A History of Co. A., First*

Ohio Cavalry, 1861–1865. A Memorial Volume, Compiled from Personal Records and Living Witnesses (Washington, OH: Press of Ohio State Register, 1898), 148; Henry C. Parsons, "Gettysburg: The Campaign Was a Chapter of Accidents," *National Tribune* (August 7, 1890); Wittenberg and Petruzzi, *Plenty of Blame to Go Around*, 89; Louis Napoleon Boudrye, *Historic Records of the Fifth New York Cavalry, First Ira Harris Guard* (Albany, NY: S. R. Gray, 1865), 65.

14.   Thomas J. Ryan, "Kilpatrick Bars Stuart's Route to Gettysburg," *Gettysburg Magazine* 27 (July 2002), 22–23; "Report of Maj. John Hammond, Fifth New York Cavalry," in *O.R.*, series one, 27 (pt. 1):1008; Rummel, *Cavalry on the Roads to Gettysburg*, 221–300; William Willis Blackford, *War Years with Jeb Stuart* (1945; Baton Rouge: Louisiana State University Press, 1993), 226.

15.   Wittenberg and Petruzzi, *Plenty of Blame to Go Around*, 89–105; "Address of General James H. Kidd, at the Dedication of Michigan Monuments upon the Battle Field of Gettysburg, June 12, 1889," in *At Custer's Side: The Civil War Writings of James Harvey Kidd*, ed. E. J. Wittenberg (Kent, OH: Kent State University Press, 2001), 9; John Esten Cooke, *Wearing of the Gray: Being Personal Portraits, Scenes and Adventures of the War* (New York: E. B. Treat, 1867), 250–53; Edward G. Longacre, *Gentleman and Soldier: A Biography of Wade Hampton III* (Nashville: Rutledge Hill Press, 2003), 144; John Krepps, "Before and After Hanover: Tracing Stuart's Cavalry Movements of June 30, 1863," *Blue & Gray Magazine* 21 (Holiday 2003), 22–23; McClellan, *Life and Campaigns of Major-General J.E.B. Stuart*, 329; "Our Special Army Correspondence—Gen. Kilpatrick's First Fight with His New Command," *New York Times* (July 4, 1863).

16.   George R. Prowell, *History of York County, Pennsylvania* (Chicago: J. H. Beers, 1907), 1:414; Scott L. Mingus, "J.E.B. Stuart Rides Through Dover, Pennsylvania," *Gettysburg Magazine* 38 (January 2008), 7; Swallow, "From Fredericksburg to Gettysburg," *Southern Bivouac* 4 (November 1885), 365; McClellan, *Life and Campaigns of Major-General J.E.B. Stuart*, 330; Edward G. Longacre, *Fitz Lee: A Military Biography of Major General Fitzhugh Lee, C.S.A.* (Cambridge, MA: Da Capo Press, 2005), 118, and *The Cavalry at Gettysburg: A Tactical Study of Mounted Operations During the Civil War's Pivotal Campaign, 9 June–14 July, 1863* (Rutherford, NJ: Fairleigh Dickinson University Press, 1986), 193; George W. Beale, *A Lieutenant of Cavalry in Lee's Army* (Boston: Gorham Press, 1918), 114; *Memoirs of the Stuart Horse Artillery Battalion: Breathed's and McGregor's Batteries*, ed. Roger Trout (Knoxville: University of Tennessee Press, 2010), 95–96.

17.   "Report of Brig. Gen. William F. Smith" (July 18, 1863), in *O.R.*, series one, 27 (pt. 2):221; *Memoirs of the Stuart Horse Artillery Battalion*, 96; Wittenberg and Petruzzi, *Plenty of Blame to Go Around*, 137; Wert, *Cavalryman of the Lost Cause*, 286.

18.   Mosby, *Stuart's Cavalry in the Gettysburg Campaign*, 183–84; Cooke, *Wearing of the Gray*, 254–55; Mingus, "J.E.B. Stuart Rides Through Dover, Pennsylvania," 14; Rummel, *Cavalry on the Roads to Gettysburg*, 303; McClellan, *Life and Campaigns of Major-General J.E.B. Stuart*, 330; "Reports of Maj. Gen. J.E.B. Stuart, C.S. Army" (August 20, 1863), in *O.R.*, series one, 27 (pt. 2): 709; *Autobiography of Major General William F. Smith, 1861–1864*, ed. H. N. Schiller (Dayton, OH: Morningside House, 1990), 67–68; Tom Huntington, *Pennsylvania Civil War Trails: The Guide to Battle Sites, Monuments, Museums and Towns* (Mechanicsburg, PA: Stackpole Books, 2007), 44; Wittenberg and Petruzzi, *Plenty of Blame to Go Around*, 153; Longacre, *Fitz Lee*, 119.

19.   Wittenberg and Petruzzi, *Plenty of Blame to Go Around*, 145–48; "Reports of Maj. Gen. J.E.B. Stuart, C.S. Army" (August 20, 1863), in *O.R.*, series one, 27 (pt. 2):697; Beale, *A Lieutenant of Cavalry in Lee's Army*, 115; Longacre, *The Cavalry at Gettysburg*, 198.

20.   Blackford, *War Years with Jeb Stuart*, 228; "The Union Cavalry Service" (July 15, 1863), in *Rebellion Record* (1864), 7:185–86; Longacre, *Gentleman and Soldier*, 147–50; J. David

Petruzzi, "The Battle of Hunterstown," in *The Complete Gettysburg Guide* (New York: Savas Beatie, 2009), 156–65; Paul M. Shevchuk, "The Battle of Hunterstown, Pennsylvania, July 2, 1863," *Gettysburg Magazine* 1 (July 1989), 99–102; Kidd, *At Custer's Side,* 10–11; *Campbell Brown's Civil War,* 206.

21. Wert, *Cavalryman of the Lost Cause,* 282; Thomas, *Robert E. Lee: A Biography,* 298, and *Bold Dragoon: The Life of J.E.B. Stuart,* 246; Mark Nesbitt, *Saber and Scapegoat: J.E.B. Stuart and the Gettysburg Controversy* (Mechanicsburg, PA: Stackpole Books, 1994), 89–91; Thomason, *Jeb Stuart,* 440. Two accounts of an icy confrontation between Lee and Stuart eventually surfaced, one describing Lee "austerely" greeting Stuart with a phlegmatic "Well, General Stuart, you are here at last," and the other a more "painful" meeting in which an angered Lee querulously demanded, "General Stuart, where have you been?" Both of these accounts contain serious anomalies. Neither Stuart nor Lee ever referred to this meeting in their official reports or in any letters. Nor did Stuart give any hint of a dressing-down by Lee in his letters in the week after Gettysburg (to the contrary, he insisted that "my cavalry has nobly sustained its reputation, and done better and harder fighting than it ever has since the war"). Moreover, the first version, with Lee "austerely" declaring, "Well, General Stuart, you are here at last," appears for the first time only in 1929, in John W. Thomason's biography of Stuart. Thomason was a career Marine officer who could be presumed to know something about military affairs, but he was not born until forty years after the battle, and cited no sources (even though he was the grandson of Longstreet's aide Thomas Goree, and interviewed members of the Stuart family for the book). The other account, which appears in numerous battle narratives (from Glenn Tucker's *High Tide at Gettysburg* to Scott Bowden and Bill Ward's *Last Chance for Victory*), is usually traced to a letter written by Thomas Munford in 1915 to Mrs. Ann Bachman Hyde, claiming to have had the whole story from Stuart's chief aide, Henry B. McClellan. But did Munford actually get this from McClellan? In 1913, Walter Kempster (who had been a lieutenant in the 10th New York Cavalry at Gettysburg) put exactly the same words into Lee's mouth, based on seeing "a letter" when Kempster had been "in Gettysburg recently" which Kempster claimed "was written by one of Stuart's brigadiers, who was present with Stuart when he reported his arrival to Gen. Lee." (*Recently* could mean almost anything, but it is significant that the 50th anniversary reunion of the armies had just taken place in Gettysburg that summer.) Even more curious, Thomas Nelson Page records the same words and the same meeting in his 1911 biography, *Robert E. Lee, Man and Soldier,* and adds some additional dialogue: "When Stuart explained, and mentioned his capture of over two hundred wagons . . . Lee exclaimed: 'Two hundred wagons! General Stuart, what are two hundred wagons to this army!'" See *Campbell Brown's Civil War,* 205; Henry B. McClellan, "Address of Major H. B. McClellan, of Lexington, Ky., on the Life, Campaigns, and Character of Gen'l J.E.B. Stuart," *SHSP* 8 (October–December 1880), 455, and McClellan, *Life and Campaigns of Major-General J.E.B. Stuart,* 332; *Campbell Brown's Civil War,* 219; *Life After J.E.B. Stuart: The Memoirs of His Granddaughter, Marrow Stuart Smith,* ed. Sean M. Heuvel (New York: Rowman & Littlefield, 2012), 142; Tucker, *High Tide at Gettysburg,* 316–17; Bowden and Ward, *Last Chance for Victory,* 422; Walter Kempster, "The Cavalry at Gettysburg" (October 1, 1913), in *War Papers Read Before the Commandery of the State of Wisconsin,* 420; Thomas Nelson Page, *Robert E. Lee, Man and Soldier* (New York: Charles Scribners, 1911), 339; Paul Shevchuk, "The Lost Hours of 'Jeb' Stuart," *Gettysburg Magazine* 4 (January 1991), 70; Robinson, *Jeb Stuart and the Confederate Defeat at Gettysburg,* 112–13; Thomas Munford to Mrs. Charles H. Hyde (July 24, 1915), Southern Historical Collection, University of North Carolina.

22. Smith, *History of the Nineteenth Regiment of Maine Volunteer Infantry, 1862–1865,* 73.

23. Léon, *Diary of a Tar Heel Confederate Soldier,* 36; Blake, *Three Years in the Army of the*

Potomac, 213–14; George Anson Bruce, *The Twentieth Regiment of Massachusetts Volunteer Infantry, 1861–1865* (Boston: Houghton Mifflin, 1906), 283–84.

24. Swallow, "The Second Day at Gettysburg," *Southern Bivouac* 4 (January 1886), 498; Berzila Inman, in Smith, *History of the 118th Pennsylvania Volunteers*, 249; Frassanito, *Early Photography at Gettysburg*, 340–41.

25. William W. Keen, "Surgical Reminiscences of the Civil War," in *Addresses and Other Papers* (Philadelphia: W. B. Saunders, 1905), 435–36; Eugene Powell, "Rebellion's High Tide— The Splendid Work the Third Day on Culp's Hill by the Twelfth Corps," *National Tribune* (July 5, 1900); Louis C. Duncan, "The Comparative Mortality of Disease and Battle Casualties in the Historic Wars of the World," *Journal of the Military Service Institution of the United States* 54 (March–April 1914), 166, 168.

26. Figes, *Crimea*, 302–3; Edgerton, *Death or Glory*, 128; Henri Dunant, *A Memory of Solferino* (Washington, DC: American National Red Cross, 1939), 70.

27. Gregory Coco, *A Vast Sea of Misery: A History and Guide to the Union and Confederate Field Hospitals at Gettysburg, July 1–November 20, 1863* (Gettysburg: Thomas Publications, 1988), ix, 129–30; Charles Edward Benton, *As Seen from the Ranks: A Boy in the Civil War* (New York: G. P. Putnam's , 1902), 31; Kiefer, *History of the One Hundred and Fifty-Third Regiment Pennsylvania Volunteers*, 99–100; Brown, *Retreat from Gettysburg*, 61–62; Wharton Jackson Green, *Recollections and Reflections*, 175–76; George G. Benedict, *Army Life in Virginia: Letters from the Twelfth Vermont Regiment and Personal Experiences of Volunteer Service in the War for the Union, 1862–63* (Burlington, VT: Free Press, 1895), 175.

28. "Our Wounded at Gettysburg—Mr. N. Davidson's Despatch," *New York Herald* (July 24, 1863); "Rebellion Echoes—The Work of Loyal Women in the War for the Union," *Gettysburg Star and Sentinel* (May 19, 1885).

29. "Report of Surg. Jonathan Letterman" (October 3, 1863), in *O.R.,* series one, 27 (pt. 1):195–96; J. B. Wescott to Joshua L. Chamberlain (February 1896), "20th Maine Infantry," in GNMP Vertical Files [#6-ME20]; Lucy Cleveland, "Dr. Baruch's Experiences as a Prisoner of War," *New York Times* (December 8, 1912); Smith, *History of the 118th Pennsylvania Volunteers*, 253; Hanifen, *History of Battery B, First New Jersey Artillery*, 80; Weygant, *History of the One Hundred and Twenty-Fourth Regiment*, 182–83; George W. New to J. B. Bachelder (September 8, 1865), in *Bachelder Papers*, 1:197–98; Craig Schneider, *The College Hospital: Pennsylvania College and the Battle of Gettysburg* (Gettysburg: Gettysburg College Civil War Era Studies, 2006), 12.

30. William Watson, *Letters of a Civil War Surgeon*, ed. Paul Fatout (West Lafayette, IN: Purdue University Press, 1996), 108; Benedict, *Army Life in Virginia*, 175; *Reminiscences of Carl Schurz*, 3:39–40; Holmes, *Acts of War*, 178–79, 181, 184–85; Decimus et Ultimus Barziza, *The Adventures of a Prisoner of War, 1863–1864*, ed. R. Henderson Shuffler (Austin: University of Texas Press, 1964), 54; Weygant, *History of the One Hundred and Twenty-Fourth Regiment*, 182–83; Rev'd H. J. Watkins, "Gettysburg War Incidents," in *1902 Spectrum* (Gettysburg College Yearbook) Special Collections, Gettysburg College; "Anonymous Mid–1930s," in *The Oxford Book of War Poetry*, ed. Tom Stallworthy (New York: Oxford University Press, 1984), 234.

31. Polley, *A Soldier's Letters to Charming Nellie*, 136; John O. Casler, *Four Years in the Stonewall Brigade* (Girard, KS: Appeal Publishing Co., 1906), 176; Robert L. Bloom, " 'We Never Expected a Battle': The Civilians at Gettysburg, 1863," *Pennsylvania History* 55 (October 1988), 183.

32. Mrs. Hugh McIlhenny, "Cobean History" (1948), GNMP Vertical Files [#1–13]; Foster, "Battle of Gettysburg" and Warren, "Recollections of the Battle of Gettysburg," Adams County Historical Society; Watkins, "Gettysburg War Incidents," 182; Alleman, *At Gettysburg; or, What a Girl Saw and Heard of the Battle*, 86–88; McCreary, "Gettysburg: A Boy's

Experience of the Battle," *McClure's Magazine* 33 (July 1909), 250; Peter C. Vermilyea, "The Effect of the Confederate Invasion of Pennsylvania on Gettysburg's African American Community," *Gettysburg Magazine* 24 (July 2001), 120; Bloom, "'We Never Expected a Battle,'" 168–69.

33. Rupp, in Bennett, *Days of "Uncertainty and Dread,"* 40–41, 48–49; Handerson, *Yankee in Gray*, 63; Timothy H. Smith, *"In the Eye of the Storm": The Farnsworth House and the Battle of Gettysburg* (Gettysburg: Farnsworth Military Impressions, 2008), 17, 33; Sheldon, *When the Smoke Cleared at Gettysburg*, 82–83, 85; McCreary, "Gettysburg: A Boy's Experience of the Battle," 247–48.

34. McCreary, "Gettysburg: A Boy's Experience of the Battle," 246; "Mrs. Gilbert's Story," *Gettysburg Compiler* (September 6, 1905); I. N. Dubboraw, "The Big Battle—A Comrade Sends Reminiscences of a Citizen at Gettysburg," *National Tribune* (December 8, 1892); John Lawrence Schick, "Battle 42 Years Ago," in GNMP Vertical Files [#8–14].

35. Alleman, *At Gettysburg; or, What a Girl Saw and Heard of the Battle*, 94; "Jennie Wade, the Heroine of Gettysburg," *Adams County Sentinel* (December 1, 1863); Frassanito, *Early Photography at Gettysburg*, 87–89; "Another Civilian Hero," *Gettysburg Star and Sentinel* (April 18, 1899); Bloom, "'We Never Expected a Battle,'" 177; Hillyer, "Battle of Gettysburg: Address Before the Walton County Georgia Confederate Veterans, August 2nd, 1904," Manuscripts, Rare Books and University Archives, Tulane University; Wilkinson and Woodworth, *A Scythe of Fire*, 254.

CHAPTER TWENTY-ONE *The general plan of attack was unchanged*

1. Jacobs, "Meterology of the Battle," *Gettysburg Magazine* 10 (January 1994), 121; "Gettysburg During the Battle—By One Who Was in the Town During the Whole," *Christian Recorder* (July 18, 1863); George Anson Bruce, *The Twentieth Regiment of Massachusetts Volunteer Infantry, 1861–1865* (Boston: Houghton Mifflin, 1906), 287–88; Kent Gramm, *Battle: The Nature and Consequences of Civil War Combat* (Tuscaloosa: University of Alabama Press, 2008), 24; "An Episode of the Battle of Gettysburg," *Catholic World* 33 (July 1881), 451–52.

2. Frederick B. Doten to J. B. Bachelder (September 22, 1870) and Theodore G. Ellis to J. B. Bachelder (November 3, 1870), in *Bachelder Papers*, 1:402, 406–7; Thompson, "A Scrap of Gettysburg," 99–100; William P. Seville, *History of the First Regiment, Delaware Volunteers* (Wilmington: Historical Society of Delaware, 1884), 83–84; Page, *History of the Fourteenth Regiment, Connecticut Vol. Infantry*, 146; Terry Crooks, "Rochester's Forgotten Regiment: The 108th New York at Gettysburg," *Gettysburg Magazine* 42 (July 2010), 101; Longacre, *To Gettysburg and Beyond: The Twelfth New Jersey Volunteer Infantry*, 129–30.

3. Bert H. Barnett, "'For an Hour and a Half We Had a Grand Fourth of July Performance': Robert E. Lee and the Cannonade of July 3," in *The Third Day: The Fate of a Nation, July 3, 1863* (Gettysburg: Gettysburg National Military Park, 2010), 95; Dickert, *History of Kershaw's Brigade*, 241; Earl J. Hess, *Pickett's Charge—The Last Attack at Gettysburg* (Chapel Hill: University of North Carolina Press, 2001), 5; "Reports of Gen. Robert E. Lee, C.S. Army" (July 31, 1863, in *O.R.*, series one, 27 (pt. 2):208; Troy Harman, *Lee's Real Plan at Gettysburg* (Mechanicsburg, PA: Stackpole Books, 2003), 64–67; H. B. McClellan, *Life and Campaigns of Major-General J.E.B. Stuart*, 337; "Battle of July Third," in Gerrish and Hutchinson, *The Blue and the Gray: A Graphic History of the Army of the Potomac and That of Northern Virginia*, 362.

4. *Campbell Brown's Civil War*, 222; Longstreet, "Lee's Right Wing at Gettysburg," in *Battles & Leaders*, 3:342; Archer, *Culp's Hill at Gettysburg*, 82.

5. James Power Smith, "General Lee at Gettysburg," *SHSP* 33 (January–February 1905), 151; Longstreet, "Lee in Pennsylvania," 429, and *Manassas to Appomattox*, 385, and "Lee's Right Wing at Gettysburg," 343; Jacobs, *Lincoln's Gettysburg World-Message*, 31; Beecham, *Gettysburg, the Pivotal Battle of the Civil War*, 262; Harman, *Lee's Real Plan at Gettysburg*, 63–64; D. Scott Hartwig, "High Water Mark Heroes, Myth and Memory," in *The Third Day: The Fate of a Nation*, 26; Bowden and Ward, *Last Chance for Victory*, 431–33, 439; Priest, *Into the Fight: Pickett's Charge at Gettysburg*, 14.

6. Walter H. Taylor, "The Campaign in Pennsylvania," in *Annals of the War*, 313; William H. J. Palmer, in T. M. R. Talcott, "The Third Day at Gettysburg," *SHSP* 41 (January–December 1916), 40; Bowden and Ward, *Last Chance for Victory*, 434; "Report of Col. E. Porter Alexander, C.S. Army" (August 3, 1863), "Report of Lieut. Gen. Ambrose P. Hill, C.S. Army" (November, 1863), and "Report of Maj. Joseph A. Engelhard, Assistant Adjutant-General, C.S. Army" (November 4, 1863), in *O.R.*, series one, 27 (pt. 2):430, 608, 658; "Afterword," in *One of Lee's Best Men: The Civil War Letters of William Dorsey Pender*, 260; Alexander, *Fighting for the Confederacy*, 244, 247; Longstreet, "Lee in Pennsylvania," 430; Jennings Cropper Wise, *The Long Arm of Lee; or, The History of the Artillery of the Army of Northern Virginia* (Lynchburg, VA: J. P. Bell, 1915), 2:661; Bradley M. Gottfried, *The Artillery of Gettysburg* (Nashville: Cumberland House, 2008), 195; Kathy Georg Harrison, *Nothing but Glory: Pickett's Division at Gettysburg* (Gettysburg: Thomas Publications, 2001), 19; Richard Rollins, "Lee's Artillery Prepares for Pickett's Charge," 44; Priest, *Into the Fight*, 181–84, 186, 200.

7. Alexander later gave conflicting estimates of the numbers of guns with which he planned to support Pickett. In 1899, he reckoned the total available artillery of Longstreet's corps on July 3rd at 62 (*Fighting for the Confederacy*, 242); but the tables submitted for Longstreet's corps after the battle show 64 guns—32 in Alexander's reserve, 18 with Pickett's division, and 14 with McLaws (*O.R.*, series one, 27 [pt. 2]:355). Fitzgerald Ross claimed that James Walton informed him that "one hundred and forty-five guns . . . were in this day placed into position, to open fire simultaneously on the enemy, preparatory to the assault which was to be made on their works" (*A Visit to the Cities and Camps of the Confederate States*, 60). Earl J. Hess puts the number at a total of 135 guns (*Pickett's Charge*, 76).

8. Alexander to J. B. Bachelder (May 3, 1876), in *Bachelder Papers*, 1:484; Adams, *The Education of Henry Adams: An Autobiography* (Boston: Houghton Mifflin, 1918), 57; Lesley J. Gordon, *General George E. Pickett in Life and Legend* (Chapel Hill: University of North Carolina Press, 1998), 14, 24, 28, 35, 75, 107; G. Moxley Sorrel, *Recollections of a Confederate Staff Officer* (New York: Neale Publishing, 1905), 54; LaSalle Pickett to Helen D. Longstreet (January 3, 1904), in Helen Longstreet, *Lee and Longstreet at High Tide: Gettysburg in the Light of the Official Records* (Gainesville, GA: privately printed, 1905), 337; Lasalle Pickett, "My Soldier," *McClure's Magazine* 30 (March 1908), 571.

9. Gordon, *General George E. Pickett in Life and Legend*, 96; Freeman, *Lee's Lieutenants*, 2:468; *Autobiography of Eppa Hunton* (Richmond: William Byrd Press, 1933), 85; Hess, *Pickett's Charge*, 40; Lee to Samuel Cooper (April 29, 1863), in *O.R.*, series one, 25 (pt. 2):758; Tucker, *Lee and Longstreet at Gettysburg*, 105; J. J. Myers, "Who Will Follow Me? The Story of Confederate General Lewis Armistead," *Civil War Times Illustrated* (July–August 1993), 35; Wayne E. Motts, *"Trust in God and Fear Nothing": Gen. Lewis A. Armistead, CSA* (Gettysburg: Farnsworth House, 1994), 39–40.

10. Col. B. L. Farinholt,"Battle of Gettysburg—Johnson's Island," *Confederate Veteran* 5 (September 1897), 469; J. W. Anderson, "Scenes About Gettysburg—A Brave Boy," *Confederate Veteran* 16 (May 1908), 230; Youngblood, "Unwritten History of the Gettysburg Campaign," 314; Kathy Georg Harrison, *Nothing but Glory*, 10–11, 13; "Capt. R. M. Stribling's Letters," *Confederate Veteran* 9 (May 1901), 215–16; Divine, *8th Virginia Infantry*, 21;

David Emmons Johnston, in Gottfried, *Roads to Gettysburg: Lee's Invasion of the North, 1863,* 179.

11. David Emmons Johnston, *The Story of a Confederate Boy in the Civil War* (Portland, OR: Glass & Prudhomme, 1914), 197–98; William D. Hewitt, "'The General Plan of Attack Was Unchanged': Robert E. Lee and Confederate Operations on July 3," in *The Third Day: The Fate of a Nation,* 20, 21; B. J. Farinholt to J. W. Daniel (April 15, 1905), John Warwick Daniel Papers, Special Collections, University of Virginia; Longstreet, "Lee in Pennsylvania," in *Annals of the War,* 442; Ross, *A Visit to the Cities and Camps of the Confederate States,* 60–61.

12. Early, "The Campaigns of Gen. Robert E. Lee," 35; Gordon, *Reminiscences of the Civil War,* 160; *Autobiography of Eppa Hunton,* 94–95, 97; Charles T. Loehr, "The 'Old First' Virginia at Gettysburg," *SHSP* 32 (January–December 1904), 40; Robert K. Krick, "James Longstreet and the Second Day at Gettysburg," in *The Smoothbore Volley That Doomed the Confederacy,* 77; Walter H. Taylor, *General Lee: His Campaigns in Virginia, 1861–1865* (Norfolk, VA: Nusbaum Book & News Co., 1906), 208–9; Louis G. Young, "Gettysburg Address" (April 3, 1900), in *Addresses Delivered before the Confederate Veterans Association of Savannah, Ga., 1898–1902* (Savannah, GA: Savannah Morning News, 1902), 40; Thomas Desjardins, *These Honored Dead,* 118.

13. Longstreet, "Lee in Pennsylvania," in *Annals of the War,* 430; W. Gart Johnson, "Reminiscences of Lee and of Gettysburg," *Confederate Veteran* (August 1893), 246; James Risque Hutter to J. W. Daniel, and J. B. Darneson, "Recollections of Some of the Incidents of the Battle of Gettysburg, Pa., July 3, 1863," in John Warwick Daniel Papers, Special Collections, University of Virginia; J. H. Moore, "Longstreet's Assault—Who Did the Grand Work at Gettysburg on the Third Day?," *Philadelphia Times* (November 4, 1882); Alexander, *Fighting for the Confederacy,* 245–46; Matthew Atkinson, "'More May Have Been Required of Them Than They Were Able to Perform': Seminary Ridge on July 3," in *The Third Day: The Fate of a Nation,* 124; Piston, *Lee's Tarnished Lieutenant: James Longstreet and His Place in Southern History,* 59–60.

14. George Shuldham Peard, *Narrative of a Campaign in the Crimea; Including an Account of the Battles of the Alma, Balaklava and Inkermann* (London: Richard Bentley, 1855), 55; Fletcher and Ishchenko, *The Battle of the Alma,* 130, 186, 196; Richard Brooks, *Solferino,* 89; Gunther Erich Rothenberg, *The Army of Francis Joseph* (Lafayette, IN: Purdue University Press, 1999), 69.

15. "The Column of Attack," *Colburn's United Service Magazine and Military Journal* 70 (1852), 200.

16. Williams to J. B. Bachelder (November 10, 1865), in *Bachelder Papers,* 1:218; George A. Thayer, "On the Right at Gettysburg," *National Tribune* (July 24, 1902); Croffut and Morris, *Military and Civil History of Connecticut,* 384–85; Henry C. Morhous, *Reminiscences of the 123rd Regiment, N.Y.S.V.: Giving a Complete History of Its Three Years Service in the War* (Greenwich, NY: People's Journal Book and Job Office, 1879), 48–49; Charles F. Morse, "The Twelfth Corps at Gettysburg," 30–31; Julian Wisner Hinkley, *A Narrative of Service with the Third Wisconsin Infantry* (Madison: Wisconsin History Commission, 1912), 85; Joseph Matchett, "46th Regiment of Infantry," in *Pennsylvania at Gettysburg,* 1:310; Alonzo Hall Quint, *The Record of the Second Massachusetts Infantry, 1861–65* (Boston: James P. Walker, 1867), 179; "Report of Henry W. Slocum" (August 23, 1863) and "Report of Brig. Gen. Alpheus Williams" (August 22, 1863), in *O.R.,* series one, 27 (pt. 1):759–60, 774–75; William L. Stork, "Gettysburg—Why Was Not the Twelfth Corps in the First Day's Fight?," *National Tribune* (September 10, 1891); Meade, *Life and Letters of George Gordon Meade,* 2:98.

17. Fox, "Slocum and His Men: A History of the Twelfth and Twentieth Army Corps," Boyle,

Soldiers True: The Story of the One Hundred and Eleventh Regiment Pennsylvania Veteran Volunteers, 125; Eugene Powell, "Rebellion's High Tide—The Splendid Work on Culp's Hill by the 12th Corps," *National Tribune* (July 5, 1900); Williams to J. B. Bachelder (November 10, 1865) and Charles P. Horton to J. B. Bachelder (January 23, 1867), in *Bachelder Papers,* 1:220, 297.

18. Morse, "The Twelfth Corps at Gettysburg," 32; Henry C. Morhous, "The Gettysburg Campaign," in *New York at Gettysburg,* 2:859; "Report of Lieut. Gen. Richard S. Ewell, C.S. Army," in *O.R.,* series one, 27 (pt. 2):447; *Campbell Brown's Civil War,* 222; Archer, *Culp's Hill at Gettysburg,* 85.

19. McKim, "Steuert's Brigade at the Battle of Gettysburg," *SHSP* 5 (June 1878), 296, 298; Henry Jacobs, "How an Eye-Witness Watched the Great Battle," Adams County Historical Society; Léon, *Diary of a Tar Heel Confederate Soldier,* 36–37; A. H. Hayward to Ambrose Hayward, Sr. (July 17, 1863), in *Last to Leave the Field: The Life and Letters of First Sergeant Ambrose Henry Hayward, 28th Pennsylvania Volunteer Infantry,* ed. Timothy J. Orr (Knoxville: University of Tennessee Press, 2010), 160; M. L. Olmsted, "On the Right at Gettysburg," *National Tribune* (December 17, 1908); Archer, *Culp's Hill at Gettysburg,* 105.

20. Robert W. Patrick, *Knapsack and Rifle; or, Life in the Grand Army* (Chicago: Continental Publishing, 1897), 231–32; Fox, "Slocum and His Men," 182; Boyle, *Soldiers True,* 127–28; SeCheverell, *Journal History of the Twenty-ninth Ohio,* 71; Morse, "The Twelfth Corps at Gettysburg," 32, 33–34; Pfanz, *Richard S. Ewell,* 319.

21. Richard A. Baumgartner, *Buckeye Blood: Ohio at Gettysburg* (Huntington, WV: Blue Acorn Press, 2003), 134.

22. Alpheus Williams to J. B. Bachelder (November 10, 1865) and Lewis A. Grant to J. B. Bachelder (August 25, 1869), in *Bachelder Papers,* 1:221, 375; Fox, "Slocum and His Men," 182, 184; Goldsborough, *The Maryland Line in the Confederate Army, 1861–1865,* 190; "Report of Brig. Gen. John W. Geary" (July 29, 1863), and "Report of Col. William R. Creighton, Seventh Ohio Infantry" (July 6, 1863), in *O.R.,* series one, 27 (pt. 1):830, 841; Richard B. Kleese, *49th Virginia Infantry* (Lynchburg, VA: H. E. Howard, 2002), 40.

23. Powell, "Rebellion's High Tide," *National Tribune* (July 5, 1900); "Report of Brig. Gen. Thomas L. Kane" (July 6, 1863), in *O.R.,* series one, 27 (pt. 1):847; Morse, "The Twelfth Corps at Gettysburg," 37; Charles P. Horton to J. B. Bachelder (January 23, 1867), in *Bachelder Papers,* 1:297; Paul Truitt, "The 7th Indiana Fighters," *National Tribune* (November 11, 1925); Lawrence Wilson, "Charge up Culp's Hill," *Washington Post* (July 9, 1899); George K. Collins, *Memoirs of the 149th Regt. N.Y. Vol. Inft., 3d Brig., 2d Div., 12th and 20th A.C.* (Syracuse, NY: G. K. Collins, 1891), 148–49. Leigh, the son of a Virginia senator, was twenty-two years old. He was reburied in Richmond after the war in Shockoe Hill Cemetery.

CHAPTER TWENTY-TWO   *Are you going to do your duty today?*

1. Meade to Margaretta Meade (July 3, 1863), George G. Meade Papers [box 1, folder 10], Historical Society of Pennsylvania; Meade, *Life and Letters of George Gordon Meade,* 2:102–3; Gibbon, *Recollections of the Civil War,* 145; Meade to Halleck (July 2, 1863), Meade to French (July 3, 1863), and "Report of Brig. Gen. John C. Robinson" (July 18, 1863), in *O.R.,* series one, 27 (pt. 1):72, 284, 290, and (pt. 3):501; Bruce, *Twentieth Regiment of Massachusetts Volunteer Infantry,* 286–87. Meade's telegram to Halleck is time-marked "8 p.m." in Meade's report in the *O.R.,* but George Meade, Jr., fixed the time in 1883 as "11 P.M." See Meade, *Did General Meade Desire to Retreat at the Battle of Gettysburg?,* 22.

2. Ernsberger, *Paddy Owen's Regulars*, 1:530, 2:575, 583; David Shields to J. B. Bachelder (August 27, 1884), in *Bachelder Papers*, 2:1068.

3. Sheldon, *The "Twenty-Seventh": A Regimental History*, 79; Gambone, *Hancock at Gettysburg*, 114; Frassanito, *Early Photography at Gettysburg*, 234–35; Smith, *Farms at Gettysburg*, 13.

4. Campbell, "'Remember Harper's Ferry': The Degradation, Humiliation, and Redemption of Col. George L. Willard's Brigade," 73–74; R. L. Murray, "Cowan's, Cushing's and Rorty's Batteries in Action During the Pickett-Pettigrew-Trimble Charge," *Gettysburg Magazine* 35 (July 2006), 39–40; Gottfried, *Stopping Pickett*, 151; Zachery A. Fry, "'Boys, Bury Me on the Field': The Forlorn and Forgotten 59th New York on Cemetery Ridge," *Gettysburg Magazine*, 36 (January 2007), 110; Lash, *"Duty Well Done: The History of Edward Baker's California Regiment (71st Pennsylvania Infantry)*, 336.

5. "Three Days' Fighting—One of Stannard's Men Tells of His First and Last Battle," *National Tribune* (August 30, 1894); Leehan, *Pale Horse at Plum Run*, 85; "2d Regiment, N.Y.S. Militia (82d Volunteers)," (July 2, 1890), in *New York at Gettysburg*, 2:664; Waitt, *History of the Nineteenth Regiment, Massachusetts Volunteer Infantry*, 234–35; "Address of Capt. John E. Reilly," in *Pennsylvania at Gettysburg*, 1:408; Robert, "The 72nd Pa.—The Trying March from Falmouth to Gettysburg," *National Tribune* (September 1, 1887); "John W. Plummer's Account," in *Rebellion Record*, ed. Moore, 10:180.

6. Gibbon, *Personal Recollections of the Civil War*, 146; Bruce, *Twentieth Regiment of Massachusetts Volunteer Infantry*, 289; Ford, *Story of the Fifteenth Regiment Massachusetts Volunteer Infantry*, 272; Frank Aretas Haskell, "Gettysburg," in *Pickett's Charge: Eyewitness Accounts at the Battle of Gettysburg*, ed. Richard Rollins (Redondo Beach, CA: Rank & File Publications, 1994), 67–69; Ernsberger, *Paddy Owen's Regulars*, 2:583; Nelson, *The Battles of Chancellorsville and Gettysburg*, 157; Walter Harrison, *Pickett's Men: A Fragment of War History* (New York: D. Van Nostrand, 1870), 95–96; Alexander, *Fighting for the Confederacy*, 253; James T. Carter, "Flag of the Fifty-Third Va. Regiment," *Confederate Veteran* 10 (June 1902), 263; Albert Walber, "From Gettysburg to Libby Prison," in *War Papers Read Before the Commandery of the State of Wisconsin*, 4:194.

7. Jacobs, *Notes on the Rebel Invasion of Maryland and Pennsylvania*, 41; Bane, *History of the Philadelphia Brigade*, 187; Waitt, *History of the Nineteenth Regiment, Massachusetts Volunteer Infantry*, 234–35; *History of the First Regiment, Delaware Volunteers*, 81; Charles W. Cowtan, *Services of the Tenth New York Volunteers, National Zouaves, in the War of the Rebellion* (New York: Charles H. Ludwig, 1882), 207; "2d Regiment, N.Y.S. Militia (82d Volunteers)," (July 2, 1890), in *New York at Gettysburg*, 2:665; Thomas Galwey, *The Valiant Hours* (Mechanicsburg, PA: Stackpole Books, 1961), 112; H. E. Jacobs, *Lincoln's Gettysburg World-Message*, 32.

8. Thomas D. Houston, "Storming Cemetery Hill—An Account of Pickett's Charge as Preserved in an Old Letter," *Philadelphia Weekly Times* (October 21, 1882); Alexander to J. B. Bachelder (May 3, 1876), in *Bachelder Papers*, 1:484–85; Alexander, *Fighting for the Confederacy*, 253–54; "Letter from Col. J. N. Walton" (October 15, 1877), *SHSP* 5 (January–February 1878), 50–51; Joseph R. Cabell to Peyton Randolph (July 11, 1863) and W. R. Aylett (July 12, 1863), in Armistead/Barton/Steuart Brigade, Pickett's Division, Letter Book, Eleanor S. Brockenbrough Library, Museum of the Confederacy; Alexander, "Causes of the Confederate Defeat at Gettysburg," *SHSP* 4 (September 1877), 102, 103.

9. "Reports of Brig. Gen. Joseph R. Davis, C.S. Army," in *O.R.*, series one, 27 (pt. 2):650.

10. J. N. Turney, "The First Tennessee at Gettysburg," *Confederate Veteran* (December 1900), 535–36; Johnston, *Story of a Confederate Boy*, 203–4; Divine, *8th Virginia Infantry*, 21; Lee E. Wallace, *3rd Virginia Infantry* (Lynchburg, VA: H. E. Howard, 1986), 36; Busey and

578 Notes to Pages 393–396

Martin, *Regimental Strengths*, 184, 298–99; Ernsberger, *Also for Glory Muster*, 44–45, 47 48, 50–51, 52, 56, 62, 65, 71, 76; Hess, *Pickett's Charge*, 38–39, 48, 72; Harrison, *Nothing but Glory*, 5–6, 13; Frederick M. Colston, "Gettysburg as I Saw It," *Confederate Veteran* 5 (November 1897), 551–52. The estimates on the numbers of men in Pickett's division, as well as in the overall attack commanded by Longstreet, have varied widely. Walter Harrison estimated that Pickett's division had only 4,700 "rank and file" (Harrison, *Pickett's Men*, 100). Charles Pickett, who served on his brother's staff, put the number at a low of 4,800 in a letter to Henry T. Owen in February 1878 (Henry Thweatt Owen Papers, Library of Virginia, Richmond, VA), and Owen himself fixed the number in 1881 as 4,761 ("Pickett at Gettysburg," in *New Annals of the War*, 300); Busey and Martin (*Regimental Strengths and Losses*, 217) set the number of Pickett's infantry at around 5,000, after subtracting the division's artillery battalion; K. G. Harrison counts "some 5,800 infantrymen," but includes in that figure "those on detail as teamsters, drovers, cooks, aids, and ambulance drivers" (*Nothing but Glory*, 4).

11.   William Henry Morgan, *Personal Reminiscences of the War of 1861–5*, 166; Clark, "Wilcox's Alabama Brigade at Gettysburg," *Confederate Veteran* 17 (May 1909), 229–30; Edmund Berkeley, in John Warwick Daniel Papers, Special Collections, University of Virginia; Alexander, "Causes of the Confederate Defeat at Gettysburg," *SHSP* 4 (September 1877), 105; Kimble, "Tennesseeans at Gettysburg—The Retreat," 460; Alexander to J. B. Bachelder (May 3, 1876) and Fry to J. B. Bachelder (December 27, 1877), in *Bachelder Papers*, 1:486, 517; Randy Bishop, *The Tennessee Brigade: A History of the Volunteers of the Army of Northern Virginia* (Bloomington, IN: Rooftop Publishing, 2007), 201; Robert A. Bright, "Pickett's Charge," *SHSP* 31 (January–December 1903), 229; Ernsberger, *Also for Glory Muster*, 85; Harrison, *Nothing but Glory*, 16, 17; Bowden and Ward, *Last Chance for Victory*, 449–50; Robertson, *18th Virginia Infantry*, 21.

12.   Edmund Berkeley, "Rode with Pickett," *Confederate Veteran* 38 (May 1930), 175; Alexander, "Causes of the Confederate Defeat at Gettysburg," *SHSP* 4 (September 1877), 105–6; "Colonel Rawley Martin's Account," *SHSP* 32 (January–December 1904), 184–85; Crocker, *Gettysburg—Pickett's Charge: Address by James F. Crocker, before Stonewall Camp, Confederate Veterans, Portsmouth, Virginia, November 7th, 1894* (Portsmouth, VA: W. A. Fiske, 1905), 14.

13.   Ernsberger, *Also for Glory Muster*, 84; Fry to J. B. Bachelder (December 27, 1877), in *Bachelder Papers*, 1:518, and "Pettigrew's Charge at Gettysburg," *SHSP* 7 (February 1879), 91–92; Frank E. Fields, *28th Virginia Infantry* (Lynchburg, VA: H. E. Howard, 1985), 25–26; Martin Hazlewood, "Gettysburg Charge," *SHSP* 24 (January–December 1896), 232, 233, 235; Hess, *Pickett's Charge*, 167–68.

14.   "Letter from Col. J. N. Walton" (October 15, 1877), *SHSP* 5 (January–February 1878), 50–51; Hess, *Pickett's Charge*, 125; Longstreet, *Manassass to Appomattox*, 390–91, and "Lee in Pennsylvania," in *Annals of the War*, 430; Alexander, "Causes of the Confederate Defeat at Gettysburg," *SHSP* 4 (September 1877), 106, and *Military Memoirs of a Confederate*, 421.

15.   Henry Knollys, *The Elements of Field-Artillery: Designed for the Use of Infantry and Cavalry Officers* (Edinburgh, U.K.: William Blackwood, 1877), 147, 151; William Miller Owen, "Recollections of the Third Day at Gettysburg," *The United Service: A Monthly Magazine Devoted to the Interests of the Military, Naval, and Civil Service* 13 (August 1885), 149, and *In Camp and Battle with the Washington Artillery of New Orleans: A Narrative* (Boston: Ticknor & Co., 1885), 248–49, 253; "Reports of Maj. B. F. Eschleman, Washington (Louisiana) Artillery" (August 11, 1863), in *O.R.*, series one, 27 (pt. 2):434; E. T. Bouldin to J. W. Daniel (May 23, 1906), John Warwick Daniel Papers, Special Collections, University of Virginia.

16.   William E. Birkhimer, *Historical Sketch of the Organization, Administration, Matériel and*

Tactics of the Artillery, United States Army (Washington, DC: James J. Chapman, 1884), 6–7; Robert K. Wright, *The Continental Army* (Washington, DC: Center of Military History, 1986), 103–4; K. Jack Bauer, *The Mexican War, 1846–1848* (New York: Macmillan, 1974), 210–11; Sears, *To the Gates of Richmond: The Peninsula Campaign,* 311, 319, 332–33; Hill, "McClellan's Change of Base and Malvern Hill," in *Battles & Leaders,* 2:394; Wise, *The Long Arm of Lee,* 1:305, 308.

17. W. W. Jacobs, "Custer's Charge—Little Hagerstown, the Scene of Bloody Strife in 1863," *National Tribune* (August 27, 1896); Teague, "Right Gone Awry," in *The Third Day: The Fate of a Nation,* 210; "Artillery Heard at Gettysburg," *Washington Daily National Republican* (July 3, 1863); "Battle of Friday—Confirmation of the News via Harrisburg," *New York Herald* (July 4, 1863); Harper, *"If Thee Must Fight,"* 251; George Clark, *A Glance Backward; or, Some Events in the Past History of My Life* (Houston, TX: Rein, 1914), 39; Gottfried, *The Artillery of Gettysburg,* 207.

18. Johnston, *The Story of a Confederate Boy,* 206; McCreary, "Gettysburg: A Boy's Experience," 246; Bennett, *Days of "Uncertainty and Dread,"* 64; John C. West to Charles S. West (July 27, 1863), in *A Texan in Search of a Fight,* 95; James Huntington, in Edward C. Browne, "Maj. Thomas Osborn's Artillery Line on July 3, 1863," *Gettysburg Magazine* 41 (July 2009), 93; Benedict, *Army Life in Virginia,* 176; Charles Blinn, diary entry for July 4, 1863, in "1st Vermont Cavalry," in GNMP Vertical Files [#6VT1-CAV]; Chauncey L. Harris to "Dear Father" (July 4, 1863), in George H. Washburne, *A Complete Military History and Record of the 108th Regiment N.Y. Vols., from 1862 to 1864* (Rochester, NY: Press of E. P. Andrews, 1894), 52; Bane, *History of the Philadelphia Brigade,* 188.

19. J. W. Anderson, "Scenes About Gettysburg—A Brave Boy," *Confederate Veteran* 16 (May 1908), 230; Leehan, *Pale Horse at Plum Run,* 87; Small, *The Sixteenth Maine Regiment,* 122; Kimble, "Tennesseans at Gettysburg—The Retreat," 460–62; Patrick, *Knapsack and Rifle,* 236; Priest, *Into the Fight,* 72–73; Andrew Cowan, "When Cowan's Battery Withstood Pickett's Splendid Charge," *Buffalo Sunday Morning News* (July 2, 1911); "This Hell of Destruction: The Benjamin Thompson Memoir, Part 2," *Civil War Times Illustrated* 12 (October 1973), 12; Kent Masterson Brown, *Cushing of Gettysburg: The Story of a Union Artillery Commander* (Lexington: University Press of Kentucky, 1993), 235; R. L. Murray, "Brig. Gen. Alexander Hays' Division at Gettysburg," *Gettysburg Magazine* 42 (July 2010), 86.

20. L. A. Smith, "Recollections of Gettysburg," 303–4; William P. Haines, *History of the Men of Co. F, with Description of the Marches and Battles of the 12th New Jersey Vols.* (Camden, NJ: C. S. McGrath, 1897), 41; Waitt, *History of the Nineteenth Regiment, Massachusetts Volunteer Infantry,* 237.

21. "The Battlefield at Gettysburg—Mr. Thomas W. Knox's Despatch," *New York Herald* (July 6, 1863); "Report of Lt. Col. Charles H. Morgan," in *Bachelder Papers,* 3:1360.

22. Hanifen, *History of Battery B, First New Jersey Artillery,* 81; *Life and Letters of George Gordon Meade,* 2:106; Hess, *Pickett's Charge—The Last Attack at Gettysburg,* 134–36; Meade to J. B. Bachelder (December 4, 1869), in *Bachelder Papers,* 1:378–79; Theodore Lyman, diary entry for September 9, 1864, in *Meade's Army: The Private Notebooks of Lt. Col. Theodore Lyman,* 32–33; "Thursday's Doubtful Issue—Friday's Victory" (July 4, 1863), in *A Radical View: The "Agate" Dispatches of Whitelaw Reid,* 2:52–54.

23. Ernsberger, *Paddy Owen's Regulars,* 2:584; David Shields to J. B. Bachelder (August 27, 1884), in *Bachelder Papers,* 2:1069; Washburn, *A Complete Military History and Record of the 108th Regiment N.Y. Vols.,* 52; "Civil War Letters of Samuel S. Partridge of the 'Rochester Regiment,'" in *Rochester in the Civil War,* Blake McKelvey, ed. (Rochester, NY: Rochester Historical Society, 1944), 43; Brown, *Cushing of Gettysburg,* 235; Small, *Sixteenth Maine Regiment,* 123–24; J. W. Chase to Samuel S. Chase (August 5, 1863), in *Yours for the Union:*

The Civil War Letters of John W. Chase, 266–67; Browne, "Maj. Thomas Osborn's Artillery Line on July 3, 1863," 101.

24.　"Remarks by Capt. John D. Rogers, 71st Pa. Vols.," in *In Memoriam, Alexander Stewart Webb,* 89; Haskell, *The Battle of Gettysburg,* 53; Benedict, *Vermont at Gettysburgh,* 14; Cook, "Personal Reminiscences of Gettysburg," 136; Scott, "Pickett's Charge as Seen from the Front Line," 6–7; David X. Junkin, *The Life of Winfield Scott Hancock: Personal, Military, and Political,* 105; Gambone, *Hancock at Gettysburg,* 118–19; Tucker, *Hancock the Superb,* 150–51; Walker, *General Hancock,* 139; Washburn, *A Complete Military History and Record of the 108th Regiment N.Y. Vols.,* 52

25.　Howard, "Campaign and Battle of Gettysburg, June and July, 1863," 63; Browne, "Maj. Thomas Osborn's Artillery Line on July 3, 1863," 101; J. B. Hardenburgh to Theodore B. Gates (October 9, 1878), in Theodore Gates Miscellaneous Manuscripts [folder 1], New-York Historical Society; Newell, *"Ours": Annals of the 10th Regiment, Massachusetts Volunteers,* 223; James Lorenzo Brown, *History of the Thirty-Seventh Regiment, Mass. Volunteers, in the Civil War of 1861–1865* (Holyoke, MA: Clark W. Bryan & Co., 1884), 185; Judson, *History of the Eighty-Third Regiment Pennsylvania Volunteers,* 136–37.

26.　Kinglake, *The Invasion of the Crimea,* 3:95; Ernsberger, *Paddy Owen's Regulars,* 2:584–88; "Letter of Brig. Gen. Alexander S. Webb to His Wife" (July 6, 1863), in *Bachelder Papers,* 1:18; "Reports of Col. Norman J. Hall, Seventh Michigan Infantry" (July 17, 1863) and "Reports of Sylvanus W. Curtis, Seventh Michigan Infantry" (August 6, 1863), in *O.R.,* series one, 27 (pt. 1):437, 449; Haskell, *The Battle of Gettysburg,* 55; Wright, *No More Gallant a Deed,* 305–6; Waitt, *History of the Nineteenth Regiment, Massachusetts Volunteer Infantry, 1861–1865,* 235–36; Rollins, "Lee's Artillery Prepares for Pickett's Charge," 50; Barnett, "Robert E. Lee and the Cannonade of July 3," in *The Third Day: The Fate of a Nation,* 99.

27.　Browne, "Maj. Thomas Osborn's Artillery Line on July 3, 1863," 94, 95; Joseph C. Mayo, "Pickett's Charge at Gettysburg" (1906), in *SHSP* 34 (Richmond, VA: Southern Historical Society, 1906), 330; James L. Speicher, *The Sumter Flying Artillery: A Civil War History of the Eleventh Battalion, Georgia Light Artillery* (Gretna, LA: Pelican, 2009), 194; Redwood, "A Boy in Gray," *Scribner's Monthly* 22 (September 1881), 646–47; Howard, "Campaign and Battle of Gettysburg, June and July, 1863," 67.

28.　Edmund Berkeley, in John Warwick Daniel Papers, Special Collections, University of Virginia; Ernsberger, *Also for Glory Muster,* 90; Kemper to E. Porter Alexander, Dearborn Confederate Collection, Houghton Library, Harvard University; Wert, *General James Longstreet,* 290; "Letter from an Unknown Member of the Quitman Guards to His Sister," in *The 16th Mississippi Infantry,* 178.

29.　McCarthy, *Detailed Minutiae of Soldier Life in the Army of Northern Virginia,* 107; John T. Winterich, "Elizabeth Allen," in *Notable American Women, 1607–1950: A Biographical Dictionary,* ed. Edward T. James (Cambridge, MA: Harvard University Press, 1971), 2:37; Joseph C. Mayo, "Pickett's Charge at Gettysburg," 331; Johnston, *The Story of a Confederate Boy,* 206, 217–18; Harrison, *Nothing but Glory,* 24, 27, 29, 30, 31.

30.　Hunton, in Bowden and Ward, *Last Chance for Victory,* 453–54; "Reports of Brig. Gen. Joseph R. Davis, C.S. Army," in *O.R.,* series one, 27 (pt. 2):650; *The Papers of Randolph Shotwell,* ed. J. G. D. Hamilton (Raleigh: North Carolina Historical Commission, 1931), 2:8; "Reports of Brig. Gen. Henry J. Hunt, Chief of Artillery" (September 27, 1863), in *O.R.,* series one, 27 (pt. 1):232; Hunt to J. B. Bachelder (January 20, 1873), in *Bachelder Papers,* 1:426. Hunt understood his role as chief of artillery to be "to make the necessary dispositions and to give all directions I considered necessary" for the artillery of the Army of the Potomac "during the rest of the battle." This was an assumption on Hunt's part: during the Chancellorsville campaign, Joe Hooker had decided to dispense with a chief of artillery, leaving the fussy, self-important Hunt to spin as an unneeded wheel at headquarters, and only with Meade's appointment on June 28th did Hunt reassert himself and begin once more behaving as the artillery chief. Or at least, that was how Meade had decided to allow Hunt to behave. There was, in truth, no actual reappointment. But Hunt insisted that Meade had told him during his wee-hours inspection of Cemetery Hill on July 2nd that the artillery "is your affair, take the proper measure to provide against the attack, and make the line safe with artillery."

31. Rittenhouse, "The Battle of Gettysburg as Seen from Little Round Top," 42–43; Henry Hunt to J. B. Bachelder (January 20, 1873), in *Bachelder Papers*, 1:428–29, 430; "Reports of Brig. Gen. Henry J. Hunt, Chief of Artillery" (September 27, 1863), in *O.R.*, series one, 27 (pt. 1):238–39; Gottfried, *The Artillery of Gettysburg*, 196–97; Hunt, "The Third Day at Gettysburg," *Battles & Leaders*, 3:372, 374.

32. "Will the infantry endure so effective a fire without some of its leaders calling out in anger, 'What is the use of our artillery if it cannot keep that of the enemy from us?,'" wrote the Prussian artillery specialist Prince Kraft zü Hohenlohe-Ingelfingen. "'Get on, you artillery, and go on firing!'" See Hunt, "The Third Day at Gettysburg," *Battles & Leaders*, 3:374; "Reports of Brig. Gen. Henry J. Hunt, Chief of Artillery" (September 27, 1863), in *O.R.*, series one, 27 (pt. 1):239; Edward H. Rogers, *Reminiscences of Military Service in the Forty-Third Regiment, Massachusetts During the Great Civil War, 1862–1863* (Boston: Rand, Avery, 1883), 67; Karl Hohenlohe-Ingelfingen, *Letters on Artillery*, trans. N. L. Walford (London: Edward Stanford, 1898), 307.

33. Gambone, *Hancock at Gettysburg*, 134–35; "Report of Lieut. Col. Freeman McGilvery" and "Report of Capt. Patrick Hart, Fifteenth New York Battery" (August 2, 1863), in *O.R.*, series one, 27 (pt. 1):884, 888; Hunt to J. B. Bachelder (January 20, 1873) and William Tecumseh Sherman (February 1882), and Patrick Hart to J. B. Bachelder (February 23, 1891), in *Bachelder Papers*, 1:432–33, 2:825–27, and 3:1798; Eric A. Campbell, "A Brief History and Analysis of the Hunt-Hancock Controversy," in *The Third Day: The Fate of a Nation*, 254, 270; Edward Longacre, *The Man Behind the Guns: A Military Biography of General Henry J. Hunt* (Cambridge, MA: Da Capo Press, 2003), 172; Charles S. Wainwright, diary entry for July 4, 1863, in *A Diary of Battle*, 253.

34. Gottfried, *The Artillery of Gettysburg*, 208; Brown, *Cushing of Gettysburg*, 241; Hunt to J. B. Bachelder (January 20, 1873), in *Bachelder Papers*, 1:428–29; Gibbon, *Personal Recollections of the Civil War*, 149–50.

CHAPTER TWENTY-THREE   *The shadow of a cloud across a sunny field*

1. Alexander, *Military Memoirs of a Confederate*, 418; Beecham, Gettysburg, *The Pivotal Battle of the Civil War*, 230; "Reports of General Robert E. Lee, C.S. Army" (January 1864), in *O.R.*, series one, 27 (pt. 2):320; Wright, *No More Gallant a Deed*, 306; Rollins, "Lee's Artillery Prepares for Pickett's Charge," 50; Murray, "Cowan's, Cushing's and Rorty's Batteries in Action During the Pickett-Pettigrew-Trimble Charge," 46, and "Brig. Gen. Alexander Hays' Division at Gettysburg," 87; John H. Rhodes, *The History of Battery B, First Regiment Rhode Island Light Artillery, in the War to Preserve the Union* (Providence, RI: Snow & Farnham, 1894), 209–13; Hess, *Pickett's Charge*, 163.

2. Alexander to J. B. Bachelder (May 3, 1876), in *Bachelder Papers*, 1:489–90, "The Great Charge and Artillery Fighting at Gettysburg," in *Battles & Leaders*, 3:364, and *Fighting for the Confederacy*, 246, 258; Rollins, "Lee's Artillery Prepares for Pickett's Charge," 50–51; Priest, *Into the Fight*, 77.

3. Twemlow, *Considerations on Tactics and Strategy*, 28; Kinglake, *Invasion of the Crimea*, 3:90;

Alexander, "The Great Charge and Artillery Fighting at Gettysburg," 364, and *Fighting for the Confederacy,* 258, 259.

4. Cowan, "Cowan's New York Battery," *National Tribune* (November 12, 1903); Alexander, "The Great Charge and Artillery Fighting at Gettysburg," 364–65, and "Causes of the Confederate Defeat at Gettysburg," 107–8; Bright, "Pickett's Charge," 263; Alexander to J. B. Bachelder (May 3, 1876), in *Bachelder Papers,* 1:489–90; Priest, *Into the Fight,* 82, 189–93; Longstreet, *Manassas to Appomattox,* 392, and "Lee in Pennsylvania," in *Annals of the War,* 431; Atkinson, "Seminary Ridge on July 3," in *The Third Day: The Fate of a Nation,* 133–34; McLaws, "Gettysburg," *SHSP* 7 (February 1879), 80; de Trobriand, *Four Years with the Army of the Potomac,* 508; Page, *History of the Fourteenth Regiment, Connecticut Vol. Infantry,* 150; Wright, *No More Gallant a Deed,* 306; Scott, "Pickett's Charge as Seen from the Front Line," 9–10; Waitt, *History of the Nineteenth Regiment, Massachusetts Volunteer Infantry,* 238.

5. Fremantle, *Three Months in the Southern States,* 264; "Notes on the 24th Michigan and Col. Henry Morrow," in *Bachelder Papers,* 1:333–34; Asa Sleath Hardman, "As a Union Prisoner Saw the Battle of Gettysburg," *Civil War Times* 51 (August 2012), 40; Henry Jacobs, "How an Eye-Witness Watched the Great Battle," Adams County Historical Society; "A.J.B.," *Emmitsburg Chronicle* (March 25, 1976), in John Allen Miller, "Signal Operations of Emmitsburg During the Civil War," Emmitsburg Historical Society.

6. Coddington, *The Gettysburg Campaign,* 502; Tucker, *High Tide at Gettysburg,* 357; Noah Andre Trudeau, *Gettysburg: A Testing of Courage* (New York: HarperCollins, 2002), 479; Winthrop Sheldon, *The "Twenty-seventh,"* 79–82; de Trobriand, *Four Years with the Army of the Potomac,* 508; Thompson, "A Scrap of Gettysburg," 102, 104; Gates, diary entry for July 3, 1863, in *The Civil War Diaries of Col. Theodore B. Gates,* 93; Capt. Winfield Scott, "Pickett's Charge as Seen from the Front Line" (1888), in *Civil War Papers of the California Commandery of the Loyal Legion,* 60:9–11; "Testimony of Major General Abner Doubleday" (March 1, 1864) and "Testimony of General John Gibbon" (April 1, 1864), in *Report of the Joint Committee on the Conduct of the War,* 4:309, 443. The conflicting descriptions of the emergence of the Confederates from Spangler's Woods raise the interesting question of whether the initial movement of Pickett's division, if not Pettigrew's and Trimble's, might have been in column rather than line. In the 24th Virginia, one captain reported that the "first movement" of Kemper's brigade out of the wood line was "by the left flank to the depth of a regt. & then by the front" (in other words, in column of regiments), while William Swallow insisted that the "nine brigades" of Pickett's division were formed "in the *direct column of attack.*" On the other side of the fields, a soldier in the 149th Pennsylvania saw Pickett's division "come out of the woods in column of fours," and Norman Hall wrote (two weeks after the battle) that the grand charge involved groups of infantry in line of battle in front and rear, but "opposite the main point of attack was what appeared to be a column of battalions." (Hall actually drew a diagram showing the main body of the Confederates attacking in column.) Charles Devens reminded the veterans of the 15th Massachusetts at the dedication of their battlefield monument at Gettysburg in 1886 that "the enemy . . . formed for the attack in two lines, which, as they move, contract their front . . . thus having the appearance and to some extent the formation of columns." Especially to the Vermont brigade, Pickett's division "looked . . . like a column and a very wide and deep one," and George Stannard "insists that it was a column . . . massed by regiments." Otis Howard, from his vantage point on Cemetery Hill, agreed with Stannard: "It was more like a closed column," spread across "a mile of frontage." See Capt. W. W. Bentley to Capt. W. Fry (July 9, 1863), in Rollins, ed., *Pickett's Charge: Eyewitness Accounts,* 163, 167; J. W. Nesbit, "Sketches and Echoes—Recollections of Pickett's Charge," *National Tribune*

(November 16, 1916); "Reports of Col. Norman J. Hall, Seventh Michigan Infantry, Commanding Third Brigade" (July 17, 1863), in *O.R.*, series one, 27 (pt. 1):437; Swallow, "The Third Day at Gettysburg," *Southern Bivouac* 4 (February 1886), 566–67; Charles Devens, "Address to the Fifteenth Regiment Association on Their Visit to the Battlefield of Gettysburg, June 1886," in *Orations and Addresses on Various Occasions, Civil and Military*, A. L. Devens, ed. (Boston: Little, Brown, 1891), 190–91; Benedict to J. B. Bachelder (December 24, 1863), in *Bachelder Papers*, 1:48–50, and *Vermont at Gettysburgh*, 16; Howard, *Autobiography*, 1:438.

7. Kemper to Rev'd A. L. Pollock, Papers of the Janney and Pollock Families, Special Collections, University of Virginia; Wallace, *3rd Virginia Infantry*, 37–39; Harrison, *Nothing but Glory*, 39, 47; Johnston, *Story of a Confederate Boy*, 207–8; "Colonel Rawley Martin's Account," 186–87; Bright, "Pickett's Charge," 229–30; *Papers of Randolph Abbott Shotwell*, 2:11; William A. and Patricia C. Young, *56th Virginia Infantry* (Lynchburg, VA: H. E. Howard, 1990), 82–83; Priest, *Into the Fight*, 83; Allen, *Under the Maltese Cross*, 173; James H. Walker, in Rollins, ed., *Pickett's Charge: Eyewitness Accounts*, 171; Henry T. Owen, "Pickett at Gettysburg," in *New Annals of the War*, 300.

8. Bright, "Pickett's Charge," 229–30; Wallace, *3rd Virginia Infantry*, 37–38; James Robbins, *Last in Their Class: Custer, Pickett and the Goats of West Point* (New York: Encounter Books, 2006), 251; Robert Emmett Curran, ed., *John Dooley's Civil War: An Irish American's Journey in the First Virginia Infantry Regiment* (Knoxville: University of Tennessee Press, 2012), 160; Divine, *8th Virginia Infantry*, 22; Mayo, "Pickett's Charge at Gettysburg," 332; Cook, "Personal Reminiscences of Gettysburg," 334. Porter Alexander, an "old friend" of Garnett's, insisted that Garnett was "buttoned up in an old blue overcoat, in spite of the heat of the day" (see Alexander, "Causes of the Confederate Defeat at Gettysburg," 108), but Henry Thweatt Owen, a captain in the 18th Virginia, countered that Garnett was wearing his "fine, new gray uniform . . . when killed in the charge at Gettysburg" (see Owen, "Error in Hon. James W. Boyd's Speech," *Confederate Veteran* 12 [January 1904], 7), as did James W. Clay of the 18th Virginia, in "About the Death of General Garnett," *Confederate Veteran* 13 (February 1906), 81.

9. Loehr, "The 'Old First' Virginia at Gettysburg," 33–34; Robert H. Moore, *The Richmond Fayette, Hampden, Thomas, and Blount's Lynchburg Artillery* (Lynchburg, VA: H. E. Howard, 1991), 78; Charles Teague, "Right Gone Awry: 'We broke, tearing back pell-mell . . . in full, breathless flight,'" in *The Third Day: The Fate of a Nation*, 205; *Papers of Randolph Shotwell*, 2:10; W. Gart Johnson, "Reminiscences of Lee and of Gettysburg," *Confederate Veteran* (August 1893), 246; Thomas D. Houston, "Storming Cemetery Hill," *Philadelphia Weekly Times* (October 21, 1882); "Captain John Holmes Smith's Account," *SHSP* 32 (Richmond, VA: Southern Historical Society, 1904), 190–91; Scott, "Pickett's Charge as Seen from the Front Line," 6–7, 11–12; Webb interview with Alexander Kelly (November 26, 1905), in *Generals in Bronze*, 154.

10. Thompson, "A Scrap of Gettysburg," 102, 104; "Report of Lieut. Col. Freeman McGilvery" and "Report of Capt. Patrick Hart" (August 2, 1863), in *O.R.*, series one, 27 (pt. 1):884, 888; "Address by Col. Andrew Cowan," in *In Memoriam, Alexander Stewart Webb*, 66; Cowan to J. B. Bachelder (August 26, 1866), in *Bachelder Papers*, 1:282–83; Allen, *Under the Maltese Cross*, 172–73; H. Seymour Hall, "At Gettysburg with the Sixth Corps" (November 6, 1896), in *War Talks in Kansas*, 264. Cadmus Wilcox estimated the distance even more closely; the "Federal artillery opened after Pickett had gone 150 yards" (Scrapbook, p. 128, Cadmus Wilcox Papers [box 1], Library of Congress).

11. "Civil War Letters of Francis Edwin Pierce of the 108th New York Volunteer Infantry," in *Rochester in the Civil War*, 170; Lt. Theron Parson's diary, in Washburn, *A Complete*

Military History and Record of the 108th Regiment N.Y. Vols., 50, 52; Scott, "Pickett's Charge as Seen from the Front Line," 9–11; "The 126th in Battle!—Heroic Valor and Its Fearful Cost!," *Geneva Gazette* (July 10, 1863).

12. Crocker, *Gettysburg—Pickett's Charge*, 16, 18; "Report of Maj. Charles S. Peyton, Nineteenth Virginia Infantry" (July 9, 1863), in *O.R.*, series one, 27 (pt. 2):386; W. B. Robertson to "Dear Mother" (July 28, 1863), in John Warwick Daniel Papers, Special Collections, University of Virginia; "To Dear Brother Evans" (December 2, 1909), in Christiancy and Pickett Family Papers [box 1, file 3], Library of Congress; "Colonel Rawley Martin's Account," *SHSP* 32 (January–December 1904), 187–88; Report of Maj. Joseph R. Cabell, 38th Virginia (July 11, 1863), Armistead/ Barton/Steuart Brigade, Pickett's Division, Letter Book, Eleanor S. Brockenbrough Library, Museum of the Confederacy.

13. Alexander, *Fighting for the Confederacy*, 262; "Report of Capt. William Davis, Sixty-Ninth Pennsylvania Infantry" (July 12, 1863) and "Report of Maj. Charles S. Peyton, Nineteenth Virginia Infantry" (July 9, 1863), in *O.R.*, series one, 27 (pt. 1):431, and (pt. 2):386; J. B. Hardenburgh to Theodore B. Gates (October 9, 1878), in Theodore Gates Miscellaneous Manuscripts [folder one], New-York Historical Society; Frey, *Longstreet's Assault—Pickett's Charge*, 126; R. L. Murray, "Brig. Gen. Alexander Hays' Division at Gettysburg," 89; Cowtan, *Services of the Tenth New York Volunteers*, 211–12.

14. Atkinson, "Seminary Ridge on July 3," in *The Third Day: The Fate of a Nation*, 117; Bright, "Pickett's Charge," 232; Waters and Edmonds, *A Small but Spartan Band*, 76; Priest, *Into the Fight*, 89; Hess, *Pickett's Charge*, 175–76; Divine, *8th Virginia Infantry*, 22, 24; Harrison, *Nothing but Glory*, 42–43; William R. Driver, "Pickett's Charge at Gettysburg" (1879), in *Papers of the Military Historical Society of Massachusetts*, 3:353–54; James Risque Hutter, in John Warwick Daniel Papers, Special Collections, University of Virginia; Reardon, *Pickett's Charge*, 21, 23; Teague, "Right Gone Awry," 207–8.

15. *Papers of Randolph Abbott Shotwell*, 2:13, 23–24; J. H. Moore, "Longstreet's Assault," *Philadelphia Weekly Times* (November 4, 1882); Joseph Hayes and Alexander Webb interview with Alexander Kelly (November 26, 1905), in *Generals in Bronze*, 135, 154; Priest, *Into the Fight*, 111–12; Swallow, "The Third Day at Gettysburg," 567; Capt. R. H. Douthat to J. W. Daniel (January 14, 1905) and Erasmus Williams, "A Private's Experience in the 14th Virginia at Gettysburg," in John Warwick Daniel Papers, Special Collections, University of Virginia; Fields, *28th Virginia Infantry*, 26; Teague, "Right Gone Awry," 211; Driver, "Pickett's Charge at Gettysburg," 355; John W. H. Porter, "The Confederate Soldier," *Confederate Veteran* 24 (October 1916), 460.

16. R. Penn Smith, "The Battle—The Part Taken by the Philadelphia Brigade in the Battle," *Gettysburg Compiler* (June 7, 1887); "Address by Col. Andrew Cowan," in *In Memoriam, Alexander Stewart Webb*, 65–66; "Colonel Rawley Martin's Account," *SHSP* 32 (January–December 1904), 188.

17. Alexander Webb interview with Alexander Kelly (November 26, 1905), in *Generals in Bronze*, 159; Anthony W. McDermott to J. B. Bachelder (June 2, 1886), in *Bachelder Papers*, 3:1410–11; Ernsberger, *Paddy Owen's Regulars*, 2:600; Swallow, "The Third Day at Gettysburg," 572.

18. Edmund Berkeley, in John Warwick Daniel papers, Special Collections, University of Virginia; Winfield Peters, "The Lost Sword of Gen. Richard B. Garnett, Who Fell at Gettysburg," *SHSP* 33 (January–February 1905), 28–29; Brown, *Cushing of Gettysburg*, 250–51; Bruce, *The Twentieth Regiment of Massachusetts Volunteer Infantry*, 293; Cowan to William Spencer (January 17, 1911), in R. L. Murray, *Hurrah for the Ould Flag! The True Story of Captain Andrew Cowan and the First New York Independent Battery at Gettysburg* (Wolcott, NY: Benedum Books, 1998), 91; Henry N. Hamilton to J. B. Bachelder (April 22, 1864) and Birkett D. Fry to J. B. Bachelder (December 27, 1877), J. B. Bachelder to Fitzhugh

Lee (December 1892), in *Bachelder Papers*, 1:179, 519, and 3:1899; "Report of Capt. Henry L. Abbott, Twentieth Massachusetts Infantry" (July 16, 1863) and "Reports of Sylvanus W. Curtis, Seventh Michigan Infantry" (July 16, 1863), in *O.R.,* series one, 27 (pt. 1):445, 450; Mayo, "Pickett's Charge at Gettysburg," 333; Fry, "The Forlorn and Forgotten 59th New York," 112; Murray, "Cowan's Cushing's and Rorty's Batteries," 52; "Address by Col. Andrew Cowan," in *In Memoriam, Alexander Stewart Webb*, 67.

19. Second Vermont Brigade, "Extract from General Stannard's diary," George G. Benedict to J. B. Bachelder (March 16, 1864), and J. L. Kemper to William Swallow (February 4, 1886) in *Bachelder Papers*, 1:55–57, 96, and 2:1192; Benedict, *Vermont at Gettysburgh*, 15–16, 17–18; Joseph Mayo, "Pickett's Charge at Gettysburg," 333; Gottfried, *Brigades of Gettysburg*, 469–70; Hess, *Pickett's Charge*, 229; Dreese, *The Hospital on Seminary Ridge*, 122.

20. Fuger, "Cushing's Battery at Gettysburg," *Journal of the Military Service Institution of the United States* 41 (January–February 1908), 408; Bane, *History of the Philadelphia Brigade*, 193; Lash, *"Duty Well Done,"* 345; B. L. Farinholt [53rd Virginia] to J. W. Daniel (April 15, 1905) and F. M. Bailey [9th Virginia] to J. W. Daniel (December 22, 1904), John Warwick Daniel Papers, Special Collections, University of Virginia; Robertson, *18th Virginia Infantry*, 23; "Address by Col. Andrew Cowan," in *In Memoriam, Alexander Stewart Webb*, 68; James T. Carter, "Flag of the Fifty-Third Va. Regiment," *Confederate Veteran* 10 (June 1902), 263; Swallow, "The Third Day at Gettysburg," 566–67. Andrew Cowan had one word for the melodramatic accounts of Cushing crying, "I will give them one more shot," or struggling to hold together his bullet-torn intestines as he pulled his final lanyard— "absurd!" See Andrew Cowan, "When Cowan's Battery Withstood Pickett's Splendid Charge," *Buffalo Sunday Morning News* (July 2, 1911) and Alfred E. Lee, *The Battle of Gettysburg*, 136.

21. "Reports of Col. Norman J. Hall" (July 17, 1863), in *O.R.,* series one, 27 (pt. 1):439; Anthony W. McDermott, *A Brief History of the 69th Pennsylvania Veteran Volunteers* (Philadelphia: D. J. Gallagher, 1887), 32; McDermott to J. B. Bachelder (August 2, 1886), in *Bachelder Papers*, 3:1411–12; Frey, *Longstreet's Assault—Pickett's Charge*, 139–40; Young, *56th Virginia Infantry*, 85–86; Twemlow, *Considerations on Tactics and Strategy*, 74; Jacob Hoke, *Historical Reminiscences of the War; or, Incidents which Transpired in and Around Chambersburg During the War of the Rebellion* (Chambersburg, PA: M. A. Foltz, 1884), 83; Fuger, "Cushing's Battery at Gettysburg," 408; Gibbon, *Personal Recollections of the Civil War*, 152, and "Testimony of General John Gibbon" (April 1, 1864), in *Report of the Joint Committee on the Conduct of the War*, 4:443–44.

22. B. L. Farinholt [53rd Virginia] to J. W. Daniel (April 15, 1905), John Warwick Daniel Papers, Special Collections, University of Virginia.

23. Brown, *Cushing of Gettysburg*, 253; Alexander Webb interview with Alexander Kelly (May 15, 1899, and October 7, 1904), in *Generals in Bronze*, 146–47, 151; Gary G. Lash, "The Philadelphia Brigade at Gettysburg," *Gettysburg Magazine* 7 (July 1992), 106–10; Alexander S. Webb to his wife (July 6, 1863) and Anthony W. McDermott to J. B. Bachelder (June 2, 1886, and September 17, 1889), in *Bachelder Papers*, 1:18–19 and 3:1412–13, 1628; Smith, "The Battle—The Part Taken by the Philadelphia Brigade in the Battle," *Gettysburg Compiler* (June 7, 1887); Gottfried, *Stopping Pickett*, 172; Hartwig, "High Water Mark Heroes, Myth and Memory," in *The Third Day: The Fate of a Nation*, 40–41; Milton Harding [9th Virginia], "Where General Armistead Fell," *Confederate Veteran* 19 (August 1911), 371.

24. Waitt, *History of the Nineteenth Regiment, Massachusetts Volunteer Infantry*, 242–43; Leehan, *Pale Horse at Plum Run*, 95–96; Smith, *History of the Nineteenth Regiment of Maine Volunteer Infantry*, 82; Lochren, "The First Minnesota at Gettysburg," 53; William E. Barrow to J. B. Bachelder (August 12, 1866), Andrew Cowan to J. B. Bachelder (August 26,

1866), A. C. Plaisted to J. B. Bachelder (June 11, 1870) and Arthur F. Devereaux to J. B. Bachelder (July 22, 1889), in *Bachelder Papers*, 1:275, 282–83, 393, and 3:1609; Bruce, *Twentieth Regiment of Massachusetts Volunteer Infantry*, 294; "Address by Col. Andrew Cowan," 66–67; Webb interview with Alexander Kelly (October 7, 1904), in *Generals in Bronze*, 151; "Testimony of General Henry J. Hunt" (April 4, 1864), in *Report of the Joint Committee on the Conduct of the War*, 4:451.

25. Waitt, *History of the Nineteenth Regiment, Massachusetts Volunteer Infantry*, 240; Leehan, *Pale Horse at Plum Run*, 95–96; A. C. Plaisted to J. B. Bachelder (June 11, 1870) in *Bachelder Papers*, 1:393; Wright, *No More Gallant a Deed*, 307–8; "Captain John Holmes Smith's Account," *SHSP* 32 (January–December 1904), 193.

26. Bingham to "Dear General," in William Palmer Collection, Western Reserve Historical Society, Cleveland; Bingham to J. B. Bachelder (January 5, 1869), in *Bachelder Papers*, 1:351–52; Bingham, "Gettysburg's Bloody Field," *Utica Observer* (June 30, 1900); Michael A. Halleran, *The Better Angels of Our Nature: Freemasonry in the American Civil War* (Tuscaloosa: University of Alabama Press, 2010), 17–30; Motts, *"Trust in God and Fear Nothing,"* 45–46.

27. Hancock interview with Alexander Kelly (July 10, 1879), in *Generals in Bronze*, 60; Gambone, *Hancock at Gettysburg*, 145; William Mitchell to J. B. Bachelder (January 10, 1866), in *Bachelder Papers*, 1:231; Steven J. Wright, " 'Don't Let Me Bleed to Death': The Wounding of Maj. Gen. Winfield Scott Hancock," *Gettysburg Magazine* 6 (January 1992), 87; Henry T. Owen, "Pickett at Gettysburg," in *New Annals of the War*, 303, 305; Tucker, *Hancock the Superb*, 155–56; Walker, *General Hancock*, 143–44.

28. Kimble, "Tennesseans at Gettysburg—The Retreat," *Confederate Veteran* (October 1910), 460–62; Louis Young, "Pettigrew's Division at Gettysburg," in *Histories of the Several Regiments and Battalions from North Carolina*, ed. W. Clark, 5:124; Fry, "Pettigrew's Charge at Gettysburg," *SHSP* 7 (February 1879), 92–93; Fry to J. B. Bachelder (January 26, 1878), in *Bachelder Papers*, 1:522–23; J. H. Moore, "Heth's Division at Gettysburg," *Southern Bivouac* 3 (May 1885), 390; Atkinson, "Seminary Ridge on July 3," in *The Third Day: The Fate of a Nation*, 115, 120–21; Bruce A. Trinque, "Confederate Battle Flags in the July 3rd Charge," *Gettysburg Magazine* 21 (July 1999), 110.

29. *Papers of Randolph Abbott Shotwell*, 2:17; Taylor, "The Campaign in Pennsylvania," in *Annals of the War*, 314; Young, "Pettigrew's Division at Gettysburg," 125; William Steptoe Christian to J. W. Daniels (October 24, 1904), in John Warwick Daniels Papers, Special Collections, University of Virginia; Hess, *Lee's Tar Heels*, 144–45, and *Pickett's Charge*, 80; Gottfried, *Artillery of Gettysburg*, 223, and "To Fail Twice: Brockenbrough's Brigade at Gettysburg," *Gettysburg Magazine* 23 (July 2000), 71–72; Swallow, "The Third Day at Gettysburg," 569–70; Thomas Osborn, "Experiences at the Battle of Gettysburg," in *Pickett's Charge: Eyewitness Accounts,* ed. Rollins, 265; Franklin Sawyer, *A Military History of the 8th Regiment Ohio Volunteer Infantry, Its Battles, Marches and Army Movements* (Cleveland: Fairbanks & Co., 1881), 131.

30. Swallow, "The Third Day at Gettysburg," 571; Moore, "Heth's Division at Gettysburg," 251; Isaac Trimble to J. B. Bachelder (February 8, 1886) and E. M. Hays to J. B. Bachelder (October 15, 1890), in *Bachelder Papers*, 2:1199, 3:1776; George D. Flowers, "The Thirty-Eighth North Carolina Regiment," *SHSP* 25 (January–December 1897), 260; Kimble, "Tennesseans at Gettysburg—The Retreat," 460–61; Alexander, *Fighting for the Confederacy*, 264; Keith Snipes, "The Improper Placement of the 8th Ohio Monument: A Study of Words and Maps," *Gettysburg Magazine* 35 (July 2006), 88; William J. Seymour, diary entry for July 3, 1863, in *The Civil War Memoirs of William J. Seymour*, 78.

31. Toombs, *New Jersey Troops in the Gettysburg Campaign*, 286; Ernsberger, *Also for Glory Muster*, 117, 124; "Letter from Lieutenant-Colonel J. McLeod Turner" (October 26, 1877),

in John W. Moore, *History of North Carolina: From the Earliest Discoveries to the Present Time* (Raleigh: Alfred Williams & Co., 1880), 2:211; Asa Sleath Hardman, "As a Union Prisoner Saw the Battle of Gettysburg," *Civil War Times* 51 (August 2012), 40; Franklin Sawyer to J. B. Bachelder (June 8, 1878, and May 11, 1880), Isaac Trimble to J. B. Bachelder (February 8, 1883), Samuel Roberts to Alexander Webb (August 18, 1883) and John L. Brady to J. B. Bachelder (May 24, 1886), in *Bachelder Papers*, 1:625, 663, 2:967, 933, and 3:1399; Sawyer, *A Military History of the 8th Regiment Ohio Volunteer Infantry*, 131–33; Longacre, *To Gettysburg and Beyond: The Twelfth New Jersey Volunteer Infantry*, 131–32; Seville, *History of the First Regiment, Delaware Volunteers*, 81–82; "Report of the Joint Committee, to Mark the Positions Occupied by the 1st and 2nd Delaware Regiments at the Battle of Gettysburg, July 2nd and 3rd, 1863," in *Journal of the House of Representatives of the State of Delaware* (Dover: Delawarean Office, 1887), 816; Murray, "Brig. Gen. Alexander Hays' Division at Gettysburg," 89.

32. Fry to J. B. Bachelder (December 27, 1877) and Isaac Trimble to J. B. Bachelder (February 8, 1883, and February 8, 1886), in *Bachelder Papers*, 1:519, 2:933, 1199; Thomas Molloy [7th North Carolina], in Hess, *Pickett's Charge*, 248–49; Scott, "Pickett's Charge as Seen from the Front Line," 13; Terry Crooks, "Rochester's Forgotten Regiment: The 108th New York at Gettysburg," 108; Ernsberger, *Also for Glory Muster*, 161, 167; William A. Love, "Mississippi at Gettysburg," *Publications of the Mississippi Historical Society* 9 (1906), 24–25; *Far from Home: The Diary of Lt. William H. Peel, 1863–1865*, ed. Ellen S. Wilds (Bloomington, IN: AuthorHouse, 2009), 66; Keith Snipes, "A Rediscovered Bachelder Letter: North Carolinians in 'Pickett's Charge,'" *Gettysburg Magazine* 37 (January 2008), 119; Lt. Octavius A. Wiggins, "Thirty-Seventh Regiment," in *Histories of the Several Regiments and Battalions from North Carolina, in the Great War 1861–'65*, ed. Clark, 2:674; Michael C. Hardy, *The Thirty-Seventh North Carolina Troops: Tar Heels in the Army of Northern Virginia* (Jefferson, NC: McFarland, 2003), 155; Fry, "Pettigrew's Charge at Gettysburg," 93; J. B.Turney, "The First Tennessee at Gettysburg," *Confederate Veteran* (December 1900), 536–37; Karlton D. Smith, "Alexander Hays and 'The Blue Birds': Brig. Gen. Alexander Hays and the Third Division, Second Corps During Longstreet's Assault," in *The Third Day: The Fate of a Nation*, 185; Robert Himmer, "Col. Hugh Reid Miller, 42nd Mississippi Volunteers, and the Pickett-Pettigrew-Trimble Assault," *Gettysburg Magazine* 35 (July 2006), 59–60.

33. Richard S. Thompson, "A Scrap of Gettysburg," 106; Seville, *History of the First Regiment, Delaware Volunteers*, 83; Ernsberger, *Also for Glory Muster*, 170; Ezra de Freest Simons, *A Regimental History: The One Hundred and Twenty-Fifth New York State Volunteers* (New York: Judson Printing, 1888), 138–39, 144; Willson, *Disaster, Struggle, Triumph*, 186; Charles Richardson to J. B. Bachelder (May 8, 1868), in *Bachelder Papers*, 1:341–42; Hays, *Under the Red Patch*, 197–98.

CHAPTER TWENTY-FOUR *As clear a defeat as our army ever met with*

1. Harrison, *Nothing but Glory*, 119–20; J. H. McNeilly, "War's Fascination," *Confederate Veteran* 24 (February 1916), 92; F. M. Colston, "Gettysburg As I Saw It," *Confederate Veteran* 5 (November 1897), 552–53.

2. Fremantle, *Three Months in the Southern States*, 266–67; Youngblood, "Unwritten History of the Gettysburg Campaign," *SHSP* 38 (January–December 1910), 317–18, and "Personal Observations at Gettysburg," *Confederate Veteran* (June 1911), 287; Frank E. Moran to J. B. Bachelder (January 24, 1882), in *Bachelder Papers*, 2:778–79; Francis Warrington Dawson, *Reminiscences of Confederate Service, 1861–1865*, ed. Bell I. Wiley (Baton Rouge:

Louisiana State University Press, 1980), 97; Swallow, "The Third Day at Gettysburg," 569; Piston, *Lee's Tarnished Lieutenant*, 62–63; Gordon, *General George E. Pickett in Life and Legend*, 116.

3. McNeilly, "War's Fascination," 92; George L. Christian to J. W. Daniel (January 4, 1898), in John Warwick Daniel Papers, Special Collections, University of Virginia; A. T. Watts, "Something More About Gettysburg," *Confederate Veteran* 6 (February 1898), 67; *A Mississippi Rebel in the Army of Northern Virginia: The Civil War Memoirs of Private David Holt*, eds. Thomas Cockerell and Michael Ballard (Baton Rouge: Louisiana State University Press, 1998), 198.

4. LaSalle Pickett, "My Soldier," 366; Charles T. Loehr, *War History of the Old First Virginia Infantry Regiment, Army of Northern Virginia* (Richmond: William Ellis Jones, 1884), 36; Bright, "Pickett's Charge," *SHSP* 31 (January–December 1903), 233–34; Capt. James Johnson (5th Florida), in *Pickett's Charge—Eyewitness Accounts*, ed. Rollins, 164; Wilson, *The Most Promising Young Man of the South: James Johnston Pettigrew and His Men at Gettysburg*, 70; Atkinson, "Seminary Ridge on July 3," in *The Third Day: The Fate of a Nation*, 125–26.

5. "Reports of Maj. Gen. J.E.B. Stuart, C.S. Army" (August 20, 1863), in *O.R.*, series one, 27 (pt. 2): 697; McClellan, *Life and Campaigns of Major-General J.E.B. Stuart*, 337; Stephen Z. Starr, *The Union Cavalry in the Civil War: From Fort Sumter to Gettysburg, 1861–1863* (Baton Rouge: Louisiana State University Press, 1979), 432–39. Yet there remain those who argue passionately for an all-encompassing significance to the Rummel farm fight, for which see Thomas Carhart, *Lost Triumph: Lee's Real Plan at Gettysburg—And Why It Failed* (New York: G. P. Putnam, 2005), and Paul D. Walker, *The Cavalry Battle That Saved the Union: Custer vs. Stuart at Gettysburg* (Gretna, LA: Pelican, 2002).

6. Longacre, *Lee's Cavalrymen*, 217–22; John B. McIntosh to J. B. Bachelder (August 27, 1885), in *Bachelder Papers*, 2:1122–23; Custer, in *Michigan in the War*, ed. John Robertson (Lansing, MI: W. S. George & Co., 1880), 409; Longacre, *Gentleman and Soldier: The Extraordinary Life of General Wade Hampton* (Nashville: Rutledge Hill Press, 2003), 150–55; Daniel Murphy, "Slashing Sabers at the Rummel Farm," *America's Civil War* (January 2005), 40–45; Alexander C. N. Pennington interview with Alexander Kelly (October 29, 1907), in *Generals in Bronze*, 256, 259; William E. Miller, "The Cavalry Battle near Gettysburg," in *Battles & Leaders*, 3:401–6; William Brooke-Rawle, "The Right Flank at Gettysburg," in *Annals of the War*, 473–84.

7. A. H. Belo [55th North Carolina], "The Battle of Gettysburg, " *Confederate Veteran* (April 1900), 168; Eric J. Wittenberg, *Gettysburg's Forgotten Cavalry Actions: Farnsworth's Charge, South Cavalry Field, and the Battle of Fairfield, July 3, 1863* (New York: Savas Beatie, 2011), 56, and "Merritt's Regular's on South Cavalry Field: Oh, What Could Have Been," *Gettysburg Magazine* 16 (January 1997), 118; Martin, *Kill-Cavalry*, 114–17; H. C. Parsons, "Farnsworth's Charge and Death," in *Battles & Leaders*, 3:393–96.

8. "Reports of General Robert E. Lee, C.S. Army" (July 4, 7, and 8, 1863), in *O.R.*, series one, 27 (pt. 2):298–300; Lee to Imboden (July 1, 1863), in *Wartime Papers of Robert E. Lee*, 537; Lee to Jefferson Davis (July 16, 1863), in *Lee's Dispatches*, 106.

9. Spencer C. Tucker, *Brigadier General John D. Imboden: Confederate Commander in the Shenandoah* (Lexington: University Press of Kentucky, 2003), 150; Brown, *Retreat from Gettysburg*, 67–69, 70–72, 72, 73, 78–79, 85, 93, 95–96, 111–12; L. T. Dickinson, "Services of a Maryland Command," *Confederate Veteran* (June 1894), 165; Mills, *History of the 16th North Carolina Regiment*, 39.

10. Eric J. Wittenberg, J. David Petruzzi, and Michael F. Nugent, *One Continuous Fight: The Retreat from Gettysburg and the Pursuit of Lee's Army of Northern Virginia, July 4–14, 1863* (New York: Savas Beatie, 2008), 5–7; "Imboden's Account of the Confederate Retreat," in

Gerrish and Hutchinson, *The Blue and the Gray: A Graphic History*, 371–72; Imboden to Lee (July 4, 1863), in *O.R.*, series one, 27 (pt. 3):966–67.

11. Youngblood, "Unwritten History of the Gettysburg Campaign," 317–18; Franklin Gaillard to his wife, July 17, 1863, in Franklin Gaillard Papers, Southern Historical Collection, University of North Carolina; Sorrel, *Recollections of a Confederate Staff Officer*, 165; Ross Stilwell, in Scott Hartwig, "'We Came Here with the Best Army the Confederacy Ever Carried into the Field': The Army of Northern Virginia and the Gettysburg Campaign," in *Gettysburg: The End of the Campaign and Battle's Aftermath* (Gettysburg: Gettysburg National Military Park, 2012), 76; Bingham to "Dear General," William Palmer Collection, Western Reserve Historical Society, Cleveland, OH.

12. Ulysses S. Grant, "The Vicksburg Campaign," in *Battles & Leaders*, 3:534; Michael Ballard, *Vicksburg: The Campaign That Opened the Mississippi* (Chapel Hill: University of North Carolina Press, 2004), 398; "A Proposed Confederate Mission," *Washington National Intelligencer* (July 9, 1863); Schott, *Alexander H. Stephens of Georgia*, 379–80; Gideon Welles, diary entry for July 6, 1863, in *Diary of Gideon Welles*, ed. J. T. Morse (Boston: Houghton Mifflin, 1911), 1:363–64; "The Retreating Rebel Army," *Pittsburgh Daily Dispatch* (July 9, 1863); George Templeton Strong, diary entry for July 4, 1863, in *Diary of the Civil War*, 328; P. H. Watson to E. M. Stanton (July 5, 1863), in *O.R.*, series one, 27 (pt. 3):552–53.

13. James Meade to William Mitchell (January 24, 1869), George G. Meade to J. B. Bachelder (December 4, 1869), Lt. John Egan to George Meade, Jr. (February 8, 1870), and Capt. George Meade to J. B. Bachelder (May 6, 1882), in *Bachelder Papers*, 1:320–21, 379–80, 389, and 2:853–55; Cleaves, *Meade of Gettysburg*, 165–66; Haskell, "The Battle of Gettysburg," 136–37, and in Gibbon, *Personal Recollections of the Civil War*, 165–66; John H. B. Latrobe, "The Pinch of the Fight at Gettysburg" (August 6, 1863), in *Picture of the Battle of Gettysburg, Painted by P. F. Rothermel, Now on Exhibition at Tremont Temple, Boston* (Philadelphia: Longacre & Co., 1871), 7; Coffin, *The Boys of '61*, 319–20; Cook, "Personal Reminscences of Gettysburg," 139.

14. Tucker, *Hancock the Superb*, 157; Gambone, *Hancock at Gettysburg*, 147–48; Hancock to Meade (July 3, 1863), in *O.R.*, series one, 27 (pt. 1):366; "Testimony of Major General Alfred Pleasonton" (March 7, 1864), "Testimony of Major General G. K. Warren" (March 9, 1864), and "Testimony of Brigadier General S.W. Crawford" (April 27, 1864), in *Report of the Joint Committee on the Conduct of the War*, 4:360, 378, 379, 380, 471; Longstreet, "Lee's Right Wing at Gettysburg," *Battles & Leaders*, 3:347; Alexander, *Fighting for the Confederacy*, 265; Thomson and Rauch, *History of the "Bucktails,"* 273–74; Benjamin F. Urban, "The Story of Gettysburg: A Great Battle as Seen By a Lancaster Boy," in *Dreaming on the Conestoga: A Collection of Sonnets Written on the Stream of My Childhood* (Lancaster: New Era Printing Co., 1911), 300; "Thursday's Doubtful Issue—Friday's Victory" (July 4, 1863), in *A Radical View: The "Agate" Dispatches of Whitelaw Reid*, 2:62, 66; Timothy J. Orr, "'Sharpshooters Made a Grand Record This Day': Combat on the Skirmish Line on July 3" and Troy Harman, "Did Meade Begin a Counteroffensive After Pickett's Charge?," in *The Third Day: The Fate of a Nation*, 73–75, 226–27, 230, 233–34, 236–37; Frank A. Bond, "Company A—First Maryland Cavalry," *Confederate Veteran* (February 1898), 80.

15. Waitt, *History of the Nineteenth Regiment, Massachusetts Volunteer Infantry*, 244–45; Page, *History of the Fourteenth Regiment, Connecticut Vol. Infantry*, 167; Rauscher, *Music on the March*, 99; Chamberlin, *History of the One Hundred and Fiftieth Regiment, Pennsylvania Volunteers*, 153.

16. P. A. Taylor, William H. Hill, and I. S. Lyon to Meade (July 4, 1863), General Orders No. 68 (July 4, 1863), Circular (July 4, 1863), and John Newton to Daniel Butterfield (July 4, 1863), in *O.R.*, series one, 27 (pt. 3):513, 516, 519, 520.

17. Brown, *Retreat from Gettysburg*, 163, 165–66, 265; Wittenberg, *One Continuous Fight*,

158, 159; Meade to Margaretta Meade (July 5, 1863), in George G. Meade Papers (box 1, folder 10), Historical Society of Pennsylvania; Herman Haupt, "The Crisis of the Civil War," *Century Magazine* 44 (September 1892), 795; "Testimony of Major General David B. Birney" (March 7, 1864), "Testimony of General A. P. Howe" (March 3, 1864), "Testimony of Major General G. K. Warren" (March 9, 1864), "Testimony of Major General George G. Meade" (March 11, 1864), and "Testimony of Major General Daniel Butterfield" (March 25, 1864), in *Report of the Joint Committee on the Conduct of the War*, 4:313, 350, 367, 378–80, 426; Meade, *Life and Letters of George Gordon Meade*, 2:116.

18. Robert Emory Park, "Sketch of the Twelfth Alabama Infantry," *SHSP* 33 (January–December 1905), 244; Samuel Pickens, diary entry for July 14, 1863, in *Voices from Company D*, 185–87; A. S. Van de Graaf, in Reardon, *Pickett's Charge*, 31; James A. Graham to W. A. Graham (July 7, 1863), in "The James A. Graham Papers, 1861–1884," ed. H. N. Wagstaff, in *James Sprunt Historical Studies*, Volume 20 (Chapel Hill: University of North Carolina Press, 1928), 151–52; J. W. Lokey, "Wounded at Gettysburg," *Confederate Veteran* (January 1914), 400; J. M. Imboden, "Lee at Gettysburg," *The Galaxy* 11 (April 1871), 510–11; Brown, *Retreat from Gettysburg*, 78–79, 93, 111–12; William Seymour, diary entry for July 5, 1863, in *The Civil War Memoirs of William J. Seymour*, 80.

19. Meade to Sedgwick (July 5, 1863), Meade to William F. Smith (July 5, 1863), Circular (July 5, 1863), Sedgwick to Meade (July 6, 1863) and Meade to Couch (July 6, 1863), in *O.R.*, series one, 27 (pt. 3):532, 535, 539, 555; "Testimony of Major General A. P. Howe" (March 3, 1864), in *Report of the Joint Committee on the Conduct of the War*, 4:314–15; Stevens, *Three Years in the Sixth Corps*, 255; Peter C. Vermilyea, "Maj. Gen. John Sedgwick and the Pursuit of Lee's Army After Gettysburg," *Gettysburg Magazine* 22 (January 2000); Early, *Lieutenant General Jubal Anderson Early, C.S.A.*, 280.

20. Samuel L. Gracey, *Annals of the Sixth Pennsylvania Cavalry* (Philadelphia: E. H. Butler, 1868), 190; "Reports of Brig. Gen. Judson Kilpatrick" (August 10, 1863), in *O.R.*, series one, 27 (pt. 1):994, Wittenberg, *One Continuous Fight*, 16–18, 53–72, 124–35, 174–88; Brown, *Retreat from Gettysburg*, 158–61; Bond, "Company A—First Maryland Cavalry," *Confederate Veteran* (February 1898), 79–80; Kimble, "Tennesseans at Gettysburg—The Retreat," 461–62; *Papers of Randolph Abbott Shotwell*, 2:33; Imboden, "The Confederate Retreat from Gettysburg," in *Battles & Leaders*, 3:425; Valuska and Keller, *Damn Dutch*, 68; Edward G. Longacre, *Lincoln's Cavalrymen: A History of the Mounted Forces of the Army of the Potomac* (Mechanicsburg, PA: Stackpole Books, 2000), 208–9.

21. Frank E. Moran to Daniel E. Sickles (January 24, 1882), in *Bachelder Papers*, 2:783; Brown, *Retreat from Gettysburg*, 91–92, 293, 298, 321–22; Lee to Mary Custis Lee (July 12, 1863), in *Wartime Papers*, 547; Lee to George E. Pickett (July 8, 1863), in *O.R.*, series one, 27 (pt. 3):983; Imboden, "Lee at Gettysburg," *The Galaxy* 11 (April 1871), 513; Alexander, *Fighting for the Confederacy*, 269; Steve French, "The Rebels at Williamsport," *Gettysburg Magazine* 27 (July 2002), 102–8; Glatthaar, *General Lee's Army*, 283; Hess, *Field Armies and Fortifications in the Civil War: The Eastern Campaigns*, 234–35.

22. Mahood, *General Wadsworth*, 191; Harry W. Pfanz, "The Gettysburg Campaign After Pickett's Charge," *Gettysburg Magazine* 1 (July 1989), 122; Mulholland, *Story of the 116th Regiment, Pennsylvania Infantry*, 149; SeCheverell, *Journal History of the Twenty-ninth Ohio Veteran Volunteers*, 75; Blake, *Three Years in the Army of the Potomac*, 225; Washburn, *Military History and Record of the 108th Regiment, N.Y. Vols.*, 48; Fox, "Slocum and His Men," 187; Andrew J. Boies, *Record of the Thirty-Third Massachusetts Volunteer Infantry: From Aug. 1862 to Aug. 1865* (Fitchburg, MA: Sentinel Publishing, 1880), 34.

23. Judson, *History of the Eighty-Third Regiment, Pennsylvania Volunteers*, 143–44; Stevens, *Three Years in the Sixth Corps*, 262; *Avery Harris Civil War Journal*, 79; Eddy, *History of the 60th Regiment, New York State Volunteers*, 266; Meade to Halleck (July 9, 1863), in *O.R.*,

series one, 27 (pt. 1):86; *Fighting with the Eighteenth Massachusetts: The Civil War Memoir of Thomas H. Mann*, 187–89.

24. Meade to Margaretta Meade (July 8, 10, and 12, 1863), in George G. Meade Papers [box 1, folder 10], Historical Society of Pennsylvania; Halleck to Meade (July 8, 1863) and Meade to Halleck (July 8, 1863), in *O.R.,* series one, 27 (pt. 3):605–6.

25. Brown, *Retreat from Gettysburg*, 320–21, 326; Ranald Mackenzie to G. K. Warren (July 12, 1863) and Lee to Stuart (July 13, 1863), in *O.R.,* series one, 27 (pt. 3):669, 1001; Channing M. Bolton, "With General Lee's Engineers," *Confederate Veteran* 30 (August 1922), 300; Jedediah Hotchkiss, diary entry for July 12, 1863, in *Make Me a Map of the Valley*, 160; Casler, *Four Years in the Stonewall Brigade*, 179–80.

26. Smith, *History of the Nineteenth Regiment of Maine Volunteer Infantry*, 90–91; Smith, "Brig. Gen. Alexander Hays and the Third Division, Second Corps," in *The Third Day: The Fate of a Nation*, 190; Slocum to Judge Leroy H. Morgan (January 2, 1864), in *The Life and Services of Major-General Henry Warner Slocum*, 84–85, 134–36; Jordan, *Red Diamond Regiment*, 83.

27. Meade to Halleck (July 10, 12, and 13, 1863), in *O.R.,* series one, 27 (pt. 1):89, 91; "Testimony of General George G. Meade" (March 5, 1864) and "Testimony of Brigadier General James S. Wadsworth" (March 23, 1864), in *Report of the Joint Committee on the Conduct of the War*, 4:336, 415; Howard interview with Alexander Kelly (April 15, 1899), in *Generals in Bronze*, 178; Wainwright, diary entry for July 13, 1863, in *A Diary of Battle*, 260; Mahood, *General Wadsworth*, 192–93; Coffin, *The Boys of '61*, 255. See also Noah Brooks' report on July 14th which also identified Pleasonton, Wadsworth, and Howard as dissenters, in *Lincoln Observed: Civil War Dispatches of Noah Brooks*, ed. Michael Burlingame (Baltimore: Johns Hopkins University Press, 1998), 58.

28. Halleck to Meade (July 13, 1863), in *O.R.,* series one, 27 (pt. 1):92; Sorrel, *Recollections of a Confederate Staff Officer*, 175; Longstreet, *Manassas to Appomattox*, 429–30; Léon, *Diary of a Tar Heel Confederate Soldier*, 40; Robert T. Hubbard, *The Civil War Memoirs of a Virginia Cavalryman*, ed. Thomas P. Nanzig (Tuscaloosa: University of Alabama Press, 2007), 103; Dickert, *History of Kershaw's Brigade*, 258; Samuel Pickens, diary entry for July 14, 1863, in *Voices from Company D*, 186–87; Hess, *Lee's Tar Heels*, 161; Brown, *Retreat from Gettysburg*, 351; Gragg, *Covered with Glory*, 216–19.

CHAPTER TWENTY-FIVE *There is bad faith somewhere*

1. Desjardin, *These Honored Dead*, 201–2; Terrence V. Murphy, *10th Virginia Infantry* (Lynchburg, VA: H. E. Howard, 1989), 80; Robertson, *18th Virginia Infantry*, 23; Divine, *8th Virginia Infantry*, 24–25, 42; Charles W. Sublett, *57th Virginia Infantry* ((Lynchburg, VA: H. E. Howard, 1985), 29.

2. J. J. Hoyle to his wife (July 15, 1863), in *Deliver Us from This Cruel War: The Civil War Letters of Lieutenant Joseph J. Hoyle, 55th North Carolina Infantry*, ed. Jeffrey M. Girvan (Jefferson, NC: McFarland, 2010), 127; George C. Underwood, "Twenty-Sixth Regiment," in *Histories of the Several Regiments and Battalions from North Carolina in the Great War, 1861–'65*, ed. Clark, 2:366; Richard B. Kleese, *49th Virginia Infantry* (Lynchburg, VA: H. E. Howard, 2002), 40; Dunbar Rowland, *The Official and Statistical Register of the State of Mississippi 1908* (Nashville: Brandon Printing, 1908), 2:442.

3. Fuller, *Personal Recollections of the War of 1861*, 70; *Confederate Veteran* 2 (May 1894), 142; Glenn W. LaFantasie, *Gettysburg Requiem: The Life and Lost Causes of Confederate Colonel William C. Oates* (New York: Oxford University Press, 2006), 101, 120–21; Michael Dreese, *Torn Families: Death and Kinship at the Battle of Gettysburg* (Jefferson, NC: McFarland,

2007), 22–23; Hess, *Lee's Tar Heels,* 157–57; R. M. Tuttle, "Unparalleled Loss—Company F, Twenty-Sixth Regiment, N.C.T., at Gettysburg, 1 July, 1863," in *Histories of the Several Regiments and Battalions from North Carolina, in the Great War 1861–'65,* ed. Clark, 5:601; Coffman and Graham, *To Honor These Men: A History of the Phillips Georgia Legion Infantry Battalion,* 301; Wyckoff, *History of the Second South Carolina Infantry,* 464, 578, 591, and *History of the 3rd South Carolina,* 420.

4.   Freeman, *Lee's Lieutenants,* 2;190–97; Divine, *8th Virginia Infantry,* 41–42; James W. Parrish, *Wiregrass to Appomattox: The Untold Story of the 50th Georgia Infantry Regiment, C.S.A.* (Winchester, VA: Angle Valley Press, 2008), 121; Tagg, *The Generals of Gettysburg,* 267–68, 338–39; E. N. Morrison, "Fifteenth Virginia Infantry," *SHSP* 33 (January–February 1905), 102; Wittenberg, *One Continuous Fight,* 284–88; Hassler, "Afterword," in *One of Lee's Best Men,* 256–59; Lee to James A. Seddon (July 17, 1863), in *O.R.,* series one, 27 (pt. 3):1016; Kimble, "Tennesseans at Gettysburg—The Retreat," 462; Robertson, *General A. P. Hill,* 228; "The Memoirs of Henry Heth, Part II," *Civil War History* 8 (September 1962), 307–8.

5.   *O.R.,* series one, 27 (pt. 2):346; Bates, *Battle of Gettysburg,* 199; Allen "General Lee's Strength and Losses at Gettysburg," *SHSP* 1 (July 1877), 34; Beecham, *Gettysburg, the Pivotal Battle of the Civil War,* 250–51; John D. Vautier, "The Loss at Gettysburg," *Southern Bivouac* 4 (March 1886), 639; Hartwig, "'We Came Here with the Best Army the Confederacy Ever Carried into the Field': The Army of Northern Virginia and the Gettysburg Campaign," 63–66; James Pleasants, in Freeman, *Lee's Lieutenants,* 2:168. In 1875, Samuel Penniman Bates, warning that "the two armies represented quantities that were constantly varying," raised the estimate of Confederate dead to 5,500, and cited reports from subsequent burials and exhumations that ran the figure as high as 7,000 (although no provision was made for identifying whether this included both killed and those wounded who subsequently died); from that, Bates estimated that the conventional ratio of killed to wounded would yield 27,500 wounded, and he accepted without question George Meade's report of having captured 13,621 prisoners—overall, Confederate losses of over 46,000. Bates's totals were brought back down to earth in 1877 by William Allan, who believed that the real figure for total Confederate casualties was 22,728, and by Robert Beecham and John D. Vautier (both of them Gettysburg veterans), who set them at 28,000. Subsequent reckonings have more or less conformed to Allan's calculations. Robert Krick, in *The Gettysburg Death Roster: The Confederate Dead at Gettysburg* (2004), favors a number only marginally different from Allan's (p. 17); Scott Hartwig (in *The Encyclopedia of the Confederacy,* 2:683) and Joseph Glatthaar, in *General Lee's Army,* are closer to Bates in claiming between 4,400 and 4,700 killed, but sharply reduce the number of wounded to between 12,000 and 13,700, and put prisoner and missing at between 5,300 and 5,800; Edwin Coddington, in *The Gettysburg Campaign* (1968), adopted the 20,451 total in Lee's report, although added a little evasively that there were "very likely more" (p. 536).

6.   Meade to Halleck (August 3 and October 1, 1863), in *O.R.,* series one, 27 (pt. 1):113, 118, 187; "General Summary of Casualties in the Union Forces in the Gettysburg Campaign, June 3–August 1, 1863," in *Pennsylvania at Gettysburg,* 1;171; Mulholland, *The Story of the 116th Regiment, Pennsylvania Infantry,* 147; Bates, *Battle of Gettysburg,* 199, and *Martial Deeds of Pennsylvania,* 345; Thomas Livermore, *Numbers and Losses in the Civil War in America, 1861–1865* (Boston: Houghton Mifflin, 1900), 103; Busey and Martin, *Regimental Strengths and Losses,* 125; "The Opposing Forces at Gettysburg," in *Battles & Leaders,* 3:440; "Testimony of Major General George G. Meade" (March 11, 1864), in *Joint Committee on the Conduct of the War,* 4:350; Gottfried, *Stopping Pickett,* 178–79.

7.   Ambrose Hayward to A. H. Hayward, Sr. (July 17, 1863), in *Last to Leave the Field,* 159; Geary to Mary Geary (July 17, 1863), in *A Politician Goes to War: The Civil War Letters of John White Geary,* ed. William A. Blair (University Park: Penn State University Press,

1995), 101; Chase to Samuel S. Chase (July 9, 1863), in *Yours for the Union*, 257, 258; Grand-champ, "The 2nd Rhode Island Volunteers in the Gettysburg Campaign," 81; Blake, *Three Years in the Army of the Potomac*, 226–27, 228–29; Hardin, *History of the Twelfth Regiment, Pennsylvania Reserve Volunteer Corps*, 163; Stevens, *Three Years in the Sixth Corps*, 264–65; Dunkelman, *Brothers One and All*, 231; diary entry for July 6, 1863, in *Inside the Army of the Potomac: The Civil War Experience of Captain Francis Adams Donaldson*, 313.

8. "The Very Latest," *Washington Sunday Morning Chronicle* (July 5, 1863) and "The Situation" (July 12, 1863); Elias Nason, *The Life and Public Services of Henry Wilson* (Boston: D. Lothrop & Co., 1881), 328–29; John L. Myers, *Senator Henry Wilson and the Civil War* (Lanham, MD: University Press of America, 2007), 112; A. Wilson Greene, "From Get-tysburg to Falling Waters: Meade's Pursuit of Lee," in *Third Day at Gettysburg and Beyond*, ed. Gary Gallagher (Chapel Hill: University of North Carolina Press, 1994), 172; Howard, *Autobiography*, 1:446; Lincoln, "Announcement of News from Gettysburg" (July 4, 1863), "To Henry W. Halleck" (July 6, 1863) and "To Jesse K. Dubois" (July 11, 1863), in *Collected Works*, 6:314, 318, and 323; John Hay, diary entries for July 11 and 14, 1863, in *Inside Lincoln's White House: The Complete Civil War Diary of John Hay*, eds. J. R. T. Ettlinger and Michael Burlingame (Carbondale: Southern Illinois University Press, 1997), 61, 62; James B. Fry, "Doubleday's 'Chancellorsville and Gettysburg,' " in *Military Miscellanies* (New York: Brentano's, 1889), 435.

9. Hay, diary entries for September 26, 1862, and July 12, 14, 15, and 19, 1863, in *Inside Lincoln's White House*, 41, 62, 63, 65; Meade to Halleck (July 14, 1863), in *O.R.*, series one, 27 (pt. 1):92; "Robert Todd Lincoln's Reminiscences, Given 5 January 1885" and Lincoln to Meade, in *An Oral History of Abraham Lincoln: John G. Nicolay's Interviews and Essays*, ed. Michael Burlingame (Carbondale: Southern Illinois University Press, 1996), 88, 153; Michael Burlingame, *Abraham Lincoln: A Life* (Baltimore: Johns Hopkins University Press, 2008), 2:512–13.

10. George H. Thacher, "Lincoln and Meade After Gettysburg," *American Historical Review* 32 (January 1927), 282–83; Brooks, *Washington in Lincoln's Time* (New York: Century Co., 1895), 95; Haupt, "The Crisis of the Civil War," 794; Welles, diary entry for July 14, 1863, in *Diary of Gideon Welles*, 1:370; Michael Burlingame, "Lincoln's Anger and Cruelty," in *The Inner World of Abraham Lincoln* (Chicago: University of Illinois Press, 1994), 189.

11. Halleck to Meade (July 14, 1863) and Meade to Halleck (July 14, 1863), in *O.R.*, series one, 27 (pt. 1):92–93; Lincoln, "To George G. Meade" (July 14, 1863), in *Collected Works*, 6:327–28.

12. Meade to Margaretta Meade (July 14, 1863), in George G. Meade Papers [box 1, folder 10], Historical Society of Pennsylvania; *Correspondence of John Sedgwick, Major-General* (Nor-folk, CT: Carl Stoeckel, 1903), 2:132; McClellan to Meade (July 11, 1863), in Meade, *Life and Letters of George Gordon Meade*, 2:134, 312; Cleaves, *Meade of Gettysburg*, 172.

13. Gideon Welles, diary entry for October 16, 1863, in *Diary of Gideon Welles*, 1:471–72; Jason Emerson, *Giant in the Shadows: The Life of Robert T. Lincoln* (Carbondale: Southern Illi-nois University Press, 2012), 82–83; Frederick D. Bidwell, *History of the Forty-Ninth New York Volunteers* (Albany, NY: J. B. Lyon, 1916), 36–37; John Watts de Peyster, "An Ideal Soldier," *National Tribune* (July 19, 1889); Valuska and Keller, *Damn Dutch*, 156–57.

14. Barthel, *Abner Doubleday*, 171; Hessler, *Sickles at Gettysburg*, 251–52; Cleaves, *Meade of Get-tysburg*, 231; "General Orders No. 10" (March 24, 1864), in *O.R.*, series one, 30 (pt. 1):722–23; John J. Hennessy, "I Dread the Spring: The Army of the Potomac Prepares for the Overland Campaign," in *The Wilderness Campaign*, ed. Gary W. Gallagher (Chapel Hill: University of North Carolina Press, 1997), 81; Sherman *Memoirs of General W. T. Sherman*, ed. Royster (New York: Library of America, 1990), 559; Steven E. Woodworth, *Nothing but Victory: The Army of the Tennessee, 1861–1865* (New York: Alfred A. Knopf, 2005), 576.

15. Sears, *Controversies and Commanders*, 216–17; Taafe, *Commanding the Army of the Potomac*, 135–36; Welles, diary entry for October 20, 1863, in *Diary of Gideon Welles*, 1:473.

16. Slocum to L. H. Morgan (January 2, 1864), in *Life and Services of Major-General Henry Warner Slocum*, 134–36; "Address by Maj. Gen. Daniel E. Sickles, U.S.A." (September 19, 1903), in *In Memoriam: Henry Warner Slocum*, 32; Crawford to Sickles (September 7, 1886), in Daniel E. Sickles Papers, New-York Historical Society; Henry Wilson, "Bills Introduced" (December 14, 1863), "Generals Hooker, Meade and Howard" (January 18, 1864), in *Congressional Globe*, 38th Congress, first session, 17, 257; Gary G. Lash, "The Congressional Resolution of Thanks for the Federal Victory at Gettysburg," *Gettysburg Magazine* 12 (January 1995), 85, 93; Tap, *Over Lincoln's Shoulder*, 178–87; "Testimony of Major General Daniel Sickles" (February 26, 1864), in *Report of the Joint Committee on the Conduct of the War*, 4:301.

17. Desjardins, *These Honored Dead*, 65–66; "The Battle of Gettysburg—Important Communication from an Eye Witness," *New York Herald* (March 12, 1864); Meade to Halleck (March 15, 1864), in *O.R.*, series one, 27 (pt. 1):128; Sauers, *A Caspian Sea of Ink*, 49–58.

18. Elihu Washburne, "Grade of General" (December 4, 1863), in *Congressional Globe*, 38th Congress, first session, 6; Meade to Margaretta Meade (February 29, 1864), in Meade, *Life and Letters of George Gordon Meade*, 2:168, 187; John Y. Simon, "From Galena to Appomattox: Grant and Washburne," in *The Union Forever: Lincoln, Grant, and the Civil War*, ed. Glenn W. LaFantasie (Lexington: University Press of Kentucky, 2012), 162.

19. Meade to Margaretta Meade (June 9, 1864), in Meade, *Life and Letters of George Gordon Meade*, 2:168, 187; Grant to Stanton (May 13, 1864), in *The Papers of Ulysses S. Grant*, Volume 10: *January 1–May 31, 1864*, ed. John Y. Simon (Carbondale: Southern Illinois University Press, 1982), 434; Gibbon, *Personal Recollections of the Civil War*, 239; Gordon C. Rhea, *The Battles for Spotsylvania Court House and the Road to Yellow Tavern, May 7–12, 1864* (Baton Rouge: Louisiana State University Press, 1997), 8; Young, *Around the World with General Grant*, 2:300; Meade to "Mr. Walker" (August 1, 1863) and to Margaretta Meade (September 3, 1863, and January 20, 1865), in George G. Meade Papers [box 2, folder 10 and box 1, folder 4], Historical Society of Pennsylvania.

20. "Great Battle in Pennsylvania—Our Forces Victorious," *Charleston Mercury* (July 8, 1863); Lee to Davis (July 4, 7, 12, and 15, 1863), in *Wartime Papers*, 539, 540, 547, 551; Jeremiah Tate to Mary Tate (July 19, 1863), in Gilder-Lehrman Collection, New-York Historical Society; Alexander, "The Great Battle of Gettysburg" (July 4, 1863), "Further Details of the Great Battle of Gettysburg" (July 7, 1863) and "P.W.A. in Virginia" (July 14, 1863), in *Writing and Fighting the Confederate War: Letters of Peter Wellington Alexander, Confederate War Correspondent*, ed. William B. Styple (Kearny, NJ: Belle Grove Publishing, 2002), 161, 166, 171, and "The Pennsylvania Campaign—A Review of Its Movements and Results," *Charleston Mercury* (July 29, 1863); James A. Graham to "Dear Mother" (July 7, 1863), "The James A. Graham Papers," 150; "The Great Battle," *Macon Daily Telegraph* (July 8, 1863).

21. McKim, *A Soldier's Recollections: Leaves from the Diary of a Young Confederate* (New York: Longmans, Green & Co., 1910), 182; Wilkinson and Woodworth, *A Scythe of Fire*, 261; Daniel Sheetz, in Dennis E. Frye, *2nd Virginia Infantry* (Lynchburg, VA: H. E. Howard, 1984), 55; Glatthaar, *General Lee's Army*, 283–84; William D. Henderson, *12th Virginia Infantry* (Lynchburg, VA: H. E. Howard, 1984), 57; John C. Timberlake, in Hess, *Pickett's Charge*, 330; Collins, *Major General Robert E. Rodes of the Army of Northern Virginia*, 296.

22. Kean, diary entries for July 7 and 19, 1863, in *Inside the Confederate Government*, 78–79, 82; Tucker, *Brigadier General John D. Imboden*, 172; W. S. Oldham, "The Last Days of the Confederacy," *DeBow's Review* 6 (October 1869), 861–62; Ted Tunnell, "A 'Patriotic Press': Virginia's Confederate Newspapers, 1861–1865," in *Virginia at War, 1864*, eds. William C. Davis and James I. Robertson (Lexington: University of Kentucky Press, 2009) 40; "From

General Lee's Army," *Richmond Enquirer* (July 21, 1863) and "The Battle of Gettysburg, Pa.," *Richmond Enquirer* (July 24, 1863); "Editor's Table," *Southern Literary Messenger* 37 (September 1863), 572; Reardon, *Pickett's Charge*, 49, 51–52.

23. Overton, *Four Years in the Stonewall Brigade*, 153–54; "The Battle of Gettysburg—They Missed Jackson," *Charleston Mercury* (August 17, 1863); Pfanz, *Richard S. Ewell*, 325–26; Miller, *John Bell Hood and the Fight for Civil War Memory*, 212; John C. West to Charles S. West (July 27, 1863), in *A Texan in Search of a Fight*, 96; Maj. T. M. R. Talcott, "The Third Day at Gettysburg," *SHSP* 41 (September 1916), 44; Reardon, *Pickett's Charge*, 32; "Battle of Gettysburg, Pa.," *Richmond Enquirer* (July 24, 1863); Gary W. Gallagher, "Confederate Corps Leadership on the First Day at Gettysburg: A. P. Hill and Richard S. Ewell in a Difficult Debut," in *Three Days at Gettysburg*, 26–27; Glatthaar, *General Lee's Army: From Victory to Collapse*, 342.

24. Mosby to Sam Chapman (March 7, 1906), in *Take Sides with the Truth: The Postwar Letters of John Singleton Mosby to Samuel F. Chapman*, ed. Pater A. Brown (Lexington: University Press of Kentucky, 2007), 55; Colonel Charles Marshall, "Events Leading up to the Battle of Gettysburg," *SHSP* (January–December 1896), 212; McLaws, "Gettysburg," *SHSP* 7 (February 1879), 75–76; McLaws to Emily McLaws (July 7, 1863), in *A Soldier's General*, 197; Wolseley, "An English View of the Civil War IV," *North American Review* 149 (September 1889), 286–88.

25. Youngblood, "Personal Observations at Gettysburg," *Confederate Veteran* 19 (June 1911), 286–87; Ross, *A Visit to the Cities and Camps of the Confederate States*, 80; Lee to Jefferson Davis (July 31, 1863), in *Lee's Dispatches*, 109; Lee to Davis (July 31, 1863), in *Wartime Papers*, 565; Davis to Lee (August 11, 1863), in *O.R.*, series one, 32 (pt. 2):640; Thomas, *Robert E. Lee*, 306.

26. Lee to Samuel Cooper (July 31, 1863, and January 1864), in *O.R.*, series one, 27 (pt. 2):307, 316; Lee, *Recollections and Letters of Robert E. Lee*, 415–16; Lee to Davis (August 8, 1863), in *Wartime Papers*, 589; Gary W. Gallagher, "Confederate Corps Leadership on the First Day at Gettysburg," 36.

27. Heth to J. W. Jones, "Letter from Major General Heth, of A. P. Hill's Corps, A.N.V.," *SHSP* 4 (October 1877), 154; Imboden, "Lee at Gettysburg," 513, and "The Confederate Retreat from Gettysburg," in *Battles & Leaders*, 3:421; Gary W. Gallagher, " 'If the Enemy Is There, We Must Attack Him': R. E. Lee and the Second Day at Gettysburg," in *Three Days at Gettysburg*, 29–30; 115; Weigley, *The American Way of War*, 116; Fellman, *The Making of Robert E. Lee*, 161–62; William Marvel, *Lee's Last Retreat: The Flight to Appomattox* (Chapel Hill: University of North Carolina Press, 2002), 189.

28. "From General Lee's Army," *Richmond Enquirer* (July 21, 1863); Cooke, *A Life of Gen. Robert E. Lee* (New York: D. Appleton, 1883), 307; McCabe, *Life and Campaigns of General Robert E. Lee* (Philadelphia: National Publishing, 1866), 395; Longstreet, "Lee in Pennsylvania," in *Annals of the War*, 414–15; J. William Jones, "The Longstreet-Gettysburg Controversy—Who Commenced It?—The Whole Matter Reviewed," *Richmond Dispatch* (February 16, 1896); Gallagher, " 'If the Enemy Is There, We Must Attack Him': R. E. Lee and the Second Day at Gettysburg," in *Three Days at Gettysburg*, 49; Mosby, *Memoirs of Colonel John S. Mosby*, 381.

29. Curtis, *History of the Twenty-fourth Michigan of the Iron Brigade*, 171–72; Buell, "Story of a Cannoneer," *National Tribune* (October 24, 1889); Capt. Alfred Lee, "Reminiscences of Gettysburg," *Ladies Repository* 25 (September 1865), 548.

30. Taylor to "Brother Dick" (July 17, 1863), in *Lee's Adjutant: The Wartime Letters of Colonel Walter Herron Taylor*, 62.

31. Rick Britton, " 'So Many Dangers Seen and Unseen': A Civil War Memoir by James Addison Leathers," *The Magazine of Albemarle County History* 59 (2001), 78–79.

32. Twemlow, *Considerations on Tactics and Strategy*, 105–6; Rafferty, "Gettysburg," in *Personal Recollections of the War of the Rebellion*, 2.

33. Davis, "The Strategy of the Gettysburg Campaign," in *Papers of the Military Historical Society of Massachusetts*, 3:442; Rossetti, "English Opinion of the American War," *Atlantic Monthly* 17 (February 1866), 133; Blake, *Three Years in the Army of the Potomac*, 222–23.

34. J. Tracy Power, *Lee's Miserables: Life in the Army of Northern Virginia from the Wilderness to Appomattox* (Chapel Hill: University of North Carolina Press, 1998), 2; Oates, *The War Between the Union and the Confederacy, and Its Lost Opportunities*, 243; Jacobs, "Notes Recounting the Battle of Gettysburg" [MS-107], in Special Collections, Gettysburg College.

35. Nicolay to Therena Bates (July 12, 1863), in *With Lincoln in the White House: Letters, Memoranda, and Other Writings of John G. Nicolay, 1860–1865*, ed. Michael Burlingame (Carbondale: Southern Illinois University Press, 2000), 118; Davis, *The Rise and Fall of the Confederate Government* (New York: D. Appleton, 1881), 2:448; Richard Henry Dana to Charles Francis Adams (March 3, 1865), in *Charles Francis Adams, Richard Henry Dana: A Biography* (Boston: Houghton Mifflin, 1891), 2:274–75.

CHAPTER TWENTY-SIX   *To Sweep & plunder the battle grounds*

1. Skelly, *A Boy's Experiences During the Battle of Gettysburg* (Gettysburg, 1932), 18; Mary McAllister account, Adams County Historical Society; Mahood, *General Wadsworth*, 189; "Squad of the 17th Conn. First Learned of Lee's Retreat at Gettysburg," *National Tribune* (October 8, 1896); Maj. Homer Stoughton to J. B. Bachelder (December 29, 1881), in *Bachelder Papers*, 2:769; Thomas L. Elmore, "Independence Day: Military Operations at Gettysburg," *Gettysburg Magazine* 25 (July 2001), 119–21.

2. Hanifen, *History of Battery B, First New Jersey Artillery*, 83; Tyson to Noble D. Preston (January 16, 1884), in "A Refugee from Gettysburg," ed. William McKenna, *Civil War Times Illustrated* 27 (November–December 1998), 74; Linn, "Journal of My Trip to the Battlefield of Gettysburg, July 1863," 60–62; Capt. George A. Thayer, "On the Right at Gettysburg," *National Tribune* (July 24, 1902); "Gettysburg During the Battle—By One Who Was in the Town During the Whole," *Christian Recorder* (July 18, 1863); Frawley, "Marching Through Pennsylvania," 101; Francis T. Hoover to Jane Ann Hedley (September 25, 1863), in Gettysburg National Military Park Vertical Files [#8–18d].

3. Abraham T. Brewer, *History* [of the] *Sixty-First Regiment Pennsylvania Volunteers, 1861–1865, Under Authority of the Regimental Association* (Pittsburgh: Art Engraving & Printing, 1911), 68, 69; Dr. George S. Osborne to J. B. Bachelder (May 14, 1885), in *Bachelder Papers*, 2:1044; Hess, *Pickett's Charge*, 345, and *The Rifle Musket in Civil War Combat*, 50; Christ, *The Struggle for the Bliss Farm*, 82, 117–18; Scott L. Mingus and Thomas M. Mingus, "'An Accident of War': York County's Civil War Damage Claims," *Journal of York County Heritage* (September 2012), 19; Sheldon, *When the Smoke Cleared at Gettysburg*, 246; "Joint Resolution of request to the Secretary of War to secure the release of certain unarmed citizens of this Commonwealth from rebel imprisonment" (March 23, 1865), in *O.R.*, series two, 8:426.

4. "Mrs. Bayly's Story of the Battle," Adams County Historical Society; "Squad of the 17th Conn. First Learned of Lee's Retreat at Gettysburg," *National Tribune* (October 8, 1896); Philip Schaff, "The Gettysburg Week," *Scribner's Magazine* 16 (July 1894), 28; Matilda Pierce Alleman, *At Gettysburg; or, What a Girl Saw and Heard of the Battle*, 99–100; Winey, *Confederate Uniforms at Gettysburg*, 80; Allen, *Under the Maltese Cross*, 191–92; Marsena

Patrick, diary entry for July 5, 1863, in *Inside Lincoln's Army*, 266–68; Sheldon, *When the Smoke Cleared at Gettysburg*, 213; Bennett, *Days of "Uncertainty and Dread,"* 75.

5. Lyon Gardiner Tyler, *Men of Mark in Virginia: A Collection of Biographies of the Leading Men in the State* (Washington, DC: Men of Mark Publishing, 1908), 4:79–81; Crocker, "Prison Reminiscences" (February 2, 1904), *SHSP* 34 (January–December 1906), 28–29, 31, and "Prison Reminiscences," *Confederate Veteran* 14 (November 1906), 503–4; Samuel Gring Hefelbower, *The History of Gettysburg College, 1832–1932* (Gettysburg: Gettysburg College, 1932), 340.

6. "Our Wounded at Gettysburg—Mr. M. Davidson's Despatch," *New York Herald* (July 24, 1863); McCreary, "Gettysburg: A Boy's Experience of the Battle," 249–50; Bennett, *Days of "Uncertainty and Dread,"* 80–81, 82–83; "U.S. Christian Commission—Incidents connected with the report of Rev. P. A. Strobel," *Christian Recorder* (September 12, 1863); Josiah Rinehart Sypher, *History of the Pennsylvania Reserve Corps: A Complete Record of the Organization* (Lancaster, PA: Elias Barr & Co., 1865), 54–55; John Y. Foster, "Four Days at Gettysburg," *Harper's New Monthly Magazine* 28 (February 1864), 385–86; "Report of Surg. Jonathan Letterman" (October 3, 1863), in *O.R.*, series one, 27 (pt. 1):198; Harper, *"If Thee Must Fight,"* 261–62.

7. "Report of Surg. Jonathan Letterman," 197; Winslow, "Report on the Operations of the Sanitary Commission During and After the Battles at Gettysburg," in *Documents of the U.S. Sanitary Commission* (New York: USSC, 1866), 2:17; Baruch, "A Surgeon's Story of Battle and Capture," *Confederate Veteran* 22 (January 1914), 545–47; Brown, *Retreat from Gettysburg*, 98, 102, 110, 113; Matt Atkinson, "'War Is a Hellish Way of Settling a Dispute': Dr. Jonathan Letterman and the Tortuous Path of Medical Care from Manassas to Camp Letterman," in *Gettysburg: The End of the Campaign*, 130; John Mumma Young, typescript "Memoirs" [VFM-169], Special Collections, Gettysburg College.

8. "College Hospital in Gettysburg," *The Land We Love*, 290–91; Colver, "Reminiscences of the Battle of Gettysburg," 179–80; Barziza, *Adventures of a Prisoner of War, 1863–1864*, 61; Linn, "Journal of My Trip to the Battlefield of Gettysburg," 62; R. J. Musto, "The Treatment of the Wounded at Gettysburg; Jonathan Letterman, the Father of Modern Battlefield Medicine," *Gettysburg Magazine* 37 (July 2007), 125–27; Maj. George L. Wood, *The Seventh Regiment: A Record* (New York: James Miller, 1865), 158–59; Bennett, *Days of "Uncertainty and Dread,"* 86–87.

9. Charles Wainwright, diary entry for July 5, 1863, in *A Diary of Battle*, 254; McCreary, "Gettysburg: A Boy's Experience of the Battle," 253; Linn, "Journal of My Trip to the Battlefield of Gettysburg," 58; Bennett, *Days of "Uncertainty and Dread,"* 86–87; Marsena Patrick, diary entry for July 5, 1863, in *Inside Lincoln's Army*, 266–68; Charles McKim, diary entry for August 5, 1863, in McKim Diary, Gettysburg National Military Park Vertical Files [#8–18e]; Sheldon, *When the Smoke Cleared at Gettysburg*, 171–72; "A Farmer's Experience—What Happened to Him During the Battle," *Gettysburg Compiler* (July 6, 1910); Blood, diary entries for July 11, 17, and 18, 1863, in Henry Boyden Blood diary, Library of Congress; "The National Necropolis—Our Heroic Dead at Gettysburg," *New York Herald* (November 20, 1863); Young, typescript "Memoirs," Special Collections, Gettysburg College; Bloom, *History of Adams County*, 182.

10. Storrs, *The "Twentieth Connecticut": A Regimental History*, 104–5; Hinkley, *Narrative of Service with the Third Wisconsin Infantry*, 91; Blake, *Three Years in the Army of the Potomac*, 219–20; Jim Weeks, "'A Disgrace That Can Never Be Washed Out': Gettysburg and the Lingering Stigma of 1863," in *Making and Remaking Pennsylvania's Civil War*, 193; Creighton, *The Colors of Courage*, 157–58; Valuska and Keller, *Damn Dutch*, 70–71.

11. Crounse, "Further Details of the Battle of Gettysburgh—Characteristics of the People of

the Town," *New York Times* (July 9, 1863) and "The Treatment of the Union Soldiers by the People of Gettysburgh," *New York Times* (July 24, 1863); Newell, *"Ours": Annals of the 10th Regiment, Massachusetts Volunteers,* 224.

12.   Benjamin Borton, *On the Parallels; or, Chapters of Inner History, a Story of the Rappahan-nock* (Woodstown, NJ: Monitor-Register Print, 1903), 177–78; Brown, *Retreat from Get-tysburg,* 83; Chase to Samuel S. Chase (August 5, 1863), in *Yours for the Union,* 268; Geary to Mary Geary (July 5, 1863), in *A Politician Goes to War,* 100; John Y. Foster, "Four Days at Gettysburg," *Harper's New Monthly Magazine* 28 (February 1864), 381; McCreary, "Get-tysburg: A Boy's Experience of the Battle," 251; Benton, *As Seen from the Ranks,* 59–60; Jenny Eyster Jacobs, "Memoir of Gettysburg Battle" (1913), in Gregory A. Coco Collec-tion, Gettysburg National Military Park Vertical Files [#b71–156]; Snipes, "The Improper Placement of the 8th Ohio Monument," 73–75.

13.   Jacobs, *Memoirs,* 61; McCreary, "Gettysburg: A Boy's Experience of the Battle," 251–52; "The National Cemetery," *Philadelphia Inquirer* (January 30, 1864); "The National Cem-etery," in *Revised Report made to the Legislature of Pennsylvania, Soldiers' National Cem-etery at Gettysburg* (Harrisburg, PA: Singerly & Myers, 1867), 175; *Adams County Sentinel* (August 25, 1863), in Frank Klement, " 'These Honored Dead': David Wills and the Sol-diers' Cemetery at Gettysburg," in *The Gettysburg Soldiers' Cemetery and Lincoln's Address* (Shippensburg, PA: White Mane Books, 1993), 4; Francis T. Hoover to Jane Ann Hedley (September 25, 1863), in Gettysburg National Military Park Vertical Files [#8–18d].

14.   Klement, " 'These Honored Dead': David Wills and the Soldiers' Cemetery at Gettys-burg," 5–7; Sheldon, *When the Smoke Cleared at Gettysburg,* 229–31.

15.   *History of Cumberland and Adams Counties, Pennsylvania* (Chicago: Warner, Beers, 1886), 172–73; Frassanito, *Early Photography at Gettysburg,* 341.

16.   "Report of David Wills" and "Report of Samuel Weaver" (March 19, 1864), in *Report of the Select Committee Relative to the Soldiers' National Cemetery* (Harrisburg, PA: Singerly & Myers, 1864), 6–7, 39–41; Creighton, *Colors of Courage,* 154–55; James M. Paradis, *Afri-can Americans and the Gettysburg Campaign* (Lanham, MD: Scarecrow Press, 2005), 57; Mark H. Dunkelman, *Gettysburg's Unknown Soldier: The Life, Death, and Celebrity of Amos Humiston* (Westport, CT: Praeger, 1999), 155; Wills to Lincoln (November 2, 1863), Abra-ham Lincoln Papers, Library of Congress; Louis A. Warren, *Lincoln's Gettysburg Declara-tion: A New Birth of Freedom* (Fort Wayne, IN: Lincoln National Life Foundation, 1964), 39–47.

EPILOGUE

1.   Welles, diary entry for July 7, 1863, in *Diary of Gideon Welles,* 1:363–64; "Great Jubilation—Speeches by the President, Secretary Stanton, Gen. Halleck and Others," *New York Times* (July 8, 1863).

2.   Lincoln, "Response to a Serenade" (July 7, 1863), in *Collected Works,* 6:319–20.

3.   Lincoln, "Address Before the Young Men's Lyceum of Springfield, Illinois" (January 27, 1838), "Fragment on Government" (1854), "Speech at Chicago, Illinois" (July 10, 1858), "Speech at New Haven, Connecticut" (March 6, 1860), and "Speech in Independence Hall, Philadelphia, Pennsylvania" (February 22, 1861), in *Collected Works,* 1:113, 2:221, 499–500, 4:24, 239.

4.   "Conversation with Hon. O. H. Browning" (June 17, 1875), in *An Oral Biography of Abra-ham Lincoln,* 5.

5.   Lincoln, "To James C. Conkling" (August 26, 1863), in *Collected Works,* 6:410.

6. Brooks, *Washington in Lincoln's Time*, 285–86; Burlingame, *Abraham Lincoln: A Life*, 2:561, 569.

7. "The National Necropilis," *New York Herald* (November 20, 1863); "The Presidential Party en Route for Gettysburg," *Daily National Republican* (November 19, 1863); Henry C. Cochrane, "With Lincoln to Gettysburg" (1907), *Gettysburg Magazine* 42 (July 2010), 117; Gerald Bennett, *The Gettysburg Railroad Station: A Brief History* (Gettysburg: Gettysburg Railroad Station Restoration Project, 2006), 17.

8. "'Gettysburg' Celebration—Our Great National Cemetery," *Philadelphia Inquirer* (November 20, 1863); "Our Great National Cemetery—Its Dedication and Consecration," *Christian Recorder* (November 28, 1863); Robert McLean, "About in Gettysburg—1863," *Gettysburg Compiler* (June 30, 1909); Warren, *Lincoln's Gettysburg Declaration*, 80–81; Everett, "The Battles of Gettysburg," in Klement, *The Gettysburg Soldiers' Cemetery and Lincoln's Address*, 217.

9. Mary Todd Lincoln interview (September 1866), in *Herndon's Informants: Letters, Interviews and Statements About Abraham Lincoln*, eds. Douglas Wilson and Rodney O. Davis (Chicago: University of Illinois Press, 1998), 360; Grow, in *Congressional Globe*, 37th Congress, first session (July 4, 1861), 4; Burlingame, *Abraham Lincoln: A Life*, 2:570; Lucas E. Morel, *Lincoln's Sacred Effort: Defining Religion's Role in American Self-Government* (Lanham, MD: Lexington Books, 2000), 46.

10. de Maistre, "Study on Sovereignty," in *The Works of Joseph de Maistre*, ed. Jack Lively (New York: Schocken, 1965), 103, 107; Crevecoeur, *Letters from an American Farmer* (New York: Duffield, 1908), 51–52.

11. Leopold, King of the Belgians, to Ferdinand Maximilian (October 25, 1861) in A. R. Tyrner-Tyrnauer, *Lincoln and the Emperors* (London: Rupert Hart-Davis, 1962), 65–67; Cobden, "The American War" (November 24, 1863), in *Speeches on Questions of Public Policy by Richard Cobden, M.P.*, eds. John Bright and J. E. T. Rogers (London: Macmillan, 1870), 2:107; Bright, "Canada" (March 13, 1865), in *Speeches on Questions of Public Policy by John Bright, M.P.*, ed. J. E. T. Rogers (London: Macmillan, 1868), 1:141; Hay, diary entry for May 7, 1862, in *Inside Lincoln's White House*, 20.

12. Warren, *Lincoln's Gettysburg Declaration*, 120; Klement, "The Music at Gettysburg," in *The Gettysburg Soldiers' Cemetery and Lincoln's Address*, 208; William H. Herndon (July 19, 1887), in Emmanuel Hertz, ed., *The Hidden Lincoln, from the Letters and Papers of William H. Herndon* (New York: Blue Ribbon Books, 1940), 192; Hay, diary entry for November 19, 1863, in *Inside Lincoln's White House*, 113; Colver, "Reminiscences of the Battle of Gettysburg," 179–80; Charles Baum, "Memoir of Lincoln's Gettysburg Address" [CWVFM-5], Special Collections, Gettysburg College.

Index

Page numbers in *italics* refer to illustrations.

Spine of Little Round Top, looking northwest: William Tipton, 1888, Adams County Historical Society

Strong Vincent: Carte de visite, Library of Congress

The Joseph Sherfy house: William Tipton, 1888, Adams County Historical Society

Wheat field lane, looking east: William Tipton, 1880, Adams County Historical Society

Confederate dead: Alexander Gardner/Timothy O'Sullivan, Library of Congress

Francis Edward Heath: Maine Department of History

Union skirmishers at Cemetery Hill: Alfred Waud, Library of Congress

Wreckage of John Bigelow's 9th Massachusetts Artillery: Timothy O'Sullivan, Library of Congress

Officers and staff of the 69th Pennsylvania: William Morris Smith, Library of Congress

Cadmus Marcellus Wilcox: Library of Congress

William Barksdale: Julian Vannerson, Library of Congress

Edward Porter Alexander: frontispiece from *Military Memoirs of a Confederate: A Critical Narrative* (1907)

Meade's headquarters: Alexander Gardner, Library of Congress

The angle, looking south: William Tipton, Adams County Historical Society

Albertus McCreary's retreat: from "Gettysburg: A Boy's Experience of the Battle," *McClure's Magazine* (July 1909)

David Emmons Johnston: frontispiece to *The Story of a Confederate Boy in the Civil War* (1914)

House of Abraham Bryan: Mathew Brady, Library of Congress

Alexander Stewart Webb: Mathew Brady, Library of Congress